Twentieth-Century
Literary Criticism

Guide to Gale Literary Criticism Series

For criticism on	Consult these Gale series
Authors now living or who died after December 31, 1959	*CONTEMPORARY LITERARY CRITICISM (CLC)*
Authors who died between 1900 and 1959	*TWENTIETH-CENTURY LITERARY CRITICISM (TCLC)*
Authors who died between 1800 and 1899	*NINETEENTH-CENTURY LITERATURE CRITICISM (NCLC)*
Authors who died between 1400 and 1799	*LITERATURE CRITICISM FROM 1400 TO 1800 (LC)* *SHAKESPEAREAN CRITICISM (SC)*
Authors who died before 1400	*CLASSICAL AND MEDIEVAL LITERATURE CRITICISM (CMLC)*
Black writers of the past two hundred years	*BLACK LITERATURE CRITICISM (BLC)*
Authors of books for children and young adults	*CHILDREN'S LITERATURE REVIEW (CLR)*
Dramatists	*DRAMA CRITICISM (DC)*
Hispanic writers of the late nineteenth and twentieth centuries	*HISPANIC LITERATURE CRITICISM (HLC)*
Native North American writers and orators of the eighteenth, nineteenth, and twentieth centuries	*NATIVE NORTH AMERICAN LITERATURE (NNAL)*
Poets	*POETRY CRITICISM (PC)*
Short story writers	*SHORT STORY CRITICISM (SSC)*
Major authors from the Renaissance to the present	*WORLD LITERATURE CRITICISM, 1500 TO THE PRESENT (WLC)*

ISSN 0276-8178

Volume 65

Twentieth-Century Literary Criticism

**Excerpts from Criticism of the
Works of Novelists, Poets, Playwrights,
Short Story Writers, and Other Creative Writers
Who Lived between 1900 and 1960,
from the First Published Critical
Appraisals to Current Evaluations**

**Nancy Dziedzic
Scot Peacock**
Editors

**Dave Galens
Thomas Ligotti
Lynn Spampinato
Brandon Trenz**
Associate Editors

GALE

DETROIT · NEW YORK · TORONTO · LONDON

STAFF

Nancy Dziedzic, Scot Peacock, *Editors*

David M. Galens, Thomas Ligotti, Lynn Spampinato, Brandon Trenz,
Associate Editors

Marlene S. Hurst, *Permissions Manager*
Margaret A. Chamberlain, Maria Franklin, Kimberly F. Smilay, *Permissions Specialists*

Diane Cooper, Edna Hedblad, Michele Lonoconus, Maureen Puhl, Susan Salas, Shalice Shah,
Permissions Associates
Sarah Chesney, Jeffrey Hermann, *Permissions Assistants*

Victoria B. Cariappa, *Research Manager*
Laura C. Bissey, Julia C. Daniel, Tamara C. Nott, Michele P. Pica,
Tracie A. Richardson, Norma Sawaya, Cheryl L. Warnock, *Research Associates*

Mary Beth Trimper, *Production Director*
Deborah L. Milliken, *Production Assistant*

Sherrell Hobbs, *Macintosh Artist*
Randy Bassett, *Image Database Supervisor*
Robert Duncan, *Imaging Specialist*
Pamela Hayes, *Photography Coordinator*

Library of Congress Catalog Card Number 76-46132
ISBN 0-7876-0779-7
ISSN 0276-8178

Printed in the United States of America
10 9 8 7 6 5 4 3 2 1

Contents

Preface vii

Acknowledgments xi

Earl Derr Biggers 1884-1933 1
American novelist, short story writer, and playwright

Benjamin Nathan Cardozo 1870-1938 19
American jurist and essayist

Erskine Childers 1870-1922 49
English novelist

Albert Einstein 1879-1955 63
German-born American physicist and philosopher

Buddy Holly 1936-1959 136
American songwriter

James Gibbons Huneker 1857-1921 155
American critic, autobiographer, and novelist

Ellen Key 1849-1926 222
Swedish educator and feminist

Frederic William Maitland 1850-1906 248
English historian

Karl Mannheim 1893-1947 294
German sociologist

Literary Criticism Series Cumulative Author Index 343

Literary Criticism Series Topic Index 423

TCLC Cumulative Nationality Index 431

Title Index to *TCLC*, Vol. 65 437

Preface

Since its inception more than fifteen years ago, *Twentieth-Century Literary Criticism* has been purchased and used by nearly 10,000 school, public, and college or university libraries. *TCLC* has covered more than 500 authors, representing 58 nationalities, and over 25,000 titles. No other reference source has surveyed the critical response to twentieth-century authors and literature as thoroughly as *TCLC*. In the words of one reviewer, "there is nothing comparable available." *TCLC* "is a gold mine of information—dates, pseudonyms, biographical information, and criticism from books and periodicals—which many libraries would have difficulty assembling on their own."

Scope of the Series

TCLC is designed to serve as an introduction to authors who died between 1900 and 1960 and to the most significant interpretations of these author's works. The great poets, novelists, short story writers, playwrights, and philosophers of this period are frequently studied in high school and college literature courses. In organizing and excerpting the vast amount of critical material written on these authors, *TCLC* helps students develop valuable insight into literary history, promotes a better understanding of the texts, and sparks ideas for papers and assignments. Each entry in *TCLC* presents a comprehensive survey of an author's career or an individual work of literature and provides the user with a multiplicity of interpretations and assessments. Such variety allows students to pursue their own interests; furthermore, it fosters an awareness that literature is dynamic and responsive to many different opinions.

Every fourth volume of *TCLC* is devoted to literary topics. These topic entries widen the focus of the series from individual authors to such broader subjects as literary movements, prominent themes in twentieth-century literature, literary reaction to political and historical events, significant eras in literary history, prominent literary anniversaries, and the literatures of cultures that are often overlooked by English-speaking readers.

TCLC is designed as a companion series to Gale's *Contemporary Literary Criticism,* which reprints commentary on authors now living or who have died since 1960. Because of the different periods under consideration, there is no duplication of material between *CLC* and *TCLC*. For additional information about *CLC* and Gale's other criticism titles, users should consult the Guide to Gale Literary Criticism Series preceding the title page in this volume.

Coverage

Each volume of *TCLC* is carefully compiled to present:

- criticism of authors, or literary topics, representing a variety of genres and nationalities

- both major and lesser-known writers and literary works of the period

- 6-12 authors or 3-6 topics per volume

- individual entries that survey critical response to each author's work or each topic in literary history, including early criticism to reflect initial reactions; later criticism to represent any rise or decline in reputation; and current retrospective analyses.

Organization of This Book

An author entry consists of the following elements: author heading, biographical and critical introduction, list of principal works, excerpts of criticism (each preceded by an annotation and a bibliographic citation), and a bibliography of further reading.

- The **Author Heading** consists of the name under which the author most commonly wrote, followed by birth and death dates. If an author wrote consistently under a pseudonym, the pseudonym will be listed in the author heading and the real name given in parentheses on the first line of the biographical and critical introduction. Also located at the beginning of the introduction to the author entry are any name variations under which an author wrote, including transliterated forms for authors whose languages use nonroman alphabets.

- The **Biographical and Critical Introduction** outlines the author's life and career, as well as the critical issues surrounding his or her work. References to past volumes of *TCLC* are provided at the beginning of the introduction. Additional sources of information in other biographical and critical reference series published by Gale, including *Short Story Criticism, Children's Literature Review, Contemporary Authors, Dictionary of Literary Biography,* and *Something about the Author,* are listed in a box at the end of the entry.

- Some *TCLC* entries include **Portraits** of the author. Entries also may contain reproductions of materials pertinent to an author's career, including manuscript pages, title pages, dust jackets, letters, and drawings, as well as photographs of important people, places, and events in an author's life.

- The **List of Principal Works** is chronological by date of first book publication and identifies the genre of each work. In the case of foreign authors with both foreign-language publications and English translations, the title and date of the first English-language edition are given in brackets. Unless otherwise indicated, dramas are dated by first performance, not first publication.

- Critical excerpts are prefaced by **Annotations** providing the reader with information about both the critic and the criticism that follows. Included are the critic's reputation, individual approach to literary criticism, and particular expertise in an author's works. Also noted are the relative importance of a work of criticism, the scope of the excerpt, and the growth of critical controversy or changes in critical trends regarding an author. In some cases, these annotations cross-reference excerpts by critics who discuss each other's commentary.

- A complete **Bibliographic Citation** designed to facilitate location of the original essay or book precedes each piece of criticism.

- **Criticism** is arranged chronologically in each author entry to provide a perspective on changes in critical evaluation over the years. All titles of works by the author featured in the entry are printed in boldface type to enable the user to easily locate discussion of particular works. Also for purposes of easier identification, the critic's name and the publication date of the essay are given at the beginning of each piece of criticism. Unsigned criticism is preceded by the title of the journal in which it appeared. Some of the excerpts in *TCLC* also contain translated material. Unless otherwise noted, translations in brackets are by the editors; translations in parentheses or continuous with the text are by the critic. Publication information (such as footnotes or page and line references to specific editions of works) have been deleted at the editor's discretion to provide smoother reading of the text.

- An annotated list of **Further Reading** appearing at the end of each author entry suggests secondary sources on the author. In some cases it includes essays for which the editors could not obtain reprint rights.

Cumulative Indexes

- Each volume of *TCLC* contains a cumulative **Author Index** listing all authors who have appeared in Gale's Literary Criticism Series, along with cross references to such biographical series as *Contemporary Authors* and *Dictionary of Literary Biography*. For readers' convenience, a complete list of Gale titles included appears on the first page of the author index. Useful for locating authors within the various series, this index is particularly valuable for those authors who are identified by a certain period but who, because of their death dates, are placed in another, or for those authors whose careers span two periods. For example, F. Scott Fitzgerald is found in *TCLC*, yet a writer often associated with him, Ernest Hemingway, is found in *CLC*.

- Each *TCLC* volume includes a cumulative **Nationality Index** which lists all authors who have appeared in *TCLC* volumes, arranged alphabetically under their respective nationalities, as well as Topics volume entries devoted to particular national literatures.

- Each new volume in Gale's Literary Criticism Series includes a cumulative **Topic Index**, which lists all literary topics treated in *NCLC, TCLC, LC 1400-1800,* and the *CLC* yearbook.

- Each new volume of *TCLC*, with the exception of the Topics volumes, includes a **Title Index** listing the titles of all literary works discussed in the volume. In response to numerous suggestions from librarians, Gale has also produced a **Special Paperbound Edition** of the *TCLC* title index. This annual cumulation lists all titles discussed in the series since its inception and is issued with the first volume of *TCLC* published each year. Additional copies of the index are available on request. Librarians and patrons will welcome this separate index; it saves shelf space, is easy to use, and is recyclable upon receipt of the following year's cumulation. Titles discussed in the Topics volume entries are not included *TCLC* cumulative index.

Citing *Twentieth-Century Literary Criticism*

When writing papers, students who quote directly from any volume in Gale's literary Criticism Series may use the following general forms to footnote reprinted criticism. The first example pertains to materials drawn from periodicals, the second to material reprinted from books.

[1]William H. Slavick, "Going to School to DuBose Heyward," *The Harlem Renaissance Re-examined,* (AMS Press, 1987); excerpted and reprinted in *Twentieth-Century Literary Criticism,* Vol. 59, ed. Jennifer Gariepy (Detroit: Gale Research, 1995), pp. 94-105.

[2]George Orwell, "Reflections on Gandhi," *Partisan Review,* 6 (Winter 1949), pp. 85-92; excerpted and reprinted in *Twentieth-Century Literary Criticism,* Vol. 59, ed. Jennifer Gariepy (Detroit: Gale Research, 1995), pp. 40-3.

Suggestions Are Welcome

In response to suggestions, several features have been added to *TCLC* since the series began, including annotations to excerpted criticism, a cumulative index to authors in all Gale literary criticism series, entries devoted to criticism on a single work by a major author, more extensive illustrations, and a title index listing all literary works discussed in the series since its inception.

Readers who wish to suggest authors or topics to appear in future volumes, or who have other suggestions, are cordially invited to write the editors.

Acknowledgments

The editors wish to thank the copyright holders of the excerpted criticism included in this volume and the permissions managers of many book and magazine publishing companies for assisting us in securing reprint rights. We are also grateful to the staffs of the Detroit Public Library, the Library of Congress, the University of Detroit Mercy Library, Wayne State University Purdy/Kresge Library Complex, and the University of Michigan Libraries for making their resources available to us. Following is a list of the copyright holders who have granted us permission to reprint material in this volume of *TCLC*. Every effort has been made to trace copyright, but if omissions have been made, please let us know.

COPYRIGHTED EXCERPTS IN *TCLC*, VOLUME 65, WERE REPRODUCED FROM THE FOLLOWING PERIODICALS:

American Literature, v. 29, March, 1957. Copyright (c) 1957 Duke University Press, Durham, NC. Reproduced by permission of the publisher.—*The Antioch Review*, v. 39, Fall, 1981. Copyright (c) 1981 by the Antioch Review, Inc. Reproduced by permission of the editors.—*The Armchair Detective*, v. 10, April, 1977; v. 22, Fall, 1989. Copyright (c) 1977, 1989 by The Armchair Detective. Both reproduced by permission of the publisher.—*The Cambridge Journal*, v. 4, October, 1950-September, 1951 for "F. W. Maitland: 1850-1950" by R. J. White. Reproduced by permission of the author.—*The Centennial Review*, v. 35, Fall, 1991 for "Albert Einstein: A Necrological Approach" by Louis Kaplan. (c) 1991 by The Centennial Review. Reproduced by permission of the publisher and the author.—*Columbia Library Columns*, v. XXXI, May, 1982. Reproduced by permission of the publisher.—*Commentary*, v. 10, September, 1950 for "Einstein: The Passion of Pure Reason" by Irving Kristol. Copyright 1950 by the American Jewish Committee. All rights reserved. Reproduced by permission of the publisher and the author.—*Current History*, v. 24, July, 1926. Copyright, 1926, by Current History, Inc. Reproduced by permission of the publisher.—*Daedalus: Journal of the American Academy of Arts and Sciences*, v. 103, Winter, 1973. Copyright (c) 1973 by the American Academy of Arts and Sciences. Reproduced by permission of Daedalus: Journal of the American Academy of Arts and Sciences.—*The French Review*, v. XIV, December, 1940. Copyright 1940 by the American Association of Teachers of French. Reproduced by permission of the publisher.—*German Life & Letters*, v. XLV, January, 1992. Reproduced by permission of the publisher.—*History Today*, v. 38, October, 1988. (c) History Today Limited 1988. Reproduced by permission of the publisher.—*Journal of Popular Culture*, v. 15, Spring, 1982. Copyright (c) 1982 by Ray B. Browne. Reproduced by permission of the publisher.—*The Midwest Quarterly*, v. XXXV, Winter, 1994. Copyright, 1994, by The Midwest Quarterly, Pittsburgh State University. Reproduced by permission of the publisher.—*Mosaic: A Journal for the Interdisciplinary Study of Literature*, v. XXII, Summer, 1989. (c) Mosaic 1989. Acknowledgment of previous publication is herewith made.—*The Nation*, New York, v. CXIV, March 22, 1922. Copyright 1922 The Nation magazine/ The Nation Company, Inc. Reproduced by permission of the publisher.—*The New Criterion*, v.V, June, 1987 for "James Huneker & America's Musical Coming of Age" by Samuel Lipman. Copyright (c) 1987 by The Foundation for Cultural Review. Reproduced by permission of the author.—*The New Republic*, v. 177, July 30, 1977. (c) 1977 The New Republic, Inc. Reproduced by permission of The New Republic.—*New Statesman*, v. LXIX, June 4, 1965. (c) 1965 The Statesman & Nation Publishing Co. Ltd. Reproduced by permission of the publisher.—*The New York Times Book Review*, May 27, 1928. Copyright (c) 1928, renewed 1956 by The New York Times Company. Reproduced by permission of the publisher.—*Orbis Litterarum*, v. 36, 1981. Reproduced by permission of the publisher.—*Scandinavian Studies*, v. 56, Autumn, 1984 for "Ellen Key and Swedish Feminist Views on Motherhood" by Torborg Lundell. Reproduced by permission of the publisher and the author.—*The Spectator*, v. 195, August 5, 1955; v. 229, September 23. (c) 1955, 1972 by The Spectator. Both reproduced by permission of The Spectator.—*Studies in Short Fiction*, v. II, Summer, 1965. Copyright 1965 by Newberry College. Reproduced by permission of the publisher.—*The University of Windsor Review*, v. IX, Fall, 1973 for "In Praise of Huneker" by Mortimer H. Frank. Reproduced by permission of the publisher and the author.

COPYRIGHTED EXCERPTS IN *TCLC*, VOLUME 65, WERE REPRODUCED FROM THE FOLLOWING BOOKS:

Earl Derr Biggers

1884-1933

American novelist, short story writer, and playwright.

INTRODUCTION

Biggers was the creator of the Hawaiian detective Charlie Chan, a character he conceived as a positive example of Asian-Americans. During the 1920s, Chinese characters in American popular fiction were often portrayed as sinister and menacing, a notable example being Sax Rohmer's villainous Fu Manchu. In response, Biggers styled Chan to be a polite and reflective policeman of Chinese origin, an American citizen who is patriotic but still retains a spiritual connection to his birthplace. Although Biggers achieved early success as a playwright, he is best remembered for his series of six mystery novels featuring Chan. The many film, radio, and television adaptations of the Chan novels kept the character alive decades after Biggers's death.

Biographical Information

Biggers was born in Warren, Ohio, on August 26, 1884. A graduate of Harvard University, he worked from 1908 to 1912 as a columnist and theater critic for the Boston *Traveler.* In 1912, Biggers married Eleanor Ladd, with whom he would later have one son. His first major work, the play *If You're Only Human,* was produced in 1912 but failed to impress audiences. More successful was Biggers's first novel, *Seven Keys to Baldpate,* which was published in 1913; a popular mystery, it was adapted for the stage by George M. Cohan, as well as for the screen as both a silent and sound film. Biggers wrote several more plays, two novels, and a number of short stories before penning the first Charlie Chan novel, *The House Without a Key.* Following the 1926 publication of the book, initially printed as a serial in the *Saturday Evening Post* (as were the five other Chan novels), Biggers moved from New York to California to work in the film industry and also to preserve his fragile health. The author saw five Hollywood films go into production based on his Chan novels, although none of them cast an Asian as the lead character. On April 5, 1933, Biggers died of heart failure in Pasadena, California.

Major Works

Biggers's best known novels feature Charlie Chan, although the detective plays only a minor role in the first of the six-novel series. While it has been suggested that Chan was modeled after two Honolulu police detectives, Chang Apana and Lee Fook, Biggers reportedly denied a direct correlation, stressing that using a Chinese policeman as a main character was a fresh idea for a mystery novel— Asians were usually cast as the villains. The first novel to prominently feature Chan was *The Chinese Parrot* (1926).

This was followed by four more book-length mysteries, including *Keeper of the Keys* (1932), the last volume of the series. Through the Chan novels in particular, Biggers built an international following, with translations of his work appearing in a dozen languages. More than thirty films and a television series were produced utilizing the character, in addition to numerous radio plays and a newspaper comic strip.

Critical Reception

Some critics do not consider Biggers's Chan mysteries to be pure detective fiction but rather melodramas which involve crime and sleuthing. Set in exotic locales, these novels often depict secondary characters who fall in love; there are also glimpses of Chan's domestic life, his happy marriage and his loving, though at times trying, relationships with his children. While the film versions of Chan are responsible for much of the figure's enduring popularity through the 1970s, more recent popular culture studies have examined Chan's stereotypical attributes. The Chan books have been criticized for their depictions of unflattering cliches associated with Asian-Americans. There are commentators, however, who view Biggers's Chan mysteries as an attempt to balance a negative stereotype with a positive one. In this respect, Biggers is credited for creating a heroic Asian character with whom readers could form an empathic connection.

PRINCIPAL WORKS

If You're Only Human   (play)   1912
Seven Keys to Baldpate   (novel)   1913
Love Insurance   (novel)   1914
Inside the Lines   (play)   1915
Inside the Lines [with Robert Welles Ritchie]   (novel) 1915
The Agony Column   (novel)   1916; also published as *Second Floor Mystery*, 1930
A Cure for Curables [adaptor, with Lawrence Whitman; from the story by Cora Harris]   (play)   1918
See-Saw [with Louis A. Hirsch]   (libretto)   1919
Three's a Crowd [adaptor with Christopher Morley; from the story "Kathleen" by Christopher Morley] (play)   1919
The House Without a Key   (novel)   1925
The Chinese Parrot   (novel)   1926
Fifty Candles   (novel)   1926
Behind That Curtain   (novel)   1928
The Black Camel   (novel)   1929
Charlie Chan Carries On   (novel)   1930
Keeper of the Keys   (novel)   1932
Earl Derr Biggers Tells Ten Stories   (short stories)   1933

CRITICISM

Burns Mantle   (essay date 1929)

SOURCE: "Novelists and the Drama," in *American Playwrights of Today*, Dodd, Mead & Company, 1929, pp. 211-29.

[*In the following excerpt, Mantle comments on Biggers's early stage career.*]

Earl Derr Biggers figures that he is one of the luckier playwrights. He quit writing novels and plays and took to writing motion picture scenarios when both the quitting and the scenario market were at their peak.

It was his last summer in New York that cured Biggers. He had had some success with plays. He had written, as far back as 1912, a comedy called *If You're Only Human* which Rose Stahl wanted to buy but which her manager, Henry B. Harris, could not see. And when *If You're Only Human* was later produced in stock Mr. Biggers met George M. Cohan. As a result of that meeting George M. bought the dramatic rights to Mr. Biggers' novel, *Seven Keys to Baldpate,* and nearly everybody knows of the success that followed that purchase. Cohan did the play,

made a vast amount of money with it and entered upon his most productive phase as a serious dramatist.

Biggers had also written a war play, *Inside the Lines,* that went fairly well in New York. Later it was played for five hundred nights in London. Then he collaborated with William Hodge on a comedy, *A Cure for Curables,* which Hodge played for two years.

"There was one line of mine in *A Cure for Curables* when it reached the boards," Earl Derr wrote from California in telling me about his adventures as a playwright, "but after careful consideration Hodge removed it."

Then came the hectic summer and the cure. Two of the Biggers' plays were on the way that summer, *See-Saw,* a story made into a musical comedy for the late Henry W. Savage, and a farce, *Three's a Crowd,* chiseled from a Christopher Morley story called "Kathleen."

The rehearsals of these two plays overlapped, I gather, and the days were exciting for the young playwright. In one case he had a producer whose custom it was to stride the stage and roar his conclusions as to what he thought should be done with the play. In the other he had one whose companions at the moment were slinking fellows who looked like bailiffs. Looked like bailiffs because, in fact, they were bailiffs.

This latter producer was from time to time selling partnerships in the Biggers' show to outsiders, hoping thereby to raise the costs of production and make secure the hotel accommodations upon which his hold was precarious. And as each new purchaser of ten per cent or five per cent came in he naturally demanded that the play be rewritten to suit him.

Between these experiences the Biggers' blood pressure mounted with the Biggers' disgust. And when the experiences were over the playwright sought the twin balms of California—the climate for his health, the motion picture factories for the re-establishment of what once had been a bank account.

To add the facts of life to the record, Earl Derr was born in Warren, O., in 1884, was graduated from Harvard with an A.B. in 1907, and became a newspaper man himself the year following. On the Boston *Traveler* he ran a humorous column and was later promoted, or at least transferred, to the drama desk. That is where he, quite naturally, became imbued with a desire to improve the drama. Many drama critics suffer the same urge but few have ever been able to do more than relieve the suffering temporarily.

Neil Ellman   (essay date 1977)

SOURCE: "Charlie Chan Carries on," in *The Armchair Detective*, Vol. 10, No. 2, April, 1977, pp. 183-84.

[*In the following essay, Ellman examines the various film characterizations of Charlie Chan and discusses the actors who have portrayed him over the years.*]

Charlie Chan Carries On is the title of the fourth novel in the series of six Charlie Chan stories written by Earl Derr Biggers during the 1920s and early 1930s. The title has additional meaning, for the character of Charlie Chan has, indeed, carried on. His popularity has outlived the memory of his creator; his name is more a household word than are the names of many of the great detectives admired by whodunit aficionados; and he continues to appear in countless television reruns of the early Chan movies, a television cartoon show for children, and numerous parodies and comedy skits. The physical image of Charlie Chan is as permanently fixed on the popular consciousness as that of Sherlock Holmes, and his recognizability far exceeds those of such fictional detectives as Sam Spade, Hercule Poirot, and Mike Hammer.

It is ironic that this should be the case, for Charlie Chan was created by an author who began his career by belittling best-sellerism, and who, before he died, resisted many efforts to popularize his creation in the mass media. Biggers had not even planned a Chan series. In the first novel, *The House Without a Key,* the detective is merely a secondary figure who does not appear until the seventh chapter; but he quickly attracted the attention of the public, which demanded to see more of him. Biggers responded with five more novels featuring the detective. As each was written, the author became more attached to his creation and more concerned with making Chan (and himself) immortal.

Nevertheless, Biggers resisted popularization through the mass media. He completely rejected an offer to have Chan appear in a comic strip, and it took the effects of the Depression for him to allow radio broadcasts of his stories. At first, he believed "radio broadcasting would make Charlie so common and well-known that he would soon be squeezed dry, and a valuable property on which I am depending for support for years to come, would be valueless" (June 30, 1932). Soon after this statement, however, Charlie Chan stories were being broadcast with Walter Connelly as his voice.

Although Biggers did feel that a successful portrayal in the movies would establish Chan "as the leading sleuth of his generation" (February 6, 1931), he feared what Hollywood might do to the character. When Conrad Veidt was being considered as the movies' first Charlie Chan, Biggers was afraid that the German actor and his German director would "scare the public to death, and brand Charlie as a sinister devil from the Orient" (January 31, 1927). When it was finally announced that Sojin, a Chinese actor, would play the role, Biggers was equally concerned, calling Sojin "a corking actor, but a long, thin, sinister chink" (March 10, 1927). The author's worst fears became reality. "The general opinion of people out here," he later explained to his publisher, "is that I ought to sue Universal for defamation of character" (February 6, 1931). Warner Baxter was the next to play Chan and the first to do it well. However, the public, as well as Biggers, was not satisfied: "The news is all about over there that Charlie cannot be cast—Fox tried every Chinese laundryman on the Coast, but never thought of trying an actor—and the issue looks like a dead one" (December 10, 1929).

A successful portrayal of Charlie Chan was finally achieved by Warner Oland, who did as much to fix the popular image of Chan as did Basil Rathbone for Sherlock Holmes. With Holmes, the image was also established through book illustrations, but with Chan this was never the case. As Biggers commented about the illustrations in his novels, "Six books and six different Charlies so far" (June 11, 1932). Oland finally took the ingredients established by Biggers and transformed them into a visual image that survives even today. While the original Chan novels are hardly ever read, the Oland portrayal keeps the image of Chan alive. It is Oland whom countless imitators have mimicked.

At first glance, it is difficult to see why Charlie Chan has survived for nearly a half-century. The original novels, as well as their sixteen movie successors, do not exploit sex or violence, and the character himself lacks much of the dynamism that contemporary fictional detectives frequently possess. Upon closer examination, however, two factors tend to explain Chan's continuing popularity—his reinforcement of a stereotype, and his domesticity.

Indeed, Charlie Chan reflects something of the occidental stereotype of Orientals. While the detective was never a Fu Manchu on the right side of the law, his sagaciousness and inexplicability reinforce rather than counter the popular image of the Oriental. In fact, in explaining his rules for writing mystery stories, Ronald A. Knox stated in 1928 that a Chinese character should never figure in a story. "Why this should be so," he tried to explain, "I do not know, unless we can find a reason for it in our Western habit of assuming that the Celestial is over-equipped in the matter of brains, and under-equipped in the matter of morals." Although such strong biases are seldom expressed today, they are still reflected in the mass media through such characterizations as the sagacious oriental servant who always manages to save the day for his employer and the sinister oriental villain who works for a communist government or international crime organization. If Charlie Chan is not sinister, he is certainly inexplicable, solving crimes with uncanny intuition and insight.

At first, Biggers played upon the stereotype, but then he hit upon a formula that subdued this approach while retaining the detective's appeal. "Sinister and wicked Chinese are old stuff," the author explained in a newspaper interview, "but an amiable Chinese on the side of law and order had never been used up to that time." Thus, the detective became more American, more Western, and more human. He became, in fact, the first "domestic" detective in fiction. The great detectives are seldom married, and even more infrequently do they have children and a home life. Chan, however, is married, has ten children, and lives a very normal life in his home on Punchbowl Hill. The movies retained this dimension of his character by utilizing his "number one son" as the equivalent of Dr. Watson in the Sherlock Holmes stories. In the novels, Chan is also portrayed as being torn between his oriental background and his occidental environment. When his cousin, Chan Lee Kim, asks him, "The foreign devil police—what has a Chinese in common with them?" Chan answers, "There are times, honorable cousin, when I do not quite understand myself."

It is this Chan, then, that Warner Oland successfully portrayed in the movies—a Chan whose speech is marked by the use of sagacious aphorisms, whose criminological methods depend more upon inexplicable intuition than on reasoning, and whose life is as normal as any man's. Oland fused these appealing characteristics with a visual image that is unforgettable and endlessly imitable.

Jon L. Breen (essay date 1977)

SOURCE: "Murder Number One," in *The New Republic,* Vol. 177, No. 3264, July 30, 1977, pp. 38-9.

[*In the following essay, Breen studies the development of Charlie Chan as a leading character in the six novels by Biggers.*]

With the exception of a couple of Dashiell Hammett characters, Sam Spade and Nick Charles, no character in detective fiction has become more famous on the basis of fewer official appearances than Earl Derr Biggers's Chinese sleuth Charlie Chan. The Honolulu policeman appeared in only six novels, beginning with *The House Without a Key* (1925), in which he is a comparatively minor character, and ending with *The Keeper of the Keys* (1932), by which time he has taken over center stage.

As with Spade and Charles, most of Chan's fame has been spread through hundreds of apocryphal cases in films, radio, television, and comic strips. As entertaining as many of these adaptations are, they have done Chan and his creator a disservice. The Charlie Chan of the six novels is a complex, multifaceted character. His screen equivalent is a smug, infallible quotation-spouter.

The greatest irony is that Chan has come to be regarded as an ethnic stereotype in some quarters. At the time of his creation, he represented a deliberate corrective to the sinister and villainous figures, most notably exemplified by Sax Rohmer's Fu Manchu, that typified the Chinese to readers of popular fiction in the '20s and before.

In an era when a popular song could present with a straight face a line like "In Limehouse, where yellow chinkies love to play," Biggers's sensitivity and commitment to racial understanding were exceptional. Early in the series, he uses the term Chinaman in third person narration, but the last book he has come to realize that the term is an offensive one to the Chinese. When a character uses the word, Chan takes it as an insult only because he knows it is intended that way.

Earl Derr Biggers was already well-established as a skilled and successful writer long before he created Charlie Chan. Born in Warren, Ohio, in 1884 and educated at Harvard, he served for several years as a columnist and drama critic for the Boston *Traveler* before the 1913 novel *Seven Keys to Baldpate* gave him his first fame. George M. Cohan would turn *Baldpate,* a light romance with a touch of mystery, into a successful stage vehicle. Biggers moved to New York to write plays of his own, as well as such novels as *Love Insurance* (1914) and *The Agony Column* (1916).

Like most successful popular writers, Biggers strongly believed in what he was doing. He claimed that editors never told him what to write, just asked him to do the best job he could. They probably didn't have to tell him, since his inclinations as a writer were so much in accord with the requirements of slick romantic fiction of the day. In his Harvard days, he was notorious among his classmates for preferring Kipling and Richard Harding Davis to Fielding, Smollett, and Richardson. According to his *New York Times* obituary, "Biggers said they read Keats to one another in the twilight at Harvard at that time, urging him to leave the room before they began."

Delicate health and the promise of film work led Biggers to move his family to California in the mid-'20s. By this time, Charlie Chan had made his debut but was not yet a world-famous character. By the time of Biggers's death in 1933, Warner Oland was solidly established as the definitive screen Chan and the Chinese sleuth occupied most of his creator's writing efforts.

All six Charlie Chan novels were serialized in the *Saturday Evening Post,* and a perusal of the illustrations charts Chan's growing fame. When *The House Without a Key* began its run in the September 24, 1925 issue, Chan did not appear in the first installment, and even when he did make his unobtrusive debut in the second installment, illustrator William Liepse was too preoccupied with the story's young lovers to offer a visual depiction of him. W. H. D. Koerner's illustrations for the second novel, *The Chinese Parrot* (1926), show Chan as youngish, not very fat and clean-shaven. The lack of a mustache is true to Biggers's descriptions of Chan—like Fu Manchu, he acquired facial hair for film work. By the appearance of the fifth novel, *Charlie Chan Carries On* (1930), artist Henry Raleigh gives us a Chan with the look of the movies about him. He has become much fatter, acquired dramatically sloping eyebrows, and grown a mustache much like Warner Oland's.

Aside from the superficial matter of a mustache, how does Chan in the books differ from Chan in the movies? He does have a large number of children, thoroughly Americanized in their speech and partially so in their values, but they stay on Punchbowl Hill. They don't dog their famous father's footsteps shouting, "Hey, Pop, I got a swell clue," nor are they ever referred to by such labels as "number-one son."

A Japanese policeman named Kashima, ambitious but inept, serves a comic relief role in some of the novels similar to that of the sons in the movies. Kashima serves to illustrate the most unattractive aspect of Chan's character. Himself the target of racial prejudice, subtle and otherwise, in all the novels, he vents his own irrational bigotry toward the Japanese on Kashima.

It is the conflict of Eastern and Western values that makes Charlie Chan an interesting character. He criticizes the ambition, the curiosity, the lack of tranquility of the Caucasian, but he sees more and more of these unworthy attributes in himself and is worried by it. Proud of his own vocabulary and command of the English language, he is upset by his offspring's use of slang. Listening to the pidgin English of a Chinese servant, he is torn between shame at the indignity of the man's condition and the feeling that somehow he has retained a basic Chinese identity that Chan has lost. Visiting the head of his family association in San Francisco, he is excoriated for his association with the "foreign devil police." Proud that his children are American citizens, he is ambivalent about his own nationality.

Chan's speech patterns change and develop in the course of the series. His first line of dialogue, "No knife are present in neighborhood of crime," illustrates a grammatical problem that will disappear by the third book in the series. In the first book, he is more given to picturesque language than to aphorisms and quotations. He says, "Is it that you are in the mood to dry up a plate of soup?" And, "Stone walls are crumbling now like dust. Through many loopholes light stream in like rosy streaks of dawn." And, at a dramatic moment, "Relinquish the fire arms . . . or I am forced to make fatal insertion in vital organ belonging to you."

In *The Chinese Parrot,* Chan must impersonate a Chinese servant, speaking such lines as, "Maybe you wantee catch 'um moah fiah, hey, boss?" It is painful to him—"All my life, I study to speak fine English words. Now I must strangle all such in my throat, lest suspicion rouse up." He draws the line at saying "velly." Only with the third novel, *Behind That Curtain* (1928), does he begin to fill the air with Chinese proverbs like "Falling hurts least those who fly low." Perhaps influenced by the movies, his quotation-spouting reaches its height in the last novel: "Only the thief oils his wheelbarrow." "The fool in a hurry drinks his tea with a fork." "Eggs should not dance with stones."

Biggers's strengths as a writer were his gently humorous style and his ability to bring his characters to life within the limits of commercial fiction. As a creator of mystery plots, he was not in a class with his contemporaries S. S. Van Dine and Ellery Queen. Though he would throw a paltry clue or two the reader's way on occasion, fair play was not manifest in most of his novels. Where Van Dine decreed there must be no love interest to detract from the ratiocination, with Biggers there was always a love interest, though it became less central as Charlie Chan's part grew larger. Only in *The Black Camel* (1929), perhaps the best all around Chan novel, is there a gathering-of-the-suspects scene of the kind familiar from the Chan films.

In the last novel of the series, perhaps showing the belated influence of Van Dine and Queen, Biggers begins to show an interest in the fair play aspect of detective story writing, carefully showcasing his clues. Had he lived to write more Chan novels, they surely would have been more tightly and deviously plotted than their predecessors and would have enhanced Biggers's reputation with such purists as Jacques Barzun and Wendell Hertig Taylor, who dismiss him with one perfunctory paragraph in their massive bibliography, *A Catalogue of Crime* (1971). But improved craftsmanship would not have changed Biggers's greatest achievement: the creation of one of the immortal fictional detectives.

Otto Penzler   (essay date 1977)

SOURCE: "Charlie Chan," in *The Private Lives of Private Eyes, Spies, Crimefighters & Other Good Guys,* Grosset & Dunlap Publishers, 1977, pp. 43-50.

[*In the following essay, Penzler provides a biography of the fictional detective Charlie Chan.*]

Sinister orientals are not often used in adventure fiction today, but a half-century ago they were one of the favorite clichés of authors who needed genuinely frightening villains. The ultimate "Yellow Peril" was, of course, the insidious Dr. Fu Manchu, but he had plenty of nasty company in the early years of the twentieth century immediately following the Boxer Rebellion and continuing right up to the Second World War. The Japanese attack on Pearl Harbor took the fun out of fictional menaces from the East.

The concept of an Oriental as a hero, or even as a major benevolent entity, was a new one in 1925 when Earl Derr Biggers created Charlie Chan to serve as a detective. One account of the genesis of Chan tells of Biggers' reading a report in a Honolulu newspaper of a local murder case being cracked by Chang Apana and Lee Fook, two Oriental policemen on the island. The idea of writing mysteries about a Chinese detective struck Biggers and he immediately wrote *The House Without a Key.*

"Sinister and wicked Chinese are old stuff," Biggers wrote, "but an amiable Chinese on the side of law and order had never been used."

Although Biggers always maintained that his Chinese detective was entirely the product of his imagination, Chang Apana, who had once visited the author at his Honolulu home, was equally convinced that he had served as the model for Charlie Chan.

Like Chan, Apana was a Chinese-American (Hawaiian) detective on the Honolulu police force, but unlike Chan, who is huge (particularly in the first book about him), he was small and slender.

Chan appears in only six books by Biggers, but they were all very popular, reprinted often, and all were serialized in *The Saturday Evening Post.* It is, however, in motion pictures that Chan is best known, appearing as the hero of more films than any other detective except Sherlock Holmes. With more than fifty films produced, Chan has been portrayed by a wide variety of actors—not one of whom has been either Chinese or Hawaiian. Two Japanese actors have taken the role of Chan, but the three who are most familiar are Caucasian: Warner Oland, Sidney Toler and Roland Winters.

Substantial differences exist between the Chan whose adventures are recorded in book form and the detective who appears so frequently on the screen. The infamous numbers one and two sons, constantly intruding themselves into the film investigations, do not appear except incidentally in the books.

Unlike the films, in which pieces of evidence are turned up with commendable regularity, the novels do not rely on physical clues as an ingredient vital to the development of the investigation. While some scraps of hard evidence are essential, the denouement is generally arrived at through Chan's understanding of human nature.

"If I understand Charlie Chan correctly," wrote Biggers,

"he has an idea that if you understand a man's character you can nearly predict what he is apt to do in any set of circumstances."

Perhaps the greatest difference between the two versions of the same character is that the Chan of the books is presented as a more complex, three-dimensional human being than the Chan of the films, where his chief distinguishing characteristic, aside from his race; is his unquenchable penchant for spewing epigrams, almost always in pidgin English.

The gentle and philosophical Chan has grown in the affection of mystery fans through the years largely because of his humanness, although it would be a mistake to underestimate the attractiveness of those witty and pertinent aphorisms. He is one of the few detectives of literature to have been paraphrased in the speech of an American president.

"Long journey always start with one short step," said Chan in 1935.

"A journey of a thousand miles must begin with a single step," said President John F. Kennedy in 1963.

Charlie Chan devotes considerable energy to two lives, each of which are extremely important to him—his professional life and his distinguished career as a policeman, and his personal life and devotion to his large, close-knit family.

His ability and reputation as "the best detective on the force" (according to Amos Winterslip at the outset of the first of Chan's recorded cases) get him a promotion from detective-sergeant to inspector by the time of his fourth recorded adventure.

Characteristically, Chan dismisses the promotion as the result of an "upheaval in local police department, and I am rewarded far beyond my humble merits."

Nevertheless, he works hard, bringing enormous zest and patience to his investigations. "Needle can be found," he says "when correct thread located."

Although he does not discuss it to the point where it becomes intrusive, Chan obviously leads a happy and active private life with his wife and family. He has nine children in 1925 and adds two more during the next five years, "which makes for a noisy house," he says in typical understatement.

His wife, a plump, jolly-looking woman, nearly as broad as Chan, has a smiling face, calm eyes, a generally placid temperament and a warm friendliness designed to make visitors feel comfortable instantly. Like her husband, she is not a native of Hawaii, but is less comfortable with the English language than Charlie, her accent running to such mutilations as "plitty tellible thing" and "mebbe you have moah tea."

Charlie had first seen her on the gleaming sand of a beach. She was, he reminisces, "as slender as the bamboo is slender, beautiful as the blossom of the plum."

All of the Chans' children are American citizens, and Charlie fears a gulf is widening between himself and them as they become more and more Americanized, making no effort to remember the precepts of their Chinese heritage. Their language is so idiomatic and slangy that it grates on his sensitive ear.

Not all of the children (eight boys, three girls) appear in his criminal cases, and he does not often speak of them, except in a general, all-inclusive manner, but those who have made their presence felt are: Rose (the oldest girl, attending college on the mainland), Evelyn (who is fifteen in 1929), Barry (the eleventh child, at whose birth Charlie is not able to be present because he has been detained by the exigencies of an investigation), and Henry (who smokes cigarettes at the breakfast table and is constantly trying to borrow the family car).

In a moment of relaxation at home, Chan is dressed in a long, loose robe of dark purple silk, seated at a table playing chess with Henry. A visitor, one of the principal figures in a murder case, calls at Chan's house, receiving a friendly welcome.

"You do my lowly house immense honor," the detective says. "This proud moment are still more proud as opportunity to introduce my eldest son." Motioning his chess opponent to step forward, the visitor notices that he is a slim, sallow boy with amber eyes—Chan himself before he put on weight.

"Mr. John Quincy Winterslip of Boston, kindly condescend to notice Henry Chan," says Charlie. "When you appear I am giving him lesson at chess so he may play in such manner as not to tarnish honored name."

Henry bows low, impressing the visitor as one of those members of the younger generation who has a deep respect for his elders. "Your father is my very good friend," Winterslip tells him, "and from now on, you are too."

Not necessarily viewing his numerous (and often trying and burdensome) sons and daughters in the same light as everyone else may, Chan considers himself unusually fortunate to have such a family. He quotes Confucius, saying, "No man is poor who have worthy son."

His house hangs "precariously" on Punchbowl Hill. Chan likes to stand at his bedroom window, which overlooks Honolulu and the sea, and reflect on his good fortune. It is particularly gratifying to him that he was able to bring his mother from China to Honolulu, so that she could spend her last years with him. She is dead now, buried on a hillside in a Chinese cemetery.

Although the house is once referred to as a cottage, it is furnished beautifully, and Chan is evidently financially secure. He is a member of the Rotary Club, and in 1930 reports having a brand new car, which he refers to as a "flivver" and which he drives fast and recklessly. In that same year, he takes a round-the-world cruise.

Born in China, Charlie Chan moved to Honolulu in 1900, when he was approximately fifteen years old, working as a houseboy in the Phillimore mansion. He was well-treated by Sally Jordan, a Phillimore daughter, who helped him get his citizenship papers, and he remains loyal to her and the rest of the family, even after becoming a famous detective—as a personal favor for them, he carries some valuable pearls (a $300,000 necklace) from Honolulu to San Francisco in 1926.

Chan takes his American citizenship seriously, as he does the language. Speaking of his adopted country, in which he has lived for twenty-five years (referring to himself as a *Kamaaina*—an old-timer), he says, "On soil of democracy you are safe from persecution."

When he affects the guise of an ignorant Chinese cook to solve the case of *The Chinese Parrot* in 1926, Chan is forced to revert to using pidgin English, which distresses him greatly. "All my life," he says, "I study to speak fine English words. Now I must strangle all such in my throat, lest suspicion rise up. Not a happy situation for me."

In Winterslip's opinion, Chan's use of the English language is "dragged from the poets."

The best-known characteristic of Chan's language is his colorful and evocative use of aphoristic wit and wisdom, his ability to find a proverb to fit any situation. In his early cases, his language is merely picturesque, but he gradually changes his style, becoming more and more philosophical as his career progresses.

Typical words of wisdom from Chan include epigrams on countless subjects, including the following:

> "Door of opportunity swing both ways."

> "Tongue often hang man quicker than rope."

> "Man who fights law always loses; same as grasshopper is always wrong in argument with chicken."

> "Owner of face cannot always see nose."

> "Theories like fingerprints—everybody has them."

> "Man without enemies, like dog without Fleas."

> "Roundabout way often shortest path to correct destination."

> "Each man thinks own cuckoos better than next man's nightingales."

> "Mind like parachute, only function when open."

> "If you want wild bird to sing, do not put him in cage."

> "He who feeds the chicken, deserves the egg."

> "To describe bitter medicine will not improve its flavor."

> "Making bedfellow of serpent no guarantee against snakebite."

> "Too late to dig well when honorable house is on fire."

> "Fresh weed better than wilted rose."

> "Make haste only when withdrawing hand from mouth of tiger."

> "Time only wasted when sprinkling perfume on goat farm."

> "Man is not incurably drowned—if he still knows he's all wet."

> "Curiosity responsible for cat needing nine lives."

> "Never hunt rabbit with dead dog."

> "If strength were all, tiger would not fear scorpion."

> "Bad alibi like dead fish—cannot stand test of time."

> "Silence big sister of wisdom."

Charlie Chan's wisdom has been demonstrated in many areas, on many occasions. His reputation is both impeccable and widespread. Sir Frederic Bruce, the former head of the Criminal Investigation Division of Scotland Yard, takes it for granted that Chan excels at his job, and he remains unimpressed. "A Chinese should make an excellent detective," he says. "The patience of the East, you know."

Chan believes more than that is involved. Although he is patient, he is also highly active. When told on his first case that the criminal must be apprehended, he calmly agrees, saying, "What will be will be."

Angrily, a lady at the scene of the crime snaps at Chan, "I know—that's your Confucius, but it's a do-nothing doctrine, and I don't approve of it."

A faint smile flickers across Chan's face. "Do not fear," he replies. "The fastest are busy, and man may do much to assist. I promise you there will be no do-nothing here." Gentle almost to a fault in most instances, he follows his statement with a warning that is—for him—almost bellicose. "Humbly asking pardon to mention it, but I detect in your eyes slight flame of hostility. Quench it if you will be so kind. Friendly cooperation are essential between us."

The only time Chan displays open hostility is when he attempts to deal with Japanese, against whom he is somewhat prejudiced.

In a restaurant, he scowls at the plate in front of him and sends for the proprietor, a suave little Japanese.

"Is it that you serve here unsanitary food?" Chan asks.

"Please deign to state your complaint," the Japanese responds.

"This piece of pie are covered with fingermarks," rebukes Chan. "The sight are most disgusting. Kindly remove it and bring me a more hygienic sector."

The proprietor picks up the offending pastry and carries it away.

"Japanese," remarks Chan, spreading his hands in an eloquent gesture.

Chan's assistant, Kashimo, is Japanese, and not overly bright. Small and anxious-looking, he tries to please his superior but is generally inefficient. On at least one occasion, he has lost the evidence—a pair of dice vital to a gambling case. When Kashimo attempts to be apologetic, Chan completely loses his patience.

"Be sorry out of my sight," he tells his hapless underling. "While you are in it my vision blurs and I feel my self-control under big strain."

Chan's racial prejudice toward the Japanese is humorless and bitter. He once states wearily, "Cooking business begins to get tiresome, like the company of a Japanese." At the end of a case, he uses judo on the murderer and grudgingly admits that it is the only thing he ever learned from the Japanese.

He has learned a great deal from others, however. A student of the English language, he also speaks Cantonese. Learned in Chinese philosophy, he is proud of his heritage and willingly dispenses his knowledge. He uses the abstract concept of ambition to distinguish a major difference between the Chinese and Caucasians (against whom he has no prejudice):

"Coarse food to eat, water to drink, and the bended arm for a pillow—that is an old definition of happiness in my country," says Chan. "What is ambition? A cancer that eats at the heart of the white man, denying him the joys of contentment. I fear I am victim of crude philosophy from Orient. Man—what is he? Merely one link in a great chain binding the past with the future. All times I remember I am one link. Unsignificant link joining those ancestors whose bones repose on a far distant hillside with the 10 children—it may now be 11—in my house on Punchbowl Hill . . . so, waiting the end, I do my duty as it rises. I tread the path that opens."

Chan feels that the success he enjoys in his career is based on "luck—always happy luck."

That assessment is, of course, far too modest. Chan does admit to being modest. "Falling hurts least those who fly low," he says. Sir Frederic concurs, saying, "And Sgt. Chan flies so low he skins the daisies."

Although that modesty may seem virtuous, it fails to explain accurately Chan's true methods of fighting crime, which have less to do with luck than with intelligence, attention to detail, and a profound understanding of human nature.

"Fingerprints and other mechanics good in books," Chan explains. "In real life not so much so. My experience tell me to think deep about human people. Human passions. Back of murder what, always? Hate, revenge, need to make silent the slain one. Greed for money, maybe. Study human people at all times."

He does not ignore physical clues, however. At the beginning of his first published case, Chan takes copious notes (possibly in shorthand) in a notebook. When the Chinese detective's superior prepares to question a witness, Chan's pencil is poised, always ready to add bits of information to his file. He describes the search for clues unpretentiously. "We grope about," he says.

When Charlie Chan gropes about, it is an amusing sight. His great bulk makes virtually any type of movement a major enterprise, although he does manage to pull it off with a certain grace. When Chan makes his entrance in *The House Without a Key*, he causes some astonished glances.

> In those warm islands, thin men were the rule, but here was a striking exception. He was very fat indeed, yet he walked with the light dainty steps of a woman. His cheeks were as chubby as a baby's, his skin ivory-tinted, his black hair close-cropped, his amber eyes slanting.

When Chan kneels to search for a clue, he is described as "a grotesque figure" who has to rise "laboriously" to his feet. When he takes a respite from the pressures of a case, he goes to the beach, presenting an enormous figure floating languidly on the water. "Little pleasant recreation," he explains. "Forget detective worries out here floating idle like leaf on stream."

In later cases, he has apparently lost weight, being described merely as "plump."

When dressed (always in western clothes, except when he is at home), Chan is entirely undistinguished, resembling every other overweight man on the island. Next to his huge stomach, his most impressive feature is his eyes.

His small, slanted eyes have the look of keen brightness that makes "the pupils gleam like black buttons in yellow light." His eyes are also the most expressive part of his face. They often "blink with pleasure," "sparkle" with amusement, shine from "some inner excitement," and widen with surprise or delight.

When he is especially pleased, his face breaks into a huge grin. Unlike the actors who have portrayed him in motion pictures, Chan wears no moustache and carefully shaves every vestige of black stubble from his cheeks.

Chan's enormous girth was not hereditary. He likes to eat, though he is generally not fond of western cooking. He enjoys drinking great quantities of tea, his favorite beverage.

In an American restaurant, he invites a visitor to join him and accept "some of this terrible provision." The coffee he calls "unspeakable" but politely offers his companion some, then grabs the check, saying, "No—pardon me—the honor of paying for this poison-tasting beverage must be mine."

Chan tries always to be polite but, he says, at times "police affairs forbid utmost courtesy."

Still, Chan is generally courteous, saying "please" and "thank you" and bowing deeply from the waist, even as he prepares to put handcuffs on a suspect. Gentle, kind and humble, he is liked by all who know him, and he is never more charming than when he "distills the wisdom of the ages" in a new and captivating epigram.

Charlie Chan's last recorded case, *Keeper of the Keys,* ends with one of his most enduring and endearing statements: "Three things the wise man does not do," he counsels. "He does not plow the sky. He does not paint pictures on the water. And he does not argue with a woman."

Thomas Godfrey (essay date 1989)

SOURCE: "Charlie Chan for Rent," in *The Armchair Detective,* Vol. 22, No. 4, Fall, 1989, pp. 359-64.

[*In the following essay, Godfrey surveys the numerous films featuring Charlie Chan.*]

> As they went out, the third man stepped farther into the room, and Miss Minerva gave a little gasp of astonishment as she looked at him. In those warm islands, thin men were the rule, but here was a striking exception. He was very fat indeed, yet he walked with the light dainty step of a woman. His cheeks were chubby as a baby's, his skin ivory tinted, his black hair close-cropped, his amber eyes slanting. As he passed Miss Minerva he bowed with a courtesy encountered all too rarely in a work-a-day world, then moved on after Hallett.
>
> "Amos," cried Miss Minerva. "That man—why he—"
>
> "Charlie Chan," Amos explained. . . . "The best detective on the force."

And so one of the most popular detectives of all time entered public consciousness and began his celebrated multimedia career. The year is 1925, the book, *The House Without a Key,* the first of six to be written by Earl Derr Biggers (1885-1933), an Ohio-born journalist and Boston-based drama critic, recently transplanted to New York.

This was not Biggers's first literary success. He had produced *Seven Keys to Baldpate* (1904) which had been turned into a Broadway success for entertainer George M. Cohan. A later book, *The Agony Column,* had placed him firmly in the mystery-suspense genre and provided him with the financial wherewithal to move to Pasadena, California, then a paradise of orange blossoms and pitasporin trees at the edge of the desert.

It was during his residency here in 1919 that he decided to take a trip to Hawaii, where he became enchanted by the then unspoiled charms of Honolulu. During this vacation, he kept abreast of police cases in the local paper and particularly the work of two native police officers, Chang Apana and Lee Fook.

With an agreement in hand for the serialization of his next novel in the *Saturday Evening Post,* he returned home and began a tale of a murder set in Honolulu. Biggers was an acute and astute observer of popular tastes. True to the convention of the time, a young couple was at the center of the plot, caught up in the investigation. Chan does not appear until the seventh chapter and then stays very much in the background as the young male visitor from Boston, who is learning about love (*circa* 1920), takes a central role in the investigation under his paternal guidance. The book moves leisurely but certainly. By modern standards, it is bland entertainment, but it was a considerable success for the *Post* and for Bobbs-Merrill, who rushed it into print. Chan quickly emerged as a popular fictional character, not surprisingly in this time of Mah Jong and chinoiserie. Biggers was immediately set to work on another work, *The Chinese Parrot,* which appeared the following year.

Pathé, the French-based film company operating in the U.S., gobbled up the film rights to *The House Without a Key,* which they made into a silent serial with Japanese-born actor George K. Kuwa as Chan, who appears late in the film, and, as in the book, creates a backdrop for romance amid the murder. It was a small role, but it was a start. A rival studio, Universal, won the bidding for the rights to the second book, which they filmed, again as a silent, in 1927, with Kamiyama Sojin, another actor of Japanese ancestry, as Chan. He was more important to the overall mystery but still supported the central romance, which served as a vehicle for two of the studio's contractees.

Behind That Curtain was the next Chan from Biggers's pen, and Fox Studios bought it immediately and filmed it with dialogue, using English actor E. L. Park as Chan. In stills, Park looks more like Erich von Stroheim than anything Biggers devised. The restructured plot was intended as a showcase for Warner Baxter, the popular actor who would soon win an Academy Award for his starring role in *The Cisco Kid.* Park was billed last and came on late. Interestingly, Boris Karloff was cast as a servant. Nobody was yet thinking of a series.

That did not occur until 1931, then Fox suddenly woke up to the realization that it had a hot property on its hands as it began work on *Charlie Chan Carries On.* It searched for a bigger name than Park's to portray the Hawaiian detective and settled on Warner Oland (1879-1938), a Swedish-born actor who had appeared on screen as an Oriental convincingly enough to impress the casting people. Oland was moved up to third billing, and the romance was pared down to support the mystery.

More than any other actor who portrayed Chan, Oland fit the description and temperament of Biggers's creation. The public response to him was enthusiastic. Fox bought up the rights to the earlier books and refilmed them with Oland now top-billed as Chan. When they had run through the books (Biggers died of a heart attack in 1933 after completing six), original plots were commissioned which eventually took Chan to Egypt, Shanghai, Paris, London, Monte Carlo, and the Berlin Olympics.

Oland took the role to heart and spoke of himself in Chanese as Chan. In 1935, he made a personal appearance tour of China, where he was reportedly well received.

In *Charlie Chan in Paris,* the first of the original stories, film adapter and mystery writer Philip Macdonald came up with a son-assistant for Charlie. The first was to be Keye Luke, a Cantonese-born artist and technical adviser at the studio on Chinese settings. He had some experience before the camera in small parts. Lee Chan was a variation on the young amateur detectives Chan had supported in the early books. Although young and enthusiastic, he was also thoughtful and respectful. Later, as the series progressed, the Chan sons would become more doltish.

Oland was, by many accounts, a heavy drinker whose health was fast deteriorating. While he was encouraged to stop drinking by the Fox production people, some of his directors felt that he gave a better performance with a few drinks in him. What seems to be methodical and purposeful deduction was often Oland groping for his lines under the influence of alcohol.

In 1937, the studio merged with Twentieth Century, and the Chans were assigned to the B-unit. Production values, writing, and acting noticeably deteriorated. Oland was failing badly. His marriage had crumbled. His concentration was shot. His characterization was now too soft and slow. In the midst of filming *Charlie Chan at Ringside,* he began to disappear for several days at a time. The studio put him on suspension. Weeks later, police found him wandering the streets of Los Angeles, confused and disheveled. Fox finally woke up to how serious his problem had become. Oland was hospitalized and dried out. A reconciliation was effected with his wife. Shooting was rescheduled.

It was too late. While vacationing in Europe, he developed pneumonia and died.

Ringside was rewritten to accommodate Fox's other series detective, Peter Lorre's Mr. Moto, and released as *Mr. Moto's Gamble* late in 1938. Keye Luke was kept in as Lee Chan. It was a strange hybrid.

The studio lost no time shopping around for a new Chan. At one time, J. Edward Bromberg, who had figured in *Charlie Chan on Broadway,* was expected to take over. Instead, they chose Missouri-born Sidney Toler (1874-1947), a character actor with a string of solid but minor credits. Wisely, some attempt was made to pick up the pace of the plots.

The refurbished series led off, rather successfully, with *Charlie Chan in Honolulu* (1939). Luke had declined to return without Oland. The now obligatory role of son-assistant was assigned to Victor Sen-Yung (a.k.a. Sen Yung), a chemical salesman who had wandered into films on a lark.

Oland had been so firmly identified with the part that many feared Toler would flop. In fact, he performs well in these earliest films, less honeyed and serene than Oland, but efficient and enthusiastic, and, judged by a rereading of Biggers's first novels, equally plausible. Unfortunately, Sen-Yung, who would appear in eighteen of the films, was more clearly juvenile comic relief than Luke had been. Yet, given this handicap, he was enjoyable.

World War II changed things. Popular tastes were running to Nazi spy thrillers and Mrs. Miniver. Twentieth Century-Fox cancelled the Moto series because of political happenings in the Pacific. Chan seemed likely to follow. The final scripts had become formula work and the sets hand-me-downs from other productions. Critics began seriously complaining of Toler's "wooden performances." After a cancellation and reprieve, Fox dropped Charlie Chan.

But moviegoers were not deprived of the Oriental detective. Executives at Monogram Studios, the king of the Poverty Row operations, picked it up. Monogram made no secret that budget was all-important. They re-used scripts with minimal rewriting. Their costume department seemed to come off the rack at Woolworth's. The distribution system was tightly wound and aimed at rural, unso-

phisticated audiences. There was a big difference between a "B" production at Fox and even something "big" at Monogram. Several film historians have contended that Monogram was incapable of making anything decent. It is hard to find an example to refute that claim.

As Toler had departed Fox with a guarantee that he would return if the series were revived, Monogram Studios brought him back, giving him new Number Three Son, Benson Fong, later a successful restaurateur. Fong was agreeable, if slow; the most Americanized of Chan's screen sons. (There had been one or two appearances by other offspring, including two actresses as Number One Daughter.)

Monogram also added black comedian Mantan Moreland as Chan's chauffeur, Birmingham Brown. In fairness to Moreland, who had an excellent knack for physical comedy, he should not be held responsible for the racially degrading, low-brow, feets-do-your-duty, fraidy-cat material he was handed by his writers. It had appeal then in the South where a large part of Monogram's audience was concentrated, but today it is liable to produce more squirms than laughs.

The Monogram quickies were cheap in every sense of the word. The sets looked like cardboard. The scripts were short and swift, filled with wild schemes and fantastic murder devices. The supporting actors often performed as if they had learned their craft from a correspondence school course. But these films were popular enough to keep the series going for another seven years. Toler, allegedly another heavy drinker who honed his characterization on a bottle, became slower and more expressionless as the series progressed. By *The Trap* (1946), he was shuffling through the part with no discernable vitality at all. Even given Monogram's failings, this last film was a painful documentation of the series's decline. Within a year, he was dead, but Charlie Chan carried on.

Bad as they had become, the Chan films were Monogram's biggest moneymaker and the studio was struggling for survival. With rising costs of production and the threat of television on the horizon, Monogram was finding that no matter how cheaply it made them, it just could not make films cheaply enough. Audience tastes had been sophisticated by wartime experiences, and the crudeness of these Poverty Row offerings appealed to fewer and fewer moviegoers.

A replacement for Toler was an urgent necessity, and they wasted no time in coming up with Roland Winters (1904-1985), a Boston-born journeyman stage actor from New York. It was a remarkable choice. He did not look Chinese at all. He did not even try. He would look straight into the camera and squint, and that was his Chinese characterization. But he was lively, the youngest Chan to date, and he was available. Monogram could not afford to wait.

He was rushed into a remake of *Mr. Wong in Chinatown* from the studio's pre-war ersatz-Chan series with Boris Karloff. Those films had been extremely crude, but Monogram's desperate executives saw no reason not to retread the scripts for the new Winters films. *The Chinese Ring* (1946) was shot with as few changes as possible. The sets were the same. Even the lines were the same. Sen-Yung, who returned, was given some of the girl reporter's speeches. What had looked far-fetched and crude in the earlier film was no better in this one, but Monogram did not seem to care.

Where Toler had been blunt, Winters was brusque. The beloved Charlie Chan epithets that Warner Oland had emoted with such globular flair were reduced to a dismissive "So much for so much."

When Monogram finished looting the Wong scripts, it started in on some old Westerns. *The Shanghai Chest* (1948), the third and perhaps best (or least dreadful) of the Winters half dozen, came from such a source. So did the increasingly dire *Mystery of the Golden Eye* (1948) and *Feathered Serpent* (1948), which followed. Keye Luke was brought back to join Sen-Yung for *Serpent* and stayed on alone in support for *Sky Dragon* (1949), the last film made on the Monogram lot. Ironically this film, from an original story line, was carried by a list of competent supporting actors: Elena Verdugo, Noel Neill, Milburn Stone, and Lyle Talbot were all headed into television in the next decade, where Winters himself turned up supporting Verdugo in the CBS sitcom *Meet Millie.*

It was finally television that put Monogram out of its misery.

And yet these films should not be completely dismissed. They were among the first features sold to television, where I initially ran into them in the mid-'50s. I particularly recall *The Scarlet Clue* with Toler (1944), set in a radio station, which featured an ingenious, if far-fetched, method of disposing of victims. I could not walk into an elevator for a month afterward. Forced to do so, I ran to the back and clutched the railing for dear life.

Moreland and Benson Fong were pure comic relief. Viewed without prejudice, their humor looked silly but harmless. It wasn't racial, it was just clowning. One was black, the other Oriental. They weren't types, they were just funny individuals. Viewed today, these films can still be seen as unsophisticated introductory detective fiction for children, though even a child will discern that the Fox stuff is better.

Chan's career continued on radio, where he was played by a number of actors, most notably Academy Award winner Ed Begley. Then, in 1958, he turned up on television as the hero of a half-hour television series, *The New Adventures of Charlie Chan.* J. Carrol Naish, a well-accomplished character actor with an impressive list of film credits, played Chan. James Hong played Number One Son Barry Chan, again mostly for comic relief.

Naish made a serious attempt at playing the celebrated detective, a marked improvement over Winters, whose portrayal had the aura of a party prank without the warmth. Naish was most effective being malicious, and a certain hardness stubbornly clings to his Charlie Chan.

But the finishing stroke was delivered by the scripts, which were unimaginative even by the television standards of the time. There was too little mystery, compounded by set-

tings that were often bare and dull. The series was not renewed.

By the '60s, Charlie Chan was in eclipse. The books were out of print and the films lay largely unavailable. Charges of racial stereotyping were raised in earnest, and in anger, about the characters. Asian-American activists found offense in the chop-suey dialogue and pseudo-chinoiserie.

In 1968, the Museum of Modern Art in New York held a retrospective of the Chan films that was startlingly successful. Universal began making a TV film called *Happiness is a Warm Clue* (originally titled *The Return of Charlie Chan*), but it waited nine years for American exposure. It was not racially offensive, just weak. Ross Martin, the versatile actor who had played Robert Conrad's partner on TV's *Wild, Wild West,* appeared as Chan in this mystery about a wealthy Greek tycoon. There were several offspring, but no revival.

Charlie Chan and the Curse of the Dragon Queen showed up in theaters in 1981, holding out the promise of Peter Ustinov as Chan. San Francisco activists were vehement in their protests, disrupting the filming, then picketing the openings. They denounced the racial misrepresentations and demanded a Chinese-American actor be given the chance to play Chan. They probably felt vindicated when they saw the results. The script was amateurish, the direction jokey, and the acting an embarrassment. *Curse* was a miserable dud. Ustinov seemed unstirred by the challenge of Chan, offering a weak variant of his Poirot. His Number One Grandson was ineffectually played by Richard Hatch, late of the TV series *The Streets of San Francisco.* His Chinese ancestry was one of the script's jokes, but no one was laughing. Audiences stayed away in droves.

Early in 1989, Key Video, the archive branch of CBS/Fox, announced their intentions to release some of the Fox Chan films. Again Chinese-American protests were heard. But Fox went ahead. The result was the Charlie Chan Collection, a selection of seven films with both Oland and Toler marketed in the same fashion as the Rathbone/Holmes series of the previous year. Each is packaged in a colorful slip-case with a foldout cover that details the mystery and outlines the suspects.

For a new generation of mystery buffs, these cassettes offer a first exposure to one of the legends of detective fiction. Five of the six novels had once appeared in a bargain omnibus edition which is now out of print. The Mysterious Press has reprinted all six titles in paperback, but a check of local outlets in the Los Angeles area finds them all but unavailable except at a few mystery bookshops, perhaps a fault of the distributor, or of the book buyers themselves.

This collection is not the first release of the Chan films on videocassette. The Winters films and some of Toler's Monogram series were briefly available from Allied Artists before its bankruptcy six years ago. These were among the first videocassettes on the market, and they disappeared before VCRs caught on as home entertainment. One of the Toler Monogram pictures, *Black Magic,* remains available on a number of the bargain video lines, as *Meeting at Midnight,* the retitling required to distinguish it from Orson Welles's 1949 foreign-made *Black Magic* about the magician Cagliostro. When the Welles film slipped into the public domain, bargain videotape manufacturers confused it with the Chan film and released it in error. The other films are still protected by copyright.

Coincidentally, another video firm, King Bee, has released several compilations of the Naish Chan television shows on cassette. You can now hold a Charlie Chan mini-retrospective in your own living room.

Sandra M. Hawley   (essay date 1991)

SOURCE: "The Importance of Being Charlie Chan," in *America Views China: American Images of China Then and Now,* Jonathan Goldstein, Jerry Israel, Hilary Conroy, eds., Lehigh University Press, 1991, pp. 132-47.

[*In the following essay, Hawley addresses Chinese stereotypes in American literature and how Biggers's character Charlie Chan figures into their history.*]

In searching for the sources of American ideas about China and the Chinese, one of the important places to look is the mystery fiction of Earl Derr Biggers, starring Charlie Chan—detective extraordinaire, Honolulu resident, half-mocked, half-mocking descendant of Confucius.

Charlie Chan's durability and widespread popularity are unrivaled by other fictional Orientals. Although only six books featuring the Hawaiian-based detective were published from 1925 to 1932 (Biggers died in 1933), Charlie Chan's renown equals that of fictional detectives like Hercule Poirot and Nero Wolfe. The charlie Chan books were all serialized in *The Saturday Evening Post,* published in hardcover editions, and reissued in paperback in 1974-75. In addition, Charlie Chan was featured in a comic strip, a radio show, a Broadway play, and some forty-nine full-length films. Students of American popular culture have called him "a national institution" and "very much a part of American folklore" [Russell Nye, *The Unembarrassed Muse* and Harold R. Isaacs, *Images of Asia*]. This popularity and longevity indicate that the Chinese detective touched a chord in the American public. Half a century is a good run for any character.

More important than longevity is his effect on images of the Chinese in American fiction. The appearance of Charlie Chan was a turning point in American portraits of and attitudes toward the Chinese people, a perceptible shift in American stereotypes of the Chinese. The older "heathen Chinee" began to yield to a new, more favorable version of the Chinese: a portrait just as stereotyped and racist, but much more human and appealing. Charlie Chan was the key figure in this transformation: he embodied concepts that became widespread and influential.

Images and perceptions of other people and other cultures reach the American public in a variety of ways: scholarly studies, travelogues, news articles, films, fiction, and most recently television. From this flow of information, accurate and otherwise, people tend to select the images that best suit their own needs as well as their own understanding. In many instances—particularly in the case of modern European nations—the amount of information is so vast that enormous selectivity is required, and an image

to fit every preconception can be developed. In many ways, the process of image formation follows what might be called a "percolator" process; ideas generated by specialists trickle down into the popular culture, often after being distilled through several filtering layers of high-school and college textbooks and classes.

In the case of China, however, this "percolator" mechanism tended to break down at the upper levels because of a limited flow of information; fictional images became much more important and influential. In American folklore and popular culture, China was long considered "inscrutable"; images of China have been wildly varied, almost schizophrenic in their content, in large part because of the extremely restricted flow of information through formal channels.

Given the lack of information generally available, Americans formed their ideas and images of Asia from any sources they could find, and in large part from the kaleidoscope of images available in fiction and film. The process of creating such images involved considerable feedback. Images too far out of line with what people believed or were willing to accept would not succeed. Thus anyone creating fictional characters had either to adopt prevailing stereotypes or to select a new image that was acceptable even if not widely used.

The popularity of Oriental characters in fiction during this period was probably to some degree the result of this desire for information about the mysterious East. *The Saturday Evening Post,* the most popular and widely read magazine of the period and the site of Charlie Chan's debut, responded to the demand for and appeal of stories with an Asian flavor. From 1920 to 1941 the *Post* published a short story with an Asian cast or setting at the rate of one every other month. The magazine serialized twenty-one novels with Asian characters or locale, approximately one a year. Only the perennial American favorite, the western, appeared with greater frequency and consistency.

In the 1920s, the dominant stereotype of the Chinese was a variation of the traditional "heathen Chinee" theme. Readers apparently still enjoyed a delicious thrill of horror at the idea of the truly diabolical Chinaman. Atrocities, mayhem, torture, and sadism were usually the result of the "warped" Oriental mind and culture and set the tone for these stories. In one *Post,* a Chinese merchant tried to smuggle a lovely young girl into the country as his bride. When his partner's wife betrayed the girl to immigration authorities, the merchant took his vengeance by pouring molten gold down the woman's throat. In another story, published in 1924, one Chinese family had already strangled three new-born daughters. When the wife of the eldest son gave birth to yet another useless girl, the youth strangled the baby and attempted to kill the wife guilty of bearing a girl. One of the most spectacularly villainous Chinese who appeared in the *Post* was Li Chang. He sought to avenge his father's death in a blaze of filial piety. Discovering that the entire crew of a ship was responsible for his father's death, Li Chang concocted a truly fiery revenge. First, he managed through devious and unscrupulous Oriental methods to infest the crew with lice. Then, playing the innocent and helpful friend, he gave the crew gasoline with which to douse and delouse themselves. When he was sure that ship and crew were thoroughly soaked, Li Chang set fire to them, eliminating lice, ship, and crew in a spectacular blaze.

The most thoroughly diabolical of Charlie Chan's predecessors was Fu Manchu, the brilliant but mad scientist and archvillain. Like Charlie Chan, Fu Manchu appealed to the American imagination: his literary life spanned thirty-five years, from the first Fu Manchu thriller in 1913 to the fortieth and last in 1948. Fu Manchu movies began appearing in 1929 and have been made as recently as 1981, while the Fu Manchu mustache became part of both folklore and football. Paperback reissues of the Fu Manchu novels appeared in 1984.

As a villain in popular fiction, Fu Manchu had no peer in malevolence or malignancy until James Bond began encountering some of his more bizarre foes. The Chinese scientist was tall, gaunt, with cat-green hypnotic eyes. He could read minds and control the aging process to the point that he enjoyed near-immortality. Opium addiction was almost his only human trait. Even his daughter, the irresistibly lovely Fah Lo Suee, was merely an adjunct to his schemes and was eventually consigned to a furnace in which Fu Manchu was casting gold according to an ancient Oriental formula.

However awesome Fu Manchu was in and of himself, he was even more terrifying because of the power he both wielded and represented. He was the leader of the Council of Seven, the dreaded and deadly Si Fan, which sought to rule the world in the name of the yellow race. Death by rare disease, mysterious poison, loathsome insect, or other vile means awaited the luckless soul who attempted to thwart Si Fan. I hold the key which unlocks the heart of the secret East, exulted Fu Manchu. "Holding that key, I command the obedience of an army greater than any ever controlled by one man. My power rests in the East, but my hand is stretched out to the West. I shall control the lost grandeur of China." In his campaign to vanquish the white race and rule the world for the Orient, Fu Manchu could call upon a spectacular assortment of traditional and exotic creatures of horror. Dacoits and other murder cults of Asia did his bidding, as did African zombies and a menagerie of ferocious and cunning beasts. In many ways, Fu Manchu was the embodiment of a white racist's nightmare.

Despite the dominance of this stereotype, there were some alterations in the image of unalloyed evil and malevolence even before the appearance of Charlie Chan. In 1922, *The Saturday Evening Post* published a short story, "Scout Wong," which presaged the coming shift of images. Young Wong, a resident of Chinatown, sees an American Boy Scout troop drilling and, enthralled by the spectacle, resolves to become a Scout himself. When he approaches the troop, the white Scouts mock him, calling him "Yellow Belly" and assuring him that no such inferior person could ever hope to become a Boy Scout. Undaunted, Wong discovers a discarded copy of the *Boy Scout Handbook* and teaches himself the code and rules. The climax of the story occurs as the Scout troop is dining in the banquet hall of the restaurant in which Wong works. Flames

sweep up through an open air duct and threaten to trap the Scouts, but Wong blocks the opening of the duct with his "yellow belly" and permits the troop to escape. He thus becomes simultaneously a hero and a Boy Scout. The tone of "Scout Wong" is patronizing, but Wong does save the white Scouts. Most of his predecessors would rather have shoved them down the air duct directly into the flames.

The American reading public was thus somewhat prepared for the debut of Charlie Chan in *The House Without a Key*, serialized in the *Post* and then published in book form in 1925. Earl Derr Biggers based his fictional detective on an actual Chinese member of the Honolulu police force, one Chang Apana. Biggers was probably also responding to an American willingness to tolerate a more sympathetic portrayal of the Chinese. The Charlie Chan films were in fact deliberately designed to refute or at least challenge the Fu Manchu image, according to their original producer.

Physically Charlie Chan was a great deal less prepossessing than Fu Manchu, and probably therefore a great deal easier to accept as a nonvillain. "He was very fat indeed, yet he walked with the light dainty step of a woman. His cheeks were as chubby as a baby's, his skin ivory-tinted, his black hair close-cropped, his amber eyes slanting." Not only unprepossessing, but downright disarming, Charlie Chan was "an undistinguished figure in his Western clothes." The expression in his eyes was "a look of keen brightness that made the pupils gleam like black buttons in the yellow light." Size and the suggestion of softness were important in the description of Charlie Chan. Earl Derr Biggers deliberately eschewed the traditional lean and hungry look for detectives to present his Oriental hero as a portly if graceful figure. The heavy-set individual is by tradition kindly, jolly, friendly, neither a threat nor a menace. Chan's size also enables the author to emphasize other characteristics commonly attributed to Asians, especially impassivity and stoicism. After all, who ever heard of a *fat* detective with the bursting nervous energy of a Holmes? In addition, his size also made Chan the ideal candidate for comparison with the Buddha, a relatively harmless touch of Orientalia. At various times Charlie Chan is described as a plain Buddha, an impassive Buddha, a serene Buddha, as immobile as a stone Buddha, and, with magnificent disregard for historical accuracy a grim and relentless Buddha.

The pleasingly plump detective's English is rather peculiar, a mixture of adroitly-used polysyllables and mangled syntax, several steps above pidgin but still exotic. A typical statement might be: "That are wrong attitude completely. Detective business made up of insignificant trifles." One verb is missing completely, the other the wrong number and person, yet the vocabulary is accurate! In Chan's dialect there is an element of condescension as well as the need to portray Charlie Chan as unusual and Oriental. Biggers carefully points out that Charlie Chan's English is different from and better than that of most other Chinese, just as Chan himself is superior to many of the Chinese portrayed in the novels. When Charlie Chan must play the role of a servant to solve a crime, he reluctantly but ostentatiously adopts a vulgar pidgin: "Maybe you wantee catch 'um moah fish, boss?" He bemoans the necessity of doing this: "All my life I study to speak fine English words. Now must strangle all such in my throat, lest suspicion rouse up. Not a happy situation for me." To sharpen the language distinctions, Chan's wife speaks broken pidgin, while his children show off their Western-style slang, often to his disgust. However, the gum-chewing, wise-cracking Number One and Number Two Sons of the movies do not appear in any of the novels.

Biographical information on Charlie Chan is scant. He is almost totally a creature of the Hawaiian and American present, with little of the Chinese past about him. He was born in China, apparently in a small village, and lived in a "thatched hut by side of muddy river." At an unspecified age he migrated from China to Hawaii, where he worked as a house-boy for a rich white family before joining the Honolulu police force. Of his personal life we know equally little; he has a wife, whose name is never mentioned, and by the midpoint of the third book eleven children, eight of them sons. "Good luck dogs me in such matters," he modestly says; "of eleven opportunities, I am disappointed but three times." Beyond this, there is no attempt to show family life in the novels, no portrait of Charlie Chan as the Chinese patriarch. The family provides a convenient prop, an occasional reminder of Charlie Chan's Chineseness, and a touch of humanity. The number of children seems less a sign of any particular sexual prowess than a shadow of the idea of the prolific Chinese hordes and perhaps even the fear prevalent in the United States in the twenties that Orientals would take over the world simply through outbreeding the whites.

There is little of China itself in any of the books. Other than casual discussions in which his early life history unfolds, Chan mentions China only twice. At one point, trying to persuade an aged servant to give evidence so that he can "see again the village where you were born—walk again the soil where your bones are to rest," he speaks fondly but briefly of China. At another point, recalling the peaceful land of his youth (which would make him over a hundred years old if Biggers adhered strictly to Chinese history), Charlie Chan remarks: "China is sick now. But as some one has so well said, many of those who send sympathy to the sick man die before him. That has happened in China's past—it will happen again." Far removed from China itself, Charlie Chan can be Chinese without being overpoweringly alien.

A somewhat warped element of Chinese culture is present in Charlie Chan's frequent resort to proverbs. Although the "Confucius says" tag of the movies is mercifully absent in the books, and Confucius himself is mentioned only three times in total, counterfeit proverbs abound. "As all those who know me have learned to their distress, Chinese have proverbs to fit every possible situation," Chan rather deprecatingly remarks. There is no attempt to present or explore Confucian philosophy or Chinese culture beyond the counterfeit proverbs. In some ways Charlie Chan's being Chinese seems little more than a convenient if somewhat exotic gimmick. Superficially Charlie Chan

may appear Chinese, but he is fundamentally stripped of any genuine Chinese culture.

The reader remains highly conscious, however, of the fact that Charlie Chan is Chinese. There are frequent references to the detective's being typical of what is expected of the Chinese, whether it be psychic powers, inscrutability, or diligence. At several points, Biggers takes care to present Chan in a mild, almost gift-shop Chinese setting. For example, the Chan family home on Punchbowl Hill is furnished with Chinese objects: carved teakwood tables, elegant porcelain vases, crimson and gold Chinese lanterns, silk paintings, and a dwarf tree. In this setting Chan greets his visitor, wearing a long scholar's robe, trousers, and felt slippers; he is "all Oriental now, suave and ingratiating but somewhat remote." However, this is the only time the detective appears in traditional Chinese costume and he is seen in his own home only twice. Otherwise his dress and milieu are Western.

Bits of Chinese and quasi-Chinese philosophy worked into the books are often presented as antithetical to, and better than, Western ideas and values. One consistently recurring theme is the virtue of patience and the idea that the Chinese more than any other race, especially the American race, recognize and esteem the virtue of patience. In a typical situation, an American girl urges Charlie Chan to move quickly to close a case. He demurs: "Patience . . . always brightest plan in these matters. Acting as champion of that lovely virtue, I have fought many fierce battles. American has always the urge to leap too quick. How well it was said, retire a step and you have the advantage." According to Chan, this attitude toward patience springs from a deeper Chinese philosophy about life and man's place in the universe:

> "Chinese knows he is one minute grain of sand on seashore of eternity. With what result? He is calm and quiet and humble. No nerves, like hopping, skipping Caucasian. Life for him not so much ordeal."

Charlie Chan also expresses a complimentary "Chinese" view of life: "Coarse food to eat, water to drink, and the bended arm for a pillow—that is an old definition of happiness in my country." It is, in fact, a statement made by Yen Hui, Confucius's disciple. The westerner's ambition and impatience have no place in the real scheme of things: "Man—what is he? Merely one link in a great chain binding the past with the future. All times I remember I am link. Unsignificant link joining those ancestors whose bones repose on far distant hillsides with the ten children—it may now be eleven—in my house on Punchbowl Hill."

Biggers tended to use such comments less as statements in their own right or as expositions of Chinese philosophy—to which they are only tenuously related—than as foils for contrast to the usually less worthy Western customs and ideas. Sometimes, Chinese and American culture are directly compared—by Americans—and Chinese culture is usually judged superior. For instance, a very proper lady and former Bostonian comments, with no more than the expected amount of condescension: "The Chinese are my favorite race. The Chinese are the aristocrats of the East. So clever and competent and honest, carrying on among the lazy riff-raff of the Orient. A grand people, Mr. Chan." Biggers doesn't let this opportunity pass. Chan replies: "Appreciation such as yours makes music to my ears. We are not highly valued in the United States, where we are appraised as laundrymen, or maybe villains in the literature of talkative films. You have great country, rich and proud, and sure of itself. About rest of world it knows little, and cares extremely less." This awareness of two different worlds is very much present in all six of the Charlie Chan books and betrays Chan into his only expression of arrogance, personal or cultural, as he greets a young and rather haughty New Englander: "Mere words cannot express my unlimited delight at meeting a representative of the ancient civilization of Boston."

Tied in with but not always directed at Charlie Chan are comments on the basic characteristics of the Chinese people. Some are banal, some condescending and some outright racist. For example, the reader is told that Chinese are night-owls, at their best after the sun sets. Chinese are also assumed to be particularly suited to be detectives. A Scotland Yard man praises Chan for unraveling an especially intricate mystery: "Sergeant, my hearty congratulations. But I know your people, and I am not surprised." In another situation, after Charlie Chan has again solved an enticing mystery, his superior pats him on the back—literally—and remarks, "A great idea, Charlie. . . . The Oriental mind . . . Rather subtle, isn't it?"

Biggers' racially tinged comments are few and mild considering American racist attitudes during the 1920s; he seems deliberately to act as a missionary for a more enlightened view of other races. When open racial prejudice does occur, it is put down immediately, and with such finality that Biggers is obviously using it as a set-piece situation. Furthermore, racial prejudice is generally the property of the more unsavory characters in the books, either the villains or the uncouth and uneducated. For example, a generally boorish Englishman, and a murderer to boot, berates his Chinese cook for exhibiting "all the worst qualities of a heathen race." Charlie responds, "A heathen race that was busy inventing the art of printing when gentlemen in Great Britain were still beating one another over head with spiked clubs." In fact, virtually the only times Charlie Chan expresses anger occur when racial slurs of this sort are expressed. Yet another supercilious Englishman, seeing the Chinese detective arrive to investigate a murder, exclaims, "Good Lord! What kind of place is this? Why don't they send a white man out here?" At this, "a rare light flared suddenly in Charlie's eyes" and he replied "in icy tones" that "the man who is about to cross a stream should not revile the crocodile's mother." Despite the somewhat Delphic quality of the instant proverb, it is clear that neither author nor character regard race as a hinderance to intelligence.

Hawaii, the setting for the first novel and for Chan's permanent home, was simultaneously remote and friendly, exotic and familiar, Asian and Western—an ideal locale for a westernized Chinese detective. The Hawaii of Earl Derr Biggers and Charlie Chan is somehow dangerous to

traditional European values, a place in which the white man must work consciously and strenuously to maintain traditional morality. It enjoys the "semi-barbaric beauty of a Pacific island" and is "too lurid to be quite respectable." Hawaii is "too sweet" according to one Bostonian who spent thirty years in the islands, "a little too much like Heaven to be altogether safe."

But this essentially alien, deceptively dangerous quality makes Hawaii the ideal setting for Charlie Chan. Like the islands, he is basically different, alien, perhaps even dangerous, but like the islands he is so pleasant that he cannot be seen as a threat. The islands are the crossroads of the Pacific, where Asian and European races, customs, and cultures meet, compete, and mingle. Charlie Chan is likewise a mixture of cultures, ideas, and values. As Hawaii is neither completely Oriental nor completely American, so too Charlie Chan is caught between the two cultures and tries to find his way through them. He is deeply troubled about becoming too American. The difficulty of remaining Chinese in a non-Chinese and pervasively American setting such as Hawaii is particularly vivid to Chan as he looks at the younger generation of his family, either his younger cousin or his own children. When he uses a particularly reprehensible bit of slang, he apologizes: "Pardon vile slang, which I acquire from my children, now being beautifully educated in American schools." Charlie Chan is both pleased and embarrassed by his cousin Willie Chan who was "attired in the extreme of college-cut clothes [and who] was an American and emphasized the fact." Willie Chan is one of the chief suppliers of slang in Charlie Chan's life and also "captain All Chinese baseball team and demon back-stopper of the Pacific." His customary greeting is a breezy "pleased to meetchu."

There is considerable ambivalence in Charlie Chan's attitude toward the Americanization of younger Chinese. He is pleased that his eleventh child will have American citizenship; "An American citizen, a future boy scout under the American flag, he should have an American name." Charlie Chan's full Chinese name is never mentioned. Yet the Americanization of his older children is a source of perplexity and even annoyance. The oldest are depicted as problems. Henry, smoking cigarettes, wearing college-cut clothes, using slang, "had been Americanized to a rather painful extent." Rose has deviated so far from Chinese tradition that she openly questions her father's judgment. Making the final transition between China and America, she plans to leave Hawaii to attend college stateside. Charlie Chan "had always been proud of the fact that they were all American citizens. But, perhaps because of this very fact, they seemed to be growing away from him. The gulf widened daily. They made no effort to remember the [Confucian] precepts and odes; they spoke the English language in a way that grated on Charlie's sensitive ear." Strongly conscious of his family and his traditions, Chan tries to envision his mother's reaction to these Americanized children. "His mother would not have approved, Charlie knew. She would have mourned for the old ways, the old customs. He mourned for them himself—but there was nothing he could do about it."

Part of Charlie Chan's ambivalence toward the Americanization of his children derives from the fact that he himself is part of the process of Americanization. He constantly tests himself to see how much he has become American and how much that has changed him. This kind of probing makes him more acceptable to American readers for two reasons. First, it implies that the American culture is innately so good and so all-pervasive that it can envelop even a tradition-minded Chinese. Second, Charlie Chan with his partially alien children and his own sense of changing values and identity was also a figure with whom Americans could sympathize, especially during the pervasive identity crisis brought on by the changing styles and values of the twenties.

Charlie Chan is keenly aware of what he considers dangerous signs of this Americanization in himself: "I will confess my shame. It seems I have circulated too long with mainland Americans. I have now, by contagion, acquired one of their worst faults. I too suffer curiosity." Interestingly, Charlie Chan views as faults characteristics that Americans tend to value such as curiosity and ambition. If not tragic flaws, they are at least devastatingly non-Chinese characteristics. Trying to explain his inability to interrogate an elderly Chinese servant, Chan admits that "a gulf like the heaving Pacific lies between us. Because he, although among Caucasians for many more years than I, still remains Chinese. As Chinese today as in the first moon of his existence. While I—I bear the brand—the label—Americanized." Chan is suddenly, acutely aware of his own dilemma, and of its cause: "I traveled with the current. I was ambitious. I sought success. For what I have won, I have paid the price. Am I an American? No. Am I then a Chinese? Not in the eyes of Ah Sing." At one point, discontent because of inaction, the Chinese detective muses to himself, "Can it be that Oriental character is slipping from me owing to fact I live so many years among restless Americans?" He concludes that "cool, calm Oriental gets too much like mainland Americans from circling in such towering society." In fact, it appears that even some of his eating habits have become Americanized. Charlie Chan orders tea with "three lumps of sugar and the breath of the lemon in passing"! These American characteristics are not necessarily happy ones for Charlie Chan, or for anyone else in his opinion. Impatience is particularly insidious in its effects upon the American: "His temples throb. His heart pounds. The fibers of his body vibrate. With what result? A year subtracted from his life."

In the last Charlie Chan novel, **Keeper of the Keys,** Biggers sets up a deliberate contrast between the Americanized detective and an old Chinese servant who has resisted Americanization and who clings to his old ways and pidgin English. In comparison to Ah Sing, Charlie Chan appears more American than the stereotyped servant. However, Charlie Chan is rarely seen with other Chinese. They are either servants in the stereotype of Ah Sing or else residents of Chinatown. Even more rarely does Charlie Chan speak Chinese. In the first of the six novels, he speaks his native language only once. Despite Biggers's references to such "Chinese characteristics" as imperturbability and psychic powers, Charlie Chan is not really very Chinese.

Unlike Fu Manchu, a mysterious and exotic Oriental, Charlie Chan is purely American in his work. He is a detective who could as easily be a resident of New York or Cleveland as of Honolulu. Hercule Poirot, Nero Wolfe, and Gideon Fell (a Belgian, a Montenegran, and an Englishman) are detectives in the same style as Charlie Chan. All employ classical methods of reasoning and logic to solve crimes. As Russell Nye points out in his discussion of American popular culture, Charlie Chan and these other detectives lived and worked in "an essentially rational world in which crime could be solved by the man of logic." As a detective—and it is important to remember that the Charlie Chan books are primarily detective fiction, not social tracts—Charlie Chan operates in a Western world of reason. He does not resort to Chinese jiggery-pokery or sleight of hand; he does not have to. Nye also points out that Charlie Chan is the first fictional detective who is in fact a professional policeman rather than a talented amateur. Disguises and amazing feats of physical prowess have almost no place in the world of Detective Sergeant Charlie Chan. Chan does go undercover once to gather evidence—he is masquerading as a Chinese cook—and resorts to an occasional wristlock on a subject, but his methods are generally nonviolent and almost totally intellectual. Furthermore, the crimes in which he becomes involved are not mysterious murders in the depths of Chinatown. They are murders in the midst of quite respectable white society.

This question of Chinese identity is one to which Biggers returns again and again, worrying it this way and that. In one novel he transports Charlie Chan from Hawaii to the mainland, but then continually sends him into Chinatown on the mainland. It is as if the author does not want to forget, and does not want his readers to forget, that Charlie Chan is Chinese—but that he also does not want this to get in the way of telling the story. Interestingly, the other major Oriental character in the series, a Japanese assistant detective named Kashimo, is the butt of racial and slapstick humor as none of the Chinese characters ever is. Kashimo's specialties seem to be hissing, fouling up evidence, and generally making life difficult for Charlie Chan and the Honolulu Police Department. The Chinese detective is even permitted an occasional jab at the Japanese. At one point, Charlie Chan observes that "cooking business begins to get tiresome like the company of a Japanese" and at another states that a twist of the wrist to disarm a suspect is "one thing I am ever able to learn from Japanese."

Charlie Chan is thus an intelligent and likeable individual who is superficially Chinese but could just as easily be American in many of his most basic traits. Sometimes the Chinese veneer is little more than a facade to create an exotic atmosphere, while at other times it is used to convey information or pseudoinformation about Chinese attitudes and to contrast them to American ideas, usually to the detriment of the American ways. There is thus a tremendous paradox in the Charlie Chan books. Charlie Chan himself is Chinese, but his methods and his milieu are American. The Chinese characteristics make him more interesting, but they are not the dominant factor in the life or being of Charlie Chan. They are more than window dressing but considerably less than the whole person. There are enough Chinese characteristics to provide color, but not so many that they overwhelm the reader or remove Charlie Chan from the reader's experience or comprehension. When American and Chinese characteristics are compared, it is usually the American rush against the Chinese calm, American ambition against Chinese acceptance and serenity. These comparisons made Charlie Chan and his culture more appealing to the individual reading the novels for relaxation and enjoyment. Earl Derr Biggers was a careful and cautious craftsman. The Charlie Chan books are vehicles for Biggers's messages, but they are small messages much more concerned with the American condition than with the Chinese. Proper Bostonians, improper Bostonians, and Englishmen of several degrees of propriety mingle with Americans in Charlie Chan's life, but there is not a single rapacious warlord or treacherous spy or even lovely sloe-eyed, boundfoot femme fatale in this essentially Western world.

Charlie Chan's outstanding characteristics—intelligence, good humor, diligence, loyalty—are valued in both Chinese and American cultures. He is Chinese only to the point to which it begins to hinder the plot or force the reader to stretch his mind, and then he becomes very much Americanized. The qualms about Americanization are interesting and express a valid point of view widely shared by the older generation of Chinese in America, but the main point seems to be that Americanization is impossible for the oldest generation of Chinese, incomplete for the generation of Charlie Chan, and inevitable for the youngest generation—not only inevitable, but also eagerly and profitably seized by the children themselves. In many ways Charlie Chan, as he realizes, is himself American.

Stereotyping and unconscious assumptions about race unquestionably appear in the Charlie Chan books. Many of the ideas about Chinese culture are skewed more or less violently, and even the admiration expressed for certain "Chinese" characteristics is often tinged with a patronizing or condescending attitude. One could argue endlessly whether a somewhat favorable stereotype is in the long run more or less harmful than a totally negative stereotype, but the argument is pointless. Both stereotypes are dangerous because they distract from reality, substitute slogans of understanding, furnish a comfortable illusion of knowledge when ignorance is the case, and mitigate against efforts at genuine understanding.

Nonetheless, stereotyped or not, the introduction of Charlie Chan marks a very real change in American images of the Chinese. Neither so villainous as Fu Manchu nor so condescendingly drawn as Scout Wong, Charlie Chan is a human being, with a family of whom he is proud (even if they occasionally dismay him), two cultures which he cannot completely reconcile within himself, a job that he performs superbly, and a set of problems and dilemmas that make him an appealing and sympathetic figure. It is

only a few years from the publication of the first Charlie Chan serial to the publication of Pearl Buck's intensely sympathetic and astonishingly successful *The Good Earth. The Good Earth,* with its heroes gallantly struggling and ultimately succeeding against overwhelming odds, might not have been readily accepted by a reading public whose primary image of the Chinese to that time had been the barbarous though fascinating Fu Manchu. Chan was the necessary bridge.

In many ways, the portraits of China and the Chinese in American fiction resemble a stratified cross section of the earth; layer rests upon layer, image succeeds image. But in a strange way, just as the archeologist or geologist can view many strata simultaneously, so the student of images of China can see the overlapping and sometimes intertwined stereotypes, one dominating a particular period but none totally erased, neither the malignancy of Fu Manchu nor the dauntless and occasionally tiresome patience of Pearl Buck's peasants. Charlie Chan occupies a vital place in this layering of images. He himself is a transitional figure, but there is a very clear demarcation between the image he presents and the images before and after him.

Charlie Chan is the most significant Chinese character in American fiction of the twenties. His success ultimately came less from his Chinese nature than from his essentially American attributes. Ironically, the most sympathetic Chinese of the period—and one of the most successful ever created—is sympathetic and successful largely because he is no longer very Chinese.

FURTHER READING

Biography

The Nation 136, No. 3537 (19 April 1933): 431.
   A brief obituary notice that remarks: "Perhaps unconsciously [Biggers] served the cause of international understanding—no slight service these days."

Criticism

Haycraft, Howard. "VIII. America: 1918-1930 (The Golden Age)." In *Murder for Pleasure: The Life and Times of the Detective Story,* pp. 159-80. New York: D. Appleton-Century Company, Inc., 1941.

   An overview of American detective fiction, with a short discussion of Biggers's Charlie Chan novels. Haycraft concludes that the Charlie Chan novels are "clean, humorous, unpretentious, more than a little romantic, and—it must be confessed—just a shade mechanical and old-fashioned by modern plot standards."

Additional coverage of Biggers' life and career is contained in the following source published by Gale Research: *Contemporary Authors*, Vol. 108.

Benjamin Nathan Cardozo

1870-1938

American jurist, essayist, and nonfiction writer.

INTRODUCTION

One of the leading legal theorists of the twentieth century, Cardozo served on the New York Court of Appeals for eighteen years prior to his appointment to the U.S. Supreme Court in 1932. Cardozo's tenure as a judge coincided with a period of ferment in American jurisprudence; rapidly changing social conditions, which generated a variety of new legal questions, and the widespread repudiation of the oracular theory of judging combined to provoke a controversy among members of the legal community over the role of the judiciary in the development of the law. Critics and biographers agree that Cardozo made a significant contribution to this debate in his legal opinions as well as in his extrajudicial writings, most notably *The Nature of the Judicial Process*, *The Growth of the Law*, and *The Paradoxes of Legal Science*, three books in which he outlined the freedoms and limitations of the judiciary in the process of legal growth and sought to develop a method of decision making that would bring public law into harmony with social need. *The Nature of the Judicial Process*, now considered a classic of judicial analysis, demystified the American court system with its frank description of how judges actually arrive at their decisions. In the later volumes, Cardozo refined his legal philosophy, continuing to focus on the dual responsibility of the judiciary to preserve continuity in the law and respond to change. Cardozo's extrajudicial writings have been consistently praised for their scholarship, candor, spirit of compromise, and liberality— qualities that also distinguished his service on the bench, making him one of the most admired and respected judges of his time. The success of Cardozo's books was also due in part to their distinction as literature. Convinced that style could not be separated from substance, Cardozo brought the judicial process to life in lucid, eloquent prose sprinkled with humor, anecdotes, and practical illustrations.

Biographical Information

Born and raised in New York City, Cardozo was the youngest son of Rebecca Nathan Cardozo and Albert Jacob Cardozo. A descendant of a long line of Sephardic Jews who had gained social prominence in New York, Cardozo could trace his American ancestry to the seventeenth century. A few years after Cardozo's birth, his father, a state supreme court judge, was implicated in Tammany Hall corruption and resigned his position under threat of impeachment. According to biographers, Cardozo was so ashamed by his father's resignation that he made it a lifetime ambition to restore his family name. Both of Cardozo's parents died when he was still very young, his

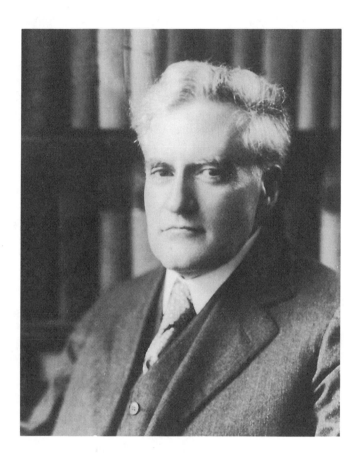

mother in 1879 and his father six years later. When he was only fifteen, Cardozo entered Columbia University. By the time he was twenty, he had earned bachelor's and master's degrees and was attending Columbia Law School. Cardozo practiced law in New York from 1891 until 1913, when he was elected a judge of the New York Supreme Court. Six weeks after the election, he received a temporary appointment to the New York Court of Appeals. Elected to the court for a full fourteen-year term in the autumn of 1917, Cardozo served as its chief judge from 1927 until 1932. It was during his tenure on the New York Court of Appeals that Cardozo first gained a reputation for successfully applying existing legal principles to changing social conditions. He joined a number of other legal scholars in pressing for judicial reform, arguing that the American judiciary was hindering social development by interpreting past laws and precedents too strictly. His opinions, which reflected his belief that judicial decisions should be based on the underlying purpose of the rule in question, rather than on its exact wording, influenced the trend in U.S. appellate judging toward increased involvement in shaping public policy. Cardozo's fame as a legal scholar was further enhanced by his extrajudicial publications, all but one of which appeared during the time he was sitting on New

York's highest court. When Oliver Wendell Holmes retired from the U.S. Supreme Court in 1932, Cardozo—the chief judge of the leading state court in the country and the author of several important books on the judicial process—was appointed by President Herbert Hoover to succeed him. His service on the Court was cut short by his death on July 9, 1938, following complications from a heart attack and a stroke. As an associate justice of the Supreme Court, Cardozo generally sided with liberals Louis Brandeis and Harlan Fiske Stone in supporting President Franklin Roosevelt's controversial New Deal measures, which were opposed by the Court majority for much of Cardozo's term of service. By 1936, however, the balance on the Court had shifted, and Cardozo's innovative approach to lawmaking was met with less resistance.

Major Works

The Nature of the Judicial Process, which consists of a course of lectures Cardozo delivered at Yale University, is generally considered his most original and influential book. In this work, Cardozo described the many various factors that influence the decisions of judges, revealing the judicial function to be a much more complicated process than merely applying existing rules to the facts of any given case or drawing logical deductions from established precedents. While acknowledging that judges are most often confronted with cases in which the law is so clear that only one outcome is feasible, Cardozo emphasized that there are "exceptional" cases requiring greater judicial discretion—those in which the law is anachronistic or its strict application would be illogical given current conditions and those in which gaps in the law exist. Cardozo was most interested in the exceptional cases, which gave judges an opportunity to exercise their "creative function." However, he was also aware of the dangers of unchecked judicial power. He called upon judges to make a conscious effort to avoid allowing personal feelings to inform their decisions, and he outlined alternative methods of decision making that he believed would preserve the continuity of the law while at the same time allow for legal growth. Summarizing his philosophy, Cardozo stated, "My analysis of the judicial process comes then to this, and little more: logic, and history, and custom, and utility, and the accepted standards of right conduct, are the forces which singly or in combination shape the progress of the law. Which of these forces shall dominate in any case, must depend largely upon the comparative importance or value of the social interests that will be thereby promoted or impaired. One of the most fundamental social interests is that law shall be uniform and impartial. There must be nothing in its action that savors of prejudice or favor or even arbitrary whim or fitfulness. Therefore in the main there shall be adherence to precedent." Cardozo elaborated on these ideas in *The Growth of the Law,* a second course of lectures he delivered at Yale, and *The Paradoxes of Legal Science,* a series of lectures he gave at Columbia. *The Growth of the Law* is primarily concerned with the question of how to choose the most appropriate method of decision making in any given case, and *The Paradoxes of Legal Science* focuses on the problem of reconciling the conflicting demands for stability and progress in the law.

To a lesser extent these issues are also discussed in *Law and Literature, and Other Essays and Addresses,* a collection most known for its title essay, in which Cardozo identifies and illustrates six different prose styles used in judicial decisions.

Critical Reception

It is generally agreed that Cardozo's enduring reputation will rest on his contribution to the modernization of legal principles. Through his progressive interpretation of the law, and of the judicial function itself, Cardozo helped to make public policy more responsive to changing social values and interests. Renowned for his legal erudition, cultured outlook, and literary style, he is also widely praised for his openmindedness and impartiality. While not all legal scholars have agreed with his analysis of the judicial process, none have denied the spirit of compromise with which he undertook his investigation.

PRINCIPAL WORKS

The Jurisdiction of the Court of Appeals of the State of New York (nonfiction) 1903; revised edition, 1909
The Nature of the Judicial Process (lectures) 1921
The Growth of the Law (lectures) 1924
The Paradoxes of Legal Science (lectures) 1928
What Medicine Can Do for Law (lecture) 1930
Law and Literature, and Other Essays and Addresses (essays and lectures) 1931
Law Is Justice: Notable Opinions of Mr. Justice Cardozo (nonfiction) 1938
Selected Writings of Benjamin Nathan Cardozo (lectures and essays) 1947

CRITICISM

Thomas Reed Powell (essay date 1922)

SOURCE: "The Behavior of Judges," in *The Nation* (New York), Vol. CXIV, No. 2959, March 22, 1922, pp. 347-48.

[*In the following essay on* The Nature of the Judicial Process, *Powell comments on Cardozo's belief that judges too often allow personal feelings and experience to inform their decisions.*]

Those who brought the Tables of Stone from Mount Sinai were not the last to thrust the lawgiver behind the mask of myth or of abstract formula. Unthinkers still assure us that ours is a government of laws and not of men, rejecting as unholy the emendation that it is a government of lawyers and not of men. Judges, they say, do but passively apply what the law in its wisdom reveals to them—or to five out of nine of them. Yet there have long been skeptics. Two hundred and four years ago Bishop Hoadley dared to say that "whoever hath an absolute authority to interpret any written or spoken laws, it is he who is truly the lawgiver, and not the person who first wrote or spoke them"; and Lord Bramwell later revealed that "one-third of a judge is a common juror if you get beneath the ermine"; to which Mr. Justice Riddell adds that "the other two-thirds may not be far different." Mr. Justice Holmes eschews fractions for biology and physics. Forty years ago he told us that "the life of the law has not been logic: it has been experience." Recently in viewing the development of a single cell he has said: "I recognize without hesitation that judges do and must legislate, but they can do so only interstitially; they are confined from molar to molecular motions." The judges of a century enjoy a range denied to the arbiter of a particular dispute; but he too has room to move about. The difference is one of degree.

Coke, an unconfirmed rumor tells us, found his Mount Sinai in his knowledge of the Latin tongue. When in need of authority for decisions he willed to reach, he would write: "As the old Latin maxim saith:"—and then he would make up the maxim. Coke may have lacked candor; but it was well that he knew what he was doing. It is from judges who know not what they do that we suffer most today—judges who think themselves constrained by principle or authority, when all that limits them is their ignorance or prejudice. This is especially unfortunate in America, where judges under the vague prescriptions of our bills of rights can veto legislation that makes a discord with their prepossessions. Modestly they may profess that it is not they that speak but the Constitution that speaketh in them; and often they are sincere, deceiving themselves when to others it is clear that they naively impute to the Constitution those personal frailties of temperament or education that long possession has made them cherish. Such judges are ignorant of the nature of the judicial process because blind to the nature and effect of their own emotional and intellectual processes. So it is that in the decisions most out of joint with the times we find ranged with the majority those judges most deficient in perception of themselves, those who link their accustomed modes of thought and feeling with something fundamental in the structure of society and find new departures so shocking that they suffer paralysis of such vision as they might in calmer mood employ. What makes a poor judge poor is as a rule less ignorance of the law than ignorance of human nature and of the nature of the judicial process.

Of such is not Judge Cardozo. The people of the State of New York are blessed in having on their highest court a man with the background, the insight, and the vision of the writer of these lectures [*The Nature of the Judicial Process*]. In reviewing them in the *Harvard Law Review* for February, Judge Learned Hand calls their author "a judge who by the common consent of the bench and bar of his State has no equal within its borders; . . . one who by the gentleness and purity of his character, his acuteness and suppleness of mind, by his learning, his moderation, and his sympathetic understanding of his time, has won an unrivaled esteem wherever else he is known." One would qualify this appreciation only by doubting whether Judge Cardozo's eminence is as solitary as it implies, and cite the appreciation itself as an index of where to look for

one of his companions in merit. Such colleagues are likely to increase in number because of the irresistible appeal of Judge Cardozo's avowal and analysis. Only the perverse or stupid can deny his wisdom that "it is when the colors do not match, when the references in the index fail, when there is no decisive precedent, that the serious business of the judge begins." And in this serious business where the judge is creator and statesman, the ancient learning in sheep and buckram is but a point of departure. That Judge Cardozo knows the other springs of wisdom is told by the titles of his chapters. He points to philosophy, to history and tradition, and to sociology. That he knows the enemies who lie in wait to taint the stream is shown by his analysis of the subconscious element in the judicial process. There is ironic wisdom in his comment that "it is often through these subconscious processes that judges are kept consistent with themselves and inconsistent with one another." Something higher than consistency with himself is demanded of a judge. In a changing world where new facts press hard on the best preserved theories, the judge must be responsive to the currents of life about him. He must strive for that sympathetic understanding that will help "to emancipate him from the suggestive power of individual dislikes and prepossessions" and "help to broaden the group to which his subconscious loyalties are due."

All this is vague enough, as no one knows better than Judge Cardozo. He tells us how much easier it is to find the ingredients to be blended than to fix the proportions of the blend. In any case where logic and history and sociology contend for mastery, whose shall be the victory or on what terms shall we have peace without victory? Judge Cardozo, like wise men generally, has no general rule. He reports battles that have been waged and shows us how the line of combat shifts from age to age. Those cast-iron obdurates who resent his analysis must yield to his recital. So measured is his judgment, so fair his portrayal, that he never would satisfy a foolish generation that searcheth for a sign. None the less he leaves us with confidence that we may with safety commit our disputes to any bench responsive to the influences he sets forth. He impresses us with his faith that "in the endless process of testing and retesting, there is constant rejection of the dross, and a constant retention of whatever is pure and sound and fine." With lawyers and judges imbued with the spirit of these lectures the lag of the law would yield much of its slack. Much as bench and bar need to go to school to Judge Cardozo, his teaching is not for them alone. The frailties of lawyers are the frailties of men, and all who form judgments are subject to passion and bias and blindness. Judge Cardozo's book would be as apt if called "The Nature of the Judgment Process." The illustrations from the law are stripped of technical raiment and will little strain and much enlighten the understanding of lesser breeds without the Law. Dwellers in darkness who shun enlightenment but love good English will do well to avoid exposure to Judge Cardozo's charm. For those who fear not wisdom there is great delight in store.

W. F. Dodd   (essay date 1922)

SOURCE: A review of *The Nature of the Judicial Process*,

in *American Political Science Review,* Vol. XVI, No. 4, November, 1922, pp. 710-11.

[*In the following essay on* The Nature of the Judicial Process, *Dodd focuses on Cardozo's explanation of the various factors that influence the decisions of appellate courts.*]

Seldom in a similar space will a student of legal institutions find so much of interest as in these lectures of Judge Cardozo [*The Nature of the Judicial Process*]. With a wealth of knowledge and a felicity of practical illustration the author outlines the influences which actually mould the judgments of appellate courts. He draws aside the veil of judicial sanctity, and shows that judges have their views determined by all the influences which control their judgment as men and as lawyers. The author's point of view is illustrated by the following quotation: "Deep below consciousness are other forces, the likes and the dislikes, the predilections and the prejudices, the complex of instincts and emotions and habits and convictions, which make the man, whether he be litigant or judge. . . . There has been a certain lack of candor in much of the discussion of the theme, or rather perhaps in a refusal to discuss it, as if judges must lose respect and confidence by the reminder that they are subject to human limitations. I do not doubt the grandeur of the conception which lifts them into the realm of pure reason, above and beyond the sweep of perturbing and deflecting forces. None the less, if there is anything of reality in my analysis of the judicial process, they do not stand aloof on these chill and distant heights; and we shall not help the cause of truth by acting and speaking as if they do. The great tides and currents which engulf the rest of men, do not turn aside in their course, and pass the judges by."

Judge Cardozo limits his discussion almost entirely to the relatively small number of cases "where a decision one way or the other, will count for the future, will advance or retard, sometimes much, sometimes little, the development of the law. These are the cases where the creative element in the judicial process finds its opportunity and power." The number of these cases is actually not small, when we include within it (as we must) the body of cases dealing with questions of constitutional and statutory construction; and these cases have an importance out of proportion to their number.

Judge Cardozo's attitude toward the various forces influencing judicial action is illustrated by the following quotation, "My analysis of the judicial process comes then to this, and little more: logic, and history, and custom, and utility, and the accepted standards of right conduct, are the forces which singly or in combination shape the progress of the law. Which of these forces shall dominate in any case, must depend largely upon the comparative importance or value of the social interests that will be thereby promoted or impaired." Judge Cardozo properly assumes that in appellate courts the eccentricities of individual judges are not so important, but tend to balance each other in the long run.

It is impossible in a brief review to do more than call attention to the excellence of this little book. Those who do not read it will miss a stimulating contribution to the discussion of our legal institutions.

James Hart   (essay date 1925)

SOURCE: A review of *The Growth of the Law,* in *Political Science Quarterly,* Vol. XL, No. 3, September, 1925, pp. 479-80.

[*In the following essay, Hart praises* The Growth of the Law *for both its readable style and its scholarly insight.*]

Judge Cardozo, of the New York Court of Appeals, has given us another book [*The Growth of the Law*] which fully comes up to the expectations of those who were fortunate enough to read his earlier lectures at Yale [*The Nature of the Judicial Process*]. Lucid in style, eclectic in philosophy, well balanced in point of view, this work is the contribution of a true scholar who sees the judicial process steadily and sees it whole. It carries further the analysis of the function of adjudication which the former volume so brilliantly began. Its phrases are pithy and shot through with imagination tempered by insight. There is a distinct touch of the artist coupled with the incisiveness of the trained thinker, the saneness of the man of affairs coupled with the sympathy of the humanist. When the author paraphrases Hamlet's famous epigram in his speech to the players, it is with appositeness but without vulgar show of learning. He assumes in the reader culture equal to his own, and leaves him to realize for himself that a judge may know his Shakespeare. The same is true of his other literary allusions.

It will be interesting to compare Judge Cardozo's definition of law with that of Professor W. W. Willoughby in the tenth chapter of his recent monumental treatise on *The Fundamental Concepts of Public Law.* It is significant that the professor of political science is a more thoroughgoing Austinian than the judge upon the bench. "A principle," says Cardozo, "or a rule of conduct so established as to justify a prediction with reasonable certainly that it will be enforced by the courts if its authority is challenged, is, then, for the purpose of our study, a principle or rule of law."

It would be unfair to the prospective reader, however, to go further into the content of this illuminating little volume. That would be an act of unkindness, for to try to separate the thought from the language in which it is expressed were to make the very thought itself to suffer. And this, forsooth, is something that can only be said of a master of style. Your true master of style is never mastered by his style, never is one who tries to make up in form what he lacks in matter. That is, of course, a veritable impossibility. He is one whose idea is so dynamic and so real that he has no trouble in expressing it in words that suggest much more than the mere words say. He not only thinks more than he says, but he possesses a subtle ability to make his reader do so, too. Such an one is Judge Cardozo.

Let the student of jurisprudence search for himself, and he will be richly rewarded. He will see sociological jurisprudence at its best. He will see it more vividly than in Pound, although Cardozo pays tribute, and justly so, to the learned Dean. He will realize that what the law needs is a "principle of growth". He will get a glimpse into the functioning of the judicial mind. He will see both stability and progress given their due weight. He will find a definition of law which is founded upon the facts of the law in action. He will discover further light upon the thesis of the author's earlier book. He will be impressed by the fact that no formula for the development of the law has been hit upon, if indeed it can be. That is a matter of trial and error by judges equipped with liberal education, training and experience, possessed of a sort of poetic imagination and the intuition of genius, and ever guided by the standards of the community and of the age on the one hand, and by the investigations of a fact-finding agency on the other. The reviewer believes that in this connection Judge Cardozo has unwittingly described himself.

Simeon Strunsky   (essay date 1928)

SOURCE: "About Books, *More or Less:* Courts and Crowds," in *The New York Times Book Review,* May 27, 1928, p. 4.

[*In the following essay on* The Paradoxes of Legal Science, *Strunsky discusses Cardozo's ideas about the creative function of the judicial process in terms of the American voting public's behavior and sentiments.*]

The presiding Judge of our New York State Court of Appeals confesses to the higher discontent which every good man brings to the practice of his profession. Judge Cardozo is not proof against the familiar belief that the grass in his neighbor's field is greener and the air on the other side of the creek is much more bracing. Why, he asks in **The Paradoxes of Legal Science** cannot I employ my rules of law with the same precision and certainty of results as the engineer with his logarithms and his stress and strain indexes? Why cannot I produce a "formula of justice" instead of having to deal with approximations obtained by rule-of-thumb? As a matter of fact, Judge Cardozo knows why he cannot, and his little book is a statement of the reasons why. But since he is an artist in his calling. I take it that any amount of good practical argument will not explain away the longing for perfection. Absolute beauty, absolute justice, absolute truth—the artist and the Judge and the scientist will take himself by the coat sleeve and show why the thing cannot be done; and he will be convinced, and he will go on to say to himself, "Yes, but why not? why not?"

In the title of the book is the answer to the nagging question. The paradoxes of legal science are implicit in the fact that the business of justice is with the paradoxes of life. The goal of juridical effort, one legal philosopher has said, is not logical perfection but compromise. What justice has been set to do, in Judge Cardozo's own summary, is to harmonize stability with progress, liberty with equality, liberty and equality with order, property rights with public welfare. How can there be a perfect formula of compromise other than that the terms of the compromise shall be observed by both parties? The parallel with the engineer's bridge, built on mathematical formulae and between two fixed points, is not a perfect one. Closer would be the comparison with the navigator's bridge, and on a ship not confined to plowing between Ambrose Channel and Cherbourg but bound for a continually shifting destination. There are rules of ship construction and there are laws of navigation. but there must always be a man on watch to compromise with emergency and with changing circumstance. When the disgruntled suitor at law repairs to the tavern and curses out the Court and remarks that the Judge can always twist the law to the Judge's own mind, he is speaking very handsomely of the man on the bench. In order to practice compromise in a changing and exceedingly complicated world the law must be always "twisted." An honest twisting of the law to the facts of life is justice.

In this statement, which I trust has not drifted into libel. lies the impossibility of the perfect formula of justice. Judge Cardozo finds that the longing for an absolute standard and guide besets the jurist hardest when the "judicial function is dynamic or creative." Diligence and memory and normal reasoning powers are sufficient to cope with a static situation, when it is a case of applying well-known rules to identical or almost identical situations. But it is precisely against the static conception of justice that the present volume is a protest. Directly or indirectly it is a plea for the creative operation of justice, for the Judge who is not content to stand by the decided things and leave it to the Legislatures to enact progress:

> We are told at times that change must be the work of statute, and that the function of the judicial process is one of conservation merely. But this is historically untrue, and were it true it would be unfortunate. Violent breaks with the past must come, indeed, from legislation, but manifold are the occasions when advance or retrogression is within the competence of Judges as their competence of Judges as their competence has been determined by practice and tradition.

Practice and tradition. There is nothing new, Judge Cardozo points out in another place, in this notion of established legal concepts bending to expediency and justice, to the shifting of the mores, to change in economic facts and relations. But what he does think is new is a present readiness on the part of Judges to "avow what they have always practiced." This I interpret to mean that not so long ago a Judge confronted by a new situation would do the right thing and pretend that the case was on all fours with Snooks v. Stokes in the seventh year of Richard II. Today the Judge is not afraid, or is growing not to be afraid, to hand down his decision because it is the right thing to do in the year 1928, and because Richard II has been dead for some time.

To what extent in the history of the law Judges have been creative and dynamic would make an interesting tale for the layman. Judge Cardozo admits that violent breaks with the past must be the work of Legislatures. But there must be instances when Judges have been ahead of the Legislatures; when laws rendered obsolete by economic evolution or rendered oppressive and cruel by a higher social ethic have been allowed to stick in the statute books by indifferent or irreconcilable Legislatures and have been mitigated by the Judges. On the whole, I take it, Judge Cardozo would not have the judicial process go in for dynamic creation ahead of the times; and that would leave some comfort for those of us—there are a great many—who are not found of lawyers and Judges. Granted, we say, that the Judge does finally bring himself to the point of admitting that the earth turns around the sun instead of the other way about; that labor unions are not conspiracies but legitimate organs of workers' self-defense; that women and children in industry need protection; that the public interest requires the restriction of private property rights in the form of zoning laws. What of it? There is not much credit in yielding to a fait accompli. saying yes to what the facts have long been asserting, refraining from the thesis that the sun do move.

Zoning laws, just referred to, would be an instance; I have taken it from Judge Cardozo's book:

> I have little doubt that a generation ago they would have been thrown out by the courts as illegitimate encroachments upon that freedom of use which is the attribute of property. I venture to express some doubt as to the fate they would have suffered even in our own day if they had come before the Supreme Court while they were yet novelties in legislation. The fact is, however, that by the time they were subjected to that challenge they were in successful operation far and wide throughout the land. The test of experience had proved them to be forces that made for conservation rather than destruction.

The sturdy critic of court and Judges would thus maintain that the judicial process is like the pre-Volstead saloon-keeper who instructed the barkeeper that Riley's credit was good for a drink if Riley had already had the drink. In the popular mind, I am afraid, the belief is still general that when Judges move they do so because they prefer to go along—at a distance—instead of being hauled. That is why an authoritative story of Judges who have gone along instead of being hauled or pushed would be educative. I don't imagine that a case can ever be made out for Judges as revolutionaries. Jurists may resent being described as a drag upon progress, but will never be averse to being described as a brake. Yet the distinction is worth keeping in mind.

In one respect—and here we are far away from Judge Cardozo's text—I do think that critics of our American courts have been harsh to the point of being unfair; and that is in protest against our celebrated divided court decisions, often in the mystic ratio of five Judges to four. I think such criticism unfair, in a minor fashion. because I have rarely come across protests by labor against a 5 to 4 decision at Washington in favor of labor, or protests by friends of free speech against similar narrow squeaks in their favor. But that, I presume, would be only human The major difficulty about critics of the 5 to 4 decision is that they resent in the courts what they accept as a matter of course in the Legislatures and in the operations of vox populi. Five Judges against four does look at first like a piece of hard luck. But that is no closer ratio than a bill which passes the House by 240 to 195 or passes the Senate by 50-odd to 40-odd, usually regarded as convincing majorities.

But much more impressive is the American people's acquiescence in the narrow squeak at the poll Grover Cleveland was first elected President by a plurality in New York State of 1,149 votes in a total of 1,125,000 votes. In the whole nation he had a plurality of 63,000 votes in a total of nearly 10,000,000 votes. Garfield "crushed" Hancock in 1880, but that was reckoning by electoral votes; actually Garfield had a plurality of 7,000 votes in the nation. In 1916 Woodrow Wilson won the Presidency by a margin of less than 4,000 votes in California; a change of less than 2,000 votes to Hughes would have given the latter California and the Presidency. More Interesting still, Mr. Cleveland was defeated in 1888, though he had a plurality of nearly 100,000 in the nation; Benjamin Harrison was a "minority" President. Compared with such narrow decisions at the polls a 5 to 4 vote in the United States Supreme Court is a landslide. Yet in its popular elections the American people has regularly accepted the breaks of the game. And it is my suspicion that people are not so indignant—at least not so permanently indignant—about close decisions in the courts as we may have been led to believe.

With all due apologies, therefore, to the shade of Alexander Hamilton, it seems to me that there is very little in the record of the American voting masses to justify apprehension of the mob getting out of hand and thus necessitating a curb by the courts on popular passions and is defense of fundamental rights of the individual. By this time it is pretty well proved that Hamilton guessed wrong when he looked to a small body like the Senate to hold the line against a mob institution like the House of Representatives. Today when somebody in the United States gets entirely out of control the chances are that he is either a member of the Workers' Communist Party or of the United States, Senate, two bodies of extremely limited membership. Nor are the courts so immune to popular sentiment as we like to believe. I trust I am not subjecting myself to the penalties of contempt when I suggest that the decisions of the United States Supreme Court on the Eighteenth Amendment and the Volstead law, uniformly in favor of both, indicate a fairly close harmony between judgment on the, bench and the popular will as expressed in the Legislatures.

If, then, it be true that the American people has never shown a desire to run amuck and go in for tyrannizing and confiscating, it follows that the "curb" of the courts upon popular passions has not been a vital factor in our history. Another way of putting it is to say that when you have a well-behaved, conservative people—and we are now reproached in some quarters for being the most conservative of modern peoples—there is less need for the courts to concern themselves overmuch with "stability." The courts can safely give part of their time and thought to progress. When you have an excitable mon you need "static" courts. When you have a self-controlled mass moving forward in decent order, the courts can afford to function creatively and dynamically, as Judge Cardozo would have them.

John Dickinson   (essay date 1929)

SOURCE: A review of *The Paradoxes of Legal Science,*

in *American Political Science Review,* Vol. XXIII, No. 1, February, 1929, pp. 200-2.

[*In the following essay on* The Paradoxes of Legal Science, *Dickinson explores Cardozo's theory that the goal of the judicial process is to reconcile opposing considerations, particularly stability and progress.*]

It may be not too much to predict that as the account now stands the chief American contributions to literature and the progress of human thought will prove to have been made in the field of jurisprudence. The writings of Holmes, Cardozo, and Pound have presented the results of a deeper probing into the operation of the legal system than had been before attempted by men bred to the common law, and have presented those results in most instances with a vividness and rare literary charm which are usually alien to the field of abstract speculation. Mr. Chief Justice Cardozo's latest volume [*The Paradoxes of Legal Science*] consisting of a course of lectures delivered in 1927 on the Carpentier Foundation at Columbia University, adds another item to the anthology of distinguished American contributions to juristic theory.

As the title of the book indicates, the central problem which engages the attention of the Chief Justice is suggested by his observation that the task of the law is to solve antinomies. "The reconciliation of the irreconcilable, the merger of antitheses, the synthesis of opposites, these are the great problems of the law . . . . We have the claims of stability to be harmonized with those of progress. We are to reconcile liberty with equality, and both of them with order. The property rights of the individual we are to respect, yet we are not to press them to the point at which they threaten the welfare or the security of the many. We must preserve to justice its universal quality, and yet leave to it the capacity to be individual and particular." Therefore the goal of juridical effort is not logical synthesis, but compromise in the effecting of reconciliations.

The Chief Justice addresses himself primarily to the great paradox involved in the need for compromise between stability and progress. It is the task of the judges to build new law, where the building of it is left in their hands, which will be adapted to the needs of society; and the needs of society are changing needs. The author lays down a working rule for judges confronted with such a task: "When changes of manners or business have brought it about that a rule of law which corresponded to previously existing norms or standards of behavior corresponds no longer to the present norms or standards, but on the contrary departs from them, then those same forces or tendencies of development that brought the law into adaptation to the old norms and standards are effective, without legislation, but by the inherent energies of the judicial process, to restore the equilibrium." "The pressure of society invests new forms of conduct in the minds of the multitude with the sanction of moral obligation, and the same pressure working upon the mind of the judge invests them finally through his action with the sanction of law." "At times the new *ethos* does not mean that there has come into being a new conception of right and wrong. It may mean nothing more than a new impatience, a new restiveness,

in the face of old abuses long recognized as wrong. Transition stages there are also when an observer can mark the law in the very process of becoming. It is throwing off a crippling dogma, and struggling for freer motion." "Our course of advance, therefore, is neither a straight line nor a curve. It is a series of dots and dashes. Progress comes *per saltum,* by successive compromises between extremes."

These compromises are effected by the judges' conception of the demands of justice. This conception must be no purely personal one, but must result from an effort to interpret the morality of the community. "Law accepts as the pattern of its justice the morality of the community whose conduct it assumes to regulate. In saying this, we are not to blind ourselves to the truth that uncertainty is far from banished. Morality is not merely different in different communities. Its level is not the same for all the component groups within the same community. A choice must still be made between one group standard and another. We have still to face the problem, At which one of these levels does the social pressure become strong enough to convert the moral norm into a jural one?" The pressure is exerted on the judges, and the choice is for them to make. "When this pressure has gone so far that it may no longer be resisted, the judges are to say. For they are the interpreters of the social mind, its will, its expectation, its desires." "In order that such a moral claim should become juridical, it must pass through. . . . the stage of declaration of right. A declaration of right is the admission by organized society that the claim is justified from the public point of view. Organized society may speak in such matters by the voice of its representatives in legislative assemblies. It may speak, at least in our Anglo-American system, by the voice of its judges."

These striking passages steer perhaps the truest and straightest course yet struck between "realists" who insist on the half-truth that social forces dictate law, and Austinians who neglect to notice that the legislative organ in making law is largely influenced by the action of such forces.

Joseph P. Pollard (essay date 1935)

SOURCE: "Introductory," in *Mr. Justice Cardozo: A Liberal Mind in Action,* Yorktown Press, 1935, pp. 7-20.

[*In the following excerpt from his full-length study of Cardozo's legal opinions, Pollard provides an overview of Cardozo's career and legal philosophy.*]

A gentle, modest man sits on the extreme left of the Chief Justice of the United States. As he listens intently to the arguments of counsel, he radiates an atmosphere of benevolence and wisdom. Everyone in the austere courtroom, judges and lawyers alike, pay him the homage of warm good-will and admiration bordering on awe. Confidence in the just decision dispels doubt. It is a feeling which could only be directed toward a man whose great talents in the law had been heralded far and wide before his accession to the high tribunal. Liberals and conservatives both see something to applaud in the record and attainments of Mr. Justice Cardozo: for humanity and honor and fair play, woven into the law through the loom of a prodigious learning, an understanding of modern human needs, and a vivid and striking power of expression, leave their mark even upon lawyers who are primarily concerned with furthering a client's dubious wants.

The American judiciary has seldom been graced with the presence of a man who combines the talents of philosopher, poet, and lawyer. Lawyers, by their very training, tend to emphasize precedent and glorify the past, and judges who are merely lawyers often fail to relate the law to the life around them, and become a hindrance rather than an aid to social development. They tend, moreover, to write their archaic views in a stuffy and heavy style, not clear even to a profession well initiated in abracadabra, and making an inexact science seem still more intangible. Thus darkness reigns, and the heavy hand of the past falls upon laymen groping for light and progress. This can only be dispelled by judges who are able to see history and tradition as a means rather than an end, who can relate past decisions to the needs of today and tomorrow, who see the law as the servant instead of the master of man, and who can make their views both clear and convincing. In this latter and far rarer group, the name of Benjamin Nathan Cardozo shines forth. By his comprehensive and understanding approach to man's troubles, and by his philosophic awareness of the functions of a judge, he is able to bring order out of the confusion which attends the solution of litigants' claims.

For eighteen years he served on the bench of the New York Court of Appeals, the most powerful and influential tribunal in the country save only the United States Supreme Court, to which he ascended upon the resignation of Justice Holmes. He came to the New York Court of Appeals in 1914 by the same route that he came to the Supreme Court in 1932—by the path of pure merit, demanded and acclaimed by those in authority who saw in him the makings of the ideal judge. Twenty years of practise at the bar, spent largely in the higher realms of arguing complex points of law in appellate courts, had convinced both governor and judges of his fitness for the task. When a vacancy on the bench occurred, Governor Glynn asked the judges to name their choice. They unanimously requested Cardozo. Glynn appreciated Cardozo's talents, but he hesitated to break the tradition which seemed to demand the appointment of some judge who had seen service on the intermediate appeals court, the Appellate Division. Cardozo's only public office had been that of trial judge in New York City for a few weeks immediately preceding the vacancy, and because of this the governor hesitated to appoint him. He asked time to consider, and when the names of other candidates were suggested to him by interested persons, he submitted these names to the Court of Appeals. They unanimously repeated their request for Cardozo. It was granted; and at the age of forty-four he started the judicial career which was to lead to high achievement. Politically a Democrat, he was elected by both Democrats and Republicans at the 1917 election for the regular term, and in 1926, judges who were both political opponents and his seniors in years of service stepped

willingly aside so Cardozo could be elevated to the position of Chief Judge. He served in that capacity, until called to Washington, in a manner to merit the high praise of Charles Evans Hughes that he was the best-qualified man ever to head the bench of New York State. And the New York Court of Appeals is unique and outstanding among state courts because called upon to deal with more important questions of commercial law than any other court in the country. Because of New York's key position as the financial center of the land, and because most business disputes are finally settled there—they cannot be appealed to Washington unless a federal question is involved—the Court of Appeals is the arbiter of many financial problems of even greater magnitude than confront the United States Supreme Court. Its decisions, consequently, are cited more often than those of any other court. And the decisions of Judge Cardozo, both in commercial cases, and in the more intimate problems of human relations, are cited more often than those of any other judge. Nor is his renown confined to courts of distant jurisdictions; in legislative halls, in law-school classrooms, and wherever the subject of law is important, Cardozo's views are spoken of with deference and admiration.

From the beginning, Cardozo gave evidence of his superior aptitude. While still a student at Columbia University, of which institution he was until recently a trustee, he wrote, as was commonly acknowledged, the most powerful English of any student there. He graduated with high honors; he mastered the study of such law as could be digested by the primitive law-school methods in vogue in the nineties. There was then no elaborate casebook system such as today calls for the resources of a penetrating and analytical student mind. There were only a few musty textbooks, promoting vague legal generalities in only a few of the fields of law. But Coke and Blackstone sufficed for the great John Marshall, and but a little more sufficed for Cardozo. Shy and diffident as a young lawyer arguing his first case before the august Court of Appeals, he yet performed the task in such a competent way that the Chief Judge singled him out after the argument and congratulated him on his able presentation of the case. After this early success in the high court, he became more and more in demand by busy lawyers who engaged him to argue their appeals for them. The way was paved for the steady rise to the heights which his talents merited.

The high esteem in which Judge Cardozo is held by those who know him, who are in a position to pay tribute to the man as well as the judge, is well illustrated by the affectionate words addressed to him by his colleagues on the Court of Appeals upon the occasion of his departure for the Supreme Court at Washington. The last consultation of the judges over which he presided was held on March 3, 1932. At the close of the consultation, he was presented with a silver loving cup, from his "friends and associates," the judges. Senior Associate Judge Cuthbert W. Pound, subsequently appointed Chief Judge by Governor Franklin D. Roosevelt, addressed Cardozo in terms which betray a warmer affection than is usually revealed in the cold type of judicial obituaries. It deserves quoting in full:

Beloved Chief Judge:

As you know, it is our custom when one of our brothers leaves us, to express in the intimacy of our own circle our affection and respect and to wish him well who goes to a hazard of new fortunes.

Such occasions are always painful, as the ties formed by years of close association are severed. None has been sadder than this parting today. Yet the sadness is so mingled with pride that we smile although our hearts are sick.

You have been a member of this court for eighteen years. All the bright spirits who were here to welcome you in 1914 have gone. For more than five years, after serving under Chief Judges Bartlett and Hiscock, you have been our head. The bar knows with what earnestness of consideration, firmness of grasp, and force and grace of utterance you have made your power felt; with what evenness, courtesy and calmness you have presided over the sessions of the court. Only your associates can know the tender relations which have existed among us; the industry with which you have examined and considered every case that has come before us; the diligence with which you have risen before it was yet dawn and have burned the midnight lamp to satisfy yourself that no cause was being neglected. At times your patience may have been tried by the perplexities of counsel and of your associates, but nothing has ever moved you to an unkind or hasty word. You have kept the court up with its calendar by promoting that complete harmony of purpose which is essential to effective work. The rich storehouse of your unfailing memory has always been open to us.

I shall not dwell upon your rare qualifications for the bench of that incomparable tribunal of statesmanship and law, the Supreme Court of the United States. You were appointed neither for political nor geographical considerations, but in defiance of them and because the whole country demanded the one man who could best carry on the great Holmes tradition of philosophic approach to modern American jurisprudence. Our loss is the gain of the high court to which you go. There will be no rest for you; no relaxation in your efforts to solve by legal formulas the problems of justice in the great field of constitutional law.

And who hath trod Olympus, from his eye
Fades not the broader outlook of the Gods.

We shall miss not only the great Chief Judge whose wisdom and understanding have added glory to the judicial office but also the true man who has blessed us with the light of his friendship, the sunshine of his smile.

Not so much honoring you, as leaving with you some reminder of our regard, we offer you this symbol of our esteem. If you miss, as you may in your new environment, the sweet serenity of your Albany life, the admiration of your brethren of some new and unexpected stroke of your genius and the tranquility of our personal and official relations, may this memento of those who love you serve to cheer and inspire you.

Through all the honors that have been heaped on him, including the many honorary degrees of universities and colleges, Judge Cardozo has maintained his congenital modesty. Addressing the alumni of New York University Law School, at a luncheon in December, 1927, he recalled the observation of Charles Francis Adams, the elder, that, as he looked back through the mists of the years, the predominant feeling was one of satisfaction that at least he had gone through life without making a conspicuous ass of himself. "That, I may say in passing, is my own paean of jubilation at the end of each judicial year." When the news of his appointment to the Supreme Court was brought to Albany, and telegrams stormed the Hotel Ten Eyck, where he maintained his Albany home for thirteen years, and clerks and bell-boys and elevator operators added their congratulations to those of friends and other admirers, he said: "I hope I shall not lose my sense of humor over all this attention," and his dark eyes twinkled out through rimless glasses.

He possesses a quiet and cultured humor, as befits the man. Even the cases which in all solemnity he decides call sometimes for a display of this priceless possession. In sustaining the conviction of a man accused of maintaining a public nuisance, by holding dances and revelry in his Manhattan catering shop, to the accompaniment of drums and brasses which annoyed neighbors a block away, he said: "Long ago it was adjudged that one dwelling in a city who with the aid of a speaking trumpet made great noises in the night time to the disturbance of the neighborhood, must answer to the King. The precedent is not one to be hastily renounced in days when trumpets have a power unknown to a simpler age." In a delightful address at the dedication of the new home of the New York County Lawyers' Association in May, 1930, he took occasion to mention the punishment which longwinded lawyers inflict upon the judges forced to listen to their prosy intonations: "Inveterate has been the habit of inordinate prolixity. From time immemorial judges have struggled fruitlessly against it, offering rewards to brevity and laying burdens on garrulity, but all to small avail. someone gave me only recently an order by the Court of Chancery made three centuries ago in which the draftsman of a verbose and impertinent replication was ordered to walk about the court with the pleading hanging about his neck and pay a fine to boot. Our methods of repression are less rigorous today, but the chancery replication was probably an innocent brochure when compared with briefs that I could offer as exhibits if the angry chancellor were here." He then mentioned how the modern courts have set limits to the time allowed an argument: "I am not advised to what extent the clipping of the wings of flight has brought suffering to counsel. My heart smites me at times at the thought of curbing them at all. After all, there is something captivating in their zeal, something human and lovable, even if a little wearing. If they wander from the point, they never do so quite so blatantly as Demosthenes or Cicero." Delivering a commencement address at the Albany Law School in 1925, Judge Cardozo congratulated the graduates on the opportunity they had had to study the law scientifically, an opportunity which had been denied to him in his student days at Columbia: "When I contrast the training that is given to the law student of today with the training that was given to me in the pre-historic days before my admission to the bar, I am filled with a spirit of envy that makes me anxious to step down and take my place in your ranks, forgetting, for the moment, that your examiners would probably refuse to pass me. . . . Take such a subject as the law of corporations; we had no instruction in it at all. Perhaps the notion was that no corporation would be foolish enough to retain us at the beginning, and that by the time such retainers came to us we could pick up the knowledge for ourselves."

Cardozo has his favorites among the jurist's craft. Chief among them is Justice Holmes, so like himself in his approach to legal problems, in his philosophy, and in his power to work magic with the written word. In his own opinions, Cardozo likes to cite the opinions of Holmes, J., and to quote excerpts from them to illustrate his point. Both judges are master of metaphor and striking phrase, both contribute literature as well as philosophy to the law. Both judges are zealous in defense of free thought and other guaranties of the Bill of Rights, and both agree that the Constitution should not be used to shield private property from legislative regulation in the public welfare. It is a natural affinity between these two of the greatest jurists in the English-speaking world. But Cardozo is also a great admirer of the late Chief Justice Taft. Taft rendered many decisions in his years on the high tribunal of which Cardozo could not approve. Taft invalidated state laws outlawing the injunction in labor disputes, he tended to glorify the Fourteenth Amendment at the expense of the state police power, he sustained the federal government in its despicable practise of tapping wires to obtain evidence to use in criminal cases. These decisions were more than a little conservative. Taft did, however, dissent from the opinion of his fellows in 1923 that minimum wage laws were unconstitutional. His innate humanity could not stomach the reactionary views of his property-conscious associates. Cardozo approved of that. And aside from a conservative approach to the problems of constitutional law, Taft was an able judge. He was extremely efficient, too, as an administrator of the affairs of the court, as a leader in procedural reform and a proponent of modern rules for the conduct of inferior federal benches. An able administrator himself, Cardozo saw much to admire in this executive ability of Judge Taft. And then Taft was, unquestionably, a human and lovable personality. Among the judges of the past, John Marshall is especially admired by Judge Cardozo. Marshall is the man to whom must go the credit for molding and strengthening a federal union, a nation, through his statesmanlike interpretation of the federal Constitution; and his great judicial achievements evoke a ready response in patriotic hearts. His epochal decisions, handed down in such imperial and magisterial manner, are cause for awe. "Those organ tones of his were meant to fill cathedrals." Cardozo also has a very high regard for the English bench, and delights in referring to English decisions, both old and modern. On that bench have been men of profound mental attainments and high integrity. Cardozo admires them for the urbanity and mellow culture revealed in their opinions; in this respect his own

opinions are acknowledged to be similar. Lord Mansfield, a judge, like Marshall, in the grand manner, is one of the highlights of the English bench, as, in more recent days, are Lords Bowen and Haldane. But Cardozo has little use for "hanging" judges like the notorious Jeffreys, or judges who prefer a "strong" decision, a decision that achieves a harsh result by applying strict logic to the development of a legal rule, regardless of justice. He likes to repeat an anecdote of Lincoln concerning a strict judge he knew: "He would hang a man for blowing his nose in the street, but he would quash the indictment if it failed to specify what hand he blew it with." The harsh martinet, the tyrant on the bench, is to be deplored. "Take such a thing as the call of the calendar and the administration of calendar rules. There is a way of doing such things as a drillmaster and a way of doing them as a man." Cardozo himself, ever courteous and kindly to lawyers, young and old, who appear before him, has never allowed the ravening official to swallow up the man.

He was a moving spirit in the formation of the American Law Institute in 1923, and has been its vice-president ever since. That Institute was organized to bring order out of the confusion of conflicting rules of law as enunciated in the courts and legislatures of forty-eight different state jurisdictions. It is the monumental task of experts in the various fields of law to gather these confusing edicts, to formulate a principle common to all, to re-state the law as the weight of authority commands. This re-statement, the result of laborious research and weeding out, has been of immense benefit to judges ever since, and the work still goes on. Cardozo's suggested reforms, his purpose of cancelling archaic rules that have no relation to the needs of life in the modern day, have been adopted in many instances. He suggested, in 1921, the formation of a ministry of justice to aid the co-operation so often lacking between courts and legislatures. Courts alone, hampered by precedent, much of which is useless, cannot always relate the law to justice. Legislatures must change many legal rules by the enacting of statutes, but legislatures, busy with so many other things in the political field, view "with hasty and partial glimpses what should be viewed both steadily and whole." There should be some responsible group, some committee, to mediate between courts and legislature, to make suggestions to the legislature to remedy the needed gaps in the rules of judge-made law. Although such a ministry was never formed, courts and legislatures no longer "move on in proud and silent isolation." For the fruit of the work of the American Law Institute, the finding out what the law is, and re-stating it in adequate and simple terms, is there for law-makers as well as judges to see, and to use in the guidance of their efforts to write statutes which will consist with justice. Even more helpful in some respects is another result of Judge Cardozo's work in law reform—the Johns Hopkins Institute of Law, organized in 1928, is studying the law functionally, searching not only for the rule that has come down from the past, but finding how that rule is adapted to the present needs of life. The result of such findings can easily be translated into law by legislative action. Co-operation within the ranks of the law itself is one important aim of Judge Cardozo's work. And co-operation between the two great professions of law and medicine, so often aloof and jealous of each other, is another. Especially in the field of criminal law is this joint effort needed. The judges need the help of the doctors in analyzing the minds of criminals so that punishment can be made to fit the crime. Happy results have already flowed from Cardozo's appeal for co-operation here. These are some of the incidents of a devotion to the law which is a devotion akin to religion, such a religion as he once explained to the members of the Jewish Institute: "The submergence of self in the pursuit of an ideal, the readiness to spend one's self without measure, prodigally, almost ecstatically, for something intuitively apprehended as great and noble, spend one's self one knows not why—some of us like to believe that this is what religion means."

As he has channelled his life in a purely intellectual course, it is not surprising that he should have found time, apart from the arduous tasks of judicial determination, to write three books which explain his broad philosophy of law and of life, books which, because of their compelling analysis of the work of judges, have influenced thought in the profession more profoundly than any writing since Holmes published *The Common Law* in 1881. These books, which are the fruits of lectures delivered at Yale and Columbia Law Schools, and which he calls "these introspective searchings of the spirit," are *The Nature of the Judicial Process,* 1921; *The Growth of the Law,* 1924; and *The Paradoxes of Legal Science,* 1928. They reveal, as Spinoza's writings reveal, the joy that lies in the pursuit of knowledge and understanding. They reveal, as Montaigne revealed, the tough mind and the gentle heart. They show the color and warmth of feeling that can be brought to the study of human nature by one who considers mysticism and idealism and spirituality as important ingredients in composing the good life. Implicit in his words is that happy blend of reason and emotion which has characterized so many benefactors of mankind. His words show his philosophy to be a practical one, as a judge's philosophy should be. Metaphysical subtleties and abstractions for their own sake have no place in it. It consists in looking at life in the large to find the guiding principle for the decision of the narrow problem before him. The law is relative, not absolute; dealing with the complexities of humanity, it must be closely related to the needs of life. It must be stable and yet must change; symmetry and uniformity should be preserved only where such symmetry and uniformity do not lead to unjust consequences. Logic of course has its place, but it also has its pitfalls. History should be seen as a liberating rather than a paralyzing force. Judges should be willing to permit experimentation and change when the beaten path falls into decay; they should remember their true function is molding the law to fit its ends; and its ends are to serve mankind, not mankind the law. Cardozo's eye is ever on the social utility of a rule of law—if a strict extension of logic or if an ancient precedent blocks progress and the attainment of justice, they should be cast aside. "Logic and history and custom have their place. We will shape the law to conform to them when we may; but only within bounds. The end which the law serves will dominate them all. There is an old legend that on one occasion God prayed, and his prayer was: 'Be it my will that my justice be ruled by my mercy.' That is a prayer which we all need to utter at times when the

demon of formalism tempts the intellect with the lure of scientific order." His gifted pen moves to a recital of the doubt which besets him as he tries, as a judge, to reconcile the interests of certainty and consistency with those of equity and fairness: "I was much troubled in spirit, in my first years upon the bench, to find how trackless was the ocean on which I had embarked. I sought for certainty. I was oppressed and disheartened when I found that the quest for it was futile. I was trying to reach land, the solid land of fixed and settled rules, the paradise of justice that would declare itself by tokens plainer and more commanding than its pale and glimmering reflections in my own vacillating mind and conscience. I found with the voyagers in Browning's *Paracelsus* that the real heaven was always beyond. As the years have gone by, and as I have reflected more and more upon the nature of the judicial process, I have become reconciled to the uncertainty, because I have grown to see it as inevitable. I have grown to see that the process in its highest reaches is not discovery, but creation; and that the doubts and misgivings, the hopes and fears, are part of the travail of mind, the pangs of death and the pangs of birth, in which principles that have served their day expire and new principles are born."

Other judges decide the cases before them by applying pure reason, fortified by precedent. Cardozo knows there is more to it than that, especially in the great field of public or constitutional law, where five to four decisions are not uncommon. Subtle, subconscious forces guide the judges, whether they know it or not: "There is in each of us a stream of tendency, whether you choose to call it philosophy or not, which gives coherence and direction to thought and action. Judges cannot escape that current any more than other mortals. All their lives, forces which they do not recognize and cannot name have been tugging at them—inherited instincts, traditional beliefs, acquired convictions; and the resultant is an outlook on life, a conception of social needs, a sense, in James' phrase of 'the total push and pressure of the cosmos,' which, when reasons are nicely balanced, must determine where choice shall fall." At least one force in that current, for Cardozo, is his Jewish origin. Twenty centuries of oppression of the Jewish race are reflected in his social-welfare decisions, as they are in those of Justice Brandeis. An awareness of what moves a judge to his decisions is matched by an awareness of the plight of the theorist in the modern maelstrom. The hazards of the work of the lonely scholar, and the complete justification for that work, are depicted in the following moving passage from *The Growth of the Law*. "The theorist has a hard time to make his way in an ungrateful world. He is supposed to be indifferent to realities; yet his life is spent in the exposure of realities, which, till illuminated by his searchlight, were hidden and unknown. He is contrasted, and to his great disfavor, with the strenuous man of action, who plows or builds or navigates or trades, yet in moments of meditation he takes the consoling knowledge to his heart that the action of his favored brothers would be futile unless informed and inspired by thoughts that came from him. Of the lot of all theorists, that of the philosopher is the sorriest. Let us heave a stone at him, say his enemies, and thus stigmatize his tribe. 'I thought the man had sense,' said the Duchess of Marlborough when she quarreled with Voltaire, 'but I find him at bottom either a fool or a philosopher.' General truths are hard to grasp. Most of us have all we can do in accumulating by dint of toil the knowledge of a few particulars. A troublesome lot, these men who are always searching for the ultimate. If we cannot understand, let us show that the superiority is ours by combining to deride."

Thus the theorist, the philosopher who shapes his shining truths from the sordid controversies of litigants. For the philosopher in his case is developed and strengthened by the judge.

Morris Raphael Cohen   (essay date 1938)

SOURCE: "Three Great Judges: Holmes, Brandeis, Cardozo," in *The Faith of a Liberal,* Transaction Publishers, 1993, pp. 20-45.

[*In the following excerpt, Cohen praises Cardozo as an inspirational force whose humanitarian philosophy, sensitivity to conflicting interests, and adaptation to changing social conditions profoundly influenced the legal profession. Cohen's commentary on Cardozo was originally published in* National Guild Quarterly *in 1938.*]

A man's philosophy, his view of life, grows out of his own experience at the same time that it reveals his work.

Perhaps the most significant fact about Justice Cardozo's career is the way in which he achieved the almost unanimous reverence and affection of the whole nation. Extreme conservatives as well as the most advanced liberals urged his appointment to the Supreme Court for the vacancy occasioned by the retirement of Justice Holmes. Surely it is significant to ask how Benjamin Cardozo came to have this hold upon our thoughts and our imaginations. And it is heartening to reflect that there is only one explanation possible, and that is in terms of the sheer merit of his service to society. Benjamin Cardozo had no political connections or group pressure to back him. He had risen by sheer individual merit to the highest position in the judicial system of the Empire State and had set an example of what a great judge can do, not only in rendering justice in the individual cases before him, but in inspiring the bench and bar to a greater and more humane conception of their obligation to the community which they serve. He was not merely the chief judge of New York State; he was also the intellectual and spiritual leader of its whole legal profession.

What was it that made it possible for him to achieve this? We know of the great charm of his personality, his essential sympathy and kindliness, indeed his courtliness in the finest sense. We know, too, of his great learning and charm of cultivated expression. But behind all this and vivifying it was his humane outlook on life.

It is significant that Justice Cardozo was one of the few of our judges who, like the late Justice Holmes, thought it important to *have* a philosophy. In the forefront of humanity's most cherished heroes, among prophets, saints, philosophers, scientists, poets, artists and inspiring national leaders, the number of lawyers does not loom large. Mankind as a whole cannot well live by bread alone, but needs sustaining and directing vision. It is hard for law-yers, bent on the affairs of the market place, to look up and see the heavens above, or to grasp entire the scheme of things in which they move. This is especially difficult in a country or epoch which, under the leadership of captains of industry and finance, worships a narrow practicality and acts as if theory could be safely ignored, if not despised. It requires, therefore, a high order of intellectual and moral energy for one who has been immersed almost all his life in the business of the law to avow and pursue an interest in its general backgrounds and ultimate outcome, following the maxim of the old Talmudic sages that he who would deal justly with the law must contemplate the eternal issues of life and death. It is because Cardozo tried to do this that he became not only a great judge, rendering justice in the individual cases before him, but also a highly beloved national figure, inspiring bench and bar to a higher and more humane conception of their duty to the community which they should serve.

The main features of Cardozo's philosophy, like those of any sound philosophy, are essentially simple, though it needs genius and energy to trace their implications and to carry them out consistently.

The first point is that law is not an isolated technique, of interest only to lawyers and to litigants, but that it is an essential part of the process of adjusting human relations in organized society.

The second point is that the law of a growing society cannot all be contained in established precedents or any written documents, important as are continuity with the past and loyalty to the recorded will of the people. In the law as a social process, the judges play a determining role, having the sovereign power of choice in their decisions. It was in this emphasis on the judicial process as selective and creative that Cardozo's thought centered.

The third point, the logical corollary to the foregoing, is that to meet his responsibility for making the law serve human needs the judge cannot rely on legal authorities alone, but must know the actual facts of the life about him, the psychologic and economic factors that determine its manifestations, and must thus keep abreast of the best available knowledge which those engaged in various social studies, researches, or investigations can supply.

These three propositions are perhaps obvious, and they may even be said to have their roots in the old liberal faith which the founders of our Republic—men like Franklin, Jefferson and James Wilson—held with fervor. But it requires vision and heroic courage to maintain these views today against the inertia and passionate errors embodied in prevalent attitudes.

To the great majority of people, law is a special technique. It is something exclusively for lawyers and their clients. I remember a class in which a student complained that he didn't see the justice of a decision in a given case. The professor replied, "This is a class in law, not in justice." Now there is of course some measure of truth in this reply. It is unfortunately true that many laws are unjust and are none the less part of our law, to be observed and analyzed. But from the historic and moral point of view this is surely not the final answer. The law arises to meet social needs and can maintain itself in the long run only if it serves those needs both justly and to the general satisfaction of the community.

There have been great judges who have clearly understood and courageously served the just needs of society without impressing their views on their fellow judges, or often persuading losing counsel of the correctness of an adverse decision, or satisfying more than a bare majority of the community whose disputes they have decided. And it is even easier for a judge to satisfy prevailing public desires without embodying in his work the qualities of righteousness which will commend it to men of other times and places. It was the peculiar genius of Cardozo that he was able to achieve to a pre-eminent degree the combination of two great gifts. He pursued righteousness without being aloof or Olympian or zealously partisan towards the controversies of his day. And at the same time, without ever subordinating his high ideals to the pressing demands of popular opinion, he was able to give a sensitive ear and eloquent tongue to the perception and expression of the conflicting interests in almost every case that came before him, so that few losing lawyers ever left his court without feeling that their cause had been accorded a fair and sympathetic hearing. Characteristic of Justice Cardozo's penetrating and engaging sympathy was his remark to losing counsel in a bitterly argued case—quoting the words of a judge of the Confederacy: "Many a good cause has been gallantly lost." The sensitivity and humility which made Justice Cardozo so anxious to satisfy all the conflicting social interests represented in any given case made it possible for a gifted intellect to formulate judicial decisions acceptable to all parties in an extraordinary number of cases. Only thus, I think, can we explain the fact that the New York bar, consisting of lawyers who had, in the main, lost as many cases as they had won before him, loved and revered Judge Cardozo with so rare a unanimity.

It was this same conciliatory sympathy and catholic understanding that made it so difficult for Justice Cardozo's colleagues on the bench to disagree with him or to fail to accord his views the deepest respect on the rare occasions when they did disagree. Thus he was able to influence the bench and bar to a far greater degree than more brilliant or learned colleagues on the Supreme Court. That the public at large appreciated the genuine liberality of Cardozo's mind is shown by the fact that no man was found to object to his appointment to the supreme tribunal of the nation.

The prevailing orthodoxy expressed some years ago by the late Senator Root and still passing as authoritative insists that the duty of the judge is simply to read and obey the statute or the Constitution and that it is no part of his business to make or change the law in any way. This assumes that the framers of a law or constitution can foresee all possible future contingencies and make definite provisions for meeting them, so that the judge can be merely a logical automaton, a sort of phonograph repeating exactly what the law had definitely declared. But this is a childish view which no student of law can maintain. The whole common law has grown out of judicial decisions, and in our constitutional law the meaning of such phrases as "due pro-

cess," "equal protection of the laws," "interstate commerce," and the like is precisely that which the courts have assigned to them.

The fundamental fallacy in the "phonograph theory" of the judicial functions, against which Justice Cardozo's entire career was an eloquent protest, is the illogical view that general principles alone can determine individual decisions. Modern logic and modern science alike demonstrate the untenability of this conception. Established legal principles may supply guiding analogies, but the decision of any individual case depends on an understanding of the actual social conditions, and of the consequences of the decision, as well as on the judge's view as to which of these consequences are best or most important. Elevation to the bench does not make a man omniscient, and the obvious fiction that courts decide only points of law prevents us from giving them adequate facilities for investigation into the relevant facts of the case, and into the larger social consequences of their decisions. In our anxiety to make judges independent of the popular will we are making them independent of the knowledge necessary to make their work satisfactory.

The consequence of judicial recognition that the judges make law is the responsibility of making it in accordance with existing conditions. Now, for judges who are intelligent enough to recognize the inadequacy of their own training in economic and social studies, it is easy to take refuge in the thought, "We are judges of the law and have nothing to do with economic or social theories." But the refuge is illusory. Those who are not aware of theory assume as facts the theories of an older generation.

A great lawyer preparing a brief in the Consolidated Gas Case told his clerks not to quote any economists later than John Stuart Mill—the judges wouldn't have heard of them. The philosophy of Cardozo makes this position impossible. Not only is law connected with other phases of human life, but human life is changing and the content of certain abstract principles must change. The principles of economics formulated two generations ago can no longer be relied on today. They must be corrected by the best available knowledge. Absolute finality is not to be found in human affairs.

It was Justice Cardozo's essential humility which made it possible for him to recognize what many of his brethren on the bench found it intolerable to admit: that he as a judge had to rely not only on past judicial decisions but on developments in the various fields of social study. He was indeed criticized for quoting nonlegal authorities in some of his judicial opinions. But the sharp distinction between legal and nonlegal authorities is an arbitrary one which no serious philosophy of law can well maintain. History celebrates the occasion when thought is wedded to fact. That is the philosophy which has made modern science so fruitful in the field of technology, and that is the philosophy which makes possible the progress of the spirit and the life of society.

Cardozo's personal career is a tribute to the fact that the United States is still a country which offers opportunity for the development of a human vision that is not restricted to any one race or creed. The validity of this liberal ideal his life illustrates and his philosophy of law illumines. At a time when there is real danger of our reverting to the medieval or barbaric view that men are to be judged entirely by their tribal descent or by their conformity to a prevailing orthodoxy, we may all be justly proud that our country is still wise enough to take advantage of the highest service which human beings can render, by recognizing and giving opportunity to merit. But the career of Cardozo suggests that this pride is not enough, and that there rests upon us the obligation to preserve this heritage at a time when liberal ideals are ignored in practice and assailed in theory. We shall be conscious of this precious responsibility so long as we hold in our national memory the lives and teachings of America's great spiritual leaders, of whom Benjamin Nathan Cardozo is not the least.

Jerome Frank   (essay date 1948)

SOURCE: "Cardozo and the Upper-Court Myth," in *Law and Contemporary Problems,* Vol. 13, No. 2, Spring, 1948, pp. 369-90.

[*Frank was an American jurist who served on the U.S. Court of Appeals for the Second Circuit from 1941 until 1957. In the following excerpt from a review of* Selected Writings of Benjamin Nathan Cardozo, *Frank faults Cardozo's description of the judicial process because it ignores the operations of trial courts.*]

> The practical is disagreeable, a mean and stony soil, but from that all valuable theory comes.
>
> [Oliver Wendell Holmes, *Holmes: His Book Notices and Uncollected Letters and Papers*]
>
> [The] first step toward improvement is to look the facts in the face.
>
> [Holmes, *Rational Basis of Legal Institutions*]

I

There has recently been published a volume, ***Selected Writings of Benjamin N. Cardozo,*** which every thoughtful lawyer and judge will want ready at hand. It will repay constant re-reading. It includes nearly all Cardozo's extra-judicial writings, notably ***The Nature of the Judicial Process,*** first published in 1921, and ***The Growth of the Law,*** first published in 1924. In these two books, one of our most eminent appellate judges set forth his legal philosophy. More important, he showed how this philosophy aided him in his judicial work, and, in that connection, disclosed some of the intimate details of upper-court techniques. I say "more important" because, before Cardozo, no judge, with the exception of Holmes, had been similarly candid. Cardozo's frankness emboldened others, lawyers and judges, to be less diffident in thinking about and commenting on courthouse ways.

He did not confine himself to a description of what appellate judges do. He told, also, what they ought and ought not do. While wisely indicating the proper limits of judicial legislation, he exhorted these judges to put moral ideals into practice. His descriptions and exhortations he both illustrated refreshingly by his own judicial opinions,

and fortified by apposite reflections on a variety of legal and non-legal philosophies.

This sort of critical self-revelation by a judge was novel and exciting. Somewhat less novelty and inventiveness appear in the contents of his own philosophy—far less than in the off-the-bench writings of his great master, Holmes, all of which contain highly original insights. Cardozo, more productive than Holmes, was also more eclectic. But, as in the case of Cicero, brilliant eclecticism became itself creative.

It was tonic that a revered judge, by no means "radical," should boldly declare, "I take judge-made law as one of the realities of life" [***The Nature of the Judicial Process***]. To be sure, this had often been said previously, once forthrightly (and with appropriate qualifications) by Holmes in a dissenting opinion to which Cardozo acknowledged his indebtedness. But many lawyers then regarded Holmes as queer and flighty. Holmes, too, had frequently noted that sometimes subconscious factors affected judges, that they sometimes decided cases intuitively, that policy attitudes, too often entertained unconsciously, influenced decisions. "The very considerations which the courts most rarely mention, and always with an apology," Holmes wrote as early as 1879, "are the secret root from which the law draws all the juices of life. We mean, of course, considerations of what is expedient for the community concerned. Every important principle which is developed by litigation is in fact and at bottom the result of more or less definitely understood views of public policy; most generally, to be sure, under our practice and traditions, the unconscious result of instinctive preferences and inarticulate convictions, but none the less traceable to public policy in the last analysis" ["Common Carriers and the Common Law," *American Law Review* (1879)]. Again, however, it was important that such a judge as Cardozo should enunciate that thesis; especially valuable was it to have Cardozo say: "Deep below consciousness are other forces, the likes and the dislikes, the predilections and the prejudices, the complex of instincts and emotions and habits and convictions, which make the man, whether he be litigant or judge. . . . There has been a certain lack of candor in much of the discussion of the theme, or rather in the refusal to discuss it, as if judges must lose respect and confidence by the reminder that they are subject to human limitations. . . . The great tides and currents which engulf the rest of men, do not turn aside in their course, and pass judges by" [***The Nature of the Judicial Process***]. Following Holmes, he sagely added: "The training of the judge, if coupled with what is styled the judicial temperament, will help in some degree to emancipate him from the suggestive power of individual dislikes and prepossessions."

Interested in matters of policy, Cardozo was fascinated by cases presenting situations where gaps in the precedents existed, or by those which invited deviation from the precedents because the old doctrines had produced unduly harsh results. He delighted in portraying the "creative function" of the judges in such instances, a function Cardozo brilliantly performed in some of his landmark opinions. Wisely, however, he warned repeatedly that those were "exceptional cases."

Perhaps Cardozo's most original suggestion was that a judge, in determining what legal rules or principles to apply in deciding a case, can and should employ four methods. Cardozo called them the methods (1) of philosophy (or analogy or logic), (2) of evolution (historical development), (3) of tradition (customs), and (4) of sociology (justice, morals, and social welfare). This suggestion stimulates the advocate who aims to persuade judges, and supplies judges with some very useful tools in decision-making. These tools, [**Selected Writings of Benjamin N. Cardozo**], to be sure, have some rough edges. As Professor Patterson says in his Preface to the four methods "were not exactly phrased or clearly delimited" by Cardozo. In particular, Cardozo's use of the word "logic" sometimes confuses, as when he speaks of a choice "between one logic and another," although what he really means, as the context shows, is this: The choice relates to the principle which becomes the major premise of the judge's logic—whether that premise be found in historical development or in tradition or in social welfare, or in a compromise between two or more of those three.

The following comments, in 1918, by Hoernlé (in a review of a book of legal essays by divers writers, a book from which Cardozo often quotes) point up this common fallacy in which Cardozo indulges: "What logician ever demanded of a lawyer a procedure yielding artificial, unreasonable, unjust results? It is the lawyer, not the logician, who has insisted . . . on torturing the ever-novel, ever-changing forms of social and industrial life into a strait-jacket of concept and rules, which are . . . treated as rigid and fixed. . . . There is no logic known to me which forbids the recognition that 'legal systems do and must grow, that legal principles are not absolute, but relative to time and place'; or which demands the ignoring of the connection between law and economics. . . . But what makes the difference . . . between the kind of thinking that is rightly denounced as formalism, logic-chopping, hair-splitting, . . . and the kind of thinking which our authors seek to secure . . . by the introduction of historical, sociological, psychological considerations? *The difference is material, not formal.* Formally, thinking is good or bad, according as the conclusion does, or does not, follow from the premises. Materially, thinking is good or bad, according as the premises from which conclusions are drawn are more or less complete as measured by the whole range of the problem, or more or less relevant to the task and the purpose in hand. What our authors criticize as bad logic is really bad premises, not a faulty technique in deducing conclusions, but a faulty subject matter. . . . What our authors call for, and seek to secure, is better premises, a fuller and completer range of *material* considerations out of which to elicit 'substantial justice'. . . . The solution depends on what view we take of the . . . factors which ought to be considered, if concrete justice is to be secured in each particular case. . . . No logician can legislate for the lawyer on such material points" [review of *The Science of Legal Method,* in *Harvard Law Review* (1918)].

But if, in company with many other legal philosophers, Cardozo sometimes went astray in his conception of logic, that was a minor fault. Despite it, these books constitute invaluable treatises on upper-court judging, treatises which almost certainly will never be equalled. I can testify that they have proved an indispensable guide to the perplexed for at least one upper-court judge, and, for him, an inexhaustible source of moral inspiration. To avoid any possible misunderstanding of the balance of this article, let me say, then, that I join whole-heartedly with the many who hail Cardozo as one of our greatest appellate judges and who appraise his books as priceless contributions to a comprehension of what appellate courts do.

By the way of preface to what follows, I quote the following: "That he [Cardozo] was a great judge, that he advanced the progress of keen thinking about the purposes and workings of the courts, is beyond question. That he was a great person, too, is undeniable. . . . Surely here was a wise and good man, entitled to veneration. But he was neither an immortal nor a mortal god. Being human, he escaped perfection. . . . No man is great in all his aspects. Diderot observed that 'everything even among the greatest of all the sons of men is incomplete, mixed, relative; everything is possible in the way of contradictions and limits; every virtue neighbors elements of uncongenial alloy; all heroism may hide points of littleness; all genius has its days of shortened vision.' Unmitigated or monolithic praise of the great departed often encourages imitation of their errors and weaknesses. . . . If it should be said that it is presumptuous for so unaccomplished a person to criticize . . . one so great as Cardozo, my answer will be this: It is a prized democratic maxim that even an alley cat may look at a king; it was an untutored boy who saw the true nature of the emperor's clothes" [Anon Y. Mous, "The Speech of Judges: A Dissenting Opinion," *Virginia Law Review* (1943)].

II

Since Cardozo, when at the bar, was principally an upper-court lawyer, and, in his long tenure on the bench, an upper-court judge (except for a few months), it would have been understandable if he had avowedly limited himself to writing of "The Nature of the Appellate Phases of the Judicial Process." In that event, these books would have deserved the all but uniform praise they have received. But I think they merit a marked criticism almost never voiced: unfortunately, Cardozo purported, without qualification, to describe the entire judicial process. Because of his reputation, the very excellence of his teachings in the narrow appellate field, to which they legitimately pertain, has tended to dampen inquiry in a far larger field where inquiry is far more necessary.

For Cardozo completely by-passed the operations of the trial courts, as if to say either that they had little significance or that their unique decisional activities and distinctive functions had no place in that process. Although, before he used the phrase, the "judicial process" had been defined to include "all the steps and proceedings in a cause from its commencement to its conclusion" [see *United States V. Murphy,* 82 F. CD. Del. (1897); *State V. Guilbert,* 56 Ohio St., 47 N. E. (1897); *Blair V. Maxbass Security Bank,* 44 N. D., 176 N. W. (1919)]. Cardozo excluded, as if non-existent, the events occurring in the trial stage of thousands of cases, events which occur in trial courts but never in upper courts: the witnesses testifying, the lawyers examining and cross-examining the witnesses, the jurors listening to the witnesses and to the arguments of the lawyers, the trial judge (when sitting without a jury) passing on the credibility of the witnesses' oral testimony. The omission of all these phenomena—familiar to every trial judge, trial lawyer, and newspaper reporters who "cover the courts"—renders Cardozo's exposition, as a description of how courts work, seriously misleading. Eminently satisfactory as an account of appellate-court ways, it is bizarre as an account of trial-court ways—as bizarre as would be an account of manners at Buckingham Palace if taken as also applicable to rush-hour behavior in the New York subways. Nor was Cardozo's misdescription inadvertent. On the contrary, as we shall see, he grew irritated when his grave omission of trial-court happenings was called to his attention, and did his best to discourage efforts to correct his description.

The omission was grave for this reason: because of it, Cardozo, with seeming justification, could give credence to a gross over-estimation of the reliability and excellence of our courthouse products. "Nine-tenths, perhaps more, of the cases that come before a court," he wrote, "are predetermined—predetermined in the sense that they are predestined—their fate established by inevitable laws that follow them from birth to death" [*The Growth of the Law*]. Substitute "upper court" for "court" in that sentence, and it is perhaps not too wide of the mark. It cannot possibly stand up, however, as a characterization of our entire court system. In most instances, when a case has already been decided by a trial court, a capable lawyer can accurately predict what, if an appeal is taken, will be the decision of the upper court. But (for reasons I shall presently canvass) no such easy prediction can be made of most trial-court decisions. Cardozo, by restricting the judicial process to appellate courts, presented a picture of the workings of our court system as, in the main, just, reliable, and steady. That highly inaccurate picture afforded smug satisfaction to much of the legal profession. For, if Cardozo was correct, the judicial process needed comparatively little improvement.

Now the truth is that, for most persons who become involved in litigation, what trial courts do has far more significance than has the performance of upper courts. For not only is the overwhelming majority of decisions not appealed, but in most of the relatively few that are appealed—probably not more than 6 per cent annually—the appellate courts accept as final the trial-court findings of fact. This they do because of a circumstance which accounts for and derives from a unique characteristic of our trial courts: a jury, or a trial judge in a non-jury case, can observe the demeanor of the orally testifying witnesses. The appellate judges cannot. Observation of witnesses' deportment is by no means an infallible method of determining the accuracy of their testimony; but, no better method having been devised, such observation of witnesses, whenever it is possible, is generally deemed essential in our legal system. Judge Learned Hand summarized views often previously expressed by our courts when he said that "that complex of sight and sound, from which we make our conclusions in a courtroom, is in large part eviscerated when reduced to the printed word" [*Petterson Lighterage & T.*

Corp. v. New York Central R. R., 126 F.2d (C. C. A.2d 1942)]. As Wigmore put it, "The witness' demeanor . . . is always assumed to be in evidence" [*Evidence*]. A "stenographic transcript," wrote Judge Ulman, ". . . fails to reproduce tones of voice and hesitations of speech that often make a sentence mean the reverse of what the mere words signify. The best and most nearly accurate record is like a dehydrated peach; it has neither the substance nor the flavor of the fruit before it was dried." [*The Judge Takes the Stand*].

It follows that the decisions of trial courts—in which courts alone can the witnesses be seen and heard—determine the fate of, say, 98 per cent of all litigated cases. That 98 per cent Cardozo usually disregarded. For him, a 2 per cent tail wagged a 98 per cent dog. It was as if a meteorologist had founded his studies of weather solely on weather conditions at the equator, or as if a physician had insisted that human health must be studied exclusively in terms of the health of twenty-year-old males. Cardozo, generalizing from wholly insufficient material, was guilty of an unwarranted extrapolation. He basically erred in considering the "facts" of cases as "data," as "given" to the courts. That is true, on the whole, in the appellate phase of that process. It is emphatically not true in its trial phase. The "facts" of cases (as I shall try to show) are not the facts as they actually occurred, not things which exist outside of court. They are usually processed by the trial courts, are their peculiar products. As Judge Olson recently said, "trials are commonly called law suits, but it often seems they might better be called fact suits" ["Observations from a Trial Bench," *Washington Law Review* (1947)].

Upper courts concern themselves chiefly with the legal rules and principles. So, too, did Cardozo in his books. As a consequence, for him the judicial process signified little more than the application to facts, already "found," of (1) established rules and principles, or (in occasional "exceptional cases") of (2) new rules and principles brought into being through the "creative" activities of the courts. The same was true of Cardozo's conception of "jurisprudence." His definitions of "law"—composed in part of ingredients taken from Holmes and from Pollock and Maitland—included non-legal materials, but did so only in so far as they contributed to such legal concepts or generalizations: "We shall unite in viewing as law," he wrote, "that body of principle and dogma which with a reasonable measure of probability may be predicted as *the* basis for judgment in pending or future controversies" [*The Growth of the Law*]. I underscore "the," as it high-lights Cardozo's perspective: The "body of principle and dogma," he is saying in effect, should alone be regarded as "the basis of judgment." Nothing is said to indicate that the ascertainment of the facts of a lawsuit also enters into the making of a judgment, so that to predict future judgments one must be able to predict what facts will be ascertained in future cases.

What I am driving at grows clearer in his other definitions: "A principle or rule of conduct so established with reasonable certainty that it *will be enforced by the courts* if its authority is challenged, is . . . a principle or rule of law" [*The Growth of the Law,* (emphasis added by Frank)]. Subsequently he expanded this statement into a general definition of "law." After noting that "that word stands for a good many notions," he added: "I find lying around loose, and ready to be embodied into a judgment according to some process of selection to be practiced by a judge, a vast conglomeration of principles and rules and usages and moralities. If these are so established as to justify a prediction with reasonable certainty that *they will have the backing of the courts* in the event that their authority is challenged, I say that they are law. . . . " [**"Jurisprudence,"** emphasis added by Frank]. It would waste time to argue whether these definitions of the hopelessly ambiguous word "law" are preferable to one of a dozen or more others. But it is distinctly worth while to point out that his definitions contain phrases which Cardozo never bothered to explain although they shriek for elucidation. I refer to the phrases, *"will be enforced* by the courts," and *"will have the backing* of the courts." If you peer behind those words, you will be gazing at an immense legal jungle (partly explored by Wigmore, in his *Principles of Judicial Proof,* and by others in books written for practicing trial lawyers), a jungle Cardozo disdained to enter—the jungle of trials and trial-court fact-finding.

Without trial-court fact-finding, judicial "enforcement" of the legal rules seldom gets under way. For a court "enforces" or "backs up" a rule only if the court, in some specific lawsuit, holds that the facts which invoke that rule are the facts of that specific case. If, and only if, the court so holds, does it apply that rule to those facts. It follows that a rule is not "enforced" unless a trial court has "found" or purports to have "found" the pertinent facts, *i.e.,* those facts to which the rule applies. It also follows that, in almost any particular case—and therefore in almost all cases—trial-court fact-finding is fully as vital as any legal rule. To the human beings whose specific lawsuits the courts decide, the determinations of the facts have the utmost significance. If the facts are found against a party, he loses. The facts of a case, as found, furnish the ticket to the decision. "No tickee, no washee." For a legal rule is only a conditional statement. It says, "If the facts are thus and so, then these legal consequences ensue."

One would suppose, then, that a study purporting to cover the judicial process, a treatise on "jurisprudence," would include an extensive discussion of the methods of trial-court fact-finding and of the influences that affect it; would explain the multitude of factors involved in it; would emphasize its ineradicable chanciness and uncertainty in most cases, due to the unavoidable fallibility of witnesses, jurors, and trial judges.

Cardozo, however, ignored those topics, and without apologies. This is the more remarkable since, in the single brief passage in which he mentions the function of facts in litigation, he acknowledges their undeniable significance: "In what I have said," he wrote in 1924 [*The Nature of the Judicial Process*], "I have thrown, perhaps too much into the background and the shadow the cases where the controversy turns not upon the rule of law, but upon its application to the facts. Those cases, after all,

make up the bulk of business of the courts. They are important for the litigants concerned in them. They call for intelligence and patience and reasonable discernment on the part of judges who must decide them. But they leave jurisprudence where it stood before." A few lines later, he says that "jurisprudence remains untouched, regardless of the outcome" of such cases.

Truly, an astonishing attitude. "Jurisprudence," as Cardozo envisions it, stands aloof from those decisions, "important to litigants," which, according to Cardozo himself, "make up the bulk of the business of the courts." Why this snobbish aloofness on the part of "jurisprudence" when so much is at stake for our citizens? Because, in Cardozo's view, "jurisprudence" is indifferent to anything other than the legal generalizations, the legal rules and principles. Since the "judicial process," for Cardozo, is substantially co-extensive with "jurisprudence," his exposition of the nature of that process likewise cold-shoulders, as unworthy of consideration, the "bulk of the business of the courts."

Having thus artificially circumscribed the judicial process (by admittedly excluding from it the bulk of judicial business), Cardozo reaches a conclusion as to its workings which necessarily is artificial but which affords him much comfort: since (1) but a small percentage of the legal rules lack certainty, and (2) certainty in the judicial process means certainty in rules, it is demonstrable (according to Cardozo's reasoning) that (3) the extent of uncertainty in the judicial process is small. This conclusion (which is correct in respect of appellate courts but otherwise false) has a logical corollary; *i.e.,* experienced, able lawyers, Cardozo implies, can usually predict court decisions with accuracy: he declared that most rules, even those which allow courts some discretion, "have such an element of certainty that, in a vast majority of instances, prediction ceases to be hazardous for the trained and expert judgment" [**"Jurisprudence"**]. In other words (so Cardozo apparently maintains) competent lawyers can predict the outcome of most lawsuits before trial.

Not only that. "Law," as Cardozo defines it, shows up as largely stable, since "law" consists of the rules. Here, apparently, is cheer for the layman, since, says Cardozo, the "law" will, on the whole, conform to the layman's "reasonable expectations" [**"Jurisprudence"**].

The fatal vulnerability of that thesis,—*i.e.,* that legal certainty and the predictability of decisions are measurable by, and correspond to, the certainty of the rules—can be made clear by exposing the error in one of Cardozo's remarks about facts. After noting that the issues in most lawsuits relate "not to the law, but to the facts," he adds: "In countless litigations, the law is so clear that the judges have no discretion." *But trial courts—juries or trial judges trying cases without juries—have an amazing discretion in finding the facts.* When, as happens in most trials, the testimony is oral and the several witnesses disagree concerning the facts, the trial court's discretion in the determination of the facts—based on a selection of some of the witnesses as credible and others as not—usually is utterly uncontrollable. Indeed, the jury system has often been praised just because juries, through general-verdict fact-finding, have a virtually unregulated power to nullify the legal rules; and much the same power is possessed by a trial judge who sits without a jury.

The exercise of this discretion will often paralyze prediction. In the first place, witnesses, being human, are humanly fallible. No one has discovered or invented any instrument or objective method by which a jury or trial judge can pick out those of the witnesses, if any, who accurately observed the facts in dispute, accurately remembered what they observed, and accurately (without bias or prejudice or perjury) report in court their memories of what they observed. Conventional jurisprudence, in turning its back on that difficulty, relies on an implicit postulate or axiom—the Truth-Will-Out Axiom, *i.e.,* that bias, mistakes and perjury are infrequent, abnormal, and that, when they occur in litigation, they are usually uncovered, so that they have slight effects on the outcome of lawsuits. That axiom, completely out of line with observable trial courtroom realities, should be repudiated. Once it is repudiated, it becomes obvious that, in the selection of portions of the testimony on which to rely, the jury or trial judge must make a guess. In this guessy choice, on which fact-finding is constructed, there inheres much inscrutable, un-get-at-able subjectivity: Not only are the reactions of the witnesses, to the past events about which they testify, shot through with subjectivity. So, also, are the reactions of juries or trial judges to the witnesses. For the juries and trial judges are themselves but fallible witnesses of the witnesses. Thus fact-finding encounters multiple subjectivity.

The truth, neglected by Cardozo & Co., is that the facts in dispute in a lawsuit are past events which do not walk into the courtroom; that those actual past "objective" events can be ascertained, at best, only through subjective reactions to the testifying witnesses' subjective reactions; and that, therefore, to speak of "finding" the "facts" is misdescriptive. Therefore, my description of the nature of a legal rule needs revision: a legal rule means, "If the jury or trial judge (expressly or impliedly) says that it believes the facts are thus and so, and if there is some substantial evidence to justify that statement of belief, then these legal consequences ensue."

No third person can tell whether such statements correctly report the beliefs of the juries or trial judges (*i.e.,* whether the statements match their private beliefs); for it is not permitted to examine or cross-examine juries and judges. But even if any such statement did correctly report such belief, no appellate judges could probe the belief to determine whether it matched the actual past facts, the "facts in themselves." For no one can formulate, in the form of rules, the bases of such a belief. The belief is "unruly," one might say. Long ago, Sir Henry Maine, in a passage which has largely escaped attention, pointed to the delicate task of a trial judge "in drawing inferences from the assertion of a witness to the existence of the facts asserted by him. It is in the passage from the statements of the witness to the inference that those statements are true, that judicial inquiries break down." It "is the rarest and highest personal accomplishment of a judge to make allowance for the ignorance and timidity of witnesses, and to see through the confident and plausible liar. Nor can any gen-

eral rules be laid down for the acquisition of this power, which has methods peculiar to itself, and almost undefinable" ["The Theory of Evidence," *Village Communities* (1872)]. Wherefore, as there is no yardstick for measuring the accuracy of a trial court's finding of facts in a case where the testimony is oral and credibility is in issue, often the discretion used in reaching that finding cannot be controlled.

You will search in vain in Cardozo's discourses on the judicial process for any mention of the huge measure of discretion vested in juries and trial judges with respect to the facts. (Indeed, nowhere did he refer to juries.) He wrote as if discretion in the judicial process consisted solely of discretion inhering in the rules or in the selection of rules. That perhaps explains why it never occurred to him to note that it is peculiarly true of jurymen and trial judges—when reacting at trials to witnesses who testify orally—that they are affected by "forces" which lie "deep below consciousness," the "likes and dislikes, the predilections and the prejudices, the complex of emotions and habits and convictions." In the upper courts, as Cardozo noted, those "forces" sometimes somewhat influence the choice of rules. In the trial courts, those "forces" influence, often immeasurably, the choice of facts which is within the wide discretion of jurors and trial judges.

Since that choice is a guess, frequently induced by inscrutable factors, the lawyer, trying to predict a decision, engages in a baffling undertaking: he is trying to predict what facts will be "found," and therefore guessing the future guess of a jury or trial judge. Moreover, before a case is tried, the lawyer's guess often must be about the future guess of a jury, or trial judge, as yet unknown to the lawyer. Necessarily, such a guess is wobbly. It would be wobbly even if all the legal rules and principles were as precise as a table of logarithms, as fixed as the North Star.

How true that is becomes obvious when one considers that in the great majority of suits (*e.g.,* negligence actions and the like) both sides agree as to the applicable rules, the disputes relating to the facts alone. In the light of such cases, it passes understanding that many distinguished legal thinkers, who are rule-obsessed (*i.e.,* who want to believe that decisions are readily foreseeable whenever the pertinent rules are precise), absurdly prattle that clear and definite rules prevent much litigation because (so say these thinkers) most men will not be so foolish as to begin suits in which the relevant rules have such definiteness. Nor can it be ignored that no legal rule, no matter how exact, precludes the injection, by one of the parties to a suit, of an issue of fact which throws open the doors to the reception of oral testimony, and thus to a choice of the "facts" by a trial judge or jury.

These choices of the "facts," resulting from the exercise of the trial courts' guessy discretion, may "leave jurisprudence untouched," but, if so, they leave it looking pretty lifeless, indeed inhuman. The legal rules and principles, the sole foundation of that artificial, ghostly, Cardozian jurisprudence, are stable for the most part, as Cardozo correctly maintains; and, often, predictions of what rules and principles the courts will employ can be fairly exact. Trained lawyers, for example, know the "jurisprudence" relevant to murder trials or automobile accident trials, and can prophesy, with a high degree of reliability, what rules will be applied in such litigation. But what of it? The layman wants to know whether those rules will be applied to the actual facts. If, in a murder case, the correct rule is applied to the wrong facts, an innocent man will be killed by the state. If a trial court, by believing a perjured witness, decides that a deed is a mortgage, the court's legal rule may be impeccable, but the wrong litigant will win.

If, as Cardozo suggests, it be the function of the courts to ensure that, in general, decisions conform to the layman's "reasonable expectations," will a layman consider that a court has discharged its obligations if the legal rules thus conform but, because of an error in fact-finding, the decision in his case does not? As I have said elsewhere: "When the actual facts of a case are not ascertained by a court, its decision may be completely erroneous while yet appearing to be correct. It matters little to a citizen, when he wrongfully loses a lawsuit, whether the decision is the product of the application of the 'wrong' legal rule to the 'right' facts, or the product of the application of the 'right' legal rule to the 'wrong' facts. It is a basic tenet of our theory of justice that cases which are substantially alike should, usually, be decided the same way—according to the same legal rules—and that cases which are substantially different should be decided differently—according to different legal rules. Defects in the ascertainment of the actual facts may result, therefore, in a denial of justice. Because of such defects, cases which, in truth, are very different may seem to the courts to be virtually identical and are decided identically. To the extent, then, that removable defects in fact-finding are not eliminated, proper and practicable individualization of cases does not occur, and avoidable injustice is done" [*If Men Were Angels*].

When one discusses legal certainty and predictability, is it not misleading to discuss merely the certainty of the rules and of predictions as to what rules courts will employ, while refusing to talk of decisions? If a man, defeated in a suit because of a mistake of the trial court about the facts, goes to jail or the electric chair, or loses his business, will it solace him to learn that there was no possible doubt concerning the applicable legal principle?

Usually a client wants his lawyer to prophesy a specific decision relating to a matter in which that particular client has a specific interest. The likelihood that the lawyer will successfully predict such a decision will vary with the stage at which he is asked for his opinion:

1. When the client, having just signed a contract, asks what are his rights thereunder, at that time neither the client nor the other party to the contract has as yet taken any steps under the contract. The lawyer's prediction at this stage must include a hazardous guess as to what each of the parties will do or not do in the future. The prediction must frequently be so full of if's as to be of little practical value.

2. After events have occurred which give rise to threatened litigation, the client may inquire concerning the outcome of the suit, if one should be brought.

a. Before the lawyer has interviewed prospective witnesses, his guess is on a shaky foundation.

b. After interviewing them, his guess is less shaky. But, unless the facts are certain to be agreed upon, the guess is still dubious, if the lawyer does not know what judge will try the case; it is more so, if there may be a jury trial, since the lawyer cannot know what persons will compose the jury.

3. After the trial, but before decision, the lawyer's prophecy may be better. For he is now estimating the reaction to the testimony of a known trial judge or a known jury. Yet, if the testimony was oral, that guessing is frequently not too easy.

4. After trial and judgment by the trial court, the guess relates to the outcome of an appeal, should one be taken. It therefore usually relates solely to the rules the upper court will apply to the facts already "found" by the trial judge or jury. At this stage, a competent, trained lawyer can often predict with accuracy. Only this last prediction situation, no others, does Cardozo discuss.

Surely his discussion is altogether too restricted. And surely those interested in the judicial process ought not to disregard such factors, producing uncertainties in decisions, as, *inter alia,* the following: perjured witnesses, coached witnesses, biased witnesses, witnesses mistaken in their observation of the facts as to which they testify or in their memory of their observations, missing or dead witnesses, missing or destroyed documents, crooked lawyers, stupid lawyers, stupid jurors, prejudiced jurors, inattentive jurors, trial judges who are stupid or bigoted or biased or "fixed" or inattentive to the testimony. Nor ought humane men ignore the fact that a party may lose a suit he should win because, in preparation for trial, he cannot afford to hire a detective, an engineer, an accountant, or a handwriting expert. Are we, judges and lawyers, to give no heed to such matters and, because of such heedlessness, to do nothing to improve, so far as practicable, the methods of fact-finding in trial courts?

III

None of these matters did Cardozo deign to consider in these books. In banishing such matters from the province of "jurisprudence," and, correlatively, in excluding them from the judicial process, he did a marked social disservice. For if they are thus ostracized, if eminent judges—setting an example to the bar—will not soil their hands with them, but regard them as legal bastards beyond the pale of proper professional notice, who will attend to them?

Someone may say in Cardozo's defense that the followed an established tradition, since few books or articles on jurisprudence had mentioned the vagaries of trials and the obstacles to prediction inhering in fact-finding. But, alas, Cardozo lent his imposing authority to the strengthening of that tradition. Worse, in 1932, in his last published address on the subject. [**"Jurisprudence"**], he severely criticized those writers who, about that time, were calling attention to the grave deficiencies and unfortunate consequences of that tradition. He ascribed to these writers "anarchical professions," expressions manifesting "a petulant contempt" of "order and certainty and rational coherence," an attempted "degradation of the principles, rules and concepts," "a tendency to exaggerate the indeterminacy . . . or chance element" in the decisions of cases, and an advocacy of the position that "conformity and order are to be spurned by the judge as no longer goods at all." He wholly disregarded the fact that several of those he thus criticized were trying to describe, not to praise, the current workings of the trial courts, that their purpose was to show that the description of the judicial process in conventional books on jurisprudence had grossly exaggerated the extent of legal certainty and had led to gross over-estimations of the capacity of lawyers to predict many decisions in particular lawsuits, because, no matter how certain most of the rules and principles might be, the fact-determinations in many lawsuits could not be foretold. He erroneously asserted that these writers regarded as desirable the amount of existing legal imprecision they described. He took their descriptions of existing conditions as manifestations of their aims and desires, of their ideals, their program. When they said, "This is the way things are," in effect he read them as saying, "This is the way things ought to be, the way we want them to be."

I shall dwell on this startling misreading, because it is the key to an understanding of Cardozo's attitude. At first glance, his strictures may appear to have been provoked by his irritation that the descriptions these writers gave of courthouse ways were strikingly at odds with his own relatively tranquil picture of the judicial process. I think, however, that the explanation is more complicated and runs thus: In this 1932 paper, he criticized all those persons unfortunately called "legal realists" but who might better have been labeled adherents of "constructive legal skepticism." Although they had in common a skeptical attitude towards traditional jurisprudence, by no means did they constitute a homogeneous movement, since they disagreed sharply with one another. Nevertheless, they may be roughly divided into two groups:

1. The first and larger group (of whom Llewellyn is representative) may conveniently be labeled "rule-skeptics." They resembled Cardozo in that they had little or no interest in trial courts, but riveted their attention largely on appellate courts and on the nature and uses of the legal rules. Some (not all) of this group (Oliphant being the most conspicuous here) espoused the fatuous notions of "behavioristic psychology." Some (not all) of these "rule-skeptics" went somewhat further than Cardozo as to the extent of the existent and desirable power of judges to alter the legal rules.

2. The second and smaller group may conveniently be labeled the "fact-skeptics." They importantly diverged not only from conventional jurisprudence but also from the "rule-skeptics." So far as appellate courts and the legal rules are concerned, the views of the "fact-skeptics" as to existent and desirable legal certainty approximated the views of Cardozo, Pound, and many others not categorized as "realists." The "fact-skeptics' " divergence sprang from their prime interest in the trial courts. Tracing the major cause of legal uncertainty to trial uncertainties, and claiming that the resultant legal uncertainty was far more extensive than most legal scholars (including the "rule-skeptics") admitted, the "fact-skeptics" urged students of our legal system to abandon an obsessively exclusive concentration on the rules.

Cardozo, in his 1932 paper, did not differentiate between the "rule-skeptics" and the "fact-skeptics." Someone might conceivably think that he deemed the "fact-skeptics" not worthy of his attention. But several times he cited the writings of at least one of them, and singled out those writings for special censure. It occasions surprise, therefore, that he said nothing responsive to the features of those writings which distinguished the views of the "fact-skeptics" from his own—the stress on the facts of cases, on juries, on trial judges, on conflicts in testimony, on the difficulties of lawyers trying to prophesy decisions in lawsuits turning on disputed fact-issues, on the frequent inability of citizens to rely on decisions because of the unknowability of future fact-findings. In this paper, Cardozo uttered not one syllable about those subjects. Why, even when specifically criticising the "fact-skeptics," he maintained such silence, I can only explain as follows: so ingrained had become his habit of assuming that legal uncertainty stemmed exclusively from rule-uncertainty, that, when the "fact-skeptics" spoke of legal uncertainty, he jumped to the conclusion that they, too, must mean solely rule-uncertainty. Wherefore, he was deaf to their reiterated assertions that they had chiefly in mind the uncertainties resulting from the contingencies which affect findings of fact.

For instance, they had said that anyone who visited trial courts would see that the outcome of most trials was chancy because of the numerous chance circumstances influencing fact-determinations; that description Cardozo translated as an expression of a preference for "the random or chance element as a good in itself . . . exceeding in value the elements of certainty and order and rational coherence." Again, as a part of their description, they had made the statement that, as trial courts have immense discretion in finding the facts of cases, those courts *can,* and sometimes do, nullify rules by deliberately or inadvertently finding the wrong facts. Cardozo interpreted that descriptive statement as disclosing a desire that a judge *should have* the power to overturn or nullify any legal rule he disliked. The "fact skeptics" had maintained that *stare decisis* often yields a certainty that is only an illusion, not primarily because of the instability of the rules, but because—even if all the rules were indubitably clear and fixed, and even if always the courts slavishly adhered to the precedents—the facts found by trial courts would frequently be unforeseeable. This, Cardozo charged, was an expression of a disdain for precedents, of a program for wiping out *stare decisis*.

In short, he did his utmost to bring into disrepute these efforts, based on observations of trial courts, to revise the traditional, misleading description of the judicial process. He stood steadfastly by his implicit position that that process and jurisprudence begin and end in the upper courts.

You see the tragic consequence of such a position: if, at any time, the legal rules and principles of a legal system are in pretty good shape, then (according to Cardozo), so also is the judicial process of that system, regardless of whether the decisions of the courts are needlessly unfair or unjust. *By shrinking the scope of the judicial process, by resisting those who would have it mean the administration of justice in all the courts, Cardozo blocked inquiry into the actual performances of courthouse government.*

Our greatest judge, Learned Hand, after a long period of service on a trial bench, remarked in 1926: "I must say that as a litigant I should dread a lawsuit beyond almost anything else short of sickness and death" ["The Deficiencies of Trials to Reach the Heart of the Matter," in *Lectures on Legal Topics*]. Cardozo took no note of that remark. If he had, it might have given him pause; for he knew that Judge Hand, in so reporting conditions in our trial courts, was not maintaining the desirability of those conditions or expressing "a petulant contempt" of "order and certainty and rational coherence." Consider this statement by Cardozo: "I sometimes think that we worry overmuch about the enduring consequences of our errors. They may work a little confusion for a time. In the end, they will be modified or corrected or their teachings ignored. The future takes care of such things" "[*The Nature of the Judicial Process*]. Apply that statement to an error about the facts in a trial, as a result of which a man loses his life's savings or is hanged. Did Cardozo mean that "the future takes care of such things?" Of course not. He was not thinking of trials and trial-court decisions but of the legal rules. His was a Hamlet-less Hamlet.

The clue to Cardozo's impatience with those who sought to include descriptions of trial-court operations in the description of the judicial process appears in several passages in his books. "Judgments themselves," he wrote, "have importance for the student so far, and so far only, as they permit a reasonable prediction that like judgments will be rendered if like situations repeat themselves. . . . When the uniformities are sufficiently constant to be the subject of prediction with reasonable certainty, we say that law exists." "[*The Growth of the Law*]. Cardozo sought solely uniformities, knowing that, if un-uniformities also exist, the predictor is in trouble; but since in most trial-court fact-finding, much of un-uniformity is present, that trouble often arises. In another passage, he said: "One of the most fundamental social interests is that law shall be uniform and impartial. There must be nothing in its action that savors of prejudice or favor or even arbitrary whim or fitfulness" [*The Nature of the Judicial Process*]. Yet decisions based on jury verdicts notoriously lack uniformity and impartiality, are replete with prejudice and fitfulness. You see why Cardozo failed to discuss them. Again, he said, "The eccentricities of judges balance one another." [*The Nature of the Judicial Process*]. So they often do in appellate courts composed of several judges. But the same cannot be said of the divers trial judges and juries when, in separate courtrooms, they hear witnesses and find facts. As I have noted elsewhere, "There is no standardization of judges and jurors so that all of them will be sure to react in identical fashion to any given body of conflicting testimony. Judges and juries vary in their respective intelligence, perceptiveness, attentiveness and other mental and emotional characteristics which are op-erative while they are listening to, and observing, witness" [*If Men were Angels*]. From all such disturbing thoughts Cardozo screened himself, by rejecting consideration of *nisi prius* courts. One cannot believe that he would have written as he did if he had had several years of experience as a trial judge. He had a blind spot. He suffered from an occupational disease to which upper-court judges are susceptible—appellate-court-itis. (That is why, one surmises, his jurisprudence omits, among other things, what might be termed "juriesprudence.")

At one point, for a moment, he almost gives the show away. He quotes Haldane's comment that his own philosophic interest in principles had been valuable to him in his practice at the bar. "It did not help in the work of cross-examination," Haldane says in these quoted comments. "I was never good at that, nor in the conduct of *nisi prius* cases. But it was invaluable in the preparation for the presentation of great questions to the Supreme Tribunals, where the judges were keen about principles and were looking out for help from the advocate." ["**Jurisprudence**"]. That hint Cardozo did not follow up. It cannot be overlooked that never does he cast a glance at the many books on trial techniques, "hints to advocates," and such. He cites Wigmore's *Evidence,* but not Wigmore's *Principles of Judicial Proof . . .* which contains a wealth of detail about vicissitudes of trials. Perhaps the secret of Cardozo's avoidance of such books is that, as Morgan suggests, they should not be read "by those who want to believe, and want others to believe, that a lawsuit is a proceeding for the discovery of truth by rational processes" [in a review of Goldstein's *Trial Technique, Harvard Law Review* (1936)]. It is worthy of remark that Chief Justice Taft, doubtless more conservative in most respects than Cardozo, did interest himself in the deficiencies of trial courts, did try to better the litigating chances in those courts of the underprivileged. What explains this difference between those two men? Probably the fact that Taft, from personal experience, knew more about the lower courts.

In the kind of courtroom where Cardozo spent most of his professional life, the atmosphere is serene—stratospheric. There, lawyers alone address the court; and they must do so with decorum, in an orderly, dignified manner. Not so in the trial courtroom. Absent there the stratospheric hush. It is, as Wigmore notes, "a place of surging emotions, distracting episodes, and sensational surprises." The drama there, full of interruptions, is turbently enacted by flesh-and-blood witnesses and lawyers. In the upper court the clashes between witnesses and counsel appear only in reposeful printed pages. Little wonder if a judge, after many years in such a serene court, grows forgetful of the unserenity characteristic of trials, develops a myopia which limits his range of vision.

Relevant here is the attitude of persons accustomed to years of near-sightedness. "When," we are told, "finally they decide for themselves that they ought to wear glasses, they are often disappointed. . . . The following conversation is fairly common: Patient: 'Doctor, I think these glasses are wrong. I can't wear them.' Doctor: 'You seem to be able to see quite clearly with them. What is wrong?'

Patient: 'I can't bear it. They make all my friends look so ugly. They have spots on their faces and their collars are dirty, and all the houses look so untidy and old. I don't like it. I don't want to see all that detail.' All one can say is that it is a pity such a patient was allowed to grow up so out of touch with reality, as this attitude of not wanting to see what is ugly may extend to one's attitude towards life and lead to a shelving of responsibility" [Mann and Pirie, *The Science of Seeing*]. This attitude of not wanting to see reality produces "shortsighted policies" [*The Science of Seeing*]. So, I think, with Cardozo. He exploited his prestige to block a movement aimed at preventing the legal profession from shelving its responsibility for conditions in the trial courts. That was indeed shortsighted policy. He had a "want to believe" and "a want to have others believe" that, on the whole, our courts employ thoroughly rational procedures. He treated his "want," his wish, as if it were a statement of existing courthouse realities. In other words, often when he said, "This is the way things are," he should have said, "This is the way things ought to be." Suppose, now, that he had so recognized, that, correcting his shortsightedness, he had perceived that his purported description of the judicial process was but a want, a wish, an ideal, an objective to be achieved by that process. What then? Then he would have converted his wishful thinking into "thinkful wishing." Then he would have felt eager to investigate our entire court system, including our trial courts, to ascertain how far it fell short of his ideal. Having ascertained, as he would have, its obvious shortcomings, he—a moralist and keen for justice—would have made detailed suggestions to bring that system closer into line with his aspirations.

The perspective which Cardozo's attitude obscured, I recently summarized in an opinion [*In re* Fried, 161 F.2d (C.C.A.2d 1947)]. as follows: "The 'substantive' legal rules, civil or criminal, embody social policies ('social value judgments'). To enforce, and thus give effect to, such policies is considered one of the principal duties of the courts. They discharge that duty, however, not at wholesale but at retail, by applying those rules in specific lawsuits to the particular facts of those respective suits as 'found' by the courts. As a 'substantive' rule merely declares that specified legal consequences will be attached to a specified state of facts, the rule should be operative only in particular instances where those facts actually occurred. Accordingly, the social policy embodied in any such rule is not actually enforced when, in deciding a case, a court, through misapprehension of what actually occurred, applies that rule to facts which in truth never existed. The whole job then miscarries: Mistakenly to apply a rule to non-existent facts—to facts mistakenly 'found'—is no less unjust, no less a defective operation of judicial administration, than to apply an erroneous 'substantive' legal rule to the actual facts. Either way, the policy expressed in the correct rule is frustrated. An error in 'finding' the facts thus yields what might be called 'injustice according to law.' The facts involved in any case are past facts. They do not walk into the courtroom. Judicial fact-finding, a human process by which a man or some men attempt to reconstruct a segment of an 'objective' past, is necessarily fallible. For it is a job of history-writing, and, like all history-writing, inescapably involves 'subjective'

factors and encounters other obstacles sometimes insurmountable. But courts cannot shirk that job. . . . Unfortunately, the major efforts of those who have tried to improve our legal system have been devoted either to improvements in other phases of 'procedure' or in the 'substantive' legal rules. Those improvements will be needlessly nullified just to the extent that the fact-finding process remains insufficiently scrutinized and, consequently, needlessly defective. Fact-finding is today the soft spot in the administration of justice. In considerable measure that is true because the reformers have largely disregarded the actual fact-finding methods used by the trial courts which, as they are the chief fact-finders, and for other reasons, constitute the most important part of our judicial system; even the procedural reformers have restricted their attention chiefly to those phases of trial court 'procedure' which manifest themselves in upper-court, and occasional trial-court, opinions. It has been too little noticed that a 'substantive legal right'—an 'interest' said to be 'legally protected' by a 'substantive' legal rule—has no practical value when a court by mistakenly mis-finding the facts— because of missing witnesses or documents, or because it believes the testimony of witnesses who in truth are inaccurate, etc.—decides that the claimant has no such 'right' or 'interest.' Doubtless, for analytic purposes, there is often much utility in formally differentiating between 'substantive' and 'procedural' rights (or 'primary' and 'secondary,' or 'antecedent' and 'remedial,' or 'telic' and 'instrumental' rights). Once, however, it is stated, in terms of this formal analysis, that a judicial decision is the 'result of the application of the [substantive] rule of law to the *facts procedurally established,*' it becomes clear that a mistaken 'procedural establishment' of the facts destroys, for court-room purposes, the asserted 'substantive right,' from which it follows that, so far as courts are concerned, the effective assertion of any 'substantive right' depends entirely on the claimant's ability to maintain his so-called 'procedural right.' The Roman lawyers perhaps sensed this truth when they spoke of the 'procedural consumption' of a 'right of action' by which it was transformed into a 'right to judgment.' In other words, for practical court purposes, no 'substantive' right exists—whether it be a right asserted by a private person or by the government in its role of vindicator of a 'substantive' criminal rule— unless a court gives an enforceable judgment in favor of the alleged right-holder; and, ordinarily, a court will not give such a judgment, even when it uses a seemingly 'correct' rule, if it goes wrong on the facts. Of course, similarly a mistake in fact-finding may cause an erroneous judgment adverse to one who defends against an asserted claim. This, perhaps, appears more clearly if we crudely schematize the formal theory of the decisional process (i.e., the theory that a judicial decision or judgment is the product of a 'substantive' legal rule applied to the facts of the case) by saying: $R \times F = D$—when R is the rule, F the facts, and D the decision or judgment. On that basis, an erroneous F will lead to an erroneous D. As the F consists of the trial court's belief as to what were the actual past facts, the F, and therefore the D, will be erroneous if the court reaches its F by reliance on inaccurate evidence.

"No matter, then, how excellent the 'substantive' legal

rules (the R's) and the social policies they embody, specific decisions will go astray, absent competent fact-finding. (Holmes, J., once said that 'the only use of the forms is to present their contents, just as the only use of a pot is to present the beer . . . , and infinite meditation upon the pot will never give you the beer.'). All of which, I think, goes to show that our trial courts should assume a larger responsibility for the ascertainment, as near as may be, of the actual facts of litigated disputes."

IV

In an address in 1931, Cardozo spoke of "the myths that gather around institutions," saying that often such "myths are really the main thing," and "greater than the reality" [**"Faith and a Doubting World"**]. Maybe those observations were revelatory. For, in all his writings, Cardozo helped to perpetuate what I would call the Upper-Court Myth, the myth that upper-court opinions are "the main thing" in courthouse government. That myth I think deplorable. It be stows upon us appellate judges too much public kudos. It obscures the transcendent importance of trial courts, and the fact that trial judges encounter far greater difficulties than we do. In part, those difficulties inhere in the character of their job; in part they derive from our antiquated trial procedures. To improve the administration of justice we need, at a minimum, to overhaul our jury system; to revise our evidence rules; to give special training for the trial bench; to augment (without displacing the essential aspects of the adversary procedure) the responsibility of government for insuring that all important and practically available evidence is presented in trials. Those and other improvements will not be achieved as long as judges of great eminence, like Cardozo, continue to induce belief in the Upper-Court Myth.

It is high time that we apply to that myth all the skills of what Samuel Butler called the Art of Covery. "This," he said, "is as important . . . as Discovery. Surely the glory of finally getting rid of and burying a . . . troublesome matter should be as great as that of making an important discovery" [*The Note-Books of Samuel Butler*].

Robert B. Downs   (essay date 1970)

SOURCE: "Legal Mind at Work: Benjamin N. Cardozo's *The Nature of the Judicial Process*," in *Books That Changed America*, Macmillan Co., 1970, pp. 207-15.

[*In the following essay, Downs examines Cardozo's legal philosophy as outlined in* The Nature of the Judicial Process, *focusing on Cardozo's analysis of the primary forces that influence the establishment of judicial principles.*]

Benjamin Cardozo was rated by Roscoe Pound, an eminent legal scholar himself, as one of the ten greatest judges produced by the American bench. The names included in the illustrious line, beginning with John Marshall, shared certain common characteristics, according to Pound: "First of all, they were great lawyers, masters of their craft, masters of the authoritative materials in which judges in the English-speaking world are expected, as a duty of their office, to find the grounds of decision, and masters

of the technique of applying those materials to the decision of cases."

Cardozo's American ancestry antedates by well over a century the beginnings of the nation. Forebears on his mother's side came from Portugal to America in 1654. His paternal ancestors left the Spanish peninsula during the expulsion of the Jews in the sixteenth century, migrating first to Holland and then to England. The founder of the American line came to the Colonies about 1752. For the next two centuries the family produced a succession of distinguished patriots and cultural leaders.

The first of the Cardozos to gain prominence—though not honor—in judicial circles was Benjamin's father, who cast an unfortunate blight on the family name. Judge Albert Cardozo was a member of the infamous Tweed Ring in New York, where his conduct finally led to charges of malfeasance and corruption being filed against him; in order to escape impeachment he resigned. It has been remarked that much of Benjamin Cardozo's life was devoted to the atonement of his father's sins.

As a child Benjamin was taught by a tutor, Horatio Alger, who later became famous as the author of the most popular books for boys of the period, in all of which the hero triumphed over poverty and adversity by courage and hard work. Benjamin was a voracious reader of the Alger thrillers, and he credited his admittance to Columbia University at the early age of fifteen to the preparation for college received from Alger.

Cardozo's rise in the legal profession was rapid and brilliant. He served successively as a justice of the Supreme Court of New York, associate judge of the Court of Appeals, and finally as associate justice of the United States Supreme Court. Throughout his career his opinions, numbering some 470 in written form, are monuments of legal scholarship. Further, they are famous for literary style—in Santayana's words "clothed in a language that lends the message an intrinsic value, and makes it delightful to apprehend, apart from its importance in ultimate theory or practice."

Aside from the opinions, scattered through the *New York Reports* and *United States Reports* from 1914 to 1938, Cardozo's writings were not voluminous. Most widely known are four small books: *The Nature of the Judicial Process, The Growth of the Law, The Paradoxes of Legal Science,* and *Law and Literature*. It is generally agreed that the most original and significant of these works, the one exerting greatest influence on the legal profession and giving laymen the clearest insight into the workings of the law, is the first, *The Nature of the Judicial Process* (1921).

The extraordinary success of *The Nature of the Judicial Process* was due in part to the charm of the author's style, but more importantly to Cardozo's careful analysis of the factors, conscious and unconscious, which guide a judge in reaching his decisions. Previous to the appearance of this unique picture of the operations of the law, there was a widely prevailing belief that the legal process consisted primarily in drawing logical deductions from established precedents. Cardozo's interpretation showed that the matter was far more complex and by implication that the case method of teaching law has distinct limitations. As viewed by Cardozo, law is a living body of principles capable of growth and change.

"The work of deciding cases," states Cardozo, "goes on every day in hundreds of courts throughout the land. Any judge, one might suppose, would find it easy to describe the process which he had followed a thousand times and more. Nothing could be farther from the truth. Let some intelligent layman ask him to explain: he will not go very far before taking refuge in the excuse that the language of craftsmen is unintelligible to those untutored in the craft." Such an answer is unsatisfying to Cardozo and no doubt to the inquirer.

Consequently, the author indulges in introspection, asking himself such searching questions as: "What is it that I do when I decide a case? To what sources of information do I appeal for guidance? In what proportions do I permit them to contribute to the result? In what proportions ought they to contribute? If a precedent is applicable, when do I refuse to follow it? If no precedent is applicable, how do I reach the rule that will make a precedent for the future? If I am seeking logical consistency, the symmetry of the legal structure, how far shall I seek it? At what point shall the quest be halted by some discrepant custom, by some consideration of the social welfare, by my own or the common standards of justice and morals?" All these varying considerations, Cardozo points out, may and should influence the judge's decisions. By "introspective searchings of the spirit" he seeks to weigh the "strange compound," to discover the relative significance of the ingredients which enter into the judicial process. It may be doubted, suggests Cardozo, whether judges ought to be allowed to brew such a compound at all; nevertheless, he says, "I take judge-made law as one of the existing realities of life. . . . Not a judge on the bench but has had a hand in the making."

The first question for which Cardozo seeks an answer is "Where does the judge find the law which he embodies in his judgment?" The rule that fits the case may be found in the Constitution or a statute. Even so, there may be gaps to fill, doubts and ambiguities to be cleared, hardships and wrongs to be mitigated or avoided. Thus arises the need for judicial interpretation. More troublesome is "the land of mystery where constitution and statute are silent, and the judge must look to the common law for the rule that fits the case." In these instances, the first step is to compare the pending case with precedents, for "in a system so highly developed as our own, precedents have so covered the ground that they fix the point of departure from which the labor of the judge begins."

If the judge relies entirely upon the Constitution, statutes, and precedents, however, no system of living law could be evolved, and judges of high courts do not view their function so narrowly. "It is when the colors do not match, when the references in the index fail, when there is no decisive precedent, that the serious business of the judge begins. He must then fashion law for the litigants before him. In fashioning it for them, he will be fashioning it for others."

The assumption is erroneous, Cardozo emphasizes, that law is unchangeable and everlasting. Nothing is stable or absolute, even principles. Decade by decade and century by century, law is being modified, with the result that "hardly a rule of today but may be matched by its opposite of yesterday." Most of the changes have been wrought by judges. Still, the search must go on for "the essential and the permanent" in the field of justice.

Four primary approaches, as applied to the judicial process, are analyzed in detail by Cardozo: (1) the method of philosophy or the rule of analogy; (2) the method of evolution or historical development; (3) the method of tradition or the customs of the community; and (4) the method of sociology or of justice, morals, and social welfare.

The first principle is based on logic, analogy, or resemblance of relations, a method which is useful in eliminating favoritism and chance, enabling the judge to reach decisions with "serene and impartial uniformity." Logical development of the law, Cardozo asserts, requires consistency: "If a group of cases involve the same point, the parties expect the same decision. It would be a gross injustice to decide alternate cases on opposite principles. If a case was decided against me yesterday when I was a defendant, I shall look for the same judgment today if I am a plaintiff. To decide differently would raise a feeling of resentment and wrong in my breast; it would be an infringement, material and moral, of my rights." Therefore, adherence to precedent must be the rule rather than the exception in courts of law.

On occasion, logical principles may conflict. As an illustration, Cardozo cites the case of a legatee who had murdered his testator. One principle would recognize that an estate must be disposed of in conformity with a legal will. Another principle is that civil courts may not add to the pains and penalties of crime. But superseding these two concepts is another principle, "its roots deeply fastened in universal sentiments of justice, the principle that no man should profit from his own inequity or take advantage of his own wrong." The court so held in deciding the case, motivated by a "compelling sentiment of justice" more powerful than the preservation and enforcement of legal rights of ownership.

Cardozo proceeds next to an examination of the historical method, or the method of evolution, as applied to law. Occasionally this approach is in conflict with the philosophical method, though more often "the effect of history is to make the path of logic clear." The law of the future should not necessarily consist of an "uninspired repetition of the present and the past," Cardozo insists, but "history, in illuminating the past, illuminates the present, and in illuminating the present, illuminates the future." The most striking example is the law of real property, wherein Cardozo holds "there can be no progress without history." The law of contract is full of history, as are "the powers and functions of an executor, the distinctions between larceny and embezzlement, the rules of venue and the jurisdiction over foreign trespass."

A third force, after history and philosophy, having a bearing upon the establishment of judicial principles, Cardozo notes, is custom. Here he quotes Blackstone, who concluded that there are three kinds of common law: "(1) General customs, which are the universal rule of the whole Kingdom, and form the Common Law, in its stricter and more usual signification. (2) Particular customs, which for the most part affect only the inhabitants of particular districts. (3) Certain particular laws, which by custom are adopted and used by some particular courts of pretty general and extensive jurisdiction." Cardozo is inclined to play down the influence of custom in the development of law, though it may be an important factor in shaping legislation. "It is, however," he remarks, "not so much in the making of new rules as in the application of old ones that the creative energy of custom most often manifests itself today. General standards of right and duty are established." In this sense custom becomes identified with "customary morality, the prevailing standard of right conduct, the *mores* of the time. . . . Life casts the moulds of conduct, which will some day become fixed as law." Thus custom is gradually transformed by the people, or their representatives, into law.

From history, philosophy, and custom, Cardozo goes on to "the force which in our day and generation is becoming the greatest of them all, the power of social justice which finds its outlet and expression in the method of sociology." "Fundamentally," he insists, "the final cause of law is the welfare of society." Even though judges may not lightly set aside existing rules, they should not indulge in formalism for its own sake but rather interpret the rules as far as possible for the public good. "When the social needs demand one settlement rather than another," Cardozo declares, "there are times when we must bend symmetry, ignore history and sacrifice custom in the pursuit of other and larger ends." This statement is an accurate reflection of the attitude of the United States Supreme Court in recent years, which Cardozo helped to shape.

Judges have greater flexibility and freedom of choice in dealing with constitutions than with statues, because "statutes are designed to meet the fugitive exigencies of the hour," while "a *constitution* states or ought to state not rules for the passing hour, but principles for an expanding future." Cardozo calls particular attention to the "great immunities" with which the Constitution surrounds the individual. How the immunities are to be defined frequently becomes a matter of judicial interpretation. Here, too, liberal views predominate among today's Supreme Court justices. As seen by Cardozo, it is the duty of the courts to examine statutes not in isolation or as abstract principles "but in the setting and the framework of present-day conditions, as revealed by the labors of economists and students of the social sciences in our own country and abroad."

The position of property under the law is clarified by Cardozo. He points out that "property, like liberty, though immune under the Constitution from destruction, is not immune from regulation essential for the common good. What that regulation shall be, every generation must work out for itself." Property has a social function to perform and legislation toward that end is an appropriate exercise of governmental power.

Altogether in the field of law, Cardozo observes, "the tendency today is in the direction of a growing liberalism. The new spirit has made its way gradually; and its progress, unnoticed step by step, is visible in retrospect as we look back upon the distance traversed. The old forms remain, but they are filled with a new content."

Summing up, Cardozo concludes:

> My analysis of the judicial process comes then to this, and little more: logic, and history, and custom, and utility, and the accepted standards of right conduct, are the forces which singly or in combination shape the progress of the law. Which of these forces shall dominate in any case, must depend largely upon the comparative importance or value of the social interests that will be thereby promoted or impaired. One of the most fundamental social interests is that law shall be uniform and impartial. There must be nothing in its action that savors of prejudice or favor or even arbitrary whim or fitfulness. Therefore in the main there shall be adherence to precedent.

In a separate chapter, Cardozo deals with "the judge as a legislator." Therein he finds that "in countless litigations, the law is so clear that judges have no discretion." Their right to legislate becomes evident when there are gaps in the law, and rules and precedents must be established. Certain general precepts, however, must be adhered to, Cardozo observes:

> The judge, even when he is free, is still not wholly free. He is not a knight-errant, roaming at will in pursuit of his own ideal of beauty or of goodness. He is to draw his inspiration from consecrated principles. He is not to yield to spasmodic sentiment, to vague and unregulated benevolence. He is to exercise a discretion informed by tradition, methodized by analogy, disciplined by system, and subordinated to "the primordial necessity of order in the social life." Wide enough in all conscience is the field of discretion that remains.

The final chapter of *The Nature of the Judicial Process* is devoted in part to a discussion of the place of precedent in our legal system. While noting valid objections to a strict adherence to precedent, Cardozo still holds that the rule should generally prevail, varying only in exceptional cases. As a practical matter, he warns that "the labor of judges would be increased almost to the breaking point if every past decision could be reopened in every case, and one could not lay one's own course of bricks on the secure foundation of the courses laid by others who had gone before him." Cardozo points out that the rule of adherence to precedent is applied with less rigidity in the United States than in England. Also, "the United States Supreme Court and the highest courts of the several states overrule their own prior decisions when manifestly erroneous," as was done in 1954, for example, when the Supreme Court ruled segregation in public schools unconstitutional, thereby reversing its own "separate but equal" dictum of 1896.

A majority of the cases which come before the courts can

reasonably be decided only one way, in Cardozo's opinion. A small percentage, however, are less clear-cut, and "these are the cases where the creative element in the judicial process finds its opportunity and power . . . where a decision one way or the other, will count for the future." It is in such instances that the judge assumes the role of a lawgiver. Looking back upon his own career, Cardozo recalls, "I was much troubled in spirit, in my first years upon the bench, to find how trackless was the ocean on which I had embarked. I sought for certainty. I was oppressed and disheartened when I found that the quest for it was futile. . . . I have become reconciled to the uncertainty, because I have grown to see it as inevitable."

Cardozo concedes that the power placed in the hands of judges is great and subject to possible abuse. He quotes Ehrlich to the effect that "there is no guaranty of justice except the personality of the judge." Below the more or less tangible factors which influence judgments are subconscious forces far more difficult to appraise. As expressed by Cardozo, "Deep below consciousness are other forces, the likes and the dislikes, the predilections and the prejudices, the complex of instincts and emotions and habits and convictions, which make the man, whether he be litigant or judge."

In conclusion, Cardozo cites with approval a statement by Theodore Roosevelt, "whose intuitions and perceptions were deep and brilliant," in the author's eyes: "The chief lawmakers in our country may be, and often are, the judges, because they are the final seat of authority. Every time they interpret contract, vested right, due process of law, liberty, they necessarily enact into law parts of a system of social philosophy; and as such interpretation is fundamental, they give direction to all law-making."

Benjamin Cardozo is most frequently bracketed with Oliver Wendell Holmes as the two pre-eminent American judges of the past fifty years. Cardozo's enduring reputation will doubtless be as an interpreter of the common law. In reviewing **Selected Writings of Benjamin Nathan Cardozo,** published posthumously, Newman Levy concluded that "no judge in our history, with the possible exception of Holmes, offered such a rare combination of legal erudition, judicial poise, and broad, humanistic culture." These qualities are demonstrated on every page of **The Nature of the Judicial Process**.

Louis Auchincloss   (essay date 1979)

SOURCE: "The Styles of Mr. Justice Cardozo," in *Life, Law and Letters: Essays and Sketches,* Houghton Mifflin Co., 1979, pp. 47-58.

[*In the following essay, Auchincloss praises Cardozo's writings for their literary qualities, using examples from his legal opinions to illustrate his various methods of decision making and his different prose styles.*]

When I went to the University of Virginia Law School in the fall of 1938, I was determined to turn my back forever on the world of letters. I had failed—I had decided grimly—because my first novel, written during my junior year at Yale, had been rejected by Scribner's. It was thus ordained, I reasoned with the violence of youth, that I should never qualify for the exotic world of art and must resign myself to a more mundane profession. Although I thought I had been humbled, there was still a note of then unconscious condescension in the attitude with which I approached my new trade. It was, in the murky depths of my deepest reflections, a second best. The world of law might have seemed to me a more "real" world—a world, to put it crudely, more fit for men, "real" men (whatever they were)—but it was still, to my naïveté, inferior to the one to which I had, however rashly, aspired.

I was in for some pleasant surprises. I soon found that the history of English jurisprudence and the growth of the common law was quite as interesting as more general histories that I had enjoyed at Yale. And cases in contracts, torts, and criminal law, where judges wrestled to fit new factual situations into ancient patterns of accepted conduct, adjusting, modifying, and sometimes making over the latter in accordance with individual theories of what "law" was or should be, fascinated me. What was a judge, describing the actions of a plaintiff or defendant in a given situation in such a way as to justify his judgment of those actions, but a novelist describing his characters so as to lend an air of verisimilitude to the moral atmosphere that he seeks to create? Perhaps I had found, like Maeterlinck's children, that the bluebird was all the while at home.

But there were aspects of the law less malleable even to an imagination as determinedly romantic as mine then was. What could it do with the flood of statute law pouring from the Congress and the state legislatures, or with the huge structure of regulations designed to interpret federal law and their appended illustrations of imagined cases where the litigants were represented by mere letters and the situations reduced to the dryest facts? Where was the possibility of drama in all of this? Where in that dreary sea of verbiage was there any prose that breathed or any detectable style? It was words, simply words, often so jumbled and obscure as to make finding the sense like hacking one's way through tangled underbrush with a machete.

The volume of such law was not then what it was to become, but the future was already marked. The masses in a world increasingly socialized were not going to allow laws affecting their daily lives to be subject to what they considered the whims of judges reared in a more individualistic society. The compulsion to legislate had already reached the point where a session of the Senate or House was labeled *good* or *bad* in accordance with the quantity of statutes passed. We were not far from the Emperor Justinian who had prohibited the judiciary from commenting on his code.

Now, of course, Justinian's effort was futile. No quantity of laws, however astutely drafted, or of regulations, however shrewdly forecast, can cover all, or even most of the situations that will arise among litigants. Judges must always exist to interpret laws. Forty years after my first term in Virginia, we have more judges, harder worked, than ever before, and in certain areas of constitutional law, notably civil rights, they are even more important. But it is still an obvious truth that when a judge's opinion may be rapidly reversed, modified, or even affirmed by a new statute or code, that opinion is going to be a less valuable precedent. As codified law, constantly modified, assimilates or rejects the decisions and opinions of the courts, these latter must become more ephemeral. We shall have no more great common law judges.

Now what is the harm of this? Probably none. I am writing subjectively. To me, a reluctant law student and a frustrated novelist, the vast, bristling black and white volume of statutory law and regulations seemed like a glacier moving ineluctably over the land to freeze below the ice the giant figures of Mansfield, Eldon, Holmes, and Cardozo, now barely discernible to the living pygmies on the surface. It was as if all my secret fears of the inevitable triumph of the philistine over the artist in our culture had been confirmed.

The figure who most helped to revive my stumbling romanticism was Benjamin Cardozo. I had seen him once on a trip to Washington when I was a boy. My father had taken me to view the Supreme Court, then sitting in the Capitol, and had pointed out the white-haired figure with the beautiful ascetic face, whispering: "*There* is the great man." One of the first books I was told to read in law school was *The Nature of the Judicial Process,* and I was immediately spellbound by a prose so formal, so majestic, so elaborate, so almost Jamesian, and yet so smooth and clear and soft. Here was a writer indeed!

I was also interested to note that he, too, was concerned that codes might "threaten the judicial function with repression and disuse and atrophy." But he did not believe that, in the long run, this would really happen. What his little book was more about was that "land of mystery" where legislation is silent and where a judge must "look to the common law for the rule that fits the case." Here indeed, as Blackstone had put it, he was the "living oracle of the law."

As I began now to study Cardozo's opinions in contracts and torts, the law became something exciting, elusive, almost mystical. It seemed to me that statutes and regulations were so much fustian of ambitious politicians and dreary bureaucrats, that we really lived in a chaos of instincts and habits and appetites and prejudices, and that law, true law (my early extravagance must be allowed), existed only in that moment when a judge fitted a particular principle to a particular set of facts, and then expired, to be remembered only in its epitaph, the judge's opinion. It was all the more important that that opinion should be beautifully constructed and expressed.

Let me try to recreate my early impressions of Cardozo by analyzing, as I saw it then, his opinion in *DeCicco* v. *Schweizer,* 221 N.Y. 431, decided by the New York Court of Appeals in 1917. No clause of a constitution or of a statute, state or federal, was here involved. The law had to be found, interpreted, and modified, by a "living oracle."

The stated facts of the case at once put me in mind of the opening of a Henry James novel. Count Oberto Gulinelli of Ferrara was engaged to be married to an American girl, presumably an heiress, one Blanche Josephine Schweizer. Her father, Joseph, evidently pleased by the prospect of this noble addition to his family, had handed his future son-in-law a written promise to pay his daughter $2500 a year after they were married. Payment was begun in 1902, immediately after the event; but in 1912 Mr. Schweizer refused to honor further his commitment. Suit was brought against him, not by his daughter or her husband, but by one DeCicco to whom the daughter had assigned her father's promise.

Alas, the romance of *The Golden Bowl* seemed already to have faded. We did not know why the father had repudiated his promise or why the daughter had sold it. The family relationship had evidently deteriorated. The fate of international marriages at the turn of the century was almost never smooth and rarely edifying.

Cardozo proceeded to review the law. It was the established rule in New York that a promise made by A to B to induce him not to break his contract with C is void because there is no consideration to support the promise. B is already under obligation to fulfill his contract with C. Mr. Schweizer had promised the Count that he would pay money to his wife if the Count carried out an engagement to which the Count was already pledged. Did not the consideration have to fail? Ah, but what if the promise had been made to B *and* C, to the Count *and* Blanche?

> The writing was signed by her parents; it was delivered to her intended husband; it was made four days before the marriage; it called for a payment on the day of the marriage; and on that day payment was made, and made to her. From all these circumstances, we may infer that at the time of the marriage the promise was known to the bride as well as the husband, and that both acted upon the faith of it.

Consideration for Mr. Schweizer's promise now becomes evident. For even if the Count and Blanche were both obliged to fulfill their contract to marry, even if neither of them had the right, acting alone, to withdraw (remember that in that day a breach of a promise to marry was still actionable), it was equally clear that, acting together, they had a right to rescind. The law had no interest in forcing two unwilling persons to wed. It was *this* right that they gave up in going to the altar on the strength of the bride's father's promise, and for this consideration the latter had now to continue to pay as he had said he would pay, even to his daughter's assignee.

But did Mr. Schweizer really intend to place such pressure on the young couple? Did he really want two reluctant persons to enter the state of matrimony for the purpose of securing a financial allowance? Cardozo said that this did not matter:

> It will not do to divert the minds of others from a given line of conduct, and then to urge that because of the diversion the opportunity has gone to say how their minds would otherwise have acted. If the tendency of the promise is to induce them to persevere, reliance and detriment may be inferred from the mere fact of performance. The springs of conduct are subtle and varied. One who meddles with them must not insist upon too nice a measure of proof that the spring which he released was effective to the exclusion of all others.

And so the shabby facts, if shabby they were: the Count seeking a dowry, the sale of the promise, the dunning of the old father, were rewoven into a hard fine rule of law that seemed to embrace the situation with some of the moral beauty of *The Golden Bowl*. Cardozo went even further, too far perhaps. He reinforced his conclusion with "those considerations of public policy which cluster about contracts that touch the marriage relation." Could he really have believed that the Schweizer-Gulinelli nuptials were for the greater good of society? Or was he establishing a basis for distinguishing the case if later situations arising in the business world should make its application unjust?

I was delighted to discover that Cardozo had written an essay entitled **"Law and Literature,"** in the very beginning of which he quoted Henry James! The great novelist was cited to support Cardozo's thesis that a judicial opinion should always be literature, that style and substance were inextricably fused in writing:

> Don't let anyone persuade you (James wrote to Hugh Walpole) . . . that strenuous selection and comparison are not the very essence of art, and that form is not substance to that degree that there is absolutely no substance without it. Form alone *takes,* and holds and preserves substance, saves it from the welter of helpless verbiage that we swim in as in a sea of tasteless tepid pudding.

Cardozo then proceeded to divide the forms, or styles, or methods if you choose, of judicial opinions into six categories. He listed them as follows: the *magisterial,* where we hear "the voice of the law speaking by its consecrated ministers with the calmness and assurance that are born of a sense of mastery and power"; the *laconic* and the *conversational,* which overlap, where the homely illustration makes its way by its appeal to everyday experience and where the doubtful precept is brought down to earth and made to walk the ground; the *refined,* which, if only held back from euphemism, lends itself to cases where there is need of delicate precision; the *demonstrative,* or persuasive, which differs from the magisterial in its freer use of illustration, analogy, history, and precedent; and the *tonsorial,* which is merely a clutter of quotations from other opinions.

Cardozo offers examples of each category by quoting other judges, but he would have done as well to limit the illustrations to his own opinions, as I shall now try to do.

Here is a good example of his magisterial style. A pacifist attacked the validity of a California statute that required all students in a state university to take a course in military science and tactics. The Supreme Court rejected the argument, and Cardozo made this statement in a concurring opinion:

> Never in our history has the notion been accepted, or even, it is believed, advanced, that acts thus indirectly related to service in the camp or field are so tied to the practice of religion as to be exempt, in laws or in morals, from regulation by the state . . . The right of private judgment has never yet been so exalted above the powers and the compulsion of the agencies of government. One who is a martyr to a principle . . . does not prove by his martyrdom that he has kept within the law.

> (*Hamilton v. Regents of the University of California,* 293 U.S. 245)

The laconic and conversational styles are often laced with maxims to illuminate the point to be made. Cardozo admired Holmes intensely for his brevity and pungency, and on this occasion emulated him almost to the point of imitation:

> Liberty of contract is not an absolute concept. It is relative to many conditions of time and place and circumstance. The Constitution has not ordained that the forms of business shall be cast in imperishable moulds.

A literary allusion can be used to give point and emphasis to statements otherwise almost too plain:

> Aviation is today an established method of transportation. The future, even the near future will make it still more general. The city that is without the foresight to build the ports for the new traffic may soon be left behind in the race for competition. Chalcedon was called the city of the blind because its founders rejected the nobler site of Byzantium lying at their feet.

Humor may be allowed to lighten the conversational style, or presumably any style save the magisterial, but, as Cardozo warns, it is chancy. He himself, as chief judge of New York, used it with good effect in a case brought by a plaintiff who had fractured his kneecap riding on a moving belt in Coney Island called "The Flopper." Cardozo, denying him relief on the eminently sensible ground that one who takes part in such a sport accepts the dangers that inhere in it insofar as they are obvious, commented:

> The antics of the clown are not the paces of the cloistered cleric. The rough and boisterous joke, the horseplay of the crowd, evokes its own guffaws, but they are not the pleasures of tranquility. The plaintiff was not seeking a retreat for meditation. Visitors were tumbling about the belt to the merriment of onlookers when he made his choice to join them. He took the chance of a like fate with whatever damage to his body might ensue from such a fall. The timorous may stay at home.

> (*Murphy* v. *Steeplechase Amusement Co.,* 250 N.Y. 479)

But the demonstrative or persuasive is Cardozo's most characteristic style. Rarely was he sure enough to use the magisterial, and his more difficult cases were beyond the laconic. Here we see him wrestling with the agonizing question of whether or not a man, sentenced by a trial court to life imprisonment for murder in the second degree, may be executed when the state, appealing his conviction, has obtained the death sentence in a second trial resulting in a verdict of murder in the first. Cardozo, writing for the majority of the Supreme Court, held that the defendant had not been placed in double jeopardy and must die:

The state is not attempting to wear the accused out by a multitude of cases with accumulated trials. It asks no more than this, that the case against him shall go on until there shall be a trial free from the corrosion of substantial legal error.

(*Palko* v. *State of Connecticut,* 58 Sup. Ct. Rep. 149)

There is here no organ note of judgment from the sky to blast the unhappy defendant. Division among the cases is readily admitted, even that the line of division, in a hasty survey, may seem "wavering and broken." Proper analysis, however, will induce a different view. Then will emerge "the perception of a rationalizing principle which gives the discrete instances a proper order and coherence."

But the defendant must not die for subtleties. The reason must be clear, and Cardozo attempts to persuade us that it is:

On which side of the line the case made out by the appellant has appropriate location must be the next inquiry and the final one. Is that kind of double jeopardy to which the statute has subjected him a hardship so acute and shocking that our polity will not endure it? Does it violate those "fundamental principles of liberty and justice which lie at the base of all our civil and political institutions"? The answer must surely be "no."

One may regret that Cardozo went on to conclude his opinion with the dictum that the second trial was not only no cruelty to the defendant but not even "vexation in any immoderate degree"! The wretched man will die, it almost seems, for the perfect balance of the law. The privilege of appeal, granted to the state by the statute in question, is no "seismic innovation":

The edifice of justice stands, its symmetry, to many, greater than before.

Another example of the careful balancing of opposing precedents and the arrival at a conclusion almost in the manner of a brief is Cardozo's opinion for the New York Court of Appeals supporting its holding to admit evidence against a defendant to a larceny charge despite the fact that this evidence has been obtained in a police search made without a warrant. "Shall the criminal go free because the constable has blundered?" Cardozo, replying to his own question in the negative, supports his position more like an advocate than a judge:

We are confirmed in this conclusion when we reflect how far-reaching in its effect upon society the new consequences would be. The pettiest peace officer would have it in his power, through overzeal or indiscretion, to confer immunity upon an offender for crimes the most flagitious. A room is searched against the law, and the body of a murdered man is found. If the place of discovery may not be proved, the other circumstances may be insufficient to connect the defendant with the crime . . . Like instances can be multiplied. We may not subject society to these dangers until the Legislature has spoken with a clearer voice . . . The question is whether protection for the individual would not be

gained at a disproportionate loss of protection for society. On the one side is the social need that crime shall be repressed. On the other, the social need that law shall not be flouted by the insolence of office. There are dangers in any choice.

(*People* v. *Defoe,* 242 N.Y. 13)

Examples of the refined style may be found anywhere in Cardozo, for his thinking is always subtle and deep. I take almost at random a passage from *Babington* v. *Yellow Taxi Corporation,* 250 N.Y. 14, which decided that a cab driver, killed in a collision after a police officer had jumped on his running board and ordered him to pursue a fleeing criminal, had died while in the performance of his duties for his employer. Cardozo cited an English statute of 1285:

The horse has yielded to the motor car as an instrument of pursuit and flight. The ancient ordinance abides as an interpreter of present duty. Still, as in the days of Edward I, the citizenry may be called upon to enforce the justice of the state, not faintly and with lagging steps, but honestly and bravely and with whatever implements and facilities are convenient and at hand. The incorporeal being, the Yellow Taxi Corporation, would have been bound to respond in that spirit to the summons of the officer if it had been sitting in the driver's seat.

Cardozo concludes his essay on law and literature by affirming that, although a judge or advocate is expounding a science, yet is he still in the process of exposition, practicing an art. The muses may look at him "a bit impatiently," but if the work is finally done they will yet "take him by the hand." I have no doubt that they have clasped Cardozo to their heart.

FURTHER READING

Criticism

Berlach, Harris. A review of *Selected Writings of Benjamin Nathan Cardozo. Jewish Social Studies* XI (1949): 86-9.
  Credits Cardozo with demystifying the judicial process.

Frankfurter, Felix. "Benjamin Nathan Cardozo." In *Of Law and Life & Other Things That Matter: Papers and Addresses of Felix Frankfurter, 1956-1963,* edited by Philip B. Kurland, pp. 185-90. Cambridge, Mass.: Belknap Press, 1965.
  Biographical sketch praising Cardozo as one of very few Supreme Court justices who have had a lasting influence on the development of the American legal system. Frankfurter served as an associate justice of the Court from 1939 until 1962.

Graves, W. Brooke. A review of *Law and Literature and Other Essays and Addresses,* by Benjamin Nathan Cardozo. *Social Science* 7, No. 4 (October 1932): 436.
  Describes the contents of *Law and Literature* and recommends the book to young people seeking information on the legal profession.

Hall, Arnold Bennett. A review of *The Growth of the Law,*

by Benjamin Nathan Cardozo. *Social Forces* IV, Nos. 1-4 (November 1925-September 1926): 202-4.

> Finds that in *The Growth of the Law* Cardozo takes a balanced, "scientific" approach to the contemporary controversy over the judiciary's freedom to participate in legal development.

Hurst, Fannie. "Benjamin Cardozo, 1870-1938." In *There Were Giants in the Land: Twenty-eight Historic Americans as Seen by Twenty-eight Contemporary Americans,* pp. 217-25. New York: Farrar & Rinehart, 1942.

> Biographical tribute hailing Cardozo as a "great liberator" whose progressive interpretation of the U.S. Constitution profoundly influenced American legal history. Hurst comments on the striking difference between the nature of Cardozo's personal life and the character of his achievements, emphasizing that, although he was a quiet, unassuming man content with a modest existence, his legal opinions, particularly those dealing with civil rights, dramatically affected the lives of the American people.

Yntema, Hessel E. A review of *Law and Literature and Other Essays and Addresses,* by Benjamin Nathan Cardozo. *American Political Science Review* XXV, No. 3 (August 1931): 749-50.

> A brief review of *Law and Literature* praising Cardozo's poetic style, openmindedness, and interest in reforming the judicial process.

Additional coverage of Cardozo's life and career is contained in the following source published by Gale Research: *Contemporary Authors*, Vol. 117.

Erskine Childers

1870-1922

(Full name Robert Erskine Childers) English novelist and nonfiction writer.

INTRODUCTION

Childers is the author of *The Riddle of the Sands,* a novel which is widely recognized as inaugurating the literary genre of English spy fiction. Published in 1903, Childers's novel was intended to be a warning, in the guise of a light adventure story, about England's vulnerability to invasion by sea. The steady popularity of *The Riddle of the Sands* is reflected in numerous reprintings throughout the decades following its initial publication and its adaptation as a film in 1979.

Biographical Information

Childers was born in London, the son of Anna Mary Henrietta Barton Childers and Robert Caesar Childers, a renowned Orientalist. Educated at Haileybury and Trinity College, Cambridge, Childers became a clerk in the House of Commons and spent weekends indulging his craving for adventure and love of the sea with solitary sails in the Thames estuary. In 1897 he made the first of six cruises along the Dutch, German, and Danish coasts and in the North Sea that provided intimate knowledge of the Frisian Islands, the setting of *The Riddle of the Sands.* Childers was among the first to join the City Imperial Volunteers for the Boer War. *In the Ranks of the C.I.V.,* his first published book, was the personal record of his experiences. He coauthored, with Basil Williams, the official history of his company, *The H.A.C. in South Africa,* and edited volume five of *"The Times" History of the War in South Africa.* He also wrote *War and the Arme Blanche* and *German Influence on British Cavalry,* two books arguing for modern weapons and training. Although of a unionist family, Childers came back from the Boer War with inclinations toward home rule for Ireland, a position which he argued in *The Framework of Home Rule.* After distinguished service in the British Army in World War I, Childers became immersed in the cause of Irish independence. A member of the Irish Treaty delegation to London in 1921, he renounced the treaty establishing the separation of Ireland into north and south and sided with Eamon de Valera in the civil war. He was captured by Free State soldiers and condemned to death. He was executed on November 24, 1922, before a Free State firing squad in Dublin.

Major Works

The main characters of *The Riddle of the Sands* are Carruthers and Davies, two young Englishmen who, while on a sailing holiday in the Baltic, North Sea, and Frisian

Sands, discover a plot on the part of Germany to invade England by sea. During the course of the narrative they struggle to solve the "riddle" of the title in order to forestall the Germans' scheme. In a long epilogue to the novel, Childers presents skeptical readers, who may fear that "a baseless romance has been foisted on them," with a half-burned "memorandum" in cipher that contains details of the German invasion plan described in the novel. "Perfect organization and perfect secrecy" underlie the riddle of the sands, writes Childers, "and no one should doubt the German capacity for executing the plan at the critical moment when Germany might have little to lose and much to gain."

Critical Reception

To its author's surprise *The Riddle of the Sands* met with immediate public and critical approval. Convinced of England's vulnerability to an invasion launched by Germany from a desolate stretch of coastline that had seemingly no strategic importance, Childers had registered his concern in an adventure story based on firsthand observations set down in logbooks in the years he had cruised those shoals. For a decade *The Riddle of the Sands* helped fuel a national debate on England's supposed state of military unreadiness. For yachtsman it remained an excellent tale of men against the sea, and in its many republications the book has continued to attract readers who admire a good spy story.

PRINCIPAL WORKS

In the Ranks of the C.I.V. (memoir) 1900
The H.A.C. in South Africa [with Basil Williams] (nonfiction) 1903
The Riddle of the Sands (novel) 1903
War and the Arme Blanche (nonfiction) 1910
The Framework of Home Rule (nonfiction) 1911
German Influence on British Cavalry (nonfiction) 1911

CRITICISM

Ian Fleming (essay date 1955)

SOURCE: "Mudscape with Figures," in *The Specator,* Vol. 195, No. 6632, August 5, 1955, pp. 199-200.

[*In the following essay, Fleming faults the spy novel* The Riddle of the Sands *for its weak thrills and lack of convincing villains.*]

Some people are frightened by silence and some by noise. To some people the anonymous bulge at the hip is more frightening than the gun in the hand, and all one can say is that different people thrill to different stimuli, and that those who like *The Turn of the Screw* may not be worried by, for instance, *The Cat and the Canary.*

Only the greatest authors make the pulses of all of us beat faster, and they do this by marrying the atmosphere of suspense into horrible acts. Poe, Stevenson and M. R. James used to frighten me most, and now Maugham, Ambler, Simenon, Chandler and Graham Greene can still raise the fur on my back when they want to. Their heroes are credible and their villains terrify with a real 'blackness.' Their situations are fraught with doom, and the threat of doom, and, above all, they have pace. When one chapter is done, we reach out for the next. Each chapter is a wave to be jumped as we race with exhilaration behind the hero like a water-skier behind a fast motor-boat.

Too many writers in this genre (and I think Erskine Childers, on whose *The Riddle of the Sands* these remarks are hinged, was one of them) forget that, although this may sound a contradiction in terms, speed is essential to a novel of suspense, and that while detail is important to create an atmosphere of reality, it can be laid on so thick as to become a Sargasso Sea in which the motor-boat bogs down and the skier founders.

The reader is quite happy to share the pillow-fantasies of the author so long as he is provided with sufficient landmarks to help him relate the author's world more or less to his own, and a straining after verisimilitude with maps and diagrams should be avoided except in detective stories aimed at the off-beta mind.

Even more wearying are 'recaps,' and those leaden passages where the hero reviews what he has achieved or ploddingly surveys what remains to be done. These exasperate the reader who, if there is to be any rumination, is quite happy to do it himself. When the author drags his feet with this space-filling device he is sacrificing momentum which it will take him much brisk writing to recapture.

These reflections, stale news though they may be to the mainliner in thrillers, come to me after rereading *The Riddle of the Sands* after an absence of very many years, and they force me to the conclusion that doom-laden silence and long-drawn-out suspense are not enough to confirm the tradition that Erskine Childers, romantic and remarkable man that he must have been, is also one of the father-figures of the thriller.

The opening of the story—the factual documentation in the preface and the splendid Lady Windermere's Fan atmosphere of the first chapters—is superb.

At once you are ensconced in bachelor chambers off St. James's at the beginning of the century. All the trappings of the Age of Certainty gather around you as you read. Although the author does not say so, a coal fire seems to roar in the brass grate; there is a glass of whisky beside your chair and, remembering Mr. Cecil Beaton's Edwardian decors, you notice that the soda-water syphon beside it is of blue glass. The smoke from your cheroot curls up towards the ceiling and your button-boots are carefully crossed at the ankles on the red-leather-topped fender so as not to disturb the crease of those sponge-bag trousers. On a mahogany bookrest above your lap *The Riddle of the Sands* is held open by a well-manicured finger.

Shall you go with Carruthers to Cowes or accompany him to the grouse-moor? It is the fag-end of the London season of 1903. You are bored, and it is all Mayfair to a hock-and-seltzer that the fates have got you in their sights and that you are going to start to pay for your fat sins just over the page.

Thus, in the dressing-room, so to speak, you and Carruthers are all ready to start the hurdle race. You are still ready when you get into the small boat in a God-forsaken corner of the East German coast, and you are even more hungry for the starter's gun when you set sail to meet the villains. Then, to my mind, for the next 95,000 words there is anticlimax.

This is a book of great renown; and it is not from a desire to destroy idols or a tendency to denigration that this review—now that, after the statutory fifty years, *The Riddle of the Sands* has entered the public domain—is becoming almost too much of an autopsy. But those villains! With the best will in the world I could not feel that the lives of the heroes (and therefore of my own) were in the least way endangered by them.

Dollmann, villain No. 1, is a 'traitor' from the Royal

Navy, whose presence among the clucking channels and glistening mudbanks of the Frisian Islands is never satisfactorily explained. His job was 'spying at Chatham, the blackguard,' and the German High Command, even in 1903 when the book was first published, was crazy to employ him on what amounts to operational research. He never does anything villainous. Before the story opens, he foxes hero No. 1 into running himself on a mudbank, but at the end, when any good villain with his back to the wall would show his teeth, he collapses like a pricked balloon and finally disappears lamely overboard just after 'we came to the bar of the Schild and had to turn south off that twisty bit of beating between Rottum and Bosch Fat.' His harshest words are, 'You pig-headed young marplots!' and his 'blackness' is further betrayed by the beauty and purity of his daughter, with whom hero No. 1 falls in love. (It is always a bad idea for the hero to fall in love with the villain's daughter. We are left wondering what sort of children they will have.)

Von Bruning, villain No. 2, is frankly a hero to the author, and is presented as such; and No. 3, Bochme, though at first he exudes a delicious scent of Peter Lorre, forfeits respect by running away across the mud and leaving one of his gum-boots in the hands of hero No. 2.

The plot is that the heroes want to discover what the villains are up to, and, in a small, flat-bottomed boat, they wander amongst the Frisian Islands (and two maps, two charts and a set of tide-tables won't convince me that they don't wander aimlessly) trying to find out.

This kind of plot makes an excellent framework for that classic 'hurdle race' thriller formula, in which the hero (despite his Fleet-Foot Shoes with Tru-Temper Spikes and Kumfi-Krutch Athletic Supporter) comes a series of ghastly croppers before he breasts the tape.

Unfortunately, in *The Riddle of the Sands* there are no hurdles and only two homely mishaps (both of the heroes' own devising)—a second grounding on a mudbank, from which the heroes refloat on the rising tide, and the loss of the anchor chain, which they salvage without difficulty.

The end of the 100,000-word quest through the low-lying October mists is a hasty, rather muddled scramble which leaves two villains, two heroes and the heroine more or less in the air, and the small boat sailing off to England with the answer to the riddle. Before 1914 this prize must have provided a satisfactory fall of the curtain, but since then two German wars have clanged about our heads and today our applause is rather patronising.

The reason why *The Riddle of the Sands* will always be read is due alone to its beautifully sustained atmosphere. This adds poetry, and the real mystery of wide, fog-girt silence and the lost-child crying of seagulls, to a finely written log-book of a small-boat holiday upon which the author has grafted a handful of 'extras' and two 'messages'— the threat of Germany and the need for England to 'be prepared.'

To my mind it is now republished exactly where it belongs—in the Mariner's Library. Here, a thriller by atmosphere alone, it stands alongside twenty-eight thrillers of the other school—thrillers where the action on the stage thrills, and the threatening sea-noises are left to the orchestra pit.

Benny Green   (essay date 1972)

SOURCE: "Brittania's Man," in *The Specator,* Vol. 229, No. 7526, September 23, 1972, pp. 472-73.

[*Green is an English jazz musician, novelist, and critic. In the following essay, Green classifies* The Riddle of the Sands *as a "call-to-arms" warning to the pre-World War British Empire.*]

The reappearance, in paperback form, of Erskine Childers's *The Riddle of the Sands* draws attention to a book which would read strangely at any time, but doubly so now that the world for which it was written has been whisked by events into the remotest past. *The Riddle of the Sands* was among the earliest, and was perhaps the best, of those Edwardian call-to-arms thrillers which acquired their tension from the British neurosis, real or imagined, regarding the possibility of some lesser breed without the law constituting a serious threat to their world dominance. It is not altogether without significance that the book appeared in 1903, soon after the painfully public exposure of the blimpish blithering of Buller and company on the veldt, or that it was written by an Englishman who had served in that war and seen for himself that resourcefulness was hardly the British High Command's long suit.

Childers's book created an immediate sensation, and retains much of its old magnetism today, although for quite different reasons. When *The Riddle of the Sands* was first published, it was part of that curious campaign of self-induced terror by which the snug and secure British liked deliciously to chill their own imperial marrow from time to time, perhaps to alleviate the tedium of a world whose sporting attention was divided between the leg-glances directed by Ranjitsinhji towards the Hove boundary and those other leg glances directed no less accurately by the King towards Mrs. Keppel. It was with a perfectly straight face that Childers established a convention destined to peter out ten years later in the unwitting bathos of Saki's *When William Came,* in which the all-conquering Kaiser is finally thwarted by the intransigence of a bunch of Boy Scouts.

No such absurdities mar the texture of *The Riddle of the Sands,* which is why its magnetism has lasted so well. For if it was originally meant to scare the British, and perhaps even stimulate them into action, by rattling the bones of the German bogey, its fascination today lies in the way the presumption of Childers's plot so precisely locates the period of its genesis; the British are Top Nation; this exalted status is in accordance with the wishes of God Almighty; the Germans are not to be trusted, all this being implied at a time when policy could still be condensed into the simple words which at one point Childers puts into the mouth of his hero:

> "We're a maritime nation; we've grown by the
> sea and live by it; if we lose command of it we
> starve. We're unique in that way, just as our

huge empire, only linked by the sea, is unique. And yet see what mountains of apathy and conceit have had to be tackled. It's not the people's fault. We've been so safe so long, and grown so rich, that we've forgotten what we owe it to. But there's no excuse for those blockheads of statesmen."

Childers presents the archetypal escapist portrait of the Public School Empire, where the caverns of Whitehall are deserted in the shooting season, and where in high summer no ennobled rump flops into the concave sanctuary of the Club armchair. Sadly, what Childers also does is to assume that all Englishmen are as interested as he is in the arts of navigation and seamanship, although to be fair, considering the nature of the tale he had to tell, it is hard to see how he could have avoided those elements altogether. *The Riddle of the Sands* is the story of how the seven-tonner 'Dulcibella' stumbles on a German plot to use the sand-channels off the Fresian Islands to expedite an invasion of Britain. There is a peripheral love interest, and a narrator who is actually called Carruthers, but the heart of the book resides in its hero Davies, who is so strong a projection of the Englishman of imperial fiction, modest, brave, above all decent, that not even the incomprehensible nautical smalltalk can obscure his outlines:

> "She was buried at once by the beam sea, and the jib flew to blazes; but the reefed stays'l stood, she recovered gamely and I held on, though I knew it could only be for a few minutes, as the centreplate was up, and made frightful leeway towards the bark."

No wonder that Arnold Bennett once confided to his journal, "Read *Riddle of the Sands*. Very annoying style."

That Davies remains representative was proved to me most unexpectedly two years ago when, in conversation with Kenneth More, and remembering *Reach for the Sky* and *North West Frontier,* I asked him if he had ever heard of Davies or thought of playing him. More told me that although he had not read Childers's book, he had received several letters drawing attention to his affinities with Davies who, by the way, remains unportrayed to this day. *The Riddle of the Sands* is interesting for another reason, in that it shows how an author can fail utterly to understand what he is doing. The yachting savoir faire which tempted Childers to turn his novel into a textbook, and which eventually led him to renegacy and violent martyrdom, very nearly foundered 'Dulcibella,' and it was only the irrepressible buoyancy of his tale that kept the whole project from sinking under the dead weight of all those luffs and jibs. This inadvertently comic situation, where a man writes one book under the delusion he is writing quite another, obtained also in that other nautical classic of the period, *Three Men in a Boat,* conceived as a river guide sanctified by gobbets of that indigestible sanctimonious swill which Jerome K. Jerome mistook all his life for religious passion. But just as Harris and George remained triumphantly pagan, so does *The Riddle of the Sands* remain triumphantly fictional.

Childers's own career proved far more hair-raising than anything he ever dreamed up for Davies. Becoming a convert to Home Rule in 1910, he took to gunrunning, and

in 1914 sailed with a thousand smuggled rifles under the very bows of the British fleet at Spithead. In 1922, having urged the Irish not to sign Lloyd George's treaty, he aligned himself with the diehards, was arrested and executed by a firing squad. And although they were Irish bullets which killed him, in a sense the finger that pulled the trigger was British; for a man whose one truly memorable act was his literary perpetuation of the stiff-upper-lip Englishman, it was a bizarre end indeed. How many authors ever end up being shot by their own hero? One consolation: had it not been for that firing squad, there would probably be no new paperback edition at all. By bringing Childers's life to so premature an end, the authorities brought forward by many years the date at which his works would come into public domain.

Anthony Masters   (essay date 1987)

SOURCE: "Erskine Childers: The Intrepid Spy," in *Literary Agents: The Novelist as Spy,* Basil Blackwell, 1987, pp. 4-14.

[*In the following essay, Masters observes how Childers's background as a yachtsman as well as his military and political experience contributed to the composition of* The Riddle of the Sands.]

> 'One of those romantic gentlemen that one reads of in sixpenny magazines, with a Kodak in his tie-pin, a sketch-book in the lining of his coat, and a selection of disguises in his hand luggage.'
>
> An early twentieth-century Englishman's idea of a spy, from Erskine Childers' *The Riddle of the Sands*

Erskine Childers was a spy by chance—a private spy, not a member of any Intelligence organization. He was a man who observed, and who then used his observations to write a successful work of fiction. He did not try to alert the authorities in any official way, but the book was taken so seriously by them that professional agents were employed to continue his observations. He had all the inner characteristics of a Buchan hero, but he did not look like one: he walked with a limp and was short and unobtrusive. Yet his sailing exploits became legendary, as did his life's tragic end, when he was found guilty of gun-running and executed. His creative, fertile mind could appreciate a potentially successful strategy, but he was not involved in a fantasy world of spies and spying. Childers was a natural spy; unlike other writers such as Ian Fleming and Howard Hunt, he observed and wrote for patriotic rather than financial reasons.

Robert Erskine Childers was born in London on 25 June 1870, the second son of Robert Caesar Childers, an eminent scholar. It was from his father, who died of consumption at the early age of thirty-eight, that Childers inherited his intense powers of concentration. From his mother he inherited his equally intense love for Ireland. Educated at Haileybury and Trinity College, Cambridge, he took his law tripos and BA in 1893. Although Childers often seemed introverted, he was able to rouse himself to splendid oratory, and this he first used to considerable effect at Cambridge when he was put up as a candidate for the presidency of the University debating society, the Magpie and Stump. He was a clerk in the House of Commons from 1895 until 1910—a period interrupted in 1900 when he became one of the first volunteers for the Boer War. He joined the Honourable Artillery Company, and was part-author of *The HAC in Africa,* published in 1903. In the First World War he joined the Royal Navy, and was swiftly promoted to lieutenant-commander. He was mentioned in dispatches and received the DSC.

Soon after he left Cambridge in 1893, Childers began spending holidays, either alone or with a friend, navigating small yachts through the English Channel or the North Sea and, in particular, along the complex and dangerous shores of the German, Danish and Baltic coasts. The most arduous cruise he ever undertook was across the North Sea, on the first of six voyages of slow discovery through the narrow and sand-locked channels of the Frisian Islands to the open Baltic Sea. During the course of these voyages he was to become familiar with the physical hazards, the bleak, haunting scenery, and a strange assortment of Dutch, Danish and German sailors and villagers. Slowly the weird landscapes and isolated peoples were to make a deep impression on his fertile and creative mind.

On 11 August 1897 Childers cast off alone on a showery, dull day, heading for Dieppe. There he picked up his brother Henry, and in easy stages they progressed through squally weather along the north-east coast of France and through the canals of Holland. Childers had never cruised under such appalling conditions, and his much loved boat, *Vixen,* was ungainly and difficult to sail. He wrote in his Journal:

> A low freeboard, a high coach-house cabin room, and a certain over-sparred appearance aloft, would unnerve the most honied tongue. In the 'salon' [the sailor] would find just enough headroom to allow him to sit upright; and before he could well help himself, the observation would escape him that the centreplate case was an inconveniently large piece of furniture. Confronted with the fo'c'sle, candour and humanity would wring from him a sigh of pity for the crew, but here he would be comforted, for there were to be no paid hands.

The two brothers crossed the Zuider Zee for Terschelling, and sailed through the desolate region of long, low, lumpy islands of white sand, which were separated from each other by difficult channels and tides. On 25 September Childers wrote in his log:

> We saw this strange region at its best this evening, the setting sun reddening gloriously over the great banks and shining ribbons of water, and bestowing pink caresses on the distant sand-hills of Rottum (inhabited, so we were told, by one lonely soul who had grown fabulously rich by the export of 'sea-bird' eggs), and the feathery line of the Frisian coast. At night we sailed off into deep water.

The intrepid pair were later towed by a tug through the Kiel Canal towards the Baltic. Then, 'the sun burst through and, unreal as a dream, after the silent expanse of the North Sea and the lonely levels of Friesland, there came the vision of a noble fiord, green hills and richly wooded banks, sloping to the blue, deep tideless waters, where, in a long, majestic curve, lay moored a line of battleships.'

In mid-October Henry had to return to England, so Childers was left to explore the fiords alone. This he did with considerable courage and independence of spirit. Although he enjoyed company in small bursts, he had enough inner resources to cope on his own for long periods. The next Easter, together with a hired hand, Childers crossed over to Holland and repeated his exploration. The journeys increased his ability for independence of thought, yet his greater confidence went unnoticed at the office as he was able to use his customary reticence as a convenient shell. But he had a special secret world—an increasingly strong inner resource—to fall back on, and he stood apart from the frenetic world of politics, which seemed to him to be dominated by egoists whose second-hand patriotic ideas and blinkered opinions deeply depressed him.

At this point he was seriously considering the possibility of writing a book about his Baltic cruises, although he had no notion at this time of an espionage theme. By January 1901, however, this strand had taken slight root, and he wrote to his Great-Aunt Flora, confiding in her the germ of a growing idea:

> I'm on a week's visit up here, shooting with the Thompsons . . . and a Miss Matthew, daughter of the Home Rule Judge . . . I have not begun that book yet. I forgot before coming away to get the diary of that cruise from the flat. An idea has struck me that a story, of which I have the germ, might be worked into it as a setting. Do you think that would be a good plan, supposing, of course, that the story was a plausible one?

Despite encouragement from Great-Aunt Flora, Childers did not immediately begin the project; he wrote to her dismally a few months later: 'I have not begun the Baltic book yet. I fear it would be no good without pictures. I also fear the story is beyond me.' By the winter of 1901, however, he was more optimistic, and wrote to his friend and fellow House of Commons Committee Clerk, Basil Williams:

> Oh, about my book, which you say I have told you nothing of. It's a yachting story, with a purpose, suggested by a cruise I once took in German waters. I discovered a scheme of invasion directed against England. I'm finding it terribly difficult, as being in the nature of a detective story there is no sensation, only what is meant to be a convincing fact. I was weak enough to 'spatchcock' a girl into it and now find her a horrible nuisance. I have not approached Reginald [Smith, of the publishers Smith and Elder] as yet.

Eventually, Childers did write the book, but was not optimistic about its fate. He felt isolated, his sisters (with whom he lived) were in Ireland and he was alone in the flat, trying to put the finishing touches to his book, at which he had been obsessively overworking—and as a result, he fell ill. Reginald Smith had promised to read the book on completion, but its author was clearly in a pessimistic mood. He was worried about the plot and style of *The Riddle of the Sands*; it was only the title he liked. Eventually, he sent the finished manuscript to Smith, who returned it, asking for drastic revisions. Childers set to work gloomily. He did not agree with all Smith's points but was prepared to work at an acceptable compromise, and this he achieved, after a great deal of painful rewriting.

Neither Smith nor Childers had the faintest idea that the book would turn out to be a great critical success. Much of this success was due to the obsession that had taken root in Childers' mind during his voyages around the sands and dykes of the Frisian Islands: he felt that Britain, once the heart of a great and prosperous empire, was all too vulnerable to invasion by sea, despite her still great naval strength. The plot of *The Riddle of the Sands* involves the accidental discovery by two English yachtsmen of German plans to turn the bleak and lonely expanses of the Frisian Islands into the springboard for an invasion of the unprotected east and south-east coasts of England. The story opens slowly, with Carruthers, an indolent young man from the Foreign Office, used to cruising in large yachts with an attentive and servile crew, joining the taciturn Davies on his small boat, the *Dulcibella,* a craft not unlike Childers' own ungainly but much loved *Vixen.*

Most friends of Childers could see much of him in Davies: unsociable, self-conscious, unpretentious, painstaking and versatile. But, in fact, Davies and Carruthers each represent one half of Childers' complex personality: Davies, the perfectionist, who loves the wild islands, and Carruthers, the intelligent if impractical man of the world. *The Riddle of the Sands* appealed to a wide spectrum of British society: yachtsmen, detective story readers and politicians. John Buchan, newly arrived colleague of Basil Williams in Lord Milner's political and administrative 'kindergarten'—as his group of bright young men were known—read it and was impressed. Perhaps the book inspired him, for it was very much in the tradition of the patriotic 'shocker' that he himself was to write. He described Childers' book as 'the best story of adventure published in the last quarter of a century . . . as for the characters, I think they are the most fully realized of any adventure story that I have ever met, and the atmosphere of grey Northern skies and miles of yeasty water and wet sands is as masterfully reproduced as in any story of Conrad's.' The book was also universally acclaimed by the reviewers, despite its awkward plotting, the statutory girl and the rather bogus Royal Navy officer turned German spy. Politicians and military strategists were particularly interested, yet were puzzled as to who Childers was and how he had arrived at such a strangely precise knowledge of the German coastline.

And they began to wonder just how vulnerable Britain's unprotected seaboard was. *Could* it be successfully invaded by an army landed from a fleet of small ships, as Childers implied? Basil Williams wrote: 'Few realized that the unobtrusive little man with the glasses and the sciatic limp was leading a double life. He let none of us know—until the information tumbled out one day, quite by chance—that his weekends were spent in the Thames estuary, sailing single-handed a scrubby little yacht.' In the book, Davies warns: 'And we aren't ready for her [Germany]; we don't look her way. We have no naval base in the North Sea, and no North Sea fleet. Our best battleships are too deep in draught for North Sea work. And, to crown it all, we were asses enough to give her Heligoland, which commands the North Sea coast.'

Childers rejected the view that Germany felt strong enough to invade England immediately; he was sure that she realized that trying to take command of the North Sea would only result in a defeat by the British Navy. He felt certain she had seen the alternative possibility of mounting an invasion in and around the Frisian Islands, and from there dispatching infantry with the lightest type of field gun in large sea-going lighters, towed by powerful, shallow-draft tugs. These would be escorted by warships that would approach the British shores at high tide.

In his postscript to the first edition in March 1903, the First Sea Lord, Admiral Sir John Fisher, wrote: 'It so happens that, while this book was in the press, a number of measures have been taken by the Government to counteract some of the very weaknesses and dangers which are alluded to above.' In fact, Sir John Fisher was to some extent understating the government's reaction. As a result of the book's publication, a Committee of National Defence was hastily created—a move which received a reassuringly warm welcome from the Commons. A site on the Forth, in Scotland, was selected for a new North Sea naval base, and a North Sea Fleet was established. Unfortunately, its ships were old-fashioned and certainly not capable of standing up to the German squadrons. A manning committee also stressed the need for a volunteer reserve, but this was only a recommendation, and made Childers considerably frustrated, for he believed that the time had come to train every Englishman in the defence of the realm. Fisher blandly pointed out that there was no fear of an imminent invasion of the British Isles. He did not seem to consider the obvious problem of the long-term invasion threat, not because Britain had total control of the sea, but because there was a very strong chance that in an even battle the command of the sea would hang in the balance for an indefinite time. But, nevertheless, a vulnerable chink in Britain's armour had been discovered by Childers' imaginative powers—an attribute that the British Secret Services would look for in writers that they were to use in the future.

Childers' military intelligence became a subject of great interest, and among many distinguished political figures who contacted him to find out more was Lord Rosebery, who wanted to know exactly how much of *The Riddle of the Sands* was fact and how much was fiction. Rosebery also urged Childers to keep on writing, for, after an invasion scare of these proportions, he was interested in how much more information Childers' imagination might reveal. Childers himself was a little bemused, for he knew he had invented the whole concept, albeit building on his own careful observations of the German coastline. But Leopold Amery, a much travelled journalist on *The Times* who had worked in Germany, the Balkans and South Africa, agreed with his assessment of German military ambitions and intentions. And it was soon after Childers wrote the book that Churchill told him that this very method of invasion had already been worked out by the Germans.

In the autumn of 1903 Leopold Amery, who was undertaking the arduous general editorship of *The Times History of the War in South Africa,* asked Childers to write volume 5. Childers had carefully studied the first two, which had been written by the now exhausted Amery. Initially he was not keen to take up the offer, but partly because his friend Basil Williams had been commissioned to write volume 4, he eventually agreed. Childers stipulated one condition: his regimental history of the Honourable Artillery Company's role on the veldt must be completed first. Despite the generous fee he would collect for the new project, he was depressed, as he knew the vast amount of work involved would take up all his spare time for at least the next three years.

The publication of *The Riddle of the Sands* eventually pushed British Naval Intelligence into action, and in May 1910 two officers were sent on a tour of the German seacoast defences and the Frisian Islands. They soon discovered that existing Admiralty charts as well as intelligence information was totally out of date, and that their only real knowledge of the mysterious Frisian Islands had been gathered from Childers' book. In fact, all Childers had done was to combine information from German and British maps and incorporate the result into the charts in his book.

The two officers, Lieutenant Brandon RN and Captain Trench RN, inspired as they were, in their espionage mission, by Childers' book, were unfortunately arrested by the Germans and given a prison sentence—a highly embarrassing situation for the British government. Pardoned by the Kaiser as a result of King George V's state visit to Germany, they were released in May 1913, seventeen months before the sentences expired. Naval Intelligence was completely reorganized as a result of this fumbling attempt at reconnaissance.

After the publication of his book Erskine Childers basked in patriotic praise; he was seen by public and politicians alike as one of the great English adventurers, despite his uncharismatic looks and personality—and the fact that he was Irish. But his passion for the Irish cause was to be his undoing; the widespread admiration for the author of what was fast becoming a classic work of espionage was to evaporate—in English eyes, at least. For some years he had been devoting more and more time to the burning issue of Irish independence, and in 1910 had become a dedicated convert to the campaign for Irish Home Rule. In July 1914 he and his wife, Mary, whom he had married in 1904, used their yacht *Asgard* to carry arms from the coast of Europe to Howth harbour, on the Irish coast, justifying this on the grounds of Asquith's Home Rule Bill, for he did not want to pursue his cause by being treacherous to a Britain now at war. Nevertheless, Childers was gradually becoming a fanatical supporter of the Irish cause, mixing more and more with extremists. In 1919 he and his family settled in Ireland, where he became principal secretary to the delegation negotiating an Irish treaty with the British government. He fiercely opposed both Mi-

chael Collins and Arthur Griffith, republicans who favoured accepting the treaty, on the grounds that it did not provide for complete independence. He believed that to separate Ulster from the rest of Ireland, which the treaty proposed, would only prolong the problem.

When the Irish Free State government was established in 1921, Childers joined the Republican Army which was created to oppose it, and became involved in the civil war between the pro-treaty and the anti-treaty forces. As a result, he found himself regarded as a traitor by both the British and the Irish Free State governments, and on 10 November 1922 Free State soldiers came and surrounded his mother's home where he was currently living. Childers was arrested but did not resist despite the fact that he was armed, as he feared for the lives of his mother and his wife. He was arrested and court-martialled in Dublin, although he refused to recognize the authority of the court. Condemned to death, he was executed at Beggars Bush barracks. Childers shook hands with each member of the firing squad before he was shot—a fate that many fought to save him from, including George Bernard Shaw.

Meanwhile, *The Riddle of the Sands* has remained in print, going into many editions, a living tribute to the vision of an intrepid explorer and a passionate individualist who not only had the imagination to pre-empt a possible enemy attack on his country but was also the first espionage writer to debate the question of the double agent and the moral validity of spying. At one point Carruthers describes the Englishman turned German agent as 'the vilest creature on God's earth'. But Davies, conscious of their own vulnerable position and anxious to expose the double agent, points out: 'Mightn't we come to be spies ourselves? . . . If he's in with . . . Germany, he's a traitor to us. If we can't do it [that is, expose Dollman] without spying, we've a right to spy.'

Roy Foster   (essay date 1988)

SOURCE: "A Patriot for Whom? Erskine Childers, a Very English Irishman," in *History Today,* Vol. 38, October, 1988, pp. 27-32.

[*In the following essay, Foster discusses Childers's tragic involvement in the Irish struggle for independence.*]

At least two books have been published called *The Riddle of Erskine Childers* and there will no doubt be more. Superficially, it is an inevitable title: the gung-ho junior imperialist from the heart of the English establishment, who published *The Riddle of the Sands* in 1903 to warn Britain of the strategic threat to her supremacy from Germany, ended his life in 1922 as an irreconcilable Irish republican, doing his best to sabotage the Anglo-Irish Treaty. His writing in the last year of his life took the form of violent and exalted propaganda for the Irregulars in the Civil War; the spy thriller had become real. He was shot by the Free State government—after a highly questionable judicial procedure—as a traitor to the new Irish regime, working to overturn it. After months on the run with the IRA guerillas, Childers was arrested in possession of a firearm—thus contravening an emergency proclamation declaring it a capital offence. But many, notably Winston

Churchill, had already identified him as primarily a traitor to his British background. Technically, this was not so; though an *engagé* Sinn Féiner from 1919, and Secretary to the Irish delegation that signed the Treaty, Childers had never actually taken arms against the British government in Ireland. But the trajectory of his career was no less dramatic for that.

Childers' ultimate destination, however, was not really a repudiation of the values in which he was reared. His father's family were firmly located in the English administrative élite—academics, professionals, some politicians (including Hugh Childers, a Gladstonian Chancellor and an early Home Rule convert). His mother was an Irish Barton—an Ascendancy Tory family with a fine house in the most beautiful part of Wicklow. Oddly described by Childers' biographer as a plain eighteenth-century house, it is anything but: a vigorous and rather grand essay in early Victorian Gothic, built in 1838 and reflecting a local tradition of prosperity, paternalism, improving landlords and model estates. A closely parallel background, some miles down the Avonmore valley, produced Charles Stewart Parnell.

The Barton house became Erskine Childers' home when he was orphaned traumatically through tuberculosis. His father, a gifted Orientalist, died in 1876 when Erskine was six, and the children were removed from their mother. Already infected, she lingered on in a sanatorium until her son was thirteen. Childers' own rather self-conscious masculinity, and his avoidance of women until his sudden and radiantly happy marriage at thirty-four, may have roots in this emotional deprivation. Despite the Wicklow background, his career followed a predictable pattern: Haileybury, Cambridge, friends like Walter Runciman and Basil Williams, service in the Boer War and later the Navy Air Arm, a House of Commons Clerkship. Liberal company and adapted Milnerite theory led him towards Home-Rule-All-Round; but the tone of his best-selling *Riddle of the Sands* indicates an unquestioning commitment to the values of the *Boy's Own Paper*. Dominion Home Rule for Ireland probably remained his ideal until 1919.

In that year, he decided to move permanently to Ireland and take up the Sinn Féin cause. As a Home Rule sympathiser in 1914, he had organised a much-publicised shipment of arms for the Irish Volunteers, intended as a public riposte to the anti-Home Rule Ulster Volunteer Force's stockpiling of weapons in the north. But for the duration of the war his energies were concentrated on imperial matters. In 1917 he acted as secretary to the ill-starred Irish Convention which attempted to pull the Home Rule chestnuts out of the fire, but there is no evidence that his ideas went any further than the Dominion Home Rule for all Ireland advocated by people like Horace Plunkett.

Childers ended the war ill, depressed and forty-eight years old. His sudden next step was a move to Ireland—strongly opposed by his wife, though she subsequently went to some trouble to conceal the fact. Galvanised by Sinn Féin's success in the 1918 election, Childers began to preach to surprised friends the pointlessness of negotiation and the iniquity of 'compromise'. Sinn Féin's tactics were still directed at pressurising international opinion at Ver-

sailles rather than shooting policemen in Ireland. But through his cousin, Robert Barton, Childers met the charismatic Michael Collins and the austere Eamon de Valera, and found new heroes.

Childers' advance in the movement was sudden, rising to Director of Publicity for the Dáil during the Anglo-Irish war, then Minister of Propaganda, and finally Secretary to the ill-starred Treaty delegation. Unable to persuade the delegates not to sign, Childers subsequently joined the Irregulars as propaganda chief and editor of *Poblacht*. He was arrested at his old home, Glendalough House, on November 10th, 1922, and shot ten days later, dying as a nationalist martyr. The exalted and implacable nature of his republicanism, and the apparent repudiation of his background, carry echoes of Maud Gonne or Bridget Rose Dugdale. But the progression was not as crude as that.

Perhaps the parallels are closer to Constance Markievicz, or for that matter Patrick Pearse and Cathal Brugha: Irish nationalists from half-English backgrounds, psychologically orphaned and ready to find an identification. The compensatory potency of Anglo-Irish nationalism needs decoding. Famously accused by Churchill of Anglophobia, Childers strenuously denied the charge: 'I die loving England', he wrote to his wife. But by then he also denied being English. After Childers' arrest, Kevin O'Higgins publicly and disingenuously hinted that he would have to be shot, but *not* 'because he was an Englishman'. The prisoner haughtily remarked that this was 'a description habitually, though incorrectly, applied to me'. By then he had opted for Irish romanticism and the martyr's niche: by deciding to make an example of him, and ignoring the battery of appeals for clemency, the Free State government gave him his wish. Though the carrying out of the death sentence appalled many, Childers' execution at Beggar's Bush barracks was in some ways a logical and even a passionately desired, ending.

It was all a long way from Trinity College, Cambridge, or Leslie Stephen's Sunday Tramps club. But in a sense the romanticism was always there. The other side of the gruff lone-sailor persona (the Davies rather than the Carruthers aspect of Childers, in *Riddle of the Sands* terms) was a rather gauche and gushing Tennyson-worshipper, who wrote to his sisters on the death of the Poet Laureate:

> His death seems to me to have just added the perfecting touch to his almost perfect life . . . You and I owe more to him than even we are faintly conscious of, I think. For my part there is hardly a good aspiration or a good emotion in me which has not either been heightened or originated by him. Now he has died there seems no change—there are his words and music still, only just with the added touch of perfection and consecration. Oh, I think such a life, such a life's work, and such a death are a treasure of unimaginable value to all English-speaking people.

The sentimental taste remained, along with a devotion to 'Rupert of Hentzau' and the like. Much later, after Childers' transformation, intellectual young republicans like Frank O'Connor were mildly shocked at their eminent comrade's taste in reading-matter: killing time in their bivouacs, when they pulled out a well-thumbed Dostoevsky, Childers became immersed in Fenimore Cooper or John Buchan.

Buchan supplies the motif for much of the Childers ethos. Himself a young Milnerite and Sunday Tramp, Buchan was deeply influenced by Childers' *Riddle,* responding then and later to the passion for small boats, espionage and doing down foreigners; Childers' lament that the book was spoiled by a love–interest is pure Buchan ('I was weak enough to "spatchcock" a girl into it and now find her a horrible nuisance'). Like a Buchan hero, Childers resolutely presented war as a public-school game: Richard Hannay might have written his letters home from the South African front with their phoney geniality and overdone sportingness. 'De Wet is the plucky one. Now that his cause is hopeless we have sworn to get him to London and give him a testimonial dinner for giving us the chance of a fight'. And like a Buchan hero, Childers chose for a wife a 'plucky' American girl, nearly as good as a man.

Erskine and Molly Childers appear most vividly as Buchan hero and heroine in the episode of the 1914 Howth gun-running, when with Mary Spring-Rice they landed a cargo of 1,500 obsolete Mauser rifles for the Irish Volunteers, precipitating a confrontation with the government. Childers was as yet unconnected with Sinn Féin, let alone the IRB: he had not met many of the hard-faced men who engineered the *Asgard*'s reception. The idea of running in nationalist arms in order to expose the government's pusillanimity regarding Ulster's defiance had occurred to several exasperated Anglo-Irish Home Rulers: Childers was at one with Mary Spring-Rich, Alice Stopford Green, Lord Ashbourne, Conor O'Brien and others. The gesture was largely symbolic. (Unlike the chillingly effective Ulster Volunteer Force's importation of 25,000 rifles and three million rounds of ammunition three months before). But it was, for Childers, a commitment to real-life romance. The secret rendezvous with foreign freighters, the demanding seamanship, the camaraderie, the hero's welcome at Howth—all were lyrically evoked by him in his last, retrospective letters to his wife. The Buchan hero had stepped into a new role; the finale would be his execution, where he tried to reject a blindfold, and insisted on shaking hands with each member of the firing-squad, to their discomfiture. His last words were an instruction to 'take a step or two forward, lads: it will be easier that way'.

It was a wasteful ending to a life of considerable talents and generous impulses; but psychologically it seems all of a piece. Inside the man of action, there was a small boy seeking to belong. The theme of separation from his mother recurs; the part his strong-minded wife played in his life, resented by many of his friends, was significant. He wrote to her as a son to a mother, and generally deferred to her judgement (the move to Ireland in 1919 was a rare piece of self-assertion). Childers' cousin Robert Barton, a member of the Treaty delegation, initially decided not to sign its terms; but when Childers approvingly told him that Molly would not have wanted him to, something snapped, and Barton signed in defiance. (He regretted it later). Childers' insecurity struck those who knew him; Michael Collins remarked, in a striking phrase, that he al-

ways did the difficult thing just because it was difficult. He forced himself through physical and mental trials; as a middle-aged naval officer and later as an Irregular guerilla, he deliberately and sometimes unnecessarily courted danger. 'I recognised Childers as a crackpot', remarked an army acquaintance who declined to join the Howth venture. 'Something always happens to crackpots. Something always goes wrong . . .'

All his life Childers 'tested' himself; all his life he looked for father-figures and gurus, being deeply and contradictorily influenced by men like Hugh Childers, Earl Roberts, Basil Williams, and Roger Casement. With de Valera, he found a faith at last:

> When all is said and done, my antecedents did of course make my *use* of the Cause infinitesimal enough by comparison with those whose sacrifices and sufferings *made* the Cause—did make me much less of an asset than I might have been had I come to the truth sooner. So all the more I value the faith and confidence you placed in me from the time of our first meeting . . . [I] would rather cut off [my] hand than weaken or injure the noblest of all Causes, or you, the greatest leader of a great Cause I have ever met.

All this helps explain the bewilderingly fast radicalising of his position from 1919—strange as it is to find him flintily refusing in 1921 just the kind of imperial Home Rule he had so recently campaigned for. Though he produced an argument based on the idea that Canada's position was not a relevant precedent, this was in fact the opposite of the case. Childers was supposedly appointed to the delegation for his expertise in imperial technicalities, but it was Collins who isolated in a private memorandum the relevant point: 'the only association which it will be satisfactory for Ireland to enter will be based, not on the present technical legal status of the Dominions, but on the real position they claim, *and have in fact secured*'. Nor did Ulster feature at the forefront of Childers' case, though he was more astute about that burked question than most.

By 1921, too, the infamous record of the Black and Tans had given republicanism the high moral ground. As editor of the *Irish Bulletin,* Childers collated and publicised every murder and atrocity committed by the other side; he had also brilliantly scaled up any military activity at all into a 'notorious' sacking or looting.

In many ways, until the recent painstaking work of scholars like Charles Townshend and David Fitzpatrick, the Anglo-Irish was has continued to be viewed through the vivid enlarging lens of the *Bulletin.* Childers had many of the qualities of a great publicist—including an ability to trim his ideological sails to a favourable wind. The tone of his terse and effective *Daily Herald* article in March 1919 about the government's military repression of strikers, and the implications for Ireland, is interesting. The piece is addressed to 'British workers' as 'a warning that the army has been transferred to the function of repressing liberties, first national, then social'; finally it appeals to James Connolly's memory and mounts an attack on 'capitalist imperialism'. This is not an approach characteristic of Childers at any other juncture; but given the conditions of 1919, it was important to keep an eye on the increasingly influential Labour Left and throw a line to Lansbury, Dutt and company. It may have influenced Churchill against Childers at least as much as his republican agitation. But at the time, the expatriot is revealed in the condemnation of Britain's current record in Ireland as equalling Germany's treatment of Belgium—still evidently for Childers the acme of repression. The echo of *The Riddle of the Sands* remains curiously resonant.

Nor was it forgotten among proGerman Irish nationalists. Much about Childers was deeply loveable, especially as a parent and a friend. But he was greatly disliked by many of his new colleagues. Arthur Griffith expansively accused him of causing the First World War, probably thinking of the celebrated 'Postscript' to the *Riddle* ('Is it not becoming patent that the time has come for training all Englishmen systematically either for the sea or for the rifle?'—a curiously Pearsean note). It must also be remembered that long before the Treaty split there was a deep divide between members of the Dáil and the IRB clique who dominated the Irish Republican Army. Though they ostensibly formed two prongs of a united offensive, their priorities and tactics were often at odds, and the movement was rent by personal rivalries—notably between de Valera, President of the Dáil, and Collins, the IRA supremo. Childers was always a Dáil man and a de Valera man, and he went with his companions when the reckoning came.

This should be borne in mind when considering the vindictive, trumped-up and essentially indefensible procedure which led to his execution: he was being judged, and prejudged, by ex-colleagues who had always disliked and often distrusted him. Both in England and in Ireland, public statements were made before his trial which effectively called for the death penalty. Summary executions of Republican Irregulars had already been carried out, but Childers' record was almost entirely that of a publicist; he claimed to his wife that he would have used his pistol to resist arrest had there not been women in the house, but he was anything but the terrorist desperado pictured by Churchill and O'Higgins. Nonetheless, a brief military trial *in camera* condemned him to death, following pressure that was essentially political, and he was executed before appeal procedures could be properly carried through. The process was hastily rationalised by old enemies on both sides of the Irish Sea.

But many of his Irregular companions in those tragic last days on the run also resented him, and referred to him contemptuously; echoes come through contemporary memoirs, though they are muffled by the battery of posthumous publications in the Childers interest—including his last letter to his wife, who guarded his shrine for decades afterwards. His psychological background as well as his intellectual conditioning present an odd strain of weakness—the weakness of inflexibility. There was about him what his much-loved Tennyson discerned in Garibaldi: 'the divine stupidity of the hero'.

As has been said, Childers was not a 'traitor' to Britain; he did not take arms in the Anglo-Irish war, though remaining engaged in press and diplomatic work on Sinn Féin's behalf and acting as a Republican Justice in the Dáil courts. Nor, unlike Pearse and Casement, did he ever support Germany. In any case, he had satisfied himself that he had transferred his allegiance. It is interesting that in *The Riddle of the Sands* the villain Dollman is presented as the epitome of corruption because he has adopted another nationality, implacably opposed to his mother country: a creature of 'malignant perfidy', according to the narrator. It is oddly prophetic of how Childers would himself be described. 'Sixteen years ago he was still an Englishman', breathes Carruthers to Davies. 'Now he's a German. At some time between this and that, I suppose, he came to grief—disgrace, flight, exile. When did it happen?'

Only six years before addressing the firing squad in 1922, Childers had been a British naval officer, appalled by the 1916 Rising. Yet at his trial he said 'I am by birth, domicile and deliberate choice of citizenship an Irishman'. This adoptive Irishness was fully meant; he chose allegiance to the Irish 'Republic' platonically declared in 1919. The theological belief in this polity as 'virtually established' implied a theological citizenship of a never-never land: Republicanism, as defined a little later in a pamphlet commemorating Austin Stack, was 'not a political formula but the [sic] way of life'. Once anchored there, it was impossible for Childers to retreat to unglamorous if pragmatic Dominion Home Rule.

Yet he was not anti-English. Churchill denounced him as 'a mischief-making murderous renegade . . . a strange being, actuated by a deadly and malignant hatred for the land of his birth'—exactly, in fact, as Carruthers described Dollman. But Childers would have said that his values, even if ostensibly subversive, actually remained true to the ideal of England betrayed by the post-war government. The same argument was adopted, for different purposes, by another disillusioned First World War airman, Oswald Mosley. Another contemporary who oddly parallels Childers is T.E. Lawrence: like him a consummate propagandist, like him caught in the overlap between acting and action, and like him driven by inner demons. Something that did not ring quite true in Childers inspired his Free State enemies ludicrously to claim that he was a British double agent all along (a twist yet again worthy of a Buchan novel). It was not that complicated—or that simple. But in all his ambiguities, insecurities, commitments and defiances, Erskine Childers remains a figure far more deeply rooted in English culture than in that of his adopted Ireland.

David Seed   (essay date 1992)

SOURCE: "Erskine Childers and the German Peril," in *German Life & Letters,* Vol. XLV, No. 1, January, 1992, pp. 66-73.

[*In the following essay, Seed notes that Childers's suggestion of German aggression in* The Riddle of the Sands, *published in 1903, was particularly insightful.*]

In 1871 *Blackwood's Magazine* published the anonymous story 'The Battle of Dorking' purporting to describe a German invasion of Britain. Subtitled 'Reminiscences of a Volunteer', this work was intended as a warning against

British complacency in the wake of the Franco-Prussian War which established Germany as Britain's main military rival in Europe. Its realism, prophetic fiction masquerading as direct factual reporting, lay in the detail with which it described the confusion following the invasion and the confrontation between British and German forces near Box Hill. Its author, Sir George Tomkyns Chesney, stressed the total lack of preparedness on Britain's part, and peppered his narrative with morals: 'we became wise when it was too late'; 'there, across the narrow straits, was the writing on the wall, but we would not choose to read it.' The British fleet is too widely dispersed to pose any real obstacle to the invaders. The army is disorganised and misled by a rumour that the enemy has landed at Harwich when it actually starts the invasion at Worthing. As the literary historian I. F. Clarke points out, 'from 1871 onwards Chesney's story showed Europe how to manipulate the new literature of anxiety and belligerent nationalism'. This work initiated a series of novels dealing with invasion—it was clearly drawn on by H. G. Wells for *The War of the Worlds,* for instance—which stress strong or weak military points in a triumphant or catastrophic manner according to the demands of propaganda.

In the years immediately following the Boer War a whole series of articles ran in British periodicals which expressed anxiety about the rapid build-up of the German navy. The *Morning Post* reported that 'there is a menace growing up in the east which cannot be ignored' and the *National Review* led an anti-German campaign by whipping up fears of a naval invasion. Three particular aspects of recent developments in Germany received attention. First in priority was the fear of Britain losing naval supremacy, specifically in the North Sea. An ex-naval officer [Thomas B. Moody] writing in the *Fortnightly Review* in 1903, for instance, traces German Anglophobia back to the war with Denmark in 1864 and makes a plea for the establishment of an east coast naval base at Filey. In the *Nineteenth Century* for the previous year Archibald S. Hurd praises the unique foresight and thoroughness of the German naval acts, contrasting the conditions they create with the state of the British navy which seems hamstrung by irrelevant traditions. The expansion of the German navy was perceived as being fuelled by the 'rooted conviction that Germany must possess colonies almost at any price', in what O. Eltzbacher saw as amounting to a national obsession. Eltzbacher was not by any means alone in treating a war between the two powers as a very real possibility: 'It is clear that the North Sea will be the theatre of war where our fate will be decided.' Expansion is also seen to be the result of the Pan-German movement which a writer in the *Quarterly Review* of 1902 explained as wanting 'nothing less than German dominion over the whole of Middle Europe, and more'. That 'more' could well include Holland because Rotterdam would possess prime strategic importance as a port situated at the mouth of the Rhine and confronting Britain.

It is vital to bear this atmosphere of suspicion and distrust in mind when trying to understand the particular impact which was made by Erskine Childers's novel *The Riddle of the Sands* when it was published in 1903. Childers had served as a volunteer in the Boer War and in 1903 held a clerkship in the House of Commons, neither of which would adequately explain the remarkable political awareness of the novel which reads like a résumé of all the fears the British press was expressing of German expansion. The novel was 'edited' by Childers as a 'record of secret service recently achieved' and describes a yachting cruise made by two university friends from Schleswig through the recently constructed Kiel Canal and around the islands of East Frisia in the course of which they stumble across a rehearsal of an invasion of Britain. Childers combines two genres, the tale of adventure and the tale of detection, into an ostensible story of sight-seeing where astonishing discoveries are made. The two friends possess simple but contrasting characters. Carruthers is the narrator, skilled at German, ignorant of seamanship; Davies is the yachtsman and the one with formulated political opinions about German imperialism. Childers initially plays the one character off against the other until Davies has convinced Carruthers of the rightness of his views and then the two friends join forces to reveal exactly what is going on in the Frisian Islands. The narrative rests on a series of realisations by Carruthers: of German military planning in general, of the strategic importance of the Ems Estuary (dividing Germany and Holland), and then—the crowning insight—of what lies behind the pretence of doing salvage work off the island of Juist:

> I was assisting at an experimental rehearsal of a great scene when multitudes of sea-going lighters, carrying full loads of soldiers, not half loads of coals, should issue simultaneously, in seven ordered fleets, from seven shallow outlets, and, under escort of the Imperial Navy, traverse the North Sea and throw themselves bodily upon English Shores.

The cruise which the two men make takes Carruthers from one moment of awareness to another.

The starting-point of the cruise in the novel is Flensburg on the eastern coast of Schleswig which had been under German administration since the 1860s. In the manuscript of the novel Childers was at pains to stress that the country was being held under a military occupation which the very buildings themselves resist. As Carruthers climbs the hill towards the site of a crucial battle between Danes and Germans the political layout of the town below becomes clear: 'higher up the hill in the newer and busier quarter German flags and German uniforms showed in still sharper contrast to the Danish element. The very cafes were hostile and distinct'. The place becomes a living embodiment of military oppression and Carruthers's sympathy immediately goes out to 'the unconquered spirit of the conquered province under the iron heel of Prussia'. Although Childers deleted both these passages, thereby toning down Carruthers's criticism of Germany, the novel nevertheless firmly retains an anti-Prussian perspective. Carruthers's reactions draw the reader's attention to Germany's colonising activities near Britain and his 'sight-seeing' mentions the sea-borne landings which led to the defeat of the Danes long before a possible analogy might be drawn with Britain.

The next important stage on the journey comes when the yacht passes through the Kiel Canal. Canal-building was a vital extension of Germany's naval effort since these artificial waterways broke the land barrier posed by Denmark and linked the Baltic with the North Sea. The other main canal referred to in the novel runs from the Ems to the Jade Estuary, cutting across the hinterland of East Frisia and offering a speedy passage to naval gunboats. When the yacht enters the Kiel Canal Carruthers sees the same warships as Childers himself saw when he sailed through it in the 1890s. The canal is revealed as a highway, a crucial artery in German communications:

> Broad and straight, massively embanked, lit by electricity at night till it is lighter than many a Great London street; traversed by great war vessels, rich merchantmen, and humble coasters alike, it is a symbol of the new and mighty force which, controlled by the genius of statesmen and engineers, is thrusting the empire irresistibly forward to the goal of maritime greatness.

It is here that the political sophistication of the novel lies, in passages like this where the German landscape is read with an eye alert to the strategic importance of canals, rivers and all the channels running between the Frisian Islands. In 1910 Childers contributed a series of articles on yachting to the *Times* and in the piece entitled 'Cruising in German Frisia' (23 August) he stressed exactly this way of responding to the landscape:

> To stand on some remote plateau of sand which the tide has laid bare in the midst of this wilderness [the Frisian coast] is to obtain a point of vantage unique of its kind in Europe. Far away at the head of the Jade is the great new naval base of Wilhelmshaven, the dynamic centre of Germany's 20th century *Welt-politik*. Up and down the fairways of the Weser and Elbe glide huge liners, cargo-steamers, and sailing-vessels from every quarter of the globe. At night the guiding lights for this great *Knoten-punkt* of traffic twinkle on the horizon, the vivid wheeling beams from Heligoland dominant in the north; while the southern sky glows faintly over distant Hamburg and Bremen.

The description is charged with political implications in suggesting a military machine focused on the naval base, facilitated by the well-lit waterways, fed by great industrial centres, and guided by the beacons of Heligoland which Britain had handed over to Germany in 1890 in return for concessions in East Africa. *The Riddle of the Sands* takes a comparatively little-known area of coastline and ingeniously demonstrates its centrality to the German war effort. Childers's insights were confirmed by an anonymous contributor to *Chamber's Journal* in 1910 who drew attention to the further developments in the canal system and the opening new shipbuilding yards on the Ems and Weser. Even the livestock of the area has its role to play, since from East Frisia 'will come the horses for the German army if ever it invades England'. This writer, Childers and the other political commentators all take it more or less for granted that conflict between England and Germany is inevitable years before the First World War broke out.

By concentrating on the maritime implications of canal and rail networks and of inland waterways, Childers distinguished his own novel from other fictitious treatments of German aggression. Although *The Riddle of the Sands* extends the tactical insights of *The Battle of Dorking*, the point of view is different since Carruthers and Davies are looking towards England, as it were over German shoulders. Chesney's narrative makes its impact from being so firmly rooted in familiar home territory, as does Saki's later novel *When William Came* (1913) which describes Britain under German occupation. Childers also avoided the sensational gimmickry of William Le Queux's *Invasion of 1910* (written with the support of Field-Marshal Lord Roberts and serialised in the *Daily Mail* in 1906) which carried fictitious proclamations addressed to the subjects of the occupying forces. Childers was a keen reader of Rudyard Kipling (referring in his novel to the latter's nautical terminology) who had been making statements about the German peril from the 1890s onwards. In 1897, for instance, Kipling pointed out the danger of war to Charles Norton, declaring: 'we are girded at and goaded by Germany'. Once war actually broke out, Kipling's anti-German feelings reached their peak and in 1916 he wrote to the *Daily Express:* 'One thing we must get into our thick heads is that whenever the German man or woman gets a suitable culture to thrive in he or she means death and loss to civilized people'. There is no suggestion in *The Riddle of the Sands* of such sweeping racial hostility, although Childers's novel bears directly on a story Kipling wrote in 1913 about the threat of invasion. 'The Edge of the Evening' (collected in *A Diversity of Creatures*) describes a gathering at a country house near the Channel. A plane—German, as it turns out—lands in the grounds of the house and is found to contain maps and aerial photographs clearly relating to a planned invasion. Childers also raises the possibility of Germans spying in England through the main personal antagonist of Davies and Carruthers, one Dollman who had served in the British navy and who now seems to be masquerading as a German officer. Dollman, it seems, has been spying around Chatham dockyard but when confronted by Childers's heroes claims to be a *British* agent. The ambiguity is erased when he takes the gentlemanly way out, of flinging himself overboard as the two are escaping with him to Holland. Personal antagonists have a symbolic role in this novel which is summed up in the original 1903 frontispiece. This depicts Kaiser Wilhelm in aggressive posture being confronted by a British opponent in an attitude of defence, his face set with determination. In 1916 Kipling published a volume of tributes (*Sea Warfare*) to the crews of British submarines, trawlers and destroyers which included, appropriately enough, an acknowledgement of Childers's technical accuracy in *The Riddle of the Sands*.

Childers's novel concludes with what purports to be the transcription of a memorandum to the German government detailing a plan of invasion which would be launched from East Frisia and which would involve a landing on the coast of Lincolnshire. The plan was of such interest to the First Lord of the Admiralty, Lord Selborne, that he asked Naval Intelligence to report to him on its feasibility. The response was a detailed explanation of how impracticable such a scheme would be. Childers's novel was so close to contemporary events that as it was going to press he had to add a postscript explaining recent developments in the area of home defence. One of Davies's complaints was that Britain possessed no standing committee to watch over its defence, and in 1903 such a committee was established. The second point the novel makes again and again is that Britain is vulnerable because it possesses no naval base on its east coast. Following public demonstrations it was announced in March 1903 that a base would be built on the Firth of Forth, thereby reducing the likelihood of attack from the North Sea. The decision had been taken in secret much earlier, but its announcement coincided happily with the publication of *The Riddle of the Sands*. Davies's third scheme was to organise the hundreds of men who like himself were skilled at navigation into a naval reserve force. Childers noted in his postscript that the idea was receiving favourable consideration and soon after his novel appeared the Naval Volunteer Reserve was indeed set up.

In 1910 *The Riddle of the Sands* was realised in a startlingly direct way. On the night of 21 August Lieutenant V. R. Brandon was arrested on the Frisian island of Borkum and charged with taking flashlight photographs of the fortifications at Borkum and Wangeroog. Some time later Captain B. F. Trench of the R.N.L.I. was also arrested in Emden. When the room he had used in the Union Hotel was searched, a number of documents were discovered under his mattress which included photographs and maps of Kiel, Wilhelmshaven and other locations on the coast with the position of buoys marked, notes on the North Sea fortifications, and details of the Kiel Canal. The story which Trench and Brandon stuck to consistently throughout their trial in the imperial court at Leipzig was that they had been making a sailing tour of Kiel, Heligoland and East Frisia in a purely personal capacity. The prosecution attacked this account, questioning the two officers about a copy of the 'naval Baedeker' (an Admiralty guide to the coastlines of different countries) which they had with them, and alleged that they were undercover agents on the basis that they had been having regular communication through coded letters with an official named 'Reggie' who was identified as a personal friend of Brandon attached to Naval Intelligence. The fact that Brandon was serving in the hydrography section of the Admiralty only appeared to confirm the prosecution's case that he and Trench were collecting details about piers, depths, etc. which would be valuable for mounting landing operations. The sections of the trial relating to Borkum were held in camera, partly because on the night of Brandon's arrest new naval floodlights were being tried out. At one point in the proceedings a copy of Childers's novel was produced and the defendants asked if they knew the book. Trench did and Brandon caused laughter in court when he declared: 'Yes I have read it—three times'. In fact the novel was more deeply implicated than was made clear at that time. When Captain William Henry Hall took over Naval Intelligence prior to the Borkum case, he made a cruise round German ports which confirmed Childers's charge that the existing Admiralty charts were inadequate, so inadequate that *The Riddle of the Sands* was used as a source of information. To rectify that situation in May 1910 Hall gave Trench and Brandon leave to tour the German coast, especially the Frisian Islands. In the event the German authorities found the case

proved and the two officers were sentenced to serve four years in a military fortress.

So much public interest was aroused by the Borkum case that Childers made a statement about it in the *Daily News* of 23 December, where he made a determined effort to stand back from partisan hysteria. The case, he implied, was an inevitable result of the very existence of armed forces:

> Let this be thoroughly understood: as long as nations maintain armaments for purposes of war, so long, as a necessary corollary, must plans, as definite and detailed as possible, be made in advance by each nation for the eventuality of war.

Childers minimised the guilt of Trench and Brandon, arguing that their one culpable act was crossing a fence to examine gun-emplacements. Their activities repeated those of Davies and Carruthers in so far as they had simply observed what was visible to any traveller and had used maps and guidebooks on open sale

> for the greatest part of the information in question is not a matter of esoteric mystery, but is easily accessible from ordinary maps, plans, charts, and books of reference which have a free international sale to any citizen of any country who wishes to obtain them.

Ironically, during the Borkum trial the prosecution tried to show that Britain was planning an invasion of Germany, no doubt with an eye to the current Anglophobia at home, whereas the very reverse was the case. Paul Kennedy has discovered a plan in the German military archives dating back to the 1890s which was very similar to that outlined in the epilogue to *The Riddle of the Sands*. Where Childers foresaw that lighters and barges would be used because of their shallow draught, the plan included steamers; and where he specified East Holland as the ideal landing-place on the Lincolnshire coast because it most closely resembled East Frisia, the German plan was directed against the coast of East Anglia. The scheme was first considered as early as 1896 but was shelved when Britain established a North Sea base.

Childers clearly intended his novel to have an effect on British naval policy and in 1906 wrote to Sir George Clarke of the Committee of Imperial Defence with a detailed memorandum on the north German coast. Among other things he proposed the construction of shallow vessels for easy loading, repeated the strategic importance of Borkum, and even suggested blocking the Kiel Canal. Unbeknown to him, Borkum was already being considered by the Committee as a possible target for invasion, but the plan was left aside until the First World War broke out, when Childers was invited to update his proposals. This he did in a document called 'The Seizure of Borkum and Juist' which found favour with Churchill but which was never put into action. The nearest Childers came to acting on his invasion plans was to participate in a Fleet Air Arm raid on Cuxhaven.

The *Riddle of the Sands* belongs to a period before Britain had a fully developed intelligence service, especially in the naval sphere. It now seems dated in its confidence that committed amateurs can function as efficiently as professionals, and yet the historical facts bear out Childers's general insights and confirm Davies's bluff assertion that 'those Admiralty chaps want waking up'. The reviewers recognised immediately that the book was written with a clear purpose in mind. In 1904 the *Westminster Gazette* explained rightly that 'it is meant to secure our national safety, and to increase the prospects of peace by making greater the risks to be faced by any nation which may contemplate the invasion of these islands'. The fact that it was immediately banned in Germany and just as quickly adopted by the Admiralty for inclusion in naval libraries only goes to show the accuracy of Childers's narrative.

FURTHER READING

Boyle, Andrew. *The Riddle of Erskine Childers.* London: Hutchinson, 1977, 351 p.
> Focuses on the seeming contradiction between Childers's service to England as a volunteer in two wars and his opposition to English rule of Northern Ireland.

Wilkinson, Burke. *The Zeal of the Convert.* Washington, D.C.: Luce, 1976, 256 p.
> First book-length biography of Childers.

Additional coverage of Childers's life and career is contained in the following sources published by Gale Research: *Contemporary Authors*, Vol. 113; and *Dictionary of Literary Biography*, Vol. 70.

Albert Einstein

1879-1955

German-born American physicist and philosopher.

INTRODUCTION

Einstein is generally acknowledged as the preeminent scientist of the twentieth century who challenged and disproved fundamental ideas concerning the physical universe. Specifically, Einstein's theory of relativity reconfigured notions of time, space, and matter that had been formulated by Isaac Newton in the seventeenth century. Ranked with Archimedes, Galileo Galilei, and Newton, Einstein is crucial for the ideas he contributed to science as well as those he helped abolish; there is not an area of intellectual life that has not been affected by his theories.

Biographical Information

Born in Ulm, Germany, on March 14, 1879, Einstein was not an especially remarkable student; in fact, his parents, who ran a company that made and sold electrical equipment, even suspected that he was mentally retarded. In 1895 his family moved to Milan, Italy, leaving him behind to finish school. Instead, Einstein stopped attending school and independently engaged in studying mathematics and other scientific disciplines. In 1896 he was admitted to the Swiss Federal Institute of Technology in Zurich. His subsequent job at the Swiss Patent Office in Bern left him time to continue scientific investigations of his own, which resulted in a series of papers, one of which was accepted as a doctoral dissertation at the University of Zurich in 1905. His discoveries proving the existence of molecules and light's dual nature—as a wave or a particle—were eclipsed by his Special Theory of Relativity. Einstein served as a professor of physics at universities in Zurich and Czechoslovakia. In 1914 he was appointed professor at the University of Berlin and director at the Kaiser Wilhelm Institute for Physics. There he developed the General Theory of Relativity and adopted his lifelong pacifist position. Einstein was awarded the Nobel Prize in 1921, in addition to many other awards. His pacifism and Zionism led to friction with the increasingly powerful National Socialists; he left Germany in 1933, settling in Princeton, New Jersey, where he taught at the Institute for Advanced Study until his retirement in 1945. With the advent of World War II, Einstein recognized the threat posed by Germany's hegemonic ambitions and advanced scientific knowledge, and actively encouraged President Franklin D. Roosevelt to develop the atomic bomb. Though he remained politically active for the last part of his life, much of it was given over to work on what he termed the grand unified theory of physics, a formulation that would define the properties of energy and matter. He was unable to achieve this goal before his death at 76 on April 18, 1955.

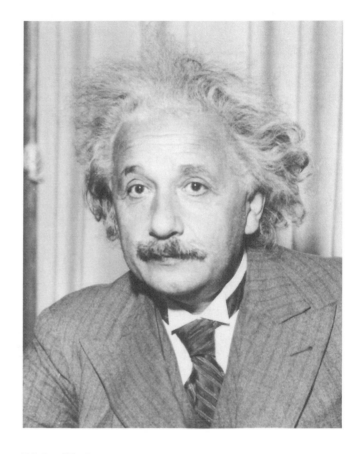

Major Works

Because of the revolutionary nature of his scientific theories, Einstein became known beyond the sphere of science. Although many fellow scientists dismissed the *Principle of Relativity* when it was first published, by the time he published *Über die spezielle und die allgemeine Relativitätstheorie* (*Relativity, the Special and the General Theory: A Popular Exposition*), the validity and importance of his work was recognized. By 1919, British astronomers had confirmed Einstein's prediction that gravity could bend light: pictures of a solar eclipse showed that the positions of star images changed in response to the gravitational effects of the sun. By the early 1930s, Einstein expanded his concerns beyond science, publishing such works as *About Zionism, Cosmic Religion, with Other Opinions and Aphorisms* and *Why War?*, which he wrote with Sigmund Freud. While Einstein was not directly involved in producing the atom bomb, his work was seminal to its development and he encouraged the bomb's use, tempering his support with the qualification that it should not be used on people. A committed pacifist, his *Essays in Humanism* and *Ideas and Opinions* reflect his determination to limit the development of nuclear arms. Later he chaired the

Emergency Committee of Atomic Scientists, which encouraged peaceful use of atomic energy.

Critical Reception

Jamie Sayen has written that Einstein "came to play a critical role in the public life of his epoch as the preeminent moral figure of the Western world." Even with his stature as a spokesman for peace and humanism, he is primarily regarded as a scientist and a philosopher. Einstein once remarked: "Politics is for the present, but an equation is something for eternity." Nonetheless, Einstein's theories—particularly the idea of relativity—have influenced virtually every aspect of twentieth-century intellectual life, from scientific study to literary criticism.

PRINCIPAL WORKS

Eine neue Bestimmung der Moleküldimensionen (nonfiction) 1905

"Entwurf einer verallgemeinerten Relativitätstheorie une eine Theorie der Gravitation" [with Marcel Grossman] (essay) 1913

"Die Grundlage der allgemeinen Relativitätstheorie" [included in *The Principle of Relativity*, 1920] (essay) 1916

Über die spezielle und die allgemeine Relativitätstheorie, gemeinverständlich [*Relativity: The Special and the General Theory: A Popular Exposition*] (nonfiction) 1917

The Principle of Relativity: Original Papers by A. Einstein and H. Minkowski (nonfiction) 1920

Äther und Relativitätstheorie [included in *Sidelights on Relativity*, 1922] (lecture) 1920

Geometrie und Erfahrung (nonfiction) 1921

The Meaning of Relativity: Four Lectures Delivered at Princeton University (lectures) 1921

Sidelights on Relativity (nonfiction) 1922

Untersuchungen über die Theorie der Brownschen Bewegungen [*Investigation on the Theory of Brownian Movement*] (nonfiction) 1922

Grundgedanken und Probleme der Relativitätstheorie (nonfiction) 1923

About Zionism: Speeches and Letters (speeches and letters) 1930

Cosmic Religion, with Other Opinions and Aphorisms (philosophy and aphorisms) 1931

The Fight Against War (nonfiction) 1933

On the Method of Theoretical Physics [reprinted in *The World As I See It*] (lecture) 1933

The Origins of the General Theory of Relativity [reprinted in *The World As I See It*] (lecture) 1933

Why War? [with Sigmund Freud] (nonfiction) 1933

Mein Weltbild [*The World As I See It*] (essays and lectures) 1934

The Evolution of Physics: The Growth of Ideas from Early Concepts to Relativity and Quanta [with Leopold Infeld] (nonfiction) 1938

Test Case for Humanity (nonfiction) 1944

The Arabs and Palestine [with E. Kahler] (nonfiction) 1944

Albert Einstein: Philosopher-Scientist [with others] [contains *Autobiographical Notes*] (nonfiction and autobiography) 1944

Out of My Later Years (essays) 1950

Ideas and Opinions (essays) 1954

Essays in Science [selected essays from *Mein Weltbild*] (essays) 1955

Grundzuge der Relativitätstheorie (nonfiction) 1956

Lettres à Maurice Solovine [*Letters to Solovine*] (letters) 1956

Einstein on Peace (nonfiction) 1960

Letters on Wave Mechanics: Schrödinger, Planck, Einstein, Lorentz (letters) 1967

Briefwechsel, 1916-1955 [with Max and Hedwig Born; *The Born-Einstein Letters: Correspondence Between Albert Einstein and Max and Hedwig Born From 1916 to 1955*] (letters) 1969

Albert Einstein, the Human Side: New Glimpses From His Archives (nonfiction) 1979

Elie Cartan-Albert Einstein: Letters on Absolute Parallelism, 1929-1932 (letters) 1979

The Collected Papers of Albert Einstein. 5 vols. (collected works) 1987-93

CRITICISM

Alfred North Whitehead   (essay date 1920)

SOURCE: "Einstein's Theory," in *Essays in Science and Philosophy*, Philosophical Library, 1947, pp. 332-42.

[*A distinguished English mathematician, philosopher, and educator, Whitehead collaborated with Bertrand Russell on the latter's* Principia Mathematica *(1910-13), a three-volume treatise on the relationship of logic to mathematics that would eventually inspire the Austrian philosopher Ludwig Wittgenstein in his ground-breaking studies. In the following essay, originally published in the* Times Educational Supplement *in 1920, Whitehead seeks to explain the major principles of Einstein's work.*]

Einstein's work may be analysed into three factors—a principle, a procedure, and an explanation. This discovery of the principle and the procedure constitute an epoch in science. I venture, however, to think that the explanation is faulty, even although it formed the clue by which Einstein guided himself along the path from his principle to his procedure. It is no novelty to the history of science that factors of thought which guided genius to its goal should be subsequently discarded. The names of Kepler and Maupertuis at once occur in illustration.

What I call Einstein's principle is the connexion between time and space which emerges from his way of envisaging the general fact of relativity. This connexion is entirely new to scientific thought, and is in some respects very paradoxical. A slight sketch of the history of ideas of relative motion will be the shortest way of introducing the new principle. Newton thought that there was one definite space within which the material world adventured, and that the sequence of its adventures could be recorded in terms of one definite time. There would be, therefore, a meaning in asking whether the sun is at rest or is fixed in this space, even although the questioner might be ignorant of the existence of other bodies such as the planets and the stars. Furthermore, there was for Newton an absolute unique meaning to simultaneity, so that there can be no ambiguity in asking, without further specification of conditions, which of two events preceded the other or whether they were simultaneous. In other words, Newton held a theory of absolute space and of absolute time. He explained relative motion of one body with respect to another as being the difference of the absolute motions of the two bodies. The greatest enemy to his absolute theory of space was his own set of laws of motion. For it is a well-known result from these laws that it is impossible to detect absolute uniform motion. Accordingly, since we fail to observe variations in the velocities of the sun and stars, it follows that any one of them may with equal right be assumed to be either at rest or moving in any direction with any velocity which we like to suggest. Now, a character which never appears in the play does not require a living actor for its impersonation. Science is concerned with the relations between things perceived. If absolute motion is imperceptible, absolute position is a fairy tale, and absolute space cannot survive the surrender of absolute position.

So far our course is plain: we give up absolute space, and conceive all statements about space as being merely expositions of the internal relations of the physical universe. But we have to take account of two very remarkable difficulties which mar the simplicity of this theoretical position. In the first place there seems to be a certain absoluteness about rotation. The fact of this absoluteness is inherent in Newton's laws of motion, and the deducted consequences from these premises have received ample confirmation. For example, the effect of the rotation of the earth is manifested in phenomena which appear to have no connexion with extraneous astronomical bodies. There is the bulge of the earth at its equator, the invariable directions of rotation for cyclones and anti-cyclones, the rotation of the plane of oscillation of Foucault's pendulum, and the north-seeking property of the gyrocompass. The mass of evidence is decisive, and no theory which burkes it can stand as an adequate explanation of observed facts. It is not so obvious how to combine these facts of rotation with any principle of relativity.

Secondly, the ether contributes another perplexity just where it might have helped us. We might have regained the right quasi-absoluteness of motion by measuring velocity relatively to the ether. The facts of rotation could have thus received an explanation. But all attempts to measure velocity relatively to the ether have failed to detect it in circumstances when, granting the ordinary hypotheses, its effects should have been visible. Einstein showed that the whole series of perplexing facts concerning the ether could be explained by adopting new formulae connecting the spatial and temporal measurements made by observers in relative motion to each other. These for-

mulae had been elaborated by Larmor and Lorentz, but it was Einstein who made them the foundation of a novel theory of time and space. He also discovered the remarkable fact that, according to these formulae, the velocity of light in vacuous space would be identical in magnitude for all these alternative assumptions as to rest or motion. This property of light became the clue by which his researches were guided. His theory of simultaneity is based on the transmission of light signals, and accordingly the whole structure of our concept of nature is essentially bound up with our perceptions of radiant energy.

In view of the magnificent results which Einstein has achieved it may seem rash to doubt the validity of a premiss so essential to his own line of thought. I do, however, disbelieve in this invariant property of the velocity of light, for reasons which have been partly furnished by Einstein's own later researches. The velocity of light appears in this connexion owing to the fact that it occurs in Maxwell's famous equations, which express the laws governing electromagnetic phenomena. But it is an outcome of Einstein's work that the electro-magnetic equations require modification to express the association of the gravitational and electro-magnetic fields. This is one of his greatest discoveries. The most natural deduction to make from these modified equations is that the velocity of light is modified by the gravitational properties of the field through which it passes, and that the absolute maximum velocity which occurs in the Maxwellian form of the equations has in fact a different origin which is independent of any special relation to light or electricity. I will return to this question later.

Before passing on to Einstein's later work a tribute should be paid to the genius of Minkowski. It was he who stated in its full generality the conception of a four-dimensional world embracing space and time, in which the ultimate elements, or points, are the infinitesimal occurrences in the life of each particle. He built on Einstein's foundations, and his work forms an essential factor in the evolution of relativistic theory.

Einstein's later work is comprised in what he calls the theory of general relativity. I will summarize what appear to me as the essential components of his thought, at the same time warning my readers of the danger of misrepresentation which lies in such summaries of novel ideas. It is safer to put it as my own way of envisaging the theory. What are time and space? They are the names for ways of conducting certain measurements. The four dimensions of nature as conceived by Minkowski express the fact that four measurements with a certain peculiar type of mutual independence are required to formulate the relations of any infinitesimal occurrence to the rest of the physical universe. These ways of measurement can be indefinitely varied by change of character, so that four independent measurements of one character will specify an occurrence just as well as four other measurements of some other character. A set of four measurements of a definite character which assigns a special type to each of the four measurements will be called a measure-system. Thus there are alternative measure-systems, and each measure-system embraces, for the specification of each infinitesimal occurrence, four assigned measurements of separate types, called the coordinates of that occurrence. The change from one measure-system to another appears in mathematics as the change from one set of variables (p1, p2, p3, p4) to another set of variables (q1, q2, q3, q4), the variables of the p-system being functions of the q-system, and *vice versa*. In this way all the quantitative laws of the physical universe can be expressed either in terms of the p-variables or in terms of the q-variables. If a suitable measure-system has been adopted, one of the measurements, say p4, will appear to us as a measurement of time, and the remaining measurements (p1, p2, p3) will be measurements of space, which are adequate to determine a point. But different measure-systems have this property of subdivision into spatial and temporal measurements according to the different circumstances of the observers. It follows that what one observer means by space and time is not necessarily the same as what another observer may mean. It is to be observed that not every change of measure-system involves a change in the meanings of space and time. For example, let (p1, p2, p3, p4) and (q1, q2, q3, q4) be the measurements in two systems which determine the same event-particle, as I will name an infinitesimal occurrence. The two measurements of time, p4 and q4, may be identical or may differ only by a constant; and the spatial set of the p-system, namely (p1, p2, p3), may be functions of the spatial set of the q-system, namely (q1, q2, q3) with q4 excluded and *vice versa*. In this case the two systems subdivide into the same space and the same time. I will call such two systems "consentient." A measure-system which has the property for a suitable observer of thus subdividing itself I will call "spatio-temporal." I am unaware whether Einstein would accept these distinctions and definitions. If he would not I have failed to understand his theory. At the same time I would maintain them as necessary to relate the mathematical theory with the facts of physical experience.

What can we mean by space as an enduring fact, within which the varying phenomena of the universe are set at successive times? I will call space as thus conceived "timeless space." All the measure-systems of a consentient spatio-temporal set will agree in specifying the same timeless space; but two spatio-temporal systems which are not consentient specify distinct timeless spaces. A point of a timeless space must be something which for all time is designated by a definite set of values for the three spatial coordinates of an associated measure-system. Let (p1, p2, p3, p4) be such a measure-system, then a point of the timeless p-space is to be designated by a definite specification of values for the coordinates in the set (p1, p2, p3), giving the same entity for all values of p4. Furthermore, according to Minkowski's conception, the life of the physical universe can be specified in terms of the intrinsic properties and mutual relations of event-particles and of aggregates of event-particles. Our problem then is narrowed down to this: how can we define the points of the timeless p-space in terms of event-particles and aggregates of event-particles? Evidently there is but one solution. The point (p1, p2, p3) of the timeless p-space must be the set of event-particles indicated by giving p4 every possible value in (p1, p2, p3, p4), while p1, p2, p3 are kept fixed to the assigned coordinates of the point. Two consequences follow from this definition of a point. In the first place, a point of timeless space is not an entity of any peculiar ultimate simplicity; it is a collection of event-particles.

Years ago, in a communication to the Royal Society in 1906 ["Mathematical Concepts of the Material World"], I pointed out that the simplicity of points was inconsistent with the relational theory of space. At that time, so far as I am aware, the two inconsistent ideas were contentedly adopted by the whole of the scientific and philosophic worlds. To say that the event-particle (p1, p2, p3, p4) occupies, or happens at, the point (p1, p2, p3) merely means that the event-particle is one of the set of event-particles which is the point. The second consequence of the definition is that if the p-system and the q-system are spatio-temporal systems which are not consentient, the p-points and the q-points are radically distinct entities, so that no p-point is the same as any q-point. A complete explanation is thus achieved of the paradoxes in spatial measurement involved in the comparison of measurements of spatial distances between event-particles as effected in a p-space and a q-space. The ordinary formulae which we find in the early chapters of text-books on dynamics only look so obvious because this radical distinction between the different spaces has been ignored.

We can now make a further step and distinguish between an instantaneous p-space and the one timeless p-space. Suppose that p4 has a fixed value, then evidently every p-point is occupied by one and only one event-particle for which p4 has this value. This event-particle has the p1, p2, p3 belonging to its p-point and also the assigned value of p4 as its four coordinate measurements which specify it. It is evident, therefore, that the set of event-particles which all occur at the assigned p-time p4 but have among them all possible spatial coordinates together reproduce in their mutual spatial relations all the peculiarities of the relations between the points of the timeless p-space. Such a set of event-particles form the instantaneous p-space occurring at the p-time p4. They are the instantaneous points of the instantaneous space. Also, all the instantaneous p-spaces, for different values of p4, are correlated to each other in pointwise fashion by means of the timeless points which intersect each instantaneous space in one event-particle. An instantaneous space of some appropriate measure-system is the ideal limit of our outlook on the world when we contract our observation to be as nearly instantaneous as possible. We may conclude this part of our discussion by noting that there are three distinct meanings which may be in our mind when we talk of space, and it is mere erroneous confusion if we do not keep them apart. We may mean by space *either* (i.) the unique four-dimensional manifold of event-particles *or* (ii.) an assigned instantaneous space of some definite spatio-temporal measure-system, *or* (iii.) the timeless space of some definite spatio-temporal measure-system.

We now turn to the consideration of time. So long as we keep to one spatio-temporal measure-system no difficulty arises; the sets of event-particles, which are the sets of instantaneous points of successive instantaneous p-spaces ("p" being the name of the measure-system), occur in the ordered succession indicated by the successive values of p4 (the p-time). The paradox arises when we compare the p-time p4 with the q-time q4 of the spatio-temporal q-system of measurement, which is not consentient with the p-system. For now if (p1, p2, p3, p4) and (q1, q2, q3, q4) indicate the same event-particle q4 can be expressed in terms of (p1, p2, p3, p4) where p4 and at least one of the spatial set (p1, p2, p3) must occur as effective arguments to the function which expresses the value of q4. Thus when we keep p4 fixed, and vary (p1, p2, p3) so as to run over all the event-particles of a definite instantaneous p-space, the value of q4 alters from event-particle to event-particle. Thus two event-particles which are contemporaneous in p-time are not necessarily contemporaneous in q-time. In relation to a given event-particle E all other event-particles fall into three classes—(1) there is the class of event-particles which precede E according to the time-reckonings of all spatio-temporal measure-systems; (2) there is the class of event-particles which are contemporaneous with E in some spatio-temporal measure-system or other; (3) there is the class of event-particles which succeed E according to the time-reckonings of all spatio-temporal measure-systems. The first-class is the past and the third class is the future. The second class will be called the class co-present with E. The whole class of event-particles co-present with E is not contemporaneous with E according to the time-reckoning of any one definite measure system. Furthermore, no velocity can exist in nature, in whatever spatio-temporal measure-system it be reckoned, which could carry a material particle from one to the other of two mutually co-present event-particles. If E1 and E2 be a pair of mutually co-present event-particles, then E1 precedes E2 in some time-systems and E2 precedes E1 in other time-systems and E1 and E2 are contemporaneous in the remaining time-systems. The properties of co-present event-particles are undeniably paradoxical. We have, however, to remember that these paradoxes occur in connexion with the ultimate baffling mystery of nature—its advance from the past to the future through the medium of the present.

For any assigned observer there is yet a fourth class of event-particles—namely, that class of event-particles which comprises all nature lying within his immediate present. It must be remembered that perception is not instantaneous. Accordingly such a class is a slab of nature comprised between two instantaneous spaces belonging to the spatio-temporal measure-system which accords with the circumstances of his observation. I have elsewhere [in "Inquiry Concerning the Principles of Natural Knowledge"] called such a class a "duration."

The physical properties of nature arise from the fact that events are not merely colourless things which happen and are gone. Each event has a character of its own. This character is analysable in two components:—(1) There are the objects situated in that event; and (2) there is the field of activity of the event which regulates the transference of the objects situated in it to situations in subsequent events. It is essential to grasp the distinction between an object and an event. An object is some entity which we can recognize, and meet again; an event passes and is gone. There are objects of radically different types, but we may confine our attention to material physical objects and to scientific objects such as electrons. Space and time have their origin in the relations between events. What we observe in nature are the situations of objects in events. Physical science analyses the fields of activity of events which determine the conditions governing the transference of objects. The whole complex of events viewed in connexion with their characters of activity takes the place of the material ether of the science of the last century. We may call it the ether of events.

Now the spatial and temporal relations of event-particles to each other are expressed by the existence in space (in whatever sense that term is used) of points, straight lines, and planes. The qualitative properties and relation of these spatial elements furnish the set conditions which are a necessary pre-requisite of measurement. For it must be remembered that measurement is essentially the comparison of operations which are performed under the same set assigned conditions. If there is no possibility of assigned conditions applicable to different circumstances, there can be no measurement. We cannot, therefore, begin to measure in space until we have determined a non-metrical geometry and have utilized it to assign the conditions of congruence agreeing with our sensible experience. Practical measurement merely requires practical conformity to definite conditions. The theoretical analysis of the practice requires the theoretical geometrical basis. For this reason I doubt the possibility of measurement in space which is heterogeneous as to its properties in different parts. I do not understand how the fixed conditions for measurement are to be obtained. In others words, I do not see how there can be definite rules of congruence applicable under all circumstances. This objection does not touch the possibility of physical spaces of any uniform type, non-Euclidean or Euclidean. But Einstein's interpretation of his procedure postulates measurement in heterogeneous physical space, and I am very sceptical as to whether any real meaning can be attached to such a concept. I think that it must be a certain feeling for the force of this objection which has led certain men of science to explain Einstein's theory by postulating uniform space of five dimensions in which the universe is set. I cannot see how such a space, which has never entered into experience, can get over the difficulty.

There is, however, another way which obtains results identical with Einstein's to an approximation which includes all that is observable by our present methods. The only difference arises in the case of the predicted shifting of lines towards the red end of the spectrum. Here my theory makes no certain prediction. A particle vibrating in the atmosphere of the sun under an assigned harmonic force would experience an increase of apparent inertia in the ratio of 1 to $3/5ga/c^2$, if vibrating radially, and in the ratio of 1 to $2/5ga/c^2$, if vibrating transversely to the sun's radius, where a is the sun's radius, g is the acceleration due to gravity, and c is the critical velocity which we may roughly call the velocity of light. If we assume that the internal vibration of a molecule can be crudely represented in this fashion, and if we may assume that the internal forces of the molecule are not themselves affected in a compensatory manner by the gravitational field, then we may expect a shifting of lines towards the red end of the spectrum somewhere between three-fifths and two-fifths of Einstein's predicted amount—namely, a shift and a broadening. But both these assumptions are evidently very ill-founded. The theory does not require that any space should be other than Euclidean, and starts from the general theory of time and space which is explained in my work already cited.

I start from Einstein's great discovery that the physical field in the neighbourhood of an event-particle should be defined in terms of ten elements, which we may call by the typical name $J\alpha\sigma$ where α and σ are each written for any one of the four suffixes 1, 2, 3, 4. According to Einstein such elements merely define the properties of space and time in the neighbourhood. I interpret them as defining in Euclidean space a definite physical property of the field which I call the "impetus." I also follow Einstein in utilizing general methods of transformation from one measure-system to another, and in particular from one spatio-temporal system to another. But the essence of the divergence of the two methods lies in the fact that my law of gravitation is not expressed as the vanishing of an invariant expression, but in the more familiar way by the expression of the ten elements $J\alpha\sigma$ in terms of two functions of which one is the ordinary gravitational potential and the other is what I call the "associate potential," which is obtained by substituting the direct distance for the inverse distance in the integral definition of the gravitational potential. The details of the methods and other results are more suitable for technical exposition.

F. S. C. Northrop   (essay date 1949)

SOURCE: "Einstein's Conception of Science," in *Albert Einstein: Philosopher-Scientist*, revised edition, edited by Paul Arthur Schlipp, The Library of Living Philosophers, 1970, pp. 387-408.

[*Northrop was an American author and educator who specialized in the fields of law, science, philosophy, and economics. In the following essay, originally published in 1949, he argues that understanding Einstein's views of the scientific method requires a well-honed "epistemological philosophy."*]

Albert Einstein is as remarkable for his conception of scientific method as he is for his achievements by means of that method. It might be supposed that these two talents would always go together. An examination, however, of statements upon scientific method by truly distinguished scientists indicates that this is far from being the case. Nor is the reason difficult to understand. The scientist who is making new discoveries must have his attention continuously upon the subject matter of his science. His methods are present, but he must have them so incorporated in his habits that he operates according to them without having to give any conscious attention to them. He is like the truly natural athlete, who performs spontaneously, but who often cannot teach others how he does it. Albert Einstein, however, is an exception to this frequently illustrated rule. He has given as much attention consciously and technically to the method of science as he has given to the theoretical foundations of physics to which he has applied scientific method.

Moreover, his analysis of scientific method has taken him beyond empirical logic into epistemology. In fact, his technical epoch-making contributions to theoretical physics owe their discovery and success in considerable part to the more careful attention which he has given, as compared with his predecessors, to the epistemological relation of the scientist as knower to the subject matter of physics as known. It happens, therefore, that to understand Albert Einstein's conception of scientific method is to have a very complete and precisely analyzed epistemological philosophy—an epistemological philosophy, moreover, which, while influenced by positivism on the one hand and ancient Greek and Kantian formal thinking on the other, departs nonetheless rather radically from both and steers a course of its own, checked at every point by actual methodological practices of scientists. The result is an epistemology which has fitted itself to an expert understanding and analysis of scientific method rather than an epistemology, such as Kantianism or positivism, which has come to science with certain epistemological premises and prescriptions and tried to fit scientific procedure to these prescriptions.

In this connection, Albert Einstein himself gives us very important advice. At the very beginning of a paper **"On the Method of Theoretical Physics"** he writes, "If you want to find out anything from the theoretical physicists about the methods they use, I advise you to stick closely to one principle: don't listen to their words, fix your attention on their deeds." Obviously this is excellent advice, and, as we shall see, Einstein has followed it, illustrating all his statements about scientific method and epistemology by specific illustrations from technical scientific theories and the technical scientific methods which they entail in their formulation, discovery and verification.

Nonetheless, his words as thus stated might easily mislead one who has not read everything which Albert Einstein has written on scientific method. One might suppose that, when he talks about fixing one's attention on the deeds of physicists, he means by "deeds" the denotatively given operations and experiments performed in a laboratory; in other words, one might suppose that he means something identical with P. W. Bridgman's operationalism.

Actually, however, Albert Einstein's meaning is almost the reverse of this, as the very next sentence in the aforementioned paper clearly indicates: "To him who is a discoverer in this field, the products of his imagination appear so necessary and natural that he regards them, and would like to have them regarded by others, not as creations of thought but as given realities."

What Einstein means here is that the full meaning of verified mathematical physics is only given in part empirically in sense awareness or in denotatively given operations or experiments, and hence involves also meanings which only the imagination can envisage and which only deductively formulated, systematic, mathematical constructions, intellectually conceived rather than merely sensuously immediate, can clearly designate. But because these deductively formulated constructions, as the scientist becomes more at home with them, so capture his imagination as to appear both "necessary and natural," and also because their deductive consequences become empirically confirmed, the tendency of the scientist is to think that they are merely denotative, empirically "given realities," rather than empirically unobservable, purely imaginatively or intellectually known, theoretically designated factors, related in very complicated ways to the purely empirically given.

This counsel by Albert Einstein is something which philosophers especially need to take seriously. If one approaches epistemology by itself, simple answers to epistemological questions often seem very satisfactory. It is obviously much more simple to affirm that all meanings in science come down to purely empirically given, positivistically immediate, denotative particulars than to hold that the source of scientific meanings is much more complicated than this. Consequently, if some philosopher, especially one with a position in a physics department, holds this simple-minded theory and asserts that this is the scientific epistemology, he can fool most philosophers, even those who are experts in epistemology. There is only one cure for this, and this cure is an examination of the technical theories of the physical sciences, their technical concepts, the specific scientific methods used actually by the scientist who introduced the concepts, and the attendant specification of the epistemological relations joining the meanings of the concepts as specified by the deductively formulated theory to meanings denotatively exhibited in empirical experience. Albert Einstein has the competence to construct such an epistemology, and he happens to have directed his attention seriously and technically to this end.

It is valuable also that Albert Einstein is a theoretical rather than an experimental physicist. The experimental physicist's business is to perform denotatively given operations. This tends to cause him to have his attention upon, and consequently to emphasize, the purely empirical, positivistically immediate side of scientific theory. It tends also to cause him to want to reduce all other meanings in science to such purely empirical, positivistically immediate operational meanings. The theoretical physicist, on the other hand, tends to approach science from the standpoint of its basic theoretical problems, as these problems are defined either by the points of difference between major theories in different parts of the science or by points of difference between the deductions from a single systematic scientific theory and propositions incompatible with these deductions, which are nonetheless called for by the experimental evidence. Thus the experimental physicist who writes on the methodology, epistemology and theory of physics tends naturally to reduce imaginatively constructed, systematically and deductively formulated scientific meanings to positivistically immediate, purely denotatively given meanings. The theoretical physicist, on the other hand, tends to see that the problems of physics are only theoretically formulatable, since facts cannot contradict each other; only the theoretically prescribed conceptualizations of the facts can contradict one another.

Albert Einstein has seen that in scientific knowledge there are two components, the one given empirically with positivistic, denotative immediacy, the other given imaginatively and theoretically and of a character quite different from the empirically immediate. In the aforementioned paper Albert Einstein makes this point unequivocally clear. After telling us to watch what physicists do, he writes as follows: "Let us now cast an eye over the development of the theoretical system, paying special attention to the relations between the content of the theory and the totality of empirical fact. We are concerned with the eternal antithesis between the two inseparable components of our knowledge, the empirical and the rational. . . ." Upon this epistemological point Albert Einstein, notwithstanding all his other major departures from Kant, is a Kantian and a Greek empirical rationalist, rather than a Humean British positivistic empiricist. Albert Einstein, at a formative period in his intellectual life, did not study Immanuel Kant's *Critique of Pure Reason* to no avail.

Furthermore, in the sentence immediately following the aforementioned quotation Einstein continues:

> We reverence ancient Greece as the cradle of western science. Here for the first time the world witnessed the miracle of a logical system which proceeded from step to step with such precision that every one of its deduced propositions was absolutely indubitable—I refer to Euclid's geometry. This admirable triumph of reasoning gave the human intellect the necessary confidence in itself for its subsequent achievements. If Euclid failed to kindle your youthful enthusiasm, then you were not born to be a scientific thinker.

There is, to be sure, the empirical, positivistically immediate, denotatively known component in scientific knowledge also. This Einstein immediately proceeds to designate:

> But before mankind could be ripe for a science which takes in the whole of reality, a second fundamental truth was needed, which only became common property among philosophers with the advent of Kepler and Galileo. Pure logical thinking cannot yield us any knowledge of the empirical world; all knowledge of reality starts from experience and ends in it. Propositions arrived at by purely logical means are completely empty as regards reality. Because Galileo saw this, and particularly because he drummed it into the scientific world, he is the father of modern physics—indeed, of modern science altogether.

In short, there must be both the postulationally designated, deductively formulated theoretic component and the inductively given, denotative, empirical component in scientific knowledge.

It might be thought from the last quotation, if nothing more by Einstein were read, that, because "knowledge of reality starts from experience and ends in it," what happens in between, as given theoretically and formulated deductively, reduces to the empirical component and hence adds to the conception of "reality" nothing of its own. The sentence, to the effect that "Propositions arrived at by purely logical means are completely empty as regards reality" might seem to suggest this. The point of the latter statement, however, is that logical implications are always carried through with expressions which contain variables;

thus in themselves they designate nothing empirical. But logical deductions proceed from expressions containing variables which are postulates, or what Albert Einstein terms "axioms." And these axioms express a systematic relatedness. Consequently, when one finds empirically, by the method of Galileo, the inductive factors which function as material constants for the variables in the postulates of the deductive system, then to this inductively given material there is contributed a systematic relatedness which pure empiricism and induction alone do not exhibit. Thus the theoretically known systematic factor, between the experience with which scientific method begins and that with which it ends, contributes something of its own to what Einstein terms the scientific "knowledge of reality." Hence, Einstein concludes: "We have thus assigned to pure reason and experience their places in a theoretical system of physics. The structure of the system is the work of reason; the empirical contents and their mutual relations must find their representation in the conclusions of the theory."

Furthermore, Albert Einstein makes it clear that it is the rationalistic, deductively formulated, structural component which is the basic thing in mathematical physics and the empirical component which is derived. This was implicit in the last sentence just quoted, when it affirmed that "the empirical contents and their mutual relations must find their representation in the conclusions of the theory." They do not find their representation in the postulates or axiomatic basis of the deductively formulated theory.

Not only do the basic concepts and postulates of theoretical physics fail to reduce to purely nominalistic, denotatively given meanings, but they cannot be derived from the empirical, or what we have elsewhere [*The Meeting of East and West*] termed the aesthetic, component in scientific knowledge by any logical means whatever; neither the logical method of formal implication nor the more Aristotelian or Whiteheadian method of extensive abstraction. Upon these points Einstein is unequivocal.

He tells us that the deductively formulated theoretic component in scientific knowledge is a "free invention(s) of the human intellect. . . ." He adds,

> Newton, the first creator of a comprehensive, workable system of theoretical physics, still believed that the basic concepts and laws of his system could be derived from experience. This is no doubt the meaning of his saying, *hypotheses non fingo*. . . . the tremendous practical success of his doctrines may well have prevented him and the physicists of the eighteenth and nineteenth centuries from recognising the fictitious character of the foundations of his system. The natural philosophers of those days were, on the contrary, most of them possessed with the idea that the fundamental concepts and postulates of physics were not in the logical sense free inventions of the human mind but could be deduced from experience by 'abstraction'—that is to say by logical means. A clear recognition of the erroneousness of this notion really only came with the general theory of relativity, which showed that one could take account of a wider range of empirical facts, and that too in a more satisfacto-

ry and complete manner, on a foundation quite different from the Newtonian. But quite apart from the question of the superiority of one or the other, the fictitious character of fundamental principles is perfectly evident from the fact that we can point to two essentially different principles, both of which correspond with experience to a large extent; this proves at the same time that every attempt at a logical deduction of the basic concepts and postulates of mechanics from elementary experiences is doomed to failure.

He adds that the "axiomatic basis of theoretical physics cannot be abstracted from experience but must be freely invented, . . . Experience may suggest the appropriate mathematical concepts, but they most certainly cannot be deduced from it." In short, the method taking one from empirically given experience to the systematic factor in scientific knowledge designated by the postulates of deductively formulated scientific theory is not that of either extensive abstraction or formal implication.

But neither is it that of any explicitly formulatable scientific method grounded in probability rather than deductive certainty. It is precisely at this point, notwithstanding his agreement with the positivists' emphasis upon empirical verification, that Albert Einstein, along with Max Planck, becomes so uneasy about positivism. The way from the empirical data to the postulates of deductively formulated physical science is a frightfully difficult one. Here, rather than anywhere else, the scientist's genius exhibits itself. The way is so difficult that no methods whatever must be barred; no sources of meaning whatever, imaginative, theoretical, of whatever kind, are to be excluded. It appears that nature covers up her basic secrets; she does not wear her heart upon her sleeve. Thus only by the freest play of the imagination, both the intuitive imagination and the non-intuitive, formal, theoretical imagination, can the basic concepts and postulates of natural science be discovered. In fact, Einstein writes, with respect to the discovery of "the principles which are to serve as the starting point . . . ." of the theoretical physicist's deductive system, that "there is no method capable of being learnt and systematically applied so that it leads to the goal."

In a paper on **"The Problem of Space, Ether, and the Field of Physics,"** Albert Einstein adds that the "hypotheses with which it [theoretical physics] starts becomes steadily more abstract and remote from experience," the greater the number of empirical facts the logical deduction from the basic postulates includes. Consequently, the "theoretical scientist is compelled in an increasing degree to be guided by purely mathematical, formal considerations in his search for a theory, because the physical experience of the experimentor cannot lift him into the regions of highest abstraction. The predominantly inductive methods appropriate to the youth of science are giving place to tentative deduction." Consequently, instead of hampering the theoretical physicist by epistemological prohibitions concerning the kind of meanings and their source permitted in his basic concepts, Albert Einstein writes that the "theorist who undertakes such a labour should not be carped at as 'fanciful'; on the contrary, he should be encouraged to give free reign to his fancy, for there is no other way to the goal." He adds: "This plea was needed . . . ; it is the line of thought which has led from the special to the general theory of relativity and thence to its latest off-shoot, the unitary field theory."

But if Einstein's dictum that the "axiomatic basis of theoretical physics cannot be abstracted from experience but must be freely invented" entails the rejection on the one hand of the positivistic, purely empirical, Humean philosophy, which would reduce all scientific meanings to nominalistic particulars, and also, on the other hand, of the Aristotelian and Whiteheadian epistemology, which, while admitting universal or nontemporal invariant meanings, would nonetheless insist upon deriving them from empirical immediacy by the method of extensive abstraction, it equally rejects the Kantian epistemological thesis that the postulated, deductively formulated systematic relatedness of scientific knowledge is a categorical *a priori*. The more systematic relatedness of space and time in scientific knowledge is as tentative, even though not given purely empirically, as is the empirical content which may be observed and correlated with factors within the space-time relatedness. This is what Albert Einstein means when he speaks of the method of theoretical physics as the method of "tentative deduction."

There is, for Albert Einstein, as for Kant, spatio-temporal relatedness in scientific knowledge, which is not to be identified with sensed relatedness. But this systematic relatedness is not a universal and necessary presupposition of any possible empirical experience. It has to be discovered by a free play of the formal, mathematical, intellectual imagination, and it has to be tested by a long sequence of deductive implications, the resultant theorems of which are correlated with observable data. Thus, although the forms of space and time, or, to speak more accurately, the form of space-time, is *a priori* in the sense that it is not given empirically and must be brought to and combined with the local, diverse, contingent, inductive data located within it, nonetheless it is not *a priori* in the Kantian sense of being a universal and necessary form of any possible empirical experience whatever.

Nor is it *a priori* in the Kantian sense that it is brought to the Humean sensuous, contingent data of science by the epistemological knower. Thus Albert Einstein writes that it "cannot be justified . . . by the nature of the intellect. . ." Instead, it belongs to and is the public physical relatedness of the public physical field of nature—in fact, it is that particular relatedness which exhibits itself as the gravitational field. Thus, in the epistemology of Albert Einstein, the structure of space-time is the structure of the scientific object of knowledge; it is not something which merely seems to belong to the object when its real basis supposedly is solely in the character of the scientist as knower.

This ultimate basis of space-time in the public, contingent, physical object of knowledge, rather than in the necessary constitution of the epistemological knower, follows from the tensor equation of gravitation in Einstein's general theory of relativity. Its ten potentials defining the gravitational field at the same time prescribe the metrical structure of space-time. Thus space-time has all the contingent character that the field strengths, determined by the contingent distribution of matter throughout nature, possess. Not even Kant would have referred these contingently distributed field strengths to the necessary constitution of the scientist as knower. The verification of the general theory of relativity indicates that there is no more justification for finding the basis of space-time in the knower.

Furthermore, this structure remains invariant for all possible physical objects which are chosen as the reference points for the empirical measurements of the astronomer or experimental physicist. Thus space-time escapes all relativity, not merely to frames of reference, but also to all the millions upon millions of human observers upon a single frame of reference such as the earth.

This means that, notwithstanding Albert Einstein's use of the word "fictitious" to designate the non-empirically given, theoretic component in scientific knowledge, this component is nonetheless not a Kantian or neo-Kantian or semantic logical positivist's subjective construct. The space-time of Einsteinian physics is the relatedness of the gravitational field of nature. It is fictitious in the sense that it is not a positivistically immediate, purely denotatively, inductively given datum; it is fictitious in the sense that it is discovered only by a free play of the scientist's imagination and not by the inductive method of extensive abstraction from empirical immediacy; it is fictitious also in the sense that it is only known positively by a leap of the imagination, a leap even of the formal, purely intellectual imagination; but it is *not* fictitious in the sense that the sole source of its being is in the knower or subject of knowledge. Instead, it constitutes and is literally the physical relatedness of the physical object of knowledge. It belongs to nature. It has its roots in nature; it is not restricted solely to the mind of man.

The foregoing consideration reminds us of the extent to which the Kantian epistemology is still working surreptitiously in the minds of even the contemporary logical positivists who suppose that they have repudiated Kant. The logical positivists thesis that anything not given with Humean, inductive, purely empirical immediacy is a mere subjective logical construct is a hangover from the epistemology of Kant, a hangover, moreover, which the contemporary mathematical physics of Einstein has unequivocally repudiated.

This is why Albert Einstein is able to make another somewhat startling affirmation. It has been noted that he emphasizes the tentative character of the hypotheses embodied in the deductively formulated, indirectly verified theory of mathematical physics. So great, in fact, is the difference between nature as theoretically designated in its systematic relatedness by deductively formulated theory and nature as given with positivistic, empirical immediacy that Einstein affirms that neither the formal, logical relation of implication nor any probability or other formulation of induction can define the method by which the scientist goes from the empirical data to the basic postulates of scientific theory. The scientist has, by trial and error and the free play of his imagination, to hit upon the basic notions. Moreover, it has been noted that these basic notions receive their verification only through a long chain of deductive proofs of theorems which are correlated with the inductive data.

With time and new empirical information the traditional basic postulates have to be rejected and replaced by new ones. Thus no theory in mathematical physics can be established as true for all time. Nor can the probability of the truth of any given theory be scientifically formulated. For there is neither an empirical frequency nor a theoretical *a priori* definition of all the possibles with respect to which any particular theory can function as a certain ratio in which the number of all the possibles is the denominator term. This was implicit in Albert Einstein's statement that there is no formulated method taking the scientist from the empirical data to the postulates of his deductively formulated theory.

Nonetheless, Einstein writes as follows: "If, then, it is true that this axiomatic basis of theoretical physics cannot be extracted from experience but must be freely invented, can we ever hope to find the right way? Nay more, has this right way any existence outside our illusions?" There could hardly be a more unequivocal formulation of the query concerning whether the systematic spatio-temporal relatedness of nature, as specified in the postulates of the theory of mathematical physics, is a mere subjective construct.

Einstein's answer is unequivocal; he answers

> without hesitation that there is, in my opinion, a right way, and that we are capable of finding it. Our experience hitherto justifies us in believing that nature is the realisation of the simplest conceivable mathematical ideas. I am convinced that we can discover by means of purely mathematical constructions the concepts and the laws connecting them with each other, which furnish the key to the understanding of natural phenomena. Experience may suggest the appropriate mathematical concepts, but they most certainly cannot be deduced from it. Experience remains, of course, the sole criterion of the physical utility of a mathematical construction. But the creative principle resides in mathematics. In a certain sense, therefore, I hold it true that pure thought can grasp reality, as the ancients dreamed.

Nor is this mere faith or conjecture on Albert Einstein's part. For we have noted previously that it is an essential point in his general theory of relativity that the form of space-time is not something having its basis in a necessary form of the intellect of the scientist as knower; instead, it is the relatedness of the gravitational potentials of the gravitational field. Thus it belongs to the object of scientific knowledge, as designated by the postulates of Einstein's general theory of relativity. When these postulates become verified through their deductive consequences, then nature as thus conceived—a gravitational field, with such and such potential distribution and such and such a space-time metric—is thereby confirmed as existing.

Albert Einstein supports this conclusion. For in the paragraph immediately succeeding the sentence last quoted he writes,

> In order to justify this confidence ["that pure

thought can grasp reality, as the ancients dreamed"], I am compelled to make use of a mathematical conception. The physical world is represented as a four-dimensional continuum. If I assume a Riemannian metric in it and ask what are the simplest laws which such a metric system can satisfy, I arrive at the relativist theory of gravitation in empty space. If in that space I assume a vector-field or an anti-symmetrical tensor-field which can be inferred from it, and ask what are the simplest laws which such a field can satisfy, I arrive at Clerk Maxwell's equations for empty space.

These considerations indicate that if we are going to make scientific theory and scientific method our criterion of the epistemology of science, then the form of space-time belongs to physical nature, not to the knower. Thus Albert Einstein's contention that "pure thought can grasp reality, as the ancients dreamed" is justified.

Moreover, the scientific method by means of which this grasp is possible is evident. It is the method of postulation, with indirect verification by way of deduced consequences. There is nothing whatever in scientific method or in the relation of the scientist as knower to the subject matter he is trying to know which prevents the scientist from formulating postulationally the properties and systematic relatedness of the thing in itself, which is the subject matter. In fact, one of the outstanding accomplishments of the general theory of relativity is its scientific demonstration that, notwithstanding all the relativity of reference frames and standpoints, inevitable in making specific measurements, science nonetheless arrives at a systematic conception of this subject matter which remains constant through all the relative standpoints.

Considerations such as these make it evident that science is much more than a weapon for utilitarian technology and prediction. It is also an instrument by means of which men are able to obtain systematic, deductively formulated, empirically verified conceptions of reality. Upon this point also Albert Einstein is explicit. He writes:

> It is, of course, universally agreed that science has to establish connections between the facts of experience, of such a kind that we can predict further occurrences from those already experienced. Indeed, according to the opinion of many positivists the completest possible accomplishment of this task is the only end of science. I do not believe, however, that so elementary an ideal could do much to kindle the investigator's passion from which really great achievements have arisen. Behind the tireless efforts of the investigator there lurks a stronger, more mysterious drive: it is existence and reality that one wishes to comprehend. . . . When we strip [this] statement of its mystical elements we mean that we are seeking for the simplest possible system of thought which will bind together the observed facts. . . . The special aim which I have constantly kept before me is logical unification in the field of physics.

In this connection it must be kept in mind, as has been previously noted, that this theoretically designated, logical unification is not a mere abstraction from purely empirical, positivistic immediacy, nor can it be logically deduced from this empirical immediacy. The postulated, deductively formulated, theoretically known component in scientific knowledge contributes something of its own. As Albert Einstein writes in his paper on **"Clerk Maxwell's Influence on the Evolution of the Idea of Physical Reality,"** "the axiomatic sub-structure of physics" gives "our conception of the structure of reality. . . ."

It may seem that Albert Einstein's conception of scientific procedure as "tentative deduction," which, because of the fallacy of affirming the consequent involved in its indirect method of verification, prevents the achievement of scientific theories which are timelessly true, enforces the conception of such theory as a mere subjective construct and invalidates his conclusion that such theory designates the character and "the structure of reality." He is fully aware of the indirect method of verification, as a subsequent quotation from him will demonstrate. He knows that the scientifically verified conceptions of this structure change with the discovery of new empirical evidence and the investigations into the theoretical problems of physics by the theoretical physicists. But this means merely that our verified scientific theories give us more and more adequate conceptions of what the character and structure of reality are. It by no means follows from the tentative character of scientific theories that they are mere subjective constructs.

Furthermore, Albert Einstein points out that it is easy to exaggerate this tentativeness. Thus, in a paper entitled **"Principles of Research"** delivered before the Physical Society in Berlin, he writes:

> The supreme task of the physicist is to arrive at those universal elementary laws from which the cosmos can be built up by pure deduction. There is no logical path to these laws; only intuition, resting on sympathetic understanding of experience, can reach them. In this methodological uncertainty, one might suppose that there were any number of possible systems of theoretical physics all with an equal amount to be said for them; and this opinion is no doubt correct, theoretically. But evolution has shown that at any given moment, out of all conceivable constructions, a single one has always proved itself absolutely superior to all the rest. Nobody who has really gone deeply into the matter will deny that in practice the world of phenomena uniquely determines the theoretical system, in spite of the fact that there is no logical bridge between phenomena and their theoretical principles; . . . Physicists often accuse epistemologists of not paying sufficient attention to this fact.

The point here is that while Poincaré is undoubtedly right theoretically in his contention that no one knows all the possible theories of reality, and hence the uniqueness of any present theory can never be established, nevertheless, for all the possible theories which scientists are able to formulate in the light of mathematical and logical investigations into the possibles, it is actually the case that mathematical physicists, using the deductive method with its indirect mode of empirical verification, are able to show

that, among the present possible theories, one is unique in its capacity to bring the widest possible range of empirical data under a single minimum set of assumptions. Moreover, it is not any subjective constructive power of the scientist which is the criterion of this uniqueness, but the correlation of the theory with the empirical data of nature. In short, the criterion of uniqueness is grounded in nature rather than in the subjective, constructive capacity of the knower of nature.

The manner in which the postulationally or axiomatically designated structure of nature is connected with the "wild buzzing confusion" of empirically given data, so that nature is found in itself to be a systematic unity, must now concern us. This connection becomes evident when one examines the method of mathematical physics as a whole. No one has stated the epistemological situation within which this method operates and to which it conforms more concisely than has Albert Einstein. In the first paragraph of his previously mentioned paper **"On Clerk Maxwell's Influence"** he writes:

> The belief in an external world independent of the perceiving subject is the basis of all natural science. Since, however, sense perception only gives information of this external world or of 'physical reality' indirectly, we can only grasp the latter by speculative means. It follows from this that our notions of physical reality can never be final. We must always be ready to change these notions—that is to say, the axiomatic substructure of physics—in order to do justice to perceived facts in the most logically perfect way. Actually a glance at the development of physics shows that it has undergone far-reaching changes in the course of time.

It will be worth our while to take up the sentences in the foregoing quotation one by one, bringing out the full content of their significance. The first sentence reads: "The belief in an external world independent of the perceiving subject is the basis of all natural science." The justification for this belief exhibits itself in Einstein's special theory of relativity.

Albert Einstein has emphasized that the key idea in this theory is the thesis that the simultaneity of spatially separated events is not given empirically. It is the case, however, as Alfred North Whitehead has emphasized, that we do immediately apprehend the simultaneity of spatially separated events. An explosion can be sensed beside one at the same time that one sees a distant flash in the sky. Clearly, these two events are separated spatially and they are sensed as occurring simultaneously. Why, then, does Einstein insist that the simultaneity of spatially separated events is not directly observed? The answer to this is that physicists want and require a simultaneity which is the same for all human beings at rest relative to each other on the same frame of reference.

Immediately sensed simultaneity does not have this characteristic. If the observer is equidistant from two events he may sense them as simultaneous. Then any observer not equidistant from the two events will not sense them as simultaneous.

It is the required public simultaneity which is one of the elements going into the notion of the external world. In fact, the concept of the external world is the scientist's terminology for the distinction between publicly valid elements in scientific knowledge and purely private factors varying from one observer to another even on the same frame of reference. Thus Einstein's contention that belief in an external world is at the basis of science is not a dogmatic selection of one epistemological theory of physical science from many possible theories, but is something grounded in distinctions required by scientific evidence itself.

In this connection it may be noted also that Alfred North Whitehead's philosophy of physics, which affirms an immediately sensed meaning for the simultaneity of spatially separated events, is far nearer to positivism than is Albert Einstein's theory. Furthermore, Alfred North Whitehead's theory that all scientific concepts are derived from "the terminus of sense awareness" by abstraction is much nearer to positivism than is the physics of Einstein, in which the theoretical concepts cannot be abstracted from or deduced from the empirical data.

Consider now Einstein's second sentence in the foregoing quotation: "Since, however, sense perception only gives information of this external world or of 'physical reality' indirectly, we can only grasp the latter by speculative means." The basis for this statement scientifically is in the method of hypothesis which deductively formulated scientific theory uses. But Albert Einstein realizes also that it follows epistemologically from Bishop Berkeley's analysis of the empirically given. Bishop Berkeley noted that all that is empirically given are sense qualities, that these are relative, private things, varying from person to person and hence relative to the mind that is apprehending them. Thus the physicist's concept of a physical object as something three-dimensional, possessing a back side which we do not sense, with right-angle corners constant through the varying sensed angles which we sense empirically is not guaranteed by positivistic, empirical observation. Even the notion of a common-sense object involves an imaginative leap by the method of hypothesis beyond pure fact. Not merely scientific objects such as electrons and electromagnetic fields, but also common-sense objects entail indirectly verified postulation.

Once this is noted, the shift of the logical positivists from the Berkeleyan sensationalism of Carnap's *Logischer Aufbau* to "physicalism" is seen to be a departure from positivism. The reason for this shift confirms the present analysis. The logical positivists wanted a scientific verification which gave objective, publicly valid meanings, not Berkeleyan solipsistic, private subjective meanings merely. But such objectivity is not given empirically; it is only given theoretically by postulation indirectly verified. This is what Einstein means when he says that "since sense perception only gives information of the external world or of 'physical reality' indirectly, we can only grasp the latter by speculative means."

His next sentence reads: "It follows from this that our notions of physical reality can never be final." The basis for this conclusion is that formal logic in scientific method runs not from the empirical data to the postulates of the deductively formulated theory but in the converse direction, from the postulates back through the theorems to the data. This means that, in scientific verification, the logic of verification is always committing the fallacy of affirming the consequent of the hypothetical syllogism. This does not entail that a theory thus verified is false. It means merely that it cannot be shown to be necessarily true. The fact that the theory is thus indirectly confirmed justifies its retention. The fact, however, that it is not related to empirical data necessarily forces one to hold it tentatively. But this is an asset rather than a liability; for otherwise we would be at a loss to explain how scientific, or even humanistic religious, theories can be empirically verified and yet shown later, with the advent of further empirical information and further theoretical investigation, to be inadequate and to require replacement by a different theory grounded in different postulates. Hence Albert Einstein's final two statements: "We must always be ready to change these notions—that is to say, the axiomatic sub-structure of physics—in order to do justice to perceived facts in the most logically perfect way. Actually a glance at the development of physics shows that it has undergone far-reaching changes in the course of time."

One additional element, often overlooked in scientific method, which Albert Einstein clearly recognizes, remains to be indicated in order to complete his conception of science. It has been noted that the basic concepts of deductively formulated scientific theory as conceived by him are neither abstracted from nor deduced from empirically given data. Consequently, they do not "reduce" to sentences about sense data, nor can they be derived from such sentences. In short, they are concepts of a kind fundamentally different from the nominalistic particulars which denote data given empirically.

This presents a problem so far as scientific verification is concerned. For, if the primitive concepts, in terms of which the deductively formulated scientific theory is constructed, gain their meanings by postulation, in terms of the formal properties of relations and other such logical constants, then the theorems deduced from the postulates of such theory must be concepts of the same character. An examination of scientific theory such as Maxwell's electromagnetic theory shows also that the concepts in the theorems refer no more to sense data than do the concepts in the postulates. They refer, instead, to numbers for wave lengths, etc. These are not sensuously qualitative things. But if this is the case, how, then, can concepts with such meanings, designating such empirically unobservable scientific structures and entities, be verified? For verification requires the relating of the theoretically designated to the positivistically and empirically immediate. This relation which must exist in scientific method remains, therefore, to be specified.

The foregoing considerations of this paper indicate that this relation, joining the theoretically designated factor in nature to the empirically given component, cannot be that of identity. What then, is the relation? In his paper **"Considerations Concerning the Fundaments of Theoretical Physics"** (*Science,* May 24, 1940), Albert Einstein answers this question as follows: "Science is the attempt to make the chaotic diversity of our sense experience correspond to a logically uniform system of thought. In this system single experiences must be correlated with the theoretic structure in such a way that the resulting coordination is unique and convincing." In other words, the relation between the theoretic component and the empirical component in scientific knowledge is the relation of correlation. Analysis of scientific method shows that this relation is a two-termed relation.

The recognition of the presence of this relation in scientific method is the key to the understanding of Albert Einstein's conception of scientific method and scientific epistemology. Because the empirical component is joined to the theoretic component by correlation, one cannot get the latter from the former by either extensive abstraction or logical implication. For, in the two-termed relation of epistemic correlation, one term does not logically imply the other, nor is the theoretic term a mere abstraction from the empirical term. And because the theoretic term cannot be derived from the empirical term, theoretic physics contributes something of its own to the scientific conception of nature and reality.

This means that the positivistic theory that all theoretical meanings derive from empirical meanings is invalid. Furthermore, the thesis that the theoretically designated knowledge gives us knowledge of the subject matter of science and of reality, rather than merely knowledge of a subjective construct projected by a neo-Kantian kind of knower, confirms the thesis that the thing in itself can be scientifically known and handled by scientific method. Thus ontology is again restored, as well as epistemology, to a genuine scientific and philosophical status.

Hence, although the positivists are wrong in their purely empirical theory of meaning in empirical science, they are right in their contention that philosophically valid propositions are scientifically verifiable propositions. The important thing is not where the meanings of scientific concepts come from, but that they be verified through their deductive consequences and attendant epistemic correlations with empirically given data, before anyone claims that they have philosophical validity as a correct designation of the nature of things.

The foregoing analysis of Einstein's conceptions of science shows that scientific concepts have two sources for their meanings: The one source is empirical. It gives concepts which are particulars, nominalistic in character. The other source is formal, mathematical and theoretical. It gives concepts which are universals, since they derive their meaning by postulation from postulates which are universal propositions.

It should be noted also that for Albert Einstein scientific method entails the validity of the principle of causality, not as conceived by Hume in terms of the hope that present sensed associations of sense data will repeat themselves, but in the sense of the mathematical physicist—the sense, namely, that with the empirical determination of the present state of a system, as defined by theoretical physics, the future state is logically implied. Albert Ein-

stein tells us that he refused to accept certain ideas of his general theory of relativity for over a period of two years, because he thought they were incompatible with this theory of causality. When this compatibility did become evident to him, he went on with the investigation and publication of the general theory of relativity. Its type of causality is a theoretically given, indirectly verified causality, not a Humean empirical one. But this point is a special, more technical case of the general thesis that scientific knowledge involves a correlation of an empirically given component with a postulationally prescribed, systematic, theoretically designated component.

Gaston Bachelard (essay date 1949)

SOURCE: "The Philosophic Dialectic of the Concepts of Relativity," in *Albert Einstein: Philosopher-Scientist*, revised edition, edited by Paul Arthur Schlipp, The Library of Living Philosophers, 1970, pp. 565-80.

[*Bachelard was an influential French philosopher and critic. Many of his writings focus on poetic imagery and its relation to the creative process, and their approach is characterized by an emphasis on psychoanalytic theory. Unlike Sigmund Freud, who regarded dreams as manifestations of an individual's motivations, Bachelard, like Carl Jung, considered dreaming to be a revelation of the collective unconscious. Bachelard thus looked to dreaming, or reverie, for certain primitive archetypes—especially the traditional elements of earth, air, fire, and water—and studied representations of each in poetic imagery. In the following essay, Bachelard discusses the ways in which Einstein's relativity created "upheavals" among many of the fundamental principles of science and philosophy.*]

I

Philosophers have removed the great cosmic drama of Copernican thought from the dominion of reality to the dominion of metaphor. Kant described his Critical philosophy as a Copernican revolution in metaphysics. Following the Kantian thesis, the two fundamental philosophies, rationalism and empiricism, changed places, and the world revolved about the mind. As a result of this radical modification, the knowing mind and the known world acquired the appearance of being relative to each other. But this kind of relativity remained merely symbolic. Nothing had changed in the detail or the principles of coherence of knowledge. Empiricism and rationalism remained face-to-face and incapable of achieving either true philosophical co-operation or mutual enrichment.

The philosophic virtues of the Einsteinian revolution could be quite differently effective, as compared to the philosophic metaphors of the Copernican revolution, if only the philosopher were willing to seek all the instruction contained in relativity science. A systematic revolution of basic concepts begins with Einsteinian science. In the very detail of its concepts a relativism of the rational and the empirical is established. Science then undergoes what Nietzsche called "an upheaval of concepts," as if the earth, the universe, things, possessed a different structure from the fact that their explanation rests upon new foundations. All rational organization is "shaken" when the fundamental concepts undergo dialectical transformation.

Moreover, this dialectic is not argued by an automatic logic, as is the dialectic of the philosopher too often. In relativity, the terms of the dialectic are rendered solid and cohesive to the point of presenting a philosophical synthesis of mathematical rationalism and "technological" empiricism. This, at least, is what we would like to show in the present article. First, we will present our view in respect to the "shaking" of some isolated concepts; then, we shall endeavor to show the value of the philosophical synthesis which is suggested by Einsteinian science.

II

As we know, as has been repeated a thousand times, relativity was born of an epistemological shock; it was born of the "failure" of the Michelson experiment. That experiment should contradict theoretical prediction is in itself not a singular occurrence. But it is necessary to realize how and why a negative result was, this time, the occasion for an immense positive construction. Those who live in the realm of scientific thinking doubtless do not need these remarks. They are nonetheless polemically indispensable for assessing the philosophical utility of relativity.

For this notion of the negative quality of experiment must not be allowed to subsist. In a well-performed experiment, everything is positive. And Albert Einstein understood this fact when he pondered over the Michelson experiment. This pseudo-negative experiment did not open upon the mystery of things, the unfathomable mystery of things. Its "failure" was not even a proof of the ineptitude of rationalism. The Michelson experiment proceeded from an *intelligent* question, a question which had to be asked. Contemporary science would be hanging "in mid-air," if the Michelson experiment had not been conceived, then actualized, then meticulously actualized in the full consciousness of the sensibility of the technique; then varied, then repeated on the floors of valleys and the peaks of mountains, and always verified. What capacity for self-doubt, for meticulous and profound doubt, for *intelligent* doubt, was contained in this will to test and measure again and again! Are we sure that Michelson died with the conviction that the experiment had been well performed, perfectly performed, with the conviction that the *negative* bases of the experiment had been reached? Thus, instead of an universal doubt, an intuitive doubt, a Cartesian doubt, technological science yields a precise doubt, a discursive doubt, an implemented doubt. It was as a consequence of this explicit doubt that the mechanistic dogmatism was shattered by relativity. To paraphrase Kant, we might say that the Michelson experiment roused classical mechanics from its dogmatic slumber.

For the negative aspect of the Michelson experiment did not deter Einstein. For him, the experimental failure of a technique thus scientifically pursued suggested the need for new theoretical information. It became indispensable to hope for a minute "Copernican revolution" in which all philosophy of reality and of reason must begin a new dialectic. In order that this dialectic may possess its full instructive value for the philosopher, it is necessary to be-

ware of sweeping philosophical designations. It is not highly instructive to say, with Meyerson, that Einstein is a *realist*. Without a doubt, Einstein submits to experience, submits to "reality." But must we not inquire: to what experience, to what reality? That of the infinitesimal decimal upon which the Michelson experiment turned, or that solid reality of the whole number, of solid, ordinary, common, gross verification? It would seem that the philosopher who acknowledges the lessons of relativity must at the very least, envisage a *new reality*. And this *new reality* enjoins him to *consider* reality *differently*.

Where, then, must the philosophy of science find its initial convictions? Must it give precedence to the lessons to be found in the beginning of experience, or in the end of experience? By building upon the first structures or upon the final structures? We shall see that the latter is correct, that it is *l'esprit de finesse* which reveals the foundations of *l'esprit geometrique*.

III

Which, then, are the concepts that are "shaken"? Which concepts undergo at the rational level, in the superb light of rational philosophy, a Nietzschean transmutation of rational values?

They are the concepts of:

> absolute space,
>
> absolute time,
>
> absolute velocity.

Is so little required to "shake" the universe of spatiality? Can a single experiment of the twentieth century annihilate—a Sartrian would say *"néantiser"*—two or three centuries of rational thought? Yes, a single decimal sufficed, as our poet Henri de Regnier would say, to "make all nature sing."

Upon what, in fact, did the notion of absolute space rest? Did it rest upon an absolute reality or upon an absolute intuition of the Kantian variety? Is it not philosophically strange that absoluteness could be attributed as well to a *reality* as to an *a priori intuition?* This double success of a raw realism and an over-simple intuitionism seems spurious. This twofold success makes a double failure. Therefore, it is necessary to investigate this double possibility of philosophical interpretation from the standpoint of the precision of modern scientific experiment. Uncriticized experience is no longer admissible. The *double philosophy* of the experience of space—realistic philosophy and Kantian philosophy—must be replaced by a *dialectical philosophy* of space, by a philosophy which is at once experimental and rational. In short, the philosophy of ultra-refined experience and the philosophy of physical theory are firmly *coupled* in relativity. The new philosophy of science will prove to be a critical philosophy more subtle and more synthetic than was Kantian philosophy in respect to Newtonian science. Relativistic criticism does not limit itself to a revolution of means of explanation. It is more profoundly revolutionary. It is more *génial*.

Thus, we come face-to-face with the fundamental assertion of Einstein: the *position* of an absolute space as the affirmation of a kind of materialization of immobility and as the residence of an unconditioned subject in the center of all the conditioned relations, is a *position* without proof. Therefore, one must—Copernican revolution at the level of an unique concept—formulate the essential relativity of the intuition of localization and the experience of localization, which simultaneously destroys two absolutes: first, the intuition of an observer has no absolute character; and secondly, the extension of an objective world has no absolute character. The essentially discursive method of reference will, therefore, always have to be explicitly considered in relation to the real phenomena studied in the extremity of scientific precision. Extreme experimental dexterity will underlie any knowledge of space. The Michelson experiment, at first sight so particular in character, will form the basis of the most far-reaching generalization.

It is, moreover, quite striking that the Michelson laboratory was, properly speaking, *cosmic*. There, the most artificial physics imaginable was referred to the space of the world. The decimal which they wished to reveal by means of the interferometer, the decimal which is of the order of three-fourths of the wavelength of a vibration of light, was related to the orbital speed of the earth, a speed of the order of eighteen miles per second. The precision of such a question posed by this technique in respect to the space of the world, this attempt to experience the immobility of space in its cosmic significance, ought to set the metaphysicians thinking who study the place of man in the world; if only these metaphysicians would give their attention to the lengthy discursive processes which lead science to build new intuitions.

IV

The new intuitions of time likewise demand lengthy preparation. They must struggle against the blinding clarity of common intuitions, and against the equally over-hasty formulation of Kantian criticism.

Here, the concept which experiences the "Nietzschean upheaval" is that of *simultaneity*. In regard to this concept, so evident, so familiar, the Einsteinian claim is pregnant. This claim collides with common sense; it is contrary to common experience; it puts in question again the very basis of classical mechanics. It demands therefore, a decisive intellectual mutation which must reverberate among the most fundamental philosophical values. More precisely, if the notion of simultaneity, which was not *criticized* by Kant, must receive a *neo-critical* examination, empiricism and rationalism must, at the same time, be *rectified* and related to each other in a new way.

To formulate a doubt concerning the notion of simultaneity is, in our opinion, to transcend the hyperbolic doubt of Cartesian philosophy. A doubt attaching to so simple, so positive, so direct a notion no longer bears the marks of a formal doubt, an universal doubt. As long as one remains within the horizons of Cartesian doubt, one is in the contingency of doubt. The Einsteinian revolution demands a necessary doubt regarding a notion which has always passed for fundamental. Concomitantly, the putting in doubt of a rational and realistic notion cannot remain provisional. Such a doubt will always carry with it a deci-

sive pedagogical effect. It will remain an imprescriptible cultural fact. Whoever, for the rest of time, would teach relativity would have to put in doubt the absolute character of the notion of simultaneity. This necessity constitutes, in some sense, an *electro-shock* for rationalistic philosophies and hardened realistic philosophies.

Granting a renunciation of the right to posit an absolute space, what is the Einsteinian claim in regard to the simultaneity of events which occur at two different points in space? Einstein demands that one define a *positive* experiment, a *precise* experiment expressible in well-defined scientific terms. There is no longer any question of retreating into the intuition of internal sensibility, whether this intuition be Kantian or Bergsonian, formalistic or realistic. One must be able to describe and institute objective experiments which enable one to *verify* this simultaneity. Immediately, a metaphysical nuance appears which the philosopher too often neglects. Here we have a *verified* reality in place of a given reality. Hereafter, if an idealist must make an initial declaration, he will be forced to do so from a point one step closer to a rationalism which is linked with reality. He cannot be satisfied with repeating after Schopenhauer: "The world is my representation"; he must say, if he is to assume the full extent of scientific thought: "The world is my verification."

More precisely, the objective world is the aggregate of facts verified by modern science, the world rendered by the conceptions verified by the science of our time. Further, *experimental verification* implies the *coherence* of the experimental method. Since a science is founded upon the Michelson experiment, this Michelson experiment must be comprehended in the very definition of simultaneity. To be sure, we are concerned with the Michelson experiment as it is, not as it was for a long time thought to be. The Michelson experiment, as it is, then, must assign reality at the outset to the convention of signaling.

Without a doubt, any number of conventions of signalling could have been adopted. One could create a meta-acoustics based upon a simultaneity verified by the transmission of sounds. But physics would gain nothing from such specialization. Hereafter, physics is cosmic. The most rapid and reliable signals which are both human and universal are light signals. The Michelson experiment discloses a privileged character which accrues to these signals. They require no support; they are not conditioned by a medium, by a transmitting ether. They are independent of the *relative* movements of the observers who utilize them. They are truly the most "reasonable" (*"rationalisables"*) of all signals. Thus, one would define the simultaneity of two events which occur in two different places in terms of an exchange of light signals and of the result, henceforth regarded as positive, of the Michelson experiment which justifies the following postulate: the velocity of light is the same in all directions irrespective of the observers who measure it, regardless of the relative motion of these observers.

This *operational* definition of simultaneity dissolves the notion of *absolute* time. Since simultaneity is linked to physical experiments which occur in space, the temporal contexture (*contexture*) is one with spatial contexture.

Since there is no absolute space, there is no absolute time. And it is due to the solidarity of space-experiments and simultaneity-experiments that a reconstitution of space and time must accompany any thorough examination of space and time. Therefore, from the standpoint of philosophy, it is evident that scientific thought requires a rebuilding of the notions of space and time in terms of their solidarity. As a consequence of this necessity to provide a new basis for space and time, relativity will emerge philosophically as a *rationalism of second order* (*rationalisme de deuxième position*), as an enlightened rationalism which necessitates a new departure.

But before building, one must destroy. One must convince oneself that any analysis which from the outset separates spatial characters and temporal characters is a crude analysis. Doubtless, such an analysis is valid for common knowledge, and no less valid for an enormous quantity of scientific thought. But for its denunciation one need only note that it masks certain well-defined problems. Looking to the new synthetic notion of space-time, henceforth indispensable for a grasp of electromagnetic phenomena, one can perceive the philosophical weakness of any attempt at vulgarization. It is not a matter of basing a synthesis upon an analysis. One must conceive the *a priori synthesis* which underlies the notion of space-time. All the tales of passing trains which signal an observer standing in a station, of aviators who smoke cigars in lengthened or contracted periods of time—to what purpose are they?—or, more precisely, for whom are they designed? Surely not for those who have not understood the *mathematical organization* of relativity. And those who have understood the *mathematical organization* of relativity require no *examples*. They install themselves in the clear and certain *algebraism* of the doctrine. It is on the basis of the synthesis of algebraism and scientific experiment that one may correctly designate the rationalistic revival implied in the doctrines of Einstein. Let us demonstrate this neo-Kantian aspect. It did not escape Léon Brunschvicg, who wrote: "The advancement on Kant (effected by these new doctrines) consisted in transporting the *a priori* synthesis from the region of intuition to the region of intellect, and this is decisive for the passage to physics."

And, in fact, any Kantian philosophy holds that space is not a concept drawn from experience of the external world, since the intuition of space is a *sine qua non* condition of experience of the external world. A similarly inverted formulation is enunciated in respect to time, which is given as the *a priori* form of internal sensibility. The *sine qua non* is the pivot of the Copernican revolution of intuitions of space and time.

And, in the same manner, in the same philosophical fashion, if one would determine the epistemological function of the space-time notion in relativistic science, one must say that the *space-time algebraic complex* is a *sine qua non* condition of the general validity of our knowledge of electromagnetism. Knowledge of electromagnetic phenomena during the nineteenth century was co-ordinated by the laws of Maxwell. Reflection upon these laws led to the conviction that they must remain *invariant* for any change of reference system. This invariance defined the transformation [formulas] of Lorentz. It established a Lorentz group which possesses the same philosophical significance for relativity geometry which the group of displacements and similitudes possesses for Euclidean geometry. Thus, it is the Lorentz transformation which underlies the notion of space-time, and the Lorentz group which forbids the separation of spatial co-ordinates and temporal coordinates. The notion of space-time takes shape in a perspective of *necessity*. To see in it a mere linguistic structure, a mere condensation of means of expression, would be to underestimate its philosophical significance. It is a conception, a necessary conception. If the rôle of the philosopher is, as we believe, to think thought, then he must think space-time in the totality of its functions, in its algebraic nature, and in its informing value for scientific phenomena.

If one adds now, that due to the operational definition of simultaneity the velocity of light enters into geometrical-mechanical references, and if one recalls that light is an electromagnetic phenomenon, one reaches the conclusion that the notion of space-time is hereafter a basic notion for an ultra-precise understanding of phenomena.

Thus, the concept of space-time, as suggested by Lorentz, as achieved by Einstein, appears as an *a priori* form, functionally *a priori,* permitting the comprehension of precise electromagnetic phenomena. It is of little importance, philosophically, that this form occurs tardily in the history of science. It is installed as functionally *primary* by the *enlightened rationalism* which constitutes one of the most clear-cut aspects of the theory of relativity. Once having aligned oneself with this enlightened rationalism, one sees that there is a *naïve rationalism* in the same sense that there is a *naïve realism*. And if one would reap all the philosophical benefits of scientific culture, one must realize psychologically the soundness of the *new foundations;* one must abandon the old points of departure, and *begin again*. At the close of the eighteenth century, in his history of astronomy, Bailly maintained that calculated astronomy procured a *peace of mind* in contrast to any theory of imaginative astronomy. Newtonian thinkers, he said, "chose to adopt the notion of attraction to fasten their imagination, to rest their thoughts."

The function of Einsteinian rationalism is likewise salutary. The algebraic notion of space-time rids us of vulgarizing images. It frees us from a falsely profound reverie upon space and time. In particular, it precludes the irrationalism associated with an unfathomable duration. The mind *rests* in the truth of its constructions.

Once the *algebraic* nature of the Einsteinian formulation is realized, one is prepared for a philosophic inversion of the abstract and concrete characters of scientific culture; or, to speak more precisely, one accedes to the *abstract-concrete* character of scientific thought. One may well say that the concept of *space-time* is more concrete, despite its intellectual character, than the two separate notions of space and time, since it consolidates two perspectives of experience. Naturally, the notion of space-time will, whenever necessary, be divided and analyzed so as to reinstate those separate functions of time and space, in view of the *simplifications* which are useful in classical mechanics. But relativity will be on guard against all *simplifications*. It *rests* upon the summit of its synthesis. From this vantage point, it judges confidently all analytical perspectives.

How shall philosophers be led to this summit? But philosophers no longer care, it seems, for synthetic thoughts. They do not wish to found knowledge upon its highest achievement. They claim to cut Gordian knots at a time when science is striving to *knit together* the most unforeseen relations, at a time when physico-mathematical science resolutely declares itself abstract-concrete.

Rather than to return ceaselessly to the base of common knowledge, as if what suffices for life could suffice for knowledge, we have the means, by pursuing Einsteinian science, to develop a terminal rationalism, a differentiating rationalism, a dialectical rationalism. This differentiation, this dialectic appears in knowledge at a second stage of approximation. In short, there occurs an inversion in [the order of] epistemological importance. The first approximation is only the opening move. Common knowledge regards it as basic, though it is only provisional. The structure of scientific understanding emerges only from refinement, through an analysis as thorough as possible of every functionality.

One may, in application, limit these functionalities, cognizant that a potentiality remains unrealized, that a sensibility is smothered. One would recognize that in quantum mechanics in numerous cases there occurs *degeneration* (*"dégénérescence"*), that is to say, extinction of a structural possibility. But the new theories yield the whole hierarchy of rationalistic and empiricist values. Classical science and common knowledge have their [respective] places in the system of epistemological values. The dialectic of relativistic mechanics and classical mechanics is an enveloping dialectic. It seems that relativity risked everything which lent certainty to the classical conception of reality, but, having risked all, lost nothing. It has retained all that was scientifically known during the last century. A shift of the finer structures reveals the ancient bonds. Thus, relativity permits a retrospective re-enactment of the entire history of mechanistic rationalism.

v

This possibility of recurring to simplified philosophies will be better understood if we can now show the notably firm nature of the coupling of rationalism and realism effected by relativity. To this end, it will suffice to consider the algebraic form, *space-time,* in its ordering functions in mechanics and electromagnetism.

Space-time is not merely a simple epistemological necessity evoked by reflection upon the conditions of invariance stipulated by the Maxwell equations. This initial synthesis propagates its ordering power. The notion of space-time conditions quadrivectors which accentuate the synthetic character of the relativistic [mode of] organization.

For example, by extending the classical conception of mechanical impulsion, which is a vector of three-dimensional space, relativity attains the conception of the impulsion of the universe as a quadrivector of four-dimensional space.

This impulsion has the three components of classical momentum as its spatial component, and energy divided by the velocity of light as its temporal component. But the quadrivector of the impulsion does not consist of a simple juxtaposition of the momentum- and energy-aspects. So powerful a conceptual fusion is achieved that the principle of the conservation of momentum and the principle of the conservation of energy are summated. In an isolated material system, the geometric sum of the quadrivectors of the impulsion remains constant when applied to different bodies in the system. Recalling that Descartes formulated his mechanics in terms of the notion of momentum whereas Leibniz advanced the notion of mechanical energy, one would perceive, from the summit of this synthesis, the historical recurrence as a profound synthesis of Descartes and Leibniz achieved by Einstein.

This same inspiration led to Einstein's discovery of the algebraic homogeneity of energy and mass. This discovery of mathematical, *rationalistic* origin had considerable *realistic* import. The mass-energy amalgam, first established for kinetic energy, clearly extends to all forms of energy. Doubtless the philosopher who thinks in words, who believes that scientific concepts have an absolute root in common notions, is shocked by the phrase "*inertia of energy.*" And yet it is this concept of the inertia of energy which marks Einsteinian science as a new science, as a conceptually synthetic science.

In effect, the realistic aspect of this mass-energy amalgam consists in none other than the union of the so different classical principles of the conservation of mass and the conservation of energy. Considered in their historical evolution, the concepts of mass and energy appear bereft of an *absolute.* Now it is necessary to establish between them a profound *relation,* an ontological relation.

In other words, in order to realize this relativization of so realistic a principle as that of the conservation of mass, one must accept once more the Copernican revolution of relativity, one must install mathematics at the *center* of experience, one must take mathematics as the inspiration of scientific experiment. For, after all, experiments as precise as those of chemistry cast no doubt upon the principle of Lavoisier. Chemistry was, in this respect, the recital of an immense success. Chemistry codified the *absolute* character of a materialism of balances. *Scientific* realism was, on this point, on a par in conviction with *naïve realism.* Let us firmly underscore that efficacious thought proceeds in the direction of rationalism s———→ realism. Primacy belongs, not to the principle of conservation (in realistic fashion), but to a principle of invariance (in rationalistic fashion). It is the conditions of invariance in the mathematical expression of the laws which permit a definition of the meaning and validity of the true *principles of conversation.* Insofar as it was thought possible to characterize the philosophy of relativity by the too-simple label of "realism" from the sole fact that relativity substantiates principles of conservation, this epistemological evolution must be the more definitively formulated. For our part, we are of the opinion that the manner of conserving is more important than what is conserved. To conserve mass and energy in a single formula is not really to ground one's faith in the reality conserved but, rather, to become conscious of the rationalistic power of the invariance of the laws.

Doubtless, experiment in its most refined, meticulous forms sanctioned the ingenious views of Albert Einstein; consequently, [the concept of the] inertia of energy possesses hereafter an undeniably realistic character. But these very *conceptions* were *original* and *inspired;* they were not psychologically *natural* and they led to scientific experiments which were quasi-*supernatural*. For example, the entirety of nuclear physics falls within the jurisdiction of the principle of *inertia of energy*. And the power of nuclear physics has been sufficiently emphasized, perhaps to the neglect of its ultra-phenomenal character. The scientist has already smashed more uranium nuclei in the space of five years than Nature in a millennium. The laboratory technician has succeeded in *implementing* by means of the atomic pile the Einsteinian principle of inertia of energy. The reality which slumbered in his materials was *provoked* by mathematically-founded experiments. Seen from the nuclear level, one might well say that matter evokes a neo-materialism in which substance and energy are interchangeable entities. Reality is no longer nature pure and simple. It must be wrought to become the object of scientific experiment. Thus, the philosophy of contemporary science as it issued from the revolutions of the beginning of the century appears as a dialectic of enlightened rationalism and elaborated realism. In order to lose none of the philosophical implications of science the two concepts of invariance and conservation must be synthesized in an *abstract-concrete* philosophy by introducing an additional unifying trait in the form of an *invariance-conservation*. Here is a philosophical *doublet* which would be mutilated by an unilateral philosophical interpretation, whether rationalistic or realistic. Science requires hereafter a bi-certitude. It must satisfy the requirements of mathematical coherence and minute experimental verification.

VI

We have followed rapidly a development of relativistic thought to a synthetic center of the science of mechanics. The synthesis on the side of electromagnetism was not less important. The components of the two tri-dimensional vectors by which classical physics defined separately the electric field and the magnetic field are recognized by relativity as the components of a single tensor. This fact endows the Maxwell-Lorentz equations with an extreme generality which goes hand in hand with an extreme algebraic condensation.

It is not the least paradoxical character of general relativity to find in the development of its doctrine this dialectic of rational condensation and extension of empirical significations. When enlightened rationalism takes hold of reality by such condensed symbols, one experiences, there too, a great peace of mind. Tensor calculus, Paul Langevin liked to say, knows relativity better than the relativist himself. Tensor calculus becomes, in some manner, charged for us with subaltern thought; it is our guarantee of forgetting nothing; it arranges for particular analyses. These symbols are in no way mystical. They are translucent to the mathematician and they render the physicist perspicacious. The unifying formulas of general relativity are

philosophical syntheses which reunite rationalism and realism.

VII

If we were to consider dialectically the *principle of equivalence* of inert mass and heavy mass, the principle which founded general relativity, we would be led to the same philosophical conclusions.

In effect, to reunite *inert mass* and *heavy mass* in a single concept amounts to amalgamating inertia, a quality inhering in a given body, and weight, a quality whose seat is, in some manner, external to the body in question. Thus, we have a prime example of the correlation of a force and a structure of space-time. This correlation inscribed in the Einsteinian principle of equivalence is greatly extended in the development of the doctrine.

Here, again, the philosopher may find instruction; for the principle of equivalence constitutes a denial of the [supposed] logical priority habitually assigned to force over against its manifestations. In fact, force is contemporaneous with phenomena. There is no circuit of being which assigns being to matter, then to its forces, then to the deformations of matter. As Eddington said [in *Space, Time and Gravitation*], "Matter is not a cause, it is an index." All exists together as the structure of space-time.

Relativity, therefore, seems to us to modify philosophically the principles of *"causalism"* in quite as thoroughgoing fashion as those of *realism*. *Abstract-concrete* philosophy will have to be formulated in terms of a new trait of metaphysical union and will have to think of scientific phenomena as *cause-functions*. There occurs an endosmosis of mathematical consequences and physical causes.

Thus, relativity ceaselessly calls scientific thought to a philosophical activity which is both *central* and *dialectic*. The traditional problem of the dualism of mind and body is posed in a precise central locus, with the benefit of an extreme sensibility. Here the most rigorous mathematician and the most meticulous physicist agree. They understand each other. They instruct each other. Thought would become empty, experience would become obscure, if one were not to accept, in the regions in which relativity functions, the synthesis of enlightened rationalism and elaborated realism.

Irving Kristol   (essay date 1950)

SOURCE: "Einstein: The Passion of Pure Reason," in *Commentary*, Vol. 10, No. 3, September, 1950, pp. 216-24.

[*Kristol is an American author and editor. In the following essay, he discusses Einstein's religious beliefs—particularly his sometimes conflicted ties to the Jewish faith—and the ways in which they ran in opposition to his devotion to reason.*]

In Philipp Frank's biography, *Einstein: His Life and Times,* we read the following anecdote:

"Einstein was once told that a physicist whose intellectual capacities were rather mediocre had been run over by a bus and killed. He remarked sympathetically: 'Too bad about his body!' "

Of course it is probable that Einstein was having his own quiet little joke, making a gesture to the public image of himself as an abstracted, bloodless intellect floating languidly in the stellar spaces. And indeed, according to Einstein's way of thinking, body is body and mind is mind, and it is hard to think of a logical reason why one should have anything to do with the other. The body grows old, but that is hardly worth a thought: Einstein believes birthday celebrations are for children. The body perishes and is buried—of what interest is this to a mature mind? ("Attending funerals is something one does to please the people around us. In itself it is meaningless.") Men are prone to make spectacles of themselves, watching the calendar, meditating on their imminent dissolution into dust, but "the true value of a human being is determined primarily by the measure and the sense in which he has attained liberation from the self."

A volume recently published in Einstein's honor [*Einstein: Philosopher-Scientist*, ed. by Paul Arthur Schilpp] contains an autobiographical sketch he wrote four years ago. It opens with the naked sentence: "Here I sit in order to write, at the age of 67, something like my own obituary." Then, with a few personal asides, there follow forty-five pages of physics and equations. The asides, to be sure, are illuminating. We learn that: "Even when I was a precocious quite young man I became vividly aware of the nothingness of the hopes and strivings that chase most men restlessly through life." Einstein's reaction to this discovery was a deep religiosity that ended abruptly at the age of twelve, giving way to a passion for science, which seemed more capable of freeing him from "the chains of the 'merely personal,' from an existence which is dominated by wishes, hopes, and primitive feelings." We are told all this briefly, in a few paragraphs quickly submerged in pages of technical discussion. But, on page 33, Einstein pulls himself up short, to dispel once and for all any confusion in the mind of the reader:

" 'Is this supposed to be an obituary?' the astonished reader will likely ask. I would like to reply: essentially yes. For the essential in the being of a man of my type lies precisely in what he thinks and *how* he thinks, not in what he does or suffers."

This, then, is how Einstein would like to see himself: no mournful pilgrim on earth, but the spirit of Pure Reason; not an anguished voice calling futilely from the depths, but a creative spirit hovering over the world of chaos; not a suffering creature, but a thinking creator, whose science is "the attempt at the posterior reconstruction of reality by the process of conceptualization," and whose duty it is "to arrive at those universal elementary laws from which the cosmos can be built up by pure deduction."

What is the path which the spirit must take to this "posterior reconstruction of reality"? On this point, Einstein is unequivocal: the path is through mathematics. And if one can "reconstruct" reality with the aid of mathematics, then it is clear that the original creation must have been according to formula. God is a mathematician, and mathematics is *imitatio Dei*. Of course, God is an exceptional mathematician and his creation is an exceptionally "well-designed puzzle." But not an insoluble puzzle, for God is just. *"Raffiniert is der Herrgott, aber boshaft ist er nicht"* ("God is subtle, but he is not malicious")—with such words Einstein consoles and encourages Princeton's mathematicians when they lounge in Fine Hall and read the inscription over the fireplace. God is not only not malicious, he is also divinely simple: "Our experience . . . justifies us in believing that nature is the realization of the simplest conceivable mathematical ideas."

And if one should inquisitively demand why God is, after all, a mathematician? Ah, that is the mystery, that "pure thought is competent to comprehend the real," that nature is intelligible.

Einstein is not involved in what have been, at different times, designated as the two major scandals of philosophy: the first, that philosophers have not yet been able to prove the existence of the external world; the second, that philosophers should ever have presumed to believe this to be their business. For Einstein, the real world simply is. *Simply—is.* For if its existence is not to be questioned by serious men, neither is its simplicity. This simplicity may not be apparent to those who are prisoners of their senses and have not been able to make the leap from the kingdom of the bodily self to the kingdom of selfless mind, which is the realm of mathematics and necessity. The world of the body's sense perception is real—but the realer world, the world of order behind the confusion of perceived existence, is the one which is also rational, that is, mathematical. When Einstein refers to the world that is both real and rational he uses the phrase "Physical Reality."

The way to Physical Reality is through the mathematical imagination, through an exercise of "musicality in the sphere of thought." Such exercises, giving birth to formulas, need to be verified by experiment in order to sift the true from the false; but this does not affect the fact that "the creative principle resides in mathematics." Sense experience is, in itself, chaotic; order is of the mind. "A theory can be tested by experience, but there is no way from experience to the setting up of a theory." The "fateful" error is to entertain the belief that scientific concepts can be abstracted out of experience. They are "free inventions of the human mind." Fortunately for us, these free inventions of the human mind are found to be congruent with those free inventions of the divine mind which make up the real and rational world of Physical Reality.

One may well ask: what manner of scientist is this? He does not fit the popular image of a white-frocked manipulator of test tubes, or speak with the familiar accents of an apostle of "scientific method." He is, for instance, flatly in disagreement with the positivist Philipp Frank, who expresses what is probably the majority opinion of philosophers of science when he writes that "science cannot discover what actually happens in the world, but can only describe and combine the results of different observations." Einstein is old-fashioned, agreeing with most classical metaphysicians, and incidentally with the man in the street, that science aims to find out what *really* happens beyond the veil of appearance. Is Einstein a crank, his head filled with anachronistic jargon about God and Physical Reality, who by sheer luck stumbled upon some useful equations? Or is the inadequacy with a misinterpretation of "scientific method"?

If we examine the phrase "scientific method," we see that there is a studied ambiguity between a "method" of discovery and a "method" of verification, with "scientific method" presumably uniting the two. But, as Morris Raphael Cohen properly emphasized many years ago: "Science knows of methods of verification, but there are no methods of discovery. If there were such, all we need would be discovered, and we would not have to wait for rare men of genius." The universe of scientific discovery is ruled by an aristocracy of talent, not a democracy of method. All theories are in principle equal before the bar of verification, but only a few can gain seats in the house of Truth, and there is no way of determining beforehand which these shall be. Genius is not reducible—to method or to anything else—and its very essence is to be uncommon, even exotic.

It is to be expected that men will be resentful of this state of affairs and attempt to circumvent it. The rise of modern science has been accompanied by an insistent philosophic effort at The Taming of the Mind. Bacon set up his inductive method, whereby a scrupulous attention to the facts and the relation between facts would make an intelligent man a scientist; Descartes proposed his analytic method, by which "all those who observe its rules exactly would never suppose what is false to be true, and would come—without fatiguing themselves needlessly but in progressively furthering their science—to the true knowledge of all that can be known"; Dewey has sought to make science's "method of inquiry" a human habit, to divert men from "meaningless" metaphysical questions, and to encourage them to good works; and, most recently, logical positivism announced that science cannot hope to plumb the nature of things, but "can only describe and combine the results of different observations," a task for which genius is dispensable, though not entirely useless.

Yet in the actual history of science, discoveries have not been the offspring of any omnipotent "method." As often as not, private fancies have been more productive than the staid virtues of sobriety and skepticism. Men of genius—Galileo, Kepler, Newton, Einstein—have stubbornly gone their own way, possessed by metaphysical ideas of God and Reality, perversely trying to plumb the depths of nature, passionate to the point of extravagance in their speculations. Descartes himself could be so certain of his method—and could make his mathematical contributions—only because he was convinced that the book of nature was in the script of geometry. The record of scientific thought gives us leave to say of science what Goethe said of poetry, that it "presupposes in the man who is to make it a certain good-natured simple-mindedness, in love with the Real as the hiding place of the Absolute."

So intimate has been the relation between scientific creativity and metaphysical (and theological) speculation, that even so astringent a thinker as Bertrand Russell has wondered at the possibility of the wellsprings of science drying up in an era which deprecates metaphysical curios-

ity. Positivists, early in this century, were too well versed in "scientific method" to believe that atoms were "real," that they were more than a convenient intellectual construct by which one could "describe and combine the results of different observations"; but the atom was split nevertheless. Afterwards, of course, the revelation of genius is taken as testimony to the virtue of "scientific method," for it is not difficult to show—after the event—that by a proper extension of "scientific method" we could have known what we did not know, and to forget that we did not know it.

To this it might be retorted: what is of importance is the *result* of Einstein's work, not the idiosyncrasies that spurred him on to the job. Science is interested in what Einstein *does,* not in what he *says.*

If this were so, then Science would be an extremely discourteous mistress—as she has indeed often appeared to be. In actual fact, the relation between what Einstein says and what Einstein does is not so easily severed. It is true that *after* Einstein has done something, his work can be repeated by other physicists and mathematicians who will have no truck with anything called Physical Reality. The General Theory of Relativity can be used by anyone; it has no metaphysical patent, any more than had Kepler's laws of planetary motion (which were also born of some very private fancies). It is also true, however, that it was Einstein who formulated the theory, and had he had none of these private fancies about Physical Reality there would not have been a General Theory of Relativity.

That it was Einstein who developed the Special Theory of Relativity in 1905 may be classified as an "accident." Physics was suffering a crisis in its foundations, experimental data refused to conform to prevailing theories, and a drastic revision of the Newtonian mechanical world view was clearly in the offing. If there had been no Einstein, someone else probably would have thought up something similar to the special theory—though precious and painful years might have been wasted. But if Einstein had not devised the General Theory of Relativity, there is a good chance that it might never have been formulated at all. For the general theory was not needed by science to explain any baffling facts. It was needed by Einstein—and by him alone—to unite the basic concepts of inertia and gravitation in one formula, in order to approximate more closely to the divine mathematical simplicity of the universe.

This intimacy between Einstein's private metaphysics and his public science is dramatically revealed in his lonely position in contemporary quantum physics. Despite the fact that his early work on photoelectric phenomena (1905)—for which he won the Nobel prize—has been extremely important in the development of quantum theory, Einstein is today an isolated and somewhat embittered figure among physicists. He believes that quantum physics has gone off the right track and has deviated from "the programmatic aim of all physics," which is the description of any situation as it really is, regardless of the act of observation. For his own part, he toiled stubbornly during the past decades to construct his recently published Unified Field Theory, which covers electromagnetic as well as gravitational fields, and which would establish—in a nearly final form—the programmatic aim of physics. Never, perhaps, has any theory by so eminent a scientist been so thoroughly ignored by his colleagues. His Unified Field Theory is not even a subject for polemic—evoking only indifference. The newspapers, of course, gave it a big play. In the laboratories, it was a topic for wisecracks. The quantum physicists feel that Einstein is exactly where he charges them with being: in a blind alley.

Einstein's reproach against quantum physics is similar—at least superficially—to that which the Catholic Church leveled against Copernicus' theory, or the conservative physicists against relativity: it is mathematically useful but not really, i.e. metaphysically, true. Einstein sees the similarity but insists that the present situation is truly unique. For while the Copernican and Newtonian revolutions radically revised man's image of nature, and the relativity theory helped to substitute a mathematical model of nature for a mechanical one, the principles of quantum physics rule out the possibility of a model altogether. And this, Einstein believes, is the suicide of physics. His theory of relativity, he says, "teaches us the connection between different descriptions of one and the same reality." But the reality is there, and *physics must describe it.*

In a letter to the physicist Max Born, in 1944, Einstein wrote: "In our scientific expectation we have grown antipodes. You believe in God casting dice and I in perfect laws in the world of things existing as real objects, which I try to grasp in a wildly speculative way."

"God casting dice" is a picturesque but not inaccurate representation of how quantum physics conceives of physical reality. The statistical probability laws of quantum mechanics are not the kind of statistical laws one meets in actuarial work, for instance. In the latter, each individual event has its cause, even if statistics gives us only an average report. In quantum physics a detailed causal analysis of atomic phenomena is not only renounced for convenience sake, but is excluded in principle. The very idea of causality does not pertain; all we know is the probability of the results of measurement at a given time.

Einstein concedes that quantum physics has made great progress with the aid of its probability statistics, but he will not admit that the present state of quantum theory is more than a stopgap. His aim is still a theory that represents "events themselves and not merely the probability of their occurrence"; he will not give up the principle of causality: he is convinced that the laws of the microscopic universe and of the macroscopic universe are continuous—nature is of one piece.

Obviously, science itself will ultimately decide whether Einstein's Unified Field Theory is relevant to the problems of modern physics—whether God casts dice or is subtle but still rational. The point here is that between Einstein as scientist and Einstein as thinker the relation is closer than some overly glib enthusiasts of "scientific method" consider decent.

Recently, the British positivist A. J. Ayer wrote (in *Partisan Review*) rather contemptuously of present-day intellectuals who turn to religion: "They want a form of expla-

nation which will say something more than merely that this is how the world works. They have to be given a reason for its working as it does. . . . It is not enough to state what happens to be true; it has to be shown that it is necessarily true."

This may be taken as a fair summary of Einstein's philosophy of science. For Einstein is one of those—again in Ayer's words—"to whom it is intolerable that facts should be contingent, that things should just happen to be as they are. . . ."

Indeed, it can be said that it is not only Einstein's philosophy of science that Ayer has described, but the philosophy of science itself. For if it were not intolerable "that facts should be contingent, that things should just happen to be as they are," why should science ever have been born? In our epoch of technology, we tend to view the aim of science as prediction and control. But this is a modern belief that would have horrified the Greeks, Copernicus, Kepler, Descartes and Newton, and which has been alien to the temper of Planck, Eddington, and Einstein, to name only a few contemporaries. For them, science has meant a passion for the rational truth which lies concealed behind all sense experience. Science in the West has been, and is, based on the assumption that what is factual and contingent has to be explained by what is rational and necessary, that statements of fact must be deduced from statements of mathematics, that matter is to be illuminated by Reason. Einstein is, *par excellence,* the scientist of the Western world, wedded to the belief that behind the particular and contingent there is the general and rational. The goal of science is a formula from which everything that ever happens can be logically and rigorously derived. Behind the All there is the One.

If we press further, and ask why Reason should have any success in comprehending Physical Reality, then, according to Einstein, we burst through science and philosophy together, and arrive at religion: "To the sphere of religion belongs the faith that the regulations valid for the world of existence are rational. . . ." This faith is not something tranquil and final; it is restless and perpetually dissatisfied, always goading Reason to convert it into a rational certitude.

God wills that the scientist—who is Reason incarnate—shall dissolve Him into demonstrable theorems. Probably the dissolution will never be final, and Einstein has uttered some forlorn sentiments on the mystery of existence. But, as Henry Margenau has acutely pointed out, in the case of Einstein "a certain pathos for the unknown, though often displayed, always intimates the ultimately knowable character of existence, knowable in scientific terms." For God may be subtle but he does not deceive.

There are, according to Einstein, three ascending stages in the development of religion: the religion of fear, the religion of morality, and the religion of the cosmos.

The religion of fear is the product of primitive, self-centered, unenlightened men, of the kind we meet in the Pentateuch. These men believed in a personal God who was involved in their destinies, who rewarded and punished his creatures. The religion of fear not only did not free men from their bodily concerns and egocentric anxieties—it made these very concerns and anxieties an occasion for God's intervention in the workings of the world.

The religion of fear is superseded by the religion of morality, as embodied in some of the Jewish prophets and elaborated by the New Testament. Knowledge itself provides only the means, not the ends of life; religion—acting through the intuition of great teachers and radiant personalities—sets up the ultimate goals of life and provides the emotional context in which they can influence the individual. Men, left to shift for themselves, would see the ends of life to be ease and happiness; such a selfish ethic, dominated by elementary instincts, is "more proper for a herd of swine." A genuinely religious person is one who has "liberated himself from the fetters of his selfish desires and is preoccupied with thoughts, feelings, and aspirations to which he clings because of their super-personal value."

The religion of morality is the highest that the great mass of men can aspire to, and it is sufficient to tame their animal spirits. But for a select few there is something finer and more noble: the religion of the cosmos. For the wise man—and this is the very definition of his wisdom—ethical behavior needs no religious sanction; sympathy and love of humanity he finds to be sufficient unto themselves. His religion, as distinct from his morality, is the result of a unique religious event, the mystical experience of the rationality of the cosmos, in which the individual is annihilated. Of this experience Einstein writes: "The individual feels the nothingness of human desires and aims and the sublimity and marvelous order which reveal themselves both in nature and the world of thought. He looks upon individual existence as a sort of prison and wants to experience the universe as a single significant whole."

This experience is not reached by any Cabalistic practices. On the contrary: the *via mystica* is nothing other than the *via scientiae*. Science, at its greatest, is identical with religion, at its most sublime. Science provokes a "profound reverence for the rationality made manifold in existence." The scientist "achieves a far-reaching emancipation from the shackles of personal hopes and desires, and thereby attains that humble attitude of mind towards the grandeur of reason incarnate in existence. . . ." And just as science leads us to true religiosity, so does true religiosity lead us to science:

"The cosmic religious experience is the strongest and the noblest, driving scientific research from behind. No one who does not appreciate the terrific exertions, the devotion without which pioneer creation in scientific thought cannot come into being can judge the strength of the feeling out of which alone such work, turned away as it is from immediate practical life, can grow.

"What deep faith in the rationality of the structure of the world, what a longing to understand even a small glimpse of the reason revealed in the world, there must have been in Kepler and Newton."

When a Boston Catholic priest took it upon himself in 1929 to warn Americans of Einstein's "atheism," Rabbi Herbert S. Goldstein cabled Einstein: "Do you believe in God?" Einstein cabled back: "I believe in Spinoza's God, who reveals himself in the harmony of all Being, not in God who concerns himself with the fate and actions of men"—a statement which so affected Rabbi Goldstein as to make him predict hopefully that Einstein "would bring mankind a scientific formula for monotheism."

Instead of the worship of the God of Abraham, Isaac, and Jacob, we have—in the tradition of Maimonides, Spinoza, and Hermann Cohen—the *amor Dei intellectualis*. Instead of the Lord of Hosts, we have the God of the philosophers—the Logos, the Reason which governs the universe, the incorporeal meaning behind the chaos of concreteness.

Reason, which worships the God of Spinoza, begins with the *proposition* "all men are mortal," and is most interested in the immortal truth of this and other propositions. Biblical faith, which worships the God of Abraham, begins with the *fact* that "all men are mortal." The truths of Reason are true even if man does not exist; they are true, as Husserl remarked, for "men, angels, monsters, and gods." Faith is less concerned with the truths of Reason than with the fate of man—the mortal, finite creature who cannot volatilize himself into Reason. Reason is what we have gained by the eating of the Tree of Knowledge: we are like unto gods, sharing in divine omniscience. Faith is the human condition experiencing itself in its most naked actuality, for with the eating of the apple there goes the Fall, and we must surely die.

The struggle between the God of Abraham and the God of Spinoza is the central theme of the spiritual history of the Western world. Out of it there comes the Old Testament and the New, Greek philosophy and Gnosticism, medieval Scholasticism and Renaissance science, German Idealism and modern atheism.

And in this conflict the Jew is tensed and sundered. For he is of the Covenant of Abraham, whom God commanded; and he has also prominently been of the opinion of Philo and Spinoza, to whom the world is the garment of Reason.

Einstein was born in 1879 into a German Jewish family whose Judaism had been pretty well eroded by the tide of assimilation. He was sent to a Catholic elementary school in Munich, and even here the fact of his being a Jew was in no way impressed on him. We are told in his autobiographical sketch about a pre-adolescent religious fervor, but it seems to have been in no way Jewish. At the Gymnasium, at the age of 14, he was instructed in the elements of Judaism; he was attracted to what he regarded as its elevated morality, repelled by its ritual codification. When Einstein was sixteen, his family moved to Milan from Munich for financial reasons; after six months, unable to bear the rigid discipline of the Gymnasium, Einstein joined them. In Milan he renounced both his German citizenship—becoming stateless—and his membership in the Jewish community; only by such a double renunciation could the rational young man show his contempt for the idols of the herd.

Einstein formally became a Jew once again in 1910 when he accepted the chair of theoretical physics at the German University in Prague. Emperor Francis Joseph believed that only members of a recognized religious denomination were qualified to teach there, so Einstein had to register as a follower of the "Mosaic creed." More than half the German-speaking population of Prague were Jews, and the city at that time was witnessing, under the general influence of Martin Buber, a Jewish intellectual renaissance. Einstein came to know and be friendly with the active leaders in this movement, especially Hugo Bergmann and Max Brod. (He met Franz Kafka, too—one wonders what they had to say to each other.) But Einstein still refused to take being a Jew seriously.

In 1921, however, Einstein publicly declared himself to be a Zionist—to everyone's surprise and the consternation of not a few. The man who was known to despise nationalism as an excrescence of the herd mentality praised Zionism as "the embodiment of the reawakening corporate spirit of the Jewish nation." What happened to bring this "conversion" about? Nothing singular or dramatic so far as we know. Indeed, it is best understood as not a conversion at all, but as a relapse—from the religion of the cosmos to the religion of morality. It was apparently not possible to sustain forever the ecstasy of Reason; one had to return to the realm of matter and men, and there the best of all possible demeanors was an exalted, abstract morality. Einstein was able to announce that he found in Judaism an admirable ethical sensibility that demanded not faith but "the sanctification of life in a suprapersonal sense." Jewish morality, like Reason (though not so nobly), turned man from himself to the sanctification of life in general. He liked to quote Rathenau to the effect that "when a Jew says he's going hunting to amuse himself, he lies."

More to the point, one feels, is the tone and inflection with which he writes of his generations of ancestors, the ghetto Jews: ". . . These obscure humble people had one great advantage over us; each of them belonged in every fiber of his being to a community in which he was completely absorbed. . . ."

Einstein's new Jewishness was not the result of his discovering a hidden Jewish self. It was, on the contrary, a new means of escaping from his self. The flight to Reason from the chaos of existence, which seemed to have succeeded so well, was now acknowledged to have been, at least in part, a failure. Something ponderable and indissoluble had been left behind: the flesh-and-blood Jew born of woman, the specific presence of the absent-minded professor. And Einstein once again fled—into Community, the ghetto, the warm mass of Jewry. What could not be transmuted into Reason would be absorbed into The Jew.

And what could not be absorbed into The Jew would be once more etherealized—this time into the World Citizen.

Einstein's political and social opinions—so naive, so superficial, so bizarre—have baffled and disturbed his many admirers. They have usually sought to explain these opinions away with the statement that there is apparently no correlation between scientific and political intelligence. But this does less than justice to Einstein, who certainly would not concede the point. Moreover, it is possible to show that Einstein's political views are closely related to his entire outlook. He has applied to society that same rage for simplicity and love for the abstract that accom-

plished so much in his theoretical physics. But men cannot be so profitably transformed into clear and logical abstractions. The result of such an effort is confusion, contradiction, and, inevitably, an unpleasant impatience on the part of the thinker.

Thus, Einstein has always been a pacifist. His pacifism is bred of an intense hatred of the military, which he regards as the bestialization of man. But in so selfless a devotion to Humanity as Einstein's, strange things happen in one's relations to men. Sometimes, indeed, one cannot see men for Humanity. So it happened that Einstein not only vigorously supported the Second World War; he also defended the indiscriminate bombing of German cities as "morally justified," and urged that the Germans be "punished as a people" for their "collective guilt."

Einstein despises capitalism because it presupposes the existence of discrete, free, and autonomous selves in competition and even conflict. The individual's position in our society is such that "the egotistical drives in his make-up are constantly being accentuated, while his social drives, which are by nature weaker, progressively deteriorate. . . . Unknowingly prisoners of their own egotism, they [individuals] feel insecure, lonely, and deprived of the naive, simple, and unsophisticated enjoyment of life." Such a simple celebration of life can only come about when men have transcended their selves into Humanity, and the chaos of existing societies has been stilled into Community. Rejecting the idea of capitalism, Einstein elects for the idea of socialism.

The ideal community is the antithesis of the self-centered individual, and the perfect community, like the purified self, can only be won through Reason. But Reason has a way of discovering the "laws of society," the observance of which constitutes freedom. So there is the not uncommon sight of the radical rationalist—for example, George Bernard Shaw or the Webbs—who is favorably disposed to a society that suppresses the "self-seeking ego" (that is, the individual) in the name of a selfless *raison d'état*. Einstein's habit of sending messages to Communist-controlled "congresses of intellectuals" does not represent any sympathy for Russian totalitarianism—which he detests—but is rather a genuflection before the socialist idea, and an act of homage to those of vigorous intellect "who get things done," especially when they wish to "do things" for "peace." An international organization of the intellectual elite influencing the policies of nations has always been one of Einstein's fondest dreams.

The escape from the self into The Jew and Humanity, however, like the flight into Reason, has failed Einstein. Though he still signs petitions and sends encouraging communications, there is abundant evidence that his heart is not in them. Einstein's melancholic loneliness is the salient feature of his personality, as it is of his face.

"My passionate sense of social justice and social responsibility has always contrasted oddly with my pronounced freedom from the need for direct contact with other human beings and human communities. I have gone my own way and have never belonged to my country, my home, my friends, or even my immediate family, with my whole heart; in the face of all these ties I have never lost an obstinate sense of detachment. . . ."

Philipp Frank comments further: "He always has a certain feeling of being a stranger, and even a desire to be isolated. On the other hand, however, he has a great curiosity about everything human and a great sense of humor, with which he is able to derive a certain, perhaps artistic pleasure from everything that is strange and even unpleasant."

And: "His attitude in intercourse with other people, consequently, was on the whole one of amusement. He saw everyday matters in a somewhat comical light. . . . The laughter that welled up from the depths of his being was one of his characteristics that immediately attracted one's attention."

Einstein has not succeeded in becoming pure spirit or pure citizen or the selfless member of an organic community. He has ended up as simply more himself, laughing at his own presumption, though not for that the more content with man's condition and man's fate.

Einstein's gaiety, his informality of dress and manner, his quick sympathy—they are of that humanism which springs, not from love of fellow men, but from compassion at the brutal fact that men exist at all. Perhaps if Einstein and Kafka—whose earthly self was amiable too, and from the same cause—had talked a while, they would have found more in common than one might expect! The Jew as Pure Reason and the Jew as Pure Alienation might have sensed in each other a kinship—perhaps even a secret identity, for the Kingdom of Reason can be as cold and infinitely empty as K.'s Kingdom of Nothingness; and both are as uninhabitable as the illusory world of the average sensual man. They might have smiled with a common irony at the world of matter and men, so complacent and blind in the ignorance of its own essential unreality. And they might have sighed, too, at being forever excluded from it.

Robert B. Downs   (essay date 1956)

SOURCE: "Harbinger of the Atomic Age," in *Books That Changed the World*, revised edition, American Library Association, 1978, pp. 374-82.

[*Downs was an American librarian, author, and editor whose professional life was committed to championing intellectual freedom and opposing literary censorship. In the following essay, originally published in the first edition of* Books That Changed the World, *he discusses various concepts rooted in Einstein's special and general theories of relativity and their impact on scientific study.*]

Albert Einstein is one of the rare figures in history who succeeded in becoming a legend of heroic proportions during his own lifetime. The more incomprehensible to the lay public his ideas appeared, the more intriguing they seemed, and the more Olympian their progenitor. As Bertrand Russell aptly remarked, "Everybody knows that Einstein has done something astonishing, but very few people know exactly what it is that he has done." To be told, though inaccurately, that there are scarcely a dozen men in the entire world who fully grasp Einstein's theories

of the universe, challenges and intrigues. The incomprehensibility of Einstein's theories stems from the complex nature of his field of operation. One point of view was expressed by George W. Gray:

> Inasmuch as the theory of relativity is presented by its author in mathematical language, and in strictness of speaking cannot be expressed in any other, there is a certain presumption in every attempt to translate it into the vernacular. One might as well try to interpret Beethoven's Fifth Symphony on a saxophone.

Nevertheless, Einstein himself, Bertrand Russell, Lev Davidovitch Landau, and others have shown that it is possible to describe the Einstein cosmos intelligibly without resort to mathematical symbolism. And a fantastic world it is, extremely upsetting to ideas firmly established for centuries, "a strange pudding for the layman to digest." We are asked, for example, to accept such incredible conceptions as these: space is curved, the shortest distance between two points is not a straight line, the universe is finite but unbounded, parallel lines eventually meet, light rays are curved, time is relative and cannot be measured in exactly the same way everywhere, measurements of length vary with speed, a body in motion will contract in size but increase in mass, and a fourth dimension—an interweaving of space and time—is added to the familiar three of height, length, and width.

Though Einstein's contributions to science have been innumerable, his fame rests primarily upon the theory of relativity, an achievement which, Banesh Hoffman concluded, "has a monumental quality that places its author among the truly great scientists of all time, in the select company of Isaac Newton and Archimedes. With its fascinating paradoxes and spectacular successes it fired the imagination of the public."

The revolution in concepts brought about by Einstein began in 1905, with the appearance in a German journal, *Annalen der Physik,* of a thirty-page paper carrying the unexciting title **"On the Electrodynamics of Moving Bodies."** At the time, Einstein was only twenty-six years of age, and serving as a minor official in the Swiss patent office. He had been born into a middle-class Jewish family at Ulm, Bavaria, in 1879. As a student, he was not precocious even in mathematics. Because of failure of the family fortune, Einstein was forced out on his own at fifteen. Emigrating to Switzerland, he was able to continue his scientific education at the Polytechnic Academy in Zurich, married a fellow student, and became a Swiss citizen. To earn a living he settled in a job making preliminary reports and rewriting inventors' applications for the patent office. His spare time was used for intensive study of the works of philosophers, scientists, and mathematicians. Soon he was ready to launch the first of a flood of original contributions to science, destined to have far-ranging repercussions.

In his 1905 paper, Einstein set forth the Special Theory of Relativity, challenging man's existing concepts of time and space, of matter and energy. The foundations for the theory were laid down in two basic assumptions. The first was the principle of relativity: all motion is relative. A familiar illustration of the principle is a moving train or ship. A person sitting in a train with darkened windows would have, if there was little commotion, no idea of speed or direction, or perhaps even that the train was moving at all. A man on a ship with portholes closed would be in a similar predicament. We conceive motion only in relative terms, that is in respect to other objects. On a vastly greater scale, the forward movement of the earth could not be detected if there were no heavenly bodies for comparisons. It should be noted that this principle was stated explicitly by Newton in his *Principia,* and was not a new contribution; Einstein merely affirmed its relevance to electrodynamics as well as in mechanics.

Einstein's second major hypothesis was that the velocity of light is independent of the motion of its source. The speed of light, 186,000 miles a second, is always the same, anywhere in the universe, regardless of place, time or direction. Light travels in a moving train, for instance, at exactly the same speed as it does outside the train. No force can make it go faster or slower. Furthermore, nothing can exceed the velocity of light, though electrons closely approximate it. The speed of light is, in fact, the only constant, unvarying factor in all of nature.

A famous experiment carried out in 1887 by two American scientists, Michelson and Morley, furnished the basis of Einstein's theory on light. They attempted to determine the velocity of the earth as it passed through the ether (a hypothetical substance which was believed to pervade all space not occupied by matter). No velocity could be determined, and most physicists abandoned the ether theory.

Einstein's paper in 1905 answered the question which had puzzled Michelson, Morley, and their fellow physicists. The essential point deduced by Einstein was that light always travels at the same velocity no matter under what conditions it is measured, and the motion of the earth in regard to the sun has no influence upon the speed of light.

Newton stated, "It may be that there is no body really at rest to which the place and motions of others may be referred." Today's scientists do not say that there is or is not such a thing as absolute motion. The question, only to be determined by experiment, is whether absolute motion can be detected. Einstein asserted that every body's movement is relative to that of another. Motion is the natural state of all things. Nowhere on earth or in the universe is there anything absolutely at rest. Throughout our restless cosmos, movement is constant, from the infinitesimally small atom to the largest celestial galaxies. For example, the earth is moving around the sun at the rate of twenty miles a second. In a universe where all is motion and fixed points of reference are lacking, there are no established standards for comparing velocities, length, size, mass, and time, except as they might be measured by relative motions. Only light is not relative, its velocity remaining changeless regardless of its source or the observer's position.

Doubtless the most difficult of all Einsteinian concepts to comprehend and the most unsettling to traditional beliefs is the relativity of time. Einstein held that events at different places occurring at the same moment for one observer do not occur at the same moment for another observer moving at a speed relative to the first. For example, two events judged as taking place at the same time by an observer on the ground are not simultaneous for an observer in a train or an airplane. Time is relative to the position and speed of the observer, and is not absolute.

As speed increases, time seems to slow down. We are accustomed to the thought that every physical object has three dimensions, but Einstein maintained that time is also a dimension of space, and space is a dimension of time. Neither time nor space can exist without the other and they are interdependent. Movement and change are constant, we live in a four-dimensional universe, with time as the fourth dimension.

Thus the two basic premises of Einstein's theory, as first presented seventy years ago, were the relativity of all motion and the concept of light as the only unvarying quantity in the universe.

In developing the principle of relativity of motion, Einstein upset another firmly established belief. Previously, length and mass had been regarded as absolute and constant under every conceivable circumstance. Now, Einstein came along to state that the mass or weight of an object and its length depend on how fast the body is moving relative to uniform motion of the observer. As an example, he imagined a train one thousand feet long, traveling at four-fifths of the speed of light. To a stationary observer, watching it pass by, the length of the train would be reduced to only six hundred feet, though it would remain a thousand feet to a passenger on the train. Similarly, any material body traveling through space contracts according to velocity. A yardstick, if it could be shot through space at 161,000 miles per second would shrink to a half-yard.

Mass, too is changeable. As velocity increases, the mass of an object becomes greater. Experiments have shown indirectly that particles of matter speeded up to 86 per cent of the speed of light weigh twice as much as they do when at rest. Movement and change and relativity had been recognized long before Einstein. The novel results of his theory come from the combination of the well-known principle of relativity with the new assumption of the constancy of the velocity of light.

Einstein's original statement of 1905, known as the special theory of relativity, is limited to uniform motion of the reference frames that are used in the description. It tells us how things look from a train moving uniformly in a straight line, but they do not tell us how things look from a rotating merry-go-round. In our cosmos, stars, planets, and other celestial bodies seldom move uniformly in a straight line. Any theory, therefore, which fails to include every type of motion offers an incomplete description of the universe. Einstein's next step, accordingly, was the formulation of his general theory of relativity, a process which required ten years of intensive application. In the general theory, Einstein studies the mysterious force that guides the movements of the stars, comets, meteors, galaxies, and other bodies whirling around in the vast universe. The general theory is valid for all kinds of observers, whether their motion is uniform or accelerated.

In his general theory of relativity, published in 1915, Einstein advanced a new concept of gravitation, making fundamental changes in the ideas of gravity and light which had been generally accepted since the time of Sir Isaac Newton. Gravity had been regarded by Newton as a "force." Einstein proved, however, that the space around a planet or other celestial body is a gravitational field similar to the magnetic field around a magnet. Tremendous bodies, such as the sun or stars, are surrounded by enormous gravitational fields. The theory also explained the erratic movements of Mercury, the planet nearest the sun, a phenomenon that had puzzled astronomers for centuries and had not been adequately covered by Newton's law of gravitation. So powerful are the great gravitational fields that they even bend rays of light. In 1919, a few years after the general theory was first announced, photographs taken of a complete eclipse of the sun conclusively demonstrated the validity of Einstein's theory that light rays passing through the sun's gravitational field travel in curves rather than in straight lines.

There followed from this premise a statement by Einstein that space is curved. Revolving planets follow the shortest possible routes, influenced by the sun's presence, just as a river flowing toward the sea follows the contour of the land, along the easiest and most natural course. In our terrestrial scheme of things, a ship or airplane crossing the ocean follows a curved line, that is the arc of a circle, and not a straight line. It is evident, therefore, that the shortest distance between two points is a curve instead of a straight line. An identical rule governs the movements of a planet or light ray.

It is not a logical deduction from Einstein's theory that space is finite. If the universe does not extend forever into space, but has finite limitations, no definite boundaries can be established. There are many cosmological models presently being considered with all sorts of different geometrical properties.

Of all the great scientific discoveries and findings coming from Einstein, his contributions to atomic theory have had the most direct and profound effect on the present-day world. Shortly after his first paper on relativity was published in 1905, in the *Annalen der Physik,* the same journal carried a short article by Einstein projecting his theory further. It was entitled **"Does the Inertia of a Body Depend on Its Energy?"** The mass-energy relation is a corollary of the special theory of relativity. At the time, he did not state that the use of atomic energy was possible. Later, he pointed out that the release of this tremendous force could be achieved according to a formula he offered, the most celebrated equation in history: $E = mc^2$. To interpret, energy equals mass multiplied by the speed of light and again by the speed of light. If all the energy in a half pound of any matter could be utilized, Einstein held, enough power would be released to equal the explosive force of seven million tons of TNT. Without Einstein's equation, as one commentator pointed out, "experimenters might still have stumbled upon the fission of uranium, but it is doubtful if they would have realized its significance in terms of energy, or of bombs."

In the famous equation $E = mc^2$, Einstein demonstrated that energy and mass are proportional to each other, differing only in state. Mass is actually concentrated energy. The formula, wrote Lincoln Barnett in a brilliant evaluation, "provides the answer to many of the long-standing mysteries of physics. It explains how radioactive substances like radium and uranium are able to eject particles at enormous velocities and to go on doing so for millions of years. It explains how the sun and all the stars can go on radiating light and heat for billions of years, for if our sun were being consumed by ordinary processes of combustion the earth would have died in frozen darkness eons ago. It reveals the magnitude of the energy that slumbers in the nuclei of atoms, and forecasts how many grams of uranium must go into a bomb in order to destroy a city."

Einstein's equation remained a theory until 1939. By that time, its author had become a resident, and was shortly to become a citizen, of the United States, for he had been driven out of Europe by the Nazis. Learning that the Germans were engaged in importing uranium and were carrying on research on an atomic bomb, Einstein wrote President Roosevelt a highly confidential letter:

> Some recent work by E. Fermi and L. Szilard, which has been communicated to me in manuscript, leads me to expect that the element uranium may be turned into a new and important source of energy in the immediate future. . . . This new phenomenon would also lead to the construction of bombs, and it is conceivable . . . that . . . a single bomb of this type, carried by boat and exploded in a port, might very well destroy the whole port together with some of the surrounding territory.

As an immediate result of Einstein's letter to Roosevelt, construction of the Manhattan atom-bomb project was started. About five years later, the first bomb was exploded at the Alamogordo reservation in New Mexico, and shortly thereafter the dreadful destruction caused by a bomb dropped on Hiroshima was instrumental in bringing the war with Japan to a quick end.

Though the atomic bomb was the most spectacular of all practical applications of the theories of Einstein, his fame was also established by another remarkable accomplishment. Almost simultaneously with his special theory of relativity in 1905, there was developed Einstein's photoelectric law, explaining the mysterious photoelectric effect. Einstein's finding was extremely important, as being one of the fundamental particles of nature—the "light-quantum" or photon—and it was also extremely important as a step toward the discovery of quantum mechanics several decades later. It was for the discovery of the photoelectric law that Einstein was awarded the Nobel Prize in physics in 1922.

In his later years, Einstein labored indefatigably on what is known as the unified field theory, attempting to demonstrate the harmony and uniformity of nature. According to his view, physical laws for the minute atom should be equally applicable to immense celestial bodies. The unified field theory would unite all physical phenomena into a single scheme. Gravitation, electricity, magnetism, and atomic energy are all forces that would be covered by the one theory. In 1950, after more than a generation of research, Einstein presented such a theory to the world. He expressed the belief that the theory holds the key to the universe, unifying in one concept the infinitesimal, whirling world of the atom and the vast reaches of star-filled space. Because of mathematical difficulties, the theory has not yet been fully checked against established facts in physics. Einstein had unshaken faith, however, that his unified field theory would in time produce an explanation of the "atomic character of energy," and demonstrate the existence of a well-ordered universe. He did not regard the theory as anything that could be tested experimentally, however, and present-day physicists are not inclined to believe that the theory will prove fruitful.

The philosophy which inspired and guided Einstein through decades of intense intellectual effort, and the rewards therefrom, were described by him in a lecture on the origins of the general theory of relativity, at the University of Glasgow in 1933.

> The final results appear almost simple; any intelligent undergraduate can understand them without much trouble. But the years of searching in the dark for a truth that one feels, but cannot express; the intense desire and the alternations of confidence and misgiving, until one breaks through to clarity and understanding, are only known to him who has himself experienced them.

On another occasion, Einstein gave evidence of the deeply spiritual side of his nature by this statement:

> The most beautiful and most profound emotion we can experience is the sensation of the mystical. It is the sower of all true science. He to whom this emotion is a stranger, who can no longer wonder and stand rapt in awe, is as good as dead. To know that what is impenetrable to us really exists, manifesting itself as the highest wisdom and the most radiant beauty which our dull faculties can comprehend only in their most primitive forms—this knowledge, this feeling is at the center of true religiousness.

Innumerable scientists have paid tribute to Einstein. Quotations from two recent reviews of his career will illustrate his unique hold on the scientific world. Paul Oehser wrote:

> Influence is a weak word for the work of Albert Einstein. The theories he advanced were revolutionary. In them was born the Atomic Age, and where it leads mankind we know not. But we do know that here is the greatest scientist and philosopher of our century, who has become almost a saint in our eyes and whose achievement is a justification of our faith in the human mind, a symbol of man's eternal quest, his reaching for the stars.

Another scientist, Banesh Hoffman, concluded:

> The importance of Einstein's scientific ideas does not reside merely in their great success. Equally powerful has been their psychological effect. At a crucial epoch in the history of science Einstein demonstrated that long-accepted ideas were not in any way sacred. And it was this more than anything else that freed the imaginations of

men like Bohr and de Broglie and inspired their daring triumphs in the realm of the quantum. Wherever we look, the physics of the 20th century bears the indelible imprint of Einstein's genius.

Concerning the present status of relativity, an international conference of theoretical physicists, at Berne, Switzerland, recently agreed that the foundations of the special and general theory have been universally accepted. Experiments have conclusively confirmed the special theory and are convincing for the general theory. The special theory has been incorporated into general physics and is used continually in atomic and nuclear physics.

For a number of years, the general theory was applied mainly to cosmology and cosmogony, but lately relativity is being applied to microphysical problems. The relationship to the quantum theory is still quite undetermined. It is apparent that general relativity provides a new approach to the ultimate properties of space and time. If true, the theory may have as much bearing on the physics of the very small as of the very large. The increasing worldwide interest in general relativity indicates that scientists believe the theory may add further to our understanding of the universe as an organic whole.

Robert Neidorf   (essay date 1959)

SOURCE: "Discussion: Is Einstein a Positivist?" in *Philosophy of Science*, Vol. 30, No. 2, April, 1963, pp. 173-88.

[*In the following essay, which originally appeared as part of a doctoral dissertation presented at Yale University in 1959, Neidorf considers whether or not Einstein's theories fit a positivistic epistemology.*]

There are in fact *two* cases to be decided, one textual and one technical. *The textual question:* Does Einstein, in his thinking and writing about the philosophy of science, advocate a positivistic (or empiricist) position? Most of the literature on this subject, both by Einstein and by commentators, turns on the special theory of relativity; accordingly, the discussion which follows will be oriented mostly towards that theory. *The technical question:* Does Einstein's work, particularly his presentation of the special theory of relativity with its associated critique of classical physics, commit one to a positivistic philosophy of science? I begin with the latter problem.

1. THE TECHNICAL QUESTION: THE CASE FOR AN AFFIRMATIVE ANSWER.

The nerve of Einstein's special theory of relativity is contained in his redefinition of simultaneity for spatially separate events. To see the sense in which Einstein appears to be applying or recommending a positivistic epistemology, we need first to examine the reasons why a *re*definition seems to be required at all. For this purpose, I shall introduce below some general (and familiar) considerations with respect to simultaneity and the measurement of time-intervals. The treatment is written initially from the Newtonian or classical standpoint, which (sadly) has almost come to be the standpoint of common sense. In so far as that standpoint is subjected to criticism, the treatment of course leans heavily on Einstein's theory, and on considerations implicitly or explicitly contained in it. The theory itself will be discussed at a later stage.

Suppose a man judges that two events, occurring at different locations, are simultaneous. He makes this judgment because (say) the sounds characteristic of each event arrive at his ear at certain given times. Taking into account the velocity of sound and the distances between himself and the event-loci, he then calculates that they went off at the same time. On the peculiarly convenient assumption that he stands midway between the event-loci, he will hear both sounds simultaneously if and only if they are in fact proceeding from simultaneous events. It is convenient to elevate this last observation into a general principle: Spatially separate events are known to be simultaneous if observers midway between them receive signals proceeding from them simultaneously. In the present case we are assuming that the signals in question are sound waves.

Now we know that this method of judging simultaneity or the lack of it (i.e. time-interval) is not in general dependable. We can list two obvious circumstances which will upset this technique. (i) If a wind is blowing, the sound waves coming from one event to the observer will be hastened, while those coming from the other will be retarded. This will delude him into thinking that the upwind event was earlier than the downwind one, even though they were "really" simultaneous. What this means is that another set of observations are relevant to the determination of simultaneity: namely, those observations by which we may determine that a wind is (or is not) blowing. (ii) Suppose the observer is midway between the event-loci at the moment the events go off, but moving from one toward the other. He will then advance to meet one wave front and retreat from the other. In the absence of any awareness of the fact that he is moving, he would then judge that one event was prior to the other, even though they were both "really" simultaneous. What this means, again, is that another set of observations are relevant to the determination of simultaneity: namely, those by which we determine that the observer is moving (or not moving) with respect to the event-loci. It is of course possible for the observer to establish his location relative to the event-loci with standard rods in advance of the simultaneity-determination. But in that case it will still have to be asked how he knows that the distance-relations have not been altered in the interim, and the means by which he knows this latter fact (or its negative) will constitute another set of data relevant to the determination of the time-interval between the events themselves.

In point of fact, the complications introduced by winds and motions are usually not a problem. We can correct for relative motions, for example, by "looking around" to be sure that no motions are in fact taking place. That is, we employ electromagnetic phenomena. Supposing, then, that we decide to make our simultaneity judgments more accurate at the outset by using light-signals (or other electromagnetic devices) instead of sound. Then, analogously to the situation with sound if I am midway between two event-loci at the time that two simultaneous flashes are fired off, I will see the corresponding flashes simultaneously. Pursuing the analogy, we see that two possible qualifications can upset the validity of this technique. Either (i) the "ether" through which the light travels may be blowing past, or (ii) I may be in relative motion with respect to the event-loci, so that additional data are required to establish the fact (if it *is* a fact) that I am still midway between them when I perceive the flashes. How can we determine whether there is an ether wind blowing, or (which comes to the same thing in the end) whether there is a motion of myself as observer with respect to the event-loci? And if either of these circumstances do obtain, how can we measure them so as to compensate for their effects?

1. To find out whether an "ether wind" is blowing we shall want to measure the apparent velocity of light as it goes past. For this purpose we can set up an auxiliary experiment such that a light-flash will set out from a point which is a known distance away, at a known time. We then note the time at which the signal arrives at our point of observation. Knowing the distance and the time-interval, it requires no sophistication to calculate the velocity of the light-signal. But the logical intolerability of this situation is evident—we wanted to employ the velocity of light to measure time-intervals between distant events, but now, in our auxiliary experiment, we are employing time-intervals between distant events to measure the velocity of light.

2. Again, suppose we want to measure the motion between us and the event-loci. For simplicity, consider only the observer and one event-locus, and assume that the motion (if any) is uniform. The general method is to arrange an auxiliary experiment in which, at known times, two light-flashes will leave the event-locus. We then note the times at which the flashes arrive at the observation-locus. This gives us a pair of time-intervals, and if there *is* a relative motion, one of the intervals will be larger than the other, and the velocity of relative motion will be calculable therefrom. But here again, we are guilty of a logical circle—we are using time-intervals to measure a motion in the auxiliary experiment, so that in the original circumstances we could use the measured motion to help in the estimation of time-intervals. If we are seeking a fundamentally valid method of estimating time-intervals between spatially-separated events, these techniques are useless.

This circularity of measurement can be broken only if there is some further meaning for time-interval or simultaneity (as applied to distant events), over and above the meaning which can be determined through the use of light-signals. That is, we seek a method of assigning time-coordinates to events which will be independent of light-velocity, just as the use of light gave us a method of assigning time-coordinates to events independent of sound-velocity. *But there is no such method.* We are able to use light as a corrective for sound because, for terrestrial purposes, light travels at an infinite velocity and sound at a very finite one. But for astronomical purposes, and in general for theoretical purposes, light too has a genuinely finite velocity. Lacking any phenomena of genuinely infinite velocity, we lack any physical means for the assignment of time-coordinates as called for in the Newtonian conception of space and time.

These results can be summarized in more abstract terms. Everything turns on the answer to this question: "What time is it over there when it is a certain time over here?" Pre-relativity physics assumes that the answer is always, "The same time." Attention then turns to the problem of assigning time-coordinates to happenings *over there*. It is observed that a time-lag always exists between the happening (over there) and the reception (over here) of a report of it. It is further observed that this time-lag is a function of certain physical processes (velocities) *which are themselves measured in terms of the time-lag*. For this reason, we have no method for measuring the time-lag independent of physical processes, and hence no independent method for assigning time-coordinates to happenings perceived over there.

The conclusion to be drawn at this stage of analysis is that there is no meaning for "simultaneity," and hence no meaning for "time-interval" and "time," independent of physical processes; the reason is that we require a physically significant procedure for the assignment of time-coordinates to spatially separate events.

2. THE TEXTUAL QUESTION: THE CASE FOR AN AFFIRMATIVE ANSWER.

It certainly seems as if the above considerations, which are central in the special theory of relativity, entail an empirical or positivistic turn, especially if the demand for "physically significant" methods be interpreted as a demand for empirical significance in terms of sensory experience. This impression can be reinforced by selections from Einstein's non-technical writings. The following, for example, is famous in this regard:

> We encounter [a] difficulty with all physical statements in which the conception "simultaneity" plays a part. The concept does not exist for the physicist until he has the possibility of discovering whether or not it is fulfilled in an actual case. We thus require a definition of simultaneity such that this definition supplies us with the method by means of which . . . he can decide by experiment whether or not both the [events in question] occurred simultaneously. As long as this requirement is not satisfied, I allow myself to be deceived as a physicist (and of course the same applies if I am not a physicist) when I imagine that I am able to attach a meaning to the statement of simultaneity.

> [Einstein, *The Principle of Relativity*]

Many of positivist persuasions have seized upon this aspect of relativity. Their interpretations of it, phrased differently, amount to the assertion that Einstein's work demonstrates the correctness of their own epistemological views, and that indeed their views are the only correct interpretation of Einstein's work. For example, Reichenbach:

> The physicist who wanted to understand the Michelson experiment had to commit himself to a philosophy for which the meaning of a statement is reducible to its verifiability, that is, he had to adopt the verifiability theory of meaning if he wanted to escape a maze of ambiguous questions

and gratuitous assumptions. It is this positivist, or let me rather say, empiricist commitment which determines the philosophical position of Einstein.

> ["The Philosophical Significance of the Theory of Relativity"]

Again, Bridgman:

> Let us examine what Einstein did in his special theory. In the first place, he recognized that the meaning of a term is to be sought in the operations employed in making application of the term.

> ["Einstein's Theories and the Operational Point of View"]

The kernel common to both of these quotations is the idea of reducing, in principle, the theoretical entities and concepts of mathematical physics to some aspect of the sense-experiences with which they are generally associated. Reichenbach's statement suggests that the entities and laws of physics are reducible to certain complex predictions concerning the frequency with which we shall have immediate experiences of a certain sort; and the laws are valid, and the entities real, if the predictions are borne out. Similarly Bridgman's statement suggests that the entire meaning of a concept is contained in the immediately sensed laboratory manipulations and operations involved whenever the concept is relevant to the physical processes under study. This general reductionist tendency can also be ascribed to Einstein by careful choice of writings. As late as 1945 he wrote:

> We are accustomed to regard as real those sense perceptions which are common to different individuals, and which therefore are, in a measure, impersonal. The natural sciences, and in particular, the most fundamental of them, physics, deal with such sense perceptions. . . . The only justification for our concepts and system of concepts is that they serve to represent the complex of our experiences; beyond this they have no legitimacy.

> [*The Meaning of Relativity*]

We can carry the proposed identification of Einstein with positivism two steps further. First, empiricist and positivist strains of thought arose in modern times partly as protest movements, directed against the abstractive excesses of "metaphysicians and theologians." In the same context with the last citation, Einstein voices the conviction that

> . . . the philosophers have had a harmful effect upon the progress of scientific thinking in removing certain fundamental concepts from the domain of empiricism, where they are under our control, to the intangible heights of the *a priori*.

Secondly, there are even hints that Einstein may belong to that school of extreme positivists (early Hume and Mach) who hold always in the forefront the "fact" that all scientific discourse is concerned with the immediate data of experience; on this view scientific and philosophic soundness is to be obtained by de-emphasizing and cutting away, whenever possible, the fictitious structure of concepts and principles with which we have unwittingly overlaid bare experience. Discussing his discovery of the special theory of relativity, Einstein wrote in later years that he was indebted to Hume and Mach for showing him the type of "critical reasoning" which he required [*Autobiographical Notes*]. And in his original presentation of the *general* theory of relativity we find the following enunciation of principle:

> No answer [to a physical question] can be admitted as epistemologically satisfactory unless the reason given is an observable *fact of experience*. The law of causality has not the significance of a statement as to the world of experience, except when *observable facts* ultimately appear as causes and effects.

> [**"The Foundation of the General Theory of Relativity"**]

3. THE TEXTUAL QUESTION: THE CASE FOR A NEGATIVE ANSWER.

We have now seen the evidence and the fundamental argument in favor of the view that Einstein is a positivist, or that Einstein's special theory of relativity somehow entails positivism. Preliminary doubts can be cast upon this thesis by a wider survey of Einstein's writings. There are available, first, some comments directed specifically against the empiricist trend in philosophy of science. In 1922, he had this to say of Mach:

> Mach's system studies the existing relations between data of experience; for Mach, science is the totality of these relations. That point of view is wrong, and, in fact, what Mach has done is to make a catalogue, not a system . . . His view of science, that it deals with immediate data, led him to reject the existence of atoms.

> [*Nature,* 18 August 1923]

Mach's scepticism in regard to atoms apparently made a great impression on Einstein, for over twenty-five years later we find him writing as follows:

> The antipathy of [Oswald and Mach] towards atomic theory can indubitably be traced back to their positivistic philosophical position. This is an interesting example of the fact that even scholars of audacious spirit and fine instinct can be obstructed in the interpretation of facts by philosophical prejudices. The prejudice—which has by no means died out in the meantime—consists in the faith that facts by themselves can and should yield scientific knowledge without free conceptual construction.

> [*Autobiographical Notes*]

This is an astounding statement. We have become accustomed to hearing this kind of accusation from members of the Vienna Circle and their followers. Those whose philosophical tastes lie in other directions may take comfort from the fact that Einstein turns their own shaft against them.

Against Hume, we find the following remarks:

> As soon as one is at home in Hume's critique one

is easily led to believe that all those concepts and propositions which cannot be deduced from the sensory raw-material are, on account of their "metaphysical" character, to be removed from thinking. For all thought acquires material content only through its relationship with that sensory material. This latter proposition I take to be entirely true; but I hold the prescription for thinking which is grounded on this to be false. For this claim—if only carried through consistently—absolutely excludes thinking of any kind as "metaphysical."

> [**"Remarks on Bertrand Russell's Theory of Knowledge"**]

These citations record Einstein's objections to any movement which tends to define away conceptual structures. The evident alternative to such views is to maintain that "thinking", as distinct from picturing and perceiving generally, is not only irreducibly relevant to the scientific enterprise, but autonomous in the sense that concepts entering constitutively into physics are neither derivable from nor exclusively determined by sensory experience. And this is just what we find Einstein claiming, in the same context with the previous citation:

> In thinking we use, with a certain "right," concepts to which there is no access from the materials of sensory experience, if the situation is viewed from the logical point of view. . . . The concepts which arise in our thought and in our linguistic expressions are all—when viewed logically—the free creations of thought which can not be inductively gained from sense-experiences. This is not so easily noticed only because we have the habit of combining certain concepts and conceptual relations (propositions so definitely with certain sense-experiences that we do not become conscious of the gulf—logically unbridgeable—which separates the world of sensory experience from the world of concepts and propositions.)

Three times Einstein uses the qualification, "from a logical point of view." This is to warn against mistaking constant association (of "certain concepts" with "certain sense-experiences") for logical identity. Einstein is not trying to cut concepts loose from experience, nor does he wish to deny that experience may—often does—seem so closely interwoven with some concept or conceptual relation as to suggest a continuity or identity between them. All that he wishes to assert—and this is a great deal—is that such intimacy is always psychological or pragmatic, never logical. Concepts, or at least the key concepts of mathematical physics, are always distinct from the sense-data with which they are customarily associated.

At this stage we have the kernel of a theory of the epistemology of science; fortunately, it has been spelled out in somewhat greater detail by Einstein himself in the 1936 article, **"Physics and Reality."** To anticipate, it will be seen that Einstein firmly recommends a dualistic epistemology, as over and against the monisms implicit in positivistic attempts to reduce theoretical structures to functions of sensory experience.

The exposition in **"Physics and Reality"** is designed to account, step by step, for the concept of the "real external world" which we develop first in common sense and later in mathematical physics. The first step is as follows:

> I believe that the first step in the setting of a "real external world" is the formation of the concept of bodily objects and of bodily objects of various kinds. Out of the multitude of our sense experiences we take, mentally and arbitrarily, certain repeatedly occurring complexes of sense impression (partly in conjunction with sense impressions which are interpreted as signs for sense experiences of others), and we attribute to them a meaning—the meaning of the bodily object. Considered logically this concept is not identical with the totality of sense impressions referred to; but it is an arbitrary creation of the human (or animal) mind. On the other hand, the concept owes its meaning and its justification exclusively to the totality of the sense impressions which we associate with it.

The main idea is quite clear: concepts are built up out of sense experience but in an arbitrary or free way. The last sentence, to the effect that the concept "owes its meaning and justification exclusively [*ausschliesslich*] to the totality of the sense impressions . . ." looks perhaps like a reductionist statement, yet runs directly counter to the assertion that the concept is "not identical" with its associated sensory materials. Apparently, Einstein is aware that the early part of the paragraph, with its emphasis on (logical) arbitrariness and freedom, might suggest that science is engaged in telling fairy stories; the point is that verification in the field of sensory experience is always required, and is to be accomplished in ways to emerge shortly. We are, after all, only in the first step.

> The second step is to be found in the fact that, in our thinking (which determines our expectation), we attribute to this concept of the bodily object a significance, which is to a high degree independent of the sense impression which originally gives rise to it. This is what we mean when we attribute to the bodily object "a real existence." The justification of such a setting rests exclusively on the fact that, by means of such concepts and mental relations between them, we are able to orient ourselves in the labyrinth of sense impressions. These concepts and relations, although free statements of our thoughts, appear to us as stronger and more unalterable than the individual sense experience itself, the character of which as anything other than the result of an illusion or hallucination is never completely guaranteed. On the other hand, these concepts and relations, and indeed the setting of real objects and, generally speaking, the existence of the "real world," have justification only in so far as they are connected with sense impressions between which they form a mental connection.

In this paragraph, the emphasis on mental aspects is strengthened, although we are warned again that a "connection" with experience is still required. The passage from the "first step" to the "second step" is roughly this: In the first stage a collection of sensory materials is selected out and made to carry a significance. The significance lies, presumably, in the very fact that *this* collection of

sense qualities enjoys a regularity of association such that a unity over and above their bare togetherness in sensation is suggested. This unity comes from us, however, not from the manifold of sensation. In the second stage, a real existence is attributed to this unified collection, such that they become the characters (in some sense) of an object supposed to have an independent and continuing existence. It is in this respect that the concept of the object begins to be "to a high degree independent of the sense impression which originally gives rise to it." The similarity of this analysis to Kantian developments is evident, and I hardly think it would be denied that the basic insight is Kant's. The advantage of Einstein's formulation here is that it suggests a mechanism of prediction and verification. "It is our thinking," he avers, "which determines our expectation." When our expectations are disappointed, we have a case where our thinking has gone wrong; and the more our expectations are fulfilled, the more confident we become that our thinking is on the right lines.

Einstein next turns briefly to the fact that the sensory manifold is open to the manipulations of mind so as to produce an "order" in it. This, he thinks, is an ultimate mystery: the comprehensibility of experience is itself incomprehensible. He then continues with the main theme:

> In my opinion, nothing can be said concerning the manner in which the concepts are to be made and connected, and how we are to coordinate them to the experiences. In guiding us in the creation of such an order of sense experiences, success in the result is alone the determining factor. All that is necessary is the *statement* of a set of rules, without which knowledge in the desired sense would be impossible.

This passage offers two significant aspects. In the first place, it reaffirms, unmistakably, the freedom of mind to construct at will, provided that the resulting constructions are adequate to the ultimate task of explicating sense experience, i.e., provided they furnish a genuinely public world of genuine predictive power. Second, a distinction is opened out between the concepts themselves and their relations to the sensory manifold. This distinction *must* be kept separate from the primary distinction between concepts and sensations, as will be seen in the sequel.

What is meant by the necessity of "the statement of a set of rules?" Presumably, such rules are required primarily for the relations of the concepts as among themselves. What then shall we say of the connections between the concepts and sensation?

> The connection of the elementary concepts of everyday thinking with complexes of sense experiences can only be comprehended intuitively and it is unadaptable to scientifically logical fixation. The totality of these connections—none of which is expressible in conceptual terms—is the only thing which differentiates the great building which is science from a logical but empty scheme of concepts. By means of these connections, the purely conceptual theorems of science become statements about complexes of sense experiences.

Here the distinction between concepts on the one hand

and their connection to experience on the other is deepened. The former are the very stuff of science, and the latter (the connections) can only be grasped intuitively; yet it is only through the latter that science is rooted in experience, i.e., it is through them that empirical verification is possible at all.

Here, Einstein's vocabulary and the evident drift of his thought are reminiscent of later epistemological developments due to Northrop and Margenau. In their view, there are two dimensions in any deductive science. One dimension consists of entities postulated for existence, with postulated properties expressible in mathematically precise ways; it may also be true that the properties are expressible *only* in mathematical ways. Further properties of, and relations among, these entities are then deducible. The other dimension consists of relations between some entities, or states of those entities, and the realm of immediate sensory experience. These relations are called "rules of correspondence" (Margenau) or "epistemic correlations" (Northrop). On this view, the postulated theory gives science its objectivity, while the epistemic correlations provide its predictive power. It seems to be no small advantage of this approach that the same view, or something very much like it, is recommended by Einstein. The principal point is the sharp distinction, already noted, between theoretical structures themselves and the rules which relate them to associated complexes of sensory experience. I do not wish, here, to aver that this theory is necessarily correct, or that it solves all problems; but it does seem to me to offer a logical minimum which any non-positivist view of the nature of scientific knowing must embody. Accordingly, I shall avail myself in what follows of the terminology of the (Einstein-) Northrop-Margenau epistemology. In particular, the phrase "epistemic correlation," as referring to relations between the two epistemological realms, will be useful. It should be noted that this view is avowedly a "bifurcation" theory, in the sense that it holds that there are two "natures" available for analysis and discrimination: the "sensed nature" of immediate experience, and the "postulated nature" of (verified) theoretical construction.

To return to Einstein, there are several points from the essay **"Physics and Reality"** which need further discussion, and which perhaps need to be taken with some caution.

(i) Although the nominal subject of his discussion is a technical science, Einstein is nevertheless seen to be speaking primarily (so far) about the "elementary concepts of everyday thinking." Apparently, he is here thinking of common-sense or "perceptual" objects: chairs, stones, people, etc. In maintaining that these are designated by concepts, he is in effect maintaining that these objects as conceived are distinct from what is given to sense-experience. This notion harks back at least to Berkeley, although he drew a very different moral from the fact. That it *is* a fact is, I should think, beyond doubt. One is reminded in this connection of Russell's "neutral monism"; desiring to draw a connection between immediate sense-experience and theoretical physics, Russell nevertheless found himself entangled in Herculean struggles, attempting to cope with the far simpler fact that we think of a

penny as a three-dimensional disc, and perceive it as a flat ellipse. The point is that Einstein, by distinguishing sharply between the perceived world and the conceived world, is not placing science in some mysterious realm whose inner workings are open only to a trained priesthood; he is thinking of science as a systematic refinement of certain methods which pervade common sense as well.

(ii) The character of science as a refinement of common sense methods emerges in subsequent passages of the essay in question. Einstein speaks of a hierarchy of concepts and relations, such that the lower levels can be logically derived from the higher levels, while the higher levels are increasingly spare, increasingly abstract, and increasingly powerful in their deductive scope. On this view, the function of science is the elaboration of increasingly abstract postulate-sets from which the rest of the structure can be deduced. The whole structure is then anchored to experience (if it *is;* and it has to be if it is to be science and not pure mathematics) through the fact that the concepts of the lower layer are epistemic correlates of certain sense experiences.

This is a sweeping vision. It shows, for example, how it is that gross perceptual objects sitting on a laboratory bench can mediate between abstractly-defined entities and certain sensory occurrences; they can do so simply because they are designated by concepts of the lower layer. But this vision needs to be qualified, since it is perhaps a little too sweeping, and too simple. It suggests, first, that the concepts of the lower layer are frozen, and this ignores the sweeping changes in theoretical understanding which can—and sometimes do—modify the "elementary concepts of everyday thinking." It is extremely doubtful that a meteorologist thinks of, say, a cloud in the same way as a resident of fifth-century Athens, although there is a good chance that the latter had a better education and a more open mind. Secondly, Einstein's spare statement encourages one to think that only concepts of a certain layer (the lowest) can be epistemic correlates. This may be usually true, but it is evidently not necessarily the case. Consider, for example, the correlation of a certain shade of blue with a certain electromagnetic frequency; the postulated phenomenon which is the epistemic correlate of the sensed blue is not designated by an "elementary concept" in Einstein's sense. Other examples are easily found, and there is no *logical* reason why epistemic correlations cannot be chosen arbitrarily, in violence to the instincts of common sense, where the demands of theory seem to require it.

(iii) Lastly, Einstein has said (see above) that the connection between concepts and sensory experience is "unadaptable to scientifically logical fixation." At first glance this is a puzzler: he appears to be saying that epistemic correlations are themselves somehow outside the range of science, whereas in one sense it is precisely the job of science to explicate that which lies "behind" or within our experience, and to specify the relations between them. There are three possible interpretations of this somewhat cryptic remark, and all are illuminating.

First, he could be using the phrase "scientifically logical fixation" to refer to the deductive relations which are exhibited in a developed science like physics. Deductions, however, are possible only with concepts, not with sensations. In order to define, as it does, a public world, the deductive conceptual structures of a science cannot contain private episodes of sensory experiences as ingredients. This is so merely because the episodes *are* private. You cannot have my sensations. To be sure, you can have sensations very much like mine, and you can know that the sensations you are having which are very much like mine *are* very much like mine, but you cannot have *mine*. What science requires is something *shareable*—and it is the concept which fulfills this need (although there may be deeper phenomenological mysteries surrounding this fact). Consequently, no concrete episode of sensory experience can legitimately appear inside the deductive structure of a science like physics. For Einstein, not only is physics *not* about sensations, but in its theoretical part it is logically indifferent to the existence of sensory experience at all. It follows that epistemic correlations between the theoretical part of science and immediate experience are likewise not candidates for direct inclusion in the main deductive structure, and can only be "comprehended intuitively."

As a second possibility, attention can be fixed on the term "unadaptable." The meaning may be that the detailed structure of concepts and epistemic correlations which obtains at some given time is theoretically open to complete logical anatomization, but presents in practice a task so prolix as to suggest that the correlations at least are "unadaptable" to such "logical fixation." If this is not Einstein's meaning, the point still seems good. A complete specification of the correlations and concepts involved in a deductive science would amount to a complete axiomatization of that science: an axiomatization, moreover, which would require *both* a specification of fundamental entities and relations *and* a specification of the epistemic correlations which (hopefully) link selected parts of the theoretical structure with immediate experience in precise ways.

As a third possibility, and again a point worth noting, Einstein may be thinking here of the "haziness" which seems to infect much if not all of our perceptual experience in varying degrees. A relation, one of whose relata is not a precisely delimitable and distinct entity, will be itself infected with the contagion of vagueness to some degree, and consequently resistive to "scientifically logical fixation." In any case, these three considerations taken together should suffice to warn us against an easy identification of all the epistemic correlations vital to the empirical grounding of any particular science at any particular time. In part, this is due to the fact that the worker in the field always tends to ignore or take for granted the epistemological and logical foundations of his science, sometimes to his peril but often to his advantage. It may then require considerable interpretation and reinterpretation before an analytically clear structure begins to emerge. Even worse, there may be contending interpretations. What remains outside contention (on this view) is the picture of an ideally logically pure science exhibiting the two dimensions of theoretical construct plus epistemic correlation, this picture functioning as a guide for criticism and analysis, and as a source of possibilities for new researches.

4. THE TECHNICAL QUESTION: THE CASE FOR A NEGATIVE ANSWER.

In a well-known remark, Einstein has warned that "if you want to find out anything from the theoretical physicists about the methods they use, . . . stick closely to one principle: don't listen to their words, fix your attention on their deeds" [**"On the Method of Theoretical Physics"**]. Accordingly, we shall now take a brief glance at the special theory of relativity in Einstein's own presentations of it. Two treatments will be examined, one technical and one "popular." It will be found that the first best exhibits the necessity for speculative freedom, and the other exhibits the necessity for holding to the distinction between concepts and epistemic correlations.

In his first relativity paper published at the beginning of the century, Einstein begins his considerations with a review of the difficulties in classical physical theory which he intended to overcome. These difficulties were of two sorts. In the first place, there were "asymmetries" of a disturbing character in Maxwell's theory of electromagnetism. If a conductor is in motion relatively to a magnet in its neighborhood, a potential difference will in general appear between the ends of the conductor. The amount of potential difference depends only on the relative motion between conductor and magnet. In the event that the conductor is stationary (in the Newtonian sense of absolute rest) while the magnet moves, Maxwell's equations specify the existence of an electrical field of force in the vicinity of the magnet; in the converse case, with magnet stationary and conductor moving, no such field occurs. This creates a muddle, for Maxwell's equations call for the existence of an entity (electrical field of force) in some circumstances and not in others, while no experimentally specifiable means of distinguishing the two sets of circumstances is at hand. (The voltage which appears depends only on the *relative* motion.) [**"On the Electrodynamics of Moving Bodies"**]

Closely related to this difficulty is another, now well-known. Electromagnetic signals (including light) are propagated with a finite and measurable velocity. When they cross an "empty space," they "move" with a fixed velocity relative to that space (or to the "ether" as its material embodiment). The earth and all things on it also so move. By measuring the relative velocity of the earth and an electromagnetic signal, the possibility is opened to a detection of the earth's motion in absolute space. The Michelson-Morley experiments were a definitive failure in this direction.

It should be noted, however, that there are troubles with the classical structure quite aside from the ether-drift experiments. The difficulty over the asymmetry of Maxwell's equations is peculiarly illuminating because of its almost purely speculative character: it expresses an intellectual unhappiness over something which has been detected in the theoretical structure of physics itself. The Michelson-Morley experiments occasioned the discovery—by Einstein—of other difficulties in explicating the physical significance of such fundamental conceptions as space and time. In no sense is it to be thought that relativity theory is invented to explain the ether-drift experiments, nor would it be possible to return to pre-relativity physics if those experiments were repeated with a positive result.

To return to Einstein's presentation. The conclusion to be drawn from both difficulties is that "the phenomena of electrodynamics . . . possess no properties corresponding to the idea of absolute rest." Of course, the same is true for the Galilean-Newtonian laws of *mechanics,* the equations for which are equally valid for all unaccelerated frames of reference, a fact sometimes referred to as the "classical principle of relativity." Alternatively, it is said that the equations of classical mechanics are invariant in form with respect to transformations leading from one unaccelerated frame of reference to another. In contrast with mechanics, classical electrodynamics (and optics) does not enjoy such invariance; to put the same point differently, the equations are not the same when referred to a system of reference at absolute rest as when referred to a system in uniform motion (as we have just seen). Einstein suggested that the laws of electrodynamics and optics should be equally "valid for all frames of reference for which the equations of mechanics hold good." And of course this desideratum can only be effected by a considerable modification of the fundamental conceptions of space and time. Again, attention is called to the highly theoretical level in which these considerations occur. It is clear that Einstein is not merely engaged in the positivistic task of reconstructing a conventional scheme of concepts (or functions) in order to bring it into harmony with a hitherto unknown and jarring datum.

The first constructive step is the elevation of the above desideratum into a postulate, known later as the "restricted principle of relativity":

1. All frames of reference, whether "at rest" or "in motion" in the classical sense, are equally valid for the description of physical processes, provided only that the "motion" (if any) is uniform.

To this is joined another postulate suggested by the results of the Michelson-Morley experiment:

2. The velocity of light *in vacuo* is constant, regardless of the state of motion of the emitting body.

Here we meet the fundamental difficulty, since these two principles appear to be contradictory, a fact which is easily seen intuitively. The apparent contradiction is removed in ways too familiar to warrant repeating. The point is that the first of these postulates (and possibly the other as well) is quite independent of direct experience; it tells us that our concepts must have a certain invariant structure, *regardless* of the experiences which confirm or disconfirm them.

The removal of the apparent contradiction between the two postulates above is of course accomplished through a redefinition of the meaning of simultaneity, and hence of space and time. Einstein begins with some considerations similar to those of section 1 of this paper, emphasizing the importance of a clear experimental or operational significance for physical ideas. He turns specifically to the problem of assigning time-coordinates to distant events. With each point in the space of some unaccelerated frame

of reference a clock is associated, and events at or near the clock receive their time-coordinates through the empirical observation of spatially contiguous simultaneities. Using two clocks "similar in all respects," we can establish local timescales associated with, say, two points A and B. "But it is not possible without further assumption to compare, in respect of time, an event at A with an event at B." We must now inquire as to the "further assumption."

From this point on, Einstein begins to build anew. As he proceeds in the construction of theory, appeal to sensation will fall further and further into the background. The leading idea in what follows is that the needed principles can and will be "established by definition."

Suppose A is a stationary point in some unaccelerated frame of reference. We wish to assign time-coordinates to events at B in such a way that these coordinates can in general be calculated from A. It is not enough that there should be a clock at B which we can inspect by telescope or get reports about, for then we should still lack any means of comparing the time-scale at B with our time-scale at A; in particular, we should not know whether the two clocks were synchronous, and we should not know how much time (measured in A's scale) elapsed while the report of the reading of B's clock was moving from B to A. Indeed, we so far have no meaning for synchronousness (simultaneity) aside from the case where the clocks are practically in the same place.

The bridge between A and B is then built with the aid of light-signals: "We establish *by definition* that the 'time' required by light to travel from A to B equals the 'time' it requires to travel from B to A." Then we imagine a light-ray departing from A, traveling to B, and being immediately reflected back to A. At A we note the time of departure and the time of return. In accordance with our "definition" we now assign to the event at B a time-coordinate mid-way between those noted at A. If, by observation or report, we find that the clock at B generally agrees with these assignments, the clocks are said to synchronize. It is *assumed* that the relation of synchronization as holding among clocks is symmetrical and transitive. From the logical point of view, the essential work in the establishment of the special theory of relativity has now been done.

It is important to be clear on the status of the "definition" just established. Everything turns on the notion that a light-signal goes from here to there and from there to here in equal times. There is no legitimate sense in which this stipulation can be directly verified. It would of course be an easy matter to reproduce the conditions of the imaginary experiment, and directly "measure" the time required for the light-rays to traverse the gap in either direction. But such "measurements" will always entail either the very principle in question, or some equally arbitrary (in the logical sense) assumption as to the comparability of separated clocks.

The theorems which emerge in the special theory, and their dramatic empirical confirmations, are a fascinating and familiar story. It is however fruitful to notice that the special theory does not seem to be complete in itself. Its success in deriving physical laws invariant with respect to all unaccelerated reference frames inevitably raises a question as to the distinction between accelerated and unaccelerated frames. Why should the former be invalid as standpoints from which to observe the physical scene? A few years later Einstein asserts, in fact, that "the laws of physics must be of such a nature that they apply to all systems of reference in any kind of motion" ["**The Foundation of the General Theory of Relativity**"]. This, the so-called general principle of relativity, is embodied in Einstein's general theory of relativity. Even there one cannot, I suppose, rest content, for this reason: there is a kind of unity between electrodynamics and mechanics at the level of the special theory (the laws of both are invariant with respect to the Lorentz transformations) which is lost in the general theory. Reestablishment of that unity at a higher level provides part of the motive for attempts to develop a "unified field theory."

The whole movement is an extension, more or less natural, of the methods of special relativity. It seeks to establish a public world of ever wider range of application, and in so doing it involves an ever greater retreat from any philosophical tradition which tends to make direct experience the archetype of knowledge. Einstein's words:

> The characteristics which especially distinguish the general theory of relativity and even more the new third stage of the theory, the unitary field theory, from other physical theories are the degree of formal speculation, the slender empirical basis, the boldness in theoretical construction and, finally, the fundamental reliance on the uniformity of the secrets of natural law and their accessibility to the speculative intellect.

[*New York Times,* 3 February 1929]

I should like now to turn to Einstein's own popular presentation of the foundations of his theory in *The Principle of Relativity*. In part, this will provide a further documentation of the argument of this section. It will also provide an opportunity to exhibit the power of the distinction between constructs and epistemic correlations (*neither* of which are to be confused with immediate experience) implicitly laid down in "**Physics and Reality.**" And lastly, the discussion of *Relativity* will provide a model of Einstein-the-supposed-positivist at work; if it is possible to understand the relevant portions of *Relativity* without supposing that Einstein is committed to some form of reductionistic empiricism, I will conclude that all the citations of section 2 of this paper have, in principle, been answered.

The discussion in *Relativity* begins with the supposition that lightning has struck a railway embankment *simultaneously* "at two places A and B far distant from each other." An imaginary reader is then asked if "there is sense in this statement" and it is supposed that he replies in the affirmative. Upon being pressed to supply the sense, the "reader" avers that "the significance of the statement is clear in itself," although some additional consideration is necessary if one is to "determine by observation whether in the actual case the two events took place simultaneously." There follows Einstein's assertion, previously quoted, that simultaneity has no meaning for the physicist or any-

one else unless the method for determining its fulfillment by observation is given.

In reply to this, the "reader" offers a new definition. He imagines an observer placed at a point midway between A and B, equipped with a V-shaped mirror by means of which he can observe both A and B at the same time. The lightning flashes are then said to be simultaneous if and only if they are seen in the mirror simultaneously. Einstein then raises the "objection" that a new presupposition has been brought in, namely, that light travels from A to M in the same time that it travels from B to M. "An examination of this suggestion," he continues, "would only be possible if we already had at our disposal the means of measuring time. It would thus appear that we are moving here in a logical circle." To this, the very wise reader is presumed to reply in the following way:

> There is only *one* demand to be made of the definition of simultaneity, namely, that in every real case it must supply us with an empirical decision as to whether or not the conception that has to be defined is fulfilled. . . . That light requires the same time to traverse the path *A—*to*—M* as for the path *B—*to*—M* is in reality neither a *supposition nor a hypothesis* about the nature of light, but a *stipulation* which I can make of my own free will in order to *arrive at a definition of simultaneity.*

This all sounds very much as if the meaning of simultaneity is to be conventionally reduced to some immediately sensed character (sensed simultaneity at the mirror). *But this would be an erroneous inference.*

In part, the difficulty derives from Einstein's language, particularly the statement that there is "only one demand" to be made of the definition in question. But the impression that we are here dealing with a reduction-definition derives mainly from the context. Einstein is displaying as clearly as possible the logically arbitrary character of the assumption that light travels at the same speed in every direction. This is clear from the last citation, and it is this purpose which is admirably served by the definition in terms of the V-shaped mirror. But we recall from the original 1905 paper that the fundamental aim in all this is to assign time-coordinates to events *at a distance.* Even in the present context, Einstein is engaged in discussing the simultaneity of the events at A and B, and these latter are unequivocally thought of as real outer events, not sense-data or functions of sense-data. This being the case, it is exceedingly hard to understand how the *meaning* of simultaneity of events at A and B can be *reduced* to a sensed simultaneity at the mirror, while the events themselves at A and B are not so reduced.

In fact, this is where we can profit from "**Physics and Reality.**" Confusion reigns here because of a failure to distinguish between the two non-sensory dimensions of the science in question. So far as the postulational structure of physics is concerned, the meaning of simultaneity is simply identity of time-coordinate, and this holds true both before and after Einstein. This conception has to be connected (*not* reduced) to experience, and this connection is effected through—if you wish—the definition in terms of the V-shaped mirror. But then the latter definition is *not* the sole meaning of simultaneity.

Again, Einstein sounds most like a positivist when he is emphasizing the necessity for having epistemic correlations; hence his constant demand that theoretically-conceived simultaneity for distant events be connected to some perceptual experience. The perceptual experience in question is a *sensed* simultaneity. In the context of **Relativity,** it is the sensed simultaneity of the two flashes seen side-by-side at the mirror. In the context of the 1905 paper, the required sensed simultaneity holds between the arrival of a signal and an observed position on the hands of a clock right along side. On the other hand, the existence of an epistemic correlation does not constitute a reduction of the concept to the perceptual experience; for the whole point is that it is through the concepts that the perceptual experiences fall into some kind of intelligible order.

Once more, the whole argument can be phrased in terms of the simultaneous events at the mirror themselves. Are these sensed events only, or is there some respect in which they are also physical events, i.e. occurrences postulated for existence whose whole nature is not exhausted by sensory components? Evidently they must also be physical events. For they bear a relevance to the distant events at A and B only because they are participants in a postulated physical process in which both pairs of events have a share. Consequently, the events at the mirror are themselves "bifurcated," i.e. they are both physical and sensed. We sense a pair of colored flashes against a shiny background, but we think of atomic or sub-atomic collisions involving light; otherwise it would be silly to suppose that events referred to the mirror are significant of a physical relation (simultaneity) between events elsewhere in space.

5. CONCLUSION: NEGATIVE.

I hope it is now clear that Einstein belonged, and rightly so, to the "metaphysical" school of the philosophy of science. Of course "metaphysical" has a pejorative meaning as well as a neutral one; in the former sense it means something like "unduly independent of experience." In *that* sense of the term, we owe to Einstein the discovery that some of our thinking about space and time had been "metaphysical," *and* we owe to him the discovery of a road leading away from the "metaphysical" to the more firmly "empirical." The hope of exhibiting these facts as clearly as possible formed part of the motive for sections I and IV of this paper.

But there is no rule restricting us to pejorative meanings unless we want to prejudice philosophical issues in advance. "Metaphysical" can also mean, vaguely speaking, "not wholly dependent upon experience." It is in this sense that Frank apparently intends the term, and it is in this sense that Einstein clearly belongs to the metaphysical school. For Einstein it is a patent fact that some kind of connection to the perceptual experience is always required for legitimate theory, but "connection to experience" does not imply *derivation from* experience, nor *reduction to* experience, nor exhibition as a conventional *function of* experience. The uncritical assumption that some such impli-

cation does hold good is responsible, I think, for much misunderstanding of Einstein.

Walter G. Creed   (essay date 1981)

SOURCE: "Is Einstein's Work Relevant to the Study of Literature?" in *After Einstein: Proceedings of the Einstein Centennial Celebration at Memphis State University, 14-16 March 1979*, edited by Peter Barker and Cecil G. Shugart, Memphis State University Press, 1981, pp. 203-11.

[*In the following essay, which was originally presented at the Einstein Centennial Celebration at Memphis State University in 1979, Creed contends that Einstein's theories may be successfully applied to the study of literature; however, Creed stresses that Einstein's belief in the fundamental value of experience in understanding and interpreting reality runs counter to much literary theory that emphasizes the importance of knowing reality only through abstract constructs such as language.*]

I am going to give a positive answer to the question my title poses: Einstein's work *is* relevant to the study of literature. But before I do, I must make some negative remarks.

First, Einstein had very little to say *directly* about literature. I know of only a few scattered comments in his letters, and these comments are rather ordinary. He was certainly not hostile to literature—in fact, he had a deep respect for writers as different as Dostoyevsky and George Bernard Shaw; but I find his remarks on literature of minor interest.

Second, although I am convinced that Einstein's physics can be relevant to literature, I find that most writers and critics have trivialized his theories in translating them into literature and criticism. The list of such trivializations is long, and most are based on the mistaken notion that the theories imply some sort of philosophical relativism. Almost no one has taken the trouble to become familiar with the theories themselves, either through Einstein's papers or other respectable expositions of them. Most have gone instead to sensational accounts like Sir James Jeans's *Physics and Philosophy*—as, for instance, Lawrence Durrell did when he took the form and philosophy for his novel-series, *The Alexandria Quartet,* from special relativity and the spacetime continuum. Critical applications of Einstein's theories have usually been no more sophisticated. Again just one example, from a critic who writes that in Thomas Mann's novel, *The Magic Mountain,* "Hans Castorp's stay in the TB sanatorium begins near the peak of the metaphoric space-time mountain. Space and time . . . set in densely. Castorp relishes time, on his arrival, minute by minute, space inch by inch; space-time, inch-minute by inch-minute."

My concern today, however, is not with the application of Einstein's physical theories to the study of literature, but with the relevance of his philosophy, particularly his philosophy of science. And this brings me to my third negative remark, which is that Einstein's work is *not* relevant to literature as long as many of the epistemological and ontological assumptions prominent in criticism today—

most of them connected in some way with contemporary science or its philosophy—are taken as final.

The first of these assumptions is that language is not merely a means of expression, used to give form to preexisting ideas, but the fundamental determinant of these ideas. Nietzsche wrote a century ago, "We have to cease to think if we refuse to do it in the prison-house of language"; and half a century ago Heidegger said, "*Language* speaks. *Man* speaks only insofar as he skillfully complies with language." Now, anyone who has struggled with language, particularly in attempting to express complex or subtle ideas, recognizes a measure of truth in these statements, though he may not want to go as far as they go. But others have gone farther, particularly twentieth-century linguists influential among literary critics. Edward Sapir, after extensive work with American Indian languages, came to the belief that our language

> powerfully conditions all our thinking about social problems and processes. Human beings do not live in the objective world alone . . . but are very much at the mercy of the particular language which has become the medium of expression for their society. It is quite an illusion to imagine that . . . language is merely an incidental means of solving specific problems of communication or reflection. The fact of the matter is that the "real world" is to a large extent unconsciously built up on the language habits of the group.

Thus the world we know—the only world we *can* know—is a world determined by our language; and this is true regardless of which language (or languages) we know.

Sapir made his statement in 1926. Much more recently, Roland Barthes, preeminent among French critics of the "structuralist" school, insisted even more strongly on the primacy of language, in an article titled "Science versus Literature." Barthes's aim was to attack the belief, fostered by science, that "language is simply an instrument" which can be "transparent and neutral" and which "is subordinate to the *matter* of science." "Every utterance," Barthes continued, "implies its own subject," and thus "objectivity is as imaginary as anything else." By its very nature, to the "science" of "writing" (structuralism in one of its several manifestations) belongs the task of "smash[ing] the theological idol set up by a paternalistic science," for "Only writing can oppose the self-assurance of the scientist" and point out to him the "sovereignty of language." Barthes directed his remarks against the scientist because he knew that every right-thinking literary critic is already well aware of language's "sovereignty."

I think it is worth stressing that Barthes is not arguing the *difficulty* of attaining objectivity but its *impossibility*. For him, the distinction Frege made in his *Grundlage* between the origin of an idea and its proof does not hold, since both are subtly controlled by psychological and social factors, the latter embedded in language itself. The British critic, Frank Kermode, made this same point in another context. Writing about "fictions"—those we live by as well as those we find in our imaginative literature, Kermode paused long enough to sweep the concepts and laws of physics in

with fictions; with, that is, those "mental structures" which are neither true nor false, subject neither "to proof [n]or disconfirmation," but only, like literary fictions, to "neglect" once they have outworn their usefulness. Kermode's justification for this (which comes, by way of Hannah Arendt, from Heisenberg and Bohr) is that the answers to the questions the physicist puts to nature are "purely human." All knowledge is, ultimately, self-knowledge.

The second assumption is that we have no valid criterion for determining what constitutes a poem or, by extension, any work of literature. A work *becomes* a poem when we decide to read and interpret it as such; otherwise it exists as a piece of prose, perhaps not even as a work of literature at all. To show how plausible this idea is, Jonathan Culler, an astute apologist and critic of structuralism, takes a short item from a French newspaper, prints it as a poem, and then shows how it can be *read* as a poem. Later he takes a short poem by William Carlos Williams and prints it as prose, and it *reads* like prose. If this view of the nature of poetry seems strange beyond belief, then think about Heisenberg's remarks on the path of the electron, which he says comes into existence only when measured and, by virtue of the limitations of measurement at the subatomic level, exists as a set of points and not as a continuous curve. The path has no existence as such until one measures it. So, neither a poem nor the path of a subatomic particle exists in and of itself, but only insofar as we decide to consider it as such. The poem and the path have no intrinsic reality. In criticism this idea leads to anarchy, to the principle that a well-turned argument is a valid argument; in physics it leads (along with other aspects of the Copenhagen interpretation) to controversies which have made quantum mechanics seem at times more like a branch of philosophy than an exact science.

The third assumption is the logical consequence of the first two. In the preface to his study of structuralism and Russian formalism, the American critic Fredric Jameson wrote "The history of thought is the history of its models." Jameson cited a number of models, including classical mechanics and the electromagnetic field, then charted the "lifetime" of a model, which "knows a fairly predictable rhythm":

> Initially, the new concept releases quantities of new energies, permits hosts of new perceptions and discoveries, causes a whole dimension of new problems to come into view, which result in turn in a volume of new work and research. Throughout this initial stage the model itself remains stable, for the most part serving as a medium through which a new view of the universe may be obtained and catalogued.

> In the declining years of the model's history, a proportionately greater amount of time has to be spent in readjusting the model itself, in bringing it back into line with its object of study. Now research tends to become theoretical rather than practical, and to turn back upon its own presuppositions (the structure of the model itself), finding itself vexed by the false problems and dilemmas into which the inadequacy of the model seems increasingly to lead it.

At length the model is exchanged for a new one.

If we substitute the term "paradigm" wherever Jameson uses "model," we get a description similar to Kuhn's view of science as moving from one set of concepts, theories, and so on to another set, without necessarily moving any closer to the truth about nature. Jameson cites *The Structure of Scientific Revolutions,* though not here and only in passing. But it is hardly coincidental that his model of the history of criticism looks so much like Kuhn's model of the history of science. Moreover, I think it would not be wrong to say that the two views have more in common than Jameson's description of "models" suggests. I refer specifically to Kuhn's sociologism, his assertion that "there is no standard higher than the assent of the relevant community" for determining which "paradigm"—or even, he implies, any problem solution—is to be considered correct.

Where does Einstein fit into this picture? Chiefly, I think, in opposition to these widespread and rather pessimistic beliefs about knowledge and reality. He believed in a real external world which one could, through daring hypotheses and patient, disciplined effort, come ever closer to knowing—not as a reflection of oneself, one's community, or even one's language, but as it really *is*. (I note in passing that Einstein committed the Nietzschean heresy, believing that he did not think within the "prison-house of language," but rather in signs and images.) And he had very good reasons for his belief; reasons which are ignored by many scientists and philosophers of science and by virtually all students of literature. This is a pity, because his belief could stand as a corrective to many of the excesses practiced (sometimes even in his name) in both philosophy and criticism these days.

I cannot explain or justify Einstein's belief in any detail today, but I can point to some of its important aspects and try to suggest why I find them compelling.

In his youth, Einstein became intensely religious for a while, then rejected religion as he began to read popular scientific books and to question the authority of the Bible and, with it, every kind of authority, most notably that of the state and the rigidly disciplined school system he was raised in. Looking back later at his brief spell as a believer, however, he saw it as "a first attempt to free myself from the chains of the 'merely personal,' from an existence which is dominated by wishes, hopes and primitive feelings." Soon after this, he realized that physics offered him a much finer opportunity to devote himself to something outside himself. "Out yonder," he wrote in one of the most striking passages of his autobiography,

> Out yonder there was this huge world, which exists independently of us human beings and which stands before us like a great, eternal riddle, at least partially accessible to our inspection and thinking. The contemplation of this world beckoned like a liberation . . . [and understanding it] swam as highest aim half consciously and half unconsciously before my mind's eye.

[*Albert Einstein: Philosopher-Scientist*]

The "religious paradise" Einstein gave up was that of conventional religion. He never again espoused a sectarian faith; but he did come to believe in what he called "cosmic religion." This religion "knows no dogma and no God conceived in man's image"; it moves beyond anthropomorphism to a view of God as nothing more—nor less—than the "sublimity and marvelous order which reveal themselves both in nature and in the world of thought." The Greeks were the first to catch a glimpse of this sublimity, and thereafter it became one of the inspiriting forces of scientific advancement. It led, after centuries, to what we now call the scientific method, and it leads as well—as Einstein's relentless fight for peace and constant concern for others amply demonstrate for one life—to release from the "prison" of "individual existence," and it allows one to "experience the universe as a single significant whole."

The study of physics, as Einstein conceived of it, and the glimpse of the "marvelous order" to which it led him seem very much like the way the study of literature was often thought of until a few decades ago. In fact, Einstein sounds a little like Matthew Arnold when he says of his "cosmic religion" that "it is the most important function of art and science to awaken this feeling and keep it alive." Much contemporary criticism, on the contrary, focuses on the work in relation to the self, glorifying individual and idiosyncratic responses rather than encouraging a view of the work and the self in relation to the world. Resting on premises akin to the linguist-structuralist concept of language in much the same way that subjectivism in physics arises from apparently objective positivist premises, it invites the reader to believe that he can know the work only as a reflection of himself.

The larger view is not easily won, as Einstein well knew from his struggles to grasp nature's secrets. But that it could be won was a conviction he held to throughout his career. Look at his world-view from another perspective. In his Herbert Spencer lecture of 1933, Einstein posed and answered a crucial question:

> If . . . it is true that the axiomatic basis of theoretical physics cannot be extracted from experience but must be freely invented, can we ever hope to find the right way? Nay, more, has this right way any existence outside our illusions? Can we hope to be guided safely by experience at all when there exist theories (such as classical mechanics) which to a large extent do justice to experience without getting to the root of the matter?

["On the Method of Theoretical Physics"]

Einstein's answer was unequivocal: "there is, in my opinion, a right way, and . . . we are capable of finding it." This answer may seem strange, coming from the very man who proved to nearly everyone's satisfaction that classical mechanics, long felt to be the one true description of the physical universe, does not get "to the root of the matter." Yet the answer is perfectly in keeping with his epistemology, which combines empiricism and rationalism, taking the best aspects of each and rejecting what is problematic.

Knowledge of the physical world is not to be sought directly, through induction, but indirectly, by way of imaginative guesses—bold theories or hypotheses guided by mathematical principles. Induction from experience will not yield the secrets of nature; first, because physics has advanced beyond the explanation of surface phenomena to the abstract laws which lie beneath them; second, because unbiased observation is not possible. "[K]nowledge cannot spring from experience alone," Einstein said, "but only from the comparison of the inventions of the intellect with observed fact."

But if induction from experience will not lead us to the general laws governing the universe, experience is nevertheless "the supreme arbiter." In fact, as Einstein said elsewhere, "all knowledge of reality starts from experience and ends in it," so that "experience is the alpha and the omega of all our knowledge of reality." The physicist, prompted to explain the phenomena of his everyday world, finds the ultimate *test* of his explanations in this same world. Thus every theory, though conceived by an imaginative act, must be constructed so as to yield, through rigorous logical deduction, empirical consequences which can be tested by anyone with the proper training and instruments. In this way Einstein combines rationalism (setting up the theory) with empiricism (testing the theory). His method demands numerous guesses and also demands that the many wrong guesses we are bound to make be dismissed. Man proposes, but nature disposes—ruthlessly. And what nature fails to dispose of, other scientists try their best to finish off.

Here, too, we have in barest outline a model for criticism. First, it suggests that we give up the notion that a poem is a poem only when we consider it as such, and that instead we attribute to it enough self-identity to keep it from dissolving into prose when we stop thinking about it. Second, the model suggests that rather than regard our interpretations as "fictions," as Kermode and others, especially the structuralists, would have us do, we take them as either true or false. More specifically, it suggests that we should make bold hypotheses, guided by formal criteria, and that we accept the fact that most of our hypotheses will be refuted by a closer reading of the text, or fail to stand up to further critical scrutiny. The model also calls for formal criteria to play a role analogous to the role mathematics and logic play in the natural sciences. I have only the vaguest notion of what these criteria might be—a few critics have begun, I think, to formulate some that may well be valid; but I am convinced that they must not perpetuate the sociologism Kuhn argues for in the sciences and which now operates pervasively and perniciously in literary criticism.

But no criterion can be accepted a priori. Einstein rejected the Kantian category of the "synthetic a priori," both explicitly, in some of his essays, and implicitly, by destroying the concepts of absolute space and time and in replacing Euclidean with Riemannian geometry as the geometry of the real world. This suggests that whatever criteria are adopted, they must be submitted to constant reappraisal in light of experience. It also suggests that no "language" has an absolute hold on us; and here I am thinking not only of spoken and written languages but of the language of mathematics. No one nowadays shares Descartes's faith in mathematics as the sole key to the physical universe, as

the language in which the Book of Nature is written. Today mathematics is widely believed to be a human invention, which grows and changes in interaction with experience. So, too, with natural languages. That these languages partially constrain and determine our view of the world and what we can say about it is, as I said earlier, true. But that they do not absolutely determine our world-view is, I think, almost self-evident—though not to many contemporary students of literature.

Einstein knew this in another context. He was well aware that "everyday thinking" is a complex affair. In his essay on **"Physics and Reality,"** he argued that the physicist, in analyzing what he does and its implications, must not restrict himself "to the examination of the concepts of his own specific field," that he cannot even get started "without considering critically a much more difficult problem, the problem of analyzing the nature of everyday thinking." Thus Einstein moved the analysis of the scientific method back to the thinking process, to the common ground from which all views of the world originate. He suggested that we do not simply observe the world, since that would result in a chaos of sense impressions. Instead, we form *concepts,* and from them build up our picture of the world:

> Out of the multitude of our sense experiences we take . . . certain repeatedly occurring complexes of sense impressions . . . and we correlate to them a concept—the concept of the bodily object. Considered logically this concept is not identical with the totality of sense impressions referred to; but it is a *free creation of the human . . . mind.*

This much corresponds to what linguists like Sapir and structuralists like Barthes say about language. But whereas they ignore the feedback process, the impact of our experience on our ideas about the world, Einstein recognizes its essential role. Concepts and their interrelationships, formed as "free mental creations," are continually compared with experience, and they are justified "only in so far as they are connected with sense impressions between which they form a mental connection."

During his lifetime, Einstein dared to challenge some of the most venerated laws of physics and principles of mathematics. Now, a hundred years after his birth, we can find in his philosophy a challenge to some of the most fashionable epistemological and ontological principles of literary criticism, as well as suggestions for formulating better principles to take their place.

Erwin Hiebert   (essay date 1984)

SOURCE: "Einstein's Image of Himself as a Philosopher of Science," in *Transformation and Tradition in the Sciences: Essays in Honor of I. Bernard Cohen*, edited by Everett Mendelsohn, Cambridge University Press, 1984, pp. 175-90.

[*In the following essay, Hiebert explores Einstein's position as a philosopher of science—as opposed to merely being a scientist—and his own views of himself as such.*]

Since antiquity, natural philosophers and scientists have expressed the conviction that the observational and experimental study of nature brings with it a good measure of intellectual and aesthetic satisfaction. Indeed, scientists on the whole claim to derive considerable personal pleasure from their work. I believe these claims are true. Now it seems plausible to assert that the machinery of human perception and cognition is both biologically structured and socially motivated to accentuate certain characteristic benchmarks of excellence in human performance. These distinctive characteristics are by no means the property of scientists. They certainly are seen to be prominent as well in the arts and humanities. Still, they are glaringly visible in the work of scientists.

To be more specific, we might mention in this context a number of criteria of excellence: structure, order, and symmetry; the power of metaphor and analogical reasoning; comprehensiveness; simplicity—or a move in the direction of efficiency and economy of thought and expression; prediction into the unknown; logical rigor and internal consistency; and elegance of conception and formulation. All of these criteria obviously occupy a position of high priority among scientists, but, of course, as already intimated, scientists by no means have a corner on them.

In view of the fact that the sciences have been conspicuously successful, from the standpoint of the criteria just mentioned, it comes as no surprise to discover that scientists and their accomplishments and methods have provided the subject matter for perennial analysis by philosophers, historians, psychologists, anthropologists, theologians, and sociologists. In spite of all the commendable analyses, dissections, and reconstructions that scientists and their methods have been subjected to, we may find it shocking to see how inadequately they deem themselves to have been analyzed by others external to their intellectual and professional framework. Indeed, scientists frequently are at a loss even to identify themselves in the analyses of outsiders who purport to be examining what goes on in their own special disciplines. Although this may be a commonly encountered phenomenon, viz., the questioning or rejection by insiders of the analyses of outsiders, perhaps it tells us that the insiders are (or think they are) playing quite a different game. At minimum they are analyzing that game in another way. In any case, we have here a number of competing perspectives.

Let me express this observation in another way. At least since the middle of the nineteenth century, scientists have become increasingly more confident that professional, working scientists, on their own, can provide the most meaningful philosophy of science that is feasible. Whether this is true or not, historians of science are increasingly anxious to understand what kind of game scientists believe they are playing. Thus, this essay focuses almost exclusively on the question of the scientist's self-image.

If, in fact, there is widespread consensus among scientists that they do not really recognize themselves in treatises devoted to analyzing their methods and their work and behavior as scientists, then it is appropriate to suggest that there may be some positive merit in studying and evaluating their own self-reflections, namely, those in which they

attempt to tell us what they do and how and why. Conceivably, some of the most pertinent questions to be explored in the philosophy of science touch on these aspects of the scientific enterprise that characterize the distinctive ways in which scientists see and understand themselves and their work.

Quite simply, what do scientists *claim* to be doing when they allege that they are engaged in scientific activity? What are the motivations, what methods (if any) are consciously cultivated; and what constitutes evidence to buttress an argument or support an explanatory hypothesis? Such questions have dimensions that can be explored profitably for the perspectives of history, psychology, the logic of science, conceptual frameworks, and various environmental contexts. But no n-dimensional analysis will help us here. We must adopt a more modest objective.

Against a specific conception of intention and outlook, viz., one that attempts to look at the scientist in the role of philosopher of science, I have undertaken a study of the self-image analysis of a number of scientists in hopes that some intrinsic pattern will emerge, if not for scientists in general, perhaps for scientists within a given discipline; and, at least within the more specialized domain of a particular science.

What I propose to do here is to examine one particular scientist's attempt to play the role of philosopher of science, namely, Albert Einstein. The rationale for this choice is that we recently celebrated Einstein's 100th birthday. Birthdays aside, the case for Einstein, his own self-image, and his view of himself as a philosopher of science provides a splendid example of the genre of questions this study purports to illuminate.

First let us mention a few landmarks in Einstein's career. In 1902, after completion of his studies at the Polytechnic in Zurich, Einstein became a Swiss citizen and worked for six years in the patent office in Bern. It was there between 1905 and 1906, when he was in his mid-twenties, that Einstein published four papers that contributed conspicuously to establishing the direction of twentieth-century theoretical physics. As is well known, these papers are models of originality, clarity, and elegance. They deal with totally diverse topics: the light quantum hypothesis, a theory of Brownian motion, an analysis of the electrodynamics of moving bodies that incorporates new views on the structure of space and time into a special theory of relativity, and a paper on the relation of the inertia and energy, or the general equivalence of the mass and energy, of a body. In one way or another, this early work of Einstein—each paper a landmark in its own right—sets the stage not only for much of his subsequent scientific work, but also for the direction of his philosophical reflections.

In 1913, after short intervals at the University of Zurich, the University of Prague, and the Polytechnic in Zurich, Einstein moved to Berlin. There, three years later, in 1916, he essentially completed his first enunciation of the general theory of relativity. The theory received its first confirmation in 1919 with the observation of the deflection of light in a gravitational field. Einstein certainly regarded his general theory of relativity as his true lifework. He said of his other contributions that they were *Gelegenheitsarbeit,* that is, performed as the occasion arose. But Max Born wrote that Einstein "would be one of the greatest physicists of all times even if he had not written a single line on relativity." In fact, Einstein received the Nobel Prize for 1921 for such *Gelegenheitsarbeit,* namely, the theory of the photoelectric effect.

In his later years Einstein turned his attention more and more to the object, methods, and limits of science. In exercising these rights, namely to pursue the philosophy of science as a scientist, Einstein was completely in step with the trends that had been set by late nineteenth-century investigators and that were being perpetuated with vigor, if not always with logical rigor, by the scientists who belonged to his generation. In his 1936 essay on physics and reality, Einstein tells us why it is not right for the physicist to let the philosopher take over the philosophy of science, especially at a time when the very foundations of science are problematic. He says: "The physicist cannot simply surrender to the philosopher the critical contemplation of the theoretical foundations: For he himself knows best, and feels more surely, where the shoe pinches." For Einstein, the philosophy of science definitely called for an in-depth knowledge of science.

On the other hand, Einstein by no means assumed that the narrow scientific specialist was qualified as a philosopher of science:

> The whole of science is nothing more than a refinement of everyday thinking. It is for this reason that the critical thinking of the physicist cannot possibly be restricted to the examination of the concepts of his own field. He cannot proceed without considering critically a much more difficult problem, the problem of analyzing the nature of everyday thinking.

Certainly here is a viewpoint that mirrors one of the central themes of Mach and the nineteenth-century critical positivists.

As already stated, our main objective is to search out such self-reflective aspects of Einstein's career as may shed light on the conception he had of himself as a philosopher of science. Before doing so, however, I would like to offer an explanation for approaching the subject in the way here indicated. It is advisable to be open and honest about one's methodology and specifically to mention at this point that the self-image study this approach entails has its own intrinsic complexities. We cannot take the time to outline them here. Suffice it to say that not the least vexatious of the difficulties encountered is that scientists, including Einstein, in analyzing their own motivations and methodological directives, are apt to construct self-images that conform to what their scientific communities expect of them. Thus, in an attempt to become philosophical and sophisticated about these matters, scientists are prone to fulfill the prophecy of philosophical climates of opinion. These may relate to such factors as a hierarchy within the sciences vis-à-vis theory and experiment, master-pupil relationships, schools of thought, centers of research activity, and so on.

So we might as well acknowledge explicitly and candidly

that there are some severe limitations imposed upon the investigator who chooses this approach, namely, to focus on what scientists *say* they are doing when they claim to be engaged in science, rather than analyzing more single-mindedly their published scientific contributions in order to discover *what they do* when they claim to be engaged in science. In relation to this issue, Einstein once said:

> If you want to find out anything from the theoretical physicists about the methods they use, I advise you to stick closely to one principle: don't listen to their words, fix your attention on their deeds. To him who is a discoverer in this field, the products of his imagination appear so necessary and natural that he regards them, and would like to have them regarded by others, not as creations of thought but as given realities.

If Einstein has suggested here that one should not listen to what scientists *say* they do, but rather look at their *works* in order to learn *what* they do, he also confessed in his autobiography (or in his obituary as he called it): "The essential in the being of a man of my type lies precisely in what he thinks, not in what he does or suffers." We discover that over the years, Einstein, as so many other scientists, surrendered to the temptation to reify his own methodological preferences into a credo that guided him in all of his work—at least that is what he seems to want to tell us. But it is not that simple.

The point that needs to be stressed in advance, with these remarks, is that what a scientist *really* does, if we may speak that way, is not revealed to the historian of science unambiguously, either by an analysis of the scientist's reflective and retrospective account of what is going on, or by an examination of the finished, formal, published, product. In my opinion, anything that contributes to the clarification of the methodological question about how science advances, or retrogresses, is fair game for the historian.

Suffice it to say that one way to search out the self-image of Einstein as a philosopher of science, and to discover the way in which he conceives of his own work and thought within the context of the scientific currents of his times, is to listen seriously to what he has to say as he reflects on these matters in so many of his essays and lectures. Besides, the historian can take advantage of Einstein, so to speak, by invading his more unbuttoned, private, and internal life, to examine the uninhibited outpourings of his soul as revealed in the correspondence and informal interchanges with his most intimate friends and invisible opponents. Although this invasion may not be quite fair to a man like Einstein, since he undoubtedly never intended to add these documents to the historical record, they in fact substantially help to answer the questions that have been posed here.

I want to assert that Einstein had two self-images of himself and his work. The self-image that dominated his early career may be characterized by an attraction to critical positivism and the empirical status of theories advocated by Ernst Mach. The other more mature, more consciously worked out self-image of Einstein, and the one I want to talk about here, was one in which Mach's sensationalism and pluralism were abandoned and replaced by a realistic, unitary, and deterministic world view that lays claim to the intuitive recognition, or near-recognition, of rock-bottom truths about nature. Concerning his mature position Einstein wrote: "My epistemological credo . . . actually evolved only much later (in life), and very slowly, and does not correspond with the point of view I held in younger years."

We might mention here, parenthetically, that Einstein's dualistic image confronts us with a paradox: Virtually all of his most creative and lasting achievements were made while he was under the influence of a philosophy that he later categorically rejected. Or had he not thought through the consequences of his philosophy for his science? In fact, why does Einstein not struggle with the question of the influence of his own philosophy of science on his scientific work?

To analyze with psychological insight and historical credibility the many reflective accounts of Einstein that reveal something substantive about his self-image as a philosopher of science is an undertaking that would be far too ambitious on this occasion. Therefore we are confronted with the more modest objective of examining the way in which Einstein was prodded into explaining his philosophical position by two of his closest colleagues and critics, namely, Arnold Sommerfeld and Max Born. In both cases we have at our disposal a substantial portion of correspondence and intellectual interchange that covers a period of almost forty years.

Sommerfeld and Einstein both were enthusiastically committed to the technical mastery and critical evaluation of everything that transpired in the intellectual realm of relativity and quantum mechanics during the revolutionary era of physics from 1900 to 1930. However no two persons could have followed the shifting scientific scenario from more diverse perspectives. We learn that Einstein, the philosopher, with cool detachment, was attracted to general overarching unitary principles and through the years became increasingly impatient with, and even hostile toward, quantum mechanics with all of its outlandish baggage of indeterminacy, statistical and probability functions, and discontinuity: He simply felt that the future of physics lay more in geometry, and therefore in continuum theory, than in particles. Intellectually independent, he continued for decades to puzzle deeply about scientific questions that most physicists had accepted as self-evident. Despite his tremendous scientific contributions, he had no school or pupils or close disciples.

By contrast, Sommerfeld, the unphilosophically disposed master of broad domains in theoretical physics, ten years older than Einstein, surrounded by an energetic and productive school of disciples in Munich, became a staunch supporter of the revolutionary quantum trends. He managed, with his unique mathematical dexterity, and his facility with intuitively clever mechanical models, to squeeze out and exploit subtle implications hidden beneath the basic principles that had been laid down by other investigators. We may add, that in the process, he formulated new problems eminently worthy of being explored on their own merits. Sommerfeld was an early en-

thusiast for both relativity and quantum theory. We shall concentrate on the Sommerfeld-Einstein discussions about quantum theory, because they demonstrate most convincingly the distinctive philosophy that Einstein generated over the years. Einstein became increasingly confident that the failure to provide a unitary continuum field theory that would encompass both macro and microphenomena provided proof positive that the quantum theorists were on the wrong track. All this, in spite of his own tremendous contributions to early quantum theory.

It was one of Einstein's early papers, the revolutionary 1905 hypotheses on light quanta, that brought him in contact with Sommerfield. They first met in Salzburg in 1909 at the Society for Natural Scientists and Physicians, where Einstein lectured on the new quantum ideas. The next year Sommerfeld traveled to Zürich to spend a week in discussions with Einstein. At the first Solvay conference in 1911, Sommerfeld explored the theoretically exciting idea that the existence of the molecule was to be taken as a function and result of the elementary quantum of action h, and not vice versa, as had been argued.

Sommerfeld early on was stirred to action by Einstein's deduction from quantum principles about vanishing heat capacities at the absolute zero of temperature. He also was encouraged by the experimental support for the quantum theory being provided by the low-temperature heat capacity measurements conducted by Nernst and his colleagues in Berlin. Sommerfeld did his best to get into the act in 1912 by requesting from Einstein an in-principle clarification of quantum ideas. Unfortunately for Sommerfeld, Einstein was largely preoccupied with gravitational theory, in spite of the fact that he did not manage to attract much attention to this work from his colleagues. It was *not* Einstein's views on relativity, but rather quantum mechanics, that was the topic of lusty debates.

In 1916, Einstein wrote to Sommerfeld;

> You must not be angry with me that I have not answered your interesting and friendly letter until now. During the last month I have experienced one of the most exciting and trying, and certainly one of the most successful times of my life.

What follows in the letter is a discussion of some of the germinal ideas and consequences of Einstein's general theory of relativity. Somewhat late, in 1916, while commenting favorably on Sommerfeld's spectral investigations and successful extension of Bohr's theory of the atom, Einstein remarked: "If only I could know which little screws the Lord God is using here." This remark I interpret to mean something like this: It is rather inconceivable that the real world is like that, namely, that atoms are quantized; but if it should turn out that the world *is* so constructed, then I must ask, is it not a bit undignified for God to have to use little screws to run the world that way?

Neither disturbed by Einstein's cavalier disregard of what was going on among quantum theorists, nor overly sensitive about the fundamental theoretical or philosophical rationale behind it all, Sommerfeld continued courageously to work out the mathematical formalism of the modified

Bohr theory with great finesse and virtuosity. Obviously impressed, Einstein responded in 1918: "If only it were possible to clarify the principles about quanta! But my hope in being able to experience that is steadily diminishing." What Einstein had been trying to show, but unsuccessfully, was that particles can be treated as stable regions of high concentration of the field.

Dubious about the direction in which quantum theory was moving, Einstein believed, by 1918, that general relativity, by contrast, was an accomplished theory. Thus he wrote:

> Behind general relativity henceforth there is nothing new to be found. In principle all has been said: Identity of inertia and mass; the metrical proportion of matter (geometry and kinematics) determined by the mutual action of bodies: and the nonexistence of independent properties of space. In principle, thereby, all has been said.

In this domain, Einstein was very certain that he had uncovered real physical truth about nature. In a letter to Sommerfeld in 1921, concerning a small supplementary addition to relativity theory that he and Hermann Weyl had published, he wrote: "I have my doubts about whether this thing has any physical worth. God makes it as he wills, and does not allow something to be put over on him." When asked to lecture on relativity, Einstein remarked that he had nothing new to say, and added: "The old stuff already is whistled by all the younger sparrows from the roof tops better than I can do it."

In 1920 Sommerfeld succeeded in explaining the multiplicity of many of the spectral lines by introducing an inner quantum number that had no physical meaning for him. "I can only further the technique of quanta," he wrote to Einstein, "you must construct their philosophy." Beginning with the work of Sommerfeld's pupil Heisenberg, in the summer of 1925, and promoted by the dramatic and ingenious contributions of Born, Jordan, Dirac, Schrödinger, Bohr, and Pauli, the elaboration of quantum theory was approached from quite different directions. It was given a formalism and mathematical structure that represents one of the most magnificent theoretical and practical accomplishments in the history of science. Much has been written about this subject and I only will mention here that in the outcome two opposing camps were created that divorced the enthusiasts for the Heisenberg-Born matrix mechanics—Born, Jordan, Dirac, Hund, and Pauli—from the supporters of the Schrödinger wave mechanics, for example, de Broglie, Planck, and Einstein. We have here the physics of the discrete versus the physics of continua.

Actually, Einstein essentially alienated himself from the direction in which quantum mechanics was headed, but felt moved now and then to take an occasional pot shot at the whole enterprise. Sommerfeld, typically engrossed in anything that would result in a practically useful and theoretically sound outcome, and philosophically uncommitted, stood outside the debate, but continued to elicit reactions from Einstein that at times revealed more about his (Einstein's) native intuitions and deep convictions that can be learned from studying his scientific papers.

In 1926 Einstein wrote to Sommerfeld:

> I have worried a great deal about searching out the relationship between gravitation and electromagnetism, but now am convinced that everything that has been done in this direction by me and others has been sterile . . . The theories of Heisenberg and Dirac, in fact, force me to admiration, but they do not smell of reality.

Or again, in another letter:

> The results of Schrödinger's theory make a great impression, and yet I do not know whether it deals with anything more than the old quantum rule, i.e., about something with an aspect of real phenomena.

Concerning Sommerfeld's monograph of 1930 on wave mechanics, Einstein said, in the same vein, that it was very nice, but that in spite of tremendous successes accomplished, the whole development and the prevailing trends did not satisfy him.

After 1930, as we well know, scientific investigations and communications suffered miserably in Germany. Research and discussion groups were splintered so severely that Sommerfeld in a reminiscent mood in 1937, wrote to Einstein (by then in Princeton) that he was consoling himself for having been able to experience personally the golden age of physics from 1905 to 1930. A decade later Sommerfeld was curious to know whether Einstein had changed his views about quantum theory.

> Perhaps you will tell me what you *now* think about continua and discontinua. Or do you take the situation to be hopeless?

Einstein replied:

> I still believe in all earnesty that the clarification of the basis of physics will come forth from the continuum [i.e., not quantum mechanics] because the discontinuum provides no possibility for a relativistic representation of action at a distance.

It is a fact that physicists more and more came to be preoccupied with the problems of quantum theory. It promised a better immediate yield. This did not deter Einstein (and others like Weyl and Eddington) from regarding reality as a continuous singularity-free manifold and from exploring a unified field theory on the model of general relativity. It was to include the laws of electromagnetism as well as those of gravitational fields.

In 1949 Einstein was seventy years old. In that year he believed that he had found the solution for which he strove for thirty years. The work was published by Princeton University Press as a new edition of ***The Meaning of Relativity***.

In a tribute for Einstein's seventieth birthday, Sommerfeld, commenting about Einstein's outstanding contributions to the field of atomic theory, remarked:

> In spite of all this, in the old question "continuum versus discontinuity" Einstein has taken his position most decisively on the side of the continuum. Everything of the nature of quanta—to

which, in the final analysis, the material atoms and the elementary particles belong also—he would like to derive from the continuum physics by means of methods which relate to his general theory of relativity. . . .

His unceasing efforts, since he resides in America have been directed toward this end. Until now, however, they have led to no tangible success. . . . By far the most of today's physicists consider Einstein's aims as unachievable, and consequently aim to get along with the dualism: wave-corpuscle, which he himself first clearly uncovered.

In December of 1951 Einstein wrote to his lifelong friend, Michele Besso:

> All these fifty years of conscious brooding have brought me no nearer to the question: What are light quanta? Nowadays every Tom, Dick and Harry thinks he knows it, but he is mistaken.

I feel that one of the most significant aspects of Einstein's attempts to formulate a unified field theory was the ease with which he rejected his own theories that did not work out. When that happened he blithely took up another approach. He did this until he died in 1955.

In 1951 Sommerfeld died at the age of eighty-three, thus terminating the discussions between the philosopher-physicist Einstein and the no-nonsense master of physics, Sommerfeld, who claimed no expertise at all in the philosophy of science but who had been anxious to exchange ideas with a colleague whose philosophy he respected.

In contrast to the picture we have sketched of Sommerfeld in Munich, as the philosophically neutral correspondent of Einstein, we have at our disposal the long-standing scientific interchange of ideas between Einstein and another physicist who was himself passionately inclined to philosophize about relativity theory and quantum mechanics at the slightest provocation. This was Max Born, in Göttingen, the physicist whose completion of Einstein's statistical interpretation of quantum theory earned him the Nobel Prize twenty-eight years after it was presented. So here in Born and Einstein we have two would-be philosophers of science wrestling intellectually with one another.

The philosophical views of Einstein and Born invariably were 180 degrees out of phase on the subject of quantum mechanics. Accordingly, an examination of their intellectual debates is all the more important because of Born's relentless efforts to entice Einstein, the independent and relatively isolated thinker, to explain and defend his position as he moved around the world and took up new positions in Prague, Zürich, Berlin, and Princeton.

Leopold Infeld tells us how Max Born first learned about Einstein's revolutionary paper—the early one on special relativity—a thirty-page work that bore the modest title, **"On the Electrodynamics of Moving Bodies."**

> When Professor Loria met Professor Max Born at a physics meeting in 1908, he told him about Einstein and asked Born if he had read the paper. It turned out that neither Born nor anyone else there had heard about Einstein. They went to the library, took from the bookshelves the seventeenth volume of *Annalen der Physik* and started to read Einstein's article. Immediately Max Born recognized its greatness and also the necessity for formal generalizations. Later, Born's own work on relativity theory became one of the most important early contributions to this field of science. Thus it was not before 1908 or 1909 that the attention of great numbers of scientists were drawn to Einstein's results.

As in the case of Sommerfeld, Born first met Einstein in Salzburg in 1909. Born characterizes the young Einstein, up through the early 1920s, as an empiricist and enthusiast for the philosophy of Hume, Mach, and Schlick. But, already in 1919, when Einstein was first ruminating about a unitary field theory that would bring gravitation and electromagnetic theory together, he was expressing a degree of discomfort about the developments in quantum mechanics. The theorists operate, he wrote, as though "the one hand is not allowed to know what the other does."

Basically at odds with the upsurge of the idea of discontinuity in physics, Einstein wrote to Born in 1920: "I do not believe that the quantum can be detached from the continuum. By analogy one could have supposed that general relativity should be forced to abandon its co-ordinate system." Einstein also was unhappy about what seemed to him the failure of the strict law of causality in quantum mechanics and the simultaneous encroachment of statistical and probability arguments. There is no doubt that by 1920, Einstein sought to hold tenaciously to continuum theory, in hopes that quantum phenomena would be absorbed somehow into the differential equations of a unified field theory.

In the 1920s and 1930s, Einstein was preoccupied mostly with general relativity. He was clarifying and perfecting its theoretical exposition and pursuing its practical consequences with great determination. But he wrote to Born that in his spare time he was "brooding . . . over the quantum problem from the point of view of relativity" because, as he said "I do not believe that (quantum) theory will be able to dispense with the continuum."

In February of 1929 in newspapers all over the world it was announced that Einstein had formulated his unified field theory in which the phenomena of electricity and magnetism were combined in a single set of equations. These ideas were reformulated and refined for twenty-five years. But during all of those years, until the last major attempt in 1949, Einstein was compelled, periodically, to admit that he was getting nowhere with his *Lieblingsidee* (viz.; the continuum) despite all attempts to analyze the issues. Now and again over the years, he felt, and announced, that he had achieved at least the glimpse of a reconciliation between relativity and quantum theory under the umbrella of continuum ideas, but these hopes were shattered one after another either by himself or others. In his letters to Born we come to see how often and how deeply Einstein was distressed about the conception of a wave-particle duality for radiation—a view he could not embrace except as a temporary crutch devoid of physical reality. In 1924 Einstein confided to Born:

My attempts to give the quantum a tangible form . . . have been wrecked time and again, but I am nowhere close to giving up hope. And if nothing works, there still remains the consolation that the failure is my fault.

In truth, the state of quantum theory in the early 1920s was one of considerable confusion. For example, there were the negative correlations with the Bohr-Sommerfeld rules. Attempts to connect quantum theory with classical mechanics were not successful. Qualitatively things worked out tolerably well, but the quantitative predictions were not impressive. Max Born certainly recognized very clearly that many technical difficulties simply escaped resolution. He referred to this state of affairs as *das Quatenrätzel* and in 1921 wrote to Einstein: "The quanta are a hopeless Schweinerei"—as he expressed himself. As already mentioned, from 1925 to 1930 we witness a series of dramatic and bold moves that reveal that the negative results of current quantum theory pushed investigators in the direction of making a sharper break with classical mechanics. This simultaneously provided a new quantum mechanics, much to the consternation of Einstein.

After 1925, Einstein and Born carried on a running commentary characterized by hard arguments in which neither could convince the other to change perspectives. Commenting about this interchange some forty years later, Born wrote:

> Einstein was fairly convinced that physics provides knowledge about the objective existence of the external world. But I, along with many other physicists gradually was converted, by experience in the domain of atomic quantum, to realize that it is not so—but rather that at every point in time we have no more than a rough approximate knowledge of the external world and that from this, according to specified rules of the probability laws of quantum mechanics, we can draw some conclusions about the unknown world.

In response to singular achievements in quantum mechanics by Born's Göttingen group (Heisenberg, Jordan, and Hund) Einstein could only respond: "Your quantum mechanics commands much attention, but an inner voice tells me that it is not yet the true Jacob. The theory offers much, but it brings us no closer to the secrets of the old one [der Alte]. In any case, I am convinced that he does not play dice." As Einstein said it: "Gott würfelt nicht." When Einstein spelled out some of the details of his attempt to establish a quantum field theory [i.e., continuum theory], Born wrote back politely that it was very interesting but not convincing. This was tit for tat.

In a letter of 1944 to Born we have a compelling illustration of Einstein's mature image of his own philosophy of science. It demonstrates convincingly how two talented scientists can be worlds apart in their interpretations of the same cognitive subject matter. Einstein writes:

> In our scientific expectations you and I have reached antipodal positions. You believe in a God who throws dice, and I believe in complete lawfulness, *viz.* in a world of something that exists objectively and that I have attempted to

snatch in a wild speculative way. I believe firmly, but I hope that a more realistic way, and especially that a more tangible evidence will be found than *I* was able to discover. The great initial success of the quantum theory cannot bring me to believe in the fundamental nature of a dice-throwing God, even if I know that my younger colleagues interpret this position of mine as the result of calcification. Someday it will be known which instinctive conception was the right one.

Born responded by saying that Einstein's expression about a dice-throwing God was totally inadequate:

> In your determined world, you must throw dice too—that is not the difference . . . First of all, you underestimate the empirical basis of quantum theory . . . and second, you have a philosophy that somehow brings the automaton of dead things in accord with the existence of responsibility and conscience.

Einstein at this point could do no better than say (1947) that he was sorry to discover that "I just cannot manage to express my position so that you will find it to be intelligible"; and then he adds the comment that the mathematical difficulties involved in trying to reach his objectives of a comprehensive unitary theory are so severe that,

> I will bite the dust before I get there . . . But concerning this I am convinced—that eventually we shall land a theory in which law-like things will not be probabilities for facts—facts such as formerly were just taken for granted. But to prove this conclusion I have no logical reasons.

And so the debate wore on and on. Einstein called Born a positivist. Born said that that was the last thing he wanted to be called by anyone. Einstein to Born: Don't you believe in the reality of the external world? Born to Einstein: Don't dodge the real issue: Do you really maintain the quantum mechanics is a fraudulent affair? Einstein to Born: You talk about the philosophy of quantum mechanics, but your remarks in essence are not philosophy at all but the manipulation under the cloak of indeterminacy to a hidden machinery of reasoning. Born to Einstein: Your position is one of metaphysics and not philosophy. That was the tone of the intellectual interchange.

We see that Einstein had formulated his own image of what the philosophy of science should be and what it should accomplish, and so had Born. Nevertheless, neither Einstein nor Born felt that they were being successful in communicating what that image was. Or were they just stubborn? At one point Wolfgang Pauli entered the debate and managed to convince Born that they had not so much disagreed, as argued from basically different premises. But it is clear to me that Pauli, in fact, also had constructed his own image of the philosophical positions that Einstein and Born represented.

I want to suggest that when Einstein died in 1955, he was holding in firm grasp essentially the world view that he had formulated in the 1920s and 1930s. What was this world view? In his lecture on the theory of relativity at King's College, London, in 1921, Einstein said:

> The theory of relativity may indeed be said to

have put a sort of finishing touch to the mighty intellectual edifice of Maxwell and Lorentz, inasmuch as it seems to extend field physics to all phenomena, gravitation included . . . I am anxious to draw attention to the fact that . . . (the theory of relativity) is not speculative in origin; it owes its invention entirely to the desire to make physical theory fit observed fact as well as possible. We have here no revolutionary act but the natural continuation of a line that can be traced through centuries. The abandonment of certain notions connected with space, time, and motion hitherto treated as fundamentals, must not be regarded as arbitrary, but only as conditioned by observed facts.

Here is a plug for the theoretical soundness and fertility of the great accomplishments of the nineteenth century.

A decade later, in an essay on the problems of space, ether, and fields, Einstein wrote:

> The theory of relativity is a fine example of the fundamental character of the modern development of theoretical science. The initial hypothesis becomes steadily more abstract and more remote from experience. On the other hand, it gets nearer to the grand aim of science, which is to cover the greatest possible number of empirical facts by logical deduction from the smallest number of hypotheses or axioms. Meanwhile, the train of thought leading from the axioms to the empirical facts or verifiable consequences gets steadily longer and more subtle.

According to Einstein the theoretical scientist is compelled in an increasing degree to be guided by purely mathematical, formal considerations in the search for a theory, because the physical experience of the experimenter cannot lead him up to the regions of highest abstraction. This is the line of thought, he says, that led from the special to the general theory of relativity and hence to its latest offshoot, the unified field theory. That unified theory, however, never came within Einstein's grasp, as he freely admitted toward the end of his life.

In the early 1930s, in an essay on the methods of theoretical physics, Einstein raised the question whether we can ever hope to find the *right* way—seeing as he believed that the axiomatic basis of theoretical physics cannot be extracted from experience but must be freely invented. In other words, has this *right* way any existence outside our illusions? Einstein's position is unequivocal:

> I answer without hesitation that there is in my opinion, a *right* way, and that we are capable of finding it. Our experience hitherto justifies us in believing that nature is the realization of the simplest conceivable mathematical ideas. I am convinced that we can discover by means of purely mathematical constructions the concepts and the laws connecting them with each other, which furnish the key to the understanding of natural phenomena. Experience may suggest the appropriate mathematical concepts, but they most certainly cannot be deduced from it. Experience remains, of course, the sole criterion of the physical utility of a mathematical construction. But the creative principle resides in mathe-

matics. In a certain sense, therefore, I hold it true that pure thought can grasp reality, as the ancients dreamed.

I believe it fair to say that Einstein's native epistemological credo comes through with remarkable consistency over the period of his last thirty to thirty-five years. I would mention first his characterization of God as a mathematician; or since Einstein did not believe in a personal God, we might better express his position by saying that natural phenomena can only be understood in depth, and natural laws can only be formulated successfully in the language of mathematics. Perhaps it is appropriate to mention in this context that Einstein's attitude changed considerably as he became increasingly preoccupied with relativity theory. Early in his career he displayed a far more skeptical attitude toward the role of mathematics in physics. Like Mach, who influenced him at that time, he must have felt that the abstract formalisms of mathematics were too closely allied with metaphysics and thus might disguise the deep *physical* significance of natural phenomena. He left such views behind when he came to recognize that his goal of achieving a more general and unitary representation of the world necessarily rested far more on sophisticated formal mathematical models than on physical terms and intuition.

Second, we see that Einstein had placed himself firmly on the side of those investigators of the classical period of physics who had expressed an unshaken faith in the ultimate conceptual unity of the physical world. In fact, in this regard he was exploring an old theme expressed cogently by d'Alembert in 1715 when he wrote: "To someone who can grasp the universe from one unified viewpoint, the entire creation would appear as a unique fact and a great truth." According to Einstein, a correct or right unitary theory of natural phenomena was conceivable and feasible, and scientists, he believed, were making steady progress in achieving that right unitary theory. Imbedded in this conception of a right theory is the belief that unambiguous progress had been achieved in moving toward the goal of constructing (discovering) a real picture, or physical representation of phenomena, that corresponds with the way things really are in nature. The right theory was equated with existence. Implied, of course, was also the conviction that the right theory is unique and not merely one of a plurality of alternative theories that might be constructed to do the job equally well.

For Einstein there was not only a right, correct, unique theory to explain the cosmos, but this theory was seen to be within our grasp. He said: "The Lord God is subtle but he is not malicious or vicious." ("Raffiniert ist der Herr Gott aber boshaft ist er nicht.") His God was a cosmic God, the God of Spinoza on a sublimated plane.

> It was not a personal God, who makes notes on whether a person behaves or misbehaves, but a cosmic God, who represents the all pervading intellect which manifests itself so marvelously in the Creation.

It was man's special mission to lay bare the marvels of that Creation.

A third point. The right unitary theory upon which Einstein placed all of his stakes, is seen to rest on a mathematical foundation that deals with fields (continua), and *not* quanta, that is, not discontinua. He felt, as he once put it,

> so long as no one has new concepts, which have sufficient constructive power, mere doubt remains; this is unfortunately my own position. Adhering to the continuum originates with me not as a prejudice, but arises out of the fact that I have been unable to think up anything organic to take its place. How is one to conserve four-dimensionality in essence (or in near approximation) and [at the same time] surrender the continuum?

For the same reasons that Einstein rejected quanta, he also put aside statistical or probabilistic arguments—because he believed that strict determinism was not to be sacrificed or even weakened.

In Einstein's fifty-year-long battle over the interpretation of quantum mechanics, one theme recurred again and again: his instinctive dislike of the idea of a probabilistic universe in which the behavior of individual atoms depends on chance. Was it likely that God would have created a probabilistic universe? Einstein felt that the answer must be no. If God was capable of creating a universe in which scientists could discern scientific laws, then God was capable of creating a universe wholly governed by such laws. He would not have created a universe in which he had to make chance-like decisions at every moment regarding the behavior of every individual particle. This was not something that Einstein could prove. It was a matter of faith and feeling and intuition. Perhaps it seems naive. But it was deep-rooted, and Einstein's physical intuition, though not infallible, had certainly stood him in good stead.

So Einstein's overall aim was a field theory that would encompass macro and micromechanics, or gravitation, electromagnetism, radiation, and atomistics including all aspects of science that pertain to the ultimate constituents of matter and their interactions at all levels. This grandiose, ambitious, and all-encompassing *Weltbild* was not one that Einstein was able to achieve despite more than twenty years of writing on the subject. Louis de Broglie summarized the position that most theoretical physicists took toward the end of Einstein's life when he commented that there exists

> a fundamental difference between gravitational and electromagnetic fields which does not allow an extension to the latter of the geometrical interpretation which succeeded in respect to the former. . . . Moreover, the nature of the electromagnetic field is so intimately bound to the existence of quantum phenomena that any non-quantum unified theory is necessarily incomplete. These are problems of formidable complexity whose solution is still in the lap of the gods.

Finally, Einstein believed, that however abstract and remote from experience the mathematical formalism of theory turned out to be, the investigator nevertheless could use experience to suggest appropriate concepts. Although the concepts themselves could not be deduced from experience, experience was still acknowledged as the sole criterion of the physical utility of the theory. That is, in the end, it was absolutely crucial that the physical theory fit the empirical facts.

To these four landmarks of Einstein's image of what he considered to be a correct philosophy of science, namely, his own, I suppose we might want to add that he obviously held in high regard the importance of philosophizing about the foundational analysis, critique, and reformation of the basic concepts that lie at the heart of a right and realistic scientific world view. How closely Einstein's image of his own views about physics borders on philosophy may be seen in the way that philosophers of science have continued to discuss his philosophy perhaps even more than physicists. I therefore would not hesitate for one moment to assert that Einstein, in a special sense, was a truly important modern philosopher and that his highly individualistic philosophical ideas and self-image have exerted an influence that, as Professor Dirac has emphasized, has changed the course of history.

We have done no more here than sketch some facets of Einstein's self-image and his conception of himself as a philosopher of science. I suggest that a parallel examination of, say, Niels Bohr or Boltzmann would land us in an entirely different ballpark. But then, there should be no doubt that Niels Bohr's views and approach to physics as well as Boltzmann's changed the course of history.

Einstein was neither systematic philosopher nor analytical philosopher. He was not given over to concerns about symbolic logic or the syntax of language or the construction of a metalanguage. He was a scientist's philosopher in the tradition of Helmholtz, Mach, Duhem, Planck, Poincaré, and Boltzmann. In spite of being worthy of being called the most revolutionary physicist of the twentieth century, he was at heart very much at home with the great scientific systems of the nineteenth century. He was, in fact, the natural philosopher par excellence. His revolutionary ideas are deeply imbedded in the three magnificent theoretical monuments of classic nineteenth-century thought, namely, mechanics, thermodynamics, and electromagnetic theory.

I do not believe that we know today whether nature is fundamentally simple and governed deep down by overarching simple general laws. Personally, philosophically, intuitively, I doubt it. That is, I doubt that scientists will ever reach rock bottom in such a way that no deeper digging is possible. To me, simplicity seems a myth and the lure of completeness deceptive. But having said this, I would want to add that whether nature is fundamentally simple or not, it probably is wise for investigators (if they want to get on with their work) to act as if it is. It is in this sense that I see Einstein's work as a guide and stimulus to scientific productivity and inventiveness.

Let me conclude with a quote from an article that Einstein wrote in 1918 for Planck's sixtieth birthday. It rather captures the spirit of Einstein's philosophy of science.

> The supreme task of the physicist is to arrive at those universal elementary laws from which the cosmos can be built up by pure deduction. There

is no logical path to these laws; only intuition, resting on sympathetic understanding can lead to them. . . . The state of mind that enables a man to do work of this kind is akin to that of the religious worshiper or the lover; the daily effort comes from no deliberate intention or program, but straight from the heart.

James D. Ziegler (essay date 1985)

SOURCE: "Primitive, Newtonian, and Einsteinian Fantasies: Three Worldviews," in *The Scope of the Fantastic–Theory, Technique, Major Authors*, edited by Robert A. Collins and Howard D. Pearce, Greenwood Press, 1985, pp. 69-75.

[*In the following essay, Ziegler argues that the* Weltanschauung—*or world-view—of any given time period necessarily places restraints on the creative imagination, but remains hopeful that the fantasy genre will benefit from the societal move from a Newtonian to an Einsteinian worldview.*]

Fantasy, as a genre of the creative imagination, can be described as a chimerical or fantastic notion, where "fantastic" connotes unrestrained extravagance in the creations of the imaginative faculty. Despite this definition, fantasy, like all other human activities, cannot be wholly unrestrained. Restraints are placed on humans not only by their biological, psychological, and social natures but by the *Weltanschauung* of their times. Thus *fantasy* must be redefined as an extravagance in the creations of the imaginative faculty within the constraints of human nature and of worldviews. I will leave to biologists, social scientists, theologians, and philosophers the problem of human nature and address the problem of restraints imposed on the creative faculty by the worldview current at the time in which fantasists create their works.

The dominant worldview before the seventeenth century is often referred to as "pre-Newtonian," a term that may also apply to peoples who have not yet accepted the Newtonian system of thought. Since such peoples may otherwise represent different cultural levels, despite basic similarities in worldview, the term *primitive* is more convenient to describe the pre-Newtonian *Weltanschauung.*

Several aspects of such a worldview stand out. There is no clear division between the divine and the human or between living and inert matter. The characteristic division is between good and evil, which are almost Manichaean in their expression. Fantasy's role in the primitive mind is primarily moral. Myths, fairy tales, folk stories, and anecdotal material reflect this view of the universe as basically a moral system. Good and evil are absolute and objective. Both fantasy and nonfantasy are attempts to answer holistic questions such as "What is Truth?" "What is good and just?" "What is life?" Whether one reads Plato or Aristophanes, these questions are implicit. Plato's account of Atlantis and Aristophanes's description of Cloudcuckooland each reflect their common preoccupation with eternal verities. Also implicit in the two accounts is a moral comparison with the "real" world. The two men, however, must locate their mythical land either in the past (Atlan-

tis) or in space (Cloudcuckooland). The descriptions must have points of similarity to the experience of humans living in the present on Earth, and these similarities must be sufficiently a part of the general worldview so that readers can comprehend and accept the moral message being conveyed. Primitive fantasy, as analyzed through the structuralist approach of Claude Lévi-Strauss, displays a striking feature: the tales are always synchronous. Even tales laid in the past can be understood only in reference to the present. The primitive mind rejects the diachronous system.

The system of thought associated with the name of Sir Isaac Newton changed, and changes, people's worldview. No longer are they engaged in a holistic approach to the world. The type of questions they now ask are: "What happens when a rock falls from a height?" "How does the blood move through the body?" "How can I exploit a vein of silver ore without the miners drowning or suffocating?" When individuals like Galileo Galilei ask these questions, they are also rejecting the synchronous approach. They are examining discrete phenomena in an attempt to satisfy immediate objectives such as allaying curiosity, healing sickness, killing enemies efficiently, and amassing wealth. Although moral questions may emerge, the phenomena themselves are not moral. The examination of the phenomena can only occur serially, resulting in a diachronous activity. The seven decades separating Galileo's *Starry Messenger* from Newton's *Principia Mathematica* encompass the revolution.

Newton's great achievement was to point out that the examination of a small segment of the universe can produce a greater knowledge of the universe itself. This can be done because the universe is the same throughout. For the next two centuries explorations of nature and humans supported Newton's conclusion. The result was the development of a closed system operating by fixed rules that could be discovered by reason based on observation. Such discovery was made possible by the objectification and quantification of the observations. Observers approached a phenomenon as external to themselves with characteristics that could be described in numerical terms. Since relationships between numbers had been known since the time of Pythagoras, phenomena could now be quantified. Such phenomena would be value free in these terms, and reason could be applied to answer the nonholistic questions in the minds of the observers.

This methodology resulted in the triumph of science—not because science proved the truth of philosophical or theological systems, but because it solved the everyday problems facing humans. Although the seventeenth century witnessed modern scientific explorations in many fields, physics dominated. In succeeding years the methods of physics were applied to other areas of human knowledge. In the process human knowledge replicated physics, further legitimating science as the only valid worldview, one that was only limited by the people's use of their innate intelligence and the tools available at the time.

In nonscientific areas the Newtonian worldview also dominated. Art, music, and literature reflect this domination. The machine became the model. Individual works by artists, musicians, and writers had to be understood as machines that demonstrated at the same time their discrete individuality and their place in the universe. Fantasy shared in this. Charles Perrault took the primitive French folk stories and transformed them into Newtonian fairy tales. In *Beauty and the Beast* Beauty is the scientist, and the Beast is nature. Through understanding, fear and revulsion give way to love and partnership. The Fairy Godmother in Cinderella can be seen as the scientist delivering humankind into the Promised Land of a better life as personified by Prince Charming. The Wicked Stepmother represents ignorance and jealousy, which are overcome by the fitting of the glass slipper upon Cinderella's foot. The glass slipper can be understood as science, Cinderella's foot as humankind. When humans accept science, they are transformed, fear and jealousy are defeated, and they live happily ever after.

Fantasy's response to the changing *Weltanschauung* may also be seen in the comparison of Cyrano de Bergerac's account of a voyage to the moon with the story of the flight of Icarus. The myth of Icarus is explicitly a moral tale. In Cyrano's account, however, individuals leave Earth for another physical object in the universe. When they arrive, that object is identifiably similar to Earth and is inhabited by similar living creatures, with similar concerns. Icarus uses wings made of feathers held together by wax; Cyrano uses rockets and beef tallow. Icarus flies too close to the sun, the wax melts, and he falls to Earth. Cyrano returns to Earth by a demon taking him to hell, which requires a passage back to Earth. Cyrano solves the problem of his return by a method lifted from the primitive worldview.

From Cyrano de Bergerac to Jules Verne, fantasists have taken the latest discoveries of Newtonian science and put humans through fantastic adventures. In all cases, however, these adventures occur in the Newtonian universe. The picaresque stories of Gil Blas, the erotic fantasies of Casanova, the lies of Baron Munchausen, the tales about Till Eulenspiegel, Jonathan Swift's satire in the account of Gulliver's travels—all are Newtonian. Fantasists joined the other, less extravagant users of the imaginative faculty in turning away from the search for the good, the true, and the beautiful to portray the real, the material, within the continuum of time.

This might appear at first to be untrue. Although fantasists such as H. G. Wells, Jules Verne, and Edward Bellamy reflect the Newtonian system, others like Mary Shelley, Edgar Allan Poe, and Bram Stoker appear to violate it. In their fantasies the premise seems to be one of deliberate flight from the Newtonian worldview. A closer reading, however, demonstrates that humans' attempt to violate the Newtonian system in these works regularly leads to disaster. Dr. Frankenstein creates a monster and is destroyed by it. Members of the Usher family attempt to survive without following the Newtonian principles and are killed off by the collapse of their house. Dracula would appear to be successful in transcending the Newtonian world; yet even he is destroyed by it in the end.

The fact that Dracula was written toward the end of the nineteenth century, and that it points to a non-Newtonian worldview, reflects what was happening in science. Scientists in the latter part of the nineteenth century were having increasing difficulties in reconciling their discoveries with Newtonian principles. Light, in particular, demonstrated properties of both matter and energy. The Newtonian system posited that matter and energy were discrete and different. The line between matter and energy became even more blurred with the work of Henri Bequerel and Wilhelm Roentgen, the discoverers of radio waves and X-rays. The development of quantum mechanics by Max Planck explained the phenomena but destroyed the barrier between matter and energy. By 1900 physicists were shifting from studying energy as an affective principle to a conception of energy as the basis of the universe.

The lack of adequate theoretical framework inhibited scientists in their attempts to explain phenomena such as radioactivity, electromagnetism, random particle activity, and osmosis. The laws of thermodynamics, which had enabled humankind to create the modern industrial society, were inadequate when applied to these phenomena. The foundations of the Newtonian system were developing cracks. The biggest crack was a growing realization that human understanding and control of nature required more than simply better observations and better tools. The seventeenth-century revolt against the then-prevailing assumption that events on Earth were punishments for sin, meliorated by God's grace, had led to the Newtonian system. It would appear that the next step would be a similar questioning of the Newtonian assumptions, with an almost infinite number of possible systems to replace the Newtonian system.

Perhaps this would have happened except for the publication of three papers by a Swiss patent office functionary in 1905-6. These papers, by Albert Einstein, although they did not have the breadth or simplicity of Newton's *Principia Mathematica,* did explain satisfactorily the discrepancies between scientific observations and the Newtonian system. In this way they are analogous to Galileo's *Starry Messenger.* Science, and humankind, then waited for the new Newton to synthesize all of the activities of scientists in the coming decades. Einstein, however, was to be the Newton of the new system, with the publication of **The General Theory of Relativity** in 1915. (The three earlier papers were published under the title **Special Theory of Relativity**.) Einstein was to spend the rest of his life in an attempt to achieve what the successors of Newton had done by developing a comprehensive system—in this case, the unified field theory. He failed, but the search is still going on, as indicated by the awarding of the Nobel Prize in physics for 1979 to men who have brought us closer to the formulation of the unified field theory. In the absence of the unified field theory Einstein's general theory of relativity expresses the contemporary worldview.

All of us are familiar with the word *relativity*. It has passed into discussions of, and inquiries into, all areas of human thought and endeavor. It has given rise to the "big-bang" theory of the universe, to situational ethics, to anarchy in the humanities. Unfortunately, most of those who use Einstein as the authority for their ideas have misused his theories. "Relativity," and its twin "uncertainty" (from Werner Heisenberg's principle), have been used to justify the rejection of absolutes, which in turn has led to the substitution of the subjective and ephemeral for the objective and eternal in nonscientific activity. Even in science the recent trend has been toward research in applied science rather than further exploration in Einsteinian problems. The present status of intellectual activity can best be summarized by statements such as this: "Since everything is relative and uncertain, whatever I express is as valid as anything else. The only criterion is the marketplace."

This approach might be acceptable if the marketplace were free. In ideas, as in goods, market research by pollsters has replaced the free exchange of intellectual endeavors. The statistician reigns supreme, and the result is presold formulas. These formulas dress up the Newtonian system in Einsteinian terminology. Whether it is *Star Trek, Star Wars,* or the latest horror flick, the Newtonian special effects demonstrate the only attempts at fantasy.

Apparently, we are aware that Einstein shattered the Newtonian worldview, but we are still unable to escape our bondage to Newton. We need some standard, and the statistician provides that standard. The computer has replaced the human brain in creating fantasy to such an extent that the brain is routinely referred to as a giant computer. But computers cannot escape the Newtonian universe, as HAL demonstrates in *2001: A Space Odyssey.* What makes HAL different is the reinjection of a primitive worldview into the Newtonian universe. In fact, much of twentieth-century fantasy appears to be the survival of the primitive worldview in the Newtonian system. This is part of the twentieth-century attempt to deal with evil, because the realities of our time are more fantastic than most of our fantasies. None of the Newtonian fantasists could imagine horrors such as World War I, Stalinism, Nazism, World War II, Viet Nam, Kampuchea, concentration camps, Gulags, modern urban terrorism, or nuclear bombs.

Only the last horror owes anything to Einstein. The others result from following Newtonian principles. But all of the horrors of the twentieth century pose a significant problem for fantasists. They have three solutions. First, they can trivialize or make banal the reality around them. This is the solution of most contemporary fantasists. Second, they can escape from the horrors of the present by creating their own world. One direction is indicated by Tolkien, another by Norman Rockwell. Third, they can illuminate the present by exaggerating its flaws and absurdities. Works such as *One Hundred Years of Solitude, The Yawning Heights,* and *Gravity's Rainbow* illustrate this solution. This third solution also reflects the Einsteinian worldview.

To support my contention, remember that both the primitive and Newtonian systems were closed systems. Einstein created an open system. To Einstein and to modern science the universe is not closed. It appears closed to the observer, but that is relative to the observer. Move the observer, and the system changes. Because energy and not mass is the basis of the universe, motion is the norm. Both the observer and the object observed are moving. The perception of the observer is determined by the relative rates of velocity involved. Another observer moving at a different velocity than the first observer would perceive the object differently. When this premise is combined with the concept of an open system, the result is uncertainty. Newtonians focused their attention upon moving particles of matter. These particles did not change as their velocities changed, because Newtonians ignored the most crucial element involved—time.

To Newton time was a constant, to be measured in the same way that mass, density, and volume are measured. To Einstein time is relative in the same way that mass, density, and volume are relative. Since mass, density, and volume change as their velocities change, time also changes—hence the popular term *fourth dimension.*

It is this use of time that differentiates most clearly the Newtonian and Einsteinian worldviews. In terms of fantasy it means that time ceases to be diachronous. Time, however, does not become synchronous, as in the primitive worldview. Instead, it becomes something defined by the moving relationships of particles of matter. This means that time in the Einsteinian universe is achronous. Matter and time are determined by velocity, which in turn is the result of energy. Einsteinian fantasists will then concern themselves with energy and will subordinate matter and time to their proper, secondary roles.

Will fantasy reflect the Einsteinian worldview? I see some evidence that this is happening. Marcel Proust, in *Remembrance of Things Past,* illustrated this to some extent; here is a work in which movement from object to object replaces movement on the continuum through time—a movement that is without velocity and is certainly not Newtonian. The surrealists, also, represent a trend toward the Einsteinian system. Although they approach reality from the standpoint of the subconscious, their work illustrates the distortions that occur when the observer is placed on a different plane than that of the Newtonian system.

In conclusion, although there are some glimmerings of the Einsteinian world-view on the horizon, successful (in monetary terms) fantasy still hews to the Newtonian world-view. It is the juxtaposition of the Newtonian and primitive views that appears to be the major alternative to straight Newtonian fantasy. We are still in the same relationship to the Einsteinian worldview as the illiterate European peasants were to the early Newtonian worldview. Before the Brothers Grimm cleaned up the German folk tales and turned them into children's stories, the forest and its creatures, including humans, were dangerous and bloody. Now that Walt Disney has completely sanitized them, the stage is set for the next breakthrough. This will come with the emergence of someone like Aristophanes or Rabelais, who can then be followed by a bowdlerizing anthologist. At present, Luis Bunuel, J. L. Borges, Thomas Pynchon, and Grigori Zinoviev are pointing the way. To seize on the essence of Einsteinian fantasy, watch *Un Chien Andalou,* read *The Yawning Heights,* and then imagine a universe in which velocity is the determinant.

Robert Hauptman and Irving Hauptman   (essay date 1987)

SOURCE: "The Circuitous Path: Albert Einstein and the

Epistemology of Fiction," in *Einstein and the Humanities*, edited by Dennis P. Ryan, Greenwood Press, 1987, pp. 125-34.

[In the following essay, Hauptman and Hauptman argue that Einstein's theories were fundamental to the development of absurdist fiction.]

> When I examine myself and my methods of thought I come to the conclusion that the gift of fantasy has meant more to me than my talent for absorbing positive knowledge.
>
> Albert Einstein

The zeitgeist and the general inferences drawn from Einstein's work come to bear most seminally on a group of philosophically oriented novelists conveniently termed absurdists, authors who believe that man is, in Heidegger's phrase, "thrown" into a world devoid of absolutes, order, and meaningfulness. The world that these novelists depict is one in which external meaning is elusive, metaphysical underpinnings are questioned, and knowledge is ephemeral. If this is the antipode of the harmonious world that Einstein demanded spiritually, it is nonetheless a valid hypostatization that follows logically from his physical theorizing. It is small consolation that the man who helped to destroy the harmony of the universe, failed to accept the consequences of his own work and spent the rest of his life attempting to prove that the universe is indeed harmonious and comprehensible. Thus to ascribe man's anguished cry entirely to a philosophical etiology, while conveniently ignoring concomitant advances in physics is rather naive. Franz Kafka, Jean-Paul Sartre, Albert Camus, and Samuel Beckett were certainly influenced by nineteenth-century philosophy but their fiction consistently reflects the world that Einstein and Heisenberg depict. A. A. Robb commenting on only one aspect, Einstein's theory of simultaneity, states that "This seemed to destroy all sense of the reality of the external world and to leave the physical universe no better than a dream, or rather a nightmare." Exactly. For Einstein's heirs nothing remains stable and the inevitable result is absurdity.

The first of the absurdists is Kafka, who, in 1910, became aware of relativity through direct contact with Einstein at the salon of Berta Fanta in Prague: ". . . he got familiar, shortly before writing his main works, with the most important matters of inquiry of the new age (for example, quantum theory and relativity theory.)" Moreover, both Sartre and Camus acknowledge their debt to Kafka. These are admittedly tenuous connections, but they certainly demand recognition. Furthermore, this [essay] does not contend that these writers were directly influenced by Einstein's work, that there is an explicit line traceable from his scientific papers to their fictional worlds. It is rather claimed that during a period that witnessed the transformation of the most basic physical concepts, it is the general zeitgeist that exercised the primary influence on the absurdists. One of the few critics to note this is S. Beynon John, who, in discussing the intellectual climate of Camus's early years, observes that,

> New scientific theories, too, seemed to challenge still further men's assumptions about the nature of experience. Among these we must count the delayed implications of Freud, and discoveries about the nature of the physical universe, especially those of Einstein. Two general conclusions were often drawn from the play of these factors. Firstly, they appeared to break up traditional values and beliefs about the nature of man and his place in the universe. Next, in the degree to which they menaced individuality or made it the prey of unconscious impulses (as with Freud), these forces seemed to impair the density of individual existence and to provoke the idea that man was adrift in an absurd universe.

It is this general Einsteinian influence that is so important for fiction.

Because Einstein's scientific methodology is based on a surprisingly well-developed epistemology and more significantly because in an indeterminate and meaningless universe epistemological questions assume unprecedented importance, it is legitimate to examine the attempts of fictional characters to acquire knowledge. But it is not the purpose of this chapter to discuss Einstein's epistemology nor to compare his perspective with ways of knowing in fictive worlds. These are autonomous realms.

> Time present and time past
> Are both perhaps present in time future,
> And time future contained in time past.

These opening lines of [T. S.] Eliot's "Burnt Norton" mirror the confusion of time in modern fiction: from Proust, Joyce, and Mann through Robbe-Grillet and Cortazar, time is manipulated into asymmetrical, simultaneous, and reversible patterns. Events are not disclosed in sequential narrative, one incident succeeding another, but rather "everything is everywhere at all times." Rudolf Arnheim perceptively remarks that

> The shattering of the narrative sequence challenges the reader or viewer to reconstruct the objective order of the events. In trying to do so, he tends to assign the scattered pieces to their place in a structurally separate system offered by Time and Space. However, if the reader or viewer would limit his effort to this reconstruction of objective reality, he would miss the entire other half of the work's structure. Although discontinuous and therefore disorderly with regard to objective reality, the presentation must also be understood and accepted as a valid sequence of its own, a flow of disparate fragments, complexly and absurdly related to one another.

Strangely enough, the novels of Kafka, Sartre, Camus, and Beckett frequently *do* unfold in a sequential fashion; that is, a distinct temporal progression can occur. On the other hand, time, for these writers, tends to be inconsequential, amorphous, alienating. As Kafka notes in his diary, "The clocks are not in unison, the inner one runs crazily on . . . the outer one limps along at its usual speed. What else can happen but that the two worlds split apart . . . ?" This disparity reinforces the chaos of a world in which the most significant things are unknowable and even the insignificant often defy comprehension. Attempts to discover are met with silence. Indeed, Camus insists that "The absurd is born of this confrontation between the human need and the unreasonable silence of the world." If one cannot know, then one cannot predict and if one cannot predict, it is difficult to know: this is a vicious circle and thus it is no surprise that the fictional worlds created here are haphazard, disharmonious, and unpredictable.

Both Kafka's *Trial* and Camus's *Stranger* are predicated on unpredictable events and unfold through the unknowable. This is, in fact, Kafka's normal perception of the world and there are potent auguries of the weltanschauung of *The Trial* and *The Castle* in Kafka's shorter fiction. In "The Judgment" George commits suicide because his father sentences him to death, but the sentence is incommensurate with his crime, which is not really knowable, particularly since it may be different for father, son, and reader. "In the Penal Colony" is a detailed account of a grotesque device used for torturing prisoners, but the offender who is about to be tormented does not know his sentence; in fact, he does not even know that he has been sentenced. Joseph K., in *The Trial,* is arrested, harassed, and ultimately executed (murdered by official thugs) without ever discovering his crime; as K. laments, "it is an essential part of the justice dispensed here that you should be condemned not only in innocence but also in ignorance." *The Trial* is K's valiant attempt to understand his position in a bizarre world, to learn what he has done, and, more important, to discover how to deal effectively with the judicial system. To this end he will try anything, but everything fails; he learns nothing of utility, and because of this he dies: knowledge is life; ignorance is death.

Kafka retells the story in *The Castle*. The orientation is different, but the goal is the same: to learn and to understand, both of which are allegorized by K's attempt to reach the castle. Of course, he never does; too many obstacles are put in his path. He fails to recognize his assistants, who have supposedly followed him to the new town. This is no surprise since they appear to be local men, not his original assistants at all. K. accepts this and acts as if they were the originals despite the evidence: " 'But if you are my old assistants you must know something about it [surveying],' said K. They made no reply. 'Well, come in. . . . ' ". The only reliable source of information is the meaningless "humming and singing" of the telephone; "Everything else is deceptive." ... Franz Kuna epitomizes Kafka's unique position:

> *The Trial* and *The Castle* are monuments to Kafka's dedication to his self-imposed task of dismantling the key assumptions underlying the idea of a harmonious order. What Einstein very much at the same time, did in physics Kafka did in the field of ethics and aesthetics.

Camus constructs *The Stranger* along similar lines: Meursault knows why he is condemned, but he does not know why he kills the Arab. And the judges, jury, and prosecutor, who think they know why Meursault is guilty, confuse the crime with his social ineptitudes. *The Stranger,* in a sense, is Camus's paean to uncertainty: "Mother died today. Or, maybe, yesterday; I can't be sure." From these opening words to the final execration, *The Stranger* insists that it is virtually impossible to know. Even the commonplace is qualified: phrases like "I suppose," "So far as I

knew," "I couldn't say," "I wasn't sure," "I can't remember," "It seemed," "I didn't know," and "I still don't know" appear in unabashed profusion. And even when Meursault *appears* to know, he actually does not, for example, when he acts as a witness for Raymond, he is merely repeating something that Raymond told him; but he does not check Raymond's story: it may be true, it probably is, but Meursault has no way of knowing. When he kills the Arab, he is dealing with a "blurred dark form" and his eyes are filled with brine and tears so that he cannot see. He shoots and then shoots four more times. He does not know why he does so. At his defense, the best he can do is to mention the sun. Meursault concludes by opening his heart "to the benign indifference of the universe." For a man who neither knows nor cares to know, this is perhaps the only solution.

The extremes of epistemological questioning are evident in Sartre's *Nausea* and Beckett's *The Unnamable*. Sartre is more concerned with the metaphysical perspective. The nausea that Roquentin feels whenever he perceives too lucidly is Sartre's metaphor for the congruency of knowledge and absurdity: the implied meaninglessness of *The Stranger* becomes explicit in Roquentin's articulated responses to his environment. Without self-knowledge and unsure of his purpose, Roquentin abandons his historical study of Rollebon, about whom little is known with certainty. *Nausea* is of particular interest in this context, because it is here that Sartre presents one of the few characters in absurdist fiction who actually has apodictic knowledge of the universe. But the self-taught man, who has acquired all of his knowledge by reading the books on the local library's shelves in *alphabetical order* (he is only halfway through), is a parody, a man for whom knowledge is of little significance:

> He has digested anti-intellectualism, manicheism, mysticism, pessimism, anarchy and egotism: they are nothing more than stages, unfinished thoughts which find their justification only in him.

Although Roquentin sees a solution to his dilemma in fictional creation (he will become a story teller) the final effect of *Nausea* is mitigated by Roquentin's belief that, "Every existing thing is born without reason, prolongs itself out of weakness and dies by chance."

In *Molloy* and *Malone Dies* Beckett depicts a quest whose epistemological significance is invariably overshadowed by metaphysical queries. But by *The Unnamable* (the final novel in the trilogy), the inexorable movement has been reversed and the metaphysical aspects give way to a 123 page litany of man's inability to know himself, his past, his desires, his physical surroundings, or his world. There are few pages upon which the narrator fails to mention his lack of knowledge and whatever he does claim to know is immediately contradicted. Metaphysical conjecturing breaks down in this epistemological quagmire. At the height of his despair Roquentin cries,

> I am. I am, I exist, I think, therefore I am; I am because I think, why do I think? I don't want to think any more, I am because I think that I don't

want to be, I think that I . . . because . . . Ugh!
I flee.

A stronger congruence of fictional worlds would be difficult to imagine. This passage provides a gloss to the Unnamable's plight. Roquentin reaches this stage and then moves on to recovery. *The Unnamable* begins and ends in similar mental gyrations. Since physically he consists (apparently) of a torso embedded in a container, there is little he can do other than think. But his goal is to "go silent," although he begins by affirming that "I shall never be silent. Never." To which he adds, some pages later, "So it is I who speak, all alone, since I can't do otherwise. No, I am speechless." He knows nothing and the reader knows even less, because it is impossible to distinguish between the truth and his mistakes, invented memories, tergiversations, and lies. No cartographer could map the narrator's progress; there is none. Early in the monologue he depicts himself at rest or in motion, the distinction is unimportant, while toward the end he laments that he is still unsure of what he is, where he is, whether vocal or silent, indeed whether he even exists. George Wellwarth sums up Beckett's position: "all knowledge is an illusion and all things are pointless—insofar as the human mind is concerned." This is the obvious conclusion and it is therefore easy to forget after all those devastating words, that *The Unnamable* ends on a positive note: "it will be I, it will be the silence, where I am, I don't know, I'll never know, in the silence you don't know, you must go on, I can't go on, I'll go on."

The four novelists discussed here depict worlds in which meaninglessness is the dominant value and the validity and significance of knowledge is highly questionable. It is the contention of this essay that this perspective can, in part, be ascribed to developments in modern science, particularly to Einstein's theorizing. That these developments logically lead to the cul-de-sac outlined above has at least been noted by the humanists. Few scientists, however, have ventured such opinions. An exception is P. W. Bridgman, the Nobel-Prize winning physicist, who in 1950 stated that,

> We are now approaching a bound beyond which we are forever estopped from pushing our inquiries, not by the construction of the world, but by the construction of ourselves. The world fades out and eludes us because it becomes meaningless. We cannot even express this in the way we would like. We cannot say that there exists a world beyond any knowledge possible to us because of the nature of knowledge. The very concept of existence becomes meaningless. It is literally true that the only way of reacting to this is to shut up. We are confronted with something truly ineffable. We have reached the limit of the vision of the great pioneers of science, the vision, namely[,] that we live in a sympathetic world, in that it is comprehensible by our minds.

If Einstein's influence on the absurdists is, at times, oblique, there is another area of fiction where it is far more salient. Many contemporary novelists have been captivated by various aspects of modern science and they make use of scientific method and metaphor often in strange and even grotesque ways. Perhaps the favorite metaphor to be

usurped from its rightful place in the physicist's arsenal is entropy. As Tony Tanner points out, the concept is virtually ubiquitous and Norman Mailer, Saul Bellow, and John Updike, inter alios, actually use the term in their fictions. Because entropy entails not merely the running down of the universe, but disorder and chaos as well, it is necessary to mention a specific manifestation. Thomas Pynchon's *Crying of Lot 49* revolves around the entropy of communication. Oedipa Maas attempts to solve the mystery of an alternate mail system, but she never learns whether the source of her knowledge is reality, hallucination, fantasy, or an extravagant perpetration; the novel concludes in ambiguity and the ultimate effect, though not as powerful, is similar to that achieved by Kafka and his heirs: one only discovers that one cannot know with certainty.

The four novels of Lawrence Durrell's *Alexandria Quartet* provide an excellent example of the novelist using an Einsteinian metaphor as a structuring principle. As Durrell puts it in his note to *Balthazar,*

> Modern literature offers us no Unities, so I have turned to science and am trying to complete a four-decker novel whose form is based on the relativity proposition.
>
> Three sides of space and one of time constitute the soup-mix recipe of a continuum. The four novels follow this pattern.
>
> The three first parts, however, are to be deployed spatially (hence the use of 'sibling' not 'sequel') and are not linked in a serial form. They interlap, interweave, in a purely spatial relation. Time is stayed. The fourth part alone will represent time and be a true sequel.

The result of this can be seen in the final novel, *Clea.* As in Faulkner's *Sound and the Fury,* events are surprised from different angles, which shows once again that knowledge is subjective and ephemeral. The philosophical position is articulated at various points in terms of "the mutability of all truth" or at its most extreme "poetic or transcendental knowledge somehow cancels out purely relative knowledge." More important, however, are the many examples of inexactitude: Capodistria's death, which turns out to be a hoax; Darley's vision of Justice, which is "an illusionist's creation"; the incredible transformation of Scobie into the Saint, El Yacoub; or the misconceptions concerning Pursewarden, who is perceived from the perspectives of Darley, the diary, his sister, his wife, and Keats. The only knowledge possible here is rather peculiar: "Sexual love *is* knowledge, both in etymology and in cold fact . . . When a culture goes bad in its sex all knowledge is impeded." While Einstein believes that there are no limits to knowledge, Durrell, using an Einsteinian structure, concludes that, with the exception of sexual knowledge, epistemological problems are unresolvable; as he observes in another context, "Under the terms of the new idea a precise knowledge of the outer world becomes an impossibility."

Stanislaw Lem's protagonists, like Kafka's, are usually searching for the solution to some enigma. *The Investigation* provides a splendid example of characters who attempt to discover order and harmony in apparent chaos. The disappearances of some corpses result in a number of tangential explanations, the most preposterous of which are couched in purely statistical terms. The result of one analysis, "the product of the distance and the time between consecutive incidents, multiplied by the temperature differential" is a constant and leads nowhere. A second statistical farrago insists that the answer to the mystery lies in the fact that the corpses disappeared in the area of England that has the lowest cancer death rate. The novel concludes with yet another hypothesis concerning truck drivers, fog, and fantasies. When confronted with this explanation, Gregory asks, "is all this true?" to which the Chief Inspector replies, "No but it might be. Or, strictly speaking, it can become the truth." These men are groping for knowledge in a world in which bodies cannot be identified with certainty; time factors are ambiguous; rumors are rampant; actions are incomprehensible; and a guilty party may not exist. Nonetheless they continue to insist on specious explanations for an unsolvable case. As Gregory declares in a moment of despair, "we human beings are the resultant of Brownian motion . . . Our knowledge is underlined by statistics—nothing exists except blind chance, the eternal arrangement of fortuitous patterns." It is perhaps superfluous to add that *The Investigation* concludes in ambiguity; there is no solution.

Concerning the reliance of statistical methods of prediction, Philipp Frank remarks, "If science could not advance beyond this stage, 'God would,' as Einstein said, 'play dice indeed.' " Robert Coover has predicated his fascinating novel, *The Universal Baseball Association, Inc. of J. Henry Waugh, Prop.*, on this supposition. J. Henry Waugh (whose initials plus the final h form the letters of the Biblical name for God, JHWH) controls a baseball game of his own creation, by rolling dice. Waugh's involvement in this board game is so intense that he fails to distinguish between it and reality; thus he alienates friends, loses his job, and imperils his own being. The game progresses according to the throw of the dice and until Damon Rutherford, Waugh's favorite player, is killed by a pitch, Waugh does not interfere. There is nothing that he can do to bring Rutherford back, but he does meddle in future games; he juggles schedules; he controls the Knickerbockers' losses; and he tampers with two rolls of the dice, which results in the death of Damon's killer. In Arlen Hansen's apt words, "God *does* play dice with the universe, but the dice are loaded." The novel concludes in a ritual reenactment of Damon's death. This mythification is Coover's subtle indication that one knows only in confusion: the player who becomes Rutherford in the reenactment is not really the earlier hero, but in the eyes of the crowd he *is,* and as such he must be sacrificed, *literally.* The ambiguity of the final pages allow for a tantalizing peroration: the reader learns nothing further of this ball player's fate, nor of Waugh's for that matter.

The preceding discussion attempts to show that Einstein's influence on novelists is both substantial and diverse. He is indirectly responsible for the world that the absurdists depict, the philosophical implications of which have had a decisive impact on the contemporary mood. Secondly, he directly influenced writers like Durrell and Coover whose fiction depends both structurally and contextually on Einsteinian metaphor. Finally, there are novelists like Vladimir Nabokov and Aldous Huxley, who merely mention Einstein or his theories in passing. Further, this essay contends that many of these novels lead to the same conclusion: in an Einsteinian universe knowledge is ephemeral, elusive, and at times unobtainable.

Dennis Bohnenkamp   (essay date 1989)

SOURCE: "Post-Einsteinian Physics and Literature: Toward a New Poetics," in *Mosaic: A Journal for the Interdisciplinary Study of Literature*, Vol. XXII, No. 3, Summer, 1989, pp. 19-30.

[*In the following essay, Bohnenkamp discusses the effects of Einstein's physics on the modern literary temperament.*]

C. P. Snow's now infamous 1959 lecture, "The Two Cultures and the Scientific Revolution," popularized the notion that science and literature held two irreconcilable world views and "had almost ceased to communicate at all." It may be true that technology, applied science and literature are often at odds, but not literature and scientific theory. Snow's allegation that "It is bizarre how very little of twentieth-century science has been assimilated into twentieth-century art" is preposterous. Even if scientists and writers do not always communicate as well as they might, there is at least a semblance of cultural continuity in any given age; the thinkers in any time share certain assumptions about the laws that govern their particular reality. Thomas S. Kuhn provides the term "paradigm" to describe this gestalt or mindset of a particular era.

It does seem that every three or four hundred years scientific revolutions take place that radically modify our picture of the universe and of ourselves. Kuhn places these paradigm shifts closer together, identifying them as "Copernican, Newtonian, chemical, and Einsteinian." The point, however, is that whatever one calls these changes in the ways in which we perceive things and wherever one places them chronologically, they influence everyone in the culture, literary as well as scientific people. These changes occur, of course, at different rates among different groups and even among different individuals. Literary artists, for example, might be quicker to learn of and adopt new modes of perception because they are risk-takers— unlike literary critics who might have a more vested ideological interest in keeping a previous paradigm in place.

My purpose in this essay is to identify the relationship between the last of Kuhn's paradigms, the Einsteinian, and its literary analogue, the Modern. Certain key ideas evolving from the Einsteinian model and that of quantum mechanics have influenced or paralleled tendencies in modern and contemporary fiction, literary theory and criticism. The influences are not necessarily direct, but an analysis of shared, interpenetrating assumptions will illuminate both the science and the literature.

I will focus especially on fiction because theories of physicists and literary fictions have much in common. Both posit hypothetical worlds. Both are judged at times by their degree of verisimilitude to what we regard as the real world. Some scientific hypotheses are valued to the degree that they can be verified, while fictions are frequently valued to the extent that they conform to a reader's experience of what is real. Both literary and scientific fictions can be esthetically pleasing; both can be disturbing. Much modern fiction is anti-realist, as is much modern science. Both describe worlds that often defy the logic of common sense. Modern literature is often nothing like life, and quantum mechanics tells us that life, the universe, reality are nothing like we think they are. Thus, I would like to suggest a new way of viewing both literary fictions and scientific theories, one which collapses their oppositions and allows them to illuminate one another. In order to do this it is necessary to suspend the idea that either is an exact representation of the phenomenal world.

If one accepts that there are some areas of similarity in the theoretical models projected by scientific theories and in created fictional worlds, then perhaps it is not too improbable to suggest that the laws governing one area, the ones most thoroughly codified (in this case, those of physics), might illuminate the other less systematized field, in this case, literature. A number of concepts evolving from Einsteinian physics and quantum mechanics provide metaphorical insights into the literature of our period. Rather than being "odd bedfellows," physics and literature are intertwined and incestuous.

. . . . .

Not long after the turn of the century, Einstein's publication of his Special Theory of Relativity (1905) raised questions that undermined the validity of the Western world's notions of reality, of common sense and of meaning. Werner Heisenberg, the quantum physicist, describes "the feeling that the ground would be cut from science"; Einstein himself felt "as if the ground had been pulled out from under one." Russell McCormach treats this disorientation fictionally in *Night Thoughts of a Classical Physicist,* the story of an aging German physicist, Professor Jakob who, presiding over the paradigm shift from the era of Newtonian causality to that of relativity, experiences such bewilderment and disappointment at the invalidation of his belief system and his life's work that he kills himself.

Radical as were the changes inherent in the Einsteinian paradigm, however, the anxieties they generated were not particularly new. A similar but more prophetic doubt permeates works like Matthew Arnold's "Dover Beach" (1867) "where the world hath neither joy nor love nor light, / Nor certitude, nor peace, nor help for pain," and Thomas Hardy's "Hap" (1866) where "Crass Casualty" and "dicing time" presage the randomness that modern physical theory institutionalizes. Similarly, Kierkegaard was undergoing fear and trembling, and Nietzsche was announcing the death of God, long before the physicists seem to have felt these effects. Yet it is one thing for poets and philosophers to experience existential "angst" and quite another for physicists to feel it. When the ancient verities collapsed for nineteenth-century doubters, they at least had science to fall back on, but when science was seeming to collapse early in the twentieth century, nothing remained.

One thing about the new paradigm that so undermined the assumptions of the Newtonian universe was the degree to which it was infected with paradox and uncertainty. Although neither Einstein's theories nor quantum mechanics describes phenomenal reality—their effects are limited to astronomic and sub-atomic systems—they do have profound implications when applied in the "real" world where Newton's Laws are thought to hold. Modern physics calls everyday reality into question, suggests that time and space are fictions, and implies that large areas of experience are simply indeterminate.

Although Einstein's ideas precede and form the basis for quantum physics, it is important to distinguish between them. Einstein retains a belief in meaning and the notion that if we keep seeking we can ultimately know the universe. His later career was spent in search of a Unified Field theory that would unite gravitation and electromagnetism and fully explain the functioning of the universe. A sizable number of physicists follow this line of thought and are pursuing connections amid the surface discontinuities of reality. Quantum theory, in contrast, exhibits much more patience with random statistical and indeterminate realities. Its ideas are less logical, less commonsensical, more paradoxical, but they appear also to be more accurate in their depiction of reality. Einstein never found the Unified Field or proved it mathematically, whereas mathematics does seem to support some of the dizzying scenarios of quantum physics—where currently there are at least eight competing visions of reality: 1) there is no deep reality; 2) reality is created by observation; 3) reality is an undivided wholeness; 4) reality consists in a steadily increasing number of parallel universes; 5) the world obeys a non-human kind of reasoning; 6) the world is made of ordinary objects and is just what it appears to be; 7) consciousness creates reality; and 8) the world is twofold, consisting of actualities and potentialities.

The most disorienting point in the relativistic view of the universe may be the discovery that time and space are neither absolute nor separable, but are locked indivisibly together in a continuum generally designated as space/time. These traditionally stable, fixed entities become relative, subjective. The ways in which we perceive them are inextricably locked into our frame of reference. Time does not flow smoothly from past to present to future; it exists in a block interpenetrated by space or perhaps in a pool or sea—not as a river, the way it is often depicted. The sequentiality and seriality that we experience in it are illusory. Similarly with space. It is neither contiguous nor uniform in Einstein's view. It is not empty nor is it a substance. The "nothing" is "something," but what it is is again dependent upon frame of reference or perspective. The Euclidean coordinates that we project upon reality may map it, but they are not reality itself. Objective reality, as Heisenberg's Uncertainty Principle underlines, can be pinned down either to position or velocity but not to both; so, the world becomes an elusive quantity. Central to the paradigm of relativity is the notion that reality, instead of lying in the objective world, lies in the act of measuring or perceiving it, in the phenomenological transaction between subject and object. As the implication of the Schrödinger's cat parable shows, however, the reality of an event is not determined until it is measured, and consequently the observer plays a major role in constituting reality. The world "out there" is colored by, if not constituted "in here."

Relativity thus collapses the subject-object dichotomy of the previous paradigm; they merge in a process that Wylie Sypher calls "methexis." In fact, in the new view, any bipolar oppositions collapse, as Bohr's theory of complementarity predicts. If light can be both a particle and a wave without contradiction depending upon the frame of reference from which it is considered, then it follows that other traditional opposites in the Relativistic paradigm also methexize. Einstein has already collapsed the distinctions between time and space, and energy and matter ($E = mc^2$). Extending this further, other dualities merge: subject-object, inside-outside, microcosm-macrocosm, ground and field, self-other, spirit and matter, male-female, etc. Reality becomes unattainable, and indeterminate. Since there are no conceptual models to aid us in visualizing relativistic ideas like the fourth dimension, all we have are metaphors—mathematics in the case of physics. Like language, however, mathematics is ever estranged, distanced from reality. The symbol never quite captures the thing; it only approximates its referent. Matter itself is seen to be a fiction. Things are not solid pieces of stuff; they are not composites in the relativistic view. Instead they are processes, interactions, particles in constant flux engaged in a "cosmic dance" or in unceasing, instantaneous interpenetration and transformation that we perceive as reality. In quantum mechanics, the world is not composed of dead or inanimate objects but is alive, in constant movement, ruled only by the laws of chance and probability.

Einstein, of course, never accepted this latter view, believing to the end that God does not play dice with the universe and seeking the ultimate meaning of it all in the Unified Field. Other more recent hypotheses about the nature of quantum reality do give at least a semblance of order. Two such models are described by Floyd Merrell in *Deconstruction Reframed*: the holographic model and Geoffrey Chew's bootstrap model. In holography, i.e., laser projection of three-dimensional images, any part of the holographic plate, no matter how small, can regenerate the whole image. Does this macrocosm within the microcosm image best describe the connections in the universe? Or is Chew's "bootstrap" theory more compelling—a theory which depicts the universe as composed not of discrete entities but as a "dynamic web of potential events in which each part contains and mirrors the structure of the whole"?

. . . . .

These paradoxical views of the universe as both discontinuous and as a seamless web do not seem to have troubled or excited physicists quite as much as writers and artists. This may be because these puzzling and paradoxical ideas do not apply directly to phenomenal reality where Newton's laws still work and common sense provides persuasive evidence. Scientists seem to be able to compartmentalize the implications of Einstein's theories and quantum mechanics in the Lilliputian and Brobdingnagian worlds

where they originated. Fiction writers, however, seem to have taken these ideas more literally and to have extended them immediately into their fictional worlds. Since their universes are fictional, and since the growing anti-realist mood of the arts at the turn of the century relieved them of the responsibility to mirror the phenomenal world, fiction writers could imaginatively incorporate some of the ideas of the new physics on the level of everyday reality. Although direct experience with physics did not always occur, a general intertextual relationship seems to have existed. The whole paradigm of Western rationalism seems to have been under fire from a number of directions. Anti-Newtonian/Cartesian sentiment was in the air. Some modern writers, among them Joyce, Mann, Durrell, Edmund Wilson, William Carlos Williams, Wallace Stevens and Evgeny Zamiatin directly acknowledge or reveal the influence of Einstein and relativity upon their thinking, while others only embed it in the epistemological assumptions of their work. They may have created their worlds under the influence of Gestalt or Freudian psychology; they may have dabbled in occultism or Eastern mythology or in primitive religion; they might have come under the sway of Nietzsche; their distensions of time may have been Bergsonian rather than Einsteinian; their unions of subject and object more Swedenborg than Heisenberg. Whatever the case, the metaphysics and the terminology of the contemporary physical paradigm are particularly useful in a literary context.

The development of the novel as a literary form seems to have paralleled the rise of the Newtonian and Darwinian paradigms. In the twentieth century, however, the death of the one heralded the death of the other. If scientists question the phenomenal world, challenge its reality, undermine its laws of cause and effect in their worlds, it is not surprising that fiction writers might do the same thing in theirs. Traditional fictional elements like plot, character, motivation, even meaning, change or recede, much as in modern physics the accustomed underpinnings of Newtonian reality collapsed.

The novel in the twentieth century has metamorphosed into forms more compatible with twentieth-century notions of reality. Modern fiction has been called many things and has taken many experimental forms, but it shares a view of the universe remarkably similar to that of the modern physicist. Modern fictions depict worlds where time and space are fluid and where they interpenetrate, where space is temporalized and time spatialized. Characters lack depth and motivation and are shifting and unstable in the same manner as objects and their backgrounds, which merge and separate ceaselessly. The reader/observer is drawn into the work as a participant; point of view is no longer stable or fixed. Meaning becomes multivocal or indeterminate.

. . . . .

One modern author whose entire body of work parallels the ideas of modern physics is James Joyce. In his early, relatively realistic works like *Dubliners, A Portrait of the Artist as a Young Man* and *Stephen Hero,* these parallels take the form of his use of the epiphany. Involving the potency of a neutral object and the sensibility of a conscious subject, the epiphany collapses the subject-object duality into an event in which the object is a sentient participant, alive in a sense. One of the mysterious findings of quantum physics is that matter is not inert or dead, but like objects in the epiphany reveals distinct signs of life.

As Joyce's literary experiment continues, his style increasingly parallels the relativistic paradigm. In *Dubliners,* despite the epiphanies, the style is predominantly naturalistic, but by the time of *A Portrait of the Artist as a Young Man* hints of stream-of-consciousness appear in its fragmentary diary excerpts and transitionless juxtapositions. These depict an interior world governed by shifting, disjointed, alogical and associational thoughts and feelings which constitute a subjective evocation of space/time given from a single perspective. Although this structure might be better explained in terms of the Freudian subconscious, it bears some affinity to the world of relativistic space/time in its apparent discontinuity.

The discourse of stream-of-consciousness can violate any of the strictures of time and place. The monologist's thoughts can move from place to place, imagined or real; actual events can be juxtaposed with fantasy, or all space/time can be represented in a single mind. If the mind can construct such an inner reality, it can also project it outward in a fictional form. Before the modern physical theories undercut our sense of the reality of the phenomenal world, this projective fiction might have been expected to conform to that world. If the world itself is only what it is because that is the way we perceive it, however, then the imaginative possibilities for fiction become almost infinite. Anything goes. What Einstein's theory does in a sense is to project the non-temporal, non-spatial reality of interiority out into the world, much as a modern novelist like Joyce does in *Ulysses* and *Finnegans Wake,* both of which, not unlike Einstein's theory or that of any scientist, try to encompass the whole of reality.

It is in *Ulysses,* however, that Joyce's method comes to maturity and shows increasing similarity to the relativist scheme. Joyce's record of a single day, 16 June 1904, has macrocosmic implications. Here Joyce does succeed in his professed aim of getting to the heart of all cities in penetrating to the heart of Dublin. As in the holographic model or the notion that the astronomical and subatomic echo one another, the universal is contained in the particular.

Stuart Gilbert describes the inhabitants of the Joycean world in the following terms:

> All these people are as they must be; they act, we see, according to some *lex eterna,* an ineluctable condition of their very existence. . . . The law of their being is within them, it is a personal heritage inalienable and autonomous. The meaning of *Ulysses,* for it has a meaning . . . is not to be sought in any of the facts of the protagonist or the mental make-up of the characters; it is, rather, implicit in the technique of the various episodes, in nuances of language, in the thousand and one correspondences and illusions with which the work is studded.

Similarly, in some contemporary physical theories, mo-

tion and change and the forces that control them are essential, intrinsic properties of things, of matter, but often the exact nature and behavior of these forces and things are indeterminate, beyond analysis, and beyond language. Both in Joyce's universe and in that of quantum mechanics, there are entities and events that make sense and others that are just the way they are and defy explanation. Both *Ulysses* and the universe are webs of relations falling in and out of patterns perceived differently by subjects with different frames of reference. On the surface, both the novel and the universe may seem discontinuous and disordered, but there are perceivable patterns of meaning. The characters and events in *Ulysses* obey a logic, but it may not be the logic we are used to.

The relativistic universe is in constant process, flux and transformation, and this is one of the significant messages of *Ulysses* and its "ineluctable modality of the visible." As Gilbert points out in his discussion of the mysticism of *Ulysses,* "a flux of transformation pervades the universe but nothing can be added or taken away"; but this universe operates on the principle that "all that exists from the smallest imaginable atom, contains within itself all the elements, the processus of the whole universe." This reflection of the holographic model or the macro/micro model of relativity shows up in the structure of the "Wandering Rocks" episode, which echoes the eighteen-part structure of the whole novel. Like the larger work, it spatializes time and presents its simultaneity, the sections cleverly interpenetrating one another in the fashion of the work as a whole. The wandering or clashing rocks from the Odyssean source themselves appear to illustrate one of the principles of relativity in that they appear to move through an optical illusion that depends upon frame of reference or point of view, an analogue perhaps of the reader's experience in confronting a plastic work like *Ulysses.*

Joyce's last work, *Finnegans Wake,* may not immediately satisfy the criteria of making sense, though it does follow another branch of quantum reality. On the surface this difficult, at times impenetrable, text seems almost meaningless. The characters have virtually hundreds of incarnations. Reality shifts instantaneously throughout all time/all space. HCE, Here Comes Everybody, is all men, Anna Livia Plurabelle all women. *Finnegans Wake* shifts languages at will. It is dominated by puns, their own kind of linguistic perspectivism, words and phrases that say different things when considered from different frames of reference. More than any other prose literature, *Finnegans Wake* severs words from their referents and emphasizes their sound. Large areas of the novel are indeterminate in terms of meaning for most readers. The design, like that of the modern conception of the universe, is so intricate, so complex, that it is inexhaustible in its content. Out of a remote corner of Dublin comes all history, all myth, all literature and all time/space. Like the space/time continuum, *Finnegans Wake* contains all.

Finnegans Wake also includes explicit references to modern physics as William York Tindall has pointed out. In one passage Joyce refers to "Winestain's theories and quantum mechanics" in a lecture by Professor Jones, the eminent spatialist. Jones attempts to assert that space is superior to time but winds up accepting the union of the two in space/time, "the grand continuum of the physicists." Apparently the influence went the other way also, because—as Anthony Zee has noted—the term for one of the hypothetical elementary particles in subatomic physics, the quark, comes from *Finnegans Wake:* "Three quarks for Muster Mark." It seems that Joyce was aware of physical theories, and the reality that underlies *Finnegans Wake* seems to be a close approximation of the notion that reality is an undivided wholeness where everything is interconnected.

. . . . .

The Relativity that underlies the Joycean universe is also to be found in most fiction in the Modernist mode. Virginia Woolf, for example, suggests the complementarity of the sexes by collapsing the male/female dichotomy in the androgyny of *Orlando*'s central character who changes sex inexplicably half way through the novel, in mid-passage between the sixteenth and twentieth centuries. Time and space congeal for Orlando as "everything was partly something else, and each gained an odd moving power from this union of itself and something else. . . . lights and shadows changed and one thing became another." Once one becomes aware of the relativistic paradigm, it becomes difficult not to see it underlying the work of those classic Modernist authors who experimented with the depiction of time and space, who present character and event as non-causal or indeterminate, or who reject the logocentric myth of objectivity. The list zigzags from Proust and Mann to Beckett, Robbe-Grillet, Nabokov, down to Borges, Garcia-Márquez, Fuentes, and back up through Pynchon, Barth and Burroughs, to name just a few.

All of Modernist literature reflects some association with the relativist mythology, though some genres do so more overtly than others. Science fiction comes to mind immediately in this connection, but another, perhaps more serious genre, one I would call "physics fiction," depends quite heavily, and quite overtly, on the mythology of relativity and quantum mechanics for its material. It is a fiction quite literally "about" physics.

At the same time that the Modernist writers' style began generally to reflect the relativistic paradigm, another group of authors began to rely even more heavily and quite overtly on it, using physics as the matter and controlling metaphor of their work. Thomas Mann's *The Magic Mountain* employs a prodigious amount of scientific theory and information to tell the story of Hans Castorp. In the microcosmic world of the International Sanitarium Berghof, Castorp debates as well as realizes the relativity of time. As his vocation changes from engineering to pure research, reality becomes increasingly problematic. The presumed oppositions of reality and fantasy merge, the distinction between sick and well blurs. Castorp confuses the identities of an attractive woman he meets at the sanitarium and a former childhood acquaintance. Mann also published an article on the implications of Einstein's theories at about the same time he was writing the novel.

Edmund Wilson also bases a novel, *I Thought of Daisy,* on the ideas of relativity as filtered through the works of Alfred North Whitehead. Daisy, the feminine interest in the novel, is like the unattainable object in the modern physical world; her essence is indeterminate, and the narrator describes her from several radically different and self-contradictory perspectives that leave the reader puzzled about what she really is like.

The practice of this kind of "physics fiction" culminates much later in the 1960s and 1970s with the work of Thomas Pynchon. His first novel, *V,* like most novels in the Modernist style, embodies the concepts of relativity on a stylistic level. Its title character goes through a number of incarnations but is ultimately indeterminate. The story is told from shifting, multiple points of view and presents the central epistemological problem posed by relativity—the conflict between order and disorder in the universe and the question of whether events in reality are connected and if so to what degree. Pynchon's other works, as many critics have noted, rely heavily on physics for their actual literal and thematic content.

One of Pynchon's early short stories, "Entropy," is a graphic representation of the Second Law of Thermodynamics, the pre-relativist view that the universe is a closed system inexorably winding down toward maximum disorder, negation, heat death. Entropy is also a prominent theme in his later works, *The Crying of Lot 49* and *Gravity's Rainbow.* Appearing in both these works as a literary character is Maxwell's Demon—a hypothetical invention created by the real nineteenth-century physicist, Clerk Maxwell, who designed the concept specifically to challenge the second law of thermodynamics. John P. Leland has described *The Crying of Lot 49* as not only being about entropy but as being entropic itself; the same may be said of *Gravity's Rainbow,* Pynchon's greatest work, which contains literally hundreds of allusions to physics. The title itself refers to the trajectory of a V-2 rocket. The novel contains equations from differential calculus and probability theory. Its whole structure embodies the conflict involved in the paradigm shift from determinism, cause and effect and control, to random chance, statistical probability and freedom. It would be virtually impossible to arrive at a full or, for that matter, adequate understanding of the novel without some grasp of the concepts of post-Einsteinian physics.

Not only Pynchon but a number of other contemporary authors write more or less directly about physics in their fiction. Several critics have pointed this out, most notably Robert Nadeau who treats the influence of modern physics in the work of Pynchon, Fowles, Barth, Vonnegut, Tom Robbins and Don Delillo; equally, N. Katherine Hayles has explored the relationship between scientific field models and the literary techniques of Pynchon, Pirsig, Nabokov and Borges among the contemporaries. To this list might be added Doris Lessing, whose *Briefing For a Descent Into Hell* (1971) explores the relativity of time and space, the notion of the interconnectedness of everything, and the reflection of the microcosm within the macrocosm in a vision approximating the holographic model. Lessing's more recent work includes a direct foray into science fiction in the multi-volumed *Canopus in Argos: The Archives.* Joseph McElroy's *Plus* (1976), the story of a disembodied brain orbiting the earth in a space capsule touches on some of the relativistic questions about subject-object, observer-observed relations, while his *Lookout Cartridge* (1974) emphasizes randomness and multiple realities in its exploration of subjects like computer circuits and non-local interaction or telepathy. Ron Loewinsohn's 1983 novel, *Magnetic Field(s),* takes not only its title but also its central concept from physics, ingeniously depicting three versions of reality linked apparently by certain inanimate objects in a complex web of interlocking involvement. Carol Hill's *Eleven Million Mile High Dancer* (1985), the story of a female astronaut, Amanda Jaworski, is constructed quite directly from the stuff of physics though in a decidedly comic way. The author extends several of the concepts of quantum mechanics into the real world. There is a cat named Schrodinger (without the umlaut) who is neither alive nor dead; allusions to physics are scattered throughout; there is an "Afterword" acknowledging the work's indebtedness to Heinz Pagel's *The Cosmic Code* and Fritzjof [sic] Capra's *The Tao of Physics,* two works popularizing the concepts of modern physics.

Two other young authors, Martin Amis in his short-story collection *Einstein's Monsters* (1987) and Tim O'Brien in *The Nuclear Age* (1985), take a more adversarial stand. Perhaps blaming the impending nuclear holocaust on the discoveries of Einstein and other physicists, these two present a bleak picture of the future. Amis in his introductory essay, "Thinkability," attacks nuclear weapons, and in stories like "Bujak and the Strong Force" and "The Time Disease" he explores some of the detrimental effects of nuclear physics. Depicting the mental deterioration of a man who has grown up in the shadow of nuclear annihilation, O'Brien divides his work into sections entitled "Fission," "Fusion" and "Critical Mass" and in each section there are sub-chapters entitled "Quantum Jumps." In his recent fiction, John Updike also makes extensive reference to contemporary physical theory; *Roger's Version* (1986) depicts, perhaps ironically, a born-again computer scientist, Dale Kohler, who attempts to find God in the most recent physics with the help of the computer.

·　·　·　·　·

Although in varying degrees, theories of physics therefore inform Modernist fiction to the extent that some knowledge of the area on the part of contemporary critics seems prerequisite. To do justice to the literature of today, the old conventional tools are not adequate. The methods of the New Critics, popularized in the 1940s and 50s and still the mainstay in many university classrooms (and high schools), seem particularly counterproductive. Newtonian/Cartesian in their approach, they reify the literary text, transforming it into an esthetic object, a "thing," and posit an ideal, objective reader who can toss aside irrelevancies and through analysis reach the correct meaning of the work. In dense, complex Modernist works this is often impossible.

Much, therefore, is to be said in support of recent critical trends. Here the text is no longer conceived of as a thing, nor is the reader viewed so readily as being able to separate him/herself from it. The reader is no longer thought of as a detached observer of the text, but is actively involved in "writing" it. The text, like Einstein's universe, is regarded as participatory. The meaning of the text, then, is seen to exist at least partially outside it: in the reader, in the values and perceptions of the "interpretive community," or in the interstices and interactions between text and reader, as phenomenologists have it. All these approaches find justification in the ideas of relativity.

Deconstruction, especially the earlier work of Jacques Derrida, also parallels the relativistic view at some key points. It too breaks down binary oppositions: signifier/signified, *language/parole,* reader/text, literature/philosophy. The deconstructor has the opposed entities "supplement" each other, whereas the relativist has them "complement" one another, but the concepts seem almost identical. The deconstructor's text, with its incompleteness, fluidity and indeterminacy, parallels the universe of quantum mechanics. In the same way that the observer participates in the composition of the relativistic universe, the deconstructing reader conspires in the writing of the text.

Although such developments in post-structuralist literary theory have extended the Einsteinian paradigm into literary criticism, I would urge that we do so in an even more systematic and consistent way.

A post-Einsteinian literary criticism would be outside ideology in its perspectivism. It would, of course, assume a perspective, but also acknowledge the subjectivity of its positions, their partiality. It would accept the multivocal nature of literary texts, as well as the hypothetical quality of interpretation, its fictionality. It would assert interpretations as dynamic models, tentative creative works themselves, dropping in the process the quest for interpretive truth. It would operate on the principle of complementarity and admit that a text can be or say two or more things at the same time depending on how one looks at it. Most important of all, such criticism would adopt the terminology of quantum mechanics and relativity to escape some of the vague, mystifying jargon of some post-structuralist theorizing. The paradigms of relativity and quantum mechanics provide us with a physics; now we need to develop a poetics that knowingly takes advantage of that model. After all, we should recall that Aristotle—the first great theoretician—was a "scientist" who constructed his "Poetics" in accordance with the laws of nature as he perceived them.

Louis Kaplan   (essay date 1991)

SOURCE: "Albert Einstein: A Necrological Approach," in *The Centennial Review*, Vol. 35, No. 3, Fall, 1991, pp. 591-606.

[*In the following essay, Kaplan contends that Einstein's* Autobiographical Notes *must be examined as a necrology-or obituary-largely because of Einstein's professional and personal connections to both the Jewish Holocaust of World War II and the atomic bombing of Hiroshima, Japan, by the United States, which Kaplan considers "the twin catastrophes at the limits of twentieth-century history and its meaning."*]

1. INTRODUCTION

This essay offers a close reading of a repeated figure in the autobiographical narrative of a survivor and a mourner whose life and work are bound up with the disasters which are evoked under the impossible names of Hiroshima and the Holocaust. Upon first impression, one might not think that an autobiographical text whose stated purpose is to review the philosophical achievements and the scientific discoveries of one of the most renowned thinkers of this century could be marked as a discourse of mourning, survival, and commemoration. But the ***Autobiographisches/Autobiographical Notes*** of Albert Einstein insists upon the generic status of *Nekrolog,* and it asks its readers at a number of points to be taken as an obituary. Whether by a throw of the dice or a divine providence, Albert Einstein always had to live with the obituaries in mind. His name and his science are inextricably linked with the corpses of the twin catastrophes at the limits of twentieth-century history and its meaning.

Einstein's necrological manoeuvres in the socio-political and ethical realms have reached the point where they have entered into cultural mythology. First, there are his complex relations to the holocaust of European Jewry. It is clear that his avid Zionism and his Jewish nationalist politics are fueled by the threat posed to European Jewry by the fascistic regimes and by Nazi Germany in particular. His early Zionist position must be viewed as necrologically motivated—as acting out of the fear of the corpses. In countless speeches and writings, his advocacy of the State of Israel counterbalances his role as a mourner and survivor of the Holocaust. For example, this fellow-sufferer delivers an eulogy to commemorate the victims of the resistance—**"To the Heroes of the Battle of the Warsaw Ghetto"** (1944). "We strive to be one in suffering and in the effort to achieve a better human society, that society which our prophets have so clearly and forcibly set before us as a goal." The messianic call of a Jewish homeland and the commemorative cry of Jewish sacrifice feed upon one another in the taking up of these prophetic terms.

But the complications are even more pronounced in Einstein's relations to the atomic bomb and his necrological actions on the brink of a nuclear disaster. On the one side, he comes as the prince of peace. He strives for a world government and for the end of all militarism. He engages in political activities designed to prevent or to guard against the piling up of the corpses. In an example of preemptive mourning, he warns of the apocalyptic possibilities of the hydrogen bomb: "If it is successful, radioactive poisoning of the atmosphere and hence annihilation of any life on earth has been brought within the range of technical possibilities." In this nightmare scenario, the necrologist is haunted by "the ghostlike character of this development" and he urges mankind to heed the necrological call before it is too late.

Nevertheless, it cannot be forgotten that the warning sirens directed at the H-bomb are counterpoised by Einstein's post-mortem position as survivor and mourner in relation to the A-bomb and the peculiar role which he played in both its conception and deliverance. After all, Einstein once wrote that infamous letter to President Roosevelt outlining the necrological powers of nuclear energy and encouraging the building of the atomic bomb. Even more problematic, there is the widespread opinion that Einstein's discoveries in the physical sciences provided the theoretical framework for the generation of the atomic bomb in the first place. Against this assertion of his responsibility, he will become quite defensive: "I do not consider myself the father of the release of atomic energy. My part in it was quite indirect. I did not, in fact, foresee that it would be released in my time. I believed only that it was theoretically possible." While he may deny the charges of paternity (i.e., that the bomb is his baby or his illegitimate son) or even the possibility that he could survive it in time, his self-professed assertion of the theoretical link (i.e., relativity) between the grim reaper of modern warfare and himself does not offer a complete release. Even an "indirect" theoretical involvement demonstrates how mourning and melancholy hang over this monstrous scene of the fathering of the atomic bomb as his own lost son.

There is another factor to bring into the necrological data base. That is the question of timing. Einstein wrote his ***Autobiographisches/Autobiographical Notes*** in 1946. This date is decisive for a necrological approach to the autobiography as a work of mourning. This puts history just one year after the bomb and the end of the Jewish slaughter. It is only in these dark lights that the Einstein survivor decided to give an accounting or eulogizing of his own life. It is a remarkable moment that has to be conceived in the terms of a historical rupture. In Einstein's brain, it is as if one era had ended and another one had begun. Poised between the mourning of one era and his survival into another, he writes his autobiography. The interruptive force of this inaugural year is also underscored when Einstein delivers a special message around the same time with a title that challenges the standard notions of timekeeping in the divide of the nuclear disaster: **"Year One—Atomic Age—A Message."**

With these catastrophic backdrops in the socio-political landscape, the cosmographic calendar, and the life and work of a unique survivor and mourner, this essay will turn to the repeated figure of mourning in the ***Autobiographisches***. This exegetical analysis focuses on the self-image of Einstein's autobiographical narrative as an obituary or *"Nekrolog."* Such an approach demands a review of the dynamics and scenography of the text at these necrological sites through the implementation of constructs from the literary critical disciplines. It restages the manner in which an intellectual biography of relativity physics inscribes itself as a subset of necrology, and the manner in which the story of a life transforms itself into the obituary pages.

II. ANOTHER HISTORIC EQUATION: AUTOBIOGRAPHY = NECROLOGY

Even when he is not deriving the formulae of relativity physics in its special or general theories, he cannot help but offer astonishing equations to the world. And in his ***Autobiographisches/Autobiographical Notes,*** Albert Einstein postulates a most important equation for the human sciences. In the process of composing his own intellectual autobiography, it turns out that an interdisciplinary contribution has been made to history and to the principles and axioms whereby the science of autobiography will have to be constituted. Substituting words for numbers, the equation will be read along the following lines: *"Autobiographisches = Hier sitze ich . . . etwas wie den eigenen Nekrolog zu schreiben"* ["Something Autobiographical = Here I sit . . . in order to write something like my own obituary"]. This is the title and the opening sentence employed by Einstein as he begins to write his autobiography. The present interpretation deduces that a sign (=) lies between them. In consequence, it concludes that Einstein begins with a pointed and epigrammatic definition of the essence of autobiography as he begins to write the story of his own life.

The story of his own life? Yet, the reclining and ironicizing Einstein teaches that the writing of one's own life is something like the writing of one's own death. Autobiography as necrology is a science of the living body's becoming-corpse. And, what is even more peculiar—this autobiographical writing will take the form of *ein Nekrolog,* an obituary—a writing of one's own life, after life and upon death. In other words, even as he begins to write his life, these words are coming from a voice beyond the grave. In terms of contemporary literary analysis, this dominant figure of autobiographical discourse is referred to as *prosopopeia,* the fiction of the voice from beyond the grave. Another voice—a necrological voice—dictates the life and mind of Albert Einstein even as Albert Einstein describes how he sat himself down to write his own story. Defamiliarizing the opening passage, the ghostly voice of necrology whispers something deadly into Einstein's ear: "There he sits in order to write something like. . . ."

This necrological approach helps to situate Einstein's move towards the impersonal in the *Autobiographisches.* In a discussion of what religion offered to him as a child, Einstein notes that it was *"ein erster Versuch . . . , mich aus den Fesseln des 'Nur-Persönlichen' zu befreien"* ["a first attempt to free myself from the chains of the 'merely personal'"]. The "merely personal" depends upon a repression of the problematic science of corpses. Placed in quotations, this marks Einstein's superimposition of an "extra-personal world" [*"ausserpersönliche Welt"*] as a necessary complement for the staging of himself as autobiographical subject. Setting up another necrological device, here the *"ausserpersönlich"* haunts even the merest of persons. The resulting neutralization provides another way to articulate the autobiographico-necrological equation. For the story of the merely personal = Here I sit in order to write something like my own (in the margins of the extra-personal).

Each of the phrases of the introductory maxim presents the paradoxes confronting the autobiographico-necrological activity. In each of its nuances, one suspects that Einstein is well aware of the black humour attending the composition of his own *"Nekrolog,"* of the necrological forces that give and take away such awareness. First, there is the matter of one's own obituary, *"den eigenen Nekrolog."* Properly speaking [*Eigentlich*], I know of no such thing as my own obituary. Of course, there is the logical impossibility of writing before one's death what can

only be written after one's death as well as the problem of writing after one's death in the first (or the last) place. Furthermore, one cannot possess ("my own") that form of inscription which attests to the dispossession and dispersion of one's own subjectivity. This oblique status of the necrological is demonstrated by the imprecise phrasing which is placed around "my own obituary." Only something like "something like" [*"etwas wie"*] can point to the living-dying state of the subject as necrologist composing "something autobiographical" or of the Einstein zombie. This borderline position and positioning of the subject has been set forth in the first three words of the text. *"Hier sitze ich. . . ."* The necrographer remains seated. He is to be imagined neither as an upstanding rigid rod nor as a straight line stretched to infinity, neither in the vertical nor in the horizontal. He is not the one who stands because he can do no other. In between is the only position possible for the necrological writings.

There has been an omission of a phrase from the first sentence of the *Autobiographisches* to be inserted at and about the proper time, *". . . um mit siebenundsechzig Jahren"* [at the age of sixty-seven]. This is the set interval of the present measured on the clock that counts historical time in the Euclidean frame of the merest of velocities. And *"um mit siebenundsechzig Jahren"* certainly places it into the chronological context *Out of His Later Years* (published in 1950). What is the relationship between this particular linear time measurement and Einstein's autobiographico-necrological equation? The clock can be set back to any arbitrarily selected point on the time line— going back seventeen, thirty-seven, forty-seven years, and so on. This is the time for reminiscence [*"Erinnerung"*]. This is memory in the making or to what will be referred in the *Autobiographisches* in "retrospect" [*"im Ruckblick"*]. Einstein recalls: *". . . der jetztige Mensch von siebenundsechzig ist nicht derselbe wie der von fünfzig, dreissig und zwanzig. Jede Erinnerung ist gefärbt durch das jetztige So-Sein, also durch einen trügerischen Blickpunkt. Diese Erwägung könnte wohl abschrecken"* [". . . today's person of sixty-seven is by no means the same as was the one of fifty, of thirty, or of twenty. Every reminiscence is colored by one's present state, hence by a deceptive point of view. This consideration could easily deter one"]. At any point in the time line or in the coloring of one's present state, one can read his age as an independent variable which in no way influences the essence of the autobiographic-necrological equation. It is a measurement to be inserted in the following manner: "Here I sit [at the age of fifty] in order to write something like my obituary"; "Here I sit [at the age of thirty] in order to write something like my obituary." It is nothing but a confirmation of how every living present always carries the signature of memoirs from beyond the grave.

Now, at the age of sixty-seven, Einstein hesitates. This is not because he fears the approach or the arrival of senility. This phenomenon could just as easily happen to the autobiographer-necrographer at the age of thirty. In these age-old considerations, Einstein raises the question of the effects of time in the faults and gaps of memory that pass between the dimming of the past and the coloring of the present and that problematize his total recall of himself by himself and by others. *"Nach einiger Überlegung fühlte ich, wie unvollkommen ein solcher Versuch ausfallen muss"* ["After some reflection, I felt how imperfect any such attempt is bound to be"]. In these opening passages, Einstein binds imperfection and the ways of error [*"die Irrwege"*] to the act of reflection, to the imperfections inherent in these reflections. The way of error leads to doubts about the validity of the truth claims of autobiographical writing. More importantly, these doubts radically question the identity of the autobiographical subject. What is the connection between today's person and the one of *x* number of years ago when the former is by no means the same as the one of ago? What is or was the truth of who he was when who he was is not who he is? Einstein's insertion of these Zeno-like paradoxes reveal that one constitutes an identity over time and the autobiographical narrative only by writing over the necrological institution of the present.

With the insertion of this deceptive variable, the equation is beginning to look much more complicated. For example, "Autobiographisches" = Here I sit [at the age of fifty] [deceptively recalling my life at the age of thirty] in order to write my obituary. While the deception factor affects the claims of the accuracy of the autobiographical record, it does not alter the essence of the equation. Rather, it shows in a profound manner how autobiography and necrology are bound to one another. The way of error demonstrates how the necrological forces invade the accounting of one's life so that the present will be colored by (something like) a putrefying and rotting cadaver.

But, still, the autobiographer as necrographer will not be deterred. He writes on: *"Aber man kann doch Manches aus dem Selbst-Erleben schöpfen, was einem andern Bewusstsein nicht zugänglich ist"* ["Nevertheless much can be gathered out of one's own experience that is not open to another consciousness"]. While he does return at this juncture to a necrological analysis, it is nevertheless necessary to understand how this conclusion in its essential affirmation of the autobiographical project depends upon necrological considerations. For the condition of possibility for the gathering of one's own experience is opened up by recalling oneself as an other. The self can only reminisce about itself [*"Selbst-Erleben"*] and constitute itself through the adoption of a specular relationship which addresses itself to and through the other. Or, as Einstein puts it in terms of the **Autobiographisches,** only "after some reflection . . ." [*"nach einiger Uberlegung"*].

In the beginning (if there was such a thing), this reflection is the first law of necrology. This is all. Recasting and inverting the Fortean epigraph through Einstein's autobiographical text, the necrologist proclaims the following law:

> **Axiom 1.** The science of the autobiographer begins with the obituary.

III. NECROLOGIZING THE *AUTOBIOGRAPHISCHES*

Having set up the basic equation of autobiography and necrology in the opening sentence of the **Autobiographisches,** one finds that Einstein's text returns to the inscription of the *"Nekrolog"* in four other instances which call for a necrological reading.

A. Scenes 2 and 3: Necrology's Interruption and Return

When the *"Nekrolog"* makes its second posthumous appearance in the **Autobiographisches,** it is linked to the dynamics of interruption. *"Nachdem ich mich nun einmal dazu habe hinreissen lassen, den notdürftig begonnenen Nekrolog zu unterbrechen . . ."* ["Now that I have allowed myself to be carried away sufficiently to interrupt my barely started obituary . . ."]. What has happened to his story? Einstein has interrupted the *Nekrolog* in order to be carried away by a number of philosophical speculations about wonder. Now he interrupts these interruptions to reflect upon the fact that it has been interrupted and in order to let himself be carried away even further so that the reader will have to excuse him for moving on to his so-called "epistemological credo": *"[S]cheue ich mich nicht hier in ein paar Sätzen mein erkenntnistheoretisches Credo auszudrücken"* ["I shall not hesitate to state here in a few sentences my epistemological credo"]. Yet, whether he knows it or not, this movement of rupture and drift reveals an Einstein at his necrographic best. He has been exposed to the interruptive force of necrology and to necrology as interruptive force. He thinks that he has interrupted the obituary. He thinks that he has drifted away from the obituary. But this is necrology in the making. It demonstrates the irreducible precedence of the interruption for the accounting of the self. This is the "barely started" space of the autobiographical subject as necrologist. It recalls the specular scene that allows him to become himself or to get carried away with himself.

Indeed, one might say that Einstein's epistemological credo also depends upon such a rupture. For the credo points to how epistemology can be located as a necrological effect. On the one side, there is *"die Gesamtheit der Sinnen-Erlebnisse, auf der andern Seite die Gesamtheit der Begriffe und Sätze, die in den Büchern niedergelegt sind"* ["the totality of sense experiences and, on the other, the totality of the concepts and propositions that are laid down in books"]. The problem, of course, is how to move from the one to the other—from experience to theory, from the world to the books. How does one open an epistemological space? It is at this juncture that Einstein makes a leap to bridge the gap: *"Die Verbindung der letzteren mit den ersteren ist rein intuitiv . . ."* ["The connection of the latter with the former is purely intuitive"]. It is not the place of a necrological approach to judge the truth or to explicate the nature of this intuitive leap. Rather, it recalls how the intuitive leap offers the means to bridge or to efface the necrological gap. After another two paragraphs of epistemological credo—*"Nun zurück zum Nekrolog"* ["And now back to the obituary"]. In both of these instances (*"Nekrolog"* 2 and 3), it would appear that Einstein tries to differentiate two parts of his text—a necrological and a non-necrological portion. This is a very odd distinction in light of the opening equation (Autobiography = Necrology) and it is a distinction that Einstein later disavows in the fourth occurrence of the *"Nekrolog."* Rather than attacking the Einstein text for these logical inconsistencies, this shift in position demonstrates how the necrological border slips through these attempts to set it into place and to master it. When one examines this excluded portion further, one finds that it outlines a history of modern philosophy. It offers *"eine Bemerkung zur geschichtlichen Entwicklung"* ["a remark as to the historical development"] on the gap between concept and experience in the thought of Hume and Kant. Indeed, these remarks inscribe "historical development" as a necrological effect. Einstein's explanation of causality reveals how the project of historical development is tied to the realm of concepts. *"Alle Begriffe, auch die erlebnisnächsten, sind vom logischen Gesichtspunkte aus freie Setzungen, genau wie der Begriff der Kausalität, an den sich in erster Linie die Fragestellung angeschlossen hat"* ["All concepts, even those closest to experience, are from the point of view of logic freely chosen posits, just as is the concept of causality, which was the point of departure for this inquiry in the first place"]. The theory-experience distinction reiterates and repeats the necrological interruption as the point of departure in the first place. Between the logical concept (e.g., "historical development") and the sensory experience lies the repetition of the interruption. Now, for the constitution of every present moment of now, there is the eternal return of a problematic point of departure:

> **Axiom 2.** Rather than interrupting or returning to necrology, necrology marks the return to the interruption.

B. Scenes 4 and 5: The Necrological Climax, or The Essentially Yes

In the ***Autobiographisches,*** the funerary speech is by no means restricted to Einstein himself. The fourth necrological instance is preceded by a paragraph that is something like a eulogy. One imagines at this juncture Albert Einstein sitting by the grave of the gravity master, Sir Isaac Newton. After pages of autobiographical reflections on the merits of the theory of relativity, Einstein backtracks in the following apologia.

> *Genug davon. Newton verzeih' mir; du fandst den einzigen Weg der zu deiner Zeit für einen Menschen von höchster Denk- und Gestaltungskraft eben noch müglich war. Die Begriffe, die du schufst, sind auch jetzt noch führend in unserem physikalischen Denken, obwohl wir nun wissen, dass sie durch andere, der Sphäre der unmittelbaren Erfahrung ferner stehende ersetzt werden müssen, wenn wir ein tieferes Begreifen der Zusammenhange anstreben.*

> [Enough of this. Newton, forgive me: you found just about the only way possible in your age for a man of highest reasoning and creative power. The concepts that you created are even today still guiding our thinking in physics, although we now know that they will have to be replaced by others father removed from the sphere of immediate experience, if we aim at a profounder understanding of relationships.]

In this testamentary homage and most intimate apology, Einstein slips into the direct and informal address of the second person ("Newton, forgive me," "you found," "you created," etc.) in his exhuming the dead hero of another physical age. In fact, this address has similarities with nec-

romancy, the art of prediction by means of communication with the dead. This address delivers the reverse side of an encounter with the fiction of the voice from beyond the grave. Far removed from Newton's immediate experience, Albert Einstein—who has reinscribed and removtivated the Newtonian text through relativity physics—assumes the role of the unknown addressee from another age. Given its position in the text, these necrological remarks counterpose Einstein's biographical eulogy of Newton with his own autobiographical necrology wherein the proceeds to put himself into Newton's place in the subsequent paragraph.

The fourth recitation brings the most astonishing results. Appropriately enough, the *"Nekrolog"* is set up to be spoken through the words of another and in the form of a question. It is rendered as a rhetorical device and placed within quotation marks. This is a singular occurrence in the ***Autobiographisches*** and a signal that something out of the ordinary is taking place. The reader is hailed as the unknown addressee in order to ask both the author and the text in this astonished tone: *"Soll dies ein Nekrolog sein?' mag der erstaunte Leser fragen"* [" 'Is this supposed to be an obituary?' the astonished reader will likely ask"]. But an even more astonished reader will likely ask: "Who asks this question?" Who asks whether this should be *ein Nekrolog?* For it is the necrological voice itself which has been inserted into Einstein's text to ask whether this is supposed to be necrology.

"Im wesentlichen ja, möchte ich antworten. Denn das Wesentliche im Dasein eines Menschen von meiner Art liegt . . ." ["I would like to reply: essentially yes. For the essential in the being of a man of my type lies . . ."]. Here the quotation is cut and the essential answer is postponed. But this is only in order to show how Einstein has already delivered and delimited necrology in its essential structure and in its structuration of the essential. The "Is this supposed to be an obituary?"—the call of and from the necrological voice—marks the questionable ontological status of the science of corpses in the being [*Dasein*] of a man of his type or in any type. This has nothing at all to do with the privileging of the *how* and the *what* of thinking over the doing or the suffering. Moreover, autobiography as necrology enacts or performs the occurrence of the "Is this supposed to be an obituary?"

"Essentially yes." What a puzzling answer! Why not yes, a simple yes, simply yes. What is the difference between *yes* and *essentially yes?* Why the insertion of this modifier? Why place what is essential as a modifier or as a supplement? Why this remainder around the yes, this hanging together with the yes? This is supposed to be an obituary. Or, to put it another way, this is how one writes necrologically, in affirming and acknowledging the other in the midst of essence.

In the advanced study of Einstein's ***Autobiographisches,*** one approaches the institution of the following principle:

> **Axiom 3.** Necrology affirms the essential and the essential modifies the affirmation.

In the final inscription of the *"Nekrolog,"* there is the attempt to give a limited and definitive definition in a declarative modality: *"Also kann der Nekrolog sich in der Hauptsache auf Mitteilung von Gedanken beschränken, die in meinem Streben eine erhebliche Rolle spielten"* ["Consequently, the obituary can limit itself in the main to the communicating of thoughts that have played a considerable role in my striving"]. Here Einstein seeks to define the autobiographico-necrological equation to the exclusion of marginal or performative effects—the playing out of the inconsiderable or on the sides, the miscommunication of a thought or of a lack of communication in general. At this juncture, it is necessary to read Einstein against himself and to listen to the necrological voice in the unconscious of the text that plays dice with his universe. The play is written on the necrological border of the *essentially yes*. This reading and role-playing involve the intertwining and the interchange of *Streben* and *Sterben,* of striving and of dying. In an autobiographico-necrological interpretation of the text, there comes a superimposition and a doubled exposure in the twists and turns of these two letters. *"Also kann sich der Nekrolog in der Hauptsache auf Mitteilung von Gedanken beschränken, die in meinem* Streben-Sterben *eine erhebliche Rolle spielten."*

IV. Necrological Opportunistics

In the **"Reply to Criticisms"** in *Albert Einstein: Philosopher-Scientist,* the essay which closes the volume which begins with the bilingual publication of the *Autobiographisches,* Einstein makes his famous remarks about the proper and improper relations between science and epistemology. While one might consider these remarks far from a biographical or an autobiographical analysis, a closer inspection reveals that these remarks contain another striking self-portrait of/by Albert Einstein. In fact, taking away certain restrictions, these comments might be placed as a supplement to the epistemological credo of the *Autobiographisches*.

> *Die äusseren Bedingungen, die fur ihn durch die Erfahrungstatsachen gegeben sind, gestatten es ihm nicht, sich beim Aufbau seines Weltbildes zu stark durch die Bindung an ein erkenntnistheoretisches System einschränken zu lassen. Daher muss er dem systematischen Erkenntnistheoretiker als eine Art bederkenloser Opportunist erscheinen. . . .*

> [The external conditions which are set for him by the facts of experience do not permit him to let himself be too much restricted in the construction of his conceptual world by the adherence to an epistemological system. He therefore must appear to the systematic epistemologist as a type of unscrupulous opportunist. . . .]

This description offers a thinly-masked case of *prosopoperia* in the conferring of a mask onto oneself. Every time that you see "he" in this quotation, you should remember that it is "I" who am speaking to you. Every time that you see "him" or "himself " in this quotation, you should not forget that it is "me" and "myself " to whom "I" am referring. Therefore, I must appear to you as a type of unscrupulous opportunist. Keeping these substitutive equations in mind (he-the scientist = I-Einstein), the remarks might be read and interpreted as an allegory for the autobiographer and for the practice of autobiography as

necrography. In other words, using some unscrupulous opportunistics, one could just as easily substitute the word "necrographer" in place of the word "scientist" in an attempt to locate "his" antecedent. In the construction of his and other conceptual worlds, the necrographer should not be restricted to any epistemological system. He is in a similar position to the scientist who experiments upon the "object" so that the facts set for him by experience and by external conditions will be subject only to the practice of an unscrupulous opportunism.

The epistemological self-portrait also establishes another specular relationship. Einstein now reads himself through the eyes of the men who practice science under the adhering label of systematic epistemology. He now imagines the necrological voice in the form of the systematic epistemologist who has come back to condemn his text. It is important to understand that the critique is linked to an inability to accept the dynamics of Einstein's necrological strategies which put epistemological systematics into question. In fact, the systematic epistemologist cannot accept the realization that he will have been made to come back in a necrological guise—as demonstrated in this passage through Einstein's text.

For the purposes of this study, it is important to outline how this brand of unscrupulous opportunism is connected with necrologics. Why is it that the necrologician will have to be an unscrupulous opportunist? This has to do with the adhesive-unadhesive status of the necrological text. As Einstein demonstrates, the autobiographical text as obituary will have been cut off (even ripped off) from the life of its addressor from the first instance. Likewise, it will be picked up in and out of every type of context by any number of unknown addressees for all time to come. In this manner, necrologics reglues the set adhesion factor of systematic epistemology. Like Albert Einstein about to begin his autobiography, the necrological text sits waiting for some speculative opportunist to come along at the opportune moment—at the moment (in) which he makes opportune—and to stake or stick his or her claim upon it. Unscrupulously, he will have found another opportunity to stage the necrological text. At this juncture, one returns to a literal meaning of both opportunist and unscrupulous as unprincipled. As in the relations between Newton and Einstein, there can be no first or final principle when given this unscrupulous structure of the necrological text and the affirmation of an unlimited supply of golden opportunities.

These two forces—the provisionally dubbed, necrologics and unscrupulous opportunism—will make it difficult to maintain the idea of a proper context. It becomes difficult to keep or to hold the autobiographical subject with the acclaimed name of Einstein within a set context. For the necrologics of the text insists upon the detaching capacity to break with every given context and to engender an infinity of new contexts without ever reaching the stuck, or the final sticking point. Necrologics removes the restrictions to the construction of conceptual worlds. It will continue to supply the demands of unscrupulous opportunists to come through its citation and its recitation. In this way, Einstein's unscrupulous opportunist outmaneuvers the fixed principles and the adherence of the systematic epistemologist.

Out of this context—and out from under a seal of approval stamped in New Jersey sometime ago—Einstein's necrological opportunistics affirms (essentially) the most appropriate and inappropriate of (auto) biographical writings. These are offered as necrographical contributions to an unscrupulous science of Einstein studies in the production of effects beyond his presence and beyond his life which no context can ever enclose.

Stephen Hawking   (essay date 1993)

SOURCE: "Einstein's Dream," in *Black Holes and Baby Universes, and Other Essays*, Bantam Books, 1993, pp. 69-83.

[*Hawking is an English physicist, author, and educator renowned for his significant contributions to contemporary scientific theory. In the following essay, which was originally presented as a lecture at the Paradigm Session of the NTT Data Communications Systems Corporation in Tokyo in 1991, he describes relativity and quantum mechanics and explains their implications for contemporary science and culture.*]

In the early years of the twentieth century, two new theories completely changed the way we think about space and time, and about reality itself. More than seventy-five years later, we are still working out their implications and trying to combine them in a unified theory that will describe everything in the universe. The two theories are the general theory of relativity and quantum mechanics. The general theory of relativity deals with space and time and how they are curved or warped on a large scale by the matter and energy in the universe. Quantum mechanics, on the other hand, deals with very small scales. Included in it is what is called the uncertainty principle, which states that one can never precisely measure the position and the velocity of a particle at the same time; the more accurately you can measure one, the less accurately you can measure the other. There is always an element of uncertainty or chance, and this affects the behavior of matter on a small scale in a fundamental way. Einstein was almost single-handedly responsible for general relativity, and he played an important part in the development of quantum mechanics. His feelings about the latter are summed up in the phrase "God does not play dice." But all the evidence indicates that God is an inveterate gambler and that He throws the dice on every possible occasion.

In this essay, I will try to convey the basic ideas behind these two theories, and why Einstein was so unhappy about quantum mechanics. I shall also describe some of the remarkable things that seem to happen when one tries to combine the two theories. These indicate that time itself had a beginning about fifteen billion years ago and that it may come to an end at some point in the future. Yet in another kind of time, the universe has no boundary. It is neither created nor destroyed. It just is.

I shall start with the theory of relativity. National laws hold only within one country, but the laws of physics are the same in Britain, the United States, and Japan. They are also the same on Mars and in the Andromeda galaxy. Not only that, the laws are the same at no matter what speed you are moving. The laws are the same on a bullet train or on a jet airplane as they are for someone standing in one place. In fact, of course, even someone who is stationary on the earth is moving at about 18.6 miles (30 kilometers) a second around the sun. The sun is also moving at several hundred kilometers a second around the galaxy, and so on. Yet all this motion makes no difference to the laws of physics; they are the same for all observers.

This independence of the speed of the system was first discovered by Galileo, who developed the laws of motion of objects like cannonballs or planets. However, a problem arose when people tried to extend this independence of the speed of the observer to the laws that govern the motion of light. It had been discovered in the eighteenth century that light does not travel instantaneously from source to observer; rather, it goes at a certain speed, about 186,000 miles (300,000 kilometers) a second. But what was this speed relative *to*? It seemed that there had to be some medium throughout space through which the light traveled. This medium was called the ether. The idea was that light waves traveled at a speed of 186,000 miles a second through the ether, which meant that an observer who was at rest relative to the ether would measure the speed of light to be about 186,000 miles a second, but an observer who was moving through the ether would measure a higher or lower speed. In particular, it was believed that the speed of light ought to change as the earth moves through the ether on its orbit around the sun. However, in 1887 a careful experiment carried out by Michelson and Morley showed that the speed of light was always the same. No matter what speed the observer was moving at, he would always measure the speed of light at 186,000 miles a second.

How can this be true? How can observers moving at different speeds all measure light at the same speed? The answer is they can't, not if our normal ideas of space and time hold true. However, in a famous paper written in 1905, Einstein pointed out that such observers could all measure the same speed of light if they abandoned the idea of a universal time. Instead, they would each have their own individual time, as measured by a clock each carried with him. The times measured by these different clocks would agree almost exactly if they were moving slowly with respect to each other—but the times measured by different clocks would differ significantly if the clocks were moving at high speed. This effect has actually been observed by comparing a clock on the ground with one in a commercial airliner; the clock in the airliner runs slightly slow when compared to the stationary clock. However, for normal speeds of travel, the differences between the rates of clocks are very small. You would have to fly around the world four hundred million times to add one second to your life; but your life would be reduced by more than that by all those airline meals.

How does having their own individual time cause people traveling at different speeds to measure the same speed of light? The speed of a pulse of light is the distance it travels between two events, divided by the time interval between the events. (An event in this sense is something that takes place at a single point in space, at a specified point in time.) People moving at different speeds will not agree on the distance between two events. For example, if I measure a car traveling down the highway, I might think it had moved only one kilometer, but to someone on the sun, it would have moved about 1,800 kilometers, because the earth would have moved while the car was going down the road. Because people moving at different speeds measure different distances between events, they must also measure different intervals of time if they are to agree on the speed of light.

Einstein's original theory of relativity, which he proposed in the paper written in 1905, is what we now call the special theory of relativity. It describes how objects move through space and time. It shows that time is not a universal quantity which exists on its own, separate from space. Rather, future and past are just directions, like up and down, left and right, forward and back, in something called space-time. You can only go in the future direction in time, but you *can* go at a bit of an angle to it. That is why time can pass at different rates.

The special theory of relativity combined time with space, but space and time were still a fixed background in which events happened. You could choose to move on different paths through space-time, but nothing you could do would modify the background of space and time. However, all this was changed when Einstein formulated the general theory of relativity in 1915. He had the revolutionary idea that gravity was not just a force that operated in a fixed background of space-time. Instead, gravity was a *distortion* of space-time, caused by the mass and energy in it. Objects like cannonballs and planets try to move on a straight line through space-time, but because space-time is curved, warped, rather than flat, their paths appear to be bent. The earth is trying to move on a straight line through space-time, but the curvature of space-time produced by the mass of the sun causes it to go in a circle around the sun. Similarly, light tries to travel in a straight line, but the curvature of space-time near the sun causes the light from distant stars to be bent if it passes near the sun. Normally, one is not able to see stars in the sky that are in almost the same direction as the sun. During an eclipse, however, when most of the sun's light is blocked off by the moon, one can observe the light from those stars. Einstein produced his general theory of relativity during the First World War, when conditions were not suitable for scientific observations, but immediately after the war a British expedition observed the eclipse of 1919 and confirmed the predictions of general relativity: Space-time is not flat, but is curved by the matter and energy in it.

This was Einstein's greatest triumph. His discovery completely transformed the way we think about space and time. They were no longer a passive background in which events took place. No longer could we think of space and time as running on forever, unaffected by what happened in the universe. Instead, they were now dynamic quantities that influenced and were influenced by events that took place in them.

An important property of mass and energy is that they are always positive. This is why gravity always attracts bodies toward each other. For example, the gravity of the earth attracts us to it even on opposite sides of the world. That is why people in Australia don't fall off the world. Similarly, the gravity of the sun keeps the planets in orbit around it and stops the earth from shooting off into the darkness of interstellar space. According to general relativity, the fact that mass is always positive means that space-time is curved back on itself, like the surface of the earth. If mass had been negative, space-time would have been curved the other way, like the surface of a saddle. This positive curvature of space-time, which reflects the fact that gravity is attractive, was seen as a great problem by Einstein. It was then widely believed that the universe was static, yet if space, and particularly time, were curved back on themselves, how could the universe continue forever in more or less the same state as it is at the present time?

Einstein's original equations of general relativity predicted that the universe was either expanding or contracting. Einstein therefore added a further term to the equations that relate the mass and energy in the universe to the curvature of space-time. This so-called cosmological term had a repulsive gravitational effect. It was thus possible to balance the attraction of the matter with the repulsion of the cosmological term. In other words, the negative curvature of space-time produced by the cosmological term could cancel the positive curvature of space-time produced by the mass and energy in the universe. In this way, one could obtain a model of the universe that continued forever in the same state. Had Einstein stuck to his original equations, without the cosmological term, he would have predicted that the universe was either expanding or contracting. As it was, no one thought the universe was changing with time until 1929, when Edwin Hubble discovered that distant galaxies are moving away from us. The universe is expanding. Einstein later called the cosmological term "the greatest mistake of my life."

But with or without the cosmological term, the fact that matter caused space-time to curve in on itself remained a problem, though it was not generally recognized as such. What it meant was that matter could curve a region in on itself so much that it would effectively cut itself off from the rest of the universe. The region would become what is called a black hole. Objects could fall into the black hole, but nothing could escape. To get out, they would need to travel faster than the speed of light, which is not allowed by the theory of relativity. Thus the matter inside the black hole would be trapped and would collapse to some unknown state of very high density.

Einstein was deeply disturbed by the implications of this collapse, and he refused to believe that it happened. But Robert Oppenheimer showed in 1939 that an old star of more than twice the mass of the sun would inevitably collapse when it had exhausted all its nuclear fuel. Then war intervened, Oppenheimer became involved in the atom bomb project, and he lost interest in gravitational collapse. Other scientists were more concerned with physics that could be studied on earth. They distrusted predictions about the far reaches of the universe because it did not seem they could be tested by observation. In the 1960s, however, the great improvement in the range and quality of astronomical observations led to new interest in gravitational collapse and in the early universe. Exactly what Einstein's general theory of relativity predicted in these situations remained unclear until Roger Penrose and I proved a number of theorems. These showed that the fact that space-time was curved in on itself implied that there would be singularities, places where space-time had a beginning or an end. It would have had a beginning in the big bang, about fifteen billion years ago, and it would come to an end for a star that collapsed and for anything that fell into the black hole the collapsing star left behind.

The fact that Einstein's general theory of relativity turned out to predict singularities led to a crisis in physics. The equations of general relativity, which relate the curvature of space-time with the distribution of mass and energy, cannot be defined as a singularity. This means that general relativity cannot predict what comes out of a singularity. In particular, general relativity cannot predict how the universe should begin at the big bang. Thus, general relativity is not a complete theory. It needs an added ingredient in order to determine how the universe should begin and what should happen when matter collapses under its own gravity.

The necessary extra ingredient seems to be quantum mechanics. In 1905, the same year he wrote his paper on the special theory of relativity, Einstein also wrote about a phenomenon called the photoelectric effect. It had been observed that when light fell on certain metals, charged particles were given off. The puzzling thing was that if the intensity of the light was reduced, the number of particles emitted diminished, but the speed with which each particle was emitted remained the same. Einstein showed this could be explained if light came not in continuously variable amounts, as everyone had assumed, but rather in packets of a certain size. The idea of light coming only in packets, called quanta, had been introduced a few years earlier by the German physicist Max Planck. It is a bit like saying one can't buy sugar loose in a supermarket but only in kilogram bags. Planck used the idea of quanta to explain why a red-hot piece of metal doesn't give off an infinite amount of heat; but he regarded quanta simply as a theoretical trick, one that didn't correspond to anything in physical reality. Einstein's paper showed that you could directly observe individual quanta. Each particle emitted corresponded to one quantum of light hitting the metal. It was widely recognized to be a very important contribution to quantum theory, and it won him the Nobel Prize in 1922. (He should have won a Nobel Prize for general relativity, but the idea that space and time were curved was still regarded as too speculative and controversial, so they gave him a prize for the photoelectric effect instead—not that it was not worth the prize on its own account.)

The full implications of the photoelectric effect were not realized until 1925, when Werner Heisenberg pointed out that it made it impossible to measure the position of a particle exactly. To see where a particle is, you have to shine light on it. But Einstein had shown that you couldn't use a very small amount of light; you had to use at least one packet, or quantum. This packet of light would disturb the particle and cause it to move at a speed in some direction. The more accurately you wanted to measure the position of the particle, the greater the energy of the packet you would have to use and thus the more it would disturb the particle. However you tried to measure the particle, the uncertainty in its position, times the uncertainty in its speed, would always be greater than a certain minimum amount.

This uncertainty principle of Heisenberg showed that one could not measure the state of a system exactly, so one could not predict exactly what it would do in the future. All one could do is predict the probabilities of different outcomes. It was this element of chance, or randomness, that so disturbed Einstein. He refused to believe that physical laws should not make a definite, unambiguous prediction for what would happen. But however one expresses it, all the evidence is that the quantum phenomenon and the uncertainty principle are unavoidable and that they occur in every branch of physics.

Einstein's general relativity is what is called a classical theory; that is, it does not incorporate the uncertainty principle. One therefore has to find a new theory that combines general relativity with the uncertainty principle. In most situations, the difference between this new theory and classical general relativity will be very small. This is because, as noted earlier, the uncertainty predicted by quantum effects is only on very small scales, while general relativity deals with the structure of space-time on very large scales. However, the singularity theorems that Roger Penrose and I proved show that space-time will become highly curved on very small scales. The effects of the uncertainty principle will then become very important and seem to point to some remarkable results.

Part of Einstein's problems with quantum mechanics and the uncertainty principle arose from the fact that he used the ordinary, commonsense notion that a system has a definite history. A particle is either in one place or in another. It can't be half in one and half in another. Similarly, an event like the landing of astronauts on the moon either has taken place or it hasn't. It cannot have half-taken place. It's like the fact that you can't be slightly dead or slightly pregnant. You either are or you aren't. But if a system has a single definite history, the uncertainty principle leads to all sorts of paradoxes, like the particles being in two places at once or astronauts being only half on the moon.

An elegant way to avoid these paradoxes that had so troubled Einstein was put forward by the American physicist Richard Feynman. Feynman became well known in 1948 for work on the quantum theory of light. He was awarded the Nobel Prize in 1965 with another American, Julian Schwinger, and the Japanese physicist Shinichiro Tomonaga. But he was a physicist's physicist, in the same tradition as Einstein. He hated pomp and humbug, and he resigned from the National Academy of Sciences because he found that they spent most of their time deciding which other scientists should be admitted to the Academy. Feynman, who died in 1988, is remembered for his many contributions to theoretical physics. One of these was the diagrams that bear his name, which are the basis of almost every calculation in particle physics. But an even more important contribution was his concept of a sum over histories. The idea was that a system didn't have just a single history in space-time, as one would normally assume it did in a classical nonquantum theory. Rather, it had every possible history. Consider, for example, a particle that is at a point A at a certain time. Normally, one would assume that the particle will move on a straight line away from A. However, according to the sum over histories, it can move on *any* path that starts at A. It is like what happens when you place a drop of ink on a piece of blotting paper. The particles of ink will spread through the blotting paper along every possible path. Even if you block the straight line between two points by putting a cut in the paper, the ink will get around the corner.

Associated with each path or history of the particle will be a number that depends on the shape of the path. The probability of the particle traveling from A to B is given by adding up the numbers associated with all the paths that take the particle from A to B. For most paths, the number associated with the path will nearly cancel out the numbers from paths that are close by. Thus, they will make little contribution to the probability of the particle's going from A to B. But the numbers from the straight paths will add up with the numbers from paths that are almost straight. Thus the main contribution to the probability will come from paths that are straight or almost straight. That is why the track a particle makes when going through a bubble chamber looks almost straight. But if you put something like a wall with a slit in it in the way of the particle, the particle paths can spread out beyond the slit. There can be a high probability of finding the particle away from the direct line through the slit.

In 1973 I began investigating what effect the uncertainty principle would have on a particle in the curved space-time near a black hole. Remarkably enough, I found that the black hole would not be completely black. The uncertainty principle would allow particles and radiation to leak out of the black hole at a steady rate. This result came as a complete surprise to me and everyone else, and it was greeted with general disbelief. But with hindsight, it ought to have been obvious. A black hole is a region of space from which it is impossible to escape if one is traveling at less than the speed of light. But the Feynman sum over histories says that particles can take *any* path through space-time. Thus it is possible for a particle to travel faster than light. The probability is low for it to move a long distance at more than the speed of light, but it can go faster than light for just far enough to get out of the black hole, and then go slower than light. In this way, the uncertainty principle allows particles to escape from what was thought to be the ultimate prison, a black hole. The probability of a particle getting out of a black hole of the mass of the sun would be very low because the particle would have to travel faster than light for several kilometers. But there might be very much smaller black holes, which were formed in the early universe. These primordial black holes could be less than the size of the nucleus of an atom, yet their mass could be a billion tons, the mass of Mount Fuji. They could be emitting as much energy as a large power station. If only we could find one of these little black holes and

harness its energy! Unfortunately, there don't seem to be many around in the universe.

The prediction of radiation from black holes was the first nontrivial result of combining Einstein's general relativity with the quantum principle. It showed that gravitational collapse was not as much of a dead end as it had appeared to be. The particles in a black hole need not have an end of their histories at a singularity. Instead, they could escape from the black hole and continue their histories outside. Maybe the quantum principle would mean that one could also avoid the histories having a beginning in time, a point of creation, at the big bang.

This is a much more difficult question to answer, because it involves applying the quantum principle to the structure of time and space themselves and not just to particle paths in a given space-time background. What one needs is a way of doing the sum over histories not just for particles but for the whole fabric of space and time as well. We don't know yet how to do this summation properly, but we do know certain features it should have. One of these is that it is easier to do the sum if one deals with histories in what is called imaginary time rather than in ordinary, real time. Imaginary time is a difficult concept to grasp, and it is probably the one that has caused the greatest problems for readers of my book. I have also been criticized fiercely by philosophers for using imaginary time. How can imaginary time have anything to do with the real universe? I think these philosophers have not learned the lessons of history. It was once considered obvious that the earth was flat and that the sun went around the earth, yet since the time of Copernicus and Galileo, we have had to adjust to the idea that the earth is round and that it goes around the sun. Similarly, it was long obvious that time went at the same rate for every observer, but since Einstein, we have had to accept that time goes at different rates for different observers. It also seemed obvious that the universe had a unique history, yet since the discovery of quantum mechanics, we have had to consider the universe as having every possible history. I want to suggest that the idea of imaginary time is something that we will also have to come to accept. It is an intellectual leap of the same order as believing that the world is round. I think that imaginary time will come to seem as natural as a round earth does now. There are not many Flat Earthers left in the educated world.

You can think of ordinary, real time as a horizontal line, going from left to right. Early times are on the left, and late times are on the right. But you can also consider another direction of time, up and down the page. This is the so-called imaginary direction of time, at right angles to real time.

What is the point of introducing the concept of imaginary time? Why doesn't one just stick to the ordinary, real time that we understand? The reason is that, as noted earlier, matter and energy tend to make space-time curve in on itself. In the real time direction, this inevitably leads to singularities, places where space-time comes to an end. At the singularities, the equations of physics cannot be defined; thus one cannot predict what will happen. But the imaginary time direction is at right angles to real time.

This means that it behaves in a similar way to the three directions that correspond to moving in space. The curvature of space-time caused by the matter in the universe can then lead to the three space directions and the imaginary time direction meeting up around the back. They would form a closed surface, like the surface of the earth. The three space directions and imaginary time would form a space-time that was closed in on itself, without boundaries or edges. It wouldn't have any point that could be called a beginning or end, any more than the surface of the earth has a beginning or end.

In 1983, Jim Hartle and I proposed that the sum over histories for the universe should not be taken over histories in real time. Rather, it should be taken over histories in imaginary time that were closed in on themselves, like the surface of the earth. Because these histories didn't have any singularities or any beginning or end, what happened in them would be determined entirely by the laws of physics. This means that what happened in imaginary time could be calculated. And if you know the history of the universe in imaginary time, you can calculate how it behaves in real time. In this way, you could hope to get a complete unified theory, one that would predict everything in the universe. Einstein spent the later years of his life looking for such a theory. He did not find one because he distrusted quantum mechanics. He was not prepared to admit that the universe could have many alternative histories, as in the sum over histories. We still do not know how to do the sum over histories properly for the universe, but we can be fairly sure that it will involve imaginary time and the idea of space-time closing up on itself. I think these concepts will come to seem as natural to the next generation as the idea that the world is round. Imaginary time is already a commonplace of science fiction. But it is more than science fiction or a mathematical trick. It is something that shapes the universe we live in.

Donald A. Crosby (essay date 1994)

SOURCE: "Einstein on Religion," in *The Midwest Quarterly*, Vol. XXXV, No. 2, Winter, 1994, pp. 186-97.

[*Crosby is an American author, educator, and minister specializing in philosophy and religion. In the following essay, he explains Einstein's religious beliefs.*]

Albert Einstein was a devoutly religious man, although he did not believe in a personal God or align himself with the teachings or practices of any particular religious community. In his lifetime he wrote and lectured on many topics other than mathematical physics, including the topic of religion. In what follows, I first discuss his view of the nature of religion in general and of the proper way of conceiving its relations to science. Then I turn to his personal religious vision, which he sometimes called "cosmic religion." I will make some critical observations as I proceed.

In two lectures delivered in 1939 and 1941, Einstein relegates religion and science to separate spheres, each with its own specific problems and concerns. He contends that when each is conceived in this way, conflict between them is impossible. Science deals solely with what *is*, with facts and relations of facts. Its task is the purely descriptive one

of discovering laws which can best explain the regularities of nature. From its sheer descriptions no valuative conclusions can be drawn. Since Einstein virtually identifies science with rationality, i.e., with conclusions supported by "experience and clear thinking," it follows that valuative judgments cannot be based on reason. They can neither be criticized nor defended in a "solid scientific way"; hence, they lie completely outside the province of scientific rationality (Einstein, *Later Years*).

Einstein recognizes, however, that human existence and activity would be impossible without the valuative choices that pervade everyday life, and he emphasizes the need for ultimate goals to give comprehensive meaning to all human pursuits, including the pursuit of scientific understanding itself. This is where religion comes into the picture. Religion, as he sees it, has nothing whatever to do with descriptions or explanations of facts. It is preoccupied exclusively with values. Its task is to express, not what is, but what *ought* to be. In particular, religion gives a vision of primary significance and value in whose context the secondary values of daily life have their relative place, importance, and justification.

Religious goals themselves "neither require nor are capable of rational justification." If this is true, what is their source? Einstein states that one must "sense their nature simply and clearly," implying that religious values are apprehended by a kind of immediate intuition. The function of religious systems is to elicit or "make clear" the fundamental aims or ideals disclosed in this act of intuition "and to set them fast in the emotional life of the individual." Religious systems accomplish this task through the medium of powerful personalities and the accumulated weight of tradition (*Later Years*).

For Einstein, then, science and religion occupy entirely separate domains, and it would be as much a mistake for science to try to encroach upon the realm of values as it would be for religion to meddle in descriptions or explanations of natural fact. He hastens to add, however, that "though the realms of religion and science themselves are clearly marked off from each other, nevertheless there exist between the two strong reciprocal relationships and dependencies" (*Later Years*). In other words, there are ways in which science has need of religion, just as there are ways in which religion must rely on science. What are these ways?

Let us consider first religion's contributions to science. Einstein thinks that there are two main contributions. First, since religion is the ultimate source of human values, and science itself cannot be the source of any values, the scientific valuation of truth and understanding must be rooted in religious intuitions. Or to put it another way, the conviction that science is important or worth doing and that a lifetime devoted to scientific inquiry is an appropriate pursuit for a human being is, at bottom, a religious conviction. Thus, the enterprise of scientific theorizing is nurtured and sustained in some decisive way by the religious postures of persons or cultures.

The second important contribution of religion to science is its provision of faith in the intelligibility and rationality of nature, a faith Einstein believes to be absolutely essential to high-level scientific investigation. Since such faith is *presupposed* by science, it must have its source elsewhere than in science. For Einstein, its source is in certain mystical feelings about nature that are deeply religious in character.

Just as there are two principal ways in which science depends on religion, so there are two major respects in which religion depends on science. The first is that religion must learn from science, if we take the term "science" in its broadest sense, "what means will contribute to the goals [religion] has set up" (*Later Years*). Scientific knowledge of the natural world is required, this is to say, if religious goals are to be successfully put into practice. Without knowledge of natural causes, there can be no control over natural effects, and the resources of nature cannot be drawn upon for the achievement of religious ends.

The second way in which religion has need of science is that scientific rationality can help to "purify" (*Later Years*) religious traditions by calling attention to the untenability of certain religious doctrines. One way this can be done is by exposing the incoherence of particular doctrines with the high ideals disclosed and insisted upon by the religious tradition itself. The doctrine of divine omnipotence, for example, is open to rational criticism on this basis. If God is omnipotent, Einstein observes,

> then every occurrence, including every human action, every human thought, and every human feeling and aspiration is also His work; how is it possible to think of holding men responsible for their deeds and thoughts before such an almighty Being? In giving out punishments and rewards He would to a certain extent be passing judgment on Himself. How can this be combined with the goodness and righteousness ascribed to Him?
>
> (*Later Years*)

Also, science's manifestation of the ordered regularity of all events, a matter lying wholly within its own province of fact, makes untenable belief in a God who rules the universe by acts of free will that are unpredictable in principle, or who exists as an independent cause of natural events alongside of natural causes. This is an issue of fact on which science and only science can decide, and the decision of science lies squarely, Einstein is convinced, on the side of "the rule of fixed [causal] necessity" (*Later Years*).

But it is at the point of this second contribution of science to religion that Einstein's analysis of the relations of the two begins to fall apart and lapse into a disturbing incoherence of its own. Does not his well-taken criticism of an omnipotent God apply just as much to his own unshakable conviction of complete causal determinism? In what sense can human beings be held responsible for their deeds and thoughts if their every deed and thought is the inevitable outcome of a causal chain stretching unbroken into the distant past? How, indeed, can goals and values function at all in a universe where human beings are incapable of choosing otherwise than they do choose, the causal conditions remaining the same? And is not science itself impos-

sible, if humans are incapable of freely choosing what seem to them to be the best theories, as assessed on the basis of the available reasons? Or how can one act responsibly toward ideals of honesty and truth in scientific inquiry, if every human act is the outcome of "the rule of fixed necessity," the dishonest ones as well as the honest ones? So far as I know, Einstein made no attempt to answer such questions. But since they bear so intimately on questions of value, is not there at least *prima facie* reason for thinking that Einstein has brought science, or what he thinks of as science, into direct conflict with the valuative domain of religion?

Another point is equally damaging to Einstein's case. It could easily be argued that belief in complete causal necessity is part and parcel of that faith in the intelligibility of nature Einstein identifies as religious in character, and hence, that it is not just a factual claim growing out of the domain of science. Ronald Clark does argue in just this way, stating that Einstein's stubborn, lifelong opposition to the indeterminacy of quantum mechanics, in the face of its wide acceptance by the scientific community and its unquestionable theoretical success, "was based . . . upon an interior assumption about the world that had much more resemblance to religious faith than to the ever-questioning skepticism of science." Einstein believed that the universe's workings were comprehensible: "therefore these workings must conform to discoverable laws; thus there was no room for chance and indeterminacy." This conviction lay behind his famous dictum contained in a letter to Max Born on December 12, 1926, that while the quantum theory "says a lot, . . . [it] does not really bring us any closer to the secret of the Old One. I, at any rate, am convinced that he does not throw dice."

So it seems that religion and science were not kept nearly so much to their own domains as Einstein's depiction of those domains would require. This suggests that those domains cannot be rigidly distinguished along the lines he has laid down. The gap between fact and value is not nearly so clean as he and other positivistically minded thinkers of his generation believed. The valuations of religion are undergirded by religious claims about the nature of things, just as scientific claims rest upon valuational assumptions of science. Lurking behind Einstein's way of distinguishing religion from science, as well as behind much of his own thinking as a physicist, were his own personal religious commitments, sometimes confused with straightforward scientific fact. To his personal religious vision we now turn. It can be briefly described under three main headings or themes.

The *first theme* of Einstein's "cosmic religion" is what he terms "that humble attitude of mind towards the grandeur of reason incarnate in existence" (*Later Years*). Or as he states the theme elsewhere, "[t]he most incomprehensible thing about the world is that it is comprehensible" (**"On Physical Reality,"** 1936; quoted by Frank, in Schilpp). This sense of the rational structure of the world and of its amenability to understanding through simple, elegant mathematical theories of sweeping breadth, was a matter of profound religious import for Einstein. It gave to his life's work the character of a pilgrimage or religious quest, its spirit akin to Johannes Kepler's exclamation, "I think God's thoughts after him!" Einstein describes this feeling best when he says:

> The most beautiful thing we can experience is the mysterious. It is the source of all true art and science. He to whom this emotion is a stranger, who can no longer pause to wonder and stand rapt in awe, is as good as dead: his eyes are closed. This insight into the mystery of life, coupled though it be with fear, has also given rise to religion. To know that what is impenetrable to us really exists, manifesting itself as the highest wisdom and the most radiant beauty which our dull faculties can comprehend only in their most primitive forms—this knowledge, this feeling, is at the center of true religiousness. In this sense, and in this sense only, I belong to the ranks of devoutly religious men.

> ("What I Believe")

The first theme of Einstein's personal religious vision, then, is this mystical feeling for nature, a reverence for its elusive vastness and complexity, but also for its discoverable logical order and intelligible structure. To penetrate even a little way into this marvelous order is to be put in touch with an "illimitable superior spirit," presence, or power which Einstein frequently refers to as "God."

But (and this brings us to the *second theme*) this God of nature, or this God who *is* nature, cannot be conceived as a personal being. Einstein sees his cosmic religion, inspired by the successes of science, as working to rid "the religious impulse of its anthropomorphisms." We can surmise that one reason for his opposition to traditional personalistic theism was that, for him, nature itself is divine, the object of highest religious veneration, whereas traditional theism subordinates nature to a transcendent Creator. Another reason, spoken of earlier, is that a personal God, acting by free will, would be capricious and unpredictable. To the extent that God's actions affect the course of natural events, to that extent those events would be unlawlike and scientifically unknowable. This would distract seriously from the first theme of cosmic religion.

Still another reason is that belief in a personal God who exercises free will invites all kinds of *ad hoc* explanations about natural occurrences, particularly those which are threatening to human beings. It panders to the worst kinds of superstitions, idle hopes, and irrational fears of humankind. This pandering, in turn, threatens to place "vast power in the hands of priests," such as prevailed prior to the age of scientific enlightenment (*Later Years*). Evidently, Einstein thinks it better to be ruled by blind laws of nature that are at least in principle comprehensible to reason than by a God whose ever-changing decisions require arbitrary and occult interpretations of a powerful priestly class.

The *third and final theme* of Einstein's cosmic religions is the ideal of selflessness. "A person who is religiously enlightened," he says, "appears to me to be one who has, to the best of his ability, liberated himself from the fetters of his selfish desires and is preoccupied with thoughts, feelings, and aspirations to which he clings because of their

super-personal value" (*Later Years*). The mystical feeling for the vastness of nature conduces to this attitude of selflessness, for it shows the individual person to be only a tiny fragment of a "huge world which exists independently of us human beings and which stands before us like a great, eternal riddle" (Einstein, in Schilpp). One is humbled by the challenge of trying to comprehend such a world and can soon lose oneself in contemplation of its beauty and immensity.

Against this backdrop, giving attention to merely selfish pursuits and concerns seemed to Einstein to be absurd. Talking late one night with his friend Leon Watters, Einstein looked intently at a picture of Watter's recently deceased wife and reflected: "[t]he individual counts for little; man's individual troubles are insignificant; we place too much importance on the trivialities of living" (quoted Clark). Einstein speaks of being impressed at an early age with the idea that persons he greatly admired seemed to have "found inner freedom and security in devoted occupation" to trying to unravel the secrets of nature (Einstein, in Schilpp). For him, the life of contemplation enables one somehow to rise above "the bondage of ego-centric cravings, desires, and fears" (*Later Years*). Such contemplation sets the fleeting existence of humans in the context of the sweeping, all-inclusive totality of universe whose fundamental principles know no alteration but are true for all time, and whose lawlike processes flow forever. "The scientist," he exults,

> is possessed by the sense of universal causation. The future, to him, is every whit as necessary and determined as the past. . . . His religious feeling takes the form of a rapturous amazement at the harmony of natural law, which reveals as intelligence of such superiority that, compared with it, all the systematic thinking and acting of human beings is an utterly insignificant reflection. This feeling is the guiding principle of his life and work, in so far as he succeeds in keeping himself from the shackles of selfish desire. It is beyond question closely akin to that which has possessed the religious geniuses of all ages.

> (*Ideas and Opinions*)

One other reason Einstein found belief in a personal God to be so distasteful was because he judged it to be inimical to this selfless ideal of religious enlightenment. Such a view pictures God as continually concerning himself with the petty affairs of individual persons, rewarding or punishing them on a day-to-day basis for their good or bad deeds, or for their successes or failures in currying his favor or avoiding his wrath (see *Ideas and Opinions*). Benedict Spinoza, whom Einstein regarded as a kindred spirit where matters religious were concerned and whom he admired as his favorite philosopher, held that belief in a personal God conduces to jealousy and self-centeredness. Spinoza argued that each person imbued with this belief will try to think out "for himself, according to his abilities, a different way of worshipping God, so that God might love him more than his fellows, and direct the whole course of nature for the satisfaction of his blind cupidity and insatiable avarice" (Spinoza). This was a view with which Einstein could readily concur. For him, as for Spinoza, to conceive of God as personal is to run directly counter to genuine religious, as well as scientific, sensibility. It belittles God's majesty and greatness, making him a manipulable pawn, and it reinforces the narrowest and most selfish impulses of humankind.

There is much that is insightful and inspiring in Einstein's cosmic religion. But I wonder if it does not tilt too far in the direction of the aesthetic or the merely contemplative to do justice to the religious impulse in all its dimensions. I do not insist that Einstein should have believed in a God who is personal and free, but that his religious vision should have elucidated some basis for the active exercise of personal freedom on the part of human beings. I say this partly because his theory of the nature of religion turns so crucially on the concept of goals and values, which seem to require the exercise of freedom for their discernment and attainment. I also say it because Einstein's own life was so exemplary in its dedication to the free pursuit of knowledge and in its deep moral concern for the freedom of the individual. Here we can be thankful for the gap in one person's life between profession and practice!

Einstein once asserted that "the highest principles for our aspirations and judgements are given to us in the Jewish-Christian religious tradition." He then went on to state that the primary religious goal articulated in that tradition is, on its purely human side, "free and responsible development of the individual, so that he may place his powers freely and gladly in the service of all mankind" (*Later Years*). But such sentiments and practices seem radically incoherent with the pessimistic resignation Einstein felt driven to by his belief in cosmic determinism. His comment on the confrontational politics of East and West during the period of the Cold War is a dramatic case in point.

> Things are going much as they did after 1918, except that there are different actors on the stage. They play as badly as they did then, but the general bankruptcy which threatens will be incomparably worse. Having lost the illusion of free will, one cannot even react in anger.

> (Einstein, letter to Otto Lehmann-Russbuldt, 1947; quoted by Michelmore)

Given the extreme difficulty, if not impossibility, of reconciling these two sides of Einstein's thought, one is led to observe of him what Frederick Copleston concluded about Spinoza: we cannot avoid the impression that he "tried to have it both ways; to maintain a thorough determinism based on a metaphysical theory, and at the same time to propound an ethic which makes sense only if determinism is not absolute" (Copleston).

It is fascinating to note that a philosopher like Immanuel Kant centered his own religious vision squarely on unshakable belief in the reality of human freedom. Only in the experience of freedom did Kant find firm basis for belief in God. Such a belief could not stem, he was convinced, from blind, causally determined forces of a nature viewed wholly through the eyes of theoretical science. Thus Kant stood at a position exactly opposite to that of Einstein as far as his view of religion was concerned, even

though, like Einstein, he conceived of nature as a deterministic system.

Uriel Tal tries to give a Kantian twist to Einstein's view of the relations of a deterministic nature, on the one hand, and human morality (along with religion), on the other, insisting that each belongs to a separate realm of thought with its own grounding and its own principles. Hence, scientific causation and determinism pose no threat to responsible human freedom. However, I find no clear evidence of such a Kantian view in Einstein's writings; evidence from them Tal adduces in trying to make this case, e.g., Einstein's 1930 dialogue with James Murphy and J. W. N. Sullivan in *Forum* magazine, seems skimpy and unconvincing. In my judgment, Einstein's thought is much closer to Spinoza's than to Kant's.

But were not Einstein and Kant each half wrong and half right? The conclusion to which I come, after reflecting on the place of religion in Einstein's thought, is that an adequate religious vision must achieve some kind of synthesis between his own outlook and that of Kant. Such a vision would conceive of God or the religious ultimate, whatever that might be, as a ground *both* of causality and freedom, of continuity and novelty. It would encourage, on the one hand, a mystical sense of the imposing order of the natural world and of respects in which the fleeting existence of each individual being is subordinate to the sublimity and sweep of its ongoing regular processes. On the other hand, it would elicit responsible awareness of a future significantly pliable to acts of human freedom and of a natural order that permits of such freedom; and it would stress the irreducible dignity and importance of each human life. The second emphasis may not fit squarely with the main thrust of Einstein's expressed ideas on religion, but it resonates with the force of his life and greatness of his spirit.

FURTHER READING

Biography

Bernstein, Jeremy. *Einstein*. New York: Penguin, 1973, 242 p.

> This introduction to Einstein pivots on the three main themes of Einstein's career—the special theory of relativity, the general theory of relativity, and quantum physics.

Clark, Ronald W. *Einstein: The Life and Times*. New York: Thomas Y. Crowell Company, 1971, 718 p.

> Overview of Einstein's personal and professional life; includes bibliography.

Frank, Philipp. *Einstein: His Life and Times*. Translated by George Rosen. Edited by Shuichi Kusaka. New York: Alfred A. Knopf, 1947, 298 p.

> Posits that understanding Einstein is a key to understanding "something of the contradictory and complicated twentieth-century world."

Hermanns, William. *Einstein and the Poet: In Search of the Cosmic Man*. Brookline Village, Mass.: Branden Press, 1983, 151 p.

Outline of Einstein's pacifist ideas, the need for what he termed "holy curiosity."

Ireland, Karin. *Albert Einstein*. Englewood Cliffs, N.J.: Silver Burdett Press, 1989, 109 p.

Examination of the effects of Einstein's work on daily life in America, aimed at young adults.

Pais, Abraham. *'Subtle is the Lord . . .': The Science and the Life of Albert Einstein*. Oxford, England: Oxford University Press, 1982, 552 p.

Primarily a scientific biography of Einstein.

Pyenson, Lewis. *The Young Einstein: The Advent of Relativity*. Bristol and Boston: Adam Hilger, Ltd., 1985, 255 p.

Discussion of Einstein's early career, including work by then-contemporaries who bore considerable influence on his thinking.

Swisher, Clarice. *The Importance of Albert Einstein*. San Diego, Calif.: Lucent Books, 1994, 128 p.

Focuses on Einstein's contributions during and after his life.

White, Michael, and Gribbin, John. *Einstein: A Life in Science*. New York: Dutton, 1994, 279 p.

An effort to show that Einstein was "as complex in personality as the theories he gave the world."

Criticism

Beller, Maria; Renn, Jürgen; and Cohen, Robert S., eds. "Einstein in Context": special issue of *Science in Context* 6, No. 1 (1993): 368 p.

An attempt to link the various research traditions and perspectives of recent Einstein studies.

Cassidy, David. *Einstein and Our World*. New Jersey: Humanities Press, 1995, 100 p.

An effort to give basic historical information as well as to "show the chief questions and debates that engage current historical scholarship."

D'Inverno, Ray. *Introducing Einstein's Relativity*. Oxford: Clarendon Press, 1992, 383 p.

Takes a dual approach to Einstein, physical and mathematical.

Fine, Arthur. *The Shaky Game: Einstein Realism and the Quantum Theory*. Chicago: University of Chicago Press, 1986, 186 p.

A collection of previously published essays that examines philosophical aspects of Einstein's work and quantum theory in several contexts.

Friedman, Alan J. and Donley, Carol C. *Einstein as Myth and Muse*. Cambridge: Cambridge University Press, 1985, 224 p.

Collaboration of a literary critic and a scientist to examine the effect of Einstein's work on twentieth-century literature.

Holton, Gerald and Elkan, Yehuda eds. *Albert Einstein. Historical and Cultural Perspectives: The Centennial Symposium in Jerusalem*. Princeton: Princeton University Press, 1982, 429 p.

Collection of papers assessing Einstein's influence on science, humanistic studies, international politics, his special relationship to Israel, and personal reminiscences.

Infeld, Leopold. *Albert Einstein: His Work and Its Influence on Our World*. New York: Charles Scribner's Sons, 1950, 135 p.

Infeld traces the scientific developments before the "Einstein revolution" and its continued reverberations.

Miller, Arthur I. *Albert Einstein's Special Theory of Relativity*. Reading, Mass.: Addison-Wesley Publishing Company, 1981, 466 p.

A biography and analysis of Einstein's first paper on electrodynamics.

Parker, Barry. *Einstein's Dream: The Search for a Unified Theory of the Universe*. New York and London: Plenum Press, 1986, 287 p.

Using Einstein's work as a foundation and a beginning, Parker analyzes the more recent discoveries that point to the prescience of Einstein's dream of a unified theory.

Paul, Iain. *Science, Theology and Einstein*. New York: Oxford University Press, 1982, 148 p.

An attempt to "persuade Christians that Einstein has something distinctive and worthwhile to offer to them."

Will, Clifford M. *Was Einstein Right? Putting General Relativity to the Test*. New York: Basic Books, 1986, 274 p.

Addressing the general reader, Will discusses the ideas, people, and machines that have drawn on Einstein's work.

Additional coverage of Einstein's life and career is contained in the following sources published by Gale Research: *Contemporary Authors*, **Vols. 121, 133;** *Major Twentieth Century Writers*.

Buddy Holly

1936-1959

(Born Charles Hardin Holley) American musician and songwriter.

INTRODUCTION

Holly was one of the most influential performers in the early development of rock music. In his brief career with the Crickets and as a solo performer from 1956 to his death in 1959, Holly gained wide attention for a unique vocal style in which he rendered the lyrics of such popular songs as "Peggy Sue" and "That'll Be the Day." His impact on the subsequent generations of musicians, including the Beatles, who adopted their name in tribute to the Crickets, extended to guitar technique and such innovations as overdubbing recording tracks and utilizing symphonic backing instruments in rock recordings.

Biographical Information

Holly was born in Lubbock, Texas. Encouraged in his early musical pursuits by his parents, he learned to play the violin and piano in addition to guitar. Holly began performing country and western music with partner Bob Montgomery as "Buddy and Bob" for local audiences while he was still in high school. He gained the notice of a Decca talent scout during performances as a supporting act for concerts by Hank Snow, Bill Haley, and Marty Robbins, which led to his first recording sessions in Nashville in 1956. However, the record company soon lost interest in Holly, and he returned to Lubbock where he formed a new band, the Crickets, featuring Jerry Allison on drums, Niki Sullivan on guitar, and Joe Mauldin on bass guitar. The group traveled to Clovis, New Mexico, to work with producer Norman Petty, with whom Holly co-wrote such songs as "Not Fade Away" and "It's So Easy"; Jerry Allison collaborated with Petty and Holly to compose "Peggy Sue" and "That'll Be the Day." Through Petty, Holly found success in the form of a recording contract for the Crickets with Decca's Brunswick subsidiary and a separate contract for Holly as a solo performer on Decca's Coral Records label. Holly's top-selling releases in 1957 included "That'll Be the Day" and "Oh, Boy!" with The Crickets and "Peggy Sue" as a solo artist. In 1958 The Crickets mounted a highly successful concert tour of England, which extended the reach of their influence. In the summer of 1958 Holly married a record studio receptionist and moved to New York City. He subsequently severed his relationship with Petty and left the Crickets to concentrate on his solo career. He hired a new group of backing musicians, including the future country star Waylon Jennings. Holly was killed in a plane crash near Ames, Iowa, on February 3, 1959, while on a promotional concert tour with J. P. Richardson ("The Big Bopper") and Ritchie Valens, who were also killed in the crash.

Major Works

Holly's continuing fame as a songwriter and rock musician rests on recordings he made in the two years preceding his death, including the albums *The Chirping Crickets* (1957) and *Buddy Holly* (1958). *The Chirping Crickets,* which was re-released after his death as *Buddy Holly and The Crickets,* contains such works as "Oh Boy!" "Not Fade Away," "Maybe Baby," and "That'll Be the Day," the song that launched Holly's enormous popularity in 1957. Recorded under the direction of producer Norman Petty, the album fused Holly's background in country music with blues and rockabilly, creating what has been termed a "Tex-Mex" sound unique to the southwestern United States. Holly had previously recorded "That'll Be the Day" in Nashville, but with Petty's guidance the tempo was heightened, and it became one of the most characteristic of Holly's hits for the nervous energy and stretched syllables of his vocal delivery. Holly's solo album, *Buddy Holly,* includes "Rave On" and the well-known "Peggy Sue," among other recordings. Typifying Holly's "hiccuping" vocal style, "Peggy Sue" is notable for its subordination of lyric to vocal interpretation as Holly repeats a woman's name over and over in different ways. In the years immediately following Holly's death numerous tribute and compilation albums were issued, principally the two-volume *The Buddy Holly Story* (1959), which combined previous hits with material that had not been included on earlier albums, including "Raining in My Heart" and "It's So Easy." Subsequent compilations of Holly's recordings have served to maintain his popularity in the decades since his death, including *The Complete Buddy Holly* (1981) and the compact disc *From the Original Master Tapes* (1985).

Critical Reception

During his brief career Holly was second in popularity only to Elvis Presley as a rock and roll performer, and, like Presley, his influence has not diminished in the decades since his death. Among the tributes to Holly that have served to extend his fame into legend, Don McLean's popular song "American Pie" (1971) describes Holly's death as "the day the music died." Various rock and country artists, including Linda Ronstadt, have continued to record Holly's songs, and he has been the subject of both theatrical and film biographies. In 1986 Holly was among the charter inductees into the Rock and Roll Hall of Fame. Assessing Holly's appeal, biographers John Goldrosen and John Beecher have concluded that "Holly was not a giant, or a god—but he was a sort of hero. Though a star, he still sounded and looked like a friend. He was one with his listeners, with one important difference: he could successfully express through his music the feelings that those listeners could not express for themselves."

PRINCIPAL WORKS

The Chirping Crickets (songs) 1957; also released as *Buddy Holly and The Crickets,* 1962
Buddy Holly (songs) 1958
That'll Be the Day (songs) 1958; also released as *The Great Buddy Holly,* 1967
The Buddy Holly Story. 2 vols. (songs) 1959-60
Reminiscing (songs) 1963
Showcase (songs) 1964
Holly in the Hills (songs) 1965
The Best of Buddy Holly (songs) 1966
Buddy Holly's Greatest Hits (songs) 1967
Giant (songs) 1969
Good Rockin' (songs) 1971
Buddy Holly: A Rock and Roll Collection (songs) 1972
Buddy Holly and The Crickets: 20 Golden Greats (songs) 1978
The Complete Buddy Holly (songs and interviews) 1981
For the First Time Anywhere (songs) 1983
From the Original Master Tapes (songs) 1985
Words of Love (songs) 1985
Legend (songs) 1986

CRITICISM

Dave Laing (essay date 1971)

SOURCE: "Listen to Me," in *On Record: Rock, Pop, and the Written Word,* edited by Simon Frith and Andrew Goodwin, Pantheon Books, 1990, pp. 326-40.

[*In the following excerpt from his 1971 study of Holly, Laing provides an analysis of the compositional structure of Holly's songs as well as the highly individual style of his performance on studio recordings.*]

Buddy Holly's music developed considerably on the records made under his own name, mostly at Petty's studio in Clovis. The backing is usually by members of the Crickets, although the record labels only said "with instrumental accompaniment." These tracks are the twelve which appeared on the album *Buddy Holly in 1958,* with the addition of four later tracks—**"Rave On," "Take Your Time," "Heartbeat,"** and **"Well All Right"**—and others not issued until after Holly's death, including **"Love's Made a Fool of You"** and two songs cut with the R&B saxophonist King Curtis: **"Reminiscing"** and **"Come Back Baby."**

The general impression given by these records is one of sparseness and simplicity, particularly in comparison with the baroque richness produced by the vocal backings on the Crickets' records. The principal elements are drums, guitar or piano, and voice, and often the drumming is pared down to a tom-tom or jelly. The songs are frequently loosely constructed, with each sung line countered by a meandering guitar line, on the call-and-response pattern of **"Not Fade Away."**

LYRICS AND SONG SHAPES

Most music in the rock 'n' roll tradition differs from other popular music and aligns itself with folk music in the relationship of the *song* to the *record.* A Cole Porter song, for example, is more than just a recording by Ella Fitzgerald. It has an independent existence beyond that particular version, and it is easy to imagine Sinatra or Crosby making their own interpretations which would be equally acceptable. No single recording of a Cole Porter song exhausts its potential, whereas the Who's recording of "My Generation" or Jerry Lee Lewis's record of "High School Confidential" does precisely that. In each case it becomes impossible to disentangle the song from the recording of it. There is much less reason for anyone else to do another version of either song, unless they were prepared to make use of the Who's or Lewis's vocal and instrumental mannerisms. Cole Porter and Jerry Lee Lewis in this sense are polar opposites, and many rock performers will be found to be at neither extreme. It is worth examining this opposition because of the light it throws on the relationship between words and music in rock 'n' roll, and in particular in Buddy Holly's work.

It is useful here to draw a tentative comparison between popular music performers and film directors as seen by critics who analyze films in terms of the auteur principle. Both *auteur* and *metteur en scène* work from a written text, but, whereas the latter does no more than faithfully transfer that text to the screen, the auteur gives it certain emphases which change its meaning.

The musical equivalent of the *metteur en scène* is the performer who regards a song as an actor does a part—as something to be expressed, something to get across. The aim is to render the lyric faithfully. An obvious example of the genre is the "protest" singer, whose work subordinates music to message. The vocal style of the singer is determined almost entirely by the emotional connotations of the words. The approach of the rock auteur, however, is determined not by the unique features of the song but by his personal style, the ensemble of vocal effects that characterize the whole body of his work.

This dichotomy also holds among popular musicians who compose their own material. Those who, like Leonard Cohen, merely transpose their lyrics into song form cannot be considered rock auteurs because their musical style is entirely determined by the words on the page. But the meaning of Jerry Lee Lewis's "Whole Lotta Shakin' Goin' On" or of Buddy Holly's **"Peggy Sue"** on disc is infinitely richer than the words of the lyric on the page. In the work of these singers, the distinction between the composition and the performance, central to classical music, breaks down. The song **"Peggy Sue"** has no real existence outside Buddy Holly's record of it.

Within rock 'n' roll, examples of two kinds of auteur can be found. Carl Perkins is a singer of the first, weaker kind, a man who can impose a distinctive personal style on his material, but whose own songs are capable of having other singers' styles imprinted on them (e.g., Elvis Presley's record of "Blue Suede Shoes"). On the other hand Bo Diddley and Jerry Lee Lewis are two singers who inscribed their styles on the songs they recorded, thus making it difficult for anyone else to perform those songs without imitating Diddley's "jungle beat" or Lewis's piano style with the famous swoop along the keyboard. Another major auteur of this kind is Buddy Holly, who found stylistic maturity at a time when it was becoming possible to play rock 'n' roll outside a rigid, conventional, 12-bar structure.

With his solo records, the shapes of Buddy Holly's songs start to match his vocal style in their originality. Short two- or three-line verse forms predominate. The effect of this in **"Words of Love"** or **"Listen to Me"** is to alter the balance between singing and instrumental work. Instead of having two large vocal sections separated by a shorter instrumental segment, these songs consist of a series of shorter singing and playing passages. . . .

"Peggy Sue" has a two-bar instrumental embellishment at the end of each verse and no "middle 8." This omission partly accounts for the unrelieved excitement of the record, since the function of the "middle 8" in most songs is to provide a breathing space from a succession of verses, just as an instrumental break does.

The structure of **"Listen to Me"** is more orthodox, although the instrumental break, in which Holly repeats the title phrase over the guitar playing, is unusually long. In **"Heartbeat,"** each line has its accompanying guitar re-

sponse, except where the song returns from the "middle 8" back to the verse. It is based upon the call-and-response pattern, which probably reached the Holly fraternity (**"Heartbeat"** is written by Petty and Bob Montgomery) through the work of Bo Diddley. One of the Holly tapes issued after his death with a backing added by Petty is of "Bo Diddley."

The themes of these songs are similar to those of the Crickets. They are all love songs, and nearly all are sung directly to the girl. **"Mailman Bring Me No More Blues"**; **"Love's Made a Fool of You"** (which is a philosophical song addressed to men in general), and "Heartbeat," where the singer soliloquizes, are the main exceptions. In addition, there are **"Ready Teddy,"** with a lyric in the "Rock Around the Clock" tradition—a general invitation to everybody to have a good time—and **"Well All Right."**

This last record is the nearest Holly and Petty ever came to making a rock 'n' roll protest lyric along the lines of Eddie Cochran's "Summertime Blues" or Chuck Berry's "Almost Grown," although there is none of the anger or irritation of those songs. The response to adult criticism of young people in **"Well All Right"** is: "Well all right / Let people say . . . " which is a shrug of the shoulders rather than a shake of the fist.

As with the Crickets' lyrics, the words of a large proportion of these solo songs are about a man trying to win a girl's love. This is the situation in **"Little Baby," "Look at Me," "Words of Love," "Listen to Me," "I'm Gonna Love You Too"** and **"Peggy Sue."** Two songs, **"Wishing"** and **"Everyday,"** are slightly different, in that the singer passively hopes that a girl will "surely come my way" instead of being involved with someone already. Instead of using his own words to win a girl, he simply hopes that fate or chance will act for him. In **"Wishing,"** he looks around for a wishing star to help him. **"Everyday"** straddles the gap between what might be called "confrontation" songs (**"Listen to Me,"** etc.) and the large body of teenage daydream songs, typified by the Everly Brothers' "All I Have to Do Is Dream," in which the real girl has been eclipsed by the girl in the singer's imagination.

Few of the Holly solo songs possess regular four-line verses, like **"That'll Be the Day."** Only **"Look at Me," "Take Your Time," "I'm Gonna Love You Too,"** and **"You're the One"** have verses of this kind. The other tracks have either two- or three-line verses, or a structure based on the 12-bar blues form, for example:

> TWO-LINE: **"Wishing," "Heartbeat," "Words of Love," "Love's Made a Fool of You"**
>
> THREE-LINE: **"Everyday," "Listen to Me"**
>
> 12-BAR BASED: **"Mailman Bring Me No More Blues," "Ready Teddy," "Rave On," "Peggy Sue," "Baby I Don't Care," "Reminiscing"**

(**"Well All Right"** has eight-line verses, four lines of which form a chorus. **"Um Oh Yeah"** has verses which vary between two and three lines.)

Of the two-line verse songs, **"Heartbeat"** and **"Love's Made a Fool of You"** have complementary guitar lines following each vocal line. **"Words of Love"** has a chorus that is the same shape as the verse. Each vocal section (verse and chorus) is therefore four lines long. The second line in each pair is half the length of the first, and the other two bars are completed with humming. . . .

Although six songs have a structure based on the 12-bar blues, only one, **"Mailman Bring Me No More Blues,"** has the classic blues form of three lines, with the second as a repetition of the first. **"Ready Teddy," "Rave On,"** and **"Peggy Sue"** have another much-used blues form, in which the two lines spread over the last eight bars crop up in every verse, as a chorus. This structure is less obvious in **"Peggy Sue"** than in **"Ready Teddy,"** where the chorus is clearly marked off from the rest of the verse. Two aspects of **"Peggy Sue"** combine to give it a spontaneous, unstructured appearance: quiet rhythm guitar work, which means that the chord changes are not emphasized, and constant repetition of the name **"Peggy Sue"** in both verse and chorus, blurring the division between the two.

The three-line verse shape of other songs also owes much to the blues, although its immediate ancestry was more likely the blues of C&W music than rhythm and blues. In both **"Everyday"** and **"Listen to Me,"** the third line is almost the same in every verse and acts as a chorus, but the effect of this line is different from the type of chorus in **"Ready Teddy."** That chorus, introduced at regular intervals, acts as a bedrock for the song, as a firm construction underlying the lyric. In **"Listen to Me"** and **"Everyday,"** however (as in **"Peggy Sue"**), the single line chorus seems to be reached each time by a less sure route, because the repeated phrases are not clearly set apart from the rest of the lyric; thus the listener hears them as a separate musical passage. The records give the impression of being one long, flowing unit, instead of songs composed of a series of structurally regular sections.

Another contributory factor to this flowing feeling is the use of rhymes: the units are very short, often only a phrase of three or four words. **"Heartbeat"** in particular has a complex rhyming scheme, with syllables echoing and bouncing off each other:

> Heartbeat why do you miss
> When my baby kisses me?
> Heartbeat why does a love kiss
> Stay in my memory?

It is worth listening to the whole sequence of rhymes, half rhymes, and echoes: do / you (line 1); why (lines 1, 3) / my (lines 2, 4) / stay (4) / ba-(2);-by / me (2) / -ry (4); does / love (3). Even the distant echo of a rhyme in the song's title contributes to the pattern.

These, then, are the features of the songs as they are before the records are made. What Buddy Holly and his backing musicians chose to make of them is the subject of the remainder of this chapter.

VOCALS

The powerful effect of Buddy Holly's singing does not come from what is normally thought of as vocal "power." In fact, his least interesting records are those in which he gives the song the full-blooded Little Richard or Elvis Presley treatment, like **"Ready Teddy"** or **"Early in the Morning."** Although he performs these songs adequately, the distinctive qualities of his singing seem to be submerged. These qualities need slower or more complicated songs than conventional rock 'n' roll tunes, to be fully effective.

Buddy Holly's singing voice was not strong, and this factor turned out to provide the basis for most of the vocal effects found on his records. Holly's voice was naturally higher-pitched than those of many rock 'n' roll singers, and lacked the body and resonance of Fats Domino or Elvis Presley. It was, in origin, like the voices of Buddy Knox, Carl Perkins, and the Everly Brothers, a typically country singing voice. Both Jimmie Rodgers and Hank Williams (the two greatest singers to fashion their own style in the C&W genre) possessed high-pitched voices, but with a wiry strength lacking in the more moping vocalizing of many of their successors.

Holly had a subtle strength allied to his relatively thin, high-pitched tone. The strength and subtlety came from a number of vocal effects or mannerisms, and a constant shifting from one to another of them, so that no phrase is sung in the same way as the preceding or the succeeding phrase. It is possible to isolate at least five distinct effects that appear frequently in the records Holly cut at Clovis as a solo artist, backed by members of the Crickets.

Contrast in pitch is the only one of his vocal mannerisms that Holly clearly borrowed from another artist, Elvis Presley. His version of "Baby I Don't Care," a song previously recorded by Presley, follows the original, where the title phrase is very low pitched. In other songs, alternate phrases are sung with contrasting pitch: in **"Mailman Bring Me No More Blues,"** the final line of the last verse, which ordinarily would have a falling cadence, is sung with the second phrase much higher than the first: "One blue letter (LOW) / Is all I can use (HIGH)." In **"Well All Right,"** the cadence at the end of the verse is the conventional falling one, but Holly overemphasizes the contrast between the high and low parts in a similar way.

In both these songs, one of the contrasting sections is made to sound "out of place" in the song. Holly sings the low part in the former song and the higher part in the latter, so that he seems to break out of the vocal range the song had set for itself: the listener is surprised by the change. This impression occurs in **"Well All Right"** because Holly's voice only sketches in the upward movement of the melody in the line "Well all right, well all right." The end of the word "right" is cut off sharply and the word itself is sung both times very softly. This contrasts with the next deeper line which is sung with greater power and assurance. In **"Mailman Bring Me No More Blues"** it is the Presley-like growl that is deliberately out of place. Contrasted high and low phrases in these records are not usually equally balanced. Holly's singing tends to place special emphasis on one of them, while the other is made to seem more integrated with the rest of the song.

More frequent than contrasts between phrases are contrasts in pitch within phrases. In **"Peggy Sue,"** Holly's voice is continually darting up and down, so that the experience of the record is like that of a roller coaster or switchback ride. In the last two lines of the second verse quoted, the underlined words are those where low pitch is accentuated by Holly's singing, and those in capital letters are the emphasized high-pitched notes: "Oh well I love you gal / Yes I LOVE you PEGGY Sue . . ." (the last word is spread over several notes, on the last two of which the voice drops).

Variations in intonation are easily discerned in Holly's singing, but are more difficult to define. **"Peggy Sue,"** Holly's most spectacular vocal performance, includes an important example in the verse preceding the guitar break. The tone of voice in which the first couple of lines are sung is new to the song; the voice is more nasal, and more "babyish," like the singing of the Crickets' **"You've Got Love."** It can be heard as a musical analogy to the private, intimate way of speaking two lovers might share; but it is only an analogy, not a representation of it. This new intonation within the record increases the tension and excitement.

In **"Peggy Sue"** the change in intonation is not related to the emotional mood or significance of the words, to reflect a particular feeling. It relates instead to the musical development of the record as a rock 'n' roll performance. Holly changes his vocal tone to take the music higher, to make it more exciting, as he would at a live performance.

The intimate intonation of Holly's voice on **"Words of Love"** has the same significance as the spoken phrases in the guitar passage of **"Listen to Me."** At one level, the latter represents Buddy Holly's dabbling in a convention found often in C&W ballads—the heart-felt recitation, but as well as addressing the girl in the lyric, "listen to me" is perhaps an injunction to the listener to notice the guitar.

Buddy Holly had a particularly individual *phrasing* technique. A large part of the art of ballad-singing lies in the singer's ability to hold a note with maximum emotional effect. Some sing in a traditional "true" manner, while others employ vibrato effects, designed to suggest choking or sobbing. Johnny Ray is the most obvious example of this last technique and he, more than anyone else, influenced young white rock 'n' roll singers of the fifties in singing ballads. Ray's style, in turn, derived from black singers, notably Roy Brown.

In the classic, early period of rock 'n' roll, the slow songs sung by Presley and others tended to be modeled on the kind of records cut by Ray and other "cry" singers. The rock ballad arrived later, at the end of the decade when rock 'n' roll seemed to become self-conscious about its lack of formal variety, with records like Ritchie Valens's "Donna."

Although Buddy Holly's best records were cut in this later period (1957-58), they stand outside the contemporary categories of beat and ballad, fast and slow, which nearly all the rest of the rock 'n' roll output of the time took for granted. His slower records are never bona fide ballads because of the way the singing on them is broken up by the guitar playing. Ballads depend on a steady buildup to a climax of joy or sadness, and consequently need at least four vocal lines uninterrupted by instrumental breaks. In comparison with the emotional explosions of most ballads, Holly's records are notably phlegmatic.

Holly puts one particular vocal technique—spreading one syllable over several beats of the music—to quite a different use from the straightforward ballad style. Holly does not actually hold the note, but substitutes several syllables for the single syllable of the lyric, in his famous "hiccup" manner. This means that his records lack the familiar effect of a long unbroken syllable held for a few beats and set off against that series of beats from the rhythm section. Instead of complementing the rhythm, Holly's staccato singing tends to imitate it and parallel it. On **"Heartbeat,"** the syllable "be" (in the "middle 8" section just before the guitar break halfway through the record) is spread out over five beats: be-uh-ee-uh-ee. In singing it, Holly's voice spirals downward to rejoin the chorus line.

Few notes are held for more than one or two beats in Holly's records, so they avoid the overpowering emotion of the ballads of that period. Holly's listeners are not overwhelmed, as they are by a ballad, but continually have their attention redirected by the frequent changes of tone, pitch, and phrasing. Holly's music is, therefore, rarely sentimental.

Variations in vocal phrasing can be described in terms of their ornamental or dramatic function within a record. The vocal embellishment at the end of each verse of **"Everyday"** ("Love like yours will surely come my way *a-bey-a-bey-bey*") is predominantly ornamental. It arises out of the rhythmic and melodic patterns of the song. On the other hand, the sound Holly adds to the end of the title line of **"Mailman Bring Me No More Blues"** is dramatic, intended to suggest sobbing, and thus adds to the situation described by the lyrics rather than the purely musical character of the song.

These two instances constitute the two extremes of Holly's technique, and many of the vocal effects on his records combine elements of both the ornamental and the dramatic function, although the dramatic function is rarely dominant. On the last verses of **"I'm Gonna Love You Too,"** his singing becomes more and more punctuated, with each word cut off and separated from the next. Sometimes an extra syllable is added (normally *-a*) to prevent two words running together. The extra syllable often coincides with Holly taking a breath and sometimes is sung falsetto. The technique has a dual role in the song: first, as Holly's response to the demands of performing the song, to bring it to a crescendo, and second, it is a more intense way of conveying the determination expressed in the words of the song. On this occasion, the dramatic and the ornamental are fused.

In **"I'm Gonna Love You Too"** Holly *sings wordlessly* for two verses, using only the sound "ah." The first begins the record, preceding the singing of the written words of the song, while the second forms a bridge between the guitar break and the next part of the lyric. The "wordless" verses thus act as an introduction to the lyric, and the syllable sung is the first syllable of the song's title: "ah'm a gonna love you too." Their effect is, in a way, like that of a stutter in ordinary speech.

The humming in **"Words of Love"** has some affinity with music as well as with words; it fills in the second half of a vocal line as a guitar phrase does in a conventional 12-bar blues. In the context of the lyric it also acts as the equivalent of the "um" sound people often use instead of "yes" to signify agreement. As a part of the lyric it gives added emphasis to the preceding words.

Buddy Holly was probably the first rock 'n' roll singer to *double-track* his voice so that he could harmonize with himself on record. The songs in which this occurs— **"Listen to Me," "Words of Love"**—provide interesting comparisons with the country-style close harmonies of Buddy and Bob on the recordings made three years earlier. In the verses of the two double-tracked records, Holly's two voices sing the same part, giving his sound a resonance that is not there on other tracks. In the middle 8 sections of these songs, however, he sings in a harmony close to the singing that he did with Bob Montgomery. But where Buddy and Bob had no distinctive sound to clearly differentiate themselves from other C&W singing teams, the later double-tracking is clearly recognizable as the mature Buddy Holly.

In addition to describing the vocal techniques that make up Buddy Holly's singing style, the aim of this section has been to suggest how that style relates to the meaning of the words Holly sings. It is clear that some records with poor lyrics turn out to be poor records, while others, with equally uninspired words, do not suffer the same fate. The difference lies in the relationship between *what* the singer is singing and the *way* he sings it in each kind of record. In the first kind, the singing style is dramatic, subordinated to the lyric: the singer is trying to get *something* across to the listener and if what he wants to express (the lyric or melody) is mediocre in itself, then the record fails, however well-executed the performance. But in records which succeed despite mediocre lyrics (and many rock 'n' roll records are of this kind), the performance achieves an autonomous character. Instead of trying to interpret the lyric, the singer uses it as a jumping-off point for his own stylistic inclinations. He uses it as an opportunity to play rock 'n' roll music, instead of regarding his role as one of portraying an emotion contained in the lyric.

The *auteur/metteur en scène* opposition already discussed is relevant here, and clearly Buddy Holly belongs in the second group of singers, although the picture is made more complex by the fact that he composed many of his own songs. Nevertheless, many of the vocal techniques he employs cannot be said to have emotional correlatives in real life. Their frame of reference is first and foremost the musical world of Holly's records. In other words, the appeal of Buddy Holly's music does not lie in what he says, in the situations his songs portray, but in the exceptional nature of his singing style and its instrumental accompaniment. In this context, it is relevant to recall that within the Holly-Petty partnership, Norman Petty wrote most of the lyrics and Holly concentrated on the music.

INSTRUMENTAL WORK

The tendency toward instrumental breaks tailored to fit closely into the rest of the song that had been apparent on the Crickets' records is taken further on the solo tracks. On the slower songs, the break is an almost exact recapitulation of the melody line (**"Everyday"**) or a repetition of a riff that runs through the whole record (**"Words of Love," "Listen to Me," "Heartbeat"**).

Norman Petty's influence on these records shows in the range of instruments that appear. Petty himself plays celeste on **"Everyday"**; piano on **"Look at Me," "Rave On,"** and **"Mailman Bring Me No More Blues"**; and organ on **"Take Your Time."** King Curtis, one of the few black musicians Holly recorded with, plays tenor sax on **"Reminiscing"** and **"Come Back Baby."** The guitar playing is by Holly himself on **"Peggy Sue," "Listen to Me,"** and the earlier records. On the tracks made after the split with the Crickets, Tommy Allsup takes the guitar breaks, notably on **"Heartbeat."**

The "dampened" style of guitar playing, which gives the instrument a dull instead of a ringing tone, is an important feature of several tracks. The clipped sound echoes Holly's own clipped, jerky style of singing. The two work together especially effectively on **"Heartbeat,"** where the basic rhythms of singing and playing have a dramatic function, to suggest a pounding heart.

Buddy Holly is able to indulge his penchant for "down-home" rock 'n' roll playing on only three of these records. **"Ready Teddy"** has a rockabilly solo, with a pattern of chords and single notes familiar from **"That'll Be the Day"** and other earlier tracks. **"Peggy Sue"** and **"Mailman Bring Me No More Blues"** have breaks that erupt in barrages of chords, with a powerful "electric" tone—not merely an acoustic guitar solo amplified, but a unique metallic sound, where each chord echoes into the next. This playing is the main feature of what has been called the Tex-Mex style, and appears on **"Words of Love," "Listen to Me," "Love's Made a Fool of You,"** and **"Heartbeat,"** as well as several Crickets tracks. The intricate pattern of "open" chords that makes up the central motif of **"Words of Love"** and **"Listen to Me"** is the apparent Mexican aspect of Holly's work. As in the rocking style, the edges of the notes are blurred so that they begin to merge into one another. Holly's guitar tone is something almost without precedent in rock 'n' roll. It is closest to the sound of the young black musicians Berry and Diddley (whose style is in turn a deliberate mutation of the Chicago blues style), and to Ritchie Valens's playing on "La Bamba," a rock 'n' roll adaptation of a traditional Mexican dance tune. It clearly has nothing to do with the more expansive and emotionally diffuse guitar work of the white country tradition and the rockabilly style. Holly's Tex-Mex style is denser and more compressed, with a correspondingly greater expressive intensity.

The guitar break on **"Love's Made a Fool of You,"** one of the lesser-known songs (which may be by Allsup), is a minor classic. It is a delicately played, thoughtful construction of single notes whose short phrases follow the line of the verse. It is like many blues guitar phrases, in that it seems to emulate the human voice.

As a descriptive term for Holly's playing, "Tex-Mex" is not very helpful because it does not take account of the major determinant of the style, which is the originality of the songs themselves. The discipline enforced on Holly—he could no longer cut loose with a raving rock 'n' roll break—made his playing more economical and more integrated into the song. In addition, much of the fineness of tone came from the technical possibilities of the Fender guitar, a model Holly was one of the first to use among rock 'n' roll players.

RHYTHM SECTION

If the guitar playing moves beyond conventional rock 'n' roll on Holly's solo records, so does Jerry Allison's drumming. On several tracks, he uses only one percussive sound to tap out a single rhythmic pattern. **"Everyday"** sounds as though he is slapping a jelly. On **"Heartbeat,"** he plays a single drum, and at the end of the track, a cowbell. The drumming on **"Listen to Me"** consists of a repeated pattern, which reinforces the guitar riff. Allison's outstanding performance is on **"Peggy Sue,"** where the drumming makes itself felt by lightness and speed rather than by a powerful regular beat. The rhythm is beaten out on bass drum and tom-tom. Together with the rhythm guitar, whose continuous light strumming understates the chord changes, it makes possible the tremendous fluidity of the record.

The rhythm guitar playing on most of the tracks is by Niki Sullivan, or probably by Holly himself where Allsup plays lead. Holly's Stratocaster is the only guitar, taking both rhythm and lead parts, on **"Peggy Sue."** In **"Well All Right"** the traditional ringing, percussive acoustic sound of the rhythm guitar dominates the beat. The break is also taken by the rhythm guitar, repeating and stressing the chords that accompany the vocal. The bass playing, as before, is resolutely conventional, and never emerges from the general sound of the rhythm section.

On most rock 'n' roll records, the rhythm section has a simple but central role: to lay down a solid beat, usually accented on the off-beat, against which singer and instrumentalist can create their irregular lines of sound, but on many of Buddy Holly's Clovis tracks, the rhythm section sets up patterns that tend to work more closely with guitar and voice, becoming more than a mere background.

THE RECORDS

It is the greater flexibility of the rhythm section that enables **"Peggy Sue"** to take off where **"Rave On"** stays on the ground. The rhythm of **"Rave On"** is a well-delineated series of beats, while **"Peggy Sue"** is a constant stream of sound. **"Rave On"** has an easy foot-tapping rhythm that is also easy to dance to, but **"Peggy Sue"** has a rhythm not clearly divided up by accentuated beats. There is a repeated rhythmic pattern in the song, but the last note of it is marked by a slight dying away of the sound merging into the next repetition of the pattern.

The traditional distinction between rhythmic section, lead voice, and instrument begins to break down in **"Peggy Sue,"** as the drums become more assertive. The notion of the stable lyric also seems to be under attack in the way that the title and certain other words and phrases appear and reappear constantly, as if Holly were improvising the

words. A further contribution to the anarchic effect has already been mentioned: the chorus line is disguised because many of its words also appear in the verse lines.

Drums, guitar, and lyrics in **"Peggy Sue"** share a repetitive quality (in **"Rave On"** they share a regularity, which is very different). The one element of the record that is not repetitive is Buddy Holly's voice, which makes use of nearly all the techniques that have already been mentioned: continually shifting pitch, tone, and phrasing. It is a great vocal performance, as Holly responds to the relentless driving of the instrumental playing and manages to make the repeated words sound fresh every time he sings them. **"Peggy Sue"** is the record that extends Buddy Holly's vocal range fully, for on verse after verse, he finds new and more ingenious ways to sing a lyric of very limited poetic resources. The song almost assumes the character of a challenge, which, perhaps, is why it is such a compelling and exhilarating record to hear.

"Peggy Sue" gives the impression of spontaneous creation. In contrast, **"Listen to Me"** and **"Words of Love"** are carefully constructed tracks, where each vocal and instrumental element fits together like the pieces of a jigsaw puzzle. Each begins with a flowing guitar riff, continuing throughout the song (**"Words of Love"**), and recurring only in the spaces between the vocal (**"Listen to Me"**). The riffs are complemented by nimble drumming patterns that are relaxed versions of Allison's playing on **"Peggy Sue."**

The interplay between voice and guitar differs on these two records. **"Listen to Me"** has an alternation of voice and guitar riff. . . . In **"Words of Love"** the voice emerges out of a continuous guitar background. The song is slower in tempo and Holly's singing is less animated. The effect of the steady guitar line is mesmeric, contributing to the calm quality of the track.

Vocally, **"Listen to Me"** contains far more of the restless side of Holly's singing. The first three lines of the verse are sung double-tracked in the familiar plangent, yearning, high-pitched way, the last line in a lower key. The greater variety in singing and playing is complemented by the loping character of the drumming, which is more active than the muted accompaniment to **"Words of Love."** Although the lyrics of both songs are very similar, the records have quite different emotional content. **"Words of Love"** projects a feeling of certainty and security, while in **"Listen to Me"** Holly seems far less sure that the girl will.

The most innovative single released by Buddy Holly before his death was the coupling of **"Heartbeat"** and **"Well All Right."** Although **"Heartbeat"** has a Latin rhythm far removed from the standard rock 'n' roll beat, the record is supple and lively. While the drums (with the ringing tone of the cowbell dominating the start and close of the record) and second guitar lay down the basic rhythm, the lead guitar fills in the breaks and plays behind the vocal so that it forms a bridge between the singer and the rhythm section. Allsup on lead guitar plays mostly dampened notes, which has the effect of emphasizing the rhythmic aspect of the notes, since they are "blunted" and without tonal variation. In contrast, the main guitar break on the record is played with the strings "open," a tone close to a steel guitar sound and that includes a number of bent notes. Here it is the actual sounds of the individual notes, rather than the rhythmic pattern they form, that is important.

There is no monolithic rhythm section behind Holly's singing on **"Heartbeat,"** but a busy complex of guitars and drums. The rhythm guitar (played by Holly himself) has an important but unobtrusive role, providing a thin, constant texture of strumming between the more exotic patterns of lead guitar and percussion. Holly's vocal depends on timing and intonation for its effect: "Heartbeat why do you *miss* / When my baby kisses *me*." In the first line there is an almost imperceptible pause after "you," and "miss" is jerked out emphatically. "Me" is pronounced curiously, in the "babyish" tone of voice. Placed at the end of the line, it holds the listener's attention during the short, dampened guitar break.

"Heartbeat" is arguably Buddy Holly's most complete record, for within it many separate elements are perfectly synchronized. Each instrument plays its different role, but meshes in with the rest, and the main instrumental and vocal motifs—the staccato rhythm and jerky singing— echo the theme of the lyric: the heavy pounding of the excited lover's heart.

The dominant instrumental sound of **"Well All Right,"** the acoustic rhythm guitar, is simple: the same chord pattern is maintained throughout the record. But it never becomes monotonous because of the subtle changes in emphasis, in light and shade, that are possible when an acoustic guitar is played harder or softer. The guitar sound moves into the foreground and recedes like waves on a shore. The drumming, in which the cymbals predominate, is related to the guitar, so that the light percussive tone melts into the equally light guitar sound.

The singing stands in the same relation to this rich instrumental sound as it does on **"Words of Love."** Instead of the music playing a minor role, to fill in the gaps between verses, the vocal seems to come out from behind the instrumental sound and to fade back into it as Holly's voice gets quieter and higher in the repetition of the title phrase.

CONCLUSION

Many of the Buddy Holly records cut in Clovis in 1957-58 diverge radically from existing rock 'n' roll song forms, both vertically (in the interaction of the instruments with each other and with the vocal) and horizontally (in the pattern of vocal and instrumental sections throughout the song). In particular, the contrast with the Crickets tracks that were made at the same time is striking.

Among the Crickets songs, the "one-track" ballads—**"An Empty Cup"** and **"Last Night"**—forced Holly's singing into a one-dimensional mold, where he had to concentrate throughout the song on achieving one specific effect. With **"Words of Love"** and the other slower solo songs, he had much more vocal play because they had broken away from the ballad genre.

Similarly, **"Peggy Sue"** stands outside the standard rock 'n' roll genre because the emphasis within it is on rhythm rather than beat. Chuck Berry sang in "Rock and Roll Music" that "It's got a backbeat, you can't lose it," but **"Peggy Sue"** lacks that accentuated backbeat, relying instead on a riff developed from Bo Diddley's style.

What distinguishes this music further from most white rock 'n' roll contemporary with it is the extent to which Holly's voice is integrated with the rest of the sound. To a considerable extent, the division between lead voice and accompaniment, in which the instrumental sound plays a subordinate role, is broken down. The fact that the musicians are now alongside him rather than in the middle distance gives Holly a stimulating musical context, with different contours on each track. On the earlier records and the Crickets tracks, Holly had been singing in an empty space, where the conventional rhythm section of the instrumental playing gave him merely rhythmic support, not musical inspiration.

The new instrumental arrangements provided the major impetus for Buddy Holly's vocal style on the solo records. Less important is the stimulus provided by the lyrics of the songs and their emotional themes. Sometimes, in fact, the characteristic emotional tone of Holly's voice goes against the apparent emotional message of the words: in **"Peggy Sue"** he sings: "If you knew Peggy Sue, then you'd know why I feel blue." It seems to be the cry of an unhappy man, but the record radiates energy and enthusiasm.

Holly's singing here and elsewhere epitomizes what Rick Nelson sings in one of his songs: "Rock and roll gets in your soul / It makes you feel so natural" ("Come On In"). Even where his singing had a dramatic function, where it interpreted the lyric, Holly was always a rock 'n' roll performer.

Richard Aquila   (essay date 1982)

SOURCE: "Not Fade Away: Buddy Holly and the Making of an American Legend," in *Journal of Popular Culture,* Vol. 15, No. 4, Spring, 1982, pp. 75-80.

[*In the following essay, Aquila examines the endurance of Holly's reputation as a songwriter and his status as a major figure in popular American culture.*]

February 3, 1959 is for many rock and roll fans a day of infamy. Don McLean, in his 1971 recording "American Pie," referred to it as "the day the music died." On that day Buddy Holly, a twenty-three-year-old rock star, was killed in the crash of a chartered single-engine airplane. Two other rock stars, Ritchie Valens and J.P. Richardson (The Big Bopper), also died in the crash. But of the three, Holly's death had the greatest impact on the music world.

Between 1957 and 1959, Buddy Holly achieved artistic and commercial success as both a solo artist and lead singer for the Crickets. Holly's distinct vocal style, sometimes referred to as Rockabilly, blended Country and Western music with Rhythm and Blues. Songs like **"That'll Be the Day," "Peggy Sue," "Maybe Baby," "Listen to Me," "Rave On," "Oh Boy"** and **"Heartbeat"** established Buddy as one of the greatest stars of early rock 'n' roll.

Today, nearly twenty years later, Holly's aura shines

brighter than ever in the galaxy of rock stars. Buddy Holly and his music live on in the minds and hearts of rock music fans. There is no doubt that Buddy Holly has achieved cult status. There are, however, several questions surrounding Holly's undying popularity. Of all the rock stars that have died, why has Buddy Holly been one of the few to achieve lasting success in the rock'n'roll world? Why was he not forgotten by most fans as were Eddie Cochran, Ritchie Valens, The Big Bopper, Johnny Horton, Johnny Burnette, and a host of others? Why did the legend about Holly develop? How did it grow? And why is Holly still so popular today? Answers to these questions will not only explain the Buddy Holly phenomenon, but they will also tell us something about the American character.

Even before Holly was buried, the legend began to grow. News of the plane crash spawned hundreds of record hops nation-wide that served as rock'n'roll memorials for Holly and the other fallen rock idols.

An ironic twist of fate brought forth one performer who was to contribute greatly to the growth of the Holly myth. When Holly's plane took off in bad weather at 1:50 A.M. from Mason City, Iowa, it was bound for Fargo, North Dakota, where Holly and his fellow musicians had a scheduled concert. When the tragic news arrived instead of the plane, a decision was made to go ahead with the rock show as a tribute to Holly and the others. Radio stations in Fargo sent out emotional pleas for local talent to replace the dead stars on the bill. An unknown singer, Robert Velline, sang several Holly tunes and sounded incredibly like Holly himself. Shortly thereafter Liberty Records signed Velline to a contract and began recording him under the name Bobby Vee.

Bobby Vee's early records captured the sound and spirit of Holly's music. Norman Petty, who recorded and produced most of Holly's hits, declared on the liner notes of Vee's first album that Bobby Vee's style and approach to music compared favorably to Holly's. The Crickets, Holly's original group, gave additional testimony to the similarity between Vee and Holly. Later the Crickets recorded an album with Vee and even toured England with him. Vee was thus given the stamp of approval by those who knew Holly best. The teenager from Fargo recorded several Holly songs for his first few albums, and eventually Vee released an entire album of Holly songs. Entitled *I Remember Buddy Holly*, it included a tribute to Holly, "Buddy's Song," that listed Holly's mother as its composer. The records put out by Vee helped keep Holly's name and music alive during the early 1960s. To this day, Vee includes a medley of Holly songs in his live performances.

Other types of records helped enshrine Buddy Holly. "Three Stars" was the first memorial song to appear, only weeks after Holly's death. There were actually two versions of the record—one by Buddy's close friend Eddie Cochran and the other by Tommy Dee. Both were maudlin and overly religious. Similar songs were released in England, with Mike Berry's "A Tribute to Buddy Holly" achieving the most popularity.

Throughout the early 1960s, the success of Holly imitators

kept Holly's name before the public eye. In 1962, Tommy Roe achieved a million-seller with "Sheila," a record that sounded remarkably close to Holly's **"Peggy Sue."** Roe admitted that it was no accident that his music was reminiscent of Holly's Rockabilly sound, since Buddy was his idol and he was trying to copy Holly's vocal style. The Surfaris also used the Holly sound successfully in their 1963 hit record, "Surfer Joe." Not to be outdone by this new generation of Holly imitators, Holly's old associates clung to Buddy's Rockabilly sound in hopes of continued success. Norman Petty produced an album, *The Buddy Holly Songbook*, by one-time Cricket Tommy Allsup. Petty also produced and recorded another Holly sound-alike hit, Jimmy Gilmer's "Sugar Shack." Petty later produced a Gilmer album entitled *Buddy's Buddy*, which contained Gilmer's versions of Holly songs. The album's cover included a portrait of Jimmy Gilmer right next to one of Buddy Holly. The Crickets also retained their ties to Holly. Their records of the early 1960s, such as **"Love's Made a Fool of You," "Teardrops Fall Like Rain"** and **"My Little Girl"** remained true to the Holly sound.

Holly's music was kept alive in yet another way. During the 1960s, Norman Petty released several "new" Buddy Holly albums. In fact, more Holly albums were issued after Buddy's death than before. The first to appear was *The Buddy Holly Story*, which was a collection of Buddy's greatest hits. The liner notes provided the listener with a biography of Holly's successful rise and tragic end. Petty followed with *The Buddy Holly Story, Volume II*. Once again some of Holly's best known songs were included, but this time the liner notes were in the form of a touching message from his widowed bride, Maria Elena Holly. Throughout the rest of the 1960s, other albums were released with titles such as *The Great Buddy Holly, Giant Buddy Holly* and *Buddy Holly Showcase* that contributed to the image of Holly's greatness. Many of the posthumous releases were recorded by Buddy between 1956 and 1959. Holly tape-recorded some of the songs in his apartment and never meant them to be heard in public. But Norman Petty took the rough tapes, overdubbed them in the studio with various musicians including Jimmy Gilmer and released them as "new" Holly records. Despite their poor quality the albums sold well, since the growing numbers of Buddy Holly fans were eager for any type of previously unreleased Holly material. Most Buddy Holly purists, however, were dissatisfied with Petty's efforts. In many cases the posthumous releases were improperly mixed and Holly's voice and guitar playing were sometimes obscured by the louder playing of Petty's studio musicians. Today the original tapes are available on a British import, *The Complete Buddy Holly*.

The Holly legend grew even larger during the mid and late 1960s, as many superstars, who were products of the British Rock Invasion paid homage to the dead star. The Beatles, who guided the musical tastes of many rock fans if not the entire direction of rock music during these years, publicly announced that some of their musical roots could be traced to Buddy Holly. The Beatles even recorded an almost identical cover version of Holly's **"Words of Love."** Other English groups likewise recorded Holly songs. The Rolling Stones had a hit with **"Not Fade**

Away." Peter and Gordon sold a million copies of **"True Love Ways."** The Hullabaloos recorded **"I'm Gonna Love You Too"** and other songs imitating the Holly sound. And Blind Faith included **"Well All Right"** on their million-selling album in 1969.

Some British rock stars carried their tribute to Holly even farther. The lead singer of Freddie and the Dreamers donned black hornrimmed glasses in an effort to look like the American star. Another group adopted Buddy's surname and as the Hollies achieved great success both in England and America.

Not to be outdone, American artists also imitated the Holly sound. In 1964 J. Frank Wilson had two hits, "Last Kiss" and "Speak to Me Baby," that copied Holly's rockabilly style. Wilson's promoters were quick to point out that not only did J. Frank sound like Buddy Holly, but he also came from Texas, as Buddy did. To further the comparison, Wilson included a version of Holly's **"That'll Be the Day"** on his first album. Skeeter Davis was another American singer who recorded Holly's material. In the mid-sixties, she released an entire album of Holly songs and even included a photograph of Buddy's parents on the album cover. Meanwhile, the Crickets continued to release records that reinforced their association with Buddy Holly. For example, in 1963, they issued *Rockin' 50s Rock And Roll,* an album that included no less than ten re-recorded Holly tunes.

By the 1970s, Holly had his permanent niche in rock music history. Yet the legend was still growing. Holly's importance to rock music was given a significant boost in 1971 when Don McLean released "American Pie." It was dedicated to Buddy Holly and maintained that American rock 'n' roll ended on the day Holly died in 1959. The song became one of the year's biggest sellers, and in the process it etched in the minds of rock 'n' roll fans the image of Buddy Holly as one of the most creative forces in rock's music history.

If American rock 'n' roll had died, Holly's music had not. In the mid seventies, ex-Beatle John Lennon released his version of **"Peggy Sue."** Another ex-Beatle, Paul McCartney, demonstrated his interest in Holly by purchasing the entire catalog of Holly songs. McCartney later helped a member of his new group, Wings, record an album of Holly songs. American artists were also busy singing Holly's songs during the 1970s. Don McLean received some air play with his version of **"Everyday."** Susan Allanson scored big with **"Maybe Baby."** And superstar Linda Ronstadt had three successive hit singles with **"I Guess It Doesn't Matter Anymore," "That'll Be the Day"** and **"It's So Easy."**

Holly's image was further enhanced with the release of other records during the 1970s. Record companies repackaged and reissued numerous collections of Holly's greatest hits. And Waylon Jennings, the outlaw of Progressive Country music and one-time bass player with Holly's back-up band, released a song-tribute to Holly called "Old Friend."

The 1970s also saw Holly become the focus for rock critics and historians. For example, several books were published that studied Holly's life and music. Two of the most informative are Dave Laing's *Buddy Holly* and John Goldrosen's *Buddy Holly: His Life and Music.*

The metamorphosis of Holly from Texas Country and rock singer to American legend was completed in 1978 with the release of a full-length motion picture, **The Buddy Holly Story**. The movie features Gary Busey in the title role and depicts Holly as the benevolent pied piper of early rock 'n' roll who met a tragic death. The movie received excellent reviews and played to large audiences across the U.S. With the artistic and commercial success of the movie, the circle was completed. The legend began with a greatest hits album called **The Buddy Holly Story,** and it was completed with a motion picture of the same name. Within twenty years, Holly had become a full-fledged American legend.

Current rock stars continue to pay homage to Buddy Holly. Rick Nelson recently released his version of Holly's **"Rave-On,"** while Bruce Springsteen often listens to Holly tapes prior to going out on stage, where he sometimes includes a powerful version of **"Rave-on."** New Wave rockers have also tapped the Holly image and sound. For example, the Holly influence is obvious in Elvis Costello's appearance or Dave Edmund's singing on **"Queen of Hearts."** Without a doubt, the Holly legend lives on in the 1980s.

Why was Holly able to achieve his legendary status? Why didn't he fade into oblivion as numerous rock stars before and after him had done? The timing of Holly's death undoubtedly had much to do with his posthumous success. Like the subject of A. E. Housman's poem "To An Athlete Dying Young," Holly died at the peak of a promising career. Afterward, rock fans were forced to look at his music differently. His recordings took on a new, dramatic aspect. No longer were they the brilliant beginnings of a musical career. The recordings now represented the total of Holly's music. His creativity and career had come to a final close. As is often the case, individuals were prepared to bestow accolades and fame on the dead artist. Many recognized his achievements. Others thought wistfully about what might have been. Fate never gave Holly the chance to fail at his art. He died a success and therefore would be remembered as such. In this way the martyred rock star joined the roster of artists whose art became even greater in death.

Obviously the quality of Holly's music also contributed to his lasting success. At his best Holly was both a craftsman and innovator within the realm of rock 'n' roll music. Holly's ability to play basic, simple, tight rock 'n' roll was the cornerstone of his career. His recordings of **"That'll Be the Day," "Oh Boy," "Maybe Baby"** and **"Peggy Sue"** are considered to be the definitive versions of the songs and are true rock 'n' roll classics. But Holly was also an experimenter. His recordings of **"Words of Love"** and "Listen to Me" show that he was far ahead of his time in the areas of studio production work and composition of more sophisticated types of rock music. Holly's greatness is underscored by the fact that his music still appeals to contemporary rock fans. As Waylon Jennings pointed out in his 1975 recording "Old Friends," rock music despite all the changes in the last twenty years keeps coming back to Holly as a source of basic rock 'n' roll.

Apart from his music Holly himself had distinctive characteristics. His vocal style, particularly the use of tone changes, voice inflection and the carrying of a syllable over several beats to form a hiccuping effect, gave Holly an identifiable sound that was copied by many singers after his death. His appearance—a tall, thin, pleasant-looking young man wearing thick, black glasses—contributed to his distinguishable image. No other rock star looked like Holly, therefore his exit from the rock stage was clearly noticeable.

Holly's appearance might have contributed to his lasting success in other ways. He was not the matinee-idol type. He didn't have the good looks of an Elvis or Fabian. He looked like an average American male. He came from a middle-class background. He wasn't handsome. And he didn't have a powerful voice. He was just like millions of American youths who wanted to be rock stars. As a result, everyone could identify with his rise to the top—and his tragic end. Furthermore, Holly was never the number one rock star in America. He was always in the second tier behind superstars like Elvis Presley and Ricky Nelson. He lacked their glitter, sex appeal and charisma. He was an underdog in a country that has always had a special place in its heart for underdogs.

Holly's lasting fame was furthered by the condition of rock 'n' roll during the early 1960s. Holly's death in 1959 removed from rock 'n' roll one of the last performers with solid, artistic credentials. By the early 1960s Elvis and Ricky were switching to middle-of-the-road music. Little Richard had retired to become a preacher. Chuck Berry was in jail and not recording. And Jerry Lee Lewis was blacklisted for marrying a thirteen-year-old girl who was his distant cousin. Most of the remaining stars were baby-faced idols like Frankie Avalon, Bobby Rydell and Johnny Tillotson. This new breed of smiling, sweatered, teen stars recorded schmaltzy songs written and produced by adults who knew little about real rock 'n' roll. By comparison Holly's reputation as a writer and performer grew even larger. This void in rock music that occurred after Holly's death solidified his position as one of the Founding Fathers and creative forces in rock 'n' roll.

The fact that Holly died a dramatic death undoubtedly contributed to the legend that developed around him. He died at a relatively young age, twenty-three, just after making it big in the music industry. Strange occurrences surrounded his death. Holly was scheduled to take a bus to Fargo, North Dakota, but at the last moment changed his plans and chartered the private plane instead. His wife had previously asked him not to fly, because she feared for his safety. Two of the rock stars killed with Holly, Ritchie Valens and J. P. Richardson, were not even supposed to be on the plane. Holly had intended to take along his back-up musicians (one of whom was Waylon Jennings), but just prior to take-off, Valens and Richardson took their place. Holly's death had a further note of tragedy. Just seven months before, Holly had married an attractive young girl named Maria Elena. At the time of his death, Buddy's wife was pregnant. Shortly thereafter she suffered

a miscarriage. One final irony accompanied the rock star's death. His last hit record, which was on the charts at the time of the plane crash, was entitled **"It Doesn't Matter Anymore."**

Admittedly, Holly's legendary status didn't just happen. The road to everlasting stardom was paved by careful planners who kept Holly's name alive through posthumous releases of Holly records, tributes, imitators, books and motion pictures. But the planners could not have been successful had there not been an audience eager for Holly material. No doubt the marketing aided the development of the Holly legend, but even without the planners, Holly probably would have achieved his legendary status anyway.

The undying popularity of Buddy Holly tells us something about the American character. It shows that the American people value excellence and creativity. At the same time, it illustrates Americans' continuing infatuation with the Horatio Algers, the dramatic and tragic figures, the underdogs and the heroes of the world. Buddy Holly represents each of these figures. If one had to select one Holly song that summed up his career, it would not be **"It Doesn't Matter Anymore."** On the contrary, it would be **"Not Fade Away."**

John Goldrosen and John Beecher   (essay date 1986)

SOURCE: "The Making of a Legend," in *Remembering Buddy: The Definitive Biography,* 1986. Reprint by Penguin Books, 1987, pp. 149-63.

[*In the following excerpt, Goldrosen and Beecher document the continued popularity and influence of Holly's songs following his death, detailing the release of "enhanced" versions of unfinished or previously unissued recordings made by Holly later in his career.*]

"The day the music died"—so Don McLean termed that cold February day in his number one song "American Pie" almost thirteen years later. He was not the first to see Holly's death as a decisive event in the history of rock 'n' roll. At the time, no one could sense fully just what the fatal accident meant for the development of the music; and yet, on three continents, the news brought an indescribable feeling of something lost—something which could never be regained. Holly was memorialized in song and several albums were issued after his death.

Within weeks of Holly's death, **"It Doesn't Matter Anymore"** climbed to number thirteen on the Hot 100 (**"Raining In My Heart"** also made the list). Coral then issued a new album, ***The Buddy Holly Story,*** which included hits from the two earlier albums as well as some singles not previously available on an LP. This release climbed high on the album chart and was in and out of *Billboard*'s list of top one hundred albums for some three-and-a-half years, eventually earning a gold record. These successes led Coral to look for other recordings by Holly which could be issued to meet the continued demand.

Few studio masters still remained unissued; and so, almost immediately, Coral turned to unmastered material which might somehow be made to sound "commercial". A pattern was set which was followed on almost all future Holly releases: Holly's demos and tapes were not released untampered, but were instead given a bigger or fuller sound through overdubbing. The results were rarely satisfactory—at least, not to the ears of Holly's fans.

The first songs subjected to this "sweetening" were the six original songs that Holly had written just before his death. Coral got the tapes of these from Maria Elena [Holly's wife] and put them in the hands of in-house producer Jack Hansen, who was Dick Jacobs's assistant. **"Peggy Sue Got Married"** and **"Crying, Waiting, Hoping"** were issued on a single in July 1959; all of the songs were released on *The Buddy Holly Story, Volume 2* (April 1960), along with the unreleased masters **"True Love Ways"** and **"Moondreams"**; **"Little Baby"**, from Holly's first album; and three songs which had been flip sides on singles: **"Well . . . All Right"**, **"Now We're One"** and **"Take Your Time"**.

Though it could not be known how Buddy himself would have arranged the material, there was a general feeling that the Coral recordings were not even close to Buddy's intentions. Vocal backgrounds (by the white pop group, the Ray Charles singers) were added to all the songs, probably with the thought of matching the vocal and instrumental blend of the Crickets recordings; however, at times Holly's own vocal is barely audible through the "background" instrumentation. All of the songs were "stretched" to some extent by repeating the instrumental break or the closing verses. All this made it necessary to obscure Holly's own guitar playing. Even so, the accompanists sometimes failed audibly in trying to follow Holly's shifting, accented rhythm.

Of the six songs, **"Crying, Waiting, Hoping"** suffered the least, **"That Makes It Tough"** and **"That's What They Say"** suffered the most, and **"What To Do"**, **"Learning the Game"** and **"Peggy Sue Got Married"** fell somewhere in between. Overall, the songs came out sounding more "pop" than anything Holly had done up to that point; and ironically enough, with the passage of years and the ignorance among newer fans about the posthumous nature of these arrangements, the songs strengthened the impression that Holly had been turning decisively away from rock 'n' roll or rockabilly and toward pop music.

The new album's sales were nowhere near those of *The Buddy Holly Story,* but there was still a clear demand for more Holly recordings. At first, Holly's family was reluctant to allow new releases. Neither Maria nor the Holleys wanted Buddy's name exploited, and they felt it would be wrong to allow Coral to issue material which would have been below Holly's own professional standards. However, the flood of letters from Holly's fans asking that all such material be issued convinced his widow and parents to allow the release of these additional recordings. The continued flow of new albums during the 1960's reflected the willingness of the fans to accept the technical limitations of the previously unissued material.

Legal complications prevented any new releases for a couple of years. At the time of Buddy's death, his recordings were scattered along the course of his musical career.

Demos made in the days of the Buddy and Bob Show were in the hands of the Holleys, Bob Montgomery, Hipockets Duncan and others in Lubbock; sides cut during the period of Holly's Decca contract were in Decca's Nashville office or in the possession of Jim Denny's Cedarwood Publishing firm; Norman Petty had masters Holly had recorded before the break between them; and Coral had a claim to anything Holly had recorded during his period on the label. (Maria had turned all her tapes over to the Holleys shortly after Buddy's death, feeling that the tapes could have only sentimental value. She had also, it should be added, assigned half of Holly's estate to his parents, even though his death without a will had left her sole heir.) The legal tangle involved in determining rights to these recordings is apparent at a glance, and would be beyond a layman's powers of explanation even if all the facts in the matter were readily available.

As part of the settlement finally reached in 1962, Norman Petty regained control of Holly's recordings. Petty's leverage in the negotiations had been that he still possessed some of Holly's material and was not obligated to give it up or allow it to be issued; but Mrs. Holley denies that this was a factor in Petty's return to authority. The main reason, she says, was simply that Norman was the person who could do the best job of producing the remaining material, since he presumably had the most familiarity with Holly's style and taste in arrangements. Also, the Holleys knew they would need someone to handle the complicated business arrangements involved, and so they turned to Norman for that aid. Under the agreement worked out, Coral remained Holly's label (and took over as well the recordings he had made on Brunswick with the Crickets), and Maria Elena, the Holleys and Petty split Holly's future royalties.

Jerry Allison comments: "I think Buddy would have been terrifically unhappy with the fact that his folks went back to Norman. I can understand why they did it—when you're in Lubbock, Texas, you don't have much choice. They didn't have any choice if they wanted to keep Buddy's name alive and keep records coming out for the fans. They couldn't go flying to New York to keep it going—if they had, they would have just gotten mixed up with some straight biz cat who just wanted to put more records out. Like, what those people had done with Buddy's last songs—that was awful, Buddy would have hated that stuff. But Norman kept it straight for the Holleys, as good as possible, and he was more into Buddy's style than those biz cats in New York. Plus the fact that he had all the tapes. So Norman got back in charge. But I think that's the last thing Buddy would have wanted."

Petty's studio band was the Fireballs, a Texas-New Mexico group most famous for their hit recordings of "Sugar Shack" and "Bottle of Wine". They were undoubtedly more capable of providing suitable backgrounds for Holly's recordings than were the musicians associated with the Decca complex in New York. Still, there were instances where there was really no reason to use any overdubbing at all.

The first album released under the new contract was *Reminiscing,* issued in early 1963 (a single of the title song had been released the previous summer). Besides the title song, the album included two songs recorded by Holly on his own tape recorded in the months before his death: "Slippin' and Slidin' " and "Wait 'Til the Sun Shines, Nellie", and eight others recorded in 1956 before the formation of the Crickets: **"Baby, Won't You Come Out Tonight"**, **"Because I Love You"**, **"I'm Gonna Set My Foot Down"**, **"Rock-A-Bye Rock"** and **"I'm Changin' All Those Changes"**, all written by Holly; "It's Not My Fault", written by Ben Hall and fellow country musician Weldon Myrick; and the rock 'n' roll classics "Bo Diddley" and "Brown-Eyed Handsome Man".

The Fireballs' best contribution on the album was to Holly's rendition of "Slippin' and Slidin' ", a recording that leaves few Holly fans indifferent. The song had been recorded originally by Little Richard in his usual wild and swinging fashion. By contrast, Holly's version is slow, quiet and rather eerie. Many fans wondered why Holly would have chosen to make a tape of this song at a pace so much slower than the original version. In 1984, MCA producer Steve Hoffman, who had become responsible for the Holly catalogue, solved the mystery. Hoffman noticed that this song had been recorded on Holly's tape recorder at 7 1/2 inches per second (IPS) while all other songs were recorded at the higher speed of 15 IPS, a speed which offers better recording quality. Hoffman also discovered some dialogue on the tape, in which Holly can be heard to say, "Play it back fast and see how funny we sound." When played back at 15 IPS, the tape sounds like the novelty records of Alvin and the Chipmunks (who had a hit in December 1958 with "The Chipmunk Song"). Apparently, Holly taped his "slow" version of "Slippin' and Slidin' " as a musical joke to entertain himself, Maria and his friends. (Personally, I always liked the slow version; and now I know that it was meant as a joke, I can only say that I *still* like it.)

Overdubbing was less restrained on "Wait' Til The Sun Shines, Nellie", an old favourite of Mrs. Holley's which Buddy had promised to record for her. Holly's practice tape, just seventy seconds long, was subjected to splicing and rearranging; the added instruments and vocals which hide these alterations obscure Holly's own performance. The whole feel of the recording is too heavy for the low-keyed and reflective mood of Holly's rendition.

"Bo Diddley" and "Brown-Eyed Handsome Man" were two demos which Holly had cut in Clovis sometime during 1956 at the suggestion of his brother Larry. Though the tunes had been recorded with a full band, the Fireballs were still used when the cuts were prepared for the *Reminiscing* album. Most of the lead guitar playing on the released version of "Bo Diddley" was, in fact, not on the original demo. All Buddy had played on his recording was a lower-pitched tremolo effect similar to Diddley's own playing on the hit version of the song; but on the overdubbed release, a whole new guitar part was added and the other instruments on Holly's original recording were also "reinforced". The changes made on Holly's recording of Chuck Berry's "Brown-Eyed Handsome Man" were less significant; the lead guitar work is entirely Holly's.

The six remaining recordings on the *Reminiscing* album

illustrate the variety of Holly's style at the time of his first Decca contract. The version of **"I'm Changin' All Those Changes"** included here is simply a shorter, alternative version of the song previously released on the Decca album of Holly's Nashville recordings. The other five, it is believed, were recorded as demo tapes for Jim Denny's Cedarwood Publishing; they were not published then, and were filed and forgotten until a search was made for unissued Holly material in the early 1960's. "It's Not My Fault" is a tune closer to country music than "Blue Days, Black Nights", Ben Hall's other effort for Holly, but the lilting beat and accented vocal effects produced by Holly give a different flavour to the country melody. **"Because I Love You"**, a slow, emotional ballad, is one of the first songs that Holly wrote himself and he gives it a beautiful and moving performance.

By sharp contrast, the three remaining tunes on the album are driving rock 'n' roll dance numbers. **"Rock-A-Bye Rock"**, **"I'm Gonna Set My Foot Down"** and **"Baby, Won't You Come Out Tonight"** demonstrate vividly Decca's failure to appreciate the talent it had on hand. These recordings *are* Buddy Holly in 1956, not as he sounded in a recording studio under the direction of older country musicians, but as he sounded with Allison, Curtis and Don Guess on the bandstand at a teenage rock 'n' roll dance. The numbers are as furious and exciting as any contemporaneous rockabilly, and lack only the polish and finesse of later recordings such as **"Rave On"** and **"Oh Boy!"**

Although the five tracks just discussed were not cut as masters, the sound quality is good, and they are still complete performances with a full band; so it is hard to understand why extra background was added to these recordings. The additions only annoy the fan who is intent on listening closely to the original performances by Holly and his group. Allison is still irked by this procedure: "The Fireballs were good boys and I really like them, and the way they played is fine for the Fireballs—but not for Buddy Holly records. I really hated that things got all mixed up—because if somebody was gonna play some drums on those things, I would have liked to play on them. I mean, I was back in Texas and back in Clovis, and Norman could have called me and said, 'Hey, you want to overdub some stuff?' And I would have loved it. But he had all these hang-ups. The Fireballs were his boys at the time. He had them play on some stuff that didn't even need it, like 'Brown-Eyed Handsome Man' and 'Bo Diddley'; and when he did it, it was like a slam at Joe B. and me, if nothing else—like 'O.K., we'll put the Fireballs in and cover them up.' Even now, it kind of bugs me to pull all those records out and listen to them and hear all that bad overdubbing."

The next album of previously unissued material was *Showcase,* released in early 1964. On this album, more of the original recordings were left intact. Two of the cuts, **"Rock Around With Ollie Vee"** and **"Girl On My Mind"**, were from the recordings Holly had made with Decca in 1956; the others (including **"Come Back Baby"**, **"Love's Made A Fool Of You"** and **"You're The One"**) appeared publicly for the first time on this album.

"I Guess I Was Just A Fool" was recorded as a demo for Decca in 1956. The song, written by Holly, is closely modelled on Elvis Presley's Sun recording of "I Forgot To Remember To Forget", which was a special favourite of Holly's. (Buddy in fact once made a demo of the Presley tune for KDAV, but the demo was destroyed when it seemed that playing it might violate Holly's Decca contract.) Holly's vocal owes something to both Presley and Hank Williams. The lead guitar on the recording was probably played by Sonny Curtis. Holly's one-minute recording of "Gone" apparently dates from about the same time—Allison guesses that it was made sometime in late 1956. This would have been, then, a couple of years before Ferlin Husky recorded the hit version of the song; the tune had in fact been written by Smokey Rogers in 1952, and a lesser known version recorded by Husky (as Terry Preston) the same year.

Four cuts on the album were versions of the early rock 'n' roll hits "Shake, Rattle and Roll", "Blue Suede Shoes", "Rip It Up" and "Honky Tonk". All of the tunes appear to have been Holly-Allison duets, recorded in late 1956 when the two were playing without a bass player or second guitarist; the original performances are, once again, obscured by overdubbing. The tapes were made on a primitive tape recorder, but regardless of the technical limitations, the recordings offer good performances. Particularly interesting is Holly's guitar playing, both on the three vocal cuts where he must accompany himself and also on the instrumental "Honky Tonk". The original recording of that tune by Bill Doggett and his combo was in two parts, issued on both sides of a 45 r.p.m. single record; Holly used figures from both parts of the Doggett original and adapted the tenor sax and guitar solos on that recording to his own style of guitar playing. On the other three cuts, Holly is clearly aware of preceding recordings of the tunes, but his guitar solos follow his own ideas on how the songs should sound.

One revealing feature of Holly's version of "Shake, Rattle and Roll" is the set of lyrics he uses. Holly would have been aware of three recordings of the song: the original version by Joe Turner; the cover of that by Bill Haley; and a version by Elvis which was first released in 1956 on an RCA single. In making his cover version, Haley changed or omitted some of Turner's original lyrics, believing them to be too suggestive for airing on pop stations, however normal they might be as rhythm & blues lyrics went. . . . [The] national pattern did not hold in Lubbock—white teenagers there listened to the original Turner recording as much as they did to Haley's cover version. Presley and Holly each use just one of Haley's verses, choosing to follow the tougher Turner wording most of the way. Their choices reflect the tastes of their peers and audiences and reveal the familiarity with Turner's recording in that part of the country.

The remaining cut on the *Showcase* album was drawn from the solo tapes Buddy had made on his own tape recorder shortly before his death. **"Ummm, Oh Yeah"**—or **"Dearest"**, as it was correctly called on a later album—had been recorded by Mickey and Sylvia, the duo whose "Love Is Strange" had been such a favourite of Holly's.

Buddy apparently intended to record both Mickey and Sylvia tunes himself, giving them a quiet, folkish flavour. The overdubbing obscures Holly's rhythm guitar playing, but the soft, restrained mood of Holly's vocal comes through clearly enough.

The following album, released in early 1965, offered a valuable glimpse of the origins of Holly's music and certainly surprised many of his fans unfamiliar with the roots of his career. ***Holly In The Hills*** (a catchy and suggestive title, to be sure, though obviously coined without much regard to the topography of the Lubbock area!) reached farther back into the past than previous albums had done, back to recordings made by Holly and Bob Montgomery in country & western and rockabilly styles. Eight of these early sides were included. The album was filled out with **"Lonesome Tears"** and **"Fool's Paradise"**, the only two Crickets recordings which had not previously appeared on albums; **"Wishing"**, one of the songs Buddy had hoped to have the Everly Brothers record; and a new version of **"What To Do"**, substituting a more adequate backing by the Fireballs for the unsatisfactory New York arrangement. In Britain, three additional Buddy and Bob tracks (**"Queen of the Ballroom"**, **"Baby It's Love"** and **"Memories"**) were used in place of **"What To Do"** and the Crickets recordings—apparently these were discovered by Hipockets Duncan after the American album had been mastered.

Exact information is lacking as to where and when the early demos were made and who played on them. Apparently, most of them were made at the Nesman Studios in Wichita Falls, while others were recorded at the Jim Beck Studio in Dallas and at KDAV's studios. The demos seem to date from 1954 to 1955, although it is possible that some were made even earlier than that. Most of the vocals on the country tunes are duets, with Montgomery handling solo choruses and Holly providing instrumental breaks—along with Sonny Curtis, who plays the fiddle on some of these recordings. Don Guess is believed to have played steel guitar on those records where it is present; Guess and Larry Welborn shared the bass playing. Holly's guitar playing is most notable on "Gotta Get You Near Me Blues", an example of his picking ability which shows why Lubbock area musicians and disc jockeys remember Buddy today as much for his fine country guitar playing as for his singing style. The two rock 'n' roll-oriented cuts, "I Wanna Play House With You" (called "Baby, Let's Play House" when Presley recorded it for Sun) and "Down The Line", demonstrate how quickly and surely Holly and his friends had moved into rockabilly in the wake of Presley's original recordings. Whatever their inexperience and amateur status, the entire group performs with a drive and energy that could make later rock 'n' roll groups envious.

Regrettably, the ***Holly In The Hills*** cuts are not totally accurate presentations of what Holly and his fellow musicians were playing in those years since, as on the earlier albums, overdubbing distorts the original sound. Most significant is the addition of drums which were not present originally on the six country-style recordings—made at a time when drums were rarely used in small country groups. Jerry Allison probably did play on "I Wanna Play House With You" and "Down The Line", even though most of the drumming heard on the finished release was provided by the Fireballs—as was some of the guitar playing.

After several years' delay (caused in part by the new popularity of older Holly records in the mid-1960's), an additional collection of Holly's home-type recordings was released in 1969 under the title *Giant*. The advent of multi-track recording equipment enabled Norman Petty to experiment more freely with the recordings; several include unusual orchestral effects, and those with backings by studio musicians have a brighter sound in which the dubbing is a bit less obvious. As with the earlier posthumous releases, though, opinions differ as to the propriety of the backings.

On "Love Is Strange", **"You're The One"** and **"Dearest"**, Petty added a string effect, actually played on an Ondeoline, a keyboard instrument, to give the songs a lush, full sound more in line with "the sound of the times". Of the three, "Love Is Strange" has perhaps the most successful arrangement; at least, it is not out of line with Holly's rendition. Still, one wonders if Holly ever would have chosen to record the piece that way. Holly gives the 1957 "calypso"-flavoured hit a surprisingly quiet, reflective treatment—the mood presented is quite different from that found in Mickey and Sylvia's original version. As for **"You're The One"** and **"Dearest"**—the original, simpler versions released on the *Showcase* album five years before were, to many fans, preferable to the new dubbed versions.

Three songs on *Giant* were early rock 'n' roll hits recorded in late 1956 under the same circumstances as the similar cuts on the *Showcase* album. They are Fats Domino's "Blue Monday", Clarence "Frogman" Henry's "Ain't Got No Home" and "Good Rockin' Tonight", which dates back to Roy Brown's 1948 rhythm & blues recording of it—Holly may have heard that at some time, but he was undoubtedly thinking of Elvis Presley's Sun version when he made his own recording. As on the *Showcase* tunes, Holly and Allison were probably the sole performers on the original tapes.

Holly recorded "Smokey Joe's Cafe" and "Slippin' and Slidin' " in late 1958 or early 1959 on the tape recorder in his apartment, accompanying himself on electric guitar (the strange guitar break after each verse on "Smokey Joe's Cafe" is Holly's own). The dubbed backing on these matches the style of Holly more closely than had the backings on earlier albums. The version of "Slippin' and Slidin' " on this album is up-tempo, unlike the "slow" version on the *Reminiscing* album.

"Have You Ever Been Lonely" was recorded at Buddy's home one day in 1956 when he and his band were practising there. As the album liner notes explain, Holly recorded it for his mother, who liked the song. Left on the tape is Holly's call, "Mother!" at the song's conclusion. It is really quite fitting that the recording was left as it is, for the tone of his voice, and the fact that he made such recordings, is testimony to the close family ties Holly had

and to the encouragement he received from them in pursuing his ambitions.

The last cut on the album was an instrumental, **"Holly Hop"**, a brief introduction to Holly's individual guitar style and some of the figures he commonly used. One Lubbock resident remembers that Holly used this instrumental as an intro to the KDAV Sunday Party show; it does sound like the sort of instrumental rock 'n' roll dance bands would use to open and close sets, so Holly might likewise have used it for his appearances at teenage dances in Lubbock. The acclaim for Holly's singing should not cause anyone to overlook his instrumental talent, though it is heard less often and is more difficult to appreciate immediately or fully.

In coming down as harshly as I have on the use of over-dubbing on Holly's posthumous albums, I have not meant to imply that the job could have been done any better. The sound on the tapes and demos was of poor quality to begin with, so the clearer, "live" sound of the overdubbing was likely to obscure the original performance, no matter what. The question which remains is, how much dubbing was really necessary? What was the intention in providing such backings—and what *should* have been the intention?

A clue to the attitude is to be found in one remark in the liner notes written by Norman Petty for *Giant*. In speaking of guitarist George Tomsco's added accompaniment to Holly's performance on **"Holly Hop"**, Petty writes: "What a combination Buddy and George, together, would have been for the music fans!" Maybe so—but should these releases have been used to make that point? Originally, the creators of the posthumous albums wanted to ensure that the record buyer did not feel cheated by being presented with home-type recordings of limited instrumentation and/or fidelity. As a solution, the records were overdubbed, with the hope of making them sound like studio recordings—thus bringing them up to contemporary standards, one might say. (Not that there was any attempt at deception—except for *The Buddy Holly Story, Volume 2,* each album's liner notes made clear the limitations of the recordings and the use of dubbing.) But too often, the original Holly recordings wound up being used as a base for something else—"Play Along With Buddy Holly" became the appearance, if not the intent, of such releases.

In attempting to create "contemporary" albums, the producers of the posthumous releases both failed to reach their own objective and lost sight of the original purpose of the series. Primarily, these albums served fans already acquainted with the recordings released during Holly's lifetime. The fans wanted the recordings never intended for release made available, regardless of the technical limitations—for they knew that Holly was an artist even when recording under casual conditions with limited intentions. Such buyers never expected the new releases to have the full sound of **"That'll Be The Day"** or **"It Doesn't Matter Anymore"**; it was enough that Buddy's performances not be discarded simply because they had not been recorded in a modern studio. Overdubbing just obscured Buddy's vocal or (especially) instrumental performance without adding much to the total recording, and the final product always *sounded* dubbed.

TWENTIETH-CENTURY LITERARY CRITICISM, Vol. 65

The object of the releases should have been to present the recordings in their original form, doing all possible to eliminate technical flaws (such as scratches on demos) without harming the sound. Where the original pieces were unfinished, they should have been left that way. As a parallel, consider the various modern LP releases of early jazz and blues recordings dating from the 1920's. Though the fidelity on these is poor by modern standards, no one suggests that new trumpet parts should be added to Louis Armstrong's recordings, or that a vocal chorus should be assigned to sing along with Bessie Smith. The buyers of these albums know what they are getting but they want the original material anyway. It is my guess that Holly's fans would have reacted in a similar fashion. It was not until twenty years after Holly's death that his record company began to approach his recordings with these considerations in mind. Recent album releases . . . have shown greater concern for the integrity of Holly's work, and have paid more attention to the tastes of the record buyers.

In Britain, Holly's popularity actually increased in the decade after his death. Recordings which had not been released prior to Holly's death or had been available only on albums were issued as singles in a steady stream through the early 1960's and continued to rise high in the charts. **"It Doesn't Matter Anymore"** was number one for three weeks in 1959, **"Midnight Shift"** was a hit later the same year, **"True Love Ways"** was a success in 1960, and in 1963 Holly's recording of "Bo Diddley" reached the top five of the singles chart, while *The Buddy Holly Story* was still among the top twenty LPs. Even as late as 1967, Holly came in seventeenth in a music weekly's popularity poll—rather remarkable when one considers how many of the paper's readers were too young to have heard Holly's music before his death.

The early recordings of Holly and the Crickets made a profound impact upon young rock 'n' roll musicians in Britain. Their notions of what a rock 'n' roll band should be were derived from the example set by the Crickets: that of a self-contained band dominated by guitar and drums, one which wrote and sang much of its own material and in which the musicians shared the spotlight. (Obviously, Holly was the leader, but it is revealing how much attention Allison and Mauldin got as well from the British fans and press during the 1958 tour.)

Today, this notion seems obvious and basic but it was not always so; Holly and the Crickets deserve much of the credit for introducing the concept and demonstrating that it could be successful. Don Everly sees this as Holly's legacy:

> His was the first musically enclosed group in which the band played and sang and did the whole thing. No one had ever really done that. I think that young kids sitting out there could say, "Well, you play the drums, I'll be the singer, and you be the guitar player and you be the bass player, and we'll be like Buddy Holly and the Crickets."

The example of Holly and the Crickets served as a direct inspiration to John Lennon and Paul McCartney.

McCartney has said, "At least the first forty songs we wrote were Buddy Holly-influenced." And Lennon drew a personal lesson from Holly: in a letter to a Holly fan, Lennon wrote, "He made it O.K. to wear glasses. I was Buddy Holly." The first recording Lennon and McCartney ever made, in their pre-Beatles days as the Quarrymen, was a version of **"That'll Be The Day"**. The name of the Beatles was coined by John Lennon in 1959—the example of the Crickets had brought other insect names to mind.

Actually, the musical style of the Beatles derived at least as much from the hard rock 'n' roll sound of Larry Williams, Chuck Berry and Little Richard, the female choral groups such as the Shirelles and the Crystals, and the duet style of the Everly Brothers. But the Beatles were influenced by the unique vocal texture of the best Crickets recordings and, most of all, by the melodic and chord patterns of Holly's songs. The latter is most noticeable in songs the Beatles wrote for other artists: "Nobody I Know" and "World Without Love", Peter and Gordon's earliest hits, and "Bad To Me" and "From A Window", recorded by Billy J. Kramer and the Dakotas. Among the Beatles' own songs, "Every Little Thing" (on the *Beatles VI* album) was very reminiscent of Holly's material, as was, strangely enough, one of their last recordings: "Here Comes The Sun"—which in rhythm and melody was not far removed from **"What To Do", "That's What They Say", "Words of Love"** or similar Holly songs.

For other British groups, the clear tenor vocals and quick driving beat of Holly's recordings were important influences. Peter and Gordon owed their early style to the duet example of the Everly Brothers and the less nasal, lower-pitched sound of Holly's singing—a combination which Holly had himself produced five years before by double-tracking his own voice on **"Wishing"**. The Searchers, one of the finest early English groups, recorded Holly's **"Listen To Me"** and **"Learning The Game"** (which they sang as "Led In The Game") on an early "live" album, and showed his influence on such songs as "Don't Throw Your Love Away" and "Every Time That You Walk In The Room". Freddie and the Dreamers, a curious, short-lived phenomenon, featured a lead singer who not only sounded like Holly and sang some of his songs, but who even *looked* like him. The list could be carried much further. But this is not to claim that Buddy Holly was the father of all British rock 'n' roll—this would be too much of a generalization. It could be said, though, that British fans and performers had the good fortune, or good taste, to be influenced by the best of the early American rock 'n' roll performers, with Holly, Chuck Berry, Little Richard, Eddie Cochran and Elvis Presley as the most influential.

The rock 'n' roll renaissance brought to the United States by the British groups in 1964 sparked new interest in the recordings of rock 'n' roll pioneers—especially when the new groups not only imitated the sound but also recorded songs made famous by the preceding generation of performers. Many younger fans learned for the first time who Chuck Berry was after hearing the Beatles sing "Roll Over Beethoven" and "Rock and Roll Music"; Buddy Holly also benefited from this sort of recognition. In 1964, **"Not**

Fade Away" was the Rolling Stones' first American release, while Peter and Gordon recorded **"Tell Me How"**. In 1965, **"Words of Love"** appeared on the *Beatles VI* album, **"It Doesn't Matter Anymore"** was recorded by Freddie and the Dreamers, **"Heartbeat"** was sung by Herman's Hermits and, most notably, **"True Love Ways"** became a top ten hit for Peter and Gordon.

The Beatles' recording of **"Words of Love"** was particularly important in making Holly's name familiar again. Their version was a fairly close imitation of Holly's original recording and was released at a time when every song on a new Beatles album attracted close and constant attention and a great deal of airplay. The Beatles' frequent mention of Holly as one of their early favourites likewise brought new attention to Holly's recordings. When **"True Love Ways"** became a hit later in the year, some disc jockeys presented special features on Holly's recordings, or periodically juxtaposed the original and new versions of the revived Holly songs.

In the United States, the influence of Holly's work in the mid- and late 1960's was reflected most genuinely in occasional outbreaks of individual performers and groups whose debt to Holly sometimes went unrecognized. The career of one such group, the Bobby Fuller Four, involved close personal and stylistic ties to early rock 'n' roll. Bobby Fuller was from El Paso and grew up listening to and admiring the recordings of Buddy Holly. Fuller corresponded with Holly's parents and, after making some local recordings on minor labels, got a contract in Los Angeles with Bob Keene, who had been Ritchie Valens's manager.

In early 1966, the Bobby Fuller Four had one of the best-selling records of the year with "I Fought The Law"—a song which had been written by Sonny Curtis and recorded by the Crickets not long after Holly's death. The song had the "Buddy Holly sound"—the rhythm, the pounding drumbeat, the tenor vocal, the chordal guitar solo, the shifting chords and triadic effects of the melody. Still, it was not an "imitation" of Holly's style—the song came from a major songwriter who composed what came naturally to him, and was played by artists in the way that was natural for them. Though the term "Tex-Mex sound" was really a promotional creation, there was still a Texas brand of rock 'n' roll, though not even the performers themselves could explain just what it was or where it came from.

Fuller's first album was one of the most danceable rock 'n' roll albums in some time. Most of the album cuts were written by Fuller, and were obviously modelled on Holly and Cochran tunes. And yet, something was lacking—the songs had the drive and feel of Holly's recordings, but lacked the lyrical content and emotional depth of those songs. Maybe Fuller would have developed as a songwriter later; but in the summer of 1966, he was found dead of asphyxiation in his car. (His death was officially ruled a suicide, despite strong evidence that he was murdered.)

The limited artistic success of the Bobby Fuller Four brings up a quite troubling and controversial element in the inheritance left by Buddy Holly to later popular performers. A line of influence can be traced from the music of Buddy Holly through that of Bobby Fuller to the much shallower sounds of Gary Lewis and the Playboys, and on to the simplistic "Bubblegum" sound of the late 1960's, typified by the Archies' "Sugar, Sugar". Some critics have therefore suggested that Holly was partially responsible for the deterioration of rock music in the decade after his death. (For an extreme and rather grotesque statement of this argument, see Nik Cohn's *Rock From the Beginning*.)

This view of Holly ignores the balanced nature of Holly's sound, and of early rock 'n' roll in general, compared to the products of the late 1960's and 1970's. Early rock 'n' roll (on through the early years of the British invasion) was able to balance the use of loud, amplified sound with the use of forms and lyric themes that had their roots deep in preceding musical styles: a heavy beat and a pretty melody were not incompatible. In the late 1960's, the unity broke down, and the disparate elements split apart. Bubblegum music was one offshoot; another was the overpowering sound of the "heavy metal" groups. While a line can be traced from Holly to the bubblegum sound, it is equally valid to see Holly's stress on a full guitar sound and heavy drumming as the basis for heavy-metal rock. (The same might be said of Eddie Cochran.) A creative artist in any field, whether it be music, literature or the fine arts, ought not to be blamed for the mediocrity or banality of those who later imitate just one element of his work, while losing the sense of balance that held it together.

Here and there in the late 1960's, a few American performers began to acknowledge the true value of Holly's music (and that of other early rock 'n' roll performers). Tom Rush's album *Take A Little Walk With Me* included his quite individualistic interpretations of several rock 'n' roll songs, including Holly's **"Love's Made A Fool Of You"**—which Rush also made a standard in his concert performances. Rush's quiet and reflective rendition of the song fully captured the spirit of the lyrics, and his instrumental accompaniment was at one and the same time quite distinct from that of the original Holly version, and yet totally appropriate to the song. Hundreds of artists have recorded Holly's songs at one time or another, but few have been as successful as Rush in producing a recording which, while the artist's own creation, fully captures the spirit of Buddy Holly's music.

In the years that followed, several other rock and folk performers acknowledged their debt to Holly or showed his influence in their songs. Bob Dylan grew up on rock 'n' roll and has said that Holly was an influence upon his style. In 1974, a *Newsweek* feature article on Dylan's national concert tour contained the following:

> Musically, he says, he doesn't consider his taste a part of the nostalgia so fashionable today in pop. "I just carry that other time around with me," he says. "The music of the late fifties and early sixties when music was at that root level— that for me is meaningful music. The singers and musicians I grew up with transcend nostalgia— Buddy Holly and Johnny Ace are just as valid to me today as then."

Bob Dylan wasn't the only singer to antagonize his folk-music following by revealing his rock 'n' roll roots. In

1970, Phil Ochs stepped out on the stage of Carnegie Hall wearing an Elvis-style gold-lamé suit and carrying an electric guitar, and played medleys of songs by Presley and Holly to a mixture of boos and cheers. (A live album of the concert was later released under the title *Gunfight At Carnegie Hall*.) In introducing his favourite Holly tunes, Ochs tried to offer an explanation to those who had come to hear him play the protest songs for which he was best known:

> I'd like to sing some songs that are just as much Phil Ochs as anything else. These songs were first recorded by somebody I hold very dear to my heart, from the 1950's—[boos and groans]—Could this be a generation gap? . . . He formed that part of my musical mind which wrote anything like "I Ain't Marching Anymore", "Changes"—that thought process came from certain people, and this is one of them: Buddy Holly. [applause and jeers] These are a collection of his songs I memorized as a kid. . . .

Another performer with roots in Holly's music was John Denver (a graduate of Texas Tech, for whatever significance that might have). Denver recorded **"Everyday"** and released it on a single in 1972; some of his most successful compositions, like "Leaving on a Jet Plane" and "Country Roads", bear the mark of Holly's influence. The Nitty Gritty Dirt Band paid their respects to Holly with a recording of **"Rave On"**. When they appeared in Lubbock in late 1971, they were amazed to find that most of their young audience didn't know who Buddy Holly was, and so they tried to enlighten the crowd by playing a medley of Holly's songs.

Critics, too, began to praise Holly and the brand of rock 'n' roll he had fashioned. Holly was the subject of articles in *Rolling Stone;* and in *Rock Encyclopedia,* Lillian Roxon had this to say about Holly:

> He was one of the giants of early rock, a figure so important in the history of popular music that it is impossible to hear a song on the charts today that does not owe something to the tall, slim bespectacled boy from Lubbock, Texas. . . . More than any other singer of that era, he brings back a time when music was fun. . . . Adults put him down with the rest of the Presley era as shock rock. Kids just remembered it was impossible not to dance, not to groove, while he sang. Most of the giants of ten years later, of the booming rock scene of the late sixties, were teenagers when Holly was king and their music reflects it. Looking back from the twin peaks of psychedelia and electronic gadgetry, he comes through fresher than ever.

No tribute to the legacy of Buddy Holly had more impact than Don McLean's "American Pie", which won gold records and spent weeks in the number one positions on the *Billboard* pop singles and LP charts in late 1971 and early 1972. Some of the symbolic lyrics could be given many (or no) explanations and, although the album was openly dedicated to Holly, the song never mentioned him by name. However, anyone familiar with the story of Buddy Holly had little trouble understanding the first verse:

> A long, long time ago,
> I can still remember, how that music used to make me smile.
> And I knew if I had the chance,
> That I could make those people dance,
> And maybe they'd be happy for a while.
> But February made me shiver,
> With every paper I'd deliver,
> Bad news on the doorstep—
> I couldn't take one more step.
> And I can't remember if I cried,
> When I read about his widowed bride,
> But something touched me deep inside,
> The day the music died.

In a matter of weeks, Holly received more publicity and recognition than he had ever received in his own lifetime. And by 1973, McLean's view of rock history had been expressed so widely and become so standard that it rated inclusion in the much-acclaimed movie, *American Graffiti.* "I can't stand that surfing shit," says hot-rodder John Milner as he turns the radio off in disgust—"rock 'n' roll's been going downhill ever since Buddy Holly died."

The resurgence of interest created by McLean's song led after some delay to Decca's release of a new collection of Holly's recordings. (By 1972, the separate Coral label had been dropped and its roster absorbed by Decca.) The new double album showed all the flaws in thinking that had affected the presentation of the posthumous releases and the selection of cuts on two previous "greatest hits" albums. What is most regrettable is that an opportunity to do better was lost. Decca originally had an independent producer, John Boylan, working on the project; plans were for a low-priced three-album boxed set containing a booklet with photographs, biographical information and a discography. All songs were to be presented in their original, undubbed forms, and the choice of songs reflected the consensus of most fans as to the best of Holly's recordings.

Then, Decca got cold feet. The plans were scrapped, and a two-album set which had been released in Germany a year before was issued instead under the title *Buddy Holly: A Rock 'n' Roll Collection*. There were no liner notes of any sort—this at a time when other companies, notably United Artists and Atlantic, were re-releasing recordings by their own rock 'n' roll artists in attractive packages with informative commentaries. The choice of selections was irrational—among the cuts not included in the new album were **"Everyday"**, **"Early In The Morning"**, **"Think It Over"**, **"True Love Ways"**, **"I'm Gonna Love You Too"** and **"It's So Easy"**. The original tapes of the posthumous releases were once more passed over in favour of the dubbed versions made with the Jack Hansen combo and the Fireballs. And, as the most astonishing boner of all, the recording of **"Love's Made A Fool Of You"** included on the new set was not Buddy Holly's own recording of it, but instead the recording cut by the Crickets shortly after Holly's departure from the group. A lot of strange things had been done to Holly's recordings over the previous thirteen years, but never before had a Buddy Holly album included a cut that Holly himself did not play on.

The new seed of interest in Holly which was planted in the

early 1970's took several years to come to fruition. When the rock 'n' roll nostalgia craze had come and gone, musicians, fans and critics began to look more closely at those few artists whose impact had been truly lasting. It was Buddy Holly as much as anyone who benefited from that attention. The late 1970's were to demonstrate the breadth of the new interest in and respect for Holly.

FURTHER READING

Biography

Goldrosen, John, and Beecher, John. *Remembering Buddy: The Definitive Biography.* New York: Penguin Books, 1986, 204 p.

Appreciative study based in part on a revised edition of Goldrosen's *Buddy Holly: His Life and Music,* published in 1975.

Criticism

Flippo, Chet. "Buddy Holly Lives!" *Rolling Stone,* No. 263 (20 April 1978): 14.

Notice of the release of *The Buddy Holly Story,* a film biography starring Gary Busey.

Friedman, Kinky. "Buddy Holly's Texas." *Rolling Stone* (19 April 1990): 103.

Offers impressions of Texan culture and the development of distinctive musical styles in Texas in the 1950s.

Gillett, Charlie. "The Independents: II." In his *The Sound of the City: The Rise of Rock and Roll,* rev. ed., pp. 96-9. New York: Pantheon Books, 1983.

Discusses Holly in a survey of rock music from 1954 to 1961. According to Gillett, "That'll Be the Day" is notable in part because it "expressed an attitude that many of its listeners wished they could be brave enough to say out loud."

Shaw, Arnold. "The Tex-Mex Sound." In his *The Rockin' '50s: The Decade That Transformed the Pop Music Scene,* pp. 185-87. New York: Hawthorn Books, 1974.

Discusses Holly, Buddy Knox, and Jimmy Bowen. Shaw notes that "That'll Be the Day" explores "the ambivalent emotions of a young man, worried that his girl would not return, and confident that she could not stay away."

Thigpen, David. "Vocal Heroes." *Harper's Bazaar* 123, No. 3,347 (November 1990): 172, 175.

Discusses the New York debut of *Buddy: The Buddy Holly Story,* a theatrical production that originated in London.

Ward, Ed; Stokes, Geoffrey; and Tucker, Ken. *Rock of Ages: The "Rolling Stone" History of Rock & Roll.* New York: Rolling Stone Press/Summit Books, 1986, 649 p.

Includes references throughout to Holly and his importance to the early development of rock music.

Additional coverage of Holly's life and career is contained in the following source published by Gale Research: *Contemporary Musicians*, Vol. 1.

James Gibbons Huneker

1857-1921

American journalist, essayist, biographer, critic, autobiographer, and novelist.

INTRODUCTION

Huneker was an influential critic and journalist who is credited with introducing American readers to many leading European writers, thinkers, artists, and composers of the late nineteenth and early twentieth centuries. A contributor to a variety of periodicals, he later collected his writings in such volumes as *Iconoclasts: A Book of Dramatists* (1905), which includes studies of Henrik Ibsen, Bernard Shaw, and Maurice Maeterlinck, and *Unicorns* (1917), which contains essays on such writers as James Joyce, George Sand, Mikhail Artzybashev, and J. K. Huysmans. Although Huneker has been criticized for lacking a coherent critical perspective, his writings are considered representative of the impressionism that characterized much of American literary journalism at the turn of the century, and, in assessing Huneker's role in the development of American criticism, Alfred Kazin has noted that "almost singled-handed he brought the new currents in European art and thought to America and made them fashionable."

Biographical Information

Huneker was born to a middle-class family in Philadelphia. He attended a private academy and later studied piano with the hope of pursuing a career as a concert pianist. In 1878 Huneker traveled for the first time to Paris, where he continued his musical training and began writing occasional pieces for the *Philadelphia Evening Bulletin*. Following his return from Europe, he taught piano in Philadelphia and contributed articles to the music journal *Etude*. In 1886 Huneker moved to New York and began writing book reviews and other critiques for the *Musical Courier*. He remained with that periodical until 1902, contributing a regular column on the arts under the name "Raconteur." During the early 1890s he also wrote music and drama reviews for the *New York Recorder*. In the ensuing decades Huneker was associated with numerous periodicals, most notably the *New York Sun, Metropolitan Magazine, Puck,* and the *New York Times,* to which he contributed as a foreign correspondent and feature writer. He died in 1921.

Major Works

Huneker's works are characterized by a cosmopolitan approach, anecdotal style, and enthusiasm for the subjects he undertook, most notably new developments in Europe-an art and literature of the fin-de-siècle period. His early reviews and essays focus on music and musicians, including the highly regarded study *Chopin: The Man and His Music* (1901). Such works as *Iconoclasts, Egoists: A Book of Supermen* (1909), and *Ivory Apes and Peacocks* (1915) comprise collections of his journalistic writings that cover an extensive range of arts and artists. He was among the first American critics to champion the dramas of Henrik Ibsen, Bernard Shaw, and August Strindberg, and *Unicorns* contains his early appreciation of James Joyce, whom he called "indubitably a fresh talent." Huneker's commentaries are often subjective and impressionistic, lacking a formal aesthetic. He praised individualism and focused his examinations on the artist's personality and on the social milieu in which the artist worked. His greatest enthusiasm was for French culture, and he wrote appreciations of Charles Baudelaire, Théophile Gautier, Paul Cézanne, and Henri Matisse, among numerous others. Huneker's favorites among contemporary American writers included Walt Whitman, Mark Twain, Edgar Allan Poe, and William Dean Howells. In addition to his critical works, Huneker also wrote a novel, *Painted Veils* (1920), and the two-volume autobiography *Steeplejack* (1920).

Critical Reception

During his lifetime Huneker was considered the preeminent literary journalist in the United States. His personal acquaintance with leading artists, composers, and writers of the period and his cosmopolitan aesthetic sensibility brought Huneker significant influence as a taste-maker in American criticism. While the informal and unsystematic style of his reviews fell out of favor with critics who advocated the social and academic critical movements that developed in the mid-twentieth century, Huneker has nevertheless been praised by such notable critics as H. L. Mencken, who described him as "one of the most charming fellows ever heard of, and the best critic of the American first line."

PRINCIPAL WORKS

Mezzotints in Modern Music (essays) 1899
Chopin: The Man and His Music (biography) 1900
Melomaniacs (essays) 1902
Overtones: A Book of Temperaments (essays) 1904
Iconoclasts: A Book of Dramatists (essays) 1905
Visionaries (essays) 1905
Egoists: A Book of Supermen (essays) 1909
Promenades of an Impressionist (essays) 1910
Franz Liszt (biography) 1911
Old Fogy: His Musical Opinions and Grotesques (essays) 1913
The Pathos of Distance: A Book of a Thousand and One Moments (essays and reminiscences) 1913
The Development of Piano Music from the Days of the Clavichord and Harpsichord to the Present Time (nonfiction) 1915
Ivory Apes and Peacocks (essays) 1915
New Cosmopolis: A Book of Images (essays) 1915
The Philharmonic Society of New York and Its Seventy-Fifth Anniversary: A Retrospect (nonfiction) 1917
Unicorns (essays) 1917
Bedouins (essays) 1920
Painted Veils (novel) 1920
Steeplejack. 2 vols. (autobiography) 1920
Variations (essays) 1921
Letters of James Gibbons Huneker (letters) 1922
Intimate Letters of James Gibbons Huneker (letters) 1924
Essays by James Huneker (essays) 1929
Americans in the Arts: Critiques by James Gibbons Huneker, 1890-1920 (essays) 1985

CRITICISM

Edward Clark Marsh (essay date 1909)

SOURCE: "James Huneker: Individualist," in *The Forum*, New York, Vol. XLI, No. 6, June, 1909, pp. 600-05.

[*In the following essay, Marsh considers the distinctive, idiosyncratic style of Huneker's literary criticism.*]

With a frankness that is altogether praiseworthy, James Huneker has affixed to his books labels which have the rare virtue of telling something about what they contain. The import of such titles as *Melomaniacs; Visionaries; Iconoclasts;* and now *Egoists,* is not cryptic. However much they may include, they will commonly be taken as barring out those manifestations of human life and thought which are reputed safe and sane. To the average man they will suggest something of morbidity; and if the average man will look further than the titles, he shall not be cheated of his expectation. It would not be easy to sum up under a single rubric all the men and subjects with which Mr. Huneker's books have dealt; their range is too wide for that. Yet they own to something in common, which marks them as having to do with a special set of phenomena. The men whose names are most frequently on the author's lips are those whom the world reckons madmen, either "sick souls," creatures of unhealthy sensibility, or the radicals, the free, independent thinkers who defy old formulas, break cherished idols and found new religions. Here, then, is one critic's specialty—since criticism must be a specialized business.

This preoccupation with themes which are taboo to the conservative is perhaps the first characteristic of the author to strike the reader of his books. But the second forthstanding characteristic involves something like a paradox. Criticism is, to be sure, for most part a business of specialization; yet the range of some of the great critics has been extraordinarily wide. One recalls at once Hazlitt's generous sympathies, Coleridge's wide reading, the learning and catholic understanding of Taine. The Frenchman, indeed, created a new standard for critics, and paved the way for such observers as the Danish Brandes, whose survey takes in the whole field of European literature. Within the restrictions of his special predilections, Mr. Huneker has followed this model. His *Iconoclasts* includes, for instance, studies of the Norwegian Ibsen, the Swedish Strindberg, the German Hauptmann, the French Hervieu, the Russian Gorky, the Italian D'Annunzio, the Belgian Maeterlinck and the Irish Shaw. But in these days of facile cosmopolitanism this sweeping of the horizon is not rare. Much more uncommon is the vertical range of Mr. Huneker's observations. He is not a critic of one art, like Arnold, nor of two or three, like Symonds and Pater, but of all the arts. George Moore has written much and well concerning music and painting, as well as literature; but among English writers I can recall no one who has passed so freely from one plane to another as Mr. Huneker, with the single exception of the brilliant Arthur Symons, with his *Studies in Seven Arts*. Indeed, the American has fairly outdone the Englishman, for he has invented new arts to criticise. Among the most astonishing of his virtuosopieces are two of his short stories, **"The Eighth Deadly Sin"** and **"The Spiral Road"**—the one an exposition of the art of perfume, the other of the art of pyrotechny. On these fantastic achievements of the future he has, with grave irony, trained his battery of technical criticism. In another of his stories, **"A Master of Cobwebs,"** he has written of his hero: "He was a critic who wrote brilliantly of music in the terms of painting, of plastic arts in the technical phraseology of music, and by him the drama was discussed purely as literature." A franker bit of satirical autobiography could not be desired.

In the development of this versatility chance has doubtless played its part; something must also be conceded to heredity. Of Austro-Hungarian descent on his father's side, his mother was a daughter of James Gibbons, an Irish agitator and poet. Mr. Huneker was educated for the Church; hence his leaning toward mysticism, and the patristic and scholastic lore with which his pages are saturated. Yet his direct approach to literature was through journalism. As a boy he wrote letters on painting and artists from Paris to American periodicals. His technical training in music was solid and thorough. He is said to be an admirable pianist. In his connection with the New York press (latterly with the *Sun* newspaper), he has been successively critic of music, the drama, and painting. His published works comprise four volumes of essays: *Mezzotints in Modern Music* (Brahms, Tchaikovsky, Chopin, Richard Strauss, Liszt and Wagner); *Overtones: a Book of Temperaments* (Richard Strauss, Parsifal, Literary Men who loved Music, The Eternal Feminine, The Beethoven of French Prose, Nietzsche the Rhapsodist, Anarchs of Art, After Wagner What? Verdi and Boito); *Iconoclasts: a Book of Dramatists* (Ibsen, Strindberg, Becque, Hauptmann, Sudermann, Hervieu, Gorky, Duse and D'Annunzio, Maeterlinck, De l'Isle Adam, Shaw); *Egoists: a Book of Supermen* (Beyle-Stendhal, The Baudelaire Legend, The Real Flaubert, Anatole France, J.-K. Huysmans, Maurice Barrès, Phases of Nietzsche, Mystics, Ibsen, Max Stirner); a book devoted to *Chopin: the Man and His Music;* and two volumes of short stories, *Melomaniacs* and *Visionaries*.

There remains a third characteristic which will have struck every one who has followed Mr. Huneker's course in letters: his independence of other critical support. For the full measure of his pioneering zeal it would be necessary to turn to the files of the newspapers in which is buried the bulk of his writing. He is given to quoting Stendhal's shrewd saying concerning romanticism, with its application to so much besides: "Romanticism is the art of presenting to people literary works which in the actual state of their habitudes and beliefs are capable of giving the greatest possible pleasure; classicism, on the contrary, is the art of presenting literature which gave the greatest possible pleasure to their great-grandfathers." Mr. Huneker has not waited for his romantics to become classics before admiring them. Fifteen years ago his columns bristled with appreciation of a young Irish playwright, then practically unknown, one Bernard Shaw. He led the fight in America for Richard Strauss while the issue was doubtful, and when the victory had been won left the laurels to others. He was the first American critic to give serious consideration to the works of Strindberg and Hervieu. At the present moment in New York the name of Claude Debussy is the rallying point of the musical radicals, and much critical pother has been raised by those who have just dis-

covered the Music of the Future; it is some years since Mr. Huneker wrote one of the best appreciations of the Frenchman that has appeared in English. Even in his latest book, which with its attention to Flaubert and Stendhal and Baudelaire, appears almost reactionary for this arch-modernist, he brings forward the French mystics Ernest Hello and Adolphe Retté, whose names have scarcely hitherto been heard on this side of the water. Path-breaking is, to be sure, a dangerous if necessary business; the man who points the way seldom enters into the Promised Land. In spite of mistakes, Mr. Huneker has lived to see many of his earlier enthusiasms justified by general agreement: to see Strauss accepted as a master, Shaw a popular playwright, Ibsen a great dramatist. If these triumphs seem obvious enough at present, they were by no means so obvious fifteen and twenty years ago.

Shall it be claimed, then, that this pioneer of radical thought has been a moulder of public opinion, a critic whose utterances have served to fix the status of the men of whom he has written, a formulator of judgments for his readers? Doubtless he has had his influence; but it would require some hardihood to maintain that he has affected profoundly the beliefs of any large section of the public. Indeed, if one may judge his theory from his practice, it may be doubted whether this has been any part of his aim. The ideal of "objective" criticism occupies little space in his mental furnishings. His judgments of men and things are frankly his own; there is no pretence of projecting them into space, and establishing for them any sort of external validity. He is not judicial. He is not dispassionate. Somewhere he has quoted approvingly Swinburne's dictum to the effect that there is no reason for writing criticism except to praise nobly. So he selects for his subjects the men with whom, on one account or another, he is strongly in sympathy. Worse still in the eyes of the official measurers of the arts, he is wont to dwell on certain phases of a man's work, to the exclusion or neglect of other sides with which his sympathy is not keen. Thus he has written much of Nietzsche; but for him the poet in Nietzsche has swallowed the philosopher. His is not the "complete" or "final" estimate of the German writer (neither, it may be remarked, is any one else's estimate). Criticism is, to use one of his own favorite metaphors, the springboard whence he projects his own views of the world. He does not adopt the time-honored formulas, and his work is often lacking in form. Also his conclusions frequently fail of definiteness. His opinions do not come in parcels neatly tied and labelled. At his best he is scarcely a court of last appeal, but only a stimulating, provocative influence; at his worst he is perverse and even incoherent, but not dull. His style is capable of becoming irritating, yet it is strong and sinewy—the reflection of a vigorous and acute intellect, original withal. If the entire critical race be divided into two classes—those who assume to do their readers' thinking for them, and those who write for the purpose of provoking thought—there will be no doubt as to the division to which Mr. Huneker belongs.

Measured by this standard, his writings have a value that is admirably illustrated by his latest book. It is in the literary field that he is most easily "placed," and *Egoists* is, with the exception of *Iconoclasts* (which dealt with writers for the stage), the first of his volumes to be devoted to literature. Because of its point of view, deliberately chosen and consistently maintained, it is organic beyond most books of essays. *A Book of Supermen:* the sub-title may be allowed, though it brings under a single category such dissimilar spirits as Walter Pater and Max Stirner. The men who form the subjects of these pages are alike in that they are strongly individual thinkers and artists. Most of them are preachers as well as practisers of individualism. In an era of socialist ideas Mr. Huneker is whole-hearted in his contempt for what he deems the sentimentalisms and sophistries of socialism. He is as stoutly individualist as he has ever been. But he is less flamboyantly defiant of the ways of the world than of yore, and he has abated the aggressive cynicism of youth. Moreover, the range of his sympathies has widened rather than contracted. Consequently he sees more sides of his subject than before. Champion of immoralists though he has been, he ranges himself more than once on the side of order and decorum. He attacks the legend of Baudelaire's Satanic wickedness, and proclaims Ibsen the austere moralist that he was. It would be hard to find a trace of iconoclasm in his admiration for Flaubert and his defence of the French author against the slanders of Maxime du Camp. This essay is, indeed, one of the most vigorous and substantial of Mr. Huneker's writings—a genuine and unaffected appreciation of a great artist. His affinity with Anatole France gives peculiar interest to his estimate of that whimsical, ironic genius. It is an admirably intimate study. His enthusiasm for the mystic Huysmans and the egoist Barrès is evidently sincere; it will not inspire an equal enthusiasm in every reader. The Ibsen is a footnote to the more elaborate study in *Iconoclasts.* The article on Max Stirner was written on the occasion of the translation into English of Stirner's book, *The Ego and His Own.* Mr. Huneker has a high opinion of the importance of this work, but the essay is not one of his successful efforts. It is sprinkled with names and citations which evidence wide reading and arouse a suspicion of consequent mental indigestion. There is a similar show of learning in the essay on Stendhal, which stands at the beginning of the volume, but there is also much more in this study. As an evaluation of Stendhal's work and his position in literary history, it is less weighty than the chapters Brandes has devoted to the same subject; but Mr. Huneker's is incomparably the more lively and interesting presentation of a somewhat baffling personality.

And here is perhaps at last the key to Mr. Huneker's most significant achievement. He is not to be understood as a critic without reference to his work as a fictionist. Literature, the arts, exist for him only in close relation with life. Whatever his medium, his attitude remains much the same. Character interests him more than events. He regards his heroes primarily as men, not as mere automatic producers of books and plays and pictures, and he probes into their psychology with the curiosity of the novelist. For the recording of his discoveries, it is relatively unimportant what medium he shall use. In this novel-writing age, it is natural that he should have essayed fiction; it is equally natural that his stories should be what they are. For a parallel to his work in this sort one must go to France. It is the fiction of ideas—for the mere story in the restricted sense, the bare narration of events, his contempt is profound. The drama in which he displays his characters is seldom externalized; it plays itself out in their souls. But the characters themselves, no matter how little they may accomplish, are real. By the same token, they are far removed from the mediocre puppets of realistic fiction. They are exceptional souls, created for the sake of what they can express. They are the spokesmen of the author's ideas—for fiction is in his hands a tool, not an end in itself. The stories in *Melomaniacs* are concerned with the aberrations of musical genius. Clever in conception, filled with fantastic wit and mordant irony, they display an astonishing insight into certain so-called morbid states of soul. Of the amazing tales in *Visionaries* a typical because extreme example is **"The Third Kingdom"**—a half-crazed monk's dream of the great world-drama, the invention of the Christian religion. It is a conception of genuine imaginative reach, and the form is hardly more than an accident. It is rather a metaphysical rhapsody than a story.

Let it be granted, then, that James Huneker is too much the critic to be a wholly successful writer of fiction. It is equally true that he is too much the fictionist to treat literature as something separate from life. To the work of criticism he brings a well-stored mind, the result of wide reading and a tenacious memory. Lacking the scholar's temper, he has erudition, though he does not always carry his learning lightly. In spite of pronounced predilections, the range of his sympathies is wide, and he is capable of healthy enthusiasms. His versatility is unquestioned, and awakens resentment in those who would confine every man to the path he may first mark out. (There is discernible a personal note in what he writes of Baudelaire: "His mistake, in the eyes of his colleagues, was to write so well about the seven arts. Versatility is seldom given its real name—which is protracted labor.") Above all, his mind is vigorous and supple, and he has the gift of telling expression. He is a *décadent* in the sense in which, as he insists, the word should alone be used: he decomposes his phrases, breaks up the old formulas, and makes new syntheses of ideas. As a critic, whether of music, the plastic arts, of poetry or fiction or philosophy, he is of those who never attain finality; but he is always stimulating, provocative of thought, and by virtue of this quality, not invariably possessed by critics, he is entitled to a distinctive place in American letters.

Current Literature   (essay date 1909)

SOURCE: "James Huneker: Super-Critic," in *Current Literature,* Vol. XLVIII, No. 1, July, 1909, pp. 57-9.

[The following essay addresses Huneker's preeminence as a literary critic.]

Brilliancy, it seems, begets brilliancy. The scintillant genius of James Huneker provokes pyrotechnics on the part of his critics. Critic of Supermen and Super-critic, his epigrammatic flashes dazzle the elect and the curious. Fitly enough, Mr. Huneker's latest book of essays [*Egoists*] is dedicated to George Brandes. What George Brandes is to the Old World James Huneker is to the New. Huneker's figure stands out in even bolder relief in America than that of Brandes in Europe. In the tiny lane of American criticism, to quote Percival Pollard, there is not even the semblance of a crowd. We can easily count our critics on our fingers; and, unless we are arrantly optimistic in our own interpretation of the word critic, we need no more than a single hand. On the hand of criticism, Mr. Pollard himself, at his best, may be compared to the little finger, Mr. Paul Elmer More, eminently sane and respectable, to the thumb, but James Huneker is the forefinger pointing the way to the new. But always pointing to Europe. Infinitely versatile Mr. Pollard calls him, and essentially cosmopolitan; but American merely incidentally. "A critic who happens also to be an American, a critic who sees, moreover, only Europe." Were it not, he complains in *Town Topics,* for Poe, a poet, also, who merely happened to be an American, and whose art had nothing essential to our soil, you might read **Egoists** and find no American art therein. If we believe we have an equal art at home, then we must censure Mr. Huneker for being, one might say, too farsighted. If we believe that we have had nothing here in that same artistic gallery, we should be content to thank our stars that we have so fine a critical spirit here as the author of the **Egoists**. "Who cannot have the rose itself," Mr. Pollard concludes, "can at least have the perfume."

A writer in *The Nation,* presumably Mr. More, is a little grieved by Mr. Huneker's apparent disembarrassment of prejudice. If a subject is only "interesting," its quality, the writer insinuates, is of no particular importance to Mr. Huneker. "As long as it is not dull, it may be anything for all he cares—odd, fantastical, curious, morbid, lunatic. . . . Naturally among other lumber he has rid himself of leading ideas and general principles. His criticism is essentially a criticism of surfaces, intersected by some critical necromancy in points." Another critic, in *America,* the new Roman Catholic weekly, more aptly describes Mr. Huneker's attitude as that of one who stands apart, contemplating all creeds and having none of his own. Yet it is libelous to maintain that Mr. Huneker lacks a fundamental conviction. "Mr. Huneker," the writer asserts, "is eloquent at times, epigrammatic frequently, interesting generally, earnest sometimes, convincing note in Huneker's dazzling chromatic scale. James Huneker, affirms Edwin Markham in the New York *American,* is more than merely colorful and decorative; he follows the Ruskin idea that ornament must spring from use. So with Mr. Huneker, epithet and epigram must sustain and illumine the argument; his gargoyles are water-spouts; his caryatids are working pillars. From a hundred fields he has gathered his honey; but one dominant mood pervades his manifold manifestations. **Iconoclasts** dealt with the modern dramatists, **Overtones** with men of strange temperament,—"the different." **Egoists** elucidates Supermen,—Stendhal, Baudelaire, Anatole France, Flaubert, Huysmans, Barrès, Ibsen and Stirner. "Mr. Huneker's sympathy," Mr. Markham explains, "is always with the thinker who breaks the stone wall of custom and shovels out a new path over the sands of the commonplace. As Mr. Chesterton, of England, celebrates the common man, so Mr. Huneker celebrates the rebel who will go his own artistic way." To quote further:

> Mr. Huneker is intent that we shall see the rebel

as he is. So Mr. Huneker takes off covering after covering to be sure that nothing obstructs the reader's view of the subject. Possibly some of us have not seen the man from this aspect or that. So turn him again; pull down that curtain, fling up this one. Metaphor, allusion, quotation, all are lavished to bring out shades of understanding, and finally we close a chapter, feeling that we have had a revelation of a personality that sheds light on all personality. . . .

In Mr. Huneker's **Iconoclasts** and **Egoists** we have descriptions of nearly all of the most radical thinkers of our restless age. Here we find the men who carry divine or demon fire—now radiating light, now scattering thick darkness. They are the Titans of the modern world. And Mr. Huneker sketches these rebellious souls with the brilliancy and boldness with which Sorolla dashes color upon his canvas.

Perhaps Mr. Huneker has preserved the full vigor of his individual genius because it has been his good fortune to write only of subjects with which he has sympathy. He has always, observes *The Times Saturday Review of Books* (New York), worked in pleasant professional byways, and each collection of essays he puts forward in book form retains the charm of spontaneity. He is no encyclopedist, seeking the records for dates and facts and collating them to give his fellow-men much information in little. Dates and facts appeal to him only when they bear directly on the inspiration and influence of the novelist, poet, philosopher, or composer or painter who holds him for the time being in thrall.

Mr. Huneker's range of interest wrings even a mead of praise from the flippant lips of *The Bookman.* The syndicate known as Andrew Lang, we are told, is popularly supposed to be omniscient in matters literary; and there are continental critics, like George Brandes (to whom **Egoists** is dedicated), who have surveyed the field of European culture, taking in the literatures of France, Germany, England, Italy, Russia, and the rest, as a whole. But the American critic, the writer insists, not content with a field as broad as the modern world, has pursued his subject into the third dimension.

> In one of his short stories he has satirized himself in the person of his hero as a man who wrote of one art in terms of another; actually, he has written of each of the arts in terms of all the others. Probably both heredity and education have contributed to this development. As a boy he had three great interests—music, painting, and literature—and before he was twenty he was in Paris, living the life of the student of those days. There he saw Flaubert, De Goncourt, De Maupassant, Daudet, Swinburne, and frequented the cafés and studios of the Impressionists and all the other rebels and outlaws of art.

One of Mr. Huneker's grandfathers was an Irish poet and also vice-president of the Fenian Brotherhood; the other a Hungarian and musician. At one time he thought of entering the Roman Catholic priesthood with the ambition of carrying off the combined laurels of Bossuet and Franz Liszt. Music has always been his master passion, and for years Mr. Huneker has been laboring on a gigantic biography of Liszt, the ideal of his boyhood and of his manhood as well. He reveals little of his personality directly in his books. In the new book, we come, again to quote from Mr. Pollard's review, upon a page of something like a revelation of self—of the human Huneker, rather than the Huneker who is merely the critical spirit temporarily embodied as a man—in the beginning of the chapter on Flaubert, where we get a momentary glimpse of a youth, a student, an artist in the Paris of 1879—whose name was Huneker. "May we not," asks Mr. Pollard, "in other books, have more than glimpses given us? For I am not of those who believe in the sphinx-like critical pose in this our day. Nor do I believe that the ego of Mr. Huneker would prove less interesting than those foreign egos he has dissected for our benefit."

Michael Monahan, in his little *Papyrus,* that storehouse of literary purples and silks, also takes Huneker to task for his all-too-elusive spirit; the real self of the author, he thinks, is hidden by too thick a veil of literary allusion. Mr. Monahan is filled with comic despair by Huneker's frequent references to Barbey d'Aurevilly. "I like best," he declares, "the pages in which there is most of *himself*. His faculty seems often clogged and impeded by an embarrassment of foreign riches without which we should have more of his own fine gold."

> Take the essay on Ibsen in this volume, a piece of work that is Huneker holograph, withal the most adequate criticism in a literary sense and the most penetrating spiritually that could be asked. Who will not say that it is worth a ton-weight of *baroque* learning and *fade* anecdotes about Baudelaire's green hair, etc., etc.? Let James reform this altogether and especially not bring all his literary pigs to market (pardon the vulgarity) on every possible occasion. It is bad literary economy to quote too much, to cite too many names, to be too clever. James has within him an angel of strength that is often put to grief by a devil of cleverness,—let him look to 't!
>
> However, this is not meant to disparage a big, brave book, rich with the stigmata of toil and thought. We like the fellow James writes about, on account of James, and we even try to believe that we like them for themselves. Yes, even Barbey d'Aurevilly!

Yet, after all, a man's literary plumage reveals, as much as it hides, his soul, and William Marion Reedy, like Monahan, one of Huneker's kin, racially and intellectually, penetrates to the man himself through his books. Here is a picture of Mr. Huneker's soul, if the style is indeed the man: "Huneker's sentences," says Reedy, "are like exploding torpedoes. He makes you think in a series of jolts and jars, but you think vividly before you come back to earth from your jump. Then you no sooner touch the ground, but you're up again." To quote further:

> He tells you about Stendhal and his curious, nervous, cynical philosophy in that singularly dry fiction of his—Stendhal, the man so afraid of being deceived that he was always deceived, even by himself, Stendhal, the predecessor of all the egotists. Likewise, he explicates for us the Bau-

delaire legend, the story of the man who strove for perfect prose, dreamed of symphonies of perfume, constructed in words, landscapes with the hard glitter of glass in moonlight and worshipped evil and wrote the poem on a corpse that flashes with the phosphorescence of putrescence. Joris Karl Huysmans, who went the route from satanist to saint and wrote descriptions of cathedrals and of music that prove the transmutation of the arts, is depicted in St. Vitus strokes. Next we have Poictevin and Maurice Barres and Ernest Hello, the latter not so unknown as Mr. Huneker thinks, for Mr. Conde Pallen has given us much of Hello in some of his Catholic literature. All these are mystics, and then we have essays in little on 'mad, naked Blake,' and upon Walter Pater.

Mr. Huneker is not so happy in his dealings with the mystics. He makes too much of a devilish racket tramping around in their towers of ivory. Imperfectly he doth attune himself to these men who have made for themselves a new and a rather hard spirituality. Poseurs all, Mr. Huneker himself must be a poseur in his attempt to get into rapport with them. He somehow doesn't quite penetrate their secret for us.

When Mr. Huneker interprets Flaubert, Nietzsche and Stirner, continues the brilliant editor of *The Mirror,* he is more at home; there is more substance in them than he can lay hands upon and out of which, in a healthy, hearty, big fashion he can wrestle their meanings. In the essays upon them, he seems to be more successful. Mr. Huneker paints for us a wonderful gallery of portraits; he ruthlessly exposes the most secret tricks of personality in his subjects; but somehow he is too big in himself to assume the attitude of adoration. That is perhaps the reason why Mr. Huneker, as Reedy suggests, without quite intending it, makes most of the men small rather than great. They are rebels, he admits, but you feel that their bravery is assumed, that these men are really afraid. To quote in conclusion:

> Nietzsche was afraid of Christ, Flaubert of a solecism, Huysmans of his own soul, Pater of red blood and the implications of his own philosophy of burning with a hard, gem-like flame, Baudelaire of committing suicide. In a sort of fugue that runs under Mr. Huneker's now plangent and then siccant style, you feel the fact that these men lack, with some exceptions, the big sincerities. You have to strain yourself to get to their complicatedly contrived points of view. They are indeed egotists, as Mr. Huneker classifies them; but not, most decidedly not supermen, even tho they did write for the few. They are abnormalities, sensitives, pathological morbidities. All seekers after the *nuances*—and after little else. They are artists, but not quite free of mere artifice.

In writing so much about people of this sort Mr. Huneker himself distorts his style into an occasional polyglotic clutter and falls into pomposities of the obvious, the axiomatic. His book is an album of human curios, of little men with swollen visions of themselves induced by rapt umbilicular self-contemplation. For all that, these fantastics have said and done things strange and often beautiful in regions beyond the prudish boundaries fixed for English and American letters, and from them our reading public may learn that there's something in art, in letters and life besides the episode in which, after many tribulations, the man gets the girl.

Wilkinson Sherren (essay date 1916)

SOURCE: "An American Speaks," in *The Bookman*, New York, Vol. XLIX, No. 294, March, 1916, pp. 189-90.

[*In the following essay, Sherren's appraisal of Huneker's* Ivory Apes and Peacocks *is influenced by Great Britain's conflict with Germany during World War I.*]

Not a ripple from the European war disturbs the surface of the essays gathered together by Mr. James Huneker, the accomplished American litterateur, who does so much to inform public taste in the United States.

Unreflecting readers of **Ivory Apes and Peacocks** might easily jump to the conclusion that he lived in a vacuum, and by some fourth dimensional trick passed from his library to concert halls and art galleries, alike unconscious of peoples half choked by squalid conditions in peace times, and massed into heroic union in the time of Armageddon.

His essays were evidently written before the struggle of titanic forces convulsed the world—certainly before the German pirate sank the *Lusitania,* for the memory of that crime would have imposed certain restrictions which are not here observed, and altered a point of view, which now displays a marvel of ante-war detachment. I refer to Mr. Huneker's essays on **"Frank Wedekind," "Max Liebemann and Some Phases of Modern German Art,"** and similar intellectual absorptions.

There are, however, many brilliant pages in **Ivory Apes and Peacocks,** which one can read with pleasure, particularly the opening essay on Mr. Joseph Conrad. It is a legitimate relief to allow Mr. Huneker to create the frame of mind necessary to the entertainment of such considerations, taking us, as they do for a while, from under the shadow of hell, flung far and wide by the Central Powers, into the indestructible sunlight.

> "The figure of Joseph Conrad," says the author, "stands solitary among English novelists as the very ideal of a pure and disinterested artist. Amid the clamour of the marketplace a book of his is a sea shell, which pressed to the ear, echoes the far-away murmur of the sea; always the sea, either as rigid as a mirror under hard blue skies, or shuddering symphonically up some exotic beach." "Conrad is a painter doubled by a psychologist; he is the psychologist of the sea—and that is his chief claim to originality . . . . Like all true artists, Conrad never preaches. His moral is in suffusion, and who runs may read."

Much, however, can be said for the writer whose passion for life sweeps him beyond the limitations of the conventional reticence Mr. Huneker would impose upon artists.

If literature is the flower of life, it is surely as well sometimes to hear what the gardener has to say, even though it may destroy the illusion that the flower came into existence of its own volition.

Ardent Whitmanites, as a corrective to any egregious tendency in their enthusiasm, may be referred to the essay entitled **"A Visit to Walt Whitman,"** a piece of destructive criticism interspersed with ill-natured anecdotes. Mr. Huneker or anyone else is quite entitled to think that Whitman's philosophy is "fudge," but it is open to question whether it is desirable or in good taste to fortify the case against Whitman by quoting what a policeman said at the Philadelphia ferry, "That old gas-bag comes here every afternoon. He gets free rides across the Delaware." It is singular that the only American Mr. Huneker writes about in this book at any length should be torn to pieces.

Mr. Huneker commands respectful attention when he writes of Russian literature. His knowledge of the subject seems to be profound, and readers who only know one or two of the Russian masterpieces can learn much from him. Here again, however, his allegiance to the method of the "disinterested artist" becomes manifest, and his admiration ceases when Tolstoy used his great art consciously for definite ends.

During the course of his acute survey of a wide field these pregnant observations occur:

> Taking Gogol as the norm of modern Russian fiction—we see the novel strained through the rich mystic imagination of Dostoievsky; viewed through the more equable, artistic and pessimistic temperature of Turgenieff, until it is seized by Leo Tolstoy, and passionately transformed to serve his own didactic purposes.

Dostoievsky is praised almost without reservation, though you are not allowed to forget how interesting a case he was for the alienist: "Tolstoy wrote of life; Dostoievsky lived it, drank its sour dregs." Even so must a novelist first grovel in mud before he can describe it? Indeed, Mr Huneker appears to believe that an artist should have no ideal outside his art, that he must be a specialised function, and no more. Were the conditions of the world ideal, something might then be said for that point of view. As things stand, however, such an attitude seems to be a denial of humanity.

Everyone who knows Mr. Huneker's work acknowledges his ability as an art critic. The amount of knowledge he manages to pack into **"The Magic Vermeer"** will convict well-informed students of ignorance of the Dutch master, beloved of Mr. E. V. Lucas, who has written delightfully about him.

Mr. Huneker also deals with other themes, to which I have not called attention, and always his level of excellence is high, and his opinions definite. He is able to define his own ignorance, and his influence is all the stronger because he nowhere allows the reader to see any of his opinions in the process of formation.

H. L. Mencken   (essay date 1917)

SOURCE: "James Huneker," in *A Book of Prefaces,* Alfred A. Knopf, 1917, pp. 151-94.

[*Mencken was one of the most influential figures in American literature from the First World War until the early years of the Great Depression. His strongly individualistic, irreverent outlook on life and his vigorous, invective-charged writing style helped establish the iconoclastic spirit of the Jazz Age and significantly shaped the direction of American literature. In the following essay, Mencken praises Huneker's enthusiasm for the arts as well as his exuberant essays on authors and composers.*]

1

Edgar Allan Poe, I am fond of believing, earned as a critic a good deal of the excess of praise that he gets as a romancer and a poet, and another over-estimated American dithyrambist, Sidney Lanier, wrote the best textbook of prosody in English [*The Science of English Verse*]; but in general the critical writing done in the United States has been of a low order, and most American writers of any genuine distinction, like most American painters and musicians, have had to wait for understanding until it appeared abroad. The case of Emerson is typical. At thirty, he was known in New England as a heretical young clergyman and no more, and his fame threatened to halt at the tea-tables of the Boston Brahmins. It remained for Landor and Carlyle, in a strange land, to discern his higher potentialities, and to encourage him to his real lifework. Mark Twain, as I have hitherto shown, suffered from the same lack of critical perception at home. He was quickly recognized as a funny fellow, true enough, but his actual stature was not even faintly apprehended, and even after *Huckleberry Finn* he was still bracketed with such laborious farceurs as Artemus Ward. It was Sir Walter Besant, an Englishman, who first ventured to put him on his right shelf, along with Swift, Cervantes and Molière. As for Poe and Whitman, the native recognition of their genius was so greatly conditioned by a characteristic horror of their immorality that it would be absurd to say that their own country understood them. Both were better and more quickly apprehended in France, and it was in France, not in America, that each founded a school. What they had to teach we have since got back at second hand—the tale of mystery, which was Poe's contribution, through Gaboriau and Boisgobey; and *vers libre,* which was Whitman's, through the French *imagistes.*

The cause of this profound and almost unbroken lack of critical insight and enterprise, this puerile Philistinism and distrust of ideas among us, is partly to be found, it seems to me, in the fact that the typical American critic is quite without any adequate cultural equipment for the office he presumes to fill. Dr. John Dewey, in some late remarks upon the American universities, has perhaps shown the cause thereof. The trouble with our educational method, he argues, is that it falls between the two stools of English humanism and German relentlessness—that it produces neither a man who intelligently feels nor a man who thoroughly knows. Criticism, in America, is a function of this half-educated and conceited class; it is not a popular art, but an esoteric one; even in its crassest journalistic manifestations it presumes to a certain academic remoteness from the concerns and carnalities of everyday. In every aspect it shows the defects of its practitioners. The American critic of beautiful letters, in his common incarnation, is no more than a talented sophomore, or, at best, a somewhat absurd professor. He suffers from a palpable lack of solid preparation; he has no background of moving and illuminating experience behind him; his soul has not sufficiently adventured among masterpieces, nor among men. Imagine a Taine or a Sainte-Beuve or a Macaulay—man of the world, veteran of philosophies, "lord of life"—and you imagine his complete antithesis. Even on the side of mere professional knowledge, the primary material of his craft, he always appears incompletely outfitted. The grand sweep and direction of the literary currents elude him; he is eternally on the surface, chasing bits of driftwood. The literature he knows is the fossil literature taught in colleges—worse, in high schools. It must be dead before he is aware of it. And in particular he appears ignorant of what is going forward in other lands. An exotic idea, to penetrate his consciousness, must first become stale, and even then he is apt to purge it of all its remaining validity and significance before adopting it.

This has been true since the earliest days. Emerson himself, though a man of unusual discernment and a diligent drinker from German spigots, nevertheless remained a *dilettante* in both aesthetics and metaphysics to the end of his days, and the incompleteness of his equipment never showed more plainly than in his criticism of books. Lowell, if anything, was even worse; his aesthetic theory, first and last, was nebulous and superficial, and all that remains of his pleasant essays today is their somewhat smoky pleasantness. He was a Charles Dudley Warner in nobler trappings, but still, at bottom, a Charles Dudley Warner. As for Poe, though he was by nature a far more original and penetrating critic than either Emerson or Lowell, he was enormously ignorant of good books, and moreover, he could never quite throw off a congenital vulgarity of taste, so painfully visible in the strutting of his style. The man, for all his grand dreams, had a shoddy soul; he belonged authentically to the era of cuspidors, "females" and Sons of Temperance. His occasional affectation of scholarship has deceived no one. It was no more than Yankee bluster; he constantly referred to books that he had never read. Beside, the typical American critic of those days was not Poe, but his arch-enemy, Rufus Wilmot Griswold, that almost fabulous ass—a Baptist preacher turned taster of the beautiful. Imagine a Baptist valuing Balzac, or Molière, or Shakespeare, or Goethe—or Rabelais!

Coming down to our own time, one finds the same endless amateurishness, so characteristic of everything American, from politics to cookery—the same astounding lack of training and vocation. Consider the solemn ponderosities of the pious old maids, male and female, who write book reviews for the newspapers. Here we have a heavy pretension to culture, a campus cocksureness, a laborious righteousness—but of sound aesthetic understanding, of alertness and hospitality to ideas, not a trace. The normal American book reviewer, indeed, is an elderly virgin, a superstitious blue-stocking, an apostle of Vassar *Kultur;* and her customary attitude of mind is one of fascinated horror. (The Hamilton Wright Mabie complex! The "white list" of novels!) William Dean Howells, despite a certain jauntiness and even kittenishness of manner, was spiritually of that company. For all his phosphorescent heresies, he was what the uplifters call a right-thinker at heart, and soaked in the national tradition. He was easiest intrigued, not by force and originality, but by a sickly, *Ladies' Home Journal* sort of piquancy; it was this that made him see a genius in the Philadelphia Zola, W. B. Trites, and that led him to hymn an abusive business letter by Frank A. Munsey, author of *The Boy Broker* and *Afloat in a Great City,* as a significant human document. Moreover Howells ran true to type in another way, for he long reigned as the leading Anglo-Saxon authority on the Russian novelists without knowing, so far as I can make out, more than ten words of Russian. In the same manner, we have had enthusiasts for D'Annunzio and Mathilde Serao who knew no Italian, and celebrants of Maeterlinck and Verhaeren whose French was of the finishing school, and Ibsen authorities without a single word of Dano-Norwegian—I met one once who failed to recognize *Et Dukkehjem* as the original title of *A Doll's House,*—and performers upon Hauptmann who could no more read *Die Weber* than they could decipher a tablet of Tiglath-Pileser III.

Here and there, of course, a more competent critic of beautiful letters flings out his banner—for example, John Macy, Ludwig Lewisohn, André Tridon, Francis Hackett, Van Wyck Brooks, Burton Rascoe, E. A. Boyd, Llewellyn Jones, Otto Heller, J. E. Spingarn, Lawrence Gilman, the late J. Percival Pollard. Well- informed, intelligent, wide-eyed men—but only four of them even Americans, and not one of them with a wide audience, or any appreciable influence upon the main stream of American criticism. Pollard's best work is buried in the perfumed pages of *Town Topics;* his book on the Munich wits and dramatists [*Masks and Minstrels of New Germany*] is almost unknown. Heller and Lewisohn make their way slowly; a patriotic wariness, I daresay, mixes itself up with their acceptance. Gilman disperses his talents; he is quite as much musician as critic of the arts. As for Macy, I recently found his *The Spirit of American Literature,* by long odds the soundest, wisest book on its subject, selling for fifty cents on a Fifth avenue remainder counter.

How many remain? A few competent reviewers who are primarily something else—Harvey, Aikin, Untermeyer and company. A few youngsters on the newspapers, struggling against the business office. And then a leap to the Victorians, the crêpe-clad pundits, the bombastic word-mongers of the campus school—H. W. Boynton, W. C. Brownell, Paul Elmer More, William Lyon Phelps, Frederick Taber Cooper *et al.* Here, undoubtedly, we have learning of a sort. More, it appears, once taught Sanskrit to the adolescent suffragettes of Bryn Mawr—an enterprise as stimulating (and as intelligible) as that of setting off fire-works in a blind asylum. Phelps sits in a chair at Yale. Boynton is a master of arts in English literature, whatever that may mean. Brownell is both L.H.D. and Litt.D., thus surpassing Samuel Johnson by one point, and Hazlitt, Coleridge and Malone by two. But the learning

of these august *umbilicarii,* for all its pretensions, is precisely the sterile, foppish sort one looks for in second-rate college professors. The appearance is there, but not the substance. One ingests a horse-doctor's dose of words, but fails to acquire any illumination. Read More on Nietzsche [*The Drift of Romanticism*] if you want to find out just how stupid criticism can be, and yet show the outward forms of sense. Read Phelps' *The Advance of the English Novel* if you would see a fine art treated as a moral matter, and great works tested by the criteria of a small-town Sunday-school, and all sorts of childish sentimentality whooped up. And plough through Brownell's *Standards,* if you have the patience, and then try to reduce its sonorous platitudes to straight-forward and defensible propositions.

2

Now for the exception. He is, of course, James Gibbons Huneker, the solitary Iokanaan in this tragic aesthetic wilderness, the only critic among us whose vision sweeps the whole field of beauty, and whose reports of what he sees there show any genuine gusto. That gusto of his, I fancy, is two-thirds of his story. It is unquenchable, contagious, inflammatory; he is the only performer in the commissioned troupe who knows how to arouse his audience to anything approaching enthusiasm. The rest, even including Howells, are pedants lecturing to the pure in heart, but Huneker makes a joyous story of it; his exposition, transcending the merely expository, takes on the quality of an adventure hospitably shared. One feels, reading him, that he is charmed by the men and women he writes about, and that their ideas, even when he rejects them, give him an agreeable stimulation. And to the charm that he thus finds and exhibits in others, he adds the very positive charm of his own personality. He seems a man who has found the world fascinating, if perhaps not perfect; a friendly and good-humoured fellow; no frigid scholiast, but something of an epicure; in brief, the reverse of the customary maker of books about books. Compare his two essays on Ibsen, in **Egoists** and **Iconoclasts,** to the general body of American writing upon the great Norwegian. The difference is that between a portrait and a Bertillon photograph, Richard Strauss and Czerny, a wedding and an autopsy. Huneker displays Ibsen, not as a petty mystifier of the women's clubs, but as a literary artist of large skill and exalted passion, and withal a quite human and understandable man. These essays were written at the height of the symbolism madness; in their own way, they even show some reflection of it; but taking them in their entirety, how clearly they stand above the ignorant obscurantism of the prevailing criticism of the time—how immeasurably superior they are, for example, to that favourite hymn-book of the Ibsenites, "The Ibsen Secret" by Jennette Lee! For the causes of this difference one need not seek far. They are to be found in the difference between the bombastic half-knowledge of a school teacher and the discreet and complete knowledge of a man of culture. Huneker is that man of culture. He has reported more of interest and value than any other American critic, living or dead, but the essence of his criticism does not lie so much in what he specifically reports as in the civilized point of view from which he reports it. He is a true cosmopolitan, not only in the actual range of his adventurings, but also and more especially in his attitude of mind. His world is not America, nor Europe, nor Christendom, but the whole universe of beauty. As Jules Simon said of Taine: *"Aucun écrivain de nos jours n'a . . . découvert plus d'horizons variés et immenses."*

Need anything else be said in praise of a critic? And does an extravagance or an error here and there lie validly against the saying of it? I think not. I could be a professor if I would and show you slips enough—certain ponderous nothings in the Ibsen essays, already mentioned; a too easy bemusement at the hands of Shaw; a vacillating over Wagner; a habit of yielding to the hocus-pocus of the mystics, particularly Maeterlinck. On the side of painting, I am told, there are even worse aberrations; I know too little about painting to judge for myself. But the list, made complete, would still not be over-long, and few of its items would be important. Huneker, like the rest of us, has sinned his sins, but his judgments, in the overwhelming main, hold water. He has resisted the lure of all the wild movements of the generation; the tornadoes of doctrine have never knocked him over. Nine times out of ten, in estimating a new man in music or letters, he has come curiously close to the truth at the first attempt. And he has always announced it in good time; his solo has always preceded the chorus. He was, I believe, the first American (not forgetting William Morton Payne and Hjalmar Hjorth Boyesen, the pioneers) to write about Ibsen with any understanding of the artist behind the prophet's mask; he was the first to see the rising star of Nietzsche (this was back in 1888); he was beating a drum for Shaw the critic before ever Shaw the dramatist and mob philosopher was born (*circa* 1886-1890); he was writing about Hauptmann and Maeterlinck before they had got well set on their legs in their own countries; his estimate of Sudermann, bearing date of 1905, may stand with scarcely the change of a word today; he did a lot of valiant pioneering for Strindberg, Hervieu, Stirner and Gorki, and later on helped in the pioneering for Conrad; he was in the van of the MacDowell enthusiasts; he fought for the ideas of such painters as Davies, Lawson, Luks, Sloan and Prendergest (Americans all, by the way: an answer to the hollow charge of exotic obsession) at a time when even Manet, Monet and Degas were laughed at; he was among the first to give a hand to Frank Norris, Theodore Dreiser, Stephen Crane and H. B. Fuller. In sum, he gave some semblance of reality in the United States, after other men had tried and failed, to that great but ill-starred revolt against Victorian pedantry, formalism and sentimentality which began in the early 90's. It would be difficult, indeed, to overestimate the practical value to all the arts in America of his intellectual alertness, his catholic hospitality to ideas, his artistic courage, and above all, his powers of persuasion. It was not alone that he saw clearly what was sound and significant; it was that he managed, by the sheer charm of his writings, to make a few others see and understand it. If the United States is in any sort of contact today, however remotely, with what is aesthetically going on in the more civilized countries—if the Puritan tradition, for all its firm entrenchment, has eager and resourceful enemies besetting it—if the pall of Harvard quasi-culture, by the Oxford manner out of Calvinism, has been lifted ever

so little—there is surely no man who can claim a larger share of credit for preparing the way. . . .

3

Huneker comes out of Philadelphia, that depressing intellectual slum, and his first writing was for the Philadelphia *Evening Bulletin.* He is purely Irish in blood, and is of very respectable ancestry, his maternal grandfather and godfather having been James Gibbons, the Irish poet and patriot, and president of the Fenian Brotherhood in America. Once, in a review of **The Pathos of Distance,** I ventured the guess that there was a German strain in him somewhere, and based it upon the beery melancholy visible in parts of that book. Who but a German sheds tears over the empty bottles of day before yesterday, the Adelaide Neilson of 1877? Who but a German goes into woollen undershirts at 45, and makes his will, and begins to call his wife "Mamma"? The green-sickness of youth is endemic from pole to pole, as much so as measles; but what race save the wicked one is floored by a blue distemper in middle age, with sentimental burblings *a cappella,* hallucinations of lost loves, and an unquenchable lacrymorrhea? . . . I made out a good case, but I was wrong, and the penalty came swiftly and doubly, for on the one hand the Boston *Transcript* sounded an alarm against both Huneker and me as German spies, and on the other hand Huneker himself proclaimed that, even spiritually, he was less German than Magyar, less "Hun" than Hun. "I am," he said, "a Celto-Magyar: Pilsner at Donneybrook Fair. Even the German beer and cuisine are not in it with the Austro-Hungarian." Here, I suspect, he meant to say Czech instead of Magyar, for isn't Pilsen in Bohemia? Moreover, turn to the chapter on Prague in **New Cosmopolis,** and you will find out in what highland his heart really is. In this book, indeed, is a vast hymn to all things Czechic—the Pilsen *Urquell,* the muffins stuffed with poppy-seed jam, the spiced chicken liver *en casserole,* the pretty Bohemian girls, the rose and golden glory of Hradschin Hill. . . . One thinks of other strange infatuations: the Polish Conrad's for England, the Scotch Mackay's for Germany, the Low German Brahms' for Italy. Huneker, I daresay, is the first Celto-Czech—or Celto-Magyar, as you choose. (Maybe the name suggests something. It is not to be debased to *Hoon-eker,* remember, but kept at *Hun*-eker, rhyming initially with *nun* and *gun.*) An unearthly marriage of elements, by all the gods! but there are pretty children of it. . . .

Philadelphia humanely disgorged Huneker in 1878. His father designed him for the law, and he studied the institutes at the Philadelphia Law Academy, but like Schumann, he was spoiled for briefs by the stronger pull of music and the *cacoëthes scribendi.* (Grandpa John Huneker had been a composer of church music, and organist at St. Mary's.) In the year mentioned he set out for Paris to see Liszt; his aim was to make himself a piano virtuoso. His name does not appear on his own exhaustive list of Liszt pupils, but he managed to quaff of the Pierian spring at second-hand, for he had lessons from Theodore Ritler (*né* Bennet), a genuine pupil of the old walrus, and he was also taught by the venerable Georges Mathias, a pupil of Chopin. These days laid the foundations for two subsequent books, the ***Chopin: the Man and His Music*** of 1900, and the ***Franz Liszt*** of 1911. More, they prepared the excavations for all of the others, for Huneker began sending home letters to the Philadelphia *Bulletin* on the pictures that he saw, the books that he read and the music that he heard in Paris, and out of them gradually grew a body of doctrine that was to be developed into full-length criticism on his return to the United States. He stayed in Paris until the middle 80's, and then settled in New York.

All the while his piano studies continued, and in New York he became a pupil of Rafael Joseffy. He even became a teacher himself and was for ten years on the staff of the National Conservatory, and showed himself at all the annual meetings of the Music Teachers' Association. But bit by bit criticism elbowed out music-making, as music-making had elbowed out criticism with Schumann and Berlioz. In 1886 or thereabout he joined the *Musical Courier;* then he went, in succession, to the old *Recorder,* to the *Morning Advertiser,* to the *Sun,* to the *Times,* and finally to the Philadelphia *Press* and the New York *World.* Various weeklies and monthlies have also enlisted him: *Mlle. New York,* the *Atlantic Monthly,* the *Smart Set,* the *North American Review* and *Scribner's.* He has even stooped to *Puck,* vainly trying to make an American *Simplicissimus* of that dull offspring of synagogue and barbershop. He has been, in brief, an extremely busy and not too fastidious journalist, writing first about one of the arts, and then about another, and then about all seven together. But music has been the steadiest of all his loves; his first three books dealt almost wholly with it; of his complete canon more than half have to do with it.

4

His first book, ***Mezzotints in Modern Music,*** published in 1899, revealed his predilections clearly, and what is more, his critical insight and sagacity. One reads it today without the slightest feeling that it is an old story; some of the chapters, obviously reworking of articles for the papers, must go back to the middle 90's, and yet the judgments they proclaim scarcely call for the change of a word. The single noticeable weakness is a too easy acquiescence in the empty showiness of Saint-Saëns, a tendency to bow to the celebrated French parlour magician too often. Here, I daresay, is an echo of old Paris days, for Camille was a hero on the Seine in 1880, and there was even talk of pitting him against Wagner. The estimates of other men are judiciously arrived at and persuasively stated. Tschaikowsky is correctly put down as a highly talented but essentially shallow fellow—a blubberer in the regalia of a philosopher. Brahms, then still under attack by Henry T. Finck, of the *Evening Post* (the press-agent of Massenet: ye gods, what Harvard can do, even to a Würtemberger!) is subjected to a long, an intelligent and an extremely friendly analysis; no better has got into English since, despite too much stress on the piano music. And Richard Strauss, yet a nine days' wonder, is described clearly and accurately, and his true stature indicated. The rest of the book is less noteworthy; Huneker says the proper things about Chopin, Liszt and Wagner, and adds a chapter on piano methods, the plain fruit of his late pedagogy. But the three chapters I have mentioned are enough; they fell, in

their time, into a desert of stupidity; they set a standard in musical criticism in America that only Huneker himself has ever exceeded.

The most popular of his music books, of course, is the ***Chopin*** (1900). Next to *Iconoclasts,* it is the best seller of them all. More, it has been done into German, French and Italian, and is chiefly responsible for Huneker's celebrity abroad as the only critic of music that America has ever produced. Superficially, it seems to be a monument of pedantry, a meticulous piling up of learning, but a study of it shows that it is very much more than that. Compare it to Sir George Grove's staggering tome on the Beethoven symphonies if you want to understand the difference between mere scholastic diligence and authentic criticism. The one is simply a top-heavy mass of disorderly facts and worshipping enthusiasm; the other is an analysis that searches out every nook and corner of the subject, and brings it into coherence and intelligibility. The Chopin rhapsodist is always held in check by the sound musician; there is a snouting into dark places as well as a touching up of high lights. I myself am surely no disciple of the Polish tuberose—his sweetness, in fact, gags me, and I turn even to Moszkowski for relief—but I have read and reread this volume with endless interest, and I find it more bethumbed than any other Huneker book in my library, saving only *Iconoclasts* and ***Old Fogy***. Here, indeed, Huneker is on his own ground. One often feels, in his discussions of orchestral music, that he only thinks orchestrally, like Schumann, with an effort—that all music, in his mind, gets itself translated into terms of piano music. In dealing with Chopin no such transvaluation of values is necessary; the raw materials are ready for his uses without preparation; he is wholly at home among the black keys and white.

His ***Liszt*** is a far less noteworthy book. It is, in truth, scarcely a book at all, but merely a collection of notes for a book, some of them considerably elaborated, but others set down in the altogether. One reads it because it is about Liszt, the most fantastic figure that ever came out of Hungary, half devil and half clown; not because there is any conflagration of ideas in it. The chapter that reveals most of Huneker is the appendix on latter-day piano virtuosi, with its estimates of such men as de Pachmann, Rosenthal, Paderewski and Hofmann. Much better stuff is to be found in ***Overtones, The Pathos of Distance*** and ***Ivory, Apes and Peacocks***—brilliant, if not always profound studies of Strauss, Wagner, Schoenberg, Moussorgsky, and even Verdi. But if I had my choice of the whole shelf, it would rest, barring the ***Chopin,*** on ***Old Fogy***—the *scherzo* of the Hunekeran symphony, the critic taking a holiday, the Devil's Mass in the tonal sanctuary. In it Huneker is at his very choicest, making high-jinks with his Davidsbund of one, rattling the skeletons in all the musical closets of the world. Here, throwing off his critic's black gown, his lays about him right and left, knocking the reigning idols off their perches; resurrecting the old, old dead and trying to pump the breath into them; lambasting on one page and lauding on the next; lampooning his fellow critics and burlesquing their rubber stamp fustian; extolling Dussek and damning Wagner; swearing mighty oaths by Mozart, and after him, Strauss—not Richard, but Johann!

The Old Fogy, of course, is the thinnest of disguises, a mere veil of gossamer for "Editor" Huneker. That Huneker in false whiskers is inimitable, incomparable, almost indescribable. On the one hand, he is a prodigy of learning, a veritable warehouse of musical information, true, half-true and apocryphal; on the other hand, he is a jester who delights in reducing all learning to absurdity. Reading him somehow suggests hearing a Bach mass rescored for two fifes, a tambourine in B, a wind machine, two tenor harps, a contrabass oboe, two banjos, eight tubas and the usual clergy and strings. The substance is there; every note is struck exactly in the middle—but what outlandish tone colours, what strange, unearthly sounds! It is not Bach, however, who first comes to mind when Huneker is at his tricks, but Papa Haydn—the Haydn of the Surprise symphony and the Farewell. There is the same gargantuan gaiety, the same magnificent irreverence. Haydn did more for the symphony than any other man, but he also got more fun out of it than any other man.

Old Fogy, of course, is not to be taken seriously: it is frankly a piece of fooling. But all the same a serious idea runs through the book from end to end, and that is the idea that music is getting too subjective to be comfortable. The makers of symphonies tend to forget beauty altogether; their one effort is to put all their own petty trials and tribulations, their empty theories and speculations into cacophony. Even so far back as Beethoven's day that autobiographical habit had begun. "Beethoven," says Old Fogy, is "dramatic, powerful, a maker of storms, a subduer of tempests; but his speech is the speech of a self-centred egotist. He is the father of all the modern melomaniacs, who, looking into their own souls, write what they see therein—misery, corruption, slighting selfishness and ugliness." Old Ludwig's groans, of course, we can stand. He was not only a great musician, but also a great man. It is just as interesting to hear him sigh and complain as it would be to hear the private prayers of Julius Caesar. But what of Tschaikovsky, with his childish Slavic whining? What of Liszt, with his cheap playacting, his incurable lasciviousness, his plebeian warts? What of Wagner, with his delight in imbecile fables, his popinjay vanity, his soul of a *Schnorrer?* What of Richard Strauss, with his warmed-over Nietzscheism, his flair for the merely horrible? Old Fogy sweeps them all into his rag-bag. If art is to be defined as beauty seen through a temperament, then give us more beauty and cleaner temperaments! Back to the old gods, Mozart and Bach, with a polite bow to Brahms and a sentimental tear for Chopin! Beethoven tried to tell his troubles in his music; Mozart was content to ravish the angels of their harps. And as for Johann Sebastian, "there was more real musical feeling, uplifting and sincerity in the old Thomaskirche in Leipzig . . . than in all your modern symphony and oratorio machine-made concerts put together."

All this is argued, to be sure, in extravagant terms. Wagner is a mere ghoul and impostor: *The Flying Dutchman* is no more than a parody on Weber, and *Parsifal* is "an outrage against religion, morals and music." Daddy Liszt is "the inventor of the Liszt pupil, a bad piano player, a venerable man with a purple nose—a Cyrano de Cognac nose." Tschaikowsky is the Slav gone crazy on vodka. He transformed Hamlet into "a yelling man" and Romeo and Juliet into "two monstrous Cossacks, who gibber and squeak at each other while reading some obscene volume." "His Manfred is a libel on Byron, who was a libel on God." And even Schumann is a vanishing star, a literary man turned composer, a pathological case. But, as I have said, a serious idea runs through all this concerto for slapstick and seltzer siphon, and to me, at least, that idea has a plentiful reasonableness. We are getting too much melodrama, too much vivisection, too much rebellion—and too little music. Turn from Tschaikowsky's *Pathétique* or from any of his wailing tone-poems to Schubert's *C major,* or to Mozart's *Jupiter,* or to Beethoven's *kleine Sinfonie in F dur:* it is like coming out of a *Kaffeeklatsch* into the open air, almost like escaping from a lunatic asylum. The one unmistakable emotion that much of this modern music from the steppes and morgues and *Biertische* engenders is a longing for form, clarity, coherence, a self-respecting tune. The snorts and moans of the pothouse Werthers are as irritating, in the long run, as the bawling of a child, the squeak of a pig under a gate. One yearns unspeakably for a composer who gives out his pair of honest themes, and then develops them with both ears open, and then recapitulates them unashamed, and then hangs a brisk coda to them, and then shuts up.

5

So much for **Old Fogy** and the musical books. They constitute, not only the best body of work that Huneker himself has done, but the best body of musical criticism that any American has done. Musical criticism, in our great Calvinist republic, confines itself almost entirely to transient reviewing, and even when it gets between covers, it keeps its trivial quality. Consider, for example, the published work of Henry Edward Krehbiel, for long the *doyen* of the New York critics. I pick up his latest book, *A Second Book of Operas,* open it at random, and find this:

> On January 31, 1893, the Philadelphia singers, aided by the New York Symphony Society, gave a performance of the opera, under the auspices of the Young Men's Hebrew Association, for the benefit of its charities, at the Carnegie Music Hall, New York. Mr. Walter Damrosch was to have conducted, but was detained in Washington by the funeral of Mr. Blaine, and Mr. Hinrichs took his place.

O Doctor *admirabilis, acutus et illuminatissimus!* Needless to say the universities have not overlooked this geyser of buttermilk: he is an honourary A.M. of Yale. His most respectable volume, that on negro folksong, impresses one principally by its incompleteness. It may be praised as a sketch, but surely not as a book. The trouble with Krehbiel, of course, is that he mistakes a newspaper morgue for Parnassus. He has all of the third-rate German's capacity for unearthing facts, but he doesn't know how either to think or to write, and so his criticism is mere pretence and pishposh. W. J. Henderson, of the *Sun,* doesn't carry that handicap. He is as full of learning as Krehbiel, as his books on singing and on the early Italian opera show, but he also wields a slippery and intriguing pen, and he could be hugely entertaining if he would. Instead, he devotes himself to manufacturing primers for the newly intellectual. I can find little of the charm of his *Sun* articles in his books. Lawrence Gilman? A sound musician but one who of late years has often neglected music for the other arts. Philip H. Goepp? His three volumes on the symphonic repertoire leave twice as much to be said as they say. Carl Van Vechten? A very promising novice, but not yet at full growth. Philip Hale? His gigantic annotations scarcely belong to criticism at all; they are musical talmudism. Beside, they are buried in the program books of the Boston Symphony Orchestra, and might as well be inscribed on the temple walls of Baalbec. As for Upton and other such fellows, they are merely musical chautauquans, and their tedious commentaries have little more value than the literary criticisms in the religious weeklies. One of them, a Harvard *maestro,* has published a book on the orchestra in which, on separate pages, the reader is solemnly presented with pictures of first and second violins!

It seems to me that Huneker stands on a higher level than any of these industrious gentlemen, and that his writings on music are of much more value, despite his divided allegiance among the *beaux arts.* Whatever may be said against him, it must at least be admitted that he knows Chopin, and that he has written the best volumes upon the tuberculous Pole in English. Vladimir de Pachmann, that king of all Chopin players, once bore characteristic testimony to the fact—I think it was in London. The program was heavy with the études and ballades, and Huneker sat in the front row of fanatics. After a storm of applause de Pachmann rose from the piano stool, levelled a bony claw at Huneker, and pronounced his dictum: "*He* knows more than *all* of you." Joseffy seems to have had the same opinion, for he sought the aid of his old pupil in preparing his new edition of Chopin, the first volume of which is all he lived to see in print. . . . And, beyond all the others, Huneker disdains writing for the kindergarten. There is no stopping in his discourse; he frankly addresses himself to an audience that has gone through the forms, and so he avoids the tediousness of the A B C expositors. He is the only American musical critic, save Van Vechten, who thus assumes invariably that a musical audience exists, and the only one who constantly measures up to its probable interests, supposing it to be there. Such a book as **Old Fogy,** for all its buffoonery, is conceivable only as the work of a sound musician. Its background is one of the utmost sophistication; in the midst of its wildest extravagances there is always a profound knowledge of music on tap, and a profound love of it to boot. Here, perhaps, more than anywhere else, Huneker's delight in the things he deals with is obvious. It is not a seminary that he keeps, but a sort of club of tone enthusiasts, and membership in it is infinitely charming.

6

This capacity for making the thing described seem important and delightful, this quality of infectious gusto, this father-talent of all the talents that a critic needs, sets off his literary criticism no less than his discourse on music and musicians. Such a book as **Iconoclasts** or **Egoists** is full of useful information, but it is even more full of agreeable adventure. The style is the book, as it is the man. It is arch, staccato, ironical, witty, galloping, playful, polyglot, allusive—sometimes, alas, so allusive as to reduce the Drama Leaguer and women's clubber to wonderment and ire. In writing of plays or of books, as in writing of cities, tone-poems or philosophies, Huneker always assumes that the elements are already well-grounded, that he is dealing with the initiated, that a pause to explain would be an affront. Sad work for the Philistines—but a joy to the elect! All this polyphonic allusiveness, this intricate fuguing of ideas, is not to be confused, remember, with the hollow showiness of the academic soothsayer. It is as natural to the man, as much a part of him as the clanging Latin of Johnson, or, to leap from art to art Huneker-wise, the damnable cross-rhythms of Brahms. He could no more write without his stock company of heretic sages than he could write without his ration of malt. And, on examination, all of them turned out to be real. They are far up dark alleys, but they are there! . . . And one finds them, at last, to be as pleasant company as the multilingual puns of Nietzsche or Debussy's chords of the second.

As for the origin of that style, it seems to have a complex ancestry. Huneker's first love was Poe, and even today he still casts affectionate glances in that direction, but there is surely nothing of Poe's elephantine labouring in his skipping, *pizzicato* sentences. Then came Carlyle—the Carlyle of *Sartor Resartus*—a god long forgotten. Huneker's mother was a woman of taste; on reading his first scribblings, she gave him Cardinal Newman, and bade him consider the Queen's English. Newman achieved a useful purging; the style that remained was ready for Flaubert. From the author of *L'Education Sentimentale,* I daresay, came the deciding influence, with Nietzsche's staggering brilliance offering suggestions later on. Thus Huneker, as stylist, owes nearly all to France, for Nietzsche, too, learned how to write there, and to the end of his days he always wrote more like a Frenchman than a German. His greatest service to his own country, indeed, was not as anarch, but as teacher of writing. He taught the Germans that their language had a snap in it as well as sighs and gargles—that it was possible to write German and yet not wander in a wood. There are whole pages of Nietzsche that suggest such things, say, as the essay on Maurice Barrès in *Egoists,* with its bold tropes, its rapid gait, its sharp *sforzandos.* And you will find old Friedrich at his tricks from end to end of **Old Fogy.**

Of the actual contents of such books as **Egoists** and **Iconoclasts** it is unnecessary to say anything. One no longer reads them for their matter, but for their manner. Every flapper now knows all that is worth knowing about Ibsen, Strindberg, Maeterlinck and Shaw, and a great deal that is not worth knowing. We have disentangled Hauptmann from Sudermann, and, thanks to Dr. Lewisohn, may read all his plays in English. Even Henry Becque has got into the vulgate and is familiar to the Drama League. As for Anatole France, his *Revolt of the Angels* is on the shelves of the Carnegie Libraries, and the Comstocks have let it pass. New gods whoop and rage in Valhalla: Verhaeren, Artzibashef, Przybyszewski. Huneker, alas, seems to drop behind the procession. He writes nothing about these second-hand third-raters. He has come to Wedekind, Schnitzler, Schoenberg, Korngold and Moussorgsky, and he has discharged a few rounds of shrapnel at the Gallo-

Asiatic petticoat philosopher, Henri Bergson, but here he has stopped, as he has stopped at Matisse, Picasso, Epstein and Augustus John in painting. As he says himself, "one must get off somewhere." . . .

Particularly if one grows weary of criticism—and in Huneker, of late, I detect more than one sign of weariness. Youth is behind him, and with it some of its zest for exploration and combat. "The pathos of distance" is a phrase that haunts him as poignantly as it haunted Nietzsche, its maker. Not so long ago I tried to induce him to write some new Old Fogy sketches, nominating Puccini, Strawinsky, Schoenberg, Korngold, Elgar. He protested that the mood was gone from him forever, that he could not turn the clock back twenty years. His late work in *Puck,* the *Times* and the *Sun,* shows an unaccustomed acquiescence in current valuations. He praises such one-day masterpieces as McFee's *Casuals of the Sea;* he is polite to the gaudy heroines of the opera-house; he gags a bit at Wright's *Modern Painting;* he actually makes a gingery curtsy to Frank Jewett Mather, a Princeton professor. . . . The pressure in the gauges can't keep up to 250 pounds forever. Man must tire of fighting after awhile, and seek his ease in his inn. . . .

Perhaps the post-bellum transvaluation of all values will bring Huneker to his feet again, and with something of the old glow and gusto in him. And if the new men do not stir up, then assuredly the wrecks of the ancient cities will: the Paris of his youth; Munich, Dresden, Vienna, Brussels, London; above all, Prague. Go to *New Cosmopolis* and you will find where his heart lies, or, if not his heart, then at all events his oesophagus and pylorus. . . . Here, indeed, the thread of his meditations is a thread of nutriment. However diverted by the fragrance of the Dutch woods, the church bells of Belgium, the music of Stuttgart, the bad pictures of Dublin, the plays of Paris, the musty romance of old Wien, he always comes back anon to such ease as a man may find in his inn. "The stomach of Vienna," he says, "first interested me, not its soul." And so, after a dutiful genuflexion to St. Stephen's ("Old Steffel," as the Viennese call it), he proceeds to investigate the paprika-chicken, the *Gulyas,* the *Risi-bisi,* the *Apfelstrudel,* the *Kaiserschmarrn* and the native and authentic *Wienerschnitzel.* And from food to drink—specifically, to the haunts of Pilsner, to "certain semi-sacred houses where the ritual of beer-drinking is observed," to the shrines at which beer maniacs meet, to "a little old house near a Greek church" where "the best-kept Pilsner in Vienna may be found."

The best-kept Pilsner in Vienna! The phrase enchants like an entrance of the horns. The best caviare in Russia, the worst actor on Broadway, the most virtuous angel in Heaven! Such superlatives are transcendental. And yet,— so rare is perfection in this world!—the news swiftly follows, unexpected, disconcerting, that the best Pilsner in Vienna is far short of the ideal. For some undetermined reason—the influence of the American tourist? the decay of the Austrian national character?—the Vienna *Bierwirte* freeze and paralyze it with too much ice, so that it chills the nerves it should caress, and fills the heart below with heaviness and repining. Avoid Vienna, says Huneker, if

you are one who understands and venerates the great Bohemian brew! And if, deluded, you find yourself there, take the first *D-zug* for Prague, that lovely city, for in it you will find the Pilsen *Urquell,* and in the Pilsen *Urquell* you will find the best Pilsner in Christendom—its colour a phosphorescent, translucent, golden yellow, its foam like whipped cream, its temperature exactly and invariably right. Not even at Pilsen itself (which the Bohemians call Plezen) is the emperor of malt liquors more stupendously grateful to the palate. Write it down before you forget: the Pilsen *Urquell,* Prague, Bohemia, 120 miles S. S. E. of Dresden, on the river Moldau (which the natives call the Vitava). Ask for Fräulein Ottilie. Mention the name of Herr Huneker, the American *Schriftsteller.*

Of all the eminent and noble cities between the Alleghenies and the Balkans, Prague seems to be Huneker's favourite. He calls it poetic, precious, delectable, original, dramatic—a long string of adjectives, each argued for with eloquence that is unmistakably sincere. He stands fascinated before the towers and pinnacles of the Hradschin, "a miracle of tender rose and marble white with golden spots of sunshine that would have made Claude Monet envious." He pays his devotions to the Chapel of St. Wenceslaus, "crammed with the bones of buried kings," or, at any rate, to the shrine of St. John Nepomucane, "composed of nearly two tons of silver." He is charmed by the beauty of the stout, black-haired, red-cheeked Bohemian girls, and hopes that enough of them will emigrate to the United States to improve the fading pulchritude of our own houris. But most of all, he has praises for the Bohemian cuisine, with its incomparable apple tarts, and its dumplings of cream cheese, and for the magnificent, the overpowering, the ineffable Pilsner of Prague. This Pilsner motive runs through the book from cover to cover. In the midst of Dutch tulip-beds, Dublin cobblestones, Madrid sunlight and Atlantic City leg-shows, one hears it insistently, deep down in the orchestra. The cellos weave it into the polyphony, sometimes clearly, sometimes in scarcely recognizable augmentation. It is heard again in the woodwind; the bassoons grunt it thirstily; it slides around in the violas; it rises to a stately choral in the brass. And chiefly it is in minor. Chiefly it is sounded by one who longs for the Pilsen *Urquell* in a far land, and among a barbarous and teetotaling people, and in an atmosphere as hostile to the recreations of the palate as it is to the recreations of the intellect.

As I say, this Huneker is a foreigner and hence accursed. There is something about him as exotic as a samovar, as essentially un-American as a bashi-bazouk, a nose-ring or a fugue. He is filled to the throttle with strange and unnational heresies. He ranks Beethoven miles above the native gods, and not only Beethoven, but also Bach and Brahms, and not only Bach and Brahms, but also Berlioz, Bizet, Bruch and Bülow and perhaps even Balakirew, Bellini, Balfe, Borodin and Boïeldieu. He regards Budapest as a more civilized city than his native Philadelphia, Stendhal as a greater literary artist than Washington Irving, "Künstler Leben" as better music than "There is Sunlight in My Soul." Irish? I still doubt it, despite the *Stammbaum.* Who ever heard of an Irish epicure, an Irish *flâneur,* or, for that matter, an Irish contrapuntist? The arts of the voluptuous category are unknown west of Cherbourg; one leaves them behind with the French pilot. Even the Czech-Irish hypothesis (or is it Magyar-Irish?) has a smell of the lamp. Perhaps it should be Irish-Czech. . . .

7

There remain the books of stories, **Visionaries** and **Melomaniacs**. It is not surprising to hear that both are better liked in France and Germany than in England and the United States. (**Visionaries** has even appeared in Bohemian.) Both are made up of what the Germans call *Kultur-Novellen*—that is, stories dealing, not with the emotions common to all men, but with the clash of ideas among the civilized and godless minority. In some of them, *e.g.,* **"Rebels of the Moon,"** what one finds is really not a story at all, but a static discussion, half aesthetic and half lunatic. In others, *e.g.,* **"Isolde's Mother,"** the whole action revolves around an assumption incomprehensible to the general. One can scarcely imagine most of these tales in the magazines. They would puzzle and outrage the readers of Gouverneur Morris and Gertrude Atherton, and the readers of Howells and Mrs. Wharton no less. Their point of view is essentially the aesthetic one; the overwhelming importance of beauty is never in any doubt. And the beauty thus vivisected and fashioned into new designs is never the simple Wordsworthian article, of fleecy clouds and primroses all compact; on the contrary, it is the highly artificial beauty of pigments and tone-colours, of Cézanne landscapes and the second act of *Tristan und Isolde,* of Dunsanyan dragons and Paracelsian mysteries. Here, indeed, Huneker riots in the aesthetic occultism that he loves. Music slides over into diabolism; the Pobloff symphony rends the firmament of Heaven; the ghost of Chopin drives Mychowski to drink; a single drum-beat finishes the estimable consort of the composer of the Tympani symphony. In **"The Eighth Deadly Sin"** we have a paean to perfume—the only one, so far as I know, in English. In **"The Hall of the Missing Footsteps"** we behold the reaction of hasheesh upon Chopin's ballade in F major. . . . Strangely-flavoured, unearthly, perhaps unhealthy stuff. I doubt that it will ever be studied for its style in our new Schools of Literature; a devilish cunning if often there, but it leaves a smack of the pharmacopoeia. However, as George Gissing used to say, "the artist should be free from everything like moral prepossession." This lets in the Antichrist. . . .

Huneker himself seems to esteem these fantastic tales above all his other work. Story-writing, indeed, was his first love, and his Opus 1, a bad imitation of Poe, by name **"The Comet,"** was done in Philadelphia so long ago as July 4, 1876. (Temperature, 105 degrees Fahrenheit.) One rather marvels that he has never attempted a novel. It would have been as bad, perhaps, as *Love Among the Artists,* but certainly no bore. He might have given George Moore useful help with *Evelyn Innes* and *Sister Teresa*: they are about music, but not by a musician. As for me, I see no great talent for fiction *qua* fiction in these two volumes of exotic tales. They are interesting simply because Huneker the story teller so often yields place to Huneker the playboy of the arts. Such things as **"Antichrist"** and **"The Woman Who Loved Chopin"** are no more, at bot-

tom, than second-rate anecdotes; it is the filling, the sauce, the embroidery that counts. But what filling! What sauce! What embroidery! . . . One never sees more of Huneker. . . .

8

He must stand or fall, however, as critic. It is what he has written about other men, not what he has concocted himself, that makes a figure of him, and gives him his unique place in the sterile literature of the republic's second century. He stands for a *Weltanschauung* that is not only unnational, but anti-national; he is the chief of all the curbers and correctors of the American Philistine; in praising the arts he has also criticized a civilization. In the large sense, of course, he has had but small influence. After twenty years of earnest labour, he finds himself almost as alone as a Methodist in Bavaria. The body of native criticism remains as I have described it; an endless piling up of platitudes, an homeric mass of false assumptions and jejune conclusions, an insane madness to reduce beauty to terms of a petty and pornographic morality. One might throw a thousand bricks in any American city without striking a single man who could give an intelligible account of either Hauptmann or Cézanne, or of the reasons for holding Schumann to have been a better composer than Mendelssohn. The boys in our colleges are still taught that Whittier was a great poet and Fennimore Cooper a great novelist. Nine-tenths of our people—perhaps ninety-nine hundredths of our native-born—have yet to see their first good picture, or to hear their first symphony. Our Chamberses and Richard Harding Davises are national figures; our Norrises and Dreisers are scarcely tolerated. Of the two undoubted world figures that we have contributed to letters, one was allowed to die like a stray cat up an alley and the other was mistaken for a cheap buffoon. Criticism, as the average American "intellectual" understands it, is what a Frenchman, a German or a Russian would call donkeyism. In all the arts we still cling to the ideals of the dissenting pulpit, the public cemetery, the electric sign, the bordello parlour.

But for all that, I hang to a somewhat battered optimism, and one of the chief causes of that optimism is the fact that Huneker, after all these years, yet remains unhanged. A picturesque and rakish fellow, a believer in joy and beauty, a disdainer of petty bombast and moralizing, a sworn friend of all honest purpose and earnest striving, he has given his life to a work that must needs bear fruit hereafter. While the college pedagogues of the Brander Matthews type still worshipped the dead bones of Scribe and Sardou, Robertson and Bulwer-Lytton, he preached the new and revolutionary gospel of Ibsen. In the golden age of Rosa Bonheur's *The Horse Fair,* he was expounding the principles of the post-impressionists. In the midst of the Sousa marches he whooped for Richard Strauss. Before the rev. professors had come to Schopenhauer, or even to Spencer, he was hauling ashore the devil-fish, Nietzsche. No stranger poisons have ever passed through the customs than those he has brought in his baggage. No man among us has ever urged more ardently, or with sounder knowledge or greater persuasiveness, that catholicity of taste and sympathy which stands in such direct opposition to the booming certainty and snarling narrowness of Little Bethel.

If he bears a simple label, indeed, it is that of anti-Philistine. And the Philistine he attacks is not so much the vacant and harmless fellow who belongs to the Odd Fellows and recreates himself with *Life* and *Leslie's Weekly* in the barber shop, as that more belligerent and pretentious donkey who presumes to do battle for "honest" thought and a "sound" ethic—the "forward looking" man, the university ignoramus, the conservator of orthodoxy, the rattler of ancient phrases—what Nietzsche called "the Philistine of culture." It is against this fat milch cow of wisdom that Huneker has brandished a spear since first there was a Huneker. He is a sworn foe to "the traps that snare the attention from poor or mediocre workmanship—the traps of sentimentalism, of false feeling, of cheap pathos, of the cheap moral." He is on the trail of those pious mountebanks who "clutter the market-places with their booths, mischievous half-art and tubs of tripe and soft soap." Superficially, as I say, he seems to have made little progress in this benign *pogrom*. But under the surface, concealed from a first glance, he has undoubtedly left a mark—faint, perhaps, but still a mark. To be a civilized man in America is measurably less difficult, despite the war, than it used to be, say, in 1890. One may at least speak of *Die Walküre* without being laughed at as a half-wit, and read Stirner without being confused with Castro and Raisuli, and argue that Huxley got the better of Gladstone without being challenged at the polls. I know of no man who pushed in that direction harder than James Huneker.

Joseph I. C. Clarke   (essay date 1921)

SOURCE: "James Gibbons Huneker," in *Journal of the American Irish Historical Society*, Vol. XX, 1921, pp. 221-28.

[*In the following essay, Clarke delineates Huneker's Gaelic background and interest in Irish writers.*]

No loss to literature, above all to American literature in recent years compares to the void left by the passing away of James Gibbons Huneker on February 10, 1921 in New York. To our ordinary mind contemplating the world of art and letters, it is the passing of the poet, the dramatist, the master story-teller, the historian, the painter, the sculptor, the singer, the actor, the musical composer, which covers the artistic personalities whose death makes men pause and lament that a fount of light and beauty to the world has disappeared. The death of James Gibbons Huneker proved that in literature there was another stamp of greatness whose effulgence fairly dazzled and delighted every man and woman capable, however poorly, of measuring it, namely, that of the critic and essayist of the seven arts—a critic and essayist who wrote with authority. Critics are the commonplace, for it is the badge of the writing tribe to be critical and to write about it: essayists are plentiful. But we measure upward in these matters until we reach an altitude of learning, knowledge, discrimination and judgment in both the critic and the essayist where greatness begins. It is characteristic of our time that

Huneker's books—seventeen volumes in all—are almost entirely built up of contributions to the periodical press of America—magazines, weeklies and daily papers—and most from the latter. It is equally notable that in the book, the ephemeral character which we associate with such origins is all but entirely missing. They are as if written for all time, dating from the hour of their production. A volume of 1899 reads as fresh and as true today as when it came from the printers. It is quite possible that to the volumes already to his credit many will hereafter be added, for after all they are only his own sifting of his output of work which was enormous. He had an incessant pen, a wonderful command of language, and he ever adorned his work, the slightest to which he touched hand, with something from the vast stores of his knowledge of the art world which no other writer in America—the world perhaps—could have in his grasp. Added to a marvellous memory, he was gifted to use a lightning recognition of likenesses or pointed dissimilarities which served to stimulate him to the luminous comparisons which are among the certificates of greatness in the working plan of criticism. The titles of most of his books do not often help one strange to his work. They are generally more ascriptive than descriptive, mostly, I presume, an endeavor on his part to strike a general note that will harmonize with some special quality emphasized in the essays and criticisms that make up the book. Here is the list:—*Mezzotints in Modern Music* (1899), *Chopin:—The Man and His Music* (1900), *Melomaniacs* (1902), *Overtones* (1904), *Iconoclasts; A Book of Dramatists* (1905), *Visionaries* (1905), *Egoists; A Book of Supermen* (1909), *Promenades of an Impressionist* (1910), *Franz Liszt* (1911), *The Pathos of Distance* (1912), *New Cosmopolis* (1915), *Ivory, Apes and Peacocks* (1915), *Unicorns* (1917), *Bedouins* (1920), *Steeplejack*, 2 vols., an autobiography (1920), *The Painted Veil* (1921). In these volumes he roams over the field of the arts, care-free, heart-free, picturing matters and men with a masterhood that here we cannot stay to describe or analyze, or to make constructive excerpts from his works by way of illustration.

The point of this brief, heartfelt tribute to the genius of Huneker in the *Journal of the American Irish Historical Society* is that for all of the Hun in the German name of Huneker, he derived a full half of his being from the Irish race, and as to scholarly bent, artistic leaning and literary predisposition, he gave the credit to his adored mother, born Mary Gibbons, a daughter of James Gibbons who saw the light in 1801 in Donegal, who "not finding the politics of his land to his taste, did what millions of his countrymen have done, emigrated to America." This was in 1820. He married Sarah Duffy and settled in Philadelphia.

James Gibbons was a leading spirit among the Irishmen and Catholics of Philadelphia during the last twenty years of his life, a zealous Fenian in the sixties, and, up to the day of his death in 1873, a determined hater of England for her misgovernment of Ireland. He was a forceful, fluent speaker, and he wrote a large sheaf of patriotic poems that were read and liked in Fenian circles. He was made a Fenian Senator, and Vice-President after the Civil War. Well I recall the zealot in his clean-shaven, eager face, his hair off his forehead, as he addressed a Fenian Convention in Philadelphia in 1869 or '70. His words burned with an inner flame. Meeting him thereafter I recall his simple human friendliness and his love of poetry. He was all Irish—an earnest soul, a man who sacrificed much and labored hard for Ireland in days of gloom and hours of hope. To his daughter, Mary Gibbons, Huneker pays beautiful tribute. Devoting a chapter of *Steeplejack* to "My Mother" he says:

> The few wits I possess came to me from my mother, who was a woman of brains, above all, of character. Before twenty she was the principal of a high school somewhere in Kensington. She saw men shot in the streets during the Know-Nothing riots of 1844, and also the burning of St. Augustine's Church on Fourth Street. She always had the faith, but these outrages on the Irish and her religion crystallized this faith. She was a pious and practical Churchwoman. Her erudition was notable. In matters of theology I never met her superior among her sex. I was inducted into the noble literature of Bossuet and Pere Lacordaire, early in my teens. [. . .]Yet she was not a bigot. She did not condemn to the everlasting bonfire dissenters from her faith.

His mother was anxious to see him enter the Church as a priest, but he says, "I hadn't the vocation." Indeed he had not—the courses of reading which he chose prove that. In this same chapter he says: "I had been confirmed at St. Malachi's by Bishop Woods, afterwards Archbishop, as I had been dedicated at St. Michael's by Bishop Gibbons, later Cardinal James Gibbons. I was taken by my mother into the Sacristy at St. Michaels and kissed the hand of that distinguished churchman."

But nothing could make a priest of him. It is quite in the character of Huneker that he should not in relating these things have told of his mother's cousinship to the great Cardinal, and hence his own, one step removed. But even now it is well to know it, and note it, and to note that the chorus of tribute and lamentation which went up all over the United States from the highest to the lowest, from our greatest officials, our university and college authorities, from the high priests of a score of creeds, down to the plainest citizen when the aged Cardinal passed away, was merely an expansion to the entire nation of the very similar, widespread personal grief that went up from the America of thought and art when the papers last February told that James Gibbons Huneker lay dead at his home in Flatbush, N. Y., after four days' illness and a month past his sixty-first birthday. Blood will tell.

I have no doubt, however, that his great musical talent came from his father, John Huneker, a man of most companionable character and artistic taste who led a blameless, useful life and provided well for his family of a wife and two sons of which James was the younger. Martin I. J. Griffin of Philadelphia, "an authority" says Huneker in *Steeplejack* "in historical research, a genealogist, particularly interested in old American Catholic families, wrote my brother, John Huneker, that Mark Honyker, in 1782, gave twenty-five pounds to enlarge St. Mary's Church. He was an uncle of John Huneker (Huneker's father). Your

family in Philadelphia goes back to 1700, and were among the earliest Catholic settlers." Huneker continues:

> A tradition is that the family originally stemmed from Hungary, then an autonomous state. An old Viennese Bible, dated 1750, spells the name Hunykyr, though we can't claim alliance with the noblest among Hungarian families, Jonas Hunyadi. Well I recollect the fear this bible aroused with its pictures of the damned in hell: indeed I conceived my first prejudices against the theological hell from these cruel illustrations.

But the Huneker blood was not all Hungarian. Huneker's father's mother was a Bowman, of English descent and there were plain Pennsylvania Dutch also among his forbears on his father's side. "My love of pictorial art was fostered at home, my passion for music stimulated in a musical atmosphere. My father was an easy-going man with a waggish disposition and a large fund of dry humor, which found expression in pithy, if not always parliamentary expressions."

Music had found expression in his father's family for generations. His grandfather, John Huneker, had been a church organist—at St. Mary's Roman Catholic Church certainly after 1806—and choir leader nearly all his life, and music was the life occupation of his great-grandfather. Of his father, Huneker tells us that he was a music lover, a singer of ballads with a rich baritone voice, a constant patron of such music as Philadelphia could sustain or procure, and entertained all prominent musicians reaching the town of the Quakers during Huneker's boyhood, such as Thalberg, Louis Moreau Gottschalk, Vieuxtemps, Olc Bull and other charmers of tone from piano or violin, men in the full light of worldwide musical fame. His father, too, was a collector in "black and white," and when in 1904 his collection was sold in New York it contained thousands of pieces of high quality:—mezzotints, line-engravings, etchings and lithographs. "That collection" says Huneker "not only educated my eye, educated me in the various schools, but it gave me the first Æsthetic thrill of my life."

Thus we see James growing towards the two great arts that, with literature were to be the main interest of his life—music and pictorial art. Meanwhile he had been attending Roth's military Academy from which he graduated from in 1873. He had been a haunter of picture galleries and an all-devouring reader from his ninth year, seeking the widest range in poetry, fiction, essays and descriptive writing. He was an impassioned piano student. Sending him to a law office, he passed his days in utter boredom. Another attempt was made to get him to work in another business. It was in vain. The Centennial Exposition of 1876 brought new and wider art-horizons to Philadelphia, and James grasped all he could learn from its pictures and sculptures in marble and metal. He fixed his mind on following his art emotions to France, to Paris with the view of making mastery of the piano his lifework. We need not follow the details of his subsequent educational history. They can be found in his fascinating *Steeplejack*. He never went to an American University. He reached Paris in October 1878 and plunged into his work, living on a sea of art enjoyment in that city of the art world, and toiling six to eight hours a day at the piano.

He did not succeed in becoming quite the master of the instrument that he had dreamed. He knew his music thoroughly, his performance was fine technically: he had a beautiful touch but public exhibition became through an abiding shyness of temperament, impossible to him. He expanded, however, in his destined ways, knowing intimately all the art wonders of the French capital and knowing and measuring its literary and art workers through intensive study of their works. He studied languages and became perfect in French, German, Italian, and burned his way through their literature. It was here he began his newspaper work, writing articles for the *Philadelphia Bulletin*. At length in about 1880 he returned to Philadelphia.

Some five years of study and piano teaching followed and in February 1886 he went to New York which for twenty-five years became his home and then, except for his annual months of Summer travel and residence in Europe—Paris, Berlin, Munich, Prague, Christiana, Stockholm, Rome, he found a hearth in the Long Island suburb of Flatbush.

In New York after a period of piano teaching in the National Conservatory of Music under Rafael Joseffy, his drift to newspaper work, which he called Bohemianism, became definite. At first he wrote for musical papers only. Then for four years he was music and dramatic critic of the N. Y. *Recorder*. Subsequently he held the same position on the N. Y. *Advertiser*—both papers long since dead. Years followed in which he did art, musical, dramatic and literary criticism for the *New York Sun* (in the time of the Laffan regime) for the *New York Times* and the *New York World*. It was the latter post which he held when going home to Flatbush from the Opera last February he had an attack of giddiness. A "cold" developed. It proved to be pneumonia, and, falling asleep four days later, he did not waken. Alas!

It was not so long before that from the endurance with which he carried the tremendous mountain of his work, not a dent on his splendid physique, his time of Bohemian revelry nigh twenty years down the wind, that he playfully wrote he would not be surprised to live fifty years further into the century. And he truly was a splendid looking man through his manhood. Tall and commanding, he stood on stalwart limbs, was broad and deep of chest with finely formed head and massive brow, dented deeply with the upright "lines of concentration" between the strongly marked eyebrows. His latter portraits show a severity of expression that came from the depths of his study, his habit of professional combat with the problems of his work rather than from the deeps of his nature which were sunny and warm and affectionate, as any who knew him could at any time prove.

It was something to have known this man, to be of those in whom at need he confided, but it is of moment that those who knew him at work and play should testify their knowledge of him. No more genial or brilliant man in everyday contact breathed. His enormous erudition was always at service, but it exacted little from others. He seemed to have no bitternesses. He had dislikes, as for instance, "canned music." It was not snobbery, but the revolt of the lifelong virtuoso to whom tone, interval, the dynamic were not for machines. Knowing as he must have come to know, his hundred superiorities, he cherished a certain shyness, an apparently real self-measuring that gave him almost the garb of humility. Yet boldness, freedom, modernity characterized his writings. His manner of flinging light across light from scores of sources and angle in illuminating a subject made his work fascinating and unique. Of European art, music, drama, literature and philosophy he knew the entire gamut, constantly increasing his store. His knowledge kept the level of the day.

No one could be more aware than he of the Celtic in his being. It was there for all men to see. His interest in the modern Irish renascence was keen. The work of William Butler Yeats, Lady Gregory, Synge, Johnson, Russell, Stephens, James Joyce, St. John Ervine and others he was familiar with, as he was the repository of Nietsche, Dostioevsky, Tolstoi, Turgeniev, Ibsen, Flaubert, De Maupassant, Bergson, Freud, Huysmans, Newman and so on in scores. In his book *Unicorns,* he has papers on James Joyce, Bernard Shaw and George Moore. He once said jestingly quoting another: "I have read everything," and it seemed so, for every writer you mentioned to him would seem already ticketed, weighed and measured in his brain. He wrote some fiction, but usually it was short and went to prove a contention of his intellect. Of late years, with many lapses, he was tending toward the faith of his early youth. Once he wrote to me that as the years went on he only saw safety in the Church. "I am a 'Hickory' Catholic" he says in *Steeplejack*. For other Christian faiths or cults he had no predilection whatever. He admired the Jewish intellect. He was hospitable to agnosticism. What he would have become we may not know.

It may be added to this brief tribute that he was married three times. His first wife was Miss Clinton, the talented sculptress. As so often happens in married life where all the conditions seem propitious, some unexpected differences are discovered. The lady had beauty, talent, charm of manner, high ideals, yet after a short term she passed out of his life—*sans rancune*. I went with him to the steamer when she was sailing to Europe after the break. There was stoicism on both sides as they said farewell. "She will be better off," he said as we walked away. "And you?" I said. "I have my work," he said. He never alluded to the lady in my hearing thereafter. The modernity of it all was something of a shock.

The greatly interesting thing to me, apart from my strong liking for the man, is that he stems so strongly from the Irish race, that he was collaterally kin to the great Cardinal James Gibbons, and like him exhibiting so many brilliant, unique facets in the great precious stone of his mind. His power of memory was of course congenital. I never knew but one other man who had it, namely Morgan Doheny, son of the dashing Irish Michael Doheny of 1848, and who also died young. James Gibbons Huneker's work will be the live evaluation of the Seven Arts during the half century bounded by his boyhood and his death.

Let me finally quote the brief opinion of H. L. Mencken, perhaps the most distinguished critic and essayist left to us. It reached the world from Baltimore when his friends and fellow-workers in New York were honoring Huneker's name, genius and lovable personality at a decorous funeral gathering at the Town Hall, which might perhaps have been more fitly held at the Cathedral. It runs:— "Huneker almost created civilized taste in the United States. Before his time criticism was three-fourths moral, and the fine arts were regarded as mere means 'to improve' the mind. He taught the young generation that beauty was an end in itself—that a first rate work of art was its own excuse for existence. The man was learned, hospitable to ideas, curious, amusing and charming. No other critic of his time, in any art, is to be mentioned in the same breath with him."

Lawrence Gilman   (essay date 1921)

SOURCE: "The Playboy of Criticism," in *The North American Review,* Vol. CCXIII, No. 785, April, 1921, pp. 556-60.

[*In the following essay, Gilman stresses Huneker's role in introducing new artistic movements to the American public.*]

"And now when the Great Moon had come, Steeplejack touched the tip of the spire, where instead of a cross he found a vane which swung as the wind listeth; thereat he marvelled and rejoiced. 'Behold!' he cried, 'thou glowing symbol of the New Man. A weathercock and a mighty twirling. This then shall be the sign set in the sky for Immoralists: A cool brain and a wicked heart. Nothing is true. All is permitted, for all is necessary.'—Thus Spake Steeplejack."

Such is the motto chosen by James Huneker to introduce his Autobiography, the last of that remarkable series of books which are now all that remains of him—save those of his writings which may be found in the newspaper files of the last quarter-century. For Steeplejack is dead, and an important chapter in the history of letters in America is closed. Mr. Huneker, in a quite definite and literal sense, began and ended a significant period in the aesthetic life of this country. He had scarcely a precursor; he was unique while he lived; and he has no successor.

Mr. Huneker's pilgrimage among the Seven Arts which he loved to patronize and expound began in the Philadelphia of 1860; it ended in Flatbush a few weeks ago. Drab outposts, it would seem; yet what a glittering web of experience and projection is hung between them! H. L. Mencken has said of Mr. Huneker that he "created civilized taste in America." There is a large infusion of truth in that somewhat too generous estimate. Only those of us who were busy with other than aesthetic activities in the 'nineties can forget the excitement stirred up by the emergence of Mr. Huneker's early books at about the time that America, under the chaperonage of Mr. McKinley, was discovering its Manifest Destiny as an exponent of pious imperialism. The United States won the Spanish War and took on Manifest Destiny and the Philippines at about the same time that Mr. Huneker steered into port his dazzling, strange, and multicolored cargo of aesthetic ivory, apes, and peacocks. It was an authentically novel adventure for

the home-keeping American reader of average intelligence and information to pick up a book by Huneker in the late 'nineties and find himself confronting a critic who was jauntily at his ease among all the fine arts known to man, and who bewildered God-fearing and "cultured" Americans, their minds going along comfortably with Hamilton Mabie and Charles Dudley Warner and Kenyon Cox and Ireneus Prime Stevenson and other illuminati of that ilk, by his casual indication of a *terra incognita* peopled by a strange race of poets, painters, music-makers, dramatists, novelists, philosophical rhapsodists, and an anonymous class impressively and with beguiling wickedness referred to by their exploiter as "anarchs," "immoralists," "melomaniacs," "iconoclasts," "visionaries," "egoists," "bedouins," and by other provocative appellations.

There were not many reading, play-going, picture-viewing, music-loving Americans at the beginning of this century who knew much about the artists who were then evolving new conceptions of color and design and sound, who were seeing man and his world with new eyes, and who were imperiously demanding of their generation fresh and unaccustomed and difficult prodigies of comprehension and appreciation. Mr. Huneker stood almost alone in America at that time as a persuasive advance agent for these new men and these unfamiliar concepts. While Hamilton Mabie and his confêres were still earnestly lecturing and essaying upon Thackeray and Dickens, trying, a little uncertainly, to estimate George Meredith, and relapsing upon Mr. James Lane Allen with obvious relief, while their musical and dramatic and pictorial brothers of the critical craft were engrossed in Brahms and Tchaikovsky, Pinero and Clyde Fitch, Sargent and Abbey, Mr. Huneker gaily conducted to public pasture (as he himself once put it) his surprising "flock of Unicorns—typifying the dreamers of dreams in the Seven Arts,"—while he produced, with sustained and amazing virtuosity, a prose kaleidoscope of latter-day artists, novelists, poets, philosophers, composers, and a miscellaneous assortment of fantasists, funambulists, madmen, mystics, and seers. For the first time, American readers felt themselves to be on familiar terms with such foreigners as Richard Strauss, Nietzsche, Flaubert, George Moore, Maeterlinck, Huysmans, Baudelaire, Stirner, De Gourmont, Rimbaud, Barrès, Picasso, Matisse, Laforgue, Wederkind, Cézanne, Van Gogh, Strindberg, Gaugin—some of them living innovators, some of them dead and enigmatic memories, but all of them remote from the experience of the average American ardently in pursuit of cultural sophistication.

And Mr. Huneker did more than import this alluring and exotic cargo. He took them about with him, made friends for them, put them up at the best clubs, found welcoming stables for his unicorns. In other words, he talked about them extremely well—with vividness, with charm, with evident affection and understanding, with a prose-style that was a new thing under the American sun: a flexible, flashing, audacious, richly communicative style, poetic and irreverent, witty and rhapsodical, swift and nervous, yet extraordinarily sumptuous and learned and ornate. It was uncompromisingly personal, pungent, racy, yet it was sophisticated to the last degree, immensely amusing and stimulating in its verbal virtuosity, its riotous gusto. To a public culture which had been timorous and parochial, a civilization which had been drab, anaemic and thin, Mr. Huneker, almost unaided, brought color and gayety and abundance.

He became at once, and always remained, the critical Playboy of the Arts. He bombarded the amazed American reader with new and startling affirmations; he was the rhapsodic celebrant of a hundred new aestheticisms; he beat the drum with vigor and eloquence, in season and out, for Strauss and Nietzsche and Blake and Flaubert, and a score of other esoteric and neglected geniuses and radical modernists in all the arts. He was the clairvoyant and eloquent interpreter of all those painters, tone-poets, novelists, essayists, philosophers, who were as yet unreceived in our intellectual society—and it is amazing to look back now, after a quarter-century, and remember how barren was that crude, oppressed, and timid civilization of ours in the later 'nineties, how ready for just such an enlivenment as Mr. Huneker brought to it.

Into the depressing drabness of our critical writing, with its incomparable paltriness and sterility, its dullness and triteness, its traditionalism and vapidity, Mr. Huneker entered with somewhat the effect of a gusty spring wind blowing through a long-closed Middle-Western "parlor."

It is assuaging to realize that that rich and generous temperament, that fine-grained and responsive intelligence, that ample and hospitable spirit, had accomplished its fertilizing, its liberating, its provocative task. There are signs in this last book of his that the sources were running dry. There is much in Mr. Huneker's story of his adventures among people and emotions that the Huneker of a decade ago would have modified or suppressed—surprising trivialities, commonplaces, conformities; much that is inconsequential and trite, and sometimes a little cheap. He has not made engrossing or illuminating or significant his studying of law, his early adventures in criticism, his visits to the Pope and to Roosevelt, his reminiscences of forgotten worthies of the stage and the concert-hall, of the Philadelphia of the 'seventies and the New York of the 'eighties and 'nineties. And he had begun to repeat himself, to thresh over old straw. It was always a defect of his style that he fell in love with certain epithets, and that these hypnotized him, dogged the footsteps of his prose, tending to make it seem artificial and self-conscious. This tendency grew upon him, so that little of his later writing was new-minted, fresh, spontaneous. He was sometimes "intoxicated by the exuberance of his own verbosity," so that he seemed to be far more concerned with the rhythms and sonorities of his prose than with its effectiveness as an instrument of precise and full communication.

He had never cared to attempt any orientation of artistic phenomena in the social scheme—his criticism was always (in the admirable phrase of that wise and exquisite American seer, Edith Wyatt) "untouched by any of the moods of a profound general consciousness." One misses in him always a realization of the need for relating individual artistic appearances to their contemporary human environment, to the great stream of general ideas and tendencies. His criticism is merely aesthetic diagnosis brilliantly and sympathetically performed in a vacuum, without any attempt to determine its human or spiritual values. No doubt he failed to discriminate between the criticism that is enriched by an acute awareness of all the interacting forces of its social setting, and the incurable American habit of discussing aesthetic phenomena in terms of a rigid and sentimental piety—the disastrous tendency which has brought into our critical writing those horrible things, the platform manner, the pulpit manner, the shield and helmet of the ethical policeman, the handcuffs of the lewd detective of the moral order. From these hideous perversions he naturally revolted with loathing. But he need not have detached himself so wholly from the deeper and wider implications of his subject-matter.

Yet, when all is said, how immeasurably valuable an influence he was! What susceptibility, clairvoyance, immediacy of response were his! He was innocent of prepossessions, infinitely flexible and generous. He was the friend of any talent fine and strange and courageous enough to incur the dislike of the mighty army of Bourbons, Puritans, and Boeotians. His critical tact was almost infallible. "Our myriad intuitions are the veiled queens who steer our course through life," says a profound and subtle mystic of today, "though we have no words in which to speak of them." But Mr. Huneker had words in which to speak of them. He has written pages that will always be cherished by those for whom criticism is one of the several ways of literature—pages of superb and gorgeous imagination, of beautiful insight, of splendid valor. He was, we have already said of him, both vivid and acute, robust and fine-fingered, tolerant yet unyielding, astringent yet tender—dynamic, contagious, perpetually lovable, inveterately alive. Remembering him, one remembers, too, one of his favorite quotations from Nietzsche: "Convictions are prisons. . . . New ears for new music. New eyes for the most remote things. . . . The pathos of distance."

George E. De Mille   (essay date 1927)

SOURCE: "Huneker," in *Literary Criticism in America: A Preliminary Survey,* 1927. Reprint by Russell & Russell, 1967, pp. 206-44.

[*In the following essay, De Mille profiles Huneker as a gifted literary critic who introduced many important European authors to North American readers.*]

I

Every now and then some criticaster, of the sort who believe that authors can be ranked and graded like pupils in a class in elementary arithmetic, sets out to answer the question, Who is the great American critic? The answers to this question have been various and surprising. Lowell has been most often mentioned, but one also hears the names of Poe, Stedman, and even Margaret Fuller. No one, however, has as yet nominated for the honor James Huneker. Indeed, of all the major American critics, Huneker has been most persistently ignored. The qualities of the man are so obvious that this demands some attempt at explanation. This neglect is no doubt partly due to his life-long connection with the daily papers—a connection that invites the academic epithet—journalistic. More of it is owing to Huneker's critical isolation. Most critics, the reader has probably noticed, speak not only for themselves, but for some group of creative writers, or some general movement of literary thought. They are party leaders, and the party helps them to fame. But Huneker belonged to no movement, advocated no reform, was touted by no clique, and it has been in the interest of no particular literary group to shout his praises. Only abroad has his importance been recognized. Remy de Gourmont, Paul Bourget, George Brandes, men whose mere awareness of the existence of an American critic meant a great deal, recorded their estimation of him in flattering terms. Nor was this undeserved. One can give him no higher praise that to say that in range of interests, in keenness of intelligence, in catholicity of taste, in brilliance of style, he reminds one constantly of the great French critics of the Nineteenth Century, of Sainte-Beuve and Taine and Le Maître.

II

He is a fascinating subject of study. All great critics are personalities; few are as interesting, as pleasing, as personal as Huneker. His essays tell us a great deal about the men he criticized, and still more about James Huneker. Every line of his prose rings with the accent of a living human voice. Every opinion he utters is of interest, not only because it is or is not true, but because he utters it. And to understand and appreciate his criticism, one must know something of the life he lived, the circumstances that shaped him, the forces that made him what he was.

James Gibbons Huneker was born in Philadelphia in 1860. His ancestry was largely Irish; his family name probably of remote Hungarian origin. His father was a well-to-do business man, who in his off hours collected etchings, haunted the theatre and the concert hall, drank brandy with Poe, and entertained at his house Thalberg and Ole Bull. The boy grew up in an atmosphere of unacademic culture. Books and music and pictures came to him, not as a discovery of late adolescence, tinged with a flavor of exoticism, but as a natural and almost essential part of everyday life. He was equally at home in Bohemia and in Belgravia.

He was brought up in the Roman Catholic Church. It may seem fantastic to connect Huneker's theological training with his qualities as a literary critic, but such a connection nevertheless exists. Tolerance, catholicity, freedom from excessive moralism, are among the most desirable of qualities in a critic. Now not one person in ten thousand, Protestant born and reared, ever escapes from the overshadowing influence of Puritanism. The literary critic born a Protestant who remains orthodox, is bound to disapprove of some of the greatest things in literature; and even though he rids himself of his dogmas in theology, he finds it almost impossible to escape them in morals. Thence comes the critical prudery that so defaces the work of Howells; even such liberals as Stedman and Lowell are restricted by it, and we find Stedman averse to Poe, and Lowell looking with disapproval at Fielding and Whitman. In lesser men than these, Puritanism leads to the oddities that make the early issues of the *North American Review* sound so often like a critical joke book.

These are the conservatives, the comparatively orthodox.

The heretics are apt to be equally biased, though in a different direction. The critic brought up under Protestantism and Puritanism who revolts violently against the religion of his forbears becomes, in ninety-nine cases out of a hundred, a violent and partisan anti-moralist. In either case the results are bad. The orthodox Puritan is blind to the shining glories of Rabelais, Cabell, and large parts of Chaucer and Shakespeare. The anti-Puritan, who is only a Puritan facing the other way, can often see no good in Emerson and Hawthorne and Tennyson.

From the one-sided excesses of both these groups the Catholic training of Huneker helped to preserve him. Vague though the liberal Catholic may become in doctrine, he retains to the end something of the religious emotion, some not-too-sharply defined theological base, some moral taste, from the safe ground of which he can view with tolerance and curiosity those whose notions do not strictly coincide with his own. Thus Huneker, never having felt the pressure of Puritanism, never felt it necessary to indulge in anti-Puritan rages. He listened with detached and intelligent interest to the sermons of literary moralists like Shaw and Ibsen. He recognized the moral instinct in human nature, and examined with curiosity and sympathy its literary manifestations. But unlike the Puritan, he never expected too much of human nature. He knew that even the saints have their days off, and he was not above a human pleasure in the contemplation of these worthies in their moments of weakness. Ribaldry—a liking for an earthy tale—is one element of the complete man; therefore we have a literature of ribaldry. Both the Puritan, who shrieks "Wipe it out," and the anti-Puritan, who demands it everywhere and then attempts to prove that it does not exist, are untrue to the facts of literature and life. Huneker did neither; he was neither prudish nor prurient. He dealt with many authors who were under the moral ban—Wedekind, George Moore, d'Annunzio—but without descending to become either an apologist or a censor. The point is worth emphasizing, because this detachment, this balance, this moral tolerance, has been sadly lacking in most of our American critics.

In 1878 Huneker, having completed his very sketchy formal education, passed a desultory year or two in a law office, and concluding at length that music was his vocation, set out for Paris to complete his musical education. The results of this foreign sojourn, coming during the formative years of Huneker's life, were greatly beneficial. It was this early visit abroad that made him the most cosmopolitan of American critics. There is, of course, an element of cosmopolitanism in nearly every great critic—some second field to which he can turn, and from which he can draw comparisons with the literature of his own time and country. With Lowell it is the Middle Ages, with Stedman the Greeks, with James the French realists, with Howells the Russians. Poe is the only exception in American criticism to this rule—but Poe is an exception to all rules. Huneker, however, was cosmopolitan in a far more thoroughgoing manner than any of these men. He was at home in more lands and literatures than any other American critic.

These earliest wander-years brought him into close contact with French literature at a time when French literature was in one of its most productive phases—at a time when its character was such as to make its influence particularly tonic on a student from America. Victor Hugo was at the height of his glory. Flaubert and Maupassant might be seen in the cafés. Zola was preaching naturalism and writing his peculiar brand of romanticism. The young musician, already a reader of Baudelaire, Stendhal, and Chateaubriand, soaked himself to saturation in the French writers of the day; from that time on, French was as natural to him as English. A constant journeying back and forth across the Atlantic kept this cosmopolitan sense alive in Huneker to the end. Thus he runs up to Christiania to interview Ibsen; spends a week-end in Kent with Conrad; argues realism with Huysmans, and Shakespeare with Maeterlinck. By such personal contacts Huneker remained always in touch with literature in the making all over Europe. And yet, unlike that other literary cosmopolitan, Henry James, he never became in any sense an expatriate, but remained to the end as American as fried chicken.

Aside from his knowledge of French literature, Huneker learned two facts of importance during his stay in Paris—that he could never become a musician worth listening to, and that he could write things for which editors were willing to pay. As a result of this enlightenment, Huneker, on his return to America, plunged into journalism, first as music critic, later as critic of literature, drama, and painting, for half a dozen New York papers. His letters are a half-comic, half-tragic record of the constant struggle to grind out his daily grist; he wrote with the printer's devil at his elbow. To some men, such a pressure to write much and rapidly would have been fatal. No doubt Huneker did turn out a great deal of criticism of no permanent value. Fortunately, however, he possessed the faculty of self-criticism. The trivial and the ephemeral in his work is safely buried in the files of the *Sun,* the *Times,* the *Herald,* where only the inordinately curious need disturb it. The fifteen volumes which he thought worthy of an appearance in book form are of as uniform and high a quality as those of the most cloistered recluse in critical history. For one thing, this journalistic effort kept him thoroughly alive—if indeed a man of such abounding vitality and such inexhaustible curiosity needed any outside influence to keep him alive—to the literary currents of his day, preventing that ossification of interest which so often overtakes critics as they pass middle age. And it strengthened his impulse to write criticism that is readable and brilliant. This brilliance, this verbal cleverness does, it is true, at times degenerate into cheapness, but it is not the cheapness of the jaded humorist. Huneker never sounds tired; his cheapness resembles rather the occasional cheapness of Dickens and Shakespeare. It is the result of a creative vitality that refused to submit to the slow patient methods of Flaubert and James.

III

Such were the influences that formed him. But what of the man himself, the personality on which these influences worked? The one great quality that irradiates every page of Huneker's criticism is his superb vitality. We are most of us such bloodless creatures that the spectacle of a literary critic so thoroughly alive at once astounds and inspires. He never exhibited a sign of mental fatigue; his spirit never drooped. His curiosity was boundless. His detachment was far removed from the bored aloofness of the typical academic critic. It was rather due to the feeling that there are so many interesting things in life that one cannot properly limit himself to any one group of interests, to any one kind of excellence. Full-blooded as few critics are, he liked best that literature which is rich in personality, teeming with life and passion. Furthermore, this personality of Huneker's spread itself at large in his writing. Such an air of high enjoyment exhales from the page that it takes possession of the reader. One is constantly, in reading Huneker, seized with a desire to go straight from the critic to the author criticized. This quality, which we find also in Lowell, is one of the rarest qualities of the great critic.

Most critics of strong vitality become leaders of movements, literary propagandists. It was Huneker's peculiar excellence to combine liveliness with detachment. An intense individualist, he abhorred movements, reforms, the uplift in all its manifestations, not because of any anti-moralistic bias, but because he hated all attempts to regiment humanity, to standardize, to take from the individual his liberty to develop his peculiarities at his own sweet will. It was his intense individualism, his dislike of the crowd, that drew Huneker to Ibsen. Ibsen was of all modern writers the one with whose philosophy Huneker was in closest agreement.

To class men, without qualifications of all sorts, as optimists or pessimists, is a silly proceeding. Temperamentally, Huneker was an optimist in the sense that, enjoying life vastly, he approved of life. But he was something more than a stomach ambulatory. His keen and searching, naturally undogmatic, restless, questioning intellect, fed on such writers as Flaubert, Conrad, Nietzsche, inevitably turned toward skeptical pessimism. Instinctively, as he admits, a yes-sayer, his mind penetrated easily the fallacies of vulgar American optimism. But although he seemed at times to doubt all things, he never appeared tortured by his doubts. Skepticism in him merely produced a wider tolerance, a greater range of vision. It gave a needed spice of sharpness to his general good nature. He even had his flashes of nihilism; he enjoyed profound pessimism, as he found it in the pages of Gorky and Strindberg. Huneker understood himself pretty thoroughly; with characteristic frankness he summed himself up in this fashion:

> I am an optimist at bottom, with a superficial
> coating of pessimism, which thaws near a piano,
> a pretty girl, or a glass of Pilsner.

A second quality combines with this purely intellectual pessimism to temper a vitality that might otherwise have become mere vigorous barbarism. It is a curious and unquestionable fact, that for all his healthy enjoyment of the world, Huneker was in some sense a mystic. Through all his Bohemian years, he was always keenly sensitive to the beauty of religion. "I love," he declared, "the odour of incense, the mystic bells, the music, the atmosphere of the altar, above all the intellectual life of the church." Frequently one may detect a critic's profoundest likings, not by the author with whom he avowedly deals, but by those whom he incidentally quotes; it is often these who lie deepest imbedded in his consciousness. Thus one may test the sincerity of Huneker's interest in the intellectual life of the church by the fact that he was constantly, in all manner of contexts, quoting Newman. It is this mystic strain which accounts for Huneker's great, perhaps exaggerated liking for Maeterlinck; and we even find him plunging into the mystic reveries of St. John of the Cross.

To the business of criticism Huneker brought, besides his magnificent personality, one of the finest critical equipments in literary history. He was by far the most versatile of American critics—one of the most versatile of all critics. Not only did he range from English and American literature to French, German, Scandinavian, Russian; literature itself was not wide enough to confine his exploring mind. Indeed, it is questionable whether literary criticism was after all his chief interest, whether his achievements in that quarter constitute his largest claim to remembrance. Music was his first love, and perhaps at all times his deepest. His first published volumes bore the title ***Mezzotints in Modern Music***. His work on Chopin, which appeared in 1900, really established him as a writer. So important an element in his personality were his musical tastes, that it is worth while to glance at them for a moment. He began as a romanticist; his taste was formed in the seventies and eighties; his prime favorite in music was always Chopin. Liszt he estimated more highly than do most musical critics. Strauss he regarded as the greatest of contemporary composers. Wagner fascinated him. One of his best essays in musical criticism was devoted to Tschaikovsky. But for popular and sentimental romanticism—the romanticism of Mendelssohn, Massenet, Meyerbeer—he had no use. He thought little of the more popular works of Chopin—the Nocturnes and most of the Valses. But a musical romanticist he in essence remained; a romanticist, however, with strong classical leanings. For the earlier and simpler classics, Mozart, Haydn, Gluck, he had little taste, comparatively speaking. They lacked the idiosyncrasy, the emotional stir, the dissonant element, which appealed to Huneker in music as in literature. But there is a profoundly classical base in any man who "begins his mornings with Bach." And Huneker's condemnation of opera,

> We would rather listen to a Beethoven string quartet played by the Flonzaleys than to all the operas ever written; the majority of them depicting soul states in a sanatorium.

is profoundly classical in its implications. And then, with the characteristic indifference of the great critic to logical consistency, he went to the opera, went and recorded with delight his reactions there. It is interesting to note his attitude toward such moderns as Schoenberg. He was at first repelled by Schoenberg, found him incomprehensible. But characteristically, he did not turn away with the usual remark that this was not music. He listened, puzzled, but curious, and finally managed to make something of the composer, though arriving at no great liking of him.

His method in musical criticism showed this same mixture of classic and romantic elements. He was always interested in the personality of the composer; this is, I suppose, a form of romanticism. He attempted to capture and express in words the emotional content of the music he discussed. But unlike the so-called literary critic of music, he never wrote programmes. His was a musical criticism for musicians, not for weak-minded amateurs who insist that music should tell them a story. His criticism of music, like Poe's criticism of literature, was highly, almost overpoweringly technical. To understand the last half of his volume on Chopin, one must read with an open score at hand; otherwise, the book is incomprehensible. It is an interesting comment on the direction of technical criticism that Huneker's criticism of music is far more technical than his criticism of literature, and that his condemnations of composers are ten times as numerous, and twenty times as absolute, as his condemnations of authors.

One finds the same qualities in his work as a critic of painting—wide knowledge, classical backbone, liking for the new, the exotic, the strange. His three idols in painting were Vermeer, Velasquez, and Rembrandt. But he was among the first in America to praise the work of Gauguin, and his pages are filled with reference to such men as Monticelli, Piranesi, Felicien Rops.

In characteristic and illuminating phrase, he labelled himself "Jack of the Seven Arts." In one issue of the *Sun* he published articles on Botticelli, on Rodin, and on *Madame Bovary*. The men who can do that sort of thing, and do it well, are not common. And for all this overpowering interest in all the arts, Huneker kept a corner of his brain free for the more coldly intellectual interests. He was enough of an amateur theologian to quote Harnack, enough of a philosopher to tilt with Bergson and William James. The chief interest of his last trip to Holland was a visit to De Vries, with whom he inspected primroses, and from whom he picked up enough of the theory of mutation to affect profoundly his thinking.

IV

All this no doubt seems far enough out of the way in a discussion of a literary critic. But as a matter of fact, it is strictly apropos. Huneker's mind was not of the sort that is divided into air-tight compartments, each containing its little isolated group of facts. He was the practitioner of a unique sort of comparative criticism. He compared, not only different literatures, but different arts. As a matter of pure theory, he denied the validity of this process, asserting that

> The respective substance of each art is different, and not even the extraordinary genius of Richard Wagner could fuse disparate dissimilarities.

And then, after making this polite bow to Professor Babbitt, he proceeded, with consistent inconsistency, to write of one art in terms of all the others. This is a dangerous process; in the hands of a tyro, a disastrous process. But Huneker makes of it something valuable. The particular function of the comparative critic is to bring together things far removed in time and space, and by a fortunate conjunction, to shed light on the things compared. Notable among such conjunctions is Huneker's parallel of Poe and Chopin—a parallel that would have occurred, I think, to no other critic, and one that sheds more light on Poe than half the volumes lately published about him. A characteristic and felicitous use of the terms of one art to illuminate a discussion of another is found in this sentence on Flaubert.

> His landscapes in the Dutch, tight, miniature style, or the large, luminous, loose manner of Holbein, or again full of the silver repose of Claude and the dark romantic beauty of Rousseau, are ravishing.

This airy leaping from literature to literature and from art to art sounds like the antics of a dilettante. But Huneker was no skimmer of surfaces. From pedantry, indeed, he was as far removed as from Puritanism. But underneath the brilliant surfaces of his essays lies a foundation of sound and thorough scholarship. There is no parading of authorities, no assumption of the ponderous manner of the academic critic. But the scholarship is there, nevertheless. The Ibsen study illustrates this point excellently. Not only had Huneker read every play of Ibsen's, including such little known works as *Catalina, Norma,* and *St. John's Night.* He had at his finger-tips the facts of Ibsen's life. He was versed in dates of production. He had apparently read all the Ibsen critics worth reading—Brandes, Jaeger, Faguet, Archer, Wicksteed, and a dozen more. Even more solidly based is the volume on Chopin, with its evidence of original investigation, with its quotations from new sources, most of all with its laborious comparison of musical editings—the nearest approach to pedantry of anything in Huneker. Not only was Huneker, when the subject called for it, definitely scholarly in method. He had as wide a background of reading as the vast majority of professional scholars. One often hears the reproach leveled at journalistic critics that, while versed in modern literature, their knowledge stops at the year 1800. From such reproach Huneker is free. His reading can only be described as immense. Within the pages of **Steeplejack**—not a critical book, but an autobiography—one finds references to almost every classic author of importance. Here is a list gathered at random from a compass of about fifty pages—Cellini, Bossuet, Rabelais, Montaigne, Goethe, Aquinas, Dante, Cervantes, Bunyan, Horace. No American critic we have considered had read so widely, and few had read so well.

In spite of his keen intellect, in spite of his great interest in ideas, Huneker had little trace, I think, of the specifically philosophical type of mind—the type of mind that seeks to organize its ideas into a system, to base its judgments on general principles which, put together, make a more or less complete philosophy of literature. Unlike his French masters, unlike most of the American critics who had preceded him, Huneker was not given to discussions of literature and criticism in the abstract. Except for one chapter in **Steeplejack,** headed "Criticism," Huneker's pronouncements on literary theory were limited to very incidental remarks dropped in the course of his examinations of specific writers. In theory, he recognizes the need of general principles of literary art. "The critic," he asserted, "should be an artist as to temperament, and he should have a credo." But as to the specific articles of this credo,

Huneker was vague. Again we find him maintaining that "there must be standards, but the two greatest are sympathy and its half-brother sincerity." Sincerity may be a standard, but sympathy is obviously an attitude in the critic, and to call it a standard is to give oneself away rather badly. It is interesting to note that while Huneker was making these remarks, he plainly had in mind two of the neo-classic critics of his own time, W. C. Brownell and Irving Babbitt, of whom he speaks in admiring terms.

But having made these gestures in the direction of critical classicism, Huneker faced about, and asserted with far more force and clearness the utter subjectivity of criticism.

> No critic has ever settled anything.
>
> Neither praise nor blame should be the goal of the critic. To spill his own soul, that should be his aim.
>
> It is his prejudices that make vital a critic's work.
>
> Humbly to follow and register his emotions aroused by a masterpiece is his function. A little humility in a critic is a wise attitude.

These assertions are plainly pure impressionism, and in almost every instance, impressionism was Huneker's method. I think we may safely attribute his occasional classical pronouncements as mere illustrations of his intellectual sympathy with convincingly stated ideas.

Two more generalizations remain to be noted, and our examinations of Huneker's light baggage of critical doctrine will be done. Interested though he always was in ideas, moral ideas included, for moralistic criticism he had not the slightest use. In his reaction—a perfectly sound reaction—against the moralizing tone that has always marked a large section of American criticism, he ran to the other extreme. "Good art," he declared, "is never obscene; the only obscene art is bad art." Particularly disgustful to Huneker was the common trick of examining the life of a writer for offences against the current notion of morality, and transferring this condemnation to his literary work. Technique, in his view, was the morality of art, and with technique criticism should most busy itself. He even, following Henry James, the one previous American critic who seems to have influenced him in any respect, objects to criticism of subject. He impatiently exclaimed, "This harping on the theme of a drama—whether pleasant or unpleasant, dull, brilliant, or truthful—is eminently amateurish." He praised the criticism of Baudelaire because "he judge more of form than theme." In this respect, Huneker approached closely the critical attitude of Poe and of Stedman. But to follow it on all occasions is to place unnecessary and belittling restrictions on criticism, and Huneker, while preeminently a critic of form, paid no attention to this limitation when it got in his way. Like the greatest critics of all times, Huneker made his doctrines to suit the occasion, and he never balked at an inconsistency. His assertion, "I don't believe in movements or schematologies, or any one method of seeing and writing," applies perfectly to his own criticism. To shift one's position in this manner exposes one to all sorts of charges from the logically minded; it is, however, another of the marks of the great critic.

V

With Huneker, as with most critics, the theory is of far less importance than the method. Huneker's method was formed by lessons from many masters. An intense individualist, he was always interested in the personality of the writer. "Psychologue" was one of his pet words; and following in the steps of Sainte-Beuve, he played the psychologue to the writers he considered. And the writers who interested him most were the writers of striking and bizarre personality. Strindberg, Neitzsche, Wedekind, Dostoieffsky, Maupassant—these are among the most brilliant of his soul-portraits. "What," he exclaimed, "is more fascinating than a peep in the laboratory of a great artist's mind?" This interest in personality sometimes extends—as in the essay on Villiers de L'Isle Adam—to writers whose actual literary output Huneker valued not at all. The very titles of his volumes reveal this individualistic tendency. ***Egoists, Iconoclasts, Bedouins, Unicorns***—the names speak for themselves.

To offset this interest in personality, which is an extreme form of Romanticism, Huneker, like a certain type of classicist, largely busied himself with questions of form and style. Like a true descendant of the great French critics, he was a stylist and a critic of style at all times. His repeated statement, "My most enduring artistic passions are for the music of Chopin and the prose of Flaubert," reveals the extent and the nature of his stylistic bent. He demanded that art should be artistic, consciously artistic. Thus we find him attacking Zola, not, like most critics of the day, for his moral ugliness, but because of his lack of finish. Eventually, this liking for the classically finished led Huneker to turn away from Whitman, one of his great early loves. But in general, Huneker's taste in style was catholic and catholicizing. Thus we find him admiring writers so far removed from him in temperament as Howells and Edith Wharton—largely because each is the master of a high prose style. He tasted with pleasure authors as far apart as Shaw and Pater, Newman and Anatole France.

Still more was Huneker concerned with form in its larger aspects—and here he became genuinely classical. It is in his dramatic criticism that this element stands out most prominently. It even leads him to say a good word for Scribe. "Scribe is a wonderful technician. From him you may learn the playwright's trade." Huneker always discussed plays from the point of view of actual stage production, passing frequently into reminiscences of performances he had witnessed—in Paris, London, Berlin, Vienna, New York. His finest work in this direction is the long article on Ibsen, in the course of which he analyzes every play of Ibsen's, so accurately and searchingly that college professors use the essay as a text for the study of Ibsen's technique. It is a revealing side-light, both on Huneker and on the practice of technical criticism in general, that Huneker's condemnations of authors are always based on technical grounds. Thus, he first finds flaws in the novels of Stendhal and the plays of Shaw. But such technical condemnations occupy a comparatively small part of Huneker's criticism.

In this technical attitude toward literature, and this technical method of criticism, Huneker was in agreement with Poe, with Stedman, with James. But unlike these men, he did not stop at technique. We have noted his interest in the writer as a person; we have noted his interest in style, in the larger aspects of form. He was equally interested in ideas, and was always careful to lay bare, usually without accepting or rejecting, the ideas of his authors. As a result of this breadth of interest, he avoided the unsatisfying narrowness of which one is often conscious when reading critics who stop at form or who deal only with ideas. One gets from Huneker a more complete and rounded picture of the author under consideration than from almost any other critic of literature.

VI

But perhaps, after all, the chief quality of the great critic is his ability to write. Huneker could write. He had the journalist's trick of turning out clean copy. It is strange to find a man whose most lasting literary passion was for the prose of Flaubert saying, with entire truthfulness, "I never rewrite my books." His stylistic excellence was not the result of long and painful labor with the file; his brilliance was the natural and rapid utterance of a brilliant mind. He enjoyed doing tricks with words; he thought in clever sentences. He wrote in sentences; sometimes in sentences only. With characteristic self-awareness, he called ***Steeplejack*** "a book of beautiful quotations." Here is an extreme instance from the same volume.

> Envy is only a form of inverted admiration. Joseph Conrad speaks of pity as a special form of contempt. Stupidity is the great humorist, says George Moore. We live too much on the surface of our being. A philosopher has said that we live forward and think backward. Sorrow is the antiseptic of sick souls. Woman, declared the Fathers of the Church (shrewd psychologists), is the most potent engine of dolour that God has given Man. The French Revolution only destroyed ruins; the social edifice had been tottering for a century. . . . Intimate friends are, as a rule, disasters. Mythomania is a malady that spares few. Its real name is religion. Walt Whitman may have been a yellow dog, but he had a golden bark. Truth is always original. But what is truth? . . . I pause for breath.

This is parody, of course; but it is almost perfect parody, and parody itself is a highly intelligent sort of criticism.

Although Huneker's manner was always staccato, in his critical works this manner was under thorough control. Disjointed though his paragraphs may appear at first reading, this effect is often an optical illusion, the result of a dazzlement produced by the too continuous sparkle and glitter of his sentences. But beneath this coating of jewels there is a rigid steel structure. Every essay has its definite mark, toward which it flies straight as an arrow.

And after all, this staccato touch lent itself excellently to the expression of Huneker's fundamental impressionism, for Huneker was at bottom an impressionist. Huneker shared with Lowell—also an impressionist at heart—the great critical gift of catching and recording the peculiar excellence of an author in pointed and memorable phrase. The thing that interested Huneker in an author was not his measuring up to or deviation from any set standard, but the author's unique quality—the thing in which he differs from all other authors. To express that uniqueness was Huneker's main critical aim. Sometimes the trick was done in a phrase. Anatole France is "a consummate flowering of the dilettante." *Les Miserables* he beautifully described as a "windy apotheosis of vapid humanitarianism." Damning, but true, was the label he applied to Massenet and his like, "the puff-paste decorative school." He neatly hit off Franz Liszt, "who composed cadenzas with orchestral accompaniment and called them concertos." Here are more lengthy specimens.

> The elemental things are his (Conrad's) chief concern, not the doings of dolls. He is not a propagandist. He never tries to prove anything.

> Gorky transfers to his pages the odor of a starving, sweating humanity, its drunkenness, its explosions of rage, guttural cries of joy, and its all too terrible animalism. . . . Gorky, for all his moral nihilism, is as superstitious as a moujik. He shakes his fist at the eternal stars, and then makes the sign of the cross.

> A latter-day pagan, with touches of the perverse, the grotesque, and the poetic; that seems to me Frank Wedekind.

> Zola is a myopic romanticist, writing in a style both violent and tumified the history of his soul in the latrines of life.

There is a danger in being able to write like that, but Huneker never committed the crime of letting the sound carry away the sense. And for all his love for sparkle and glitter, Huneker could and did write pages of as solid and sensible exposition as any man of the Eighteenth Century.

VII

Insatiable in curiosity, cosmopolitan in training, writing in a style to stimulate the interest of the most jaded reader, filled with a highly communicable enthusiasm, Huneker made an incomparable literary pioneer. He has been reproached for his coldness toward American writers. Writing from an international viewpoint, he naturally had little use for those American writers who loomed large in our eyes during the last century only because of our literary isolation. But both the American writers whom he mentions and those of whom he omits to speak are evidence of his power of selection, his ability to pick out the best. It is just for those American writers to whose reputations time has added that he shows due admiration. We have noted his early devotion to Poe. Emerson seems to have influenced him profoundly. He quoted Thoreau with appreciation. Whitman he liked at first, later partly outgrew, but eventually accepted. Of his connection with the critical work of Henry James we have spoken. And these are the American writers to whom European criticism has paid most attention. Furthermore, Huneker retained to the end an interest in American literature in the making. No better illustration of his catholicity can be found than his esteem for Howells, who was in so many ways the very antithesis of Huneker. And he noted with appreciation the appearance of such ultra-moderns as Edgar Saltus and Carl Van Vechten.

Toward English writers his attitude was always that of a discoverer. Back in 1888—the early date is significant—he was directly responsible for the first appearance in this country of an article by Shaw. He fought for George Moore when Moore was critically anathema in America. He was one of the first American critics to see that Havelock Ellis was something more than a technical psychologist. He hailed the dawn of the Irish Renaissance. He saw merit in James Joyce.

But others might have discovered these men for us. Huneker's special contribution was to make us better acquainted with contemporary continental literature. *Iconoclasts,* which appeared in 1905, was the first piece of criticism in this country to give serious attention to the continental dramatists. It was also the first book by a major American critic to consider the drama as a subject for criticism. His studies in French literature make up a good half of his critical volumes. From Germany he brought back Nietzsche, Hauptmann, Sudermann, Wedekind; from Austria, Schnitzler; from Russia not only the better known men—Tolstoy, Turgeniev, Dostoieffsky, but such unheard of writers in that day as Gorky and Artzibascheff. Merely to list the names of the foreign authors worth knowing with whom he helped to make us acquainted would fill a page.

This is a critical virtue, but it runs close to a critical defect. Huneker liked the thrill of discovery. He had a penchant for the new, the different, the outré. And one feels at times, that like Charles Lamb before him, he liked an author better for not being soiled by the admiration of the crowd. Thus he has been reproached for not keeping his eye fixed on the best things in literature, for preferring a second rate novelty to a greater but better known author. There is some truth in this, but also some justification for the attitude. Huneker wrote at the end of a century of great critical activity. Lowell and Hazlitt and Arnold and dozens of lesser men had already written almost ad nauseam on Chaucer and Shakespeare and Dante; and I suspect Huneker felt that all had been said on the major classics. Thus he deliberately turned to the equally necessary task of widening the literary horizon. I doubt whether he would have bettered Lowell on Spenser, and I am sure Lowell could not have written half so well on Shaw and Conrad. It was part of Huneker's work to correct the tendency of the greater critics to forget that literature was a living thing, that classics were still being written.

Catholicity, catholicism—the words constantly spring to one's lips when one speaks of Huneker. Now catholicity means something more than mental or critical spinelessness. The critic who likes everything is good for nothing. And Huneker, great as was his faculty of appreciation, far apart as were many of the things he liked, was never indiscriminate. His roving spirit paid no attention to the scholastic name-fences that hem in the admirations of lesser men. Classic and romantic, moral and immoral, realist and naturalist, hedonist and puritan—all were one to him, provided the author had something to say and knew how to say it. He could understand all kinds of excellence, but excellence of some kind there must be to win his approval.

For the second-rate, the cheaply sentimental, the unintelligent, the badly-written, he had no use. And even in the authors whom he most liked, he was keen to distinguish between the good and the less good. He smelled sentimentalism in Chopin, deplored the lack of healthy earthiness in "preacher George" Shaw—"Beefsteak, old Scotch ale, a pipe, and Montaigne, are what Shaw needs for one year"—noted the over-symbolism of *The Wild Duck,* soundly castigated Tolstoy for his anti-artistic heresy. He might have written excellent destructive criticism, armed as he was with knowledge, analytic power, humor, and the gift of slashing phrase. But his geniality and his utter lack of the reformer's zeal led him rather to pass over in silence the authors whose crimes outweighed their virtues. What critical fault-finding he did was only for the purpose of separating the real excellence of an author from the weaknesses and errors that block our clear view of that excellence. And it is a tribute to his discrimination that unlike Poe, he never lavished praise on an author undeserving of critical attention.

At the opposite pole of criticism from those critics who like a writer as he approaches some preconceived standard in the critic's mind, Huneker looked at each writer who was worth considering at all, not for resemblances, but for differences. What he wanted in an author was that author's individuality. And like a good critic, he threw logical consistency to the winds, and shifted his point of view from author to author. The essays composing the volume *Iconoclasts* are perhaps the finest illustration in the whole field of criticism of this Protean flexibility of spirit. With Ibsen, we find Huneker talking of individualistic philosophy and the technique of the drama. He turned to Strindberg, and it was Strindberg himself that interested him, the massive, neurotic, tortured soul. The essay on Henri Becque is a rather coldly analytic discussion of characters and themes; the study of Hauptmann warm and humanitarian in tone. Into Shaw he poured volley after volley of arrow-pointed sentences, employing Shaw's own tricks of paradox, verbal gymnastics, wit, surprise. The succeeding essay, on Gorky, is a complete antithesis. Sombre in tone, savoring curiously the profound pessimism of the Russian, it is a fugue on the opening theme, "De profundis ad te clamavi." He praised Sudermann for his technical virtuosity, d'Annunzio for his evocations of passion, Maeterlinck for his twilight mysticism. The very style changed, as Huneker endeavored to accommodate his spirit to that of the author reviewed. A more catholic volume, a volume manifesting appreciation of more varieties of literary excellence, a volume that comes nearer to the critical ideal of judging an author in the light of his own aims, purposes, personality, exists, I think, nowhere.

VIII

From the main currents of American criticism, Huneker stood rather aloof. Some connection he had, as we have noted, with the work of previous American critics. Something of his individualistic attitude was probably derived from Emerson. Much of his attitude toward technical criticism came directly from Henry James, but Huneker consistently avoided the Jamesian restrictions on the range of the critic. At times he veered slightly toward the new humanistic school, ultimately derived from Lowell, and represented in that day by Babbitt and Brownell, though in general his critical attitude was the very opposite of theirs. But the main critical movement of the earlier part of Huneker's critical life was in the direction of dogmatic realism, a movement that, reverting to the methods of the Eighteenth Century, attempted to fix the novel by laying down for it a strict set of literary laws, and by damning all novelists who declined to comply. From the aims and methods of this movement Huneker turned with complete aversion. Not that he was an anti-realist; it was merely that he refused to be bound by the rules of any school of literary art, realistic, naturalistic, veritistic, or what you will. With the rather heavily serious moral attitude of the realistic school Huneker was also in complete disagreement. He represented rather that general tendency toward the liberalizing of literary opinion, both in matters of form and in questions of morals, that we have noted as one of the leading tendencies in American criticism from 1815 on.

Owing to the very nature of his work, its vagueness in theory, its eclecticism of spirit, Huneker left no immediate critical descendants. Traces of his influence can indeed be found in many quarters. His interest in the drama was, I think, one of the many contributing factors in that renaissance of the American drama which began in the nineties and flowered only yesterday. His literary cosmopolitanism left its mark on nearly all succeeding American critics, most notably perhaps on Ernest Boyd, who seems at times a conscious imitator of Huneker. His impatience with moral attitudes in literary criticism has been adopted by the literary radicals of Mr. Mencken's school, men from whom he is in many respects far removed. But in general we may say that Huneker stands as a great critical monolith at the opening of the Twentieth Century.

To understand all schools and to belong to none; to appreciate the good in literature under a thousand varying forms; to experience constant and unwearied delight in reading, and to express that delight, that gusto, in contagious terms; to penetrate, with lightning keenness, the secret of an author's power; to reveal that secret in dazzling and unforgettable phrase—these are the achievements of a great critic. And above all these, to flash constantly upon the reader glimpses of a personality as rare, as fascinating, as that of any author whom he discusses, is to write criticism that is in itself literature. There are moods in which one is disposed to call Huneker the greatest of American critics. This is probably excessive. At any rate, he stands, with Lowell and Poe and James, in the very front rank of American criticism.

Granville Hicks　(essay date 1929)

SOURCE: "The Passing of James Huneker," in *The Nation,* New York, Vol. CXXIX, No. 3364, December 25, 1929, p. 780.

[*Hicks was an American literary critic whose famous study* The Great Tradition: An Interpretation of American Literature since the Civil War (1933) *established him as the foremost advocate of Marxist critical thought in Depression-era America. Throughout the 1930s he argued for a more socially engaged brand of literature but after 1939 sharply denounced communist ideology and adopted a less ideological posture in critical matters. In the following essay, Hicks disputes the reasoning behind Huneker's impressionistic criticism while praising the author for the gusto of his opinions.*]

Reading Huneker's essays today, one feels creeping over one the revolting suspicion that James Huneker, that great iconoclast, godfather of Mencken and all the Menckenites, was nothing but a sort of Hamilton Wright Mabie with a perverse streak of naughtiness and with somewhat better luck in choosing the objects of his enthusiasm. His own heresies seem tame, and the heresies of his chosen supermen take on in his presentation an equal mildness. The *enfant terrible* of the last generation disappears, and in his place we behold a garrulous, gossipy, erudite gentleman with a taste for Pilsner and a gentle fondness for wild men.

This is, of course, ridiculous, and one banishes the suspicion with an apology for ever having allowed it to intrude upon one's consciousness. Huneker was head and shoulders above most contemporary critics. His learning should have made the academicians blush; his perception of the importance of such figures as Ibsen, Huysmans, Strauss, and a dozen others was prompt and unhesitating; the vigor with which he recommended his favorites was sincere and persuasive. While Mabie spouted set speeches on Wordsworth and Longfellow, and commemorated on his White Lists the names of the more trivial and innocuous novels of his day, Huneker was casting his net into the sea of international literature and catching in it real fish instead of minnows.

All this one must gladly grant, and yet it is difficult to assert that Huneker is any less completely dead than Mabie and those other contemporaries above whom, looked at in relation to his period, he looms so vastly. The truth of the matter is that Huneker, whatever he may have been able to say to his own generation, has singularly little to say to ours. It is not very illuminating to learn that Shaw has a sentimental side, that de Maupassant's style is hard but graceful, or that Laforgue was a fantastic chap. (Edmund Wilson, by the way, says more that seems really important about Laforgue in a couple of paragraphs in an essay on another subject than Huneker manages to say in fifteen pages.) There is little coherence in the essays, and there is much repetition. There are few ideas, and those few are seldom developed with satisfying thoroughness and originality. What we do find in the essays is the quality for which Huneker was famed—gusto. He liked what he liked, and he wrote about it with inextinguishable enthusiasm and relish, with much smacking of lips and licking of chops. After reviewing forty or fifty separate works by Brahms, he can still make his adjectives wag their tails in glee; and even his harshest judgments are almost invariably capped with paragraphs of eulogy. His chronicles of his heroes' lives are quite as heartily appreciative as his criticisms, and they occupy rather more space.

But gusto is not enough; in fact gusto, taken by itself, can only become tiring. In sound criticism we respond to a certain force of reason and insight, even when we disagree with particular opinions. Huneker, however, is satisfying only so long as we share his views, and one suspects that his present admirers would be the first to call him an empty fellow if he had praised. Tennyson and Browning instead of Nietzsche and Stendhal. If criticism is to survive, it must be by virtue of the intellectual and imaginative resources of the critic. The adventures of a soul, even among masterpieces, are worth recording only if the soul itself has some intrinsic worth beyond that lent by enthusiasm and erudition.

If Huneker's rejoicings fail to move us today, it is partly because fashions in criticism have changed. This change Mr. Mencken notes in his introduction to the essays, commenting on it with a melancholy made pathetically striking by its setting in the midst of the pyrotechnic glories with which he does honor to Huneker's memory. "All the young critics of today," Mr. Mencken writes, "turn away from his innocent delight in all lovely and amusing things to seek inspiration in the moral sitz-baths of More, Babbitt and Company." And again: "There is a swing back to the pious, intellectual flummery that he abhorred." There is a swing, certainly, whether backward or forward. Not only is Huneker deserted but also Mencken himself; and many of the young critics proceed from Babbitt's humanism to Anglo-Catholicism, Neo-Thomism, and other dogmas from which Huneker would have shrunk in horror. The explanation lies, one cannot but believe, precisely in the inadequacies of the school of criticism of which Huneker was a major representative. The impressionistic critic can explode in a series of ecstasies; he can indulge in a running comment on the virtues of the piece under consideration; he can stray leisurely along the by-paths of biography and gossip; or he can expose the effervescent workings of his own soul. All these performances seem today rather jejune. There is a demand that criticism proceed from a well-stocked mind, from a mind that can recognize implications and tendencies, that can grapple with ideas as well as emotions.

The danger that the pendulum will swing too far is apparent: it is more than a danger; it is almost a certainty. We already have critics who think that a smattering of almost any dogmatic theory is sufficient equipment for the literary life. But at the same time there is a sharpening of perception, a struggle to create standards, an increased attention to the object of criticism instead of the feelings of the critic. Huneker seems stale. We can recognize his capacity for the kind of thing he sought to do, his brilliance, his independence; but his work is seen to be—O, damning phrase!—of merely historical importance.

Van Wyck Brooks   (essay date 1932)

SOURCE: "James Huneker," in *Sketches in Criticism,* E. P. Dutton & Co., Inc., 1932, pp. 230-35.

[*An American critic and biographer, Brooks is noted chiefly for his studies of such writers as Mark Twain, Henry James, and Ralph Waldo Emerson, and for his influential commentary on the history of American literature. In the following essay, Brooks remembers Huneker as a prototypical American writer attracted to European culture.*]

Do you remember the roses in the Luxembourg Gardens,

those roses, at once so opulent and so perfect, that blossom against the grey stone of the old balustrades? But one does not forget them: it is as if in some unique fashion they fulfilled the destiny of all the roses. What one perhaps does forget is the sacrifice they represent. Who can estimate the care lavished upon the organisms that bear those blossoms, which are indeed the fruit of a ruthless and incessant pruning? They have scarcely known what it is to sprawl in the sunshine; every stalk, every tendril has submitted to the most rigorous of disciplines. It is a Spartan life, in short, which those plants have led; all their energy has been canalized to a single end. But what a sumptuous end! A good part of our delight in it springs from our having witnessed there the perfect fulfillment of an intention.

That is the French way, with roses and with artists. Our American way is different. We believe, before everything else—and with reason, heaven knows, considering our laborious history—in "having a good time." For us the leaves and the tendrils have as much right to a place in the sun as the blossoms. But what becomes of the blossoms? They are small, too often, defective and short-lived; for nine-tenths of the energy of the organism has been used up in "living." I am thinking, on the one hand, of those French critics with whom James Huneker invites a comparison, and, on the other, of Huneker himself. The life disclosed in his autobiography, **Steeplejack**—how full it is, how abounding, how generous, and yet, from another point of view, how wasted! Nothing is more appealing about Huneker than his humility. "I have written," he says, "of many things, from architecture to zoology, without grasping their inner substance. I am a Jack of the Seven Arts, master of none." Remembering all we owe to him, we cannot quite accept that protestation; yet it does suggest his status in relation to his own by no means extravagant ideal. Huneker was not an Anatole France, a Jules Lemaître, a Remy de Gourmont, but who will deny that he had the making of one? Where their works were at once so opulent and so perfect, his, on the whole, were defective and short-lived; and this was because of the dissipation of energy to which his autobiography bears witness. Nothing is more touching than the account he gives of his periodical efforts to stop the "leakage of moral gas" in his career; and certainly no one has ever been more conscious of the creative ideal than he. And if one dwells upon this aspect of so rich a life, it is merely because it so perfectly illustrates the American view of art as a by-product of "having a good time."

Huneker, in fact, was an American of the Americans: they waste their breath who attempt to prove that there was anything "foreign" in his love of beer and music, anything exotic in his real fibre. He tells us that his cosmopolitanism "peeled off like dry paint from a cracked wall when President Wilson proclaimed our nation at war." He seems always to have been cheerfully adaptable and happily adjusted to the ways of his country and its beliefs and assumptions. Fully a third of his book deals with his boyhood in Philadelphia; and there was never a boyhood that more fully meets the qualifications of Professor Brander Matthews for a true-blue American critic, namely, that he should have had firecrackers on the proper occasions and played baseball in a vacant lot. His shudders at the memo-

ry, now of the lurid Madame Blavatsky, now of a Black Mass that he witnessed in Paris, his acquiescence in Roosevelt's "amazement" at the fact that, having been in Paris when he was twenty-one, he had not given up his studies and rushed home to cast his first vote, reveal all the ingenuousness of heart, the childlike acceptance of common sense, that mark our countrymen among the peoples of the world. And then there was his inconsecutiveness and his impulsiveness ("I fly off with ease on any tempting tangent, also off my handle"), his breakneck style, his breezy familiarity with all things sacred and profane, his joy in collecting celebrities as a boy collects their autographs, and finally that homesickness for Europe which makes half the charm of his writing—that endowing of everything, philosophic, religious, moral, artistic, so long as it is European, with a rosy veil of romance. Huneker, in fact, was very much, at bottom, the man of the tribe, the *homme sensuel moyen*, both in the general and in the national sense; and, perceiving this, we can understand more readily why he never quite got possession of himself. In retrospect, that engaging personality strikes one as a sort of national symptom.

For one might almost say that Huneker was a scapegoat for the repressions of a desiccated Puritanism. Starve a people too long, fail to educate its eye, its ear, its palate, drive its senses back, tell it to be satisfied with eating straw, to hold its tongue, to ignore its preferences, not to let its fancy stray, not even to have a fancy, to keep its nose to the grindstone, and sooner or later you will have an eruption. Mediævalism had its eruption in Rabelais, Victorian England had its eruption in the art of the eighteen-nineties, the Middle West is having its eruption today in Greenwich Village. Our whole American generation indeed is having its eruption, and Huneker foreshadowed this eruption. One thinks of him as in some way incarnating the banked-up appetite of all America for the colour and flavour, the gaiety and romance, the sounds and smells of Continental Europe, which our grim commercialism, fortified by Mark Twain's humour, had led us to ridicule and decry, and as going forth to devour it like a cake. Huneker, in a word, was Europe-struck, and his gusto and voracity had behind them the momentum of a nation's hunger. And so it was that, although he had grown up in a singularly free and artistically friendly atmosphere, he could not stop and discriminate, but ran about riotously like a kitten in a field of catnip. Everything in Europe was magical to him, Offenbach as well as Mozart, Chartres Cathedral and the Strauss waltzes, the Brussels beer and the graves of the philosophers: it was all just one blazing Turner sunset. America, in fact, in Huneker, was making up for lost time. He fell on his knees and fairly ate Europe, as Nebuchadnezzar in his madness ate the grass.

It is thus that Huneker might be figured in a sketch of the successive phases of America's artistic development. He is our *Yellow Book,* more violent and promiscuous than England's, as our repressions had been greater; and it is difficult not to see him as a victim for all the sins our countrymen have committed against art. "I have no grievances," he says. "I am what I made myself; therefore I blame myself for my shortcomings." A frank and charming attitude, and one for which we honour him, even as we shall continue to enjoy his writings; for he kept to the end the zest of a hungry crow in a newly sown cornfield. Yet we cannot but think how different the results would have been if the sprawling vine of his talent had been planted in a riper soil and had had the right gardeners to tend it. In short, he is one of those barbaric natural forces, incompletely personalized and differentiated, that stand for us in lieu of a literature, and show us how rich we are in the sheer raw material of creative energy. Half of that creative energy is ice-bound, half of it spills over in a tropical exuberance, but it *exists,* awaiting the apparatus of civilization. Meanwhile, to them that love much (even if they love too many, as Heine said), much is forgiven; and who has loved more than James Huneker? "I can love, intensely love, an idea or an art," he remarks. "I am a Yea-Sayer." It is true; and, thanks to this love, he will always seem to us as much a creator as a victim of America.

Eliot G. Fay   (essay date 1940)

SOURCE: "Huneker's Criticism of French Literature," in *The French Review,* Vol. XIV, No. 24, December, 1940, pp. 130-37.

[*In the following essay, Fay focuses on Huneker's reviews of works by such French authors as Gustave Flaubert.*]

Several years ago I attempted a study of American criticism of French literature. I wanted to discover which American critics had written most copiously and most discerningly about the literature of France. I began by excluding from my study, perhaps a little arbitrarily, those writers who appeared to me to be book reviewers or literary historians, rather than critics. And I excluded also those critics whose work, since they were still alive, remained unfinished.

It soon became apparent that almost all the criticism of the kind I had in mind was written between 1865 and the present time. Criticism is one of those literary forms which invariably develop last. First comes the creative impulse, to be followed later by the urge to analyze. Therefore it is not surprising that American writers produced but little criticism of any kind during the Colonial Period. From 1815 to 1865 there were, of course, good critics. But they did not seem much interested in French literature. Emerson's essay on Montaigne, in *Representative Men,* and Lowell's essay on Rousseau, in *Among My Books,* are among the few exceptions to the rule.

After the Civil War a number of able critics turned their eyes toward France. The earliest of these is Henry James, whose book *French Poets and Novelists* appeared in 1878. James was followed by Brander Matthews, author of *French Dramatists of the Nineteenth Century,* published in 1901. Then came James Huneker, with *Egoists,* in 1909, and Irving Babbitt, with *Masters of French Criticism,* in 1912. These are the outstanding American critics of French literature. A secondary list would include Lafcadio Hearn, Vance Thompson, Amy Lowell, and Stuart P. Sherman.

Henry James is the most voluminous American critic of French literature, having contributed to American and British periodicals more than ninety essays on the subject. Brander Matthews is the pioneer in French drama during the second half of the nineteenth century, and the author of an important *Life of Molière.* Irving Babbitt is the official interpreter of French critics. He is also, of course, the chief authority on *Rousseau and Romanticism.* James, Matthews, and Babbitt all practice, however, that kind of criticism which is sometimes called "dogmatic". They assume that life and art are founded on certain definite principles, and that these principles are very clearly perceptible to themselves. A much less sanguine, and therefore far more stimulating, critic is James Huneker. Huneker is always the brilliant impressionist. Like Anatole France in *La Vie Littéraire,* he "relates the adventures of his soul in the midst of masterpieces."

. . . . .

In *Steeplejack,* his autobiography, James Gibbons Huneker states that his mother taught him in his teens "to love the noble literature of Bossuet and of Lacordaire." "I lay the blame on the Exposition of 1879," he says, "for my subsequent running away to Paris." When Huneker left Philadelphia to sail for France he was eighteen. He bought a fourth-class passage on a French Line steamship for the alluring price of twenty-eight dollars. He was going to Paris ostensibly to study music. It was his sojourn there, however, that was largely responsible for his determination to become a critic, not only of music, but also of literature and the other arts.

Upon his arrival in Paris the young man was temporarily overwhelmed. His French, he had already discovered on shipboard, was not the language spoken in France. The Latin Quarter was not the same as that described in Murger's *Vie de Bohème.* Some friends of his parents undertook to show him the city, but in the end their mania for visiting churches irked him beyond endurance. He decided to take matters into his own hands, and rented a room on the top floor of an old house in the Rue Puteaux.

Huneker's room contained a bed, a wash-stand, a wardrobe, a stove, and an antiquated upright piano. He practiced playing from six to ten hours every day. All the other lodgers objected, and one old lady told him that his playing reminded her of the time, eight years earlier, when Paris had been bombarded by the Prussians. In the meantime he was often hungry. On such occasions he would sometimes go to bed and lie there with a heavy volume of Chopin's music on his stomach.

On November 14, 1878, Huneker sent a letter to the Philadelphia *Evening Bulletin.* It was printed, and from then until the following summer he sent a letter to the paper every week. Each letter netted him five dollars. When his monthly check arrived, he would eat his fill of steak *à la Chateaubriand* and Brussels sprouts, accompanied by a bottle of Burgundy wine.

Huneker saw Victor Hugo half a dozen times. He thought him "a commonplace old gentleman, with a white clipped beard and the inevitable umbrella of the prudent Parisian." Hugo usually rode on the top of an omnibus, and was always saluted by bared heads. "It's Monsieur Hugo, the great poet," whispered a conductor as the illustrious Frenchman nimbly mounted to the *impériale*. His eyes alone proclaimed the fire of genius. "They burnt in his head like lamps."

One day, at the Café Sylvain, Huneker spied Guy de Maupassant. The burly young fellow was enjoying a glass of beer. He looked decidedly uninteresting. On another day, in the Rue Saint-Lazare, Gustave Flaubert went striding by. He was "huge, veritable Viking, with the long, drooping mustache of a trooper, and big blue eyes in a large red face."

One of the literary figures whom Huneker found most fascinating was Villiers de l'Isle-Adam. Of him he writes: "He was the greatest liar I ever met. . . . He was an accomplished monologuist, and needed but a vinegar-cruet as an audience." Huneker marvelled at his novel, *l'Eve future,* whose heroine was a woman made of steel springs, and whose hero was no one less than Thomas A. Edison.

Huneker frequented not only the Louvre but also the Trocadéro, being deeply interested in contemporary art. Among the reigning painters in 1878 were Meissonnier, Carolus-Duran, and Cabanel, "whose Venus painted with a brush dipped in soft soap," he says, "may be seen smiling on a couch of sea-foam at the Philadelphia Academy of Fine Arts." He was much impressed by Carolus-Duran, the teacher of John Singer Sargent, "with his velvet jacket, lace collar and cuffs, dark, handsome head, and eyes sparkling with diabolic verve."

Meanwhile poor Huneker was refused admission to the Paris Conservatory of Music. He prepared for his examination by going to church daily for a week. But God declined to overlook his technical shortcomings. "Quelle barbe!" exclaimed one of the ladies present, when he made his first appearance with a fluffy blond beard attached to the end of his chin. He was much too frightened to play his best. Consequently he failed to pass the examination.

A little later Huneker went to Italy to consult the director of the conservatory at Bologna. On the way back to Paris he spent three days in the vicinity of Lake Geneva. There he visited Rousseau's birthplace, the cathedral where Calvin preached, and Voltaire's estate at Ferney. Once more in Paris, he soon deserted it in favor of Auteuil, where he was welcomed by his friend Vance Thompson, the American poet and author of *French Portraits.* Thompson lived in a villa which had been purchased by the great Boileau in 1685. Auteuil had been the home of Benjamin Franklin, and of that Madame Helvétius whom Franklin wished to marry. The place was fraught with memories of Lamartine, Hugo, Balzac, George Sand, Musset, and the Goncourt brothers.

At length Huneker returned to America. In 1886, determined to become a writer, he went to live in New York. But later he revisited Europe many times. And never, up to his death in 1921, did he lose his interest in the poets, dramatists, and novelists of France.

. . . . .

Nearly all of Huneker's essays on French literature first came out in papers like *The Philadelphia Bulletin, The*

New York Sun, and *The New York Times.* Some, however, appeared originally in *The Atlantic Monthly, Smart Set, The North American Review,* and *Scribner's Magazine.* The best were subsequently reprinted, together with other essays, in the many volumes published by the author between 1904 and 1921.

Following, in chronological order, are the names of the volumes that contain Huneker's essays on French literature: ***Overtones, Iconoclasts, Egoists, The Pathos of Distance, Ivory, Apes and Peacocks, Unicorns, Bedouins,*** and ***Variations***. These books include chapters on Balzac, Maeterlinck, Anatole France, Barrès, Huysmans, Stendhal, Baudelaire, Flaubert, Gautier, Verlaine, Bergson, George Sand, and several others less well known. Approximately twenty French writers are discussed. Most of them belong to the second half of the nineteenth century, and more than half are novelists.

"My favorite book," says Huneker, "is ***Egoists***." It is, at any rate, in ***Egoists*** that we find six of the author's most important essays on French literature. It contains chapters on Stendhal, Baudelaire, Flaubert, Anatole France, Huysmans, and Barrès, not to mention Ernest Hello and Francis Poictevin. By studying five of these chapters, beginning with the one on Stendhal, we can obtain some insight into the critic's method as applied to novelists.

Huneker wrote the Stendhal essay thirty years ago, before Henry Beyle was widely known in the United States as one of the great masters of the French psychological novel. He refers to Stendhal as "the most personal of writers," "the Superman of his day," and as "the Paul Pry of psychologists." "The queen of Stendhal women," he affirms, "is Gina, *la duchesse* Sanseverina. . . . That loveable lady, with the morals of a *grande dame* out of the Italian Renaissance, will never die. A more vital woman has not swept through literature since the Elizabethans." But he adds that "love for Stendhal was without a Beyond. . . . (He) left the soul out of his scheme of life. . . . For this reason his windows do not open upon eternity."

Part of Huneker's enthusiasm for Gustave Flaubert resulted from their chance encounter, already mentioned, in the streets of Paris. In his essay he calls Flaubert "the most artistic of novelists" and "a man in love with beautiful sounds." "It is almost touching," he thinks, "in these times when a man goes into the writing business as if vending tripe, to recall the example of Flaubert, for whom art was more sacred than a religion. . . . Dual in temperament, he swung from an almost barbaric Romanticism to a cruel analysis of life that made him the pontiff of the Realistic school. . . . Since *Madame Bovary* French fiction, for the most part, has been Flaubert with variations."

Huneker begins his essay on Anatole France by making the usual comparison with Renan, whose gifts of "irony and pity" France inherited. "Pagan in his irony, his pity wholly Christian, Anatole France has in him," asserts the critic, "something of Petronius and not a little of Saint Francis." "Few writers," he continues, "swim so easily under such a heavy burden of erudition. . . . The full flowering of France's knowledge and imagination in things patristic and archeologic is to be seen in *Thaïs,* a masterpiece of color and construction. A monument of erudition, thick with pages of jewelled prose, *Thaïs* is a book to be savored slowly and never forgotten. . . . Smooth in his transitions, replete with sensitive rejections . . . a lover and a master of large luminous words . . . the very marrow of the man is in his unique style."

Huneker's essay on Huysmans, like the one on Stendhal, was to some extent the work of a pioneer. From the writings of Huysmans, the critic observes, "pessimism is never absent; his firmament is clotted with black stars. . . . The soul in its primordial darkness interests him, and he describes it with the same penetrating prose as he does the carcass of an animal. . . . Of superior interest is (Huysmans') struggle up the ladder to (spiritual) perfection. This painful feat is slowly accomplished in *la Cathédrale, l'Oblat,* and *Lourdes.*"

In his essay on Maurice Barrès, Huysmans first describes that writer's philosophy during the earlier part of his career. "The proper study of Maurice Barrès," according to the critic, "was Maurice Barrès. . . . He boldly proclaimed the *culte du moi.* . . . The impressionism which permeates (*Le Jardin de Bérénice*) is a veritable lustration for those weary of commonplace modern fiction. . . . With the advent, in 1897, of *les Déracinés,* a sharp change in style may be noted. It is the sociological novel in all its thorny efflorescence."

. . . . .

The passages quoted above represent James Huneker's criticism of five French novelists of the nineteenth century. What, having perused these passages, is one to conclude with regard to the critic's grasp of his subject and with regard to the manner in which his impressions are recorded? This is a question which cannot, of course, be answered to the satisfaction of everyone. Moreover it is a problem whose solution is of special rather than of general interest. I believe, nevertheless, that one or two characteristics of Huneker's criticism are easily ascertainable and perhaps worth mentioning.

Anyone who studies the criticism of French literature produced by Henry James, by Brander Matthews, and even by Irving Babbitt becomes aware of a certain element which is totally lacking in the criticism of Huneker. I refer to the tendency, especially marked in the case of Henry James, to introduce into the judgment of a work of art the question of morality. This is something that Huneker virtually never does. For better or for worse he judges a piece of literature on its merits as an artistic production, without regard to whether or not it seems to bolster up this or that preconceived standard of human behavior.

No reader of Huneker's criticism can fail to be impressed with the man's astonishing background. His criticism is, to an extraordinary degree, allusive. In discussing a certain writer he invariably refers to other writers who preceded him. He refers to still other writers, the man's contemporaries, who were working in foreign lands and in foreign languages. Not content with this, he introduces painters and musicians, past and present, domiciled in every country of Europe. Such allusions would be worthless were they culled from an encyclopedia. But in the case

of Huneker one knows that he is perfectly acquainted, through untiring study, with the men and works whereof he speaks.

One of the most remarkable things about Huneker's criticism is his literary style. It is far from possessing the meticulous perfection or the suave urbanity to be found in that of Henry James. It is, however, a forceful style, replete with life and color. It is the style of a man who is not only sensitive to beauty, but who is also able to react to beauty, or to ugliness, with refreshing youthfulness and vigor. Huneker is original, if not always discreet, in his choice of metaphors. He it was who called Brunetiére a "constipated critic," and Bergson "the playboy of western philosophy."

Oscar Cargill   (excerpt date 1941)

SOURCE: "The Intelligentsia," in *Intellectual America: Ideas on the March,* 1941. Reprint by The Macmillan Company, 1948, pp. 399-536.

[*An American educator, historian, and literary critic, Cargill edited critical editions of the works of such major American authors as Henry James, Frank Norris, Walt Whitman, and Thomas Wolfe. In the following excerpt, Cargill examines the novel* Painted Veils *in order to understand the crisis of faith Huneker experienced late in his life.*]

One purveyor of European ideas to Americans in this period was both a cosmopolitan and a man of taste. This was James Gibbons Huneker, the Philadelphia Irishman of whom H. L. Mencken has written so well, not in *A Book of Prefaces,* but in the Introduction to the *Essays* which he selected and edited for Scribner's in 1929. As any one knows who has read *Steeplejack* (1918) or *Painted Veils* (1920), Huneker at the end of his critical and creative life was horribly oppressed by a sense of personal failure. In the autobiography the self-condemnation is complete and abysmal:

> . . . I love painting and sculpture: I may only look, but never own either pictures or marbles. I would fain be a pianist, a composer of music: I am neither. Nor a poet. Nor a novelist, actor, playwright. I have written of many things from architecture to zoology without grasping their inner substance. I am Jack of the Seven Arts, master of none. . . .

This, says Mencken, was "the worst critical judgment in a lifetime of critical judgments." Yet he himself substantially supports Huneker's view of himself when he admits that the critic's chief defect was "excess of eclecticism." The vice was so rare, however, in the latter half of the nineteenth century in America that it is easily forgiven, and we are not inclined to believe that it alone depressed Huneker. The novel *Painted Veils* tells a different story, and to it we turn in our quest for an explanation of the funereal gloom in which Huneker shrouded himself.

Painted Veils is a narrative of the adventures of a young aesthete, "Ulrick Invern, a writer, incidentally a critic," whose well-to-do Irish father was secretary at the American legation in Paris, where Ulrick and his brother Oswald were born. Of this brother Oswald, Huneker has written a short story entitled **"The Supreme Sin"** which appears in that volume largely given over to the praise of Mary Garden, entitled *Bedouins* (1920). Oswald, described as a painter and diabolist in *Painted Veils,* in this short story is duped into attending a black mass at which the officiating priest, Van Zorn, is parent of the girl whom Oswald loves. When, at the height of the ceremony, Diabolus is evoked, what should appear but the beautiful image of his loved one; terrified, the young man saves himself by calling on the Son of Mary, and the vision vanishes. The last we hear of Oswald he is leading the monkish life in the deserts of Arabia. This short story, despite certain capricious involutions, comes directly from a reading of Huysmans. Its simpler outline makes it possible for us, if we are not well read in diabolism, to perceive Huneker's meaning in *Painted Veils*. For whereas the idea that the devil is a woman is treated facetiously in **"The Supreme Sin,"** it is given much more credence in the novel.

Ulrick Invern, brother to Oswald and protagonist in *Painted Veils,* tastes only disillusionment from his sampling of women. Three ladies afford him the gamut of experience: Mona Milton, the marrying kind; Dora, a high-class prostitute; and Esther, or Istar, Brandes, an opera star. Mona, he discovers, loves him only because through him she may have the children for whom she hungers; premature birth, however, kills their illegitimate child, and she, without a pang apparently, gives up Ulrick to marry a rounder who makes her a contented mother. About Dora, Ulrick has no illusions—she loves merely professionally, and one man is as good as another. It is his burning for Istar Brandes, however, that finally destroys him. Over this young woman he presumes he has some sway because he had rescued her from an orgy of a religious sect when she was nobody, but in the end he discovers this is his greatest error. Repulsed by the crowd around her after her triumphant return from Europe and her engagement at the Metropolitan, Ulrick flees to Dora, but is pursued by Istar who takes Dora from him for her own delight, and Ulrick discovers she is the sum of his other two mistresses, a self-centered Lesbian.

One final revelation is necessary, however, before Ulrick fully understands the entire nature of feminine passion. He has had a friend throughout the course of his story, Mel Milton, who has stood by him through thick and thin,—even when Ulrick seduced his sister his friendship remained unshaken. To be sure, Milton, who is studying for the priesthood, is a tedious platitudinarian, but he has the virtue of realizing that he is tedious. Nevertheless he is concerned for his friend's soul. "A woman's heart contains treasures of affection. Don't waste them. . . . I'm a bore, but right is sometimes on the side of the stupid, and victory doesn't always perch on the banners of the intellectually elect." Mel Milton, however, is seduced in the end by Istar Brandes, and Ulrick learns several things in one crowded lesson. First, that his friend whom he has always called Milton is really named Melchizedek (*king of righteousness*) and belongs to the eternal priesthood (see Heb. 7:2). And secondly, when he calls Istar a beast, that lady informs him that she had enjoyed relations with Brother Rainbow, the negro head of the religious cult from which

he had supposed he rescued her, and thus his earliest conjecture (made after reading Reinach's *Orpheus*) that the chief source of religion is fornication, is confirmed. The whole significance of the Melchizedek-Istar relationship dawns on him with paralyzing effect. Istar is Ashtaroth, symbol of all worship, who, when the final veil is removed, is seen to be sexual adoration. This is too much for the idealistic Ulrick who drinks himself to death in Paris.

Ulrick's friends never attribute his death, however, to disillusioned idealism. Alfred Stone, cynical reviewer and acquaintance of Ulrick's, has a theory which is generally accepted. According to this view, Ulrick, whose mind was "a crazy-quilt, mince pie and Chopin," failed to strike root in America because the American spiritual atmosphere was too "tonic" for his decadent ideas. "His *Fleurs du Mal* wilted. So did he. He hadn't the guts to last." Returning to Paris, he died of an evil inherited from his father ("our old enemy, Spirochaeta Pallida, I suspect," Stone sneers). This judgment is superbly ironic to the reader who knows the facts. That reader, however, cannot but see that Ulrick Invern and James Gibbons Huneker are one, and that *Painted Veils* is really an *apologia pro vita sua*—one of the most remarkable ever written. Invern acknowledges the same masters as Huneker: the Goncourt brothers, Huysmans, Gourmont, Barrès, and Nietzsche. Invern, like Huneker, had tried to practice criticism in America; both men were dismissed as fantastic and decadent. The parallels go very far—even down to Huneker's admiration for Mary Garden as a "superwoman" and Invern's early fascination in Esther Brandes. *Painted Veils,* properly appreciated, is a defense of the artist-critic as a misunderstood idealist. Huneker freely acknowledges his absorption in decadence and diabolism—but whither do these paths lead? In a preposterous epilogue Huneker maintains that the thirst of Petronious Arbiter for an absolute in evil (in the popular view the thirst of Invern-Huneker) is the same as the God-intoxicated craving of Thomas à Kempis for the Infinite. "On the vast uncharted map of mysticism extremes may meet, even mingle . . . *Credo quia impossible est . . .*"

Huneker was sixty when he wrote *Painted Veils* and he was dying. He wanted to make his peace with the Church. In his lifetime he had condemned as the seven deadly virtues: humility, charity, meekness, temperance, brotherly love, diligence, and chastity. He had cultivated the seven arts: poetry, music, architecture, painting, sculpture, drama, and dancing. If he wished to save his soul, he must show the course of his life ultimately moral. The path of Petronius and the path of Thomas must merge in the end; the extremes of art and religion must meet somewhere in eternity. Wherefore Ulrick Invern is shown a martyr and Istar becomes "the Great Singing Whore of Modern Babylon"—the United States. But to make his allegory complete and to save his soul Huneker has to adopt a wholly medieval, but thoroughly orthodox, attitude towards woman. She is still the source of evil in the world, and if churchmen are corrupt, it is her influence. The author of Genesis, St. Paul, and Huneker are in agreement about her, but not Jesus and Pope Pius XI. *Painted Veils* is not a pretty book; in fact, it is a rather cowardly book, and we are not surprised that H. L. Mencken is discreetly silent about it. Yet it is an extraordinarily ingenious book: dependent on both Huysmans and Saltus, it is better than either, more neatly patterned, sounder in its knowledge of literature and music, more disturbing in its decadence and diabolism. As a piece of moral writing, it is quite as significant as *Mont-Saint-Michel and Chartres,* though it is inferior to it as prose. Its consequence, so far as Huneker is concerned, is to reveal his perturbation, at the close of his life, not over his eclecticism, but at his lack of moral significance and purpose.

Fortunately, James Gibbons Huneker was little occupied with his immortal soul during the course of his lifetime. There is nothing egocentric about either *Iconoclasts* (1905) or *Egoists* (1909), his most popular critical books, nor in his studies of Chopin and Liszt, nor in *Old Fogy* (1913). There is instead a joyous sampling of whatever the seven arts had to offer to a man of fine sensibility and good breeding. To understand Huneker one has to look into his boyhood home—as exceptional a home for the Philadelphia of the 'sixties as was the Dublin home of Bernard Shaw's childhood. Here congregated the artists and musicians whom his father knew; here flourished the interest in French literature that his mother felt a necessary prerequisite for her conception of his ultimate profession of priest. It is to be doubted if any contemporary of Huneker's read, as a child, not only the sermons of Lacordaire, Bourdaloue, Madame de Swetchine, and Eugénie de Guérin, but also in the works of Pater, Arnold, Swinburne, Rossetti; Poe, Gautier, Rabelais, Montaigne, Goethe, Aquinas, Emerson, Schopenhauer, and Whitman. His runaway flight to Paris (with his parents' connivance) in 1876 seems an inevitable sequel to such a childhood. That he should have come back to teach appreciation of the seven arts to Americans is more of a miracle.

Name almost any important name in art, music, or literature in Scandinavia, Germany, France, or England in the latter half of the nineteenth century, and it is a safe bet that James Gibbons Huneker was the first to write intelligently upon that artist in America. He was the most important early crusader here for Ibsen, Shaw, Sudermann, Hauptmann, Huysmans, Stendhal, Maeterlinck, Richard Strauss, Anatole France, Barrès, Stirner, and Nietzsche. Probably his newspaper articles and his *Promenades of an Impressionist* (1910) did more to clarify in the public mind what the French impressionist painters were up to than the writings of any other critic. He believed Monet one of the greatest men of the nineteenth century, and his commendation of Monet and Cézanne gave both men an immense reputation here. Today, as we survey Huneker's work, we are perhaps inclined to see the influence of the French Decadents predominant in it, but it is doubtful if Huneker, under full sail, was more aware of the wind from that quarter than from Germany, Scandinavia or England. Yet out of two French novels on art—Zola's *L'œuvre* and Goncourt's *Manette Salomon*—Huneker got whatever he had of method in criticism. He aimed at Impressionism, but he had such a lively curiosity about the personalities of his subjects that frequently his criticism amounted to no more than racy gossip, gossip that spread enchantment over whatever he discussed. Mencken says that his talk "made his books seem almost funereal": one has to take

this as hyperbole, for it is incredible that one could talk that much better than these chatty, engaging volumes. Yet Huneker's books are not properly criticism. He was too amiable—as Mencken points out—to do a good job of critical dissection. Repeatedly he calls himself a disciple of Gourmont. "My dear friend and master, the late Rémy de Gourmont," is his tribute in *Bedouins*. But when he was charged with the lack of a unifying theme in *Egoists* and sought to defend himself by claiming that this lack of unity illustrated the practice of "dissociation," he showed that he had no clear idea of Gourmont's principle. If not a critic, James Gibbons Huneker remains the merchant prince of all the importers of European ideas at the turn of the century. Never cordial towards the Russians, whose pessimism and moral depth oppressed him, and overcautious in regard to Americans (Whistler, Whitman, and Poe are all whom he chose to praise), he selected almost unerringly people of real importance to discuss. He was, above everything else, a gifted connoisseur.

Charles I. Glicksberg   (essay date 1951)

SOURCE: "James Gibbons Huneker," in *American Literary Criticism: 1900-1950,* Hendricks House, Inc., 1951, pp. 60-3.

[*An American critic and educator, Glicksberg has written widely on American literature. In the following essay, he criticizes Huneker for not developing a theory of aesthetics upon which to base opinions.*]

Born in Philadelphia on January 31, 1860, Huneker was fortunate in having parents who were sincerely devoted to the arts of music and painting. His early passionate interest in literature precluded the thought of preparing him, as his mother wished, for the priesthood. He studied law for some years at the Law Academy in Philadelphia, but he was not destined for that profession. Unable to shake off his deep passion for the arts, particularly music, he went to Paris, where he studied music at the Sorbonne. There he discovered that he lacked the fundamental talent to become a professional musician. In the meantime, he had developed an appreciation of the beauty and importance of impressionistic art. After returning to the United States, he continued his musical studies and taught the piano for a period of ten years at the National Conservatory in New York City. But it was in journalism that he found his true vocation. From 1891 to 1895 he acted as music and dramatic critic for the *New York Recorder;* from 1895 to 1897 he served as music and dramatic critic on the staff of the *Morning Advertiser.* He worked, too, for such papers as the *New York Sun,* the *New York Times,* and the New York *World.* He ranged far and wide, writing copiously on literary and artistic themes or on any subject that engaged his attention. He traveled frequently to Europe, where he met distinguished personalities in the fields of art and literature and where he gained much of the material that went into the making of his numerous essays and books. His first published book, *Mezzotints in Modern Music,* came out in 1899.

Huneker was constantly under the spur of journalistic necessity, compelled to turn out reams of copy for the printer's devil. Consequently a great deal of his work suffered because it was dashed off hastily, with great vigor but without deep reflection. Another reason for the rapid collapse of his reputation lies in the very qualities that assured him quick recognition during his lifetime: his flamboyant style, his vivid personality, his impressionistic method. A robustious personality, loving life greatly, he is genuinely responsive to every authentic manifestation of beauty and originality. Though he calls himself a steeplejack of the seven arts, he is neither an amiable dilettante nor a journalistic amateur. His talents and his exuberant temperament were admirably suited to perform what he considered the prime function of criticism: to stimulate, to awaken in the reader a desire to return with heightened appreciation and interest to the original work of art.

His work, however, lacks fundamental insight and unity of design. Its impressionistic ardors and ecstasies afforded an excellent medium for the expression of a vital personality. Characteristic of the man is the pride he takes in his iconoclastic assaults, his explorations and discoveries. Though his criticism lacked a central, organic principle, it was suffused by a healthy egotism and a contagious enthusiasm. His critical verdicts are personal opinions, since they are not based on a philosophical foundation; they are no more than the record of his tastes, his temperamental preferences and aesthetic impressions. But he had an enormous hunger for all kinds of experiences, all the varied colors and consummations that life has to offer. His criticism, free from moral preconceptions, is notable for its catholicity, its cosmopolitanism, its air of genial and generous tolerance. Therein undoubtedly lies his salient virtue as a critic. A critic, he contends, must be endowed with the saving quality of humility, so that he will register with devout fidelity the emotions aroused in him by a masterpiece. Whatever other gifts the critic may possess, he must be sympathetic and sincere.

Huneker acquired fame by writing with inexhaustible zest about unrecognized or unknown European geniuses, and succeeded in communicating the distinctive quality that characterized their work. Though he was a splendid purveyor of the best of European culture, his cardinal mistake was that he did not take the work of criticism with sufficient seriousness. Regarding it as preeminently an art, not a science, he had, like Mencken, a profound contempt for most aesthetic theories. A work was beautiful and quiveringly alive, one responded to it intuitively, and that was the ultimate secret and quintessence of criticism.

His impressionistic writing was at least read and made its influence widely felt. Untrammeled by gentility or tradition, he was caught up by the creative turmoil and travail of his time. With soaring rhetoric, cascading wit, and a remarkable capacity for journalistic improvisation, he introduced American readers to a motley band of European artists, musicians, poets, philosophers, and novelists. He penned critical essays on such figures as Hauptmann, Sudermann, Gorky, Nietzsche, Remy de Gourmont, Strindberg, Shaw, Flaubert, Anatole France, Baudelaire, Villiers de l'Isle Adam, Ibsen, Stirner, Cézanne, George Sand, Rodin, Wagner, Walt Whitman, James Joyce,

Huysmans, Verlaine, Conrad, Artzibashev, Degas, Matisse, Renoir, Debussy.

What was signally missing in his work was a principle of evaluation which could distinguish between the first- and the second-rate. If a work was imbued with immense vitality, that was all he cared about. Since he never succeeded in working out a rounded body of aesthetic ideas, he had no theory of criticism to guide him. An arch-individualist, he gave us no more than the history of his soul adventuring among masterpieces. Distrusting the abstract categories of philosophy, he did not put much faith in the analyses dictated by pure reason. Concentrated beauty and the diverse intuitive visions of life embodied in art—these were enough for him. Genius was more important than the counters of logic. Though he realized the danger of impressionism when carried to extremes, he did not always avoid it himself. For example, writing on Huysmans, he pens such a vague sentiment as: "He is the virtuoso of the phrase. He is a performer on the single string of self. He knows the sultry harmonics of passion."

But if he failed to formulate a consistent theory of criticism, a fairly consistent aesthetic *attitude* does emerge from his writing. An uncompromising individualist (though he loved in life to rub shoulders with all sorts and conditions of men), he preferred, in the hieratic realm of the arts, the aristocratic genius, the superman. Altruism and humanitarianism were spurious catchwords. He distinguished between true individualism, which is marked by a state of integrity and enlarged, luminous self-consciousness, and the materialistic self-seeking which often mistakenly passes for individualism.

He was opposed to fiction of a doctrinaire stamp, fiction that was too neatly labeled realistic, naturalistic, sociological, or political. Fiction is fundamentally a fine art. The notion of "democratic" art, he declares irritably, is a snare and a curse. There is only good art. The novel with a purpose lacks validity both as a document and as a work of art. Life and literature must be wedded. Fiction must strike deep roots in the soil of experience. In **"Cross-Currents in Modern French Literature,"** he denounces the blight of provincialism in America, its sterile insularity. There is no excuse for provincialism in criticism.

> "A critic will never be a catholic critic of his native literature or art if he doesn't know the literatures and arts of other lands, paradoxical as this may sound. We lack aesthetic curiosity. Because of our uncritical parochialism America is comparable to a cemetery of clichés."
>
> [Huneker, *Unicorns*]

Huneker probably drew his own portrait, with mock-seriousness, in **"The Critic Who Gossips."** It begins, significantly enough, with this confession: "He has a soul like a Persian rug." This gossip-ridden type of critic is fonder of anecdotes than of history. Huneker himself achieved no coherent philosophy of life and with the exception of *Painted Veils* and *Steeplejack,* his autobiography, he produced no single, unified book. In reply to the charge preferred by Percival Pollard that he bowed before the idols of European culture and neglected American culture and art, he asserted that he had gained his living for nearly four decades by writing about the painting, music, literature, and sculpture of his countrymen. Yet the names he is most proud of, the writers with whom he corresponds most frequently, were not Americans but Europeans—English, Celtic, German, French, Scandinavian. All the arts won his hearty allegiance. Because of his rich technical knowledge and capacity for appreciation he could compare not only the literatures of various countries but also the different arts, persevering in his efforts to achieve a synthesis of the seven arts and to interpret one art in terms of another.

His criticism flowed from the richness and vitality of his temperament, but as an impressionist he had no critical ideas of importance to propound and no sound method to formulate. Subjective in his criticism, he denied that criticism was equipped to solve any literary problems. The critic, even at his best, can no more help being prejudiced than he can jump out of his own skin. Beyond setting down the emotions aroused in him by a masterpiece he cannot hope, and should not try, to go. He should concern himself with the technical accomplishment of a work of art, its mastery of form and perfection of style, but even here Huneker did not care to be consistent. Mencken insists that the younger critics owe Huneker a great debt of gratitude for clearing the ground of the rotting lumber of the old criticism.

Arnold T. Schwab   (essay date 1957)

SOURCE: "James Huneker's Criticism of American Literature," in *American Literature*, Vol. 29, No. 1, March, 1957, pp. 64-78.

[*In the following essay, Schwab surveys Huneker's critical writings on American authors, including Walt Whitman, Henry James, and Theodore Dreiser.*]

American critics and literary historians have generally accepted the notion that James Gibbons Huneker was largely indifferent to the literature of his own country. He was, to be sure, primarily interested in writers whose ideas and methods were of world-wide significance or whose temperaments appealed to him; many of these happened to be European. To maintain, however, that he was oblivious to the literary scene at home and to the talents of American authors is to perpetuate an injustice that disturbed Huneker and has long deserved correction.

Since he reprinted in his numerous collections a total of only six essays on American writers of belles lettres, one article on the American novel, and a few passages dealing with American literature, one must examine the New York newspapers and magazines in which much of his writing is buried to learn the full extent of Huneker's interest in that literature. Especially revealing are the files of the *Musical Courier* from February, 1889, to October, 1902, during which period he wrote a weekly column of miscellaneous criticism headed "The Raconteur." The newspapers on which he worked for thirty years—the *Recorder, Morning Advertiser, Sun, Times,* and *World*—also contain a sizable body of opinion on American literature, as does his department, "The Seven Arts," in *Puck* (1914-1917).

The gentility of the 1890's was regnant when Huneker, something of a Bohemian in private life and a sophisticate in literary taste, attacked "morality yowlers" such as Elbridge Gerry and Anthony Comstock, whom he ridiculed, for example, in the *Morning Advertiser* on April 3, 1896. On September 8, 1897, he poked fun at moralistic critics like Maurice Thompson (*Musical Courier*), and on December 19, 1900, he protested against the "simpering attenuations and Miss Nancy reticences" of American novelists (*MC*). "The eradication of the Puritan microbe will be no easy task," he wrote on October 5, 1996, "taught as we are in our arid schools and universities that the entire man ends at his collar bone" (*Times*). But Huneker was not always pessimistic; on August 21, 1895, for example, he remarked that "artists like Henry Fuller, Mary Wilkins and a few others [were] pointing the way to one of the richest literary finds in the world, for remember the United States is yet undiscovered" (*MC*).

It appears that Huneker was thoroughly familiar with the work of Poe, Whitman, Clemens, Howells, and Henry James. He was always proud that Poe, an acquaintance of Huneker's father and his first literary idol, had played so important a part in European letters. On December 21, 1892, Huneker compared Poe and Chopin at length, deplored the waste of Poe's talent in the commercial America of his time, commented on the lack of impurity or licentiousness in his writings, described his personality and temperament, and briefly traced his influence on Continental literature (*MC*). On November 1, 1893, five months after the publication of the results of a poll sponsored by the *Critic,* which revealed that no book by Poe had been included among the ten greatest books published in America, nor among the thirty-nine which received the highest number of votes, Huneker wished that America would appreciate Poe as much as France did (*MC*). On February 27, 1901, he stated that Poe was "the victim of Yankee college professors who found him lacking the patriotism of Whittier, the humor of O. W. Holmes, the sanity of Lowell and the human qualities of Longfellow!" (*MC*). On May 8 of the same year he exulted that Emerson's "jingle man" was the "best known . . . abroad of any American author, his works the most translated" (*MC*), while on September 17, 1902, he lauded James A. Harrison's important edition of Poe (MC), whom he discussed again on December 29, 1906 (*Times,* Book Review).

As a young man, Huneker was so impressed by *Leaves of Grass* that he once called on Whitman in Camden in 1878; later he occasionally encountered the poet outside Philadelphia's Academy of Music after a concert and escorted him to the Camden ferry street-car. In 1887 Huneker publicly praised Whitman's frankness, though he had reservations about the poems. On May 13, 1891, he listed Whitman among the great personalities then living in America. "[He] represents a primal force," Huneker wrote, "but in the best of [his] work, despite its rugged sincerity, there is always an unfinished quantity" (*MC*). On the following November 1 a long, complimentary article on Whitman by Huneker appeared in the *Recorder;* here he condemned America's neglect of Whitman, deprecated the "violently unfair" attacks made against him, praised his "peculiar magnetic qualities," and briefly discussed his poetry.

Whitman, he concluded, was "one of the greatest natural forces in American literature". It was essentially this article, I believe, that Huneker referred to when he recalled in 1911 that he had written Whitman's obituary for the New York *Home Journal;* a search in the latter publication—for which Huneker occasionally wrote about the time he was on the *Recorder*—reveals no such obituary that can be identified as his. (The Huneker Collection at Dartmouth College contains an unlabeled clipping of what seems to be the *Recorder* article, with marginal corrections and additions in Huneker's handwriting, one of which reads: "The poet lies at death's door in Camden, N. J." This suggests that he revised the November 1 piece—perhaps when Whitman was critically ill in late December, 1891—intending to use it as an obituary; it may have been put aside when the poet lingered on for several months. The unsigned obituary which appeared in the *Recorder* on March 27, 1892, is probably not Huneker's).

By July 13, 1898, however, Huneker had reacted against Whitman. He still felt that some of the poems—"When Lilacs Last in the Dooryard Bloom'd," "Rise O Days from Your Fathomless Deeps," "O Captain! My Captain!," "Give Me the Splendid Silent Sun," and certain passages from "Song of Myself"—were "the finest things America has given to the nations"; but he now believed that the "slush, trash, nonsense, obscenity, morbid eroticism, vulgarity and preposterous mouthings well nigh spoil one's taste for what is really great in *Leaves of Grass.* . . ." He called Whitman "a poseur of gigantic . . . proportions" and maintained that "despite his roaring masculinity, [Whitman] had a streak of the effeminate in him" (*MC*).

The remark about Whitman's sexuality suggests that Huneker had become convinced by his reading of studies by various writers that Whitman was an invert. The eccentricities of the artistic personality had long fascinated Huneker, and he had steeped himself in the literature of abnormal psychology. As far as I can discover, he was the first *American* critic to refer openly to Whitman's homosexual leaning. He was more explicit on November 21, 1914—after the publication of monographs by Bertz and Rivers—when he observed that passages in *Leaves of Grass* "fully warrant unprejudiced psychiatrists in styling this book the bible of the third sex" (*Puck*). It was this side of Whitman—together with the latter's optimistic faith in the masses, which Huneker thought naive—that seemed to antagonize the generally tolerant critic. The exact nature of Whitman's sexuality is still, of course, a major crux, but though Huneker probably implied more about the poet's habits than the evidence supports, he undoubtedly helped to focus attention on an aspect of Whitman which subsequent American critics, following the work of Continental scholars like Catel and Schyberg, have not been able to ignore.

A far more representative American than Whitman, Huneker thought, was Mark Twain, most of whose best work had been completed before Huneker began to criticize American literature. Though he frequently quoted the humorist's quips and anecdotes, he realized that Twain was more than a mere funny-man. "Mr. Clemens is one of the most original writers that America has produced and more of an artist than is generally believed," he remarked on June 28, 1899. "The public was slow to recognize his power in fields [other than humor]. I pin my faith to *Huckleberry Finn.* For me it is the great American novel, even if it is written for boys" (*MC*).

Huneker frequently mentioned or quoted William Dean Howells. On January 30, 1901, for example, he heartily seconded Howells's attack on historical romancers and echoed the older critic's plea for realistic fiction (*MC*). "There are only two schools of writers," Huneker wrote on the following May 29th, "—those who know how to write and those who do not. Mr. Howells belongs to the former" (*MC*). By this time Huneker had forgotten that on January 22, 1896, he had wistfully recalled the "love, lust and cruelty . . . and power" in Howells's early international novel, *A Foregone Conclusion,* written, Huneker said, when Howells's world was not "bounded by backyards" (*MC*).

On April 5, 1903, however, in one of his most important uncollected essays on American literature, Huneker took issue with Howells's famous statement concerning the tragic note in American fiction. American life *was* full of tragedy, Huneker maintained, but our novelists and dramatists were avoiding the dark issues. Yet Howells himself, Huneker explained, was not

> strait-laced, prudish, narrow in his views, but he puts his foot down on the expression of the tragic, the unusual, the emotional. With him, charming artist, it is a matter of temperament. . . . Mr. Howells, with his jewelled art, his miniatures of men and women, his delicate phrasing of elemental truths, has influenced his juniors more than he knows. But where he is reticent, they are flabby, where he paints with sure though dainty touches, their pictures are faded, insincere.

> *(Sun)*

Though Howells seemed old-fashioned to the younger generation—which, to be sure, was encouraged by Huneker to expect stronger meat in fiction—Huneker continued to admire him:

> Compare the so-called "realistic" novels of Mr. Howells . . . with the fiction of the moment [he wrote on August 12, 1910]. What a falling off. . . . To the Jack Londons who are carrying off the sweepstakes of fiction Mr. Howells is no doubt a superannuated writer. Would that there were more like Mr. Howells in the continence of his speech, in the nobility of his ideals, wholesomeness of his judgment, and delicacy of perception of character.

> *(Sun)*

On January 2, 1915, Huneker advised readers and writers to "return to the fiction of Mr. Howells and there learn sense of proportion, continence of expression, the art of exquisitely simple prose, and vital characterization." "It will be to his novels," Huneker added, "that the historians will go for a truthful study of men and women and manners during the last quarter of the Nineteenth Century in

New England and elsewhere and not to the vermillion prose of the present crowd of melodramatists between covers . . ." (*Puck*). On July 16, 1916, he again paid his respects to Howells in an article on "The Great American Novel," which brought him a letter from Howells, who had discussed the same subject four years earlier. (Huneker came to the same conclusion: there could be no such thing as *the* great American novel; it would be "in the plural—thousands perhaps." "Native talent, subtle and robust, we possess in abundance," he wrote. "Thus far it has cultivated with success its own parochial garden—which is as it should be" [*Times*].)

Huneker probably put his finger on the most important reason for the decline of Howells's reputation as a novelist when he gently disagreed with him on the question of tragedy in this country. "Years ago," Huneker remarked on August 29, 1915, "Mr. Howells said we could never write of America as Dostoievsky did of Russia, and it was true enough at the time; nor, would we ever tolerate the nudities of certain Gallic novelists. Well, we have, and I am fain to believe that the tragic issues of American life should be given fuller expression . . ." (*Times*). Today the concern with the tragic vision and the obsession with evil have operated against Howells. Huneker seems to have foreseen something of this trend, just as he emphasized those qualities which may eventually produce a Howells revival: the comprehensiveness and faithfulness of his portrait of America.

Another American, whose revival is one of the most remarkable facts of our literary history, outranked Howells in Huneker's estimation. More than forty years before the rediscovery of Henry James, Huneker was proclaiming him America's greatest contemporary novelist and perhaps her keenest critic. He devoted more space to James than to any other American writer, and probably quoted him more often than any novelist except Flaubert.

By the mid-nineties the popularity James had won with *Daisy Miller* and *The Portrait of a Lady* had practically vanished, leaving him only a small cult of readers. Yet on September 25, 1895, Huneker wrote that "our greatest artist lives in London. When he publishes we poke fun at his exquisite style and cadenced prose. I mean, of course, Henry James" (*MC*). On the following January 1 Huneker, who, despite his antipathy to socialism, had hobnobbed with East Side radicals and was exceedingly well-read on the subject of anarchy—he later wrote editorials on it for the *Sun*—singled out the poorly received *The Princess Casamassima* as James's masterpiece thus far (*MC*). On March 17, 1896, Huneker remarked that *The Spoils of Poynton* was "full of humanity and delicate strokes of art and observation," although its theme was "caviare to the general reader" (*MC*). On the following December 9 Huneker defended the expatriated novelist against charges of "un-Americanism":

It is so convenient [he wrote] to say of Henry James that . . . American men interest him not, American women delight him not. Yet what American writer has given us such absolutely tempting and truthful national types? . . . The master of living American novelists, I am tempted to say the greatest of American fictionists until I remember Hawthorne, sits serenely at his desk in London and writes perfect prose and carves for us the Americans at home and abroad.

(*MC*)

Year after year Huneker reviewed James's novels. *What Maisie Knew* was the "masterpiece of the season," he wrote on December 1, 1897, "surely the most remarkable analysis of a child's soul the world has ever enjoyed" (*MC*). Mentioning James's *The Other House* in the same article, he disagreed with those who deprecated James's choice of subject rather than criticizing the execution of the work. On October 19, 1898, Huneker noted that "In the Cage" was "a miracle of workmanship" though slight in theme and curiously involved in style (*MC*). Two months later *The Two Magics* won his unqualified praise; frankly admitting, on December 14, that he did not fully understand the allegory in "The Turn of the Screw," he commented: "Never in the history of the supernatural has such a story been written. . . . Anything more morbid would be hard to conceive. Yet the treatment is never morbid; it is uplifting, almost comforting, and comfort the reader needs . . ." (*MC*). On February 26, 1902, Huncker stated that James took "the purely physical point of view" for his thesis in *The Sacred Fount,* and that the reviewers of the book feared to look the "Jamesian proposition squarely in the eye" (*MC*).

On September 24 of the same year, Huneker wrote at length on *The Wings of the Dove*, indicating his awareness of James's accomplishments in technique:

All the old time conventional chapter endings are dispensed with; many are suspended cadences. All barren modulations from event to event are swept away—unprepared dissonances are of continual occurrence. There is no descriptive padding—that bane of second class writers; nor are we informed at every speech of a character's name. The elliptical method Mr. James has absorbed from Flaubert. . . . Nothing is forestalled, nothing is obvious and one is forever turning the curves of the unexpected; yet while the story is trying in its bareness, the situations are not abnormal.

He acknowledged, entertainingly, that the novel was not easy to read: "The style is crackjaw—a jungle of inversions, suspensions, elisions, repetitions, echoes, transpositions, transformations, neologisms, in which the heads of young adjectives gaze despairingly and from afar at verbs that come thundering in Teutonic fashion at the close of sentences leagues long." But Huneker believed that the reward was eminently worth the effort, and he concluded prophetically: "It is fiction of the future: it is a precursor of the book our children and grandchildren will enjoy when all the hurly-burly of noisy adventure, of cheap historical tales and still cheaper drawing-room struttings shall have vanished from fiction" (*MC*).

After James's death, Huneker eulogized him on June 24, 1916, commented on the influence of his fiction, lamented his neglect in America, and again predicted that time would right the injustice (*Puck*). Though Huneker maintained here that "a Puritan tempered by European culture" lurked in James, he decided, by the following December 17, that James did not possess the New England conscience, that he should not be identified with the cases he studied, and that he was actually our "first great unmoralist" (*Sun*). Less than a year before his own death, Huneker twice reviewed James's posthumously published letters.

Of the American writers of his own generation, Huneker gave most attention to Edgar Saltus, Henry B. Fuller, and Edith Wharton. Judging from their present reputation, he seems to have overrated the once popular Saltus and Fuller. On May 10, 1899, he reviewed Mrs. Wharton's first book, *The Greater Inclination,* noticing her indebtedness to Henry James but finding also in these short stories a "very neat, telling style of her own" and a delicate sense of humor; he thought that some day she would write a "strong novel" (*MC*). He was disappointed by her first novelette, *The Touchstone;* her characterization, formal sense, and psychology were at fault, he observed on May 2, 1900, and her style too much like James's (*MC*). In 1905 Huneker seemed to like *The House of Mirth,* though ten years later, on May 8, 1915, he called it her "least artistic work" (*Puck*). A section of an essay in **Ivory Apes and Peacocks** deals with Undine Spragg, the disagreeable heroine of *The Custom of the Country* (1913). And on November 7, 1920, Huneker praised Mrs. Wharton's evocation of the New York of the 1870's in *The Age of Innocence* (*World*).

As for the younger writers, Huneker knew Stephen Crane for some years, but a careful search has failed to uncover any evidence that he reviewed Crane's books. Yet their friendship did not prevent the critic from publishing—on August 3, 1898—what he identified as a reprint from the Buffalo *Enquirer* but what may actually be an original parody (it could not be found in the newspaper) of Crane's colorful war correspondence (*MC*). On June 13, 1900, shortly after Crane's death, Huneker described his friend as "a good fellow and a promising writer. Without the sustained power or formal gifts of Frank Norris, [he] would nevertheless have made a strong book some day." Huneker did Crane a service by recommending here an *Evening Sun* article by Acton Davies as the most authoritative account of Crane's much-maligned personality (*MC*).

Huneker greeted Frank Norris's *McTeague* more cordially than most American critics did. Norris, he observed on July 12, 1899, was

> a realist and employs the Zola tonality, but he will grow away from the note-taking bird's-eye view school and touch the hem of higher issues. Of all the young American writers he has the keenest vision and a strong, natural style. . . . The book has its shocking, even its coarse pages,

but the humor, so grim, so hearty, so Rabelaisian, redeems them. . . . Norris is bound to make a stir.

> (*MC*)

On April 10, 1901, Huneker remarked that *Moran of the Lady Letty, Blix,* and *A Man's Woman* were all clever but unfinished sketches, but with *The Octopus* Norris had "partially fulfilled" his promise. It was the "biggest novel of the purely American type" since *The Rise of Silas Lapham,* he said, and indeed Norris had "a temperamental force, an exuberance of imagination, a swing that Mr. Howells never possessed." Despite its faults—too much blood-spilling, an ending marred by political polemics, unnecessary length, and obvious traces of Hardy, Tolstoy, and Zola—Huneker believed that the book placed its author in the front rank of fiction writers (*MC*). He corresponded with Norris and continued to laud his work.

Although I have not been able to find it, Huneker claimed that he wrote a favorable review of Theodore Dreiser's *Sister Carrie,* which, he said, had been sent to him by Norris. For "sheer similitude," Huneker remarked on June 27, 1914, the novel had "no equal in American fiction" (*Puck, LXXV,* 21), and on November 5, 1916, he stated that Dreiser had not excelled his portrait of Carrie (*Sun*). At Dreiser's request, Huneker read the manuscript of *Jennie Gerhardt* in 1911 and suggested various changes:

> It's a big book [he wrote Dreiser]. . . . I'm not yet certain whether I like it better than *Sister Carrie.* . . . What made me happy while reading it was the fact that it attempted to prove nothing. . . . A moving and vivid picture of life, nothing else. . . . Your story is very human, simply conceived, probable, sympathetic—though not invariably well-told. Your prose style is still opaque, moves too slowly, lacks rhythmic variety; and is too "literary". . . . Despite this handicap the story shines through; the characterization is masterly—hard to beat—the sequence of events logical. Your fashionable women are not well realized. I like Lester's brother—the real, cold American business man, hard as nails. . . . To make an essentially weak girl sympathetic, without pulling out all the lachrymose stops of pity and indignation, is a difficult undertaking. Of course, there will be a yowl of woe from the dyspeptic moral critics. With a few exceptions you have kept your hands off the girl and not disfigured the book by moralic reflections. But these exceptions spring to the eye and they made me groan. . . . It interrupts the swing of the narrative. . . . Another bad thing, perhaps the most offensive (to me, understand) in the book is your *epilogue.* Again, in the name of Flaubert and Maupassant, why? Your ending, on what musicians would call a suspended harmony, is superb. . . . Don't spoil [it] for the sake of moralizing no matter how symmetrical or ethical that moralizing may be. Your story ends there. Let it end there. . . . There is page after page in *Jennie* that recalls the best of the Russians. I admire your courage in tackling such a purely American theme, and giving it such a dreary setting. . . . Local color is perfect. . . . Again I say a big book, eloquent in

its humanity, *too long;* too many repetitions (you ride certain words to death, such as *big*), and the best fiction I have read since that of Frank Norris.

Dreiser said that he followed some of Huneker's suggestions, though he retained part of the epilogue; when the novel was eventually reprinted, however, the epilogue was dropped.

Huneker apparently wrote no notice of *Jennie Gerhardt,* and he was living in Europe when Dreiser's third novel, *The Financier,* was published. But on June 3, 1914, he informed Dreiser that he had just read *The Titan*—which Dreiser had sent Huneker at the latter's request—and that he had reviewed the "powerful book" for *Puck.* "I find Frank C. Y. [*sic*] a bit older," he wrote Dreiser, "a little heavier in the going—but that's a tribute to your time sense and the atmosphere of characterization. I look for the no. 3 of the trilogy. Emilie-Berenice promises a rare development. Keep it up old man! You've won, even if you will 'do' those terrible epilogues and moral codas!" "Before he sails," Huneker added, "I shall get *The Titan* and *The Financier* to Georg Brandes . . ." (then visiting America). The review of *The Titan* appeared on June 27:

> Dreiser is a master of numbers, crowds, confusion, and swarming cities. . . . [He] captured the precise air of Philadelphia, and in his new book he suggests the raw Chicago of the seventies and eighties with exactitude. . . . He dots his i's and crosses his t's; yet with all the crass realism, there is a bigness about the work which overshadows its petty faults. The height, depth, breadth, and mass of this ugly, but very significant and modern fictional architecture may repel at first, but in the end impresses by sheer sincerity
>
> (*Puck*).

Huneker thought much less of Dreiser's next novel, *The "Genius."* It was far too long, he maintained on February 12, 1916, and its hero a "shallow bore" and a "wooden Indian as to character after he leaves the Middle West to settle in New York" (*Puck*). Dreiser was "without an ear for prose or an eye for form," Huneker wrote their mutual friend Mencken on the following April 11. After Mencken had urged him, several months later, to defend Dreiser against charges of obscenity, Huneker responded on November 5 by remarking that *The "Genius"* was "moral to the sermonizing point" (*Sun*). Believing that the only immoral book was a badly written one, he could not wholeheartedly join Mencken's crusade despite his dislike of censorship. This may have led to a coolness between Huneker and Dreiser, for a passage printed in the serialized version of *Steeplejack,* but omitted in the book, was rather sharp:

> Dreiser we must accept with his faults full-blown. He is dull yet powerful at times. Israel Zangwill was right when he called *Sister Carrie* the best fiction of that year over here. *Jennie Gerhardt* is more individual. . . . Since then his uncompleted Trilogy . . . and *The "Genius"* have not put *Jennie Gerhardt* in the background, though *The Titan* is potentially big. I agree with

H. L. Mencken that Dreiser's *A Hoosier Holiday* is the most readable of his books. Nevertheless the Zola influence is not to be denied, it has mortised his work with materialism. Theodore Dreiser has a ponderous style and he lacks vision.

> [Philadelphia *Press*]

Huneker's criticism of many minor American short-story writers, essayists, and especially novelists was extensive, if usually brief. On December 9, 1896, for example, he found fault with the style of the veritists and disagreed with their delineation of the American type; (*MC*); novels dealing with rural characters and written in dialect had little attraction for him. Yet on April 28, 1897, he praised Mary Hartwell Catherwood's *The Spirit of an Illinois Town* (*MC*). Distrusting reformers, indifferent to politics except for his aversion for socialism, and opposed to polemic tracts in the guise of fiction, Huneker naturally had little sympathy for the Muckrakers, and his attack on Upton Sinclair, Jack London, and others of this group, printed in the *Sun* on September 23, 1908, is one of his most outspoken articles on American literature:

> The "new" novelists [he wrote] may write more carefully than the Beadle school—though we doubt it—but they still deal with the same raw material, the material of cheap melodrama. Their handling of love episodes has much of the blaring brass band quality—and quantity—of old fashioned Italian opera. . . . Our gay mud slingers only think of raising an immediate row. Success for them means a vilely written book of socialistic farrago, full of the crimes of the rich and the virtues of the poor.

On August 12, 1910, he again ridiculed the fiction of popular "lay preachers" (*Sun*).

If Huneker did not criticize American verse at length during the nineties, he nevertheless directed his readers to some of the best poets of a rather barren period, chiefly by reprinting poems in "The Raconteur." On December 9, 1891, for example, he reprinted Emily Dickinson's "I'm Nobody! Who Are You?" with the comment that she had "a delicacy of expression like Chopin's . . . and her soul, timidly ardent and coy in color, repressed itself within the bounds of a few shyly passionate phrases that are as fragmentary as Sappho's, but nearly as precious" (*MC*). Edwin Arlington Robinson's "Luke Havergal" headed Huneker's column as early as June 8, 1898 (*MC*), and poems by Richard Hovey, Lizette Woodward Reese, and William Vaughn Moody appeared there around the turn of the century. Later, however, Huneker, whose taste in poetry was formed in the heyday of Swinburne and the Pre-Raphaelites, was not sympathetic toward the free verse movement. Whitman's "jigsaw jingle," he stated on January 2, 1921, "the speech of a man with the hiccoughs, . . . is imitated the land over by the younger, hoarser choir, with the result . . . that a new school of poetry and prose (?) has been founded in which epilepsy and sterility are the dominating characteristics" (*World*).

Huneker's important criticism of American playwrights is far too extensive to be discussed here; as a New York drama critic for at least eight years—on the *Recorder,*

Morning Advertiser, Sun, and the *Metropolitan Magazine* (with occasional comments on the theater in *Puck*)—he wrote countless columns on Herne, Gillette, Thomas, Fitch, Belasco, Moody, and lesser-known American dramatists. Likewise, I can only mention as evidence of his interest in American literary criticism his friendship with and praise of many of his colleagues—Percival Pollard, Vance Thompson, Brander Matthews, William C. Brownell, George Jean Nathan, and H. L. Mencken.

I do not wish to exaggerate the scope of Huneker's criticism of American literature. The best of it was generally restricted to novelists flourishing around the turn of the century; a systematic approach to the major figures in the entire range of our literature is not to be discovered in his essays. Moreover, his prejudice against some New England writers—salutary as it may have been when Longfellow, Whittier, Holmes, and Lowell were considered the equals of Emerson, Hawthorne, and Thoreau—disqualified him as an objective critic of the main stream of the American literary tradition. And his aristocratic bias and generally conservative taste in poetry prevented him from doing full justice to Whitman and the free-verse school.

Within his limits, however, and particularly in his special province, the contemporary novel, Huneker was remarkably perceptive and prophetic. Very few of his American swans turned out to be geese; recent criticism has largely confirmed his judgment of Howells, James, Norris, and Dreiser. This, I submit, is no mean achievement for a critic—and especially for one allegedly oblivious to the writings of his countrymen. Surely it is time that our literary historians dispelled the legend of James Huneker's indifference to American literature.

Annette T. Rottenberg   (essay date 1965)

SOURCE: "Aesthete in America: The Short Stories of James Gibbons Huneker," in *Studies in Short Fiction,* Vol. II, No. 4, Summer, 1965, pp. 358-66.

[*In the following essay, Rottenberg assesses the short stories by Huneker collected in the volumes* Melomaniacs, Visionaries, *and* Bedouins.]

In 1964 **Painted Veils,** The only novel which Huneker ever wrote, appeared in a paperback reprint as a "classic of American realism," the sign of a belated revival, perhaps; but the short stories, collected in **Melomaniacs** (1902) and **Visionaries** (1905), as well as a few in **Bedouins** (1920), have never been reissued and remain virtually forgotten and unread. Mencken, who thought Huneker unequalled as a critic of music and literature, might have said deservedly so—"I can see no great talent for fiction *qua* fiction in these two volumes of exotic tales," (a judgment with which Huneker, with his proverbial modesty and good humor, agreed, although he could not forbear calling these books his favorites, precisely "because they were despised and rejected.") But there were other verdicts, among them those of Frank Norris, who praised them, asserting that Huneker had achieved "originality without grossness," and Benjamin De Casseres, an extravagant admirer of Huneker in everything, who compared him to

Baudelaire, Laforgue, Poe, and D'Aurevilly. Neither Mencken's indifference nor De Casseres' exaggeration is altogether just. It is true that the reader who looks for "a classic of American realism" in these fifty-odd short stories will be disappointed, but he will discover instead the charm of anachronism, enlivened by the presence of gifted and eloquent creatures whose habitats are the salon and the studio and by flights of invention which encompass the metaphysical, the playful, and the horrific.

Today Huneker has a small but justifiable claim on the student of American literary history. Standing outside the main stream, he anticipated ideas and aesthetic developments of subsequent generations—a fact which becomes increasingly evident as the tenets of naturalistic realism give way. There is nothing in these stories to suggest that he was contemporary with Crane, Norris, Howells, or Dreiser, although he is related to James and Wharton. His antecedents are not Balzac or Turgenev. (He tried to imitate Flaubert, but pessimism and the depiction of social reality were not his forte.) Among the realists, he is a fabulist and a romantic; among the naturalists, a neo-gothic fantasist. Almost alone among American writers, he links us with the aesthetic movements of France and England.

In America there were virtually no echoes of the *fin-de-siècle* voices which had spoken with such authority and influence first in France and then in England. Huneker, a professional advocate and interpreter of European music, painting, and literature, was in an ideal position to exploit in his own fiction the "aesthetic satanism" of the Continent, a vision characterized by preoccupation with (though not necessarily belief in) the existence of sin, the denial of Christ, demonology and the occult, woman as a manifestation of ancient and preternatural forms of corruption, the three-sided relationship between art, madness, and depravity.

Mencken's word *exotic* explains, at least in part, the appeal of Huneker's gothic tales. (". . . grotesque, bizarre, satanic, Latin to the mirror," said De Casseres, "endowed with a forbidden and blasphemous beauty.") [*James Gibbon Huneker*] The ideas which absorbed Huneker were rarely handled by American writers of the period. One large group of stories—in which we recognize the shades of *The Monk*—concerns spiritual corruption among members of the clergy who engage in the study of esoteric doctrine. They are drawn not toward worldliness but toward pagan cults, indecent rituals, and worship of the Antichrist. In a second group of stories Huneker attempts to dramatize what might be called the gospel of the East as expounded by Nietzsche (a gospel which has lately been treated with profound seriousness by Herman Hesse.) "There can be nothing good, as we know it, nor anything evil, in the eye of the Omnipresent and the Omniscient," says the Oriental proverb that is the epigraph to **"The Spiral Road,"** one of his best stories. (De Casseres insisted that Huneker himself lived by such a credo: "Good and evil were also mere words to Huneker. Experience was Grace." But there is nothing in the autobiography or the letters to support this somewhat sensational view.)

Huneker was equally at home in a special corner of the contemporary world. Like George Moore, whose eccentricities of style he sometimes imitated, he was fascinated by the life of the artist and the effects of creative energy and worldly ambition on the performer and his circle. It was a subject which Huneker understood to the depths of his being, both as a musician *manqué* and a lifelong friend of the great and the not-so-great. Only Henry James has treated the artist with such imaginative concern. Most of Huneker's artists are musicians, more especially singers. The public performances and private musicales, the professional training, the social life in the cafés, the enmities and love affairs, are often brilliantly and sometimes humorously delineated. Oddly enough, Huneker saw music as a demonic force, capable of inducing madness or crime, or of inflicting psychological torture. De Casseres wrote that "his one theme is Genius," but the characters in Huneker's stories display artistic temperament rather than genius. Occasionally Huneker also reveals his interest in what he himself called the Ibsen girl, the emancipated woman who was then in literary fashion and whose principal role consisted in haranguing her listeners, or so it seemed.

To speak first of Huneker's limitations; they are partly a function of his own less than perfect artistry and partly those of his chosen genre in which the result of any lapse may be a descent into absurdity. The milieu is strongly literary; among the attenuated creatures of this rather bloodless world, overwrought by their struggles with their art or their gods, Huneker sometimes comes close to self-parody, as when in **"The Eternal Duel"** he comments on the hatred of the wife for her husband, "who had invaded the citadel of her soul and conqueror-like had filched her virgin zone." But such departures are infrequent, and the more serious failures owe something to Huneker's attempting in his gothic tales to take up residence in a universe which he did not fully understand. It is only fair to add that at the turn of the century most American writers, dedicated to the interpretation of the material and social reality, would have found it difficult or impossible to enter this "No-Man's Land," as Huneker called it.

For many of Huneker's ideas there was a source much closer to home than Baudelaire, Huysmans, or E. T. W. Hoffmann. This source was Poe, to whom Huneker referred as "with Chopin, my earliest passion." In **"Poe and His Polish Contemporary,"** Huneker asked, ". . . but was he [Poe] as American as Hawthorne and Emerson were Americans?" The similarities are less significant than perhaps Huneker knew. For some of the stories (*e.g.,* **"The Vision Malefic," "The Lord's Prayer in B,"** and **"The Spiral Road"**) he borrowed the familiar physical and emotional trappings: the macabre landscape near the sea, the gloomy house inhabited by a madman with sinister designs on the world, a medieval cloister in which depraved monks torture their victims or profane their own gods, even the Negro as a symbol of evil in **"Hall of the Missing Footsteps"** and *Painted Veils.* The terror experienced by the protagonists in these haunted surroundings is very reminiscent of Poe, but Huneker does not emulate his master in what we take to be among the most powerful of Poe's effects, "a shift from a belief in evil spirits as things that come to plague us from outside to a consciousness of terrors inside us that merely take possession of our

minds." [Edmund Wilson on Algernon Blackwood in *Classics and Commercials*]

In Huneker there is—not always, but too often—a curious failure to pursue the implications of a mortal fear, a tendency to draw back at the last moment, and to offer an explanation which is either reassuring or at worst merely ludicrous. It is not at all clear that Huneker means to reassure. It seems reasonable to infer that he was far from being able to plumb the depths of human perversity and therefore to dramatize them effectively. Obviously Huneker did not feel himself seized, as Poe did, by the horrors of a tormented psyche; he was fascinated by the subterranean passions, especially those generated by religion and art, and by the aberrations of genius, but he never felt threatened by them.

One or two examples will make this clear. In the story **"Pan"** ("For the Great Pan is alive again," says the introductory quotation) the young woman Lora is strangely affected by the gypsy music of a band to which she is listening in a café, "sheer madness of the blood," and by one of the musicians in the band.

> She imagined a determined Hungarian prairie, over which dashed disordered centaurs brandishing clubs, driving before them a band of satyrs and leaping fauns. The hoofed men struggled. At their front was a monster with a black goat-face and huge horns; he fought fiercely the half-human horses . . . most melancholy were the eyes of the defeated Pan—the melancholy eyes of Arpad Vihary. . . .

The story ends as it began, with a quotation: "Had the great god Pan passed her way?" suggesting a refulgent paganism, an occult world whose powers can be summoned to release us from the imperatives of Christian morality. But the encounter between Lora and the musician at the end violates these mysterious intimations. The great god Pan turns out to be a poor circus freak, and there is something faintly absurd in the references to his inability to sit down, a fact which is supposed to betray his animal identity.

"Hall of the Missing Footsteps" creates the lurid setting which derives from Poe, and even the fairy-tale device of the place forbidden to the protagonist. ("Make any excuse but do not set foot on its ebon floor.") Here Huneker emphasizes the relationship between music and the occult or the diabolical.

> Riding over the black and white rocks of his keyboard, he felt as if in the clutches of an unknown force. He discerned death in the distance—death and the unknown horror—and was powerless to resist. Still the galloping of unseen feet, horrible, naked flesh, that clattered and scraped the earth; the panting, hoarse and subdued, of a mighty pack, whose thirst for destruction, for revenge, was unslaked.

But the force of this representation of the terror worked by music is diminished when we learn that the musician has been drugged and that the source of the evil is physiological rather than metaphysical.

We are aware—now more than ever, perhaps, with the current attention to Genet and Burroughs—that the literary satanist is often a practitioner as well as an observer of the events he reproduces; and we are permitted to wonder, I think, whether involvement, both physical and emotional, is the indispensable passport to success as an artist of the perverse. Certainly Huneker's own life was, so far as we can tell, thoroughly conventional, and the standards of that life do, in fact, take precedence over the professed literary values. The truth is that, despite his borrowing of *fin-de-siècle* themes, despite his evident debt, both acknowledged and unacknowledged, to Nietzsche, despite his preoccupation with sin and the helplessness of those who are confronted by it, either as victims or reformers, despite the morbid sensuality of his settings, Huneker is unmistakably puritanical in his approach to and withdrawal from these neo-Romantic concerns. A moral bias shows in his repeated dramatization of the strongly-rooted (puritan and philistine) belief that artists are more liable to corruption than other men; that art, in fact, may be an instrument of the devil; and that women, especially actresses—"overdecorated and underdressed creatures, daubed like idols" [**"The Purse of Aholibah"**]—are sources of spiritual destruction. In addition, the fallen artist always suffers an unhappy fate, which Huneker regards with pity and horror—and sometimes amusement. The sense of release that the sinful ought to experience—if, indeed, there is joy in perversity—is curiously absent in the short stories. (The case is different in *Painted Veils,* where it is clear that the heroine, Easter, having been wholly converted to satanism, is in no danger of earthly retribution.) Such a story as Happiness in Crime by D'Aurevilly (with whom Huneker was compared by De Casseres), the account of a murder whose perpetrators as a consequence enter into a life of profound and lasting happiness, suggests a cynicism of which Huneker was probably incapable.

In this respect, of course, Huneker is not different from his European counterparts. For all their affirmations about the ethical independence of the artist and the necessity, in Graham Hough's words, "for judging religion, morals and society by aesthetic standards," the influence of 19th century Christianity pervades their art. Pater pointed out what should have been evident even to Wilde's enemies, that *The Picture of Dorian Gray,* far from being "immoral" and "obscene," as the defense attorney at the famous trial in 1895 described it, might properly be construed as a tract strictly enjoining the practice of vice and crime. And such an interpretation would have been valid for dozens of other art objects of the period as well.

Huneker's virtues, like his limitations, are influenced by the nature of his themes and the techniques which they elicit. These themes, as we have seen, reflect Huneker's aesthetic predilections—a belief in the autonomy of art and the equation of art with beauty. As a critic Huneker agreed with James that "life without rearrangement" was the "strenuous force [which] keeps Fiction upon her feet"—he assigned to Tolstoy, Turgenev, Flaubert, Dostoyevsky, and Conrad the first places in his hierarchy of novelists—but as a writer Huneker, also like James, preferred to inhabit a rarefied dimension where truth rather than reality prevailed and where the creatures of his own pen represented all that was exquisite, sensitive, and articulate. In his best stories Huneker contributes what has been rare in American short fiction, a virtuoso display of intellection on the part of both the author and his creation. Whatever is at work in the mind of the protagonist—prejudices, arguments, doubts, and convictions—may, in fact, constitute the real action of the story. In long and excited dialogues, or monologues, the speakers search for answers to abstruse philosophical or aesthetic dilemmas. These disquisitions are always lively, often sparkling, witty, and epigrammatic. They reflect Huneker himself at his best, a spirited, urbane, and supremely well-informed observer.

But to Huneker, as to Huysmans, who inspired Huneker to write **"The Eighth Deadly Sin,"** a strange story about the power of perfume, it is taste rather than intellectual prowess that serves as a criterion of sensibility; and he is at pains to make us aware of the preferences that govern the lives of his characters and by which they are meant to be judged. In describing their rooms, Huneker chooses to catalogue, not the tables and chairs but the literary and historical figures of whom portraits and by whom books and art objects abound.

> Her living room [says the opening sentence of **"A Sentimental Rebellion"**] was a material projection of Yetta Silverman's soul. . . . On one wall hung the portraits of Herzen, Bakounine and Kropotkin. . . . Other images of the propaganda were scattered over the walls: Netschajew—the St. Paul of the Nihilists—Ravachol, Octave Mirbeau, Jean Grave, Reclus, Spies, Parsons, Engels, and Lingg—the last four victims of the Haymarket Affair, and the Fenians, Allen, Larkin, and O'Brien, the Manchester martyrs. Among the philosophers, poets, and artists were Schopenhauer, Tolstoy, Max Stirner—a rare drawing—Ibsen, Thoreau, Emerson—the great American individualists—Beethoven, Zola, Richard Strauss, Carlyle, Nietzsche, Gorky, Walt Whitman, Dostoievsky, Mazzini, Rodin, Constantin Meunier, Shelley, Turgenieff, Bernard Shaw, and finally the kindly face and intellectual head of the lawyer who so zealously defended the Chicago anarchists . . . together with much revolutionary literature, poems, pamphlets, the works of Proudhon, Songs Before Sunrise, by Swinburne, and a beautiful etching of Makart's proletarian Christ. . . .

Carried to extremes, refinement of taste becomes a hallmark of eccentricity, then of perversity; and it is not surprising that, as a disciple of the neo-Romantics, Huneker should cause his characters to express a preference for perversity over banality.

> The Devil? [cries Oscar Inven in **"The Supreme Sin"**]. Any belief but the dull, cynical unfaith of his existence, any conviction, even a wicked one, any act of the will, rather than the motiveless, stagnant days he was leading.

One may question whether such a choice does not offer—as perhaps it did to Huysmans, Wilde, Swinburne, and others—a cheap and ready way to escape the difficulties inherent in giving life to the prosaic. But no cry could strike a more responsive note in present-day readers than that of Oscar Inven. In the arts, to say nothing of other areas of life, the quest for knowledge, sensation, experience, even delirium, is reflected in the proliferation of experiments, many of them designed only to awaken or to shock, which descend from earlier experiments of the writers and painters who were contemporary with Huneker. Such artists represent a break with the traditional observers of the world; they are characterized by the kind of imagination which Warren and Welleck [*in The Theory of Literature*] call "diffluent," that of "the symbolist poet or writer of Romantic tales (Tieck, Hoffmann, Poe) who starts from his own emotions and feelings, projecting them through rhythms and images."

Huneker's gothic stories, despite their failure to arouse genuine terror, are impressive excursions into a dreamlike world that is essentially poetic. In his use of the fanciful, never a strong element in American fiction (Hawthorne and Poe apart), Huneker often manages to combine whimsy and immense theatricality, a pastiche not meant, in my view, to be taken seriously as an explication of the human condition but designed rather as a good show. In **"The Spiral Road,"** an outstanding example of the type, mankind is to be liberated through a new art of universal appeal—an art richer than painting, sculpture, or literature, less restricted than music. This art is pyrotechny! At the end the inventor and his niece ride across the night sky (by means unknown) in a fiery chariot which is part of an apocalyptic fireworks display witnessed by thousands of spectators on the beach. Huneker delights in such effects, which sometimes suggest the visions of Blake, without the personal mysticism.

> In a flare of light sounded the trumpets of destiny; eternity unrolled before me, and on the vast plain I saw the bones of the buried dead uniting, as men and women from time's beginning arose in an army, the number whereof is unthinkable. And oh! Abomination of desolation, the White Horse, not *Kalki* the tenth incarnation of Vishnu, but the animal foretold in their Apocalypse, came through the lightnings, and in the whirlwinds of flame and thunder, I saw the shining face of Him, the Son of Man!

> ["The Iron Fan"]

Huneker does not, as we have seen, dwell exclusively among the symbolist poets or the tellers of romantic tales; his stories of artists are mirrors, slightly tinted, it is true, held up to a precious but still recognizable society. If his themes are no longer new, Huneker's treatment nevertheless endows them with undeniable vitality which owes almost everything to the flamboyant charm of his style and to the wit and elegance of the dialogues between his characters. "Prose," he said, "is like music, every word, every letter must be placed for sound, color, nuance." It is Huneker's style which persuades us from time to time that we are in the presence of an authentic artist who, like Stevenson, might have outdone himself had he been interested in the depths rather than the shallows of human life. Mencken, deriding **"The Woman Who Loved Chopin,"** called it a second-rate anecdote, then added, ". . . it is the

filling, the sauce, the embroidery that counts. But what filling! what sauce! what embroidery!"

It is unlikely that Huneker's fiction can be revived in any meaningful sense. He was not a major writer, and he left no descendants—with the possible exceptions of Cabell and Elinor Wylie. But as almost the only representative in America of the aesthetic adventure, he deserves a modest place in the canon of our short story writers. And at least once in a while it is gratifying to encounter, as we do in Huneker, an obviously contrived but scintillating invention reflecting a vision of life different from the one we have become accustomed to.

Mortimer H. Frank (essay date 1973)

SOURCE: "In Praise of Huneker," in *The University of Windsor Review*, Vol. IX, No. 1, Fall, 1973, pp. 100-12.

[*In the following essay, Frank commends Huneker for his devotion to the arts and intuition about significant artists.*]

For the first two decades of this century, James Huneker was probably America's most prolific critic of the European and American creative scene. Although his early training was in music, Huneker's interests ranged over all the arts and led to his becoming a critic for New York's major magazines and newspapers and, between 1899 and 1921, to his publishing the remarkable total of sixteen volumes—one novel, two collections of short stories, biographies of Liszt and Chopin, and eleven collections of critical essays. His judgments won praise from many, including William Butler Yeats, Bernard Berenson, and Bernard Shaw, and one admirer, Edmund Wilson, acknowledged Huneker's influence on his own work. At the height of Huneker's fame, his friend, H. L. Mencken, published a laudatory article, "James Huneker." Responding to this praise, Huneker wrote to Mencken: "As for the 'J.H.' (James Huneker) it is despairingly exaggerated—why, *warum, pourquoi, perche?* A newspaperman in a hell of a hurry writing journalese is not to be dumped in a seat of the mighty so easily." [*Letters of James Huneker*, 1922]

This self evaluation was to prove prophetic, and today only two of Huneker's books—*Chopin* (New York, 1900) and *Ivory Apes and Peacocks* (New York, 1915)—are in print. Moreover, scholars sneeringly view him as a journalist, a popularizer, an appreciator without critical standards. That he had standards, however, is implicit in his letter to Mencken; clearly Huneker saw the difference between first-class writing and the kind that may result from the exigencies of newspaper deadlines, and when he put a newspaper article between covers, he took care to revise it. Thus much of his criticism, in addition to its historical significance, has the cogency of an informed, well-planned argument.

James Gibbons Huneker was born in Philadelphia in 1857. His father, a well-to-do house painter with intellectual leanings, had wanted his son to become a lawyer, but the son, who was immersed in studying the piano and reading voraciously and who had greatly upset his father by visiting the likes of Walt Whitman in nearby Camden, New Jersey, had no intention of sacrificing a life in the arts to the world of torts and briefs. In 1878 Huneker left Philadelphia for Paris where he continued his piano studies in the hope of making a career as a virtuoso. Although he came to realize that he lacked the technical equipment to fulfill this hope, his Paris stay was to prove invaluable, giving him first-hand contact with European artistic life and the opportunity to comment about it in letters written to the Philadelphia *Bulletin*. These formed the foundation for his career in journalism. Returning to America in 1879, he settled ultimately in 1886 in New York City, teaching piano at The National Conservatory and writing free-lance articles for newspapers and magazines. The favorable reception of his first book, ***Mezzotints in Modern Music*** (New York, 1899), led to prominent positions on New York's major newspapers, The *Times,* The *Sun,* and The *World* for which he wrote music, drama, and literary criticism. Often he was sent by these papers to Europe, assignments that enabled him to meet among others Joseph Conrad, Claude Debussy, and Richard Strauss. The many books Huneker wrote during this time did not prevent his remaining an active journalist throughout his life, and his last publication was a brief review for The *World* of the Boston Symphony Orchestra's Carnegie Hall concert on February 5, 1921. Four days later, Huneker died.

Eight years after his death Mencken collected some of his essays in a memorial volume [***Essays by James Huneker*** 1929]; in its introduction Mencken noted: "The young professors who write literary history for sophomores seldom mention him today, but there was more in him than all their N. P. Willises and Charles Dudley Warners—nay than in their Lowells and Howellses." Doubtless this praise is tinged with Mencken's iconoclasm and some lack of objectivity that must have resulted from the friendship he shared with Huneker. Indeed, Howells and Huneker had mutual admirations, Tolstoy and Henry James among them, but Huneker was from a later generation than Howells and travelled newer roads. Edmund Wilson, in a position to write more objectively than Mencken, saw in Huneker's criticism the only comments of the time "of any real value . . . on the artistic life of Europe." [*A Literary Chronicle: 1920-1950,* 1956]

Wilson's and Mencken's praise notwithstanding, many factors explain Huneker's declining reputation. For one thing his output is uneven, and some of his pieces, although valuable in their day, are now dated. Many, however, are not, but with their careless factual inaccuracies, occasionally slipshod style, and irreverent tone seem unscholarly. What "scholar," after all, would call a play "art with a capital F"? But all this simply comes down to is that Huneker's work, although lacking the formal dress of scholarship, is nevertheless infused with its spirit. Allusive and suggestive, his essays differ from traditional scholarship as the imaginative professor differs from his traditional colleague. The latter often gives a well-ordered lecture, apparently covering everything and providing his students with the illusion that his subject has been wrung dry; the former, in contrast, makes no attempt to present a seemingly all-inclusive, Harvard-outline-styled talk. Instead he speaks around his subject, stimulating a variety of ideas and opening new channels of thought that kindle his students' imaginations. Huneker's criticism is often of

this order. It abounds with ideas, which when carefully gleaned, suggest further thought. A good case in point are these remarks about James's *Wings of the Dove:*

> The fiction of the future! It is an idea that propounds itself after reading the *Wings of the Dove.* Here at last is the companion work to the modern movement in music, sculpture, and painting. Why prose should lag behind its sister arts I do not know; possibly because every drayman and pothouse politician is supposed to speak it. But any one who has dipped into that well of English undefiled, the seventeenth-century literature, must realize that today [1904] we write parlous and bastard prose. It is not, however, splendid, stately rhythmic prose that Mr. James essays or ever has essayed. For him the "steam-dried" style of Pater, as Brander Matthews cruelly calls it, has never offered attractions. . . . It is from the great effortless art of the Russian master [Turgenev] that Mr. James mainly derives. But Turgenev is only one form of an influence, and not a continuing one. Hawthorne it was in whom Mr. James first planted his faith; the feeling that Hawthorne's love of the moral problem still obsesses the living artist is not missed in his newer books. The Puritan lurks in James, though a Puritan tempered by culture, by a humanism possible only in this age. Mr. James made the odious work, and still more odious quality of cosmopolitanism a thing of rare delight. In his newer manner, be it never so cryptic, his Americans abroad suffer a rich sea change, and from Daisy Miller to Milly Theale is the chasm of many years of tempered culture. . . . Perhaps it is her [Daisy's] latest sister, Milly, whose dovelike wings hover about the selfish souls of her circle, that is the purer embodiment of an artistic dream. [*Overtones,* 1904]

This may not be exhaustive criticism (many of Huneker's ideas are amplified later in the essay), but with a couple of hundred words and writing as a contemporary observer without the benefit of "scholarship" to draw upon, Huneker calls to mind a spate of ideas, summarizing the traditions that influenced James and the continuity of tradition in James's heroines, specifying the break with tradition in James's late prose style, and recognizing the clear moral line James draws between Milly Theale and the debased society in which she is forced to plunge.

And it must be remembered that these are the insights of a man whose profession was rooted in music. But this, perhaps, is what makes Huneker's achievements special: his musical bent, rather than confining him, encouraged exploration into various areas of creativity, sparking his interest in literature and art. How his work was consequently affected is best illustrated by letting Huneker speak for himself. The passage that follows comes from **"The Greater Chopin"** (*Mezzotints in Modern Music*) and comprises the essay's fifth section.

In the city of Boston, January 19, 1809, a son was born to David and Elizabeth Poe. On March 1, 1809, in the little village of Zela-zowa-Wola, twenty-eight miles from Warsaw, in Poland, a son was born to Nicholas and Justina Chopin. The American is known to the world as Edgar Allan Poe, the poet; the Pole as Frederic Francois Chopin, the composer. October 7, 1849, Edgar Poe died neglected in Washington Hospital at Baltimore, and October 17, 1849, Frederic Chopin expired in Paris surrounded by loving friends. Poe and Chopin never knew of each other's existence yet—a curious coincidence—two supremely melancholy artists of the beautiful lived and died almost synchronously.

It would be a strained parallel to compare Chopin and Poe at many points yet the chronological events referred to, are not the only comparisons that might be made without the fear or flavor of affection. There are parallels in the soul-lives as well as in the earth-lives of these two men—Poe and Chopin seem ever youthful—that may be drawn without extravagance. True, the roots of Chopin's culture were more richly nurtured than Poe's, but the latter, like a spiritual air plant, derived his sustenance none know how. Of Poe's forbears we may hardly form any adequate conception; his learning was not profound, despite his copious quotations from almost forgotten and recondite authors; yet his lines to Helen were written in boyhood. The poet in his case was indeed born, not made. Chopin, we know, had careful training from the faithful Elsner; but who could have taught him to write his opus 2, the variations over which Schumann rhapsodized, or even that gem, his E flat nocturne—now, alas! somewhat stale from conservatory usage?

Both these men, fledged in their gifts, sprang from the Jovian brain and, while they both improved in the technics of their art, their individualities were at the outset as sharply defined as were their limitations. Read Poe's "To Helen", and tell me if he made more exquisite music in his later years. You remember it:

Helen, thy beauty is to me
Like those Nicéan barks of yore
That gently, o'er a perfumed sea,
The weary, way-worn wanderer bore
To his own native shore.

On desperate seas long wont to roam,
Thy hyacinth hair, thy classic face,
Thy naïad airs have brought me home
To the glory that was Greece,
And the grandeur that was Rome.

I refrain from giving the third verse; but are not these lines remarkable in beauty of imagination and diction when one considers they were penned by a youngster scarcely out of his teens!

Now glance at Chopin's earlier effusions, his opus 1, a rondo in C minor; his opus 2 already referred to; his opus 3, the C major polonaise for 'cello and piano; his opus 5, the Rondeau à la Mazur in F; his opus 6, the first four mazourkas,

perfect of their kind; opus 7, more mazourkas; opus 8, the G minor trio, the classicism of which you may dispute; nevertheless it contains lovely music. Then follow the nocturnes, the concerto in F minor, the latter begun when Chopin was only twenty, and so on through the list. Both men died at forty—the very prime of life, when the natural forces are acting freest, when the overwrought passions of youth had begun to mellow and yet there were several years before the close, a distinct period of decadence, almost deterioration. I am conscious of the critical claims of those who taste in both Poe's and Chopin's later music the exquisite quality of the over-ripe, the savor of morbidity.

Beautiful as it is, Chopin's polonaise-fantaisie opus 61, with its hectic flush—in its most musical, most melancholy cadences—gives us a premonition of death. Composed three years before he died, it has the taint of the tomb about it and, like the A minor mazourka, said by Klindworth to be Chopin's last composition, the sick brain is heard in the morbid insistence of the theme, of the weary "wherefore?" in every bar. Is not this iteration like Poe's in his last period? Real "Ulalume" with its haunting, harrowing harmonies:

Then my heart it grew ashen and sober,
As the leaves that were crisped and sere—
As the leaves that were withering and sere.
         . . . . .
In terror she spoke, letting sink her
Wings until they trailed in the dust—
In agony sobbed, letting sink her
Plumes till they trailed in the dust—
Till they sorrowfully trailed in the dust.

This poem, in which sense swoons into sound, has all the richness of color, the dangerous glow of the man whose brain is perilously near the point of unhingement.

Poe then, like Chopin, did not die too soon. Morbid, neurotic natures, they lived their lives with the intensity that Walter Pater declares is the only true life. "To burn always with his hard, gem-like flame," he writes "to maintain this ecstasy, is success in life. Failure is to form habits."

Certainly Chopin and Poe fulfilled in their short existences these conditions. They burned ever with the flame of genius and that flame devoured their brains as surely as paresis. Their lives, in the ordinary Philistine or Plutus-like sense, were failures; uncompromising failures. They were not citizens after the conjugal manner nor did they accumulate pelf. They certainly failed to form habits and, while the delicacy of the Pole prevented his indulging in the nightside Bohemianism of the American, he nevertheless contrived to outrage social and ethical canons. Poe, it is said, was a drunkard, though recent researches develop the fact that but one glass of brandy drove him into delirium. Possibly like Baudelaire, his disciple and translator, he indulged in some deadly drug or perhaps congenital derangement, such as masked epilepsy, or some cerebral disorder, colored his daily actions with the semblance of arrant dissipation and recklessness.

There are two Poes known to his various friends. A few knew the one, many the other; some knew both men. A winning, poetic personality, a charming man of the world, electric in speech and with an eye of genius—a creature with a beautiful brain, said many. Alas! the other; a sad-eyed wretch with a fixed sneer, a bitter, uncurbed tongue that lashed alike friend and foe, a sot, a libertine, a gambler—God! what has not Edgar Allan Poe been called! We all know that Griswold distorted the picture, but some later critics have declared that Poe, despite his angelic treatment of his cousin-wife Maria Clemm, was not a man of irreproachable habits.

This much I have heard; at the time Poe lived in Philadelphia, where he edited a magazine for Burton or Graham—I forget which—my father met him several times at the houses of Judge Conrad and John Sartain, the latter the steel engraver. Poe, my father has repeatedly told me, was a slender, nervous man, very reticent, very charming in manner, though, like Chopin, disposed to a certain melancholy hauteur; both men were probably poseurs. But after one glass of wine or spirits Poe became an uncontrollable demon;—his own demon of perversity; and poetry and blasphemy poured from his lips. John Sartain has told of a midnight tramp he took with Poe, in the midst of a howling storm, in Fairmount Park, Philadelphia, to prevent him from attempting his life. This enigmatic man, like Chopin, lived a double life, but his surroundings were different and this particular fact must be accented.

America was not a pleasant place for an artist a half century ago. William Blake the poet-seer wrote: "The ages are all equal but genius is always above its age." Poe was certainly above his age—a trafficking time in the history of the country, when commerce ruled and little heed was given to the beautiful. N. P. Willis, Poe's best friend, counsellor and constant helper, wrote pale proper verse while Poe made a bare living by writing horrific tales wherein his marvellous powers of analysis and description found play and pay. But oh! the pity of it all! The waste of superior talent—of absolute genius. The divine spark that was crushed out, trampled in the mud and made to do duty as a common tallow dip! One is filled with horror at the thought of a kindred poetic nature also being cast in the prosaic atmosphere of this country; for if Chopin had not had success at Prince Valentine Radziwill's soirée in Paris in the year 1831 he would certainly have tried his luck in the New World, and do you not shudder at the idea of Chopin's living in the United States in 1831?

Fancy those two wraiths of genius, Poe and Chopin, in this city of New York! Chopin giving piano lessons to the daughters of wealthy aristocrats of the Battery, Poe encountering him at some conversazione—they had conversaziones then—and propounding to him Heine-like questions: "Are the roses at home still in their flame-hued pride?" "Do the trees still sing as beautifully in the moonlight?"

They would have understood one another at a glance. Poe was not a whit inferior in sensibility to Chopin. Balzac declared that if Chopin drummed on a bare table, his fingers made subtle-sounding music. Poe, like Balzac, would have felt the drummed tears in Chopin's play, while Chopin in turn could not have failed to divine the tremulous vibrations of Poe's exquisitely strung nature. What a meeting it would have been, but again, what inevitable misery for the Polish poet!

A different tale might be told if Poe had gone to Paris and enjoyed some meed of success! How the fine flower of his genius would have bloomed into fragrance if nourished in such congenial soil! We would probably not have had, to such a desperate extent the note of melancholia, so sweetly despairing or despairingly sweet, that we now enjoy in his writings—a note eminently Gothic and Christian. Goethe's "Nur wer die Sehnsucht Kennt" is as true of Poe as of Heine, of Baudelaire, of Chopin, of Schumann, of Shelley, of Leopardi, of Byron, of Keats, of Alfred de Musset, of Senancour, of Amiel—of all that choir of lacerated lives which wreak themselves in expression. One is well reminded here of Baudelaire who wrote of the ferocious absorption in the pursuit of beauty, by her votaries. Poe and Chopin all their lives were tortured by the desire of beauty, by the vision of perfection. Little reckoned they of that penalty which must be paid by men of genius, and has been paid from Tasso to Swift and from Poe and Baudelaire to Guy de Maupassant.

Frederic Chopin's culture was not necessarily of a finer stamp than Edgar Poe's, nor was his range wider. Both men were narrow in sympathies though intense to the point of poignancy and rich in mood-versatility. Both were born aristocrats; purple raiment became them well and both were sadly deficient in genuine humor—the Attic salt that conserves while mocking itself. Irony both possessed to a superlative degree and both believed in the rhythmical creation of lyrical beauty and in the harm of evanescence. Poe declared, in his dogmatic manner, that a long poem could not exist. He restricted the poetical art in form and length, and furthermore insisted that "Beauty of whatever kind in its supreme development invariably excites a sensitive soul to tears." The note of melancholy was to him the one note worthy the singing. And have we not a parallel in Chopin's music?

He is morbid, there is no gainsaying it and, like Poe, is at his best in smaller art forms. When either artist spreads his pinions for symphonic flights, we are reminded of Matthew Arnold's poetical description of Shelley "beating in the void his luminous wings in vain." Poe and Chopin mastered supremely, as Henry James would say, their intellectual instruments. They are lyrists and their attempts at the epical are usually distinguished failures.

Exquisite artificers in precious cameos, these two men are of a consanguinity because of their devotion to Our Ladies of Sorrow, the Mater Lachrymarum, the Mater Suspiriorum and the Mater Tenebrarum of Thomas De Quincey. If the Mater Malorum—Mother of Evil—presided over their lives, they never in their art became as Baudelaire, a sinister "Israfel of the sweet lute." Whatever their personal shortcomings, the disorders of their lives found no reflex beyond that of melancholy. The notes of revolt, of anger, of despair there area but of impurity, no trace whatsoever. Poe's women—those ethereal creatures whose slim necks, willowy figures, radiant eyes and velvet footfalls, encircled in an atmosphere of purity—Poe's women, while not being the womanly woman beloved of William Wordsworth, are after all unstained by any morbidities.

Poe ever professed in daily life, whatever he may have practised, the highest reverence for "das ewig Weibliche" and not less so Chopin, who was fastidious and a very stickler for the more minute proprieties of life. Am I far fetched in my simile when I compare the nature of Poe and Chopin! Take the latter's preludes for example, tiny poems, and parallel them to such verse of Poe's as the "Haunted Palace", "Eulalie", "Annabel Lee", "Eldorado", "The Conqueror Worm" or that incomparable bit, "Israfel":

> In Heaven a spirit doth dwell
> Whose heart-strings are a lute
>   None sing so wildly well
>   As the Angel Israfel.

Poe's haunting melodies, his music for music's sake, often remind us of Chopin. The euphonious, the well sounding, the wohlklang, was carried almost beyond the pitch of endurance, by both artists. They had however some quality of self-restraint as well as the vices of their virtues; we may no longer mention "The Raven" or "The Bells" with equanimity, nor can we endure listening to the E flat nocturne or the D flat valse. In the latter case repetition has dulled the ears for enjoyment; in the former case the obvious artificiality of both poems, despite their many happy conceits, jars on the spiritual ear. The bulk of Chopin's work is about comparable to Poe's. Neither man was a copious producer and both carried the idea of perfection to insanity's border. Both have left scores of imitators but in Poe's case a veritable school has been founded; in Chopin's the imitations have been feeble and sterile.

Following Poe we have unquestionably Algernon Charles Swinburne, who is doubly a reflection of Poe, for he absorbed Poe's alliterative system, and from Charles Baudelaire his mysticism, plus Baudelaire's malificence, to which compound he added the familiar Swinburnian eroticism. Tennyson and Elizabeth Barrett-Browning felt Poe's influence, if but briefly, while in France and Belgium he has produced a brood of followers beginning with the rank crudities of Gaboriau, in his detective stories, modelled after "The Murder in the Rue Morgue";

the Belgian Maeterlinck, who juggles with Poe's motives of fear and death, Baudelaire, a French Poe with an abnormal flavor of Parisian depravity super-added and latterly that curious group, the decadents, headed by Verlaine, and Stephen Mallarmé. Poe has made his influence felt in England too, notably upon James Thomson, the poet of "The City of Dreadful Night" and in Ireland, in the sadly sympathetic figure of James Clarence Mangan. Of Chopin's indirect influence on the musical world I would not care to dilate fearing you would accuse me of exaggeration. Liszt would not have been a composer—at least for the piano, if he had not nested in Chopin's brain. As I said before, I certainly believe that Wagner profited greatly by Chopin's discoveries in chromatic harmonies, discoveries without which modern music would yet be in diatonic swaddling clothes.

On one point Poe and Chopin were as dissimilar as the poles; the point of nationality. Poe wrote in the English tongue but beyond that he was no more American than he was English. His milieu was unsympathetic, and he refused to be assimilated by it. His verse and his prose depict character and situations that belong to no man's land— to that region East of the moon and West of the sun. In his "Eldorado" he poetically locates the country wherein his soul dramas occur. Thus he sings:

> "Over the mountains
>   Of the moon
> Down the valley of the shadow,
>   Ride, boldly ride,"
>   The shade replied,
> "If you seek for Eldorado."

His creations are mostly bodiless and his verse suggests the most subtle imagery. Shadow of shadows, his prose possesses the same spectral quality. Have you read those two perfect pastels—"Silence" and "Shadow"? If not, you know not the genius of Edgar Allan Poe. Chopin is more human than Poe, inasmuch as he is patriotic. His polonaises are, as Schumann said, "cannons buried in flowers." He is Chopin and he is also Poland though Poland is by no means Chopin. In his polonaises, in his mazourkas, the indefinable Polish Zal lurks, a drowsy perfume. Chopin struck many human chords; some of his melodies belong to that Poe-like region wherein beauty incarnate reigns and is worshipped for itself. This then is the great dissimilarity between the artist in tone and the artist in words. Poe had no country; Chopin had Poland. If Chopin's heart had been exposed "Poland" might have been found blazoned upon it.

But, if Poe lacked political passion he had the passion for the beautiful. Both men resembled one another strangely, in their intensity of expression. Both had the power of expressing the weird, the terrific, and Chopin in his scherzi, thunders from heights that Poe failed to scale. The ethical motif was, curiously enough, absent in both and both despised the "heresy of instruction." Art for art's sake, beauty for beauty's sake alone, was their shibboleth.

Criticism of this kind may no longer be in vogue, but style is ephemeral and imagination permanent. The free play that Huneker gave his imagination in comparing Poe and Chopin is in many ways typical of his work. Of course the defects of that work—factual errors and impressionistic subjectivity about music—are present, but so too are its virtues: indirectly Huneker had contact with Poe and Chopin, his father having known Poe and Huneker himself having studied piano with Chopin's most famous pupil, George Mathias. In short, Huneker was "that man"; he "was there," providing a first-hand contact with tradition that today can be experienced only vicariously. Close to Poe's time, Huneker recognized how the intellectual climate of Poe's period was unconducive to Poe's special talents. What is more Huneker saw how Poe and Chopin shared a mastery of morbid miniature. Naturally, it is easy to disdain Huneker's fantasies of a meeting between Poe and Chopin and of how each might have fared in the other's country. But from such fantasies emerge realities, and one is reminded of how Europe, on the foundation of centuries of tradition, was far more able than the stripling United States to nourish the artistic temperament.

Ultimately this Poe-Chopin comparison illustrates that Huneker, unlike today's "scholar," was no specialist; his one abiding belief was in art, not of course with an *F*, but with an *A*. What interested him most was the glory of the creative process, the way in which one mind created order, how that mind had been influenced by another and then became an influence itself. Thus he saw Chopin's antecedents in Bach and Wagner's in Chopin's, the vapidity of Liszt's virtuoso piano pieces, Brahms as a Beethovenian classicist, and Wagner's influence on Schoenberg. He was well ahead of his time in granting Johannes Brahms, Claude Debussy, Joseph Conrad, Bernard Shaw, Henrik Ibsen, and Henry James a place among the immortals. After hearing the world premiere of Schoenberg's *Pierrot Lunaire* in 1912 and thoroughly disliking it, he nonetheless analyzed the score carefully, an analysis that led him to predict with astonishing accuracy "the old tonal order changed forever." [*Ivory Apes and Peacocks*]

To appreciate Huneker's accomplishments one has only to ask who is today's Huneker? Who is the critic picking from among today's novelists, playwrights, and composers the ones who will survive in seventy-five years? Viewed in this light Huneker's achievements are substantial. And equally important he exemplified something that today is evanescent: he was not "a Chopin man," "a James man," or "a Shaw man"; he was his own man living deeply in the artistic life of his time. Reading Huneker puts us in touch with that life and serves as a reminder of how criticism itself may be imaginative and creative.

Arno Karlen   (essay date 1981)

SOURCE: "Huneker and Other Lost Arts," in *The Antioch Review*, Vol. 39, No. 4, Fall, 1981, pp. 402-21.

[*In the following essay, Karlen contemplates Huneker's drift into obscurity following his death and expresses the need to resurrect Huneker's reputation.*]

If you could resurrect a few writers of the past for one evening's conversation, which ones would you choose? A fascinating game, and not a new one. More than a half century ago, James Gibbons Huneker wrote of "the whimsical notion of Charles Lamb that he would rather see Sir Thomas Browne than Shakespeare. . . . I have often wondered if the most resounding names in history are the best beloved."

I have a few favorites of my own. I'd rather talk with Kuprin than Tolstoi, with John Aubrey than John Milton. And if I had to pick a few American writers, Huneker himself would be among them. On a scale of literary greatness he must be ranked below Hawthorne or Hemingway, but I'd rather have him come alive for one night, to sit with him at Luchow's as he piled up a dozen or so empty beer steins, outdrinking and outtalking Mencken, George Jean Nathan, the Ashcan artists, and his other grateful, dazzled protégés. He went for hours, whole nights—according to witnesses the most brilliant conversation they ever heard—on the art and lives of Chopin, Schoenberg, Artsybashev, Schnitzler, Goya, Laforgue, Lincoln, Brillat-Savarin, and Picasso, on sex and religion and philosophy, genetics and history, Philadelphia and Prague, the finest beers and best museums of Europe. Often he spoke of his friends and acquaintances—Conrad, Crane, Dreiser, Shaw, de Gourmont, Huysmans, Wedekind, Glackens, Sloan, William Steichen, Teddy Roosevelt, Mary Garden, and virtually every major musical figure of a half-century. The talk was witty, ribald, and as exciting as his best prose.

That prose is strangely neglected now. It is a scandal of ignorance and lapsed taste that it's missing from anthologies of American writing. Huneker wrote twenty volumes of criticism, essays, biography, autobiography, and fiction, and far more that remains uncollected. He was the finest music critic America ever produced, perhaps the best in the English language. No other American has also been a first-rate critic of literature, drama, and painting. Huneker is the closest we have come to a Taine or de Gourmont, a man of letters and the arts who spread his net in every direction without foolishly tearing it, and an artist in his own right.

Edmund Wilson said that Huneker shaped Wilson's entire generation. Perhaps not Eliot, Pound, or Wilson himself changed so many people's artistic knowledge and sensibility. Huneker introduced America to the revolution of the modern movement in Europe and to America's first lonely moderns. He blazed the path here for Nietzsche, Ibsen, Mussorgsky, Conrad, Hauptmann, Joyce, Munch, the post-Impressionists, the early masters of photographic art; a list of his critical firsts comprises a numbing catalogue. As Mencken said, his first judgments were good an amazing number of times, and "his solo has always preceded the chorus."

A few academic critics complained that Huneker was merely a popularizer. They were utterly wrong. He was a first-rate pianist, piano teacher, and musicologist; his music criticism makes Shaw's seem a wash of witticisms with music as the subject. He made his own discoveries in the arts—for instance, of Wedekind's plays and Munch's prints when they first appeared in Europe. Authors such as Dreiser sought his advice on their manuscripts—and often, wisely, followed it. He wrote one of the most scandalously successful novels of his time; not a great one, but it is still interesting and amusing. He did all this in the process of wringing a living from newspapers and magazines, often thousands of words a day to fill his columns and meet piles of alimony and medical bills. And this was at a time when most critics and scholars, let alone the general public, lagged decades behind his knowledge and taste.

Huneker abruptly lost center stage in the thirties; since then he has hardly been out of the wings. How did a man of such learning, charm, and gusto fall into a limbo of footnotes and passing mentions? The usual answer to such a question is, "Literary tastes change." True, tastes change with decades and generations, and many fine artists sink into a well of disregard till some distant period revives them. But that generalization, by briefly explaining everything, clarifies too little. Why does this artist fade but not that one? Lesser writers than Huneker have held their place better. This is a matter to which I will return. For the moment let me suggest that Huneker and certain other artists are ignored because their very virtues make today's public edge away uneasily. It tells more about us than about a Huneker.

Huneker's fascination with personality made it hard for him to separate an artist and his work; he would scorn today's purely textual critics as dry parasites on the warm body of art. Certainly his own background shaped his artistic and intellectual development. He was born prematurely and puny, and was therefore coddled and a bit spoiled from infancy on. Even as a burly and vigorous man, the reigning American critic of all the arts, he had the sensitivity, narcissism, and bravado so common in children who felt they were their mothers' favorites.

The Huneker home was alive with interest in the arts. The elder Huneker, a prosperous printer, collected engravings and loved the theater. He and his friends, many of them artists, exchanged tales of the gifted people they had known in Philadelphia, from Poe to Junius Brutus Booth. Mrs. Huneker, an intellectually acute and ambitious former school teacher, encouraged James to study music and eventually guided her son's writing apprenticeship, editing his work and helping him get it published. She was also a devout Catholic and hoped James would distinguish himself in the priesthood. But James rebelled against the regimentation of Catholic academies. In 1872, at the age of fifteen, he left school with an abiding scorn for institutions and formal scholarship.

It became a rankling question: What would James do for a living? He was interested in music, natural science, literature, the theater, art, but he would not go on with school. He studied painting. For a while he worked in a foundry. Then he and the family settled on apprenticeship in a law office, but the law left him stunningly bored. He returned secretly to the piano, which he had studied as a child. Soon he was playing seriously, sometimes four hours a day, before and after work. It was a late start for a musician, but he studied with a passion nothing else had wakened in him. After six dispiriting years at law offices, he staked his

future on music and left for Paris in hope of meeting Liszt and of entering the Conservatoire.

Plagued always by anxiety over public performance, Huneker played poorly at the examination and was accepted only as an auditor. He caught only a glimpse of Liszt in the street. But he did study privately with a student of Liszt, then with Georges Mathias, a student of Chopin. And during this first of what would be a score of visits to Europe, he stumbled towards his vocation.

The culture Huneker found in Paris made America seem a backward, prim province. This country did not then have the great art collections, orchestras, and literary life we have taken for granted for decades. It's easy now to indulge in nostalgic affection for the Mauve Decade in which Huneker became a major writer, but it was a time of class-bound, moralistic gentility in the arts. The Floradora Girls may have had great things by the standards of the day, and Diamond Jim may have flashed his rocks and not given a damn for obesity and cholesterol. But it wasn't charming that Henry James, his first wave of popularity gone, lived in London unmissed by much of America. While William Harding Davis passed for fine reading, and Civil War melodramas for good theater, academic and popular critics alike still saw Poe and Whitman as moral blights, the literary equivalent of syphilis. Few Americans had heard of Baudelaire, Ibsen, Nietzsche, Wagner, Manet. Zola and even Stendhal, to the few who'd read them, were dangerous imports, if not outright pornography. Furthermore, the nineties were not gay to hordes who labored in mills, mines, and sweatshops, and a cliff of fastidious avoidance faced the few writers who dared write about them.

Restless, iconoclastic, always churning with curiosity and vitality, Huneker discovered in Paris Monet, Renoir, Maeterlinck, Huysmans, de Gourmont, the American Edward MacDowell, German philosophers, Russian novelists. He learned that the modern movement was, like the Renaissance, international, and his own homeland was still blind to it. When not studying and restudying his gods, Flaubert and Bach and Chopin, he read, rushed to theaters and galleries and cafés. And as he unwitting prepared to be America's first cosmopolitan critic, he began a left-handed career as a writer—sending pieces home to the Philadelphia *Evening Bulletin* on events and the arts in Paris.

After about a year in Europe, Huneker returned to Philadelphia. There for another six years he continued advanced music studies and squeezed out a living as a piano teacher and occasional writer for newspapers and magazines. At thirty he still refused to admit once and for all that he lacked the extra virtuoso edge of a concert soloist; he had not made a strong mark as a writer. So, not having succeeded greatly at anything, including making a living, he took a plunge. In 1886 he moved to New York, determined to find a place as a writer and critic while he continued at the piano.

Huneker found that place quickly. Not only because he had talent and wit. It helped that he was a brilliant talker, an enthusiast, a generous and tactful colleague to writers and musicians. It helped that to pay the bills he could write, write, write. For almost fifteen years he produced a daily column of gossip and comment that made him a popular raconteur and observer. Having also established himself by the 1890s as a first-rank music critic, he moved on to drama, literature, and painting. He also wrote on travel, science, beer, Vermeer, any of the myriad things that caught his interest and excitement. He also wrote short stories and prose poems, especially as he moved from newspapers to such magazines as *Atlantic Monthly, Smart Set,* and *North American Review.*

By the turn of the century, when Huneker was becoming the nations's most read and respected critic, publishers began gathering his best work in books. When he died, in 1921, he had had twenty published. The essays in such volumes as **Egoists** and **Iconoclasts** had introduced Americans to Hauptmann, Sudermann, Przybyszevsky, Maeterlinck, Verhaeren, Gorky; they spread the gospel of Nietzsche, Conrad, Shaw, Ibsen. He championed Strindberg, Gauguin, Manet, Dégas, and Munch when much of Europe still laughed or fumed at them. Huneker was occasionally called an importer of European culture; his disciple, critic Benjamin De Casseres, called him the end of the nineteenth century in Europe and the beginning of the twentieth in America. But Huneker was one of the first spokesmen here for Stephen Crane, Frank Norris, Theodore Dreiser, H.B. Fuller, Sloan, Glackens, Prendergast, Griffes, and MacDowell, and he led the fight to establish Poe and Henry James as artists of world stature. Van Wyck Brooks began *The Confident Years,* his account of the end of the Anglo-Saxon genteel tradition, with Huneker's arrival in New York in 1886.

It isn't enough to give Huneker a posthumous medal for trailblazing and leave his books thinly scattered in usedbook stores. He still opens the eyes, sharpens the ears, primes the mind—and raises one's spirits. His essays affirm Pound's dictum that literature is news that stays news. The discovery of Munch, Conrad, and Schoenberg is no longer news, but Huneker's discovery of them is.

Here I cannot even fully survey Huneker's life and work. The life, full of fascinating encounters and a tangled succession of wives and lovers, is described well in a biography by Arnold T. Schwab. **Steeplejack,** the autobiography Huneker wrote near his life's end, is still engrossing. So, despite its flaws, is his one novel, **Painted Veils**. It was considered too wicked for bookstores in 1920 and had to be published privately—which made it a *succès de scandale*. Like most of Huneker's fiction, it draws on his own life and the lives of artists he knew. It shows sporadic talent for character-drawing and less for plot. Today it holds up as a portrait of the Bohemian 1890s and for a scattering of vivid scenes and monologues. Few of Huneker's short stories bear reprinting now, but it should be said that they were always more congenial to European readers, who have a tradition of *Kultur-Novellen,* the fiction of ideas. Three of Huneker's most popular books when he lived were **Chopin, Old Fogy,** and **Ivory Apes and Peacocks**. Each is a minor American classic, and each a good introduction to Huneker.

Old Fogy is Huneker at play, pouring out opinions on music and musicians, anecdotes about great artists he had known, the composing and performing styles of a century. Though the tone sometimes falls into forced jocularity, **Fogy** remains an education for musician, critic, and listener. And by looking at specific cases in one art, it suggests an approach to all the arts.

Essays signed Old Fogy appeared for years in *Etude* magazine; when they were collected in 1913 in a book allegedly edited and introduced by Huneker, few can have doubted their authorship. Fogy was, according to Huneker's preface, an effusive, sometimes cranky old eccentric, once a pupil of Liszt, who had retired to a "little villa on the Wissahickon Creek" that he had named for Dussek (to a Philadelphian this rings a bit like "chateau Chopin on the Chicago"). Fogy usually expressed Huneker's views, but in irritable moments he became a parody of Huneker's fellow critics.

Fogy on Berlioz: "Berlioz is called the father of modern instrumentation. That is, he says nothing in his music, but says it magnificently."

On Tchaikovsky: "Tchaikovsky studied Liszt with one eye; the other he kept on Bellini and the Italians. What might have happened if he had been one-eyed I cannot pretend to say." And elsewhere, "His *Manfred* is a libel on Byron, who was a libel on God."

On playing Bach: "Yes, you may indulge in *rubato*. I would rather hear it in Bach than in Chopin. Play Bach as if he still composed—he does. . . ." As Fogy explained, to the extent that any subsequent composer understood Bach, he built well.

Huneker's preface related that Fogy's playing was accomplished but rarely inspired. "Solidly schooled . . . but when excited he revealed traces of a higher virtuosity than was to have been expected. . . . His touch was dry, his style neat. A pianist made, not born, I should say." It is Huneker's slightly ungenerous description of himself. A distinguished keyboard teacher, he had good advice to give.

On when to practice: "The morning hours are golden. Never waste them . . . on mechanical finger exercise. Take up Bach, if you must unlimber your fingers and your wits . . . any time will do for gymnastics."

On preparing as an artist: "This season there will be a race between Rosenthal and Sauer, to see who can vomit the greater number of notes. . . . In my time a piano artist read, meditated, communed much with nature, slept well, ate and drank well, saw much of society, and all his life was reflected in his play."

On touch: "The springiest wrist . . . cannot compensate for the absence of an elastic finger-stroke. It is what lightens up and gives variety and color to a performance. You [cannot] neglect touch—touch, the revelation of the soul."

Fogy said that every pianist who had a beautiful touch sat low before the keyboard. Dohnányi sat high and played down on the keys; his touch was hard as steel. "Pachmann's playing is a notable example of plastic beauty. He seems to dip his hands into musical liquid instead of touching inanimate ivory. . . ."

If Fogy's lectures on Bachian structure and wrist position

were only for pianists, they would not have become intellectual staples to literate America. They direct a listener's discrimination and take him into the artist's workshop to reveal the roots of artistic effects in specific techniques, the path between an idea and its execution.

The praise of Vladimir de Pachmann, the great interpreter of Chopin, deserves special notice. It came after a bitter feud between him and Huneker, and it shows Huneker's capacity to reeducate himself. Pachmann was short, bearded, full of twitches, grimaces, and affectations at the keyboard. He could seem both virulent and effeminate; once he offered to make up an argument with his manager with a kiss and instead bit him in the neck. Huneker had no use for all this, in fact considered it a blot on the musical profession, and broke his rule against putting personal recriminations in print. He said Pachmann's "Bach was worse than his bite," covered him with scorn, and finally dubbed the writhing little pianist a "Chopinzee," and the epithet followed Pachmann all his life.

Finally Pachmann accosted Huneker in Luchow's and reviled him until the critic rose and calmly emptied a stein of beer over the pianist's shirt-front. Pachmann made such a scene that the manager of Luchow's insisted he apologize. Pachmann went back to Huneker's table and shrieked, "Skunk! I apologize, skunk!"

Huneker was obliged to continue reviewing Pachmann's concerts. Once Pachmann saw him in the audience and announced he would play some Chopin even Huneker didn't know. He played a lovely but unfamiliar piece and asked Huneker how he liked it. The critic called back from his seat, "I never like any composition played backwards, especially Chopin." Pachmann laughed, clapped his hands, and said, "You are very bright man, Huneker. Now I play it right for you." Which he did.

Reluctantly the two men came to respect and even like each other. Perhaps Pachmann improved; it is more likely that Huneker, who had not publicized the Luchow incident, saw past Pachmann's exasperating mannerisms to his exquisite musicianship. Once this happened, Huneker never stopped praising Pachmann in print. Eventually he invited Pachmann to his home for dinner, and the pianist afterward gave Huneker a private concert that lasted five hours, until three in the morning.

The personal vituperation was uncharacteristic of Huneker, but the ability to change his mind was typical. This is wonderfully clear in *Ivory Apes and Peacocks*. Music is a small part of the book, but the essay on Schoenberg is a beautiful example of Huneker taking the reader along on his exploration of new territory.

When Huneker prepared to hear Schoenberg's music, he wanted to study the score, but it was not available yet in New York, so he went cold to hear *Pierrot Lunaire*.

> What did I hear? At first, the sound of delicate china shivering into a thousand luminous fragments. In the welter of tonalities that bruised each other as they passed and repassed, in the preliminary grip of enharmonics that almost made the ears bleed, the eyes water, the scalp to freeze, I could not get a central grip on myself. . . .

But, he said, when he finally surrendered himself to the composer, "I couldn't let go the skein of the story for fear that I might fall off somewhere into a gloomy chasm and be devoured by chromatic wolves." And how did Schoenberg hold the listener? By clever, acrid orchestration and adept counterpoint; a talent for expressing sorrow and desolation; "a series of points, dots, dashes, or phrases that sob and scream, despair, explode, exalt, blaspheme." One thing was certain, said Huneker, "the old tonal order has changed for ever." This music was not, as most people said, mad or disordered, but "as logical as a highly wrought mosaic . . . few men are so conscious of what they are doing, and few modern composers boast such a faculty of attention."

There was a gentle Schoenberg whose music Huneker would discover a little later. For the moment he had to say, "If such music-making is ever to become accepted I long for Death the Releaser. More shocking still would be the suspicion that in time I might be persuaded to like this music, to embrace, after abhorring it. . . ." And that was what happened. Not long after that essay, Huneker wrote another saying that his first impressions of Schoenberg "were neither flattering to his composition nor to my indifferent critical acumen. . . . He is significant in the reaction against formal or romantic beauty. I said the same more than a decade ago of Debussy." Preserve an open mind, he warned, for a decade hence Schoenberg might prove as conventional a member of musical society as the other "recent anarchs" Debussy and Richard Strauss.

The two essays on Schoenberg in *Ivory Apes and Peacocks* show the critic listening, fighting habit, seeking the music's own logic, and finding it. The conclusion he reached still seems to me just: "Every composer has his aura; the aura of Arnold Schoenberg is, for me, the aura of sublime ugliness, of hatred and contempt, of cruelty, and of the mystic grandiose. He is never petty . . . and he has the courage of his chromatics." Though he gave Schoenberg his due, Huneker never became aesthetically enthralled by his music; if that be a shortcoming, it is a virtue that Huneker never made a cult of the music or read nonexistent beauties into some of it, as did many others who championed it on theoretical or revolutionary principles. Only Thomas Mann, in *The Magic Mountain,* caught for me as Huneker did Schoenberg's mixture of method and mysticism, and the feelings of obsession, rage, and loathing that lurk in some of it.

In *Ivory Apes and Peacocks* many Americans first heard of Bartok, Kodály, Stravinsky, the Cubists, Ensor, Fénéon, Satie; of Gauguin, Strindberg, Blok, Korolenko, Andreyev, Reger, and Roussel. They also took some interesting vicarious trips—for instance, across the river from Philadelphia to Camden with teenage Jim Huneker to meet Walt Whitman. They discovered with him in Munich, in 1901, an art gallery the public called the Chamber of Horrors, and filled with laughter and sounds of disgust. There Huneker recognized the genius of young Munch and bought one of the artist's works. More from this volume:

On Hugo Wolf: "Hugo Wolf was a song writer who perilously grazed genius, but he rotted before he was ripe."

On Laforgue: "All victories are alike; defeat alone displays an individual profile. [Laforgue's] urbanity never deserted him, though it was an exasperated urbanity. His art was an art of the nerves. . . . Like Chopin or Watteau, he danced on roses and thorns."

On Conrad: "Reticence is a distinctive quality of this author; after all, isn't truth an idea that traverses a temperament?"

If one had to pick one piece from this book to anthologize, it would be **"Three Disagreeable Girls."** It is the one Huneker began by asking which people from the past one would want to meet. He continued:

> What is the name of your favorite heroine? Whom should you like to meet in that long corridor of time leading to eternity, the walls lined with the world's masterpieces of portraiture? I can answer for myself that no Shakespearian lovely dame or Balzacian demon in petticoats would ever be taken off the walls by me. They are either too remote or too unreal, though a word might be said of Valérie Marneffe. In the vasty nebula of the Henry James novel there are alluringly strange women, but if you summon them they fade and resolve themselves into everlasting phrases. . . . But Emma Bovary might come if you but ardently desired. And the fascinating Anna Karenina. Or Becky Sharp with her sly graces.

Sly Becky, he said, was the first of a generation of disagreeable heroines, of whom the three most stunning recent examples were Hedda Gabler, Mildred Lawson (in George Moore's *Celibates*), and Undine Spragg (in Edith Wharton's *The Custom of the Country*). They were widely seen as repellent examples of the "new woman"—jargon rather like ours, and no better. Huneker insisted, "The 'feminist' movement is not responsible for them; there were disagreeable females before the flood [and] Hedda boldly carved out of a single block stands out as the very Winged Victory of her species." For convenience she had married a boring man. She was charmless never, but disagreeable always—sly, morbid, cowardly, with a largely cerebral interest in the forbidden. She saw suicide as her only escape, and "really it was the most profound and significant act of her life, cowardly as was the motive. She was discontented, shallow, the victim of her false upbringing." She and Eiljert "could have consorted with Emma Bovary and found her 'ideals' sympathetic." Finally, if she had not been attractive, and pathetic for her misspent life and death, she would be quite unendurable.

> I believe if Hedda Gabler had hesitated and her father's pistol hadn't been hard by, she would have recovered her poise and deceived her husband. I believe that if Emma Bovary had escaped that snag of debt she would have continued to tool Charles. And I believe Mildred Lawson married at last and fooled herself into the belief that she had a superior soul, misunderstood by the world and her husband. There is no telling how vermicular are the wrigglings of mean

souls. Mildred was a snob, therefore mean of soul; and she was a cold snob, hence her cruelty.

Huneker noted that although Mildred Lawson's creator was openly hostile to the "new woman," he was too good an artist to use a character as a dialectic battering ram. The important truth about Mildred is that she is selfish, and "at the end her selfishness strangles the little soul she possesses. . . . She despises conventional men, and is herself compact of conventionality. . . . As in the case of Hedda Gabler, it is her social conscience that keeps her from throwing her bonnet over the moon, not her sense of moral values; in a word, virtue by snobbish compulsion."

Nor was Edith Wharton's Undine Spragg disagreeable because she was, in today's cliché, "liberated"—and certainly she was not liberated because she made a few flying visits to Bohemia during her race to the social finishing line. It was because she remained, behind her loveliness and her flirting with trendy ideas, greedy and shallow. "No emotional experience would leave a blur on her radiant youth, because love for her is a sensation, not a sentiment . . . she was bored as a wife, and like Emma Bovary found in adultery all the platitudes of marriage."

Huneker concludes, the new woman isn't necessarily disagreeable, and in any case none of these antiheroines is a new woman. All are compromisers and vulgarians. Hedda, like Mildred, "lacked the strength either to renounce or to sin." Undine Spragg lacked both the courage and the brains to be downright wicked. "She is only disagreeable and fashionable, and she is as impersonal and monotonous as a self-playing pianoforte."

Huneker was skeptical about what he saw as women "claiming the earth and adjacent planets," but he recognized that "new freedom and responsibilities have evolved new social types." And he himself had lived unconventionally, among gifted and unconventional friends—including many gifted and independent women. He had no patience for near-misbehavior, prudery, and cant, no time for soulful whiners male or female. And, present-day reviewers take note, he was too intelligent, and too good an artist, to estimate a novel and its characters on the basis of ideology. Always fascinated by the labyrinth of inner self, he insisted on looking at these three antiheroines as individuals, not political emblems. He saw that their flaws were ancient, familiar ones, which have changed only in how they are rationalized. To judge "new women," one would have to look elsewhere. When one did, the questions would be the same as in the past: decency, courage, an intelligent heart.

Huneker's second book, published in 1900, ***Chopin: The Man and His Music,*** contains a few factual errors, and parts of it are a bit overblown—Old Fogy himself chided the author of ***Chopin*** for sins of rhetoric. Yet it remains, as Chopin scholar Herbert Weinstock said, "unique and uniquely lively among the vast literature on Chopin," a fine example of seeing an artist clearly through clouds of habit and inherited opinion. Most listeners and many musicians still haven't grasped its message.

Huneker, having studied with a student of Chopin, knew

first-hand how the composer actually played and taught. He had edited, phrased, and fingered all of Chopin's then-known work. In those days, as is still largely true, much of Chopin's best was played rarely, and the same few pieces misplayed so that they seemed sentimental and trivial. Few artists have been so regularly torn to tatters or coated with syrup. Huneker wanted to write a book that would "not bow down before that agreeable fetish of sawdust and molasses . . . created by silly sentimentalists and rose-leaf poets."

After giving a brief life of Chopin, Huneker analyzed each of the waltzes, scherzi, polonaises, mazurkas, nocturnes, ballades, études, and sonatas. He covered everything from fingering, phrasing, and pedal work to interpretation. True, Chopin was occasionally an arch salon composer, sometimes lugubrious or sentimental (though no more often than, say, Beethoven). What people managed to keep missing was the extraordinary range of moods he touched in his short pieces. He could be suave, sinister, ironic, heroic, prankish, with the ruggedness of Beethoven and the serenity of Mozart. Many of the more musically and emotionally complex pieces are shunned because they are "too difficult for the vandal with an average technique," others because they tax the interpretive art of the finest performer. Huneker wrote of the second *Etude* in A minor, opus 10: "It takes prodigious power and endurance to play this work . . . and no little poetry. It is open air music, storm music, and at times moves in processional splendor. Small souled men, no matter how agile their fingers, should avoid it." Chopin, he made the reader realize, was often like a tornado seen through the wrong end of an opera glass.

Huneker's view of Chopin is astringent, and quite correct. Chopin was never an avid supporter of Romanticism. He was aloof, hated extravagance, sought reserve in both his life and his music. His musical lineage ran through Hummel to Mozart and Bach; to prepare for a concert he usually shut himself up to play Bach, Bach, Bach. His preludes could have been written only by a devout student of Bach. And he did for the mazurka and scherzo and polonaise what Bach did for earlier forms, brought them to formal perfection.

Chopin's innate classicism was misunderstood because he was the most daring harmonic innovator since Bach. He spun music into new, extended, dispersed harmonies, creating "ascending and descending staircases of chromatics like Piranesi's marvellous aerial architectural dreams." Chopin also changed the arts of the pedal and of keyboard touch. Here was the source of the revolution carried on by Wagner, Strauss, Debussy, and later composers. But critics of Chopin's day heard the suspensions, anticipations, and forbidden acrid harmonies as formlessness.

We know how Chopin played and taught. A student recorded, "He required adherence to the strictest rhythm, hated all lingering and lagging, misplaced rubatos, as well as exaggerated ritardandos. 'Je vous prie de vous asseoir,' he said, on such an occasion, with gentle mockery." Some listeners claimed that Chopin departed from the beat; actually, he played with rubato in the true sense—stealing time from one note or phrase but never failing to return

it later in the passage. Huneker hits the heart of the matter:

> The tempo rubato is probably as old as music itself. It is in Bach, it was practiced by the old Italian singers. Mikuli says that no matter how free Chopin was in his treatment of the right hand in melody or arabesque, the left kept strict time. Mozart and not Chopin it was who first said: "Let your left hand be your conductor and always keep time." . . . Chopin was a very martinet with his pupils if too much license of tempo was taken. His music needs the greatest lucidity in presentation, and naturally a certain elasticity of phrasing. Rhythms need not be distorted, nor need there be absurd and vulgar haltings, silly and explosive dynamics. Chopin sentimentalized is Chopin butchered. He loathed false sentiment, and a man whose taste was formed by Bach and Mozart . . . could never have indulged in exaggerated, jerky tempi, in meaningless expressions. Come, let us be done with this fetish of stolen time, of the wonderful and so seldom comprehended rubato . . . If you wish to play Chopin, play him in curves . . . [the music] must be delivered in a flowing, waving manner, never square or hard, yet with every accent showing like the supple muscles of an athlete beneath the skin.

That, of course, was why Fogy had said he would rather hear rubato in Bach than in Chopin—to reach the real Chopin, not the flossy caricature that passes for Chopin. Then, despite the sometimes tortured mood and feverish harmonies, one never lost the structure that gave it all coherence. A few times I have experimented with teaching advanced writing workshops by playing recordings of several different pianists performing the same short Chopin piece (always the splendid Lipatti—if only Huneker had lived to hear him!). In discussing style in writing, one can always be seduced away by subject matter or the mannerisms of an individual or period. Listening to music and picking out whether it is the tempo, the pedal, the touch, whatever, that produces a different style puts the concrete, technical aspects of style in the forefront. Some students have found it eye-opening, and I like to think Huneker would have enjoyed the idea.

Today it takes effort to get people to "advance" to some of Huneker's views of eighty years ago. Looking back, one wonders how he got away with it—shoveling his favorite egoists and iconoclasts at America, standing for frankness despite censorship "that seeks to elevate literature in this 'free' land to the dignity of a laundry." Yet he did not suffer revenge from gangs of Comstockian figleafers, respectable philistines, and harrumphing professors. He didn't even scare off readers with his knowledge; he handed it out, they asked for more.

To say America was ready for a Huneker is the sort of waste-basket explanation that passes because it has an element of truth. But there were some other prescient critics, and among them were good writers. None (except Pound, a generation younger) had Huneker's gift for language—his long, leisurely, confiding sentences alternating with brisk staccatos, the galloping range of allusions and metaphors, the easy assurance without pedantry. Finally, though, the most important reason was the man himself.

Huneker had mastered two arts and knew others well. But instead of delivering sentence from a high bench, he invited the reader into the artist's workshop, the artist's mind and heart, to be his partner in discovery. He did so with humility, for he had known failure—by his middle thirties had settled for being a distinguished rather than an exceptional pianist, but never stopped playing, studying, teaching. Few men have let go of a dream with so much grace, so little bitterness. Huneker's essays and fiction often turn on ambition, greatness, and failure, and they are sometimes tinged with wistfulness; but unlike so many aspiring artists turned critic, Huneker never harried and belittled achievement. He rejoiced in others' artistry.

Furthermore, Huneker was—there is no better word—a gentleman. He was sometimes boisterous, roosterish, and could be justly hard-edged; for instance, he began a review of a soprano's chilly rendition of *Aida,* "Last night there was skating on the banks of the Nile." But those he criticized respected and even liked him—even de Pachmann ended up liking him (Shaw was the notable exception). They knew that he was not against the artist, but on the side of art, without anger or vengefulness. He laughed at ignorance, priggishness, and poor performance, and tried to praise what was good, rather than cudgel what was not.

Finally, there was the infectious zest that overwhelmed his shortcomings. He felt the critic's job was not to outdo colleagues in cruel deftness, but to discover fire and then strike fire in his readers. He could make anything seem delightful and fascinating, for as De Casseres said, "The psychical root of James Huneker was ecstasy."

Certainly Huneker had shortcomings. The newspaper writer must grip readers every day, year after year, or feel the feet of hungry competitors climbing his back. He always faces the pitfalls of haste and overproduction—an effervescence that doesn't rise naturally from the material but seems pumped in. Sometimes, even in the anthologized essays, you feel him filling the bottom of the column or working up forced muscularity. Even ***Steeplejack*** and ***Painted Veils*** were written in gusts of thousands of words a day, to meet serialization deadlines. And when Huneker consciously sought poetic prose, he sometimes became florid and arch, showing the influences of Huysmans and Edgar Saltus more than the Flaubert he idolized, and falling into the clichés of 1890s' "nonconformism." He made two criticisms of Lafcadio Hearn that, as he knew, sometimes fitted himself:

> His mania for the word caused him to neglect the sentence; his devotion to the sentence closed for him any comprehensive handling of the paragraph; he seldom wrote a perfect page. . . . A man after nearly two thousand years of Christianity may say to himself: "Lo! I am a pagan." But all the horses from Dan to Beersheba cannot drag him back to paganism, cannot make him resist the "pull" of his hereditary faith.

And Huneker had his stopping points—Matisse, Picasso, the Cubists, Schoenberg. He recognized their importance, but there were limits to his enjoyment of them. Huneker

said that "one must get off somewhere," and he got off where art seemed to him to lose heart and humanity. He was a big step ahead of his contemporaries, a half-step behind the revolution of the next generation. But his refusal to jump on revolutionary bandwagons was often rightheaded. He saw the artistic limits of Futurism. The Futurists, he said, fought for a fresh and innocent eye, but one cannot will innocence; and they attempted to express in paint what should be expressed in literature or with a moving-picture camera. Most of all, he disliked their anarchic anger, their will to destroy, their cultish ideology. Huneker hated preaching and systems, and if that limited him, it saved him from foolish patriotisms and narrowness. Remember the words of Cocteau: "Stravinsky said to me one day that you have to be indulgent with listeners, since if he had been presented with his current works the year before, he would have shrugged his shoulders." Huneker didn't embrace Stravinsky and Picasso in 1910, but he was among the few who did more than shrug.

I can't resist this gifted, ebullient, yet profoundly sensible man who seemed to love art more than himself. A man whose first memories were the fall of Richmond and Lincoln's cortege, who ended his autobiography with his first airplane ride and then with sitting down to practice "certain compositions of my beloved Chopin to master which eternity itself would not be too long. . . . I once more place the notes on the piano desk. Courage!"

Well, later decades found him resistible. The forgetting began in the decade after his death. Mencken, who humbly looked up to Huneker as king of the critical hill, is more read and better remembered. The comparison is revealing. Mencken is memorable, but not a better writer than Huneker and without Huneker's breadth or depth of culture. The quality that so endeared Mencken to readers in the teens and twenties was a spirit of opposition that too often slipped into rancor without wit. Though often generous, Mencken was always glad for a chance to deliver a diatribe, swing a verbal knout. His brassy, relentless pugnacity could become monotonous—the shouting of contempt at easy targets.

It may have been Mencken's shortcomings as much as his virtues that gave him popularity in a decade that enjoyed hostile flippancy—as recent decades have enjoyed varieties of "coolness." Perhaps Huneker's lasting virtues—his emphasis on quality, his civility, decency, refusal to wound or to preach—worked against him. High-spirited and good-spirited, he was an iconoclast but never the shrill village atheist. Certainly he did not fit the intellectual and artistic preoccupations of the thirties—often more political than aesthetic. And after the Second World War, critics proud of their purely textual rigor were fashionable; to them, Huneker, if they read him, seemed subjective, self-indulgent, and not fully respectable.

The four most distinguished American critics of this century have been Huneker, Pound, Eliot, and Wilson. Huneker and Wilson have resemblances; I see more scope and depth in Huneker. Huneker lacks Pound's ripping intellect, his cleansing express trip through culture; he also lacks Pound's tics, rages, and obsessiveness. Both writers always make me want to read aloud to a friend, for they make criticism an art. Eliot, I suspect, however brilliant and original, will ultimately date more than the others as a critic (though not as a poet), for he had a rather constricted temperament.

Many academics who have deified Eliot and his offspring and consider Huneker unrigorous may one day stand corrected. Some seem to most prize solemnity, tunnel vision, and specialized jargon with which to hammer, screw, and ream literature into what they consider correct shape. Huneker would have advised them, I suspect, to drink and eat better, spend more time talking to cabbies and cops and gamblers, to read for pleasure, enjoy sex, and then bring their entire humanity back to their work.

And where are the specialists of literature, the writers of texts and anthologies and syllabi? Some, unfortunately, justify de Gourmont's description of them to Huneker, "coprolites of the ideal." In search of subjects for Ph.D. theses, they unearth some rather meager talents of the American past, but if you ask about Huneker, they say, "Sorry, not in my field," or, "Sorry, not a major figure." That is, he committed the sin of writing in the wrong decade or genre, or beyond their narrow competence.

I suggest they take a look at what they are missing—a delightful man who stands in the front rank of American criticism and the fine second rank of American writing. He still faces the resistance bred of sixties and seventies hipness, cool, and anti-intellectualism. Huneker, thank God, is anything but cool, and he takes for granted a reader who, if he doesn't know, wants to know. The same defensive edginess and avoidance has often greeted work by Saul Bellow, Edward Dahlberg, and still, to this day, Henry James.

So it is not just random changes of fashion that account for Huneker's being ignored. The same is true of many other fine artists of the past half-century. Alexander Kuprin's novel *Yama* went through many editions here in the thirties, but few know it now—not *War and Peace,* but livelier than Sarah Orne Jewett, J. D. Salinger, and some other favorites of those who claim to master and doctor our literature. An uneven book, sometimes sloppy but quivering with vitality, joy, grief, and wonder, and perhaps too nakedly passionate—not erotic, though it is about prostitutes, but passionate—for some people's comfort.

Where is the passionate but spare and hard *Christ in Concrete,* by Pietro di Donato? When I last spoke to the author, a few years ago, he was sometimes making his living as a plasterer. Thousands of his thirties readers don't know he's still writing. Maybe he isn't comfortably mushy enough for nostalgic revivers of "ethnic" novels.

Some novels by George Gissing have finally been brought back in print, but where is the fine, sad little book, *The Private Papers of Henry Ryecroft?* Its pessimism is genuine. Gissing won't let us off the hook with cheap nihilism or unearned cynicism. Quietly, brutally, he lays out an earned pessimism, and apparently that makes him too "minor" for attention in a devoutly optimistic land.

Where is the novel *At Swim-Two-Birds,* by Flann O'Brien?

Unsanctified by syllabi or mass paperback publishers. Yet it is a wildly funny and brilliant book that reels to the edge of melancholy and back to laughter again.

Where, for that matter, are some of the writers Huneker discovered for America—Schnitzler, Sudermann, de Gourmont? Known but largely unread. Perhaps these books, like Huneker's, challenge us to be ashamed of low emotional voltage and intellectual slack. Perhaps many readers today are afraid to be seized, thrilled, frightened, enlightened. What we need is another James Gibbons Huneker. But we haven't had one for so long that we've forgotten what it's like.

Paul E. Cohen   (essay date 1982)

SOURCE: "A Riot of Obscene Wit," in *Columbia Library Columns,* Vol. XXXI, No. 3, May, 1982, pp. 19-28.

[*In the following essay, Cohen discusses the merit and notoriety of* Painted Veils.]

"The other day Huneker came into my office with the ms. of his novel," wrote H. L. Mencken in 1919 about *Painted Veils,* the holograph manuscript of which is now in the Solton and Julia Engel Collection. "The thing turned out to be superb—the best thing he has ever done. But absolutely unprintable. It is not merely ordinarily improper; it is a riot of obscene wit." The novel was the work of James Gibbons Huneker, the well-known journalist and critic who at age sixty-two had written his first full-length work of fiction. "The old boy has put into it every illicit epigram that he has thought of in 40 years," Mencken went on, "and some of them are almost perfect. I yelled over it."

Huneker had actually submitted the novel to him hoping it might be serialized in *Smart Set,* the sophisticated literary journal Mencken edited with George Jean Nathan. However, Mencken exhibited an essentially prudish nature when he found the work too full of "lascivious frills and thrills" for his journal and turned it down with the prediction that the "pornographic novel will never be published." This was 1919, after all, the very year James Branch Cabell's *Jurgen* was barred from bookshops by the New York Society for the Suppression of Vice, the same organization which had previously banned Theodore Dreiser's *The Genius.* "If we printed [*Painted Veils*]," Mencken joked, "we'd get at least 40 years."

The publishing problem Huneker had created was probably driven home to him after he read *Jurgen* which he "marvelled over—at the notion of it being obscene." *Painted Veils* is not a bawdy book; it has no coarse or vulgar language and no graphic accounts of carnal pleasures. Nevertheless, it is still possible to understand Mencken's refusal to serialize the book. The characters in the novel make love with frequency—and in a variety of complex combinations—and epigrammatic comments about sex dominate in such a way that it is possible to lose sight of other elements of the narrative. Huneker considered the work "frankly erotic" and boasted to Mencken: "There are enough happenings to amuse the choicest company at a bordel."

The racy story was set in New York City during the late

nineteenth century among the musicians, artists, decadents and dilettantes Huneker had known two or three decades earlier. From all accounts, there could have been no better spokesman for this *fin de siècle* group than Huneker himself who was described by the poet Benjamin De Casseres as "the incarnation of the cultured bohemianism of the glamorous days when the city was young, irresponsible, Dionysian." He had taken the city by storm in the late 1880s, according to Alfred Kazin, "driving a dozen horses and tumbling over between them. He had more energy, knew more people, retailed more gossip, wrote more books, drank more beer, and disseminated more information on the artistic personality than almost any other journalist of his time." Kazin could have added that Huneker had probably had more love affairs than most of his contemporaries as well.

Trained as a musician, first in Philadelphia and later in Paris, Huneker's success in journalism came as a result of his failure to become a piano virtuoso. He turned to writing original and witty articles on music in which he popularized many modern European composers including Richard Strauss. Later he wrote lively essays on drama, art and literature which showed the influence of such authors as Joris Karl Huysmans, Rémy de Gourmont, and Edmond and Jules de Goncourt. These are the writers Huneker had admired in Paris and all of them appear briefly as characters in his *roman á clef.*

Huneker's career as journalist writing for a number of New York dailies is chronicled in *Steeplejack* (1918), an autobiography completed shortly before he began *Painted Veils.* "I would fain be a pianist, a composer of music," the frustrated author forlornly divulged in these memoirs. "I am neither. Nor a poet. Nor a novelist, actor, playwright. I have written many things from architecture to zoology without grasping their inner substance. I am Jack of the Seven Arts, master of none." Throughout his life, Huneker had proudly called himself a "man-of-letters," a phrase once employed to describe the kind of roving literary journalism he practiced. As academics and specialists started taking over much of this literary writing, "men-of-letters" began to lose their influence and the phrase itself became pejorative. As Huneker approached sixty, he seemed aware of the changing literary climate which was making his profession obsolete; apparently this realization strengthened his conviction that his own career had been a dismal failure.

He was especially depressed that summer of 1919 when he started his novel. In addition to being disillusioned, he was in dire financial and physical straits, having just returned from the hospital where he had been operated on for the removal of a cyst from his bladder. Furthermore, and perhaps more devastating for the rakish writer, he was now impotent, a condition he had complained to his doctor about as early as 1911. By 1919, he admitted that he had altogether given up what he liked to call "horizontal refreshment": "Fornication is forgotten—and thank the lord." It was in these trying circumstances that Huneker sat down to write the most lurid book of his time—and he wrote it at breakneck speed.

"Ill as I was from bladder trouble—5 months on the water wagon now—I composed and wrote a novel—100,000 words," he told De Casseres. "I wrote it in 7 weeks, less 2 days—wrote it with the tears in my eyes from age; and in revenge" Huneker hoped that his female readers would find the work especially erotic—if not thoroughly arousing. Had Huneker become an "exhibitionist in print?" Was he seeking alternative techniques to stimulate women now that he was *"non compos penis,"* as Mencken playfully described the unfortunate condition? Perhaps by writing *Painted Veils* Huneker was simply working out his sexual inadequacies or gratifying some of his needs.

In the novel, Huneker retold the story he had written in his autobiography—but from a different perspective. He claimed that he left out of his memoirs accounts of his love life because "I didn't wish the publishers to go to jail." But in *Painted Veils* all of the "suppressed complexes" come to the surface: "I've traced a parallel route frankly dealing with sex; also with the development of a young man deracinated because born in Paris and suffering." That character is Ulrick Invern, "a writer, incidentally a critic" who lives ambivalently on the fringes of the artistic world of New York City. He is trapped between the advice of Rémy de Gourmont, who encouraged him in Paris to return to America, and Edgar Saltus, who told him he should have remained in Paris. "Apart from his studies nothing interested [Ulrick] like sex," and much of the novel is about his essentially unfulfilling—though nonetheless intriguing—relationships with three fetching women whom Huneker characterized as "hot and hollow."

Easter Brandes, a narcissistic singer, has the strongest hold on Ulrick, and she is caught early in the book admiring her naked reflection in a mirror: "she bowed low to her image, kicked her right leg on high, turned her comely back, peeped over her shoulder, mockingly stuck out her tongue as she regarded with awe—almost—the delicately modelled buttocks." Ulrick also has a love affair with Mona Milton, a concupiscent woman who "wished that her soul could be like a jungle at night, filled with the cries of monstrous sins." Finally, the young protagonist passes some of his time with Dora, a classy prostitute who is a "treasure-trove for an erotic man."

The central incident of the narrative occurs at a Holy Roller revival in Zaneburg, New Hampshire, where Ulrick and Easter meet for the first time. A Negro preacher named Brother Rainbow presided over this religious gathering which degenerated into an orgy. During the frenzy, the lights go out, and Ulrick and Easter each have sex. Ulrick presumes that his partner had been Easter and as a result he pursues her throughout the book with a stronger passion than he can ever muster for the other women he meets. At the end of the novel, however, he learns the truth about the incident: "In the darkness we all got mixed up," Easter informs him. She had been raped by Brother Rainbow while Ulrick's companion had been the preacher's white assistant, Roarin' Nell.

"The story itself is largely true," Huneker told the incredulous John Quinn, a famous lawyer and collector who called the novel "Painted Whores." "I know—and knew—[Easter]. She is a composite of—well, I'll tell you some day. Mona is in town today: and the little slut, Dora, still lives and ceased fornication." H. L. Mencken thought he knew the names of two women who may have provided the inspiration for Easter, and he wrote about them to Dr. Fielding Hudson Garrison, a mutual friend and well-known medical historian: "I suspect that Huneker's heroine is chiefly Sibyl Sanderson, with touches of Olive Fremstad. Before the collapse of his glands he was in the intimate confidence of both of them." Mencken was more or less correct, though Mary Garden, Sibyl Sanderson's protégée, was probably a stronger influence than Sanderson's herself. All three were glamorous opera singers whose love affairs sometimes attracted as much attention as their singing. Olive Fremstad, who also provided Willa Cather with the model for the heroine of her *Song of the Lark,* is the only one of the three with whom Huneker was ever linked romantically.

Huneker likened his heroine to the mythological Istar, a Babylonian goddess of sex and war, and patterned the novel on an obscure poem by Epopee d'Izdubar, "Istar's Descent into Hdes," from which he quotes the passage entitled "Painted Veils." There Istar travels through seven gates on her way through hell. At each one, she is stripped of an article of clothing until "At the seventh gate, the warder . . . took off the last veil that covers her body." The seven arts which Huneker practiced are represented by the seven veils which symbolically drape the seven sins to which he so often gleefully yielded. The gates of the poem also provided Huneker with the structure for his work which is divided into seven chapters called "gates."

As the characters progress through these gates, hypocrisy is stripped from them and at the end their true natures are revealed. "Hypocrisy is, as you say, necessary to screen certain unpleasant realities," Ulrick's friend Mel informs him. "It is a pia fraus; painted veils. Painted lies." Easter is an innocent, small-town singer at the first gate of the novel; by the time she reaches the sixth gate she is a dazzling opera star who has become "Istar, the Great Singing Whore of Modern Babylon." She is completely immoral, has taken up lesbianism, and has seduced Dora, the prostitute. Ulrick's best friend, a priest, has also fallen victim to her; instead of being corrupted by a religious man—as she was by Brother Rainbow—she has become a seducer of the cloth.

Easter's activities have a debilitating effect on Ulrick though his troubles seem more complex than simple dissatisfaction with her. Ulrick never appears satisfied—or even very successful—in his relationships with women. "He had ardently longed for this meeting," Ulrick thought during an embrace with Mona, "and now he was acting like a cowardly eunuch." As her passions increased, he "resisted her tumultuous onset blushing like a virgin." He behaved no better with Dora when he "turned his head away as she repeatedly kissed him." Even with Easter: "he kissed her on the mouth, but the champagne odour was repugnant." Ulrick's unhappiness and dissatisfaction are closely linked to his sexuality, and he may have been suffering a form of impotence not unlike his creator's. "All is lacking, if sex is lacking," Ulrick had disclosed to Easter, "or if the moisture of the right man is lacking." The revelation that it was Roarin' Nell, not Easter, with whom

he had coupled at the Holy Roller meeting horrified Ulrick, and he subsequently drank himself to death in Paris.

"As to my novel . . . it will shock you," Huneker wrote to William Crary Brownell, the urbane literary adviser to Scribner's, in a letter discussing the possibility of publishing the book with that firm. Charles Scribner had once told Huneker that he would tolerate anything Huneker chose to print, but obviously Scribner never expected a book "inscribed in all gratitude to the charming morganatic ladies, *les belles impures,* who make pleasanter this vale of tears for virile men. What shall it profit a woman if she saves her soul but loseth love?" The novel, in fact, was such a departure from his other work, which consisted largely of critical essays and studies of Chopin and Liszt, that Huneker had had the foresight to send the manuscript to other publishers, not only to Mencken but also to Alfred Knopf and Horace Liveright.

Scribners did like the book, however, or at least Huneker hyperbolically reported that they had told him "not in this generation have they read fiction so original, brilliant, *human,* or so well composed and written!" And they offered to publish it, but only in an expurgated edition "for a purer public" than Huneker wanted to reach on the first go-round. "As to the bowdlerization, nothing is decided upon," Huneker told T. R. Smith, Boni and Liveright's editorial assistant. "The story can stand on its merits without the humorous elements; of obscenity, vulgarity or indecency, there is not a trace; only extreme frankness and the sex side dealt with as if by a medical expert. Might I say gynecologist."

Boni and Liveright accepted the book complete with the "omphalic trimmings." As Dreiser's publisher, this firm had already had experience with controversial books, but even they would not issue the book in a trade edition. Huneker nevertheless entered into negotiations with Horace Liveright with high expectations of success, and a signed, private printing was scheduled for October 1920 ("if the police, prompted by the Society for the prevention of cruelty to imbeciles, don't intervene"). "I should like you to see the publisher's contract," he appealed to John Quinn. "I need money and I'm going to get it." In a letter to Horace Liveright about that contract, Huneker tried to anticipate contingencies which might arise: "And please mention English edition; and my rights to translations, dramatic and movie rights. I'll interpolate this claim if it is not included. As to probable date of payments; $1000 when the book appears, balance of $800 as soon as possible. I'll sign 1200 sheets; I wish there were 1500."

There were no translations, no expurgated editions, no movies, no plays, not even any lawsuits. But that first printing, offered only by subscription, quickly sold out in a ten-dollar edition printed expressly for, according to Mencken, "the admittedly damned." Issuing it this way entailed few risks, and an expensive, small printing had the additional virtue of appealing to collectors of pornography. While Mencken would not fall into that category, he was nevertheless one of the recipients. Pasted into his copy, now in the H. L. Mencken Room of the Enoch Pratt Free Library, is a card which reads: "To my old friend, the Attila of American criticism, and the salt of the earth generally, this book of senile scabrous morality is inscribed with the regards of James Huneker." Huneker also sent Mencken another card stating that the title should be changed to *Painted Tails;* he instructed Mencken to affix this to his copy as well, but apparently it was lost.

Had the book been more thoughtfully written—or perhaps only more slowly written—and skilfully developed, it might have won a less tentative place for itself in the annals of American literature. Huneker seemed well aware of the work's limitations when he wrote "No book, no matter what the length of its incubation, can be art, that is actually written in 7 weeks, less 2 days." Nevertheless, Harry Levin called *Painted Veils* the book which "ushered in the twenties," and the novel has been praised by others including Oscar Cargill who declared it an *"apologia pro vita sua*—one of the most remarkable ever written."

Painted Veils has also enjoyed short periods of popularity. In 1928, six years after Huneker's death, Horace Liveright successfully reissued it and in 1953 an Avon paperback edition is said to have had the astonishing sale of 200,000 copies. However, it did not have the *succès de scandale* Huneker might have anticipated after Mrs. N. P. Dawson used a superlative to describe it in the *New York Globe:* "There are disgusting scenes in *Painted Veils* that 'outstrip' anything that has ever been put in print before" (December 24, 1920). Nor did it gain the importance Columbia professor Vernon Loggins predicted in 1937 in *I Hear America,* In a discussion of three writers—Huneker, F. Scott Fitzgerald, and Carl Van Vechten—Loggins wrote: "But of all the books of sophistication published in America during the twenties the one which now seems most likely to last is James Gibbons Huneker's *Painted Veils.*"

Samuel Lipman (essay date 1987)

SOURCE: "James Huneker & America's Musical Coming of Age," in *The New Criterion,* Vol. V, No. 10, June, 1987, pp. 4-14.

[*In the following essay, Lipman details Huneker's writings about music.*]

Imagine a small child, said by some to be musically precocious, sitting at a Steinway grand piano more than forty years ago, vainly attempting to show interest in practicing some small pieces of Chopin. The California sun was shining outside, the day was short, and the practice hours were long. The demands of a doting mother and of a piano teacher of the old Russian school were strict even when not severe, and to the child the prospect of a lifetime of practice just possibly someday making perfect seemed dull indeed.

But wait. As the child stared sadly at the music before him, he found something more in those assorted yellow-bound volumes published by G. Schirmer than mere notes, the uninvited causes of his labors; there were words, too, enchanting descriptions of the Polish composer's music. Indeed, the greatness and romance the child could hardly find emerging from his own exertions he found in the words the kind publisher had provided:

During the last half of the nineteenth century two men became rulers of musical emotion, Richard Wagner and Frédéric-Francois Chopin. The music of the Pole is the most ravishing in the musical art. Wagner and Chopin; the macrocosm and the microcosm. Chopin, a young man, furiously playing his soul out upon the keyboard, the soul of his nation, the soul of his time, is the most individual composer who ever set humming the looms of our dreams. . . . Chopin is not only the poet of the pianoforte, he is the poet of music. . . .

There were exciting words, too, for the child about the individual pieces which sat so resistantly on the music-desk of the piano. Descriptions of the pieces the child was attempting to play were understandably the first sought out; here, alas, the child was disappointed, for the commentator's major efforts were devoted to those works of Chopin's beyond the child's technical command and physical grasp. But what magical comments there were for other, indubitably more exciting, compositions, compositions which, with practice, might well be performable when weak fingers were stronger and small hands were larger. Of the C-sharp minor Waltz, opus 64, no. 2, for example, the child read:

The veiled melancholy of the first theme has seldom been excelled by the composer. It is a fascinating lyric sorrow, and the psychologic motivation of the first theme in the curving figure of the second theme does not relax the spell. A space of clearer skies, warmer, more consoling winds are in the D flat interlude; but the spirit of unrest soon returns. The elegiac note is unmistakeable in this veritable soul dance.

The reader need remain in suspense no longer. The child so eager to read that the practice hours might pass more quickly was I; more important, the writer of the delicious and educative words that caused my time to move so profitably was James Huneker, a critic not just of music but of literature, drama, and painting, a critic whose historical position as our leading evangelist of the arts remains as firm today as it was at the time of his death in Brooklyn in 1921 at the age of sixty-four.

The coming of intellectual age which Huneker's florid notes in the Schirmer Chopin edition helped hasten for me parallels in a small way the major contribution he is credited with making toward the maturity of American cultural taste in the years before World War I. Indeed, the present received opinion of Huneker was voiced by H. L. Mencken, who liked to see himself as a prophetic figure in America's passage from provincialism to cosmopolitanism. In 1917, Mencken wrote of Huneker:

If the United States is in any sort of contact today, however remotely, with what is aesthetically going on in the more civilized countries—if the Puritan tradition, for all its firm entrenchment, has eager and resourceful enemies besetting it—if the pall of Harvard quasiculture, by the Oxford manner out of Calvinism, has been lifted ever so little—there is surely no man who can claim a larger share of credit for preparing the way. . . .

Mencken's claim is a large one, one which invites consideration of its truth in its own time. It also invites consideration for its relation to our putatively different musical life today. And so my task here will be to examine Huneker's critical career, chiefly with reference to music, but with examples from his writings about the other arts as well, to see just how far forward Huneker did indeed bring our attitudes toward high culture; I shall be concerned also to evaluate just what this artistic coming of age meant for the exact nature of American musical taste then—and now.

James Huneker was born in Philadelphia in 1857, the son of middle-class parents, German or Hungarian on his father's side, Irish on his mother's. Part of his inheritance was Fenian, for his maternal grandfather was a prominent Irish patriot who had emigrated from Country Donegal in 1820; part was music loving and art loving, for his father knew the pianists Sigismond Thalberg and Louis Moreau Gottschalk and the violinist Henri Vieuxtemps. The senior Huneker also owned a large collection of mezzotints, line engravings, etchings, and lithographs, including work by Lucas van Leyden, Dürer, and Rembrandt. His mother, a devout Roman Catholic who had been a schoolteacher before her marriage, wrote well and read omnivorously. Encouraged by his mother, from his earliest days the young Huneker got on well with Jews, studying Hebrew toward a possible future vocation as a priest. In much later life he responded to an Irish streetcar conductor who described the attractive and hilly neighborhood through which the vehicle was passing as "Kike's Peak" with the words: "God was ever good to the Irish and to his own."

The young Huneker didn't have an easy time in school, and made abortive attempts at becoming a railroad engineer, a lawyer, and a piano salesman. He had more success reading literature, quickly becoming acquainted with the work of Poe, Baudelaire, Gautier, and Flaubert. In the spring of 1878 Huneker visited Whitman in nearby Camden, but his father, aware of Whitman's dubious reputation, quickly put an end to the relationship. He was fascinated by the theater, which was in lively shape in Philadelphia in those pre-film and pre-television days. But his real love was music. He took piano lessons, and reveled in the locally produced chamber-music evenings, during which professional musicians played to an enthusiastic audience of amateurs. And while still in his teens, he started to write. His first effort, published in the *Evening Bulletin,* was a report of one such concert.

The 1876 Centennial Exposition in Philadelphia whetted the young Huneker's appetite for travel and experience of the wider world. To his already remarkably cosmopolitan upbringing he now added a year of piano studies in Paris at the end of the 1870s. Though later in life he taught piano in New York at Jeannette M. Thurber's National Conservatory of Music (upon the recommendation of Rafael Joseffy, the Chopin authority and pupil of Liszt), as a student Huneker wasn't good enough to gain admittance to the Paris *Conservatoire*; instead he had to content himself with auditing the class of Georges Mathias, a student of Chopin himself. As it has done for so many susceptible young Americans in the past two centuries, Paris opened

Huneker's mind even further to the new in music, literature, and the visual arts.

Huneker, of course, was hardly cut out by either nature or nurture to be an expatriate. But when he returned to the United States he found Philadelphia dull, despite its many musical activities. By now a writer for Theodore Presser's *Etude* magazine, Huneker cast longing eyes toward New York, then as now the center of American music. Finally, in 1886, he moved to New York, there to embark on the career of free-lance critic, which was to describe his way of life and thought for the next thirty-five years.

In New York, Huneker was caught up in a musical maelstrom. The new Metropolitan Opera House on Broadway and Thirty-ninth Street had opened in 1883 with a performance of Gounod's *Faust*; by 1892 all of Wagner's major works (save *Parsifal*) had been given there, and in the 1890s Metropolitan casts for both German and Italian operas reached a level of international distinction only rarely equaled since. In orchestra life, there were numerous and regular concerts by the New York Symphony under the leadership of the Damrosch family, and by the New York Philharmonic under Theodore Thomas in the 1880s and Anton Seidl in the 1890s. After 1887, the Boston Symphony played as many concerts annually in New York as did the Philharmonic. The opening of Carnegie Hall in 1891 was marked by a visit from Tchaikowsky, who conducted there his *Marche Solonnelle,* the Third Orchestral Suite, and the B-flat minor piano concerto. European artists were beginning to live in New York as well. Joseffy, who was born in Hungary, settled in New York after his 1879 debut under Leopold Damrosch; in the early 1890s the great Lithuanian-born pianist Leopold Godowsky established residence in New York, where he taught at the New York College of Music; from 1892 to 1895 the Czech composer Antonin Dvorák was the Director of the celebrated National Conservatory.

In the year of Huneker's arrival he attended the American premiere of Wagner's *Tristan und Isolde* at the Metropolitan Opera House, paying for a top-gallery ticket by pawning his overcoat. For all his many literary interests, music was his life. Soon after coming to New York he told a story in the *Etude* of a pianist on his deathbed who, asked by a priest whether he were a Catholic or a Protestant, answered: "Father, I am a pianist." In recounting this story, Arnold Schwab, Huneker's invaluable and indefatigable biographer, remarks that Huneker's reply "illustrates his own attitude toward religion"; it seems at least as likely that it illustrates Huneker's own attitude toward music and the piano.

For the next decade and more Huneker bathed in the heady cultural waters of a New York now beginning to combine the economic progress of a century of American independence with the contributions of the successive waves of immigrants—Irish, German, Central European, Balkan, Mediterranean, and Jewish—who were now placing their imprints on our nation. He reveled in the life of the little family hotels, where excellent table d'hôte dinners could be found in the company of artists and intellectual dreamers. Always a lover of Pilsner beer, he was a great saloon-goer, and there too he sampled New York's melting pot. As Huneker's biographer writes: "At Justus Schwab's greasy saloon near the German neighborhood of Tompkins Square, Huneker hobnobbed with French communards, Spanish and Italian refugees, German socialists, and Russian politicals."

All this time Huneker continued to write prolifically for newspapers and periodicals, as he was to do for the rest of his life. By 1899 he was ready to publish *Mezzotints in Modern Music,* his first of some twenty-one books. Two of these books were collections of previously published short fiction, three (among them a short history of the New York Philharmonic) were journalistic hack jobs, one consisted of two volumes of memoirs, and one was a remarkable novel, published shortly before he died. The remainder of Huneker's books were collections of essays on European subjects, based upon his free-lance articles, many of them on recent and romantic music but many also on the new dramatists of the 1890s, modern and classical painters, French and English literature, and the philosophy of Nietzsche.

Echoing in its title his father's collection of black-and-white art, *Mezzotints in Modern Music* established the framework for a critical career of remarkable intellectual consistency. It begins with a ringing article called **"The Music of the Future."** Curiously for a hot-headed lover of the new in art, but significantly for his critical development, Huneker's projected future seems to belong to Johannes Brahms, not Richard Wagner. In praising Brahms, then perceived as Wagner's archenemy and artistic opposite, Huneker puts his facility for purple prose at the service of an unwavering classic position:

> Brahms reminds one of those medieval architects whose life was a prayer in marble; who slowly and assiduously erected cathedrals, the mighty abutments of which flanked majestically upon mother earth, and whose thin, high pinnacles pierced the blue; whose domes hung suspended between heaven and earth, and in whose nave an army could worship, while in the forest of arches music came and went like the voices of many waters.

Elsewhere in *Mezzotints in Modern Music* Huneker is nothing if not eclectic. He writes at length about Tchaikowsky, Richard Strauss and Nietzsche, Chopin, Liszt, and Wagner, mixing praise and reservations. Even when Huneker's reservations are quite severe, the prevailing tone is one that encourages the reader to seek out the music for himself. Thus in the case of Tchaikowsky, when Huneker finds himself unable to understand the second and third movements of the *Pathétique* Symphony—he describes the five-four meter of the second as "a perverted valse, but one that could not be danced to unless you owned three legs"—he still can find the movement "delightfully piquant music," and call the "touch of Oriental color in the trio . . . very felicitous." And for the famous last movement, Huneker pulls out all the stops of exalted *fin de siècle* literary morbidity:

> Since the music of the march in the Eroica, since the mighty funeral music in Siegfried, there has

been no such death music as this "adagio lamentoso," this astounding torso, which Michel Angelo would have understood and Dante wept over. It is the very apotheosis of mortality, and its gloomy accents, poignant melody and harmonic coloring make it one of the most impressive of contributions to mortuary music. It sings of the entombment of a nation, and is incomparably noble, dignified and unspeakably tender. It is only at the close that the rustling of the basses conveys a sinister shudder; the shudder of the Dies Irae when the heavens shall be a fiery scroll and the sublime trump sounds its summons to eternity.

Huneker waxes enthusiastic about Richard Strauss's 1896 tone poem *Also sprach Zarathustra,* clearly relishing the linkage between Strauss's music and Nietzsche's iconoclastic philosophy. For Huneker the composition is

> the gigantic torso of an art work for the future. Euphony was hurled to the winds, the Addisonian ductility of Mozart, the Théophile Gautier coloring of Schumann, Chopin's delicate romanticism, all were scorned as not being truthful enough for the subject in hand, and the subject is not a pretty or sentimental one. Strauss, with his almost superhuman mastery of all schools, could have written with ease in the manner of any of his predecessors, but, like a new Empedocles on Aetna, preferred to leap into the dark, or rather into the fiery crater of truth.

Overall, Huneker stresses Strauss's achievements in gaining control over "the indefiniteness of music," and in giving "an emotional grab to pure abstractions." In the end, Huneker is under no illusion that in the union between the superman-poet and superman-composer there can be any winner but the music. His words once again emphasize a belief in the primacy of music:

> Poor, unfortunate, marvelous Nietzsche! But it is Strauss mirroring his own moods after feeding full on Nietzsche, and we must be content to swallow his title, "Also sprach Zarathustra," when in reality it is "thus Spake Richard Strauss!"

From Strauss, Huneker moves back to Chopin, thus embarking on a course he was to take often in his life. Always determined to defend Chopin against charges that he was a sentimental miniaturist, Huneker looks for "the greater Chopin," the classic master of noble forms and large emotions. This Chopin he finds in such then less-played works as the F-sharp major Impromptu, the three Polonaises (those in F-sharp minor, A-flat major, and the Polonaise-Fantasy in A-flat minor), the Preludes, and the Scherzi. Quick to find the equivalents between creators in different arts, Huneker compares Chopin with Poe. For him they both were

> [e]xquisite artificers in precious cameos . . . of a consanguinity because of their devotion to Our Ladies of Sorrow, the Mater Lachrymarum, the Mater Suspiriorum and the Mater Tenebrarum of Thomas de Quincey. If the Mater Malorum—Mother of Evil—presided over their lives, they never in their art became as Baudelaire, a sinis-

ter "Israfel of the sweet lute." Whatever their personal shortcomings, the disorders of their lives found no reflex beyond that of melancholy.

If Huneker loves Chopin, he only likes Liszt. Somewhere he sees Liszt as a mountebank both spiritual and musical. Even when describing the B-minor Sonata, the Liszt piano work he most admires, he cannot help remarking on the composer's insincerity. This insincerity is shown in the appearance of "the sigh of sentiment, of passion, of abandonment which engenders the notion that when Liszt was not kneeling before a crucifix, he was before a woman." Huneker is fascinated by Liszt's path-breaking Transcendental Etudes and Concert Etudes, but it is significant that he ends his *Mezzotints* chapter on etudes for the piano by advising pianists to "play the Chopin études, daily, also the preludes, for the rest trust to God and Bach. Bach is the bread of the pianist's life; always play him that your musical days may be long in the land."

Finally, of course, there is Wagner. Huneker is at great pains to separate the composer from his literary utterances:

> Keep in your mind that Wagner the artist was a greater man than Wagner the vegetarian, Wagner the anti-vivisectionist, Wagner the revolutionist, the Jew hater, the foe of Meyerbeer and Mendelssohn, and greater than Wagner the philosopher.

Huneker finds Wagner "a poet of passion," though he does not admire the composer's librettos. In a mixed tribute to the composer, Huneker closes *Mezzotints* with a kind of surrender: "We are the slaves of our age, and we adore Wagner because he moves us, thrills and thralls us. His may not be the most spiritual art, but it is the most completely fascinating."

Huneker's second book is devoted to Chopin. Called *Chopin: The Man and His Music,* the book, published in 1900, attempts to serve as biography, study of the composer's psychology, and a brief description of each piece in his oeuvre. What Huneker achieves in this book is not scholarship, reasoned consideration of his idol, or even a real book; rather he is here the piano *aficionado,* the worshiper at the sacred fount of the keyboard. For him, the Etudes are "Titanic Experiments"; the Preludes are "Moods in Miniature"; the Nocturnes describe "Night and its Melancholy Mysteries"; the Ballades are "Faëry Dramas"; the Polonaises are "Heroic Hymns of Battle"; the Mazurkas are "Dances of the Soul"; the Scherzi are "Chopin the Conqueror." The end of the book is a tribute to the immortality of art and the artist, thrown into the void of the future:

> He did not always succeed, but his victories are the precious prizes of mankind. One is loath to believe that the echo of Chopin's magic music can ever fall upon unheeding ears. He may become old-fashioned, but, like Mozart, he will remain eternally beautiful.

Huneker's two books of short fiction, the 1902 *Melomaniacs* and the 1905 *Visionaries,* convey by their titles something of the overheated, extravagant, and bizarre atmosphere of the stories they contain. The most significant

influence on Huneker's style—in addition to Poe—was Joris Karl Huysmans, whose 1884 novel *A rebours* still seems a century later the most important example of *l'esprit décadent*. To the classic symbolist—and later decadent—brew of voluptuousness, febrile nervosity, indulgence in drugs and alcohol, obsessive seeking after sensation, and Satanism, Huneker adds the triumph of music as queen of the arts by putting in melomania—a crazed involvement in music whereby the art of tone becomes an all-consuming, destructive passion.

In these forty-four stories (several more are scattered through the books of essays), Huneker presents an asylum gallery of artists, along with the trapped members of their families. His protagonists are varied, though curiously repetitious. A composer creates a music so emotionally powerful that its performance in Paris causes a conflagration that destroys the city. A pianist, now surviving by playing in a cheap restaurant, tells of his drunken and botched debut, caused by his awareness the evening before that his coming failure would kill his parents. A soothsayer creates a new art—the eighth deadly sin—out of perfumes. A mad Russian scientist uses fireworks to make a world-conquering beauty, but the fireworks get out of control and kill the watching thousands. An Irish priest is taken to a Greek Orthodox baby who turns out to be the Antichrist; by baptizing the child the priest destroys the creature's spell. Perched between the mock-serious and the dead-serious, these stories now seem too artificial to compel attention, but in their day they must have caused many a maiden—and bachelor too, for that matter—to shiver. Again, they testify to the gathering strength of art as a religious mania. Despite their slight value as literature, Huneker's stories do make clear an important change in turn-of-the-century opinion about the significance of music and the other arts: from merely expressing tragedy, they have progressed to causing it.

Increasingly, the word "anarch" becomes central for Huneker, who lays stress upon the idea of the great artistic creator as totally self-governing. Thus *Overtones,* his 1904 collection of essays, is dedicated to Strauss, whom Huneker calls in the dedication "An Anarch of Art." Strauss's overlordship is shown in his "cold, astringent voluptuousness." Huneker goes on to write:

> He himself may be a Merlin,—all great composers are ogres in their insatiable love of power,—but he has rescued us from the romantic theatric blight; and a change of dynasty is always welcome to slaves of the musical habit.

Once again it is curious that in the foregoing quotation Huneker rejects Wagner's unification of the arts in favor of that expression in music alone for which he admired Brahms, and for which he now credits Strauss. This quotation is of interest too for its comfortable Nietzschean division of the world into master and slaves—in this case the master who composes and the slaves who have the musical habit.

It is no surprise when, in *Overtones,* Huneker goes on to reject Wagner's *Parsifal* as absolute music and to find in the opera a "lack of absolute sincerity . . . the work of a man who had outlived his genius." In this judgment of

Parsifal, Huneker is only walking in the footsteps of Nietzsche, who followed a period of Wagner idolatry with the most vitriolic rejection of *Der Meister* on record. In Nietzsche's condemnation of Wagner's causing music to be taken over by the drama, Huneker finds corroboration for his own conviction that "music pure and simple, for itself, undefiled by costumes, scenery, limelights, and vocal virtuosi, is the noblest music of all."

Elsewhere in *Overtones* Huneker scorns Mendelssohn as a writer of "Bach watered for general consumption." Continuing the fight of the Nineties over Max Nordau's *Degeneration*—a rejection of modern art (and artists) as depraved—he asserts that "there are no sane men of genius." He rejects Verdi's music written before *Aida* as brainless, though promising and potent—but he praises *Falstaff* to the skies. He admires Debussy's new *Pelléas et Mélisande,* though without finding it successful as absolute music. He ends with a plea for "intellectual music" without "metaphysical meanings," and his proffered model is Mozart's G-minor Symphony: "in its sunny measures is sanity."

Neither the 1905 *Iconoclasts* nor the 1909 *Egoists* deals with music at all. *Iconoclasts* is concerned with the contemporary European dramatists—first among them Ibsen—and in particular with plays containing a social message. Because my main concern here is with Huneker as a music critic, it is perhaps only necessary to remark that in his fulsome praise for Ibsen he seems to have one standard, that of realism, for drama, and another, that of beauty, for music:

> Love me, love my truth, the playwright says in effect; and we are forced to make a wry face as we swallow the nauseous and unsugared pill he forces down our sentimental gullets.

Egoists carries the subtitle "A Book of Supermen," and is chiefly interesting for its articles on nineteenth-century French writers, including Stendhal, Baudelaire, Flaubert, Anatole France, Huysmans, and Maurice Barrés—in addition to Nietzsche and Stirner. The book treats these disparate creatures as supreme individualists, and though it gives them high praise for their ability to follow their own way, Huneker seems to be making an attempt to gain rational control of an artistic movement all too easily allowed to luxuriate, as it had in his own short fiction, in its own willfulness. Thus, in the essay on Baudelaire, he attacks the idea that artists are dissipated creatures:

> What the majority of mankind does not know concerning the habits of literary workers is this prime fact: men who work hard, writing verse— and there is no mental toil comparable to it— cannot drink, or indulge in opium, without the inevitable collapse. The old-fashioned ideas of "inspiration," spontaneity, easy improvisation, the sudden bolt from heaven, are delusions still hugged by the world. To be told that Chopin filed at his music for years, that Beethoven in his smithy forged his thunderbolts, that Manet toiled like a labourer on the dock . . . is a disillusion for the sentimental.

And with Nietzsche, too, Huneker, if not actually changing his opinion on the philosopher's stature as a superman and an "anarch," seems to qualify his position:

> No longer is he a bogey man, not a creature of blood and iron, not a constructive or an academic philosopher, but simply a brilliant and suggestive thinker who, because of the nature of his genius, could never have erected an elaborate philosophic system, and a writer not quite as dangerous to established religion and morals as some critics would have us believe.

The 1910 *Promenades of an Impressionist* is concerned with painting. The use of "impressionist" in the title does not refer to the painters of that school but to Huneker's characteristic device of critical impressionism, the recording of his reactions and feelings as aroused by the art he was considering. The book opens with a discussion of the post-Impressionist Cézanne, whom Huneker respects but cannot warm up to. As would happen when he came to face the new music of Arnold Schoenberg, Huneker is careful to make the distinction between truth and beauty:

> Stubborn, with an instinctive hatred of academic poses, of the atmosphere of the studio, of the hired model, of "literary," or mere digital cleverness, Cézanne has dropped out of his scheme harmony, melody, beauty—classic, romantic, symbolic, what you will!—and doggedly represented the ugliness of things. But there is a brutal strength, a tang of the soil that is bitter, and also strangely invigorating, after the false, perfumed boudoir art of so many of his contemporaries.

In *Promenades,* Huneker gives a sign that, as the appreciator of the new, he is increasingly conscious that a critic can in his life represent only one moment of artistic revolution, and that the critic's role too will be superseded. Thus, he compares Cézanne's still lifes to those of the eighteenth-century painter Chardin:

> Chardin interprets still-life with realistic beauty; if he had ever painted an onion it would have revealed a certain grace. When Paul Cézanne paints an onion, you smell it. Nevertheless, he has captured the affections of the rebels and is their god. And next season it may be someone else.

Huneker's lurking rejection of the new in art becomes clear when he writes of Frans Hals: "How thin and insubstantial modern painting is if compared to this magician. . . ."

From this point on, it is difficult not to feel that, with one glorious exception at the very end of his life, Huneker's remaining books mark a downward curve. The 1911 *Franz Liszt* is a congeries of quotations from contemporaries of the composer and lists of his pupils and descriptions of their playing. Despite praise for Liszt's emancipation of instrumental music through his contributions to the symphonic poem, much of the book is merely a hymn to the piano, Liszt's graceful contribution to which, Huneker realizes, "will die hard, yet die it will." Of Liszt's arrangements and paraphrases, Huneker writes: "One may show off with them, make much noise and a reputation for virtuosity, that would be quickly shattered if a Bach fugue were selected as a text."

The very title of the 1913 *Pathos of Distance,* taken from Nietzsche, admirably conveys the tone of retrospection which will now increasingly characterize Huneker's writing, and marks, along with the consideration of Schoenberg two years later in *Ivory Apes and Peacocks,* the limits of Huneker's wholehearted acceptance of the new. In *The Pathos of Distance,* Huneker admires post-Impressionism, but without paying it the ultimate honor:

> Rhythmic intensity is the key to the new school; line, not colour is king. Not beauty, but, as Rodin said, character, character is the aim of the new art.

While Huneker could find room in his pantheon for Cézanne, Gauguin, Van Gogh, and Matisse, he could find no such place for the Cubists:

> The catalogue of the Tenth Autumn Salon [Paris, 1912] shows. . . few masterpieces, much sterile posing in paint, any quantity of mediocre talent, and in several salles devoted to the Cubists and others of the ilk any amount of mystification, charlatanry, and an occasional glimpse of individuality. I am in sympathy with revolutionary movements in art, but now I know that my sympathies have reached their outermost verge.

In the 1915 *Ivory Apes and Peacocks* Huneker seems willing to accept the music of Schoenberg's *Pierrot Lunaire* as something the future may embrace, though it is plain that his tolerance of it owes entirely to the demands of reason and not to love:

> I fear and dislike the music of Arnold Schoenberg. . . . the aura of Arnold Schoenberg is, for me, the aura of subtle ugliness, of hatred and contempt, of cruelty, and of the mystic grandiose. He is never petty. He sins in the grand manner of Nietzsche's Superman, and he has the courage of his chromatics. If such music-making is ever to become accepted, then I long for Death the Releaser. More shocking still would be the suspicion that in time I might be persuaded to like this music, to embrace, after abhorring it. . . . I have been informed that the ear should play a secondary role in this "new" music; no longer through the porches of the ear must filter plangent tones, wooing the tympanum with ravishing accords. It is now the "inner ear," which is symbolic of a higher type of musical art. A complete dissociation of ideas, harmonies, rhythmic life, architectonic is demanded. To quote an admirer of the Vienna revolutionist: "The entire man in you must be made over before you can divine Schoenberg's art". . . . Cheer up, brethren! Preserve an open mind. It is too soon to beat reactionary bosoms, crying aloud, Nunc dimittis! Remember the monstrous fuss made over the methods of Richard Strauss and Claude Debussy. I shouldn't be surprised if ten years hence Arnold Schoenberg proves quite as conventional a member of musical society as those two other "anarchs of art."

Unfortunately, this laudable optimism that a new generation will make up its mind favorably about currently problematic art rings false in the light of Huneker's own unwillingness to praise any new music as he had praised the new music of his youth. The new music was not what he loved; he did not love Stravinsky, Kodály, and Bartok, of whom Huneker can say no more than that they "are not to be slighted." Even more clearly, his beloved music was not that of Prokofiev: Huneker, though he later was to find some of the composer's miniature piano pieces "piquant," in a 1918 review (quoted in the Arnold Schwab biography) thought his music "volitional and essentially cold," marked by "intrinsic poverty of ideas," and written by a "psychologist of the uglier emotions—hate, contempt, rage—above all, rage—disgust, despair, mockery, and defiance." Even in the case of his once-adored Richard Strauss, Huneker is unable to go beyond *Salome, Elektra,* and *Der Rosenkavalier. Ariadne auf Naxos,* the premiere of which in the original Max Reinhardt version he attended in Stuttgart in 1912, he found a misfire, and for the probable success of Strauss in the future he is forced to fall back upon the composer's undoubted success in the past.

Though in *Ivory Apes and Peacocks* and the subsequent 1917 *Unicorns* Huneker is still capable of praise for new literature—he admires Conrad, Wedekind, the now forgotten Russian novelist Michael Artzibashef, and Joyce—his musical world seems to have closed in. He has nothing to say in his books about any American composer save Edward MacDowell, and only in the case of a few performers—the pianists Godowsky and Vladimir de Pachmann, and the singer Mary Garden—can he manage something like the old enthusiasm.

Indeed, what I have earlier called Huneker's increasing mood of retrospection comes to a climax in his last book, the post-humously printed *Variations,* which appeared in 1921. In a chapter entitled "A Mood Reactionary," presciently anticipating today's sophisticated musical opinion, Huneker writes in his own name what he had only written before as a spoof under the pseudonym of "Old Fogy":

> Berlioz, Tchaikowsky and R. Strauss are not for all time.

> The truth is that musical art has gone far afield from the main travelled road, has been led into blind alleys and dark forests. . . . [W]ho has "improved" on Bach, Handel, Haydn, Mozart, Gluck, Beethoven, Schubert, Schumann, Chopin? Name, name, I ask. What's the use of talking about the "higher average of today?" How much higher? You mean that more people go to concerts, more people enjoy music, than fifty years or a hundred years ago. Do they? I doubt it. Of what use all our huge temples of worship if the true gods of art no longer be worshipped therein? Numbers prove nothing. . . . The multiplication of orchestras, opera-houses, singing-societies, and concerts are not indicative that general culture is achieved. Quality, not quantity, should be the shibboleth. The tradition of the classics is fading, soon it shall vanish. We care little for the masters. Modern music worship is a fashionable fad. People go to listen because

they think it is the mode. Alack and alas! that is not the true spirit in which to approach the Holy of Holies, Bach, Handel, Mozart, and Beethoven. Oremus!

And lest the words I have just quoted be taken as no more than the passing mood of a prolific writer, the final words of *Variations,* in all their simplicity, convey all too well the mood of Huneker's musical last will and testament:

> A good comrade, a loving husband and father, the giant tenor of his generation, Enrico Caruso is dead. But to his admirers, he remains the dearest memory in this drab, prosaic age.

Two books more of James Huneker remain to be considered: *Steeplejack,* the memoirs which appeared in book form in 1920 after their newspaper publication two years earlier, and *Painted Veils,* his 1920 novel. *Steeplejack* is a charming book, full of reminiscences and amplified gleanings from previously published material. The anecdotes it contains are wonderful, and one of them at least deserves immortality:

> I made Monsignor laugh [on a visit to the Vatican in 1905] when I retailed that venerable tale about Liszt's repentance and withdrawal from the world to the Oratory of the Madonna del Rosario on Monte Mario, an hour from Rome. Pope Pio Nono conferred upon the Magyar pianist the singular honor of personally hearing his confession and receiving the celebrated sinner into the arms of Mother Church. (Perhaps the delightful old Pope was curious.) After the first day and night, Liszt was still on his knees, muttering into the exhausted ears of the unhappy Pontiff the awful history of his life and loves. Then, extenuated, Pio Nono begged his penitent: "Basta! Caro Liszt. Your memory is marvellous. Now go to the piano and play there the remainder of your sins."

But even more important than *Steeplejack's* anecdotes are the revelations it contains about his own approach to work as a critic. In an attack upon Swinburne's statement that the chief attraction of the profession of criticism should be the possibility of giving noble praise, Huneker points out that the poet "had the most vitriolic pen in England," and then goes on to remark:

> . . . neither praise nor blame should be the goal of the critic. To spill his own soul, that should be his aim. Notwithstanding the talk about objective criticism, no such abstraction is thinkable. A critic relates his prejudices, nothing more. It is well to possess prejudices. They lend to life a meaning.

But Huneker's mature thoughts on criticism are concerned with more than his own individual impressionist style. He knows too, and marvelously expresses, the universal truth that a critic is at the mercy of the artistic quality of that about which he writes:

> I was slowly discovering that to become successful, a critic can't wait for masterpieces, but must coddle mediocrity. Otherwise, an idle pen. Big talents are rare, so you must, to hold your job,

praise conventional patterns. And that way leads to the stifling of critical values.

Huneker's novel, *Painted Veils,* begins with a *fin de siècle* epigraph, redolent of the diabolism with which Huneker had played for so many years:

Now the Seven Deadly Virtues are: Humility, Charity, Meekness, Temperance, Brotherly Love, Diligence, Chastity. And the Seven Deadly Arts are: Poetry, Music, Architecture, Painting, Sculpture, Drama, Dancing.

The novel tells the story of an American opera singer, greatly gifted in voice and ambition, and a rich American expatriate. The opera singer, meant to suggest Istar, the Assyrian goddess of love, knowing nothing of virtue, chooses the deadly art of music and lets nothing human or divine stand in the way of her career. The American expatriate, her lover and a sometime music critic whose life in many ways parallels Huneker's knows the good, but allows himself to be the cause of the ruin of others. The opera singer, after a lifetime of sexual license, remains "the greatest Isolde since Lilli Lehmann . . . Istar, the Great Singing Whore of Modern Babylon." Her American lover dies in Paris in the final stages of syphilis. Long after the novel's many bawdy incidents have been forgotten, the reader retains a strong and moving impression that for Huneker, as for so many Catholics on the Continent, art has been the other, and reverse, face of God. In this, his last book published during his lifetime, Huneker returned, in symbolic expression if not in actual observance, to the devout Catholicism of his family.

As this consideration of James Huneker comes to its end, the real nature of his contribution to the cultural taste of his America, and to the cultural taste of our America, becomes clear. There can be no doubt that he was a vivid and effective messenger, not just for the various arts of the 1890s but in a wider sense for the European gospel of art and aestheticism. Whatever may have been his contribution to the advancement of American taste in literature and drama, it seems that in the visual arts he recoiled personally from the implications of much of the new painting from post-Impressionism onward. The fact that in the service of the gospel of the new he felt it necessary to praise that which he could not love suggests an earlier origin for today's spurious doctrine of the artistic "cutting edge." It also suggests the importance of Huneker's role, and that of his historical reputation, in fostering that doctrine.

In the case of music, his recoil from the avant-garde very likely returned him to a taste that went little further than Chopin. In this he functioned not to bring American opinion over to the side of the new music of the Eighties and Nineties, which in any case had achieved wide popularity on its own by the coming of the twentieth century, but rather to solidify that antecedent worship of the classic German composers and Chopin which to this day marks the orientation of cultivated music lovers.

A word is in order, too, about Huneker's literary achievement. Unlike his music-critic colleagues (and friends) H. E. Krehbiel, Richard Aldrich, and Lawrence Gilman, Huneker was an exciting writer. In this day of the increasing penetration of criticism—especially music criticism—

by the academy, Huneker's work strikes me as possessing, and conveying, the golden value of artistic involvement. In the best sense, his style was always oriented to action, leading the reader toward ever more vital thought about and experience of art.

It must not be forgotten that James Huneker began his critical career as a musician and pianist, and a musician and a pianist he remained to the end of his life. When Mencken's philistine-bashing boosterism of Huneker's contribution to advanced taste in America is properly forgotten, I hope that I at least, in tribute to my childish hours of attention to Huneker while sitting at the piano, will remember his words from the closing paragraph of **Steeplejack:**

> I can't play cards or billiards. I can't read day and night. I take no interest in the chess-board of politics, and I am not too pious. What shall I do? Music, always music! There are certain compositions by Chopin to master which eternity itself would not be too long . . . I once more place the notes on the piano desk . . . How many years have I not played that magic music? Music the flying vision . . . music that merges with the tender air . . . its image melts in shy misty shadows . . . the cloud, the cloud, the singing, shining cloud . . . over the skies and far away . . . the beckoning cloud. . . .

FURTHER READING

Byrne, Norman T. "James Gibbons Huneker." *Scribner's Magazine* LXXI, No. 3 (March 1922): 300-03.
    Profiles Huneker, concluding that his "chief value lies . . . not in his works, which with the exception of the study of Chopin will probably be forgotten comparatively soon, but in his having, in the freshness of his method, paraded before the American public his ideas on an art of which they were all but totally ignorant."

DeCasseres, Benjamin. *James Gibbons Huneker.* New York: Joseph Lawren, 1925, 62 p.
    Laudatory, impressionistic survey of Huneker's works, with a bibliography of primary and secondary sources.

———. "Foreword." In *Intimate Letters of James Gibbons Huneker,* edited by Josephine Huneker, n.p. New York: Liveright Publishing Corp., 1936.
    Appreciative commentary noting: "No matter what or whom [Huneker] was writing about he was writing about Huneker. He saw all genius as one of the facets of himself."

Gilman, Lawrence. "The Book of the Month: Huneker's Letters." *North American Review* CCXVI, No. 805 (December 1922): 843-48.
    Favorable review of *Letters of James Gibbons Huneker,* calling Huneker's correspondence "buoyant, brave, delightful."

Hind, C. Lewis. "James Gibbons Huneker." In his *More Authors and I,* pp. 159-64. New York: Dodd, Mead and Co., 1922.

Personal profile offering a favorable assessment of Huneker's journalistic style.

Huneker, James. "Huneker on Huneker." *American Mercury* 1, No. 1 (January 1924): 22-6.
    Reprints letters from the period 1908 to 1920 addressed to music critic Edward Ziegler of the *New York Herald* and editor Maxwell E. Perkins of Charles Scribner's Sons, among others.

Kazin, Alfred. "American Fin de Siècle." In his *On Native Grounds: An Interpretation of Modern American Prose Literature,* pp. 63-6. New York: Harcourt, Brace and Co., 1942.
    Identifies Huneker as the embodiment of fin-de-siècle impressionism in American literary journalism. According to Kazin: "Impressionism was often nonsense; but it also marked the apprenticeship of the modern critical spirit in America."

Matthiessen, F. O. "Sherman and Huneker." In his *The Responsibilities of the Critic: Essays and Reviews* edited by John Rackliffe, pp. 154-59. New York: Oxford University Press, 1952.
    Discusses Huneker's critical style in terms of the work of the American critic Stuart P. Sherman, finding the work of the latter to be "the more permanently valuable." According to Matthiessen, Huneker's essays "appear rather like disjointed passages of conversation, . . . full of charm and gusto, playing gaily over the surfaces, but communicating very little of exactly what quality distinguishes one work from another, and defining almost nothing."

Mencken, H. L. "Huneker: A Memory." In his *Prejudices: Third Series,* pp. 65-83. New York: Alfred A. Knopf, 1922.
    Offers personal reminiscences of Huneker and assesses his influence in the development of American literary criticism. According to Mencken, Huneker is best remembered for bringing to American criticism the idea that "art is no longer, even by implication, a device for improving the mind. It is wholly a magnificent adventure."

———. "Introduction." In *Essays by James Huneker,* edited by H. L. Mencken, pp. ix-xxiii. New York: Charles Scribner's Sons, 1929.
    Characterizes Huneker as "one of the most charming fellows ever heard of, and the best critic of the American first line," praising Huneker's pioneering critical affirmation of many European artists and thinkers.

Roosbroeck, G. L. van. Review of *Essays by James Huneker,* edited by H. L. Mencken. *Romanic Review* XXII, No. 1 (January-March 1931): 62-4.
    Characterizes Huneker as the "most candid and competent" of the group of fin-de-siècle literary journalists who introduced American readers to such European artists, composers, and authors as Friedrich Nietzsche, Richard Strauss, Paul Cézanne, Arthur Rimbaud, and Vincent Van Gogh, among others.

Schwab, Arnold T. "Georg Brandes and James Huneker: A Cosmopolitan Friendship." *Modern Language Forum* XXXVIII, Nos. 3-4 (September-December 1953): 30-49.
    Traces Huneker's relationship with the Danish critic Georg Brandes, to whom Huneker had dedicated *Egoists* in 1909. Schwab reprints extant correspondence between the two critics in its entirety.

————. *James Gibbons Huneker: Critic of the Seven Arts.* Stanford, Calif.: Stanford University Press, 1963, 384 p.

> Features detailed accounts of the compositional background, publishing history, and critical reception of Huneker's works.

Smith, Bernard. "The Twentieth Century." In his *Forces in American Criticism: A Study in the History of American Literary Thought,* pp. 266-301. New York: Harcourt, Brace and Co., 1939.

> Characterizes Huneker's critical essays as receptive and enthusiastic though lacking in philosophical depth and discrimination. According to Smith, Huneker embodied "a type, a perfect symbol of his age. . . . In both the man and the writer—in his cosmopolitanism, his contempt for small-town righteousness, his sensuality, and his grim, inflexible individualism—the 'smart set' and their zealous apes could find a delightful reflection of their profoundest impulses."

Additional coverage of Huneker's life and career is contained in the following source published by Gale Research: *Dictionary of Literary Biography*, **Vol. 71.**

Ellen Key

1849-1926

Swedish educator and feminist.

INTRODUCTION

Sometimes called the "great-aunt of radical Europe," Key is best known as a pacifist and feminist whose ideas influenced social policies both in her native Sweden and throughout the western world. Key maintained a nearly mystical view of maternity, and her feminist theories elevated motherhood—whether it involved actual childbearing or "mothering" society's ills by agitating for peace—to a place of central importance in the psychological and social realization of women. She also believed that international reconciliation of differences would eventually lead to a recognition of war as barbaric, much as slavery or cannibalism had been recognized as such, and to its abolition. She was a popular lecturer and the recipient of many accolades from her contemporaries, who praised her energy and inspiration.

Biographical Information

Born on December 11, 1849 in Västervik, Sweden, Key was the daughter of a politician and estate-owner. In 1868 her family moved to Stockholm, where Key was trained as a teacher. She began publishing in Swedish periodicals during the 1880s, expressing social and political views, particularly those on women's individualism and property rights, that were criticized by conservatives as tantamount to advocating atheism and free love. Key continued teaching until 1900, then turned to lecturing and writing full-time, producing some thirty books over the course of her life. From 1903 to 1909 she left Sweden to live abroad, where she was welcomed by fellow progressives, particularly in Germany. Key was disappointed by Germany's militarism in World War I and by the refusal of French and German feminist organizations to send delegates to The Hague, Holland, to support a peace movement founded by women. By 1910 she had returned to Sweden. After World War I, Key called for reconciliation between the nations involved in the conflict and appealed to outraged mothers to lead a revolt that would bring about lasting world peace. Key died on April 25, 1926.

Major Works

In her best-known book, *Barnets århundrade* (*The Century of the Child*), Key took a critical stance toward prevailing educational theories and assailed traditional sex roles in and out of marriage. Her anti-authoritarian approach to education exerted a powerful influence in Scandinavian public schools. In *Lifslinjer* (*Life-Lines*), she discussed the vibrant intellectual life available to independent-minded and strong-willed women. The philosophy of morals of

that work reflected Key's emphasis on duty, self-discipline, faithfulness, and beauty. She followed this work with *Kvinorörelsen* (*The Woman Movement*), an exposition of her belief in women's power, and *Kriget, freden och framtiden* (*War, Peace and the Future*), a full accounting of her pacifist views.

PRINCIPAL WORKS

Individualism och Socialism (nonfiction) 1895
Missbrukad Kvinnokraft [*The Strength of Women Misused*] (nonfiction) 1896
Kvinnopsykologi och kvinnlig logik (nonfiction) 1896
Tankebilder [*Thought Pictures*] (nonfiction) 1898
Människor (nonfiction) 1899
Barnets århundrade [*The Century of the Child*] (nonfiction) 1900
Lifslinjer. 3 vols. [*Life-Lines*] (nonfiction) 1903-6
Kvinorörelsen [*The Woman Movement*] (nonfiction) 1909
Love and Marriage (nonfiction) 1911

Kriget, freden och framtiden [*War, Peace and the Future*]
   (nonfiction)   1914
En djupare syn på kriget   (nonfiction)   1916
Allsegraren. 2 vols.   (nonfiction)   1918-24

CRITICISM

The New York Times Book Review   (essay date 1909)

SOURCE: "When the Child Gets His Rights," in *The New York Times Book Review*, March 6, 1909, p. 128.

[*In the following review, the anonymous author praises* The Century of the Child, *noting, however, that many of Key's assertions will already be taken for granted by American readers because of the direction of the women's movement in the United States at the time of the work's publication in English.*]

Among the books of serious import that have been published in Germany during the last year or two, none has attracted wider attention or caused more general discussion than Ellen Key's **The Century of the Child**. It has won the consideration of the Kaiser, has gone through more than twenty editions, and has been published in several other European countries. The author was formerly among the foremost champions of the feminist movement in Germany, but she severed her connection with the cause of woman's emancipation because she had come to believe that it was working on a wrong basis, and that the best good of the sex and of the race demanded a different conception of woman's nature and a different attitude toward her mission in the world.

The author declares that she has not renounced her belief in the right of woman to choose her own way in life, to work out her own individual destiny, but she contends that in all this woman must guard herself, and must be protected by society, from the necessity of engaging in any work that would injure or interfere with the maternal function, if she is or expects ever to be a mother. In that category Ellen Key puts work outside the home, whether professional or industrial, and any occupation that would tend to make much draft upon her energy. Nevertheless, she believes that it is for the good both of the individual and of society that every able-bodied person, men and women alike, should work, should have some money earning occupation which would afford economical independence.

"I do not believe," she says, "that social development will maintain the old ideal of the father as the one who takes care of the family. I hope, rather, that the new conception of having every individual look after himself will gain more ground." And in recognition of the immense value to society of the mother's business as conservator of the family and trainer of the children, while this occupation lasts "society must guarantee her existence." "It is plain," she goes on, "that nothing is now more needed than such plans of social order, such programmes of education, as

will give the mother back to her children and to her home."

The book takes its title from a sentence in the drama *The Lion's Whelp*, wherein one of the characters, speaking near the end of the last century, says: "The next century will be the century of the child, just as this century has been the woman's century. When the child gets his rights morality will be perfected." The primary rights of the child for which the author contends are the right to be born of loving, harmonious parents, healthy and strong in body and sound in brain and soul, into a home where it is welcome and into the arms of a mother willing and able to care for, to train and teach it through its childhood.

The granting of its rights to the child, before and after its birth, she expects will have upon mankind such developing, humanizing, uplifting effect as it has never before known. "It must be the general conviction," she declares, "that the new instincts, the new feelings, the new thoughts, the new ideas, which mothers and fathers pass on into the flesh and blood of their children will transform existence. . . . Only when woman heeds the message which life proclaims to her, that through her salvation must come, will the face of the earth be renewed."

The author makes a number of practical suggestions—that is, theoretically practical—for the bringing about of this result. She would have woman taught, or compelled, if necessary, to give up all methods of dressing, working, living that interfere with the developing and maintaining of a strong, healthful body, in order that she may have a good physical inheritance to transmit to her offspring; she would have the law exercise supervision over marriages, so that the physically or mentally unsound may be restrained from multiplying their infirmities; and she would have women, at the age when men in Europe serve their years of military service, obliged by law to pass through a period of equal length in which they would be trained in the care and nurture of children and in all the duties of motherhood.

Several chapters are devoted to an exposition of the author's ideas on the mental, moral, and physical training of young children. She does not believe in herding children in kindergartens and schools, and she has many upsetting things to say of kindergarten methods. But she never disputes an established method without having something else to offer in its place. She thinks that all young children ought to have most of their training, of all sorts, in the home and at the hands of their mother, or, at least, under her supervision, and she brings forward many physiological and psychological arguments to support her contention.

Ellen Key is evidently deeply in earnest over the principles she advances in this book. Her argument is not always all that could be desired. It is often sloppy in method and expression, and it lacks the clear-cut, incisive manner of the logical mind. She has observed much and read widely, but she has often lacked discrimination in the one and has been too credulous in the other. Her statements, for instance, about certain developments in America will doubtless be convincing enough in Germany, but in this country will not enhance the credibility of her statements about things elsewhere. To American readers she will seem often to be beating a man of straw, because here the woman movement has taken a different direction from that which it is following in Germany.

Caroline L. Hunt   (essay date 1909)

SOURCE: A review of *The Century of the Child*, in *The Dial*, Chicago, Vol. XLVI, No. 550, May 16, 1909, pp. 325-27.

[*In the following review of* The Century of the Child, *Hunt offers a favorable opinion, but laments what she considers Key's "bitterness of spirit" apparent in the work.*]

Abundant food for thought and unlimited material for discussion are to be found in Ellen Key's ***The Century of the Child,*** which has just been translated from the Swedish—or, more correctly, has just come to English readers through the German by double translation. The original was published in 1900, and took its title from a saying of one of the characters in *The Lion's Whelp*: "The next century will be the century of the child, just as this century has been the woman's century."

It is unfortunate that the author's most radical views, and those that are likely to be thought subversive of morality, are set forth in the opening chapter, which concerns marriage and parenthood; for many readers will be turned aside at this point and miss the chapters on Education which are the most valuable part of the book. Those who have patience with the matrimonial heresies of this chapter, and will read further, are likely to discover that they were at the beginning introduced to the writer's greatest weakness as well as to her greatest strength. Her strength lies in her abstract ideals for the conditions under which children should be born and educated; her weakness, in her apparent inability to recognize and her obvious unwillingness to acknowledge the part which religious and social institutions have had in preparing the world for these ideals and their realization. We learn from biographical sketches of Ellen Key, that she has severed her connection with all organized social movements. Her book indicates that she has done this with a bitterness of spirit that makes her an unfair critic.

To illustrate: The "woman's rights movement" seems to her to stand only for an effort on the part of women to secure, solely for their own satisfaction, educational advantages and admission to professions and fields of activity from which they have been excluded in the past. There is within the movement, as she sees it, no solidarity of spirit except that which has a distinctly selfish purpose. To this understanding we may not offer objection; for every person has a right to his own definition of a term so elastic as the "woman's rights movement." We may, however, dissent when women as a class, or any class of women, are held responsible for the demoralizing effect of modern factory life upon working women and upon the homes of working people. These effects can in fairness be charged only to our industrial system, and not to the ambitions of a sex.

If it is true that the adherents of the woman's rights movement as Ellen Key knows it are hopelessly blind to the fact that "the passion to discover truth must be accompanied by the passion to use it for the welfare of mankind," that they are not interested in protective legislation for women and children nor in supporting organized efforts of working women to improve their own conditions, then there is for her only one possible line of action; *i.e.*, to sever her connection with the movement and then to work alone or to form new associations for the purpose of gaining opportunity to work effectively in the interests of humanity. Individual development, however, must precede social usefulness; and the woman's rights movement, even in the narrowest conception we have of it, has secured for women the education and the training necessary for efficient organized work in behalf of education, the home, and the child. That the coming century is to be the century of the child partly *because* the century just passed was the woman's century, is a fact which Ellen Key fails to recognize.

It is much the same with her treatment of Socialism. It is unfair to commend unreservedly a plan for pensioning mothers during the time their children need their care, without referring to the fact that this is one of the cardinal principles of Socialism; unfair, also, to accuse Socialists as a whole of obstructing protective legislation, a charge which can be fairly brought against a small section of the party only.

The writer's attitude toward marriage is much the same as her attitude toward the woman's rights movement and Socialism. With her high ideals for "the common living of man and woman," she apparently fails to credit the institution of marriage and the legal protections which have been thrown about it with having fostered and promoted these ideals.

But while we object to many of the conclusions of the book, our hearts go out in sympathy to the author, who, a keen observer of life, saw that at the opening of this century (the twentieth after Christ) "the passions of men were still aroused in economic and in actual warfare," that "despite all the tremendous development of civilization in the century just passed, man had not yet succeeded in giving to the struggle for existence nobler forms," and that "Christian people continued to plunder one another and call it exchange, to murder one another *en masse* and call it nationalism, to oppress one another and call it statesmanship." No wonder she was led to criticize the conditions under which the succeeding generations of this slowly developing race have been educated, and also the conditions under which they have been born.

The chapters on Education redeem the rest of the book, although they contain much that is inapplicable to our system of public instruction, for we have abolished many of the abuses that are mentioned. Like Ellen Key, however, we are still seeking a kind of education which will give to the world "new types of people with higher ideals,—travellers on unknown paths, thinkers of yet unthought thoughts, people capable of the crime of inaugurating new ways"; and we acknowledge that we have in her not only a companion in ideals but a leader in methods. Her chapters on Education are masterly contributions to the literature of pedagogy, the result of a profound sympathy with and an understanding of child nature, and of long experience in child-training.

Except to those who insist upon rejecting as a whole, if they cannot accept as a whole, any book that embodies a call to action, *The Century of the Child* offers abundant inspiration. The truth is that it contains a definite programme for woman's future work, organized as well as unorganized, in the interest of the child. This, to be sure, can be read as a whole only by patching together bits that are scattered about among the denunciations of peoples and institutions; but the book itself is probably much more readable than it would be if the programme were presented in orderly and systematic fashion.

Havelock Ellis   (essay date 1910)

SOURCE: An introduction to *Love and Marriage* by Ellen Key, translated by Arthur G. Chater, G. P. Putnam's Sons, 1911, pp. vii-xvi.

[*Ellis was a pioneering sex psychologist and a respected English literary figure. His most famous work is* The Psychology of Sex (1897-1928), *a seven-volume study containing case histories of sex-related psychological abnormalities, which was greatly responsible for changing British and American attitudes toward sexuality. In addition to his writings on psychology, Ellis edited a series of English dramas and retained an active interest in literature throughout his life. In the following essay, originally published in 1910, and later published as an introduction to the 1911 English translation of Key's* Love and Marriage, *Ellis provides a critical biography of Key.*]

Ellen Key, whose most important book [*Love and Marriage*] is here for the first time presented in English, is no stranger in the English-speaking world. Her *Century of the Child* has already found many appreciative readers in America as well as in England. Ellen Key is descended from a Scotch Highlander, Colonel M'Key (probably of the famous MacKay clan) who fought under Gustavus Adolphus, and she attaches no little significance to this ancestry. She has always interested herself in English matters, and is well acquainted with the life and literature of Great Britain; but she belongs first and foremost to Scandinavia.

She was born in 1849 in the Swedish province of Smaland, on a country estate of her father. He had played a distinguished part in the Swedish parliament as an avowed radical, but his wife was a representative of an old and noble family. Ellen, their eldest child, was marked from an early age by her love of nature and of natural things. This devotion to nature may be considered hereditary, for her great-grandfather was an ardent disciple of Rousseau, and a special admirer of Rousseau's famous treatise on Education. He gave to his son the name of Émile, which was handed down to Ellen Key's father. It was perhaps owing to the Rousseau tradition that the young girl was initiated from childhood in swimming, rowing, riding, and other exercises then usually reserved for boys. At the same time, she loved music and devoured books including Scott's novels

and Shakespeare's plays. An early enthusiasm was for Goethe's *Hermann and Dorothea*; it may be said, indeed, that the ideal of natural, beautiful, and harmonious living for which that book stands has never left Ellen Key. She was educated for the most part at home by German, French, and Swedish teachers, but it may easily be believed that a girl of so much individuality of character, so impetuous and so independent, proved a difficult child to manage and was often misunderstood. One may divine as much from the sympathetic attitude towards children and the reverence for their healthy instincts, which are revealed in *The Century of the Child*. Fortunately young Ellen had a wise and discerning mother, to whom she owned much; with a fine intuition, this mother overlooked her daughter's indifference to domestic vocations and left her free to follow her own instincts, at the same time exercising a judicious influence over her development. While still a young girl, the future author, inspired by Björnson and other Scandinavian writers, conceived the idea of devoting herself to the study of the condition of the people and wrote several novels on peasant life. A remark of her mother's—that her daughter surely could not be meant to write novels, because the main questions for her were "the questions of her own soul"—opened her eyes to the truth that fiction could not be her vocation. But she was very far from knowing what her life's work was to be, and her dreams were of love and motherhood, not of a career.

With Björnson she was throughout in friendly relationship. He had recognised her fine abilities before she even began to write, and she on her side was full of admiration for his genius, strength, and goodness. The other world-famous writer of Scandinavia Ellen Key learned to know through his work at the age of eighteen, when her mother presented to her *Love's Comedy, Brand,* and *Peer Gynt*; this also was an influential event in her life. Among writers to whom she was later attracted were Elizabeth B. Browning, George Eliot, John Stuart Mill, Herbert Spencer, and John Ruskin.

At the age of twenty-three, Ellen Key began those constant excursions to all the great centres of Europe, which may be said never since to have ceased, at first in the company of her father, whose secretary, confidant, and almost co-worker she had become, and she was thus gradually led to writing for journals. A love of art seems to have been a primary inspiration of these early journeys, for at this time Ellen Key was fascinated by the art of painting as she has always been by the greater art of living, and her wide knowledge of pictures has often happily illuminated her later writings. After 1880, however, when her father, as the result of an agricultural crisis, lost his property, she was compelled, at the age of thirty, to choose a career and for a time became a teacher in a girls' school. She had always been attracted to teaching and many years earlier, at the instigation of Björnson, had studied the school system of Denmark. At a later period she gave courses of lectures in literature, history, and æsthetics. For twenty years she occupied the Chair of History of Civilisation in Sweden at the Popular University of Stockholm.

The early years of her career as a teacher seem to have been a period in Ellen Key's life of much struggle, hardship, and mental depression due to personal sorrows. Amongst these were the deaths in rapid succession of several distinguished women with whom she was closely associated, Sophie Kowalevsky, Anna Charlotte Leffler, and (by suicide) Ernst Ahlgren. She had not yet reached full development nor found her true place in the world. Although her abilities, when she was still a girl of twenty, had been discerned by a distinguished Swedish woman's rights advocate, Sophie Adlersparre, who encouraged her to write for her journal, she has always been shy and diffident, with none of the self-confident qualities, which an outsider might be tempted to attribute to her, of an imposing Corinne. She published no book till she had reached middle-age—most of her best books belong to the present century—and though she had so far overcome her timidity as to discuss literary and æsthetic questions before a public audience, she had yet scarcely touched openly on those dangerous and difficult questions which arouse fierce antagonisms. It required some assault on her most cherished convictions to arouse her latent courage. This occurred when an old Swedish law against heresy was revived in order to send to prison some young men who had freely argued the consequences, as they conceived them, of the Darwinian doctrine in religion and sexual morals. There is nothing so sacred to Ellen Key as the right to personal opinion and personal development; the sight of any injustice or oppression has always moved her profoundly, and on this occasion she sprang forward into the fray like a lioness in defence of her cubs. She is, in the opinion of Georg Brandes, "a born orator," and she publicly brought her eloquence to the service of the cause she had at heart. Her discussion of the question was marked by moderation, skill, and learning, but her attitude on this occasion served to define publicly her real position. Henceforward the conventionally respectable elements of Swedish society felt justified, according to the usual rule, in dealing out reckless and random abuse to the daring pioneer. She, on her side, retained her serenity, remaining a true woman, with much of the mother in her and something of the child, but before long her literary activities developed along her own native lines, and in full maturity she frankly approached the essential questions of life and the soul. A considerable series of volumes began rapidly to appear, often rather informal in method and personal in style, but freely following the author's thought and feeling, full, not only of ardent enthusiasm but of fine intuition and mellow wisdom. In 1903 was begun the publication of her most extensive work, *Lifslinjer* (Lines of Life), of which work the first two volumes constitute [*Love and Marriage*]. . . . A few years later appeared *The Century of the Child* and in 1909 *The Woman's Movement,* by many regarded as the best statement which has been made of that movement in its widest bearings. Ellen Key has also published a long series of essays on literary personalities—C. J. L. Almquist, the Brownings, Anna Charlotte Leffler, Ernst Ahlgren, etc.—who have appealed to her as illustrating some aspect of her own ideals. The latest of these is a lengthy study or Rahel Varnhagen.

Ellen Key is a Scandinavian and may perhaps even be said to be a typical figure of the country whose foremost woman she is. Moreover, she loves her own land and is resolved to spend the rest of her life in a house she proposes to build in a beautiful part of the country, Alvastra, near Lake Wetter, close to the ruins of the first Swedish monastery, a spot already sacred through its associations with the great Swedish saint, Brigitta. But the prophet is a prophet everywhere except in his own country. It is easy to find estimable Swedes who are far from anxious to claim the honour which Ellen Key reflects on their land. It is in Germany that her fame has been made. To-day the Germans, and not least the German women, awaking from a long period of quiescence, are inaugurating a new phase of the woman movement. The first phase of that movement dates from the eighteenth century, and its ideals were chiefly moulded by a succession of distinguished English women who claimed for their sex the same human rights as for men: the same right to be educated, the same right to adopt the occupation they were fitted for, the same political rights. In the course of a century these claims, although not yet completely realised, have gradually been more and more generally conceded as reasonable.

At the same time, however, it began to be seen that these demands, important as they are, by no means cover the whole ground, while, taken separately, they were liable to lead in a false direction; they tended to masculinise women and they ignored the claims of the race. In their ardour for emancipation, women sometimes seemed anxious to be emancipated from their sex. Thus it was not enough to claim woman's place as a human being—especially in an age when man was regarded as the human being *par excellence*—but it also became necessary to claim woman's place in the world as a woman. That was not, as it might at first seem, a narrower but a wider claim. For on the merely human basis women were reduced to the level of competitive struggle with men, were allowed to bring no contribution of their own to the solution of common problems, and, worst of all, their supreme position in the world as mothers of the race was altogether ignored. So that the assertion of the essential rights of women as women meant at the same time the assertion of the rights of society and the race to the best that women have to give. It was certainly by no accident that the Germans, who once before led the evolution of Europe by their triumphant assertion of the fundamental human impulses and have since been pioneers in social organisation, should take the leading part in the inauguration of this new phase of the woman movement.

The publication of Ellen Key's books corresponded in date with the recent tendency of the Germans to bring to bear on the questions of sex their characteristic Teutonic thoroughness and practicality. It is not surprising, therefore, that this Swedish woman, with her many-sided vision of the world, her daring yet serene statement of the secrets of human hearts, should be treated as the natural leader of the movement on its most womanly side. Love, as Ellen Key regards it, is at the core of the woman question, and these opening volumes of *Lifslinjer* are, above all, a contribution to the woman question, a modern and more mature version of that *Vindication of the Rights of Woman* which Mary Wollstonecraft had set forth a century earlier.

In England, and the same may be said of America, we are yet but at the beginning of this new phase of the woman movement. We have been mainly concerned with the rights of women to be like men; we are only now beginning to understand the rights of women to be unlike men, rights which, as Ellen Key understands them, include, although they go beyond, the rights embodied in the earlier claims. The dogmatic fanatics of every party, it is true, cannot endure Ellen Key; they cannot understand her, though she understands them, and even regards them with a certain sympathetic tolerance, as we should expect from a disciple of Montaigne and Shakespeare and Goethe. She is many-sided and is quite able to see and to accept both halves of a truth. In one of her earliest essays she showed how individualism and socialism, which some people suppose to be incompatible, are really woven together, and in the same way she now shows that eugenics and love—the social claims of the race and the individual claims of the heart—are not opposed but identical. Similarly, she declares that to build up, to help, to console is the greatest of women's rights; but, she adds, they cannot adequately exercise that right unless they also possess the right of citizenship—so disconcerting the narrow partisan on each side. In matters of detail we may at many points reserve our opinion. Ellen Key is, above all—like Olive Schreiner, to whom she is, in some respects, akin—the prophet of a movement which transcends merely isolated measures of reform. Her writings are the candid expression of her intimate self. In this book [*Love and Marriage*], especially, we feel that we are in the inspiring presence of a woman whose personality is one of the chief moral forces of our time.

The New York Times Book Review   (essay date 1911)

SOURCE: A review of *Love and Marriage,* in *The New York Times Book Review*, March 26, 1911, pp. 165, 171.

[*In the following review, the anonymous author admires Key's straightforward approach to human emotion and sexuality in* Love and Marriage.]

A Swede who had his own part in the period of "storm and stress" in his native land, and has since in the course of cosmopolitan wanderings acquired an almost Stevensonian aptness in the use of English, declared of Ellen Key, the pioneer of the insurrection of women in Sweden, that she dealt in "winged words," and as a lecturer fairly flung well-aimed facts at her hearers. Something of the quality of style so described remains even in the translation of a part of Miss Key's notable work *Lifslinjer,* which is now, after a lapse of eight years since the appearance of the original, published here with the title *Love and Marriage*. Those eight years represent, perhaps, the interval between the stage of progress of the so-called women's movement in America and that in the nations of northern Europe. There, in the nature of things, the problems of readjustment arising out of the present "industrial" phase of civilization have earlier become acute, partly owing to the greater complexity of the social fabric which was suddenly exposed to the strain of these new conditions, and partly because the northern European populations had already reached—and passed—that "saturation point" which is with us even now only a matter of the very near future.

These interesting scientific questions aside, Miss Key, who at the age of sixty-two years is still actively engaged in her life's work, is estimated by Mr. Havelock Ellis, in his preface to the present volume, as "a personality which is one of the chief moral forces of our time." Her writings, he proceeds, "are the candid expression of her intimate self." They have about them, too, in spite of the brave candor and forthright recognition of facts which is not their least characteristic, a certain quality of the poet and the seer which it is not necessary to ascribe entirely to Miss Key's Scottish ancestry, though the progenitor of her family did happen to be a Highlander—one Col. McKey who fought under the renowned Gustavus Adolphus. There are seers and poets also in Scandinavia.

Perhaps the clearest way to put it is to say that this Swedish woman uses, in the frankest and broadest treatment of the complex questions of sex as related to legal forms of marriage and divorce and customary standards of so-called morals, true and false, the utmost idealism of aim and point of view. The resulting conclusions—where any are drawn—are quite as apt to rebuke the modern feminist of the extreme type, as to shock Mrs. Grundy. On the one hand, for instance, Miss Key is clear that the present marriage form is outgrown and inadequate as the sole contrivance, for mating men and women; on the other, she is equally clear that the notion of emancipating woman at large from the care of her children and collecting the nation's offspring in state nurseries under the supervision of "professional mothers," is fatal and foolish.

Again, she declares with entire frankness that strict monogamy has remained, and will remain for a long time to come, an unrealized ideal. She even admits that there is as yet no proof that it is the best thing for the race, and allows grounds, both in biology and economics, for the practical difference in the standards of morality for men and women. It is at the point of the economic basis that she would attack the problem of bringing the practical standards closer together. Evolution is already at work, she thinks, in the same direction: And it is just in that which conventional moralists most fear—in the growing freedom of love to make its own choice and decide its own questions of morals—that she sees the evidence—and the line—of that evolution.

What she insists upon—and what all the new moralists insist upon—is that the present classification of things as moral and immoral needs radical revision. What she strives to do is to bring home the realization that there are things condoned, legalized, and even blessed by the church, which are infinitely more dangerous to the race, to society, to the nation, to the family and to the individual, than certain unions without wedlock and births without benefit of clergy.

Thus, she discusses the right of woman to motherhood—even asserts the right of unmarried woman to motherhood in certain circumstances, which are not as exceptional as they ought to be—in the same spirit that she discusses the other question of the right to exemption from motherhood which the earlier type of the emancipated woman was so eager to claim, and which the merely frivolous type of woman of fashion has shown herself more and more disposed to assume without argument or defense. She finds the exemption justified, of course, in certain exceptional cases, but she is not less convinced that motherhood is not merely the destiny, but the highest privilege, of womanhood, and that with all the approximation of the mental attitude of the two sexes that comes of woman's new and growing activities, woman should and must remain a specialist. Nay, even her social and civic activities Miss Key pictures as tending in direction of the exercise of a "collective motherliness." The women who choose, or have thrust upon them, "careers" rather than child-bearing, should find employment, she says, which makes use of the mother in them, and does not allow that special endowment to go quite to waste.

Thus you have a wise woman, mellow and singularly sane for the prophet of a new era, telling the truth as she sees it, and telling it such plain words, taking account of things so intimate and delicate, that quotation in an article like this can be indulged in only sparingly. Even the paraphrase, indeed, must often sacrifice definition and force to discretion. However, a few passages may be quoted. Here is one:

> The feminine fiction of the present day reminds one of a relief on a sacrificial altar in the Roman forum, where the ox, the sheep and the pig proceed in file to meet the knife. Hecatombs of these animals—in the likeness of husbands or lovers—are now sacrificed to Eros by the new woman. It may not be very long before the vow of fidelity is exchanged for an oath of silence, and the marriage contract contains a provision that, in case of a rupture, love-letters are not to be used as literature.

Again, Miss Key remarks upon the fallacy of the notion—fostered, she declares, by the Christian Church—that "While God walked in Paradise and founded marriage, the Devil went about in the wilderness and instituted love." Her doctrine is that the tendency—which all who care for the race must aid—is to make these twain, marriage and love, not two, but one. The true morality will come when that "dualism is vanquished by monism." And with it, perhaps, as evolution educates "love's selection" toward the point where each chooses infallibly his own one perfect mate, we shall attain the ideal monogamy.

Meantime, "the new man lives in the dream of the new woman, and she in a dream of the new man. But when they actually find one another, it frequently results that two highly developed brains analyze love, or that two worn-out nervous systems fight out a disintegrating battle over love. The whole thing usually ends in each of them seeking peace with some surviving incarnation of the old Adam and the eternal Eve." The same healthy sense of life and fact lurks in Miss Key's dictum that the "wise virgins' deadly sin against love is that they disdained to learn of the foolish ones the secret of fascination; that they would know none of the thousand things that bind a man's senses or lay hold of his soul; that they regard the power to please as equivalent to the betray." She writes also, not without pungency:

> So long as "pure" women take pleasure in the cruel sport of the cat; so long as with the facile changes of the serpentine dancer, they evade the responsibilities of their flirtations; so long as they delight in provoking jealousy as a homage to themselves; so long will they be helping to brew the hell-broth around which men will celebrate the witches' Sabbath in the company of the bat-winged bevies of the night.

It need hardly be said, even for the benefit of those who do not know her work, that Miss Key champions woman's suffrage.

Current Opinion (essay date 1913)

SOURCE: "Charlotte Gilman's Reply to Ellen Key," in *Current Opinion*, Vol. LIV, No. 3, March 1913, pp. 220-21.

[*In the following essay, the anonymous author contrasts the feminist views of Key with those of the noted American writer Charlotte Perkins Gilman, most widely known today for her early-twentieth century feminist short story "The Yellow Wallpaper."*]

In her recent powerful attack on "amaternal" feminism, Ellen Key, the great Swedish thinker, singles out the words of Charlotte Perkins Gilman, our American feminist philosopher, as presenting the strongest antithesis to her own, and expounding a theory of life which she opposes as dangerous and destructive; the most vital point of difference being their conception of motherliness. Mrs. Gilman's ideal is social motherhood, Ellen Key's a more intensely individual mother. Each writer expresses her thought with unrivalled poetic fervor. Moreover, they represent the two deepest contending forces in the woman movement to-day. "If Ellen Key is right," says Mrs. Gilman, in the February number of her magazine, *The Forerunner,* "then I am absolutely and utterly, foolishly and mischievously, wrong."

Mrs. Gilman states briefly the position defined by Ellen Key as follows: "The object of our life is the improvement of human beings; the improvement of human beings is best attained by the right birth and rearing of children. To this end we need the full development of the individual character of both men and women through education, association, freedom, work and love. To this end also we need the consecration of the individual mother to her children."

Her own position Mrs. Gilman proceeds to define as primarily that of a humanist, not a feminist. "The object of our life," she affirms, "is the improvement of social relations; the improvement of social relations is best attained by the right performance of social functions, i.e., all forms of human work which benefit society. To this end we need the full development of individual service in both men and women, through education, association, freedom, work and love—human love. To this end also we need a social motherhood."

In Ellen Key's opinion, the entire activity of women in industrial life and also in the professions (she excepts politics) is merely a means of earning a livelihood or of egoistic self-expression. Motherhood, she maintains, is a woman's true vocation. She assumes that the best education of the child requires the continuous exclusive devotion of the individual mother. Mrs Gilman, on the contrary, contends that the rapidly enlarging range of woman's activity is a social duty, and not a personal one; that the best education of the child requires, in addition to the love and care of its mother, the work of specialists in child culture. She writes:

> The reason why women need the fullest freedom in human development—and this means not merely education but action—is two-fold: it is needed because women are half the people of the world and the world needs their service *as people,* not only as women; and secondly (here I think Ellen Key agrees to a certain extent) that women as women, i.e., as mothers, need full human development to transmit it to their children.
>
> Doing human work is what develops human character. Human work is specialized activity in some social function—any art, craft, trade or profession that serves society.
>
> What society most lacks to-day is the capacity of individuals to feel and think *collectively,* to grasp social values, to recognize, care for and serve social needs, to see in the common business of life not personal expression or personal aggrandizement but social service. The reason we lack this capacity is that half the world has been denied the means to develop it. Women, in specializing as human beings in some trade or profession, are serving both the individual and the collective needs of their children; they help make a better world, and they make better children.

There has been much misapprehension in the past of Mrs. Gilman's position. Even Ellen Key, it would seem, confuses her ideas with those of certain egoistic feminists in Europe who depreciate the function of motherhood. "Never once," says Mrs Gilman, "in writing, or from platform or pulpit, have I denied the right and duty, the joy and pride of every normal woman to be a mother, to bear her children, to suckle her children, to provide—assisted by the father—the best conditions for their offspring. What I do deny absolutely is that the individual mother is, or ever can be, all-sufficient as an educator of humanity." She continues:

> The individual animal mother is so sufficient because animals do not specialize as we do. One conspicuous quality of humanity is its profound personal distinctions. A kitten or a cub is a kitten or a cub—and may be efficiently cared for by its mother; but each child varies from the other, and from its parents, in ever-widening degree, and for the understanding and right handling of this human quality our children need not only love but the widest experience.
>
> This experience is forever denied the mother.
>
> Not only are some women far better fitted for child-care by their natural talents than other women; not only are some women far better fitted for it by opportunities of training; but this remains the hopeless impossibility: so long as each woman takes all the care of her children herself,

> no woman on earth *can ever have the requisite experience.*
>
> The human child needs first and always the mother's love, but he needs in ever-increasing addition to this the love and care and service of those socially specialized to this great end.

Mrs. Gilman goes on to point out what she considers another vitally important error in Ellen Key's assumption (which is a very common one) that when a woman is engaged in a profession or industry, she can not give due love and care to her husband and children. This rests, of course, on another assumption, that the home of to-day is unchangeable, that it must always remain as it is at present—"a group of undifferentiated industries," demanding all the woman's time and strength. Mrs. Gilman's ideas on this subject are well known. A kitchenless home, with highly specialized care and education of children beginning at their birth, does not seem to her impossible of human attainment. "For the necessary time required for the work of the world," she writes, "father, mother and child may be outside of the home, and yet when father, mother and child return—it is home indeed."

To Ellen Key's ideal of a home which requires the life devotion of a mother-priestess, Charlotte Gilman opposes an ideal of social service for both man and woman made possible by a new and better kind of home. Against the growth of the highly evolved emotion of social service, she finds "no single deterrent influence more sinister, more powerful, than the persistence of this ancient root-form of society, this man-headed, woman-absorbing, child-restricting, self-servicing home." What we need, Mrs. Gilman concludes, is not a more intense but a larger maternal love.

V. Jefferson Watts   (essay date 1913)

SOURCE: "Knowledge and Morals," in *Scientific American Supplement*, Vol. LXXV, No. 1946, April 19, 1913, pp. 246-47.

[*In the following essay, Watts excoriates Key for what he considers her unscientific approach.*]

Ellen Key, the famous Swedish writer, in her masterpieces *Love and Ethics* and *Love and Marriage,* claims that to the loveless marriages, to the narrow, medieval conventionalism of society that condones such marriages and places the ban of social ostracism upon the unfortunate woman who through love has become a mother out of wedlock, and at the same time gives social recognition to the man, the fellow participator in the crime, and to those individuals who console themselves with the baser substitutes for love, to all of these are due the distorted social conditions and evils of the present day.

She furthermore claims that, inasmuch as sex instinct is the primal force in life about which all other forces revolve and on which all issues depend, all forces, such as will, judgment, reason, as well as all issues, even society, should subserve to the sex instinct. Then there will be no more unhappy marriages, no more divorces, no more social evil; then will it be possible to create a more highly developed race of human beings. In other words, when soul mate finds soul mate, mutual recognition taking place by reason of the sex instinct, then must society and the Almighty recognize such a union, in spite of the Seventh Commandment, that a more perfect race may be created.

"Love can exist without marriage, but marriage cannot exist without love." She maintains that she does not advocate "free love"; that her philosophy is the mean between the two extremes of the loveless marriage, legal prostitution, and free love, illegal prostitution. She insists that her philosophy requires no ceremony to make love lasting, for the fetters of her philosophy are more binding than any words pronounced by a minister of Christ, because her philosophy permits of but one supreme love in a lifetime.

Ellen Key may truly be classed as the propounder of a philosophy which, though secretly believed in and followed by the more daring of womankind and always advocated by certain types of men to gain their ends with women since the beginning of time, would make Socrates, the founder of philosophy and likewise of the purest code of morals after Christ, turn in his grave!

In her attempt to reveal woman's nature, in her endeavor to find a remedy for the sex evils of the age, in her effort to adjust woman to the changing conditions and yet not have her efface herself or her God-given duties in her own sphere, Ellen Key has offered this love philosophy to perplexed woman as a solution for her own problems and incidentally for those of man, and she has offered society an immoral and most decidedly impractical panacea for its ills. To meet these changing conditions, woman's chastity must undergo a revaluation, and this revaluation is nothing more nor less than old-fashioned adultery, for the sole purpose of gratifying the sex instinct, even as do the beasts of the field. Ellen Key has not offered her disciples any other crown of glory here—certainly none in the hereafter—than transitory physical happiness—there could be no mental or moral; and as for compensation for the loss of their own self-respect and the respect of their fellow beings, to say nothing of that of a Higher Power, evidently they are left to work out their own salvation.

If the mother of Alexander Hamilton had voiced her inmost thoughts before she died, would she have said that the revaluation of her chastity compensated her for all that she gave up? Here was a woman who, according to the laws then extant in the West Indies, could not be divorced. She loved this Hamilton and he loved her and they lived together as man and wife—"one supreme love in a life-time," according to Ellen Key. He was an ideal lover but he did not prove an ideal husband. The prosaic of life entered in upon the love dream, as it always has and always will, and the result of their awakening to the commonplaces of life was the shattering of their love dream, and man-fashion, Hamilton left the woman he had seduced to bear the brunt of the disgrace alone. And here is one great flaw in Ellen Key's philosophy—she does not take into account the practical, everyday side of marriage, she deals only with the ideal; and she also overlooks the fact that after the first few weeks or months of wild abandon, this same practical element becomes predominant; she also ignores the fact that, whereas passion generally

endures throughout married life, love does not, unless fed by the constant fires of variety, congeniality and mutual understanding.

If the victims of Aaron Burr could speak, what tales of anguish and sorrow would they not reveal! And yet they revalued their chastity, according to Ellen Key!

Dolly Madison, in the *First Lady of the Land,* shows that she values her chastity too highly to intrust it even in wedlock to a libertine. And yet her love for him would, in Ellen Key's estimation, have justified her in marrying him. Here is another flaw in her philosophy—she does not take into consideration the fact that men must be fit to assume the responsibilities of marriage and parenthood, if a more highly developed race of human beings is to be created. Dolly Madison had strength of character enough to make physical attraction subservient to judgment, because she knew that she did not dare to intrust herself and her probable offspring to a *roué*. In other words, she had the "betterment of the species and the good of humanity at heart as well as her own happiness."

That there are so many loveless marriages, so many disappointing ones, so many divorces and so many affinities, shows that there is something radically wrong with the system of marriage; but the fault is not in the institution itself, it is in the woeful lack of preparation and education, mental, moral and physical, of the contracting parties. And those who are directly responsible for the present chaos are the parents, for bringing up their children in ignorance, and indirectly the state for allowing all sorts of promiscuous and unregulated marriages. But in spite of the chaos, there is a way out that will eventually lead to peace and order in the state marital. However, this way does not lie through the destruction of marriage as an institution, as Ellen Key would have us believe, but in the preservation and upbuilding of this sacred institution through education.

By making sex instinct the controlling force in life instead of reason and judgment, by placing the sensual above all moral and social obligations, Ellen Key is not only not solving the sex problems and eradicating the sex evils of the age, but she is paving the way for a more licentious free love than we have at present.

Enlarging the scope of any evil can never eradicate that evil nor even lessen it, any more than the willful spreading of a disease can check the ravages of that disease. Neither will it help matters to call that evil by another name for the purpose of gilding it. The only way to circumvent any evil is (1) to get at the underlying causes; (2) to make a careful study of the conditions that engender such an evil and cause it to flourish; (3) to eradicate the obnoxious conditions; and (4) to supply a practical and effectual remedy.

The cause of the sex evils of the present day is not, as Ellen Key would have us believe, the ignorance of the existence of passion, or sex instinct, or of its primal purpose, but the causes are (1) the ignorance of the difference between love and passion; (2) the inability to control this force passion, so that love, which is passion regenerate, may come into its own; (3) the ignorance of the elements of real love that must be the foundation of any lasting marriage, such as respect, congeniality, etc.; (4) the ignorance of the mental, moral and physical requirements that are necessary for the happiness and well-being of all who contemplate matrimony and parenthood; (5) the ignorance of the importance of the prenatal period in molding the disposition, features, character, of the prospective child and future citizen; (6) the ignorance of the care of the child and its proper bringing up; (7) the ignorance of the derogatory influence, mentally, morally and physically, of hereditary taints of insanity and sexual diseases upon the offspring, even unto the third and fourth generation.

The conditions which engender these evils and cause them to flourish are (1) the unwillingness of parents to assume the responsibilities of parenthood and instruct their children in the meaning of life and in all matters pertaining thereto, instead of letting them pick up their information on the streets, in alleys, or in even more objectionable places, from all sorts of malicious sources, thereby causing them to get a distorted view of life and placing them in the way of every kind of moral danger; (2) the false modesty and fear of criticism that keeps teachers, superintendents and school boards, especially in the smaller cities, towns and villages, from insisting that graded courses in sex hygiene, scientific mating and parenthood be a part of every school curriculum from the kindergarten to the senior year of high school—the course in sex hygiene used in some of the high schools, while it is a step in the right direction, is by no means comprehensive enough; (3) the prudishness or thoughtlessness of otherwise public spirited citizens that prevents their urging through their respective congressmen and assemblymen laws that will provide for comprehensive and compulsory sex instruction in all State universities, public and parochial schools and an additional course for parents; (4) the indifference of city, State and Federal governments toward the future welfare of citizens and nation, by not taking the initiative in providing laws for the temporary control and ultimate prevention of the social evil, the marriage and divorce evils, and the diseases attendant upon these evils; (5) the lack of co-operation between the churches in regard to these evils and their lack of provision for warding them off; (6) the hesitancy on the part of religious institutions and organizations generally, to add a course in sex hygiene to their religious curriculum; (7) there are no courses in the science of life in our higher institutions of learning; (8) there is no Department of Eugenics at Washington to demand certain standards for qualification for matrimony; to provide for universal education so that these standards may be attained; to provide medical attendance in all vice districts in all localities until such districts can be entirely eliminated; to investigate the economic causes for vice and to eradicate them; to put an end to the white salve traffic as England is doing; to institute State matrimonial bureaus on the French principle, with an added department for fallen women, and also one for the control of sexual diseases on the German principle; to force pre-marital medical examination in every city and State in the Union; to establish a single standard of morals by providing severe, laws for the masculine offenders; to make race breeding a matter of scientific importance and national issue as is the case in some of the leading countries of Europe.

These obnoxious conditions can be eradicated and the evil greatly lessened, if the intelligent people, irrespective of class, creed or politics or nationality, will unite in a nation-wide crusade, well organized and co-operative, against these conditions. The ensign of this crusade must be knowledge, and the weapons universal education in the science of life, and these weapons must be wielded by government, clergy and laity. Marriage must no longer be considered a haphazard state of deliverance, but a business into which both parties must put the best they have in health, morals, love, responsibility, etc., so that the profits, happiness and noble offspring may be the highest possible—an institution with a firm economic basis together with lofty ideals, which can only be preserved as its participants are duly qualified mentally, morally and physically. The knowledge of the science of life—or how to be born, how to grow up, how to love, how to marry, how to create and how to rear—will provide this qualification, just as it will cure the sex evils and distorted conditions of the age.

"Knowledge is power and power is life!" Never was there truer maxim and never did maxim more aptly fit the case in hand. It was the knowledge of the ancients that made possible the almost universal tendency toward education in science and the arts in this present day, and it was the knowledge and perseverance of the few that eventually lifted the veil of ignorance of the Middle Ages and paved the way for modern achievement; and it is the knowledge of the scientists and students of humanity regarding the awful consequences to individual and nation of these unchecked sex evils that is arousing them to the necessity of providing a practical and lasting cure for these sex evils as the root of all other evils; and it will be knowledge, discriminate at first because of prejudice, and gradually universal, as these narrow prejudices are overcome and the Science of Life takes its rightful place in the home along with the other moral and material guides that properly belong in man's household, that will make woman value her chastity too highly to become a mother out of wedlock or to intrust it in wedlock to a libertine, fit or unfit. It is knowledge that will eventually put the ban of social ostracism on the double standard of morals, a process already begun in Queen Mary's Court; it is also knowledge gleaned from the pages of science of life that will reveal to man the important relation of the trinity, mind and body and soul, to matrimony, which is virtually the mental, moral and physical union of one man and one woman in holy wedlock for the purpose of continuing the race; and it is this same knowledge that will make possible the conservation of energy of both sexes for the entrance into "the most holy thing in nature," marriage, and through marriage, the creation of a perfect race of human beings. It is knowledge that will teach man to choose his mate, not by the sex instinct alone, but by love, of which sex instinct is a part, plus congeniality, wherein respect and morals shall also have their say. It is knowledge that will give man a realizing sense of the necessity of a proper mental, moral and physical condition at the time of generation—for the child is the instantaneous photograph of the condition of the father at this time—and it is knowledge that will compel woman to give heed to her mental, moral and physical condition during the nine months of pregnancy and to use her judgment in regard to all outside influences that are brought to bear on her at that time, and also in regard to her own thoughts and desires—for great statesmen, lawyers, musicians, artists, are not so much a matter of coincidence as they are the direct result of painstaking and unceasing study, determined exercise of will and cultivation of taste during the prenatal period; neither are criminals, drunkards or degenerates so much a matter of chance, heredity or environment, as they are the product of the uncontrolled thought or wish of the mother during pregnancy or of the bestial condition of the father at the time of generation; and cripples and imbeciles are not so much the result of unfortunate circumstances as they are the direct result of an unsuccessful attempt at abortion on the part of the mother. It is knowledge that makes travail safe and almost painless and does away with the desire to practise abortion, which is due mostly to the ignorant fear of women of becoming mothers. It is knowledge that teaches the young mother to care for her baby easily and scientifically; that teaches her that the way to control her child is through obedience and the way to keep this control is through confidence; then when she faces the delicate situation of fitting the girl and boy for marriage and parenthood—her husband also has his duty to perform—her task is lighter and the result more beneficial, and she has then fulfilled her highest obligation to God and man!

It is only the knowledge of the terrible ravages of indulgence on mind, body and morals, and the supplement of mental and physical labor that will enable both sexes to refrain from this vicious practice. It is only the knowledge of the causes, symptoms, means of transmission, and of the number of years necessary to effect a complete cure of syphilis, the suffering entailed by the treatment, as well as the danger of allowing this disease to remain in the blood, both to the sufferer himself and to all those who ignorantly or carelessly come in contact with him, even after a local cure has been effected, that will teach humanity that self-control is of more value to health and happiness than the gratification of desire at the probable price of contracting this dread disease, which leaves its imprint, in the form of scrofula, infantile paralysis and bridgeless noses, etc., on the children of the offender and on his children's children, even unto the third and fourth generation. It is the knowledge of the innocent means of transmission of this disease that will make people more careful in the use of public places and appliances which of necessity must be patronized. It is knowledge that will teach man the secret of longevity and youth. And it is knowledge that will enable man to distinguish real love from passion; that will enable him to realize the potent force of congeniality in keeping down the affinity and divorce evils and in eventually rooting them out. And it is knowledge of this science of life that will finally reinstate the sanctity of the home which through ignorance has been so rudely defiled. It is knowledge that will put an end to the white slave traffic, because heretofore it has been the ignorance of the victims that has made their seduction to this nefarious business possible, either by kidnapping or drugging. It is knowledge that will keep the too trusting and unwary girl from surrendering herself to her lover, or to be more accurate, her seducer, under promise of marriage, because through knowledge she will learn to recognize all such overtures for her virtue as insults, mere tricks to bring about her ruin, and she will

come to understand as her knowledge increases that no man seeks to seduce any woman through love, but through passion, and having gained his desire, his former passion turns to hate and loathing because unaccompanied by reverence or respect; and the woman who has fallen a victim to that passion, finding herself abandoned by the man she loved, sinks by degrees, varying according to temperament, to the lowest depths. It is knowledge that will teach both man and woman that to understand love, they must first understand that passion is but an element of love, an atom, but not love entire, even as will, judgment, respect, reverence, congeniality, are elements or atoms of love, and that all of these are necessary to form the sublime molecule, love. Knowledge also teaches man that the road to real love lies through the conquest of passion and that the only road to the happy marriage lies through real love.

Ellen Key's philosophy might do very well for an ideal race of human beings who were pure enough to be above passion or to be without it, but for the all too human race of men and women that inhabit this earth, whose everyday existence is one constant struggle with the arch enemy, passion, and whose success or failure depends upon their subjugation of it, this philosophy is very misleading and impractical. What erring humanity needs is education to enable it to withstand this enemy and to make it subservient to will and judgment. Herein lies another flaw in Ellen Key's philosophy—that sex instinct, which in man or beast is the primitive instinct for mating, and which, untutored and uncontrolled, is primarily a force for evil; this sex instinct she has made the controlling force in life, instead of love, which is the quintessence of controlled passion, and which is the greatest force for good in life.

It seems hardly possible that any philosopher could claim that the sex evils and distorted conditions are due to the lack of the recognition of the potency of the sex instinct, when on every side we see the most alarming and revolting evidences of its unrestrained sway. Alas! it is not the ignorance of the existence of this sex instinct or of the force of it that is the root of all the evils of the present day, and of the distorted social conditions, but the ignorance of the proper control of this instinct and the conservation of it for its rightful purpose. It likewise seems impossible that a philosopher who had the real good of humanity at heart could advocate the "burning of an ideal love into the heart of the youth with letters of fire—to give him real moral strength," and in the same breath advocate the casting off of all moral and social restraint to passion and thus destroy society's bulwark, woman's chastity, and the offspring's protection, marriage. That is but a contradictory philosophy which does not eradicate the sex evils, nor even lessen them, neither does it solve the sex problems, it only enlarges their scope for evil and promises nothing to its disciples but social and moral death! Burn the knowledge of the science of life into the heart of the youth with letters of fire—that will give him real moral strength; and burn it into the hearts of as many of erring humanity as it is possible for institutions, organizations and individuals in their respective jurisdictions to reach, and let the Government burn it into the heart of the nation through a new Department of Eugenics at our capital at Washington!

The love we all pray for, long for and so seldom realize in its fullest measure, is not attained, either because by dreaming of an impossible ideal love we overlook real love, or by thinking that we will never experience real love, we ignorantly or willfully accept its baser substitute, passion, in place of the purer gem. What is it and how shall we know it in contradistinction from its unrefined element, passion?

Love in its highest sense is that feeling of pre-eminent devotion and tenderness, founded on respect, mutual understanding and sympathy, a feeling so pure that it will guard the object of its affection from all physical and moral harm and will endow it with a sacredness which, though allied to the physical, will transcend the animal and raise it to the plane of the spiritual. Such a love could only have for its goal matrimony, and for its ultimate purpose the creation of a perfect race.

"Knowledge is power and power is life!" And the power and the life are within your reach if you will but stretch forth your hand and grasp them, and having grasped them, will you not, in the spirit of mercy that "blesseth him that gives and him that takes, that is mightiest in the mightiest," stretch forth your hand and help to lift the darkness of ignorance and prejudice from the masses that are as yet groping for the light?

Amalie K. Boguslawsky (essay date 1914)

SOURCE: "Ellen Key—Idealist," in *The Dial*, Chicago, Vol. XVI, No. 662, June 16, 1914, pp. 47-8.

[*In the following essay, Boguslawsky asserts that although many of Key's contentions are idealistic, her ideas regarding parenthood and child care are rooted in practicality.*]

Always since the Galilean lived his revolutionary message—to reform man and not methods—every step in the world's ethical and moral progress has been inspired by the standard-bearer of a new idealism. With the wane of each century, the idealism which demanded the ascetic renunciation of earthly joys has been more sternly challenged, until a higher conception of true life-values is leading us back to the Greek ideal of beauty and happiness as the basis of a life-giving harmony.

Ellen Key's credo, "the enhancement of life through love, joy, and beauty in things small and great," implies much more than the joy of living. To her, happiness means "to love, work, think, suffer, and enjoy on an ever higher plane." She expounds her gospel in a glowingly picturesque and even startling way, and those who read coming events in to-day's idealistic tendencies believe that she has established the three truths on which our moral future will be based: 1, The futility of legislation and economic readjustments for bringing about the regeneration of the race; 2, The wisdom of courageous truthtelling as regards vital issues; 3, A truer recognition of the sacredness of human relations.

As a forerunner in urging the vital reforms for which we are fighting to-day, Ellen Key has always insisted on freedom for the new type of beings who are developing as a result of the transvaluation of moral standards that must

eventually bring about a betterment of the species. The closing sentence in her most indignantly contested book, *Love and Marriage,* proves her intent to let her theories be a stepping-stone to changed and bettered marriage conditions, and not a plan for immediate action: "Those who believe in a humanity perfected by love must learn to count in thousands of years, not in centuries, much less in decades."

Why, then, do we hear all this hue and cry about Ellen Key's "immoral" precepts? To see danger in her reversal of accepted standards in sexual ethics is as misleading as was the popular interpretation of the high-handed exit of Ibsen's Nora. It would be just as absurd to accuse her of suggesting free love as a solution for marital tangles as it was to blame Ibsen for the panacea which "misunderstood women" found in his open-door theory. Both these idealists are counting in "thousands of years" for the consummation of their hope of social advance through the ennoblement of natural impulses.

In demanding new forms, Ellen Key asks freedom "for the only love worthy the name," the sanctified, self-sacrificing love that is life's highest spiritual expression: self-sacrificing only in the sense of giving and demanding the highest happiness in love. All other love she considers desecration, whether in marriage or out of it. "Her greatest victory is that pure-minded young men have made their own her demands of true morality," said one admirer on the occasion of her sixtieth birthday. The new type of woman which is being evolved from this supreme test of her theories will be the corner-stone upon which the new creed of a higher freedom for both man and woman will rest. Fewer Priscillas, ever ready to bear the marriage yoke, will worship man as the lord of creation, and more Brunhildes will defend the fiery wall of newly-won privileges which protects the cherished freedom of their personality.

On the other hand, Ellen Key proves the possibility of making practical ideals fit to-day's needs in her plea for the rights of the child. What a neglected factor the child has been in our demand for the right to develop our own individuality! We are only beginning to concede his right to be well born and well equipped, physically and morally, for the task of finding his true place in the great scheme of existence.

What the dreamer Rousseau began, the centuries are slowly bringing to a splendid fruition. With two inspired women like Maria Montessori, who is freeing children's souls, and Ellen Key, fighting against our effete conception of the moral law, in the vanguard, we are slowly realizing our possibilities in making the most perfect development of the individual the basis of social advancement.

In *The Century of the Child,* a powerful leaven in the great social upheaval now going on, Ellen Key bases her plea for less training and more opportunity for free action on the premise that mankind can rise to its highest fulfillment only through the most perfect development of human impulses and the best training of the faculties. To this end she would change Froebel's dictum, "Let us live for the children," to the admonition, "Give the children a chance to live." "Aim to leave your child in peace, interfere as little as possible, try to remove all impure impressions, but above all else *perfect yourself* and let your personality, aided by reality in all its rude simplicity, become a factor in the child's development." Nietzsche expresses this essence of the educational wisdom of the ages more tersely: "See that through thee the race progresses, not continues only. *Let a true marriage help thee to this end.*"

Ellen Key's arraignment of our present method of predigested instruction, of artificial spurs to endeavor, and of over-vigilance and protective pampering is a strong negative plea for more natural methods of training children. She thinks an adult person would lose his reason if some Titan should try to train him by the methods ordinarily employed with children. Like all right-minded people, she considers corporal punishment detrimental to the development of courage, energy, and self-reliance. She quotes the opinion of an educator who claims that many nervous little liars simply need good nourishment and outdoor life; and she holds the "good" school, with its over-insistence on versatility, responsible for the nervousness of our day.

The child should be trained to exercise his own powers: trained—not allowed to exercise them as he wills. Herein lies the misconception that leads many ultra-modern parents to give the reins into the child's own hands. We are in danger now of passing the Scylla of restrictive methods only to founder on the Charybdis of unrestricted liberty. Even the radical Ellen Key advises strict discipline for young children "as a pre-condition to a higher training." During the first and most important formative period she insists upon absolute obedience.

Our present system of training often limits the natural capacities of the child and shields him from life's real experiences. In answer to the assertion that splendid men and women have grown up under a system of repression and punishment, she argues that parents were consistent and unbending in earlier days: not over-indulgent and severe by turns, guided by nerves and moods, as are many parents of to-day.

"We need new homes, new schools, new marriages, new social relations for those new souls who are to feel, love, and suffer in ways infinitely numerous, that we now cannot even name," is her insistent plea.

Home influence, its settled, quiet order, and its call for tasks conducive to the happiness and the comfort of the family, is underestimated as an educational factor of great value. As soon as humanity awakens to the consciousness of "the holiness of generation," Ellen Key's ideal of a better parenthood will be realized. The mothers of the future must live according to her eugenic creed: to enhance life and to create higher forms. To this end she would consecrate woman as the priestess of life, who regards motherhood as a vocation of high worth, not as an incident or as an irksome task to be avoided.

In *Motherliness and Education for Motherhood,* she asks woman to concentrate her divergent interests in order to make herself more efficient for her most important duties, and she urges reform measures to so aid the working mother that she may devote more attention to her children. Another suggestion, to make a course in caring for children, in health culture and nursing, obligatory for girls, is a more rational demand than the European law for compulsory military duty, and would surely be productive of better results. The ethical as well as the practical value of efficiency is being recognized in the business world, in professional and educational life. Why not in the highest of all vocations—parenthood?

The Woman Movement challenges those of Ellen Key's adversaries who claim that she opposes woman's emancipation: for her the most important woman question is the highest development of the individual woman. "Motherhood," she assures us, "will exact all the legal rights without which woman cannot, in the full sense of the word, be either child mother or community worker." Her glowing faith in the perfectibility of human nature, her courage in braving false interpretations of her creed, and her prophetic understanding of our most urgent spiritual needs give her the right to shed a blinding light on matters tabooed by those who fear the truth. She is not a disillusionist for courageous souls. Anyone who reads *Life Lines* understandingly is impressed by the author's tremendous sense of righteousness, and by the optimism of her prophecies.

In her biographies of noted women the forward-seeking vision in their lives and in their work is a typically modern note. Rahel Varnhagen has never before been drawn with the ultra-modern touch that reveals her aspiring soul as a strong influence in spurring on great men to unusual deeds of intellectual valor.

A humanitarian in the widest sense, Ellen Key disapproves of many forms of charity, while she insists upon the right of every human being to develop his best possibilities through an inspiring environment and a chance to express himself in his work. She once heard a young working-girl say: "It is not your better food and finer clothes we mostly envy, but it is the many intellectual enjoyments which are so much more within your reach than ours." The organization of the Tolstjerna circles was the result of this plaint. Women of wealth and culture, with a sympathetic understanding, met working girls on terms of equality. Ellen Key's beautiful home will belong to these girls in the future. Only four of them are to occupy it at one time; she wants them to be honored members of a family, not dwellers in an institution. The home is her sanctuary. All her "revolutionary" doctrines are directed towards its perfection by making men and women better able to guard its sacred flame and render it worthy to be the cradle of a new race of beings and a nobler civilization.

Raymond Bellamy   (essay date 1915)

SOURCE: A review of *The Renaissance of Motherhood*, in *The American Journal of Sociology*, Vol. XX, No. 4, January, 1915, pp. 541-43.

[*In the following review, Bellamy provides a short summary and a favorable review of* The Renaissance of Motherhood.]

The author condenses the thoughts of [*The Renaissance*

of Motherhood] into the following words which appear in the preface:

> In this book I have spoken of the social means possible for calling forth a renaissance of motherhood. I have proposed the study of eugenics; a year of social service as preparation for motherhood; state pensions for mothers. . . . But the real renaissance must come through an education of the feelings. . . . No renaissance is possible before mothers and teachers . . . prepare the girls' hearts for love and motherhood. . . . And then will come indeed the new religion of the new century, the century of the child, now only a hope in the soul of some dreamers.

Part I: Women and Morals.—In this section the author takes the stand without question that women have stronger intuitions and weaker powers of reason than men. Women as a rule have advanced the ethical evolution, but have occasionally had a retarding effect, as, for example, when the Icelandic women urged their men to avenge manslaughter by death rather than to accept fines. Woman's ethical conservatism has given a training in habits which finally became instincts in regard to what is right. This thought is met repeatedly throughout the book and one is led to believe that the author holds to the inheritance not only of acquired physical characteristics but also of acquired habits of thought. The feelings of sympathy and therefore morality have undoubtedly grown out of the family life. Woman has always considered it "moral" to submit to the social customs of the day even though it meant that she should be eaten or be compelled to kill her own child. Woman's chastity has not, as a rule, originated in "woman's nature," but has developed because she was considered as property. Nevertheless, "Because of her motherhood, woman's sexual nature gradually became purer than man's." It is now the task of society to eradicate all traces of the earlier times when women and children were the property of men and to bring about a perfect equality in the marriage union.

"Sexual slavery in matrimony, never discountenanced by the church, intensified in women all the vices which man later called 'woman's nature.'" A woman could win comfort and support only by pleasing a man and therefore all her efforts were bent in the direction to please. Because woman was regarded as property, her morality came to be judged only by her sexual life, and this accounts for her general lack of responsibility in business. But women are now coming to insist that even in the sexual field individual conscience and not traditional ideals is to determine conduct. "At present we are living in a chaos where ancient and low instincts, in women as in men, fertilized with new and high ideas, have given birth to many monstrous forms of life." Out of this is to arise the new morality which is to have expression in two ways: one is the individual's right to self-assertion in love, and the other society's right to limit this self-assertion for the welfare of the race. "Eugenics will finally become just as deep-rooted an instinct as the duty to defend the home country against outer foes."

Part II: Motherliness.—It has been natural to sing of the beauty and power of motherliness and the race has never doubted but that it could rely on the warmth of motherliness "as for millions of years we can yet rely on the warmth of the sun." But today the unlooked-for has happened and there are many women who refuse to become mothers while others are advocating that the children be cared for entirely outside of the home. It is only by regaining this lost motherliness that woman may hope to reach her highest development. The monotonous work of the factory, office, or store cannot possibly bring a greater degree of happiness, freedom, or honor than the broad usefulness of the home where woman is sovereign.

Part III: Education for Motherhood.—The bright pictures which have been painted will become realized only after some hundreds of years. "The modern woman's view of motherhood . . . is not calculated to nourish optimism." All "reforms" must fail if not accompanied by some real betterment of human nature. All plans for community homes and institutional care of the children are not only destined for failure, but, "If Satan announced a prize competition for the best means of increasing hatred on earth, this reform proposition ought to receive first prize." From the point of view of the new religion, intelligent parenthood will as far exceed professional work as justice, mercy, and charity exceed mint, anise, and cumin. As a part of the reorganized educational system, girls and boys alike are to receive a year's training in social service. The age of marriage for women should be raised to twenty-one and the year before this given to this social service. This should be divided into three courses: first, a course in national and domestic economics; second, a theoretic course in hygiene; and third, a theoretic course in the physical and psychical duties of a mother before and after the birth of the child. These courses should be supplemented by practical training in the care of children. This thorough education, if it be added to a real awakening to the beauty of motherhood, will bring about the renaissance and secure for woman her highest development.

Nancy M. Schoonmaker   (essay date 1926)

SOURCE: "Ellen Key's Ideals of Love and Marriage," in *Current History*, Vol. 24, No. 4, July, 1926, pp. 529-32.

[*In the following essay, Schoonmaker eulogizes Key and provides an overview of her views.*]

With the passing of Ellen Key, who died at her home in the south of Sweden on April 25, 1926, there is brought vividly to mind again the contribution which this woman was privileged to make to the thought of her age. The seventy-seven years of her life fell in a time when great currents of progress and change were sweeping over the world. Born in an age and country in which the reactionary forces were altogether dominant, before such forces had even been made fully articulate by resisting such opposition as later massed against them for their eventual overthrow, she lived to see laws and customs and the thought of the world liberalized to an almost incredible extent.

In her young girlhood, if she had cared to look into the matter—as perhaps she did—she would have discovered, for instance, that the laws governing marriage were so entirely one-sided and unjust to woman that at least one illustrious Swedish gentleman of her acquaintance chose a common-law marriage rather than ask his life companion to subject herself to the humiliating conditions of the legal ceremony. She lived to see her country so modify its laws governing this institution, marriage, divorce, property rights, guardianship of dependent children, illegitimacy, as to deserve the distinction of carrying perhaps the best such laws in the world. She lived to see woman emerge into full political equality; she lived to see the child escape from the injustices of repression into a larger freedom of development; she lived to see her world and ours, both given more or less openly to the conviction that the legal, the proprietary and the other social conveniences were the essentials in determining the morality of an erotic relationship, come into a new consciousness of love and love alone as the single moral motivating force back of marriage.

In all the movements looking to these changes Ellen Key had a part. It was in the early years of such reforms when those who led were called upon to endure criticism and contempt. Of these Ellen Key was given her full share. On one occasion at least this criticism and contempt poured upon her from within the woman movement when she gave utterance to what seemed at the time a sudden reversion to the old doctrine of restricted womanhood. But so far has the world progressed that, before her death, Ellen Key rather suffered our neglect because she had begun to seem almost old-fashioned.

Her slant toward liberalism came as a family heritage. It was an ancestor seven generations back, Lieut. Col. James McKey, Scotch in spirit and pronunciation, who, at the close of the Thirty Years War, migrated to Sweden. For three generations the family kept the "Mc." For twice as many generations they made their mark upon the life of their times. In the record of them there breaks out again and again evidence that the strain is rich and fertile. Squires, statesmen, judges, warriors, men of esthetic and literary gifts step through the pages of Ellen Key's background. And the high-bred Swedish wives which the Scotch McKeys took unto themselves brought their gift also to the blend. The women of the family no less than the men seem to have been marked by originality of thought, strength of conviction, courage of expression. It was Ellen Key's great-great-grandmother who was a champion of women's rights. It was Ellen Key's own mother, with royal blood in her veins, who entirely shared the liberal opinions of her husband, who gave the keenest sympathy and insight to his undertaking to found a new agrarian party, who followed with deepest comprehension his work as a member of the Riksdag and who early saw in her daughter the promise of unusual ability.

The liberal opinions of her parents were partly responsible for the extreme simplicity of the home in which Ellen grew up with her brothers, one of whom was christened George Washington Key, in honor of a certain distant hero whom these wide-visioned parents saw and recognized. Every available penny of the family income was being poured into the venture of liberal political organization, but never to the point of depriving the family of books, books of all kinds, esthetic, philosophical, literary, with which the house overflowed. There was also intimate association with the notable men of the time.

In her early girlhood Ellen Key was the intimate companion of her father; a few years later she acted as his secretary. She thought of this association always as one rich in significance and opportunity for her. When her father's plans for political reform failed, carrying down with them the bulk of his estate, it became necessary for Ellen to seek self-support. She left the country which she loved so deeply and found a position in a liberal school in Stockholm. In many ways this association was a pleasant one for her, and she remained in the school for nineteen years. It was a work for which by nature and by training she was well fitted, for back of the intellectual life which she had always lived was what amounted to a passionate devotion to children. But for all that, these years of teaching were not entirely happy ones. She was oppressed by city life, homesick for the country in which she had been brought up, and tormented also by the urge to write. There was also a religious crisis to be lived through. She had been trained to too great intellectual freedom and activity to find blind faith an easy matter. In the process of seeking to establish God upon a foundation of reason she lost her way and passed into a period of complete agnosticism. Her faith in a personal God never came back, but she did return to a recognition of the Deity as the force beneficent and allwise, not to be measured and bound by the human intelligence, but to be fully trusted and worshipped as the guiding principle of all life.

During these years as a teacher she began also to lecture, at first before groups of working women upon political subjects; and later, as her reputation grew, before all manner of audiences. A Socialist in politics, she found herself also linked up with various liberal movements, among them the women's organizations. But her allegiance was no mere blind following. It was at a meeting of the Woman's Congress in Copenhagen in 1896 that she attacked the ruling ideals of the suffrage movement. Choosing for her subject **"The Abuse of Woman's Strength,"** she charged the suffragists will forgetting the claims of woman as a sex being; she criticized the indiscriminate rush into men's occupations, and exalted the maternal function as the sole legitimate work for woman. To the women assembled to listen to her it seemed an absolute reversion to all that against which they were fighting. It was heresy of the blackest sort. She was throwing the weight of her influence not for them but against them. At that period in Ellen Key's development there is no doubt that woman was reacting sharply against the whole domestic function and occupation and saw freedom and individuality as to be secured only outside the home, in the wage-earning professional world.

The criticism which she received at that time affected Ellen Key profoundly. Shortly afterward she resigned from the school, went to live in Germany and gave herself more and more to writing. Though she never retracted from her position that marriage and motherhood is for woman the supreme expression, we find her at pains to make clear that this conviction did not at all interfere with her desire to see woman come into educational and political and economic freedom. But her attack upon the suffrage movement at the time when that movement so greatly needed her support was not easy to forgive. Among the older Scandinavian suffragists she remained even to the time of her death the "wise fool."

BOOKS ON WOMAN'S POSITION

Ellen Key came late to her literary maturity. In Germany, at the age of 54, she began the series of essays which were later to make up her first book. One has only to glance at the titles of these essays and books to find the key to her chief interests. *Love and Marriage, The Woman Movement, The Morality of Women, The Century of the Child, Renaissance of Motherhood, The Younger Generation, Love and Ethics,* show her mind playing more and more around the problem of woman's ideal place in an ideal world.

In her writing, just as in her speaking, she found herself driven always to a merciless expression of all the light that was in her. She did not know how to compromise, to play for popularity, to say what seemed to her half truths. It seemed to be a matter in which her own personal honor was involved. She could not stop short of the last step. She seemed compelled to carry to its last end the development of any precept which she accepted and laid down. It is the habit of mind of the scientist, and turned upon physical, chemical facts it carries, in these modern times, no offense. We exact no denials from our modern Galileos. But Ellen Key was delving into social problems; she was turning the sharp light of her logic upon such uncharted, in-the-air matters as love; she was looking at marriage not from the established point of view of accepted morality and law, but from some new angle. Deeply concerned with what she called the erotic happiness of the individual—not because she loved the individual to the hurt of society, but because she believed that society, the race, could only thus gain its best service from the individual, she was looking at the whole sex relationship with judicial, unbiased coldness. And the alarming thing was that she was asserting, not that it was something outside the law, but that the man-made law concerning the sex relationship was often enough directly at variance with the deeper law of nature or God, as one chooses to call it, which lies back of the reproductive process.

Starting with the premise that love and not law must be the moral determining motive, she drew her first corollary: Marriage is immoral without love; then the second: Love is moral without marriage. It was not that she counseled the common disregard of the legal marriage ceremony. But she felt that too much stress had been laid upon it, that it had been the cloak for too much immorality. She believed that the duty the individual owed to his love was his first and greatest duty, that individual love was "the most important factor in evolution, the deepest determining force," "that not legitimacy but the quality of children must be the standard by which the morality of a union is measured," that out of such unions of love, whether or not with the benefit of clergy or law, would come the race of supermen and superwomen. "The woman of the future," she says, "the phrase charms like a song,"—the woman of the future and her child, begotten in love, through

whom, she believed, would come the spiritual transformation of the world. In order to accomplish this world task, woman must be made free. She must have political rights, economic rights, not as an end in themselves, but as a means to better motherhood. And most of all she must have, wed or unwed, the right to her love and her child.

UNMARRIED MOTHER'S RIGHTS

Like the idealist she was, she threw this challenge at the world. She declared openly for the rights of the unmarried mother. It was this declaration which brought down upon her the harshest criticism it was given her to endure. From all over the world rose the storm of protest. As she had before been charged with being against woman in her struggle for freedom, she was now declared to be against society, the home, the Bible, decency. But she stood firm upon the ground she had taken. Love and love alone can make any union moral. Marriage is immoral without love; love is moral without marriage. In book after book she elaborated this doctrine; year after year she went on talking about it until in our day we have come to feel that it is not after all a doctrine pregnant with power to overthrow society. Perhaps our alarm vanished when we discovered that it remained a theory, not generally put into practice; perhaps we saw that the emphasis needed to be put rather upon love *within* than *without* marriage.

At all events, in the later years of her life Ellen Key saw whatever of general condemnation there had been of herself and her theories settle back into appreciation and honor. Even her Government paid its tribute when it offered her the land upon which her villa stands, this built from the returns of her books which have been translated into many languages and sold all over the world. A more beautiful place could hardly have been found for one to round out one's life. On the brow of a cliff, sloping down by jagged rocks to a great lake, "my sea," she called it, set round by great trees, she found days of quietness and peace. From every civilized country men and women made pilgrimages to her, sometimes to lay their personal problems before her, sometimes to offer her gifts and do her honor. Whoever came found always the warmest welcome, the sort of human affection that must express itself in the touch of her hand.

Great student of love and marriage though she was, it was never given her to know the love of a wife or of a mother. But it was something markedly akin to maternal love that she poured out upon the individual whom she touched and upon the world which she looked out upon. No one who has seen her there in her high home can ever forget the something noble in the poise of her head with its halo of white hair, the quiet strength of her shoulders, the intense vivid youthful interest which she kept to the last in all that the world was doing and thinking, and most of all her abiding faith in the wonder and goodness of life. "We who are now living and working," she said, "will soon be shadows. But our dreams are already moving with white feet in the light of the dawn."

Charles N. Genno   (essay date 1981)

SOURCE: "The Importance of Ellen Key's 'Die Entfaltung der Seele durch Lebenskunst' for Musil's Concept of the Soul," in *Orbis Litterarum*, Vol. 36, No. 4, 1981, pp. 323-31.

[*In the following essay, Genno discusses the influence of Key's works on the writings of the early-twentieth century Austrian novelist Robert Musil.*]

Robert Musil's preoccupation with the state of modern man's soul, which once prompted the noted critic Ernst Blass to dub him, in a rather feeble pun, "ein Entdecker von Neu-Seelland," is evident throughout the entire corpus of his writings. A major recurrent theme in his novels, short stories, essays and plays is the superficiality of twentieth-century man, attributable paradoxically to "zu wenig Verstand in den Fragen der Seele." For centuries, according to Musil, men of science have been envisioning a new humanity, which never materializes because, in their ceaseless effort to create it, they have somehow lost contact with the soul.

Critics have been quick in pointing out the indisputable importance of men like Plato, Ralph Waldo Emerson, Friedrich Nietzche, and Ernst Mach for Musil's concept of the soul. But one major influence on his earliest attempts to theorize about it has been sadly neglected: the famous Swedish feminist Ellen Key.

In his introduction to the English edition of Ellen Key's best known book *Love and Marriage* (1911), Havelock Ellis justly called her "one of the chief moral forces of our time." Unfortunately, she is all but forgotten today, but at the turn of the century her lectures in many countries and her writings stirred a controversy over her feminist ideas on social relationships, comparable to that over Susan B. Anthony's in America.

Ellen Key was born in 1849 in the Swedish province of Småland, the descendant of a Scottish Highlander, Colonel M'Key, who had fought bravely under Gustavus Adolphus in the Thirty Years' War. She completed her early education for the most part on the country estate of her father, an avowed radical in the Swedish parliament, under the tutelage of French, German and Swedish educators. From earliest childhood on, she evinced a strong love of nature and of natural things, attributable in part to her Rousseauian education. Her great-grandfather had been an ardent admirer of Rousseau's famous treatise on Education. He gave his son the name of Emile, which was handed down to Ellen's father, another avid disciple of Rousseau.

In 1880, compelled to seek employment after her father lost his wealth as the result of an agricultural crisis, Ellen Key became a teacher in a girl's school. Some years later she was given the Chair of History of Civilization in Sweden at the Popular University of Stockholm, where she remained for twenty years. Nearly all of her books, which concern themselves with the essential questions of life and the soul, were written only after she had reached middle-age. The first volume of her most ambitious work, *Lines of Life,* appeared in 1903. It was followed a few years later by *The Century of the Child* and, in 1909, by *The Woman's Movement*.

It is interesting to note that Ellen Key's fame was not established in Sweden or England, but in Germany. Robert Musil first read her essay **"Die Entfaltung der Seele durch Lebenskunst"** in the June, 1905 edition of *Die neue Rundschau*. Some time afterwards he noted in his diary the tremendous impact that this essay had made on his thinking. "Ihre Idee, die Seele zum Gegenstand des Studiums zu machen, war für mich erlösend," he wrote. A close reading of the essay is extremely elucidating for any study of Musil's views on the soul.

In **"Die Entfaltung der Seele durch Lebenskunst"** Ellen Key undertook the ambitious task of tracing the historical development of the concept of *Lebenskunst,* or 'the art of living.' It is not surprising that Musil, who regarded his own literary activities as primarily a vehicle for expounding his theories on the art of living, was fascinated by her astute observations.

The essay begins with a discussion of the efforts of the ancient Greeks at the time of Heraclitus to reconcile art with life. She argues that their government as well as the education of their youth were comprehended by them as a form of creative art and that their own style of living chiseled their personalities according to the lofty ideal of the 'beautiful Good': "Sowohl die Staatsregierung wie die Erziehung der Jugend wurden von den höchststehenden Hellenen als schaffende Kunst aufgefaßt, und ihre eigene Lebensführung meißelt ihre Persönlichkeiten nach dem Ideal der 'schönen Güte' aus." The Greek ideal of the 'art of living' was to become the model for the Renaissance period and, later, for Goethe. In their striving to form beautiful people through teaching and environment the men of the Renaissance were in essential agreement with the principal tenet of the Platonic philosophers: that the soul through beauty and goodness achieves divinity, for beauty and goodness are the essence of being.

According to Ellen Key, the *point de départ* of Romanticism was the feeling which its adherents shared with Goethe of the unity between God and nature, life and art. To a far greater degree than Goethe, however, the Romantics were sensitive to the inner unity of souls. For them, the experience of true love represented the highest gradation of the soul: "Sie fühlten, daß die Liebe—sobald sie sich zur höchsten Sympathie erhoben hat—die höchste Steigerung der Seele ist." Before Romanticism disintegrated into a school of grotesqueness, reaction and obscurantism, it bequeathed to the modern world its own profound feeling and a burning desire for existence in a state of realized beauty, in a 'third kingdom' where love and beauty are worshiped and reason has become the servant of the spirit. The great mistake of the Romantics, Ellen Key thought, was in believing that they could dispense with reason altogether.

The essay contains a number of references to writers in whose works the author finds confirmation for some of her own theories about the soul. Goethe is clearly a favourite. She maintains that concern for 'the art of living' pervades all his works in the conscious striving of his protagonists for something higher: "Er faßte das Leben nie als bloßes Dasein allein auf, sondern als ein Leben, während dessen der Weltverlauf unbewußt und der Menschengeist zielbewußt eine immer höhere Steigerung erreicht." In Schiller's writings she finds appealing the belief that only through an aesthetic education can the lost harmony of the ancient Greeks be recovered. She praises Otto Ludwig for having proven the need to recognize uniformity of human nature as the goal in art, education and social intercourse, and for insisting that beauty, in the profoundest sense of the word, is as essential to the soul as oxygen to the body. Thomas Carlyle also receives mention for having recognized, along with Goethe, that our subconscious is the source of all great powers. More important for the argument, however, are the comments about Carlyle's friend, Ralph Waldo Emerson, whose major preoccupation was the soul, its expansion and exercise of power. His doctrine of self-culture assumes a steadily ascending development in the individual, a truer, more intensified and healthier life through a growing feeling of unity with existence. Self-culture means the simultaneous release of all great potentialities for living, resulting in a heightening of thought, feeling and will.

Having acknowledged varying degrees of indebtedness to others through discussion of their ideas, Miss Key towards the end of the essay expounds her own views on the soul and the art of living. The perceptive reader will notice, however, the strong influence of Nietzsche and Emerson in her arguments. The individual with soul, she claims, feels that all souls are alive in his own and that the greatest thinkers can only explain to him what he has already experienced within himself. The man with soul can only thrive through maintaining his individuality. To conform means to lose touch with his most prized possession: his soul.

Perfection of the soul is defined as a link or connection among all our various capabilities. Wherever one quality dominates, the soul is damaged. Reason is a particularly dangerous quality because of its propensity to make distinctions and to dissect things. Soul is defined as, "das Fluidum, das die Fähigkeiten vereinigt."

Ellen Key believed that not only the body, but also the soul was a product of evolution. In the essay the argues that its present state is the result of millions of years of trial and error. Whenever its development is impeded, both the individual and the race suffer. It is the task of the forerunner of the future to prevent this. And who is this forerunner? According to the feminist author, the future is first seen "in der Dichtung, in der Kunst und in der Frauenseele." She cites the famous Italian actress Eleonora Duse as one whose life reveals the bliss of fullness of soul and its torment. Will the lonely new soul of the future be able to live at all under existing conditions? As a partial response to her own question, she advocates an educational programme for the new soul which will transform human passions into flames of the soul and which will strengthen intellectual powers and aesthetic judgment. The primacy of the soul in our lives must be recognized: "Seelenzustände sind die einzigen, wirklichen, die einzigen überall existierenden Werte; Seelenmacht, die einzige, wirklich umgestaltende Macht." To protect the soul, phantasy and feeling must be defended against the enemy, pure reason. In the perfect *Lebenskünstler* complete har-

mony will reign between his inner and outer ego and among all his various powers. All facets of the soul will work together to elevate each other. For such rare individuals this elevation of the soul represents the only form of happiness.

At this juncture in the essay the nexus between the perfection of the soul and the experience of love is established. The individuals is never capable of fulfilling all the conditions for perfection of his soul as completely as when he is in love. Through this experience he enters into what Ellen Key calls the third realm, "das dritte Reich—das Reich der Seele." She believes that it is easier for women to reach this ideal state because their nature is more unified and their emotional life is richer. She envisions a new world order in which sexual differences and huge age gaps will play a much less important role in our lives. She describes it as a society in which "den neuen Menschen, Männern wie Frauen, Jungen wie Alten, Vereinten wie Einsamen gemeinsam ist, daß das, was sie vom Leben wollen, nur ist, daß sein Saitenspiel einen immer tieferen, reineren, volleren Ton gewinne—selbst wenn dieser aus einer Violine singt, die aus Splittern zusammengefügt wurde."

The concluding paragraphs of the essay are an encomium to the soul. The purpose of life, the author proclaims, is life itself. Only when the soul is master in the house of life will the monster called social order sink into oblivion, allowing the soul finally to create its own higher existence.

. . . . .

In the course of perusing this rather lengthy, though by no means exhaustive summary of **"Die Entfaltung der Seele durch Lebenskunst,"** the reader who is conversant with Robert Musil's writings will have recognized numerous interesting similarities between Ellen Key's theories on the soul and his. At the time of its appearance he was twenty-five years old, on the threshold of his literary career. His first major work, *Die Verwirrungen des Zöglings Törless,* appeared the following year, in 1906. In it the eponymous hero announces that his mission in life is "eine Aufgabe der Seele." This task of reestablishing contact with one's lost soul became a central theme in all Musil's subsequent writings. Thomas, the main character in his play *Die Schwärmer* (1921), serves as the author's propagandist when he analyzes for his brother-in-law Josef the cause of modern man's spiritual crisis:

> "Sieh um dich! Unsre Kollegen fliegen, durchbohren Berge, fahren unter Wasser, zucken vor keiner noch so tiefen Neuerung ihrer Systeme zurück. Alles, was sie seit Jahrhunderten machen, ist kühn als Gleichnis einer ungeheuren, abenteuerlichen neuen Menschlichkeit. Die niemals kommt. Denn ihr habt über eurem Tun längst die Seele vergessen."

The scope of the paper does not allow a thorough discussion of Musil's concept of the soul. The theme receives its fullest treatment, of course, in his *magnum opus Der Mann ohne Eigenschaften*. In the early pages of the novel the essayist Musil, in one of his frequent interjections as independent conveyer of his thoughts, criticizes the excessive degree of specialization and mechanization in the modern world by describing the average man's vision of Utopia:

> Eine solche soziale Zwangsvorstellung ist nun schon seit langem eine Art überamerikanische Stadt, wo alles mit der Stoppuhr in der Hand eilt oder stillsteht. Luft und Erde bilden einen Ameisenbau, von den Stockwerken der Verkehrsstraßen durchzogen. Luftzüge, Erdzüge, Untererdzüge, Rohrpostmenschensendungen, Kraftwagenketten rasen horizontal, Schnellaufzüge pumpen vertikal Menschenmassen von einer Verkehrsebene in die andre . . . Fragen und Antworten klinken ineinander wie Machinenglieder, jeder Mensch hat nur ganz bestimmte Aufgaben, die Berufe sind an bestimmten Orten in Gruppen zusammengezogein, man ißt während der Bewegung, die Vergnügungen sind in andern Stadtteilen zusammengezogen, und wieder anderswo stehen die Türme, wo man Frau, Familie, Grammophon und Seele findet.

The chief theoreticians of the soul in the novel are Ulrich and his cousin Ermelinda Tuzzi or, as he calls her, Diotima. Besides the obvious affinities with Plato's and Hölderlin's Diotima and her own ideal, Frau von Stein, the character owes much to the influence of Ellen Key's ideas on Musil. At the beginning of the novel Diotima is preoccupied with her plan to unite her concept of spirit with present social conditions. To combat the maladies of this soulless epoch, which suffers from the dominance of logic and psychology, she makes her salon the headquarters for the Parallel Action, which she hopes will restore a lost spiritual depth to society. Diotima's driving ambition is to bring the soul into the spheres of power, to reinstate culture in the present age of civilization. Through her infatuation with the Pressian industrialist Arnheim, she becomes interested in the relationship of love to the soul. Like Ellen Key, she becomes convinced that love and the soul are inextricably bound together, and hopes to use Arnheim as a means to regain access to her soul. She mentions to him the superstitious belief, traceable to Plato's *Phaidros,* that in a period every thousand years the spirit and reality are united in chosen individuals, allowing them to enter into the kingdom of the soul. She and Arnheim prove to be incapable of bridging the gap between reality and this ideal concept of love.

Of all the characters in *Der Mann ohne Eigenschaften* Ulrich is the one who is best equipped to experience the full possibilities of the soul. His year's leave of absence from life is designed to help him to restore the lost harmony between his outer and inner worlds which he has known as a child. By studying the writings of various mystics, he comes to the realization that love and the soul are inseparable. Through the experience of love with his sister Agathe, he, too, attempts to enter into the Thousand Years' Kingdom of the soul. The difference between the two essays lies in the degrees of intensity. While Diotima and Arnheim are satisfied with merely theorizing about it, Ulrich and Agathe's "journey into Paradise" is a bold attempt to realize the kingdom of the soul. Their failure is attributable largely to a civilization which has placed insurmountable impediments in the way of a meaningful relationship between the individual and nature.

Through the above comments the question to what extent Musil made actual use of Ellen Key's theories has partially been answered. It is clear that he shared her views on the ethical mission of the artist. In his "Rede zur Rilke-Feier" (1927) he stated that the poet's mission, as he saw it, was the "Entfaltung der Schöpfung und der Möglichkeiten des Geistes." He was also in total sympathy with her stance on the problem of individuality and the need for self-culture. In his essay "Der Anschluß an Deutschland" (1919) he draws a distinction between two types of culture; the first he calls 'geistige Kultur,' the second, 'Lebensform, der gute Stil.' The first is the home of original, free thought, the realm of the individual. The second is the realm of conformity. He contends that the second should grow out of the first, but finds that in the twentieth century the two are almost always separated. This rupture is most clearly delineated in *Der Mann ohne Eigenschaften,* where attempts by various individuals to combine them result in a maze of conflicting inner beliefs which resolve themselves usually in external conformity and inner chaos. All Musil's individuals, in their quest for self-culture, share a sense of isolation, an unwillingness to accept any clearly defined professional status, a cold, ironic attitude towards society, a burning desire for truth and exactitude, and an unrelenting drive to find a formula for living a rich and full existence.

Ellen Key's assertion in **"Die Entfaltung der Seele"** that the man who possesses soul must by necessity lack definite qualities in order to realize all his potentialities— "Überall, wo eine Eigenschaft herrscht, ist weniger Seelenvollheit"—provided Musil with one of the central ideas in *Der Mann ohne Eigenschaften,* as the title of the novel indicates. In chapter 61 of Book One he equates the concept of Utopia with possibilities: "Utopien bedeuten ungefähr so viel wie Möglichkeiten; darin, daß eine Möglichkeit nicht Wirklichkeit ist, drückt sich nichts anderes aus, als daß die Umstände, mit denen sie verflochten ist, sie daran hindern, denn andernfalls wäre sie ja nur eine Unmöglichkeit." The utopist's task is to come to grips with reality with its multiplicity of potentialities.

Another important part of Ellen Key's discourse on the soul, which relates directly to Musil's works, is the nexus she finds between man's animal instincts and the soul: "Ja, die Menschen der Seele fühlen sich den Tieren näher als den Verstandesmenschen, weil sie bei den ersten finden, was sie bei den letzteren vermissen." This idea is echoed again and again in Musil's writings. Törless's involvement with the prostitute Bozena, his homosexual affair with Basini, and his association with his perverse fellow students, Reiting and Beineberg, are all important contributions to his spiritual growth, as he announces to the bewildered faculty caput after his attempted flight from the school. In *Tonka,* the last and most successful of the three tales in *Drei Frauen* (1924), a young chemistry student becomes romantically involved with a young woman who has been reared in a sexually promiscuous environment. When she becomes pregnant, he calculates that conception must have occurred during one of his lengthy periods of absence. Besides this, she has contracted a venereal disease, while he is completely healthy. Torn between the almost certain proof of her infidelity, based on scientific statistics, and the slim possibility of some supernatural explanation, he chooses the rational interpretation. Only after her death can he accept her innocence. Through Tonka the young offspring of the age of science and logic becomes aware of the possibility of a new truth outside the empirical world. His inability to trust her completely while she was alive has prevented him from experiencing the same perfection of soul which she possessed. In the two tales of *Die Vereinigungen* (1911) and in the Moosbrugger episode in *Der Mann ohne Eigenschaften* other salient variations of this important theme are found.

In drawing the reader's attention to various parallels between Ellen Key's concept of the soul and Robert Musil's, it has not been my intention to convey the idea that the latter was in total agreement with everything in **"Die Entfaltung der Seele durch Lebenskunst."** On the one hand, he was lavish in his praise of it: "Ihre Grundidee—mehr Seele, oder überhaupt Seele—ist ausgezeichnet. Ihre Idee, die Seele zum Gegenstand des Studiums zu machen, war für mich erlösend." On the other hand, he recognized a number of contradictions in her definition of the soul and her advice on how to nurture it. He criticized her equation of 'fullness of life,' (which means the realization of all its possibilities), with 'harmony,' arguing that the two do not necessarily go hand in hand. Fullness of life, he felt, had to be combined with the simplification of life. Contemporary society was so full of paradoxes and contradictory tendencies that a full, varied existence within the boundaries of its institutions would not bring the individual into closer contact with his soul. Only closer contact with the laws of nature could achieve that. Finally, while he agreed essentially with her polemic against reason in the essay, he felt that she had gone too far in her attack and had shown no awareness of the difficulties associated with it. In spite of these minor objections, Musil was very conscious of the great debt that he owed to this remarkable woman. The important influence that she exerted on him can be observed throughout his writings.

Torborg Lundell   (essay date 1984)

SOURCE: "Ellen Key and Swedish Feminist Views on Motherhood," in *Scandinavian Studies*, Vol. 56, No. 4, Autumn, 1984, pp. 351-69.

[*In the following essay, Lundell explores the role of mothers in Swedish feminism and in Key's writings.*]

During the nineteenth century the concept of family and the role of woman as mother changed in Sweden as in most other countries in Europe. As the century progressed, more and more literature and public discussions dealt with the joys of motherhood and means of promoting motherhood and motherliness. A "cult of motherhood" aimed primarily at middle class women flourished together with a "cult of true womanhood." Motherhood was regarded as woman's most natural, highest, and noblest state. Failure to succeed in motherhood meant failure as a woman. But as Eleanor Riemer and John C. Fout point out in *European Women: A Documentary History 1789-1945,* proponents of the motherhood cult who claimed to uphold tradition actually defined what

woman's behavior and attitudes *should* be, rather than describing what they actually were (or had been). Feminists too embraced the cult of motherhood, though they did not necessarily see it as woman's only role. Primarily they wanted motherhood to be appreciated by society—not denigrated, but seen as an important social contribution.

With this exaltation of the mother role there came the view that the mother represented moral ideals, the most important quality she could, and must, transmit to her children. As a Swedish male literary critic said in the mid-century: the task of mothers was "fostra en sedligare, friare och lyckligare generation än vi själva." No small task indeed and one that, with its implication of constant vigilance and sacrifice of the mother's own time and interests, was imposed upon women at the same time as women's roles and aspirations were rapidly changing. This led to conflicts for many women who could not integrate their personal experience with an ideology that stressed the joys of motherhood as woman's only *raison d'être*.

This ideal for the middle class woman/mother soon carried over to the working class. Here the underlying thought was not to create a mission for a group of women who, with the development of industrialism and capitalism, had lost their status as contributors to the family's economic well being. Instead the intention was "arbetarklassens förädling genom återupprättandet af hemmets och familjelifvets helgd," as a writer in the woman's magazine *Dagny* phrased the issue. Whereas the middle class woman had been displaced by the change in economic structure, the working class woman was abused by it, and it became an issue for the Social Democratic party to improve her situation. So, for example, did August Babel, the father of the German Social Democrats, look forward to a home life for the working class where the family would not be split by "slavery for wages."

The nature of motherhood, then, during the nineteenth century became a political, economic, and moral issue with the general assumption that all women should somehow fit into the same structural model of motherhood: mothers served ideally at home all the time. This was most vigorously advocated by Ellen Key, the foremost writer and philosopher on motherhood in Sweden around the turn of the century. Her views on this and other issues regarding women put her in an international context. She was, for example, influential in the creation of the "Mutterschutz" movement in Germany. She also shared many of Havelock Ellis' views. This inquiry is, however, limited to the Swedish scene. While she can be accused of having romantic and unrealistic views on motherhood, her program for full-time motherhood and its social implication still, in parts, contains ideas too radical to have been instituted even in today's progressive Sweden. However, she also acknowledges, though she does not dwell upon, the need for *flexibility* in our views on how individual women could or should integrate motherhood into their lives.

Furthermore, Key's main concern was the ideal form of motherhood for the working-class woman who, for economic reasons, often could not devote herself to full-time motherhood. This does not mean that she is an anti-feminist romantic who would confine women to motherhood, Cheri Register claims in "Motherhood at Center: Ellen Key's Social Vision." Instead, her writings "enlarged the scope of feminist activity" by focusing on the specifically feminine aspects of women's situation and its implications for woman's place in society. This led her to criticize the woman's movement in *Missbrukad Kvinnokraft och Naturenliga arbetsområden för kvinnor* (1896) because she felt it had become dogmatic in its attempt to bring women's lives on equal footing with men's, i.e., equal right to (professional) education and work outside the home, which, of course, also was more a concern for the middle-class woman.

Instead, Key argues, motherhood itself is a "kall" (profession). "Vi måste i våra kulturplaner," she says in *Barnets århundrade,* "utgå därifrån att moderskapet är väsentligt för kvinnans natur och det sätt på vilket hon uppfyller detta kall, är av största vikt för samhället." Consequently, she argues further in *The Renaissance of Motherhood* that motherhood must be made economically secure and recognized "as a public work to be rewarded and controlled by society." This is essential because, as she says in *Kärleken och Äktenskapet,* the State lacks nurturing qualities. Therefore it is necessary to allow what Key calls "the milk of human kindness" to flow into the social sphere. As Cheri Register points out, Key identified the problems of society as a "tension between the private and personally human and the public and university human."

To eliminate this tension and its negative impact on the quality of life in society, Key argues, motherly qualities must be made socially important and the values they represent, emotion and love, must be brought to bear on social legislation and structure. If motherliness becomes a socially important value this would raise women's status and contribute to a more satisfying life for everyone.

At this time, a woman, the working class woman and the under-educated middle class woman, "had at best to choose between a mediocre performance in a spiritually deadening job and motherhood deprived of social support and prestige," Register points out. At worst she did not have a choice; she had to work. It is doubtful whether motherhood at the time (at least the proper patriarchal form of motherhood) was deprived of prestige since this is the time when motherhood was held forth as the highest and noblest occupation for women, but there was certainly no economic support for motherhood.

The necessity of economic support for women to enable them to function as mothers was discussed at length by Key in *Barnets århundrade*. To her, women's economic means of survival were less a matter of individual independence from male dominance than a question of undisturbed performance of the mother role. Therefore, she did not favor facilitating paid work outside the home as a desirable means to accomplish women's economic independence. Instead, she proposed publicly-financed payments for women raising children. In this respect, Register notes, she differed from "the standard feminist position which saw paid work as a vital expression of the right to control one's own life." On the other hand, Key claimed that " 'individens självbestämningsrätt' är en ihålig fras inom ett på storindustri byggt samhälle och dubbelt ihåligt när

den gäler kvinnan." This is why, Key argued, we must alter the conditions that increasingly deprive women of the happiness of motherhood, and children of the care of a mother. Her feelings in this respect are most strongly worded in *The Renaissance of Motherhood*: "The socially destructive, racially wasteful and soul-withering consequence of the working mother outside the home must cease." Consequently she did not approve of day care centers.

Still, it was not to "imprison women in immanence," Register argues, but to "transform social existence" that Key espoused a "right to motherhood." However, motherhood must be free "from patriarchal legal and moral strictures," i.e., legitimate motherhood must exist independent of marriage. These were, of course, shocking ideas at the time as they were when expressed by Alexandra Kollantay in 1918 in post-revolutionary Russia. Kollantay then argued that motherhood is to be regarded as a social function and therefore should be protected by the state regardless of marital status. She later reveals in the Swedish feminist journal *Tidevarvet* that she was much criticized for her "new morals." Clearly, a notion of motherhood, however sacred in the rhetoric of state and church, was sacred only when performed according to patriarchal rules, be it in revolutionary Russia or bourgeois Sweden.

To accomplish her ideal of "right to motherhood," Key advocated that every mother should be supported by society during each child's first three years. This support was to cover only essential cost of living expenses but it was to be regarded as an unquestionable right because "varje mor [har] rätt till samhällets underhåll då hon bär samhållets viktigaste börda."

In *The Renaissance of Motherhood,* Key outlines the prerequisites for this support: The woman must be of legal age, have completed a year of training in child care, be caring for the child herself or have arranged for equivalent care (another full-time mother-figure, one presumes), and she was not to have enough wealth or income to provide for herself. Obviously, Key did not believe in instinctual mother care but in an education to motherhood—which was consistent with her view of motherhood as a socially redeemable task. Women undergoing training for motherhood she saw as being in the same position as men completing their mandatory military training and therefore equally deserving of social support during this period. It would thus be possible for all women to acquire proper education for motherhood, regardless of marital or economic status. This measure, she believed, would reduce the working-class woman's burden and also eliminate the middle-class woman's desire to seek other employment to attain economic independence.

The fact that Key did indeed have radical ideas on how to improve the mother's status and economic security, must, however, be reconciled with the fact that she also showed strong ambivalence (by feminist standards) towards women in general and motherhood in particular. This leads the Swedish expert on Ellen Key, Ronny Ambjörnsson, to emphasize that she was not a feminist but a socialist and social reformer. She also belongs rhetorically to the nineteenth century, with its taste for sentimental and hyperbolic language which might alienate a reader of today. In her popular essay **"Samhällsmoderlighet"** she vacillates between realistic evaluation of women's individuality in relation to motherhood, romantic ideals of the life of woman as mother, and muddled speculations about the nature of woman's character.

Consider, for example, her notion about men's and women's place and function in society as it relates to motherliness. She ascribes to the general school of thought of the day which saw in the "nature" of each sex a limitation of its activities and talents, and consequently a predetermined division of labor. But she also believed that society could improve and develop to a higher state only through transformation of the nature of each sex. This transformation starts in the home, Key argues, with the education women give the new generation. The values learned at home will then influence the laws, the way in which work is organized and the patterns of consumption. However, since women, especially the "best," are supposed to be full-time mothers and not enter public life until later in life, society would still be dominated by men, though they would have been taught to respect motherly values and needs. Naturally, this social vision, sounding like enlightened patriarchalism, is hard to reconcile with more ambitious feminist ideals regarding the future of women.

Society should in fact, Key implies, already show more progress towards being organized according to the principles advocated by her, considering the glorification of motherhood that was taking place during the nineteenth century. For the lack of progress she blames women themselves. Society is still lacking in genuine motherliness because, she says, most women still cheat when they serve as children's caretakers, lovers, wives, homemakers. Within each field "sakna de konst och vetenskap, klarsyn och omtanke." However, personal, economic and social circumstances might also prevent women from performing as ideal or even acceptable mothers. This was voiced as early as 1844 by Anders Lagergren, parson in Strängnäs, in his motion to institute a school for girls because he found that "långt ifrån alla mödrar förstod sig på att uppfostra barn . . . Många mödrar led av fattigdom, dålig hälsa och så tung arbetsbörda att de inte hade någon energi kvar till att uppfostra sina döttrar." His motion was denied because the home was seen as being too important and necessary for the daughter (regardless of the dire facts, it seems). This is also the time when a remarkably large number of infants were suffocated while sleeping with their mothers—a trend that would continue for a long time. Curiously, Lagergren's wording of the problem is more compassionate than Key's, who seems more impatient with the state of affairs. The necessity of education of women is always a strong underlying assumption in Key's philosophy about motherhood. But she is primarily interested in an education for women that is relevant to motherhood because she also believes that not all signs are favorable for the hope that woman will be able to "genomgå akademier och sköta statstjänster utan skada för snabbheten i blick, finheten i iakttagelse, givmildheten i själ som väsen."

Even if we excuse such dated notions about the nature of women, it is hard to look realistically upon Key's further visions about women's abilities to engage in full-time motherhood while at the same time infusing society with motherly qualities. We have, for example, Key's vivid scene from a working-class home picturing how the ideal mother will merge her involvement in motherhood with her interest in public life. As family mother, the politically interested woman (and this is the woman Key seems to have in mind most of the time), will be forced to choose between participating in activities outside the home, which will be unfortunate for the home and the children, and staying at home, which will be painful to herself and her need of independence. She can sacrifice her personal pleasures, not her duties. (It is important to note that Key accepts and embraces the belief that motherhood does mean *sacrifice* of a woman's individual needs—what she calls "enskilda nöjen.") What happens then when the worker's wife wants to go to an election rally with her husband? Who shall take care of the children?

> Tjänare finns inga. Grannhustrun? Också hon vill gå på mötet. Barnkrubban? Den är stängd om aftnarna ty även dess föreståndarinna har allmänintressen! Det finns således ingen annan väg än att denna hustru måste nöja sig med mannens omdöme.

However shocking this might sound to a modern feminist, we must not forget that Key was not only preaching the "right to motherhood," but also advocating love as the only legitimate basis for a relationship with children. A love, that is, which meant merging of soul and body, a love one might conclude which made husband and wife perfectly and absolutely in tune with each other politically as well as personally. Still, she did not argue that the wife should leave the children in their father's care while she went to the rally and told him how to vote. Nor did she encourage female bonding by suggesting that women take turns babysitting each other's children so that at least some of them could attend the meeting.

Key may be even more unrealistic in her estimation of what a woman as mother will have the energy to do during her period of active motherhood. A woman ought to stay home from meetings and decline public service as long as she is needed in the home on a full time basis, Key argues. However, she must, at the same time, "behålla känning med alla stora tidsrörelser och hålla sig andligt vaken för att framledes kunna bli omedelbart verksam." She must do this not for her own sake, though, but because only in this way will she become, in a deep sense, "livsstegrande" to her husband and children. And Key is not talking about a single child but preferably about four siblings.

It is thus not without reason that Key, who never married or had children, nor for that matter ever had to struggle with a working class limitation of economic means, has been accused of talking about something she knew nothing about. The most well-known spokeswoman for this type of criticism of Ellen Key's ideas is Elin Wägner, writer and feminist who stands as the heir to Key's position in Swedish culture. Elin Wägner's great admiration for Ellen Key did not exclude her critique of those parts of Key's work which she found weak in argument and characterized by an idealization of reality.

Ellen Key's and Elin Wägner's relationship has been explored by Ingrid Claréus, who notes that, in a long article in *Tidevarvet* at the time of Ellen Key's death in 1926, Elin Wägner summarizes her opinion of Key's stand on the issue of motherhood. She argues against Key's thesis that woman's task was to humanize love and bring up the next generation. Ellen Key had found this to be such an important task that she could not understand why women wanted to work outside the home. But Wägner points out that Key does not look realistically upon the fact that to be happy, women must be able to choose their partner in love and to do that they must be economically independent.

In spite of her criticism of Key's ideas, Wägner's vision of future society is not substantially different from Key's, though somewhat more optimistic. Key may have been talking at length about "samhällsmoderlighet" but she did not think that women had enough intelligence and opportunity to realize this ideal. Wägner, however, believed in a radical change in society where women's influence would indeed affect the world and create the new world state. She envisaged a new type of matriarchy where motherliness would rule and men would be changed by the women, where there would be "moderliga" men. In this respect they both belong to the tradition of Fredrika Bremer and her belief in woman's innate goodness, her talent to create and promote life, her motherliness which embraces everything and which has the capacity to create peace and freedom in the world.

In fact, it was the peace movement, more than the question of the status and economics of motherhood, that involved and united the feminists of that time. Ellen Key brings together mother qualities and the peace movement as the means whereby women can change the world. She writes in **Missbrukad Kvinnokraft** that woman has an important mission, both as mother at home and mother in society. Her humanism should undermine "det etablerade samhället med dess vertikala lojaliteter." This could be done through work for peace, which she calls "undermineringsarbete," towards a more humane society. Key deplored the waste of energy and mother care when mothers "med allt större allvar och ansvarskänsla, föda och fostra det nya släktet," and work to improve the next generation physically and mentally, only to see their sons killed on the battlefield.

We note again Key's emphasis on the quality of mothering as a means for societal improvement and thus an asset to society. The importance she places on quality also lies behind her disapproval of child care centers (*barnkrubba*) which were nothing but parking places for working-class children while their mothers worked. Middle-class children, on the other hand, attended nursery schools (*barnträdgård*) with educational goals, their mothers being concerned about proper education for their children. Here again we meet the fact that motherhood ideologies are unavoidably intertwined with class questions. Ellen Key's socialist ambitions and views on motherhood are interdependent, and that makes it hard for her to formulate an altogether consistent philosophy on mother-

hood. One can agree with her conviction that full-time motherhood is a more stimulating occupation than a menial job, but is it more stimulating than intellectual and creative work? And what about an adult woman's needs to interact with other adults? Key argues that the rewards and importance of motherhood more than balanced any sacrifice of personal interests by the mother. Then again, she did allow for individual *flexibility* in mothering. For example, she did acknowledge, without condemning, that there exist mothers who, as she says, "av ett eller annat skäl ej kan eller vill ägna sig åt barnens skötsel och fostran." Such mothers, she suggests, could work outside the home and "Skaffa sig en ersättare vid deras vård." Other feminists were more willing to go along with this latter conclusion. Also, they were inclined to regard mothers' interests outside child care not as "pleasures" but as rights.

In *Tidevarvet* of 1936 we find, for example, an article justifying children's stay in a child-care facility because it benefits the mother:

> Är det inte emellertid så att ur *nödvändigheten* att lämna bort barnen till barnkrubban eller barnträdgården har vuxit fram insikten om betydelsen av att någon tid på dygnet ha barnen även under denna ålder . . . under inflytande av pedagogisk expertis . . . Så, menar vi, kan och bör allt flera områden helt eller delvis läggas över från husmodern till experten för att hon inom sitt hem eller utom, skall få erfara det som gör en människa fri: att på någon punkt vara helt samlad, helt kunnig, helt i sitt esse.

In other words, she is free from domestic and motherly chores to pursue her own work and interests.

These feminist concerns about the rights of the mother were raised at a time when the Social Democratic party had taken the first steps towards social and economic appreciation of motherhood to offset a serious decline in birthrate. Gunnar and Alva Myrdal are credited with formulating the ideology and policy which promoted the belief that since society is dependent on a rising birth rate for its survival, it would also have to assume some of the economic responsibility for motherhood. They also recognized that women were more likely to reproduce if conditions for motherhood were favorable. As Cheri Register points out, this ideology is inspired by Ellen Key's ideas, though they were not acknowledged as such.

The next major work discussing the role of women as mothers with impact on the Swedish scene was Alva Myrdal's and Viola Klein's, *Women's Two Roles* (1956). They formulated five points as basis for a discussion about the complex interaction between social and personal factors inherent in the fact that only women become mothers:

> 1 Women, as the childbearing sex, present specific social problems. This fact has, in particular, to be taken into account in the evaluation of their creative contribution to society.
>
> 2 As a result of this maternal function, women's adjustment to the social changes brought about by the Industrial Revolution, especially the separation of work from home, has been retarded.

3 The mental health and happiness of coming generations depend, to an extent which we have today only begun to understand, on the love and security which maternal care provides during early childhood. In this sense, women bear a special responsibility for the future quality of our people.

4 The general increase in longevity which characterizes this century has had a more marked effect on women than men.

5 Under present conditions with an average family of only slightly more than two children and reasonable amenities, an average housewife can be considered to be employed full time on tasks which are necessary for homemaking only during a quarter to one third of her normal adult life.

We note that Myrdal and Klein perpetuate Ellen Key's ideas though they have been cloaked in a more social scientific language. Women are still seen as carrying the sole responsibility for child care (and homemaking). Women, not men, have two roles, home and work, and one comes before the other. It is primarily the longer life span that makes it necessary for women to plan for work outside the home at some later point in life. This is regarded as necessary not only for personal satisfaction but for social good:

> Modern mothers who make no plans outside the family for their future will not only play havoc with their own lives, but will make nervous wrecks of their overprotected children and their husbands.

But their rationale is different from Key's. Myrdal and Klein imply that women should work for therapeutic reasons—not, as Key argued, because women/mothers possess resources that will benefit society.

Woman is mother first, woman second, and person third, in an implied pattern of hierarchy that Myrdal and Klein share with Key. Still there are signs of a development towards contemporary thinking, that of shared responsibilities and realization of female (and male) potentials in a wider range of activities. In the 1956 edition of *Women's Two Roles,* Myrdal and Klein state: "Nowadays not even the most ardent feminist would deny that the claims of children to their mother's time and attention come first in the order of priorities." This sentence was deleted in the 1968 revised edition. Furthermore, even in the 1956 edition, they quote at length Margaret Mead's observation that:

> The specific biological situation of the continuing relationship of the child to its biological mother and its need for care by human beings are being hopelessly confused in the growing insistence that child and biological mother, or mother surrogate, must never be separated, that all separating even for a few days is inevitably damaging, and that if long enough it does irreversible damage. This . . . is a new and subtle form of antifeminism in which men—under the guise of exalting the importance of maternity—are tying women more tightly to their children

than has been thought necessary since the invention of bottle feeding and baby carriages.

There are other signs of an ideology in transition expressed in *Women's Two Roles.* The trend here is to find a balance between woman's child-caring responsibilities and her personal working needs and talents, or to find a way to make women feel that they lead a useful life beyond the child raising years. The ideal promoted in this book is a mother who is at home during a child's first three years, then works 4-6 hours a day while the child attends preschool and, as the child grows, increases her work hours outside the home. This will prepare her for her own liberation from the children when she is about 45 years old, which, then, would be a blessing for herself, the family, and the society. But not all women are expected to follow this pattern and the element of flexibility present already in Key's work is here more firmly established. The authors warn more about the dangers of an unfulfilled housewife/mother who feels that she lacks contacts and intellectual stimulation by staying home and caring for her children, than about the dangers of a mother who is working outside the home, provided, of course, that the child can be lovingly taken care of by another person (who still is assumed to be another woman).

Complicating the mother role is the fact that women are not exclusively mothers even if they do stay at home to care for their children. They must also take care of the house, make a home, and serve a husband's needs. Many such tasks may be uncongenial to a woman's talents, interests and qualifications, even though she may prefer to care for her children full time than to work outside the home. It is thus not the child care but the care of house and husband in addition that may be a major source of discontent for women/mothers.

This domestic aspect of motherhood Ellen Key only mentions in passing and with a romantic rather than practical view. She sees women as transmitters of aesthetic values, as promoting a sense of beauty by decorating the home, but she ignores the potential drudgery of daily housework. Myrdal and Klein look more realistically upon the fact that this aspect of full-time motherhood may contribute to making it a potentially unfulfilling occupation. Both they and Key are concerned with the lack of economic security and social status connected with full time motherhood/housework. But Myrdal and Klein are not as radical as Key in their proposed solution to this problem. They do not suggest what amounts to state paid wages for mothers, as does Key. Instead they want to facilitate women's reentry to remunerative working life.

In the 1970s the question of economic security and social status in relation to motherhood was approached from a new angle. The discussion was no longer dealt exclusively with women's roles as mothers, but also with men's roles as fathers. Behind the discussion lies the philosophy, formulated with the rise of modern feminism, that nurturing qualities should be encouraged in both sexes, and that in striving towards equality between the sexes, each sex must enter the traditional realm of the other sex: women the breadwinning and men the nurturing.

The introduction of a nine-month paid maternity leave

(now twelve months with some restrictions) in the 1970s, facilitated more flexible parenting. Still, it is primarily women who parent. Even the ten-day paid leave of absence in connection with birth to which fathers are entitled was, according to a 1980 study covering 6,000 men, used fully by only 10%. Negative attitudes on the part of coworkers and employers, especially in the private sector, play a large role in keeping parental obligations traditionally separated. Also, because domestic work is considered as part of mothering tasks, men who opt to share child care also necessarily share in housework. This new philosophy was formulated by the well-known feminist Eva Moberg, who argued in 1970 that the state should expand its services radically to enable women to earn a living and acquire a good professional education. She also emphasized that men and women should share equally in work outside the home and care for home and children. She sees this sharing as a step towards the goal of a complete human role or existence for both sexes. But by and large, feminist views on motherhood are no longer promoted by individual women but by groups or government appointed committees. The feminist Grupp 8 issued a manifesto urging day care for all children from 6 months to 7 years of age and employment insurance for mothers unable to work because of lack of day care centers. This view, of course, imposes *one* value system for all mothers, just as Ellen Key did, though the doctrine is different from that of Key who, we remember, argued generally that women should stay home with their small children.

In announcing the establishment of a committee for equality between men and women, then Prime Minister Olof Palme did, however, consider the needs both of women working outside the home and those working in the home. His guidelines of December 1972 contained the following:

> I första hand gäller det att hävda kvinnans rätt till arbete . . . Ungdoms-och vuxenutbildningen måste medverka till att en arbetsfördelning, byggd på jämställdhet mellan män och kvinnor främjas på arbetsmarknaden och i hemmen. En sådan arbetsfördelning ställer stora krav på barntillsyn, annan service i bostadsområdena och en vidgad plats för gemenskap utanför hemmen och i samhällslivet och av olika former av service kräver uppmärksamhet.

Still, in the committee's report released in May 1973, it is work outside the home that is seen as the key to women's equality: "Kvinnans rätt till trygghet genom eget förvärvsarbete hävdas allt starkare." But this demand runs parallel to demands for shortening the workday to six hours, so that:

> varje människa ska kunna ha heltidsarbete och samtidigt möjlighet till god kontakt med barn . . . För barnens skull behövs en kortare arbetsdag . . . Föräldrar och barn måste hinna umgås med varandra varje dag . . . Barnen behöver även män att lära sig av och samspela med. Därför är det viktigt att också männen får kortare arbetsdag liksom att fler män knyts till förskolan.

We note then that motherhood as such is not recognized as a social asset that deserves economic reward corresponding to its value for the survival of society. What is actually proposed to satisfy women's needs to pursue their interests and utilize their talents and education outside the home is put in terms of children's needs rather than women's needs or even society's need for motherliness.

It seems that even today, feminists are not comfortable with promoting an issue in terms of women's needs. There are women's "rights" and children's "needs." We are, in other words, not that liberated from a view we can trace back to Ellen Key and her tradition—namely that mothers are expected to put their own interests or needs second to what is perceived to be the interest of the child, or, if not second, they are at least not to emphasize their own interests. For example, present policy still dictates that day-care centers should be located where the child lives and not in connection with either parent's workplace. This presumably is good for the child, who then will have the same playmates outside the day care center and in, and who will avoid commuting. There is not enough consideration given to the adult woman/mother's needs which may be better served by a day-care center at her workplace or, for that matter, at the father's. For we should be aware of that in spite of the trend towards sharing of total responsibilities, the fact remains that it is still in most cases the mother who takes the child to the day-care center, not to mention the fact that there are a great number of single mothers. Besides, a location near the mother's workplace would also make it more convenient for the mother to continue breastfeeding after returning to work, an aspect of children's needs, mothering, and location of day care center that does not seem to have entered into the discussion. Since 1973 mothers are, after all, legally entitled to nurse or pump out their milk during working hours. We may well ask whether the catering to the presumed "good of the child" in reality means the good of the male child because the female child soon learns, or learns at least when she becomes a mother, that her needs even today are to be subordinated to another's needs, here expressed in social priorities set by male-dominated bodies of government.

For example, the Kungliga Biblioteket's attempt to create day care facilities for the library personnel failed because the Stockholm "kommun" did not want to spend money for the benefit of children from other "kommuner." In fact, this type of bickering on the "kommun" level has not been unimportant in creating the present lack of day care flexibility. Also, the political aspect of the location of day care centers in, for example, corporate space, has been debated in recent years.

A certain lack of *flexibility* in contemporary ideology and policy setting tracts is dependent in part also upon the fact that though the traditional division of labor between men/fathers and women/mothers which confined each sex to separate work places and areas of authority is largely eliminated, the child is still not welcome in the traditionally male-dominated working world. This creates a problem for mothers as well and, perhaps, some "mothering" fathers. I think that if, for example, male scholars had to travel with a three-year old on a research trip as I did to Sweden in the spring of 1982, we would soon have a new philosophy about day care policy. We would get excellent, reasonably priced drop-in child care facilities at libraries, archives and other work places. During my stay I found only one such place, in Stockholm, and that was in a large department store. The only conclusion I can draw from the present situation in Sweden is that the public sphere recognizes the public need of parents only as shoppers. Had it not been for the understanding, motherly librarians in three university towns, and, in all fairness, the other users of the facilities, men and women, my public identity as a professor could not have been integrated with my private identity as a mother as well as it was. And for this I think I have to thank as yet unformulated trends towards an ideology which will argue that society should be opened up for children as well as for women. This ideally would lead to a less forbidding gap, in terms of physical space, between work/public sphere and home-child/private sphere. As Sheila Kitzinger comments in *Women as Mothers,* after observing that several men were working at the University of Stockholm with babies on their backs, "When parenthood is shared not only do fathers come into the home, but babies go out of it more and mobility becomes a prime requisite. The gulf between home and work place disappears."

But this will allow for only one way of mothering with economic security and social status, that of the working woman. This is the type of woman/mother which is the model for the Social Democratic Party which represents the dominant feminist view. Speaking for women who would rather be mothers and homemakers are the Center Party and the Conservative Party each proposing a child care benefit, which would be taxable and qualify a person for pension points. This is a view very similar to Ellen Key's though she receives no credit for this today. We sense her spirit also behind recent proposals for parental education except for the fact that fathers are to be involved in this too. Key's basic ideas obviously still have relevance today though her socialist-oriented ideology now, ironically, is promoted by the conservative parties. For a radical approach to motherhood, Key's radicalism has been substituted for a radical path more in keeping with the time and its emphasis on equality. Motherhood must be shared.

This is the view of the Swedish Equal Opportunities Ombudsman, Inga-Britt Törnell. Being asked whether she believed that men and women could ever be completely equal in working life considering the fact that women bear the children, she said: "If men are prepared to accept their part in looking after the children, then I think it is perfectly possible." To promote the birth of more children in Sweden, now suffering from the lowest birth rate since 1931, the Social Democratic minister of Social Affairs, Karin Söder, recently saw the solution not in making motherhood more attractive in a stereotypical way, but in making fatherhood more like motherhood. "The men must take on a larger responsibility for the care of the children."

Legally, too, the view of motherhood is undergoing a change. Professor of Law Ulla Jacobsson noted in 1979 that "actual social phenomena may be said to support the motherhood principle" (explaining the courts' tendency to decide custody cases in favor of the mother). However, she continues:

> But these social realities are in the process of change. For every step forward toward a more equal sharing of roles by women and men both at home and at work, there is less basis for the principle that mother is best. Given a specific custody case, the probability that the woman will be the better custodian than the man is decreasing, and the motherhood principle is becoming harder and harder to defend.

> If the courts are to reject the idea that the mother has a *natural preference* as custodian, and instead take as their point of departure *social realities,* then it is necessary to investigate how matters stand in each particular case and to give the woman and the man the same starting position in the judicial process.

One major trend of feminist view seems to lean towards a total merging of father and mother roles—and wisely so, if the intent is to accomplish the goal of social motherliness promoted by the feminist tradition since Fredrika Bremer. When each parent feels responsible for and actively takes part in the upbringing of children, nurturing qualities will become as important as other qualities necessary to run a society. This way there will be an impact of motherly qualities on the mainstream of social policy-making process. This is what Ellen Key envisaged, though she might not approve of the way in which her vision might be fulfilled today.

FURTHER READING

Biography

Claréus, Ingrid. "Ellen Key and Her Strand." *Scandinavian Review* 71, No. 1 (March 1983): 38-45.
    Strand, Key's final residence, is described as a perfect reflection of her aesthetic and a refuge for women graduate students and scholars.

Nyström-Hamilton, Louise. *Ellen Key: Her Life and Her Work.* New York and London: G. P. Putnam's Sons, 1913, 177 p.
    An attempt to "give a true picture of the woman, not a study of her literary works." This work also includes discussion of Key's work as it relates to her personal life.

Criticism

Mudgett, Bruce. Review of *The Woman Movement. The Annals of the American Academy* 48, No. 137 (July 1913): 278.
    Praises Key for recognizing that women's rights involve more than suffrage.

"Ellen Key." *The Nation* 122, No. 3174 (5 May 1926): 493-94.
    Obituary notice that criticizes Key for presenting "futile and subtle resistance" to other feminist views, while observing that her death "obliterates a great figure among the women of today."

Frederic William Maitland

1850-1906

English historian and lawyer.

INTRODUCTION

Maitland was the preeminent English legal historian of the late nineteenth century. In such works as *The History of English Law before the Time of Edward I* (1895), which he coauthored with Sir Frederick Pollock, Maitland traced the development of common law, which comprises the body of law based on custom, precedent, and judicial decisions rather than on written statutes and which forms the basis of the modern English and American judicial systems. Maitland's prolific scholarship includes volumes on medieval property laws, public institutions, constitutional law, canon law, the history of malice aforethought, and judicial cases dating back to the thirteenth century. In addition, through his role as a founder and literary director of the Selden Society, Maitland was instrumental in publishing numerous primary sources to aid scholarship in the area of legal history.

Biographical Information

Maitland was born in London in 1850. He was educated at Eton College and Trinity College, Cambridge, taking a B.A. in 1873 and a master's degree in 1876. He considered an academic career but, having failed to win a fellowship in history, began law studies at Lincoln's Inn, London, in 1872. Maitland was called to the bar in 1876 and entered a legal firm in London, where he specialized in conveyances, the drawing of deeds and leases for transferring ownership of real property. While working as a barrister in the late 1870s and early 1880s he began contributing articles on historical topics to the *Westminster Review* and the *Law Magazine and Review*. In 1884 he left legal practice to return to Cambridge as a reader in English law. During this period he was instrumental in founding the Selden Society, a group devoted to publishing primary materials for the study of English law, and in 1888 he was named Downing Professor of the Laws of England, a position he held for the remainder of his life. From 1899 onward Maitland spent winter months in the Canary Islands, where he died in December 1906.

Major Works

During the twenty years of Maitland's publishing activity he completed a broad range of works, including numerous volumes of primary materials that he annotated and edited. Until the late-Victorian period, the source materials for the study of English legal history remained largely unknown although readily available in public records offices in England. Maitland is credited with initiating interest in these court records and other public documents through

his early works, including *Pleas of the Crown for the County of Gloucester in 1221* (1884) and other records of judicial cases from the twelfth and thirteenth centuries. In his works Maitland traced ideas and general principles that by the nineteenth century had become seminal in English law back to their roots in particular events and court cases. His *History of English Law before the Time of Edward I* presents an exhaustive survey of Angevin law—law under the rule of the Plantagenet monarchs who reigned in England from 1154 to 1399—and focuses on technical aspects of such areas as matrimonial law, class distinctions, criminal law, and contract law, among other topics. *Domesday Book and Beyond* (1897) extends Maitland's earlier efforts to an examination of the English manorial system using as source material the "Domesday book," a survey of English life in 1086. Another area that Maitland had examined in *History of English Law* was the relationship between church and state in medieval England, and in *Roman Canon Law in the Church of England* (1898) he argued that, contrary to the position outlined by the Royal Commission on Ecclesiastical Courts in 1883, English ecclesiastical courts of the Middle Ages did uphold papal law. Among other works, Maitland's lectures were published in such volumes as *Township and Borough* (1898), *English Law and the Renaissance* (1901), and *The Constitutional History of England* (1908).

Critical Reception

Both Maitland's original works and those he compiled were instrumental in uniting the study of law with the study of English history, which in the nineteenth century had largely been focused on the monarchy and struggles over governing power. Later historians have broadened scholarly inquiry into subjects that Maitland first brought to the fore, and the primary materials that were made available through his efforts continue to serve scholars in researching legal history. Assessing Maitland's influence, W. S. Holdsworth commented in the 1930s that "In an age of great historians I think that Maitland was the greatest, I think that he was the equal of the greatest lawyers of his day, and that, as a legal historian, English law from before the time of legal memory has never known his like."

PRINCIPAL WORKS

Pleas of the Crown for the County of Gloucester in 1221 [editor] (law) 1884
Justice and Police (history) 1885
Bracton's Note Book. 3 vols. [editor] (law) 1887

Select Pleas of the Crown, Vol. I: 1200-1225 [editor] (law) 1888

Why the History of English Law Is Not Written (lecture) 1888

Select Pleas in Manorial and Other Seignorial Courts, Vol. I: Reigns of Henry III and Edward I [editor] (law) 1889

The Court Baron [editor, with W. P. Baildon] (history) 1891

The History of English Law before the Time of Edward I. 2 vols. [with Frederick Pollock] (history) 1895; revised edition, 1898

Select Passages from the Works of Bracton and Azo [editor] (law) 1895

Domesday Book and Beyond: Three Essays in the Early History of England (history) 1897

Magistri Vacarii Summa de Matrimonio [editor] (law) 1898

Roman Canon Law in the Church of England (history) 1898

Township and Borough (lecture) 1898

Political Theories of the Middle Ages [translator] (history) 1900

The Charters of the Borough of Cambridge [editor, with Mary Bateson] (history) 1901

English Law and the Renaissance (lecture) 1901

*Year Books of Edward II. 4 vols. [editor] (law) 1903-7

The Life and Letters of Leslie Stephen (biography and letters) 1906

The Constitutional History of England (lectures) 1908

Equity; also, The Forms of Action at Common Law (lectures) 1909

The Collected Papers of Frederic William Maitland. 3 vols. (lectures, essays, and history) 1911

A Sketch of English Legal History [with Francis C. Montague] (history) 1915

Selected Essays (essays) 1936

Selected Historical Essays (essays) 1957

Frederic William Maitland, Historian: Selections from His Writings (history and essays) 1960

Letters of Frederic William Maitland (letters) 1965

Letters to George Neilson (letters) 1976

*Volume IV of this work was completed by G. J. Turner.

CRITICISM

P. Vinogradoff (essay date 1907)

SOURCE: "Frederic William Maitland," in *The English Historical Review*, Vol. XXII, No. 86, April, 1907, pp. 280-89.

[*In the following obituary tribute, Vinogradoff provides a personal retrospective of Maitland's life and work.*]

A Greek myth tells us of a king at whose touch all objects, however homely, were turned into gold. We do not see such transformations nowadays, but we know another king at whose touch every living being, however noble, is turned into dust. King Death has touched with his wand one of the most subtle and profound thinkers of our time, and stores of patiently accumulated knowledge, marvellous designs of a creative intellect have disappeared for ever from this world of ours. The best thing we have to do is to look for moral support to the example of the fallen champion, to his indomitable energy and absorbing devotion to his task through a life of pains and forebodings which might have crippled a less courageous nature. Of late years he was walking in the shadow of death in a more manifest sense than most of us, but he was too proud and strong to slacken in his efforts.

It is not my intention in the present notice to give anything like a complete account and estimate of Maitland's achievement; it is too early yet to condense its value in a short summary, and in one way or another all students of English law and history must realise constantly the importance of his bequests in the course of their own work. I should like merely to tell the readers of his Review of some impressions created by his personality and his writings in the mind of one who has had many opportunities to study both. It has been my privilege to stand very near Maitland in the early stage of his career, and since then our friendly intercourse has never been interrupted, in spite of the fact that I lived most of the time in another country and our personal interviews were not very frequent. I met him the first time at a friend's house in London in the beginning of 1884. It was at a dinner party, at which Sir Henry Maine was present. Maitland did not take much part in the talk, and listened modestly, but when we went home together we had some interesting conversation on the subject of our studies. He said, among other things—and he often repeated to me afterwards—that he would much rather devote his life to the historical study of English law than watch in his chambers in Lincoln's Inn for the footsteps of the client who never comes. Since that day we met often, and I always look with a peculiar feeling on the **Gloucester Pleas of the Crown,** the **Note Book of Bracton,** the **Rolls of King's Ripton,** and many pages of my own book on *Villainage.* They recall to my mind endless talks on remote problems of legal and social history; there are many personal traits about them which the duty of addressing a large audience of strangers has not entirely wiped out.

I am, perhaps, dwelling too long on these recollections, which concern chiefly myself. To his ever increasing public of readers and pupils the great scholar stood also in a kind of special, personal relation through his style, the literary presentment of his subject. The French saying, *Le style c'est l'homme,* seems true in more ways than one. A writer's style is not only a significant expression of his character and moods; it constitutes a sort of medium between him and his audience; it may attract and electrify, or, on the contrary, it may jar on them. It is not for me to speak of the idiomatic pith, the boldness, and picturesqueness of Maitland's style; but I may be allowed to dwell on a feature which has been often noticed by more competent judges: one of the qualities which contributed most to attract his readers and to dispose them towards admiration and persuasion was the wealth of humour that pervaded all his writings, in spite of their severe aims and their highly technical details. It is certainly not of smoothly polished classical patterns that one is reminded when reading brilliant pages on Anglo-Saxon hides, medieval modes of pleading, or German juridical theories. The poignant sense of the irony of life makes one rather think of Shakespeare, the continual shifting of colour and light of Sterne, the coruscating epigram of Meredith. One may take illustrations almost at random, and I do not try to select an especially happy one by quoting a passage from the introduction to Gierke's *Political Theories of the Middle Age*.

> The Realist's cause would be described by those who are forwarding it as an endeavour to give scientific precision and legal operation to thoughts which are in all modern minds and which are always displaying themselves especially in the political field. We might be told to read the leading article in to-day's paper and observe the ideas with which the writer 'operates': the will of the nation, the mind of the legislature, the settled policy of one State, the ambitious designs of another: the praise and blame that are awarded to group-units of all sorts and kinds. We might be asked to count the lines that our journalist can write without talking of organisation. We might be asked to look at our age's criticism of the political theories and political projects of its immediate predecessor and to weight those charges of abstract individualism, atomism, and macadamisation that are currently made. We might be asked whether the British Empire has not yet revolted against a Sovereign that was merely Many (a Sovereign Number as Austin said) and in no sense really One, and whether 'the People' that sues and prosecutes in American courts is a collective name for some living men and a name whose meaning changes at every minute. We might be referred to modern philosophers: to the social tissue of one and the general will, which is the real will, of another. Then, perhaps, we might fairly be charged with entertaining a deep suspicion that all this is a metaphor: apt perhaps and useful, but essentially like the personification of the ocean and the ship, the storm and the stormy petrel.

One of the most marked peculiarities of such a style is its vividness, the power of closing abstract reasoning into forms taken from the living world of shapes and sounds. The wealth of concrete illustration was not suggested in this case merely by artistic taste. It corresponded to a constant striving of the mind to obtain a full and close grasp of the subject studied. Powerful though he was in abstract speculation and dialectic analysis, what Maitland wanted most was to trace ideas to their embodiment in facts, to sketch their ramifications and complications in practice. Therefore he never fell a prey to those scholastic formulae in which analytical jurists often delight. It is interesting to watch him in close proximity to prominent German jurists.

He much admired the work of Gierke, for instance, and fully appreciated the part played by the 'Germanists' in the remodelling of their country's private law. Of late years he had begun studying very attentively the German civil code, and even, I believe, to translate portions of it in his spare moments. But the reading of his preface to the *Political Theories of the Middle Age* suggests interesting comparisons with the main text of the German writer; the latter is, after all, a masterly exposition of formulae and principles, while the English introduction tries to reduce all theories to their practical consequences, and to sketch their evolution in all the complexity of their natural environment. Of Jellinek's dogmatic constructions and of his deductive 'Study of the State' Maitland never had occasion to speak; but in a recent production of one of Jellinek's pupils, Hatschek's Handbook of English Public Law, much is said about coincidences with Maitland's views in regard to English public bodies as representing 'passive unions' (*passive Verbände*) in contrast with 'active' ones. There is good reason to believe that this pitting of abstract categories against one another did not meet with Maitland's approval, and the latter's masterly analysis of the life of English townships and parishes, boroughs and counties, certainly does not lend itself to such scholastic distinctions. He laid stress on their responsibilities in regard to the State, but did not consider them as produced by outside pressure or void of active interests and life. In this case, as in the study on trusts, Maitland was chiefly concerned to show by what legally imperfect and clumsy means the need for corporate organisations is sometimes met in practice, and how slowly a clear conception of the principles of an institution ripens in the course of its historical life. A London club or an Inn of Court serves the purposes of a social or collegiate group, although the technical principle of the corporation is absent in this and in many other similar cases. Even so the vill and the county were certainly groups with independent cohesion and real interests; but it was important to show to what extent their self-government was determined, among other things, by the requirements of central government. It may perhaps be urged that Maitland's statements are somewhat eccentric in form and influenced by his desire to avoid commonplaces, but they do not fit into the pigeon-hole of the *passiver Verband*.

Even so the attention bestowed on the concrete, the interest for first-hand evidence, the disinclination to deal in other people's words made it impossible for our scholar to sympathise either with the old-fashioned doctrines of Austinian jurisprudence which he found to be 'naturerightly'—that is, outside the frame of space and time—or with grandiloquent 'sociology,' piling up hollow terms and pretentious generalisations on very slight foundations of fact. He was emphatically *an historian,* a student of actual development in the past. Although his work never stuck in details for their own sake, it will always remain an example of what a thorough grasp of details and keen investigation of all the particulars of a case can mean in the research of scientific truth. For a teacher of this kind the drudgery of special disquisitions did not exist, because every minute observation connected itself with other observations on the lines of a profound insight into general processes. He shared the enthusiasm of the naturalist who is not repelled by the mean or the insignificant, for whom such terms have, in truth, no meaning; so he thoroughly realises that a microscopic study of tissues, a patient observation of the structure and doings of infinitesimal *protozoa* as essential as the description of mighty and beautiful specimens. And Maitland was not scared when, in order to read and to publish Year Books, he, the jurist, had to build up a grammar of corrupt law French and to fathom the inadvertences and blunders of fourteenth-century legal students taking hurried notes in court.

On the other hand he was not likely to rest content with supposed juridical notions of a permanent nature. Wielding the sharp scalpel of the lawyer with consummate ability within given surroundings, he was never oblivious of the relative and changeable character of the first principles from which legal analysts have to evolve their arguments. The most fascinating task of the legal historian was to watch the gradual modification of legal rules, the half-instinctive adaptation of legal theory to the promptings of business or to the interests represented by conflicting social forces. We should claim on behalf of the Year Books that

> . . . they show us a marvellous deal of the play of those moral and economic forces of which legal logic is the instrument, and, often, if we may say, the reluctant instrument. Our old lawyers were fond of declaring 'that the law will suffer a mischief rather than an inconvenience,' by which they meant that it will suffer a practical hardship rather than an inconsistency or logical flaw. But . . . we are forcibly told where the mischief lies, where the shoe pinches, even when we are also told that the unconformist foot that will not fit the shoe is a bad foot and ought to be pinched. And then, as we compare case with case, we see that more commodious shoes are made for growing feet: logic yields to life, protesting all the while that it is only becoming more logical.

The touch of irony so characteristic of Maitland's style is certainly not the product of literary manncrism. Its effectiveness depends on habits of mind, which led him to approach most subjects in a sceptical mood. He seems to be wandering in a strange world, crowded with fancies and shams. He is constantly on the alert against traditions kept up out of sheer indolence of mind, against political and religious prejudice, against complex theories devoid of foundation in reality. And his criticism generally illustrates the maxim, *Suaviter in modo, fortiter in re.* With all reverence to acknowledged authorities he is often able to show that many of their constructions are hollow, and do not stand a searching examination. In the essays on **Canon Law,** for instance, Maitland, though dissenting from all churches, supports in substance the contentions of Roman catholic scholars against a kind of antedated Anglicanism favoured by Bishop Stubbs. The genuine respect felt by Maitland for this eminent man did not prevent the critic from exposing pitilessly the gaps and inconsistencies of the evidence appealed to. One of the motives for drawing a remarkable parallel between Azo and Bracton was the desire to enter a protest against a view propounded by Maine with more assurance than discretion in regard to the influence of the civilian on the English lawyer. Altogether the principles and methods of the school of comparative jurisprudence as expounded by Maine did not find much favour with our scholar. He was too exacting in his handling of evidence and too distrustful of general assumptions to let pass without a challenge wide statements more often supported by allusions than by definite proofs. Moreover it seemed to him that one of the leading ideas of the school—namely, the view that different nations pass approximately through the same stages of evolution—was fundamentally wrong. Races and nations do not travel by the same roads and at the same rate; each chooses its own direction and traverses the country at a different speed. The interest of history lies in taking note of these different records and not in grinding down characteristic varieties to colourless uniformity.

On several very important points Maitland criticised the teaching of investigators hailing from the comparative school. He was, for instance, opposed to the idea of a primitive collectivism shaping the early land law of Indo-European nations, and of England in particular. He looked at the old English townships from a point of view acquired in the course of a study of medieval law in its express manifestations. They appeared to him chiefly as organisations for the collection of dues, the assumption of responsibilities, and the management of some economic concerns with but a slight legal admixture. Communalism evaporates at the touch of legal doctrine, as he puts it. No evidence of a township moot as distinct from the manorial court is forthcoming; the doctrine of corporation appears altogether unfit to explain the ties between villagers. Economic and legal development starts from the notion of 'mine' and not from that of 'ours.'

What may be called Maitland's antiquarian individualism brought him into collision with the teaching about tribal as well as about agrarian communities. Evidence supplied by Celtic material never seemed quite satisfactory to him; it was too illogical, too incoherent, presented in too uncritical a manner. And the fundamental conception of agnatic kinship was dissolved for him by the consideration that relationship through women, necessarily divergent, appears as the earliest form of relationship. Thus Maitland was always inclined to follow individualistic lines when explaining ancient society, although he admitted that the influence of groups made itself felt, to a certain extent, in a loose and extralegal way. Fustel de Coulanges's clear-cut individualism did not suit him. He often said, in conversation, that the great French *savant* had probably never vouchsafed to look at the map of an open-field country.

Although Maitland's teaching thus ran counter to some of the views held by Maurer and the Germanists on the one hand, Maine and the comparative jurists on the other, he was in no way at one with the exaggerated reaction produced by these views. Neither wholesale Romanism, with the derivation of the manor from the Roman villa, nor the device of treating Old English society as a ring of slave-holders gradually losing their grasp over their dependents was to his taste. He refused to consider the Saxon conquest as achieved by a handful of chieftains without followers, and declared emphatically in favour of the prevalence of Germanic tradition in Old English development. As for the free elements of the population and the rise of the manorial system, his treatment of the problem reckoned materially with the heterogeneous character of Old English society and the degradation of an originally free class.

It is not my object in the present instance to enter into any discussion of Maitland's views on subjects which have called forth protracted literary controversies. I have had occasion to state that I dissent from some of his doctrines on these points. Others may urge objections on their side. But no one can deny, I think, that the sharpness of Maitland's criticism, his high standard of evidence, the thoroughness of his methods of investigation have done more to clear up the difficult problems in question than most dutiful repetitions of time-honoured theories. Whatever may be the ultimate outcome of the controversy, neither the doctrine of early collectivism nor that of tribal development, nor that of gradual emancipation can afford to disregard the exact study of documents and the close reasoning brought to bear on the problems by the late Downing professor. And although the comparative method has certainly not been exploded by his distrust for its applications, those who have to make use of it may do worse than take a warning from his protest against the sliding analogies and sweeping generalisations which are least permissible to a school which claims to do its work on scientific principles.

A touch of good-humoured sarcasm was perhaps more appropriate to Maitland's countenance than other expressions. Some of his most striking appreciations of persons and institutions savour of a rather irreverent frame of mind. But he would go far wrong who supposed, on the strength of sceptical and sarcastic passages, that the sharp glance of the great scholar was apt to discover nothing but the seamy, the incongruous aspect of things. Maitland had gifts of devotion and enthusiasm which acted as a powerful set-off to his Mephistophelian faculties. No one of the dissonances of history escaped his ear, but he did not fail either to catch the strange harmony of the concert. The grand way in which he clung to study and mastered knowledge enabled him to realise fully the majesty of history as a whole. Two favourite passages close the general introduction to the *Study of the Year Books*. They were not composed but treasured by him, and they are indeed an honour both to those who wrote them and to the one who took them up as noble *dicta*. One is of Justice Holmes, the other of Albert Sorel. I may be allowed to quote at least one of them.

> When I think thus of the law I see a princess, mightier than she who once wrought at Bayeux, eternally weaving into her web dim figures of the ever lengthening past—figures too dim to be noticed by the idle, too symbolic to be interpreted except by her pupils, but to the discerning eye disclosing every painful step and every world-shaking contest by which mankind has worked and fought its way from savage isolation to organic social life.

In every special case, in the treatment of any great doctrine, or institution, or epoch, Maitland has a manner of starting with disconcerting critical observations and of noticing at the outset contradictions and confusion, but then he feels his way, as it were, like a musician running his fingers over the keys in an improvised prelude, towards leading ideas and harmonious combinations. Read his chapters on such subjects as military tenure, or inheritance, or

municipal institutions: the dry material becomes curiously attractive through the reflexion of a kind of organic process in the mind of the scholar creating order and sense in the midst of confusion.

Nor were the interests of this thinker solely directed to the study of impersonal evolution. The kindest and most generous of men in personal intercourse, he was keenly appreciative of any merit or achievement of those with whom he came in contact. He was always on the look-out for genuine research, and acknowledged his debts in regard to those from whom he had learnt with ungrudging warmth. The article in the *Quarterly Review* on Liebermann's *Anglo-Saxon Laws* must have brought the proudest reward to the Berlin editor for his masterly work, and many other scholars can look with gratification on sentences in Maitland's books which weigh more than undiscerning praise. I was often struck by the fact that a man of so critical a mind was often almost too apt to admire books which he had just finished reading. He recovered soon enough from some of his *engouements,* if I may be allowed to use the untranslatable French expression; but they showed, as it seems to me, that his artistic nature was apt to take for a time the strain of a fine performance, and that critical dissent came almost as an afterthought. Criticism was not less effective for that, but it was never spoiled by the niggardly obtuseness which seeks not to estimate but to harm.

Maitland's learning was anything but insular. He followed with keen interest and unfailing judgment the main currents of legal and historical literature on the continent. In regard to some of his best known theories there may be traced the influence of suggestions received from fellow-workers' writings. We have to note, for instance, how his views as to corporations were influenced by Gierke; in what a remarkable way he developed for England Keutgen's garrison explanation of the rise of boroughs; how he adopted and strengthened Ficker's and Heusler's teaching on early kingship. Thus, although not addicted to comparative legal history in the general sense of the word, he fully realised the importance of analogies for suggesting explanations and filling up gaps in the evidence.

It would be out of the question to state in a short notice, written under the impression of a recent death, what the principal achievements of such a life's work have been. Scholars of the twenty-first century will be in a better position to pronounce a verdict in this respect, as we are nowadays better able to speak of Selden and Blackstone than their own contemporaries. But some lines of appreciation are so clearly indicated even now that it seems natural to allude to them. It is no exaggeration to say that we have known and lost the greatest historian of the law of England, one who not only surpassed all predecessors in this domain but is not likely to be surpassed soon in the course of succeeding generations. As the principal contributor to the monumental *History of English Law,* as the editor of Bracton's **Note Book** and the **Year Books of Edward II,** as the writer of innumerable and invaluable articles for learned periodicals, Maitland has practically remodelled our knowledge of English law at the most important period of its existence. To realise his achievement in this respect one need only think of the standard books of the pre-Maitlandian age—the uncritical, scanty compilation of Reeves and Finlason, the brilliant but all too brief sketch of O. W. Holmes, the fragmentary and ill-balanced attempts of Palgrave and Sir J. Stephen. What we have now is the production of a writer steeped in the original lore of medieval common law. Bracton and Martin of Pateshull would certainly not have rejected him as a colleague, and, on the other hand, he stands hand in hand with the leading representatives of European learning at the eventful turn from the nineteenth century to the twentieth.

His intimate knowledge of the thirteenth-century world brought him much nearer to the life of the middle ages than any one else can pretend to be, and we cannot wonder that the great lawyer reveals himself as a great historian. In *Domesday Book and Beyond* he took up a task which led him to examine some of the most complicated and contested problems of social history, and here again his trained and piercing eye did not fail not only to discover new facts, but to co-ordinate them in an unexpected manner. I cannot help thinking that one of the limitations inherent in human work is noticeable in the natural bent of a mind exercised on common-law problems to explain earlier periods mainly in the light of a conflict between individualistic rights and forces. And the standards of criticism and evidence are perhaps too stringent for the case of primitive institutions and the confused fermentation of nationalities in the making. But I need not dwell on disputed points. Even what has been said in these few pages may be sufficient to recall to the memory of European scholars that we have to mourn a real leader of thought. Lawyers, historians, and sociologists are equally indebted to him—lawyers because of his subject, historians because of his methods, sociologists because of his results.

Ernest Barker   (essay date 1937)

SOURCE: "Maitland as a Sociologist," in *Sociological Review,* Vol. XXIX, No. 2, April, 1937, pp. 121-35.

[*In the following essay, Barker discusses the sociological aspects of Maitland's historical writings.*]

Frederic William Maitland, the grandson of Samuel Maitland, a historian of the Dark Ages who was famous a hundred years ago, was born in 1850 and died at the end of 1906. Educated at Eton and at Trinity College, Cambridge, he was called to the bar in 1876; but devoting himself to the study of law rather than its practice (as Jeremy Bentham had done before him), he came back to Cambridge in 1884 as Reader of English Law, and in 1888 he was elected Downing Professor of the Laws of England. In the twenty-two years of his teaching and writing in Cambridge, from the age of 34 to the age of 56, he achieved a volume of work, and accumulated a store of influence, which made him one of the great forces of his generation, and indeed a great force to-day. The wonder is all the greater when we reflect that he suffered from ill-health for the greater part of his working life, and, for the last eight years, was regularly compelled to fly to the South every winter. Perhaps the flame burned all the brighter because the vital reserves were always being summoned to feed the wick.

He was primarily a lawyer, or, more exactly, a legal historian. But he interpreted law in that broad and generous sense which makes it the general framework of social life—a framework partly created by the needs and aspirations of society, but partly, and in turn, reacting on those needs and aspirations, and helping to determine their form and their development. In this sense it may be said that the study of law was a thing which became in his hands a sociological study. He went beyond legal rules and procedure to the social content of law. Legal history became for him a history of the manor, regarded as a social institution or group; it became a history of township and borough, similarly regarded: it became, at the last, a history of the whole general institution which we call the group or society, in all its various forms.

In the last ten years of his life, from 1896 to 1906, he was more and more fascinated by the problem of the group. In 1897 he published *Domesday Book and Beyond,* in which he dealt with the society of the manor. In the autumn of 1897 I heard him deliver at Oxford, in a voice of which I have never forgotten the magic, some lectures on the societies of Township and Borough, which were published under that title in 1898. He had moved to the general problem of the group at large by 1900. In that year appeared a little volume, *The Political Theories of the Middle Age,* translated from Gierke's German, but armed with an introduction, dealing with what I have called the general problem of the group, which perhaps exerted more influence, if not on legal at any rate on general contemporary thought, than anything else which he wrote. It influenced the thought of Dr. Figgis about the Church; it was cited by the Webbs in the introduction to the 1911 edition of their *History of Trade Unionism:* it was a mine for all who were interested in groups—groups ecclesiastical or groups economic or any manner of group. But the little volume of 1900 was not the only publication of Maitland's last years which bore on this problem. He wrote a number of other essays and articles of which it was also the theme. Some were lectures or papers read to clubs; one was an article contributed to a German legal periodical; two were articles contributed to our own *Law Quarterly Review.* They were all collected in the third volume of his *Collected Papers,* which appeared in 1911. They have now been republished in a little volume, under the title of *Selected Essays,* which appeared at the end of last year. If one desires to find the quintessence of "Maitland as a Sociologist," it is to be found in that volume, along with his introduction to *The Political Theories of the Middle Age.*

Before I turn to Maitland's theory of the group, which may be called his specific contribution to sociology, there is something which may properly be said, and indeed must necessarily be said, about the sociological method which he followed in the writing of legal and constitutional history. I have said "the sociological method": I might more exactly, using a prefix of which the lawyers are fond, have said "the quasi-sociological method," intending thereby a method which is not specifically sociological, but is the sort of method, or analogous to the sort of method, which would be used by the sociologist. What I mean is that Maitland interpreted the manor, and feudalism, and the Middle Ages in general, intrinsically and by their own light, as a sociologist would seek to do—not extrinsically and through the spectacles of a later and different age, which is what the historian may do when he is not imbued with a tincture of sociology. This, to my mind, is the difference between Maitland and Stubbs. Great as Stubbs was, he wrote his *Constitutional History of England* in spectacles—the spectacles of Victorian Liberalism, which are all the more curious on his nose when one remembers that he was a natural Tory. Maitland wore no spectacles. He saw the Middle Ages *sub specie temporum suorum*—in the light of their own social conditions and their own stock of social ideas. We may call this gift which he had the gift of sympathetic imagination; but it is more than that—it is the gift of a sympathetic *scientific* imagination, and the science which inspires the gift is the science of sociology. "To make discoveries," he said, "we must form new habits of mind, and the thoughts of men in the past must once more become thinkable to us." This leads me to another of his sayings, which I have never forgotten (though I quote it purely from memory, and therefore probably misquote it), that to understand the Middle Ages we must think ourselves back into a mediæval haze. "Too often," he wrote, in words which express the idea behind that saying with a measured exactitude, "we allow ourselves to suppose that, could we but get back to the beginning, we should find that all was intelligible, and should then be able to watch the process whereby simple ideas were smothered under technicalities and subtleties. But it is not so. Simplicity is the outcome of technical subtlety: it is the goal, not the starting-point. As we go backwards, the familiar outlines become blurred; the ideas become fluid, and instead of the simple we find the indefinite."

This line of thinking and of interpretation brought many revolutions. You will all remember Maine's *Ancient Law* and Maine's theory of the patriarchal origin of society. What has Maitland to say? "Maine's patriarch, who is a trustee, who represents a corporation, looks to me suspiciously modern. He may be a savage, but he is in full evening dress." That is one thing he had to say: and it is devastating. There was also another. He held that there was no one sort of origin, and no one sort of sequence of development. "When this evidence about barbarians gets into the hands of men who . . . have been taught by experience to look upon all the social phenomena as interdependent, it begins to prove far less than it used to prove. Each case begins to look very unique, and a law which deduces that 'mother right' cannot come after 'father right,' or that 'father right' cannot come after 'mother right,' or which would establish any similar sequence of 'states,' begins to look exceedingly improbable." Maitland was deeply convinced of the truth that there was no one line of progress, and that human societies did not grow logically by similar or identical processes of immanent development. Societies were interdependent: there was always a process of the diffusion of culture from one society to another: one society, borrowing from another which was an advance of itself, might make a sudden leap which would be inexplicable except in terms of such diffusion and borrowing. "Our Anglo-Saxon ancestors did not arrive at the alphabet or at the Nicene Creed by traversing a long series of 'stages': they leapt to the one and the other."

I may seem to have strayed into anthropology, and to have taken Maitland with me in my straying. Let me return to history which is more indubitably history, and let me refer you to Maitland's treatment of feudalism. There are, he says, still some historians who talk of feudalism as if it were a disease of the body politic. Well, no doubt there were some things in the Middle Ages, things properly called feudal, which came of evil and made for evil. But take feudalism by and large; use the term in a wide sense (as a sociologist would); and how does it appear? "If we use the term in this wide sense, then (the barbarian conquests being given to us as an unalterable fact) feudalism means civilization, the separation of employment, a division of labour, the possibility of national defence, the possibility of art, science, literature, and learned leisure; the cathedral, the scriptorium, the library, are as truly the work of feudalism as is the baronial castle." Here is a thing which seems to me well said. It shows how the history of law became in Maitland's hands, as Mr. Fisher has said, "a contribution to the general history of human society." The same lesson appears when we look at his account of one of the institutions of feudalism (in the wide sense of the word), the mediæval manor. How did it come to pass that the villagers followed that curious system of scattered strips in the three great open fields of arable land which surrounded their village dwellings? Had a lord done all this planning and parcelling? Hardly. How would it suit his interest, and how could he induce stubborn villagers to accept his ruling? Does it not look as if the body of villagers wanted each member to take the rough with the smooth, and no man to get off better than any other? They did not mind if this made cultivation difficult and diminished their returns. "They sacrificed the cause of efficiency on the altar of equality." There is insight into the nature of man, and especially into the nature of village society, in that epigram.

But it is time that I turned to what I have called Maitland's specific contribution to sociology—his general theory of the group. I have said that the theory of the group was engaging his attention in the last ten years of his life. I always remember one sentence (I think it recurred more than once) in those lectures on *Township and Borough* which I attended in 1897. "Borough community is corporate: village community is not." The question of the nature of corporativeness, if I may use that word, was stirring his mind. What, he was asking himself, is a group or a society of men, at its highest point of identity, when it is somehow one and the plurality of its members is somehow merged into the unity of one body—one *corpus* or corporation? That is a question which you cannot answer without ranging up and down the scale, from the loosest of cohesions to the tightest of corporations. Where does the change come—the magical change that gives you the corporate body? In what does the change consist, and who is it that produces the change? Is it the authority of the State and the fiat of the *princeps*? Or do corporations make themselves, and do they become what they are by their own proper motion?

It was partly the reading of Gierke's great book on the German *Genossenschaft* which had stimulated these questionings. It was partly also some issues which were being raised in this island about 1900. One of them was the Scottish Church case, which began in 1900 and was finally decided by the House of Lords, so far as the law of the matter went, in 1904. This was a case which raised the question of the identity of a Church. Another issue was that of the legal position of Trade Unions—the question whether a Trade Union was in any sense corporate and in any way liable therefore to be treated as a single body responsible for its acts and the acts of its agents—which was being raised in the English courts and led to the Taff Vale decision of 1901. But it was not only the reading of Gierke and the nature of contemporary events which stimulated Maitland's mind: it was also the course of his own study. He was dealing with the history of English law and English legal institutions. Now whatever else we may say about England, it has certainly been a paradise of groups. They begin in old Anglo-Saxon frith-gilds (mutual insurance societies, as I should call them, for the safer commission and the surer compensation of cattleraids), if they are not even earlier than the frith-gilds: they continue, through mediæval religious gilds, mediæval societies of lawyers called Inns of Court, seventeenth-century Free Churches, seventeenth-century East India and other companies, down to modern groups such as Lloyd's, the Stock Exchange, the Trade Union, the London club (such as the Athenæum), and, as I am in private duty bound to mention, this Institute of Sociology which I am now addressing. These riches fascinated Maitland. They may well fascinate any Englishman. How shall we count them, and in what denominations and under what categories shall we classify them?

I have said that these riches fascinated Maitland. He told them over and over, from the far past to the multitudinous present with all its rapid and large increase of corporate or quasi-corporate groups. I cannot do better than quote Mr. Fisher, his brother-in-law and biographer. "Trade Unions and joint-stock companies, chartered boroughs and mediæval universities, village communities and townships, merchant guilds and crafts, every form of association known to mediæval or modern life came within his view, as illustrating the way in which Englishmen attempted 'to distinguish and reconcile the manyness of the members and the oneness of the body.' An enquiry of this kind was something entirely new in England." I am not sure if it was entirely new—I remember, for example, Toulmin Smith's book on English Gilds—but it was certainly new in its scope, its zest, and its depth. Perhaps the fact that he was a member of Lincoln's Inn, and had worked in one of the old mediæval English legal societies, still living and active, and (what is more) had studied and written about the achievement of the lawyers who had also worked in these societies in bygone days—perhaps this stimulated his love for the theme of the group. Certainly he had a deep interest in the lawyer-group, which is a peculiar fact of our English life. (At any rate I know of nothing like our Inns of Court in any other country.) There is a lively passage about them, and the men who inhabited them during the Middle Ages, in the introduction which he wrote to a volume of the Year Books. "They are gregar-

ious, clubbable men, grouping themselves in hospices which become schools of law . . . arguing, learning, and teaching, the great mediators between life and logic, a reasoning, reasonable element in the English nation."

A great mediator between life and logic—this is what Maitland himself was, when he dealt with the understanding of the group. The subject suited his own philosophical bent: he had been trained in the Mental and Moral Sciences Tripos, and had taken a first class in that Tripos in 1872. I am not sure that he did not lean too much to logic, at the expense of life, in his interpretation of the group at that highest point of its identity at which it becomes a corporation. He was affected by Gierke's theory: he thought that a corporation was a real person. He believed that the change which was reached in the scale of group-being, when you come to the corporation, was the emergence of a new person, with a mind and will of its own; and he believed that this person was real—as real, unless I am mistaken, as you and I are real. I cannot follow that interpretation; but I will not go into the reasons which hold me back from following. . . . Here I will only say that real group-persons terrify me, but leave me still a sceptic. When I am told, for instance, that the nation "is an organism, with a being, ends, and means of action superior to those of the individuals, separate or grouped, who compose it" (and that is what I am told in the Italian Charter of Labour of 1927), I can only say that that is not what a nation is, or ever can be, to me. The group at its highest, when it almost seems to merge plurality into unity, is still to me so many individual human beings. What raises it to its highest is not the emergence of a real new personality, over and above the personalities of its members: it is simply the height or quality of the common purpose which individual persons agree in holding and willing—the width, the depth, and the permanence of that purpose. Purpose is all; and it is by their purposes that I should judge, range, classify, and also criticize, groups.

Having said these words, and having implied, as I confess that I have, that Maitland seems to me to have overexalted the being of the corporate group, and to have contributed, in some measure, to the group-cult of our days (not that it is so marked in England as it is elsewhere), I now pass on—very gladly, and with far more zest in agreement than I have in my disagreement—to say some words about Maitland's contribution to the general understanding of our English groups and societies. There are two things which I wish to say. One concerns the idea of the group—and more particularly the corporate group, the group which acts as a single body or *corpus,* 'and moveth altogether if it move at all'—as it acts in the sphere of our national politics, or, in other words, in the sphere of the State. The other concerns the idea of the group—the group generally, corporate or unincorporate, whether it moves with the oneness of the body or the manyness of the members—as it acts in the sphere of our social life, or, in other words, in the sphere of Society.

In the sphere of our politics we have long had one idea of a corporation which seemed to Maitland curious, and indeed unfortunate. This is the idea of the king as a corporation sole, a corporation with only one member, to wit, himself. I would not necessarily dismiss altogether this idea of the corporation sole, curious as it may seem—though I do not like it in its particular application to the king. I have met and stayed with a corporation sole in Massachusetts—Dr. Lawrence Lowell, who is a corporation sole in respect of the Lowell Lectures, of which he holds the funds and for which he makes the arrangements. That corporation sole invited me to lecture, and paid me a generous remuneration: I have no quarrel with it. But I feel differently, taught by Maitland, about the idea of the king as a corporation sole. Dr. Lawrence Lowell, as a corporation sole, has not got into the way of anything else. He has not stopped the emergence of some other and truer idea of a corporation in the same sphere in which he is one. The idea of the king as a corporation sole *has* got into the way of something else. It has stopped the emergence—or rather not stopped, but blurred and confused the emergence—of the great and true idea that all the people of England, as members of one body, including the king their head, and carrying the king on their shoulders with them, are the true and only corporation of England in the sphere of politics. This is not Republicanism (the king is still there as head of the body): it is good old mediæval theory, and it was a theory still known to our lawyers in the sixteenth century. A Chief Justice was declaring in 1522, "A corporation is an aggregation of head and body: not a head by itself nor a body by itself; and it must be, consonant to reason, for otherwise it is worth naught." That is good sense; and it is a pity that it was ever forgotten, and that the king became a corporation sole, or "head by itself." It caused a good deal of trouble; and it is still causing trouble to-day. When I see the king, in the change lately made in the Coronation Oath, made to speak about "My possessions." I see that the corporation sole, or head by itself, is still floating about. And I murmur to myself that any possessions, any rights, any duties, in the sphere of our national politics, really appertain and belong to a corporation aggregate, of which you and I are members along with the king our head—not we alone, nor he alone, but all of us together. That is the true political corporation—the true owner of the possessions, rights, and duties common to the people; and if a word is wanted for it, the right word, as Maitland said (and it is a good old sixteenth-century word), is the word Commonwealth. It is a word which has been borrowed for the Empire, to which, I venture to think, it does not really belong. The Empire is not a commonwealth, but a number of allied and kindred commonwealths. And one of these commonwealths is the commonwealth of this island.

It is in the sphere of social life, and in regard to the groups, corporate or unincorporate, which move in that sphere, that Maitland has, I think, taught us most. There is a word or term morphology which Goethe, I believe, introduced into science. It is defined as a branch of biology which is concerned with the form of animals and plants, and with the factors which govern or influence that form. Using that word, I should say that Maitland was a master of social morphology. He studied the forms of society, in mediæval, modern, and contemporary times, and he studied the factors (above all the legal factors) which have governed or influenced, or are governing or influencing, these forms. The great factor which he studied was the English law of Trust. A trust, I may remind you, is in its origin (it begins in 1400 or thereabouts) a legal act by which a landowner, tied by the law of primogeniture, contrives to release some of his property, and to vest it in trustees who will hold it in trust, to the use and for the benefit of his younger sons and his daughters. Very good, you will say, but what has that got to do with social morphology or with the growth of societies? Very much, Maitland will tell us: at any rate in England and so far as English law is concerned. As the law of Trust develops, it is found that a growing society can take advantage of it as easily as the solitary dying landowner. The members of a society collect subscriptions; they vest them in a permanent body of trustees, who can always be renewed by fresh election or by simple co-optation; the trustees hold the subscriptions, and any other funds or property, to the use and for the benefit of the society; and lo and behold, the society is a going concern, with the necessary buildings, and the necessary general resources, for the achievement of the common purpose by which it is held together. The society needs no incorporation, which might put it at the mercy of the State, since the State might refuse to grant it: it only needs to "trustify" itself, which it can do by going to any lawyer, and when it has done that it can trust the Lord Chancellor, who sees to the observance of trusts, to keep the trustees in order. In this way, as Maitland showed, and showed by a wealth of examples, the trust has been with us, for the last three or four hundred years, a great "instrument of social experimentation." It has been a dominant factor in the history of our social morphology. The Free Churches have availed themselves of it; Trade Unions have availed themselves of it; commercial and industrial companies have availed themselves of it; clubs, literary and philosophical societies, whatever you like, have all availed themselves of it. The pulsation of social life has caught at a legal instrument, and used it, "by kind permission" of the law, for the achievement of its own objects. That reminds me of a saying of Maitland, which I think is apposite. "The one thing that it is safe to predict is that in England social-political will take precedence of jurisprudential considerations." In other words, we let the growth of English society catch at our law, mould our law, use our law for its purposes. Blessings on the law which has been so amenable. Blessings above all on the law of Trust, which has listened so readily to social persuasion. We owe to it more than we know.

We owe to it, for example, a great deal of our religious and what I may call our economic liberty. Where would Free Churches and Trade Unions have been if it had not been for our law of Trust? It is difficult to imagine the answer, or to detect the dim and dusty retreat to which they might otherwise have been condemned. Wesleyans owe much to John Wesley: they also owe something to the Lord Chancellor. It was in firm reliance on the Lord Chancellor that John Wesley set his seal, in 1784, to a document declaring the trusts on which he held certain lands and buildings in various parts of England. That document secured the Wesleyan Church in the free and unfettered, yet guaranteed, enjoyment of all its scattered chapels and their various funds. It is natural for Maitland to say, reflecting on these facts, "All that we English people mean by religious liberty has been intimately connected with the making of trusts." If by religious liberty we mean not merely the liberty of the individual, but the liberty of the religious society, and if we realize that a religious society, in order to possess liberty, must be free to own and control its buildings and its funds, we shall readily see that religious liberty is closely connected with the law of Trust. The trust was a screen behind which a religious society could lie perdu, in unmolested security; or again, to use another of Maitland's metaphors, it was a backstair—a blessed wide backstair—up which religious society could climb to the height of being corporate (or shall I say "quasi-corporate?" at any rate corporate enough for every practical purpose) without needing to be incorporated.

What protected the Free Churches, and indeed any Church that sought the protection, was ready to protect also the Trade Union. Trade Unions owe much to many brave labour leaders: they also owe something, just like the Wesleyans, to the Lord Chancellor. Nor need we stop at them. The whole general history of our social morphology is intertwined with the trust. "Behind the screen of trustees, and concealed from the direct scrutiny of legal theories, all manner of groups can flourish: Lincoln's Inn, or Lloyd's, or the Stock Exchange, or the Jockey Club, a whole Presbyterian system, or even the Church of Rome with the Pope at its head." . . . "So wide was that blessed back-stair."

But I must come to an end. If I try to summarize the chief idea, which I want to leave in your minds, I should do so in this way. Sociology runs into law, and is intertwined with the concepts of the lawyers. We should have societies without lawyers; but the forms which societies take are largely dependent on the boxes which lawyers provide for their reception and incubation. Our English law has provided a generous box; and that has helped the germination of our English societies. But the interesting thing about the box which is called Trust is that it was not provided for societies. It was provided, as we have seen, for something else; but the box which the lawyers made for something else was found by societies, and turned by them (of course with the aid and connivance of the lawyers) to another purpose—the purpose of social experimentation. A most interesting thing, as I say; and it leads us on to reflect upon another interesting thing. The Marxists say that the interest of a dominant social class precipitates law, and precipitates it in its own favour. Does it? The story which Maitland tells shows, indeed, that the interest of the feudal landowner originally precipitated the law of trust; but it also shows another thing—that the law thus precipitated ultimately came to serve a very different and a vastly greater social interest, the interest of little struggling village chapels and of striving and fighting Trade Unions. Now a Marxist would admit that a law once precipitated for one purpose may come incidentally, by acquiring a sort of independent life, to serve other purposes. But will that admission cover the story which Maitland tells? Hardly. A law which in the great range of its application, for the last three or four centuries, has served purposes almost the opposite of those of its origin, at any rate in so far as class-interest is concerned, is a law which cannot be explained by the principle of class-interest. Class-interest may have started it; but it has escaped from the interest which start-

ed it, and run magnificently wild. The growth of our English society, the poor as well as the rich, has poured itself into this box of trust. The law of Trust has been impartially accommodating: it has aided equally the growth of different social interests, or, if it has aided any one interest particularly, it has aided particularly the interest of the poor. Anyhow, it has aided, as Maitland says, the general process of social experimentation. That is a great thing, perhaps the greatest of all things, if you believe, as I do, that the process of social experimentation is prior to the State, is greater than the State, and must be served and preserved by the State.

We may therefore thank Maitland, with a deep gratitude, for the light he has shed on the social growth of our people. Perhaps it is also a light on the normal growth of all peoples. Perhaps we may even add that it is a light which should guide future growth. Free social experimentation—in the field of religious life, which cries aloud to-day for such ventures; in the field of economic life, which knows no panacea but demands every experiment of remedy—free social experimentation . . . what can be greater?

G. M. Young   (essay date 1937)

SOURCE: "Maitland," in *Daylight and Champaign: Essays,* revised edition, Rupert Hart-Davis, 1948, pp. 271-77.

[In the following essay, Young evaluates Maitland as a historian.]

Some years ago it was proposed in Cambridge to issue, with due comment and annotation, Maitland's Collected Papers. 'The Syndics of the University Press did not, however, see their way to a new edition on these lines, and another project was suggested. This was to select certain of the papers likely to be most useful to students in law, history, and politics, to edit them and publish them in one volume. . . . The editors venture to think that they (the students to wit) have here all that is of practical use to them; and they have put them upon their inquiry as to where they can find the rest.' In other words, if you want to get marks, you will read Maitland's *Selected Essays*: if you want to waste your time, you will read Maitland.

I cannot think this attitude accords either with the function of an Academic Press, or the respect which a university ought to show to the memory of a master. Granted that some of Maitland's work, now forty years old and more, is 'touched with obsolescence', no passage of time can dull the genius which vibrates in every paragraph he wrote. As Bentley said of Bishop Pearson, 'the very dust of his writings is gold'. But it does not follow that the dust heap is the proper place for them: and such an edition as Professor Hazeltine and his colleagues first proposed would be not only a noble memorial to a scholar of incomparable inspiration, but a history of the progress of the studies in which he was a master. I hope it will still be undertaken. After all, Syndics are not like other publishers. They can always cover their losses by bringing out a Prayer Book in red white and blue, or a new Bible with camera studies of Behemoth and the Pygarg.

Someone may ask what right I have to speak, and I fully admit that much of Maitland's work is above my head. But it so happens, thanks to a good teacher, that on one subject which he treats of I am not altogether uninformed, and never shall I forget the evening when I took down **Domesday and Beyond;** and read, and read, till the owl in the fir tree began audibly to wonder why the lamp was still burning; the little breezes that stray down the dene from Wansdyke turned chilly; and the dawn came. I have just opened it again, and if I do not shut it quickly, this paper will not get written to-day, or to-morrow: no great loss, perhaps, were it not that I have one or two things to say about Maitland which I believe to be worth saying, and, at this particular time, needful to be said. In passing, I invite the Syndics (and Delegates) to look at the last paragraph of that book—and blush, if Delegates (and Syndics) can.

But before I go any further, I should like to define to myself the character of Maitland's mind: and the first thing that strikes me is its companionable quality. He is never telling you: he is always, most genially and modestly, arguing, never so far ahead that you cannot follow, with a deliberate invitation at every turn to tell him something of your own, and an unforced humour playing over the whole debate. Our intelligent Press periodically sets as a competition: Whom would you most like to take a country walk with? The entrants must be much less modest or self-conscious than I am, because, of their two favourites, I doubt if Dr. Johnson would have thought me worth talking to, and I am sure I should cut but a poor figure after ten miles' unmitigated Socrates. I should without hesitation choose Maitland, not so much for anything he might have to say, as to observe his gift of entering into 'the business, projects, and current notions of right and wrong' in other ages; and his power of 'making the thoughts of our forefathers, their common thought of common things, thinkable' once more.

By taking the history of law and institutions for his province, Maitland planted himself in the position where his genius for thinking other men's thoughts could operate with most effect. Law, as he understood it, is fundamentally a system of common thought about common things: the things and the thoughts, the actual doings, for example, of a villain or a trade unionist, and the reflections thereon of Bracton or the judges in the Taff Vale Case, reacting on each other, and modifying each other into a pattern of such shifting intricacy that the most comprehensive vision will not take in the whole pattern, and the keenest eye will misread some of the incidents. They say now that his theory of the defensive origin of the boroughs is 'wrong', or, what is worse, 'imaginative'; and I am reminded of the warning in my school edition of *Julius Caesar:* 'Do not talk about Shakespeare's mistakes: they are probably your own.' But very likely his critics are right. As he says himself, 'the new truth generally turns out to be but a quarter truth, and yet one which must modify the whole tale': and in a world so perplexingly contrived as this is, a frank and joyous acknowledgement of ignorance is the only way of wisdom. 'We must go into the twilight, not haphazard, but of set purpose, and knowing well what we are doing'; and, when all the other classes have been abolished, there will

remain the distinction between those who know that all hypotheses, interpretations, creeds, programmes, and what not, are questions, and those who suppose them to be answers.

At no time did this truth need to be more frequently or emphatically restated than to-day, and I am glad that the Syndics have allowed the editors to print the essay on the Body Politic, written apparently for a dining club, in which Maitland delivered his profession of faith, and his warning against the facile acceptance of systems. So entirely does he seem to belong to our own world, that it is with surprise one remembers that he was born in 1850, and was nine years old when Macaulay died. But he grew up in a time when systems were the mode, when Auguste Comte had turned the history of the world into a commodious suburban residence—theology on the ground floor, metaphysics above, and the clear light of positivism shining in at the top floor windows: and young Darwinians, going far beyond anything that Darwin would have countenanced, were tracing the development of society with as much assurance as if they had been there all the time: just as, with not less confidence, their grandfathers had propounded the Scheme of Redemption or the Wage Fund Theory, and their grandchildren now propound the materialistic conception of history.

So long as historic systems are in vogue, so long that warning voice will be needed. How plausible they all are, each in its day! How much they explain that was dark before! How easy they make things! How much trouble they take off our minds! Very well: then answer this question on any system you like. In the nineteenth century, the European nations borrowed from us the criminal jury which they had abandoned, and we had kept. Why had we kept it? Try it on Positivist or Evolutionary or Materialistic principles, and see where you get to. Maitland's answer comes with a flash which makes even his editors blink. 'Tut tut,' their footnote says, 'this is a built-up area, and he went through at thirty-one.' I do not know whether the answer is right, but I quote it as the best example in this volume of the soar and swoop which marks Maitland out as the most inspiring of all historical companions. He made of history the Gay Science. To account for a detail of legal history, he lifts to the third century, and watches the Manichean heresies streaming for a thousand years along the Mediterranean coasts to Languedoc. But we were an Orthodox Island. Therefore the Church had no need here to enforce the inquisitorial process proper for the detection of heresy. Therefore we kept the jury. And the next moment he is on the ground, searching the year-books for such grains of truth as that a use in law is not a *usus* but an *opus,* and that medieval lawyers sometimes liked to show their superior education by spelling it *oeps.*

The swiftness with which Maitland moves over the field, and the microscopic observation which never seems to weary on the longest flight, together make him, it seems to me, an almost faultless example of what Bacon called the *intellectus purus et aequus,* 'never distracted by study of particulars and never lost in contemplation of the entirety', the *intellectus simul capax et penetrans,* over which the Idols of the Cave and the Theatre have no power. This volume has set me reading again his *Canon Law in the Church of England,* which of all his works I have always most admired for the logical dexterity with which the argument is sustained, and most enjoyed for the dainty and respectful malice with which he plants his barbs in the great Bishop. Here he is fencing with an equal, exchanging secret professional jokes between the bouts. In his *Constitutional History* and the chapter on the Elizabethan Settlement of Religion, which some may regard as his masterpiece, he is speaking tutorially. Elsewhere, and for the most part, he is the explorer reporting his travels as he goes. It is unfortunate for his fame—which he would not in the least have minded—and, what is more to be regretted, for his influence, that so much of his work was involved in technical matters. But I doubt if he left a page, I am sure he did not leave an essay, which has not startled some fit reader, not so much by the range or the precision, as the appropriateness of the learning revealed—the right detail coming exactly at the right moment—or made him glow with that sense of confident and delighted energy which only the highest genius can communicate. And they who have received it will impart it as they can.

Goethe (or someone else) said of (Winckelmann, I think, but I see that this quotation is not going to be so impressive as I intended): 'Man lernt nichts, aber man wird etwas.' One learns nothing, but one becomes something. I certainly do not think it any more desirable that we should all become historians than that we should all take courses in dentistry, plumbing, and cookery. But it is, I believe, of some concern to the Commonwealth that we should all brush our teeth, wash with reasonable regularity, and eat well-chosen food well prepared, and in the same sense and degree a right historical attitude seems to me of special consequence in an age when a wrong attitude is being so diligently inculcated for partisan ends. The materialistic conception of history is no more than the sectarian perversion of the great and truly philosophic doctrine—first adumbrated by the French and English historians of the eighteenth century—that all historic forces are interconnected. But historic forces have their seat in human observation, reflection, and purpose: 'in business, projects, and common notions of right and wrong': they act through the minds of men, they reveal themselves in—at the last analysis they are—their 'common thought of common things'. There they must be looked for, and there only will they be found. And of Maitland we can say that, in his chosen field, no man ever searched more diligently, and no man ever saw so much.

R. J. White   (essay date 1951)

SOURCE: "F. W. Maitland: 1850-1950," in *The Cambridge Journal,* Vol. 4, October, 1950-September, 1951, pp. 134-43.

[*In the following essay, White offers an appraisal of Maitland's work on the centenary of his birth.*]

It is strange to think that Maitland should have joined the centenarians. His genius has always seemed to lie in just those qualities of mind and spirit that should protect a man from the centenary-mongers, Wisden-watchers, and monumental masons of the memory. Yet, so it is. Maitland was born a century ago, and the word has gone round, and the plums of Fisher's little *Life* of 1910 have been pulled out and offered to us as substitutes for thinking about Maitland in 1950. Bletchley Junction threatens to become a terminus.

The perspective is still too short for anything like a final appraisal of the man and his work, but something more might already be attempted than the recitation of examples of his notorious wit or the affixing of a few unexamined labels. The wit and the *beaux yeux* can be taken for granted. That he was a wholly delightful human being could be adduced from almost any single page of his prose, for in his case, as in few others, the style was verily the man. The customary labels can safely be left to writers in the little magazines that specialize in the award of alphas and betas, majors and minors, to their betters. What is wanted is a series of documented inquiries into Maitland's place in the history of history, in order to see him in the progress of studies. What is attempted here is a prolegomena to such inquiries: an assessment of the kind of mind that Maitland brought to the problems of history.

Maitland, we have to remind ourselves, was born in the hey-day of Lord Palmerston and the Great Exhibition; he was eighteen when Mr Gladstone formed his first Administration; he grew up with *Essays and Reviews,* the *Origin of Species,* and *In Memoriam.* When he died at Quiney's Hotel in Las Palmas, a few days before Christmas 1906, the great Liberal victory seemed to have set the seal on the forward-looking forces of Edwardian England; and although prophetic minds—Maitland's among them—had seen in the South African War the ghastly shape of things to come, the Hundred Years' Peace still hung over Europe. The horse-trams still rumbled along King's Parade, beer was tuppence a pint and tobacco fourpence an ounce, and there were still young women to carry coals and do the washing-up at £30 a year for married dons. England, and most of all Cambridge, was still a good place for a scholar and a gentleman, although Maitland, who was both, had had to winter in the Canaries since 1898. Cycling up and down the hills of Las Palmas to the derision of the chiquillos, or stretched out on a chaise-lounge with a straw-hat and a pipe copying Year Books, while Mrs. Maitland haggled over vegetables at the house-door in torrential Spanish, he nevertheless found life in exile 'downright wickedly pleasant'. That, after all, is how we see him: the Edwardian don with the quiff, the cut-away starched collar, the guardsman's moustache, and the eyes of an invalid-poet. Something of the bright-eyed sadness of R. L. Stevenson, something of the military bearing of Elgar; the brave and fragile English man of letters, condemned to a premature death. Some one had once predicted that he would turn out 'a kind of philosophic Charles Lamb'.

Maitland left off being Charles Lamb while he was still up at Trinity. Lamb went out with the piano, the racing-oar and the cinder-track. There came in the tireless pioneer of a certain kind of scholarship: the man who was to do for legal history what his grandfather, Samuel Roffey Maitland, had done for ecclesiastical history: 'to teach men, e.g. that some statement about the thirteenth century does not become the truer because it has been constantly re-peated, that "a chain of testimony" is never stronger than its first link'. Thus F. W. Maitland defined the achieve-ment of Samuel Roffey in 1891, and in so doing he was de-fining his own task as he saw it. He was to write books which were to render impossible a whole class of existing books, and like Samuel Roffey, he was to write them for the few: those few who would be, as he put it, 'just the next generation of historians . . . ' What he admired about S. R. M., more even than his style and his matter, was his method: his rigorous application of the canons of evi-dence. The ideal of scholarship upheld by S. R. M. had been confirmed for his grandson by his beloved master at Cambridge, Henry Sidgwick: 'An unattainable ideal, per-haps, but a model of perfect work.' No dogma, no indoc-trination, no 'school'; but the freest and boldest thought set forth with the utmost candour, sobriety and circum-spection; the maximum of ascertainable and communica-ble truth attended with all those reservations and qual-ifications, exceptions and distinctions, 'which suggest themselves to a subtle and powerful mind'. Possessed of such an ideal of scholarship, and an almost virgin field of discovery, 'he did' (to apply F. W. M.'s words on S. R. M. to F. W. M. once more) 'what was wanted just at the mo-ment when it was wanted, and so has a distinct place in the history of history in England'.

That is where F. W. Maitland's place is, and must be; not in the calendar of 'Great Historians', but in the history of history. It will always be useless to advise people to 'read Maitland' as one advises them to 'read Gibbon' or to 'read Macaulay'. It is useless to pretend that anyone but a schol-ar, or at least a person of scholarly habits and intention, is ever going to read Maitland's works as they will sit down and read Gibbon's *Decline and Fall* or Macaulay's *History of England*. Mr G. M. Young's famous reference to the evening when he took down **Domesday Book and Beyond** 'and read, and read, till the owl in the fir-tree began audibly to wonder why the lamp was still burning, and the little breezes that stray down the dene from Wans-dyke turned chilly, and the dawn came . . . ' is a tribute to the scholarly tastes of Mr Young rather than a recom-mendation of Maitland as a popular spell-binder. For one thing, there can hardly be a Collected Edition, and there will certainly never be a 'Penguin'. He has nothing to say to the Common Reader who requires his history to be gen-eralized into broad outlines and movements, and in some sense relevant to what he calls 'the contemporary situa-tion'. He had not very much to say even to the world that attends Inaugurals. His own Inaugural, as Downing Pro-fessor of the Laws of England, was largely devoted to pointing out the spadework awaiting the modest pioneer of English legal history, in readiness for 'the great man when he comes . . . ' When, at the death of Lord Acton, Arthur Balfour offered him the Regius Chair at Cam-bridge, he declined not only because he was a sick man but because he would have been expected to address himself to the World at Large, and he doubted very much whether he 'had anything to say to the W. at L.' He was relieved to have escaped the crowds that came to hear Bury. 'I don't think that I should like full houses and the limelight. So I go back to the Year Books. Really, they are astonish-ing. . . . '

He knew that he was a pioneer, that he was finding a way into a largely unexplored territory, making use of a whole world of new material, and that his work must necessarily be provisional, exploratory, even (for a great part) editori-al. With the modesty and devotion of the pioneer, he was content to be the servant of the great historian of the fu-ture. It is typical that almost the last and greatest of his works should have been to edit and translate the Year Books of Edward II, with full *apparatus criticus* and a priceless Anglo-French Grammar and Syntax. 'Someday' he observed, 'they will return to life once more at the touch of a great historian.' He was like a man who comes upon a mountain, a mine, or a dark continent. He was con-stantly pointing to the vast heap, the depths, or the dark-ness of the 'beyond', and calling upon the pioneers to join him; pulling out exciting specimens of ore and cracking open their veins with the neatest of scholastic hammers; even inventing a grammar and syntax for the lingo of the natives. And the great trek into the beyond had begun in a hansom-cab.

Not Gibbon's immortal moment among the ruins of the Capitol will outlive Maitland's Sunday morning in the Parks at Oxford, when, sprawling on the grass beside Paul Vinogradoff, he heard for the first time of the almost virgin treasures of the Public Record Office awaiting the studious artisan of English medieval history. Not the vesper-hymns of barefooted friars, but the Sabbath bells of Protestant North Oxford, and a pupil of Mommsen wagging his little beard and talking the queer English he had picked up from a study of the Bible and the *Pink 'Un*. A Sunday tramp—that pedestrian delight of Victorian dons—a lounge in a Park—and, next day, a cab-ride from Paddington: the shade of Gibbon shudders and turns pale. But this is Sun-day, May 11th, 1884. Not Rome, but the Gothic North, awaits its historian. It waited just twenty-four hours. On Monday afternoon, Maitland was in the Record Office transcribing the earliest Plea-roll of the County of Gloucester. By the end of the year, **Pleas of the Crown for the County of Gloucester** was in print—a small, uncomely volume, but a landmark in the history of history. It was dedicated to Paul Vinogradoff. Another man might have been 'interested' by Vinogradoff's talk of treasure. Anoth-er man might have gone to see—in a fortnight, or in six months, or when he had time. Maitland went the next day. He went, not because he was merely interested, or curious, or speculative, but because his imagination had caught fire. He had seen the very life of a vanished age peep at him from a pile of parchment. 'I often think' he was to write to Vinogradoff, when he was Downing Professor of the Laws of England, 'what an extraordinary piece of luck for me it was that you and I met upon a "Sunday Tramp". That day determined the rest of my life.'

But the passion, the potentiality, was there long before the words of Vinogradoff awakened it. The Plea-rolls of the County of Gloucester found Maitland in a much more im-portant sense than he found them. Coleridge used to say that 'in the Bible there is more that *finds* me than I have experienced in all other books put together'. The compari-son is not irreverent if, as Coleridge believed, the imagina-tion is the creative principle in man, the faculty by which he shares in the divine creativity. Whether the imagination is awakened by the history of the House of Israel or by the history of the County of Gloucester may be mightily important to a theologian, but the Divine has a habit of working in ways that are hidden from divines. 'If it be but luck that sends us to Gloucester' Maitland observed, 'still the lot has fallen to us in a fair ground . . . *Deus in medio ejus; non commovebitur.*' In Maitland, the ground for visitation was well prepared. He was no rootless intellectual ready to feel vague emotions about 'the past'. He had history in his blood, and he had a patrimony in a beloved soil. All the best history begins as local history, and Maitland knew and loved the county of Gloucester. He belonged to the Cotswold country and 'Squire Maitland's lands'. The grey stone manor-house of Brookthrope looked out to the Malvern Hills where on another May morning, five hundred years before Maitland's vision in the Oxford Parks, William Langland too had seen a Fair Field Full of Folk. For that, after all, is what Maitland saw in 1884 in the plea-rolls of 1221. 'A picture' he called his book, 'or rather, since little imaginative art went to its making, a photograph of English life as it was early in the thirteenth century . . . What is visible in the foreground is crime, and crime of a vulgar kind—murder and rape and robbery. This would be worth seeing were there no more to be seen, for crime is a fact of which history must take note, but the political life of England is in a near background . . .' And there they all are, the vanished folk: sheriffs and famous men, 'a sufficiency of abbots and priors . . . the great landowning families . . . a crowd of men neither rich nor famous . . . reeves, smiths, millers, carpenters in abundance . . . pledges, witnesses, finders of dead bodies, suspected persons, and so forth . . . a section of the body politic . . .' Such a view, after all, owes more to the imagination than Maitland, in his modesty, was prepared to admit.

The quality of Maitland's imagination should not be misunderstood. It was intensely concrete; or, one should rather say, it was an imagination *for* the concrete. It had nothing of the vague, otherseeking quality of the romantic. It was neither elegiac, nor nostalgic, nor escapist. He did not go in search of the past as something strange, mysterious, different, or remote. It was not a matter of going to discover or experience something 'there'—something 'past' in the sense of dead, cut off, finished; something that once was and that is no longer; something the more attractive just *because* it was once and is no longer. Nor was he in search of the 'practical past'—the past that explains or justifies or condemns the present, although he could hardly have been a historian at all without being aware of the relevance of the past in the world of present experience. Of course the past 'led up to' the present, in the broad sense that there must always be, conventionally, a before and after in any temporal view of things. History as process was not invalidated for him by a philosophy of experience; indeed, he was so little a philosopher *explicité* that he could assume, with the happy ignorance of the born historian, the validity of a philosophy of history as the story of the progressive reason of mankind. I say 'assume' because his work is shot through and through with the happy gleams of a progressive rationality that he hardly ever adumbrated. Far too sensitive to the enormous complexity of things to accept the crudities of historical causation as

they appear in the work of the great liberal-rationalist tradition to which he nevertheless belonged, he yet saw the human race under the order of a broadly progressive rationality. 'Towards definition' might have been his motto; with a never-failing note of caution against simplicity.

That is where the concrete nature of his imagination made Maitland the greatest of his line. 'The history of law must be the history of ideas.' Yes, but ideas exist in the minds of men, and ideas are about things (*pace* the philosopher), and the main thing they are about is money, or money's worth—notably, in land. Men had talked for long enough about the military and political character of feudalism, and about the 'feudal system' as a system of law and obligation. Maitland thought it was time to talk about it in terms of economics, too—in terms of landed property, its uses, and its unequal distribution. 'There seems to me a tendency to lay too much stress on the military and political, too little on the economic side of feudalism.' Legal ideas do not exist in their own right but as the vesture of the substantial, and it was the substantial form beneath the vesture that Maitland watched in its every posture and its endless flexibility . . . And more than that. He saw always the specific example of the substantial. It is right to have our 'idea of a feudal state'. But it is much more right to attend to 'the concrete actual realities to which it answers, the Germany, France, England of different centuries . . .' Not the generality of the General Eyre, which might have been mistaken for a Governor of Jamaica, but *the* Eyre held before the King's Justices at Gloucester in the year of Grace, A.D. 1221, was what interested him. Nor is it even 'the King's Justices' that we see, but the Abbot of Reading, Simon, and the Abbot of Evesham, Randolf, and—most famous of all—Martin Pateshull— 'so strong, so sedulous, that he wears out all his fellows . . . for every day he begins work at sunrise and does not stop until nightfall . . . The amount of hard riding, let alone justice, that he had done is almost beyond belief'. And the places: not the Hundreds, Towns and Manors of the County of Gloucester, but Campden and Slaughter, Grumbaldsash and Wick. Maitland knew where they were: he had gone there to find them. 'Many questions are solved by walking. *Beati omnes qui ambulant.*' That was his way in his first book. It was his way in his last—the great edition of the Year Books of Edward II. 'What they desired'—the lawyers of the thirteenth century, and Maitland of the nineteenth—'was the debate with the lifeblood in it . . . They wanted to remember what really fell from Bereford, C. J., his proverbs, his sarcasms: how he emphasized a rule of law by *Noun Dieu* or *Par Seint Piere!*' It is almost a symbol of Maitland's method that Edith of Wackford came into Court with the disputed pig in her arms. The pig is always there, in Maitland's arms. One can almost hear its individual grunt. But, unlike any pig of Carlyle (his only rival in concrete particularity), one only hears it once.

Now this attachment to the concrete, as we have it in Maitland, must be carefully distinguished from 'the human touch' or the 'eye for the telling detail' by which the purveyors of 'social history' sell their wares. Maitland never employs the concrete and living instance simply because it is picturesque or strange. The taste for what Coleridge stigmatized as 'the contingent and the transitory' must always be part of the make-up of a historian, and mere vulgar curiosity about what he mistakenly calls 'other times' plays a greater part among his motives and incentives than he is sometimes willing to admit. Without something of the antiquarian to weight his feet he will be the more likely to perish among the -isms and -ologies of the conceptualists. But the desire to get past Carlyle's imaginary 'Time-curtains' and to lay hands on the 'genuine flesh-and-blood Rustic of the year 1651', unless it is controlled by a strong sense of that totality of human experience which must inform and suffuse our every experience of particularity, will lead only to a nostalgic and fruitless trifling with the superficies of history. This is the ever-present danger which attends much that goes by the equivocal name of 'social history', and Maitland was preserved from its menace not only by his legal training but by his conscious intentions. He was, by both profession and bent, a dealer in the 'public'. Ideas, to him, are never private ideas, always institutional. Crime, unlike sin, is a public concern, and it is controlled not by conscience but by institutions. Greed and jealousy, lust and beer, he observes, are monotonous; the tale requires to be diversified by the activity of officials and institutions in order to become the stuff of history. Hence the priceless miniature biographies of Gerard of Athée and Engelard of Cigoné, King John's rascally but highly competent Sheriffs of Gloucestershire. Their exactions diversify the tale of common crime, and 'mere social history is enlivened by a touch of politics'. The tiny gust of sarcasm contained in such a phrase says volumes for Maitland's attitude to any such definition of social history as 'History with the politics left out'.

Maitland's power of realizing the concrete in its multitudinous variety is matched only by his power of persuading the reader that multiformity is not a synonym for chaos, but is the very semblance of life as he knows it in its ultimate rationality. Neither in nature nor in history (to make a distinction without division) is seeming chaos to be subdued by the imposition of law. It is to be subdued only by our apprehension of the law which subsists within them. Maitland was content with his partial glimpsing of the inner logic of things. Everywhere we find him patiently assisting its appearance. Of course, he will say, there is 'progress', in the sense of an endless process of individuation, but the moral being sometimes crawls, sometimes runs, or for a time it doubles on its tracks. 'No doubt, from one point of view, namely that of universal history', he observed, of the Dark Ages, 'we do see confusion and retrogression . . . Lines that have been traced with precision are smudged out, and then must be traced once more.' When the barbarian hordes invade a Roman province, we shall say—if we take a narrower view—that 'their legal thought gradually goes to the bad, and loses distinctions which it has once apprehended'. The endless process of education of the human spirit, which is history, may seem to be halted, but it never ceases. 'In course of time men will evolve formulas which will aptly fit their thought.' The barbarians take what they need of their inheritance and use it as they will. 'This is as it should be. Men are learning to say what they really mean.' Again, of the large process known as the feudalizing of Europe, it is possible—from the narrow view of this place and that—to re-

gard it as 'a disease of the body politic' producing 'phenomena which come of evil and make for evil'. But in the widest sense, looking at several centuries of time, 'feudalism will appear to us as a natural and even a necessary stage in our history'. It will mean the civilization of an epoch, a moving, changing form of society; and the England of the eleventh century will show itself to be nearer to the England of the nineteenth, when compared to the England of the seventh century—by just four hundred years. That Maitland had to say this in 1897, and that we no longer need to have it said to us, is one measure of the difference that he made to our thinking.

History, then, for Maitland, is not a straight line, not a chain of cause and effect, least of all a triumphal procession from darkness into light. It is the image of the life of nature itself: a web in which every thread is connected with every other. So are those other images of nature, *The Ancient Mariner* and the Fifth Symphony. It is how the poet or the musician is more habituated to see the world than are most historians: even as Thomas Hardy saw it—a vast web which quivers in every part when one part is shaken, 'like a spider's web if touched'. It is not how Michelet or Mill, Macaulay or Maine, see it. Sometimes it seems, indeed, as if the nature of history has always been best known to those who do not write it. Maitland, the dissenter from all churches who restored the ecumenical law of Rome at the expense of Ecclesia Anglicana; the Liberal who could criticize the Liberalism of 1884 on behalf of the Shallows and the Silences of real life; the rationalist who spent his life in trying to get under the skin of the Ages of Faith; this Maitland is the great exception, and it was his unique combination of scientific scholarship with the intuitive knowledge of a great artist that made him the finest historical intelligence that the English-speaking world has produced. Perhaps his passion for music, which was second only to his passion for the law, had something to do with it. He read a score with the same facility and delight with which he read the Year Books. The same exercise of the mind was involved in both; the immediate apprehension of inner logic and organic wholeness. He did not find the principle of unity in Providence, or a Great Mathematician, or the Life Force, or even a Divine Lord Chancellor. The most that he would allow himself was a reference, untroubled by Hegelian ramifications, to the progressive rationality of mind. One feels that he was, of all historians, the nearest to knowing what history is, and this because he never tried to impose a philosophy upon it but was content to experience it.

So Maitland gives us the seamless web. It was he who, in the first sentence of the *History of English Law,* gave us the very similitude. 'Such is the unity of all history that any one who endeavours to tell a piece of it must feel that his first sentence tears a seamless web . . . The web must be rent; but, as we rend it, we may watch the whence and whither of a few of the several and ravelling threads which have been making a pattern too large for any man's eye.' The thread which he chose to watch—or, as Henry James would say, his 'pattern in the carpet'—was that of the law, the evolution of the ideas by which men have juridically regulated their relationships to each other in face of a common environment. The history of the law was not the whole of history, but it was, to Maitland, the formal construction which showed the changing life of mankind most immediately and at its most vital moments. The best way to get to know a nation, he once said, is to go and watch a murder trial in its courts. 'The great mediators between life and logic' he found not in a people's philosophers, or priests, or scientists, but in its practising lawyers. Bracton's book on the laws of England marked and made 'a critical moment in the history of English law, and therefore in the essential history of the English people'. The Pleas of the Crown for the County of Gloucester should be welcome 'not only to some students of English law, but also . . . to some students of English history'. He inserted the clause: 'if such a distinction be maintainable'—and it is evident that he thought it was not. By following this thread, of all others, Maitland did not pretend that men would be able to see the whole pattern of history: that was too large for any man's eye. But he did think that it would bring us nearest to all the rest, providing that we remember always that the law is the vesture of the non-legal forces at work in society. The history of the law should lead us to look beyond the sphere of the legal, to the exigencies which government's physical livelihood, to the mysterious impingements of human personalities, and to the complex interplay of the game of politics. Maitland was not indulging in the cobbler's propaganda on behalf of leather. In fact, he was always emphasizing how many other things than a good lawyer a good historian of the law must be. He emphasized it best by being those things himself.

Maitland may be said to have strengthened the tradition by which the History of England, as taught at our Universities, has been for so long equated with Constitutional History. That tradition still flourishes, despite attempts to replace it with undifferentiated English History. It is a good tradition, and has served us well. Here is something for which England is famous—her unique contribution to civilized living. Not only is it right and proper that Englishmen should be trained to understand this, their heritage, but the very process of training them to understand it involves a discipline unrivalled outside the Classics and Mathematics. Maitland's name is indissolubly connected not only with this tradition of studies. It is even more intimately connected with the 'legalistic' character of English Constitutional History as it is taught. His Lectures on Constitutional History remain at the head of the Reading List for the subject endorsed by the Faculty at Cambridge. Hallam and Dicey, Holdsworth and Jennings, they are there, too. And this is right and proper. English Constitutional History has not only been largely written by lawyers: it has largely been made by them. Judges, barristers, inns of court and law schools have been the champions and breeding grounds of those liberties which the Constitution exists to defend and vindicate. It was very well, and very natural, for Jeremy Bentham to talk one hundred and fifty years ago of 'Judge and Co.' as public enemy number one. It was fortunate for us that the inns bred Bentham as well as Burke. As Maitland was fond of saying, 'Law Schools make tough law'—tough enough for every enemy of liberty down to the High Court of Chancery itself. The question now is whether that toughness will prove sufficient to meet the challenge of administrative tyranny in the name of 'the sovereign people'. As long as those who have charge of our destinies are bred in the 'legalistic' tradition of our Constitution and its history, the danger facing us will at least be under surveillance. It is right that the rivals of that tradition—economists, sociologists, psychologists, and the rest—should stake their claims, and make them good, for inclusion in the general story. But it is also right for them to remember that, so long as the sword sleeps in our civil life, the field of battle where the great issues are fought must ever be where it has ever been—the ancient purlieus of litigation.

In so far as the legalistic tradition in our constitutional history owes anything to Maitland, it owes a broader and deeper conception of what such terms as 'law' and 'constitutional history' ought to contain. Maitland taught us what Savigny taught him, and what his plunge into Plea-rolls, Bracton, and the Year Books confirmed in enthralling detail: that law is the product of social needs, a rational concept of human relationships arising from the total history of a people. He taught us, again, that the history of a people lies within the greater framework of a civilization. He knew and loved the unique characteristics of England as a developing society within medieval Europe. He cherished its differences and devoted some of his subtlest pages to their analysis. But he was always aware, and his reader is always made aware, of a wider framework of reference. The first edition of the *History of English Law* began with the Saxons; the second edition began with Rome. That wonderful opening chapter, added in 1898, was the work of Maitland alone, and it lifts the whole work on to the plane, if not of the universal, at least into the orbit of metropolitan Europe. Again, take the opening passage of his chapter on the Anglican Church Settlement and Scotland, in the second volume of the *Cambridge Modern History*. His concern is with a small rough spot on the rim of sixteenth-century Europe. He is to show us the Scotland of Melville and Knox. But he takes his stand first at Rome, the central point of the Counter-Reformation, and thence looks outwards to 'what was shaping itself in the northern seas'. Only then, when we have seen 'two small Catholic powers traditionally at war with each other, the one a satellite of the Habsburg luminary, the other a satellite of France' does he carry us down in a swoop upon his subject proper—'that wonderful scene, the Scotland of Mary Stuart and John Knox . . . such glorious tragedy . . . such modern history', the scene where 'the fate of the Protestant Reformation was being decided, and the creed of unborn millions in undiscovered lands was being determined'. It is history in the making that we are shown. We are not told what was done, and why. We are shown it in the doing.

A reading of Maitland's chapter in the *Cambridge Modern History* leaves no doubt in one's mind that he would have succeeded brilliantly as a historian of the 'extended' subject—as a so-called 'narrative historian' who takes for his subject the total history of a people or a civilization, say *The History of England,* or *The History of Europe.* Nor can there be any doubt that he believed such work was still possible and desirable. What he chiefly admired in the work of his master, Stubbs, was 'the immense scope of the book . . . the enormous mass of material that is being used, and the ease with which this immense weight is moved and controlled . . . the excellent and (to the best of my belief) highly original plan which by alternating "analytical" and "annalistic" chapters weaves a web so stout that it would do credit to the roaring loom of time.' Polyglot history—although he participated in it—made him wonder. 'It will be a very strange book, that History of ours', he wrote, when he had sent off his contribution to Lord Acton's miscellany. He thought that if contributors failed, and Lord Acton had to write all twelve volumes himself (which he could have done without turning a hair) it might not be a matter of the worst coming to the worst but of the best coming to the best. And finally, Maitland always thought of himself as a pioneer whose work might help to make possible 'the great historian of the future'. Even that masterpiece of monographic art, *Domesday Book and Beyond,* was a 'provisional answer' which could be 'forgotten' when Paul Vinogradoff's *Villeinage in England* should appear; while the monumental *History of English Law* is described in the Introduction as concerned more with the advancement of knowledge than with symmetry of design. 'The time for an artistically balanced picture of English medieval law will come: it has not come yet.'

Maitland's work is peppered with these anticipatory and suspensory references. 'The time will come . . . The sun will rise, not a doubt of it . . . The great historian of the future . . . He that should come . . . the great man for the great book . . . ' Nearly half a century has passed since Maitland died, and the time has not come, and the great historian of synthesis is still to seek. History is deeper than ever in the morass of monographs, learned articles, revisions, and wait-a-bits. The University student is fed increasingly on Mr X's article on this, and Mr Z's excursus on that. Paradoxically enough, it is a situation to which Maitland himself contributed more than most. An age which has outlived his liberal-rationalist confidence in the progressive reason, his attachment to the objective pursuit of truth, and his happy faith in the arrival of another master of history on the grand scale, has sought increasingly to shuffle off its larger responsibilities by an obsessive concern with quantitative inquiries and provisional judgments. His warnings against over-simplification and hasty dogmatism have run to seed. What he learnt from Henry Sidgwick in the way of intellectual caution and qualification has become a disease. Maitland himself observed the symptoms. Unless a man were Sidgwick himself, he would say, 'there does seem a chance that while he is choosing, he may fall a prey to the insidious disease that is called "scholar's paralysis".' Can anyone doubt that that is what we have come to, fifty years after? To open almost any historical monograph of the mid-twentieth century is like opening a door upon a quicksand.

The fact is that Maitland was living and thinking in the sunset of the tradition of 'general history'—the tradition that began properly with Hume and Gibbon and bids fair to end with Trevelyan. He was very nearly the last of that great Liberal intelligentsia (the horrid word is inescapable) which slowly but surely substituted History for the Classics as the central discipline of a humane education. His brother-in-law, Herbert Fisher, was to write what will

probably prove to be the last one-man *History of Europe,* of any standing, a work that confesses its author's inability to discover any pattern in historical phenomena, and, at its worst, evokes the last false echo of the Gibbonic sonorities. 'What these gentlemen need,' Karl Marx was wont to remark of the deviationists, 'is philosophy'. It is what historians need, now. It is what Maitland had, implicitly in heart and spirit, if not explicitly on tongue and pen, and what made his work, monographical as it had necessarily to be at the stage of historical studies in which he worked, the very image of life. The methods of the master are not enough. The lesson of the master has still to be learnt. Which means that Maitland's successor can only be another Maitland, and even one Maitland in a century is perhaps more than we have a right to expect.

Robert Livingston Schuyler   (essay date 1960)

SOURCE: Introduction to *Frederic William Maitland: Historian,* edited by Robert Livingston Schuyler, University of California Press, 1960, pp. 1-45.

[*In the following excerpt, Schuyler provides an overview of Maitland's works.*]

During Maitland's lifetime he came to be generally regarded by those best qualified to judge his work as the greatest historian English law had ever known, and in the half century that has passed since his death his stature as a legal historian has not diminished. His writing, however, was not confined to the field of legal history. Whatever its subject, it is permeated with a spirit that is the essence of the historical mind. He has a message for everyone who is interested in history, whether professionally or not and no matter in what branch of history or in what particular subjects. His own interests and the character of his historical materials were such that he was often led to offer opinions on questions to which final answers could not be given, though in doing so he was, characteristically, not opinionated. It is not surprising that some of his views have been disputed by other scholars, in his own day and since. But his writings retain their power to stimulate and inspire, even where later investigations, not a few of them stemming from ideas which he himself threw out, have made it necessary to qualify opinions that he advanced. What a distinguished historian of our day, Sir Frank Stenton, has said about one of his books could be said equally well of others, that "the vitality of Maitland's writing, the acuteness of his mind and above all the interest which he could impart to the austerest of technical problems, have made *Domesday Book and Beyond* a source of inspiration which is hardly affected by changes of opinion about its subject-matter." The extent and variety of his historical output seem the more remarkable in view of the brevity of his career as a professional historian—it lasted little more than twenty years—and the fact that much of his time and energy during that short period was consumed in the performance of academic duties. In a bibliography compiled by one of his warm admirers and published soon after his death (A. L. Smith, *Frederic William Maitland: Two Lectures and a Bibliography*) there are listed more than one hundred thirty items, including the books he wrote, the volumes of legal records and other source materials he edited, with introductions which in many cases amount to historical treatises, articles he contributed to various journals, and some of his book reviews.

Maitland was a lawyer, and he is generally thought of, and rightly so, as primarily a historian of English law. But law was not the earliest of his intellectual pursuits. His habits of thought were not formed in the discipline of legal study, which, as law has been taught and learned, has not been calculated to develop a historical mind. He gave evidence of historical interests before he became a lawyer, and it would be a mistake to think of him as essentially a lawyer who just happened to become interested in the history of his subject. He was, rather, what his friend and collaborator Sir Frederick Pollock called him, "a man with a genius for history, who turned its light upon law because law, being his profession, came naturally into the field." One of Maitland's students at Cambridge was George Macaulay Trevelyan, who was to become perhaps the most popular historian of his day in England. He has told us that Maitland used medieval law as a tool to "open . . . the mind of medieval man and to reveal the nature and growth of his institutions." Maitland was a potential historian who became temporarily, and not very willingly it would seem, a practicing lawyer.

Anyone who has read more than a very little of Maitland will be impressed, as all students of his writings have been, by his concreteness and attention to detail. He had a healthy distrust of the glittering generality that disdains illustration. "People can't understand old law," he once remarked, "unless you give a few concrete illustrations; at least I can't." In the introduction to his **Pleas of the Crown for the County of Gloucester** he says that "a large stock of examples, given with all their concrete details, may serve to produce a body of flesh and blood for the ancient rules which . . . are apt to seem abstract, unreal, impracticable." His writings are alive with the doings of men, even though the men must sometimes be left unnamed. He never forgot that laws and institutions and ideas have no existence, no life and evolution of their own, apart from human beings. In his obituary article on Maitland, Vinogradoff wrote: "Although his work never stuck in details for their own sake, it will always remain an example of what a thorough grasp of details and keen investigation of all the particulars of a case can mean in the research of scientific truth."

Maitland, however, was not bogged down in detail and incapable of generalization. The combination of broad views and minute investigation, of what Macaulay called landscape painting and map making in the writing of history, is one of his marked characteristics. Generalization is not confined to surveys of wide scope that he wrote, such as his masterly summary of the results of research which was published as a preliminary chapter in the second edition of "Pollock and Maitland" and entitled "The Dark Age in Legal History," and his article on the history of English law, published in the eleventh edition of the *Encyclopaedia Britannica*. It is much in evidence in his technical writings also, sometimes in epigrammatic remarks which drive points home and clinch arguments. These are never mere purple patches, sewn on just for ornament.

Though primarily a legal historian, Maitland was not a narrowly legal historian. His major specialty was the history of the English common law, but the common law did not develop in isolation from other bodies of law, from equity, for example, administered in the Court of Chancery, and from canon law, administered in the ecclesiastical courts, and he was led to study the history of these other legal systems. Nor was his curiosity confined to the domain of legal history as a whole. He realized that specialization, division of labor, is necessary for the advancement of knowledge, but no historian has perceived more clearly that the various departments into which the whole of history, *considered as knowledge about the past,* has been divided for convenience and utility are not severally self-sufficient or self-explanatory. No historian has felt more sensitively that this departmentalization of knowledge does not correspond to anything in history, *considered as the flow of events in the past,* to anything inherent in the historic process itself—that it tends, on the contrary, to obscure relationships which have always existed in that process as an undivided whole. For Maitland there was nothing sacrosanct about the boundaries of the various departments of history, and they ought not to be thought of as barriers. He counted it for righteousness in his friend Leslie Stephen that he was "a great contemner of boundaries, whom no scheme of the sciences, no delimitation of departments, would keep in the highway if he had a mind to go across country." Maitland knew that the historian of law should often visit other historical bailiwicks—the economic, social, religious, political, for example—for enlightenment and explanation, and, conversely, that specialists in other historical domains ought on occasion to cross the frontiers of legal history.

In the formative period of his mental life Maitland read widely in different branches of philosophy, but the bent of his mind was historical, and perhaps he was too essentially and wholeheartedly the historian to take very kindly to the philosophy of history. His writings, at any rate, may be searched in vain, I believe, for references to so-called historical laws, determinism of any variety (providential, economic, racial, geographic, or any other), controlling social forces, or *Zeitgeister.* He did not misspend time and energy in the attempt to establish "fundamental causes." He knew that causation in history is always multiple and complex and that among historical antecedents there are always events that look like historical accidents, events which it seems impossible to account for as even probable results of *their* known antecedents. He never brushed aside as vain or useless conjectures as to what might have happened if some preceding occurrence had not occurred, never condemned conjectures on the part of historians in response to hypothetical questions contrary to historical facts. Without such conjectures, indeed, it would seem to be impossible to estimate the significance of events and personalities in history, and he himself at times engaged in them. For example, in a passage in "Pollock and Maitland" dealing with the results of the Norman Conquest in English legal history he asks whether a charter of liberties would ever have been granted in England if William the Conqueror had left only one son. And again, in his **English Law and the Renaissance,** when he is speaking of what he regarded as England's narrow escape from a "reception" of Roman law in the middle years of the sixteenth century, he says that "if there had been a Reception—well, I have not the power to guess and you have not the time to hear what would have happened; but I think that we should have had to rewrite a great deal of history."

Maitland's mind, like those of other great historians, was of strongly critical cast. The exercise of private judgment, which made him in religion a dissenter from dissent, became early an integral part of the man.

—*Robert Livingston Schuyler*

Maitland's mind, like those of other great historians, was of strongly critical cast. The exercise of private judgment, which made him in religion a dissenter from dissent, became early an integral part of the man, and a right which was a necessity for him in his own mental life he assumed to be a right of others. He took no false pride in his own opinions and welcomed criticism of them. In the estimation of H. A. L. Fisher, who knew him both as man and as historian, "no one was more entirely free from self-importance or from any desire to defend, after they had become untenable, positions which he had once been inclined to maintain." He was forever asking himself questions, nor was his curiosity confined to matters of obvious importance. An inconspicuous "&c." in the title of English sovereigns gave rise to an article which showed that what looked trivial on the surface originated in a deliberate stroke of statesmanship. Maitland's ingenuity and imaginative power in textual criticism are widely in evidence in his writings, notably in his editions of documentary materials. Impressive illustrations can be found in his introduction to the Selden Society's edition of *The Mirror of Justices*. This was a medieval law book, or what purported to be such, which enjoyed a high reputation from the days of Sir Edward Coke in the seventeenth century to the nineteenth century. It does not seem to have been a success in its own day or in the Middle Ages generally. It was not printed until 1642. In some way Coke, who died in 1634, acquired a manuscript copy of the book which, says Maitland, he devoured with his habitual "uncritical voracity" and pronounced to be "a very ancient and learned treatise of the laws and usages of this Kingdom." He incorporated in his *Institutes* many stories that he had found in this book, and since generations of English lawyers were brought up on Coke's *Institutes, The Mirror of Justices* passed into English legal tradition as a great authority. Maitland was not the first to cast doubts on its reliability, but he went much further in that direction than earlier critics had gone. His object was to find out from internal evidence when and why the book was written and what kind of book it was. His discussion of these questions is a first-rate illustration of historical detective work combined with flights of imagination.

Independence of judgment brought Maitland at times into conflict with opinions and schools of thought which were widely accepted and had the support of great names. A case in point resulted from a study that he made of Roman canon law in English ecclesiastical courts in the Middle Ages, the results of which are set forth in his *Roman Canon Law in the Church of England* (1898). He came to conclusions contrary to the opinion held by the High Anglican party in the Church of England, which enjoyed the approval of the great Stubbs and the endorsement of a Royal Commission on Ecclesiastical Courts in a report made in 1883. According to this view Roman canon law, or papal law, had not been binding on ecclesiastical courts in medieval England unless accepted by the church in England. This was, as Pollock remarked, "a patriotic, a comfortable and, above all, an anti-Roman doctrine. . . ." Vinogradoff called it "a kind of ante-dated Anglicanism." Maitland came to the opposite opinion, namely, that papal canons were treated by the English ecclesiastical courts as being, of their own force, binding law. Binshop Stubbs himself was convinced by Maitland's arguments. Yet Maitland, though not overawed by great names, was not polemical by preference. He did not seek controversy or rejoice in it, like some of his predecessors, contemporaries, and successors. He wrote many book reviews, in which there was much constructive criticism, but petty fault-finding was distasteful to him. He disliked it in others and never practiced it himself; he was habitually considerate toward other scholars. His historical criticisms, according to Vinogradoff, exemplified the maxim *suaviter in modo, fortiter in re*. Only if he thought that injustice had been done did he show signs of strong feeling, and then he could be devastating. A good example of this is his shattering refutation of an ill-advised and unfair attack which Sir Henry Maine, a renowned jurist and historian, had made on Bracton.

Maitland was skillful in summarizing the results of research in attractive form, and some of his writing was intended for the general public that takes some interest in history, but the writings that best exhibit his historical genius were addressed to more specialized classes of readers. Though he was devoid of the intellectual snobbishness that prizes knowledge the more when it is esoteric, it would be correct to call him a historian's historian rather than a general reader's historian. He was eager to advance learning and to aid other scholars and encourage them to labor, not in *his* vineyard (for no historian could be less monopolistic or proprietary in his attitude toward his field of specialization) but in the vineyard with him. His perception of historical problems awaiting solution and of work that needed to be done in aid of historical scholarship made him extraordinarily fertile in suggestion. He not only made great contributions to historical knowledge by his own investigations but also stimulated others to make further contributions by theirs. He regarded it a crime against history for the historian to eliminate from his finished product, in the name of art, the evidences and processes of reasoning on which it had been based. He spoke with playful sarcasm of England as a land "where men are readily persuaded that hard labour is disagreeable and the signs of hard labour are disgusting." He gave high praise to historians who took their readers into their confidence and showed them historianship behind the scenes. Of Bishop Stubbs he said: "No other Englishman has so completely displayed to the world the whole business of the historian from the winning of the raw material to the narrating and generalising." Like Stubbs he was a mighty contributor to historical knowledge, and a historical editor who carried the editorial art to its highest levels. No other series of introductions to historical sources deserves to be placed above theirs.

That Maitland's appeal has not been to the general reading public is explained largely, no doubt, by the nature of his subject matter. The historian of ideas and institutions—and this essentially is what he was—has never enjoyed the popular favor accorded to the narrative historian. "The History of Institutions cannot be mastered—can scarcely be approached—without an effort." Such is the majestic sentence with which Stubbs began the preface to his *Constitutional History of England*. One cannot imagine *Domesday Book and Beyond* displacing the latest best-selling novel on dressing tables in young ladies' boudoirs, the ambition that Macaulay cherished for his *History of England*. The kind of history to which Maitland devoted his best efforts requires for its appreciation more active response on the reader's part, greater mental exertion, and a higher degree of sympathetic imagination than the metallic rhetoric of Macaulay or the glowing prose of John Richard Green. It is also, as Maitland perceived, more risky than narrative history. "Would Gibbon's editor," he asked, "find so few mistakes to rectify if Gibbon had seriously tried to make his readers live for a while under the laws of Franks and Lombards?"

Maitland, however, conclusively refutes the notion, widespread though it seems to be, that there is some kind of incompatibility between deep learning and good writing, for he was a master in the expression of thought in English prose. Contemporaries who were familiar with his writings were impressed by his literary qualities and noted his gift for making unpromising subjects interesting. A generation after his death the editors of a collection of his articles coupled what they called "the matchless attraction of his style" with "the brilliant scholarship and originality of thought which he brought to bear upon every topic that he handled." He had no set method, nor any single manner, of writing. He was eloquent (though never pompous) or homely (though never vulgar) or gay (though never flippant) as his subject or his mood moved him. He was interested in words, took them seriously, chose them with care, and liked to manipulate them. Humor is a salient trait in his writing, humor "abounding in delightful surprises," says Pollock, "overflowing even into the titles of learned papers, breaking out in footnotes with rapid allusive touches." Vinogradoff speaks of "the wealth of humour that pervaded all his writings, in spite of their severe aims and their highly technical details." An example of the kind of refreshment that the reader gets in Maitland's technical papers occurs in an article on **"The Corporation Sole,"** in which, having occasion to speak of a gift of land "to God and the church of St. Peter of Westminster," he remarks, "We observe that God and St. Peter are impracticable feoffees." There were darts of sarcasm and irony in his quiver, and he knew how to discharge them with

telling effect, but his darts, however pointed, were never poisoned, and they were rarely aimed at individuals. His writings are full of epigrammatic phrases and remarks. He often made use of analogy and metaphor, though recognizing that they are often misleading and generally unsafe as a basis for argument. Maitland is not always crystal clear. He often had to deal with ideas that were indefinite and hazy and with facts that were complicated, and it is one of his merits as a historian that he does not make them seem clear and simple. He knew that overdefiniteness and oversimplification are faults in a historian. Some of the classical expositions of "the feudal system" and "the manorial system" are likely to make medieval society look simpler than it was, but, he said, "we think it part of our duty to insist that the facts which the lawyers of the thirteenth century had to bring within their theories were complicated." Hazy ideas and complicated facts are not the easiest subject matter for lucid exposition. Then there are difficulties in expounding technical matters, and much of Maitland's writing is technical. But these considerations apart, he seems sometimes to be unduly allusive, occasionally even intentionally inexplicit, perhaps because he assumes too much knowledge on the part of his readers.

Maitland is not always crystal clear. He often had to deal with ideas that were indefinite and hazy and with facts that were complicated, and it is one of his merits as a historian that he does not make them seem clear and simple.

—Robert Livingston Schuyler

During the entire course of man's thinking and talking and writing about the past of his species throughout what has been called "the history of history," conditions and events of later times have cast their shadows behind them. This after-mindedness, to give it a short name, has usually been present-mindedness and has been through the ages the most potent breeder of anachronism, the most persistent cause of historical distortion. If Francis Bacon had lived in our times instead of the seventeenth century, he might have included it among those "idols" on which he discoursed in his *Novum Organum,* those false notions and erroneous conceptions, deeply embedded in the human mind, which impede the advance of knowledge. Its antithesis is, let us call it, historical-mindedness, which sees, or tries to see, past events and ideas and institutions in their contemporary context. Historical-mindedness, in this sense, was alien to prevailing habits of thought before belief in evolution came to condition thinking about the past, and acceptance of the philosophy of evolution did not become widespread before the nineteenth century. Once in a while before then a voice had been raised against after-mindedness, but it was a voice crying in the wilderness. In England there was Sir Henry Spelman, for example, an early seventeenth-century historian (in the days when historians used to be called "antiquaries") of remarkable learning, considering the resources available to him, and of great originality, whose main interests were in English legal and ecclesiastical history. In the opening paragraph of a tract entitled *Of Parliaments* Spelman took occasion to criticize earlier antiquaries for their present-mindedness: "When States are departed from their original Constitution, and that original by tract of time worn out of Memory, the succeeding Ages, viewing what is past by the present, conceive the former to have been like to that they live in; and framing thereupon erroneous Propositions, do likewise make thereon erroneous Inferences and Conclusions." Then, four or five generations after Spelman, there was John Reeves, also a legal historian and also impressed by the prevailing after-mindedness of his predecessors. He said as much in a preface to the first volume of his multivolume *History of the English Law,* published in 1783, and hopefully announced a new plan of his own. Spelman and Reeves, however, like most men who have been "ahead of their times," had little if any effect upon traditional attitudes and points of view.

John Fiske, an enthusiastic devotee of the doctrine of evolution as well as a celebrated American popularizer of history, emphasized the need of freeing the mind from "bondage to the modern map," a phrase which he borrowed from the English historian Edward A. Freeman, in order to understand what the European mariners of the fifteenth and sixteenth centuries were seeking. "The ancient map," he said in the preface to his *Discovery of America,* "must take its place. . . . In dealing with the discovery of America one must steadily keep before one's mind the quaint notions of ancient geographers. . . . It was just these distorted and hazy notions that swayed the minds and guided the movements of the great discoverers." Bondage to the modern map, however, has been only one phase of bondage to the modern in general from which the study and writing of history have suffered so much. The process of emancipation from this bondage needed, and still needs, to be extended to all branches of history—to the history of institutions and ideas no less than the history of geographical discovery. Maitland's clear and steady perception of this need in historiography was, it seems to me, the most distinguishing trait in his historianship. It pervades his writings. A good example is to be found in the introduction to his edition of the roll of one of the later parliaments of Edward I, published in 1893. This was, as a medievalist of our day has called it, "a magnificent attack on after-mindedness." It threw a flood of light on the nature of early parliaments, showing how different they were from parliaments of later times, though scholars were slow to appreciate its importance in parliamentary history.

Historical-mindedness, Maitland early came to realize, is very difficult in the field of early custom and law. It is much harder to find out what our remote ancestors thought—and for him the history of law ought to be a history of ideas—than to find out what implements they made. Speaking of work that had been done in particular phases of legal history—the history of real property law, of criminal law, etc.—he says: "Everywhere the investigator finds himself compelled to deal with ideas which are not the ideas of modern times. These he has painfully to reconstruct, and he cannot do so without calling in question much of the traditional learning. . . ." Again and again Maitland tells us, in one connection and another, that the emergence of modern ideas ought not to be antedated, that history ought not to be hurried. "Against many kinds of anachronism we now guard ourselves. We are careful of costume, of armour and architecture, of words and forms of speech. But it is far easier to be careful of these things than to prevent the intrusion of untimely ideas. . . . If, for example, we introduce the *persona ficta* too soon, we shall be doing worse than if we armed Hengist and Horsa with machine guns or pictured the Venerable Bede correcting proofs for the press." In history, as in logic and mathematics, a *reductio ad absurdum* can be effective in refuting a fallacy. "It is reported," Maitland wrote in one of his early book reviews, "that London auctioneers deem no house worthy to be called a 'mansion' unless it has backstairs; therefore, every *mansion* mentioned in any document of the twelfth century must have had backstairs. This may be strange reasoning, but it is hardly stranger than to take a piece of Coke and illustrate Domesday with it."

Again and again, explicitly and implicitly, Maitland warns us against forcing modern ideas on the Middles Ages. The problem in hand may be the status of the *servus* of Domesday Book. Was he thought of as a thing or as a person—or as neither? "We may well doubt," says Maitland, "whether this principle—'The slave is a thing, not a person'—can be fully understood by a grossly barbarous age. It implies the idea of a person, and in the world of sense we find not persons but men." Modern legal conceptions are in general too definite, modern legal distinctions too sharply drawn, to suit medieval facts. "As we go backwards the familiar outlines become blurred; the ideas become fluid, and instead of the simple we find the indefinite." Thus in modern law a sharp distinction is drawn between a corporation and a group of co-owners. But "we may suspect . . . that in a remote past these two very different notions, namely, that of land owned by a corporation and that of land owned by a group of co-owners, were intimately blent in some much vaguer notion that was neither exactly the one nor exactly the other. . . ." Again, a sharp distinction has been drawn by modern historians between "alodial ownership" and "feudal tenure," but it ought not to be pushed too far back for, in the eleventh century, as Maitland pointed out, men were said to hold land of others *in alodio.* "To whatever quarter we look, the law [in the late thirteenth century] seems to be emerging into clearness out of a confused and contentious past. The courts are drawing a line between franchises and feudal rights; but it is no easy task, and violence must be done to the facts and the theories of former times."

Maitland knew that after-mindedness is not an exclusively modern phenomenon. He knew that men in *all* ages had trodden that primrose path which has always led to anachronism and distortion of *earlier* ages. Medieval lawyers, in whose thinking he was especially interested, were thoroughly afterminded, as was shown, for example, in the law of villeinage in the thirteenth century—"it seems to betray the handiwork of lawyers who have forced ancient facts into a modern theory."

Domesday Book and Beyond is, as its title suggests, an example of the retrogressive method in history, the method of working back from the later known to the earlier unknown, of which Frederick Seebohm, among English historians, was a conspicuous exponent; and Maitland gave Seebohm high praise for the insights he was able to gain from his method. The question may properly be asked whether this method was consistent with Maitland's teaching against after-mindedness. There was, obviously, a danger that in using Domesday Book to lighten the darkness that lay beyond it, anachronism and distortion would result. He was fully alive to this danger; we have his word for it that "the method which would argue from what *is* in one century to what *was* in an earlier century, requires of him who employs it the most circumspect management." He looked upon the retrogressive method as one to be resorted to only for want of a better, only where adequate contemporary evidence was lacking. It was not for him the ideal method. In studying parliamentary history in its beginnings "it is hard to look at the thirteenth century save by looking at it through the distorting medium of the fourteenth," hard but not impossible. "We must judge the [parliament] rolls of Edward I's reign on their own merits without reference to the parliament rolls of his grandson's, or of any later, reign."

"The verdict of history" is a trite phrase, but it is seldom if ever found in Maitland. It has a connotation of finality that is alien to his approach to history. Even in the realm of ethics there are no absolutes for a relativist. Bracton, for example, ought not to be accused of plagiarism because he did not conform to modern standards in acknowledging indebtedness to others. In his time nobody did. "Literary communism" was the order of the day. A contrast may be noted between Maitland and Lord Acton in their conceptions of the attitude toward human behavior in the past appropriate to the historian. The two men were colleagues at Cambridge, where Acton was Regius Professor of Modern History from 1895 till his death in 1902. There was friendship and mutual respect between them. Acton discussed his plan for the *Cambridge Modern History* with Maitland and invited him to contribute to it, which Maitland did; and Maitland recognized Acton's colossal erudition and wrote an appreciative, though not uncritically laudatory obituary article on him. In his Inaugural Lecture as Regius Professor Acton exhorted his hearers "to try others by the final maxim that governs your own lives, and to suffer no man and no cause to escape the undying penalty which history has the power to inflict on wrong." He paid little heed to what he himself called "the time test," but for Maitland "the time test" was the essential consideration in forming historical judgments about anybody or anything.

Retrojection of the present into the past should be guarded against as far as possible—but how far was it possible?

> If we speak, we must speak with words; if we think, we must think with thoughts. We are moderns, and our words and thoughts can not but be modern. Perhaps, as Mr. Gilbert once

suggested, it is too late for us to be early English. Every thought will be too sharp, every word will imply too many contrasts. We must, it is to be feared, use many words and qualify our every statement until we have almost contradicted it.

And how "in some yet distant age men will see or fancy that they see the time in which we live, is a question that even the most ignorant of us should not readily answer." The ideal of historical-mindedness, of objectivism, may not be fully attainable, but ought not a man's reach to exceed his grasp? At any rate it did not occur to Maitland to build a philosophy of historiography upon the difference between the two.

A mind as acute as Maitland's, and historically conditioned as his was, could not fail to be constantly concerned with the meanings of words, with ambiguities in their meanings, with changes that have come over their meanings in the course of time.

—*Robert Livingston Schuyler*

A mind as acute as Maitland's, and historically conditioned as his was, could not fail to be constantly concerned with the meanings of words, with ambiguities in their meanings, with changes that have come over their meanings in the course of time. It might seem to be of little historical importance whether in Domesday Book a man was said to hold land under (*sub*) a lord or of (*de*) a lord, but this was not Maitland's view. For an understanding of early English landholding much hinges, he believed, on a distinction between the two Latin prepositions. He tells us that "*sub* lays stress on the lord's power, which may well be of a personal or justiciary, rather than of a proprietary kind, while *de* imports a theory about the origin of the tenure; it makes the tenant's rights look like derivative rights:—it is supposed that he gets his land from his lord." Again, a single word may carry more than a single meaning. *Dominus,* for example, may signify a slaveowner, but it may also mean a feudal suzerain; *dominium* may mean ownership or rule, or a blend of the two.

The problem that lies at the heart of semantics arises from the identification of, or confusion between, the words, the verbal labels, or *symbols,* used for objects, qualities, ideas, and, in general, whatever talk or writing is about, and the objects, qualities, and ideas to which the symbols refer, the *referents,* as semanticists call them. In reality there is, of course, no direct and inherent connection between the word and what it refers to, as Locke was at pains to point out in his *Essay concerning Human Understanding.* A rose by any other name would smell as sweet. But a tacit assumption that a direct connection between symbol and referent actually exists is deeply ingrained in the human mind. Words used as symbols for what is indefinite and vague, for abstractions such as righteousness, justice, liberty, and the like, evoke widely different referents in different minds, and effective communication is thereby impaired, or blocked. Agreement regarding the referent may be called the goal of semantics. Maitland did not employ the vocabulary of semantics, which is not strange since the term itself was only beginning to come into English usage as the name of the science of meaning toward the close of his life. Yet he was a pioneer in what might be called historical semantics, a fertile field which has been only slightly cultivated by historians, though lexicographers, with their obsolete definitions of words, have long been professionally concerned with it.

A vivid appreciation of the instability of meaning attached to many words was one of Maitland's major perceptions. The word *landlord* is an instance in point. "We make one word of it," he remarked, "and throw a strong accent on the first syllable. The lordliness has evaporated; but it was there once. Ownership has come out brightly and intensely; the element of superiority, of government, has vanished." His sensitivity to varying shades of meaning attached to a word is illustrated by the pains he took to show that in Bracton's day the word *manerium* (manor) was not a technical term of law, susceptible of precise definition. As a historian of law he was impressed by the fact that lawyers had taken their terms from popular speech and given them technical meaning and definition. This was the case with the word *seisin,* for example. Sometimes a word continued to have both a technical meaning for lawyers and a vaguer meaning for laymen—a source of possible ambiguity.

Maitland did an immense amount of translation, and the way of translators is hard, as he early discovered. How, for instance, ought Latin terms in Domesday Book to be rendered into English?

> If we translate *miles* by *soldier* or *warrior,* this may be too indefinite; if we translate it by *knight,* this may be too definite, and yet leave open the question whether we are comparing the *miles* of 1086 [the year of the Domesday Survey] with the *knight* of unconquered [i.e., Anglo-Saxon] England or with the knight of the thirteenth century. If we render *vice-comes* by *sheriff,* we are making our sheriff too little of a *vicomte.* When *comes* is before us we have to choose between giving Britanny an *earl,* giving Chester a *count,* or offending some of our *comites* by invidious distinctions.

Nor could the semantic problem be evaded in translating from a modern language. Thoroughly at home in German, which he had learned in childhood and for which he had a strong liking, he sometimes had to be satisfied with the least inadequate English rendering of a German expression. He came to the conclusion that an English translation of the work of a German lawyer could, at best, never be entirely satisfactory: "To take the most obvious instance, his *Recht* is never quite our *Right* or quite our *Law.*" Sometimes a German word seemed to him preferable to its not quite equivalent English counterpart. He was led to speculate on the comparative semantic merits of the German and English languages for legal history. The German historian, he concluded, had at his disposal more

clearly defined terms and sharper concepts than the English historian, but this was not an unmitigated advantage for it might lead him to construct theories about early times too sharp to be true. Still he could see possibilities that are "concealed from us in our fluffier language; and the sharp one-sided theory will at least state the problem that is to be solved."

When judged in relation to the state of knowledge and the standards of learning in English legal history when Maitland entered that field, he appears as a towering figure. Personal affection and profound respect did not impair the judgment of Sir Frederick Pollock when he wrote in an obituary article on his old friend and collaborator:

> It is not easy to convey an adequate notion of Maitland's work to those who have not themselves labored in the same field. It is still less easy for any one to appreciate the difficulties or the success who does not remember the conditions under which he started. . . . Looking back some twenty-five years, we see the early history of the Common Law still obscure, insulated, a seeming chaos of technical antiquities. Historians excusably shrank from it, and the lawyers who really knew much of it could almost be counted on one's fingers. . . . This was the world which Maitland's genius transformed. . . . So complete has the transformation been that our children will hardly believe how uncritical their grandfathers were, and on what palpable fictions they were nourished. . . . Maitland commanded the dry bones to live, and henceforth they are alive.

James R. Cameron   (essay date 1961)

SOURCE: "Maitland as Historian," in *Frederick William Maitland and the History of English Law,* 1961. Reprint by Greenwood Press, 1977, pp. 3-25.

[*In the following excerpt from a study of Maitland that was first published in 1961, Cameron offers an analysis of Maitland's concept of history.*]

[Maitland] came to history from the study of law, and the interrelationship of these two strains is evident throughout his writings. I do not mean to imply that Maitland was a narrow legal historian; this is far from the truth. Traditionally a lawyer is conservative in judgment and looks to the past only to find precedents for a case or evidence to sustain a preconceived opinion. Training in law normally does not result in historical-mindedness. Sir Frederick Pollock, who collaborated with Maitland in planning and writing **The History of English Law Before the Time of Edward I,** has described Maitland as "a man with a genius for history, who turned its light upon law because law, being his profession came naturally into the field."

Maitland was certainly aware of the hazards of his profession, and he did not fall into the pattern of many lawyers who have written on history both before and since his time. He warns us that "we must not be in a hurry to get to the beginning of the long history of law." The historian of law, like any historian for that matter, must guard carefully against reading ideas of a later time into an earlier period and *vice versa*. Maitland warns us against the fallacy of believing that merely because our remote ancestors were simple folk they had simple law: "Simplicity is the outcome of technical subtlety; it is the goal not the starting point. As we go backwards the familiar outlines become blurred; the ideas become fluid, and instead of the simple we find the indefinite." Extreme caution must be exercised in order to prevent reading our own ideas into the words used by our forebears. Medieval historians must be at least amateur etymologists. By way of example, Maitland tells us that "if we introduce the *persona ficta* too soon, we shall be doing worse than if we armed Hengest and Horsa with machine guns or pictured the Venerable Bede correcting proofs for the press."

For Maitland the earliest English law could not be distinguished from custom. The conscious separation of law from morals and religion was a slow and gradual process. "The history of law must be a history of ideals." The historian of law must strive to determine not only what men have said and done but what men have thought. In England this task gains significance from the fact that the connected and distinguishable legal life of the nation goes back to the time of Edward I. Undoubtedly this was an important factor not only in influencing Maitland to undertake his monumental work but also in defining the scope of the *History of English Law Before the Time of Edward I*. Although this work bears the joint authorship of Frederick William Maitland and Sir Frederick Pollock, Pollock wrote a preface in which he protested that although it had been jointly planned, Maitland had done by far the greater portion of both the actual research and the writing. Miss Cam tells us that Maitland wrote all of this work except the chapter on Anglo-Saxon law.

Since Maitland was primarily a historian of English law, he recognized the importance of the divisions of labor in order that the advancement of knowledge might be facilitated. For him the history of law was an integral part of the history of England; indeed, "it was the key to the whole story." He recognized that it was necessary to go outside of his own special field of interest in order to gain a complete understanding or explanation of the material under consideration. He readily acknowledged that the history of English towns "must not be merely the history of legal arrangements. The trade winds blow where they list, and defy the legislator." Maitland undoubtedly gave more assistance to those laboring in neighboring vineyards than he received, by pointing out that "legal documents, documents of the most technical kind, are the best, often the only evidence that we have for social and economic history, for the history of morality, for the history of practical religion." He certainly deserves some of the credit for the fact that medievalists today use legal documents as sources for social and economic history to a far greater extent than they did in the nineteenth century.

Maitland's legal training caused him to be suspicious of generalizations. In instances in which generalizations were essential, he illustrated his general principles by applying them to specific cases. As Sir Paul Vinogradoff has suggested, "What he wanted most was to trace ideas to their embodiment in facts." Maitland's ability to relate legal terms to personal experiences and meaningful patterns of thought is illustrated by his explanation of the meaning of the Anglo-Saxon term *sake:*

> It is still in use among us, for though we do not speak of a sake between two persons, we do speak of a man acting for another's sake, or for God's sake, or for the sake of money. In Latin therefore *sake* may be rendered by *placitum:* "Roger has sake over them" will become "Rogerius habet placita super eos"; Roger has the right to hold pleas over them. Thus easily enough *sake* becomes the right to have a court and do justice.

It was Maitland's extensive knowledge of source material which enabled him to use this manner of exposition. He tried to use words to paint an image which would be correct and also intelligible to his readers. Although he preferred a concrete or case-related type of exposition, he was neither unable nor unwilling to resort to generalization when it was necessary or desirable. This becomes immediately apparent to anyone who reads his article on the Elizabethan settlement in the *Cambridge Modern History* or his article on the history of English law which appears in the *Encyclopaedia Britannica*. Even in his more technical writings, however, "he exhibited the rare combination of mastery of detail and high generalizing power."

Maitland's concern for the history of English law was central to his whole professional career. Nearly everything that he wrote or edited was directly related to this general subject. Although he was probably not aware of it at the time, his inaugural lecture as Downing Professor of the Laws of England set the theme for his academic career. He tells us in the first place that the history of English law was not written because its study was isolated from every other study. Secondly, although English lawyers were exposed to a little knowledge of the history of English law, this was primarily medieval law as interpreted by modern courts to suit modern cases. This was hardly the historical method, nor did it lead to a very rapid increase in the knowledge of the history of law. Maitland pointed out that only a few of the men who chose the legal profession would succeed in it, and he suggested that some of those who failed would be admirably prepared to pursue the history of law. This sounds like practical advice from one who knew whereof he spoke. Mr. Rogers, with whom Maitland read law for several years, wrote that although Maitland possessed "the clearest grasp of legal points and the utmost lucidity of expression, . . . I doubt if he would have succeeded as a barrister" because "he was the most retiring and diffident man that I ever knew."

A Sunday afternoon stroll, on May 11, 1884, with the Russian scholar, Paul Vinogradoff, has been credited, by Maitland's biographer, with first calling to Maitland's attention the abundance of written records at the Public Record Office, from which the history of English law might be derived. Several more recent writers have pointed out that Maitland had already been working in the Public Record Office before the supposedly climactic day described by Fisher. Professor Plucknett has distorted Fisher's account to mean that Maitland's encounter with Vinogradoff was responsible for "Maitland's sudden conversion to legal history." This interpretation can be readily disproved merely by referring to the Maitland bibliography at the end of [*Frederic William Maitland and the History of English Law*] which indicates that Maitland's publications on legal history go back five years prior to this encounter. Actually Fisher merely stated that Maitland had told him personally of that Sunday talk:

> . . . how from the lips of a foreigner he first received a full consciousness of that matchless collection of documents for the legal and social history of the middle ages, which England had continuously preserved and consistently neglected, of an unbroken stream of authentic testimony flowing for seven hundred years, of tons of plea-rolls from which it would be possible to restore an image of long-vanished life with a degree of fidelity which could never be won from chronicles and professed histories. His vivid mind was instantly made up; on the following day he returned to London, drove to the Record Office, and being a Gloucestershire man . . . asked for the earliest plea-roll of the county of Gloucester.

We know that Maitland and Vinogradoff first met on a "Sunday tramp" arranged by Leslie Stephen on January 20 of the year in question. The facts would best be served if we assumed that it was on this first encounter that Vinogradoff shared the triumph of his discovery with his newfound friend. In recounting this event many years after it actually occurred, Maitland was probably confused in his own mind about the actual day. Undoubtedly the source of his knowledge was of far greater importance to Maitland than the exact day of the event. We have every reason to believe that Vinogradoff was the first to appreciate the value of the records stored in the Public Record Office. Maitland dedicated his first volume of legal records to him. In a later letter to his friend, Maitland referred to this incident as "that day [which] determined the rest of my life." One must conclude that it was Vinogradoff who first pointed out to Maitland the treasure in the Public Record Office. If this is so and Maitland was using the Record Office in February, then Vinogradoff must have confided in Maitland at their first meeting in January.

Maitland was also inspired by his grandfather, Samuel Roffey Maitland, and by his friend Frederick Pollock. In a letter to his sister, Maitland evaluated his grandfather's writings. It is of some interest to note that most of the things which he said about his grandfather's writings could be said with equal validity about his own.

> It is a book for the few, but then those few will be just the next generation of historians. It is a book which "renders impossible" a whole class of existing books. . . . One has still to do for legal history something of the work which Samuel Roffey Maitland did for ecclesiastical history . . . to teach men that some statement about the thirteenth century does not become the truer because it has been constantly repeated.

Most of Maitland's writings revolve about the hub of English law. His earliest works were editions of legal records which he felt it was necessary to scrutinize in order to evaluate properly the workings of the early legal system.

The earliest court records which were available were those of the thirteenth century. He was forced, therefore, to begin at that point and to work in both directions. He first gave his attention to working backwards to the earlier period. In this, he followed the method of Frederick Seebohm. It was necessary to spend much time analyzing the records of the Domesday survey. Although certain general results were incorporated in the *History of English Law,* Maitland found it necessary to extend his views in a separate and subsequent volume, **Domesday Book and Beyond**. He was aware of the danger his method entailed, but realizing that there was none other available, he proceeded with extreme caution to decipher this enigmatic period. If all of his conclusions have not stood up, they have at least provided a stimulus to other scholars. The Ford Lectures for 1897 were a by-product of this research. Maitland's monumental work ground to a halt at the reign of Edward I because there was so much to be prepared and explored before a synthesis could be produced. He turned to decipher the Year Books, but found it necessary to prepare a grammar of Norman French before he could proceed. He probably overestimated the value of the Year Books, but even this conclusion could not be reached before he and others had laid the groundwork by their investigations.

Professor Schuyler tells us that Maitland has meant more to him than any other historian, "not primarily for the subjects he dealt with, but for his methods, his insights, and his superb historical sense. Maitland also set a standard for scholarship in reviewing the work of another author. If a scholar is to persuade those of his readers who are really worth convincing, he must give them not bare theories but "the very terms of the original documents candidly, accurately, and at length." Maitland practiced what he preached in this regard, for his works contain many Latin citations and his footnotes are liberally sprinkled with Latin quotations. This method precludes any concern for historical philosophy by its dedication to historical truth. Nor was Maitland content when he merely used documents, for these documents must be subjected to rigid examination. It was by this method that he determined that the Year Books were not official records maintained by the court but were the notebooks of young law students who were attending the court sessions. In a similar manner he became convinced that Henry II, by the Assize of Clarendon, instituted the inquest or the presentment jury. Henceforth, a jury could be summoned when there was no litigation in order to provide the king with desired information.

In little more than twenty years, and with Maitland severely hampered half the time by pleurisy, "a flood of books, articles, and reviews flowed from his pen, of a sustained high quality and, at times, brilliance unequalled in English historiography." "He left no rough edges and he touched nothing he did not adorn." A recent editor of Maitland's essays remarked that "nothing that he wrote can ever be tarnished by time in the matchless attraction of his style or in the brilliant scholarship and originality of thought which he brought to bear upon every topic that he handled." The writing style of Maitland would never rival that of Macaulay, Trevelyan, or Churchill in popular appeal, for two reasons. In the first place, the subject matter which formed the basis of his conclusions was of little interest to any but lawyers and scholars; and secondly, he was not writing for the masses. Nevertheless, he was able to express himself simply, clearly, and forcefully. His article in the *Cambridge Modern History* revealed that he was capable of writing for a much wider audience when he pleased.

Maitland's work as a researcher and editor enabled him to bring to his writing "that firmness of hand which nothing but original research can give." Since his conclusions are based so squarely upon his sources, they cannot be ignored regardless of their validity. It was his firm conviction that a good work of scholarship should possess value even though all of the conclusions of the writer should prove to be false. The keenness of Maitland's mind and the originality of his thought are evident in most of his writings. His works are permeated with suggestions which deserve, and in many cases have received, close examination and further exposition. As was to be expected, some of his suggestions have proved to be fruitful while others have fallen by the wayside. The originality of his thought and the soundness of his scholarship are undoubtedly two of the outstanding characteristics discovered in his writings.

"The best of gamekeepers is a converted poacher, and the best historians of law have been converted lawyers." The same qualities of mind which made him admirably suited to be a solicitor stood him in good stead in his approach to the history of law. Maitland's ability to analyze is revealed in his effort to decipher the nature of the organization of the institutions of Anglo-Saxon society from the evidence of the Domesday survey. His analytical mind was aware of the value, if not the necessity, of comparing English with Continental developments. He noted that during the reign of Henry II, England took the lead among the states of Europe "in the production of law and of a national legal literature." Next, he went on to contrast Glanvill's treatise with the absence of any counterpart in either Germany or France. In yet another place, he pointed out that English medieval law could be illustrated at numberless points by the contemporary law of France and Germany. The comparative method held an important place in both Maitland's mind and his writings. His analytical skill is well exemplified in "The History of a Cambridgeshire Manor," in which he sets forth the chronological development of the manor of Wilburton belonging to the church of Ely from about 1350 through the sixteenth century. His highly developed powers of synthesis can be illustrated by his description of a typical manor, which he summarizes as follows:

> Thus we may regard the typical manor (1) as being *qua* vill, an unit of public law, of police and fiscal law, (2) as being an unit in the system of agriculture, (3) as being an unit in the management of property, (4) as being a judicial unit. But we have now to see that hardly one of these traits can be considered as absolutely essential.

The quest for historical truth was uppermost in Maitland's scholarship. He tried to divest himself of all prejudice and preconceptions and so lose himself in the documents of the period he was studying that he would be able to think the thoughts of medieval men after them. Professor Schuyler went so far as to declare, "I doubt whether any medievalist has ever made a more earnest and sustained effort to get inside the medieval mind." Maitland's constant and relatively successful effort to approach the sources with an open mind led him to see many things which others had missed and to challenge beliefs which others had uncritically accepted. It was while reading the *Provinciale* of William Lyndwood that Maitland became aware of a contradiction between the ideas of this fifteenth-century churchman and those attributed to fifteenth-century churchmen by the *Report of the Ecclesiastical Courts Commission*. Maitland's lack of enthusiasm for any particular church or theological position gave him an impartiality and an open-mindedness which was generally not to be found in church historians. He was able to document and support his conclusions so satisfactorily that even Bishop Stubbs, who had helped in the preparation of the Report, accepted his conclusions.

The quest for historical truth must involve thoughts as well as words. Maitland not only was a clear thinker but possessed an unusual knack of turning a clever phrase and, with a characteristic wit, driving home the point which would clinch his argument:

> If we speak, we must speak with words; if we think, we must think with thoughts. We are moderns and our words and thoughts can not but be modern. Perhaps, as Mr. Gilbert once suggested, it is too late for us to be early English. Every thought will be too sharp, every word will imply too many contrasts. We must, it is to be feared, use many words and qualify our every statement until we have almost contradicted it.

His concern for truth inevitably led to extreme care in his choice and use of words in order that he might convey the exact sense or meaning that he had grasped. This has made it relatively easy for those who have differed with him to take issue with him, for no one has ever professed ignorance of the meaning or intention of Maitland's words. "Maitland's ear for gradations in the scale of meaning was extraordinarily sensitive; it would be difficult, in any of his writings, to find cases of semantic flatting or sharping." His daughter tells us that he was very careful in dealing with words and always said or thought the words to himself as he read or wrote. He even went so far as to recite his lectures to himself as he paced back and forth, in order to make certain that what he said sounded as he intended that it should. One of the qualities which contributed most to attract his readers was the "wealth of humor that pervaded all his writings, in spite of their severe aims and their highly technical details." One cannot read Maitland's writings for very long without coming across one of his "happy pointed phrases." His humor is not an ornamental adjunct but generally concludes an argument in which he sums up his case in the manner of "a wise and kindly judge who takes into account all the extenuating circumstances and as he looks at the culprit feels 'there, but for the grace of God, stands Richard Baxter.' " His introduction to *Mirror of Justices* is probably the best extended example of his use of humor in effectively handling an involved and complicated problem involving the book's authorship, purpose, and value.

After a decade of private law practice, Maitland, in 1884, returned to Cambridge as a Reader of English Law. The publication of *Pleas of the Crown for the County of Gloucester* earlier in the year had won for him wide recognition as a scholar. He was to remain at Cambridge first as Reader and then as Downing Professor of the Laws of England for the remainder of his life. He confided to his friend Vinogradoff on many occasions "that he would much rather devote his life to the historical study of English law than watch his chamber in Lincoln's Inn for footsteps of the client who never comes." Maitland had attracted the attention of Frederick Pollock as early as 1879 when Maitland published an article on **"The Law of Real Property."** Pollock found in Maitland a kindred mind; and a friendship developed, which, among other things, resulted in the *History of English Law*.

Soon after settling at Cambridge, Maitland recognized that his vision of writing the history of English law was so broad that a co-operative effort would be required to do the editing and produce the monographs which would form the foundation for such a work. He therefore instituted the organization of the Selden Society in 1887 "to encourage the study and advance the knowledge of the history of English law." It has been said that without Maitland's genius, learning, and devotion the Selden Society would not have existed. There is no question but that he was its prime mover, and he was its first literary editor. Eight of the twenty-one volumes issued by the society during his lifetime came from his pen, and another was almost completed at his death. . . .

Maitland was not only a scholar but also a professor. His inheritance of a modest estate from his grandfather enabled him not only to marry in 1886 while living on the slender stipend of a Reader but also to "incur the expense involved in the preparation and publication of some of his most important work." We know of his lectures through both the witness of his students and posthumous publication. As Miss Cam has pointed out, it is to be regretted that Maitland is known to so many students mainly through his lectures on constitutional history which were written in 1888 and published after his death against his declared judgment. His lectures had the same general characteristics which distinguished his writings. They were "original, illuminating, suggestive, and stimulating in what they had to say, which was carefully prepared" and read in a slow, distinct voice which enabled the student to take full notes. Maitland did not shirk his nonteaching professorial duties, but carried them out with the same thoroughness and loyalty that marked his other academic activities.

Maitland's chief impact upon the teaching of history was "his presentation of Henry II as founder of the common law, and with it of the English monarchy as the guardian of justice to all." Today it is universally recognized that Maitland's introduction to the Parliamentary Roll of 1893, it attracted little attention until 1910, when Charles McIlwain's *High Court of Parliament* appeared. The implications and suggestions of Maitland's introduction have produced a major revision in the accepted views on the nature and the origin of Parliament. This introduction is an outstanding example of Maitland's critical approach to his documents. It seems strange that he did not return to this subject, but his failure to do so might be explained by suggesting that he considered it to be a constitutional rather than a legal issue and therefore outside the realm of his prime concern. The failure of scholars to grasp the implications of this introduction—that the history of Parliament must be rewritten—may be attributed to the seeming tentativeness of Maitland's approach. In only one instance did he suggest that he had ventured to differ from what seemed to be the general opinion of scholars, and he even questioned whether this difference was real or apparent. At the time that Maitland wrote, it was necessary to emphasize the curial nature of Parliament. Those who pursued this course, including Maitland himself, underestimated the political aspects of a parliament. We are now able to obtain a more balanced estimate of the nature and function of Parliament than was possible heretofore.

Maitland's character and personality are reflected in the reviews which he wrote of the works of others and by his own reactions to what others said or wrote about his own work. His judgments on the writings of others were as astute as those which he made on the documents that formed the basis of his own writings. He had a critical mind which enabled him to read with insight, and yet even his criticisms usually reflected a kindliness of manner. He was called upon to write reviews of thirty-three books, mostly for the *English Historical Review*. He declined the invitation of Reginald L. Poole to review other books because of personal feelings about their authors. Maitland began his reviews by pointing out the strong points or major contributions of the work under consideration before mentioning its shortcomings. He was never afraid to state what appeared to him to be the truth merely because it went against accepted opinion; in fact, he seemed to take delight in challenging views which were hallowed by tradition. His manner was entirely different, however, when it came to dealing with individuals. Although he set forth his revisionary views concerning English canon law in a forthright manner, he was disturbed when he heard that Bishop Stubbs had taken personal offense at his words. Maitland's views on English canon law were first revealed in a series of articles in the *English Historical Review*. As he was bringing his essays together to republish them in book form, he wrote to Reginald Poole:

> I hope and trust that you were not very serious when you said that the Bishop was "sore." I feel for him a respect so deep that if you told me that the republication of my essays would make him more unhappy than a sane man is whenever people dissent from him, I should be in great doubt what to do. It is not too late to destroy all or some of the sheets. I hate to bark at the heels of a great man whom I admire but tried to seem, as well as to be, respectful.

When it came to having his own work reviewed, Maitland preferred to have the most competent critic examine it. In submitting two of the volumes which he prepared for the Selden Society to the *English Historical Review—The Mir-*

ror of Justices and ***Bracton and Azo***—he asked that a professed Romanist be asked to review them. He disclaimed any knowledge of Roman law and wanted to know "whether I have been guilty of many 'howlers'—in short I want to know the worst." But he was not one to sit idly by while his works were subjected to an ill-founded attack. The Reverend Malcolm MacColl, canon of Ripon, entered into controversy with Maitland on the subject of canon law. Maitland's reply was a devastating one which removed the Anglican position from serious contention thereafter. Round took exception to some of the views expressed in ***Domesday Book and Beyond***. But this did not upset Maitland's equilibrium, for he recognized the weakness of his position. In a letter to Poole, he wrote: "It grieves me that you should brood over my Domesday. Of all that I have written that makes me most uncomfortable. I try to cheer myself by saying that I have given others a lot to contradict." Earlier, he had taken the unusual steps of writing a letter to James Tait concerning the latter's review of ***Domesday Book and Beyond***. In it he expressed his appreciation for the critical nature of the review, which went far toward establishing Tait's reputation as one of the best historical scholars in England. This was typical of Maitland's encouragement to young scholars. Professor W. W. Buckland pointed out that Maitland was tolerant of slips and even ignorances in a younger scholar and illustrated the point by relating a personal experience.

The British educational system of Maitland's day did not place great emphasis upon what today we should call graduate study; therefore, Maitland's lectures were directed primarily toward undergraduates who were preparing for the Tripos. This system had two effects upon Maitland which were different from what his experience would have been had he been teaching in either the United States or Germany. First, he had few students whom he could prepare to assist him in his work or to follow him in realizing the vision which no man could complete in one lifetime. Nevertheless, he did hold a few advanced classes in paleography and diplomatics for the study of medieval English charters. He contended that in sixty hours he could train a student to read medieval documents with "fluency and exactitude." Second, Maitland was not the founder of any formal "school" although his views on the Parliament of 1305 are often considered the beginning of a distinct school of thought upon that subject. Mary Bateson was the only pupil of his who followed directly in her master's footsteps, but unfortunately her untimely death preceded Maitland's. Her industry and judgment rivaled that of Maitland. Her scholarship and her work as an editor brought her recognition as one of the best medievalists in England, and for this she gave credit to the "counsel and direction of Professor Maitland."

Maitland certainly had a broad vision of the history of English law. He expressed the hope that he would be able to bring "the English law of the thirteenth century into line with the French and German law of the same age." He felt that it would be impossible to evaluate adequately the true character of English law apart from the larger context of European law. He took pains to try to determine what was known to Glanvill and Bracton, but he was equally interested in contemporary scholarship among French, German, and American scholars. He indicated that he was trying to do for English law what many had already done for French and German law. He seemed to be one of the first English scholars to appreciate the work of American scholars. He was instrumental in getting Bigelow's book on *Torts* accepted in his law school and even an English edition of it published by the Cambridge University Press. Perhaps it was Maitland's early appreciation of American scholars which contributed in part at least to acclaim of him among scholars in the United States. He corresponded with several American professors and received them when they visited England.

The breadth of Maitland's vision for his subject explains why he was not able to complete the exposition of the history of English law. When he began his study, he carried the account back to Anglo-Saxon times on the strength of his Domesday studies and the research of other experts on local history. Maitland himself contributed a history of ancient Cambridge. He was able to carry his account forward to the time of the beginning of the Year Books. He felt that a critical edition of the Year Books was essential to the carrying forward of his main interest. This could not be done without a thorough knowledge of the Anglo-Norman French in which the records were made. Maitland investigated this language so thoroughly that a contemporary philologist, M. Paul Meyer, recommended his introduction to the first volume of the ***Year Books of Edward II*** to all students of medieval French.

K. B. McFarlane   (essay date 1965)

SOURCE: "Mount Maitland," in *New Statesman,* Vol. LXIX, No. 1786, June 4, 1965, pp. 882-83.

[*In the following essay, McFarlane reviews* The Letters of Frederic William Maitland.]

F. W. Maitland's posthumous reputation has run an oddly uneven course. When he died in 1906 his university received what was surely a letter with few if any precedents: an official address of condolence from the Chancellor and Masters of Oxford. Did her ancient sister perhaps feel that Cambridge, having already lost so much learning, wanted loyalty? Those seven lines of obituary in the *Cambridge Review,* when set beside the *Oxford Magazine*'s two columns, were few enough to incite odious comparisons. The charitable theory that the depth of the silence equalled the depth of the shock is not borne out by the other evidence. Maitland had been much honoured when alive and yet *The Times* considered that a third of a column measured his deserts. It is easy to understand Thomas Seccombe's indignation at 'the shallowness of the ripple in the general consciousness caused by the passing of England's greatest historian since Gibbon and Macaulay.' In the half century that followed, despite his reputation among scholars, Maitland's publishers, no doubt for the best of reasons, have not shown themselves over-anxious to keep his most important works in print. His public can never have been large.

Being a stoic as well as incorrigibly modest, he would have thought this no occasion for complaint. Well aware of the shallows and silences of real life, he might not even have resented the further disservice that awaited him: an official biography, justly described by its compiler as a 'sketch', which was perfunctory and none too accurate. When one remembers what the ailing Maitland, putting aside unfinished work, did for his old friend Leslie Stephen, it is hard to forgive that miserable sketch. Its consequences are probably now irreparable. Maitland rates his own abilities as a biographer ridiculously low and the best-selling days of his masterly *Leslie Stephen,* if it ever had any, were soon over. But the very least he had done was to give the permanence of print to a mass of Stephen's letters before they could be destroyed or lost. Though Herbert Fisher published a small selection of Maitland's letters, a good few of which have since vanished, he seems to have made no real attempt to trace, still less to use, the many that must still have been in existence when he compiled his book. Today the originals known to survive number only just over 450. All are printed in full in Mr Fifoot's scholarly and handsome edition [*The Letters of Frederic William Maitland*], along with some 50 other letters or parts of letters of which copies have been traced.

If Seccombe meant to suggest that Maitland's greatness as a historian fell short of the heights attained by Gibbon and Macaulay, he did his friend an injustice. Probably he wished only to indicate how select was the company to which Maitland belonged. Few with any right to an opinion would find fault with that estimate for claiming too much. As we look back over the whole range from a distance, we can see that the summit of Mount Maitland overtops them all. What other English historian has combined such exact scholarship with so much imaginative insight, intellectual grasp, and brilliance in exposition? Outside Britain his only rival is Mommesen.

Consider what he achieved in that miraculous decade which followed the publication of the three volumes of *Bracton's Note-Book* in the autumn of 1887. He had scarcely read the proofs that summer when he fell ill. This was the first recorded attack of the tuberculosis which, together with diabetes, was to make the rest of his life precarious and to force him to winter abroad away from his books from 1898 onwards. It was not long before he was made aware of his doctor's verdict. As he wrote to Vinogradoff in March 1889,

> I very much want to see you again and I don't know that I can wait for another year: this I say rather seriously and *only to you*. Many things are telling me that I have not got unlimited time at my command and I have to take things very easily.

Yet in those 10 years he edited three and a half volumes for the Selden Society, one for the Pipe Roll Society and the *Memoranda de Parliamento* for the Rolls Series, as well as overseeing the editorial work of others. At the same time he wrote the *History of English Law* but for one chapter, *Domesday Book and Beyond* and *Township and Borough,* as well as 18 considerable articles and many shorter ones for such journals as the *English Historical Review.*

Judged purely on quantity this was astonishing enough for a man obliged to 'take things very easily' and with other calls on his time. His three books alone contained little short of a million words. And not one too many. If, as we are told, some readers found Maitland's works fatiguing it was not their bulk but their brilliance that was not to be borne. Only the dullard could find Maitland dull and then for no better reason than because he too is required to think. Here was a writer who could be highly technical and a delight to read, a fine artist with a powerful analytical mind and a remarkable flair for the concrete instance that made the past live. Some have found his writings too allusive, but even those who cannot recognise the allusion—it might be to a contemporary music hall song or to Macaulay's weighing a book by Edward Nares—are left in no doubt about Maitland's meaning. Recognition merely adds a bonus of enjoyment. Maitland is allusive not to show off but because he overestimates his reader's knowledge.

After 1897 the pace of his production inevitably slackened, but not the quality. There was the same learning, weighty but winged, the sparkle, the lucidity, the same sureness of finger in disentangling historical knots. In the immense output of less than 20 years there are few pages that do not bear the stamp of Maitland's highly individual and, it would seem, effortless genius. He wrote like a brilliant talker; we are told that his talk was brilliant and that his public speeches were long remembered and quoted.

That is the chief reason why his letters are so disappointing. They might have been written by almost any competent scholar. This impression is intensified by their subject-matter. What survives is in the main the professional correspondence, with successive secretaries of the Selden Society, with Frederick Pollock, with Reginald Lane Poole, then editor of the *English Historical Review,* with a group of American legal historians, with H. A. L. Fisher, Paul Vinogradoff and the prickly J. H. Round. Communication with the last of these was broken off—inevitably, though to Maitland's rueful surprise—after a devastating but urbane review of Round's *Commune of London.* These business letters are full of inquiries and comments on work in progress that will interest scholars active in the same fields; and they will be of great value to some future historian of English historiography. They will not excite or entertain the student of character, still less the casual reader. Only when illness had removed Maitland to Funchal or the Canaries do his letters, in particular those to Henry Jackson, become descriptive and discursive. Even then, they are not outstandingly good of their kind.

Maitland could not, of course, write clumsily or obscurely. It is his manly Victorian reticence that prevents him from being a good letter-writer. It seems to have been impossible for those reared in the liberal, moral, agnostic Cambridge of Henry Sidgwick and Leslie Stephen to 'speak out' about their deeper feelings. The Oxford Tractarians and their allies had spoken out too much. Maitland's was the generation of 'no flowers by request'. He was conscious of the stiffness, but he could not overcome it. 'I am cursed with shyness,' he writes, 'I am tongue-tied.' As a correspondent he had gagged himself. The rare humour is somewhat schoolboyish. Even his comments on the suicide of a close associate show an unpleasant want of feeling. No doubt his actions were generous, but the expression of sentiment is ruled out. One begins to long for the mawkishness and introspection of the Newman circle.

Another reason for disappointment is the total absence of letters written before 1880, when Maitland was 30. The two letters from Eton to a sister throw no light on his intellectual development. There are none at all from the undergraduate or the student of Lincoln's Inn. This is all the more serious since no attempt seems to have been made after his early death to collect information from his school and university contemporaries. Maitland was President of the Union at Cambridge, an 'Apostle', a 'Sunday Tramp', a running Blue and a member of the 'Scratch Eight', a London dining-club for 'talking nonsense and mistaking it for philosophy'. Many of those intimate with him survived him. Our first real glimpse of him, as a pupil in chambers, shows him fully grown.

> 'He had not been with me a week,' his master wrote long after, 'before I found that I had in my chambers such a lawyer as I had never met before. I have forgotten, if I ever knew, where and how he acquired his mastery of law; he certainly did not acquire it in my chambers; he was a consummate lawyer when he entered them.'

It seems that we shall never know how that and the other miracles happened. The young man who 'would have been an honour to the Bench' had he suddenly been made a judge, seems to have become a great historian in the same wholly mysterious way. He tells us himself that 'the idle whim of an idle undergraduate' took him into Henry Sidgwick's lecture-room in his second year at Trinity. The result was his appearance at the head of the first class in the Moral and Mental Science Tripos some 18 months later. A word from Vinogradoff, the visiting Russian medievalist, seems to have turned him equally suddenly into a historian. As far as training went, no one could have been more of an amateur.

Having got over one's disappointment, some pleasure can be derived from catching echoes of the famous style, especially when contemporary issues touched his own special studies. 'Yes', he writes from Grand Canary in 1899,

> the 'crisis in the church' or what of it may be heard in the Hesperides, interests me in various ways . . . I see that the Right Reverend Father in God whom we used to know as GFB has passed the word that the Canon Law is a pathless wilderness. My Lord of London said to me something of the same kind. I think that these highly prudent prelates will discourage their young men from excursions over ground which, whether I am right or wrong, is certainly full of ugly holes for Anglicans. To express a tolerant contempt for lawyers will be the popular and the sage course. Lawyers have written a great deal of nonsense in all ages: the middle not excepted. Besides, the medieval Canon Law is not a subject about which strictly orthodox Romanists can write with freedom, or, if they are at all learned, with pleasure.

Hardly enough for the reader to cry *'aut Maitland aut diabolus'*, but a faint reminder of a familiar voice. Though

never slovenly in anything he wrote, Maitland does up his buttons when he writes a letter. He was 'F. W. Maitland' even to a sister, and, of course, to all his friends.

Mr Fifoot has done his editorial work splendidly, providing just the right amount and kind of annotation. But one obscure allusion has defeated him. 'I am hoping,' wrote Maitland,

> for a day at Cheltenham if only Fitzroy F. will attend to business. Could I do anything for you there and save an additional gua? No, not gua, only £1. On one occasion the elder F. returned the shilling to me, but pocketed the sovereign. Bless him!

To anyone who visited the Phillipps Library in the old days the footnote 'T. Fitzroy Fenwick of Cheltenham, who was concerned with antiquarian publications' will seem almost the best joke in the book. It is gratifying to catch so excellent an editor nodding.

H. E. Bell   (essay date 1965)

SOURCE: "The Characteristics of Maitland's Work," in *Maitland: A Critical Examination and Assessment,* Harvard University Press, 1965, pp. 3-16.

[In the following excerpt, Bell examines the defining characteristics of Maitland's works.]

Historiography—the study of the ways in which men have applied themselves to the problem of writing history—has become a fashionable, perhaps too fashionable, subject. For the professional, in history as in any other craft, there must always be an interest in seeing how the greatest practitioners have gone about their business; but whether that interest is sufficient to justify the mass of work that has recently appeared on historiography is not so certain. In particular, an extended study of an individual historian would seem to be justifiable only in one of two circumstances: he must either have been, in some sort, a public figure in his own age, whose historical writing influenced political action of his time, or alternatively he must have introduced and developed ideas and techniques of permanent significance in the writing of history.

Maitland's work possessed qualities and characteristics that made it permanently influential on English historical scholarship.

The most obvious of these was its wide range. It is not merely that Maitland's researches stretched from the age of the Saxon settlement to the sixteenth century: it is that within that long period his interests were catholic and his knowledge encyclopaedic. A scholar who is going to write big, wide-ranging books must possess the facility of working quickly. Holdsworth, for instance, did not find it necessary to use accumulated notes, but wrote straight from his authorities, and in this sort of connection Maitland was exceptionally fortunate in having a quite remarkable visual memory: Fisher drew a charming portrait of him, smoking and reading his black-letter law books far into the night, never taking a note, yet being able to retain whatever he wanted. But, of course, the breadth of his scholarship was dependent on more than a happy technical facility: it resulted rather from his effort to reconstruct the ideas and motives of the ages that he studied. Because he succeeded so far in this, because, in G. M. Trevelyan's phrase, he "was using mediaeval law as the tool to prise open to our view the mind of mediaeval man", his writings have as much significance for economic, social and constitutional, as for purely legal, history.

Indeed, to describe Maitland simply as a legal historian is inadequate unless the description is accompanied by recognition of the fact that his work utterly changed both the techniques and scope of English legal history. A system like the English common law—

> That codeless myriad of precedent,
> That wilderness of single instances—

in which the principle of *stare decisis* had become basic, was necessarily dependent on history of a sort: few nineteenth century lawyers would have maintained, as did Sir Edward Clarke, that there was no apparent reason why any law book or document more than forty years old should be preserved. Nevertheless, much that passed for legal history was uncritical. Preoccupation with statement of the rule was rarely balanced by scientific inquiry into the contemporary circumstances that had brought it about; above all, too often anachronisms were perpetrated and comparatively modern concepts imposed where they did not belong, on the law of an earlier age. Nor had the promising start made by the seventeenth-century antiquaries towards the exploitation of the public records been effectively developed, despite the work of the Record Commission. As late as 1888 Maitland wrote to M. M. Bigelow of the Boston University School of Law, "I can't tell why it is, but certainly you seem to care a deal more for legal history on your bank of the Atlantic than we do here. It is a malarrangement of the universe which puts the records in one continent and those who would care to read them in another." And even in America this interest was only recent.

The means by which Maitland remedied the inadequacies of the older legal history, and indeed revolutionized the study of the subject, are discussed in detail elsewhere in [*Maitland: A Critical Examination and Assessment*]. In the present context, however, it is well to emphasize two characteristics of his historical writing about law—widely different from each other, but both probably deriving from his early philosophical training. The first is his constantly repeated effort to penetrate to the inner meaning of the words used in his sources; the second is his eye for the great central concepts of the common law in different phases of its development.

With regard to the former, Professor R. L. Schuyler is right to entitle one section of his recent little Maitland Reader "The Meaning of Words", for, as he claims in his introduction, Maitland was a pioneer in historical semantics. This is not, of course, to suggest that he used the technical vocabulary of semantics (he had technical terms enough, of another sort, on his hands); on the contrary, his approach to word study was simple, sometimes it seems almost light-hearted. Frequently his way into the meaning of a word was through some significant surviving

modern use of it. Thus, seeking to explain the term *sake* in the phrase *sake and soke,* he said—"It is still in use among us, for though we do not speak of a sake between two persons, we do speak of a man acting for another's sake, or for God's sake, or for the sake of money." Nor was his approach to the all-important *seisin* different. "To this day", he reminded his readers, "we call the person who takes possession of land without having title to it a 'mere squatter'; we speak of 'the sitting tenant', and such a phrase as 'a country seat' puts us at the right point of view." Or yet again, dealing with the *borh,* "the term *borrow*", he pointed out, "tells us of a time when men rarely, if ever, lent without receiving sufficient *borh*". Yet no man was more clearly aware than Maitland of the changing meaning of the same word throughout the centuries, and he took infinite pains to establish the right meaning in a particular context, stressing especially the confusion that might arise when the same word was used in both a general and a severely technical way.

As for his interest in the great concepts of the law, which brought him into the field of jurisprudence, one outstanding example will suffice—his preoccupation with "juristic persons", the trust and the corporation. As early as 1890 he wrote to Pollock about this—"for six weeks past I have had 'juristic persons' on my mind, have been grubbing for the English evidence and reading the Germans, in particular Gierke's great book". His studies on this topic informed much of what Maitland wrote on the borough; they led to his translation of Gierke's **Political Theories of the Middle Ages** in 1900, and in the years just after the turn of the century to a notable series of original papers. At one stage he proposed "Hic jacet persona ficta" for his own epitaph. Much of Maitland's most subtle scholarship was turned on to this work: as W. W. Buckland claimed, he was "at his best where law and philosophy meet".

For the common law, on the history of which he had spent so much of his effort, Maitland came to have an admiration that was akin to love. About its achievements he wrote, on occasion, moving prose that stands as literature in its own right. "High technique", he wrote in the introduction to his first Year Book, "is admirable whenever and wherever it is seen"—and he had the subtlety of mind to appreciate, as well as the literary skill to celebrate, that technique. Sir Charles Ogilvie, indeed, accuses him of admiring it too much—to the detriment of equity's share in justice and the belittling of civil-law procedure. Yet Maitland maintained a critical awareness of those points at which the common law was, or rather became, confused and inadequate. His first published article was a forthright demand for reform of real property law. In this paper, which appeared in the *Westminster Review* in 1879, he showed that he had no liking for medieval survivals for their own sake. "We have never fairly cleared up that great medieval muddle which passes under the name of feudalism," he wrote twenty years later, "and until that be done, English Law cannot be stated in terms that would befit the modern code of a self-respecting nation." Or again, copyhold tenure got short shrift from him. "The tenure still exists", he warned his law students, "a horrible nuisance as you will learn at large some day." Nor did he readily submit to the tyranny of authority: he was especially, and repeatedly, critical of the great Sir Edward Coke.

Returning to Maitland's significance for other sorts of history than the purely legal, we may make a negative point, which is that he was not a narrative historian. That his interests and inclinations leant towards a different sort of history is clear from the occasional comments he made on historians in the course of his correspondence. Gardiner he found hard to enjoy, and in a letter to Fisher right at the end of his life, "Oman", he said, "writes well but his is not the sort of history that I care for". He himself had been asked to do the 1066-1215 volume in Longmans' *History of England,* but he had not accepted the invitation. Only once amongst all his writings did he turn to narrative history—in his chapter on the Anglican Settlement and the Scottish Reformation in the *Cambridge Modern History.* Where his talent really lay was in a sort of descriptive analysis, characterized by a concreteness that led A. L. Smith to compare him to Macaulay. More light-heartedly (and perhaps Maitland would have preferred it that way), his friend Leslie Stephen said that he sometimes feared Maitland had got permanently into the wrong century.

Because he asked the right questions, Maitland greatly stimulated further study—not merely in general terms but along lines that he himself has specifically suggested. He did not, like his German professorial contemporaries, surround himself with research pupils, each with his assigned task within a framework of the professor's devising.

—H. E. Bell

Connected with his analytical power was his remarkable ability for formulating an historical issue or, in simpler terms, for asking the right questions. This Maitland regarded as one of the most important of the historian's functions: for instance, at the outset of **Domesday Book and Beyond** he said "some of the legal problems that are raised by it [Domesday Book], especially those which concern the time of King Edward, have hardly been stated, much less solved. It is with some hope of stating, with little hope of solving them that we begin this essay. If only we can ask the right questions we shall have done something for a good end." Because he asked the right questions, Maitland greatly stimulated further study—not merely in general terms but along lines that he himself has specifically suggested. He did not, like his German professorial contemporaries, surround himself with research pupils, each with his assigned task within a framework of the professor's devising. He did not even, as his friend Vinogradoff was later to do in Oxford, develop the seminar system—though perhaps what the seminar was for Vinogradoff the Selden Society was for Maitland. Where Maitland's influence really lay, however, and indeed where it

still lies, is through his books and the pointers to further investigation that they contain. This matter is particularly worthy of stress, because the later chapters of the present book will often concern theses of Maitland's that subsequent scholarship has caused to be abandoned and overturned. It is important not to leave the impression that this derogates from his greatness: on the contrary, it represents precisely the sort of progress in scientific historical inquiry that he envisaged and that his own work stimulated.

To reinforce what has been said about this aspect of Maitland's influence, it is worth while to give some examples of his pointing the path taken by subsequent scholars. It would not be unfair, for instance, to term Professor M. M. Postan's distinguished paper on the Chronology of Labour Services as, in some sort, a gloss on Maitland's sentence in **Domesday Book and Beyond,** "We dare not represent the stream of economic history as flowing uninterruptedly from a system of labour services to a system of rents." Or again, in a footnote to the same book, Maitland commented that the anatomy of Domesday Book deserved examination by an expert: that was precisely what happened in 1953, and the findings of the experts who made the anatomical examination are reported in the official publication *Domesday Re-Bound.* Thirdly, Maitland's expressed wish that the broad features of Domesday Book should be set out in a series of statistical tables is in process of realization in Professor H. C. Darby's Domesday geography studies. So far our examples have been taken from **Domesday Book and Beyond,** but Maitland's other great books, and especially the **History of English Law,** supply comparable pointers that have been followed to advantage by half a century's historians. Such is his recognition of the lack of a separate concept of public law in medieval times, underlined and brilliantly illustrated by Professor T. F. T. Plucknett. Because of the persistent influence that he has enjoyed in this sort of way, a study of Maitland brings us into contact with much of the most vital recent work on medieval English history.

So far we have not considered Maitland's literary presentation of his work, and yet as a characteristic of his achievement it was important. The fact that he not merely said good things, but said good things well, no doubt increased his influence on those who studied his writings. He never minimized difficulties or sought to oversimplify or to overclarify where some confusion was implicit in his sources. Only he tried, and rarely failed, to make what he was writing about sound interesting. His lucid, urbane style helped, and so did his wit. Of the high seriousness of his attitude there can be no doubt, and it would be a travesty to represent him as a joker. He was, however, the least pompous of men, with, as has been said, nothing of the *régent parcheminé* about him. Each of his readers is entitled to his own private anthology of Maitland's witticisms: first place in my anthology of them would be filled by his description of the feudal system being introduced into England by Sir Henry Spelman and Sir Martin Wright, and a close second what he had to say about the School of Pythagoras and that odd little triangle of ground behind St John's College, Cambridge, until recently owned by Merton College, Oxford, "endowed by its founder, by Walter Merton himself, with strips that he had purchased for reasons that I dare not guess". Or again, in **Township and Borough** there is his charming distinction between *villa* and *villata*—"Whatever else Oxford may be, it is a *villa,* a town; and whatever else the community of Oxford may be, it is a *villata,* a township. A township should no more mean a little town than a fellowship should mean a little fellow!" In only one connection did Maitland perhaps overelaborate his witticisms—when they took the form of pseudo-pleadings or other semi-humorous adaptations of medieval common form.

Maitland's translations, too, were sometimes extremely witty. He rendered William of Drogheda's *cautelae* as "tips", "wrinkles", "dodges". *Ivit domum pedibus et manibus* he translated "went home on all fours". To the sentence in a deposition *Et dicit quod quidam parvus nuntius Willelmi Marescalli cum butonibus venit, etc.,* he appended the succinct footnote "Can this be an early appearance of the boy in buttons?"

Reference to his translations serves to recall how very much of Maitland's working time was spent in editing records and other manuscripts. The techniques that he developed in that connection were marked by great common sense and a total absence of *mystik* and expertise for its own sake. At the outset of his career he had himself sat down, without paleographical knowledge, and puzzled out his Gloucester roll of 1221, and he believed that others could do the same. He repeatedly made light of the difficulty of reading legal manuscripts—"anyone who knows some law and some Latin will find that the difficulty disappears in a few weeks". He used to contend that in sixty hours spent over facsimiles he could turn out a man who would be able to read medieval documents with fluency and exactitude. This recalls Stubbs's impatience with those who pleaded difficulty in reading charters—"Five minutes", he asserted with some exaggeration, "would suffice for mastering the writing if you would only take the trouble to apply your minds to it." In these days of readerships in palatography and of university diplomas in archives it is well to remember the common-sense contentions of these great practitioners.

Similarly, when it came to the presentation of documents in print, Maitland's attitude was eminently sensible. In his introductions to the various texts he edited he took care to make clear the way in which he had worked. For instance, in the introduction to his first Year Book, "we shall, by the use of brackets," he wrote, "try to give the reader a fair opportunity of judging how defective is the editor's knowledge of old French and old law", or, more succinctly, "Fidelity with a leaning to correctness should be our aim." In adopting the method of extending medieval abbreviations he followed the preference of the old antiquaries Selden and Madox, and rejected the use of special record type with which the Record Commission had experimented. "An appetite for abbreviated documents may come in time", he said in the introductory volume to **Bracton's Note Book**. "Even record type may be pronounced unsatisfying; readers will not be content until they can see the very upstrokes and downstrokes reproduced by photography; but to suppose that such an appetite exists at the present day, would be a foolish dream; to

provide food for it, would be waste of money." About the same date, too, he wrote along similar lines to Maxwell Lyte in connection with the scheme that had been mooted for republication of the old printed Year Books.

Such, in general terms, were the principal characteristics of Maitland's work.

G. R. Elton   (essay date 1985)

SOURCE: "The Historian," in *F. W. Maitland,* Yale University Press, 1985, pp. 19-55.

[*In the following excerpt, Elton outlines Maitland's approach to writing history.*]

In Maitland's day historians, especially English historians, virtually never reflected on their activities. Most of them wrote history—or failed to commit their knowledge to paper—because they enjoyed doing so, and they did not feel called upon to philosophize about it; at most they would stake claims for the role their calling played in the formation of public men. Philosophers accepted the triumph of historical studies which had followed in the wake of the renewal of the methods of enquiry that in the course of the nineteenth century had spread from Germany to all of Europe. Sprung from the rise of romanticism and nationalism which had originated in the later eighteenth century, the dominance of historical studies as the best way to understand humanity was later reinforced by Darwinian theories of evolution which seemed to demonstrate that all creation rested on historical principles. True, other social studies were beginning to make themselves felt. Anthropology directed the influential, though in the end misleading, work of Sir Henry Maine, and theoretical sociology, operating by analysis of the present without much regard for roots and antecedents, began to make itself felt through such writers as Auguste Comte and Herbert Spencer. Nor was there much debate about methods in that positivist age: diligent reading of the sources, assisted by a conventional view of human nature (Freud had still to cast his baleful shadow) and plain common sense, was mostly regarded as adequate. Some historians went to the archives, as James Anthony Froude did; such others as Edward Augustus Freeman made do with what was in print. Guides to the student, full of the distillation of experience and over-methodizing everything, appeared in German and French, but not in English. The ideal goal was generally held to be the large, mainly narrative, description of a segment of time, of the past of a nation, or of such an institution as the papacy. William Stubbs, Regius professor at Oxford and afterwards bishop there, received special admiration because after years of labour devoted to the editing of chronicles he triumphantly produced his three volumes of the *Constitutional History of England* (1874-8). Stubbs drew his line at 1485, and indeed professionally respected history tended to be medieval. The search for origins, so powerful a stimulus to the historical studies of the seventeenth century, had revived in an age which regarded Victorian England as the outstanding culmination of a long development in human government, power and civilization.

Maitland distrusted generalizations, or rather the glibness

with which large generalizations were made, and if he never wrote the 'great book' in the manner of Stubbs or Froude it was because he saw no point in doing so until historians had gone much more deeply into the sources. It is notable that this admirer of the German historians never pronounced the conventional encomium on Ranke which one finds scattered through much comment at the time; perhaps more surprisingly, he seems never to have encountered Jakob Burckhardt whose interest in the general history of civilization rather than politics he shared. Most of his asides on history reveal only his genuine modesty about himself. He thought that he lacked the ability to write great books of the conventional kind, a performance he was content to leave to others. He expressed sincere admiration for Stubbs's achievement, even though he knew well enough that he was engaged in destroying many of the foundations of that Tory scholar's whiggish synthesis. And in spite of his philosophical training he rarely put thoughts on his concept of history on paper.

Only in his inaugural lecture, **'Why the History of English Law Remains Unwritten',** did he come close to a statement of his credo. He explained the absence of a history of the law in part by means of the isolated position occupied by lawyers: they who, unlike other scholars, could understand and use the materials were not interested in using them historically and never looked around at other forms of intellectual enterprise. Yet 'history involves comparison': the closed exploration of a single system cannot produce history. This is very true: much history always was and continues to be hampered by such isolation, and one of the chief virtues of historical studies lies in the breakdown of unconscious assumptions when they come up against alternative circumstances and convictions. Much of the impact of Maitland's work stood linked to his knowledge of the legal history of other countries. Furthermore, to him historical enquiry demanded the subversion of what had been said before: 'An orthodox history seems to me a contradiction in terms . . . If we try to make history the handmaid of dogma she will soon cease to be history.' Another very true observation which a great many modern historians would do well to heed.

Such views arise in part from a naturally sceptical temperament (essential to the good historian) which questions everything until genuine proof is proffered, but in Maitland this inclination received reinforcement from his never ceasing awareness of the vast reservoir of historical materials that remained unexplored. Piled up in the archives, so far unread and even more commonly unedited, he saw the deposits of men's experience and deeds—not just the letters which most historians knew about but records legal, financial, economic, of men's thoughts: how could anyone understand an age without their use? How could one continue to write history out of chronicles, aided only by a few samples of those archives that happened to have been put into print? His understanding of the historian's labours was dominated by his awareness of those mountains of writs, rolls, accounts and so forth stored (mostly) at the Public Record Office, all waiting to be read and analysed. 'Hoarded wealth,' as he told his audience, which enjoyed the lecture but had no idea what the professor was

talking about, 'yields no interest.' He wished that wealth to be put in circulation.

The interest, he knew well enough, would not materialize in constitutional histories (Stubbs) or narrative accounts of the Tudor age (Froude): 'Perhaps,' he cried out, 'there are countries in which the writing of historical monographs has become a nuisance; but surely it is better to have too many than none at all.' When he said this there existed almost no monographs written by Englishmen about the history of their law and government; such work as had been done came from Germany and the United States. A year later, introducing a very learned account of **'The Materials for English Legal History',** he recorded the words of 'a distinguished English lawyer' who was prepared to leave the writing of a history of English law to 'some of the antiquarian scholars of Germany and America' since Englishmen would lack 'the patience and learning to attempt it'. Gentlemen at most write pretty little essays; they leave it to dull foreigners to get their hands dirty in the dust of the archives. As usual Maitland was too courteous to express the contempt for such attitudes which he clearly felt and which helped to fuel those twenty-odd years of feverish work on the sources.

One other remark in that inaugural lecture deserves attention here. Aware that one of the obstacles to good legal history lay in the lawyer's necessary preoccupation with the current meaning of the law, he stated 'that a thorough training in modern law is almost indispensable for anyone who wishes to do good work on legal history'. That was probably truer in his day than it has since become; the many reforms of the last hundred years have terminated so much of the old law that present-day lawyers tend to be more bewildered by what they encounter in the middle ages or the sixteenth century than assisted by their legal expertise. But Maitland's reason was specific: the legal historian would 'often have to work from the modern to the ancient, from the clear to the vague, from the known to the unknown'. That method he was to employ particularly in ***Domesday Book and Beyond,*** but it can be traced through a great deal of his work. It has its dangers; it can harden the teleological attitudes and manners of reflection habitual with lawyers; we shall see that Maitland did not always escape them. But he was right in thinking this way of proceeding frequently unavoidable as well as highly illuminating.

As Maitland always insisted, in the middle ages the materials of history were mainly the materials of the law; to him the history of the law constituted a preliminary step towards the history of medieval people in general. The accident of his training and the nature of the sources that captivated him thus took him into what some have called the narrow limits of legal history. The vast bulk (though by no means all of it) of medieval historical material is indeed the product of the law and its courts. Maitland, however, understood what has not always been grasped so clearly since, namely that those records enshrine the lives of individuals and communities in all sorts of aspects— that properly understood they could be used to recover the real fullness of those lives. A short passage in his inaugural lecture in a way constitutes his own programme of work which even for the middle ages, not to mention later sectors of English history, remains uncompleted:

> Think for a moment what lies concealed within the hard rind of legal history. Legal documents, documents of the most technical kind, are the best, often the only evidence we have for social and economic history, for the history of morality, for the history of practical religion. Take a broad subject—the condition of the great mass of Englishmen in the later middle ages, the condition of the villagers. That might be pictured for us in all truthful detail; its political, social, economic, moral aspects might all be brought out; every tendency of progress or degradation might be traced; our supply of evidence is inexhaustible: but no one will extract its meaning who has not the patience to master an extremely formal system of pleading and procedure, who is not familiar with a whole scheme of actions with repulsive names. There are large and fertile tracts of history which the historian as a rule has to avoid because they are too legal.

The first part of this pronouncement—wise as well as exacting—has quite often been heeded by scholars who thought the second needlessly persnickety; very few have brought to the use of legal records in the search for history other than legal that understanding of the law which alone unlocks the records. Maitland did. Yet examples still abound of the errors lurking in wait for those who think that the materials of the law, especially when in print, can be understood by common sense; and those errors get aggravated when scholars commit the other sin condemned by Maitland—when history is made to serve dogma. Legal records are indeed a repository of knowledge stretching far beyond the reconstruction of the history of law, but they cannot well be used by the ignorant and innocent. However, as Maitland knew and said, that means only that the ignorant should learn, the innocent grow wise, not that the records should be left unstudied.

Thus Maitland in effect declared that in the first instance the historian must grasp the law that produced those records, which means the law of that day in its own right and operation. This comprehension determined his evident strategy: he needed to understand before he could write. In consequence, a great part of the corpus of his work consists of preparatory labours leading up to the coping stone of either a genuine synthesis or at least a powerful suggestion how the synthesis will come out. This is a manner of proceeding which only a man of his phenomenal speed and memory can afford to practise if those coping stones are ever to be reached. His astounding capacity for holding things in the mind also appears in his obedience to his own dictum that history calls for comparisons. Maitland not infrequently described himself as ignorant of other laws and other countries, and no doubt by the side of his knowledge of the common law his understanding of other systems looked pale. However, his work, and especially his footnotes, contradict these well-meant expressions of modesty. In his discussion, for instance, of **'The Early History of Malice Aforethought'**, an essay published as early as 1883, he showed himself well acquainted with the laws of Germany and France; a later

paper on the esoteric theme **'Possession for Year and Day'** displayed a special knowledge of the ancient laws of those countries. Evidence abounds of his enormously wide reading in several languages: there are a good few scholars of his day who would now be totally forgotten but for their appearance in his footnotes. The author of **Roman Canon Law in the Church of England** knew a great deal about that system, and although the book did not appear until 1898 it included essays written as early as 1886. Maitland knew enough of it—of its sources and its implications—to understand why the high-church men of his own day thought it wiser to cultivate their ignorance of it. As for the civil or Roman law, though he regularly professed himself to be but indifferently learned in it and certainly never acquired a full mastery, he knew its sources and could direct others to the right books: he knew it better than he thought or said. He no sooner made the acquaintance of a Scots lawyer than he eagerly enquired after the old law of that country. No man more diligently struggled to avoid the insularity of the common law; much of the enduring strength of his learning derives from his well-instructed ability to see the history of that law three-dimensionally in a world which held those other laws as well.

The mainstay of that strength, however, lay in his determination really to understand his sources—their contents and their limitations. Though he never explained his working methods they jump from the page as one reviews his labours. London was in his day probably a little more accessible from Cambridge than it is now, but even so there were problems of distance and travel, especially in a busy term time. But Maitland spent a great many hours—sometimes any spare moment he could snatch from other engagements in the capital—at the Public Record Office; quite manifestly, as casual remarks show, he saw a very wide range of manuscripts from feet of fines and plea rolls to letters patent and state papers, some of which never got used in his writings. He had an advantage over the present day: at that time the P.R.O. attracted few people and produced documents at enviable speed. True, the two fat volumes of **The History of English Law** appear to rest entirely on records in print (listed at the start in three and a half crowded pages), but—apart from the fact that a knowledge of unprinted and uncited manuscripts lay behind much that was said—quoting only print was made possible in great part by his own previous editorial labours—especially **Bracton's Note-Book, Memoranda de Parliamento,** and several Selden Society volumes. His edition of the **Note-Book**—identified by him as the collection of cases on which the author of that famous thirteenth-century treatise rested his description of the law of England—constituted his major breakthrough to an understanding of the treatise itself; and this remains crucial even if we have to think him mistaken, as shortly we shall see he was, about both Bracton and the *Note-Book*. What matters here is the manner of working—from the sources, through preliminary labours to the great work. Maitland's lesser writings frequently combine the character of research programmes with the preliminary sorting out of problems; and one reason for his long influence lies in the fact that he himself was not given the time to follow up all the lines he opened.

**Maitland's lesser writings frequently
combine the character of research
programmes with the preliminary sorting
out of problems; and one reason for his
long influence lies in the fact that he
himself was not given the time to follow
up all the lines he opened.**

—G. R. Elton

The story of Maitland's long love affair with the Year Books is instructive. Like every other lawyer with an interest in history, he knew, of course, about these collections of cases put together annually from about the reign of Edward I onwards. That is to say, he was familiar with the mainly pretty poor editions in black-letter, published in the sixteenth century. He revelled in their immediacy and reality—the record of arguments and discussion in court, of *obiter dicta* and jokes and (rarely) grounds given for decisions. He also knew their serious shortcomings—texts often corrupted and contents quite insufficiently explained. Then on Wednesday, 21 April 1886, he was approached by Henry Maxwell Lyte (deputy keeper of the public records, then the title of the head of the P.R.O.) with the suggestion that the Year Books needed a modern edition. This would in fact appear to have been the first personal contact between the two men. By Saturday Maitland had thought the problem through to the point of being able to submit a full-scale programme of editing and publication, a programme which he then found himself committed to initiating in person. The surviving volumes for Edward I had already been edited, very poorly, for the Rolls Series (1866-79), while an encouraging start had been made in the same series on the reign of Edward III. Maitland therefore proposed to tackle the extensive collection for Edward II. He asked to be allowed to wait until he had finished *Bracton's Note-Book,* but in fact a great many other engagements intervened before, in 1903, he was able to produce his first Year Book edition. However, when at last he found time for the task he not only produced a model edition but prefaced it with another of those preparatory exercises he knew to be essential to a true understanding: he reconstructed at length the grammar and vocabulary of the medieval Law-French in which the Books were written. Since the use of this specialized jargon had been abolished by statute in 1731, understanding of it had become a lost art: only Maitland's remarkable excursus into philology made the proper use of those invaluable materials possible.

In his introduction the editor further settled the real character of the Year Books (a point he himself had still been uncertain about even two years earlier): he showed them to have been students' compilations made from notes in court, and not, as had been supposed on ancient authority, semi-official collections of cases made for the use of judges and counsel. At the same time he set out the arguments for their use by historians in ways that have become clas-

sic. Here, as he told us, we find the living language and practice of the law—a guide not only to the law but to the very life of the nation. I think myself that, though he was on the right lines, his enthusiasm exaggerated the profit likely to be got from that source: it does tell us more about law than about life. Even so, Maitland's enthusiasm helps to explain why he never continued writing the history of English law beyond the reign of Edward I. No one was more convinced than he that this could not be done until the Year Book material had been properly digested, which meant first properly edited. It added a whole new dimension to the sources available to the legal historian, enabling him to see the law in operation and not only as defined in edicts or collected in codes. He himself edited two more volumes in the three remaining years of his life, the last brought out after his death by G. J. Turner, whose combination of fine scholarship and indolence had often driven Maitland to distraction. For a while the Selden Society's Year Book series continued active, and from 1914 the Ames Foundation at Harvard joined in with editions for Richard II's reign. But the gaps remain enormous: twenty-three volumes now cover only the first twelve of Edward II's twenty regnal years, and we have only three volumes edited for Richard II's twenty-two, not to mention the bare sprinkling of volumes for the fifteenth century. The drive behind the editing of Year Books has slackened: it is widely held that a man can do more important work and earn a greater repute by less laborious exercises. Yet it is true that Maitland diagnosed their value pretty correctly and that they remain underused.

Thus equipped, Maitland tackled the task of writing real history. Reading the sources properly and solving their problems may seem so obvious a preparatory stage that it hardly deserves so much comment. It is nothing of the sort: great reputations have been made, both before Maitland's day and after, by men who fudged both the reading and the analysis of their sources; because Maitland was a medievalist, it has proved easier for this state of affairs to endure in the post-medieval period. The strength behind Maitland's astounding endurance lay in the fact that—instinctively, it seems, for he had no guide or model—he chose to work correctly. Another source of that strength, however, may be found in his careful restriction of his area of operations. Maitland wrote so much, nearly all of it of genuine importance, that one can forget his decision to limit himself in time. Not for him the writing of sixteen volumes covering all the history of English law from Anglo-Saxon times to 1875, which remarkable achievement Sir William Holdsworth produced solely out of printed materials. (It is said that he saved time by never taking a note but worked at his desk at All Souls, surrounded by terraces of books with marking slips in them.) Not for Maitland either the often slender and sometimes credulous foundation of evidence and interpretation employed by Holdsworth, whose great work has for years been as much an obstacle as an aid to the correct understanding of the themes he treated. Maitland was, in effect, content to be the historian of English law from the Conquest to the reign of Edward I—quite a sufficient era to study from the sources, in all conscience. Of course, he did extend his range on occasion—back into pre-Conquest England, or into the fifteenth century for the canon law, or less successfully into the supposed Renaissance of the sixteenth—but in the main he stayed with the ages of Glanvill and Bracton which it was his achievement to show forth as the formative and decisive era in the history of the common law.

There was another limitation in his method which assisted the concrete definition and solidity of his work but does not seem to have been noticed before. Though many of his essays, particularly the earlier ones before he fully realized the nature of his sources, ranged across stretches of time and varieties of materials, his great books took their origin from concentration on one particular source, usually an ancient treatise. The method recalls the principle of the old 'readings' at the Inns of Court for which the lecturer chose a single statute and built up his exposition of the law by tracking developments upon one section after another through the subsequent case-law. *The History of English Law* ('Pollock and Maitland') took its origin from a study of the treatise ascribed to Henry de Bracton; it is not without significance that the section on pre-Norman England was Pollock's sole contribution. *Domesday Book and Beyond* announces the principle in its title: an analysis of Domesday Book was used to extrapolate law and society backwards, from (as Maitland had advised in his inaugural lecture) the known to the unknown. The treatise on the canon law contained, as already mentioned, a collection of essays on various aspects of the subject, but its core consisted of a study of William Lyndwood's fifteenth-century *Provinciale*. In his Ford lectures at Oxford, *Township and Borough,* the single book was replaced by the single town, and a pretty small one at that: he used medieval Cambridge to recreate the realities of medieval urban and rural conditions. It may be doubted whether any other great historian ever so regularly received inspiration from a restricted and restricting source, only to burst out of it by pursuing the suggestions he found there into a whole range of sources and problems. The method helps to explain Maitland's astonishing productivity. Concentrate a well-stocked mind upon a single compilation, apply to it the kind of precise reasoning and concrete imagination Maitland possessed, and useful, even powerful, results will come forth far more rapidly than they do to the historian who reads a whole body of source materials with a mind to finding out what actually happened. Both are thorough, but one starts from inspiration and the other from perspiration—not a new crack, I know, but distinctly apposite here. Maitland's ability to discern patterns of existence and development—that skill with which he rapidly ordered an inchoate mass of details, and which has convincingly been linked to his training as a lawyer—owed a great deal to his habit of working outwards from a central source.

Maitland's skill in producing a convincing shape of the past is the more remarkable because he in effect avoided the most common and most traditional of expository schemes. He wrote no, or almost no, narrative, and he regarded himself as incapable of telling a story in the usual manner. When during the planning of *The History of English Law* Pollock tried to persuade him to write a short outline history of that law at least covering the middle ages, Maitland retorted with an explanation of his approach to the writing of history. He himself, he said, could not forget the many problems which ignorance placed in the way of the treatment proposed: he needed to analyse and dispose of them first. But he encouraged Pollock to go ahead and write 'a famous book'. He could not pass over complex issues 'in a few brief paragraphs—if I am to write about it I can not but write at length.' 'I quite see that a brief history of English law is much wanted and might be written, but I also see that I can not write it.' He did actually change his mind sufficiently to produce eighty pages of such 'Outlines of English Legal History, 560-1600' for a once famous collection of essays on English social history. Its author, were he not known, is unmistakable on every page, but the sum total leaves a good deal to be desired. Episodic and epigrammatical, it solves far fewer of the problems along the road than it seems to think, and once Maitland leaves his familiar stamping ground to look at the fifteenth and sixteenth centuries he loses most of his sovereignty. His accounts, for instance, of Parliament and Star Chamber, though they contain some of his typical flashes of insight, are really caricatures. This happened because here Maitland was of necessity forced to rely on other people's views which he had not had the time to test against the sources: where he happens to know some piece of evidence properly he at once corrects vulgar error, but this happens rarely in that gallant, and misconceived, survey.

Analysis, not narrative, constituted Maitland's organizing principle for the writing of history.

—G. R. Elton

Thus analysis, not narrative, constituted Maitland's organizing principle for the writing of history. His admiration for Stubbs, he said, grew every day, and with that model of the long narrative before him he felt quite unable to think of emulating it. He really did not believe that he could write continuous narrative. Now in a way this is absurd: no one could tell a story better than Maitland, as his daughter (among others) testified. *The History of English Law* teems with brief tales that transform abstract analysis into the living experience of real people. Take just one example, the explanation of the survival in Kent of the peculiar custom known as gavelkind (partible inheritance among male heirs). Where others might have laboriously set out the law of this exception to the rule and perhaps speculated about the endurance of ancient custom, Maitland in two pages written in the present tense brings the men of Kent—tenants as well as lords—vividly before us in what is in effect a tale of their dealings with one another, and by the end we understand why gavelkind survived there at a time when primogeniture was sweeping the board everywhere else. Thus if Maitland really believed himself to be incapable of narrative history he was wrong; it was his purpose—his determination to understand and explain before he told—not his deficiencies that pointed the way to essentially analytical techniques. His disavowals should perhaps be read in the context of his time. While narrative nowadays ranks rather low in the estimation of professional historians, in the age of Stubbs and Froude, of Freeman and Gardiner the notion that real historians tell great (and lengthy) stories still prevailed. This was not the only aspect of professional history in which Maitland proved himself to be the first of the moderns.

Maitland's method has its dangers which shall be discussed in a moment. But in the first place it made Maitland into the enduring writer of history that he became. The history he wrote concerned itself with highly technical issues and used materials and terms of art that are not accessible to the general reader; indeed, too few historians have bothered to master them since. In Maitland's hands they created lasting orthodoxies. The age of Henry II as the foundation era of settled government and the common law; the age of Bracton as the era of codification and consolidation, as English custom underwent scrutiny by eyes trained in the law of Rome; the lore of the forms of action as the essence of medieval jurisprudence; the analysis of society in terms of tenures; the discovery of Anglo-Saxon social and economic arrangements by working backwards from 1086; the medieval Parliament as a court rather than a political assembly; the dominance of papal law in the English church down to the Reformation; the vital significance of the Year Books—all these and many more commonplaces of our understanding of the English middle ages were created in Maitland's two decades of almost feverish activity. A hundred years of teaching have anchored them in concrete so well set that every effort of doubt or modification calls for dynamite.

Once Maitland had found his vocation he treated it as a solemn duty which, being the most unsolemn of men, he somewhat shamefacedly admitted he enjoyed enormously. When he assured the editors of a technical collection of legal cases that they had given him hours of unalloyed pleasure, we believe him literally where with anyone else we might suspect hypocrisy; his book on the canon law, he said, brought him more fun than 'any other job I ever did'. In fact, that he enjoyed himself all the time both researching and writing springs from just about every page he wrote. This is among historians by no means a common experience, even among the active sector of the profession; far more of them will recognize the truth of A. F. Pollard's remark about 'the toil of producing research which it is only a pleasure to pursue'. Maitland enjoyed both the seeking of the truth—in materials immensely more difficult and indeed repellent than Pollard, careful avoider of manuscripts, ever studied—and the telling of it.

A striking irony lies embedded in Maitland's long ascendancy over the territory which he not only made his own but also persuaded others to regard as the central region of medieval history. The man who declared that an orthodox history was a contradiction in terms created despite himself an orthodoxy so enduring that even his latter-day critics speak as though in the presence of a god whose wrath might still strike them down. We have no English historian before him whose work is still treated as though

it was the latest, even the last, word, and among his immediate successors only T. F. Tout and a little later Sir Frank Stenton are still read for the serious, by now much criticized, content of their books. Sir Charles Firth, A. F. Pollard, Sir Maurice Powicke, Sir Lewis Namier, Sir John Neale (knighthoods came to historians after Maitland's day), all great names once and still respected for what once they did: but no one refers to them as though despite their tiresome departure to the grave they were living colleagues and fellow-workers. That is how we treat Maitland. Some on that list—especially the last two—actually wished to create orthodoxies and enduring truths. They failed where Maitland, modestly unconvinced that final answers are possible for historians, became an oracle whose sayings, it seems, do enshrine such impossible truths. Why?

Some points are obvious but also rather superficial. There is the manifest fact that Maitland knew what he was talking about, had done a vast deal of work, and seemed always able to distinguish speculation from certainty. Criticizing Maitland has in part proved so difficult because of the caution with which he formulated his answers, a caution not at first apparent in the transparent lucidity of his style. However, there were two very special reasons which assisted in the prolonged survival of his work. In his own line, he has never until very recently had numerous successors, able to take up his questions and his sources, and able to develop his themes beyond the point to which he had taken them. And secondly, he wrote better than any serious historian of England has ever done, before or since his time. It is virtually impossible to be bored by Maitland even at his most technical, and seeing how very boring even good historians can be this gives him a remarkable advantage. Without any intention of playing the advocate, he insensibly persuades, even enslaves, by the beauty of his style. These two points need a little more analysis.

Why have there been so few historians of the law—real historians of quality, I mean? For a time it seemed as though only one of rank was to be permitted to every generation, the staff passing, after an interval, from Maitland to Theodore Plucknett (*difficilis descensus . . . ?*) and then to Samuel Thorne, though of late the great revival of legal history has at last picked up the message and inspiration of Maitland. This has led to a major extension of the territory covered by sound legal history and almost inevitably has brought with it the discovery that even Maitland needs revising, at the periphery and in the centre. By real historians of the law I mean scholars who can satisfy both historians and lawyers that they understand their themes. Maitland's inaugural lecture proves that he knew the fundamental problem well enough. Practitioners and historians concern themselves with the same body of materials, but in it they seek totally different things.

> A lawyer finds on his table a case about rights of common which sends him to the Statute of Merton. But is it really the law of 1236 he wants to know? No, it is the ultimate result of the interpretations set on the statute by the judges of twenty generations . . . What the lawyer wants is authority and the newer the better; what the

historian wants is evidence and the older the better.

No two breeds of learned men differ more widely in their acquired mental characteristics, and the accident that they operate on the same sources disguises the essential irreconcilability of their concerns. I have always found it much easier to understand the thought processes of physicists or biologists, analysing their problems empirically, than those of lawyers seeking guidance for present action from decisions and sayings whose very words have quite probably changed their meaning several times over the centuries. Their circumstances certainly have. The lawyers' teleological preoccupation, in which all things past have meaning only insofar as they can be shown to have led to a present use, beset English history for centuries: historians were led to believe that their task lay in explaining the present rather than the past.

The distance between minds that wish to know what seven centuries have made of the Statute of Merton, and those who wish to know what the makers of the statute thought they were doing, is so great as to be ordinarily unbridgable. Men who have an instinctive grasp of the law and its ways stand at the opposite end of the spectrum from men who have an instinctive grasp of the past and its ways. Yet, as Maitland understood and demonstrated, the medieval past and its ways have mainly to be reconstructed from sources produced by the law and its operation. Small wonder that a true historian who can cope with the law of the past is a rare thing, even though I could now name a dozen who have really learned to tie the ends of the spectrum together; small wonder that an exceptional historian like Maitland, who to the uncommon double skill added wonderful gifts as a scholar and writer, found himself elevated to a plinth on which the word *veritas* was engraven by generations of admirers.

As for Maitland's style, much has been written about it, most of it true. It combines earnestness and wit, charm and sinew, in a manner so personal that any attempt to learn from it would be idiocy. We are often warned not to imitate Maitland, and no one has ever seriously tried to do so, but it has to be confessed that a solid diet of reading Maitland does have its effects. All of a sudden one finds oneself using the first person plural (one of Maitland's most obtrusive hallmarks), starting sentences with 'Now, . . .', introducing concrete metaphors by way of explanation. Maitland, in his innocence, works insidiously. Yet resistance is very necessary; more than most historians, Maitland testifies to the truth that the style is the man. Those usually short, often vibrating, sentences, the avoidance of learned circumlocutions and even long words as such; the manner in which the royal 'we' gathers the reader into the company of the writer; the constant illumination of abstract or general notions by anchoring them in the experience of real people; the frequent (possibly unconscious) echoes from a whole cultural reservoir filled with, among other things, the Bible; the wit which, because it grows naturally from the discourse, remains funny to this day; and the courtesy which renders the not infrequent stabs of the stiletto painless: all these compass Maitland the man, a man both wise and artless. It seems that Maitland was in no sense a conscious stylist, a careful and

particular carpenter of words and architect of sentences: nobody who wrote so much so fast could have been. True, he wrote even his lectures out in full and practised them before delivery, a delivery which depended upon the presence of a script. This might argue against spontaneity and for painful labour, but the conclusion would be false. Indeed, it is rather that Maitland's manner of lecturing explains his style: whether speaking or writing, he was always talking to the reader as much as to a listener. It is because his written words bring the sound of his voice even to generations that could never hear him that he remains so alive, so immediate, so insidious a writer.

One genre of writing, rarely commented on in thinking about Maitland, will help to explain further. One of the duties of the learned is to review the work of others, and Maitland did a certain amount of this: not all that much because what in his wake was to become a flood of medieval monographs, in his own day was still but a trickle. Still, he wrote a number of notices all of which show the same characteristics: generous acknowledgment of the reviewed author's attainment, plain but courteous correction of error, and an elegant conciseness. Models of their kind, in a way, for reviews must neither evade the duty to advance the state of scholarship nor do so with savagery, but as a rule a bit anodyne. Once, however, Maitland removed the baffles. He was reviewing John Horace Round's *The Commune of London and Other Studies* (1899), and he felt obliged to speak out about that sinister, touchy and quarrelsome controversialist's manner and defects. The result was a unique piece of learning mixed with invective, the more devastating because it spoke quietly, with irony and a touch of condescension. It shows what Maitland could do when really roused. He took Round to task for never producing a real book but only collections of disparate papers, a habit which, Maitland said, gave grounds unhappily to those who thought that serious research stood in the way of writing history, and he topped this by citing Renan's remark that no one can be at one and the same time a good controversialist and a good historian. Then he cut loose. Round had made a nasty crack about a minor error of Kate Norgate's to the effect that 'one must not be severe on a lady's Latin'; finding a German name misspelt in the book before him did not, said Maitland, make him point out that the author's 'acquaintance with the German tongue is but gentlemanly'. Round, still pursuing his endless feud with the long-dead Freeman, refered to a little *clique* of Oxford historians who had 'endeavoured, without scruple and with almost unconcealed anger, to silence me at any cost'; 'they must be simple folk down there at Oxford,' said Maitland, 'to think that Mr Round will ever be silent' about his own rightness and the wrongs committed by his adversaries. Round's whine that 'in England, at the present, there is neither inducement nor reward' for original research calls forth the retort that anyone writing in Round's antiquarian fashion must expect to remain unread by the general public: 'We know of no country in the world where there is any pressing demand for short studies of disconnected themes.' And on he went to dissect the book, mixing open admiration for its excellences with precise critique of its deficiencies. As Maitland should have expected, the review caused deep offence, and what had been a quite regular correspondence between the two eminent scholars came to an end. Maitland foresaw 'that I shall now have J.H.R. as an assailant for our joint lives'. But it is plain that he had no regrets. He abominated Round's manners, which he had had occasion to deplore before when Round had attacked the misfortunate Hubert Hall, a scholar who had invited the tiger-cat's assault by producing a far from perfect edition: 'If all that R. says is true, I still think that he is using language which should be reserved for cases of a different sort . . . Poor Hall has a fluffy mind but never scamps work, besides being (but this alas is irrelevant) the most unselfish man I have ever known.' Maitland evidently thought Round's behaviour intolerable in a fellow scholar, and when finally provoked said so. It was in fact virtually impossible to live in the same world as Round without causing him in the end to take offence: to him, the taking of offence was the elixir of life. He who had hitherto flattered Maitland 'absurdly' no doubt felt particularly shattered by an attack from that quarter, but I think that Maitland enjoyed the opportunity to execute justice on a persistent offender. I certainly hope he did.

In the last twenty years or so, a good deal of Maitland's work has at last been accorded the honour of proper criticism; at last his unwanted orthodoxy has gone, leaving behind his true achievement, to be assessed in the historian's manner which he wished to teach to others.

—G. R. Elton

Maitland's greatness and the elements that went to the making of it should thus not be doubted. However, it is no service to him to turn admiration into adulation. It was no service to his own convictions to set him up for orthodoxy and for decades to cite him as scripture. He never believed himself to be a god or even to be humanly perfect in his ways, and we should not evade the duty to say something about the weaknesses or errors that may—are bound to—accompany his transcendent skills. In the last twenty years or so, a good deal of his work has at last been accorded the honour of proper criticism; at last his unwanted orthodoxy has gone, leaving behind his true achievement, to be assessed in the historian's manner which he wished to teach to others.

There have before this been attempts to evaluate Maitland's work against revisions and departures since his day; they have been marked by a careful listing of changing views and all avoidance of the possible reasons why Maitland, so formidably persuasive in his judgments, might here or there have erred. They have also usually and rightly recognized that Maitland's habitual caution allowed him to qualify even very positive assertions in such a way as to prepare the road for his revisers. I shall confine myself to some major issues, taking it for granted that a century of research will bring with it some modifications here and there.

The 'garrison theory' of the origin of English boroughs (that they started as places fortified against Danish invaders), a theory he put forward in ***Domesday Book and Beyond*** as well as in ***Township and Borough,*** and which his disciples came to overwork, was criticized in a famous review by James Tait who then took some forty years to bring out his definitive, and very soporific, statement on the matter. Maitland, it is clear, underestimated the part which trade and merchants played in the rise of towns; he never proved himself more the lawyer than in his relative neglect of economic influences. Maitland's disparaging judgment of the law-book called *Fleta* (compiled early in the fourteenth century)—'an edition of Bracton much abridged and "brought up to date" by references to the earlier statutes of Edward I'—has been thoroughly overthrown by H. G. Richardson and G. O. Sayles (Maitland worshippers) in their edition of that work. Maitland's conviction that Domesday Book was what he called a 'geld-book'—a register of potential payers of the tax called danegeld—arose mainly from the state of Domesday studies in his day; it has been proved to be both wrong and seriously misleading. Errors of that kind, in themselves inevitable, do affect a historian's general interpretation both of the sources and of the history he gets from them, but they do not affect the greatness of Maitland's achievement over all, nor did those critics suppose that they did. Here I shall also omit a discussion of the one work which has been almost universally rejected—Maitland's Rede lecture on ***English Law and the Renaissance***. . . . But there remain three issues which seem to reach further and deserve a closer look: Maitland's teaching on writs and the forms of action; Maitland's assessment of Bracton; and Maitland's analysis of the law of the twelfth century.

Maitland in effect taught us that the system of writs by means of which actions were started constituted the essential structure of the medieval law. This interpretation seemed to be directly derived from the compendia produced at the time: both the commentators (Glanvill, Bracton and so forth) and the practitioners (in the so-called Register of Writs) built their analysis of the law around these forms of action. In this law of procedure Maitland identified the predominant jurisprudence of the middle ages; as he once said, the medieval law reversed the natural course of justice, for whereas justice demands that for every wrong there shall be a remedy, the middle ages held that where there is no remedy no wrong has been committed. If there is no writ appropriate to a complaint, the complainant can have no recourse to the law. It matters little that he was wrong to doubt the existence of an 'official' Register kept in the Chancery or did not give sufficient place to the history of the judicial writ before the age of Henry II: those are the normal details of disputable research. The former mistake stemmed from the fact that Maitland did not have as large a sample of versions of the Register at his disposal as did later scholars; the second from his excessive respect for Henry II and relative ignorance of both Anglo-Saxon England and pre-Conquest Normandy. In both instances, the correctors acknowledge his inspiration. They would also do well to admire his far-seeing caution: thus a page in *The History of English Law* leaves the door wide open for the sort of revision since carried out by R. van Caenegem.

Of far greater importance is the fact that Maitland ignored the plaint by bill, the bringing of an action not by original writ but by a form of petition in which the plaintiff could set out his grievance and pray for remedy. This, of course, made it possible for any alleged sufferer of a wrong to approach the king's court in search of justice, and indeed some of the forms of action owed their development to the provision of new remedies for wrongs raised by bill. Maitland knew this but the growing reluctance of Chancery to make new writs persuaded him to suppose that actions by bill disappeared from the courts and the common law not later than about the end of the fourteenth century as the Register of Writs settled into a final and immutable form; he held that in the later middle ages actions by bill belonged solely to the chancellor's court. This may be true of Common pleas but it is not true for the law at large. Not only was procedure by plaint freely used in the reign of Henry III; it remained available in the King's Bench to the end of the middle ages and beyond. Its willingness to hear plaintiffs by bill as well as by writ enabled that court to recover from the late-medieval slump in business that it experienced and to take over much litigation that earlier would have gone to other courts.

More surprising than this failure to remember the bill was Maitland's treatment of trespass. Here, too, his understanding of the Register obscured his vision. Trespass troubled medieval lawyers by not fitting too well into any of their established categories. Here was a civil remedy for wrongs not very different from the crimes pursuable at the crown's suit. Its peculiarities are well summed up in the fact that unlike other forms of action it could command an enforcement procedure which culminated in outlawry, a means otherwise reserved to pleas of the crown (felonies). The lawyers' inability to cope with trespass lay at the heart of the deplorable underdevelopment of the medieval criminal law. Maitland saw the writ bobbing about the Register like a homeless waif, now accommodated here and now farmed out there, and he thus called it an intruder still not properly at home in the law by the end of the sixteenth century. And he had virtually nothing to say about its offspring, trespass on the case, or simply case. Yet as a practitioner at the bar he must have been well aware that such actions as assumpsit (the basis of contract law) or trover (the basis of fraudulent conversion) stemmed from case, and he should have seen that in the fifteenth century case opened the law to new actions almost as freely as procedure by bill had done. In his lectures to students of the law he came very close to saying it all. But he failed to draw the inferences. By ignoring bills and playing down case, Maitland for generations convinced historians that the late-medieval common law had 'ossified', so that it needed action by new courts (Chancery, Star Chamber) as well as Parliament to supply litigants with chances of redress in much altered circumstances. As we shall see, he thus totally missed one of the most remarkable events in the history of the common law as it renewed itself from within in response to need. The fundamental cause of this mixture of error and blindness would seem to have lain in his trust in the Register of Writs as an authoritative and complete statement of the law.

The problem of Henry de Bracton, supposed author of the great treatise ascribed in Maitland's day to about the middle of the thirteenth century, is highly complex, and a brief summary must distort its subtleties. Bracton was central to Maitland's work: an inspiration and guide whose book he knew inside out. One of his greatest feats of historical research produced the three-volume edition of what he called *Bracton's Note-Book,* a collection of cases which he identified as Bracton's source-book for his treatise. The reconstruction seemed the more convincing because Maitland found some of the cases so collected marked for transcription on the plea rolls. Maitland also convinced himself that though the author of the treatise had some acquaintance with the law of Rome he was insufficiently learned in it to have used it for the systematizing of English law: thus the ordered and advanced state of the law described in Bracton implied a highly developed achievement for the native law of England. Of all this very little now stands. The destroyer has been one of Maitland's greatest admirers, Samuel E. Thorne of Harvard University, who gave twenty years of his life to a final edition and accurate translation of 'Bracton'. Thorne has demonstrated that the treatise as we have it did not come from one hand; several 'redactors' (whose existence Maitland had tentatively allowed for) had been at work on it and the text handed down to us was produced after the accession of Edward I in 1272 (Bracton died in 1268). Thorne has also shown it to be much more likely that the original work of collecting and collating was not done by the Henry of tradition but either by his master and teacher, William Ralegh, or by Ralegh's own revered mentor, Martin of Pateshull: a splendid trinity of leading judges in direct personal descent. The *Note-Book,* as Thorne shows, bears a far more distant relation to the contents of 'Bracton' than Maitland supposed, and the famous marginal notes on the plea rolls belong to many hands and possibly several centuries. Furthermore, and perhaps most to the detriment of the story as told by Maitland, Thorne has proved that those common-law judges knew the Roman *Code* very well, and that such order and system as they could manage to provide for the law of their own country derived from Rome. As for the law of England revealed in the treatise, it has turned out to lack system, to be often internally contradictory, and so to fall well short of the excellence discerned by Maitland. Some of that inadequacy, however, may well have been introduced by those later redactors who seem to have managed to muddle their predecessors' acquaintance with the Roman law as much as they introduced confusion into the law of England.

Now Thorne, who for some years after he published these formidable findings used to wear a button in his coat that read 'Bracton Lives', would be distressed if it were thought that he had in some way dethroned Maitland. On the contrary, his admiration for his predecessor remains undimmed, and he is more conscious than anyone of the care Maitland took to qualify his judgments when he knew he stood on shaky ground. Nevertheless, this recent history of Bracton's book amounts to more than ordinary revision in the course of advancing research. It is a major upheaval. We still await what may become of it all, but it looks to me as though much of the beautiful clarity of 'Pollock and Maitland', the apparent perfection of logic and sense upon which the iron grip of the work has rested, may well shatter as the lesson is absorbed that this supposedly comprehensive statement of English law 'in the age of Bracton' is instead a complex mixture of sense and doubts, a cumulated and only partially digested corpus strung along the only available lines of order, namely those confounded forms of action. Maitland had to use the printed form of Bracton produced in 1569 and reprinted with defects in 1640; he knew very well how inadequate this was and several times called for a new edition. Considering what he had to work with, his achievement remains astounding. That is not in question: what must now be asked is whether the product resulting from such handicaps can really, a hundred years after its appearance, still dominate all studies of English law in the middle ages.

This question is raised in its starkest form by the latest scholar to take his axe to the forest oak. Van Caenegem, Sayles, Thorne all remained and remain devotees of Maitland, even though they have found him wanting in some very important ways. Our last critic, however, though he too remains respectful and is liable to emphasize the temerity of his heretical views, has found real chinks in Maitland's armour. This is S. F. C. Milsom, who very appropriately practises legal history from a chair in Maitland's own university and like Maitland began his career as a lawyer. The matters at issue turn upon highly technical points of the law and its record, and Milsom does not make things easier by an allusive and elliptical style, but they reach right down into our view of medieval society. The essence of his revisionist attack lies in his allegation that Maitland failed to give proper weight to the social structure of a feudal or seigneurial world: he overestimated the governing control of the king's courts and undervalued the independence of the local lords' courts. As Maitland saw it, Henry II's legislation (if that is what it was) replaced feudalism by centralized government when he offered better and swifter justice to complainants disturbed in their rights of possession by, as it were, interlopers; he identified seisin—the thing complainants sought to protect or recover—as equal to possession vested in them by grant or inheritance. In his world there were two contestants at law—he who claimed the land and he who sat on it—fighting out the rights of it before a relatively impartial court; unable to get what they held to be their just rights they took advantage of the king's offer in what Maitland called the possessory assizes (especially the assizes of novel disseisin and of mort d'ancestor) to help them to a solution of their problems. The picture Maitland drew of that world had a beautiful coherence and consistency, but it was the world as it emerged in his thirteenth-century sources read backwards and extended into the very different age that went before.

Milsom, on the other hand, argues for what he calls a three-dimensional world in which claimant, tenant (he who happens to hold at the relevant point in time) and lord are all involved in every such dispute, a world in which seisin is not a quality settled in the occupier of the land but an action of the lord's who invests another with seisin and thus at his pleasure makes him the rightful occupier for the time being. Originally seisin was not equal to the concept of possession in the Roman law, as Maitland maintained (and as in due course it became), but the definition of a relationship created by the lord when he admits another to hold land of him. The assizes are not 'possessory', a term that Maitland invented for them, and are not primarily intended to transfer actions to the king's court; they are means for restoring the proper course of the tenant's rights by urging the lord to do justice and not to abuse his power. When the king's writ instructed the sheriff to see to it that a dispute was settled by the lord it meant precisely that; the ancillary sanction—if the lord refuses have the parties before the king's justices—was originally a warning of what might happen, not the primary purpose of the action. Only as both tenant and lord began to see advantages in using the king's court did these assizes become regular means of starting litigation at the centre. Disseisin did not, in the twelfth century, imply forcible dispossession by another: Milsom rightly emphasizes that if this had been so, life at the time would have been impossibly violent and uncertain, seeing how often the assize issued. The traditional picture presupposes a degree of lawlessness not otherwise apparent in the record, as dispossessors again and again entered upon another's land and forced him to recover at law what was his own. Rather, disseisin represents the failure of the lord to bestow seisin where by the custom of his own court it should go; the claimant is not trying to recover lands taken from him but asks that what by binding custom should be his should not be conferred upon another. His right of seisin is defined in the relationship between vassal and lord and signified in a piece of land: that is the way the age thinks of the matter. But if the lord breaks the rules—for instance, by passing over an heir and granting seisin to another—the offended party is unlikely to find a remedy in the local court and seeks an order from the king, telling the lord to do the right thing. Milsom, of course, works this out in great detail and for all the so-called possessory assizes.

In the end, the two pictures differ in emphasis rather than essentials, but the difference is nonetheless great. As Milsom sees it, Maitland antedated the settled and sophisticated state of the law by a hundred years at least, whereas in his view the feudal relationships predominated down to the end of the twelfth century over the king's rule, with lords reigning in their lands and the royal courts at most offering *adhoc* assistance to an aggrieved party against his lord. Out of that assistance grew certainties of possession enforced by the king's courts, but this happy state was not achieved until the powerful realities of the feudal chain of command had been polished away through the increasing interference from above and the work of generations of lawyers who systematized a centralized structure out of the confused and particularized interaction in which what the lords said counted and kings were confined to urging those powerful men to behave by the rules. The difference between Maitland and Milsom may be illustrated by their views concerning the law of inheritance. Maitland regarded it as effectively settled by the middle of the twelfth century: a tenant could use the king's court to compel his lord to grant seisin to a man who claimed by right of his ancestor's seisin. The lord has thus lost all control over who should hold of him once he had made the original grant to a man who came to have heirs. According to Milsom, this was the end product of a long process during which the lord claimed and exercised his right to place seisin where he saw fit, applying accepted rules but himself deciding what in a given case those rules meant, and making a decision against which there could be no present or future appeal. It was this long process that Maitland drastically foreshortened, thereby giving us quite the wrong view of that earlier and genuinely feudal society. Maitland's splendid quip that the feudal system was introduced into England by Sir Henry Spelman (a seventeenth-century historian) and flourished best in the eighteenth century is a perfectly sound rebuff to those who treat the English kingdom as 'feudal' down to the Tudor age—as many then did, and Marxists still do. But it does overlook the likelihood that it took more than one king, even a Conqueror, to triumph over the social structure and world of ideas within which he had been able to conquer England in the first place.

To sum up: as Milsom says, when Edward I came to the throne 'the world was as Maitland saw it', but he was mistaken in thinking that its notions and commonplaces had remained unchanged for 200 years. Needless to say, we can again find signs that Maitland was not unaware of this: he once admitted that when placing himself in the last quarter of the thirteenth century he was 'dealing with institutions that are already decadent. The feudal scheme of public law has seen its best or worst days.' However, it is really misleading to identify 'the feudal scheme' with any law that can properly be called public (lords' law and king's law were both private and particular to cases as they arose), and also he backdated its decay markedly too far and thus endowed Henry II with an anachronistic attitude to the duties, functions and potential of a king.

I have dwelt at length on what might appear to be a very esoteric dispute because Milsom seems to me to have put his finger on some real weaknesses in Maitland's historical method. No attempt has yet been made to assess this new interpretation, and for all I know Milsom may not in the end prevail: though I must say that he makes excellent sense to one who is historian without any training in the law. His account incorporates the fact of continuous change in ways that Maitland's fails to do, which means that it fits the experience of the historian but not of the lawyer. Maitland, of course, was a historian too and knew all about change through time, but as we shall see he could unconsciously fall victim at times to his lawyer's training.

Enough has in any case been said to show that Maitland's towering achievement differs from the Bible: his works are not law or revelation. We can be quite sure that of all the people involved he would have been the first to insist on this fact. The thought that he might have brought the history of the law to a standstill by the authority of his writings would have horrified him, and we shall have occasion to point to his influence as the sower of seeds rather than

the builder of permanent structures. What he did build, of course, was monumental enough to last a very long time, and his gift for seeing difficulties and weaknesses in his own arguments (another of the true historian's gifts that he possessed) assisted in his monolithic survival. No one more frequently hinted at qualifications and possibilities which, pressed by time, he could not pursue further. Monoliths, excellent objects for worship, are of little use to the study of history. It is therefore important to realize that much work has been done since his time, that the history of England and its law does not now stand where it stood on the day that F. W. Maitland was alive and dead, and that he was quite correct in thinking himself not perfect. What matters next is to identify the sources of his imperfections, such as they were, because understanding them adds further to the lessons which Maitland taught to historians.

Maitland's towering achievement differs from the Bible: his works are not law or revelation. We can be quite sure that of all the people involved he would have been the first to insist on this fact.

—*G. R. Elton*

Much of the revision done since Maitland's day simply represents the progress of research, commonly under inspirations received from him. New sources are opened up, old ones studied afresh; new theories open vistas, old ones return to make sure that the road leads through real country, not the fantasies of the dogmatizers; all historical understanding grows out of debates and dialectics which ensure that no question can ever be thought of as finally settled, while every question so handled comes by devious routes ever close to some effective truth. Many of the detailed corrections and revisions applied to Maitland's edifices in the last hundred years are of this mundane and respectable kind. It has also become plain that even he, master as he was of accurate speed, at times worked too fast. He read enormously and remembered tenaciously, and he had an exceptional gift for associating disparate and scattered detail in an all-embracing mind, but no one can see everything. His fundamental error over Bracton owed much to the fact that he had seen only some of the extant manuscripts: since putting this matter right called for several people's labours over seventy years, the shortcoming is no blame to him and worth mentioning only as a warning to those—some still survive—who will not believe that he could ever have failed to know everything relevant to his work. As Maitland kept telling people, the Public Record Office holds mountains of stuff which need to be worked through before anything resembling certainty can be achieved; what remains so impressive are both his awareness of the unexplored ranges and the amount he managed to do with the parts of them that he had himself been able to explore.

This is not, however, the whole story. Why did he stop the history of English law round about 1300? One reason seems to have been his quite genuine desire to get the book done before Pollock could insist on contributing any more to it, a reason which Milsom fairly enough calls bizarre. If one man, even a giant, had to be able to manage that, the timespan needed limiting. There was also the fact, of which he showed himself very well aware, that from the beginning of the fourteenth century the state of the sources alters drastically; with the arrival of the Year Books and the proliferation of plea rolls the writing of legal history assumes a very different dimension, quite unmanageable by one man. Look at the long row of Selden Society volumes—ninety-seven by now and nearly all attendant upon the times that followed the age of Bracton! Much of the history of English law in the later middle ages is written there.

However, Maitland who usually avoided dubious and sweeping statements twice spoke in terms which ring an alarm bell: this should not be ignored. Perhaps the most shocking thing (shocking to the historian) he ever wrote was the explanation of his interest in the land law of Henry III's day: that interest 'will lie in this, that it is capable of becoming the land law of the England, the America, the Australia of the twentieth century'. Quite obviously that was not what drove him to wrestle with seisin, tenure and all the rest: so why did he say it? And in another place he defended as 'sound and truthful' the legal tradition that English law after Edward I had been of an unbroken continuity, so much so that what applied under Edward III was still in effect alive in his own day. He acknowledged that his conviction was 'not all true' but allowed 'it to be in the main . . . truthful'. It is a little ironic that in that very passage Maitland should speak of 'the besetting sin . . . of antedating the emergence of modern ideas', since now it appears that he himself antedated the emergence of old ideas. Even before the destruction of the inherited system in the second half of the nineteenth century, any conviction that little or nothing had changed since 1300 was entirely untrue, but it was what later lawyers salvaged from Sir Edward Coke's faith in an immemorial law and what they preserved by the manner in which they approached their sources and wrote their history. As Milsom says, 'You look on centuries of material generated on the premise that nothing much must be seen to have changed, and write a book saying that nothing much changed.' Maitland usually knew better: he understood the need to look at the past with no thought for its future. But that was not the way lawyers thought, nor the way that most historians of Maitland's day thought who wished to trace 'developments' to their contemporary condition. Maitland, who helped to teach us the error of those ways, stood at the beginning of an era: he worked out principles for others to learn from. No wonder that on occasion he fell victim to the predominant climate surrounding him. Thus, his concentration on the thirteenth century was assisted by a conviction that in that age the law that he knew received its classic formation and the foundations which remained for centuries. That is to say that despite himself he was capable of falling into the teleological error.

The damaging consequences of those rare slips received support from two other facets of his method. We have noted his practice of starting from one central source—from Bracton, from Domesday, from Lyndwood—and we have also had occasion to notice that this practice in part derives from the lawyer's training which accustoms a man to finding a major authority surrounded by commentaries and glosses. Much of Maitland's work answers to that description. The practice works in law because the great lawyer automatically constructs comprehensive answers out of the raw materials so offered, and Milsom, with reason, has pointed out the effect of such proceedings upon Maitland whose exceptional clarity of mind constructed exceptionally coherent and convincing 'pictures' (synthesizing schemes). But the structural principle thus obtained is imposed upon, not extracted from, the confusions of the real world: 'That,' as Milsom puts it, 'is how the law works, and largely how it changes. The change is in the premises from which a matter is approached'—and by himself changing the premises he proceeds to change the picture. However, this is not how history works or changes: the historian may well come to alter the existing picture by questioning its premises, but he should not replace one set of premises by another until he has searched the record with as much freedom from organizing systems as he can manage—the more the very much better. Though Maitland did a great deal of precisely that, at times, in order to present his findings, he had recourse to the lawyer's method, and it could get him into trouble.

Because Maitland knew so much his premises often worked and his pictures withstood the pressure of later research, though how much that endurance owed to the lucidity and concreteness with which they were described is something that only the future will show, now that Maitland is at last ceasing to be the god whose word must never be questioned. It is, however, already apparent that one of his preferred ways of working contributed to the risk of teleological error which like all of us he ran at all times and avoided more commonly than most of us. He believed that dark ages can be illuminated by working backwards from a position upon which light has dawned. This was expressly what he meant to do in ***Domesday Book and Beyond,*** where 'beyond' means 'before', but he followed much the same precept when he approached the history of the law since the Conquest to 1278 by taking his stand with the outcome and tracking back to the origins. He did marvels with that method, and only the expansion of the archives has rendered it supererogatory in most cases, but it is one with a teleological thread built in. The past must be led up to a known present, and in the journey one encounters very grave dangers that the known present may get unhistorically projected backwards. In addition, such parts of the past as did not make it into the known present are liable to get discarded. Maitland's demonstrable errors—well, for the present highly doubtful expositions—concerning seisin, the role of the crown, the disappearance of seigneurial justice, the prehistory of the established writ system, all owe more than a little to this backward-working technique. Of course, Maitland knew that the historian should work forward without thinking about the outcome, but he rightly thought that there are problems in history where the state of the evidence prohibits such proper methods; he knew his risks but did not always see when he had failed to avoid them. Milsom is probably right in his allegation that even Maitland, who kept emphasizing the fact that unchanging terms keep on changing the contents of their meaning, had difficulties on occasion, when faced with terms like tenure or inheritance, in realizing how much the overtones of the thirteenth century had already changed what those identical words had meant a hundred years earlier.

Lastly, Maitland's sources—virtually all of them products of the king's government—together with some convictions and preoccupations of his own day could induce him to overestimate the power, initiative and ingenuity of the realm's central bodies—to predate centralized kingship and unifying principles. Centralized kingship and unifying principles form one of the main threads of English law and English history: no wonder that this lawyer-historian was perhaps a little too ready to see them at work a little too early or too successfully. I speak as a non-lawyer historian who in his time has been overimpressed by the work of a centralizing monarchy. It is, I think, becoming clear that neither Henry II nor his agents were so consciously engaged in providing a royal law in supersession of diversified customs as Maitland tended to suppose. Of course, once again he was the first to express doubts. Writing to an American colleague in 1889, he could not help thinking 'that the law of the King's courts is only a part of the law, and that the lawyers in those courts, having to do only with the remedies there given get into a way of speaking about "property" which really is misleading'. It could be charged that when the **History of English Law** came out six years later too little of this true insight appeared in it.

Criticizing Maitland is a dangerous game: so often one finds that he has been there first, and he wrote so much that it is far too easy to miss something. No wonder that the worshippers have had their own way for so long. Yet it is necessary to point out that even he could err quite dramatically at times because his method, the source of such learned success, had its weaknesses. In his day few people analysed even their own historical methods beyond such obvious needs as the study of original documents properly understood, the elimination of forgeries, correct dating of the undated. Maitland, it would seem instinctively (being that sort of scholar), did most things right and always remained uncertain about much that he wrote about: he knew that the search for total knowledge, total certainty, meant only total silence. The intermediate answer is what needs to be offered, and he did not expect his intermediate answers to sit unchallenged for so long. Nevertheless, reliance on a single source with the rest gathered predictably around it, together with a predilection for a clarity far beyond the powers of those who in the circumstances of their own day made the law of which he spoke, could at times produce errors not explicable solely by an inevitable inability to read everything or singlehandedly in a brief lifetime to do the work of dozens in a century. Even Maitland erred—and only of Maitland among all English historians through the ages is it even necessary to record the fact.

FURTHER READING

Biography

Fifoot, C. H. S. *Frederic William Maitland: A Life.* Cambridge, Mass.: Harvard University Press, 1971, 313 p.

Biographical study intending to "evoke Maitland himself, his qualities of mind and spirit as these are revealed in his writings, among his friends . . . and in the midst of his family."

Criticism

Cam, Helen M. "Introduction." In *Selected Historical Essays of F. W. Maitland,* edited by Helen M. Cam, pp. ix-xxix. Cambridge: Cambridge University Press, 1957.

Discusses Maitland's subjects, techniques, and influence, and outlines the selection of material in the volume, which, according to Cam, is "designed to render more accessible those shorter writings of Maitland's which have the greatest intrinsic value for students of history and best illustrate his distinctive qualities."

Gooch, G. P. "Acton and Maitland." In his *History and Historians in the Nineteenth Century,* rev. ed., pp. 354-75. London: Longmans, Green and Co., 1952.

Includes an introductory survey of Maitland's works and career, citing him as "the most brilliant and original of English institutional historians."

Holdsworth, W. S. "Maitland." In his *The Historians of Anglo-American Law,* pp. 130-56. New York: Columbia University Press, 1928.

Traces Maitland's intellectual development, personality, and position in English law and history.

——. "Maine, Maitland, and Pollock." In his *Some Makers of English Law: The Tagore Lectures, 1937-38,* pp. 265-90. Cambridge: Cambridge University Press, 1966.

Discusses the historical tradition in English law and the rise of the historical school among English lawyers of the late nineteenth century as exemplified by Maitland, Henry Maine, and Frederick Pollock.

Lapsley, G. "Editorial Note to 'Introduction to Memoranda de Parliamento, A.D. 305,' by F. W. Maitland." In *Maitland: Selected Essays,* edited by H. D. Hazeltine, G. Lapsley, and P. H. Winfield, pp. 1-13. Cambridge: Cambridge University Press, 1936.

Discusses developments in parliamentary studies since Maitland.

Ogle, Arthur. *The Canon Law in Medieval England: An Examination of William Lyndwood's "Provinciale," in Reply to the Late Professor F. W. Maitland.* 1912. Reprint. New York: Burt Franklin, 1971, 220 p.

Opposes Maitland's treatise on Canon Law and its use as a basis for arguing the disendowment of the Welsh Church.

Smith, A. L. *Frederic William Maitland: Two Lectures and a Bibliography.* Oxford: Clarendon Press, 1908, 71 p.

Discusses such topics as Maitland's historigraphical methods, perspective, and prose style, concluding with an estimate of his influence within the context of the modern historical study of law.

Stephenson, Carl. "Commendation and Related Problems in *Domesday*." In his *Mediaeval Institutions: Selected Essays,* edited by Bryce D. Lyon, pp. 156-83. Ithaca, N.Y.: Cornell University Press, 1954.

    Discusses Maitland's interpretations in *Domesday Book and Beyond* of the relationship between lord and land-holder in pre-Norman England.

Karl Mannheim

1893-1947

German sociologist.

INTRODUCTION

Mannheim is credited as one of the founders of sociology as a systematic, coherent, and unified science. He firmly believed that as a scientific discipline sociology could help resolve the conflicts of modern society through a "sociology of knowledge." Mannheim differentiated between two different areas of knowledge: the knowledge that derives from scientific data and class-based knowledge, such as religious, philosophical, and traditional forms of knowledge. Both his predecessor Max Weber and his contemporary Georg Lukács exerted strong influence on Mannheim's work. His contributions also advanced the sociology of education, political sociology, and modern social structure.

Biographical Information

Mannheim was born in Budapest, Hungary, on March 27, 1893, the only child of a German mother and Hungarian father. After the fall of the Hungarian Republic of Councils in 1919, Mannheim left Hungary for Germany. His academic career included studies at the universities of Budapest, Freiburg, Paris, and Berlin. In the early 1920s he moved to Heidelberg, where he earned his doctorate at the University of Heidelberg. By 1930 he was a lecturer at the University of Frankfurt. After Hitler came to power in 1933, Mannheim took a position at the London School of Economics, and in 1945 he was appointed to the chair of sociology of education at the University of London. He was a popular lecturer and public figure in his adopted country. Mannheim died on January 9, 1947.

Major Works

From 1910 to 1916 Mannheim corresponded with Hungarian philosopher and literary historian Georg Lukács, an influence evident in Mannheim's key work, *Ideologie und Utopie (Ideology and Utopia)*. In it he argued that although knowledge is integral to humankind's adaptation and survival in the world, it is the environment that determines the kind of knowledge people have. He labeled ideas that serve to protect the established elite "ideologies," and descibed as "utopias" those ideas that aim to better the lot of the less fortunate. Mannheim's decision to leave Germany for England prompted his collection of essays *Mensch und Gesellschaft im Zeitalter des Umbaus (Man and Society in an Age of Reconstruction)*, in which he argued against National Socialism as exploitative of a global crisis in the institutions that comprise liberal civilization. *Diagnosis of Our Time*, his subsequent collection of lectures and essays, expanded on the concepts of social planning introduced in his previous work while also arguing

for a reevaluation of Christianity and the creation of a new system of values. In *Freedom, Power, and Democratic Planning*, Mannheim expanded on the ideas of his two previous books and added an analysis of power, which he viewed as the most pressing problem of the postwar period. Although he was a strong advocate of social planning, he believed in a "fundamental democratization" that would produce an informed public capable of demanding the dissolution of government when necessary.

PRINCIPAL WORKS

Lelek es Kultura   (nonfiction)   1918
Die Strukturanalyse der Erkenntnistheorie   (nonfiction) 1922
Ideologie und Utopie [Ideology and Utopia]   (nonfiction) 1929
Die Gegenwartsaufgaben der Soziologie: Ihre Lehrgestalt (nonfiction)   1932
Rational and Irrational Elements in Contemporary Society (nonfiction)   1934
Mensch und Gesellschaft im Zeitalter des Umbaus [Man and Society in an Age of Reconstruction]   (essays) 1935
Diagnosis of Our Time   (essays)   1943
Freedom, Power, and Democratic Planning   (essays) 1950
Essays on the Sociology of Knowledge   (essays)   1952
Essays on Sociology and Social Psychology   (essays) 1953
Essays on the Sociology of Culture   (essays)   1956
Systematic Sociology: An Introduction to the Study of Society   (essays)   1957
An Introduction to the Sociology of Education [with W. A. C. Stewart]   (essays)   1962
From Karl Mannheim   (essays)   1971
Strukturen des Denkens [Structures of Thinking]   (nonfiction)   1980
Konservatismos: Ein Betrag zur Soziologie des Wissens [Conservatism: A Contribution to the Sociology of Knowledge]   (nonfiction)   1984

CRITICISM

Kenneth Burke   (essay date 1936)

SOURCE: "The Constants of Social Relativity," in *The Philosophy of Literary Form: Studies in Symbolic Action,* third edition, University of California Press, 1973, pp. 404-6.

[*In the following essay, which was originally published as a review of* Ideology and Utopia *in 1936, Burke examines Mannheim's concept of a "sociology of knowledge."*]

Discouraged by the ways in which the perspectives of different people, classes, eras, cancel one another, you may decide that all philosophies are nonsense. Or you may establish order by fiat, as you bluntly adhere to one faction among the many, determined to abide by its assertions regardless of other people's assertions. Or you may become a kind of referee for other men's contests, content to observe that every view has some measure of truth and some measure of falsity. If they had asserted nothing, you could assert nothing. But in so far as they assert and counterassert, you can draw an assertion from the comparison of their assertions.

Professor Karl Mannheim's "sociology of knowledge" is a variant of the third of these attitudes. He would begin with the *fact of difference* rather than with a *choice among the differences*. But in erecting a new perspective atop the rivalries of the old perspectives, he would subtly change the rules of the game. For the new perspective he offered would not be simply a *rival perspective;* it would be a *theory of perspectives*. In so far as it was accurate, in other words, its contribution would reside in its ability to make the *perspective process* itself more accessible to consciousness.

Faction A opposes Faction B. To do so as effectively as possible, it "unmasks" Faction B's "ideology." Faction B may talk nobly about "humanity" or "freedom," for instance. And Faction A discloses the "real meaning" of these high-sounding phrases in terms of interests, privileges, social habits, and the like. Faction B retaliates by unmasking Faction A's ideology.

Each faction exposes, as far as possible, the conscious and unconscious deception practiced by the ideologists of rival camps. But in the course of exposing the enemy, a faction comes upon principles that could be turned upon itself as well. Hence, it can spare its own members from the general censure only by "pulling its punch." And precisely at this point there enter the opportunities for a "sociology of knowledge," if only the sociologist can so change the rules of the game that he finds no embarrassment in completing and maturing this "unmasking" process.

This he does in the easiest way imaginable. Whereas the ideologists of the opposing factions "point with alarm" to the fact that there is a difference between the face value of an opponent's idea and its real value in social commerce, the sociologist starts out by taking such discrepancies for granted. He begins with the assumption that an idea must be "discounted" by the disclosure of the interests behind it. Hence, he can treat the difference between the face value of an ideology and its behavior in a social context not as an "unmasking" but as an "explanation" or "definition" of the ideology. Thus, instead of being startled to find that an idea must be discounted, and taking this fact as the be-all and end-all of his disclosures, he assumes at the start the necessity of discounting, and so can

advance to the point where he seeks to establish the *principles of discounting*.

Such, at least, is the reviewer's way of understanding Professor Mannheim's point in tracing a development from the "unmasking of ideologies" to the "sociology of knowledge." And his [*Ideology and Utopia*] presents a great wealth of material to guide the sociologist who would define ideologies in terms of their social behavior. Incidentally, in his gauging of the case, he suggests reasons why members of the intelligentsia are not a perfect fit for strict political alignment. Their working capital is their education—and in so far as they accumulate this capital to its fullest, they venture far beyond the confines of some immediate political perspective. He does not use this thought, however, to disprove the value of political affiliation. On the contrary, he suggests that there are ways in which this somewhat "classless" ingredient in the "capital" of the intelligentsia may serve to broaden and mature the outlook of the stricter partisans, and enable them to take wider ranges of reality and resistance into account.

As for the key terms, ideology and utopia, their "discounting" in social textures makes it impossible for the reader to follow them as absolute logical opposites. In general, the term ideology is used to connote "false consciousness" of a conservative or reactionary sort—while utopia stresses the same phenomenon in the revolutionary category. If conditions have so changed, for instance, that the landed proprietor has become a capitalist yet "still attempts to explain his relations to his laborers and his own function in the undertaking by means of categories reminiscent of the patriarchal order," he is thinking by "ideological distortion." And the "spiritualization of politics" in the thinking of the Chiliasts is treated as a typical utopia, surviving even in the thought of anarchists like Bakunin. However, although the conservative is not naturally given to utopian imaginings, being content to accept the *status quo,* the competitive pressure of revolutionary utopias spurs him to the construction of counter-utopias. Hegel's romantic historicism, erected in opposition to the liberal idea, is given as a prime example. Perhaps the following quotation illustrates the difference most succinctly:

> As long as the clerically and feudally organized medieval order was able to locate its paradise outside of society, in some other-worldly sphere which transcended history and dulled its revolutionary edge, the idea of paradise was still an integral part of medieval society. Not until certain social groups embodied these wish-images into their actual conduct, and tried to realize them, did these ideologies become utopian.

The book is concerned with the ramifications and subtilizations of this distinction, and with a theory of knowledge to be drawn from the plot of history as charted in accordance with these terms. The discussion being conducted largely in abstractions, the book will probably not endear itself to the general reader—but anyone interested in the relation between politics and knowledge should find it absorbing. Perhaps we could venture to summarize the case this way: whereas the needs of the forum tend to make sociology a subdivision of politics, Professor Mannheim is contributing as much as he can toward making politics a subdivision of sociology.

Louis Wirth   (essay date 1936)

SOURCE: Preface to *Ideology and Utopia: An Introduction to the Sociology of Knowledge,* by Karl Mannheim, translated by Louis Wirth and Edward Shils, Harcourt Brace & Company, 1936, pp. viii-xxx.

[*In the following essay, Wirth outlines the central ideas in* Ideology and Utopia *in the context of modern sociological thought.*]

The original German edition of **Ideology and Utopia** appeared in an atmosphere of acute intellectual tension marked by widespread discussion which subsided only with the exile or enforced silence of those thinkers who sought an honest and tenable solution to the problems raised. Since then the conflicts which in Germany led to the destruction of the liberal Weimar Republic have been felt in various countries all over the world, especially in Western Europe and the United States. The intellectual problems which at one time were considered the peculiar preoccupation of German writers have enveloped virtually the whole world. What was once regarded as the esoteric concern of a few intellectuals in a single country has become the common plight of the modern man.

In response to this situation there has arisen an extensive literature which speaks of the "end," the "decline," the "crisis," the "decay," or the "death" of Western civilization. But despite the alarm which is heralded in such titles, one looks in vain in most of this literature for an analysis of the basic factors and processes underlying our social and intellectual chaos. In contrast with these Professor Mannheim's work stands out as a sober, critical, and scholarly analysis of the social currents and situations of our time as they bear upon thought, belief, and action.

It seems to be characteristic of our period that norms and truths which were once believed to be absolute, universal, and eternal, or which were accepted with blissful unawareness of their implications, are being questioned. In the light of modern thought and investigation much of what was once taken for granted is declared to be in need of demonstration and proof. The criteria of proof themselves have become subjects of dispute. We are witnessing not only a general distrust of the validity of ideas but of the motives of those who assert them. This situation is aggravated by a war of each against all in the intellectual arena where personal self-aggrandizement rather than truth has come to be the coveted prize. Increased secularization of life, sharpened social antagonisms and the accentuation of the spirit of personal competition have permeated regions which were once thought to be wholly under the reign of the disinterested and objective search for truth.

However disquieting this change may appear to be, it has had its wholesome influences as well. Among these might be mentioned the tendency toward a more thoroughgoing self-scrutiny and toward a more comprehensive awareness of the interconnections between ideas and situations than had hitherto been suspected. Although it may seem like grim humour to speak of the beneficent influences arising out of an upheaval that has shaken the foundations of our social and intellectual order, it must be asserted that the spectacle of change and confusion, which confronts social science, presents it at the same time with unprecedented opportunities for fruitful new development. This new development, however, depends on taking full cognizance of the obstacles which beset social thought. This does not imply that self-clarification is the only condition for the further advancement of social science, as will be indicated in what follows, but merely that it is a necessary precondition for further development.

I. The progress of social knowledge is impeded if not paralysed at present by two fundamental factors, one impinging upon knowledge from without, the other operating within the world of science itself. On the one hand the powers that have blocked and retarded the advance of knowledge in the past still are not convinced that the advance of social knowledge is compatible with what they regard as their interests, and, on the other hand, the attempt to carry over the tradition and the whole apparatus of scientific work from the physical to the social realm has often resulted in confusion, misunderstanding, and sterility. Scientific thought about social affairs up to now has had to wage war primarily against established intolerance and institutionalized suppression. It has been struggling to establish itself against its external enemies, the authoritarian interest of church, state and tribe. In the course of the last few centuries, however what amounts at least to a partial victory against these out side forces has been won, resulting in a measure of toleration of untrammelled inquiry, and even encouragement of free thought. For a brief interlude between the ears of medieval, spiritualized darkness and the rise of modern secular dictatorships, the Western world gave promise of fulfilling the hope of the enlightened minds of all ages that by the full exercise of intelligence men might triumph over the adversities of nature and the perversities of culture. As so often in the past, however, this hope seems now to be chastened. Whole nations have officially and proudly given themselves up to the cult of irrationality, and even the Anglo-Saxon world which was for so long the haven of freedom and reason has recently provided revivals of intellectual witch hunts.

In the course of the development of the Western mind the pursuit of knowledge about the physical world resulted after the travail of theological persecution, in the concession to natural science of an autonomous empire of its own Since the sixteenth century, despite some spectacular exceptions, theological dogmatism has receded from one domain of inquiry after another until the authority of the natural sciences was generally recognized. In the face of the forward movement of scientific investigation, the church has yielded and time after time readjusted its doctrinal interpretation so that their divergence from scientific discoveries would not be too glaring.

At length the voice of science was heard with a respect approximating the sanctity which formerly was accorded only to authoritarian, religious pronouncements. The revolutions which the theoretical structure of science has undergone in recent decades have left the prestige of the scientific pursuit of truth unshaken. Even though in the last five years the cry has occasionally been raised that science was exerting a disruptive effect upon economic organization and thus its output should therefore be restricted, whatever slowing down of the pace of natural science research has taken place during this period is probably more the result of the decreasing economic demand for the products of science than the deliberate attempt to hamper scientific progress in order to stabilize the existing order.

The triumph of natural science over theological and metaphysical dogma is sharply contrasted with the development in the studies of social life. Whereas the empirical procedure had made deep inroads on the dogmas of the ancients concerning nature, the classical social doctrines proved themselves more impervious to the onslaught of the secular and empirical spirit. This may in part have been due to the fact that the knowledge and theorizing about social affairs on the part of the ancients was far in advance of their notions about physics and biology. The opportunity for demonstrating the practical utility of the new natural science had not yet come, and the disutility of existing social doctrines could not be convincingly established. Whereas Aristotle's logic, ethics, aesthetics, politics, and psychology were accepted as authoritative by subsequent periods, his notions of astronomy, physics, and biology were progressively being relegated to the scrapheap of ancient superstitions.

Until early in the eighteenth century political and social theory was still under the dominance of the categories of thought elaborated by the ancient and medieval philosophers and operated largely within a theological framework. That part of social science that had any practical utility was concerned, primarily, with administrative matters. Cameralism and political arithmetic, which represented this current, confined themselves to the homely facts of every-day life and rarely took flights into theory. Consequently that part of social knowledge which was concerned with questions most subject to controversy could scarcely lay claim to the practical value which the natural sciences, after a certain point in their development, had achieved. Nor could those social thinkers from whom alone an advance could come expect the support of the church or the state from whom the more orthodox wing derived its financial and moral sustenance. The more secularized social and political theory became and the more thoroughly it dispelled the sanctified myths which legitimized the existing political order, the more precarious became the position of the emerging social science.

A dramatic instance of the difference between the effects of and the attitude toward technological as contrasted with social knowledge is furnished by contemporary Japan. Once that country was opened to the streams of Western influence the technical products and methods of the latter were eagerly accepted. But social, economic, and political influences from the outside are even to-day regarded with suspicion and tenaciously resisted.

The enthusiasm with which the results of physical and biological science are embraced in Japan contrasts strikingly with the cautious and guarded cultivation of economic,

political, and social investigation. These latter subjects are still, for the most part, subsumed under what the Japanese call *kikenshiso* or "dangerous thoughts." The authorities regard discussion of democracy, constitutionalism, the emperor, socialism, and a host of other subjects as dangerous because knowledge on these topics might subvert the sanctioned beliefs and undermine the existing order.

But lest we think that this condition is peculiar to Japan, however, it should be emphasized that many of the topics that come under the rubric of "dangerous thought" in Japan were until recently taboo in Western society as well. Even to-day open, frank, and "objective" inquiry into the most sacred and cherished institutions and beliefs is more or less seriously restricted in every country of the world. It is virtually impossible, for instance, even in England and America, to inquire into the actual facts regarding communism, no matter how disinterestedly, without running the risk of being labelled a communist.

That there is an area of "dangerous thought" in every society is, therefore, scarcely debatable. While we recognize that what it is dangerous to think about may differ from country to country and from epoch to epoch, on the whole the subjects marked with the danger signal are those which the society or the controlling elements in it believe to be so vital and hence so sacred that they will not tolerate their profanation by discussion. But what is not so easily recognized is the fact that thought, even in the absence of official censorship, is disturbing, and, under certain conditions, dangerous and subversive. For thought is a catalytic agent that is capable of unsettling routines, disorganizing habits, breaking up customs, undermining faiths, and generating scepticism.

The distinctive character of social science discourse is to be sought in the fact that every assertion, no matter how objective it may be, has ramifications extending beyond the limits of science itself. Since every assertion of a "fact" about the social world touches the interests of some individual or group, one cannot even call attention to the existence of certain "facts" without courting the objections of those whose very *raison d'être* in society rests upon a divergent interpretation of the "factual" situation.

II. The discussion centring around this issue has traditionally been known as the problem of objectivity in science. In the language of the Anglo-Saxon world to be objective has meant to be impartial, to have no preferences, predilections or prejudices, no biases, no preconceived values or judgments in the presence of the facts. This view was an expression of the older conception of natural law in accord with which the contemplation of the facts of nature, instead of being coloured by the norms of conduct of the contemplator, automatically supplied these norms. After the natural law approach to the problem of objectivity subsided, this non-personal way of looking at the facts themselves again found support for a time through the vogue of positivism. Nineteenth century social science abounds in warnings against the distorting influences of passion, political interest, nationalism, and class feeling and in appeals for self-purification.

Indeed a good share of the history of modern philosophy

and science may be viewed as a trend, if not a concerted drive, toward this type of objectivity. This, it has been assumed, involves the search for valid knowledge through the elimination of biased perception and faulty reasoning on the negative side and the formulation of a critically self-conscious point of view and the development of sound methods of observation and analysis on the positive side. If it may appear, at first glance, that in the logical and methodological writings on science the thinkers of other nations have been more active than the English and Americans, this notion might well be corrected by calling attention to the long line of thinkers in the English-speaking world who have been preoccupied with these very same problems without specifically labelling them methodology. Certainly the concern with the problems and pitfalls involved in the search for valid knowledge has constituted more than a negligible portion of the works of a long line of brilliant thinkers from Locke through Hume, Bentham, Mill, and Spencer to writers of our own time. We do not always recognize these treatments of the processes of knowing as serious attempts to formulate the epistemological, logical, and psychological premises of a sociology of knowledge, because they do not bear the explicit label and were not deliberately intended as such. Nonetheless wherever scientific activity has been carried on in an organized and self-conscious fashion, these problems have always received a considerable amount of attention. In fact, in such works as J. S. Mill's *System of Logic* and Herbert Spencer's brilliant and much neglected *Study of Sociology,* the problem of objective social knowledge has received forthright and comprehensive treatment. In the period that followed Spencer this interest in the objectivity of social knowledge was somewhat deflected by the ascendancy of statistical techniques as represented by Francis Galton and Karl Pearson. But in our own day the works of Graham Wallas and John A. Hobson, among others, signalize a return to this interest.

America, despite the barren picture of its intellectual landscape that we so generally find in the writings of Europeans, has produced a number of thinkers who have concerned themselves with this issue. Outstanding in this respect is the work of William Graham Sumner, who, although he approached the problem somewhat obliquely through the analysis of the influence of the folkways and mores upon social norms rather than directly through epistemological criticism, by the vigorous way in which he directed attention to the distorting influence of ethnocentrism upon knowledge, placed the problem of objectivity into a distinctively concrete sociological setting. Unfortunately his disciples have failed to explore further the rich potentialities of his approach and have largely interested themselves in elaborating other phases of his thought. Somewhat similar in his treatment of this problem is Thorstein Veblen who, in a series of brilliant and penetrating essays, has explored the intricate relationships between cultural values and intellectual activities. Further discussion of the same question along realistic lines is found in James Harvey Robinson's *The Mind in the Making,* in which this distinguished historian touches on many of the points which the present volume analyses in detail. More recently Professor Charles A. Beard's *The Nature of the Social Sciences* has dealt with the possibilities of ob-

jective social knowledge from a pedagogical point of view in a manner revealing traces of the influence of Professor Mannheim's work.

Necessary and wholesome as the emphasis on the distorting influence of cultural values and interests upon knowledge was, this negative aspect of the cultural critique of knowledge has arrived at a juncture where the positive and constructive significance of the evaluative elements in thought had to be recognized. If the earlier discussion of objectivity laid stress upon the elimination of personal and collective bias, the more modern approach calls attention to the positive cognitive importance of this bias. Whereas the former quest for objectivity tended to posit an "object" which was distinct from the "subject," the latter sees an intimate relationship between the object and the perceiving subject. In fact, the most recent view maintains that the object emerges for the subject when, in the course of experience, the interest of the subject is focused upon that particular aspect of the world. Objectivity thus appears in a two-fold aspect: one, in which object and subject are discrete and separate entities, the other in which the interplay between them is emphasized. Whereas objectivity in the first sense refers to the reliability of our data and the validity of our conclusions, objectivity in the second sense is concerned with relevance to our interests. In the realm of the social, particularly, truth is not merely a matter of a simple correspondence between thought and existence, but is tinged with the investigator's interest in his subject matter, his standpoint, his evaluations, in short the definition of his object of attention. This conception of objectivity, however, does not imply that henceforth no distinction between truth and error is ascertainable. It does not mean that whatever people imagine to be their perceptions, attitudes, and ideas or what they want others to believe them to be corresponds to the facts. Even in this conception of objectivity we must reckon with the distortion produced not merely by inadequate perception or incorrect knowledge of oneself, but also by the inability or unwillingness under certain circumstances to report perceptions and ideas honestly.

This conception of the problem of objectivity which underlies Professor Mannheim's work will not be found totally strange by those who are familiar with that current of American philosophy represented by James, Peirce, Mead, and Dewey. Though Professor Mannheim's approach is the product of a different intellectual heritage, in which Kant, Marx, and Max Weber have played the leading roles, his conclusions on many pivotal issues are identical with those of the American pragmatists. This convergence runs, however, only as far as the limits of the field of social psychology. Among American sociologists this point of view has been explicitly expressed by the late Charles H. Cooley, and R. M. MacIver, and implicitly by W. I. Thomas and Robert E. Park. One reason why we do not immediately connect the works of these writers with the problem complex of the present volume is that in America what the sociology of knowledge deals with systematically and explicitly has been touched on only incidentally within the framework of the special discipline of social psychology or has been an unexploited by-product of empirical research.

The quest for objectivity gives rise to peculiarly difficult problems in the attempt to establish a rigorous scientific method in the study of social life. Whereas in dealing with the objects in the physical world the scientist may very well confine himself to the external uniformities and regularities that are there presented without seeking to penetrate into the inner meaning of the phenomena, in the social world the search is primarily for an understanding of these inner meanings and connections.

It may be true that there are some social phenomena and, perhaps, some aspects of all social events that can be viewed externally as if they were things. But this should not lead to the inference that only those manifestations of social life which find expression in material things are real. It would be a very narrow conception of social science to limit it to those concrete things which are externally perceivable and measurable.

The literature of social science amply demonstrates that there are large and very definite spheres of social existence in which it is possible to obtain scientific knowledge which is not only reliable but which has significant bearings on social policy and action. It does not follow from the fact that human beings are different from other objects in nature that there is nothing determinate about them. Despite the fact that human beings in their actions show a kind of causation which does not apply to any other objects in nature, namely motivation, it must still be recognized that determinate causal sequences must be assumed to apply to the realm of the social as they do to the physical. It might of course be argued that the precise knowledge we have of causal sequences in other realms has not as yet been established in the social realm. But if there is to be any knowledge at all beyond the sensing of the unique and transitory events of the moment, the possibility of discovering general trends and predictable series of events analogous to those to be found in the physical world must be posited for the social world as well. The determinism which social science presupposes, however, and of which Professor Mannheim treats so understandingly in this volume, is of a different sort from that involved in the Newtonian celestial mechanics.

There are, to be sure, some social scientists who claim that science must restrict itself to the causation of actual phenomena, that science is not concerned with what should be done, not with what ought to be done, but rather with what can be done and the manner of doing it. According to this view social science should be exclusively instrumental rather than a goal-setting discipline. But in studying what is, we cannot totally rule out what ought to be. In human life, the motives and ends of action are part of the process by which action is achieved and are essential in seeing the relation of the parts to the whole. Without the end most acts would have no meaning and no interest to us. But there is, nevertheless, a difference between taking account of ends and setting ends. Whatever may be the possibility of complete detachment in dealing with physical things, in social life we cannot afford to disregard the values and goal of acts without missing the significance of many of the facts involved. In our choice of areas for research, in our selection of data, in our method of investiga-

tion, in our organization of materials, not to speak of the formulation of our hypotheses and conclusions, there is always manifest some more or less clear, explicit or implicit assumption or scheme of evaluation.

There is, accordingly, a well-founded distinction between objective and subjective facts, which results from the difference between outer and inner observation or between "knowledge about" and "acquaintance with," to use William James's terms. If there is a difference between physical and mental processes—and there seems to be little occasion to talk this important distinction out of existence—it suggests a corresponding differentiation in the modes of knowing these two kinds of phenomena. Physical objects can be known (and natural science deals with them exclusively as if they could be known) purely from the outside, while mental and social processes can be known only from the inside, except in so far as they also exhibit themselves externally through physical indexes, into which in turn we read meanings. Hence insight may be regarded as the core of social knowledge. It is arrived at by being on the inside of the phenomenon to be observed, or, as Charles H. Cooley put it, by sympathetic introspection. It is the participation in an activity that generates interest, purpose, point of view value, meaning, and intelligibility, as well as bias.

If then the social sciences are concerned with objects that have meaning and value the observer who attempts to understand them must necessarily do so by means of categories which in turn depend on his own values and meanings. This point has been stated time and again in the dispute which has raged for many years between the behaviourists among the social scientists who would have dealt with social life exclusively as the natural scientist deals with the physical world, and those who took the position of sympathetic introspectionism and understanding along the lines indicated by such a writer as Max Weber.

But on the whole, while the evaluative element in social knowledge has received formal recognition, there has been relatively little attention given, especially among English and American sociologists, to the concrete analysis of the role of actual interests and values as they have been expressed in specific historical doctrines and movements. An exception must be made in the case of Marxism which, although it has raised this issue to a central position, has not formulated any satisfactory systematic statement of the problem.

It is at this point that Professor Mannheim's contribution marks a distinctive advance over the work that has hitherto been done in Europe and America. Instead of being content with calling attention to the fact that interest is inevitably reflected in all thought, including that part of it which is called science, Professor Mannheim has sought to trace out the specific connection between actual interest groups in society and the ideas and modes of thought which they espoused. He has succeeded in showing that ideologies, i.e. those complexes of ideas which direct activity toward the maintenance of the existing order, and utopias—or those complexes of ideas which tend to generate activities toward changes of the prevailing order—do not merely deflect thought from the object of observation, but also serve to fix attention upon aspects of the situation which otherwise would be obscured or pass unnoticed. In this manner he has forged out of a general theoretical formulation an effective instrument for fruitful empirical research.

The meaningful character of conduct does not warrant the inference, however, that this conduct is invariably the product of conscious reflection and reasoning. Our quest for understanding arises out of action and may even be consciously preparatory for further action, but we must recognize that conscious reflection or the imaginative rehearsal of the situation that we call "thinking" is not an indispensable part of every act. Indeed, it seems to be generally agreed among social psychologists that ideas are not spontaneously generated and that, despite the assertion of an antiquated psychology, the act comes before the thought. Reason, consciousness and conscience characteristically occur in situations marked by conflict. Professor Mannheim, therefore, is in accord with that growing number of modern thinkers who, instead of positing a pure intellect, are concerned with the actual social conditions in which intelligence and thought emerge. If, as seems to be true, we are not merely conditioned by the events that go on in our world but are at the same time an instrument for shaping them, it follows that the ends of action are never fully stable and determined until the act is finished or is so completely relegated to automatic routines that it no longer requires consciousness and attention.

The fact that in the realm of the social, the observer is part of the observed and hence has a personal stake in the subject of observation is one of the chief factors in the acuteness of the problem of objectivity in the social sciences. In addition we must consider the fact that social life and hence social science is to an overwhelming extent concerned with beliefs about the ends of action. When we advocate something, we do not do so as complete outsiders to what is and what will happen. It would be naïve to suppose that our ideas are entirely shaped by the objects of our contemplation which lie outside of us or that our wishes and our fears have nothing whatever to do with what we perceive or with what will happen. It would be nearer the truth to admit that those basic impulses which have been generally designated as "interests" actually are the forces which at the same time generate the ends of our practical activity and focus our intellectual attention. While in certain spheres of life, especially in economics and to a lesser degree in politics, these "interests" have been made explicit and articulate, in most other spheres they slumber below the surface and disguise themselves in such conventional forms that we do not always recognize them even when they are pointed out to us. The most important thing, therefore, that we can know about a man is what he takes for granted, and the most elemental and important facts about a society are those that are seldom debated and generally regarded as settled.

But we look in vain in the modern world for the serenity and calm that seemed to characterize the atmosphere in which some thinkers of ages past lived. The world no longer has a common faith and our professed "community of interest" is scarcely more than a figure of speech. With the loss of a common purpose and common interests, we have also been deprived of common norms, modes of thought, and conceptions of the world. Even public opinion has turned out to be a set of "phantom" publics. Men of the past may have dwelled in smaller and more parochial worlds, but the worlds in which they lived were apparently more stable and integrated for all the members of the community than our enlarged universe of thought, action, and belief has come to be.

A society is possible in the last analysis because the individuals in it carry around in their heads some sort of picture of that society. Our society, however, in this period of minute division of labour, of extreme heterogeneity and profound conflict of interests, has come to a pass where these pictures are blurred and incongruous. Hence we no longer perceive the same things as real, and coincident with our vanishing sense of a common reality we are losing our common medium for expressing and communicating our experiences. The world has been splintered into countless fragments of atomized individuals and groups. The disruption in the wholeness of individual experience corresponds to the disintegration in culture and group solidarity. When the bases of unified collective action begin to weaken, the social structure tends to break and to produce a condition which Emile Durkheim has termed *anomie,* by which he means a situation which might be described as a sort of social emptiness or void. Under such conditions suicide, crime, and disorder are phenomena to be expected because individual existence no longer is rooted in a stable and integrated social milieu and much of life's activity loses its sense and meaning.

That intellectual activity is not exempt from such influences is effectively documented by this volume, which, if it may be said to have a practical objective, apart from the accumulation and ordering of fresh insights into the preconditions, the processes, and problems of intellectual life, aims at inquiring into the prospects of rationality and common understanding in an era like our own that seems so frequently to put a premium upon irrationality and from which the possibilities of mutual understanding seem to have vanished. Whereas the intellectual world in earlier periods had at least a common frame of reference which offered a measure of certainty to the participants in that world and gave them a sense of mutual respect and trust, the contemporary intellectual world is no longer a cosmos but presents the spectacle of a battlefield of warring parties and conflicting doctrines. Not only does each of the conflicting factions have its own set of interests and purposes, but each has its picture of the world in which the same objects are accorded quite different meanings and values. In such a world the possibilities of intelligible communication and *à fortiori* of agreement are reduced to a minimum. The absence of a common apperception mass vitiates the possibility of appealing to the same criteria of relevance and truth, and since the world is held together to a large extent by words, when these words have ceased to mean the same thing to those who use them, it follows that men will of necessity misunderstand and talk past one another.

Apart from this inherent inability to understand one another there exists a further obstacle to the achievement of consensus in the downright obstinacy of partisans to refuse to consider or take seriously the theories of their opponents simply because they belong to another intellectual or political camp. This depressing state of affairs is aggravated by the fact that the intellectual world is not free from the struggle for personal distinction and power. This has led to the introduction of the wiles of salesmanship into the realm of ideas, and has brought about a condition where even scientists would rather be in the right than right.

III. If we feel more thoroughly appalled at the threatening loss of our intellectual heritage than was the case in previous cultural crises it is because we have become the victims of more grandiose expectations. For at no time prior to our own were so many men led to indulge in such sublime dreams about the benefits which science could confer upon the human race. This dissolution of the supposedly firm foundations of knowledge and the disillusionment that has followed it have driven some of the "tender minded" to romantic yearning for the return of an age that is past and for a certainty that is irretrievably lost. Faced by perplexity and bewilderment others have sought to ignore or circumvent the ambiguities, conflicts, and uncertainties of the intellectual world by humour, cynicism, or sheer denial of the facts of life.

At a time in human history like our own, when all over the world people are not merely ill at ease, but are questioning the bases of social existence, the validity of their truths, and the tenability of their norms, it should become clear that there is no value apart from interest and no objectivity apart from agreement. Under such circumstances it is difficult to hold tenaciously to what one believes to be the truth in the face of dissent, and one is inclined to question the very possibility of an intellectual life. Despite the fact that the Western world has been nourished by a tradition of hard-won intellectual freedom and integrity for over two thousand years, men are beginning to ask whether the struggle to achieve these was worth the cost if so many to-day accept complacently the threat to exterminate what rationality and objectivity has been won in human affairs. The widespread depreciation of the value of thought on the one hand and its repression on the other hand are ominous signs of the deepening twilight of modern culture. Such a catastrophe can be averted only by the most intelligent and resolute measures.

Ideology and Utopia is itself the product of this period of chaos and unsettlement. One of the contributions it makes toward the solution of our predicament is an analysis of the forces that have brought it about. It is doubtful whether such a book as this could have been written in any other period, for the issues with which it deals, fundamental as they are, could only be raised in a society and in an epoch marked by profound social and intellectual upheaval. It proffers no simple solution to the difficulties we face, but it does formulate the leading problems in a fashion that makes them susceptible of attack and carries the analysis of our intellectual crisis farther than has ever been done before. In the face of the loss of a common conception of the problems and in the absence of unanimously accepted criteria of truth, Professor Mannheim has sought to point out the lines along which a new basis for objective investi-

gation of the controversial issues in social life can be constructed.

Until relatively recently, knowledge and thinking, while regarded as the proper subject matter of logic and psychology, were viewed as lying outside the realm of social science because they were not considered social processes Whereas some of the ideas that Professor Mannheim presents are the result of the gradual development in the critical analysis of thought processes and are an integral part of the scientific heritage of the Western world, the distinctive contribution of the present volume may turn out to be the explicit recognition that thought, besides being a proper subject matter for logic and psychology, becomes fully comprehensible only if it is viewed sociologically. This involves the tracing of the bases of social judgments to their specific interest-bound roots in society, through which the particularity, and hence the limitations, of each view will become apparent. It is not to be assumed that the mere revelation of these divergent angles of vision will automatically cause the antagonists to embrace one another's conceptions or that it will result immediately in universal harmony. But the clarification of the sources of these differences would seem to be a precondition for any sort of awareness on the part of each observer of the limitations of his own view and at least the partial validity of the views of the others. While this does not necessarily involve the holding of one's interests in abeyance, it does make possible at least a working agreement on what the facts in an issue are, and on a limited set of conclusions to be drawn from them. It is in some such tentative fashion as this that social scientists, even though they are in disagreement on ultimate values, can to-day erect a universe of discourse within which they can view objects from similar perspectives and can communicate their results to one another with a minimum of ambiguity.

IV. To have raised the problems involved in the relations between intellectual activity and social existence squarely and lucidly is in itself a major achievement. But Professor Mannheim has not rested at this point. He has recognized that the factors at work in the human mind impelling and disturbing reason are the same dynamic factors that are the springs of all human activity. Instead of positing a hypothetical pure intellect that produces and dispenses truth without contaminating it by the so-called non-logical factors, he has actually proceeded to an analysis of the concrete social situations in which thought takes place and intellectual life is carried on.

The first four parts of the present volume demonstrate the fruitfulness of this sociological approach concretely and offer an exemplification of the methods of the new discipline, the formal foundations of which are sketched in Part V under the title, "The Sociology of Knowledge." This new discipline historically and logically falls within the scope of general sociology conceived as the basic social science. If the themes that Professor Mannheim has treated are systematically developed, the sociology of knowledge should become a specialized effort to deal in an integrated fashion, from a unifying point of view and by means of appropriate techniques, with a series of subject matters which hitherto have been only cursorily and discretely touched upon. It would be premature to define the exact scope which this new discipline will eventually take. The works of the late Max Scheler and of Professor Mannheim himself have, however, gone sufficiently far to allow of a tentative statement of the leading issues with which it must concern itself.

Of these the first and basic one is the social-psychological elaboration of the theory of knowledge itself, which has hitherto found a place in philosophy in the form of epistemology. Throughout the recorded history of thought this subject has haunted the succession of great thinkers. Despite the age-old effort to resolve the relationship between experience and reflection, fact and idea, belief and truth, the problem of the interconnection between being and knowing still stands as a challenge to the modern thinker. But it no longer is a problem that is the exclusive concern of the professional philosopher. It has become a central issue not merely in science, but in education and politics as well. To the further understanding of this ancient enigma the sociology of knowledge aspires to make a contribution. Such a task requires more than the application of well-established logical rules to the materials at hand, for the accepted rules of logic themselves are here called into question and are seen, in common with the rest of our intellectual tools, as parts and products of the whole of our social life. This involves the searching out of the motives that lie back of intellectual activity and an analysis of the manner and the extent to which the thought processes themselves are influenced by the participation of the thinker in the life of society.

A closely allied field of interest for the sociology of knowledge lies in the reworking of the data of intellectual history with a view to the discovery of the styles and methods of thought that are dominant in certain types of historical-social situations. In this connection it is essential to inquire into the shifts in intellectual interest and attention that accompany changes in other phases of social structure. It is here that Professor Mannheim's distinction between ideologies and utopias offers promising directives for research.

In analysing the mentality of a period or of a given stratum in society, the sociology of knowledge concerns itself not merely with the ideas and modes of thinking that happen to flourish, but with the whole social setting in which this occurs. This must necessarily take account of the factors that are responsible for the acceptance or the rejection of certain ideas by certain groups in society, and of the motives and interests that prompt certain groups consciously to promote these ideas and to disseminate then among wider sections.

The sociology of knowledge furthermore seeks to throw light on the question of how the interests and purposes of certain social groups come to find expression in certain theories, doctrines, and intellectual movements. Of fundamental importance for the understanding of any society is the recognition accorded to the various types of knowledge and the corresponding share of the resources of society devoted to the cultivation of each of these. Equally significant is the analysis of the shifts in social relationships brought about by the advances in certain branches of knowledge such as technical knowledge and the increased mastery over nature and society that the application of this knowledge makes possible. Similarly the sociology of knowledge, by virtue of its concern with the role of knowledge and ideas in the maintenance or change of the social order, is bound to devote considerable attention to the agencies or devices through which ideas are diffused and the degree of freedom of inquiry and expression that prevails. In connection with this attention will be focused upon the types of educational systems that exist and the manner in which each reflects and moulds the society in which it operates. At this point the problem of indoctrination, which has recently received so much discussion in educational literature, finds a prominent place. In the same manner the functions of the press, of the popularization of knowledge and of propaganda receive appropriate treatment. An adequate understanding of such phenomena as these will contribute to a more precise conception of the role of ideas in political and social movements and of the value of knowledge as an instrument in controlling social reality.

Despite the vast number of specialized accounts of social institutions, the primary function of which centres around the intellectual activities in society, no adequate theoretical treatment of the social organization of intellectual life exists. One of the primary obligations of the sociology of knowledge consists, therefore, in a systematic analysis of the institutional organization within the framework of which intellectual activity is carried on. This involves, among other items, the study of schools, universities, academies, learned societies, museums, libraries, research institutes and laboratories, foundations, and publishing facilities. It is important to know how and by whom these institutions are supported, the types of activity they carry on, their policies, their internal organization and interrelations, and their place in the social organization as a whole.

Finally, and in all of its aspects, the sociology of knowledge is concerned with the persons who are the bearers of intellectual activity, namely the intellectuals. In every society there are individuals whose special function it is to accumulate, preserve, reformulate, and disseminate the intellectual heritage of the group. The composition of this group, their social derivation and the method by which they are recruited, their organization, their class affiliation, the rewards and prestige they receive, their participation in other spheres of social life, constitute some of the more crucial questions to which the sociology of knowledge seeks answers. The manner in which these factors express themselves in the products of intellectual activity provides the central theme in all studies which are pursued in the name of the sociology of knowledge.

In *Ideology and Utopia,* Professor Mannheim presents not merely the outlines of a new discipline which promises to give a new and more profound understanding of social life, but also offers a much-needed clarification of some of the major moral issues of to-day. It is in the hope that it will make some contribution to the solution of the problems which intelligent people in the English-speaking world are facing that the present volume has been translated.

T. S. Eliot   (essay date 1940)

SOURCE: "Man and Society," in *The Spectator,* Vol. 164, No. 5841, June 7, 1940, p. 782.

[*In the following review of* Man and Society in an Age of Reconstruction, *Eliot praises Mannheim's insight and intellectual honesty.*]

Dr. Karl Mannheim is a sociologist, indeed, one of the most distinguished of living sociologists; and this massive work [**Man and Society in an Age of Reconstruction**] has the inexorable formality and complete apparatus (with seventy-three pages of bibliography) that one expects of continental scholarship. It is also difficult reading; though the difficulty of Dr. Mannheim's style is not due to any imperfection of English, and not, as with much American writing in this field, to the employment of a technical jargon. The vocabulary is that of any educated person. The difficulty of reading is due rather to a conscientious thoroughness, which prevents the author from passing any point until he has considered it from every aspect, and keeps the impatient reader marching at his own slow pace; it is also due to a judicial and remarkably impartial temper of mind, which refuses to present the difficult as if it were simple, or to allow prejudice or emotion to usurp the province of thinking.

It would seem at first, therefore, that this book is one which should be reviewed only by a professional sociologist for the benefit of other sociologists. If that were so, it would hardly be reviewed in these columns, and certainly not by this reviewer. This is, in fact, a book which everyone seriously interested in the future of our society ought to read; and being the work of a mind not only powerful and learned, but intelligent and widely cultivated, and possessed of urbanity and wisdom, it is profitable reading quite independently of our prejudices either for or against the science of which the author is an exponent. The value of reading it is not dependent upon our accepting any particular conclusions, but resides rather in giving us a widened consciousness of the contemporary situation; this is, indeed, one of that small number of books an acquaintance with which becomes "experience." To compare it with any other book published within the last few years must be misleading, but I hope that it will at least be read by all those to whom the names of Borkenau and Peter Drucker have significance.

I cannot attempt any account of the whole field that the book covers; the most that one can do is to suggest the assumptions from which it starts. The dilemma of modern society is the apparent necessity of choice between freedom and organisation. The future of totalitarian society may seem very doubtful; its structure may be very brittle, its cohesion superficial; its ability to preserve even the level of civilisation which it inherited may vanish; but it has undoubted advantages of efficiency in the present, and might conceivably succeed in bringing all other forms of social order to its own condition, even though that condition be deplorable. To Mannheim, as to many other thoughtful minds, the totalitarian order is only a local attempt to cope with a malady which infects the whole world; it is a specific which only alters the phase of the disease. Society cannot be restored to the nineteenth century situation; it must alter its aims. Society cannot return to any earlier degree of simplicity; it can only proceed to a more intelligent and thorough organisation. But freedom of some kind is also essential for human beings; so the problem is, in what areas of life are we to have organisation and control, and in what areas are we to have freedom of action by voluntary associations and by individuals? Hence the phrase, which Dr. Mannheim has put into currency, "planning for freedom."

Such is a very crude summary of the premises of the book. Incidental to their elaboration is a great deal of very penetrating analysis of the contemporary situation and its origins. The first impression of the reader on reviewing the author's elaborate armament of social techniques, social controls and scientific authority may be one of panic; or he may be unfairly biased by memories of one or another of Mr. Wells's flimsier inventions. Overcome by the prospect of all this planning, the reader may wonder whether the "freedom" will not become illusory, and whether, human nature being what it is, the result will be any more tolerable than what has already been produced in Germany. One reason why people may respond in this way is that most of us, however radical, progressive or open-minded we flatter ourselves to be, have an unconscious determination towards the past: we tend to escape into the past and into the future at the same time, and refuse to acknowledge that the present is what it is and not another thing. But there is a rejoinder of another kind. Dr. Mannheim is quite clear in understanding that "techniques" such as he is concerned with are neutral. He is quite ready to admit that they can be used for evil purposes as well as good. But there, he would say, they are: for better or worse, we have a "mass" society; and if we do not study how to use the techniques for good, then we must certainly be prepared to see them used for evil. And when we have read and pondered his whole discussion we must face the question: "What is the alternative?" It can only be, I believe, that which we may call the "dark age attitude"— waiting, perhaps for many generations, for the storm of the machine age to blow over; retiring, with a few of the best books, to a small self-contained community, to till the soil and milk the cow. That, like extreme pacifism, is an attitude with which there is no argument. But if we still look for any other attitude to adopt we must adjust our minds to consider Mannheim's proposals with equanimity.

One reason why this book is so substantial and impressive is the consistency with which the author confines himself to his terms of reference: this may cause misunderstanding on the part of those who hastily assume that he ought to be doing something that he has not attempted. And even if we understand the limitations I do not suggest we shall all accept his analysis everywhere. For instance, in his very important discussion of the nature of *élites* he speaks of selection on the basis of *blood, property* and *achievement,* as if these represented a simple progression from an aristocratic, through a bourgeois, to a mass society. It might be argued, I think, that in the most productive periods of civilisation there had been all three, and that they had overlapped and partly fused. It is perhaps owing partly to the disintegration of *élites* that we may be considered to have no effective *élite* at all at the present time. But Dr. Mannheim reminds us that "we have no clear idea how the selection of *élites* would work in an open mass society in which only the principle of achievement mattered"; he has no more illusions about the future than about the past. He only asks the questions: "What is the actual situation?" and "What, if we are to do anything, should we do about it?" That his answers are in terms of sociology, and not in those of religion, ethics, economics or political idealism, is a limitation which only affirms the value of the book.

John Middleton Murry   (essay date 1949)

SOURCE: "Karl Mannheim," in *Katherine Mansfield and Other Literary Studies,* Constable, 1959, pp. 152-62.

[*In the following essay, Murry evaluates Mannheim's contribution to modern social thought.*]

One thing was certain to those who had the privilege of direct contact with Karl Mannheim: that his was an eminent mind. It stood above others; it comprehended more; saw the great issues of our time in a wider perspective. More than this, he was pervaded with the sense of their urgency. The degree of his detachment was balanced by the degree of his identification. If he had stood aloof in order to understand, it was only in order that he might participate in the struggle with a full consciousness of what was, and was not possible: he was a master-strategist—the wisest I have known of the forces of light. And he was heroic. One felt that he was profoundly tired, his heart as it were soaked through with the weariness of bitter disappointment; yet he was indefatigable, determined to spend himself to the uttermost, in his mission of spreading awareness of the human predicament and creating the capacity of response to its demands.

It is beyond my competence to attempt an objective appraisal of his obviously great contribution to sociological thought. I can do no more than elucidate some of the constant stimulus he applied to my own mind. And here I must premise that I found myself, from the beginning of my contact with him, in instinctive sympathy with his mode of thinking. Though the range and resources of his knowledge were far superior to my own, from the outset he confirmed in me a conviction that the prevalent social and political thinking of today was too abstract or too rigid or too emotional. It was not engaging with the events themselves. The crying need was for minds which could think on many levels at once. In Mannheim I responded to one who had made himself a master of this flexibility of thought, and who encouraged me in my stumbling efforts to attain it. He had a rare genius for the Socratic midwifery appropriate to an age of sickeningly swift and radical change: for helping to bring to birth a new mode of thought that should be at once instrumental and directive in the process of our time.

The names he gave to this were not entirely happy. Neither "planned thinking", nor "thinking at the level of planning", were calculated to ring a bell in the unprepared mind. He more nearly hit the mark with his slogan, "Planning for Freedom". That, at least, defined the main purpose of the new mode of thinking, in a phrase which contained the element of paradox necessary to distinguish it; and since it is of the essence of the new thinking that it should be purposeful in a new sense, the slogan comes near to fulfilling the function of a definition. Moreover, it indicates a relation which Mannheim's thinking certainly had to that of Marx. Marx's dictum: "The philosophers have interpreted history, it is our task to change it", was the first parent of the school of thought of which Mannheim was the brilliant exponent. But Mannheim had profited, as no orthodox Marxist could possibly do, by the subsequent experience of mankind. He was totally immune from the dogmatism of positing a single motivation of social change, though he allowed full weight to the economic. But he saw, very clearly, that Marx's thinking was conditioned by a particular social situation, which had passed away.

In substance his thesis, as compared to Marx's, was that the social revolution had occurred, in Russia and Germany, to the disastrous accompaniment of revolutionary violence, but it had taken place no less in other highly industrialized societies. The political and social problem was to avert dictatorship, which was a crude surgical operation on society—in itself a confession of failure—rather a rational and remedial adjustment. For such a rational adjustment the democracies were equipped. The problem was to induce them to make proper use of their equipment. To conceive of the situation, as the Communists do *de fide,* as one in which dictatorship must succeed, while the democracies must fail, in solving the problem, is to misconceive it entirely. The fact is that "the democracies have not yet found a formula to determine which aspects of the social process should be controlled by regulation, and the dictatorships cannot see that interfering with everything is not planning".

Thus, the concept of "revolution" is itself misleading and irrelevant. Revolution is a consequence and not a cause. It is the consequence of the sudden disintegration of socially established attitudes which results from collective insecurity: it is the concomitant and index of the failure of a society to make a rational adjustment to the profound changes in its technical and structural foundations. Where such adjustment is not made, collective insecurity follows, and the irrationality of revolution and war erupts from the depths of a national or international society which has not discovered how to organize and integrate the impulses to violence. To Mannheim we may go for the deeper and disquieting obverse of Mr Churchill's world-famous epigram: "Never was so much owed by so many to so few" '

> There has seldom been a generation which was
> less willing for petty sacrifice and more likely to
> pay the supreme one without even knowing why.

That was, I believe, written in 1935; and it was, alas, to be prophetic even of many of those who earned Mr. Churchill's famous eulogy.

Out of this context emerges the meaning of Mannheim's concept of "planning". It is the outcome and purpose of the thinking of rational beings who have achieved a higher level of consciousness. Higher than what? Than the uncoordinated, unsynthesized thinking of the specialized sciences, or the dogmatic religious psychologies of the nature of Man, conceived in abstraction from society. No doubt, Mannheim himself could be charged with dogmatism when he asserts, pretty peremptorily, that man is transformable, and implies all human ideologies have a social origin. But the reply is that, self-evidently, Man is Man-in-Society; and conscious control of society is the form necessarily taken by any realistic effort towards human self-control. There is no danger, provided we understand clearly that control of society is essentially a means—the only means—to secure and enlarge the freedom of man, by preventing him from remaining the slave of blind social forces, which seem to him impersonal precisely because they are generated by his own "free" activities. "Planning" is the activity of consciousness whereby man escapes from the bondage of false freedom, which is the freedom to destroy himself by defect of consciousness, into a authentic freedom: the condition established for him by a society which is consciously and conscientiously self-regulated. "Planning" is thus—to use one of Mannheim's own definitions—"foresight deliberately applied to human affairs so that the social process is no longer merely the product of conflict and competition". Not, of course, a Utopia in which conflict and competition are totally eliminated from the social process, but where they are regulated and confined to spheres in which they are socially beneficent.

At this point it becomes evident that Mannheim's primary objective was to educate his contemporaries into a new conception of freedom. Not to reconcile them to the misleading notion that planning, in the current sense of the word, was compatible with freedom (that is to say, some planning with some freedom, both of the old and familiar style) but to persuade them to a radical change of both concepts, so that planning and freedom were understood to be complementary and interdependent. In a kind of primitive and elemental way men do understand this. They appreciate the necessity of government, in order to secure any real freedom at all; they appreciate the necessity of self-government, or democracy, in order that their freedom may be enlarged, and made more rational, by their willing consent to their own government. But at this point there is, or there threatens to be, a hiatus. Men continue to demand and to exercise freedoms of a type that are obsolete and anachronistic, because they set in motion impersonal social forces which undermine the collective security and open the gates to the irruption of mass-irrationality. Contemporary examples of such insistence on anachronistic freedoms are the self-contradictory demand of Russia for entire national sovereignty, or the demand of the English coal-miners for a yet further increase in wages unrelated to any increase in output. The one directly diminishes the collective security of the world-society; the other, by intensifying the pressure towards domestic inflation, diminishes the collective security of the country.

Against dangers of this kind, Mannheim saw but one prophylactic: an increase in human rationality expressed in a new understanding of freedom. Of the way to achieve these he was certain: it was by a more comprehensive science of society based on a more objective analysis and a new synthesis. By that effort, the new and necessary type of thinking would be evolved, which would be essentially dynamic, comporting a change in the thinker himself and setting him the task of changing others. Primarily, he envisaged the task as the education of an élite—the aristocracy within democracy without which it is an unworkable system—into a new understanding of modern society, and of the nature of the contemporary social process.

> If anything creative emerges from the general disillusionment of an age which has witnessed the practical deterioration of the ideals of Liberalism, Communism and Fascism, it can only be a new experimental attitude in social affairs, a readiness to learn from all the lessons of history. But one can only learn if one has belief in the power of reason. For a time it was healthy to see the limitations of the ratio, especially in social affairs. It was healthy to realize that thinking is not powerful if it is severed from the social context and ideas are only strong if they have their social backing, that it is useless to spread ideas which have no real function and are not woven into the social fabric. But this sociological interpretation of ideas may also lead to complete despair, discouraging the individual from thinking about issues which will definitely become the concern of the day. This discouragement of the intelligentsia, which may lead them to too quick a resignation of their proper function as the thinkers and forerunners of a new society, may become even more disastrous in a social setting where more depends on what the leading élites have in mind than in other periods of history. The theory that thought is socially conditioned and changes at different periods in history is only instructive if its implications are fully realized and applied to our own age.

This suggests the one radical criticism which can be made of Mannheim's thought: that it ends in a universal relativism. I am sure the criticism cannot be sustained, though I could wish that Mannheim himself had more explicitly formulated the assumptions which he accepted as self-evident. He rebuts the criticism in this passage by saying that the theory that thought is socially conditioned is only instructive if its implications are realized and applied to our own age: which must mean that we are called upon consciously to submit our own thought to a social conditioning, to apply it to the actual social reality *in statu mascendi* and thereby to compel it to transcend itself, or pass beyond the limitations imposed by a habit of abstraction and specialization. That, no doubt, in itself involves a moral choice; it is, as von Hügel would have said, a *costing* emancipation of thought. But that alone does not appear to guarantee that it will help the cat to jump the right way. What *is* the right way? Is there, on Mannheim's principles, any means of determining that? I am sure there is, although (as I say) I would prefer that he himself should have been more explicit about it. It is indicated in his declaration that one can only learn from all the lessons of history "if one has belief in the power of reason". The emphasis is on *power*. Another more direct indication is contained in a passage which is more fully quoted below. "Freedom of thought will not be established"—in a society planned for freedom—"because it is a virtue in itself, but because the unhampered exchange of opinion is the only guarantee of social progress".

Thus, the condition of rationality is the unhampered exchange of opinion. That alone is a rational society in which this condition is deliberately secured, by means appropriate to the real condition of the society, and only a rational society is capable of progress. From those propositions it seems to follow that progress is an advance in rationality. And rationality—the reason in the power of which one must believe—requires for its manifestation freedom of thought and expression. To maintain this, a rational society must proscribe those who would abolish or diminish this freedom.

Still, it may be said, we are not given a clear definition either of rationality or its power. Probably, no further definition is really possible. The *power* of reason will consist, mainly, in the power of such a society to appeal to the human reason as a manifest good, and to elicit the moral action of men in support and defence of it, as the sole guarantee of a continuous advance in truth and justice. In regard to this normative ideal—of the society "planned for freedom"—Mannheim's relativism amounts to no more than the recognition that "the chances of achieving this new society are, to be sure, limited. It is not absolutely predetermined. But this is where our new freedom begins." Man is free to reject or achieve it; to reject it through ignorance, or to achieve it through fuller consciousness. But he has only to understand the human predicament, and the social situation, to devote himself to the task of achieving it. That is the effect of the "power of reason" in himself, and he must believe that it has the like power in others.

The purpose of sociology as Mannheim understood and practised it is to defend and strengthen the rational society. To that end the historical consciousness must be contemporary and dynamic. Marx expressed that truth in terms which are now crude and treacherous because they derived from a social situation which is past. The need is now for a dynamism that is truly contemporary, which takes account both of the fundamentally changed situation since the Communist Manifesto and of the processes which have caused that change. It is one of the tragedies of our time—perhaps the greatest—that the Communists of the West have been unwilling to make the adjustment to reality. They have clung to an outmoded orthodoxy which has led them to an absurdly partial interpretation of events, and a complete failure in rational anticipation: for which they have striven to compensate by an opportunism so outrageously cynical that it has corroded the very foundations of rationality. The degeneration of the profound insight of Marx into the fanatical religious doctrine that Stalinist Russia can do no wrong is one of the most astonishing phenomena of an astonishing age.

Of course, that phenomenon also needs to be understood, not merely condemned. The moral vacuum which this preposterous orthodoxy has come to occupy arises from the lack of a faith adequate to the real social situation; and that lack is largely due to the persistence of the ideology of a purely negative Liberalism which left fundamental

doctrines to be decided by individual caprice, and deplored even a conscious affirmation of the principles of the social consensus on which it was founded. The distinctive economic doctrines of Liberalism have been entirely discarded, but the negative ideology persists at a time when the changed social structure imperatively demands a doctrine that is, if not more positive than itself, at least in sufficient harmony with it to give it relevant and effective guidance. This failure of the British intelligentsia, deeply infected by the anarchy of Liberalism, to produce a positive ethic (and metaphysic) of co-operation, has helped to create the situation in which the sinister combination of fanaticism and cynicism, which goes by the name of Communism, not merely corrupts the young but, by its influence on men who hold key-positions among the workers, does much to hamper the incoherent effort of the nation to assert its own will to live.

It was, I think, no accident that Karl Mannheim, the central European, by birth a Hungarian, a German by choice in the pregnant days of the Weimar Republic, was driven to take refuge in this country, and became one of its most devoted citizens, and gave himself unsparingly to the work of making it conscious of its opportunity and its danger. I should describe his life-work, unhesitatingly, as an effort to give his adopted country a doctrine at once worthy of its best traditions, and moulded exactly on its real condition. Obviously, such a description is teleological. When his own decisive thinking was done, Mannheim was still a German, whose self-imposed duty it was to give the nascent democracy of the Weimar Republic a conscious philosophy. But the necessity which drove him to England was implicit in his own activity. England had become the only possible home for the peculiar synthesis of rationality and freedom for which he stood: the only country where it might be achieved. And it says something for England that shortly before his death he had been appointed to one of the "key-positions" by which he rightly set such store.

To educate the educators was his mission: to carry men's minds beyond the barren and unprofitable antithesis between planning and freedom, to make them aware at once that the rational control of society was necessary—in order that man, the really existent man, and not the atomistic figment of nostalgic fantasy, might control himself and his destiny—and that this control was the indispensable condition of freedom—real freedom and not the specious substitute for it that still fascinates so many backward-looking imaginations.

> There are certain basic virtues which are essential to the maintenance of a planned society, and it is necessary that we should use all the resources of our education to create them. These basic virtues are not very different from those which the ethics of all world-religions, among others Christianity, have held to be vital: co-operation, brotherly help and decency. This education is primarily needed to destroy the psychological anarchy of liberal capitalism, which is based on the artificial cultivation of certain exaggerated attitudes. One of these is the mania for competition, which springs not from the desire for objective achievement and community service, but from sheer self-centredness or very

often from neurotic anxiety. A democratically planned society must thoroughly develop the new forms of freedom, but once developed it must defend them with the same zeal that any society shows in defence of its fundamental principles. Democracy ought to instruct its citizens in its own values instead of feebly waiting until its system is wrecked by private armies from within. Tolerance does not mean tolerating the intolerant. Once integration and equilibrium have been achieved in the sphere of elementary human relationships, there must be very far-reaching liberty on the higher planes of our spiritual life, especially freedom for intellectual discussion. But freedom of thought will not be established merely because it is a virtue in itself but because the unhampered exchange of opinion is the only guarantee of social progress.

Democracy, too, has its orthodoxy: but it is an orthodoxy which at the simple level of the essential social consensus is but workaday epitome of the ethical teaching of all high-religions, and at a higher level of consciousness is understood to be the indispensable condition of the continuance of man's search for truth and freedom. If social progress is to be progress indeed, and not mere biological process, freedom must be understood as the willing consent to establish the social conditions of freedom. The obstinate endeavour to perpetuate forms of freedom which were appropriate only to a past condition of society—such for example as the freedom to do altogether as one likes with one's own, or the much vaunted consumer's choice—coming, as they do, into direct conflict with the organization necessary to keep society alive, only makes for confusion and inefficiency and a lowering of the standard of life which vastly diminishes the total freedom of society. What is true of the capitalist is equally true of the working-class, which adheres to the equally obsolete principle of selling its labour for the highest price it can extract from a seller's market. That price-control without wages-control is irrational, as we are now learning, is only one of the many exemplifications of one of Mannheim's basic axioms: that partial planning is worse than no planning at all. The "freedoms" which the partial planner treats as sacrosanct, through ignorance or timidity, then become self-destructive.

The vital freedoms of democracy can be preserved and extended in modern society. Of that Mannheim was convinced. But he was equally convinced that there is only one way to do it: that is, consciously to organize society in such a fashion that these freedoms are guaranteed. The question for him, was whether existing democracy was capable of the effort—the small conscious sacrifice that would avert the great unconscious one. That depended primarily on the capacity of the democratic élites for a radical change in their modes of thought. It is at this point that Mannheim, though a Jew, came into intimate harmony with the most responsible Christian thinking of our day, which regards as the *note* of Christianity the willingness to suffer such a radical change in those habitual postulates of social thought which Mannheim distinguished as *principia media*: the principles which are of an age and not for all time, as they almost invariably are imagined to be.

The future is open. The impassioned objectivity of Mannheim's study of the social mechanism served merely to reinforce his convictions of this basic freedom of social man to choose and create his own destiny. But this freedom could not be exercised by abstract idealism: it was realized only in relevant and responsible action, that is to say, action which proceeded from a clear knowledge of those points and structures in society where positive influence was possible, and applied itself to some one of them. Herein lay at once the likeness and the extreme difference between Mannheim's thought and Marx's. All that Marx had—in unconscious deference to the *principia media* of his age—taken for granted as permanent in the structure of capitalist society, Mannheim had submitted to a searching analysis based upon bitter experience. He turned the tables on Marx by demonstrating the Utopianism of his "scientific socialism". Yet he was the first to acknowledge the profound genius of his predecessor, of whom—in the positive and creative sense—he was one of the greatest disciples. A comparison and a contrast between the fate and fortune of these two German-Jewish refugees, with almost a century between them, imposes itself: one fled from the collapse of German liberalism in the 1840's, the other from the collapse of German Social Democracy (of which Marx was the deity) in the 1930's. I would like to think that, in making Mannheim Professor of Education at London, England instinctively showed its recognition of what is necessary at this time of revolutionary change. It gave Marx freedom; it gave Mannheim the freedom and the task of teaching it how to preserve the freedom that it gave. None was better fitted to fulfil it. *Multis ille bonis flebilis occidit.*

Helmut R. Wagner   (essay date 1952)

SOURCE: "Mannheim's Historicism," in *Social Research,* Vol. 19, No. 3, September, 1952, pp. 300-24.

[*In the following essay, Wagner analyzes the concept of a "sociology of knowledge" as developed in* Ideology and Utopia.]

With increasing recognition of the need for broader theoretical orientations, American sociologists have become increasingly interested in the problems of a sociology of knowledge. In pursuing this interest they have not fallen back on earlier American "armchair" traditions—on such heritages, for example, as Summer's theory of ethnocentricity, Keller's evolutionary extensions of it, Veblen's combination of class interpretation with a theory of social-evolutionary stages, Robinson's critique of social conceptions and thought control. Rather, attention has been fixed on a series of European theoreticians, among them such positivistic thinkers as Pareto and Durkheim and such "idealistic" philosophers as Scheler. The dominant influence, however, has been that of karl Mannheim.

Actually, this influence stems from but one publication, the three essays combined in the English edition of ***Ideology and Utopia***. This book represents Mannheim's most persistent effort toward an all-inclusive sociology of knowledge. Ontology, epistemology, and logic are here subsumed under a theory of the social conditioning of thought—a theory that serves both as a basis for a general sociology and as a potential instrument of social change. The radicalism as well as the scope of this undertaking is challenging. It seems that Mannheim has set the stage for the highly controversial discussions concerning a sociology of knowledge to take place on all conceivable levels: philosophical-epistemological; logical-methodological; sociological-empirical; political-activistic.

These discussions have involved philosophers and logicians of different schools, as well as social theoreticians and researchers of diverse interests. Their extent and tone seem to indicate, first, that Mannheim has challenged widely accepted postulates, and second, that he has posed problems that demand attention, even though they may have been only obliquely approached. Such problems are numerous: the social preconditions of human cognition; the social processes of the origination and distribution of knowledge on the commonsense level; the formation of social and political ideologies; the influence of social factors on the formulation of scientific theories and the steering of scientific interests; the selection of particular items of research for popularization, and the transformation of specialized into general knowledge on the scientific level; the eventual limitations imposed on cognitive processes by the particularities of cultural situations and social structures; the subtle influences that "feeling tone," "climate of opinion," and the "relative natural aspect of the world" exert in different social units on the general ideas and orientations of thinkers and researchers, on their operational frame of reference, and on both the direction of their inquiries and the interpretation of their findings.

It shall not be asserted here that Mannheim has seen these problems with that clarity which would be a first condition for their solution; nor can it be taken for granted that he has pointed out reliable ways for solving them. In fact, he has been assailed on almost every point, and often with cogent arguments. Most of his critics, however, have confined themselves to a discussion of certain individual postulates, without duly considering the universal theoretical context in which they have been offered: thus most of the philosophical criticism advanced against him reads like a spirited continuation of the age-old controversies concerning the certainty of philosophical truths and the relativism of knowledge. And well-meaning supporters of Mannheim have often conceived of his theories as instructions for empirical sociological research; consequently they have run into seemingly glaring contradictions between different parts and postulates of *Ideology and Utopia* for which the only apparent explanation that could be advanced was the confusion of the author.

Neither friends nor foes have sufficiently understood that Mannheim's sociology of knowledge represents—if we refrain from harping on occasionally ambiguous formulations or other minor details—a quite consistent system of social thought, and one that can be properly understood only in its total spirit, with due consideration of Mannheim's general philosophical intent. To grasp this is no easy matter, however, for thinkers who have grown up in an intellectual atmosphere rather remote from the particular social-philosophical traditions out of which this sociol-

ogy of knowledge arose. It is for this reason that I shall here trace the outlines of Mannheim's system of a sociology of knowledge, as contained in and implied by the essays in *Ideology and Utopia,* and appraise this system with regard to its possible significance for a modern sociological theory which is not bound by its underlying orientations and presuppositions.

I

Mannheim's sociology of knowledge cannot be viewed as a frame of reference for empirical inquiry as long as we understand the latter term to mean procedures based on nominalistic considerations, such as have been developed by Max Weber, or on pragmatic approaches, such as may be traced to John Dewey, or on any of the currently recognized ways of selecting, collecting, appraising, and interpreting data according to research hypotheses which are thereby subjected to empirical test. To be sure, Mannheim demanded that every "idea" be judged by "its congruence with reality." But the concept of reality, as he understood it, was so much at variance with the prevailing presuppositions of social research that he planned to construct a different epistemological system which, he hoped, would allow a justification of his theoretical postulates.

Rejecting a Platonic as well as a "mechanistic" concept, Mannheim spoke of the "dynamic character of reality," that is, the everchanging aspects of the world within the flux of social evolution, and the varying pictures of it gained by different groups of social actors within this process. Thus "reality" is not only an embodiment of social existence within the ongoing historical process, but also the necessarily restricted or partial comprehension of that existence by members of individual groups or social strata. This comprehension tends to become more inclusive, and the historical process itself drives toward the point from which it will become possible to reveal its immanent meaning.

Mannheim's conception of reality is thus historicistic. In fact, his whole sociology of knowledge is closely related to those interpretations of the social process which have been philosophically postulated by Hegel and sociologically reinterpreted by Marx. In the tradition of a Hegelian-Marxian historicism, he wrote *Ideology and Utopia* as an attempt to offer new solutions where Marx's imposing ideas had obviously failed. Mannheim's sociology of knowledge is understandable only as a historicistic system. If it lacks the intrinsic coherence and the compelling logic of his predecessors' systems, it is because he tried to avoid their most contested assumptions, to modify their excessive claims, to salvage historicism from destruction by its many adversaries, and to open up new lanes for its future development, including new fields for its application.

His central preoccupation was interest in a basic change of modern society. Like Marxism, Mannheimian sociology of knowledge was meant to serve both as a theoretical instrument of political engineering and as a philosophical promise of social salvation. This dual purpose governs the whole system, defining the meaning of its concepts, indicating the tone of its interpretations, and serving as final point of reference for the criteria by which its basic postulates can be vindicated and validated. In other words, Mannheim's sociology of knowledge is more than a sociology of social thought. It is a historicistic theory of "knowledge" in the service of an idea directed toward basic social change.

II

This becomes strikingly clear in Mannheim's conception of knowledge. Here he excluded from consideration all forms of mathematical reasoning, but he made no basic distinctions between the remaining types of cognition, although he had definite ideas as to their epistemological order of rank. Priority he gave to what he called political sociology, having as its focal point the "relation between theory and practice." Although not quite established as yet, it represents "a quite different form of knowledge from one customarily conceived"—that is, a governing one. The fact that it is in contradiction to the present-day conception of science should be only "a stimulus to the revision of our conception of science as a whole."

Mannheim advanced three reasons in justification of this quite extraordinary demand. Politics as a science, he argued first, is directly connected with, and emerges from, the Social Process, and thus is the most adequate expression of Social Becoming; in simpler words, social existence finds its most elementary, and therefore most genuine, expression in the spheres of political thinking. Secondly, politics was for Mannheim the basic instrument for the assertion of social groups within the social process; whatever political thoughts emerge from group existence, they become expressions of group or class desires—or, as [Jacques J.] Maquet has expressed it, "means of combat in the pursuit of collective objectives" and instruments of "adaptation to the conditions of the struggle for domination." In these ways, thirdly, political thinking reverses itself into political action, and political "practice," in turn, represents itself as a potential instrument for a volitional change of the social process.

Thus the claim of priority for political sociology is based on historicistically cogent reasons. Whether that claim would withstand examination on the grounds of a scientific methodology is another matter. But if we eliminate from present consideration the problem complex of "political practice," and concentrate on the cognitive aspects of this sociology of knowledge, we are left with a theory that may be summarized as follows.

Knowledge emerges out of the social process in the struggle of social groups for self-assertion and political survival. Thus active existence within the dynamic structures of a society is the source of socially relevant cognition. Being immersed in the social process, a group possesses, first of all, a common undertone of sentiments or, as Mannheim called it, a collective unconscious. This unconscious, it seems, acts as a driving force behind the social assertions of the group, and at the same time becomes the basis from which the elements of the group's *Weltanschauung* develop. The collective *Weltanschauung* appears as a product of a common historical fate, and unites the group spiritually; common people simply "absorb" it, but even "the

profound insight of the genius" stems from the same grounds.

The *Weltanschauung* governs the "thought style" of the group, the mode in which its members conceive of the "world" from the vantage point of their particular social position. The outlook thus attained consists of an interpretation of the group's "world," a conception of its place in society and history, a hierarchy of group values and norms, and, in general, a partly emotionally charged, partly rationalized total frame of reference of the collectivity. The more or less systematic verbalization of this *Weltanschauung* appears as the ideology of the group. And knowledge, finally, is the system of rational explanations and rules for all types of action which emerge from the application of these spontaneous orientations to the practical matters of group existence—primarily to its self-maintenance and assertion.

The theory, as presented so far, leans heavily on the Marxian conception of ideology and class consciousness. But Mannheim's conception of knowledge, being tied up with the *Weltanschauung* of a social group and thus with its collective unconscious anchored directly in the stream of an unfolding social process, represents cognition only as an indirect manifestation of historicistic group existence—as a rationalization of that existence for the social-technical purposes of an essentially political activity.

This functionality of knowledge eludes positivistic interpretation not only with regard to its historicistic genesis. In addition, the rationality of the means applied is not matched by rational ends. Rather, it is governed by a historical teleology: a social group, or class, tends to conceive of its role in society in terms of a "mission," as defined by its *Weltanschauung* and expressed in its "utopia," that is, in its ideological anticipation of a state of society which is to be brought about, and which thus transcends given realities as well as given knowledge.

This conception of knowledge explains Mannheim's rejection of the conventional conception of science. It reveals the incompatibility of his type of reasoning with that expressed in rules of procedure governing the practical fields of social research. And it clarifies his attempt to place a "science of politics" at the top of a hierarchy of all fields of knowledge.

III

Mannheim's conception of knowledge is embedded in his historicistic ontology. Operating on the basis of a Hegelian theory of emanation, he was confronted with two problems of a crucial character.

One concerns the modes, and also the possibilities, of theoretically recognizing the process of social becoming and its spontaneous ideological products out of the conditions of the process itself. The explanation had to be intrinsic; that is, Mannheim's sociology of knowledge itself had to appear as product, or emanation, of the same social process which it was meant to interpret, or which it had "discovered". Consequently Mannheim attempted to distinguish his own position from that of Marx by effecting a transition from what he called the partial to the total conception of ideology. The partial conception claims absolute validity for one's own theory, while disposing of the thoughts of others as ideological mystifications of the realities of class existence. The total conception admits the relativism of its own postulates, that is, their explanation in terms of the social conditions of their genesis.

This, however, brings the second problem to the fore. Mannheim was not willing to accept the position taken by those skeptical philosophers who disclaim the possibility of a philosophical or scientific certainty in favor of a universal relativism. On the contrary, he was seriously concerned with an ultimate vindication of his theories, and he made considerable efforts to show that his sociological system was capable of producing valid knowledge. Epistemologically, Mannheim rejected a universally relativistic position. Thus he was forced to fall back on ontological assertions, and these were derived essentially from Hegel's conception of history as the process of a gradual self-recognition of the Objective Mind of the World Spirit.

Mannheim, like his historicistic predecessors, saw himself at a crucial stage within the historical process. "It is only now," he maintained, "that the new historical sense is beginning to penetrate and a dynamic concept of ideology can be conceived of."

The emergence of modern mass society, accompanied by a "process of democratization," leads to a confrontation of different ideologies with equal claims to validity. Sociology of knowledge has thus been prepared for politically. Intellectually, it has been initiated by the emergence of epistemology as an investigation of the conditions and possibilities of cognition, by the rise of the "psychogenetic approach" as a mode of explaining thought, and finally by the adoption of techniques for debunking ideologies and reducing ideas to their social preconditions. Through the cumulative effects of these three critiques of knowledge it has finally become possible to construct a sociological system which allows a systematic comprehension of the actual conditions for the formation and assertion of social thought, and knowledge in general.

Having comprehended this unique situation, Mannheim had only to develop a corresponding methodology that would allow him to describe the social processes underlying the genesis and functioning of ideologies and knowledge. He did this with the help of a few conceptual tools and a particular procedure. As regards the tools, I have already discussed the rationally ascending order of the concepts of group unconscious, *Weltanschauung,* ideology, and knowledge. Methodologically, the series is completed by the concept of thought system. On the other hand, the link between social existence and thought system is accomplished by the operational tool of imputation.

A thought system, in Mannheim's sense, is a construct. In contrast to a *Weltanschauung,* which emanates spontaneously out of the social ground of group existence, a thought system is the systematic creation of a sociologist of knowledge. Neither the individual members of a group nor their abstract sum total "can legitimately be considered as bearers of this ideological thought system as a whole." The latter has to be constructed out of such dis-

crete elements as those to be found in the utterances of group members or in the writings of intellectuals who make themselves the ideological mouthpieces of certain social classes. [In a footnote, the critic explains: "It was Mannheim's contention, for example, that in Germany the whole ideology of conservatism had to be created by hired intellectuals, since the conservative classes were incapable of formulating their own world views and outlook. See his essay, **'Das Konservative Denken,'** in *Archiv für Sozialwissenschaft und Sozialpolitik,* vol. 57 (1927) nos. 1 and 2."]

This process of construction consists in tracing back particular statements to the *Weltanschauung* out of which they have apparently arisen. Thus Mannheim was confident that he could make explicit the whole thought system that is implicit in the discrete segments of ideologies. He spoke of uncovering the "underlying unity of outlook." But this is only a part of the task. If the *Weltanschauung* remains hidden behind discrete segments of thoughts, rather than being manifest in comprehensive and closed systems of ideology, and if these discrete segments are produced not only by group members but also by intellectuals who attach themselves to the group, the process of construction has to be extended from the thought system to the group itself.

Mannheim did not develop a theory of social stratification, even though he leaned toward an acceptance of the Marxian class concept. His social groups remain undefined and indefinite, and appear as intangible as his *Weltanschauungen.* In this connection it is of interest to note that in his only comprehensive, and highly interesting, representation of an ideology, that of German conservatism, he did not deal with the actual conditions and situations of the classes whose world view he constructed. It is clear, however, that if he had decided to do so, he would have wound up with exactly the same process of construction with which he attempted to reduce discrete segments of thought to "implicit" *Weltanschauungen.*

Mannheim established the link between his key concepts of thought system and social group by his procedure of imputation. This methodological device was derived not so much from Max Weber's ideal-typical procedures as from the sophisticated dialectics of Georg Lukacs. The latter, a radical Marxian theoretician, defined class consciousness as the consciousness "which men in a definite position in life *would* have if they were *capable of completely comprehending* that position." It is the men in possession of the superior knowledge of Marxism who "completely comprehend" class positions, construct ideological systems adequate to them, and impute these systems to classes which likewise exist only as historicistic potentialities.

Mannheim's central concern, like that of Lukacs, was the imputation of the construct of thought system to the construct of class. Both constructs, whatever they denote, are extremely remote from the historicistic-existential assumptions of his ontology. They have no connection with the asserted immediateness of concrete social experience, they lead to no direct comprehension of social realities, and to no spontaneous revelation of intrinsic meanings.

The imputation of social thought to social reality is practically the opposite of emanation and discovery.

IV

The inherent relativism of Mannheim's sociology of knowledge is evident not only from his considerations on the historicity of human thought, that is, its dependence on, and limitation by, the historically created conditions prevailing in a specific culture at a specific time. On the contrary, his emphasis was on the relativity of human thought with regard to position in social space. In a stratified society, he reasoned, thought products and knowledge are expressions of group or class situations. It is not only the content of ideologies that varies from group to group within the same society; also the members of different groups see and comprehend even the same things with different eyes. Their "thought styles" are as different as their thought systems.

Group and class ideologies, in their dual function as thought systems and thought styles, have been called *Aspektstrukturen,* roughly translatable as universes of discourse. They represent the common frames of reference of the group members. Within these frames, meaningful discussions are possible; errors of thought may be eliminated as accidental deviations from the common outlook, and truth may be established by reference to universally recognized group values. Usually, universes of discourse are conceived of as the unquestioned sources and preconditions of valid knowledge. The detached observer, however, is aware that a number of universes of discourse exist, and he may recognize their partial correctness as well as their particular social slant. This particular nature of universes of discourse, which opens up a view upon the social "world" as seen from a specific social angle, has been described as perspectivism.

If a sociologist of knowledge decides to adhere to a non-evaluative treatment of his subject matter, he must establish the partiality, the perspectivism, of all socially encountered group ideologies, without attempting to construct postulates that would be valid for all of them. A recognition of perspectivism leads to the acceptance of a universal relativism, and thereby excludes the establishment of a generally valid knowledge.

Such relativism, however, would have defeated Mannheim's philosophical intentions, which demanded a validation of his system. Thus he spoke not of relativism but of relationism, meaning that social thoughts, while related to the positions of their bearers, are not equally relative. On the contrary, they can be evaluated as to their possible contribution to social knowledge. Mannheim established an "evaluative conception of ideology" which was to make it possible to recognize valid components of perspectivistic thought systems. Further manipulation was to make it possible to recombine these into systems of knowledge which, with regard to their comprehension of the whole of society as well as their own understanding, would transcend single universes of discourse.

In investigating successive ideologies Mannheim asserted a "necessary regularity" in their sequence, a regularity leading to an understanding of the "inner meaning of history" itself. Relationism here refers to the gradual and partial unfolding of genuine social insights, and is therefore a way toward valid knowledge. In a somewhat similar way he held that the elements of a higher social cognition, as contained in various contemporaneous thought systems, are merged into systems of greater comprehension and correctness. Thus Mannheim assumed an inherent tendency, in the development of ideologies, toward a socially total and non-perspectivistic knowledge.

Methodologically, he was faced with the task of showing how his sociology of knowledge, as a system of social inquiry, could serve as an instrument for the systematic liquidation of the ontologically postulated relativism, and how it could establish generally valid knowledge within the framework of his epistemological assumptions. In other words, he had to answer the question how sociology of knowledge is possible in the face of his historicistic presuppositions.

V

Mannheim's argumentation, in agreement with the structure of his sociological system, had to follow two lines. Holding that thought is connected with and dependent on the social position of its proponents, he had to search for a social position within the class structure of a stratified society from which it would be possible to view the historical variations and the contemporaneous multiplicity of thought systems with sufficient detachment to evaluate them properly. And holding that universes of discourse are of a perspectivistic and partial character, he had to design methods by which the occupants of the aforementioned detached position would be able to recognize and manipulate the partial segments of knowledge contained in given thought systems in such a way as to arrive at a socially universal knowledge. The first problem, in Robert Merton's terminology, is that of supplying the "structural warranties" of Mannheim's theory. The second concerns warranties of a methodological character.

For the structural warranties Mannheim referred to the "socially unattached intelligentsia." Modern intellectuals occupy a sphere between the struggling classes of their society, and are not bound by those classes' vested interests. Given to intellectual pursuits, they are inclined to honor the code of objectivity which guides the reasoning of scientists, in contrast to the bias that permeates the thinking of the men who fight for economic and political gains.

Mannheim realized, of course, that most intellectuals are socially attached, and render services to the big classes. But he believed that they are in a position to gain a group consciousness of their own, and to become aware of the possibilities of their situation. These possibilities are unique. The intellectuals may achieve "things which are of indispensable significance for the whole social process," foremost among them the "discovery of the position from which a total perspective would be possible," that is, from which the totality of the social process could be comprehended. Even when they are attached to political parties, they could manage to arrive at a universal understanding of the society which they try to influence from a specific position. This too is the particular "mission" of the intelligentsia.

Mannheim spoke here of potentialities rather than of actualities. His expectations are strongly reminiscent of those that the Marxians attach to the class of their choice. The workers, reason the Marxians, have a historical mission to fulfil which they have not yet fully grasped but which they will attend to in the near future, under the guidance of those exceptional intellectuals who, for the first time in history, have discovered the intrinsic meaning of the Historical Process and can thus not only foresee its ulterior goal but also recognize those social forces that will bring it about.

Under the disillusioning influence of the political experiences that he shared with his European contemporaries during the years 1918 to 1924, Mannheim recognized the collapse of the Marxian hopes. But since he did not intend to abandon the scheme of his historicistic expectations, he shifted the "historical mission" from the proletarian class to his "socially unattached intelligentsia." Since the failure of the former it has become the latter, he believed, which occupies the crucial position within modern society, a position that offers all possibilities for the solution of the great problems of our time. At present this mission has been grasped by only a small group of exceptional intellectuals. But the progress of society itself, and its exposure to the shock of severe crises, make it likely that the whole intelligentsia will become aware of it. Theirs is the power to recognize the interests of the whole society, as against the partisan interests of the parties. And theirs is the power to transform their knowledge into political practice, by penetrating into the ranks of the political factions "in order to compel them to accept their demands."

In this, Mannheim paid homage to another principle of militant Marxism, that of the "unity of theory and practice." For the creators of the new "politics as science" there is no time for contemplation: in order to understand the dynamics of social development they have to participate, whether pro or con, in the "struggle for the ascendance of the lower strata," thus immersing themselves in "the dynamic unfolding of conflicting forces" out of which alone the knowledge aspired for can arise. By means of his political activities the Mannheimian "political scientist" attains contact with the elementary stream of social becoming.

This outlook sheds light on another of Mannheim's ideas, one that has been widely overlooked. He devoted long pages of his *Ideology and Utopia* to representing the development of the "utopian mentality," and this effort culminated in a search for the possibilities of a new social utopia, that is, a prophetic outlook on the future which would be inspiration and guide for those social forces aiming at a basic change of their society—a society which, in 1929, was drifting toward the dangerous rapids of economic collapse, depression, fascism, and a new world war.

Mannheim used the concept of utopia in a different sense from its usual meaning. For him it denoted not a striving for the impossible, but an ideological anticipation of the future of society. In Marxian theory, he held, the "utopian mentality" reached its highest and most adequate stage so far; also, Marxism marked the turning point from speculation to science. Henceforth it will be possible to erect a sociological system that will not only serve as a "key science" but also represent the utopia of our time.

As yet, this utopia does not exist, but the situation seems to be ripe for it, and the sociologists of knowledge have to take part in the coming struggle between a "complacent tendency to accept the present" and the new "utopian trends." In a way, the future of humanity depends on the emergence of these trends. Thus Mannheim alerted the intelligentsia to "the necessity of being continuously prepared for a synthesis in a world which is attaining one of the high points of its existence."

All this should show that Mannheim's "socially unattached intelligentsia" enters the historical stage as a historical potentiality, indeed as an almost chiliastic expectation. Agreement or disagreement with this idea of the intelligentsia and its mission is no sociological matter, but a matter of *Weltanschauung* and belief. As far as sociology of knowledge is concerned, Mannheim has in no way demonstrated that this idea supplies the structural warranties of his theory. What remains is not the intelligentsia as a socially functioning group, but isolated social philosophers presenting his historicistic theories and expectations in the form of a particular sociological system.

VI

This leaves Mannheim's sociology of knowledge as an intellectual system and a rational instrument for attaining knowledge. Thought systems are characterized by their partiality and their relationism. Their content, however, may be systematically manipulated by thinkers who decide to detach themselves from their ideological subject matter.

Social detachment may take place on the level of common-sense experience: the member of a closed community who moves into another environment becomes acquainted with different modes of living and thinking, and is thus in a position to compare their respective values and limitations; hence formerly absolute beliefs become relativated. Or a community may undergo such changes that previous outlooks become obsolete, and are replaced by new ones; the old beliefs are then recognized as having been historically conditioned rather than absolute. Finally, a community may become so differentiated that contrasting modes of interpretation confront one another, one of them becoming dominant.

What appears in such processes may be systematized into a sociological procedure. By conscious detachment a sociologist of knowledge may categorize the perspectivistic outlooks that apply to, and are valid in, a given social area. This is called particularization, that is, a definition of the range and limits of the perspectives contained in ideologies. As soon as thought systems are properly particularized, they are fit for further manipulation by way of selection and synthesis.

Synthesis takes place on several levels, and in different areas. It may be possible to ascertain the "common denominator" of two neighboring universes of discourse, and to translate the terms of the one into those of the other. Or two perspectives may be of different value, and then it may be possible to select the better one as a starting point for further synthesis. If particularization of ideas is carried out with sufficient detachment, it amounts to a neutralizing of the factors making for a situational determination of thought. Thus a sociologist of knowledge may not only arbitrate between divergent views, but also proceed to integrate some of their elements into a higher system of social knowledge. In such a procedure, sociology of knowledge shifts from the descriptive to the theoretical level. From comparison of the substantive assertions of different thought systems, and integration of their content, it proceeds toward a synthesis of thought styles, a synthesis with a broadened "categorical formal scope."

Mannheim saw theoretical synthesis as a kind of rational parallel to the ideological syntheses that go on in a highly dynamic and highly differentiated society by way of group contacts and interpenetration in different spheres, especially in the sphere of political action, interaction, conflict, and cooperation. The sociologist of knowledge, so to speak, executes intellectually what occurs spontaneously within the social process he observes. Here too the link between theoretical reflection and social existence is maintained, and stressed.

The syntheses that are reached, whether through the activities of social groups or through the theoretical elaborations of sociologists of knowledge, cannot be taken as final. They are progressive steps toward further and more comprehensive syntheses, and thus are only transitory phases within the process of Social Becoming. Mannheim may have seen this process itself as unending, and an ultimate synthesis as the limitary point of human thought tending toward infinity. On the other hand, he displayed great confidence in his sociological system, regarding it as at least a reliable instrument for an optimal synthesis of social knowledge. This, again, remains an unsubstantiated evaluation. Its plausibility depends entirely on the acceptance of Mannheim's historicistic presuppositions. If social thought is an emergent of the social process and a manifestation of social existence, then it may be said that Mannheim's system is an adequate means of interpreting what emerges.

VII

Mannheim's sociology of knowledge tends to be self-contained. It is based on a system of historicistic assumptions, and it can be used to reinforce these assumptions by quasi-methodological procedures. The philosophical assumptions justify the gnosiological means, and the gnosiological means vindicate the historicistic assumptions.

If this cycle is broken—for example, by a treatment of Mannheim's sociology of knowledge as an empirical system—difficulties arise which seem to be of a forbidding nature. Thus the methodological manipulation of the processes of synthesis poses questions that have not been satisfactorily answered by Mannheim, questions as to sociologically acceptable criteria and methodologically acceptable procedures of validation. This difficulty may be made

evident by a short survey of the criteria of validation contained in his sociology of knowledge.

First, Mannheim was of the opinion that the genesis of propositions has an effect on their validity But as to the nature and extent of this effect he was deliberately imprecise. A proposition, according to him, can be validated by reference to "dynamic criteria," that is, by reference to its "situational adequacy," its usefulness for the practical assertion of a group. On the other hand, the fact that an idea "works" does not establish its "truth." Thus Mannheim's "dynamic criteria" cannot stand on their own feet. If single propositions are to be validated within his system, this can be done only by a delegation of meaning, or by subsuming them under more inclusive postulates. This would be a strictly non-empirical procedure, and it would cause individual propositions to participate in the historicistic meanings that attach to the total system. As a result of this particular methodological situation, generally accepted procedures of validation are not applicable to statements contained in Mannheim's sociology of knowledge.

Second, it is a basic tenet of Mannheim's sociology of knowledge that a group's specific position within the social structure tends to condition its intellectual outlook. The perspective inherent in a given universe of discourse is a direct expression of social position—a social-existential factor. It is for this reason that the persons sharing a thought system are able to ascertain the validity of observations, propositions, and ideas within their own socially defined range. The criterion for establishing this partial validity is unanimity of observation and conclusion. Knowledge derived in this way may be said to be authentic for the universe of discourse under consideration, but it must be stated that here the criterion of unanimity has no logical relation to processes of validation. All it allows one to establish is the existence of common beliefs and the absence of deviating opinions: whether the former constitute "truths" and the latter "errors" is not dependent on the unanimity of the group members' judgment. At best, unanimity could establish the "social adequateness" of a prevailing view; but this is tautological. Again the "truth content" of opinions can be determined within Mannheim's system only by delegating the "validity" ascribed to the given thought system as a whole, with the latter conceived of as a particular station in the historicistic development of a certain idea (for example in the dialectical progression of the "utopian mentality").

Third, the possibility of a non-perspectivistic and thus universal knowledge would have been demonstrated if Mannheim had shown that there is a particular and unique position within the social structure, the occupants of which are situationally equipped to overlook and comprehend the totality of the social process. He believed that he established such a stratum in his "socially unattached intelligentsia," but this proves to be a historicistic construction without empirical counterpart. Mannheim failed to link his theoretical system to the existence of a specific social group.

Fourth, a comprehensive or overall social insight may be gained through various means of synthesis. In so far as such syntheses are accomplished by conscious intellectual effort they may be subjected to what Maquet has called the criterion of objectivity. But since this turns out to be only another name for the criterion of unanimity, which we have already disposed of, nothing new is added by applying it to a unification of several perspectives. For selecting the "best perspective" among several, Mannheim suggested "empirical fruitfulness" as a measure: the best perspective is that which reveals the "decisive features of the object." This suggestion begs the question, however: what is regarded as most fruitful depends on the purpose in hand and the frame of reference used. In this case the frame of reference has to exist outside the perspective under consideration. Thus the selection of a "best perspective" for purposes of synthesis, or of the "best elements" out of several perspectives, must rest on acceptance of a preestablished theory. The suggested procedure seems to be subject to, or dependent on, an acceptance of Mannheim's sociological system.

Fifth, Mannheim offered a particular mode of validation in regard to his concept of utopia. In his view, utopias are anticipations of future states of society; consequently they can be validated by the course of historical events. Unfortunately, however, such a validation occurs only ex post facto. Only the historian can ascertain what ideologies have helped to "shatter" a previously existent reality and have thus proved themselves to have been utopias. Moreover, Mannheim's representation of the four stages in the development of the "utopian mentality" produces results that are a far cry from even such ex post facto verification. The "orgiastic chiliasm" of the peasant Anabaptists proved unfounded, and many of its proponents perished; the rest did not manage to "make history." The "liberal-humanitarian idea" of the "ascendant bourgeoisie" was only vaguely formulated, and, to say the least, it is a considerable exaggeration to speak of the realization of the "idea of freedom" within liberal society. The "conservative idea" of the old ruling classes was created in ideological defense against liberal critics, as an attempt to glorify and justify the present by appeal to the past; it was in itself an ex post facto creation, pointing backward, not forward, and by Mannheim's own definition it cannot be accepted as a utopia. And finally the "socialist utopia" has not materialized either; its Bolshevist variation has led to social constellations completely outside the Western cultural sphere to which Mannheim's reasoning applies, while its social-democratic variation has been reduced to a basically conservative reform movement. Thus if any general methodological significance attaches to Mannheim's notion of utopia, it has not been demonstrated by his historical representation.

Sixth, and finally, although Mannheim hesitated to work out the epistemological system that is needed as a foundation for his sociology of knowledge, he operated in fact—partly implicitly, partly explicitly—on the assumptions of a historicistic theory of knowledge. Ultimately all his criteria for the validation of his gnosiological propositions can be reduced to a single historicistic postulate: socially valid cognition and knowledge are emergents of the social process. Acceptance of his argumentation presupposes acceptance of this postulate.

In brief, then, while Mannheim has touched on a series of questions that are relevant for modern sociology, the solutions he has provided within his historicistic frame of reference are open to question. Certainly they are hardly acceptable by social researchers who believe that the interpretation of social processes must be based on established observational methods within the fields of social experience. And even for inquiry into the sociological aspects of ideologies and of knowledge—their forms, foci, dispersion, and limitations—it might be advisable to select a theoretical basis less dependent on historicistic presuppositions than that offered in Mannheim's system.

Theodor W. Adorno   (essay date 1967)

SOURCE: "The Sociology of Knowledge and Its Consciousness," in *Prisms,* translated by Samuel Weber and Sherry Weber, The Mit Press, 1981, pp. 35-49.

[*In the following essay, Adorno focuses his discussion on* Man and Society in an Age of Reconstruction.]

The sociology of knowledge expounded by Karl Mannheim has begun to take hold in Germany again. For this it can thank its gesture of innocuous skepticism. Like its existentialist counterparts it calls everything into question and criticizes nothing. Intellectuals who feel repelled by 'dogma', real or presumed, find relief in a climate which seems free of bias and assumptions and which offers them in addition something of the pathos of Max Weber's self-conscious and lonely yet undaunted rationality as compensation for their faltering consciousness of their own autonomy. In Mannheim as in his polar opposite, Jaspers, many impulses of Weber's school which were once deeply embedded in the polyhistoric edifice come to light. Most important of these is the tendency to suppress the theory of ideologies in its authentic form. These considerations may justify returning to one of Mannheim's older books, ***Man and Society in an Age of Reconstruction***. The work addresses itself to a broader public than does the book on ideology. It cannot be held to each of its formulations. All the greater, however, is the insight it offers into the influence of the sociology of knowledge.

The mentality of the book is 'positivistic'; social phenomena are taken 'as such' and then classified according to general concepts. In the process social antagonisms invariably tend to be glossed over. They survive merely as subtle modifications of a conceptual apparatus whose distilled 'principles' install themselves autocratically and engage in shadow battles: 'The ultimate root of all conflicts in the present age of reconstruction can be seized in a single formula. All down the line tensions arise from the uncontrolled interaction of the "laisser-faire principle" and the new principle of regulation.' As if everything did not depend on who regulates whom. Or, instead of specific groups of people or a specific structure of society, 'the irrational' is made responsible for the difficulties of the age. The growth of antagonisms is elegantly described as 'the disproportionate development of human capacities', as though it were a question of personalities and not of the anonymous machinery which does away with the individual. Right and wrong are glossed over in like manner; the 'average man' is abstracted from them and assigned an ontological 'narrow-mindedness' which 'has always been there'. Of his 'experimental self-observation'—the term is borrowed from more exact sciences—Mannheim frankly confesses: 'All these forms of self-observation have the tendency to gloss over and neglect individual differences because they are interested in what is general in man and its variability.' Not, however, in his particular situation and in the real transformations he undergoes. In its neutrality the generalizing order of Mannheim's conceptual world is kindly disposed to the real world; it employs the terminology of social criticism while removing its sting.

The concept of society as such is rendered impotent from the outset by a language which invokes the exceedingly compromised term, 'integration'. Its occurrence is no accident. Mannheim's use of the concept of the social totality serves not so much to emphasize the intricate dependence of men within the totality as to glorify the social process itself as an evening-out of the contradictions in the whole. In this balance, theoretically, the contradictions disappear, although it is precisely they which comprise the life-process of 'society': 'Thus it is not immediately evident that an opinion which prevails in society is the result of a process of selection which integrates many similarly directed expressions of life.' What disappears in this notion of selection is the fact that what keeps the mechanism creaking along is human deprivation under conditions of insane sacrifice and the continual threat of catastrophe. The precarious and irrational self-preservation of society is falsified and turned into an achievement of its immanent justice or 'rationality'.

Where there is integration, elites are never far away. The 'cultural crisis' to which, in Mannheim, terror and horror are readily sublimated becomes for him the 'problem of the formation of elites'. He distills four processes in which this problem is supposed to crystallize: the growing number of elites and the resulting enfeeblement of their influence, the destruction of the exclusiveness of elite groups, the change in the process of selection of elites, and the change in their composition. In the first place, the categories employed in this analysis are highly questionable. The positivist who registers the facts *sine ira et studio* is ready to accept the phrases which conceal the facts. One such phrase is the concept of the elite itself. Its untruthfulness consists in the fact that the privileges of particular groups are presented teleologically as the result of some kind of objective process of selection, whereas in fact no one has selected these elites but themselves. In his use of the concept of the elite Mannheim overlooks social power. He uses the notion 'descriptively', in the manner of formal sociology. This allows him to shed only as much light as he wishes on each particular privileged group. At the same time, however, the concept of the elite is employed in such a way that the present emergency can be deduced from above, from some equally 'neutral' malfunctioning of the elite-mechanism, without regard to the state of political economy. In the process Mannheim comes into open conflict with the facts. When he asserts that in 'mass democratic' societies it has become increasingly easy for anyone to gain entrance into any sphere of social influence and that the elites are thereby deprived of 'their exclusive char-

acter, which is necessary for the development of intellectual and psychological impulses', he is contradicted by the most humble prescientific experience. The deficient homogeneity of the elites is a fiction, one related to those of chaos in the world of values and the disintegration of all stable forms of order. Whoever does not fit in is kept out. Even the differences of conviction which reflect those of real interests serve primarily to obscure the underlying unity which prevails in all decisive matters. Nothing contributes more to this obfuscation than talk of 'the cultural crisis', to which Mannheim unhesitatingly adds his voice. It transforms real suffering into spiritual guilt, denounces civilization, and generally works to the advantage of barbarism. Cultural criticism has changed its function. The cultural philistine has long ceased to be the man of progress, the figure with which Nietzsche identified David Friedrich Strauss. Instead, he has learned profundity and pessimism. In their name he denies the humanity which has become incompatible with his present interests, and his venerable impulse to destruction turns against the products of the culture whose decline he sentimentally bemoans. To the sociologist of the cultural crisis this matters little. His heroic *ratio* does not even refrain from turning the trite thesis of the demise of the formative power of European art since the end of the Biedermeyer period against modern art in a manner which is both romantic and reactionary.

Accepted along with elite theory is its specific colouration. Conventional notions are joined by naïve respect for that which they represent. Mannheim designates 'blood, property, and achievement' the selection principles of the elites. His passion for destroying ideologies does not lead him to consider even once the legitimacy of these principles; he is actually able, during Hitler's lifetime, to speak of a 'genuine blood-principle', which is supposed to have formerly guaranteed 'the purity of aristocratic minority stocks and their traditions'. From this to the new aristocracy of blood and soil it is only a step. Mannheim's general cultural pessimism prevents him from taking that step. As far as he is concerned, there is still too little blood. He dreads a 'mass democracy' in which blood and property would disappear as principles of selection; the all too rapid change of elites would threaten continuity. He is particularly concerned with the fact that things are no longer quite right with the esoteric doctrine of the 'genuine blood-principle'. 'It has become democratic and quite suddenly offers to the great masses of the population the privilege of social ascendancy without any achievement.' Just as the nobility of the past was never any more noble than anyone else, the aristocracy of today has neither an objective nor a subjective interest in really relinquishing the principle of privilege. Elite theory, happy in the invariant, unites different levels of what sociologists today call social differentiation, such as feudalism and capitalism, under the heading 'blood- and property-principle'; with equally good humour it separates what belongs together, property and achievement. Max Weber had shown that the spirit of early capitalism identifies the two, that in a rationally constituted work process the capacity for achievement can be measured in terms of material success. The equation of achievement and material success found its psychological manifestation in a readiness to make success as such a fetish. In Mannheim this tendency appears in sublimated form as a 'status drive'. In bourgeois ideology property and achievement were first separated when it became obvious that 'achievement' as the economic *ratio* of the individual no longer corresponded to 'property' as its potential reward. Only then did the bourgeois truly become a *gentilhomme*. Thus, Mannheim's 'mechanisms of selection' are inventions, arbitrarily chosen co-ordinates distanced from the life-process of actual society.

Conclusions can be drawn from them which bear a fatal resemblance to the lax conceptions of Werner Sombart and Ortega y Gasset. Mannheim speaks of a 'proletarianization of the intelligentsia'. He is correct in calling attention to the fact that the cultural market is flooded; there are, he observes, more culturally qualified (from the standpoint of formal education, that is) people available than there are suitable positions for them. This situation, however, is supposed to lead to a drop in the social value of culture, since it is 'a sociological law that the social value of cultural goods is a function of the social status of those who produce them'. At the same time, he continues, the 'social value' 'of culture necessarily declines because the recruiting of new members of the intelligentsia extends increasingly to lower social strata, especially that of the petty officialdom. Thus the notion of the proletarian is formalized; it appears as a mere structure of consciousness, as with the upper bourgeoisie, which condemns anyone not familiar with the rules as a 'prole'. The genesis of this process is not considered and as a result is falsified. By calling attention to a 'structural' assimilation of consciousness to that of the lowest strata of society, he implicitly shifts the blame to the members of those strata and their alleged emancipation in mass democracy. Yet stultification is caused not by the oppressed but by oppression, and it affects not only the oppressed but, in their essentials, the oppressors as well, a fact to which Mannheim paid little attention. The flooding of intellectual vocations is due to the flooding of economic occupations as such, basically, to technological unemployment. It has nothing to do with Mannheim's democratization of the elites, and the reserve army of intellectuals is the last to influence them. Moreover, the sociological law which makes the so-called status of culture dependent on that of those who produce it is a textbook example of a false generalization. One need only recall the music of the eighteenth century, the cultural relevance of which in the Germany of the time stands beyond all doubt. Musicians, except for the *maestri,* primadonnas, and *castrati* attached to the courts, were held in low esteem; Bach lived as a subordinate church official and the young Haydn as a servant. Musicians attained social status only when their products were no longer suitable for immediate consumption, when the composer set himself against society as his own master—with Beethoven. The reason for Mannheim's false conclusion lies in the psychologism of his method. The individualistic facade of society concealed from him the fact that its essence consists precisely in developing forms which undergo a process of sedimentation and which reduce individuals to mere agents of objective tendencies. Its disillusioned mien notwithstanding, the standpoint of the sociology of knowledge is pre-Hegelian. Its recourse to a group of organizers, in the case of Mannheim's 'law', to the bearers of culture,

is based on the somewhat transcendental presupposition of a harmony between society and the individual. The absence of such harmony forms one of the most urgent objects of critical theory, which is a theory of human relations only to the extent that it is also a theory of the inhumanity of those relations.

The distortions of the sociology of knowledge arise from its method, which translates dialectical concepts into classificatory ones. Since in each case what is socially contradictory is absorbed into individual logical classes, social classes as such disappear and the picture of the whole becomes harmonious. When, for instance, in the third section of the book Mannheim distinguishes three levels of consciousness: chance discovery, invention, and planning, he is simply trying to interpret the dialectical scheme of epochs as that of the fluidly changing modes of behaviour of socialized man in general, in which the determinant oppositions disappear: 'It is of course clear that the line which divides inventive thinking, which is rationally striving to realize immediate goals, from planned thinking is not a hard and fast one. No one can say for certain at what degree of foresight and at what point in the widening radius of conscious regulation the transition from inventive to planned thinking takes place.' The notion of an unbroken transition from a liberal to a 'planned' society has its correlative in the conception of that transition as one between distinct modes of 'thinking'. Such a conception awakens the belief that the historical process is guided by an inherently univocal subject embodying the whole of society. The translation of dialectical into classificatory concepts abstracts from the conditions of real social power upon which alone those levels of thought depend. 'The novel contribution of the sociological view of the past and the present is that it sees history as an area open to experimentation in regulatory intervention'—as though the possibility of such intervention always corresponded to the level of insight at the time. Such a levelling off of social struggles into modes of behaviour which can be defined formally and which are made abstract in advance allows uplifting proclamations concerning the future: 'Yet another way remains open—it is that unified planning will come about through understanding, agreement, and compromise, i.e. that the state of mind will triumph in the key positions of international society which hitherto has been possible only within a given national group, within whose enclaves peace was established by such methods.' Through the idea of compromise the very contradictions which were supposedly resolved through planning are retained; the abstract concept of planning conceals them in advance and is itself a compromise between the laissez-faire principle which is preserved in it and the insight into its insufficiency.

Dialectical concepts cannot be 'translated' into the categories of formal sociology without their truth being impaired. Mannheim flirts with positivism to the extent that he believes himself able to rely on objectively given facts, which, however, in his rather lax manner he describes as 'unarticulated'. These unarticulated facts can then be put through the sociological thought-machine and thus elevated to general concepts. But such classification according to ordering concepts would be an adequate cognitive process only if the facts, which are assumed to be immediately given, could be abstracted from their concrete context as easily as it would appear to the naïve first glance. It is not adequate, however, if social reality has, prior to every theoretical ordering glance, a highly 'articulated' structure upon which the scientific subject and the data of his experience depend. As analysis advances, the initial 'facts' cease to be descriptive, self-contained data, and sociology is all the less at liberty to classify them to suit its needs. That 'facts' must undergo this correction as the theoretical understanding of society proceeds means not so much that new subjective ordering schemes must be devised, as it would seem to naïve experience, as that the data which are presumably given embody more than mere material to be processed conceptually, namely, that they are moulded by the social whole and thus 'structured' in themselves. Idealism can be overcome only when the freedom to conceptualize through abstraction is sacrificed. The thesis of the primacy of being over consciousness includes the methodological imperative to express the dynamic tendencies of reality in the formation and movement of concepts instead of forming and verifying concepts in accordance with the demand that they have pragmatic and expedient features. The sociology of knowledge has closed its eyes to this imperative. Its abstractions are arbitrary as long as they merely harmonize with an experience which proceeds by differentiating and correcting. Mannheim does not allow himself the logical conclusion that the 'unbiased' registration of facts is a fiction. The social scientist's experience does not give him undifferentiated, chaotic material to be organized; rather, the material of his experience is the social order, more emphatically a 'system' than any ever conceived by philosophy. What decides whether his concepts are right or wrong is neither their generality nor, on the other hand, their approximation to 'pure' fact, but rather the adequacy with which they grasp the real laws of movement of society and thereby render stubborn facts transparent. In a co-ordinate-system defined by concepts like integration, elite, and articulation, those determining laws and everything they signify for human life appear to be contingent or accidental, mere sociological 'differentiations'. For this reason, sociology which generalizes and differentiates seems like a mockery of reality. It does not recoil before formulations like 'disregarding the concentration and centralization of capital'. Such abstractions are not 'neutral'. What a theory regards and what it disregards determines its quality. Were 'disregarding' sufficient, one could, for instance, also analyse elites by observing such groups as the vegetarians or the followers of Mazdaznan and then refine this analysis conceptually until its manifest absurdity disappeared. But no corrective could compensate for the fact that the choice of basic categories was false, that the world is not organized according to these categories. All correctives notwithstanding, this falseness would shift the accents so fundamentally that reality would drop out of the concepts; the elites would be 'groups of the Mazdaznan form' which happened to be characterized in addition by the possession of 'social power'. When at one point Mannheim says that 'in the cultural sphere (properly also in the economic) there has never been an absolute liberalism, that alongside of the undirected working of the social forces there has always ex-

isted, for instance, regulation in education', he is obviously trying to establish a differentiating corrective to the belief that the principle of laissez-faire, long ago exposed as ideology, ever prevailed in an unrestricted manner. But through the choice of an initial concept which is to be differentiated only afterwards the crucial issue is distorted: the insight that even under liberalism the principle of laissez-faire served only to mask economic control and that accordingly the establishment of 'cultural goods' was essentially determined by their conformity with the ruling social interests. The insight into a basic matter of ideology evaporates into mere finesse; instead of directing itself to the concrete in the first place without hypostatizing indispensable general concepts, the method seeks to conciliate by demonstrating that it remembers the concrete too.

The inadequacies of the method become manifest in its poles, the law and the 'example'. The sociology of knowledge characterizes stubborn facts as mere differentiations and subsumes them under the highest general units; at the same time, it ascribes an intrinsic power over the facts to these arbitrary generalizations, which it calls social 'laws', such as the one relating cultural goods to the social status of those who produce them. The 'laws' are hypostatized. Sometimes they assume a truly extravagant character: 'There is, however, a decisive law which rules us at the present moment. Unplanned spheres regulated by natural selection on the one hand and deliberately organized areas on the other can exist side by side without friction only *as long as the unplanned spheres predominate*' [Mannheim's italics]. Quantified propositions of this form are no more evident than those of Baaderian metaphysics, over which they have the advantage only of a lack of imagination. The falseness of Mannheim's hypostasization of general concepts can be grasped precisely at the point where he interjects the 'principia media' to which he debased the laws of dialectical movement: 'However much we must take the *principia media* and the corresponding concepts ("late capitalism", "structural unemployment", "lower middle-class ideology", etc.) as concrete expressions of a special historical setting, it should nevertheless be borne in mind that what we are doing is differentiating and individualizing abstract and general determinants (general factors). The *principia media* are in a certain sense nothing but temporary groups of general factors so closely intertwined that they operate as a single causal factor. That we are essentially dealing here with general factors in an historical and individual setting is evident from our example. Our first observation implies the general principle of the functioning of a social order with freely contracting legal personalities; the second, the psychological effect of unemployment in general, and the last, the general law that hopes of social advancement tend to affect individuals in a way which obscures their real social position.' It is just as mistaken, Mannheim continues, to believe that conceptions of man in general are valid in themselves as 'to neglect or ignore the general principles of the human psyche within the concrete modes of behaviour of these historical types'. Accordingly, the historical event seems to be determined in part by 'general', in part by 'particular' causes which together form some sort of 'group'. This, however, implies the confusion of levels of abstraction with causes. Mannheim sees the decisive weakness of dialectical thought in its misunderstanding of 'general forces'—as if the commodity forms were not 'general' enough for all the questions with which he deals. 'General forces', however, are not independent in opposition to 'particular' ones, as though a concrete event were 'caused' once by a causal proposition and then again by the specific 'historical situation'. No event is caused by general forces, much less by laws; causality is not the 'cause' of events but rather the highest conceptual generality under which concrete causal factors can be subsumed. The significance of the observation Newton made on the falling apple is not that the general law of causality 'acts' within a complex which includes factors of a lower degree of abstraction. Causality operates only in the particular and not in addition to it. Only to this extent can the falling apple be called 'an example of the law of gravity'; the law of gravity is as much dependent on the falling of this apple as vice-versa. The concrete play of forces can be reduced to schemata of varying levels of generality, but it is not a question of a conjunction of 'general' and 'particular' forces. Mannheim's pluralism, of course, which conceives what is crucial as merely *one* perspective among many, is hardly eager to give up its sums of general and particular factors.

The fact, baptized in advance as a 'unique situation', thereby becomes a mere example of these forces. Dialectical theory, in contrast, can no more accept the concept of the example as valid than could Kant. Examples function as convenient and interchangeable illustrations; hence they are often chosen at a comfortable distance from the true concerns of mankind today, or they are pulled, as it were, out of a hat. But they are quickly forced to pay the consequences. Mannheim writes, for instance: 'An illuminating example of the disturbances which can arise from substantial irrationality may be seen where, for example, the diplomatic staff of a state has carefully thought out a series of actions and has agreed on certain steps, when suddenly one of its members falls prey to a nervous collapse and then acts contrary to the plan, thereby destroying it.' It is useless to portray such private events as 'factors'; not only is the 'radius of action' of the individual diplomat romantically overestimated, but also unless the blunder itself served the course of political developments stronger than the diplomats' considerations it could be corrected in five minutes over the telephone. Or, with the pictorial vividness of a children's book, Mannheim writes: 'As a soldier I must control my impulses and desires to a quite different degree than as a free hunter, whose acts are only periodically purposive and who will only occasionally need to take hold of himself—for instance, at the moment when he has to fire at his prey.' As is generally known, the occupation of hunter has in recent years been replaced by the sport of hunting, but even the sportsman who takes hold of himself only 'at the moment when he has to fire at his prey', apparently in order not to be started by the crack of his own rifle, will hardly bag much, probably frighten away his prey, and perhaps not even find it. The insignificance of such examples is closely related to the influence the sociology of knowledge has had. Selected for their subjective neutrality and therefore inessential in advance, the examples serve to distract. Sociology originated in the impulse to criticize the principles of the soci-

ety with which it found itself confronted; the sociology of knowledge settles for reflections on hunters dressed in green and diplomats in black.

The direction in which, in terms of content, the formalism of such conceptualization tends reveals itself when programmatic demands are voiced. An 'optimum' for the thorough organization of society is demanded, but no thought is given to the gap that would have to be breached to attain such an optimum. If things are only put together rationally, everything will fall into place. Mannheim's ideal of a 'desired direction' between 'unconscious conservatism' and 'misdirected utopianism' corresponds to this: 'We can see at the same time, however, the general outline of a possible solution to the present tension, namely a sort of authoritarian democracy making use of planning and creating a stable system from the present conflict of principles.' This is in accordance with the stylistic elevation of the 'crisis' to a 'human problem', in which Mannheim shows himself in agreement with modern German anthropologists, his declaration against them notwithstanding, and with the existentialist philosophers. Two characteristics more than all others, however, reveal the conformism of Mannheim's sociology of knowledge. First, it remains concerned with symptoms. It is thoroughly disposed to overestimate the significance of ideologies as opposed to what they represent. It placidly shares with them precisely that equivocal conception of 'the' irrational to which the critical lever should be applied: 'We must, moreover, realize that the irrational is not always harmful but that, on the contrary, it is among the most valuable powers in man's possession when it acts as a driving force towards rational or objective ends, creates cultural values through sublimation and cultivation, or, as pure élan, heightens the joy of living without breaking up the social order by lack of planning.' There are no further hints as to the nature of this irrational, which is said to produce cultural values through cultivation, although such values are by definition the product of cultivation, or to 'heighten' the joy of living, which is irrational anyway. In any case, however, the equation of the instincts with the irrational is ominous, for the concept is applied in 'value-free' manner both to the libido and to the forms its repression takes. The irrational seems to endow ideologies with substantiality in Mannheim. They receive a paternal reproof but are left intact; what they conceal is never exposed. But the vulgar materialism of prevailing praxis is closely related to this positivistic tendency to accept symptoms uncritically, this perceptible respect for the claims of ideology. The facade remains intact in the glow of amenable observation, and the ultimate wisdom of this sociology is that no impulse could arise within the interior which could seriously threaten to proceed beyond its carefully marked bounds: 'In actual fact the existing body of ideas (and the same applies to vocabulary) never exceeds the horizon and the radius of activity of the society in question.' Whatever 'exceeds' the limits, to be sure, can easily be seen as 'adjustment to the emotional evocation of spiritual values, etc.'. This materialism, akin to that of the family head who considers it utterly impossible for his offspring to have a new thought, since everything has already been thought, and hence recommends that he concentrate on earning a respectable living, this seasoned and arrogant materialism is the reverse image of the idealism in Mannheim's view of history, an idealism to which he also remains true in other respects, especially in his conceptions of 'rationality' and progress, an idealism according to which changes in consciousness are even capable of lifting 'the structural principle of society off its hinges from the inside out, so to speak'.

The real attraction of the sociology of knowledge can be sought only in the fact that those changes in consciousness, as achievements of 'planning reason', are linked directly to the reasoning of today's planners: 'The fact that the complex actions of a functional, thoroughly rationalized society can be thought through only in the heads of a few organizers assures the latter of a key position in society.' The motif which becomes apparent here extends beyond the consciousness of the sociology of knowledge. The objective spirit, as that of those 'few organizers', speaks through it. While the sociology of knowledge dreams of new academic fields to conquer, it unsuspectingly serves those who have not hesitated a moment to abolish those fields. Mannheim's reflections, nourished by liberal common sense, all amount to the same thing in the end—recommending social planning without ever penetrating to the foundations of society. The consequences of the absurdity which has now become obvious and which Mannheim sees only superficially as a 'cultural crisis', are to be mollified from above, that is, by those who control the means of production. This means, however, simply that the liberal, who sees no way out, makes himself the spokesman of a dictatorial arrangement of society even while he imagines he is opposing it. Of course, the sociology of knowledge will reply that the ultimate criterion for judging planning is not power but reason and that reason includes the task of converting the powerful. Nevertheless, since the Platonic philosopher-kings it has been clear what such a conversion involves. The answer to Mannheim's reverence for the intelligentsia as 'free-floating' is to be found not in the reactionary postulate of its 'rootedness in Being' but rather in the reminder that the very intelligentsia that pretends to float freely is fundamentally rooted in the very being that must be changed and which it merely pretends to criticize. For it the rational is the optimal functioning of the system, which postpones the catastrophe without asking whether the system in its totality is not in fact the optimum in irrationality. In totalitarian systems of every kind, planning directed at maintaining the system leads to the barbarous suppression below the surface of the contradictions it inevitably produces. In the name of reason the advocates of planning turn power over to those who already possess it in the name of mystification. The power of reason today is the blind reason of those who currently hold power. But as power moves towards the catastrophe it induces the mind which denies it with moderation to abdicate to it. It still calls itself liberal, to be sure, but for it freedom has already become 'from the sociological point of view nothing but a disproportion between the growth of the radius of effective central control on the one hand and the size of the group unit to be influenced on the other'. The sociology of knowledge sets up indoctrination camps for the homeless intelligentsia where it can learn to forget itself.

Edward Shils   (essay date 1973)

SOURCE: Review of *Ideology and Utopia*, in *Daedalus: Journal of the American Academy of Arts and Sciences*, Vol. 103, No. 1, Winter, 1973, pp. 83-9.

[*In the following essay, Shils discusses the social and historical circumstances under which Mannheim wrote* Ideology and Utopia.]

Karl Mannheim was extraordinarily sensitive to his national and continental environment and to his own time. He read widely; he had a lively curiosity and a quickly moving imagination which enabled him to respond to many kinds of events. From 1914 until his death in 1947 at the age of fifty-four he had only about a decade of relative calm: 1925 to 1929 in Germany and 1933 to 1939 in Great Britain. The rest of his adult life was spent in the midst of war, revolution, and uncivil commotion. A sociologist of such a sensitive imagination could not have avoided perceiving these unrelenting and pitiless conflicts and making them into a theme of central importance in his thought.

Ideologie und Utopie was published in 1929 when disorder began once more in the Weimar republic. In 1931, when disorder was at its height, he published an article entitled *"Wissenssoziologie"* in a German encyclopedia of sociology. In 1935, very shortly after his settlement in England, he wrote a long essay which attempted to place the two former writings in the wider setting of the plurality of intellectual outlooks which had developed in Europe since the Reformation, to assimilate his new interest in psychoanalysis into his earlier Hegelian, Marxian and Weberian sociology, and to find a way out of the relativism in which he was entrapped and most ill-at-ease. In 1936, all three of these writings were published in English translation. The long essay formed the introductory chapter, the three chapters of *Ideologie und Utopie* followed, and the encyclopedia article constituted the concluding chapter. The result was a book which, full of the contradictions and uncertainties of Mannheim's thought, was an adequate expression of his tentacularly rich and sympathetic mind.

For better or for worse, Mannheim was, in his intellectual disposition, a thoroughgoing sociologist. He had a profound distaste for individualism; he believed not only that the individual was a frail reed but that he scarcely existed as a thinking reed. Mannheim began his intellectual career at the end of the First World War under the powerful influence of the Hegelian conception of the objective spirit. As a Hegelian, he was also a historicist. He believed that every society and epoch had its own intellectual culture, of which every single work produced in it was a part. In this imposing medium the individual mind and its works were only instances of the "objective spirit" or culture into which they were born. The individual's mind, the individual's imagination, the individual's power of reason and observation were only fictions. The idealistic tradition attributed primary reality to the trans-individual complex of ideas; the individual was no more than a creature of this trans-individual reality. The properties of the individual could be derived from this reality; the individual imposed and added little or nothing to it. The movement of this cosmos of symbols through history bore no trace of the individual's mental powers.

Yet even this view was not wholly acceptable to Mannheim. Although it denied the power of the individual it still accorded too much autonomy to the realm of the mind, even to the collective mind, to a realm of ideas possessing an inner, selfdeveloping dynamic force of its own. Marxism offered Mannheim the intellectual opportunity to escape from idealism because it had so much in common with idealism. Marxism too was historicist; it too was holistic; it too denied the primacy of the individual. But unlike idealism, it denied the primacy of the intellectual sphere. It refused to accept the idealistic view that ideas—the realm of symbols—have an internal force of their own which presses them to develop in a direction which is inherent in them. It was this anti-intellectualism which led Mannheim to add Marxism to his intellectual parentage.

I think that Mannheim was never an avowed Marxist. He was generally sympathetic with socialistic ideas but he never, as far as I know, associated himself publicly with the Social Democratic Party in Germany even though many of his friends and close associates did. He took pains to distinguish himself from Marxism but he never concealed his appreciation of it. Whereas he often spoke disparagingly of idealism, he did not speak in the same way of Marxism. Yet he wanted to go deeper than Marxism seemed capable of going.

Nonetheless, Mannheim never succeeded in emancipating himself either from Marxism or from idealism. The Marxian influence was dominant in his fundamental belief in the primacy of the nonintellectual stratum of being and in the peripheral significance of intellectual activity. The sociology of knowledge was intended to go beyond Marxism. Although he regarded it as a mark of superiority of the sociology of knowledge that it regarded "not merely classes, as a dogmatic type of Marxism would have it," as the determinant of "thought-models" but went beyond Marxism to include "generations, states, groups, sects, occupational groups, schools, etc.," he immediately went on to say:

> We do not intend to deny that of all the above-mentioned social groupings and units, class stratification is the most significant, since in the final analysis all the other social groups arise from and are transformed as parts of the more basic conditions of production and domination.

To his undivested idealism and Marxism, he added, in the early 1930's, a very generalized admixture of psychoanalysis. To the power of culture and "social" or "existential position," he joined, in the early 1930's, the "collective unconscious" as one more counteragent to the autonomy of the observing, imagining and reasoning mind.

II

The upshot of these powerful influences was the "sociology of knowledge" and the closely associated critique of objectivity. The sociology of knowledge was intended to be a study of the dependence of outlooks, theories, doctrines etc. on the "social position of the knower." It was intended to demonstrate that whatever human beings believe they know about the world is dependent on their circumstances

and fortunes in society; their knowledge and beliefs are, according to the sociology of knowledge, overpoweringly bound by the outlook which they have inherited and by the force of their social position. Mannheim never defined "social position" any more than he defined the "existential connectedness" of knowledge (*Seinsverbundenheit des Wissens*) but his intention was clear: thought was always a creature of social circumstance, never the creator of thought or social circumstance. Inherited outlooks were adduced to show the limited power of the individual mind, never to show the limits of the powers of social or class position.

He went to great exertions to distinguish the sociology of knowledge from the "theory of ideology." The latter did no more than attribute error to deliberate deception, falsification, masking, and self-blinding; in its way, the "theory of ideology" left intact the fundamental capacities of the individual mind and this was not reconcilable with Mannheim's idealistic, historicist, and environmentalist postulates. According to Mannheim, the theory of ideology left the epistemological foundations of empiricism intact; it assumed that men possessed the powers to discern the truth but failed to do so intentionally because they anticipated advantages from avoiding the acknowledgment of the truth. The theory of ideology postulated the existence of an apparatus of perception and reasoning common to human beings; the failure of this apparatus to bring forth identical results in everyone was attributable to "mistakes" and to the power of passions and interests which diverted this apparatus from its proper operation. Still, the potentialities were there in the individual.

The sociology of knowledge, however, according to Mannheim, worked at the deeper levels of the mind. In accordance with the historicist idealistic tradition, the diversity of beliefs which men have about themselves, their societies, and the world are accounted for by the diversity of the conceptual or categorical apparatus which they bring to bear on the "facts." (Facts always troubled Mannheim methodologically and he expressed his uneasiness by quotation marks.) Among various epochs, classes, etc., these conceptual or categorical apparatuses are incomparably and even unassimilably different from each other; their distinctiveness extends to conceptions of causation and time, criteria of valid evidence, models of explanation, etc. These distinctive apparatuses are different from each other because of the different social situations, social positions, existential conditions, life situations, etc., in which the individual carriers of these apparatuses live. The discovery of these affinities between the outlooks and the social situations and the derivation of the former from the latter are the tasks of the sociology of knowledge.

One sees straightaway how persistent was the power of Marxism over Mannheim's thought even when he thought he had transcended it. The weaknesses of this sort in the sociology of knowledge were the same as those of the Marxian sociology of knowledge. They were first, the assertion without evidence of correlations between vaguely defined independent and equally vaguely defined dependent variables without any plausible theoretical linkages between the two to compensate for the absence of empirical evidence; and second, the reduction of intellectual activities to an epiphenomenal status.

As a result of the first weakness, the sociology of knowledge never became established as a productive part of sociology. The subject was doomed to remain at the point of programs and prolegomena but it produced no results. There were of course other reasons. Most sociologists of the generation immediately after Mannheim lacked the sophisticated knowledge of intellectual history needed to undertake satisfactory work in the field and, if they had possessed such sophistication, the undertaking would in time have appeared unfeasible to them. Since it is a denial of the constitution of intellectual activity to regard such activity as having no character other than that imposed on it by the social situation of those engaged in it, serious sociologists who began it in good faith would surely have seen through it. How could one study any object and try to discover the truth about it if, from the very beginning, one was convinced that one's conclusions were inevitably determined not by the application of criteria of truth to carefully observed evidence but rather by one's own social circumstances, such as class position? In its Mannheimian form the sociology of knowledge was doomed to discredit but Mannheim's failure even to provide models of the theoretical linkage meant that it never reached the stage of undergoing the saving revision which systematic research might have provided. The result was therefore a stillbirth.

Curiosity and imagination, observational and reasoning power, learning and systematic study in the form of observation, erudition, or experiment had no place in Mannheim's sociology of knowledge. Nothing new could be said by the performers of intellectual activities studied by the sociology of knowledge. All they could do was to respond to their life situations in ways which did not call upon their individual intellectual powers. Any appearance of individuality in an intellectual work was nothing more than a result of a variation or idiosyncrasy of the social position or situation of the intellectual actor.

So eager was Mannheim to protect the view that intellectual action had no autonomous power that it was sufficient for him to find one trait which he could assert to be dependent on the social position of the intellectual actor for him to assume triumphantly that all the rest of the intellectual actor's work was equally dependent on that situation. If it could be shown, or at least asserted with a show of plausibility, that a problem had been formulated in response to a newly emergent and practically significant situation, then Mannheim regarded that as evidence that the entire intellectual undertaking—the analysis of the problem, the hypothesis formulated to render it, the mode of gathering evidence, and the conclusion—was determined by the "existential condition of the knower."

There was something in what Mannheim said but it was much less and much different from what he thought. His insistent dislike of idealism made it impossible for him to acknowledge in principle that intellectual traditions are significant, although by no means exclusive, determinants of intellectual action; it was his dislike of the immanent interpretation of the history of intellectual works—nowadays called "internalist"—which drew him into the sociological—or "externalist"—camp. He remained there until he ceased to concern himself with the sociology of knowledge; the appearance of the English version, *Ideology and Utopia,* marked his departure from the subject.

His espousal of a historicist Marxian variant of a sociological approach, his desire to escape from idealism, and his dislike of individualism were, in combination, an insuperable hindrance to the development of Mannheim's sociology of knowledge. These commitments prevented him from admitting in principle that the cognitive powers of human beings have in some historically very important cases an autonomous motivation and a constitutive set of properties which operate in all societies and in all epochs; he provided no place for the fact that human beings possess curiosity and imagination and reasoning and observational powers, and that the results of these are precipitated into works which are then crystallized into traditions. He failed to acknowledge in his theory that intellectual traditions have real influence on subsequent intellectual works—although in his own explanations he repeatedly invoked intellectual traditions as *ad hoc* explanations—and that intellectual traditions change and grow, and that they do so when the human beings who come under their influence are impelled by practical desire or intellectual propensity to deal with problems which have not been adequately dealt with by the tradition in its hitherto accepted form.

His sociology of knowledge remained more Marxist than it need have and than was good for it. It is not that the Marxian view of the determination of intellectual actions and works by class position is wholly wrong or utterly irrelevant. But it covers only a very small part of the phenomenon and it does that very crudely. Although Mannheim sometimes suggested in passing that institutional structures and roles other than class were of importance, he regarded them as really secondary or inconsequential. He had little sense for the social institutional processes which are directly involved in the transmission, establishment, and acceptance of knowledge. Although he wrote an interesting essay on the role of competition in the intellectual sphere, he had little understanding for the competition of ideas and the processes of selection through which some find acceptance and others are relegated to obscurity or oblivion. Competition was for him "a representative case in which extratheoretical processes affect the emergence and the direction of the development of knowledge," but he interpreted that to mean that "diverse interpretations of the world. . . . when their social background is uncovered, reveal themselves as the intellectual expressions of conflicting groups struggling for power." He did not mean intellectuals struggling for the acceptance of their ideas or works; he meant nonintellectuals struggling for power over society. He never tried to disclose the mechanisms by which these political and economic conflicts are transferred into the competition of interpretations of the world. Had he tried, he might have discovered that he was on the wrong track. Alternatively, had he worked backwards from the competition of interpretations in specific instances, he might have contributed to the development of a sociology of knowledge which showed a realistic awareness of the fact that knowledge is an independent value and possesses a type of reality which the Marxian theory in its usual form could not accommodate.

In this connection it may be noted that although Mannheim often used the pragmatist or instrumentalist idiom in accordance with which "a theory is wrong if in a given practical situation it uses concepts and categories which, if taken seriously, would prevent man from adjusting himself at that historical stage," he found no place for the investigation of the role of the cognitive element in action or of the influence of natural and social science in society. He did not do so because, having to his own satisfaction got rid of his idealistic old man of the sea, he went to the opposite extreme of denying the dignity and partial autonomy of the sphere of cultural things, including scientific knowledge and the other symbolic constructions of the imaginative and rational powers of the human mind.

III

This derogatory attitude toward knowledge found a fitting expression in Mannheim's relativism. Now, whereas moral relativism seems utterly self-evident to the intellectual stratum in its present state of mind, although its members are not at all reluctant to act as dogmatic moral preachers to the whole human race, cognitive relativism is another matter. Those who shirk the acquisition of knowledge might find a congenial self-justification in cognitive relativism, but not those who seek to acquire knowledge. Mannheim was an honest and serious man and he wanted his assertions to be believed because of their truthfulness and not because they were connected with his existential position and that of his audience. He was in fact profoundly embarrassed by the difficulty into which he was brought by his relativism. He tried to find various ways out. One was through the conception of a "freely floating intelligentsia" which by virtue of its detachment from partisanship could construct a synthesis of the partial views attained from partisan positions. He did not follow this up although it had possibilities of fruitfulness; I surmise that he did not do so because it was contradictory to his dominant beliefs about the ineluctible pervasiveness of the extra-intellectual determinants of knowledge. The other alternative he sought was "relationism," a proposition which he left extremely ambiguous and hence compatible both with the relativism of which he unwillingly saw the defects and with the "objectivism" which his "sociologistic" prejudice rendered unacceptable to him.

IV

All this notwithstanding, *Ideology and Utopia* has remained continuously in print in the United States and Great Britain for nearly forty years. In recent years, it has found admirers among the newer breed of misologists, and there is no doubt that in his vague and portentious declarations there can be found authority, couched in the somber tones of a German intellectual of his time, for disparaging the whole enterprise of science and learning.

Yet that alone does not quite exhaust the grounds of his persistent appeal. Perhaps they lie in the gravity of his mood, in his large epochal perspective, and in the impression which he always gave in his personal bearing and in the overtones of his writings that, despite the repeated assertions to the contrary in those writings, the quest for truthful understanding is one of the grandest and worthiest activities in which human beings can engage in this life. It is a great pity that he spent a substantial part of his too short life arguing for a hopelessly wrong position which his own demeanor refuted.

Bhikhu Parekh (essay date 1973)

SOURCE: "Social and Political Thought and the Problem of Ideology," in *Knowledge and Belief in Politics: The Problem of Ideology,* Robert Benewick, R. N. Berki, Bhikhu Parekh, eds., George Allen & Unwin Ltd, 1973, pp. 57-87.

[*In the following essay, Parekh provides an outline of the place of rationalism in the history of philosophy and examines Mannheim's approach to the "crisis of rationality" that is often identified with the modern era.*]

The most influential conception of rationality in Western thought, a conception that is *prima facie* highly plausible and has a good deal of attraction for intellectuals, goes back to the pre-Socratics and finds its noblest expression in the philosophy of Plato and Aristotle. On this, what for convenience I shall call the traditional view of rationality, thinking was essentially a contemplative activity in which the human mind soared above the contingencies of human existence and comprehended its subject matter without being influenced by any extra-rational factors issuing from the thinker's psychological or social background. Thinking, in other words, was regarded as a direct and unmediated encounter between the thinking mind and its objects of thought. The traditional view of rationality also drew a fairly neat distinction between theory and practice. Unlike the world of practice which arose from human wants and desires and thus from a lack of human self-sufficiency, theorizing was regarded as an unconstrained, free, and indeed useless activity in which the human mind was guided by nothing other than the disinterested desire to seek the truth. Aristotle expressed the distinction well when he described practice as an essentially human, and theory as an essentially divine, activity. As God is self-sufficient, he could not want or desire anything and could only be defined as self-thinking thought. Man therefore was believed to be most god-like when he was engaged in theorizing. Aristotle carried the argument to its logical conclusion when he suggested that the theoretical reason, *nous,* could not be inherent in the human organism but came from 'outside' and was immortal. It was simple and changeless, and since it dealt with pure forms and did not depend on physical sensations and images to provide it with its subject matter, it was self-sufficient. As the theoretical reason was thus detachable from the human body, it was believed to be totally uninfluenced by its physical and social environment.

Man, on the traditional view of rationality, was essentially a theoretical being whose primary concern was to discover and contemplate the truth. In his pursuit of truth he was guided by nothing other than the disinterested concern to reach the truth. As practical interests distorted and corrupted thought, man, it was believed, could pursue the truth only if he had no interest in the practical outcome of his pursuit. The more the human reason was dissociated from passions and desires, the more it was considered capable of attaining the truth. It is worth noting that for Plato, Aristotle, Descartes and even Spinoza, desires and passions were not original properties of the human soul but the 'disturbances' it suffered as a result of its union with the body and which it could and should constantly endeavour to transcend. Not only was the human reason not influenced by human passion, it was not influenced by the surrounding society or the social position of the thinker either. That the thinker existed in a particular society was considered a historical contingency that in no way affected the operations of his reason. When the socially transcendent human reason discovered truths, they were naturally believed to be eternally valid.

While some of the beliefs of the traditional view of rationality were questioned by many Christian theologians, the first full-scale challenge to it was not mounted until the dawn of the modern era. The challenge came from two related but essentially different directions.

The first attack was based on a psychological theory of human action that was initiated by Hobbes, refined by Locke, and perfected by the thinkers of the French Enlightenment. Man, it was argued, was essentially a practical being whose main concern in life was to pursue his happiness, to make the world a habitable place. Reason, it was argued further, was set in motion by human desires; indeed, it was created by desires, so that the more a man desired, the greater the stimulus he had to think and therefore the greater his reason. As Voltaire, in his *Treatise of Metaphysics,* remarked, 'the passions are the wheels which make all these machines go'. Vauvenargues reflected the same attitude in his *Introduction to the Knowledge of the Human Mind* when he concluded that the true nature of man did not lie in reason but in the passions. Helvetius observed in his *Treatise on Man* that reason in itself was inert and was set in motion only by desires. As reason thus arose and operated within the overall context of practical interests and desires, its essential task was considered to be to serve passions, to find the best means of gratifying them. It was argued, further, that of all human passions the concern for personal interest was the 'most powerful, most important, most uniform, most lasting and most general' (Bentham). It was believed to be natural to man to 'prefer himself to mankind'; indeed, it was argued that this desire comes with us 'from the womb' and 'never leaves until we go into the grave' (Adam Smith). Now if a man was a creature compelled by his very nature to pursue his own interest, and if reason was only a means to satisfying human desires, it was very difficult to see how human thought could be other than self-interested. Not only in all his conscious activities but even in his unconscious desires and motivations man could not but be guided by considerations of self-interest. And this applied not merely to his practical activity but also to his intellectual activities.

The second major attack on the traditional theory of rationality came from the historicist school of which Hegel was the greatest philosopher. Kant had already paved the way for this line of attack by denying the objective and ontological unity of the world on which the traditional theory was based. He took the view that the world in itself had no order, no internal principles of unity, and that it was the perceiving subject who imposed order on his experiences and created a coherent perceptual universe out of the chaos of experience. However, as Kant had assumed that the human mind had an inherent structure, and that the principles it imposed were universally common, his view did not lead to epistemological subjectivism. But it did raise some acute problems. He had assumed that the human mind had fixed categories of understanding, without explaining how they came to be there in the first instance. He had further treated the human mind as if it somehow stood outside society and was not a product or even an integral part of society. He had also not asked if the human mind and its categories always remained the same or if they were subject to historical evolution.

Trying to meet the difficulties that Kant's epistemology had raised, Hegel argued that man was essentially a social creature, and society essentially a historical product. He thought that each society had a unique modality of consciousness, a *Volkgeist* that permeated and unified all its parts and gave it an internal unity and distinctive identity. The *Volkgeist,* further, was a manifestation of the world spirit, representing a particular stage in its successive historical manifestations. Hegel's philosophy implied that human thought was culturally and historically conditioned and could not transcend the categories and assumptions of its time. It implied further that human thinking was not an individual but a social activity, that man thought not as an individual but as a member of his society, and that the relationship between the human mind and its object was necessarily culturally mediated.

Both the psychological and the historicist attacks on the traditional theory of rationality were coordinated by Marx, which is why he is such a central figure in the discussion of ideology. Marx married liberal psychology to Hegel's historicism. Like Hegel he too divided history into several epochs, but unlike him his principle of division was not cultural but economic. Human thought for him was determined by interests as the liberals had argued; but he defined interest not in individual but in socio-historical terms. Each individual thought, he believed, in terms of the categories characteristic of his class, and what made him a representative of his class was the fact he continued to wrestle with the same problems at the theoretical level that preoccupied other members of his class in actual life. He remained unable, Marx thought, to transcend the categories and assumptions of his class because ultimately, to put it somewhat crudely, it was not in his interest or in the interest of his class that he should do so. Such limited and distorted thought Marx called ideology.

The psychological and the historicist attacks on the traditional theory of rationality created a serious intellectual crisis and generated 'the problem of ideology'. They managed to cast serious doubts on the traditional theory, and yet what they proposed to put in its place destroyed human rationality and capacity ever to reach the truth. If self-interest was the ultimate spring of human conduct it was difficult to see how it did not permeate and distort thought, how a man could accept truths that went against his interest. One could of course argue that truth and interest always harmonized, or that it was in man's interest to pursue truth. But this was, to say the least, a highly questionable assumption and it in no way relieved the tension between liberal psychology and liberal epistemology. Similarly if all thought was historically conditioned as Hegel had argued, the idea of the Absolute could not make any sense, and even if it did, it was difficult to see how the historically limited mind of Hegel could claim to grasp the ways of the Absolute in their totality. Similarly, Marx too could not argue that while all thought was class determined he had somehow transcended the categories of his class or that interest had not distorted his thought. And therefore if they were to be consistent both he and Hegel had to argue that truth was relative to historical epoch or class, that man could never attain objective and universally valid truths, that there were as many different types of rationality as there were societies and classes, and that therefore mankind did not constitute a rational community capable of mutual comprehension.

The essence of the problem of ideology then was, and is, whether the historically, sociologically and psychologically naive traditional theory of rationality could be revised without destroying rationality altogether. In other words, can one bring down human reason from its seat in high heavens (as Greeks had imagined it) to the earth and locate it firmly and securely in the human world without losing it in the process? Or can the dignity and power of reason be secured only by pretending that it is a divine and transcendent faculty? In short, can reason be human (or humanized) without ceasing to be reason?

Of a number of attempts made to deal with this crisis of rationality, Mannheim's was one of the most significant. He saw the problem that Weber did not. And he did not feel committed to defending Marx and Hegel in a way that Lukács did. While he did not resolve the problem, he did face up to it and opened up an interesting line of inquiry. It will therefore be rewarding to consider in some detail his analysis and proposed resolution of the problem. In the next two sections I shall outline his position and criticize what appears to be a fundamental weakness in an otherwise stimulating analysis. In the final section I shall sketch very briefly the outlines of a theory of rationality that incorporates many of Mannheim's basic insights and avoids his mistakes.

I

Following Marx, Mannheim argues that human thought arises and operates in a definite social milieu. The process of knowing in his view is 'decisively' influenced at 'critical' points by 'extratheoretical' or 'existential' factors. To every social situation, he argues, there pertains a definite point of view: a definite perspective on the world, a definite conceptual framework, a definite set of beliefs about man and society, a definite set of 'basic categories of thought', a definite standard for evaluating and validating knowledge. As he puts it [in ***Ideology and Utopia***], 'mental structures are inevitably differently formed in different social and historical settings'. It is the social context that de-

termines the way an individual defines and uses concepts, the way he contrasts them with other concepts, the sorts of concepts that are absent from his thought, the dominant models of his thought, the level of his abstraction and his theory of reality. Mannheim explains in some detail how this is so.

It is because their different social backgrounds give rise to different perspectives that two different persons, both reasoning accurately, judge the same object and define the same word very differently. Thus to a nineteenth-century German conservative, freedom meant the right of each estate to live according to its own privileges, while to a contemporary liberal, it meant precisely the absence of these privileges. That each side saw only one aspect of the concept is 'clearly and demonstrably connected with their respective positions in the social and political structure'. Similarly, conservatives generally use morphological categories of thought that enable them to grasp the totality of experience as a whole, whereas left-wing groups, concerned to change things, generally atomize a situation into its component elements in order that they can reassemble them anew. Take again, the differences in the thought-models of different individuals and groups. While the success of the natural sciences created a general desire to study social phenomena in mechanistic-atomistic terms, it is significant, thinks Mannheim, that not all the groups in society accepted their dominance. The landed nobility, the displaced classes and the peasantry were generally disinterested in and even resentful of any attempt to study society in scientific terms. This was so because the world view that the natural sciences represented 'belonged to a mode of life other than their own', was alien to their 'life-situation'. Mannheim offers a similar explanation of the difference in the level of intellectual abstraction of different individuals and groups. Why is it, he asks, that Marxism, which is so keen to trace the ideological origins of its opponents' thought, did not develop a general theory on this basis? And replies that this was because of the Marxists' subconscious reluctance to think out the implications of their insight to a point where they would have a 'disquieting effect' on their own position. In other words Marx did not develop a general theory of ideology because it would have shown that his own ideas were as ideological as those of his opponents.

In Mannheim's view, men are members of various groups and confront the world both practically and intellectually as members of these groups. As they think *with* some groups and *against* some others, thinking is basically a social, a collective, activity.

—*Bhikhu Parekh*

The recognition of the 'infiltration of the social position of the investigator into the results of his study', Mannheim argues, entails a rejection of nearly all the basic assumptions of the traditional theory of rationality. Its biggest mistake was to detach human thinking from its social and activist context. It had naively assumed that thinking was a solitary and uniquely individual activity. In Mannheim's view, on the other hand, men are members of various groups and confront the world both practically and intellectually as members of these groups. As they think *with* some groups and *against* some others, thinking is basically a social, a collective, activity. 'Strictly speaking it is incorrect to say that the single individual thinks. Rather it is more correct to say that he participates in thinking further what men have thought before him'. Thinking, further, is not a contemplative but a practical activity and is integrally connected with the human need to respond to the world. Its problems, concepts, forms of thought are not *sui generis* or excogitated out of the human mind but arise in the course of transforming and grappling with the world. Thinking and acting, theory and practice, are not separate activities but two somewhat different dimensions of a single composite activity. Theory arises out of and reacts on practice, just as practical concerns generate and transform, and are in turn transformed by, theory.

As the traditional theory of rationality is based on false assumptions concerning the nature of thought, Mannheim goes on, its notions of truth and objectivity need to be radically revised. If all thought is practical, the idea of a disinterested pursuit of truth does not make any sense. And if all thought is socially determined the idea of absolute and universally valid truth does not make any sense either. To suggest that some forms of thought and criteria of validity are universally true is naive in the extreme. 'Such simple and unsophisticated ideas in their purity and naivety are reminiscent of some intellectual Eden that knows nothing of the upheaval of knowledge after the fall'. The discovery that thought is immersed in the life of society, that it has 'social and activist roots', has already been made, and it is no longer possible to go back to the cosy and comforting but essentially invalid rationalism of the traditional theory of rationality. One can, of course, keep pointing to a few basic propositions of logic and mathematics and even of some of the natural sciences as examples of universally valid truth and continue chanting slogans about the dignity and purity of human thought. But that is no answer to a man who, deeply perplexed and bewildered by the sheer multiplicity and chaos of social and political thought, asks how 'the partisanship, the fragmentariness of our vision' can be transcended and how we can deal with the 'undoubted' fact that human ideas are profoundly conditioned by deep psychological and social forces. It is no use talking to him about the formal consistency or inconsistency of a theory, since his query is about the diversity of substantive interpretations of facts. And it is no use either to refer him to the verificationist criteria for evaluating different theories, since the social and political facts to which an appeal is being made can themselves be interpreted and described in so many different and conflicting ways. To put the point differently, the recognition of the 'inherently ideological character of all thought', of the fact that the 'thought of all parties in all epochs is of an ideological character', has destroyed 'man's confidence in human thought in general'. And the fundamental problem that

any well-considered theory of rationality must answer is as to how one can deal with this crisis in human self-confidence, without taking recourse to the already discredited Platonic, Cartesian and other forms of abstract rationalism, or to self-destructive scepticism and irrationalism, or to an 'ill-considered and sterile form of relativism . . . increasingly prevalent today'.

Mannheim's own answer to the crisis created by the knowledge of the existential determination of truth is along the following lines. Just as in personal life one acquires mastery over blind and unconscious impulses by first becoming aware of them, and then consciously controlling them, so too in his pursuit of knowledge man can acquire objectivity, not by ignoring or holding 'in abeyance' his interests and evaluations but only by recognizing and accepting them. And just as a patient needs a psychoanalyst to make him aware of his unconscious impulses and to help him to come to terms with and even conquer them, a society needs a sociologist of knowledge. The task of the sociologist of knowledge is threefold. First, he is to interpret and organize people's complex and chaotic ideas into coherent and intelligible perspectives. Second, he is to interpret and analyse these perspectives and classify them into a few basic styles of thinking. Having done this he is to take the third and final step of going 'behind' these basic styles of thinking, relating them to their relevant social backgrounds and showing how each perspective is existentially determined. This three-stage inquiry Mannheim calls sociology of knowledge. And its method of operation he calls 'relationism', that is, relating isolated ideas to a perspective, a perspective to a thought style, and relating the latter in turn to a life-situation. Relationism then is Mannheim's answer to relativism, and sociology of knowledge is his answer to ideology.

By analysing the life-experiences within which a perspective arises and from which it derives its meaning, the sociologist of knowledge, in Mannheim's view, is able to comprehend its inner significance and rationality. He is also able to show to its adherents why they think the way they do, why they emphasize certain experiences and not others, why they value certain things and not others, why they use words and concepts one way rather than another. By thus demonstrating to them how their perspective reflects and articulates a *Weltanschauung* appropriate to their particular social position, he is able both to show them the one-sidedness of their perspective and to make them receptive to the insights of other perspectives. In seeing how various perspectives differ and why, the sociologist of knowledge, further, is able to go beyond them all and is in a position to create a higher level of abstraction that offers a 'common denominator', a common vocabulary and a common body of standards for translating the insights and results of one perspective in terms of another. He is able, in other words, to develop 'a more comprehensive basis of vision', a dynamic and synthetic viewpoint that encompasses, explains and integrates conflicting perspectives.

Sociology of knowledge, Mannheim maintains, does no more than provide a common framework within which different perspectives can engage in a dialogue. Since a mere empirical demonstration of the origin of an idea tells us nothing about its validity, sociology of knowledge is not equipped to assess the validity of ideas, which, as the traditional theory of rationality had insisted, remains the preserve of epistemology. However, sociology of knowledge is not entirely irrelevant to epistemology. The knowledge of the origin of an idea clarifies its meaning and indicates how it is intended to be taken. It informs us, further, about the scope of the statement, the area of experience it is intended to cover; by thus indicating how its truth or falsity is to be ascertained, it guides us in deciding *how* it is to be validated and *within what limits* it is to be considered valid. In other words sociology of knowledge 'particularizes' the 'scope and the extent' of the validity of an idea or a theory. In Mannheim's cryptic and vague phrase, the value of the findings of the sociology of knowledge 'lies somewhere . . . between irrelevance to the establishment of truth on the one hand, and entire adequacy for determining the truth on the other'.

Since Mannheim is convinced that there is a 'close' relationship between the origin of an idea and its validity, between sociology of knowledge and epistemology, he argues that the 'fundamental presuppositions' of the traditional conception of epistemology should be radically revised. The 'self-sufficiency of epistemology', accepted as a self-evident truth by the traditional theory of rationality, is a myth. The traditional conception of epistemology is derived from the natural sciences; and since the historical-social perspective of the investigator is irrelevant to the validity of the knowledge acquired in these sciences, traditional epistemology has remained unhistorical and abstract. When therefore it is applied to the social sciences where the social position of the investigator is of utmost importance it leads to distortion. What we need to do therefore is to evolve a historically orientated epistemology that takes full account of the concrete interplay between existence and knowledge. Once the traditional epistemology is revised, says Mannheim, its notions of truth and objectivity have to be revised as well. Different perspectives have different insights into social reality and all we can hope for is to encourage a debate among them and arrive at a broader and richer insight, an insight that is more comprehensive and richer than any of them but not one that can pretend to represent 'truth as such'. A true social or political theory is not one that no one can deny but one that most men can accept. The idea of 'absolute truth' or 'truth in itself' is therefore inapplicable to the study of man. Besides, as a richer and more satisfactory conception of social reality can only be attained by integrating partial and narrower conceptions of reality, an 'indirect approach through social history' is in the end far more fruitful than 'a direct logical attack'. Truth, that is to say, is reached not by falsifying and knocking down theories but by understanding their social context, appreciating their partial insights, and incorporating them in a wider perspective.

II

Mannheim spoils a good thesis by exaggerating it. He says much that is interesting and valid and with which, as will become apparent in the next section, I agree. As we shall see later he is right to emphasize the social and activist context of social and political thought and to draw attention to some of the problems created by the remarkably different ways in which people see the same reality. He is right to criticize the traditional theory of rationality for its historical and sociological *naïveté;* and he is no less right to criticize Hegel and Marx for emphasizing the historicity of all thought but claiming inconsistently that their own theories somehow represented absolute truth. He is also right to see the narrowness of Marx's economism, and to want to define the category of social factors much more widely. Mannheim's own proposal for a sympathetic analysis and systematic synthesis of conflicting social and political theories does suggest a way out of the pluralist impasse and opens up an interesting line of inquiry. His basic mistake, however, was twofold. First, while he was right to see that human thought, especially social and political thought, cannot be dissociated from human interests, values, anxieties, cultural biases, etc., he went wrong in arguing that it was determined by any or all of them. In other words, he confused the fact that man is culturally conditioned with the dubious view that man is socially determined, and rejected only the economistic version of the determinist thesis, but not the thesis itself. Mannheim's second basic mistake was to confuse pluralism with relativism, the undoubted fact that different people see reality differently with the dubious view that they see different realities and that truth and reality are relative. These mistakes led his otherwise stimulating analysis into blind alleys.

Although Mannheim's entire analysis hinges on his basic thesis that knowledge is determined by social background, he never clearly defines any of the key terms involved. He does not explain what he means by knowledge.

—*Bhikhu Parekh*

Although Mannheim's entire analysis hinges on his basic thesis that knowledge is determined by social background, he never clearly defines any of the key terms involved. He does not explain what he means by knowledge. It is not clear, for example, if he means the total body of information that an individual has or only the systematic body of theoretical knowledge. That your name is John and that Paris is the capital of France can in one sense be called knowledge, but Mannheim clearly does not want to say that this type of knowledge is relative to different perspectives. By knowledge therefore he must be taken to mean systematic and organized knowledge. Even here, however, he qualifies his thesis by saying that not all but 'most of the domains of knowledge' are existentially determined. How the distinction between different types of knowledge is made and why only some of them are considered socially determined is nowhere explained. He is not even certain what domains of knowledge are existentially determined. He is clear that 'historical, political and social sciences' and 'ordinary thought' are determined and 'exact sciences' are not. But his attitude to logic is ambiguous. At times he suggests that its 'laws' are immune from social determination; but at other times he argues that even formal logic is acceptable and appears plausible only to certain types of society or to certain sections of it.

Not only does he not give a coherent account of what type of knowledge is determined and why, he also does not explain what precisely he means by determinism. Sometimes knowledge is said to be 'casually' determined; sometimes it is said to be 'conditioned' by existential factors; sometimes it is said to be 'closely connected' with or 'in harmony' with or 'in accord' with them; sometimes it 'corresponds' to them; while at other times, as is more often the case, he is content to remark that it is 'no accident' that ideas and social background correspond. Mannheim could, of course, argue, as in fact he does, that these and other expressions do not reflect any ambiguity in his thought but only represent different *types* and *levels* of correlation that can exist between thought-process and life-situation. Thus in some cases ideas are determined by social factors; in other cases, they are only conditioned by them; and in some other cases they only correspond to them. This would be a plausible thesis to maintain, but then it would mean that Mannheim is not justified in talking about existential *determination* of knowledge, since determination refers to but one particular type of relationship and an extremely strong one at that. What is more, in those cases where ideas are said to accord with or correspond to existential factors, he would not really be establishing any meaningful correlation between them, since merely to show that certain ideas happen to be vaguely associated with certain social backgrounds is not to say anything of real significance. Mannheim needs to show that this association is not a mere coincidence but due to the influence of social factors.

Mannheim, again, does not show what existential factors determine ideas, why they and not others should be singled out, and why they have this kind of influence. Unlike Montesquieu he does not assign any influence to climatic, geographical and other natural factors without showing why. One would have thought that they too are 'existential' factors. He is also not clear whether or not psychological factors 'determine' thought and to what degree. At times he assigns key role to 'collective-unconscious, volitional impulses' and argues that thought requires an 'emotional-unconscious undercurrent to assure the continuous orientation for knowledge in group life'. In his view it is 'impulsive, irrational factors' that furnish 'the real basis' for the development of society and of ideas. Knowing, he maintains, 'presupposes a community of knowing which grows primarily out of a community of experiencing prepared for in the subconscious'. Since the collective unconscious of a group has such a powerful influence on its ideas he devotes nearly eighteen pages to the discussion of how to control it. For the most part, however, Mannheim is not happy with such psychological accounts; and while stressing their importance, he seems to want to explain them in sociological terms, generally taking the view that uncon-

scious psychological influences are themselves the result of social forces.

But when it comes to specifying social factors he is, again, ambivalent. Sometimes he takes every possible type of social grouping to be a determinant of ideas, and emphasizes the role of family, childhood experiences, occupational groups, etc. At other times, he follows Marx in regarding the class as all-important. At yet other times he stresses 'political interests' as existentially very important. Sometimes he moves away from groups altogether and resorts to that capacious umbrella of social forces, social structure as a whole, and even the entire historical epoch as the existential determinants of ideas. Thus he says at various places that the rationalistic manner of thinking arose in the modern society because it was 'in accord with the needs of an *industrial society*', that the post-Romantic generation adopted a revolutionary view of society because it was 'in accord with the needs of *the time*', that psychic energies and forms of thought are transformed by 'social forces'. To say that social factors determine ideas is not really to say anything meaningful, unless one shows how the social factors are themselves interrelated. Now either Mannheim should pick up one of them as all-important, or he should establish a pattern of interaction among them. He does neither. He is tempted to take the familiar Marxist line, but fights shy of its reductionism and naive economism. The result is that he keeps emphasizing different factors as they suit his argument, leaving his theory of social determinism incredibly chaotic.

Mannheim's basic thesis then is muddled. He does not clarify what types of ideas are determined by what types of existential factors; and he is not clear either on whether they are determined or conditioned or stimulated by them or whether they simply happen to correspond to them. What is worse his concern to establish his thesis leads him to make highly dubious assertions. Explaining why Marx did not develop a sociology of knowledge, he argues that it was because he did not want, albeit unconsciously, to jeopardize his own claim to represent an absolutely true theory of society. But how does Mannheim know that this was Marx's unconscious reason? Why cannot one admit that Marx did genuinely believe, however wrongly, that while the ideas of some classes were determined by interests, his own were not? Perhaps he was inconsistent, but what evidence does Mannheim have to jump to the conclusion that this inconsistency sprang from Marx's unconscious desire to distort the truth to bolster his scientific claims? Mannheim asserts, again, that much of modern sociology shies away from dealing historically and concretely with the problems of society and remains abstract and formalistic because it is afraid that otherwise its own internal contradictions, and those of capitalism itself, might become visible to others. The bourgeois discussion of freedom, Mannheim again insists, has always concentrated on political but never on social and economic freedom, because the bourgeoisie are fearful that this might pose a threat to their interests. In no case does he offer any evidence that this was or is really the intention of the parties concerned. He does not show, for example, that formalistic sociology is really committed to the defence of capitalism, or that the adoption of an historical approach will necessarily lead it to criticize it. The reasoning in each case is deductive and speculative and one could just as plausibly offer a totally different account of the phenomenon concerned.

Even if Mannheim's thesis could be correctly formulated, it would have to be rejected on a number of grounds. If all thought is existentially determined, so is the thought that all thought is existentially determined, and therefore has no general validity. Again, a society is a system of roles and reciprocal relationships which cannot be sustained if its members do not have similar ideas on their position in society and the rights and duties it entails. In other words the existence of an organized society becomes impossible to explain if its members have different ideas corresponding to their different social backgrounds. Again, Mannheim's view rests on a naive conception of the nature of ideas. It assumes that as social conditions change ideas change automatically; but this is to treat ideas like a baggage that one can pick up and put down at will. It also implies that men cannot change their ideas unless they change their social group, and this not only denies all intellectual value to education, discussion, criticism, introspection and disturbing personal experiences, but also makes it impossible to explain the familiar fact that people do change their ideas without changing their social position.

Even though Mannheim's account of ideology and rationality is untenable, what he says about sociology of knowledge makes some very interesting points. His view that the knowledge of the life-situation of a person is useful in understanding his social and political ideas is valid and his belief that it is possible to work out a realm of debate where competing viewpoints can carry on a dialogue and come better to appreciate their partialities opens up an interesting line of inquiry. Even though he does not establish any clear relationship between the origin and the validity of an idea, he does manage to suggest that the two are related, although not in quite the way he proposes. His plea for both an historically orientated epistemology in social and political thought, and for a revision of the notions of objectivity and truth as they apply to the study of man, is blacked up by some very powerful arguments.

The point, however, is that his sociology of knowledge is impossible if his theory of ideology is correct. In other words, paradoxically, his cure is only effective if his diagnosis is wrong. It is not at all clear how it is possible for holders of different perspectives ever to argue if their categories of thought and forms of consciousness are determined existentially. As each perspective is a self-enclosed world and no one can get out of it, the possibility of a dialogue is foreclosed. This applies to the sociologist of knowledge as well who, despite Mannheim's rather naive theory of 'socially unattached intellectuals', is as much a prisoner of his existentially determined perspective as anyone else, and therefore cannot have the ability to reconstruct other perspectives faithfully or to relate them to their adherents' life situation or provide a 'common denominator' between them. Further if different perspectives are to criticize each other, they must have *some* common standards to which they can appeal and whose general va-

lidity they must accept. This means that objective standards that Mannheim had earlier rejected and that indeed generated the problem of ideology in the first instance have now to be brought back through the backdoor, as he actually does in his reference to 'the direct examination of facts'. But once they are brought back, it becomes possible for different perspectives to communicate and criticize each other directly; and therefore sociology of knowledge is no longer necessary to provide a common vocabulary or a common realm of discourse. In other words, if all social and political thought is ideological, sociology of knowledge is impossible; if, on the other hand, it is not ideological, sociology of knowledge is not necessary to play the redemptive role that Mannheim assigns it.

III

Mannheim then has failed to provide a satisfactory theory of social and political rationality. As he mistakenly took a determinist and relativist view of social and political thought he remained unable to explain how social thought could be improved, how men could debate and discuss, how the partial insights of conflicting social and political theories could be synthesized. The problem for any well-considered theory of rationality, therefore, is how it can come to terms with the plurality of social and political thought without getting misled into determinist and relativist blind alleys. Below is sketched very briefly and tentatively the outline of one possible way of conceiving rationality.

We can take it as true that a human being does not exist in a vacuum but is a member of a society by whose cultural milieu he is necessarily conditioned. He grows up with its values, prejudices and categories of thought that are often too deep even for consciousness. His language too directs his perceptions and thoughts along definite channels. He occupies a definite position in society that delimits his range of experiences, and therefore influences the view he will be inclined to take of his fellow-men, the beliefs he will find plausible, the weight he will attach to an argument or to an account of human behaviour. The cultural ethos of his society moulds and shapes his mind; it disposes him to look at the world in a certain way and gives his consciousness a quality, a tone, a content, a rhythm, a structure. His reason, which is only the way his consciousness operates, is thus firmly and securely located in the culture of his community and is not a natural or transcendent faculty but a cultural capacity. Human mind, further, is a complex totality in which reason, passion, desire are all closely intertwined. It cannot therefore be broken up into separate parts each of which operates in isolation from the rest. Just as human feelings and emotions are not primeval raw forces but are already permeated by reason, so also human reason is immersed in the individual's values, interests, anxieties and aspirations. To abstract it from them is to distort it, to miss its inspiring and guiding principles. Thinking in short, is not a cerebral or a mental process but a total human response, and it is not the human reason, nor the human mind, but the total human being who thinks and reasons. Further, man faces the world not in his sovereign loneliness but as a cultural being, as a being with a complex of values and attitudes. This is indeed what is involved in being human. *Contra* Mannheim he can, of course, change or modify some or most or even all of his values and attitudes but it is impossible to imagine a human being who has no definite way of looking at man and society, who is not orientated to the world in some definite way.

Intellectual inquiries differ in the way they involve the total human person. In the inquiries like logic and mathematics that are purely formal, one proposition follows from another with deductive rigour, leaving no room for preference or interpretation, and therefore human values and prejudices do not enter. In the natural sciences where there is room for interpretation and discretion, they do enter, but to a limited degree and not in a way that affects the substance of the theories developed. Thus whether or not the universe is a deterministic system and allows 'free will', whether or not it leaves room for God, whether its ultimate constituents are isolated and singular atoms or whether they constitute a 'community' are issues that do affect the scientist's personal values, emotions, world view, and therefore influence the way he describes his conception of the universe or what theories he finds persuasive and appealing. One has only to consider, for example, the way some scientists refuse to accept a deterministic conception of the universe, or the way they talk about the 'community' of atoms, or define the notions of absolute space and time. Again, not every scientific hypothesis can be completely verified, and a scientist has to decide if evidence for it is *sufficiently* strong and probability sufficiently high. And here one of the factors influencing his judgements is his view of the seriousness of the consequences issuing from making a mistake in accepting the hypothesis. Thus, for example, if the hypothesis under consideration was that a toxic ingredient was present in a drug in lethal quantity, the scientist would want a relatively high degree of confirmation before accepting it.

The study of man is of a very different kind. Being a study of men like himself whose actions provoke attitudes of approval or disapproval, praise or condemnation, it *activates* the theorist's cultural values in a way that the study of nature or number does not. Human actions have a meaning that is not obvious and straightforward and has to be teased out. And this can only be done on the basis of what one expects men to be like, what one's experiences of men are like. What one says is capable of influencing others, and therefore involves one's interests and values. One likes to see a certain type of world, a certain pattern of interpersonal relationship, and since theory is one mode of action one's theories and interpretations are unavoidably coloured by one's anxieties and aspirations as the testimonies of Plato, Augustine, Hobbes, further, Rousseau and Marx make so abundantly clear. A theorist, further, has a certain way of looking at the world. He is either a pessimist or an optimist; he either loathes conflict or welcomes it. And these attitudes influence his selection of facts, the importance he assigns them and the way he feels inclined to relate them. Again, his language is already charged with the ethos of his community and directs his thought, and therefore his choice and manner of relating facts, in a certain definite way. A language that offers no means of describing or referring to men separately from their caste or

other social groupings would make it most difficult to develop a theory, e.g. of methodological or ontological individualism and would incline its users to look for only those aspects of human conduct in which individuals cooperate and act in a concerted manner.

Apart from this general fact that human prejudices, values, interests, attitudes, are activated by the study of man in a way they are not by other types of study, there are also several other reasons why the study of man is culturally conditioned. Unlike natural events human beings are historical creatures. They have a past that endures in the present; they are subject to historical change; and they can and do organize their personal and social life in so very different ways. Our moral life, for example, is a precipitate of several moralities: the Greco-Roman, Judaic, Christian, feudal and the contemporary bourgeois and socialist moralities. All these strands have given rise to a highly complex pattern of moral conduct that is by no means a coherent structure. What is more they are combined differently in different sections of society or by different individuals and generate unique patterns of moral conduct. A moral philosopher is no exception and therefore he will tend to offer an account of moral life that is faithful to his own moral experiences. But his moral experiences are not others' moral experiences; and therefore an account that strikes him as natural, accurate, obvious, true, strikes another as one-sided and even false. Kantian moral theory, for example, offers a perfectly valid account of the moral experiences of men who live a life of duty for duty's sake and generally take a legalistic attitude to life. But it cannot but strike as odd to those who take life less rigorously, who would bend a rule at the first available opportunity to make others happy. This does not mean that the Kantian moral theory is valid for some and not for others, but rather that it is able to account for certain types of moral experiences much better than others, and that therefore those to whom the former types of experience come naturally will be persuaded of its truth in a way that others would not be. *Contra* Mannheim it does not mean either that a moral philosopher cannot imagine what different types of moral experiences are like and take account of them in constructing his moral theory. However, imagination, like reason, is not some abstract faculty but is culturally conditioned and therefore there are limits to what a man can imagine. When a moral or social theorist tries to comprehend another society or an unfamiliar experience, he does not approach it with a blank mind but with a mind already accustomed to looking at man and society in a specific way. He can certainly stretch his imagination and revise his preconceptions, but there are limits to how far he can go. And even when he can imagine unfamiliar experiences, he needs to interpret and make sense of them, and here his own cultural assumptions and categories inescapably enter.

In social and political thought there is also the further question of theoretical discretion in conceptualizing experience. A concept can best be understood on the analogy of a beam of light; it has an unmistakable centre but a nebulous and hazy circumference and therefore covers a wide range at either end of which it merges into other concepts. An analysis of a concept therefore involves determining both its centre (its paradigmatic usage) and its range (that is, its permissible usages). Take, for example, the concept of man. We know how to use this concept and have generally no difficulty recognizing human beings. But suppose walking through the jungles of Africa I come across a tiny insect who greets me and strikes off an extremely pleasant conversation about the beauty of the jungle and its wild life, the misery and poverty of Africans, etc. How am I to describe this creature? It behaves like a man, and therefore I could call it a man. But it looks like an insect, and therefore I could refuse to call it a man. There is no reason why I could not take either view, and in each case I would be no more or no less objective or right than the person taking the opposite view. The same sort of problem comes up in less bizarre cases. Is the so-called psychic 'violence' violence or not? Is exploitation violence as the New Left insists? Or should the term violence be reserved only for the use of physical force? Is Aristotle's proportional equality to be called equality? Is the Greek city-'state' a state? Or is the term to be reserved only for the modern post-Renaissance state? Is university politics politics? Or is the term to be reserved only for the conduct of the affairs of the state? There are good and bad reasons for each side of the controversy, and therefore a theorist has a discretion. Depending on how he uses each of the countless concepts that go to compose his theory, he will describe, interpret and relate the relevant phenomena differently.

Theories about man and society then are culturally conditioned and reflect the cultural orientation of their originators. Hence they appear plausible to those sharing their underlying cultural values and attitudes; to those who take a different view of man and society, they appear less convincing and persuasive. Not that they are true for one group and false for another, but rather that they appear true, self-evident, to one group but not to another. That all theories about man and society are permeated by their creators' cultural biases and values, and that they appear more plausible and persuasive to some but not to others, can be established not only on the basis of a philosophical analysis of the nature of thinking but also by showing empirically how there is hardly any social or moral or political theory that does not, as it were, give away its originator's identity.

Max Weber is one of the clearest examples of a thinker who believed that a social scientist could and should offer, and that he himself did offer, 'an unconditionally valid type of knowledge' that, in his favourite phrase, 'must be acknowledged as correct even by a Chinese'. Ignoring the vulgar Nazi criticism of his writings as essentially 'Jewish', the crude Communist attack on him as a man concerned to make out a case for charismatic leadership and thereby for the Führer, and ignoring also the rather crude neo-liberal attack on him as a man whose writings were inspired by a Machiavellian worship of power and German imperialism, it is still possible to show that underlying Weber's sociological writings is a definite cultural bias, a definite *Weltanschauung,* a clearly identifiable body of moral values. He is an old-fashioned liberal who prizes individual liberty, above all the freedom of conscience, the freedom to make one's moral choices oneself. One of the important reasons why he separated fact and value was

not that this might corrupt the objectivity of science but rather that it might create moral experts and give the scientist a power to prescribe moral values that might detract from the individual's unique moral status and dignity. It is also this that explains his interest in and intense concern about the consequences of bureaucratization. Consider, for example, his following description of it:

> . . . each man becomes a little cog in the machine and, aware of this, his one preoccupation is whether he can become a bigger cog . . . it is horrible to think that the world could one day be filled with those little cogs, little men clinging to little jobs and striving towards bigger ones . . . this passion for bureaucracy is enough to drive one to despair. It is as if we were deliberately to become men who need order and nothing but order, who become nervous and cowardly if for one moment this order wavers, and helpless if they are torn away from their total incorporation in it. That the world should know men but these; it is in such an evolution that we are already caught up, and the great question is therefore not how we can promote and hasten it, but what we can oppose to this machinery in order to keep a portion of mankind free from this parcelling-out of the soul, from this supreme mastery of the bureaucratic way of life.

This is not a value-free statement but the remark of a man firmly committed to individual liberty. His liberalism comes out in a variety of other ways as well. As a secular rationalist he denies that the world is intrinsically rational; and as a good pluralist, he sees different religions as so many equally valid attempts to make some sense of it. Similarly he regards different moral systems as more or less equally valid ways of organizing moral life. Again, as a good liberal he takes the individual as the ultimate social reality, an unanalysable 'atom' of sociology, and issues the methodological prescription that any property involving reference to a collectivity must ultimately be resolved into concepts referring to actions of identifiable individuals. Again, he subscribes to the liberal view of man as an essentially rational being in whom irrationality is a deviation, an aberration, and deduces the methodological prescription, embodied in his theory of ideal type, that all 'irrational, affectually determined, elements of behaviour' should be treated 'as factors of deviation from a conceptually pure type of action'. Even without consulting a 'Chinese', someone who takes a different view of man and society, a Marx or a Tawney or a Samuelson, for example, would quarrel with many of Weber's interpretations and explanations and offer a different account of the nature and rise of bureaucracy or capitalism or Protestantism or Calvinism.

Not only that Weber, the champion of 'unconditionally valid knowledge', himself does not produce a body of knowledge that 'even a Chinese' must accept; no other political or social scientist has so far done so either. Don Martindale has shown in detail how many of the allegedly value-neutral sociological theorists rest on unmistakable normative foundations. Henry Murray and David McClelland have shown how theories of personality project their authors' personal and cultural orientations. Charles

Taylor has analysed Lipset's *Political Man* in considerable detail and shown how underlying his analysis is an unmistakable liberal preference for a society in which conflict is not suppressed but brought out into the open and integrated into the social framework, in which economic inequality is reduced, in which there is a large middle class and whose members are prepared to settle their differences by compromise and bargain. After a careful survey of the researches on the Negro problem in America, Myrdal concluded that 'there is no piece of research on the Negro problem which does not contain valuation, explicit or implicit'. J. W. Bennett has shown in a most interesting article how researches into the Pueblo culture describe and account for the same basic facts so very differently. Thompson, Benedict and others describe Hopi life as harmonious, organic, spontaneous, and involving minimum physical force; Goldfrank and Eggam, on the other hand, emphasize its deep social conditioning, its harshness, its coerciveness, and the emotional price it exacts from its members. These and other differences, as Bennett has shown, arise not from any carelessness in empirical research on the part of either group of writers, but essentially from the basic differences in their values, their attitudes to life, their cultural background, their prejudices, that lead them to select different facts, or to order the same facts differently, or to interpret and elucidate their meanings differently. Bertrand Russell was not entirely wrong when, commenting on the studies of the behaviour of rats by American and British psychologists, he remarked how American and British rats seemed to him to behave almost exactly as the Americans and Britishers did in their ordinary life. It is not difficult either to show how the study of the Third World by developmental experts says more about them than about the countries they study.

Since social and political theories are unavoidably selective, partial and culturally conditioned, the only way to improve them is to force them to explain themselves, to articulate and justify their assumptions and choice of concepts, to defend their interpretations of facts and show why other interpretations are mistaken. By criticizing a theory we can show how it rests on dubious assumptions, or how its concepts are muddled, or how it does not account for certain types of experience and how it becomes incoherent and muddled when it tries to give a plausible account of them, or how it draws illegitimate inferences or is internally inconsistent. In other words the institutionalization of criticism, as Popper has rightly emphasized, is the basic precondition of improving social and political theories.

If our earlier account of social and political theory is correct, Popper's theory of criticism, however, needs to be modified in several important respects. Popper argues that a theory can be falsified if it does not conform to facts. This does not take account of the twofold fact that facts can be interpreted differently and that facts themselves can be so very different. As we saw earlier, Kant's moral theory gives a satisfactory account of certain types of moral experience but not others. It would be wrong to say that the latter falsify his theory; rather they demonstrate how it is partial and limited, how its explanatory power and truth-content are limited. Similarly to a Bentham tak-

ing an egoistic view of man Jesus's martyrdom is as much an act of self-love or self-interest as Shylock's demand for a portion of flesh or Hitler's slaughter of Jews. This certainly goes against our ordinary evaluations of Christ's motives, but it would not do to use this as a 'fact' that falsifies Bentham's moral psychology, no more than our ordinary feeling that the earth is flat could be invoked to reject the scientific theory that the earth is round. Our ordinary evaluations can be wrong, or while admitting them at one level Bentham might rightly want to deny them at another.

The only way we can criticize Bentham's account of Christ's behaviour is by examining if and how he can show why self-love takes so very different forms in the cases of Shylock and Jesus, what secret pleasure Christ is pursuing in his martyrdom, why Bentham takes the view that man is necessarily an egocentric creature, how he would knock down other interpretations of human conduct, etc. In other words, facts do not falsify a social and political theory in a way that the discovery that there is no cat in my room falsifies the assertion that there is. Rather they impugn the validity of a theory by showing how in the course of explaining them it is forced to become more and more muddled, incoherent, ambiguous, bizarre. Facts destroy a social or political theory not so much by falsifying it as by undermining its integrity and credibility, by making it incoherent. In some sense this is like the way a lawyer proves a hostile witness a liar. He presents him with an inconvenient fact and asks him to explain it. The latter might be able to explain it away, in which case the lawyer presents him with another awkward fact. He might be able to explain away this fact as well, and then the lawyer presents him with yet another disturbing fact. And so on until the man is cornered, exposed, rendered incoherent. Hobbes or Bentham or Weber or Hegel, too, cannot be refuted, but cornered by being patiently presented with inconvenient facts at each stage of the argument. The more general methodological point of this example is that coherence correspondence dichotomy needs to be revised in discussing social and political thought, since the most effective way to criticize a social theory is not merely to expose its formal inconsistencies or to show that it does not correspond to facts but rather to use *facts* to demonstrate its incoherence, to use *empirical* evidence to demonstrate its *logical* weakness.

The second important respect in which Popper's theory of criticism needs to be modified is directly related to the peculiar character of social and political thought. As social and political facts can be interpreted differently and given different meanings and significance, our concern here, as Mannheim has argued, is to understand each other, to benefit from each others' insights, and ideally to acquire as comprehensive and rich a vision of social life as possible, a vision to which each theory makes a contribution and which unites all contestants at a deeper level of understanding. What one needs, therefore, is not a boxing match between different theories where each gets a point for every punch it lands and the victory goes to the one who deals a knock-out blow, as Popper's rather aggressive metaphors suggest, but a sympathetic and imaginative dialogue in which each contestant tries to learn from the rest.

In this process of helping each theory to understand what makes others tick, what they really mean, and why they have an appeal for their adherents, something like Mannheim's sociology of knowledge has a useful role. Even the sociology of knowledge, however, is a somewhat crude tool and needs to be supplemented by literature, art and philosophy that can present the insights of each theory in an imaginative way and increase their mutual comprehension. As social and political knowledge grows not merely by criticism but also by sympathy and imagination, as one's concern here is not to knock down a theory but to absorb and incorporate its insight into an ever-widening vision, a theory that aims only to devise methods of falsification is one-sided and misses out one of the crucial dimensions of social and political debate.

Popper's theory of criticism needs to be modified in another respect as well. We saw earlier how social and political thought is integrally tied up with interests, values, prejudices. The civil climate of criticism that presupposes the willingness to expose oneself to others' relentless probing and to learn from their criticisms can hardly be sustained in a society where participants are involved in a ruthless struggle for survival or supremacy. Since social and political theory inevitably has, or can be seen to have, *some* practical implications, its discussion inevitably arouses fears and suspicions and introduces into calm academic discussion the all too familiar urgency of the market place. Marx is right that in a society characterized by clashes of sectional interests, the tendency to distort ideas is likely to be great. Mannheim's point that participants in a debate can better understand each other the greater the similarity of their experiences, is also appropriate here. In other words the pursuit of objectivity and truth requires the creation of a society from which violent clashes of interest have been eliminated, where there is less acute division of labour and specialization of thought so that people have the disposition and the ability to view their disciplines in a wider context, where there is considerable social mobility so that individuals have a chance to see their society and life from different perspectives, where there is equality of educational opportunity so that no intellectual inquiry is dominated by people sharing a uniform life-style. This is indeed the basic lesson we can learn from ideologists, that just as ideas are closely tied up with individual interests and values, so also is the search for truth and objectivity tied up with the creation of a humane society.

By criticism and sympathetic imagination social and political theories can be improved. But we need to be careful how we describe the process of improvement. Popper himself and many others have described it as getting closer to the truth, implying that one day we might reach the truth, the absolute truth as Popper calls it. Now because social and political thought is necessarily partial, selective, culture-bound, the idea of absolute truth does not make sense. An absolutely true theory would be one that can *never* be faulted, that accounts for the total diversity of relevant experience without distorting or overlooking *any* element in it, that uses concepts with which *no one* can quarrel, that rests on *no* assumptions that the theorist has not clearly articulated and defended. It is difficult to imagine what such a theory can even look like. Since values enter into the theorist's interpretation and explanation of his subject matter, an absolutely true social theory is possible only if we have an absolutely true moral theory, a set of absolutely true moral values; but such a moral theory is not available for obvious reasons. Just as the notion of absolute truth does not make sense, the notion of progressive approximation to it has to be rejected as well for the simple reason that there is nothing *towards* which one can be said to be moving or to which one can be said to be getting closer. The spatial metaphor carries the danger of inducing the belief that if we keep trying hard we would one day get to the truth. In other words it conveys the mistaken notion that the pursuit of truth is a journey that has a terminus, a destination that will one day be reached. It was this imagery that probably led Mill, Hegel, Marx and others to believe that progress will or must one day reach perfection. Theories, like society, can certainly be improved; but as they can *always* be improved, there is no terminus where improvement can be assumed to come to an end. Even as there cannot be an absolutely perfect society, a society in which there are no deficiencies whatsoever, for somewhat different reasons there cannot be an absolutely objective or absolutely true social theory either.

Because no theory about human behaviour can ever pretend to absolute truth and objectivity, there is no theory that cannot be criticized. But precisely because *every* social theory can be criticized and shown to be partial, culture-bound and narrowbased, no social theory can be rejected simply because it is open to criticism; otherwise no social theory would ever deserve acceptance. Since *no* theory can be absolutely true, one can only judge it in *comparative* terms, that theory being better which is less open to criticism than its rivals. To continue with our analogy, theories are like societies; if one demanded to live only in a society that was flawless, one would never find a society worth living in. One must be content to judge a society as better or worse than others that exist or are practically possible. Similarly, one theory is better than another and deserves acceptance if it is less partial, less discretionary, less culture-bound than its rivals.

A choice between social and political theories however is not always as clear-cut as this. Of a social theory, as of any other theory, we make a number of demands. It should not ignore any relevant fact; it should not distort facts; it should define its concepts clearly; it should be internally consistent; it should be imaginative and open up fruitful lines of inquiry; it should be structurally neat and tidy. Like moral ideals that cannot all be achieved, these demands cannot all be met. In tightening up its concepts or in achieving comprehensiveness, a theory may lose in empirical richness. In trying to be 'absolutely accurate', it might become as chaotic as the reality itself, losing in coherence what it gains in suggestiveness. As no theory possesses all the qualities one ideally expects in it, beyond a certain point the choice between them is a matter of individual discretion. There is also another point. Extreme and one-sided theories have often contributed far more to the growth of knowledge than those prosaic and balanced theories that see all sides of the question and never manage to rise above the level of common sense. Their uncompromising intransigence and unconcealed and fierce partiality force other practitioners of the discipline to reassess their assumptions, and stimulate and raise the level of intellectual debate. Objectivity, therefore, is not the only or even always the highest virtue in a theory. If a discipline is dominated by a single body of assumptions that its professionally socialized practitioners unconsciously assume to be self-evidently true, there is much to be said for advancing or accepting an extreme theory in order to stir them into critical self-examination and to encourage a radical reappraisal of the conceptual tools of the discipline. Since objectivity and impartiality are achieved as a result of the clash of subjectivity and partiality, falsehood and extremism often make most worthwhile contributions to the discovery of truth.

David Kettler, Volker Meja, and Nico Stehr (essay date 1984)

SOURCE: "Politics as a Science," in *Karl Mannheim,* Ellis Horwood Limited, 1984, pp. 14-32.

[*In the following excerpt, Kettler, Meja, and Stehr focus on the political aspects and implications of Mannheim's sociological writings.*]

MANNHEIM AND LIBERAL POLITICAL THOUGHT

Karl Mannheim often commented on the social condition of the outsider, who stands on the margin of an integrated social field, or on the boundary between two or more. No condition could have been more familiar to him. While the position of a Jewish student and young intellectual in the Budapest of 1910 may have been 'marginal' only when viewed from the nationalist perspective easy enough for this circle to dismiss, he twice in his life underwent the experience of exile and twice had to find a voice and a language appropriate to a newcomer. He left Hungary in 1919, after the failures of the progressive liberal and Soviet regimes; and he fled Germany for England in 1933, after the National Socialist decree deprived him of the Frankfurt professorship which he had only recently gained.

But it was not only the force of circumstances which brought him repeatedly to the boundary. Already as a young man in Budapest he had chosen an intellectual place for himself between proponents of reform based on social science, led by Oscar Jászi, and advocates of cultural renovation grounded on an essentially aesthetic philosophy, under George Lukács. And later, during his German academic career, he long prided himself on standing between sociology and philosophy, as well as between the exciting world of intellectuals' criticisms and the exacting world of academic rigour. Mannheim's English writings include reflections on the role of the refugee, and on his special mission as a mediator between European and Anglo-Saxon intellectual modes; and he aimed his work at creating conjunctions between sociology and education, between the preoccupations of practical reformers and those of the university.

Mannheim was by no means content simply to enjoy the ironic distance and special insights which the boundary condition is sometimes thought to provide. He believed that it also creates a unique opportunity to mediate between antithetical forces and to work for syntheses, and, indeed, that it implies a mission to do so. In his accounts of the sociology of knowledge, the enquiry for which he is best known, he emphasizes that the very possibility of such an approach to ideas and culture depends on the existence of a social stratum whose members have lived in diverse cultural and social settings and are now situated where they can experience that diversity. But the point of their intellectual labours is not to be, according to Mannheim, an impressionistic relish of variety, but rather a restoration of a common spirit and joint direction to the society as a whole.

This very preoccupation with bridging mutually alien worlds, overcoming conflicts, and cultivating comprehensive unities gives a certain political cast to his thought, or at least provides one source of his interest in political thinking. Mannheim's two best-known works both treat materials of primary interest to political writers. In ***Ideology and Utopia,*** he subjects complexes of political ideas to sociological interpretation, and in ***Man and Society in an Age of Reconstruction*** he proposes a design for reorganizing the social order so as to overcome the crisis afflicting public life. In both books, however, he disregards many of the primary concepts of political discourse and many of the issues discussed in political theory. In these writings, questions of rational public policy displace questions of legitimate authority, justice, citizenship, or the best constitution. In Mannheim's work we find ideology and sociology instead of political theory, and, especially in his later writings, 'elites' instead of governors, techniques of social control instead of law, command or coercion, questions of integration and coordination instead of power and resistance. Nevertheless, it is justified to see Karl Mannheim as a sociological political theorist.

Some writers have objected that Mannheim's thought represents the negation of political theory rather than, in any serious sense, its continuation and adaptation. But the defining feature of theoretical political thought is not the moral problem of obligation or the question of the best constitution or any other such theme. It would be more appropriate to consider as part of the history of political theory any sustained attempt to depict a structured relationship between politics and knowledge; and it would be best to recognize that various attempts will differ markedly as to the concepts and problems which appear central, as to the approaches which seem appropriate, and as to the criteria for correct answers to the questions raised.

Questions about what persons can know and how they can know it have special weight in political enquiry. They refer, for example, to that 'recognition' without which authority is inconceivable; they refer to responsibility; and they refer to the 'rationality' which the most varied political theories locate somewhere in political life and which is supposed somehow to vindicate the coercion and violence which are everywhere a feature of that life. When political theorists are quite secure in their answers to questions about the nature of knowledge, they are likely to construct new questions which presuppose those answers—as with subtle enquiries about natural law, and the like. But if the problems of knowledge themselves require new solutions, then the traditional topics are likely to be recast so as to reflect these more basic considerations.

The theme of knowledge enters upon our understanding of political theory at two levels. First, there are the difficulties likely to arise in showing that political thought constitutes a structure of knowledge and not merely an assemblage of opinions and assertions. And second, there are the questions which arise from the tasks assigned to knowledge within the political world. Mannheim thought that a sociological approach, grounded on the special boundary position of the social type of the 'intellectuals', could break through the impasse he found blocking advance in this domain. What appears to Mannheim as a Copernican new insight into the nature of political knowledge requires a substantial reformulation of traditional political concepts and relationships. The sociology of knowledge offers itself as at once a thorough critique of the prevailing tradition of political thought, charging it with having illusions about political knowledge and about its knowledge about that knowledge, and as an adequate approach to solving the constitutive problems of that tradition. Beyond the sociology of knowledge, then, Mannheim offers ways of knowing what must be known in political life.

Mannheim's earliest work, it must be said, displays little interest in what he then took to be the political domain as such. There he is most concerned to counter the inclusion of all ethical and aesthetic questions within a comprehensive positivist system, which dismisses any responses which cannot be comprehended by the methods of that approach. Envisioning instead a pluralist universe of discrete spheres and spiritual enterprises, he seeks to restore the legitimacy of the older humanist concerns by assigning each its place within distinctive cultural enquiries. In the context of these discussions, the political sphere appears comparatively uninteresting, as an arena for the adjustment of narrow interests devoid of spiritual meaning. But Mannheim soon moves away from this position.

The conception of political thinking which he eventually develops claims a wider field than had conventionally been assigned to it and comes, in fact, to comprehend most thinking other than the strictly technical. At first, though, in the methodological reflections leading up to the sociology of knowledge, he takes practical political knowledge in the narrower sense of humanist statesmanship as paradigm for all qualitative, non-positivist thinking. On the basis of this model of the thought which most interests him, he increasingly stresses the need to understand and develop ideas dealing with matters considered political in the narrow sense while seeking to relocate them in a broader sociological context. He leaves no doubt that he means thereby to incorporate and to correct the treatments accorded political matters by earlier political thinkers. The aim is a knowledge about political thinking and about substantive political matters which builds on the effective political knowledge of practitioners, but which also covers many social and philosophical matters not hitherto recognized as integral to such knowledge.

The sociological interpretation of much philosophy and sociology, paradoxically, reveals the political character of the thought-activities these disciplines document, when, as Mannheim urges, 'political' is taken in a broad sense to refer to all 'activity aiming at the transformation of the world' in accordance with a structured will. When Mannheim traces his own work to the philosophical tradition of Hegel or to the sociological tradition of Max Weber, accordingly, he is not denying its political character, because he usually treats these intellectual achievements as ways of coping with the demands voiced and the issues defined by liberal, conservative, and socialist political ideologies. To view Mannheim in the context of political thought, then, is to take him as he commonly saw himself.

To locate Mannheim in the political field, we begin with a typically ambiguous note he wrote to himself at some time during the mid-30s: 'Disproportionate development between attitudes and thought: in my understanding I have discerned that liberalism is obsolete, but my attitudes are still at a liberal level'. About a decade before he wrote this note, in his work on conservative thought, Mannheim assigned special importance to a distinction analogous to that between attitudes and thinking. He there distinguishes between the determinate patterns of consciousness through which men mediate their experiences of the world and their conceptualized thinking. He takes the former as embodying formative will; they constitute the animating principles of a 'style'. 'Structural analysis' of a doctrine, he then argues, involves the discovery of the stylistic principle which gives it structure and therewith direction. The 'style' is a plan. In that work, then, he also takes up the possibility of thought which does not rest upon such a structured mode of experiencing, but he treats it as a surface phenomenon, incapable of securing authentic knowledge. Anything like a 'disproportion between thinking and attitudes', from this earlier point of view, would imply an inauthentic condition requiring a shift to bring thought more nearly in line with experiential modes.

As indicated by the language of the note quoted, there was some change in Mannheim's thinking in the years intervening between the two writings. His adoption of the term 'attitudes' is associated with a heightened rationalism, a greater propensity to refer such core beliefs or structuring influences to irrational processes which critical thinking must somehow counter and overcome. But strong ambivalence remains.

Mannheim recognizes the liberal response to the world as a primary reference point for his thought. Like John Dewey, whom he came greatly to admire, he distinguishes between an old liberalism and a new, and dismisses only the former as anachronistic and philosophically inadequate. In his practical political creed, at least, he builds on the tradition of the liberal and reformist movement which was led in the Budapest of his youth by Oscar Jászi. His many departures from that tradition, even when they are adaptations to what he takes to be historical imperatives, can best be understood as part of a search for an inclusive and philosophically grounded way of comprehending liberal calls for reason, reconciliation, responsibility, and personal development. Writing to Jászi in 1936, in response to some criticisms Mannheim says:

> I am an old follower of yours and the impres-

sions of my youth of the purity of your character are so profound that all reproofs I find paternal and they touch me deeply. . . . I find the basic difference between the two of us in one thing. In my opinion, both of us are 'liberal' in our roots. You, however, wish to stand up against the age with a noble defiance, while I, as a sociologist, would like to learn by close observation the secret (even if it is infernal) of these new times, because I believe that this is the only way that we can remain masters over the social structure, instead of it mastering us. To carry liberal values forward with the help of the techniques of modern mass society is probably a paradoxical undertaking; but it is the only feasible way, if one does not want to react with defiance alone. But I am also familiar with such a way of reacting, and it is probably only a matter of time until I join you in it.

When Mannheim arrived at the University of Budapest in 1912, he followed a well-established organizational path which took him from the Galileo Circle, then a club for reform-minded students, to its sponsoring group, a lodge of Freemasons named for a liberal revolutionary, and to the activities of the Social Scientific Society. The reformers avowed themselves 'socialists' rather than 'individualists' on questions of economic organization, but they stressed that their consequent advocacy of state planning and regulation had nothing in common with notions of class struggle or class revolution, not to speak of the dictatorship of the proletariat or the end of the state. The state, they thought, must be strong, liberal, parliamentary, and democratic. Oscar Jászi had written in 1908:

> To raise humanity to the highest conceivable level of morality, science, aesthetics, and hygiene—that is the objective. The way to it is through the ever more complete mastery by the human spirit over things. The main idea of socialism, planful cooperation all along the line, is doubtless a more scientific idea than the main idea of individualism. . . . But at the same time there must not be missing that quantum of freedom which determines goals, makes discoveries possible, changes antiquated conditions, precludes arbitrary rule, and makes possible the advancement of the best.

In support of these objectives, the reform group lent its support to the Socialist Party in campaigns for democratic suffrage and political liberalization. Democratization was reconciled with the requirements for 'scientific' policy by confidence in the influence of a dedicated and enlightened intelligentsia. Their authority was to be exercised, above all, through popular enlightenment. At the opening of a 'Free School for Social Studies', soon to be expanded into a program of Workers' Schools supported by the socialist trade unions, Jászi emphasized the non-partisan but also political character of this activity:

> We must . . . make every effort to work out a new morality, a new ethics in place of the decaying old religious or metaphysical one. A new morality, founded on science and human solidarity. . . . One more word about the road to this end. We are convinced that this road can only be the road of free inquiry. The road knows neither dogmas nor party-truths. No socialist party-truths either, it goes without saying.

And indeed, radical intellectuals repeatedly praised these schools for helping to moderate the unreasoning socialist enthusiasms of the masses. While the Socialist leadership saw in the Workers' Schools an instrument for organizing and mobilizing the hitherto unpolitical industrial workers, the lecturers themselves hoped for a different kind of popular education, and they stressed the complex and technical character of problems encountered in managing social change, implying that solutions of these problems require leadership by the well-educated. Shortly before the First World War, Jászi founded the Radical Party. Speaking to a membership meeting, he said:

> Guidance for the ideal politician can only come from the Platonic ideal: an age must come when public life is controlled by philosophers, when men of complete theoretical knowledge and complete moral purity take the lead.

For a few months after the Austro-Hungarian military collapse in 1918, Jászi and many of his closest associates participated in the National Council which attempted to govern Hungary. Characterizing the first proclamation of that body, Jászi subsequently claimed

> that every line is impregnated with a sincerely democratic and socially progressive spirit, and that in the reforms demanded we went to the utmost limits attainable at the then-existing state of the country's economic and cultural development . . . rule in the state by laboring peasants and worker-masses, under the leadership of the genuine, truly creative intellectuals.

Mannheim soon rejected the philosophical and cultural premises which underlie these formulations. But variations on the substantive themes recur throughout his work; and, in the late thirties, he practically reasserts the whole creed as his own. This provides one fundamental reason for placing his work in the liberal tradition.

PHILOSOPHICAL PROBLEMS OF LIBERALISM

The characterization of the liberal tradition offered in thus sketching the practical political creed which was Mannheim's point of departure and of reference will not satisfy those who define liberalism in terms of 'negative freedom' or 'distrust of political power' or 'individual consent'. But an adequate conception of liberalism as a tradition precludes abstracting some ideas from Locke's *Second Treatise,* Smith's *Wealth of Nations,* or Mill's *Liberty* and treating these as touchstones. The story of liberalism is a story of adjustments in these elements, as they are put in new contexts designed to meet changing conceptions of theoretical knowledge as well as developments in other studies taken as relevant. This is quite apart from the effects of changing political circumstances, which are not of immediate concern.

For the liberal reformers of Mannheim's youth, the most important studies were sociological, and in that discipline the followers of Spencer could not maintain their influence against the impact of French and German investigations.

Mannheim complicated the situation by emphasizing the importance of other historical and cultural studies. But he did this not least because he became convinced that the liberalism of Jászi sacrificed vital interests of personal fulfilment because of its deference to a social science he considered positivist and hostile to spirituality. That is, after all, a liberal objection to the prevalent form of liberalism.

Mannheim's reservations have to do with the philosophical framework for liberalism rather than with the practical political creed. The central question turns on the character of scientific political knowledge. An important study by Robert Denoon Cumming on John Stuart Mill and the constitution of liberalism as a tradition has called attention to the profound difficulties which confront modern attempts to think philosophically about liberalism. Cumming suggests that liberalism since Mill has been preoccupied with method, that it has been taken up with a process of adjusting a creed to a set of considerations about ways of holding, discussing, and legitimating political opinions. Taking Mill as the representative liberal, Cumming identifies two central features of liberal ventures in political philosophy: first, the liberal political thinker defines his own intellectual situation as a period of 'transition' or 'crisis' requiring a major reinterpretation of the 'tradition' made up of certain ethical ideals and political ideas; second, the modern liberal believes that in political thought as in politics conflicts are not 'insurmountable', that they represent 'differences of opinion . . . resolvable by some kind of transition and adjustment'.

In the work of John Stuart Mill, these two assumptions run through an assemblage of essays, treatises, and journalistic reports which confront the interrelated methodological issues which Mill himself identifies as central to his concerns:

> In politics, though I had no longer accepted the doctrine of [James Mills's] *Essay on Government* . . . as a scientific theory, though I ceased to consider representative democracy as an absolute principle, and regarded it as a question of time, place, and circumstances; though I now looked upon the choice of political institutions as a moral and educational question more than one of material interests . . . ; nevertheless, this change in the premises of my political philosophy did not alter my practical political creed as to the requirements of my own time and country. I was as much as ever a radical and democrat for Europe, and especially for England.

The three central issues recognized by Mill, then, are:

> (1) the relationship between political ideas and the requirements of scientific theory: can political ideas be recast so as to reveal them as the outcome of scientific enquiry, or, if not, how can they be thought of as matters for rational discourse and choice?

> (2) the matter of appropriateness to time, place, and circumstances: is a theory of history the proper context for moral and political decision, and if so, would this not imply a relativism destructive of the humanist interest in what is proper to human nature?

> (3) the question of the extent to which political teachings, as pedagogical components of a pedagogical political order, are themselves matters of 'moral cultivation' and education: are political discussions themselves to be governed by their pedagogical effects on the discussants and auditors, as in rhetorical conceptions of political knowledge, and, if so, what is to prevent political ideas from becoming either wholly unrealistic or starkly manipulative?

Mill did not solve these problems, and Cumming concludes that liberalism appears condemned to 'a certain eagerness for elaborating . . . methodological precepts and remedial programs for the construction of the science of politics—without actually constructing it'.

The liberal thinkers represented by Jászi believed that they could meet the difficulties raised by Mill:

(1) They thought that science, in the broad sense in which they understood it, generates and vindicates their doctrine. As suggested by Jászi's distinction between 'scientific principles' and 'ethical purity', the needed knowledge may be distributed between distinct sciences of means and ends. Methods of knowing may differ with regard to differing classes of objects, but in principle the whole forms a unified structure comprising universally valid relationships between the subjects and objects of knowledge and it provides the means for answering objectively and without prejudice the questions humankind must address. Formulations of both kinds of knowledge, moreover, are equally theoretical, logical, and demonstrable to unbiased intelligence. For these continental liberals, in short, idealist philosophy provides a conception of knowledge which appears to overcome the difficulties created for Mill by his empiricism, while still comprehending the empirically founded social sciences.

When scientific intelligence addresses itself to the social and political realm, according to this theory, it discovers itself as underlying principle. Things make sense by virtue of the fact that they have been ordered by knowledge. There are two qualifications. The knowledge constituting the empirical social world may be radically imperfect and incomplete; the progress of reason requires whole epochs. And things may sometimes proceed in ways that make no sense, simply on the strength of force and ignorance. Civilization is a progressive task, not a metaphysical given. All this appears as philosophically informed supposition in Kant's *Idea for a Universal History,* but now seems to these thinkers a matter of scientific knowledge, arising from the sociological enquiry initiated by Comte and Spencer. As knowledge becomes more complete, the directing of affairs by those who know becomes ever more feasible, but also more necessary.

Knowledge can have effect in the world, they believe, because those who possess it can with the help of scientific method and philosophy become certain of their own knowledge. Those who will benefit from it, moreover, can accept its authority because popular education will persuade them of its legitimacy and because they will directly experience the benefits of an alliance against those they know to be their oppressors. Democratization, accordingly, destroys the power of obscurantist privilege and opens the way to rational solutions. The dark fears of the tyranny of the majority which distracted J. S. Mill are now seen as due to a failure to appreciate the cumulative character of social rationalization, the ways in which achieved social changes condition needs and beliefs. Industrial workers disciplined by their role in complex industrial processes and organized in strategy-minded unions, for instance, need not be feared as a mob threatening to civilization. Jászi always thought that the experience with the Marxist social movements prior to the Russian Revolution had confirmed the masses' will and ability to subordinate themselves to men of knowledge, notwithstanding what he took to be some mystical elements in the doctrine and some atavisms in conduct. Knowledge can be power because power depends on opinion and opinion can be cultivated. Like their counterparts in Germany, England, France, and the United States, the Hungarian reformers thought they were witnessing the emergence of a popular scientific culture.

(2) In great measure, then, the liberals of the generation before Mannheim referred the difficulties which distressed their predecessors to the special limitations afflicting theory and practice in earlier times. But this does not mean that they made the validity of theoretical knowledge relative to time and place, a function of variable parallelograms of forces. While development and progress are vital elements in the social sciences and while the attainment of knowledge itself progresses over time, in their view, normative criteria are timeless and universal in principle. In the last analysis, Jászi maintained, the formal norms of validity rest on what must be presupposed for a rational and free humanity. Political knowledge will consequently identify different problems and possibilities at different times and places, but the ends in relation to which they are construed as problems or possibilities are themselves universal, and the standards which qualify those identifications as knowledge are valid without reference to historical change.

(3) Similarly, the alleged antinomies between the pedagogical and cognitive functions of theory, between the contributions of knowledge to spiritual and to instrumental progress, morality and happiness, are ascribed to a confused or defeatist frame of mind. Participation in knowledge, Jászi thought, gives self-command and command over events. Knowledge can be inculcated in degrees and by stages, and the simplifications required by popularization in no way need jeopardize the standards constituting genuine theoretical knowledge.

A high level of material civilization, if wrought by free social actors, according to this doctrine, affords resources for cultural creativity and leisure for cultural appreciation. There is no clash between organization for modern innovative productivity and moral improvement. The choices between contrasting emphases which had appeared as dilemmas during the harsh early years of the new civilization, now appear compatible, matters of preferences and timing. Persistent agonizing over the choices is now charged to obscurantist propagandists whose hostility to progress in fact stems from a care for privilege or,

at best, from a certain sensibility appropriate enough to poetic genius but lacking all claims on reason.

There are important strategic questions concerning the relationships between moral education and intellectual interests for these thinkers, but they can be answered by political knowledge if asked in rational and specific ways. The questions are not viewed as threats to the structure of knowledge itself. In this respect, as in others, the combination of idealist philosophy and positivist sociology appeared to Jászi and his followers to have enabled their liberalism to overcome the philosophical impasse which blocked Mill.

This summary of the ways in which these Central-European liberals handled the issues which Cumming showed us in Mill is not meant as a caricature. But anyone familiar with Thomas Mann's *Magic Mountain* will doubtless hear the accents of the progressive Freemason, Settembrini, in all this and may well turn away with impatient disdain. That reaction is mistaken. It is in any case not helpful for understanding Mannheim. He is, of course, deeply moved by the sorts of considerations the dark Jesuitical Bolshevik, Nephta, puts before the ingenuous Hans Castorp in the novel. But he does not imagine that these negations are solutions; nor is he prepared to rest in the Olympian distance.

The topics of Mannheim's studies clearly indicate his lifelong preoccupation with the constitutive problems of liberal political thinking, and this provides a second, more profound, reason for emphasizing his relationships to liberalism. Mannheim cannot accept the theory of knowledge advanced by the liberals and consequently reopens the questions they had resolved with its help. (1) Beginning with his doctoral dissertation on epistemology, he recurrently sought to relate the theoretical materials with which he was involved to the philosophical delineation of knowledge and especially to the requirements of scientific theory. (2) The themes of history and historicism are even more pervasive, as are (3) his efforts to specify the ways in which the cultural and pedagogical character of theoretical beliefs and utterances affects their characteristics as theory.

Mannheim always described his own work as a work of transition necessitated by a crisis in the liberal tradition and order, and he made it his avowed objective to develop a synthesis which would acknowledge and comprehend the partial legitimacy of each of the bitterly contending and mutually incomprehending parties making up the theoretical and political fields. His writings throughout display in classical form the characteristic preoccupations which Cumming leads us to expect in liberal thinking.

THE LIBERAL FOUNDATIONS OF 'SYNTHESIS'

In the work of his maturity, Mannheim was greatly influenced by certain aspects of Marxian socialist theory, and he recognized a number of other contestants in the ideological field as well, but his deeper analyses constantly come back to a fundamental opposition between 'liberal' (or progressive) and 'conservative' political thinking and to the need for synthesis between them. In his major historical study of conservative thought, Mannheim offers a revealing contrast between the formative principles of liberal and conservative thinking. Although that work is artfully designed to communicate with conservative readers, the further development of Mannheim's theorizing builds more on the liberal side of the comparison.

Mannheim claims that liberalism is conditioned by a consciousness of the possible, not the actual; that it experiences time as the beginning of the future, not as the end of the past or as eternal now. Things to be understood are put in the context of a projected future or in essential relationship to some universal ideal norm, not in the context of their past or of some immanent tendency. Liberals, according to Mannheim, think of their fellows as contemporaries, as associates in a temporal continuum, not as compatriots sharing some communal space with past and future. Structuralism, Mannheim observes, is a liberal way of organizing knowledge: the liberal seeks to understand things as rationalized and manipulable. The conservative, in contrast, pursues interpretive apprehension and appreciation. Liberals, moreover, experience the world in an abstract way, expressible in theoretical terms, while conservatives respond to concrete, unanalysed complexities. Tied to this, in Mannheim's view, is the liberal's vision of complex entities as assembled from additive individual units and his perception of time as a cumulation of discrete moments.

Mannheim stresses the one-sidedness of the theories based upon liberal experiences and he insists upon the corrective value of conservatism; but the liberal elements are clearly more fundamental to his overall design. Defining situations in terms of the 'next step', structural analysis, theoretical comprehension, the perception of generations and contemporaneity are the major presuppositions of his subsequent work. From that perspective, the critiques of rationalism, ahistorism, and individualism indicate areas requiring adjustment. The liberal elements are the basic ones.

This becomes even clearer in the essay on politics as a science. In it, Mannheim portrays the demand for a science of politics as a major product of bourgeois liberal-democratic thought, while associating himself with that demand quite unequivocally in the essay as a whole. Mannheim observes that liberalism created the 'systemic location' for a science of politics, just as it formed institutions which it imagined would rationalize political conflict, such as parliaments, electoral systems, and the League of Nations. As expounded in the liberal political tradition itself, Mannheim contends, all of these conceptions are afflicted by a misleading 'intellectualism' which grossly overvalues the cognitive power and practical efficacy of abstract thinking oriented to universal laws. What is needed, Mannheim argues, is a more adequate conception of what it means to master the political world by reason and to govern political practice by reason. But he clearly does not advocate an abandonment of the underlying design.

In the original German text of 1929, the continuity between Mannheim's thesis and the basic liberal project is made graphic by Mannheim's use of the term *Plattform*. In criticizing the liberal theory of knowledge, Mannheim

remarks, 'it was thus the foremost preoccupation of this style of thought to create a purified platform consisting of knowledge which is universally valid, comprehensible, and communicable'. Such knowledge, Mannheim contends, cannot be. But there can be a science of politics after all and a 'platform' where it will operate. Moreover, he claims, this locus of political knowledge involves persons whose wills are free from constraints, who have political choice or decision before them.

The spatial metaphor is important here. Mannheim is talking about a place to stand, a place where knowledge and choice matter and which in some way commands political life. Older liberal conceptions of scientific politics and parliament are aspects of an inadequate design for such a platform. Mannheim's proposal for political education offers a different design:

> But isn't it desirable and possible to have a form of political awakening which speaks to the comparatively free will which is already and should increasingly become the element upon which modern intellectuals rest? Aren't we simply giving up on a weighty achievement of European history if we fail to make the effort, just at the critical moment, as the party machine threatens, to strengthen the tendencies striving to found political decision on comprehensive orientation? Is political awakening only possible in the form of conditioning? Isn't a will which incorporates criticism also a will, and even a higher form of will, which we may not so readily renounce? . . . Or is only preparation for insurrection to be deemed political action? Isn't the continuous transformation of men and conditions also action? . . . And can it be that only the will which seeks dynamic equilibrium, which has comprehensive vision, lacks a tradition and form of cultivation appropriate to it? Isn't it really in the general interest to create new centres of political will, quickened by critical conscience? There must be a platform where that which is necessary for such a critical orientation . . . can be taught, in a way which presupposes people still searching for solutions, people who have not as yet committed themselves.

But if the difficulties which Mill had identified have not been solved by the proposals of Jászi and his generation, how can the comprehensive vision for such a science come about and gain validity as well as political effect? Mannheim originally intended the essay on politics as a science as starting point for *Ideology and Utopia*, his best-known work, and it is the treatment of ideology elaborated in that study which is supposed to provide the 'organon' for such a science.

Mannheim persistently pursued the hunch that sociology of knowledge is somehow central to any strategy for creating a *rapprochement* between politics and reason, and this pursuit connects his diverse essays in that discipline. Throughout, he believed that such sociology has an important transformative effect on its practitioners: sociology of knowledge calls intellectuals to their vocation of striving for synthesis. It changes their relationship to the parties contending in society, giving them distance and overview. But Mannheim's conception of the specific ways in which such sociology might affect the state of political knowledge fluctuated and changed. There are three main versions:

(1) Sociology of knowledge as a pedagogical but also political mode of encountering and acting upon the other forces making up the political world, serving as mediating force reorienting all vital participants in the political process and generating the synthesis which makes possible the 'next step' in a sequence of human activities having intrinsic value;

(2) sociology of knowledge as an instrument of enlightenment, related to the dual process of rationalization and individuation identified by Max Weber, and comparable to psychoanalysis, acting to free men and women for rational and responsible choices by liberating them from subservience to hidden forces they cannot control because they do not recognize them, and by enabling them to gauge realistically the consequences of their actions; and

(3) sociology of knowledge as a weapon against prevalent myths and as a method for eliminating bias from social science, so that it can master the fundamental public problems of time and guide appropriate political conduct.

Before 1932, Mannheim's work fluctuates between the first two versions: afterwards, and especially after 1933, the third plays a substantially greater role. All three versions can best be understood in the context of the quest for an adequate philosophical mode for liberalism. The shifts in emphasis among them in the course of his English career depend on his accommodation to patterns of thinking in his new English-speaking audiences, on changes of Mannheim's diagnosis of the main obstacles to effective political knowledge, as well as on his changed assessment of the prospects for knowledge, planning and rational rule. With his later conception of 'thought at the level of planning', he comes close to claiming success in the search for a science able to 'contribute', as he writes to Louis Wirth upon the outbreak of the war in 1939, 'both to the interpretation of the appalling events and to the right action'.

FURTHER READING

Criticism

Baum, Gregory. *Truth Beyond Relativism: Karl Mannheim's Sociology of Knowledge*. Milwaukee: Marquette University Press, 1977, 83 p.

> Argues for applying Mannheim's theory of the sociology of knowledge to theological method and ecclesiology.

Bauman, Zygmunt. "Understanding as the Work of History: Karl Mannheim." In his *Hermeneutics and Social Science*, pp. 89-110. New York: Columbia University Press, 1978.

> Views Mannheim's work as an outgrowth of Max Weber's. Bauman concludes that unlike Weber and Karl Marx, Mannheim sought objective truth outside the "logic of history."

Bogardus, Emory S. "Mannheim and the Sociology of

Knowledge." In his *The Development of Social Thought*, pp. 605-19. Westport, Conn.:Greenwood Press Publishers, 1960.

> Discussion of the sociology of knowledge as a basis for "social reconstruction" and Mannheim's "major" role in the development of this branch of sociology.

Carr, Edward H. "Karl Mannheim." In his *From Napoleon to Stalin and Other Essays*, pp. 177-83. London: The MacMillan Press, Ltd., 1980.

> Contends that Mannheim's importance to British sociology is linked to his "immense talent for synthesis."

Congdon, Lee. "Karl Mannheim as Philosopher." *The Journal of European Studies* 7, No. 25 (March 1977): 1-18.

> Argues for Mannheim's contribution to modern philosopical thought, particularly in his call for a "historicized ontology."

Hartung, Frank E. "Problems of the Sociology of Knowledge." *Philosophy of Science* 19, No. 1 (January 1952): 17-32.

> Charges that Mannheim's formulation of the sociology of knowledge does not state how the existential determination of thought can be demonstrated.

Hinshaw, Virgil G., Jr. "The Epistemological Relevance of Mannheim's Sociology of Knowledge." *The Journal of Philosophy* XL, No. 3 (4 February 1943), pp. 57-72.

> Observes that there is no epistomological branch of the sociology of knowledge and that the sociologist of knowledge is a scientist, not a philosopher.

Jay, Martin. "The Frankfurt School's Critique of Karl Mannheim and the Sociology of Knowledge." In his *Permanent Exiles: Essays on the Intellectual Migration from Germany to America*, pp. 62-78. New York: Columbia University Press, 1985.

> Argues that Mannheim's work on the connections between culture and society was influenced by his friend and mentor, Georg Lukács.

Loader, Colin. *The Intellectual Development of Karl Mannheim: Culture, Politics and Planning*. London: Heinemann, 1981 261 p.

> Study of Mannheim designed to trace "an intellect developing through several sociocultural contexts."

Meja, Volker and Kettler, David. "Cultural Politics in Karl Mannheim's Sociology." In *From Karl Mannheim*, edited by Kurt H. Wolff. New Brunswick, New Jersey: Transaction Publishers, 1993.

> Maintains that Mannheim's work should be studied without reference to political labels.

Merton, Robert K. "Karl Mannheim and the Sociology of Knowledge." In his *Social Theory and Social Structure*, pp. 542-62. New York: The Free Press, 1968.

> Considers Mannheim's sociology of knowledge as both an outgrowth of and a reaction to the work of his immediate predecessors, including Emile Durkheim and Lucien Lévy-Bruhl.

Remmling, Gunter W. "Karl Mannheim: A Revision of an Intellectual Portrait." *Social Forces* 40, No. 1 (October 1961): 23-30.

> An attempt to clarify Mannheim's contribution to modern sociology by delineating the changes in his thinking through four distinct phases.

Robinson, Daniel S. "Karl Mannheim's Sociological Philosophy." *Personalist* 29, No. 2 (Spring 1948): 137-48.

Examines Mannheim's philosophy of history and his effort to analyze the historical changes he lived through.

Sagarin, Edward and Kelly, Robert J. "Karl Mannheim and the Sociology of Knowledge." In *The Legacy of the German Refugee Intellectuals*, edited by Robert Boyers, pp. 273-83. New York: Schocken Books, 1972.

An overview of the intellectual, social, and political influences that led to the formulation of Mannheim's sociology of knowledge.

Simonds, A.P. "What Is the Sociology of Knowledge?" In his *Karl Mannheim's Sociology of Knowledge*, pp. 23-48. Oxford: The Clarendon Press, 1978.

An analysis of the nature and purpose of Mannheim's examination of the link between knowlege and society.

Wagner, Helmut R. "The Scope of Mannheim's Thinking." *Social Research* 20, No. 1 (Spring 1953): 100-09.

Reviews of Mannheim's *Essays on the Sociology of Knowledge* and *Freedom, Power, and Democratic Planning* as examples of the scope of Mannheim's thinking and confirmation of the central importance of *Ideology and Utopia* in his writings.

Twentieth-Century
Literary Criticism

Cumulative Indexes
Volumes 1-65

How to Use This Index

The main references

> **Calvino, Italo**
> 1923-1985.....CLC 5, 8, 11, 22, 33, 39,
> 73; SSC 3

list all author entries in the following Gale Literary Criticism series:

BLC = *Black Literature Criticism*
CLC = *Contemporary Literary Criticism*
CLR = *Children's Literature Review*
CMLC = *Classical and Medieval Literature Criticism*
DA = *DISCovering Authors*
DC = *Drama Criticism*
HLC = *Hispanic Literature Criticism*
LC = *Literature Criticism from 1400 to 1800*
NCLC = *Nineteenth-Century Literature Criticism*
PC = *Poetry Criticism*
SSC = *Short Story Criticism*
TCLC = *Twentieth-Century Literary Criticism*
WLC = *World Literature Criticism, 1500 to the Present*

The cross-references

> See also CANR 23; CA 85-88;
> obituary CA 116

list all author entries in the following Gale biographical and literary sources:

AAYA = *Authors & Artists for Young Adults*
AITN = *Authors in the News*
BEST = *Bestsellers*
BW = *Black Writers*
CA = *Contemporary Authors*
CAAS = *Contemporary Authors Autobiography Series*
CABS = *Contemporary Authors Bibliographical Series*
CANR = *Contemporary Authors New Revision Series*
CAP = *Contemporary Authors Permanent Series*
CDALB = *Concise Dictionary of American Literary Biography*
CDBLB = *Concise Dictionary of British Literary Biography*
DLB = *Dictionary of Literary Biography*
DLBD = *Dictionary of Literary Biography Documentary Series*
DLBY = *Dictionary of Literary Biography Yearbook*
HW = *Hispanic Writers*
JRDA = *Junior DISCovering Authors*
MAICYA = *Major Authors and Illustrators for Children and Young Adults*
MTCW = *Major 20th-Century Writers*
NNAL = *Native North American Literature*
SAAS = *Something about the Author Autobiography Series*
SATA = *Something about the Author*
YABC = *Yesterday's Authors of Books for Children*

Literary Criticism Series
Cumulative Author Index

A. E. . . . . TCLC 3, 10
See also Russell, George William

Abasiyanik, Sait Faik 1906-1954
See Sait Faik
See also CA 123

Abbey, Edward 1927-1989 . . . . . . CLC 36, 59
See also CA 45-48; 128; CANR 2, 41

Abbott, Lee K(ittredge) 1947- . . . . . . CLC 48
See also CA 124; CANR 51; DLB 130

Abe, Kobo 1924-1993 . . . . . CLC 8, 22, 53, 81
See also CA 65-68; 140; CANR 24;
DAM NOV; MTCW

Abelard, Peter c. 1079-c. 1142 . . . CMLC 11
See also DLB 115

Abell, Kjeld 1901-1961 . . . . CLC 15
See also CA 111

Abish, Walter 1931- . . . . CLC 22
See also CA 101; CANR 37; DLB 130

Abrahams, Peter (Henry) 1919- . . . . . CLC 4
See also BW 1; CA 57-60; CANR 26;
DLB 117; MTCW

Abrams, M(eyer) H(oward) 1912- . . . CLC 24
See also CA 57-60; CANR 13, 33; DLB 67

Abse, Dannie 1923- . . . . CLC 7, 29; DAB
See also CA 53-56; CAAS 1; CANR 4, 46;
DAM POET; DLB 27

Achebe, (Albert) Chinua(lumogu)
1930- . . . . . CLC 1, 3, 5, 7, 11, 26, 51, 75;
BLC; DA; DAB; DAC; WLC
See also AAYA 15; BW 2; CA 1-4R;
CANR 6, 26, 47; CLR 20; DAM MST,
MULT, NOV; DLB 117; MAICYA;
MTCW; SATA 40; SATA-Brief 38

Acker, Kathy 1948- . . . . CLC 45
See also CA 117; 122

Ackroyd, Peter 1949- . . . . CLC 34, 52
See also CA 123; 127; CANR 51; DLB 155;
INT 127

Acorn, Milton 1923- . . . . CLC 15; DAC
See also CA 103; DLB 53; INT 103

Adamov, Arthur 1908-1970 . . . . . . CLC 4, 25
See also CA 17-18; 25-28R; CAP 2;
DAM DRAM; MTCW

Adams, Alice (Boyd) 1926- . . . CLC 6, 13, 46
See also CA 81-84; CANR 26, 53;
DLBY 86; INT CANR-26; MTCW

Adams, Andy 1859-1935 . . . . TCLC 56
See also YABC 1

Adams, Douglas (Noel) 1952- . . . CLC 27, 60
See also AAYA 4; BEST 89:3; CA 106;
CANR 34; DAM POP; DLBY 83; JRDA

Adams, Francis 1862-1893 . . . . NCLC 33

Adams, Henry (Brooks)
1838-1918 . . . . . . TCLC 4, 52; DA; DAB;
DAC
See also CA 104; 133; DAM MST; DLB 12,
47

Adams, Richard (George)
1920- . . . . CLC 4, 5, 18
See also AAYA 16; AITN 1, 2; CA 49-52;
CANR 3, 35; CLR 20; DAM NOV;
JRDA; MAICYA; MTCW; SATA 7, 69

Adamson, Joy(-Friederike Victoria)
1910-1980 . . . . CLC 17
See also CA 69-72; 93-96; CANR 22;
MTCW; SATA 11; SATA-Obit 22

Adcock, Fleur 1934- . . . . CLC 41
See also CA 25-28R; CAAS 23; CANR 11,
34; DLB 40

Addams, Charles (Samuel)
1912-1988 . . . . CLC 30
See also CA 61-64; 126; CANR 12

Addison, Joseph 1672-1719 . . . . LC 18
See also CDBLB 1660-1789; DLB 101

Adler, Alfred (F.) 1870-1937 . . . . . . TCLC 61
See also CA 119

Adler, C(arole) S(chwerdtfeger)
1932- . . . . CLC 35
See also AAYA 4; CA 89-92; CANR 19,
40; JRDA; MAICYA; SAAS 15;
SATA 26, 63

Adler, Renata 1938- . . . . CLC 8, 31
See also CA 49-52; CANR 5, 22, 52;
MTCW

Ady, Endre 1877-1919 . . . . TCLC 11
See also CA 107

Aeschylus
525B.C.-456B.C. . . . . CMLC 11; DA;
DAB; DAC
See also DAM DRAM, MST

Afton, Effie
See Harper, Frances Ellen Watkins

Agapida, Fray Antonio
See Irving, Washington

Agee, James (Rufus)
1909-1955 . . . . TCLC 1, 19
See also AITN 1; CA 108; 148;
CDALB 1941-1968; DAM NOV; DLB 2,
26, 152

Aghill, Gordon
See Silverberg, Robert

Agnon, S(hmuel) Y(osef Halevi)
1888-1970 . . . . CLC 4, 8, 14
See also CA 17-18; 25-28R; CAP 2; MTCW

Agrippa von Nettesheim, Henry Cornelius
1486-1535 . . . . LC 27

Aherne, Owen
See Cassill, R(onald) V(erlin)

Ai 1947- . . . . CLC 4, 14, 69
See also CA 85-88; CAAS 13; DLB 120

Aickman, Robert (Fordyce)
1914-1981 . . . . CLC 57
See also CA 5-8R; CANR 3

Aiken, Conrad (Potter)
1889-1973 . . . CLC 1, 3, 5, 10, 52; SSC 9
See also CA 5-8R; 45-48; CANR 4;
CDALB 1929-1941; DAM NOV, POET;
DLB 9, 45, 102; MTCW; SATA 3, 30

Aiken, Joan (Delano) 1924- . . . . CLC 35
See also AAYA 1; CA 9-12R; CANR 4, 23,
34; CLR 1, 19; DLB 161; JRDA;
MAICYA; MTCW; SAAS 1; SATA 2,
30, 73

Ainsworth, William Harrison
1805-1882 . . . . NCLC 13
See also DLB 21; SATA 24

Aitmatov, Chingiz (Torekulovich)
1928- . . . . CLC 71
See also CA 103; CANR 38; MTCW;
SATA 56

Akers, Floyd
See Baum, L(yman) Frank

Akhmadulina, Bella Akhatovna
1937- . . . . CLC 53
See also CA 65-68; DAM POET

Akhmatova, Anna
1888-1966 . . . . CLC 11, 25, 64; PC 2
See also CA 19-20; 25-28R; CANR 35;
CAP 1; DAM POET; MTCW

Aksakov, Sergei Timofeyvich
1791-1859 . . . . NCLC 2

Aksenov, Vassily
See Aksyonov, Vassily (Pavlovich)

Aksyonov, Vassily (Pavlovich)
1932- . . . . CLC 22, 37
See also CA 53-56; CANR 12, 48

Akutagawa Ryunosuke
1892-1927 . . . . TCLC 16
See also CA 117

Alain 1868-1951 . . . . TCLC 41

Alain-Fournier . . . . TCLC 6
See also Fournier, Henri Alban
See also DLB 65

Alarcon, Pedro Antonio de
1833-1891 . . . . NCLC 1

Alas (y Urena), Leopoldo (Enrique Garcia)
1852-1901 . . . . TCLC 29
See also CA 113; 131; HW

Albee, Edward (Franklin III)
1928- . . . . . . CLC 1, 2, 3, 5, 9, 11, 13, 25,
53, 86; DA; DAB; DAC; WLC
See also AITN 1; CA 5-8R; CABS 3;
CANR 8; CDALB 1941-1968;
DAM DRAM, MST; DLB 7;
INT CANR-8; MTCW

Alberti, Rafael 1902- . . . . CLC 7
See also CA 85-88; DLB 108

Albert the Great 1200(?)-1280 . . . . CMLC 16
See also DLB 115

Alcala-Galiano, Juan Valera y
See Valera y Alcala-Galiano, Juan

Alcott, Amos Bronson 1799-1888 . . **NCLC 1**
See also DLB 1

Alcott, Louisa May
1832-1888 . . . . **NCLC 6; DA; DAB;**
DAC; WLC
See also CDALB 1865-1917; CLR 1, 38;
DAM MST, NOV; DLB 1, 42, 79; JRDA;
MAICYA; YABC 1

Aldanov, M. A.
See Aldanov, Mark (Alexandrovich)

Aldanov, Mark (Alexandrovich)
1886(?)-1957 . . . . **TCLC 23**
See also CA 118

Aldington, Richard 1892-1962. . . . . . **CLC 49**
See also CA 85-88; CANR 45; DLB 20, 36,
100, 149

Aldiss, Brian W(ilson)
1925- . . . . **CLC 5, 14, 40**
See also CA 5-8R; CAAS 2; CANR 5, 28;
DAM NOV; DLB 14; MTCW; SATA 34

Alegria, Claribel 1924-. . . . . **CLC 75**
See also CA 131; CAAS 15; DAM MULT;
DLB 145; HW

Alegria, Fernando 1918-. . . . . **CLC 57**
See also CA 9-12R; CANR 5, 32; HW

Aleichem, Sholom . . . . **TCLC 1, 35**
See also Rabinovitch, Sholem

Aleixandre, Vicente
1898-1984 . . . . **CLC 9, 36; PC 15**
See also CA 85-88; 114; CANR 26;
DAM POET; DLB 108; HW; MTCW

Alepoudelis, Odysseus
See Elytis, Odysseus

Aleshkovsky, Joseph 1929-
See Aleshkovsky, Yuz
See also CA 121; 128

Aleshkovsky, Yuz . . . . **CLC 44**
See also Aleshkovsky, Joseph

Alexander, Lloyd (Chudley) 1924- . . **CLC 35**
See also AAYA 1; CA 1-4R; CANR 1, 24,
38; CLR 1, 5; DLB 52; JRDA; MAICYA;
MTCW; SAAS 19; SATA 3, 49, 81

Alfau, Felipe 1902-. . . . . **CLC 66**
See also CA 137

Alger, Horatio, Jr. 1832-1899 . . . . . **NCLC 8**
See also DLB 42; SATA 16

Algren, Nelson 1909-1981 . . . . **CLC 4, 10, 33**
See also CA 13-16R; 103; CANR 20;
CDALB 1941-1968; DLB 9; DLBY 81,
82; MTCW

Ali, Ahmed 1910- . . . . **CLC 69**
See also CA 25-28R; CANR 15, 34

Alighieri, Dante 1265-1321 . . . . **CMLC 3, 18**

Allan, John B.
See Westlake, Donald E(dwin)

Allen, Edward 1948-. . . . . **CLC 59**

Allen, Paula Gunn 1939- . . . . **CLC 84**
See also CA 112; 143; DAM MULT;
NNAL

Allen, Roland
See Ayckbourn, Alan

Allen, Sarah A.
See Hopkins, Pauline Elizabeth

Allen, Woody 1935- . . . . **CLC 16, 52**
See also AAYA 10; CA 33-36R; CANR 27,
38; DAM POP; DLB 44; MTCW

Allende, Isabel 1942- . . . . **CLC 39, 57; HLC**
See also AAYA 18; CA 125; 130;
CANR 51; DAM MULT, NOV;
DLB 145; HW; INT 130; MTCW

Alleyn, Ellen
See Rossetti, Christina (Georgina)

Allingham, Margery (Louise)
1904-1966 . . . . **CLC 19**
See also CA 5-8R; 25-28R; CANR 4;
DLB 77; MTCW

Allingham, William 1824-1889 . . . **NCLC 25**
See also DLB 35

Allison, Dorothy E. 1949- . . . . **CLC 78**
See also CA 140

Allston, Washington 1779-1843. . . . **NCLC 2**
See also DLB 1

Almedingen, E. M. . . . . **CLC 12**
See also Almedingen, Martha Edith von
See also SATA 3

Almedingen, Martha Edith von 1898-1971
See Almedingen, E. M.
See also CA 1-4R; CANR 1

Almqvist, Carl Jonas Love
1793-1866 . . . . **NCLC 42**

Alonso, Damaso 1898-1990 . . . . **CLC 14**
See also CA 110; 131; 130; DLB 108; HW

Alov
See Gogol, Nikolai (Vasilyevich)

Alta 1942- . . . . **CLC 19**
See also CA 57-60

Alter, Robert B(ernard) 1935-. . . . . . **CLC 34**
See also CA 49-52; CANR 1, 47

Alther, Lisa 1944-. . . . . **CLC 7, 41**
See also CA 65-68; CANR 12, 30, 51;
MTCW

Altman, Robert 1925-. . . . . **CLC 16**
See also CA 73-76; CANR 43

Alvarez, A(lfred) 1929-. . . . . **CLC 5, 13**
See also CA 1-4R; CANR 3, 33; DLB 14,
40

Alvarez, Alejandro Rodriguez 1903-1965
See Casona, Alejandro
See also CA 131; 93-96; HW

Alvarez, Julia 1950-. . . . . **CLC 93**
See also CA 147

Alvaro, Corrado 1896-1956 . . . . **TCLC 60**

Amado, Jorge 1912- . . . . . **CLC 13, 40; HLC**
See also CA 77-80; CANR 35;
DAM MULT, NOV; DLB 113; MTCW

Ambler, Eric 1909-. . . . . **CLC 4, 6, 9**
See also CA 9-12R; CANR 7, 38; DLB 77;
MTCW

Amichai, Yehuda 1924- . . . . . . **CLC 9, 22, 57**
See also CA 85-88; CANR 46; MTCW

Amiel, Henri Frederic 1821-1881 . . **NCLC 4**

Amis, Kingsley (William)
1922-1995 . . . . . **CLC 1, 2, 3, 5, 8, 13, 40,**
44; DA; DAB; DAC
See also AITN 2; CA 9-12R; 150; CANR 8,
28; CDBLB 1945-1960; DAM MST,
NOV; DLB 15, 27, 100, 139;
INT CANR-8; MTCW

Amis, Martin (Louis)
1949- . . . . **CLC 4, 9, 38, 62**
See also BEST 90:3; CA 65-68; CANR 8,
27; DLB 14; INT CANR-27

Ammons, A(rchie) R(andolph)
1926- . . . **CLC 2, 3, 5, 8, 9, 25, 57; PC 16**
See also AITN 1; CA 9-12R; CANR 6, 36,
51; DAM POET; DLB 5, 165; MTCW

Amo, Tauraatua i
See Adams, Henry (Brooks)

Anand, Mulk Raj 1905-. . . . . **CLC 23, 93**
See also CA 65-68; CANR 32; DAM NOV;
MTCW

Anatol
See Schnitzler, Arthur

Anaya, Rudolfo A(lfonso)
1937- . . . . **CLC 23; HLC**
See also CA 45-48; CAAS 4; CANR 1, 32,
51; DAM MULT, NOV; DLB 82; HW 1;
MTCW

Andersen, Hans Christian
1805-1875 . . . . **NCLC 7; DA; DAB;**
DAC; SSC 6; WLC
See also CLR 6; DAM MST, POP;
MAICYA; YABC 1

Anderson, C. Farley
See Mencken, H(enry) L(ouis); Nathan,
George Jean

Anderson, Jessica (Margaret) Queale
. . . . **CLC 37**
See also CA 9-12R; CANR 4

Anderson, Jon (Victor) 1940- . . . . **CLC 9**
See also CA 25-28R; CANR 20;
DAM POET

Anderson, Lindsay (Gordon)
1923-1994 . . . . **CLC 20**
See also CA 125; 128; 146

Anderson, Maxwell 1888-1959 . . . . . **TCLC 2**
See also CA 105; DAM DRAM; DLB 7

Anderson, Poul (William) 1926- . . . . **CLC 15**
See also AAYA 5; CA 1-4R; CAAS 2;
CANR 2, 15, 34; DLB 8; INT CANR-15;
MTCW; SATA-Brief 39

Anderson, Robert (Woodruff)
1917- . . . . **CLC 23**
See also AITN 1; CA 21-24R; CANR 32;
DAM DRAM; DLB 7

Anderson, Sherwood
1876-1941 . . . . **TCLC 1, 10, 24; DA;**
DAB; DAC; SSC 1; WLC
See also CA 104; 121; CDALB 1917-1929;
DAM MST, NOV; DLB 4, 9, 86;
DLBD 1; MTCW

Andier, Pierre
See Desnos, Robert

Andouard
See Giraudoux, (Hippolyte) Jean

Andrade, Carlos Drummond de . . . . . . **CLC 18**
See also Drummond de Andrade, Carlos

Andrade, Mario de   1893-1945 . . . . . **TCLC 43**

Andreae, Johann V(alentin)
   1586-1654 . . . . **LC 32**
See also DLB 164

Andreas-Salome, Lou   1861-1937 . . . **TCLC 56**
See also DLB 66

Andrewes, Lancelot   1555-1626 . . . . **LC 5**
See also DLB 151

Andrews, Cicily Fairfield
See West, Rebecca

Andrews, Elton V.
See Pohl, Frederik

Andreyev, Leonid (Nikolaevich)
   1871-1919 . . . . **TCLC 3**
See also CA 104

Andric, Ivo   1892-1975 . . . . **CLC 8**
See also CA 81-84; 57-60; CANR 43;
   DLB 147; MTCW

Angelique, Pierre
See Bataille, Georges

Angell, Roger   1920- . . . . **CLC 26**
See also CA 57-60; CANR 13, 44

Angelou, Maya
   1928- . . . . **CLC 12, 35, 64, 77; BLC; DA;
      DAB; DAC**
See also AAYA 7; BW 2; CA 65-68;
   CANR 19, 42; DAM MST, MULT,
   POET, POP; DLB 38; MTCW; SATA 49

Annensky, Innokenty Fyodorovich
   1856-1909 . . . . **TCLC 14**
See also CA 110

Anon, Charles Robert
See Pessoa, Fernando (Antonio Nogueira)

Anouilh, Jean (Marie Lucien Pierre)
   1910-1987 . . . . . . **CLC 1, 3, 8, 13, 40, 50**
See also CA 17-20R; 123; CANR 32;
   DAM DRAM; MTCW

Anthony, Florence
See Ai

Anthony, John
See Ciardi, John (Anthony)

Anthony, Peter
See Shaffer, Anthony (Joshua); Shaffer,
   Peter (Levin)

Anthony, Piers   1934- . . . . **CLC 35**
See also AAYA 11; CA 21-24R; CANR 28;
   DAM POP; DLB 8; MTCW; SAAS 22;
   SATA 84

Antoine, Marc
See Proust, (Valentin-Louis-George-Eugene-)
   Marcel

Antoninus, Brother
See Everson, William (Oliver)

Antonioni, Michelangelo   1912- . . . . . **CLC 20**
See also CA 73-76; CANR 45

Antschel, Paul   1920-1970
See Celan, Paul
See also CA 85-88; CANR 33; MTCW

Anwar, Chairil   1922-1949 . . . . **TCLC 22**
See also CA 121

Apollinaire, Guillaume . . **TCLC 3, 8, 51; PC 7**
See also Kostrowitzki, Wilhelm Apollinaris
   de
See also DAM POET

Appelfeld, Aharon   1932- . . . . **CLC 23, 47**
See also CA 112; 133

Apple, Max (Isaac)   1941- . . . . **CLC 9, 33**
See also CA 81-84; CANR 19; DLB 130

Appleman, Philip (Dean)   1926- . . . . . **CLC 51**
See also CA 13-16R; CAAS 18; CANR 6,
   29

Appleton, Lawrence
See Lovecraft, H(oward) P(hillips)

Apteryx
See Eliot, T(homas) S(tearns)

Apuleius, (Lucius Madaurensis)
   125(?)-175(?) . . . . **CMLC 1**

Aquin, Hubert   1929-1977 . . . . **CLC 15**
See also CA 105; DLB 53

Aragon, Louis   1897-1982 . . . . **CLC 3, 22**
See also CA 69-72; 108; CANR 28;
   DAM NOV, POET; DLB 72; MTCW

Arany, Janos   1817-1882 . . . . **NCLC 34**

Arbuthnot, John   1667-1735 . . . . **LC 1**
See also DLB 101

Archer, Herbert Winslow
See Mencken, H(enry) L(ouis)

Archer, Jeffrey (Howard)   1940- . . . . **CLC 28**
See also AAYA 16; BEST 89:3; CA 77-80;
   CANR 22, 52; DAM POP;
   INT CANR-22

Archer, Jules   1915- . . . . **CLC 12**
See also CA 9-12R; CANR 6; SAAS 5;
   SATA 4, 85

Archer, Lee
See Ellison, Harlan (Jay)

Arden, John   1930- . . . . **CLC 6, 13, 15**
See also CA 13-16R; CAAS 4; CANR 31;
   DAM DRAM; DLB 13; MTCW

Arenas, Reinaldo
   1943-1990 . . . . **CLC 41; HLC**
See also CA 124; 128; 133; DAM MULT;
   DLB 145; HW

Arendt, Hannah   1906-1975 . . . . **CLC 66**
See also CA 17-20R; 61-64; CANR 26;
   MTCW

Aretino, Pietro   1492-1556 . . . . **LC 12**

Arghezi, Tudor . . . . **CLC 80**
See also Theodorescu, Ion N.

Arguedas, Jose Maria
   1911-1969 . . . . **CLC 10, 18**
See also CA 89-92; DLB 113; HW

Argueta, Manlio   1936- . . . . **CLC 31**
See also CA 131; DLB 145; HW

Ariosto, Ludovico   1474-1533 . . . . **LC 6**

Aristides
See Epstein, Joseph

Aristophanes
   450B.C.-385B.C. . . . . **CMLC 4; DA;
      DAB; DAC; DC 2**
See also DAM DRAM, MST

Arlt, Roberto (Godofredo Christophersen)
   1900-1942 . . . . **TCLC 29; HLC**
See also CA 123; 131; DAM MULT; HW

Armah, Ayi Kwei   1939- . . . . . **CLC 5, 33; BLC**
See also BW 1; CA 61-64; CANR 21;
   DAM MULT, POET; DLB 117; MTCW

Armatrading, Joan   1950- . . . . **CLC 17**
See also CA 114

Arnette, Robert
See Silverberg, Robert

Arnim, Achim von (Ludwig Joachim von
   Arnim)   1781-1831 . . . . **NCLC 5**
See also DLB 90

Arnim, Bettina von   1785-1859 . . . . **NCLC 38**
See also DLB 90

Arnold, Matthew
   1822-1888 . . . . . **NCLC 6, 29; DA; DAB;
      DAC; PC 5; WLC**
See also CDBLB 1832-1890; DAM MST,
   POET; DLB 32, 57

Arnold, Thomas   1795-1842 . . . . . . **NCLC 18**
See also DLB 55

Arnow, Harriette (Louisa) Simpson
   1908-1986 . . . . **CLC 2, 7, 18**
See also CA 9-12R; 118; CANR 14; DLB 6;
   MTCW; SATA 42; SATA-Obit 47

Arp, Hans
See Arp, Jean

Arp, Jean   1887-1966 . . . . **CLC 5**
See also CA 81-84; 25-28R; CANR 42

Arrabal
See Arrabal, Fernando

Arrabal, Fernando   1932- . . . **CLC 2, 9, 18, 58**
See also CA 9-12R; CANR 15

Arrick, Fran . . . . **CLC 30**
See also Gaberman, Judie Angell

Artaud, Antonin (Marie Joseph)
   1896-1948 . . . . **TCLC 3, 36**
See also CA 104; 149; DAM DRAM

Arthur, Ruth M(abel)   1905-1979 . . . . **CLC 12**
See also CA 9-12R; 85-88; CANR 4;
   SATA 7, 26

Artsybashev, Mikhail (Petrovich)
   1878-1927 . . . . **TCLC 31**

Arundel, Honor (Morfydd)
   1919-1973 . . . . **CLC 17**
See also CA 21-22; 41-44R; CAP 2;
   CLR 35; SATA 4; SATA-Obit 24

Asch, Sholem   1880-1957 . . . . **TCLC 3**
See also CA 105

Ash, Shalom
See Asch, Sholem

Ashbery, John (Lawrence)
   1927- . . . . . . **CLC 2, 3, 4, 6, 9, 13, 15, 25,
      41, 77**
See also CA 5-8R; CANR 9, 37;
   DAM POET; DLB 5, 165; DLBY 81;
   INT CANR-9; MTCW

Ashdown, Clifford
See Freeman, R(ichard) Austin

Ashe, Gordon
See Creasey, John

Ashton-Warner, Sylvia (Constance)
   1908-1984 . . . . **CLC 19**
See also CA 69-72; 112; CANR 29; MTCW

Asimov, Isaac
    1920-1992 ... **CLC 1, 3, 9, 19, 26, 76, 92**
    See also AAYA 13; BEST 90:2; CA 1-4R;
    137; CANR 2, 19, 36; CLR 12;
    DAM POP; DLB 8; DLBY 92;
    INT CANR-19; JRDA; MAICYA;
    MTCW; SATA 1, 26, 74

Astley, Thea (Beatrice May)
    1925- .... **CLC 41**
    See also CA 65-68; CANR 11, 43

Aston, James
    See White, T(erence) H(anbury)

Asturias, Miguel Angel
    1899-1974 .... **CLC 3, 8, 13; HLC**
    See also CA 25-28; 49-52; CANR 32;
    CAP 2; DAM MULT, NOV; DLB 113;
    HW; MTCW

Atares, Carlos Saura
    See Saura (Atares), Carlos

Atheling, William
    See Pound, Ezra (Weston Loomis)

Atheling, William, Jr.
    See Blish, James (Benjamin)

Atherton, Gertrude (Franklin Horn)
    1857-1948 .... **TCLC 2**
    See also CA 104; DLB 9, 78

Atherton, Lucius
    See Masters, Edgar Lee

Atkins, Jack
    See Harris, Mark

Attaway, William (Alexander)
    1911-1986 .... **CLC 92; BLC**
    See also BW 2; CA 143; DAM MULT;
    DLB 76

Atticus
    See Fleming, Ian (Lancaster)

Atwood, Margaret (Eleanor)
    1939- ..... **CLC 2, 3, 4, 8, 13, 15, 25, 44,
    84; DA; DAB; DAC; PC 8; SSC 2; WLC**
    See also AAYA 12; BEST 89:2; CA 49-52;
    CANR 3, 24, 33; DAM MST, NOV,
    POET; DLB 53; INT CANR-24; MTCW;
    SATA 50

Aubigny, Pierre d'
    See Mencken, H(enry) L(ouis)

Aubin, Penelope 1685-1731(?) .... **LC 9**
    See also DLB 39

Auchincloss, Louis (Stanton)
    1917- ...... **CLC 4, 6, 9, 18, 45; SSC 22**
    See also CA 1-4R; CANR 6, 29;
    DAM NOV; DLB 2; DLBY 80;
    INT CANR-29; MTCW

Auden, W(ystan) H(ugh)
    1907-1973 ...... **CLC 1, 2, 3, 4, 6, 9, 11,
    14, 43; DA; DAB; DAC; PC 1; WLC**
    See also AAYA 18; CA 9-12R; 45-48;
    CANR 5; CDBLB 1914-1945;
    DAM DRAM, MST, POET; DLB 10, 20;
    MTCW

Audiberti, Jacques 1900-1965 ...... **CLC 38**
    See also CA 25-28R; DAM DRAM

Audubon, John James
    1785-1851 .... **NCLC 47**

Auel, Jean M(arie) 1936- .... **CLC 31**
    See also AAYA 7; BEST 90:4; CA 103;
    CANR 21; DAM POP; INT CANR-21

Auerbach, Erich 1892-1957 ...... **TCLC 43**
    See also CA 118

Augier, Emile 1820-1889 .... **NCLC 31**

August, John
    See De Voto, Bernard (Augustine)

Augustine, St. 354-430 ..... **CMLC 6; DAB**

Aurelius
    See Bourne, Randolph S(illiman)

Aurobindo, Sri 1872-1950 .... **TCLC 63**

Austen, Jane
    1775-1817 ..... **NCLC 1, 13, 19, 33, 51;
    DA; DAB; DAC; WLC**
    See also CDBLB 1789-1832; DAM MST,
    NOV; DLB 116

Auster, Paul 1947- .... **CLC 47**
    See also CA 69-72; CANR 23, 52

Austin, Frank
    See Faust, Frederick (Schiller)

Austin, Mary (Hunter)
    1868-1934 .... **TCLC 25**
    See also CA 109; DLB 9, 78

Autran Dourado, Waldomiro
    See Dourado, (Waldomiro Freitas) Autran

Averroes 1126-1198 .... **CMLC 7**
    See also DLB 115

Avicenna 980-1037 .... **CMLC 16**
    See also DLB 115

Avison, Margaret 1918- .... **CLC 2, 4; DAC**
    See also CA 17-20R; DAM POET; DLB 53;
    MTCW

Axton, David
    See Koontz, Dean R(ay)

Ayckbourn, Alan
    1939- ...... **CLC 5, 8, 18, 33, 74; DAB**
    See also CA 21-24R; CANR 31;
    DAM DRAM; DLB 13; MTCW

Aydy, Catherine
    See Tennant, Emma (Christina)

Ayme, Marcel (Andre) 1902-1967 ... **CLC 11**
    See also CA 89-92; CLR 25; DLB 72

Ayrton, Michael 1921-1975 .... **CLC 7**
    See also CA 5-8R; 61-64; CANR 9, 21

Azorin .... **CLC 11**
    See also Martinez Ruiz, Jose

Azuela, Mariano
    1873-1952 .... **TCLC 3; HLC**
    See also CA 104; 131; DAM MULT; HW;
    MTCW

Baastad, Babbis Friis
    See Friis-Baastad, Babbis Ellinor

Bab
    See Gilbert, W(illiam) S(chwenck)

Babbis, Eleanor
    See Friis-Baastad, Babbis Ellinor

Babel, Isaak (Emmanuilovich)
    1894-1941(?) ...... **TCLC 2, 13; SSC 16**
    See also CA 104

Babits, Mihaly 1883-1941 .... **TCLC 14**
    See also CA 114

Babur 1483-1530 .... **LC 18**

Bacchelli, Riccardo 1891-1985 ..... **CLC 19**
    See also CA 29-32R; 117

Bach, Richard (David) 1936- .... **CLC 14**
    See also AITN 1; BEST 89:2; CA 9-12R;
    CANR 18; DAM NOV, POP; MTCW;
    SATA 13

Bachman, Richard
    See King, Stephen (Edwin)

Bachmann, Ingeborg 1926-1973 ..... **CLC 69**
    See also CA 93-96; 45-48; DLB 85

Bacon, Francis 1561-1626 .... **LC 18, 32**
    See also CDBLB Before 1660; DLB 151

Bacon, Roger 1214(?)-1292 ...... **CMLC 14**
    See also DLB 115

Bacovia, George. .... **TCLC 24**
    See also Vasiliu, Gheorghe

Badanes, Jerome 1937- .... **CLC 59**

Bagehot, Walter 1826-1877 ...... **NCLC 10**
    See also DLB 55

Bagnold, Enid 1889-1981 .... **CLC 25**
    See also CA 5-8R; 103; CANR 5, 40;
    DAM DRAM; DLB 13, 160; MAICYA;
    SATA 1, 25

Bagritsky, Eduard 1895-1934 ..... **TCLC 60**

Bagrjana, Elisaveta
    See Belcheva, Elisaveta

Bagryana, Elisaveta. .... **CLC 10**
    See also Belcheva, Elisaveta
    See also DLB 147

Bailey, Paul 1937- .... **CLC 45**
    See also CA 21-24R; CANR 16; DLB 14

Baillie, Joanna 1762-1851 .... **NCLC 2**
    See also DLB 93

Bainbridge, Beryl (Margaret)
    1933- .... **CLC 4, 5, 8, 10, 14, 18, 22, 62**
    See also CA 21-24R; CANR 24;
    DAM NOV; DLB 14; MTCW

Baker, Elliott 1922- .... **CLC 8**
    See also CA 45-48; CANR 2

Baker, Nicholson 1957- .... **CLC 61**
    See also CA 135; DAM POP

Baker, Ray Stannard 1870-1946 ... **TCLC 47**
    See also CA 118

Baker, Russell (Wayne) 1925- ...... **CLC 31**
    See also BEST 89:4; CA 57-60; CANR 11,
    41; MTCW

Bakhtin, M.
    See Bakhtin, Mikhail Mikhailovich

Bakhtin, M. M.
    See Bakhtin, Mikhail Mikhailovich

Bakhtin, Mikhail
    See Bakhtin, Mikhail Mikhailovich

Bakhtin, Mikhail Mikhailovich
    1895-1975 .... **CLC 83**
    See also CA 128; 113

Bakshi, Ralph 1938(?)- .... **CLC 26**
    See also CA 112; 138

Bakunin, Mikhail (Alexandrovich)
    1814-1876 .... **NCLC 25**

Baldwin, James (Arthur)
1924-1987 ..... **CLC 1, 2, 3, 4, 5, 8, 13, 15, 17, 42, 50, 67, 90; BLC; DA; DAB; DAC; DC 1; SSC 10; WLC**
See also AAYA 4; BW 1; CA 1-4R; 124; CABS 1; CANR 3, 24; CDALB 1941-1968; DAM MST, MULT, NOV, POP; DLB 2, 7, 33; DLBY 87; MTCW; SATA 9; SATA-Obit 54

Ballard, J(ames) G(raham)
1930- .... **CLC 3, 6, 14, 36; SSC 1**
See also AAYA 3; CA 5-8R; CANR 15, 39; DAM NOV, POP; DLB 14; MTCW

Balmont, Konstantin (Dmitriyevich)
1867-1943 .... **TCLC 11**
See also CA 109

Balzac, Honore de
1799-1850 .... **NCLC 5, 35, 53; DA; DAB; DAC; SSC 5; WLC**
See also DAM MST, NOV; DLB 119

Bambara, Toni Cade
1939-1995 ...... **CLC 19, 88; BLC; DA; DAC**
See also AAYA 5; BW 2; CA 29-32R; 150; CANR 24, 49; DAM MST, MULT; DLB 38; MTCW

Bamdad, A.
See Shamlu, Ahmad

Banat, D. R.
See Bradbury, Ray (Douglas)

Bancroft, Laura
See Baum, L(yman) Frank

Banim, John 1798-1842 .... **NCLC 13**
See also DLB 116, 158, 159

Banim, Michael 1796-1874 ...... **NCLC 13**
See also DLB 158, 159

Banks, Iain
See Banks, Iain M(enzies)

Banks, Iain M(enzies) 1954- .... **CLC 34**
See also CA 123; 128; INT 128

Banks, Lynne Reid .... **CLC 23**
See also Reid Banks, Lynne
See also AAYA 6

Banks, Russell 1940- .... **CLC 37, 72**
See also CA 65-68; CAAS 15; CANR 19, 52; DLB 130

Banville, John 1945- .... **CLC 46**
See also CA 117; 128; DLB 14; INT 128

Banville, Theodore (Faullain) de
1832-1891 .... **NCLC 9**

Baraka, Amiri
1934- .... **CLC 1, 2, 3, 5, 10, 14, 33; BLC; DA; DAC; DC 6; PC 4**
See also Jones, LeRoi
See also BW 2; CA 21-24R; CABS 3; CANR 27, 38; CDALB 1941-1968; DAM MST, MULT, POET, POP; DLB 5, 7, 16, 38; DLBD 8; MTCW

Barbauld, Anna Laetitia
1743-1825 .... **NCLC 50**
See also DLB 107, 109, 142, 158

Barbellion, W. N. P. .... **TCLC 24**
See also Cummings, Bruce F(rederick)

Barbera, Jack (Vincent) 1945- ..... **CLC 44**
See also CA 110; CANR 45

Barbey d'Aurevilly, Jules Amedee
1808-1889 .... **NCLC 1; SSC 17**
See also DLB 119

Barbusse, Henri 1873-1935 .... **TCLC 5**
See also CA 105; DLB 65

Barclay, Bill
See Moorcock, Michael (John)

Barclay, William Ewert
See Moorcock, Michael (John)

Barea, Arturo 1897-1957 .... **TCLC 14**
See also CA 111

Barfoot, Joan 1946- .... **CLC 18**
See also CA 105

Baring, Maurice 1874-1945 .... **TCLC 8**
See also CA 105; DLB 34

Barker, Clive 1952- .... **CLC 52**
See also AAYA 10; BEST 90:3; CA 121; 129; DAM POP; INT 129; MTCW

Barker, George Granville
1913-1991 .... **CLC 8, 48**
See also CA 9-12R; 135; CANR 7, 38; DAM POET; DLB 20; MTCW

Barker, Harley Granville
See Granville-Barker, Harley
See also DLB 10

Barker, Howard 1946- .... **CLC 37**
See also CA 102; DLB 13

Barker, Pat(ricia) 1943- .... **CLC 32, 94**
See also CA 117; 122; CANR 50; INT 122

Barlow, Joel 1754-1812 .... **NCLC 23**
See also DLB 37

Barnard, Mary (Ethel) 1909- .... **CLC 48**
See also CA 21-22; CAP 2

Barnes, Djuna
1892-1982 ... **CLC 3, 4, 8, 11, 29; SSC 3**
See also CA 9-12R; 107; CANR 16; DLB 4, 9, 45; MTCW

Barnes, Julian 1946- .... **CLC 42; DAB**
See also CA 102; CANR 19; DLBY 93

Barnes, Peter 1931- .... **CLC 5, 56**
See also CA 65-68; CAAS 12; CANR 33, 34; DLB 13; MTCW

Baroja (y Nessi), Pio
1872-1956 .... **TCLC 8; HLC**
See also CA 104

Baron, David
See Pinter, Harold

Baron Corvo
See Rolfe, Frederick (William Serafino Austin Lewis Mary)

Barondess, Sue K(aufman)
1926-1977 .... **CLC 8**
See also Kaufman, Sue
See also CA 1-4R; 69-72; CANR 1

Baron de Teive
See Pessoa, Fernando (Antonio Nogueira)

Barres, Maurice 1862-1923 ...... **TCLC 47**
See also DLB 123

Barreto, Afonso Henrique de Lima
See Lima Barreto, Afonso Henrique de

Barrett, (Roger) Syd 1946- .... **CLC 35**

Barrett, William (Christopher)
1913-1992 .... **CLC 27**
See also CA 13-16R; 139; CANR 11; INT CANR-11

Barrie, J(ames) M(atthew)
1860-1937 .... **TCLC 2; DAB**
See also CA 104; 136; CDBLB 1890-1914; CLR 16; DAM DRAM; DLB 10, 141, 156; MAICYA; YABC 1

Barrington, Michael
See Moorcock, Michael (John)

Barrol, Grady
See Bograd, Larry

Barry, Mike
See Malzberg, Barry N(athaniel)

Barry, Philip 1896-1949 .... **TCLC 11**
See also CA 109; DLB 7

Bart, Andre Schwarz
See Schwarz-Bart, Andre

Barth, John (Simmons)
1930- ...... **CLC 1, 2, 3, 5, 7, 9, 10, 14, 27, 51, 89; SSC 10**
See also AITN 1, 2; CA 1-4R; CABS 1; CANR 5, 23, 49; DAM NOV; DLB 2; MTCW

Barthelme, Donald
1931-1989 ...... **CLC 1, 2, 3, 5, 6, 8, 13, 23, 46, 59; SSC 2**
See also CA 21-24R; 129; CANR 20; DAM NOV; DLB 2; DLBY 80, 89; MTCW; SATA 7; SATA-Obit 62

Barthelme, Frederick 1943- .... **CLC 36**
See also CA 114; 122; DLBY 85; INT 122

Barthes, Roland (Gerard)
1915-1980 .... **CLC 24, 83**
See also CA 130; 97-100; MTCW

Barzun, Jacques (Martin) 1907- ..... **CLC 51**
See also CA 61-64; CANR 22

Bashevis, Isaac
See Singer, Isaac Bashevis

Bashkirtseff, Marie 1859-1884 ... **NCLC 27**

Basho
See Matsuo Basho

Bass, Kingsley B., Jr.
See Bullins, Ed

Bass, Rick 1958- .... **CLC 79**
See also CA 126; CANR 53

Bassani, Giorgio 1916- .... **CLC 9**
See also CA 65-68; CANR 33; DLB 128; MTCW

Bastos, Augusto (Antonio) Roa
See Roa Bastos, Augusto (Antonio)

Bataille, Georges 1897-1962 .... **CLC 29**
See also CA 101; 89-92

Bates, H(erbert) E(rnest)
1905-1974 ...... **CLC 46; DAB; SSC 10**
See also CA 93-96; 45-48; CANR 34; DAM POP; DLB 162; MTCW

Bauchart
See Camus, Albert

Baudelaire, Charles
1821-1867 .... **NCLC 6, 29, 55; DA; DAB; DAC; PC 1; SSC 18; WLC**
See also DAM MST, POET

Baudrillard, Jean 1929- .... **CLC 60**

Baum, L(yman) Frank 1856-1919 . . . TCLC 7
See also CA 108; 133; CLR 15; DLB 22;
JRDA; MAICYA; MTCW; SATA 18

Baum, Louis F.
See Baum, L(yman) Frank

Baumbach, Jonathan 1933- . . . . . . CLC 6, 23
See also CA 13-16R; CAAS 5; CANR 12;
DLBY 80; INT CANR-12; MTCW

Bausch, Richard (Carl) 1945- . . . . . . CLC 51
See also CA 101; CAAS 14; CANR 43;
DLB 130

Baxter, Charles 1947- . . . . CLC 45, 78
See also CA 57-60; CANR 40; DAM POP;
DLB 130

Baxter, George Owen
See Faust, Frederick (Schiller)

Baxter, James K(eir) 1926-1972 . . . . CLC 14
See also CA 77-80

Baxter, John
See Hunt, E(verette) Howard, (Jr.)

Bayer, Sylvia
See Glassco, John

Baynton, Barbara 1857-1929 . . . . . . TCLC 57

Beagle, Peter S(oyer) 1939- . . . . CLC 7
See also CA 9-12R; CANR 4, 51;
DLBY 80; INT CANR-4; SATA 60

Bean, Normal
See Burroughs, Edgar Rice

Beard, Charles A(ustin)
1874-1948 . . . . TCLC 15
See also CA 115; DLB 17; SATA 18

Beardsley, Aubrey 1872-1898 . . . . . NCLC 6

Beattie, Ann
1947- . . . . CLC 8, 13, 18, 40, 63; SSC 11
See also BEST 90:2; CA 81-84; CANR 53;
DAM NOV, POP; DLBY 82; MTCW

Beattie, James 1735-1803 . . . . NCLC 25
See also DLB 109

Beauchamp, Kathleen Mansfield 1888-1923
See Mansfield, Katherine
See also CA 104; 134; DA; DAC;
DAM MST

Beaumarchais, Pierre-Augustin Caron de
1732-1799 . . . . DC 4
See also DAM DRAM

Beaumont, Francis
1584(?)-1616 . . . . LC 33; DC 6
See also CDBLB Before 1660; DLB 58, 121

Beauvoir, Simone (Lucie Ernestine Marie
Bertrand) de
1908-1986 . . . . CLC 1, 2, 4, 8, 14, 31, 44,
50, 71; DA; DAB; DAC; WLC
See also CA 9-12R; 118; CANR 28;
DAM MST, NOV; DLB 72; DLBY 86;
MTCW

Becker, Carl 1873-1945 . . . . TCLC 63:
See also DLB 17

Becker, Jurek 1937- . . . . CLC 7, 19
See also CA 85-88; DLB 75

Becker, Walter 1950- . . . . CLC 26

Beckett, Samuel (Barclay)
1906-1989 . . . . . . CLC 1, 2, 3, 4, 6, 9, 10,
11, 14, 18, 29, 57, 59, 83; DA; DAB;
DAC; SSC 16; WLC
See also CA 5-8R; 130; CANR 33;
CDBLB 1945-1960; DAM DRAM, MST,
NOV; DLB 13, 15; DLBY 90; MTCW

Beckford, William 1760-1844 . . . . NCLC 16
See also DLB 39

Beckman, Gunnel 1910- . . . . CLC 26
See also CA 33-36R; CANR 15; CLR 25;
MAICYA; SAAS 9; SATA 6

Becque, Henri 1837-1899 . . . . NCLC 3

Beddoes, Thomas Lovell
1803-1849 . . . . NCLC 3
See also DLB 96

Bedford, Donald F.
See Fearing, Kenneth (Flexner)

Beecher, Catharine Esther
1800-1878 . . . . NCLC 30
See also DLB 1

Beecher, John 1904-1980 . . . . CLC 6
See also AITN 1; CA 5-8R; 105; CANR 8

Beer, Johann 1655-1700 . . . . LC 5

Beer, Patricia 1924- . . . . CLC 58
See also CA 61-64; CANR 13, 46; DLB 40

Beerbohm, Henry Maximilian
1872-1956 . . . . TCLC 1, 24
See also CA 104; DLB 34, 100

Beerbohm, Max
See Beerbohm, Henry Maximilian

Beer-Hofmann, Richard
1866-1945 . . . . TCLC 60
See also DLB 81

Begiebing, Robert J(ohn) 1946- . . . . . CLC 70
See also CA 122; CANR 40

Behan, Brendan
1923-1964 . . . . CLC 1, 8, 11, 15, 79
See also CA 73-76; CANR 33;
CDBLB 1945-1960; DAM DRAM;
DLB 13; MTCW

Behn, Aphra
1640(?)-1689 . . . . . . LC 1, 30; DA; DAB;
DAC; DC 4; PC 13; WLC
See also DAM DRAM, MST, NOV, POET;
DLB 39, 80, 131

Behrman, S(amuel) N(athaniel)
1893-1973 . . . . CLC 40
See also CA 13-16; 45-48; CAP 1; DLB 7,
44

Belasco, David 1853-1931 . . . . TCLC 3
See also CA 104; DLB 7

Belcheva, Elisaveta 1893- . . . . CLC 10
See also Bagryana, Elisaveta

Beldone, Phil "Cheech"
See Ellison, Harlan (Jay)

Beleno
See Azuela, Mariano

Belinski, Vissarion Grigoryevich
1811-1848 . . . . NCLC 5

Belitt, Ben 1911- . . . . CLC 22
See also CA 13-16R; CAAS 4; CANR 7;
DLB 5

Bell, James Madison
1826-1902 . . . . TCLC 43; BLC
See also BW 1; CA 122; 124; DAM MULT;
DLB 50

Bell, Madison (Smartt) 1957- . . . . . . CLC 41
See also CA 111; CANR 28

Bell, Marvin (Hartley) 1937- . . . . . CLC 8, 31
See also CA 21-24R; CAAS 14;
DAM POET; DLB 5; MTCW

Bell, W. L. D.
See Mencken, H(enry) L(ouis)

Bellamy, Atwood C.
See Mencken, H(enry) L(ouis)

Bellamy, Edward 1850-1898 . . . . . . NCLC 4
See also DLB 12

Bellin, Edward J.
See Kuttner, Henry

Belloc, (Joseph) Hilaire (Pierre)
1870-1953 . . . . TCLC 7, 18
See also CA 106; DAM POET; DLB 19,
100, 141; YABC 1

Belloc, Joseph Peter Rene Hilaire
See Belloc, (Joseph) Hilaire (Pierre)

Belloc, Joseph Pierre Hilaire
See Belloc, (Joseph) Hilaire (Pierre)

Belloc, M. A.
See Lowndes, Marie Adelaide (Belloc)

Bellow, Saul
1915- . . . . . . CLC 1, 2, 3, 6, 8, 10, 13, 15,
25, 33, 34, 63, 79; DA; DAB; DAC;
SSC 14; WLC
See also AITN 2; BEST 89:3; CA 5-8R;
CABS 1; CANR 29, 53;
CDALB 1941-1968; DAM MST, NOV,
POP; DLB 2, 28; DLBD 3; DLBY 82;
MTCW

Belser, Reimond Karel Maria de 1929-
See Ruyslinck, Ward
See also CA 152

Bely, Andrey . . . . TCLC 7; PC 11
See also Bugayev, Boris Nikolayevich

Benary, Margot
See Benary-Isbert, Margot

Benary-Isbert, Margot 1889-1979 . . . CLC 12
See also CA 5-8R; 89-92; CANR 4;
CLR 12; MAICYA; SATA 2;
SATA-Obit 21

Benavente (y Martinez), Jacinto
1866-1954 . . . . TCLC 3
See also CA 106; 131; DAM DRAM,
MULT; HW; MTCW

Benchley, Peter (Bradford)
1940- . . . . CLC 4, 8
See also AAYA 14; AITN 2; CA 17-20R;
CANR 12, 35; DAM NOV, POP;
MTCW; SATA 3

Benchley, Robert (Charles)
1889-1945 . . . . TCLC 1, 55
See also CA 105; DLB 11

Benda, Julien 1867-1956 . . . . TCLC 60
See also CA 120

Benedict, Ruth 1887-1948 . . . . TCLC 60

Benedikt, Michael 1935- . . . . CLC 4, 14
See also CA 13-16R; CANR 7; DLB 5

Benet, Juan 1927-. . . . . CLC 28
See also CA 143

Benet, Stephen Vincent
1898-1943 . . . . TCLC 7; SSC 10
See also CA 104; DAM POET; DLB 4, 48,
102; YABC 1

Benet, William Rose 1886-1950 . . . TCLC 28
See also CA 118; DAM POET; DLB 45

Benford, Gregory (Albert) 1941-. . . . CLC 52
See also CA 69-72; CANR 12, 24, 49;
DLBY 82

Bengtsson, Frans (Gunnar)
1894-1954 . . . . TCLC 48

Benjamin, David
See Slavitt, David R(ytman)

Benjamin, Lois
See Gould, Lois

Benjamin, Walter 1892-1940 . . . . . TCLC 39

Benn, Gottfried 1886-1956. . . . . TCLC 3
See also CA 106; DLB 56

Bennett, Alan 1934-. . . . . CLC 45, 77; DAB
See also CA 103; CANR 35; DAM MST;
MTCW

Bennett, (Enoch) Arnold
1867-1931 . . . . TCLC 5, 20
See also CA 106; CDBLB 1890-1914;
DLB 10, 34, 98, 135

Bennett, Elizabeth
See Mitchell, Margaret (Munnerlyn)

Bennett, George Harold 1930-
See Bennett, Hal
See also BW 1; CA 97-100

Bennett, Hal . . . . CLC 5
See also Bennett, George Harold
See also DLB 33

Bennett, Jay 1912-. . . . . CLC 35
See also AAYA 10; CA 69-72; CANR 11,
42; JRDA; SAAS 4; SATA 41, 87;
SATA-Brief 27

Bennett, Louise (Simone)
1919- . . . . CLC 28; BLC
See also BW 2; CA 151; DAM MULT;
DLB 117

Benson, E(dward) F(rederic)
1867-1940 . . . . TCLC 27
See also CA 114; DLB 135, 153

Benson, Jackson J. 1930-. . . . . CLC 34
See also CA 25-28R; DLB 111

Benson, Sally 1900-1972 . . . . CLC 17
See also CA 19-20; 37-40R; CAP 1;
SATA 1, 35; SATA-Obit 27

Benson, Stella 1892-1933. . . . . TCLC 17
See also CA 117; DLB 36, 162

Bentham, Jeremy 1748-1832 . . . . . NCLC 38
See also DLB 107, 158

Bentley, E(dmund) C(lerihew)
1875-1956 . . . . TCLC 12
See also CA 108; DLB 70

Bentley, Eric (Russell) 1916-. . . . . . . CLC 24
See also CA 5-8R; CANR 6; INT CANR-6

Beranger, Pierre Jean de
1780-1857 . . . . NCLC 34

Berendt, John (Lawrence) 1939-. . . . CLC 86
See also CA 146

Berger, Colonel
See Malraux, (Georges-)Andre

Berger, John (Peter) 1926- . . . . . . CLC 2, 19
See also CA 81-84; CANR 51; DLB 14

Berger, Melvin H. 1927-. . . . . CLC 12
See also CA 5-8R; CANR 4; CLR 32;
SAAS 2; SATA 5, 88

Berger, Thomas (Louis)
1924- . . . . CLC 3, 5, 8, 11, 18, 38
See also CA 1-4R; CANR 5, 28, 51;
DAM NOV; DLB 2; DLBY 80;
INT CANR-28; MTCW

Bergman, (Ernst) Ingmar
1918- . . . . CLC 16, 72
See also CA 81-84; CANR 33

Bergson, Henri 1859-1941. . . . . TCLC 32

Bergstein, Eleanor 1938-. . . . . CLC 4
See also CA 53-56; CANR 5

Berkoff, Steven 1937-. . . . . CLC 56
See also CA 104

Bermant, Chaim (Icyk) 1929- . . . . . . CLC 40
See also CA 57-60; CANR 6, 31

Bern, Victoria
See Fisher, M(ary) F(rances) K(ennedy)

Bernanos, (Paul Louis) Georges
1888-1948 . . . . TCLC 3
See also CA 104; 130; DLB 72

Bernard, April 1956- . . . . CLC 59
See also CA 131

Berne, Victoria
See Fisher, M(ary) F(rances) K(ennedy)

Bernhard, Thomas
1931-1989 . . . . CLC 3, 32, 61
See also CA 85-88; 127; CANR 32;
DLB 85, 124; MTCW

Berriault, Gina 1926-. . . . . CLC 54
See also CA 116; 129; DLB 130

Berrigan, Daniel 1921-. . . . . CLC 4
See also CA 33-36R; CAAS 1; CANR 11,
43; DLB 5

Berrigan, Edmund Joseph Michael, Jr.
1934-1983
See Berrigan, Ted
See also CA 61-64; 110; CANR 14

Berrigan, Ted. . . . . CLC 37
See also Berrigan, Edmund Joseph Michael,
Jr.
See also DLB 5

Berry, Charles Edward Anderson 1931-
See Berry, Chuck
See also CA 115

Berry, Chuck. . . . . CLC 17
See also Berry, Charles Edward Anderson

Berry, Jonas
See Ashbery, John (Lawrence)

Berry, Wendell (Erdman)
1934-. . . . . CLC 4, 6, 8, 27, 46
See also AITN 1; CA 73-76; CANR 50;
DAM POET; DLB 5, 6

Berryman, John
1914-1972 . . . . . . CLC 1, 2, 3, 4, 6, 8, 10,
13, 25, 62
See also CA 13-16; 33-36R; CABS 2;
CANR 35; CAP 1; CDALB 1941-1968;
DAM POET; DLB 48; MTCW

Bertolucci, Bernardo 1940- . . . . CLC 16
See also CA 106

Bertrand, Aloysius 1807-1841 . . . . NCLC 31

Bertran de Born c. 1140-1215. . . . . CMLC 5

Besant, Annie (Wood) 1847-1933 . . . TCLC 9
See also CA 105

Bessie, Alvah 1904-1985. . . . . CLC 23
See also CA 5-8R; 116; CANR 2; DLB 26

Bethlen, T. D.
See Silverberg, Robert

Beti, Mongo. . . . . CLC 27; BLC
See also Biyidi, Alexandre
See also DAM MULT

Betjeman, John
1906-1984 . . . CLC 2, 6, 10, 34, 43; DAB
See also CA 9-12R; 112; CANR 33;
CDBLB 1945-1960; DAM MST, POET;
DLB 20; DLBY 84; MTCW

Bettelheim, Bruno 1903-1990 . . . . . . CLC 79
See also CA 81-84; 131; CANR 23; MTCW

Betti, Ugo 1892-1953 . . . . TCLC 5
See also CA 104

Betts, Doris (Waugh) 1932-. . . . CLC 3, 6, 28
See also CA 13-16R; CANR 9; DLBY 82;
INT CANR-9

Bevan, Alistair
See Roberts, Keith (John Kingston)

Bialik, Chaim Nachman
1873-1934 . . . . TCLC 25

Bickerstaff, Isaac
See Swift, Jonathan

Bidart, Frank 1939-. . . . . CLC 33
See also CA 140

Bienek, Horst 1930-. . . . . CLC 7, 11
See also CA 73-76; DLB 75

Bierce, Ambrose (Gwinett)
1842-1914(?) . . . . TCLC 1, 7, 44; DA;
DAC; SSC 9; WLC
See also CA 104; 139; CDALB 1865-1917;
DAM MST; DLB 11, 12, 23, 71, 74

Biggers, Earl Derr 1884-1933 . . . . . TCLC 65
See also CA 108

Billings, Josh
See Shaw, Henry Wheeler

Billington, (Lady) Rachel (Mary)
1942-. . . . . CLC 43
See also AITN 2; CA 33-36R; CANR 44

Binyon, T(imothy) J(ohn) 1936- . . . . CLC 34
See also CA 111; CANR 28

Bioy Casares, Adolfo
1914- . . . CLC 4, 8, 13, 88; HLC; SSC 17
See also CA 29-32R; CANR 19, 43;
DAM MULT; DLB 113; HW; MTCW

Bird, Cordwainer
See Ellison, Harlan (Jay)

Bird, Robert Montgomery
1806-1854 . . . . NCLC 1

Birney, (Alfred) Earle
1904-. . . . . CLC 1, 4, 6, 11; DAC
See also CA 1-4R; CANR 5, 20;
DAM MST, POET; DLB 88; MTCW

Bishop, Elizabeth
    1911-1979 ...... **CLC 1, 4, 9, 13, 15, 32;**
                     DA; DAC; PC 3
    See also CA 5-8R; 89-92; CABS 2;
    CANR 26; CDALB 1968-1988;
    DAM MST, POET; DLB 5; MTCW;
    SATA-Obit 24

Bishop, John 1935-.............. **CLC 10**
    See also CA 105

Bissett, Bill 1939-......... **CLC 18; PC 14**
    See also CA 69-72; CAAS 19; CANR 15;
    DLB 53; MTCW

Bitov, Andrei (Georgievich) 1937-... **CLC 57**
    See also CA 142

Biyidi, Alexandre 1932-
    See Beti, Mongo
    See also BW 1; CA 114; 124; MTCW

Bjarme, Brynjolf
    See Ibsen, Henrik (Johan)

Bjornson, Bjornstjerne (Martinius)
    1832-1910 .... **TCLC 7, 37**
    See also CA 104

Black, Robert
    See Holdstock, Robert P.

Blackburn, Paul 1926-1971 ...... **CLC 9, 43**
    See also CA 81-84; 33-36R; CANR 34;
    DLB 16; DLBY 81

Black Elk 1863-1950 .... **TCLC 33**
    See also CA 144; DAM MULT; NNAL

Black Hobart
    See Sanders, (James) Ed(ward)

Blacklin, Malcolm
    See Chambers, Aidan

Blackmore, R(ichard) D(oddridge)
    1825-1900 .... **TCLC 27**
    See also CA 120; DLB 18

Blackmur, R(ichard) P(almer)
    1904-1965 .... **CLC 2, 24**
    See also CA 11-12; 25-28R; CAP 1; DLB 63

Black Tarantula, The
    See Acker, Kathy

Blackwood, Algernon (Henry)
    1869-1951 .... **TCLC 5**
    See also CA 105; 150; DLB 153, 156

Blackwood, Caroline 1931-1996 ... **CLC 6, 9**
    See also CA 85-88; 151; CANR 32;
    DLB 14; MTCW

Blade, Alexander
    See Hamilton, Edmond; Silverberg, Robert

Blaga, Lucian 1895-1961 .... **CLC 75**

Blair, Eric (Arthur) 1903-1950
    See Orwell, George
    See also CA 104; 132; DA; DAB; DAC;
    DAM MST, NOV; MTCW; SATA 29

Blais, Marie-Claire
    1939- .... **CLC 2, 4, 6, 13, 22; DAC**
    See also CA 21-24R; CAAS 4; CANR 38;
    DAM MST; DLB 53; MTCW

Blaise, Clark 1940-.............. **CLC 29**
    See also AITN 2; CA 53-56; CAAS 3;
    CANR 5; DLB 53

Blake, Nicholas
    See Day Lewis, C(ecil)
    See also DLB 77

Blake, William
    1757-1827 .... **NCLC 13, 37, 57; DA;**
                     DAB; DAC; PC 12; WLC
    See also CDBLB 1789-1832; DAM MST,
    POET; DLB 93, 163; MAICYA;
    SATA 30

Blake, William J(ames) 1894-1969 ... **PC 12**
    See also CA 5-8R; 25-28R

Blasco Ibanez, Vicente
    1867-1928 .... **TCLC 12**
    See also CA 110; 131; DAM NOV; HW;
    MTCW

Blatty, William Peter 1928-......... **CLC 2**
    See also CA 5-8R; CANR 9; DAM POP

Bleeck, Oliver
    See Thomas, Ross (Elmore)

Blessing, Lee 1949-.............. **CLC 54**

Blish, James (Benjamin)
    1921-1975 .... **CLC 14**
    See also CA 1-4R; 57-60; CANR 3; DLB 8;
    MTCW; SATA 66

Bliss, Reginald
    See Wells, H(erbert) G(eorge)

Blixen, Karen (Christentze Dinesen)
    1885-1962
    See Dinesen, Isak
    See also CA 25-28; CANR 22, 50; CAP 2;
    MTCW; SATA 44

Bloch, Robert (Albert) 1917-1994... **CLC 33**
    See also CA 5-8R; 146; CAAS 20; CANR 5;
    DLB 44; INT CANR-5; SATA 12;
    SATA-Obit 82

Blok, Alexander (Alexandrovich)
    1880-1921 .... **TCLC 5**
    See also CA 104

Blom, Jan
    See Breytenbach, Breyten

Bloom, Harold 1930- .... **CLC 24**
    See also CA 13-16R; CANR 39; DLB 67

Bloomfield, Aurelius
    See Bourne, Randolph S(illiman)

Blount, Roy (Alton), Jr. 1941- ..... **CLC 38**
    See also CA 53-56; CANR 10, 28;
    INT CANR-28; MTCW

Bloy, Leon 1846-1917............ **TCLC 22**
    See also CA 121; DLB 123

Blume, Judy (Sussman) 1938-... **CLC 12, 30**
    See also AAYA 3; CA 29-32R; CANR 13,
    37; CLR 2, 15; DAM NOV, POP;
    DLB 52; JRDA; MAICYA; MTCW;
    SATA 2, 31, 79

Blunden, Edmund (Charles)
    1896-1974 .... **CLC 2, 56**
    See also CA 17-18; 45-48; CAP 2; DLB 20,
    100, 155; MTCW

Bly, Robert (Elwood)
    1926- .... **CLC 1, 2, 5, 10, 15, 38**
    See also CA 5-8R; CANR 41; DAM POET;
    DLB 5; MTCW

Boas, Franz 1858-1942........... **TCLC 56**
    See also CA 115

Bobette
    See Simenon, Georges (Jacques Christian)

Boccaccio, Giovanni
    1313-1375 .... **CMLC 13; SSC 10**

Bochco, Steven 1943-............. **CLC 35**
    See also AAYA 11; CA 124; 138

Bodenheim, Maxwell 1892-1954 ... **TCLC 44**
    See also CA 110; DLB 9, 45

Bodker, Cecil 1927-.............. **CLC 21**
    See also CA 73-76; CANR 13, 44; CLR 23;
    MAICYA; SATA 14

Boell, Heinrich (Theodor)
    1917-1985 .... **CLC 2, 3, 6, 9, 11, 15, 27,**
             32, 72; DA; DAB; DAC; SSC 23; WLC
    See also CA 21-24R; 116; CANR 24;
    DAM MST, NOV; DLB 69; DLBY 85;
    MTCW

Boerne, Alfred
    See Doeblin, Alfred

Boethius 480(?)-524(?) .... **CMLC 15**
    See also DLB 115

Bogan, Louise
    1897-1970 .... **CLC 4, 39, 46, 93; PC 12**
    See also CA 73-76; 25-28R; CANR 33;
    DAM POET; DLB 45; MTCW

Bogarde, Dirk .... **CLC 19**
    See also Van Den Bogarde, Derek Jules
    Gaspard Ulric Niven
    See also DLB 14

Bogosian, Eric 1953- .... **CLC 45**
    See also CA 138

Bograd, Larry 1953-.............. **CLC 35**
    See also CA 93-96; SAAS 21; SATA 33

Boiardo, Matteo Maria 1441-1494 .... **LC 6**

Boileau-Despreaux, Nicolas
    1636-1711 .... **LC 3**

Bojer, Johan 1872-1959.......... **TCLC 64**

Boland, Eavan (Aisling) 1944-... **CLC 40, 67**
    See also CA 143; DAM POET; DLB 40

Bolt, Lee
    See Faust, Frederick (Schiller)

Bolt, Robert (Oxton) 1924-1995 .... **CLC 14**
    See also CA 17-20R; 147; CANR 35;
    DAM DRAM; DLB 13; MTCW

Bombet, Louis-Alexandre-Cesar
    See Stendhal

Bomkauf
    See Kaufman, Bob (Garnell)

Bonaventura.................... **NCLC 35**
    See also DLB 90

Bond, Edward 1934-....... **CLC 4, 6, 13, 23**
    See also CA 25-28R; CANR 38;
    DAM DRAM; DLB 13; MTCW

Bonham, Frank 1914-1989........ **CLC 12**
    See also AAYA 1; CA 9-12R; CANR 4, 36;
    JRDA; MAICYA; SAAS 3; SATA 1, 49;
    SATA-Obit 62

Bonnefoy, Yves 1923-........ **CLC 9, 15, 58**
    See also CA 85-88; CANR 33; DAM MST,
    POET; MTCW

Bontemps, Arna(ud Wendell)
    1902-1973 .... **CLC 1, 18; BLC**
    See also BW 1; CA 1-4R; 41-44R; CANR 4,
    35; CLR 6; DAM MULT, NOV, POET;
    DLB 48, 51; JRDA; MAICYA; MTCW;
    SATA 2, 44; SATA-Obit 24

Booth, Martin 1944-.............. **CLC 13**
    See also CA 93-96; CAAS 2

Booth, Philip 1925-............... **CLC 23**
See also CA 5-8R; CANR 5; DLBY 82

Booth, Wayne C(layson) 1921-..... **CLC 24**
See also CA 1-4R; CAAS 5; CANR 3, 43;
DLB 67

Borchert, Wolfgang 1921-1947..... **TCLC 5**
See also CA 104; DLB 69, 124

Borel, Petrus 1809-1859........ **NCLC 41**

Borges, Jorge Luis
1899-1986 ... **CLC 1, 2, 3, 4, 6, 8, 9, 10,**
13, 19, 44, 48, 83; DA; DAB; DAC;
HLC; SSC 4; WLC
See also CA 21-24R; CANR 19, 33;
DAM MST, MULT; DLB 113; DLBY 86;
HW; MTCW

Borowski, Tadeusz 1922-1951...... **TCLC 9**
See also CA 106

Borrow, George (Henry)
1803-1881 .... **NCLC 9**
See also DLB 21, 55, 166

Bosman, Herman Charles
1905-1951 .... **TCLC 49**

Bosschere, Jean de 1878(?)-1953... **TCLC 19**
See also CA 115

Boswell, James
1740-1795 ...... **LC 4; DA; DAB; DAC;**
WLC
See also CDBLB 1660-1789; DAM MST;
DLB 104, 142

Bottoms, David 1949-............. **CLC 53**
See also CA 105; CANR 22; DLB 120;
DLBY 83

Boucicault, Dion 1820-1890...... **NCLC 41**

Boucolon, Maryse 1937(?)-
See Conde, Maryse
See also CA 110; CANR 30, 53

Bourget, Paul (Charles Joseph)
1852-1935 .... **TCLC 12**
See also CA 107; DLB 123

Bourjaily, Vance (Nye) 1922- .... **CLC 8, 62**
See also CA 1-4R; CAAS 1; CANR 2;
DLB 2, 143

Bourne, Randolph S(illiman)
1886-1918 .... **TCLC 16**
See also CA 117; DLB 63

Bova, Ben(jamin William) 1932-.... **CLC 45**
See also AAYA 16; CA 5-8R; CAAS 18;
CANR 11; CLR 3; DLBY 81;
INT CANR-11; MAICYA; MTCW;
SATA 6, 68

Bowen, Elizabeth (Dorothea Cole)
1899-1973 ...... **CLC 1, 3, 6, 11, 15, 22;**
SSC 3
See also CA 17-18; 41-44R; CANR 35;
CAP 2; CDBLB 1945-1960; DAM NOV;
DLB 15, 162; MTCW

Bowering, George 1935-........ **CLC 15, 47**
See also CA 21-24R; CAAS 16; CANR 10;
DLB 53

Bowering, Marilyn R(uthe) 1949-... **CLC 32**
See also CA 101; CANR 49

Bowers, Edgar 1924- .... **CLC 9**
See also CA 5-8R; CANR 24; DLB 5

Bowie, David..................... **CLC 17**
See also Jones, David Robert

Bowles, Jane (Sydney)
1917-1973 .... **CLC 3, 68**
See also CA 19-20; 41-44R; CAP 2

Bowles, Paul (Frederick)
1910- .... **CLC 1, 2, 19, 53; SSC 3**
See also CA 1-4R; CAAS 1; CANR 1, 19,
50; DLB 5, 6; MTCW

Box, Edgar
See Vidal, Gore

Boyd, Nancy
See Millay, Edna St. Vincent

Boyd, William 1952-........ **CLC 28, 53, 70**
See also CA 114; 120; CANR 51

Boyle, Kay
1902-1992 ..... **CLC 1, 5, 19, 58; SSC 5**
See also CA 13-16R; 140; CAAS 1;
CANR 29; DLB 4, 9, 48, 86; DLBY 93;
MTCW

Boyle, Mark
See Kienzle, William X(avier)

Boyle, Patrick 1905-1982.......... **CLC 19**
See also CA 127

Boyle, T. C. 1948-
See Boyle, T(homas) Coraghessan

Boyle, T(homas) Coraghessan
1948- .... **CLC 36, 55, 90; SSC 16**
See also BEST 90:4; CA 120; CANR 44;
DAM POP; DLBY 86

Boz
See Dickens, Charles (John Huffam)

Brackenridge, Hugh Henry
1748-1816 .... **NCLC 7**
See also DLB 11, 37

Bradbury, Edward P.
See Moorcock, Michael (John)

Bradbury, Malcolm (Stanley)
1932- .... **CLC 32, 61**
See also CA 1-4R; CANR 1, 33;
DAM NOV; DLB 14; MTCW

Bradbury, Ray (Douglas)
1920- .... **CLC 1, 3, 10, 15, 42; DA;**
DAB; DAC; WLC
See also AAYA 15; AITN 1, 2; CA 1-4R;
CANR 2, 30; CDALB 1968-1988;
DAM MST, NOV, POP; DLB 2, 8;
INT CANR-30; MTCW; SATA 11, 64

Bradford, Gamaliel 1863-1932..... **TCLC 36**
See also DLB 17

Bradley, David (Henry, Jr.)
1950- .... **CLC 23; BLC**
See also BW 1; CA 104; CANR 26;
DAM MULT; DLB 33

Bradley, John Ed(mund, Jr.)
1958- .... **CLC 55**
See also CA 139

Bradley, Marion Zimmer 1930-..... **CLC 30**
See also AAYA 9; CA 57-60; CAAS 10;
CANR 7, 31, 51; DAM POP; DLB 8;
MTCW

Bradstreet, Anne
1612(?)-1672 ...... **LC 4, 30; DA; DAC;**
PC 10
See also CDALB 1640-1865; DAM MST,
POET; DLB 24

Brady, Joan 1939- .... **CLC 86**
See also CA 141

Bragg, Melvyn 1939- .... **CLC 10**
See also BEST 89:3; CA 57-60; CANR 10,
48; DLB 14

Braine, John (Gerard)
1922-1986 .... **CLC 1, 3, 41**
See also CA 1-4R; 120; CANR 1, 33;
CDBLB 1945-1960; DLB 15; DLBY 86;
MTCW

Brammer, William 1930(?)-1978 .... **CLC 31**
See also CA 77-80

Brancati, Vitaliano 1907-1954..... **TCLC 12**
See also CA 109

Brancato, Robin F(idler) 1936-..... **CLC 35**
See also AAYA 9; CA 69-72; CANR 11,
45; CLR 32; JRDA; SAAS 9; SATA 23

Brand, Max
See Faust, Frederick (Schiller)

Brand, Millen 1906-1980.......... **CLC 7**
See also CA 21-24R; 97-100

Branden, Barbara .... **CLC 44**
See also CA 148

Brandes, Georg (Morris Cohen)
1842-1927 .... **TCLC 10**
See also CA 105

Brandys, Kazimierz 1916-......... **CLC 62**

Branley, Franklyn M(ansfield)
1915- .... **CLC 21**
See also CA 33-36R; CANR 14, 39;
CLR 13; MAICYA; SAAS 16; SATA 4,
68

Brathwaite, Edward Kamau 1930-... **CLC 11**
See also BW 2; CA 25-28R; CANR 11, 26,
47; DAM POET; DLB 125

Brautigan, Richard (Gary)
1935-1984 .... **CLC 1, 3, 5, 9, 12, 34, 42**
See also CA 53-56; 113; CANR 34;
DAM NOV; DLB 2, 5; DLBY 80, 84;
MTCW; SATA 56

Brave Bird, Mary 1953-
See Crow Dog, Mary
See also NNAL

Braverman, Kate 1950- .... **CLC 67**
See also CA 89-92

Brecht, Bertolt
1898-1956 ...... **TCLC 1, 6, 13, 35; DA;**
DAB; DAC; DC 3; WLC
See also CA 104; 133; DAM DRAM, MST;
DLB 56, 124; MTCW

Brecht, Eugen Berthold Friedrich
See Brecht, Bertolt

Bremer, Fredrika 1801-1865 ..... **NCLC 11**

Brennan, Christopher John
1870-1932 .... **TCLC 17**
See also CA 117

Brennan, Maeve 1917-............. **CLC 5**
See also CA 81-84

Brentano, Clemens (Maria)
1778-1842 .... **NCLC 1**
See also DLB 90

Brent of Bin Bin
See Franklin, (Stella Maraia Sarah) Miles

Brenton, Howard 1942-........... **CLC 31**
See also CA 69-72; CANR 33; DLB 13;
MTCW

Breslin, James 1930-
See Breslin, Jimmy
See also CA 73-76; CANR 31; DAM NOV;
MTCW

Breslin, Jimmy .... CLC 4, 43
See also Breslin, James
See also AITN 1

Bresson, Robert 1901- .... CLC 16
See also CA 110; CANR 49

Breton, Andre
1896-1966 ..... CLC 2, 9, 15, 54; PC 15
See also CA 19-20; 25-28R; CANR 40;
CAP 2; DLB 65; MTCW

Breytenbach, Breyten 1939(?)- .. CLC 23, 37
See also CA 113; 129; DAM POET

Bridgers, Sue Ellen 1942- .... CLC 26
See also AAYA 8; CA 65-68; CANR 11,
36; CLR 18; DLB 52; JRDA; MAICYA;
SAAS 1; SATA 22

Bridges, Robert (Seymour)
1844-1930 .... TCLC 1
See also CA 104; CDBLB 1890-1914;
DAM POET; DLB 19, 98

Bridie, James .... TCLC 3
See also Mavor, Osborne Henry
See also DLB 10

Brin, David 1950- .... CLC 34
See also CA 102; CANR 24;
INT CANR-24; SATA 65

Brink, Andre (Philippus)
1935- .... CLC 18, 36
See also CA 104; CANR 39; INT 103;
MTCW

Brinsmead, H(esba) F(ay) 1922- .... CLC 21
See also CA 21-24R; CANR 10; MAICYA;
SAAS 5; SATA 18, 78

Brittain, Vera (Mary)
1893(?)-1970 .... CLC 23
See also CA 13-16; 25-28R; CAP 1; MTCW

Broch, Hermann 1886-1951 .... TCLC 20
See also CA 117; DLB 85, 124

Brock, Rose
See Hansen, Joseph

Brodkey, Harold (Roy) 1930-1996 .. CLC 56
See also CA 111; 151; DLB 130

Brodsky, Iosif Alexandrovich 1940-1996
See Brodsky, Joseph
See also AITN 1; CA 41-44R; 151;
CANR 37; DAM POET; MTCW

Brodsky, Joseph .. CLC 4, 6, 13, 36, 50; PC 9
See also Brodsky, Iosif Alexandrovich

Brodsky, Michael Mark 1948- ..... CLC 19
See also CA 102; CANR 18, 41

Bromell, Henry 1947- .... CLC 5
See also CA 53-56; CANR 9

Bromfield, Louis (Brucker)
1896-1956 .... TCLC 11
See also CA 107; DLB 4, 9, 86

Broner, E(sther) M(asserman)
1930- .... CLC 19
See also CA 17-20R; CANR 8, 25; DLB 28

Bronk, William 1918- .... CLC 10
See also CA 89-92; CANR 23; DLB 165

Bronstein, Lev Davidovich
See Trotsky, Leon

Bronte, Anne 1820-1849 .... NCLC 4
See also DLB 21

Bronte, Charlotte
1816-1855 .... NCLC 3, 8, 33; DA;
DAB; DAC; WLC
See also AAYA 17; CDBLB 1832-1890;
DAM MST, NOV; DLB 21, 159

Bronte, Emily (Jane)
1818-1848 .... NCLC 16, 35; DA; DAB;
DAC; PC 8; WLC
See also AAYA 17; CDBLB 1832-1890;
DAM MST, NOV, POET; DLB 21, 32

Brooke, Frances 1724-1789 .... LC 6
See also DLB 39, 99

Brooke, Henry 1703(?)-1783 .... LC 1
See also DLB 39

Brooke, Rupert (Chawner)
1887-1915 .... TCLC 2, 7; DA; DAB;
DAC; WLC
See also CA 104; 132; CDBLB 1914-1945;
DAM MST, POET; DLB 19; MTCW

Brooke-Haven, P.
See Wodehouse, P(elham) G(renville)

Brooke-Rose, Christine 1926- ...... CLC 40
See also CA 13-16R; DLB 14

Brookner, Anita
1928- .... CLC 32, 34, 51; DAB
See also CA 114; 120; CANR 37;
DAM POP; DLBY 87; MTCW

Brooks, Cleanth 1906-1994 ..... CLC 24, 86
See also CA 17-20R; 145; CANR 33, 35;
DLB 63; DLBY 94; INT CANR-35;
MTCW

Brooks, George
See Baum, L(yman) Frank

Brooks, Gwendolyn
1917- ...... CLC 1, 2, 4, 5, 15, 49; BLC;
DA; DAC; PC 7; WLC
See also AITN 1; BW 2; CA 1-4R;
CANR 1, 27, 52; CDALB 1941-1968;
CLR 27; DAM MST, MULT, POET;
DLB 5, 76, 165; MTCW; SATA 6

Brooks, Mel .... CLC 12
See also Kaminsky, Melvin
See also AAYA 13; DLB 26

Brooks, Peter 1938- .... CLC 34
See also CA 45-48; CANR 1

Brooks, Van Wyck 1886-1963 ...... CLC 29
See also CA 1-4R; CANR 6; DLB 45, 63,
103

Brophy, Brigid (Antonia)
1929-1995 .... CLC 6, 11, 29
See also CA 5-8R; 149; CAAS 4; CANR 25,
53; DLB 14; MTCW

Brosman, Catharine Savage 1934- .... CLC 9
See also CA 61-64; CANR 21, 46

Brother Antoninus
See Everson, William (Oliver)

Broughton, T(homas) Alan 1936- ... CLC 19
See also CA 45-48; CANR 2, 23, 48

Broumas, Olga 1949- .... CLC 10, 73
See also CA 85-88; CANR 20

Brown, Charles Brockden
1771-1810 .... NCLC 22
See also CDALB 1640-1865; DLB 37, 59,
73

Brown, Christy 1932-1981 .... CLC 63
See also CA 105; 104; DLB 14

Brown, Claude 1937- .... CLC 30; BLC
See also AAYA 7; BW 1; CA 73-76;
DAM MULT

Brown, Dee (Alexander) 1908- .. CLC 18, 47
See also CA 13-16R; CAAS 6; CANR 11,
45; DAM POP; DLBY 80; MTCW;
SATA 5

Brown, George
See Wertmueller, Lina

Brown, George Douglas
1869-1902 .... TCLC 28

Brown, George Mackay
1921-1996 .... CLC 5, 48
See also CA 21-24R; 151; CAAS 6;
CANR 12, 37; DLB 14, 27, 139; MTCW;
SATA 35

Brown, (William) Larry 1951- ...... CLC 73
See also CA 130; 134; INT 133

Brown, Moses
See Barrett, William (Christopher)

Brown, Rita Mae 1944- ..... CLC 18, 43, 79
See also CA 45-48; CANR 2, 11, 35;
DAM NOV, POP; INT CANR-11;
MTCW

Brown, Roderick (Langmere) Haig-
See Haig-Brown, Roderick (Langmere)

Brown, Rosellen 1939- .... CLC 32
See also CA 77-80; CAAS 10; CANR 14, 44

Brown, Sterling Allen
1901-1989 .... CLC 1, 23, 59; BLC
See also BW 1; CA 85-88; 127; CANR 26;
DAM MULT, POET; DLB 48, 51, 63;
MTCW

Brown, Will
See Ainsworth, William Harrison

Brown, William Wells
1813-1884 .... NCLC 2; BLC; DC 1
See also DAM MULT; DLB 3, 50

Browne, (Clyde) Jackson 1948(?)- ... CLC 21
See also CA 120

Browning, Elizabeth Barrett
1806-1861 ..... NCLC 1, 16; DA; DAB;
DAC; PC 6; WLC
See also CDBLB 1832-1890; DAM MST,
POET; DLB 32

Browning, Robert
1812-1889 .... NCLC 19; DA; DAB;
DAC; PC 2
See also CDBLB 1832-1890; DAM MST,
POET; DLB 32, 163; YABC 1

Browning, Tod 1882-1962 .... CLC 16
See also CA 141; 117

Brownson, Orestes (Augustus)
1803-1876 .... NCLC 50

Bruccoli, Matthew J(oseph) 1931- .. CLC 34
See also CA 9-12R; CANR 7; DLB 103

Bruce, Lenny .... CLC 21
See also Schneider, Leonard Alfred

Bruin, John
See Brutus, Dennis

Brulard, Henri
See Stendhal

Brulls, Christian
See Simenon, Georges (Jacques Christian)

Brunner, John (Kilian Houston)
1934-1995 . . . . **CLC 8, 10**
See also CA 1-4R; 149; CAAS 8; CANR 2,
37; DAM POP; MTCW

Bruno, Giordano 1548-1600 . . . . **LC 27**

Brutus, Dennis 1924- . . . . **CLC 43; BLC**
See also BW 2; CA 49-52; CAAS 14;
CANR 2, 27, 42; DAM MULT, POET;
DLB 117

Bryan, C(ourtlandt) D(ixon) B(arnes)
1936- . . . . **CLC 29**
See also CA 73-76; CANR 13;
INT CANR-13

Bryan, Michael
See Moore, Brian

Bryant, William Cullen
1794-1878 . . . . . **NCLC 6, 46; DA; DAB;**
DAC
See also CDALB 1640-1865; DAM MST,
POET; DLB 3, 43, 59

Bryusov, Valery Yakovlevich
1873-1924 . . . . **TCLC 10**
See also CA 107

Buchan, John 1875-1940 . . . **TCLC 41; DAB**
See also CA 108; 145; DAM POP; DLB 34,
70, 156; YABC 2

Buchanan, George 1506-1582 . . . . **LC 4**

Buchheim, Lothar-Guenther 1918- . . . **CLC 6**
See also CA 85-88

Buchner, (Karl) Georg
1813-1837 . . . . **NCLC 26**

Buchwald, Art(hur) 1925- . . . . **CLC 33**
See also AITN 1; CA 5-8R; CANR 21;
MTCW; SATA 10

Buck, Pearl S(ydenstricker)
1892-1973 . . . . **CLC 7, 11, 18; DA; DAB;**
DAC
See also AITN 1; CA 1-4R; 41-44R;
CANR 1, 34; DAM MST, NOV; DLB 9,
102; MTCW; SATA 1, 25

Buckler, Ernest 1908-1984 . . . . **CLC 13; DAC**
See also CA 11-12; 114; CAP 1;
DAM MST; DLB 68; SATA 47

Buckley, Vincent (Thomas)
1925-1988 . . . . **CLC 57**
See also CA 101

Buckley, William F(rank), Jr.
1925- . . . . **CLC 7, 18, 37**
See also AITN 1; CA 1-4R; CANR 1, 24,
53; DAM POP; DLB 137; DLBY 80;
INT CANR-24; MTCW

Buechner, (Carl) Frederick
1926- . . . . **CLC 2, 4, 6, 9**
See also CA 13-16R; CANR 11, 39;
DAM NOV; DLBY 80; INT CANR-11;
MTCW

Buell, John (Edward) 1927- . . . . **CLC 10**
See also CA 1-4R; DLB 53

Buero Vallejo, Antonio 1916- . . . **CLC 15, 46**
See also CA 106; CANR 24, 49; HW;
MTCW

Bufalino, Gesualdo 1920(?)- . . . . **CLC 74**

Bugayev, Boris Nikolayevich 1880-1934
See Bely, Andrey
See also CA 104

Bukowski, Charles
1920-1994 . . . . **CLC 2, 5, 9, 41, 82**
See also CA 17-20R; 144; CANR 40;
DAM NOV, POET; DLB 5, 130; MTCW

Bulgakov, Mikhail (Afanas'evich)
1891-1940 . . . . **TCLC 2, 16; SSC 18**
See also CA 105; DAM DRAM, NOV

Bulgya, Alexander Alexandrovich
1901-1956 . . . . **TCLC 53**
See also Fadeyev, Alexander
See also CA 117

Bullins, Ed 1935- . . **CLC 1, 5, 7; BLC; DC 6**
See also BW 2; CA 49-52; CAAS 16;
CANR 24, 46; DAM DRAM, MULT;
DLB 7, 38; MTCW

Bulwer-Lytton, Edward (George Earle Lytton)
1803-1873 . . . . **NCLC 1, 45**
See also DLB 21

Bunin, Ivan Alexeyevich
1870-1953 . . . . **TCLC 6; SSC 5**
See also CA 104

Bunting, Basil 1900-1985 . . . . **CLC 10, 39, 47**
See also CA 53-56; 115; CANR 7;
DAM POET; DLB 20

Bunuel, Luis 1900-1983 . . **CLC 16, 80; HLC**
See also CA 101; 110; CANR 32;
DAM MULT; HW

Bunyan, John
1628-1688 . . . . . . **LC 4; DA; DAB; DAC;**
WLC
See also CDBLB 1660-1789; DAM MST;
DLB 39

Burckhardt, Jacob (Christoph)
1818-1897 . . . . **NCLC 49**

Burford, Eleanor
See Hibbert, Eleanor Alice Burford

Burgess, Anthony
CLC 1, 2, 4, 5, 8, 10, 13, 15, 22, 40, 62,
81, 94; DAB
See also Wilson, John (Anthony) Burgess
See also AITN 1; CDBLB 1960 to Present;
DLB 14

Burke, Edmund
1729(?)-1797 . . . . **LC 7; DA; DAB; DAC;**
WLC
See also DAM MST; DLB 104

Burke, Kenneth (Duva)
1897-1993 . . . . **CLC 2, 24**
See also CA 5-8R; 143; CANR 39; DLB 45,
63; MTCW

Burke, Leda
See Garnett, David

Burke, Ralph
See Silverberg, Robert

Burke, Thomas 1886-1945 . . . . **TCLC 63**
See also CA 113

Burney, Fanny 1752-1840 . . . . **NCLC 12, 54**
See also DLB 39

Burns, Robert 1759-1796 . . . . **PC 6**
See also CDBLB 1789-1832; DA; DAB;
DAC; DAM MST, POET; DLB 109;
WLC

Burns, Tex
See L'Amour, Louis (Dearborn)

Burnshaw, Stanley 1906- . . . . . **CLC 3, 13, 44**
See also CA 9-12R; DLB 48

Burr, Anne 1937- . . . . **CLC 6**
See also CA 25-28R

Burroughs, Edgar Rice
1875-1950 . . . . **TCLC 2, 32**
See also AAYA 11; CA 104; 132;
DAM NOV; DLB 8; MTCW; SATA 41

Burroughs, William S(eward)
1914- . . . . **CLC 1, 2, 5, 15, 22, 42, 75;**
DA; DAB; DAC; WLC
See also AITN 2; CA 9-12R; CANR 20, 52;
DAM MST, NOV, POP; DLB 2, 8, 16,
152; DLBY 81; MTCW

Burton, Richard F. 1821-1890 . . . . **NCLC 42**
See also DLB 55

Busch, Frederick 1941- . . . **CLC 7, 10, 18, 47**
See also CA 33-36R; CAAS 1; CANR 45;
DLB 6

Bush, Ronald 1946- . . . . **CLC 34**
See also CA 136

Bustos, F(rancisco)
See Borges, Jorge Luis

Bustos Domecq, H(onorio)
See Bioy Casares, Adolfo; Borges, Jorge
Luis

Butler, Octavia E(stelle) 1947- . . . . . **CLC 38**
See also AAYA 18; BW 2; CA 73-76;
CANR 12, 24, 38; DAM MULT, POP;
DLB 33; MTCW; SATA 84

Butler, Robert Olen (Jr.) 1945- . . . . . **CLC 81**
See also CA 112; DAM POP; INT 112

Butler, Samuel 1612-1680 . . . . **LC 16**
See also DLB 101, 126

Butler, Samuel
1835-1902 . . . . . . **TCLC 1, 33; DA; DAB;**
DAC; WLC
See also CA 143; CDBLB 1890-1914;
DAM MST, NOV; DLB 18, 57

Butler, Walter C.
See Faust, Frederick (Schiller)

Butor, Michel (Marie Francois)
1926- . . . . **CLC 1, 3, 8, 11, 15**
See also CA 9-12R; CANR 33; DLB 83;
MTCW

Buzo, Alexander (John) 1944- . . . . . . **CLC 61**
See also CA 97-100; CANR 17, 39

Buzzati, Dino 1906-1972 . . . . **CLC 36**
See also CA 33-36R

Byars, Betsy (Cromer) 1928- . . . . **CLC 35**
See also CA 33-36R; CANR 18, 36; CLR 1,
16; DLB 52; INT CANR-18; JRDA;
MAICYA; MTCW; SAAS 1; SATA 4,
46, 80

Byatt, A(ntonia) S(usan Drabble)
1936- . . . . **CLC 19, 65**
See also CA 13-16R; CANR 13, 33, 50;
DAM NOV, POP; DLB 14; MTCW

Byrne, David 1952- . . . . **CLC 26**
See also CA 127

Byrne, John Keyes 1926-
See Leonard, Hugh
See also CA 102; INT 102

Byron, George Gordon (Noel)
1788-1824 ..... **NCLC 2, 12; DA; DAB;**
DAC; PC 16; WLC
See also CDBLB 1789-1832; DAM MST,
POET; DLB 96, 110

C. 3. 3.
See Wilde, Oscar (Fingal O'Flahertie Wills)

Caballero, Fernan 1796-1877..... **NCLC 10**

Cabell, James Branch 1879-1958 ... **TCLC 6**
See also CA 105; DLB 9, 78

Cable, George Washington
1844-1925 .... **TCLC 4; SSC 4**
See also CA 104; DLB 12, 74; DLBD 13

Cabral de Melo Neto, Joao 1920-... **CLC 76**
See also CA 151; DAM MULT

Cabrera Infante, G(uillermo)
1929- .... **CLC 5, 25, 45; HLC**
See also CA 85-88; CANR 29;
DAM MULT; DLB 113; HW; MTCW

Cade, Toni
See Bambara, Toni Cade

Cadmus and Harmonia
See Buchan, John

Caedmon fl. 658-680............. **CMLC 7**
See also DLB 146

Caeiro, Alberto
See Pessoa, Fernando (Antonio Nogueira)

Cage, John (Milton, Jr.) 1912- ..... **CLC 41**
See also CA 13-16R; CANR 9;
INT CANR-9

Cain, G.
See Cabrera Infante, G(uillermo)

Cain, Guillermo
See Cabrera Infante, G(uillermo)

Cain, James M(allahan)
1892-1977 .... **CLC 3, 11, 28**
See also AITN 1; CA 17-20R; 73-76;
CANR 8, 34; MTCW

Caine, Mark
See Raphael, Frederic (Michael)

Calasso, Roberto 1941- .... **CLC 81**
See also CA 143

Calderon de la Barca, Pedro
1600-1681 .... **LC 23; DC 3**

Caldwell, Erskine (Preston)
1903-1987 .... **CLC 1, 8, 14, 50, 60;**
SSC 19
See also AITN 1; CA 1-4R; 121; CAAS 1;
CANR 2, 33; DAM NOV; DLB 9, 86;
MTCW

Caldwell, (Janet Miriam) Taylor (Holland)
1900-1985 .... **CLC 2, 28, 39**
See also CA 5-8R; 116; CANR 5;
DAM NOV, POP

Calhoun, John Caldwell
1782-1850 .... **NCLC 15**
See also DLB 3

Calisher, Hortense
1911- .... **CLC 2, 4, 8, 38; SSC 15**
See also CA 1-4R; CANR 1, 22;
DAM NOV; DLB 2; INT CANR-22;
MTCW

Callaghan, Morley Edward
1903-1990 ..... **CLC 3, 14, 41, 65; DAC**
See also CA 9-12R; 132; CANR 33;
DAM MST; DLB 68; MTCW

Callimachus
c. 305B.C.-c. 240B.C......... **CMLC 18**

Calvino, Italo
1923-1985 ..... **CLC 5, 8, 11, 22, 33, 39,**
73; SSC 3
See also CA 85-88; 116; CANR 23;
DAM NOV; MTCW

Cameron, Carey 1952- .... **CLC 59**
See also CA 135

Cameron, Peter 1959-............. **CLC 44**
See also CA 125; CANR 50

Campana, Dino 1885-1932........ **TCLC 20**
See also CA 117; DLB 114

Campanella, Tommaso 1568-1639.... **LC 32**

Campbell, John W(ood, Jr.)
1910-1971 .... **CLC 32**
See also CA 21-22; 29-32R; CANR 34;
CAP 2; DLB 8; MTCW

Campbell, Joseph 1904-1987 .... **CLC 69**
See also AAYA 3; BEST 89:2; CA 1-4R;
124; CANR 3, 28; MTCW

Campbell, Maria 1940-....... **CLC 85; DAC**
See also CA 102; NNAL

Campbell, (John) Ramsey
1946- .... **CLC 42; SSC 19**
See also CA 57-60; CANR 7; INT CANR-7

Campbell, (Ignatius) Roy (Dunnachie)
1901-1957 .... **TCLC 5**
See also CA 104; DLB 20

Campbell, Thomas 1777-1844 .... **NCLC 19**
See also DLB 93; 144

Campbell, Wilfred................ **TCLC 9**
See also Campbell, William

Campbell, William 1858(?)-1918
See Campbell, Wilfred
See also CA 106; DLB 92

Campion, Jane................... **CLC 95**
See also CA 138

Campos, Alvaro de
See Pessoa, Fernando (Antonio Nogueira)

Camus, Albert
1913-1960 .... **CLC 1, 2, 4, 9, 11, 14, 32,**
63, 69; DA; DAB; DAC; DC 2; SSC 9;
WLC
See also CA 89-92; DAM DRAM, MST,
NOV; DLB 72; MTCW

Canby, Vincent 1924-............. **CLC 13**
See also CA 81-84

Cancale
See Desnos, Robert

Canetti, Elias
1905-1994 .... **CLC 3, 14, 25, 75, 86**
See also CA 21-24R; 146; CANR 23;
DLB 85, 124; MTCW

Canin, Ethan 1960-............... **CLC 55**
See also CA 131; 135

Cannon, Curt
See Hunter, Evan

Cape, Judith
See Page, P(atricia) K(athleen)

Capek, Karel
1890-1938 ...... **TCLC 6, 37; DA; DAB;**
DAC; DC 1; WLC
See also CA 104; 140; DAM DRAM, MST,
NOV

Capote, Truman
1924-1984 ...... **CLC 1, 3, 8, 13, 19, 34,**
38, 58; DA; DAB; DAC; SSC 2; WLC
See also CA 5-8R; 113; CANR 18;
CDALB 1941-1968; DAM MST, NOV,
POP; DLB 2; DLBY 80, 84; MTCW

Capra, Frank 1897-1991........... **CLC 16**
See also CA 61-64; 135

Caputo, Philip 1941-............. **CLC 32**
See also CA 73-76; CANR 40

Card, Orson Scott 1951- .... **CLC 44, 47, 50**
See also AAYA 11; CA 102; CANR 27, 47;
DAM POP; INT CANR-27; MTCW;
SATA 83

Cardenal, Ernesto 1925-..... **CLC 31; HLC**
See also CA 49-52; CANR 2, 32;
DAM MULT, POET; HW; MTCW

Cardozo, Benjamin N(athan)
1870-1938 .... **TCLC 65**
See also CA 117

Carducci, Giosue 1835-1907...... **TCLC 32**

Carew, Thomas 1595(?)-1640....... **LC 13**
See also DLB 126

Carey, Ernestine Gilbreth 1908-.... **CLC 17**
See also CA 5-8R; SATA 2

Carey, Peter 1943-............ **CLC 40, 55**
See also CA 123; 127; CANR 53; INT 127;
MTCW

Carleton, William 1794-1869...... **NCLC 3**
See also DLB 159

Carlisle, Henry (Coffin) 1926-...... **CLC 33**
See also CA 13-16R; CANR 15

Carlsen, Chris
See Holdstock, Robert P.

Carlson, Ron(ald F.) 1947-........ **CLC 54**
See also CA 105; CANR 27

Carlyle, Thomas
1795-1881 .. **NCLC 22; DA; DAB; DAC**
See also CDBLB 1789-1832; DAM MST;
DLB 55; 144

Carman, (William) Bliss
1861-1929 .... **TCLC 7; DAC**
See also CA 104; DLB 92

Carnegie, Dale 1888-1955 .... **TCLC 53**

Carossa, Hans 1878-1956........ **TCLC 48**
See also DLB 66

Carpenter, Don(ald Richard)
1931-1995 .... **CLC 41**
See also CA 45-48; 149; CANR 1

Carpentier (y Valmont), Alejo
1904-1980 .... **CLC 8, 11, 38; HLC**
See also CA 65-68; 97-100; CANR 11;
DAM MULT; DLB 113; HW

Carr, Caleb 1955(?)-.............. **CLC 86**
See also CA 147

Carr, Emily 1871-1945.......... **TCLC 32**
See also DLB 68

Carr, John Dickson 1906-1977 ...... **CLC 3**
See also CA 49-52; 69-72; CANR 3, 33;
MTCW

Carr, Philippa
See Hibbert, Eleanor Alice Burford

Carr, Virginia Spencer 1929- ...... **CLC 34**
See also CA 61-64; DLB 111

Carrere, Emmanuel 1957- .... **CLC 89**

Carrier, Roch 1937- ..... **CLC 13, 78; DAC**
See also CA 130; DAM MST; DLB 53

Carroll, James P. 1943(?)- .... **CLC 38**
See also CA 81-84

Carroll, Jim 1951- .... **CLC 35**
See also AAYA 17; CA 45-48; CANR 42

Carroll, Lewis .... **NCLC 2, 53; WLC**
See also Dodgson, Charles Lutwidge
See also CDBLB 1832-1890; CLR 2, 18;
DLB 18, 163; JRDA

Carroll, Paul Vincent 1900-1968.... **CLC 10**
See also CA 9-12R; 25-28R; DLB 10

Carruth, Hayden
1921- ...... **CLC 4, 7, 10, 18, 84; PC 10**
See also CA 9-12R; CANR 4, 38; DLB 5,
165; INT CANR-4; MTCW; SATA 47

Carson, Rachel Louise 1907-1964... **CLC 71**
See also CA 77-80; CANR 35; DAM POP;
MTCW; SATA 23

Carter, Angela (Olive)
1940-1992 ...... **CLC 5, 41, 76; SSC 13**
See also CA 53-56; 136; CANR 12, 36;
DLB 14; MTCW; SATA 66;
SATA-Obit 70

Carter, Nick
See Smith, Martin Cruz

Carver, Raymond
1938-1988 ... **CLC 22, 36, 53, 55; SSC 8**
See also CA 33-36R; 126; CANR 17, 34;
DAM NOV; DLB 130; DLBY 84, 88;
MTCW

Cary, Elizabeth, Lady Falkland
1585-1639 .... **LC 30**

Cary, (Arthur) Joyce (Lunel)
1888-1957 .... **TCLC 1, 29**
See also CA 104; CDBLB 1914-1945;
DLB 15, 100

Casanova de Seingalt, Giovanni Jacopo
1725-1798 .... **LC 13**

Casares, Adolfo Bioy
See Bioy Casares, Adolfo

Casely-Hayford, J(oseph) E(phraim)
1866-1930 .... **TCLC 24; BLC**
See also BW 2; CA 123; DAM MULT

Casey, John (Dudley) 1939- .... **CLC 59**
See also BEST 90:2; CA 69-72; CANR 23

Casey, Michael 1947- .... **CLC 2**
See also CA 65-68; DLB 5

Casey, Patrick
See Thurman, Wallace (Henry)

Casey, Warren (Peter) 1935-1988 ... **CLC 12**
See also CA 101; 127; INT 101

Casona, Alejandro .... **CLC 49**
See also Alvarez, Alejandro Rodriguez

Cassavetes, John 1929-1989 .... **CLC 20**
See also CA 85-88; 127

Cassill, R(onald) V(erlin) 1919- . **CLC 4, 23**
See also CA 9-12R; CAAS 1; CANR 7, 45;
DLB 6

Cassirer, Ernst 1874-1945 .... **TCLC 61**

Cassity, (Allen) Turner 1929- .... **CLC 6, 42**
See also CA 17-20R; CAAS 8; CANR 11;
DLB 105

Castaneda, Carlos 1931(?)- .... **CLC 12**
See also CA 25-28R; CANR 32; HW;
MTCW

Castedo, Elena 1937- .... **CLC 65**
See also CA 132

Castedo-Ellerman, Elena
See Castedo, Elena

Castellanos, Rosario
1925-1974 .... **CLC 66; HLC**
See also CA 131; 53-56; DAM MULT;
DLB 113; HW

Castelvetro, Lodovico 1505-1571..... **LC 12**

Castiglione, Baldassare 1478-1529 ... **LC 12**

Castle, Robert
See Hamilton, Edmond

Castro, Guillen de 1569-1631........ **LC 19**

Castro, Rosalia de 1837-1885 ..... **NCLC 3**
See also DAM MULT

Cather, Willa
See Cather, Willa Sibert

Cather, Willa Sibert
1873-1947 .... **TCLC 1, 11, 31; DA;
DAB; DAC; SSC 2; WLC**
See also CA 104; 128; CDALB 1865-1917;
DAM MST, NOV; DLB 9, 54, 78;
DLBD 1; MTCW; SATA 30

Catton, (Charles) Bruce
1899-1978 .... **CLC 35**
See also AITN 1; CA 5-8R; 81-84;
CANR 7; DLB 17; SATA 2;
SATA-Obit 24

Catullus c. 84B.C.-c. 54B.C. ..... **CMLC 18**

Cauldwell, Frank
See King, Francis (Henry)

Caunitz, William J. 1933- .... **CLC 34**
See also BEST 89:3; CA 125; 130; INT 130

Causley, Charles (Stanley) 1917- ..... **CLC 7**
See also CA 9-12R; CANR 5, 35; CLR 30;
DLB 27; MTCW; SATA 3, 66

Caute, David 1936- .... **CLC 29**
See also CA 1-4R; CAAS 4; CANR 1, 33;
DAM NOV; DLB 14

Cavafy, C(onstantine) P(eter)
1863-1933 .... **TCLC 2, 7**
See also Kavafis, Konstantinos Petrou
See also CA 148; DAM POET

Cavallo, Evelyn
See Spark, Muriel (Sarah)

Cavanna, Betty .... **CLC 12**
See also Harrison, Elizabeth Cavanna
See also JRDA; MAICYA; SAAS 4;
SATA 1, 30

Cavendish, Margaret Lucas
1623-1673 .... **LC 30**
See also DLB 131

Caxton, William 1421(?)-1491(?)..... **LC 17**

Cayrol, Jean 1911- .... **CLC 11**
See also CA 89-92; DLB 83

Cela, Camilo Jose
1916- .... **CLC 4, 13, 59; HLC**
See also BEST 90:2; CA 21-24R; CAAS 10;
CANR 21, 32; DAM MULT; DLBY 89;
HW; MTCW

Celan, Paul ...... **CLC 10, 19, 53, 82; PC 10**
See also Antschel, Paul
See also DLB 69

Celine, Louis-Ferdinand
.... **CLC 1, 3, 4, 7, 9, 15, 47**
See also Destouches, Louis-Ferdinand
See also DLB 72

Cellini, Benvenuto 1500-1571 .... **LC 7**

Cendrars, Blaise .... **CLC 18**
See also Sauser-Hall, Frederic

Cernuda (y Bidon), Luis
1902-1963 .... **CLC 54**
See also CA 131; 89-92; DAM POET;
DLB 134; HW

Cervantes (Saavedra), Miguel de
1547-1616 .... **LC 6, 23; DA; DAB;
DAC; SSC 12; WLC**
See also DAM MST, NOV

Cesaire, Aime (Fernand)
1913- .... **CLC 19, 32; BLC**
See also BW 2; CA 65-68; CANR 24, 43;
DAM MULT, POET; MTCW

Chabon, Michael 1965(?)- .... **CLC 55**
See also CA 139

Chabrol, Claude 1930- .... **CLC 16**
See also CA 110

Challans, Mary 1905-1983
See Renault, Mary
See also CA 81-84; 111; SATA 23;
SATA-Obit 36

Challis, George
See Faust, Frederick (Schiller)

Chambers, Aidan 1934- .... **CLC 35**
See also CA 25-28R; CANR 12, 31; JRDA;
MAICYA; SAAS 12; SATA 1, 69

Chambers, James 1948-
See Cliff, Jimmy
See also CA 124

Chambers, Jessie
See Lawrence, D(avid) H(erbert Richards)

Chambers, Robert W. 1865-1933... **TCLC 41**

Chandler, Raymond (Thornton)
1888-1959 .... **TCLC 1, 7; SSC 23**
See also CA 104; 129; CDALB 1929-1941;
DLBD 6; MTCW

Chang, Jung 1952- .... **CLC 71**
See also CA 142

Channing, William Ellery
1780-1842 .... **NCLC 17**
See also DLB 1, 59

Chaplin, Charles Spencer
1889-1977 .... **CLC 16**
See also Chaplin, Charlie
See also CA 81-84; 73-76

Chaplin, Charlie
See Chaplin, Charles Spencer
See also DLB 44

Chapman, George 1559(?)-1634...... **LC 22**
See also DAM DRAM; DLB 62, 121

Chapman, Graham 1941-1989 . . . . . . CLC 21
See also Monty Python
See also CA 116; 129; CANR 35

Chapman, John Jay 1862-1933 . . . . . TCLC 7
See also CA 104

Chapman, Lee
See Bradley, Marion Zimmer

Chapman, Walker
See Silverberg, Robert

Chappell, Fred (Davis) 1936- . . . . CLC 40, 78
See also CA 5-8R; CAAS 4; CANR 8, 33;
DLB 6, 105

Char, Rene(-Emile)
1907-1988 . . . . CLC 9, 11, 14, 55
See also CA 13-16R; 124; CANR 32;
DAM POET; MTCW

Charby, Jay
See Ellison, Harlan (Jay)

Chardin, Pierre Teilhard de
See Teilhard de Chardin, (Marie Joseph)
Pierre

Charles I 1600-1649 . . . . LC 13

Charyn, Jerome 1937- . . . . CLC 5, 8, 18
See also CA 5-8R; CAAS 1; CANR 7;
DLBY 83; MTCW

Chase, Mary (Coyle) 1907-1981 . . . . . . DC 1
See also CA 77-80; 105; SATA 17;
SATA-Obit 29

Chase, Mary Ellen 1887-1973 . . . . CLC 2
See also CA 13-16; 41-44R; CAP 1;
SATA 10

Chase, Nicholas
See Hyde, Anthony

Chateaubriand, Francois Rene de
1768-1848 . . . . NCLC 3
See also DLB 119

Chatterje, Sarat Chandra 1876-1936(?)
See Chatterji, Saratchandra
See also CA 109

Chatterji, Bankim Chandra
1838-1894 . . . . NCLC 19

Chatterji, Saratchandra . . . . TCLC 13
See also Chatterje, Sarat Chandra

Chatterton, Thomas 1752-1770 . . . . LC 3
See also DAM POET; DLB 109

Chatwin, (Charles) Bruce
1940-1989 . . . . CLC 28, 57, 59
See also AAYA 4; BEST 90:1; CA 85-88;
127; DAM POP

Chaucer, Daniel
See Ford, Ford Madox

Chaucer, Geoffrey
1340(?)-1400 . . . LC 17; DA; DAB; DAC
See also CDBLB Before 1660; DAM MST,
POET; DLB 146

Chaviaras, Strates 1935-
See Haviaras, Stratis
See also CA 105

Chayefsky, Paddy . . . . CLC 23
See also Chayefsky, Sidney
See also DLB 7, 44; DLBY 81

Chayefsky, Sidney 1923-1981
See Chayefsky, Paddy
See also CA 9-12R; 104; CANR 18;
DAM DRAM

Chedid, Andree 1920- . . . . CLC 47
See also CA 145

Cheever, John
1912-1982 . . . . . . CLC 3, 7, 8, 11, 15, 25,
64; DA; DAB; DAC; SSC 1; WLC
See also CA 5-8R; 106; CABS 1; CANR 5,
27; CDALB 1941-1968; DAM MST,
NOV, POP; DLB 2, 102; DLBY 80, 82;
INT CANR-5; MTCW

Cheever, Susan 1943- . . . . CLC 18, 48
See also CA 103; CANR 27, 51; DLBY 82;
INT CANR-27

Chekhonte, Antosha
See Chekhov, Anton (Pavlovich)

Chekhov, Anton (Pavlovich)
1860-1904 . . . . . TCLC 3, 10, 31, 55; DA;
DAB; DAC; SSC 2; WLC
See also CA 104; 124; DAM DRAM, MST

Chernyshevsky, Nikolay Gavrilovich
1828-1889 . . . . NCLC 1

Cherry, Carolyn Janice 1942-
See Cherryh, C. J.
See also CA 65-68; CANR 10

Cherryh, C. J. . . . . CLC 35
See also Cherry, Carolyn Janice
See also DLBY 80

Chesnutt, Charles W(addell)
1858-1932 . . . . TCLC 5, 39; BLC; SSC 7
See also BW 1; CA 106; 125; DAM MULT;
DLB 12, 50, 78; MTCW

Chester, Alfred 1929(?)-1971 . . . . CLC 49
See also CA 33-36R; DLB 130

Chesterton, G(ilbert) K(eith)
1874-1936 . . . . TCLC 1, 6, 64; SSC 1
See also CA 104; 132; CDBLB 1914-1945;
DAM NOV, POET; DLB 10, 19, 34, 70,
98, 149; MTCW; SATA 27

Chiang Pin-chin 1904-1986
See Ding Ling
See also CA 118

Ch'ien Chung-shu 1910- . . . . CLC 22
See also CA 130; MTCW

Child, L. Maria
See Child, Lydia Maria

Child, Lydia Maria 1802-1880 . . . . NCLC 6
See also DLB 1, 74; SATA 67

Child, Mrs.
See Child, Lydia Maria

Child, Philip 1898-1978 . . . . CLC 19, 68
See also CA 13-14; CAP 1; SATA 47

Childers, (Robert) Erskine
1870-1922 . . . . TCLC 65
See also CA 113; DLB 70

Childress, Alice
1920-1994 . . CLC 12, 15, 86; BLC; DC 4
See also AAYA 8; BW 2; CA 45-48; 146;
CANR 3, 27, 50; CLR 14; DAM DRAM,
MULT, NOV; DLB 7, 38; JRDA;
MAICYA; MTCW; SATA 7, 48, 81

Chislett, (Margaret) Anne 1943- . . . . CLC 34
See also CA 151

Chitty, Thomas Willes 1926- . . . . CLC 11
See also Hinde, Thomas
See also CA 5-8R

Chivers, Thomas Holley
1809-1858 . . . . NCLC 49
See also DLB 3

Chomette, Rene Lucien 1898-1981
See Clair, Rene
See also CA 103

Chopin, Kate
. . . . TCLC 5, 14; DA; DAB; SSC 8
See also Chopin, Katherine
See also CDALB 1865-1917; DLB 12, 78

Chopin, Katherine 1851-1904
See Chopin, Kate
See also CA 104; 122; DAC; DAM MST,
NOV

Chretien de Troyes
c. 12th cent. - . . . . CMLC 10

Christie
See Ichikawa, Kon

Christie, Agatha (Mary Clarissa)
1890-1976 . . . . . . CLC 1, 6, 8, 12, 39, 48;
DAB; DAC
See also AAYA 9; AITN 1, 2; CA 17-20R;
61-64; CANR 10, 37; CDBLB 1914-1945;
DAM NOV; DLB 13, 77; MTCW;
SATA 36

Christie, (Ann) Philippa
See Pearce, Philippa
See also CA 5-8R; CANR 4

Christine de Pizan 1365(?)-1431(?) . . . . LC 9

Chubb, Elmer
See Masters, Edgar Lee

Chulkov, Mikhail Dmitrievich
1743-1792 . . . . LC 2
See also DLB 150

Churchill, Caryl 1938- . . . CLC 31, 55; DC 5
See also CA 102; CANR 22, 46; DLB 13;
MTCW

Churchill, Charles 1731-1764 . . . . LC 3
See also DLB 109

Chute, Carolyn 1947- . . . . CLC 39
See also CA 123

Ciardi, John (Anthony)
1916-1986 . . . . CLC 10, 40, 44
See also CA 5-8R; 118; CAAS 2; CANR 5,
33; CLR 19; DAM POET; DLB 5;
DLBY 86; INT CANR-5; MAICYA;
MTCW; SATA 1, 65; SATA-Obit 46

Cicero, Marcus Tullius
106B.C.-43B.C. . . . . CMLC 3

Cimino, Michael 1943- . . . . CLC 16
See also CA 105

Cioran, E(mil) M. 1911-1995 . . . . CLC 64
See also CA 25-28R; 149

Cisneros, Sandra 1954- . . . . . . CLC 69; HLC
See also AAYA 9; CA 131; DAM MULT;
DLB 122, 152; HW

Cixous, Helene 1937- . . . . CLC 92
See also CA 126; DLB 83; MTCW

Clair, Rene . . . . CLC 20
See also Chomette, Rene Lucien

Clampitt, Amy 1920-1994 . . . . CLC 32
See also CA 110; 146; CANR 29; DLB 105

Clancy, Thomas L., Jr. 1947-
See Clancy, Tom
See also CA 125; 131; INT 131; MTCW

Clancy, Tom. . . . . **CLC 45**
See also Clancy, Thomas L., Jr.
See also AAYA 9; BEST 89:1, 90:1;
DAM NOV, POP

Clare, John 1793-1864 . . . . . . **NCLC 9; DAB**
See also DAM POET; DLB 55, 96

Clarin
See Alas (y Urena), Leopoldo (Enrique
Garcia)

Clark, Al C.
See Goines, Donald

Clark, (Robert) Brian 1932- . . . . **CLC 29**
See also CA 41-44R

Clark, Curt
See Westlake, Donald E(dwin)

Clark, Eleanor 1913-1996 . . . . **CLC 5, 19**
See also CA 9-12R; 151; CANR 41; DLB 6

Clark, J. P.
See Clark, John Pepper
See also DLB 117

Clark, John Pepper
1935- . . . . **CLC 38; BLC; DC 5**
See also Clark, J. P.
See also BW 1; CA 65-68; CANR 16;
DAM DRAM, MULT

Clark, M. R.
See Clark, Mavis Thorpe

Clark, Mavis Thorpe 1909- . . . . **CLC 12**
See also CA 57-60; CANR 8, 37; CLR 30;
MAICYA; SAAS 5; SATA 8, 74

Clark, Walter Van Tilburg
1909-1971 . . . . **CLC 28**
See also CA 9-12R; 33-36R; DLB 9;
SATA 8

Clarke, Arthur C(harles)
1917- . . . . . . **CLC 1, 4, 13, 18, 35; SSC 3**
See also AAYA 4; CA 1-4R; CANR 2, 28;
DAM POP; JRDA; MAICYA; MTCW;
SATA 13, 70

Clarke, Austin 1896-1974. . . . . **CLC 6, 9**
See also CA 29-32; 49-52; CAP 2;
DAM POET; DLB 10, 20

Clarke, Austin C(hesterfield)
1934- . . . . **CLC 8, 53; BLC; DAC**
See also BW 1; CA 25-28R; CAAS 16;
CANR 14, 32; DAM MULT; DLB 53,
125

Clarke, Gillian 1937- . . . . **CLC 61**
See also CA 106; DLB 40

Clarke, Marcus (Andrew Hislop)
1846-1881 . . . . **NCLC 19**

Clarke, Shirley 1925- . . . . **CLC 16**

Clash, The
See Headon, (Nicky) Topper; Jones, Mick;
Simonon, Paul; Strummer, Joe

Claudel, Paul (Louis Charles Marie)
1868-1955 . . . . **TCLC 2, 10**
See also CA 104

Clavell, James (duMaresq)
1925-1994 . . . . **CLC 6, 25, 87**
See also CA 25-28R; 146; CANR 26, 48;
DAM NOV, POP; MTCW

Cleaver, (Leroy) Eldridge
1935- . . . . **CLC 30; BLC**
See also BW 1; CA 21-24R; CANR 16;
DAM MULT

Cleese, John (Marwood) 1939- . . . . . **CLC 21**
See also Monty Python
See also CA 112; 116; CANR 35; MTCW

Cleishbotham, Jebediah
See Scott, Walter

Cleland, John 1710-1789 . . . . **LC 2**
See also DLB 39

Clemens, Samuel Langhorne 1835-1910
See Twain, Mark
See also CA 104; 135; CDALB 1865-1917;
DA; DAB; DAC; DAM MST, NOV;
DLB 11, 12, 23, 64, 74; JRDA;
MAICYA; YABC 2

Cleophil
See Congreve, William

Clerihew, E.
See Bentley, E(dmund) C(lerihew)

Clerk, N. W.
See Lewis, C(live) S(taples)

Cliff, Jimmy. . . . . **CLC 21**
See also Chambers, James

Clifton, (Thelma) Lucille
1936- . . . . **CLC 19, 66; BLC**
See also BW 2; CA 49-52; CANR 2, 24, 42;
CLR 5; DAM MULT, POET; DLB 5, 41;
MAICYA; MTCW; SATA 20, 69

Clinton, Dirk
See Silverberg, Robert

Clough, Arthur Hugh 1819-1861. . **NCLC 27**
See also DLB 32

Clutha, Janet Paterson Frame 1924-
See Frame, Janet
See also CA 1-4R; CANR 2, 36; MTCW

Clyne, Terence
See Blatty, William Peter

Cobalt, Martin
See Mayne, William (James Carter)

Cobbett, William 1763-1835 . . . . . **NCLC 49**
See also DLB 43, 107, 158

Coburn, D(onald) L(ee) 1938- . . . . . . **CLC 10**
See also CA 89-92

Cocteau, Jean (Maurice Eugene Clement)
1889-1963 . . . . **CLC 1, 8, 15, 16, 43; DA;
DAB; DAC; WLC**
See also CA 25-28; CANR 40; CAP 2;
DAM DRAM, MST, NOV; DLB 65;
MTCW

Codrescu, Andrei 1946- . . . . **CLC 46**
See also CA 33-36R; CAAS 19; CANR 13,
34, 53; DAM POET

Coe, Max
See Bourne, Randolph S(illiman)

Coe, Tucker
See Westlake, Donald E(dwin)

Coetzee, J(ohn) M(ichael)
1940- . . . . **CLC 23, 33, 66**
See also CA 77-80; CANR 41; DAM NOV;
MTCW

Coffey, Brian
See Koontz, Dean R(ay)

Cohan, George M. 1878-1942 . . . . . **TCLC 60**

Cohen, Arthur A(llen)
1928-1986 . . . . **CLC 7, 31**
See also CA 1-4R; 120; CANR 1, 17, 42;
DLB 28

Cohen, Leonard (Norman)
1934- . . . . **CLC 3, 38; DAC**
See also CA 21-24R; CANR 14;
DAM MST; DLB 53; MTCW

Cohen, Matt 1942- . . . . **CLC 19; DAC**
See also CA 61-64; CAAS 18; CANR 40;
DLB 53

Cohen-Solal, Annie 19(?)- . . . . **CLC 50**

Colegate, Isabel 1931- . . . . **CLC 36**
See also CA 17-20R; CANR 8, 22; DLB 14;
INT CANR-22; MTCW

Coleman, Emmett
See Reed, Ishmael

Coleridge, Samuel Taylor
1772-1834 . . . . . **NCLC 9, 54; DA; DAB;
DAC; PC 11; WLC**
See also CDBLB 1789-1832; DAM MST,
POET; DLB 93, 107

Coleridge, Sara 1802-1852 . . . . **NCLC 31**

Coles, Don 1928- . . . . **CLC 46**
See also CA 115; CANR 38

Colette, (Sidonie-Gabrielle)
1873-1954 . . . . . . **TCLC 1, 5, 16; SSC 10**
See also CA 104; 131; DAM NOV; DLB 65;
MTCW

Collett, (Jacobine) Camilla (Wergeland)
1813-1895 . . . . **NCLC 22**

Collier, Christopher 1930- . . . . **CLC 30**
See also AAYA 13; CA 33-36R; CANR 13,
33; JRDA; MAICYA; SATA 16, 70

Collier, James L(incoln) 1928- . . . . . **CLC 30**
See also AAYA 13; CA 9-12R; CANR 4,
33; CLR 3; DAM POP; JRDA;
MAICYA; SAAS 21; SATA 8, 70

Collier, Jeremy 1650-1726. . . . . **LC 6**

Collier, John 1901-1980. . . . . **SSC 19**
See also CA 65-68; 97-100; CANR 10;
DLB 77

Collins, Hunt
See Hunter, Evan

Collins, Linda 1931- . . . . **CLC 44**
See also CA 125

Collins, (William) Wilkie
1824-1889 . . . . **NCLC 1, 18**
See also CDBLB 1832-1890; DLB 18, 70,
159

Collins, William 1721-1759 . . . . **LC 4**
See also DAM POET; DLB 109

Collodi, Carlo 1826-1890 . . . . **NCLC 54**
See also Lorenzini, Carlo
See also CLR 5

Colman, George
See Glassco, John

Colt, Winchester Remington
See Hubbard, L(afayette) Ron(ald)

Colter, Cyrus 1910- . . . . **CLC 58**
See also BW 1; CA 65-68; CANR 10;
DLB 33

Colton, James
See Hansen, Joseph

Colum, Padraic 1881-1972......... **CLC 28**
See also CA 73-76; 33-36R; CANR 35;
CLR 36; MAICYA; MTCW; SATA 15

Colvin, James
See Moorcock, Michael (John)

Colwin, Laurie (E.)
1944-1992 .... **CLC 5, 13, 23, 84**
See also CA 89-92; 139; CANR 20, 46;
DLBY 80; MTCW

Comfort, Alex(ander) 1920-......... **CLC 7**
See also CA 1-4R; CANR 1, 45; DAM POP

Comfort, Montgomery
See Campbell, (John) Ramsey

Compton-Burnett, I(vy)
1884(?)-1969 ..... **CLC 1, 3, 10, 15, 34**
See also CA 1-4R; 25-28R; CANR 4;
DAM NOV; DLB 36; MTCW

Comstock, Anthony 1844-1915 .... **TCLC 13**
See also CA 110

Comte, Auguste 1798-1857....... **NCLC 54**

Conan Doyle, Arthur
See Doyle, Arthur Conan

Conde, Maryse 1937-......... **CLC 52, 92**
See also Boucolon, Maryse
See also BW 2; DAM MULT

Condillac, Etienne Bonnot de
1714-1780 .... **LC 26**

Condon, Richard (Thomas)
1915-1996 .... **CLC 4, 6, 8, 10, 45**
See also BEST 90:3; CA 1-4R; 151;
CAAS 1; CANR 2, 23; DAM NOV;
INT CANR-23; MTCW

Congreve, William
1670-1729 .... **LC 5, 21; DA; DAB;**
DAC; DC 2; WLC
See also CDBLB 1660-1789; DAM DRAM,
MST, POET; DLB 39, 84

Connell, Evan S(helby), Jr.
1924-.................... **CLC 4, 6, 45**
See also AAYA 7; CA 1-4R; CAAS 2;
CANR 2, 39; DAM NOV; DLB 2;
DLBY 81; MTCW

Connelly, Marc(us Cook)
1890-1980 .... **CLC 7**
See also CA 85-88; 102; CANR 30; DLB 7;
DLBY 80; SATA-Obit 25

Connor, Ralph.................... **TCLC 31**
See also Gordon, Charles William
See also DLB 92

Conrad, Joseph
1857-1924 .... **TCLC 1, 6, 13, 25, 43, 57;**
DA; DAB; DAC; SSC 9; WLC
See also CA 104; 131; CDBLB 1890-1914;
DAM MST, NOV; DLB 10, 34, 98, 156;
MTCW; SATA 27

Conrad, Robert Arnold
See Hart, Moss

Conroy, Pat 1945-............. **CLC 30, 74**
See also AAYA 8; AITN 1; CA 85-88;
CANR 24, 53; DAM NOV, POP; DLB 6;
MTCW

Constant (de Rebecque), (Henri) Benjamin
1767-1830 .... **NCLC 6**
See also DLB 119

Conybeare, Charles Augustus
See Eliot, T(homas) S(tearns)

Cook, Michael 1933-............. **CLC 58**
See also CA 93-96; DLB 53

Cook, Robin 1940-............... **CLC 14**
See also BEST 90:2; CA 108; 111;
CANR 41; DAM POP; INT 111

Cook, Roy
See Silverberg, Robert

Cooke, Elizabeth 1948-........... **CLC 55**
See also CA 129

Cooke, John Esten 1830-1886..... **NCLC 5**
See also DLB 3

Cooke, John Estes
See Baum, L(yman) Frank

Cooke, M. E.
See Creasey, John

Cooke, Margaret
See Creasey, John

Cook-Lynn, Elizabeth 1930- .... **CLC 93**
See also CA 133; DAM MULT; NNAL

Cooney, Ray .... **CLC 62**

Cooper, Douglas 1960-............ **CLC 86**

Cooper, Henry St. John
See Creasey, John

Cooper, J. California................ **CLC 56**
See also AAYA 12; BW 1; CA 125;
DAM MULT

Cooper, James Fenimore
1789-1851 .... **NCLC 1, 27, 54**
See also CDALB 1640-1865; DLB 3;
SATA 19

Coover, Robert (Lowell)
1932- .. **CLC 3, 7, 15, 32, 46, 87; SSC 15**
See also CA 45-48; CANR 3, 37;
DAM NOV; DLB 2; DLBY 81; MTCW

Copeland, Stewart (Armstrong)
1952- .... **CLC 26**

Coppard, A(lfred) E(dgar)
1878-1957 .... **TCLC 5; SSC 21**
See also CA 114; DLB 162; YABC 1

Coppee, Francois 1842-1908 ...... **TCLC 25**

Coppola, Francis Ford 1939-....... **CLC 16**
See also CA 77-80; CANR 40; DLB 44

Corbiere, Tristan 1845-1875 ..... **NCLC 43**

Corcoran, Barbara 1911-.......... **CLC 17**
See also AAYA 14; CA 21-24R; CAAS 2;
CANR 11, 28, 48; DLB 52; JRDA;
SAAS 20; SATA 3, 77

Cordelier, Maurice
See Giraudoux, (Hippolyte) Jean

Corelli, Marie 1855-1924........ **TCLC 51**
See also Mackay, Mary
See also DLB 34, 156

Corman, Cid..................... **CLC 9**
See also Corman, Sidney
See also CAAS 2; DLB 5

Corman, Sidney 1924-
See Corman, Cid
See also CA 85-88; CANR 44; DAM POET

Cormier, Robert (Edmund)
1925- ..... **CLC 12, 30; DA; DAB; DAC**
See also AAYA 3; CA 1-4R; CANR 5, 23;
CDALB 1968-1988; CLR 12; DAM MST,
NOV; DLB 52; INT CANR-23; JRDA;
MAICYA; MTCW; SATA 10, 45, 83

Corn, Alfred (DeWitt III) 1943-.... **CLC 33**
See also CA 104; CANR 44; DLB 120;
DLBY 80

Corneille, Pierre 1606-1684.... **LC 28; DAB**
See also DAM MST

Cornwell, David (John Moore)
1931- .... **CLC 9, 15**
See also le Carre, John
See also CA 5-8R; CANR 13, 33;
DAM POP; MTCW

Corso, (Nunzio) Gregory 1930-... **CLC 1, 11**
See also CA 5-8R; CANR 41; DLB 5, 16;
MTCW

Cortazar, Julio
1914-1984 ...... **CLC 2, 3, 5, 10, 13, 15,**
33, 34, 92; HLC; SSC 7
See also CA 21-24R; CANR 12, 32;
DAM MULT, NOV; DLB 113; HW;
MTCW

CORTES, HERNAN 1484-1547..... **LC 31**

Corwin, Cecil
See Kornbluth, C(yril) M.

Cosic, Dobrica 1921-.............. **CLC 14**
See also CA 122; 138

Costain, Thomas B(ertram)
1885-1965 .... **CLC 30**
See also CA 5-8R; 25-28R; DLB 9

Costantini, Humberto
1924(?)-1987 .... **CLC 49**
See also CA 131; 122; HW

Costello, Elvis 1955-.............. **CLC 21**

Cotter, Joseph Seamon Sr.
1861-1949 .... **TCLC 28; BLC**
See also BW 1; CA 124; DAM MULT;
DLB 50

Couch, Arthur Thomas Quiller
See Quiller-Couch, Arthur Thomas

Coulton, James
See Hansen, Joseph

Couperus, Louis (Marie Anne)
1863-1923 .... **TCLC 15**
See also CA 115

Coupland, Douglas 1961-..... **CLC 85; DAC**
See also CA 142; DAM POP

Court, Wesli
See Turco, Lewis (Putnam)

Courtenay, Bryce 1933-........... **CLC 59**
See also CA 138

Courtney, Robert
See Ellison, Harlan (Jay)

Cousteau, Jacques-Yves 1910-...... **CLC 30**
See also CA 65-68; CANR 15; MTCW;
SATA 38

Coward, Noel (Peirce)
1899-1973 .... **CLC 1, 9, 29, 51**
See also AITN 1; CA 17-18; 41-44R;
CANR 35; CAP 2; CDBLB 1914-1945;
DAM DRAM; DLB 10; MTCW

Cowley, Malcolm 1898-1989 .... **CLC 39**
See also CA 5-8R; 128; CANR 3; DLB 4,
48; DLBY 81, 89; MTCW

Cowper, William 1731-1800....... **NCLC 8**
See also DAM POET; DLB 104, 109

Cox, William Trevor 1928- ... **CLC 9, 14, 71**
See also Trevor, William
See also CA 9-12R; CANR 4, 37;
DAM NOV; DLB 14; INT CANR-37;
MTCW

Coyne, P. J.
See Masters, Hilary

Cozzens, James Gould
1903-1978 .... **CLC 1, 4, 11, 92**
See also CA 9-12R; 81-84; CANR 19;
CDALB 1941-1968; DLB 9; DLBD 2;
DLBY 84; MTCW

Crabbe, George 1754-1832....... **NCLC 26**
See also DLB 93

Craddock, Charles Egbert
See Murfree, Mary Noailles

Craig, A. A.
See Anderson, Poul (William)

Craik, Dinah Maria (Mulock)
1826-1887 .... **NCLC 38**
See also DLB 35, 163; MAICYA; SATA 34

Cram, Ralph Adams 1863-1942.... **TCLC 45**

Crane, (Harold) Hart
1899-1932 .... **TCLC 2, 5; DA; DAB;**
DAC; PC 3; WLC
See also CA 104; 127; CDALB 1917-1929;
DAM MST, POET; DLB 4, 48; MTCW

Crane, R(onald) S(almon)
1886-1967 .... **CLC 27**
See also CA 85-88; DLB 63

Crane, Stephen (Townley)
1871-1900 .... **TCLC 11, 17, 32; DA;**
DAB; DAC; SSC 7; WLC
See also CA 109; 140; CDALB 1865-1917;
DAM MST, NOV, POET; DLB 12, 54,
78; YABC 2

Crase, Douglas 1944- .... **CLC 58**
See also CA 106

Crashaw, Richard 1612(?)-1649...... **LC 24**
See also DLB 126

Craven, Margaret
1901-1980 .... **CLC 17; DAC**
See also CA 103

Crawford, F(rancis) Marion
1854-1909 .... **TCLC 10**
See also CA 107; DLB 71

Crawford, Isabella Valancy
1850-1887 .... **NCLC 12**
See also DLB 92

Crayon, Geoffrey
See Irving, Washington

Creasey, John 1908-1973.......... **CLC 11**
See also CA 5-8R; 41-44R; CANR 8;
DLB 77; MTCW

Crebillon, Claude Prosper Jolyot de (fils)
1707-1777 .... **LC 28**

Credo
See Creasey, John

Creeley, Robert (White)
1926- ..... **CLC 1, 2, 4, 8, 11, 15, 36, 78**
See also CA 1-4R; CAAS 10; CANR 23, 43;
DAM POET; DLB 5, 16; MTCW

Crews, Harry (Eugene)
1935- .... **CLC 6, 23, 49**
See also AITN 1; CA 25-28R; CANR 20;
DLB 6, 143; MTCW

Crichton, (John) Michael
1942- .... **CLC 2, 6, 54, 90**
See also AAYA 10; AITN 2; CA 25-28R;
CANR 13, 40; DAM NOV, POP;
DLBY 81; INT CANR-13; JRDA;
MTCW; SATA 9, 88

Crispin, Edmund .... **CLC 22**
See also Montgomery, (Robert) Bruce
See also DLB 87

Cristofer, Michael 1945(?)- .... **CLC 28**
See also CA 110; DAM DRAM; DLB 7

Croce, Benedetto 1866-1952 ...... **TCLC 37**
See also CA 120

Crockett, David 1786-1836 .... **NCLC 8**
See also DLB 3, 11

Crockett, Davy
See Crockett, David

Crofts, Freeman Wills
1879-1957 .... **TCLC 55**
See also CA 115; DLB 77

Croker, John Wilson 1780-1857 .. **NCLC 10**
See also DLB 110

Crommelynck, Fernand 1885-1970 .. **CLC 75**
See also CA 89-92

Cronin, A(rchibald) J(oseph)
1896-1981 .... **CLC 32**
See also CA 1-4R; 102; CANR 5; SATA 47;
SATA-Obit 25

Cross, Amanda
See Heilbrun, Carolyn G(old)

Crothers, Rachel 1878(?)-1958..... **TCLC 19**
See also CA 113; DLB 7

Croves, Hal
See Traven, B.

Crow Dog, Mary.................. **CLC 93**
See also Brave Bird, Mary

Crowfield, Christopher
See Stowe, Harriet (Elizabeth) Beecher

Crowley, Aleister.................. **TCLC 7**
See also Crowley, Edward Alexander

Crowley, Edward Alexander 1875-1947
See Crowley, Aleister
See also CA 104

Crowley, John 1942-.............. **CLC 57**
See also CA 61-64; CANR 43; DLBY 82;
SATA 65

Crud
See Crumb, R(obert)

Crumarums
See Crumb, R(obert)

Crumb, R(obert) 1943-............ **CLC 17**
See also CA 106

Crumbum
See Crumb, R(obert)

Crumski
See Crumb, R(obert)

Crum the Bum
See Crumb, R(obert)

Crunk
See Crumb, R(obert)

Crustt
See Crumb, R(obert)

Cryer, Gretchen (Kiger) 1935-...... **CLC 21**
See also CA 114; 123

Csath, Geza 1887-1919.......... **TCLC 13**
See also CA 111

Cudlip, David 1933- .... **CLC 34**

Cullen, Countee
1903-1946 ...... **TCLC 4, 37; BLC; DA;**
DAC
See also BW 1; CA 108; 124;
CDALB 1917-1929; DAM MST, MULT,
POET; DLB 4, 48, 51; MTCW; SATA 18

Cum, R.
See Crumb, R(obert)

Cummings, Bruce F(rederick) 1889-1919
See Barbellion, W. N. P.
See also CA 123

Cummings, E(dward) E(stlin)
1894-1962 ...... **CLC 1, 3, 8, 12, 15, 68;**
DA; DAB; DAC; PC 5; WLC 2
See also CA 73-76; CANR 31;
CDALB 1929-1941; DAM MST, POET;
DLB 4, 48; MTCW

Cunha, Euclides (Rodrigues Pimenta) da
1866-1909 .... **TCLC 24**
See also CA 123

Cunningham, E. V.
See Fast, Howard (Melvin)

Cunningham, J(ames) V(incent)
1911-1985 .... **CLC 3, 31**
See also CA 1-4R; 115; CANR 1; DLB 5

Cunningham, Julia (Woolfolk)
1916- .... **CLC 12**
See also CA 9-12R; CANR 4, 19, 36;
JRDA; MAICYA; SAAS 2; SATA 1, 26

Cunningham, Michael 1952- .... **CLC 34**
See also CA 136

Cunninghame Graham, R(obert) B(ontine)
1852-1936 .... **TCLC 19**
See also Graham, R(obert) B(ontine)
Cunninghame
See also CA 119; DLB 98

Currie, Ellen 19(?)-............... **CLC 44**

Curtin, Philip
See Lowndes, Marie Adelaide (Belloc)

Curtis, Price
See Ellison, Harlan (Jay)

Cutrate, Joe
See Spiegelman, Art

Czaczkes, Shmuel Yosef
See Agnon, S(hmuel) Y(osef Halevi)

Dabrowska, Maria (Szumska)
1889-1965 .... **CLC 15**
See also CA 106

Dabydeen, David 1955- .... **CLC 34**
See also BW 1; CA 125

Dacey, Philip 1939- .... **CLC 51**
See also CA 37-40R; CAAS 17; CANR 14,
32; DLB 105

Dagerman, Stig (Halvard)
1923-1954 .... **TCLC 17**
See also CA 117

Dahl, Roald
1916-1990 . . . . . . **CLC 1, 6, 18, 79; DAB;**
DAC
See also AAYA 15; CA 1-4R; 133;
CANR 6, 32, 37; CLR 1, 7, 41;
DAM MST, NOV, POP; DLB 139;
JRDA; MAICYA; MTCW; SATA 1, 26,
73; SATA-Obit 65

Dahlberg, Edward 1900-1977. . . **CLC 1, 7, 14**
See also CA 9-12R; 69-72; CANR 31;
DLB 48; MTCW

Dale, Colin. . . . . **TCLC 18**
See also Lawrence, T(homas) E(dward)

Dale, George E.
See Asimov, Isaac

Daly, Elizabeth 1878-1967. . . . . **CLC 52**
See also CA 23-24; 25-28R; CAP 2

Daly, Maureen 1921- . . . . **CLC 17**
See also AAYA 5; CANR 37; JRDA;
MAICYA; SAAS 1; SATA 2

Damas, Leon-Gontran 1912-1978 . . . **CLC 84**
See also BW 1; CA 125; 73-76

Dana, Richard Henry Sr.
1787-1879 . . . . **NCLC 53**

Daniel, Samuel 1562(?)-1619. . . . . . . **LC 24**
See also DLB 62

Daniels, Brett
See Adler, Renata

Dannay, Frederic 1905-1982 . . . . . . **CLC 11**
See also Queen, Ellery
See also CA 1-4R; 107; CANR 1, 39;
DAM POP; DLB 137; MTCW

D'Annunzio, Gabriele
1863-1938 . . . . **TCLC 6, 40**
See also CA 104

Danois, N. le
See Gourmont, Remy (-Marie-Charles) de

d'Antibes, Germain
See Simenon, Georges (Jacques Christian)

Danticat, Edwidge 1969- . . . . **CLC 94**
See also CA 152

Danvers, Dennis 1947-. . . . . **CLC 70**

Danziger, Paula 1944- . . . . **CLC 21**
See also AAYA 4; CA 112; 115; CANR 37;
CLR 20; JRDA; MAICYA; SATA 36,
63; SATA-Brief 30

Da Ponte, Lorenzo 1749-1838 . . . . **NCLC 50**

Dario, Ruben
1867-1916 . . . . **TCLC 4; HLC; PC 15**
See also CA 131; DAM MULT; HW;
MTCW

Darley, George 1795-1846. . . . . . . **NCLC 2**
See also DLB 96

Darwin, Charles 1809-1882 . . . . . . **NCLC 57**
See also DLB 57, 166

Daryush, Elizabeth 1887-1977. . . . **CLC 6, 19**
See also CA 49-52; CANR 3; DLB 20

Dashwood, Edmee Elizabeth Monica de la
Pasture 1890-1943
See Delafield, E. M.
See also CA 119

Daudet, (Louis Marie) Alphonse
1840-1897 . . . . **NCLC 1**
See also DLB 123

Daumal, Rene 1908-1944. . . . . **TCLC 14**
See also CA 114

Davenport, Guy (Mattison, Jr.)
1927- . . . . **CLC 6, 14, 38; SSC 16**
See also CA 33-36R; CANR 23; DLB 130

Davidson, Avram 1923-
See Queen, Ellery
See also CA 101; CANR 26; DLB 8

Davidson, Donald (Grady)
1893-1968 . . . . **CLC 2, 13, 19**
See also CA 5-8R; 25-28R; CANR 4;
DLB 45

Davidson, Hugh
See Hamilton, Edmond

Davidson, John 1857-1909. . . . . . . **TCLC 24**
See also CA 118; DLB 19

Davidson, Sara 1943-. . . . . **CLC 9**
See also CA 81-84; CANR 44

Davie, Donald (Alfred)
1922-1995 . . . . **CLC 5, 8, 10, 31**
See also CA 1-4R; 149; CAAS 3; CANR 1,
44; DLB 27; MTCW

Davies, Ray(mond Douglas) 1944- . . **CLC 21**
See also CA 116; 146

Davies, Rhys 1903-1978. . . . . **CLC 23**
See also CA 9-12R; 81-84; CANR 4;
DLB 139

Davies, (William) Robertson
1913-1995 . . . . . **CLC 2, 7, 13, 25, 42, 75,**
91; DA; DAB; DAC; WLC
See also BEST 89:2; CA 33-36R; 150;
CANR 17, 42; DAM MST, NOV, POP;
DLB 68; INT CANR-17; MTCW

Davies, W(illiam) H(enry)
1871-1940 . . . . **TCLC 5**
See also CA 104; DLB 19

Davies, Walter C.
See Kornbluth, C(yril) M.

Davis, Angela (Yvonne) 1944- . . . . . . **CLC 77**
See also BW 2; CA 57-60; CANR 10;
DAM MULT

Davis, B. Lynch
See Bioy Casares, Adolfo; Borges, Jorge
Luis

Davis, Gordon
See Hunt, E(verette) Howard, (Jr.)

Davis, Harold Lenoir 1896-1960. . . . **CLC 49**
See also CA 89-92; DLB 9

Davis, Rebecca (Blaine) Harding
1831-1910 . . . . **TCLC 6**
See also CA 104; DLB 74

Davis, Richard Harding
1864-1916 . . . . **TCLC 24**
See also CA 114; DLB 12, 23, 78, 79;
DLBD 13

Davison, Frank Dalby 1893-1970 . . . **CLC 15**
See also CA 116

Davison, Lawrence H.
See Lawrence, D(avid) H(erbert Richards)

Davison, Peter (Hubert) 1928- . . . . . **CLC 28**
See also CA 9-12R; CAAS 4; CANR 3, 43;
DLB 5

Davys, Mary 1674-1732. . . . . **LC 1**
See also DLB 39

Dawson, Fielding 1930-, ... **CLC 6**
See also CA 85-88; DLB 130

Dawson, Peter
See Faust, Frederick (Schiller)

Day, Clarence (Shepard, Jr.)
1874-1935 . . . . **TCLC 25**
See also CA 108; DLB 11

Day, Thomas 1748-1789. . . . . **LC 1**
See also DLB 39; YABC 1

Day Lewis, C(ecil)
1904-1972 . . . . **CLC 1, 6, 10; PC 11**
See also Blake, Nicholas
See also CA 13-16; 33-36R; CANR 34;
CAP 1; DAM POET; DLB 15, 20;
MTCW

Dazai, Osamu . . . . **TCLC 11**
See also Tsushima, Shuji

de Andrade, Carlos Drummond
See Drummond de Andrade, Carlos

Deane, Norman
See Creasey, John

de Beauvoir, Simone (Lucie Ernestine Marie
Bertrand)
See Beauvoir, Simone (Lucie Ernestine
Marie Bertrand) de

de Brissac, Malcolm
See Dickinson, Peter (Malcolm)

de Chardin, Pierre Teilhard
See Teilhard de Chardin, (Marie Joseph)
Pierre

Dee, John 1527-1608 . . . . **LC 20**

Deer, Sandra 1940-. . . . . **CLC 45**

De Ferrari, Gabriella 1941-. . . . . **CLC 65**
See also CA 146

Defoe, Daniel
1660(?)-1731 . . . . **LC 1; DA; DAB; DAC;**
WLC
See also CDBLB 1660-1789; DAM MST,
NOV; DLB 39, 95, 101; JRDA;
MAICYA; SATA 22

de Gourmont, Remy(-Marie-Charles)
See Gourmont, Remy (-Marie-Charles) de

de Hartog, Jan 1914-. . . . . **CLC 19**
See also CA 1-4R; CANR 1

de Hostos, E. M.
See Hostos (y Bonilla), Eugenio Maria de

de Hostos, Eugenio M.
See Hostos (y Bonilla), Eugenio Maria de

Deighton, Len . . . . **CLC 4, 7, 22, 46**
See also Deighton, Leonard Cyril
See also AAYA 6; BEST 89:2;
CDBLB 1960 to Present; DLB 87

Deighton, Leonard Cyril 1929-
See Deighton, Len
See also CA 9-12R; CANR 19, 33;
DAM NOV, POP; MTCW

Dekker, Thomas 1572(?)-1632. . . . . . . **LC 22**
See also CDBLB Before 1660;
DAM DRAM; DLB 62

Delafield, E. M. 1890-1943 . . . . **TCLC 61**
See also Dashwood, Edmee Elizabeth
Monica de la Pasture
See also DLB 34

de la Mare, Walter (John)
1873-1956 .... **TCLC 4, 53; DAB; DAC; SSC 14; WLC**
See also CDBLB 1914-1945; CLR 23; DAM MST, POET; DLB 162; SATA 16

Delaney, Franey
See O'Hara, John (Henry)

Delaney, Shelagh 1939- .... **CLC 29**
See also CA 17-20R; CANR 30; CDBLB 1960 to Present; DAM DRAM; DLB 13; MTCW

Delany, Mary (Granville Pendarves)
1700-1788 .... **LC 12**

Delany, Samuel R(ay, Jr.)
1942- .... **CLC 8, 14, 38; BLC**
See also BW 2; CA 81-84; CANR 27, 43; DAM MULT; DLB 8, 33; MTCW

De La Ramee, (Marie) Louise 1839-1908
See Ouida
See also SATA 20

de la Roche, Mazo 1879-1961 ...... **CLC 14**
See also CA 85-88; CANR 30; DLB 68; SATA 64

Delbanco, Nicholas (Franklin)
1942- .... **CLC 6, 13**
See also CA 17-20R; CAAS 2; CANR 29; DLB 6

del Castillo, Michel 1933- .... **CLC 38**
See also CA 109

Deledda, Grazia (Cosima)
1875(?)-1936 .... **TCLC 23**
See also CA 123

Delibes, Miguel .... **CLC 8, 18**
See also Delibes Setien, Miguel

Delibes Setien, Miguel 1920-
See Delibes, Miguel
See also CA 45-48; CANR 1, 32; HW; MTCW

DeLillo, Don
1936- ..... **CLC 8, 10, 13, 27, 39, 54, 76**
See also BEST 89:1; CA 81-84; CANR 21; DAM NOV, POP; DLB 6; MTCW

de Lisser, H. G.
See De Lisser, Herbert George
See also DLB 117

De Lisser, Herbert George
1878-1944 .... **TCLC 12**
See also de Lisser, H. G.
See also BW 2; CA 109

Deloria, Vine (Victor), Jr. 1933-.... **CLC 21**
See also CA 53-56; CANR 5, 20, 48; DAM MULT; MTCW; NNAL; SATA 21

Del Vecchio, John M(ichael)
1947- .... **CLC 29**
See also CA 110; DLBD 9

de Man, Paul (Adolph Michel)
1919-1983 .... **CLC 55**
See also CA 128; 111; DLB 67; MTCW

De Marinis, Rick 1934- .... **CLC 54**
See also CA 57-60; CAAS 24; CANR 9, 25, 50

Dembry, R. Emmet
See Murfree, Mary Noailles

Demby, William 1922-....... **CLC 53; BLC**
See also BW 1; CA 81-84; DAM MULT; DLB 33

Demijohn, Thom
See Disch, Thomas M(ichael)

de Montherlant, Henry (Milon)
See Montherlant, Henry (Milon) de

Demosthenes 384B.C.-322B.C. ... **CMLC 13**

de Natale, Francine
See Malzberg, Barry N(athaniel)

Denby, Edwin (Orr) 1903-1983 ..... **CLC 48**
See also CA 138; 110

Denis, Julio
See Cortazar, Julio

Denmark, Harrison
See Zelazny, Roger (Joseph)

Dennis, John 1658-1734........... **LC 11**
See also DLB 101

Dennis, Nigel (Forbes) 1912-1989 .... **CLC 8**
See also CA 25-28R; 129; DLB 13, 15; MTCW

De Palma, Brian (Russell) 1940-.... **CLC 20**
See also CA 109

De Quincey, Thomas 1785-1859 ... **NCLC 4**
See also CDBLB 1789-1832; DLB 110; 144

Deren, Eleanora 1908(?)-1961
See Deren, Maya
See also CA 111

Deren, Maya .... **CLC 16**
See also Deren, Eleanora

Derleth, August (William)
1909-1971 .... **CLC 31**
See also CA 1-4R; 29-32R; CANR 4; DLB 9; SATA 5

Der Nister 1884-1950............ **TCLC 56**

de Routisie, Albert
See Aragon, Louis

Derrida, Jacques 1930-........ **CLC 24, 87**
See also CA 124; 127

Derry Down Derry
See Lear, Edward

Dersonnes, Jacques
See Simenon, Georges (Jacques Christian)

Desai, Anita 1937- ...... **CLC 19, 37; DAB**
See also CA 81-84; CANR 33, 53; DAM NOV; MTCW; SATA 63

de Saint-Luc, Jean
See Glassco, John

de Saint Roman, Arnaud
See Aragon, Louis

Descartes, Rene 1596-1650 .... **LC 20**

De Sica, Vittorio 1901(?)-1974 ..... **CLC 20**
See also CA 117

Desnos, Robert 1900-1945 .... **TCLC 22**
See also CA 121; 151

Destouches, Louis-Ferdinand
1894-1961 .... **CLC 9, 15**
See also Celine, Louis-Ferdinand
See also CA 85-88; CANR 28; MTCW

Deutsch, Babette 1895-1982 .... **CLC 18**
See also CA 1-4R; 108; CANR 4; DLB 45; SATA 1; SATA-Obit 33

Devenant, William 1606-1649 ...... **LC 13**

Devkota, Laxmiprasad
1909-1959 .... **TCLC 23**
See also CA 123

De Voto, Bernard (Augustine)
1897-1955 .... **TCLC 29**
See also CA 113; DLB 9

De Vries, Peter
1910-1993 .... **CLC 1, 2, 3, 7, 10, 28, 46**
See also CA 17-20R; 142; CANR 41; DAM NOV; DLB 6; DLBY 82; MTCW

Dexter, John
See Bradley, Marion Zimmer

Dexter, Martin
See Faust, Frederick (Schiller)

Dexter, Pete 1943-............ **CLC 34, 55**
See also BEST 89:2; CA 127; 131; DAM POP; INT 131; MTCW

Diamano, Silmang
See Senghor, Leopold Sedar

Diamond, Neil 1941- .... **CLC 30**
See also CA 108

Diaz del Castillo, Bernal 1496-1584 .. **LC 31**

di Bassetto, Corno
See Shaw, George Bernard

Dick, Philip K(indred)
1928-1982 .... **CLC 10, 30, 72**
See also CA 49-52; 106; CANR 2, 16; DAM NOV, POP; DLB 8; MTCW

Dickens, Charles (John Huffam)
1812-1870 ...... **NCLC 3, 8, 18, 26, 37, 50; DA; DAB; DAC; SSC 17; WLC**
See also CDBLB 1832-1890; DAM MST, NOV; DLB 21, 55, 70, 159, 166; JRDA; MAICYA; SATA 15

Dickey, James (Lafayette)
1923-......... **CLC 1, 2, 4, 7, 10, 15, 47**
See also AITN 1, 2; CA 9-12R; CABS 2; CANR 10, 48; CDALB 1968-1988; DAM NOV, POET, POP; DLB 5; DLBD 7; DLBY 82, 93; INT CANR-10; MTCW

Dickey, William 1928-1994 ...... **CLC 3, 28**
See also CA 9-12R; 145; CANR 24; DLB 5

Dickinson, Charles 1951-.......... **CLC 49**
See also CA 128

Dickinson, Emily (Elizabeth)
1830-1886 .... **NCLC 21; DA; DAB; DAC; PC 1; WLC**
See also CDALB 1865-1917; DAM MST, POET; DLB 1; SATA 29

Dickinson, Peter (Malcolm)
1927- .... **CLC 12, 35**
See also AAYA 9; CA 41-44R; CANR 31; CLR 29; DLB 87, 161; JRDA; MAICYA; SATA 5, 62

Dickson, Carr
See Carr, John Dickson

Dickson, Carter
See Carr, John Dickson

Diderot, Denis 1713-1784 .... **LC 26**

Didion, Joan 1934-..... **CLC 1, 3, 8, 14, 32**
See also AITN 1; CA 5-8R; CANR 14, 52; CDALB 1968-1988; DAM NOV; DLB 2; DLBY 81, 86; MTCW

Dietrich, Robert
See Hunt, E(verette) Howard, (Jr.)

Dillard, Annie 1945-........... **CLC 9, 60**
See also AAYA 6; CA 49-52; CANR 3, 43;
DAM NOV; DLBY 80; MTCW;
SATA 10

Dillard, R(ichard) H(enry) W(ilde)
1937-........................ **CLC 5**
See also CA 21-24R; CAAS 7; CANR 10;
DLB 5

Dillon, Eilis 1920-1994........... **CLC 17**
See also CA 9-12R; 147; CAAS 3; CANR 4,
38; CLR 26; MAICYA; SATA 2, 74;
SATA-Obit 83

Dimont, Penelope
See Mortimer, Penelope (Ruth)

Dinesen, Isak....... **CLC 10, 29, 95; SSC 7**
See also Blixen, Karen (Christentze
Dinesen)

Ding Ling....................... **CLC 68**
See also Chiang Pin-chin

Disch, Thomas M(ichael) 1940-... **CLC 7, 36**
See also AAYA 17; CA 21-24R; CAAS 4;
CANR 17, 36; CLR 18; DLB 8;
MAICYA; MTCW; SAAS 15; SATA 54

Disch, Tom
See Disch, Thomas M(ichael)

d'Isly, Georges
See Simenon, Georges (Jacques Christian)

Disraeli, Benjamin 1804-1881 .. **NCLC 2, 39**
See also DLB 21, 55

Ditcum, Steve
See Crumb, R(obert)

Dixon, Paige
See Corcoran, Barbara

Dixon, Stephen 1936-..... **CLC 52; SSC 16**
See also CA 89-92; CANR 17, 40; DLB 130

Dobell, Sydney Thompson
1824-1874 .... **NCLC 43**
See also DLB 32

Doblin, Alfred................... **TCLC 13**
See also Doeblin, Alfred

Dobrolyubov, Nikolai Alexandrovich
1836-1861 .... **NCLC 5**

Dobyns, Stephen 1941-........... **CLC 37**
See also CA 45-48; CANR 2, 18

Doctorow, E(dgar) L(aurence)
1931- ..... **CLC 6, 11, 15, 18, 37, 44, 65**
See also AITN 2; BEST 89:3; CA 45-48;
CANR 2, 33, 51; CDALB 1968-1988;
DAM NOV, POP; DLB 2, 28; DLBY 80;
MTCW

Dodgson, Charles Lutwidge 1832-1898
See Carroll, Lewis
See also CLR 2; DA; DAB; DAC;
DAM MST, NOV, POET; MAICYA;
YABC 2

Dodson, Owen (Vincent)
1914-1983 .... **CLC 79; BLC**
See also BW 1; CA 65-68; 110; CANR 24;
DAM MULT; DLB 76

Doeblin, Alfred 1878-1957........ **TCLC 13**
See also Doblin, Alfred
See also CA 110; 141; DLB 66

Doerr, Harriet 1910- .... **CLC 34**
See also CA 117; 122; CANR 47; INT 122

Domecq, H(onorio) Bustos
See Bioy Casares, Adolfo; Borges, Jorge
Luis

Domini, Rey
See Lorde, Audre (Geraldine)

Dominique
See Proust, (Valentin-Louis-George-Eugene-)
Marcel

Don, A
See Stephen, Leslie

Donaldson, Stephen R. 1947-....... **CLC 46**
See also CA 89-92; CANR 13; DAM POP;
INT CANR-13

Donleavy, J(ames) P(atrick)
1926- .... **CLC 1, 4, 6, 10, 45**
See also AITN 2; CA 9-12R; CANR 24, 49;
DLB 6; INT CANR-24; MTCW

Donne, John
1572-1631 .... **LC 10, 24; DA; DAB;**
DAC; PC 1
See also CDBLB Before 1660; DAM MST,
POET; DLB 121, 151

Donnell, David 1939(?)-........... **CLC 34**

Donoghue, P. S.
See Hunt, E(verette) Howard, (Jr.)

Donoso (Yanez), Jose
1924- .... **CLC 4, 8, 11, 32; HLC**
See also CA 81-84; CANR 32;
DAM MULT; DLB 113; HW; MTCW

Donovan, John 1928-1992 .... **CLC 35**
See also CA 97-100; 137; CLR 3;
MAICYA; SATA 72; SATA-Brief 29

Don Roberto
See Cunninghame Graham, R(obert)
B(ontine)

Doolittle, Hilda
1886-1961 ..... **CLC 3, 8, 14, 31, 34, 73;**
DA; DAC; PC 5; WLC
See also H. D.
See also CA 97-100; CANR 35; DAM MST,
POET; DLB 4, 45; MTCW

Dorfman, Ariel 1942-.... **CLC 48, 77; HLC**
See also CA 124; 130; DAM MULT; HW;
INT 130

Dorn, Edward (Merton) 1929-... **CLC 10, 18**
See also CA 93-96; CANR 42; DLB 5;
INT 93-96

Dorsan, Luc
See Simenon, Georges (Jacques Christian)

Dorsange, Jean
See Simenon, Georges (Jacques Christian)

Dos Passos, John (Roderigo)
1896-1970 ..... **CLC 1, 4, 8, 11, 15, 25,**
34, 82; DA; DAB; DAC; WLC
See also CA 1-4R; 29-32R; CANR 3;
CDALB 1929-1941; DAM MST, NOV;
DLB 4, 9; DLBD 1; MTCW

Dossage, Jean
See Simenon, Georges (Jacques Christian)

Dostoevsky, Fedor Mikhailovich
1821-1881 ..... **NCLC 2, 7, 21, 33, 43;**
DA; DAB; DAC; SSC 2; WLC
See also DAM MST, NOV

Doughty, Charles M(ontagu)
1843-1926 .... **TCLC 27**
See also CA 115; DLB 19, 57

Douglas, Ellen .... **CLC 73**
See also Haxton, Josephine Ayres;
Williamson, Ellen Douglas

Douglas, Gavin 1475(?)-1522........ **LC 20**

Douglas, Keith 1920-1944 .... **TCLC 40**
See also DLB 27

Douglas, Leonard
See Bradbury, Ray (Douglas)

Douglas, Michael
See Crichton, (John) Michael

Douglass, Frederick
1817(?)-1895 .... **NCLC 7, 55; BLC; DA;**
DAC; WLC
See also CDALB 1640-1865; DAM MST,
MULT; DLB 1, 43, 50, 79; SATA 29

Dourado, (Waldomiro Freitas) Autran
1926- .... **CLC 23, 60**
See also CA 25-28R; CANR 34

Dourado, Waldomiro Autran
See Dourado, (Waldomiro Freitas) Autran

Dove, Rita (Frances)
1952- .... **CLC 50, 81; PC 6**
See also BW 2; CA 109; CAAS 19;
CANR 27, 42; DAM MULT, POET;
DLB 120

Dowell, Coleman 1925-1985........ **CLC 60**
See also CA 25-28R; 117; CANR 10;
DLB 130

Dowson, Ernest (Christopher)
1867-1900 .... **TCLC 4**
See also CA 105; 150; DLB 19, 135

Doyle, A. Conan
See Doyle, Arthur Conan

Doyle, Arthur Conan
1859-1930 .... **TCLC 7; DA; DAB;**
DAC; SSC 12; WLC
See also AAYA 14; CA 104; 122;
CDBLB 1890-1914; DAM MST, NOV;
DLB 18, 70, 156; MTCW; SATA 24

Doyle, Conan
See Doyle, Arthur Conan

Doyle, John
See Graves, Robert (von Ranke)

Doyle, Roddy 1958(?)-............. **CLC 81**
See also AAYA 14; CA 143

Doyle, Sir A. Conan
See Doyle, Arthur Conan

Doyle, Sir Arthur Conan
See Doyle, Arthur Conan

Dr. A
See Asimov, Isaac; Silverstein, Alvin

Drabble, Margaret
1939- .... **CLC 2, 3, 5, 8, 10, 22, 53;**
DAB; DAC
See also CA 13-16R; CANR 18, 35;
CDBLB 1960 to Present; DAM MST,
NOV, POP; DLB 14, 155; MTCW;
SATA 48

Drapier, M. B.
See Swift, Jonathan

Drayham, James
See Mencken, H(enry) L(ouis)

Drayton, Michael 1563-1631........ **LC 8**

Dreadstone, Carl
See Campbell, (John) Ramsey

Dreiser, Theodore (Herman Albert)
 1871-1945 . . . . **TCLC 10, 18, 35; DA;
                                        DAC; WLC**
 See also CA 106; 132; CDALB 1865-1917;
  DAM MST, NOV; DLB 9, 12, 102, 137;
  DLBD 1; MTCW

Drexler, Rosalyn 1926- . . . . **CLC 2, 6**
 See also CA 81-84

Dreyer, Carl Theodor 1889-1968. . . . **CLC 16**
 See also CA 116

Drieu la Rochelle, Pierre(-Eugene)
 1893-1945 . . . . **TCLC 21**
 See also CA 117; DLB 72

Drinkwater, John 1882-1937 . . . . . . **TCLC 57**
 See also CA 109; 149; DLB 10, 19, 149

Drop Shot
 See Cable, George Washington

Droste-Hulshoff, Annette Freiin von
 1797-1848 . . . . **NCLC 3**
 See also DLB 133

Drummond, Walter
 See Silverberg, Robert

Drummond, William Henry
 1854-1907 . . . . **TCLC 25**
 See also DLB 92

Drummond de Andrade, Carlos
 1902-1987 . . . . **CLC 18**
 See also Andrade, Carlos Drummond de
 See also CA 132; 123

Drury, Allen (Stuart) 1918- . . . . **CLC 37**
 See also CA 57-60; CANR 18, 52;
  INT CANR-18

Dryden, John
 1631-1700 . . . . **LC 3, 21; DA; DAB;
                                 DAC; DC 3; WLC**
 See also CDBLB 1660-1789; DAM DRAM,
  MST, POET; DLB 80, 101, 131

Duberman, Martin 1930- . . . . **CLC 8**
 See also CA 1-4R; CANR 2

Dubie, Norman (Evans) 1945- . . . . . . **CLC 36**
 See also CA 69-72; CANR 12; DLB 120

Du Bois, W(illiam) E(dward) B(urghardt)
 1868-1963 . . . . . . **CLC 1, 2, 13, 64; BLC;
                                      DA; DAC; WLC**
 See also BW 1; CA 85-88; CANR 34;
  CDALB 1865-1917; DAM MST, MULT,
  NOV; DLB 47, 50, 91; MTCW; SATA 42

Dubus, Andre 1936- . . . **CLC 13, 36; SSC 15**
 See also CA 21-24R; CANR 17; DLB 130;
  INT CANR-17

Duca Minimo
 See D'Annunzio, Gabriele

Ducharme, Rejean 1941- . . . . **CLC 74**
 See also DLB 60

Duclos, Charles Pinot 1704-1772 . . . . . **LC 1**

Dudek, Louis 1918- . . . . **CLC 11, 19**
 See also CA 45-48; CAAS 14; CANR 1;
  DLB 88

Duerrenmatt, Friedrich
 1921-1990 . . . . . . **CLC 1, 4, 8, 11, 15, 43**
 See also CA 17-20R; CANR 33;
  DAM DRAM; DLB 69, 124; MTCW

Duffy, Bruce (?)- . . . . **CLC 50**

Duffy, Maureen 1933- . . . . **CLC 37**
 See also CA 25-28R; CANR 33; DLB 14;
  MTCW

Dugan, Alan 1923- . . . . **CLC 2, 6**
 See also CA 81-84; DLB 5

du Gard, Roger Martin
 See Martin du Gard, Roger

Duhamel, Georges 1884-1966 . . . . **CLC 8**
 See also CA 81-84; 25-28R; CANR 35;
  DLB 65; MTCW

Dujardin, Edouard (Emile Louis)
 1861-1949 . . . . **TCLC 13**
 See also CA 109; DLB 123

Dumas, Alexandre (Davy de la Pailleterie)
 1802-1870 . . . . **NCLC 11; DA; DAB;
                                        DAC; WLC**
 See also DAM MST, NOV; DLB 119;
  SATA 18

Dumas, Alexandre
 1824-1895 . . . . **NCLC 9; DC 1**

Dumas, Claudine
 See Malzberg, Barry N(athaniel)

Dumas, Henry L. 1934-1968 . . . . . **CLC 6, 62**
 See also BW 1; CA 85-88; DLB 41

du Maurier, Daphne
 1907-1989 . . . . **CLC 6, 11, 59; DAB;
                                        DAC; SSC 18**
 See also CA 5-8R; 128; CANR 6;
  DAM MST, POP; MTCW; SATA 27;
  SATA-Obit 60

Dunbar, Paul Laurence
 1872-1906 . . . . . . **TCLC 2, 12; BLC; DA;
                                 DAC; PC 5; SSC 8; WLC**
 See also BW 1; CA 104; 124;
  CDALB 1865-1917; DAM MST, MULT,
  POET; DLB 50, 54, 78; SATA 34

Dunbar, William 1460(?)-1530(?) . . . . **LC 20**
 See also DLB 132, 146

Duncan, Lois 1934- . . . . **CLC 26**
 See also AAYA 4; CA 1-4R; CANR 2, 23,
  36; CLR 29; JRDA; MAICYA; SAAS 2;
  SATA 1, 36, 75

Duncan, Robert (Edward)
 1919-1988 . . . . **CLC 1, 2, 4, 7, 15, 41, 55;
                                                PC 2**
 See also CA 9-12R; 124; CANR 28;
  DAM POET; DLB 5, 16; MTCW

Duncan, Sara Jeannette
 1861-1922 . . . . **TCLC 60**
 See also DLB 92

Dunlap, William 1766-1839 . . . . **NCLC 2**
 See also DLB 30, 37, 59

Dunn, Douglas (Eaglesham)
 1942- . . . . **CLC 6, 40**
 See also CA 45-48; CANR 2, 33; DLB 40;
  MTCW

Dunn, Katherine (Karen) 1945- . . . . . **CLC 71**
 See also CA 33-36R

Dunn, Stephen 1939- . . . . **CLC 36**
 See also CA 33-36R; CANR 12, 48, 53;
  DLB 105

Dunne, Finley Peter 1867-1936. . . . **TCLC 28**
 See also CA 108; DLB 11, 23

Dunne, John Gregory 1932- . . . . **CLC 28**
 See also CA 25-28R; CANR 14, 50;
  DLBY 80

Dunsany, Edward John Moreton Drax
 Plunkett 1878-1957
 See Dunsany, Lord
 See also CA 104; 148; DLB 10

Dunsany, Lord. . . . . **TCLC 2, 59**
 See also Dunsany, Edward John Moreton
  Drax Plunkett
 See also DLB 77, 153, 156

du Perry, Jean
 See Simenon, Georges (Jacques Christian)

Durang, Christopher (Ferdinand)
 1949- . . . . **CLC 27, 38**
 See also CA 105; CANR 50

Duras, Marguerite
 1914-1996 . . **CLC 3, 6, 11, 20, 34, 40, 68**
 See also CA 25-28R; 151; CANR 50;
  DLB 83; MTCW

Durban, (Rosa) Pam 1947- . . . . **CLC 39**
 See also CA 123

Durcan, Paul 1944- . . . . **CLC 43, 70**
 See also CA 134; DAM POET

Durkheim, Emile 1858-1917 . . . . . . **TCLC 55**

Durrell, Lawrence (George)
 1912-1990 . . . . **CLC 1, 4, 6, 8, 13, 27, 41**
 See also CA 9-12R; 132; CANR 40;
  CDBLB 1945-1960; DAM NOV; DLB 15,
  27; DLBY 90; MTCW

Durrenmatt, Friedrich
 See Duerrenmatt, Friedrich

Dutt, Toru 1856-1877 . . . . **NCLC 29**

Dwight, Timothy 1752-1817 . . . . . . **NCLC 13**
 See also DLB 37

Dworkin, Andrea 1946- . . . . **CLC 43**
 See also CA 77-80; CAAS 21; CANR 16,
  39; INT CANR-16; MTCW

Dwyer, Deanna
 See Koontz, Dean R(ay)

Dwyer, K. R.
 See Koontz, Dean R(ay)

Dylan, Bob 1941- . . . . . . **CLC 3, 4, 6, 12, 77**
 See also CA 41-44R; DLB 16

Eagleton, Terence (Francis) 1943-
 See Eagleton, Terry
 See also CA 57-60; CANR 7, 23; MTCW

Eagleton, Terry . . . . **CLC 63**
 See also Eagleton, Terence (Francis)

Early, Jack
 See Scoppettone, Sandra

East, Michael
 See West, Morris L(anglo)

Eastaway, Edward
 See Thomas, (Philip) Edward

Eastlake, William (Derry) 1917- . . . . . **CLC 8**
 See also CA 5-8R; CAAS 1; CANR 5;
  DLB 6; INT CANR-5

Eastman, Charles A(lexander)
 1858-1939 . . . . **TCLC 55**
 See also DAM MULT; NNAL; YABC 1

Eberhart, Richard (Ghormley)
 1904- . . . . **CLC 3, 11, 19, 56**
 See also CA 1-4R; CANR 2;
  CDALB 1941-1968; DAM POET;
  DLB 48; MTCW

Eberstadt, Fernanda 1960- . . . . CLC 39
See also CA 136

Echegaray (y Eizaguirre), Jose (Maria Waldo)
1832-1916 . . . . TCLC 4
See also CA 104; CANR 32; HW; MTCW

Echeverria, (Jose) Esteban (Antonino)
1805-1851 . . . . NCLC 18

Echo
See Proust, (Valentin-Louis-George-Eugene-)
Marcel

Eckert, Allan W. 1931- . . . . CLC 17
See also AAYA 18; CA 13-16R; CANR 14,
45; INT CANR-14; SAAS 21; SATA 29;
SATA-Brief 27

Eckhart, Meister 1260(?)-1328(?) . . CMLC 9
See also DLB 115

Eckmar, F. R.
See de Hartog, Jan

Eco, Umberto 1932- . . . . CLC 28, 60
See also BEST 90:1; CA 77-80; CANR 12,
33; DAM NOV, POP; MTCW

Eddison, E(ric) R(ucker)
1882-1945 . . . . TCLC 15
See also CA 109

Edel, (Joseph) Leon 1907- . . . . . . CLC 29, 34
See also CA 1-4R; CANR 1, 22; DLB 103;
INT CANR-22

Eden, Emily 1797-1869 . . . . NCLC 10

Edgar, David 1948- . . . . CLC 42
See also CA 57-60; CANR 12;
DAM DRAM; DLB 13; MTCW

Edgerton, Clyde (Carlyle) 1944- . . . . CLC 39
See also AAYA 17; CA 118; 134; INT 134

Edgeworth, Maria 1768-1849 . . . NCLC 1, 51
See also DLB 116, 159, 163; SATA 21

Edmonds, Paul
See Kuttner, Henry

Edmonds, Walter D(umaux) 1903- . . CLC 35
See also CA 5-8R; CANR 2; DLB 9;
MAICYA; SAAS 4; SATA 1, 27

Edmondson, Wallace
See Ellison, Harlan (Jay)

Edson, Russell . . . . CLC 13
See also CA 33-36R

Edwards, Bronwen Elizabeth
See Rose, Wendy

Edwards, G(erald) B(asil)
1899-1976 . . . . CLC 25
See also CA 110

Edwards, Gus 1939- . . . . CLC 43
See also CA 108; INT 108

Edwards, Jonathan
1703-1758 . . . . LC 7; DA; DAC
See also DAM MST; DLB 24

Efron, Marina Ivanovna Tsvetaeva
See Tsvetaeva (Efron), Marina (Ivanovna)

Ehle, John (Marsden, Jr.) 1925- . . . . CLC 27
See also CA 9-12R

Ehrenbourg, Ilya (Grigoryevich)
See Ehrenburg, Ilya (Grigoryevich)

Ehrenburg, Ilya (Grigoryevich)
1891-1967 . . . . CLC 18, 34, 62
See also CA 102; 25-28R

Ehrenburg, Ilyo (Grigoryevich)
See Ehrenburg, Ilya (Grigoryevich)

Eich, Guenter 1907-1972 . . . . CLC 15
See also CA 111; 93-96; DLB 69, 124

Eichendorff, Joseph Freiherr von
1788-1857 . . . . NCLC 8
See also DLB 90

Eigner, Larry . . . . CLC 9
See also Eigner, Laurence (Joel)
See also CAAS 23; DLB 5

Eigner, Laurence (Joel) 1927-1996
See Eigner, Larry
See also CA 9-12R; 151; CANR 6

Einstein, Albert 1879-1955 . . . . TCLC 65
See also CA 121; 133; MTCW

Eiseley, Loren Corey 1907-1977 . . . . . CLC 7
See also AAYA 5; CA 1-4R; 73-76;
CANR 6

Eisenstadt, Jill 1963- . . . . CLC 50
See also CA 140

Eisenstein, Sergei (Mikhailovich)
1898-1948 . . . . TCLC 57
See also CA 114; 149

Eisner, Simon
See Kornbluth, C(yril) M.

Ekeloef, (Bengt) Gunnar
1907-1968 . . . . CLC 27
See also CA 123; 25-28R; DAM POET

Ekelof, (Bengt) Gunnar
See Ekeloef, (Bengt) Gunnar

Ekwensi, C. O. D.
See Ekwensi, Cyprian (Odiatu Duaka)

Ekwensi, Cyprian (Odiatu Duaka)
1921- . . . . CLC 4; BLC
See also BW 2; CA 29-32R; CANR 18, 42;
DAM MULT; DLB 117; MTCW;
SATA 66

Elaine . . . . TCLC 18
See also Leverson, Ada

El Crummo
See Crumb, R(obert)

Elia
See Lamb, Charles

Eliade, Mircea 1907-1986 . . . . CLC 19
See also CA 65-68; 119; CANR 30; MTCW

Eliot, A. D.
See Jewett, (Theodora) Sarah Orne

Eliot, Alice
See Jewett, (Theodora) Sarah Orne

Eliot, Dan
See Silverberg, Robert

Eliot, George
1819-1880 . . . . . NCLC 4, 13, 23, 41, 49;
DA; DAB; DAC; WLC
See also CDBLB 1832-1890; DAM MST,
NOV; DLB 21, 35, 55

Eliot, John 1604-1690 . . . . LC 5
See also DLB 24

Eliot, T(homas) S(tearns)
1888-1965 . . . . . CLC 1, 2, 3, 6, 9, 10, 13,
15, 24, 34, 41, 55, 57; DA; DAB; DAC;
PC 5; WLC 2
See also CA 5-8R; 25-28R; CANR 41;
CDALB 1929-1941; DAM DRAM, MST,
POET; DLB 7, 10, 45, 63; DLBY 88;
MTCW

Elizabeth 1866-1941 . . . . TCLC 41

Elkin, Stanley L(awrence)
1930-1995 . . . . . . CLC 4, 6, 9, 14, 27, 51,
91; SSC 12
See also CA 9-12R; 148; CANR 8, 46;
DAM NOV, POP; DLB 2, 28; DLBY 80;
INT CANR-8; MTCW

Elledge, Scott . . . . CLC 34

Elliott, Don
See Silverberg, Robert

Elliott, George P(aul) 1918-1980 . . . . . CLC 2
See also CA 1-4R; 97-100; CANR 2

Elliott, Janice 1931- . . . . CLC 47
See also CA 13-16R; CANR 8, 29; DLB 14

Elliott, Sumner Locke 1917-1991 . . . CLC 38
See also CA 5-8R; 134; CANR 2, 21

Elliott, William
See Bradbury, Ray (Douglas)

Ellis, A. E. . . . . CLC 7

Ellis, Alice Thomas . . . . CLC 40
See also Haycraft, Anna

Ellis, Bret Easton 1964- . . . . CLC 39, 71
See also AAYA 2; CA 118; 123; CANR 51;
DAM POP; INT 123

Ellis, (Henry) Havelock
1859-1939 . . . . TCLC 14
See also CA 109

Ellis, Landon
See Ellison, Harlan (Jay)

Ellis, Trey 1962- . . . . CLC 55
See also CA 146

Ellison, Harlan (Jay)
1934- . . . . CLC 1, 13, 42; SSC 14
See also CA 5-8R; CANR 5, 46;
DAM POP; DLB 8; INT CANR-5;
MTCW

Ellison, Ralph (Waldo)
1914-1994 . . . . CLC 1, 3, 11, 54, 86;
BLC; DA; DAB; DAC; WLC
See also BW 1; CA 9-12R; 145; CANR 24,
53; CDALB 1941-1968; DAM MST,
MULT, NOV; DLB 2, 76; DLBY 94;
MTCW

Ellmann, Lucy (Elizabeth) 1956- . . . . CLC 61
See also CA 128

Ellmann, Richard (David)
1918-1987 . . . . CLC 50
See also BEST 89:2; CA 1-4R; 122;
CANR 2, 28; DLB 103; DLBY 87;
MTCW

Elman, Richard 1934- . . . . CLC 19
See also CA 17-20R; CAAS 3; CANR 47

Elron
See Hubbard, L(afayette) Ron(ald)

Eluard, Paul . . . . TCLC 7, 41
See also Grindel, Eugene

Elyot, Sir Thomas 1490(?)-1546 . . . . . LC 11

Elytis, Odysseus 1911-1996..... **CLC 15, 49**
See also CA 102; 151; DAM POET; MTCW

Emecheta, (Florence Onye) Buchi
1944-............... **CLC 14, 48; BLC**
See also BW 2; CA 81-84; CANR 27;
DAM MULT; DLB 117; MTCW;
SATA 66

Emerson, Ralph Waldo
1803-1882 ..... **NCLC 1, 38; DA; DAB;
DAC; WLC**
See also CDALB 1640-1865; DAM MST,
POET; DLB 1, 59, 73

Eminescu, Mihail 1850-1889..... **NCLC 33**

Empson, William
1906-1984 .... **CLC 3, 8, 19, 33, 34**
See also CA 17-20R; 112; CANR 31;
DLB 20; MTCW

Enchi Fumiko (Ueda) 1905-1986.... **CLC 31**
See also CA 129; 121

Ende, Michael (Andreas Helmuth)
1929-1995 .... **CLC 31**
See also CA 118; 124; 149; CANR 36;
CLR 14; DLB 75; MAICYA; SATA 61;
SATA-Brief 42; SATA-Obit 86

Endo, Shusaku 1923-..... **CLC 7, 14, 19, 54**
See also CA 29-32R; CANR 21;
DAM NOV; MTCW

Engel, Marian 1933-1985.......... **CLC 36**
See also CA 25-28R; CANR 12; DLB 53;
INT CANR-12

Engelhardt, Frederick
See Hubbard, L(afayette) Ron(ald)

Enright, D(ennis) J(oseph)
1920-................... **CLC 4, 8, 31**
See also CA 1-4R; CANR 1, 42; DLB 27;
SATA 25

Enzensberger, Hans Magnus
1929-...................... **CLC 43**
See also CA 116; 119

Ephron, Nora 1941-.......... **CLC 17, 31**
See also AITN 2; CA 65-68; CANR 12, 39

Epsilon
See Betjeman, John

Epstein, Daniel Mark 1948-........ **CLC 7**
See also CA 49-52; CANR 2, 53

Epstein, Jacob 1956-............. **CLC 19**
See also CA 114

Epstein, Joseph 1937-............. **CLC 39**
See also CA 112; 119; CANR 50

Epstein, Leslie 1938-............. **CLC 27**
See also CA 73-76; CAAS 12; CANR 23

Equiano, Olaudah
1745(?)-1797............. **LC 16; BLC**
See also DAM MULT; DLB 37, 50

Erasmus, Desiderius 1469(?)-1536.... **LC 16**

Erdman, Paul E(mil) 1932-........ **CLC 25**
See also AITN 1; CA 61-64; CANR 13, 43

Erdrich, Louise 1954-.......... **CLC 39, 54**
See also AAYA 10; BEST 89:1; CA 114;
CANR 41; DAM MULT, NOV, POP;
DLB 152; MTCW; NNAL

Erenburg, Ilya (Grigoryevich)
See Ehrenburg, Ilya (Grigoryevich)

Erickson, Stephen Michael 1950-
See Erickson, Steve
See also CA 129

Erickson, Steve................... **CLC 64**
See also Erickson, Stephen Michael

Ericson, Walter
See Fast, Howard (Melvin)

Eriksson, Buntel
See Bergman, (Ernst) Ingmar

Ernaux, Annie 1940-............. **CLC 88**
See also CA 147

Eschenbach, Wolfram von
See Wolfram von Eschenbach

Eseki, Bruno
See Mphahlele, Ezekiel

Esenin, Sergei (Alexandrovich)
1895-1925 .... **TCLC 4**
See also CA 104

Eshleman, Clayton 1935-........... **CLC 7**
See also CA 33-36R; CAAS 6; DLB 5

Espriella, Don Manuel Alvarez
See Southey, Robert

Espriu, Salvador 1913-1985........ **CLC 9**
See also CA 115; DLB 134

Espronceda, Jose de 1808-1842... **NCLC 39**

Esse, James
See Stephens, James

Esterbrook, Tom
See Hubbard, L(afayette) Ron(ald)

Estleman, Loren D. 1952-......... **CLC 48**
See also CA 85-88; CANR 27; DAM NOV,
POP; INT CANR-27; MTCW

Eugenides, Jeffrey 1960(?)-........ **CLC 81**
See also CA 144

Euripides c. 485B.C.-406B.C. .... **DC 4**
See also DA; DAB; DAC; DAM DRAM,
MST

Evan, Evin
See Faust, Frederick (Schiller)

Evans, Evan
See Faust, Frederick (Schiller)

Evans, Marian
See Eliot, George

Evans, Mary Ann
See Eliot, George

Evarts, Esther
See Benson, Sally

Everett, Percival L. 1956-......... **CLC 57**
See also BW 2; CA 129

Everson, R(onald) G(ilmour)
1903-....................... **CLC 27**
See also CA 17-20R; DLB 88

Everson, William (Oliver)
1912-1994 .... **CLC 1, 5, 14**
See also CA 9-12R; 145; CANR 20; DLB 5,
16; MTCW

Evtushenko, Evgenii Aleksandrovich
See Yevtushenko, Yevgeny (Alexandrovich)

Ewart, Gavin (Buchanan)
1916-1995 .... **CLC 13, 46**
See also CA 89-92; 150; CANR 17, 46;
DLB 40; MTCW

Ewers, Hanns Heinz 1871-1943 ... **TCLC 12**
See also CA 109; 149

Ewing, Frederick R.
See Sturgeon, Theodore (Hamilton)

Exley, Frederick (Earl)
1929-1992 .... **CLC 6, 11**
See also AITN 2; CA 81-84; 138; DLB 143;
DLBY 81

Eynhardt, Guillermo
See Quiroga, Horacio (Sylvestre)

Ezekiel, Nissim 1924-............. **CLC 61**
See also CA 61-64

Ezekiel, Tish O'Dowd 1943-....... **CLC 34**
See also CA 129

Fadeyev, A.
See Bulgya, Alexander Alexandrovich

Fadeyev, Alexander.............. **TCLC 53**
See also Bulgya, Alexander Alexandrovich

Fagen, Donald 1948-.............. **CLC 26**

Fainzilberg, Ilya Arnoldovich 1897-1937
See Ilf, Ilya
See also CA 120

Fair, Ronald L. 1932-............. **CLC 18**
See also BW 1; CA 69-72; CANR 25;
DLB 33

Fairbairns, Zoe (Ann) 1948- .... **CLC 32**
See also CA 103; CANR 21

Falco, Gian
See Papini, Giovanni

Falconer, James
See Kirkup, James

Falconer, Kenneth
See Kornbluth, C(yril) M.

Falkland, Samuel
See Heijermans, Herman

Fallaci, Oriana 1930-............. **CLC 11**
See also CA 77-80; CANR 15; MTCW

Faludy, George 1913-............. **CLC 42**
See also CA 21-24R

Faludy, Gyoergy
See Faludy, George

Fanon, Frantz 1925-1961..... **CLC 74; BLC**
See also BW 1; CA 116; 89-92;
DAM MULT

Fanshawe, Ann 1625-1680 .... **LC 11**

Fante, John (Thomas) 1911-1983 ... **CLC 60**
See also CA 69-72; 109; CANR 23;
DLB 130; DLBY 83

Farah, Nuruddin 1945-....... **CLC 53; BLC**
See also BW 2; CA 106; DAM MULT;
DLB 125

Fargue, Leon-Paul 1876(?)-1947 ... **TCLC 11**
See also CA 109

Farigoule, Louis
See Romains, Jules

Farina, Richard 1936(?)-1966 .... **CLC 9**
See also CA 81-84; 25-28R

Farley, Walter (Lorimer)
1915-1989 .... **CLC 17**
See also CA 17-20R; CANR 8, 29; DLB 22;
JRDA; MAICYA; SATA 2, 43

Farmer, Philip Jose 1918-....... CLC 1, 19
See also CA 1-4R; CANR 4, 35; DLB 8;
MTCW

Farquhar, George 1677-1707........ LC 21
See also DAM DRAM; DLB 84

Farrell, J(ames) G(ordon)
1935-1979 .... CLC 6
See also CA 73-76; 89-92; CANR 36;
DLB 14; MTCW

Farrell, James T(homas)
1904-1979 .... CLC 1, 4, 8, 11, 66
See also CA 5-8R; 89-92; CANR 9; DLB 4,
9, 86; DLBD 2; MTCW

Farren, Richard J.
See Betjeman, John

Farren, Richard M.
See Betjeman, John

Fassbinder, Rainer Werner
1946-1982 .... CLC 20
See also CA 93-96; 106; CANR 31

Fast, Howard (Melvin) 1914- ...... CLC 23
See also AAYA 16; CA 1-4R; CAAS 18;
CANR 1, 33; DAM NOV; DLB 9;
INT CANR-33; SATA 7

Faulcon, Robert
See Holdstock, Robert P.

Faulkner, William (Cuthbert)
1897-1962 ..... CLC 1, 3, 6, 8, 9, 11, 14,
18, 28, 52, 68; DA; DAB; DAC; SSC 1;
WLC
See also AAYA 7; CA 81-84; CANR 33;
CDALB 1929-1941; DAM MST, NOV;
DLB 9, 11, 44, 102; DLBD 2; DLBY 86;
MTCW

Fauset, Jessie Redmon
1884(?)-1961 .... CLC 19, 54; BLC
See also BW 1; CA 109; DAM MULT;
DLB 51

Faust, Frederick (Schiller)
1892-1944(?) .... TCLC 49
See also CA 108; DAM POP

Faust, Irvin 1924-................ CLC 8
See also CA 33-36R; CANR 28; DLB 2, 28;
DLBY 80

Fawkes, Guy
See Benchley, Robert (Charles)

Fearing, Kenneth (Flexner)
1902-1961 .... CLC 51
See also CA 93-96; DLB 9

Fecamps, Elise
See Creasey, John

Federman, Raymond 1928- ...... CLC 6, 47
See also CA 17-20R; CAAS 8; CANR 10,
43; DLBY 80

Federspiel, J(uerg) F. 1931-........ CLC 42
See also CA 146

Feiffer, Jules (Ralph) 1929-.... CLC 2, 8, 64
See also AAYA 3; CA 17-20R; CANR 30;
DAM DRAM; DLB 7, 44;
INT CANR-30; MTCW; SATA 8, 61

Feige, Hermann Albert Otto Maximilian
See Traven, B.

Feinberg, David B. 1956-1994..... CLC 59
See also CA 135; 147

Feinstein, Elaine 1930-............ CLC 36
See also CA 69-72; CAAS 1; CANR 31;
DLB 14, 40; MTCW

Feldman, Irving (Mordecai) 1928-.... CLC 7
See also CA 1-4R; CANR 1

Fellini, Federico 1920-1993 ..... CLC 16, 85
See also CA 65-68; 143; CANR 33

Felsen, Henry Gregor 1916- .... CLC 17
See also CA 1-4R; CANR 1; SAAS 2;
SATA 1

Fenton, James Martin 1949-....... CLC 32
See also CA 102; DLB 40

Ferber, Edna 1887-1968........ CLC 18, 93
See also AITN 1; CA 5-8R; 25-28R; DLB 9,
28, 86; MTCW; SATA 7

Ferguson, Helen
See Kavan, Anna

Ferguson, Samuel 1810-1886..... NCLC 33
See also DLB 32

Fergusson, Robert 1750-1774 .... LC 29
See also DLB 109

Ferling, Lawrence
See Ferlinghetti, Lawrence (Monsanto)

Ferlinghetti, Lawrence (Monsanto)
1919(?)-........ CLC 2, 6, 10, 27; PC 1
See also CA 5-8R; CANR 3, 41;
CDALB 1941-1968; DAM POET; DLB 5,
16; MTCW

Fernandez, Vicente Garcia Huidobro
See Huidobro Fernandez, Vicente Garcia

Ferrer, Gabriel (Francisco Victor) Miro
See Miro (Ferrer), Gabriel (Francisco
Victor)

Ferrier, Susan (Edmonstone)
1782-1854 .... NCLC 8
See also DLB 116

Ferrigno, Robert 1948(?)-.......... CLC 65
See also CA 140

Ferron, Jacques 1921-1985 ... CLC 94; DAC
See also CA 117; 129; DLB 60

Feuchtwanger, Lion 1884-1958 ..... TCLC 3
See also CA 104; DLB 66

Feuillet, Octave 1821-1890 ...... NCLC 45

Feydeau, Georges (Leon Jules Marie)
1862-1921 .... TCLC 22
See also CA 113; DAM DRAM

Ficino, Marsilio 1433-1499 .... LC 12

Fiedeler, Hans
See Doeblin, Alfred

Fiedler, Leslie A(aron)
1917-.................. CLC 4, 13, 24
See also CA 9-12R; CANR 7; DLB 28, 67;
MTCW

Field, Andrew 1938-.............. CLC 44
See also CA 97-100; CANR 25

Field, Eugene 1850-1895 .... NCLC 3
See also DLB 23, 42, 140; DLBD 13;
MAICYA; SATA 16

Field, Gans T.
See Wellman, Manly Wade

Field, Michael .... TCLC 43

Field, Peter
See Hobson, Laura Z(ametkin)

Fielding, Henry
1707-1754 ...... LC 1; DA; DAB; DAC;
WLC
See also CDBLB 1660-1789; DAM DRAM,
MST, NOV; DLB 39, 84, 101

Fielding, Sarah 1710-1768.......... LC 1
See also DLB 39

Fierstein, Harvey (Forbes) 1954- ... CLC 33
See also CA 123; 129; DAM DRAM, POP

Figes, Eva 1932-.................. CLC 31
See also CA 53-56; CANR 4, 44; DLB 14

Finch, Robert (Duer Claydon)
1900-..................... CLC 18
See also CA 57-60; CANR 9, 24, 49;
DLB 88

Findley, Timothy 1930- ...... CLC 27; DAC
See also CA 25-28R; CANR 12, 42;
DAM MST; DLB 53

Fink, William
See Mencken, H(enry) L(ouis)

Firbank, Louis 1942-
See Reed, Lou
See also CA 117

Firbank, (Arthur Annesley) Ronald
1886-1926 .... TCLC 1
See also CA 104; DLB 36

Fisher, M(ary) F(rances) K(ennedy)
1908-1992 .... CLC 76, 87
See also CA 77-80; 138; CANR 44

Fisher, Roy 1930-................ CLC 25
See also CA 81-84; CAAS 10; CANR 16;
DLB 40

Fisher, Rudolph
1897-1934 .... TCLC 11; BLC
See also BW 1; CA 107; 124; DAM MULT;
DLB 51, 102

Fisher, Vardis (Alvero) 1895-1968.... CLC 7
See also CA 5-8R; 25-28R; DLB 9

Fiske, Tarleton
See Bloch, Robert (Albert)

Fitch, Clarke
See Sinclair, Upton (Beall)

Fitch, John IV
See Cormier, Robert (Edmund)

Fitzgerald, Captain Hugh
See Baum, L(yman) Frank

FitzGerald, Edward 1809-1883 .... NCLC 9
See also DLB 32

Fitzgerald, F(rancis) Scott (Key)
1896-1940 .... TCLC 1, 6, 14, 28, 55;
DA; DAB; DAC; SSC 6; WLC
See also AITN 1; CA 110; 123;
CDALB 1917-1929; DAM MST, NOV;
DLB 4, 9, 86; DLBD 1; DLBY 81;
MTCW

Fitzgerald, Penelope 1916-... CLC 19, 51, 61
See also CA 85-88; CAAS 10; DLB 14

Fitzgerald, Robert (Stuart)
1910-1985 .... CLC 39
See also CA 1-4R; 114; CANR 1; DLBY 80

FitzGerald, Robert D(avid)
1902-1987 .... CLC 19
See also CA 17-20R

Fitzgerald, Zelda (Sayre)
1900-1948 . . . . **TCLC 52**
See also CA 117; 126; DLBY 84

Flanagan, Thomas (James Bonner)
1923- . . . . **CLC 25, 52**
See also CA 108; DLBY 80; INT 108;
MTCW

Flaubert, Gustave
1821-1880 . . . . **NCLC 2, 10, 19; DA;**
DAB; DAC; SSC 11; WLC
See also DAM MST, NOV; DLB 119

Flecker, Herman Elroy
See Flecker, (Herman) James Elroy

Flecker, (Herman) James Elroy
1884-1915 . . . . **TCLC 43**
See also CA 109; 150; DLB 10, 19

Fleming, Ian (Lancaster)
1908-1964 . . . . **CLC 3, 30**
See also CA 5-8R; CDBLB 1945-1960;
DAM POP; DLB 87; MTCW; SATA 9

Fleming, Thomas (James) 1927- . . . . **CLC 37**
See also CA 5-8R; CANR 10;
INT CANR-10; SATA 8

Fletcher, John 1579-1625 . . . . . . **LC 33; DC 6**
See also CDBLB Before 1660; DLB 58

Fletcher, John Gould 1886-1950 . . . **TCLC 35**
See also CA 107; DLB 4, 45

Fleur, Paul
See Pohl, Frederik

Flooglebuckle, Al
See Spiegelman, Art

Flying Officer X
See Bates, H(erbert) E(rnest)

Fo, Dario 1926- . . . . **CLC 32**
See also CA 116; 128; DAM DRAM;
MTCW

Fogarty, Jonathan Titulescu Esq.
See Farrell, James T(homas)

Folke, Will
See Bloch, Robert (Albert)

Follett, Ken(neth Martin) 1949- . . . . **CLC 18**
See also AAYA 6; BEST 89:4; CA 81-84;
CANR 13, 33; DAM NOV, POP;
DLB 87; DLBY 81; INT CANR-33;
MTCW

Fontane, Theodor 1819-1898 . . . . . **NCLC 26**
See also DLB 129

Foote, Horton 1916- . . . . **CLC 51, 91**
See also CA 73-76; CANR 34, 51;
DAM DRAM; DLB 26; INT CANR-34

Foote, Shelby 1916- . . . . **CLC 75**
See also CA 5-8R; CANR 3, 45;
DAM NOV, POP; DLB 2, 17

Forbes, Esther 1891-1967 . . . . **CLC 12**
See also AAYA 17; CA 13-14; 25-28R;
CAP 1; CLR 27; DLB 22; JRDA;
MAICYA; SATA 2

Forche, Carolyn (Louise)
1950- . . . . **CLC 25, 83, 86; PC 10**
See also CA 109; 117; CANR 50;
DAM POET; DLB 5; INT 117

Ford, Elbur
See Hibbert, Eleanor Alice Burford

Ford, Ford Madox
1873-1939 . . . . **TCLC 1, 15, 39, 57**
See also CA 104; 132; CDBLB 1914-1945;
DAM NOV; DLB 162; MTCW

Ford, John 1895-1973 . . . . **CLC 16**
See also CA 45-48

Ford, Richard 1944- . . . . **CLC 46**
See also CA 69-72; CANR 11, 47

Ford, Webster
See Masters, Edgar Lee

Foreman, Richard 1937- . . . . **CLC 50**
See also CA 65-68; CANR 32

Forester, C(ecil) S(cott)
1899-1966 . . . . **CLC 35**
See also CA 73-76; 25-28R; SATA 13

Forez
See Mauriac, Francois (Charles)

Forman, James Douglas 1932- . . . . . . **CLC 21**
See also AAYA 17; CA 9-12R; CANR 4,
19, 42; JRDA; MAICYA; SATA 8, 70

Fornes, Maria Irene 1930- . . . . . . **CLC 39, 61**
See also CA 25-28R; CANR 28; DLB 7;
HW; INT CANR-28; MTCW

Forrest, Leon 1937- . . . . **CLC 4**
See also BW 2; CA 89-92; CAAS 7;
CANR 25, 52; DLB 33

Forster, E(dward) M(organ)
1879-1970 . . . . . **CLC 1, 2, 3, 4, 9, 10, 13,**
15, 22, 45, 77; DA; DAB; DAC; WLC
See also AAYA 2; CA 13-14; 25-28R;
CANR 45; CAP 1; CDBLB 1914-1945;
DAM MST, NOV; DLB 34, 98, 162;
DLBD 10; MTCW; SATA 57

Forster, John 1812-1876 . . . . **NCLC 11**
See also DLB 144

Forsyth, Frederick 1938- . . . . . . **CLC 2, 5, 36**
See also BEST 89:4; CA 85-88; CANR 38;
DAM NOV, POP; DLB 87; MTCW

Forten, Charlotte L. . . . . **TCLC 16; BLC**
See also Grimke, Charlotte L(ottie) Forten
See also DLB 50

Foscolo, Ugo 1778-1827 . . . . **NCLC 8**

Fosse, Bob . . . . **CLC 20**
See also Fosse, Robert Louis

Fosse, Robert Louis 1927-1987
See Fosse, Bob
See also CA 110; 123

Foster, Stephen Collins
1826-1864 . . . . **NCLC 26**

Foucault, Michel
1926-1984 . . . . **CLC 31, 34, 69**
See also CA 105; 113; CANR 34; MTCW

Fouque, Friedrich (Heinrich Karl) de la Motte
1777-1843 . . . . **NCLC 2**
See also DLB 90

Fourier, Charles 1772-1837 . . . . . . **NCLC 51**

Fournier, Henri Alban 1886-1914
See Alain-Fournier
See also CA 104

Fournier, Pierre 1916- . . . . **CLC 11**
See also Gascar, Pierre
See also CA 89-92; CANR 16, 40

Fowles, John
1926- . . . . . . **CLC 1, 2, 3, 4, 6, 9, 10, 15,**
33, 87; DAB; DAC
See also CA 5-8R; CANR 25; CDBLB 1960
to Present; DAM MST; DLB 14, 139;
MTCW; SATA 22

Fox, Paula 1923- . . . . **CLC 2, 8**
See also AAYA 3; CA 73-76; CANR 20,
36; CLR 1; DLB 52; JRDA; MAICYA;
MTCW; SATA 17, 60

Fox, William Price (Jr.) 1926- . . . . . **CLC 22**
See also CA 17-20R; CAAS 19; CANR 11;
DLB 2; DLBY 81

Foxe, John 1516(?)-1587 . . . . **LC 14**

Frame, Janet . . . . **CLC 2, 3, 6, 22, 66**
See also Clutha, Janet Paterson Frame

France, Anatole . . . . **TCLC 9**
See also Thibault, Jacques Anatole Francois
See also DLB 123

Francis, Claude 19(?)- . . . . **CLC 50**

Francis, Dick 1920- . . . . **CLC 2, 22, 42**
See also AAYA 5; BEST 89:3; CA 5-8R;
CANR 9, 42; CDBLB 1960 to Present;
DAM POP; DLB 87; INT CANR-9;
MTCW

Francis, Robert (Churchill)
1901-1987 . . . . **CLC 15**
See also CA 1-4R; 123; CANR 1

Frank, Anne(lies Marie)
1929-1945 . . . . **TCLC 17; DA; DAB;**
DAC; WLC
See also AAYA 12; CA 113; 133;
DAM MST; MTCW; SATA 87;
SATA-Brief 42

Frank, Elizabeth 1945- . . . . **CLC 39**
See also CA 121; 126; INT 126

Frankl, Viktor E(mil) 1905- . . . . **CLC 93**
See also CA 65-68

Franklin, Benjamin
See Hasek, Jaroslav (Matej Frantisek)

Franklin, Benjamin
1706-1790 . . . . . **LC 25; DA; DAB; DAC**
See also CDALB 1640-1865; DAM MST;
DLB 24, 43, 73

Franklin, (Stella Maraia Sarah) Miles
1879-1954 . . . . **TCLC 7**
See also CA 104

Fraser, (Lady) Antonia (Pakenham)
1932- . . . . **CLC 32**
See also CA 85-88; CANR 44; MTCW;
SATA-Brief 32

Fraser, George MacDonald 1925- . . . . **CLC 7**
See also CA 45-48; CANR 2, 48

Fraser, Sylvia 1935- . . . . **CLC 64**
See also CA 45-48; CANR 1, 16

Frayn, Michael 1933- . . . . . . **CLC 3, 7, 31, 47**
See also CA 5-8R; CANR 30;
DAM DRAM, NOV; DLB 13, 14;
MTCW

Fraze, Candida (Merrill) 1945- . . . . . **CLC 50**
See also CA 126

Frazer, J(ames) G(eorge)
1854-1941 . . . . **TCLC 32**
See also CA 118

Frazer, Robert Caine
See Creasey, John

Frazer, Sir James George
See Frazer, J(ames) G(eorge)

Frazier, Ian 1951-............... CLC 46
See also CA 130

Frederic, Harold 1856-1898...... NCLC 10
See also DLB 12, 23; DLBD 13

Frederick, John
See Faust, Frederick (Schiller)

Frederick the Great 1712-1786...... LC 14

Fredro, Aleksander 1793-1876..... NCLC 8

Freeling, Nicolas 1927- .... CLC 38
See also CA 49-52; CAAS 12; CANR 1, 17,
50; DLB 87

Freeman, Douglas Southall
1886-1953 .... TCLC 11
See also CA 109; DLB 17

Freeman, Judith 1946-............ CLC 55
See also CA 148

Freeman, Mary Eleanor Wilkins
1852-1930 .... TCLC 9; SSC 1
See also CA 106; DLB 12, 78

Freeman, R(ichard) Austin
1862-1943 .... TCLC 21
See also CA 113; DLB 70

French, Albert 1943- .... CLC 86

French, Marilyn 1929-...... CLC 10, 18, 60
See also CA 69-72; CANR 3, 31;
DAM DRAM, NOV, POP;
INT CANR-31; MTCW

French, Paul
See Asimov, Isaac

Freneau, Philip Morin 1752-1832.. NCLC 1
See also DLB 37, 43

Freud, Sigmund 1856-1939 .... TCLC 52
See also CA 115; 133; MTCW

Friedan, Betty (Naomi) 1921-...... CLC 74
See also CA 65-68; CANR 18, 45; MTCW

Friedlander, Saul 1932-........... CLC 90
See also CA 117; 130

Friedman, B(ernard) H(arper)
1926-........................ CLC 7
See also CA 1-4R; CANR 3, 48

Friedman, Bruce Jay 1930-.... CLC 3, 5, 56
See also CA 9-12R; CANR 25, 52; DLB 2,
28; INT CANR-25

Friel, Brian 1929-........... CLC 5, 42, 59
See also CA 21-24R; CANR 33; DLB 13;
MTCW

Friis-Baastad, Babbis Ellinor
1921-1970 .... CLC 12
See also CA 17-20R; 134; SATA 7

Frisch, Max (Rudolf)
1911-1991 ..... CLC 3, 9, 14, 18, 32, 44
See also CA 85-88; 134; CANR 32;
DAM DRAM, NOV; DLB 69, 124;
MTCW

Fromentin, Eugene (Samuel Auguste)
1820-1876 .... NCLC 10
See also DLB 123

Frost, Frederick
See Faust, Frederick (Schiller)

Frost, Robert (Lee)
1874-1963 .... CLC 1, 3, 4, 9, 10, 13, 15,
26, 34, 44; DA; DAB; DAC; PC 1; WLC
See also CA 89-92; CANR 33;
CDALB 1917-1929; DAM MST, POET;
DLB 54; DLBD 7; MTCW; SATA 14

Froude, James Anthony
1818-1894 .... NCLC 43
See also DLB 18, 57, 144

Froy, Herald
See Waterhouse, Keith (Spencer)

Fry, Christopher 1907-....... CLC 2, 10, 14
See also CA 17-20R; CAAS 23; CANR 9,
30; DAM DRAM; DLB 13; MTCW;
SATA 66

Frye, (Herman) Northrop
1912-1991 .... CLC 24, 70
See also CA 5-8R; 133; CANR 8, 37;
DLB 67, 68; MTCW

Fuchs, Daniel 1909-1993 .... CLC 8, 22
See also CA 81-84; 142; CAAS 5;
CANR 40; DLB 9, 26, 28; DLBY 93

Fuchs, Daniel 1934-............. CLC 34
See also CA 37-40R; CANR 14, 48

Fuentes, Carlos
1928-...... CLC 3, 8, 10, 13, 22, 41, 60;
DA; DAB; DAC; HLC; WLC
See also AAYA 4; AITN 2; CA 69-72;
CANR 10, 32; DAM MST, MULT,
NOV; DLB 113; HW; MTCW

Fuentes, Gregorio Lopez y
See Lopez y Fuentes, Gregorio

Fugard, (Harold) Athol
1932-.... CLC 5, 9, 14, 25, 40, 80; DC 3
See also AAYA 17; CA 85-88; CANR 32;
DAM DRAM; MTCW

Fugard, Sheila 1932- .... CLC 48
See also CA 125

Fuller, Charles (H., Jr.)
1939-............ CLC 25; BLC; DC 1
See also BW 2; CA 108; 112;
DAM DRAM, MULT; DLB 38;
INT 112; MTCW

Fuller, John (Leopold) 1937-....... CLC 62
See also CA 21-24R; CANR 9, 44; DLB 40

Fuller, Margaret .... NCLC 5, 50
See also Ossoli, Sarah Margaret (Fuller
marchesa d')

Fuller, Roy (Broadbent)
1912-1991 .... CLC 4, 28
See also CA 5-8R; 135; CAAS 10;
CANR 53; DLB 15, 20; SATA 87

Fulton, Alice 1952-.............. CLC 52
See also CA 116

Furphy, Joseph 1843-1912....... TCLC 25

Fussell, Paul 1924-............... CLC 74
See also BEST 90:1; CA 17-20R; CANR 8,
21, 35; INT CANR-21; MTCW

Futabatei, Shimei 1864-1909..... TCLC 44

Futrelle, Jacques 1875-1912 ...... TCLC 19
See also CA 113

Gaboriau, Emile 1835-1873...... NCLC 14

Gadda, Carlo Emilio 1893-1973 .... CLC 11
See also CA 89-92

Gaddis, William
1922-..... CLC 1, 3, 6, 8, 10, 19, 43, 86
See also CA 17-20R; CANR 21, 48; DLB 2;
MTCW

Gaines, Ernest J(ames)
1933-......... CLC 3, 11, 18, 86; BLC
See also AAYA 18; AITN 1; BW 2;
CA 9-12R; CANR 6, 24, 42;
CDALB 1968-1988; DAM MULT;
DLB 2, 33, 152; DLBY 80; MTCW;
SATA 86

Gaitskill, Mary 1954-............. CLC 69
See also CA 128

Galdos, Benito Perez
See Perez Galdos, Benito

Gale, Zona 1874-1938 .... TCLC 7
See also CA 105; DAM DRAM; DLB 9, 78

Galeano, Eduardo (Hughes) 1940-... CLC 72
See also CA 29-32R; CANR 13, 32; HW

Galiano, Juan Valera y Alcala
See Valera y Alcala-Galiano, Juan

Gallagher, Tess 1943-.... CLC 18, 63; PC 9
See also CA 106; DAM POET; DLB 120

Gallant, Mavis
1922-...... CLC 7, 18, 38; DAC; SSC 5
See also CA 69-72; CANR 29; DAM MST;
DLB 53; MTCW

Gallant, Roy A(rthur) 1924- .... CLC 17
See also CA 5-8R; CANR 4, 29; CLR 30;
MAICYA; SATA 4, 68

Gallico, Paul (William) 1897-1976 ... CLC 2
See also AITN 1; CA 5-8R; 69-72;
CANR 23; DLB 9; MAICYA; SATA 13

Gallo, Max Louis 1932-........... CLC 95
See also CA 85-88

Gallois, Lucien
See Desnos, Robert

Gallup, Ralph
See Whitemore, Hugh (John)

Galsworthy, John
1867-1933 ...... TCLC 1, 45; DA; DAB;
DAC; SSC 22; WLC 2
See also CA 104; 141; CDBLB 1890-1914;
DAM DRAM, MST, NOV; DLB 10, 34,
98, 162

Galt, John 1779-1839........... NCLC 1
See also DLB 99, 116, 159

Galvin, James 1951-.............. CLC 38
See also CA 108; CANR 26

Gamboa, Federico 1864-1939...... TCLC 36

Gandhi, M. K.
See Gandhi, Mohandas Karamchand

Gandhi, Mahatma
See Gandhi, Mohandas Karamchand

Gandhi, Mohandas Karamchand
1869-1948 .... TCLC 59
See also CA 121; 132; DAM MULT;
MTCW

Gann, Ernest Kellogg 1910-1991.... CLC 23
See also AITN 1; CA 1-4R; 136; CANR 1

Garcia, Cristina 1958-............ CLC 76
See also CA 141

Garcia Lorca, Federico
1898-1936 . . . **TCLC 1, 7, 49; DA; DAB;
DAC; DC 2; HLC; PC 3; WLC**
See also CA 104; 131; DAM DRAM, MST,
MULT, POET; DLB 108; HW; MTCW

Garcia Marquez, Gabriel (Jose)
1928- . . . . **CLC 2, 3, 8, 10, 15, 27, 47, 55,
68; DA; DAB; DAC; HLC; SSC 8; WLC**
See also AAYA 3; BEST 89:1, 90:4;
CA 33-36R; CANR 10, 28, 50;
DAM MST, MULT, NOV, POP;
DLB 113; HW; MTCW

Gard, Janice
See Latham, Jean Lee

Gard, Roger Martin du
See Martin du Gard, Roger

Gardam, Jane 1928- . . . . **CLC 43**
See also CA 49-52; CANR 2, 18, 33;
CLR 12; DLB 14, 161; MAICYA;
MTCW; SAAS 9; SATA 39, 76;
SATA-Brief 28

Gardner, Herb(ert) 1934- . . . . **CLC 44**
See also CA 149

Gardner, John (Champlin), Jr.
1933-1982 . . . . . **CLC 2, 3, 5, 7, 8, 10, 18,
28, 34; SSC 7**
See also AITN 1; CA 65-68; 107;
CANR 33; DAM NOV, POP; DLB 2;
DLBY 82; MTCW; SATA 40;
SATA-Obit 31

Gardner, John (Edmund) 1926- . . . . . **CLC 30**
See also CA 103; CANR 15; DAM POP;
MTCW

Gardner, Miriam
See Bradley, Marion Zimmer

Gardner, Noel
See Kuttner, Henry

Gardons, S. S.
See Snodgrass, W(illiam) D(e Witt)

Garfield, Leon 1921- . . . . **CLC 12**
See also AAYA 8; CA 17-20R; CANR 38,
41; CLR 21; DLB 161; JRDA; MAICYA;
SATA 1, 32, 76

Garland, (Hannibal) Hamlin
1860-1940 . . . . **TCLC 3; SSC 18**
See also CA 104; DLB 12, 71, 78

Garneau, (Hector de) Saint-Denys
1912-1943 . . . . **TCLC 13**
See also CA 111; DLB 88

Garner, Alan 1934- . . . . **CLC 17; DAB**
See also AAYA 18; CA 73-76; CANR 15;
CLR 20; DAM POP; DLB 161;
MAICYA; MTCW; SATA 18, 69

Garner, Hugh 1913-1979 . . . . **CLC 13**
See also CA 69-72; CANR 31; DLB 68

Garnett, David 1892-1981 . . . . **CLC 3**
See also CA 5-8R; 103; CANR 17; DLB 34

Garos, Stephanie
See Katz, Steve

Garrett, George (Palmer)
1929- . . . . **CLC 3, 11, 51**
See also CA 1-4R; CAAS 5; CANR 1, 42;
DLB 2, 5, 130, 152; DLBY 83

Garrick, David 1717-1779 . . . . **LC 15**
See also DAM DRAM; DLB 84

Garrigue, Jean 1914-1972 . . . . **CLC 2, 8**
See also CA 5-8R; 37-40R; CANR 20

Garrison, Frederick
See Sinclair, Upton (Beall)

Garth, Will
See Hamilton, Edmond; Kuttner, Henry

Garvey, Marcus (Moziah, Jr.)
1887-1940 . . . . **TCLC 41; BLC**
See also BW 1; CA 120; 124; DAM MULT

Gary, Romain . . . . **CLC 25**
See also Kacew, Romain
See also DLB 83

Gascar, Pierre . . . . **CLC 11**
See also Fournier, Pierre

Gascoyne, David (Emery) 1916- . . . . **CLC 45**
See also CA 65-68; CANR 10, 28; DLB 20;
MTCW

Gaskell, Elizabeth Cleghorn
1810-1865 . . . . **NCLC 5; DAB**
See also CDBLB 1832-1890; DAM MST;
DLB 21, 144, 159

Gass, William H(oward)
1924- . . . **CLC 1, 2, 8, 11, 15, 39; SSC 12**
See also CA 17-20R; CANR 30; DLB 2;
MTCW

Gasset, Jose Ortega y
See Ortega y Gasset, Jose

Gates, Henry Louis, Jr. 1950- . . . . . . **CLC 65**
See also BW 2; CA 109; CANR 25, 53;
DAM MULT; DLB 67

Gautier, Theophile
1811-1872 . . . . **NCLC 1; SSC 20**
See also DAM POET; DLB 119

Gawsworth, John
See Bates, H(erbert) E(rnest)

Gay, Oliver
See Gogarty, Oliver St. John

Gaye, Marvin (Penze) 1939-1984 . . . **CLC 26**
See also CA 112

Gebler, Carlo (Ernest) 1954- . . . . **CLC 39**
See also CA 119; 133

Gee, Maggie (Mary) 1948- . . . . **CLC 57**
See also CA 130

Gee, Maurice (Gough) 1931- . . . . **CLC 29**
See also CA 97-100; SATA 46

Gelbart, Larry (Simon) 1923- . . . **CLC 21, 61**
See also CA 73-76; CANR 45

Gelber, Jack 1932- . . . . **CLC 1, 6, 14, 79**
See also CA 1-4R; CANR 2; DLB 7

Gellhorn, Martha (Ellis) 1908- . . **CLC 14, 60**
See also CA 77-80; CANR 44; DLBY 82

Genet, Jean
1910-1986 . . . **CLC 1, 2, 5, 10, 14, 44, 46**
See also CA 13-16R; CANR 18;
DAM DRAM; DLB 72; DLBY 86;
MTCW

Gent, Peter 1942- . . . . **CLC 29**
See also AITN 1; CA 89-92; DLBY 82

Gentlewoman in New England, A
See Bradstreet, Anne

Gentlewoman in Those Parts, A
See Bradstreet, Anne

George, Jean Craighead 1919- . . . . . . **CLC 35**
See also AAYA 8; CA 5-8R; CANR 25;
CLR 1; DLB 52; JRDA; MAICYA;
SATA 2, 68

George, Stefan (Anton)
1868-1933 . . . . **TCLC 2, 14**
See also CA 104

Georges, Georges Martin
See Simenon, Georges (Jacques Christian)

Gerhardi, William Alexander
See Gerhardie, William Alexander

Gerhardie, William Alexander
1895-1977 . . . . **CLC 5**
See also CA 25-28R; 73-76; CANR 18;
DLB 36

Gerstler, Amy 1956- . . . . **CLC 70**
See also CA 146

Gertler, T. . . . . **CLC 34**
See also CA 116; 121; INT 121

Ghalib . . . . **NCLC 39**
See also Ghalib, Hsadullah Khan

Ghalib, Hsadullah Khan 1797-1869
See Ghalib
See also DAM POET

Ghelderode, Michel de
1898-1962 . . . . **CLC 6, 11**
See also CA 85-88; CANR 40;
DAM DRAM

Ghiselin, Brewster 1903- . . . . **CLC 23**
See also CA 13-16R; CAAS 10; CANR 13

Ghose, Zulfikar 1935- . . . . **CLC 42**
See also CA 65-68

Ghosh, Amitav 1956- . . . . **CLC 44**
See also CA 147

Giacosa, Giuseppe 1847-1906 . . . . . . **TCLC 7**
See also CA 104

Gibb, Lee
See Waterhouse, Keith (Spencer)

Gibbon, Lewis Grassic . . . . **TCLC 4**
See also Mitchell, James Leslie

Gibbons, Kaye 1960- . . . . **CLC 50, 88**
See also CA 151; DAM POP

Gibran, Kahlil
1883-1931 . . . . **TCLC 1, 9; PC 9**
See also CA 104; 150; DAM POET, POP

Gibran, Khalil
See Gibran, Kahlil

Gibson, William
1914- . . . . **CLC 23; DA; DAB; DAC**
See also CA 9-12R; CANR 9, 42;
DAM DRAM, MST; DLB 7; SATA 66

Gibson, William (Ford) 1948- . . . **CLC 39, 63**
See also AAYA 12; CA 126; 133;
CANR 52; DAM POP

Gide, Andre (Paul Guillaume)
1869-1951 . . . . **TCLC 5, 12, 36; DA;
DAB; DAC; SSC 13; WLC**
See also CA 104; 124; DAM MST, NOV;
DLB 65; MTCW

Gifford, Barry (Colby) 1946- . . . . **CLC 34**
See also CA 65-68; CANR 9, 30, 40

Gilbert, W(illiam) S(chwenck)
1836-1911 . . . . **TCLC 3**
See also CA 104; DAM DRAM, POET;
SATA 36

Gilbreth, Frank B., Jr. 1911-....... CLC 17
See also CA 9-12R; SATA 2

Gilchrist, Ellen 1935-.. CLC 34, 48; SSC 14
See also CA 113; 116; CANR 41;
DAM POP; DLB 130; MTCW

Giles, Molly 1942-.............. CLC 39
See also CA 126

Gill, Patrick
See Creasey, John

Gilliam, Terry (Vance) 1940-....... CLC 21
See also Monty Python
See also CA 108; 113; CANR 35; INT 113

Gillian, Jerry
See Gilliam, Terry (Vance)

Gilliatt, Penelope (Ann Douglass)
1932-1993 .... CLC 2, 10, 13, 53
See also AITN 2; CA 13-16R; 141;
CANR 49; DLB 14

Gilman, Charlotte (Anna) Perkins (Stetson)
1860-1935 .... TCLC 9, 37; SSC 13
See also CA 106; 150

Gilmour, David 1949-............. CLC 35
See also CA 138; 147

Gilpin, William 1724-1804....... NCLC 30

Gilray, J. D.
See Mencken, H(enry) L(ouis)

Gilroy, Frank D(aniel) 1925-........ CLC 2
See also CA 81-84; CANR 32; DLB 7

Ginsberg, Allen
1926- ...... CLC 1, 2, 3, 4, 6, 13, 36, 69;
DA; DAB; DAC; PC 4; WLC 3
See also AITN 1; CA 1-4R; CANR 2, 41;
CDALB 1941-1968; DAM MST, POET;
DLB 5, 16; MTCW

Ginzburg, Natalia
1916-1991 .... CLC 5, 11, 54, 70
See also CA 85-88; 135; CANR 33; MTCW

Giono, Jean 1895-1970......... CLC 4, 11
See also CA 45-48; 29-32R; CANR 2, 35;
DLB 72; MTCW

Giovanni, Nikki
1943- ...... CLC 2, 4, 19, 64; BLC; DA;
DAB; DAC
See also AITN 1; BW 2; CA 29-32R;
CAAS 6; CANR 18, 41; CLR 6;
DAM MST, MULT, POET; DLB 5, 41;
INT CANR-18; MAICYA; MTCW;
SATA 24

Giovene, Andrea 1904-............. CLC 7
See also CA 85-88

Gippius, Zinaida (Nikolayevna) 1869-1945
See Hippius, Zinaida
See also CA 106

Giraudoux, (Hippolyte) Jean
1882-1944 .... TCLC 2, 7
See also CA 104; DAM DRAM; DLB 65

Gironella, Jose Maria 1917-....... CLC 11
See also CA 101

Gissing, George (Robert)
1857-1903 .... TCLC 3, 24, 47
See also CA 105; DLB 18, 135

Giurlani, Aldo
See Palazzeschi, Aldo

Gladkov, Fyodor (Vasilyevich)
1883-1958 .... TCLC 27

Glanville, Brian (Lester) 1931- ...., CLC 6
See also CA 5-8R; CAAS 9; CANR 3;
DLB 15, 139; SATA 42

Glasgow, Ellen (Anderson Gholson)
1873(?)-1945 .... TCLC 2, 7
See also CA 104; DLB 9, 12

Glaspell, Susan (Keating)
1882(?)-1948 .... TCLC 55
See also CA 110; DLB 7, 9, 78; YABC 2

Glassco, John 1909-1981 .... CLC 9
See also CA 13-16R; 102; CANR 15;
DLB 68

Glasscock, Amnesia
See Steinbeck, John (Ernst)

Glasser, Ronald J. 1940(?)-........ CLC 37

Glassman, Joyce
See Johnson, Joyce

Glendinning, Victoria 1937-........ CLC 50
See also CA 120; 127; DLB 155

Glissant, Edouard 1928-........ CLC 10, 68
See also DAM MULT

Gloag, Julian 1930- .... CLC 40
See also AITN 1; CA 65-68; CANR 10

Glowacki, Aleksander
See Prus, Boleslaw

Gluck, Louise (Elisabeth)
1943- .... CLC 7, 22, 44, 81; PC 16
See also CA 33-36R; CANR 40;
DAM POET; DLB 5

Gobineau, Joseph Arthur (Comte) de
1816-1882 .... NCLC 17
See also DLB 123

Godard, Jean-Luc 1930-........... CLC 20
See also CA 93-96

Godden, (Margaret) Rumer 1907-... CLC 53
See also AAYA 6; CA 5-8R; CANR 4, 27,
36; CLR 20; DLB 161; MAICYA;
SAAS 12; SATA 3, 36

Godoy Alcayaga, Lucila 1889-1957
See Mistral, Gabriela
See also BW 2; CA 104; 131; DAM MULT;
HW; MTCW

Godwin, Gail (Kathleen)
1937- .... CLC 5, 8, 22, 31, 69
See also CA 29-32R; CANR 15, 43;
DAM POP; DLB 6; INT CANR-15;
MTCW

Godwin, William 1756-1836...... NCLC 14
See also CDBLB 1789-1832; DLB 39, 104,
142, 158, 163

Goethe, Johann Wolfgang von
1749-1832 .... NCLC 4, 22, 34; DA;
DAB; DAC; PC 5; WLC 3
See also DAM DRAM, MST, POET;
DLB 94

Gogarty, Oliver St. John
1878-1957 .... TCLC 15
See also CA 109; 150; DLB 15, 19

Gogol, Nikolai (Vasilyevich)
1809-1852 .... NCLC 5, 15, 31; DA;
DAB; DAC; DC 1; SSC 4; WLC
See also DAM DRAM, MST

Goines, Donald
1937(?)-1974 .... CLC 80; BLC
See also AITN 1; BW 1; CA 124; 114;
DAM MULT, POP; DLB 33

Gold, Herbert 1924-....... CLC 4, 7, 14, 42
See also CA 9-12R; CANR 17, 45; DLB 2;
DLBY 81

Goldbarth, Albert 1948-........ CLC 5, 38
See also CA 53-56; CANR 6, 40; DLB 120

Goldberg, Anatol 1910-1982 .... CLC 34
See also CA 131; 117

Goldemberg, Isaac 1945-.......... CLC 52
See also CA 69-72; CAAS 12; CANR 11,
32; HW

Golding, William (Gerald)
1911-1993 .... CLC 1, 2, 3, 8, 10, 17, 27,
58, 81; DA; DAB; DAC; WLC
See also AAYA 5; CA 5-8R; 141;
CANR 13, 33; CDBLB 1945-1960;
DAM MST, NOV; DLB 15, 100; MTCW

Goldman, Emma 1869-1940...... TCLC 13
See also CA 110; 150

Goldman, Francisco 1955-......... CLC 76

Goldman, William (W.) 1931-.... CLC 1, 48
See also CA 9-12R; CANR 29; DLB 44

Goldmann, Lucien 1913-1970 ...... CLC 24
See also CA 25-28; CAP 2

Goldoni, Carlo 1707-1793 .... LC 4
See also DAM DRAM

Goldsberry, Steven 1949-.......... CLC 34
See also CA 131

Goldsmith, Oliver
1728-1774 ...... LC 2; DA; DAB; DAC;
WLC
See also CDBLB 1660-1789; DAM DRAM,
MST, NOV, POET; DLB 39, 89, 104,
109, 142; SATA 26

Goldsmith, Peter
See Priestley, J(ohn) B(oynton)

Gombrowicz, Witold
1904-1969 .... CLC 4, 7, 11, 49
See also CA 19-20; 25-28R; CAP 2;
DAM DRAM

Gomez de la Serna, Ramon
1888-1963 .... CLC 9
See also CA 116; HW

Goncharov, Ivan Alexandrovich
1812-1891 .... NCLC 1

Goncourt, Edmond (Louis Antoine Huot) de
1822-1896 .... NCLC 7
See also DLB 123

Goncourt, Jules (Alfred Huot) de
1830-1870 .... NCLC 7
See also DLB 123

Gontier, Fernande 19(?)- .... CLC 50

Goodman, Paul 1911-1972.... CLC 1, 2, 4, 7
See also CA 19-20; 37-40R; CANR 34;
CAP 2; DLB 130; MTCW

Gordimer, Nadine
1923- .... CLC 3, 5, 7, 10, 18, 33, 51, 70;
DA; DAB; DAC; SSC 17
See also CA 5-8R; CANR 3, 28;
DAM MST, NOV; INT CANR-28;
MTCW

Gordon, Adam Lindsay
　1833-1870 .... NCLC 21

Gordon, Caroline
　1895-1981 ... CLC 6, 13, 29, 83; SSC 15
　See also CA 11-12; 103; CANR 36; CAP 1;
　DLB 4, 9, 102; DLBY 81; MTCW

Gordon, Charles William 1860-1937
　See Connor, Ralph
　See also CA 109

Gordon, Mary (Catherine)
　1949- .... CLC 13, 22
　See also CA 102; CANR 44; DLB 6;
　DLBY 81; INT 102; MTCW

Gordon, Sol 1923- .... CLC 26
　See also CA 53-56; CANR 4; SATA 11

Gordone, Charles 1925-1995 ...... CLC 1, 4
　See also BW 1; CA 93-96; 150;
　DAM DRAM; DLB 7; INT 93-96;
　MTCW

Gorenko, Anna Andreevna
　See Akhmatova, Anna

Gorky, Maxim .... TCLC 8; DAB; WLC
　See also Peshkov, Alexei Maximovich

Goryan, Sirak
　See Saroyan, William

Gosse, Edmund (William)
　1849-1928 .... TCLC 28
　See also CA 117; DLB 57, 144

Gotlieb, Phyllis Fay (Bloom)
　1926- .... CLC 18
　See also CA 13-16R; CANR 7; DLB 88

Gottesman, S. D.
　See Kornbluth, C(yril) M.; Pohl, Frederik

Gottfried von Strassburg
　fl. c. 1210- .... CMLC 10
　See also DLB 138

Gould, Lois .... CLC 4, 10
　See also CA 77-80; CANR 29; MTCW

Gourmont, Remy (-Marie-Charles) de
　1858-1915 .... TCLC 17
　See also CA 109; 150

Govier, Katherine 1948- .... CLC 51
　See also CA 101; CANR 18, 40

Goyen, (Charles) William
　1915-1983 .... CLC 5, 8, 14, 40
　See also AITN 2; CA 5-8R; 110; CANR 6;
　DLB 2; DLBY 83; INT CANR-6

Goytisolo, Juan
　1931- .... CLC 5, 10, 23; HLC
　See also CA 85-88; CANR 32;
　DAM MULT; HW; MTCW

Gozzano, Guido 1883-1916 .... PC 10
　See also DLB 114

Gozzi, (Conte) Carlo 1720-1806 .. NCLC 23

Grabbe, Christian Dietrich
　1801-1836 .... NCLC 2
　See also DLB 133

Grace, Patricia 1937- .... CLC 56

Gracian y Morales, Baltasar
　1601-1658 .... LC 15

Gracq, Julien .... CLC 11, 48
　See also Poirier, Louis
　See also DLB 83

Grade, Chaim 1910-1982 .... CLC 10
　See also CA 93-96; 107

Graduate of Oxford, A
　See Ruskin, John

Graham, John
　See Phillips, David Graham

Graham, Jorie 1951- .... CLC 48
　See also CA 111; DLB 120

Graham, R(obert) B(ontine) Cunninghame
　See Cunninghame Graham, R(obert)
　B(ontine)
　See also DLB 98, 135

Graham, Robert
　See Haldeman, Joe (William)

Graham, Tom
　See Lewis, (Harry) Sinclair

Graham, W(illiam) S(ydney)
　1918-1986 .... CLC 29
　See also CA 73-76; 118; DLB 20

Graham, Winston (Mawdsley)
　1910- .... CLC 23
　See also CA 49-52; CANR 2, 22, 45;
　DLB 77

Grahame, Kenneth
　1859-1932 .... TCLC 64; DAB
　See also CA 108; 136; CLR 5; DLB 34, 141;
　MAICYA; YABC 1

Grant, Skeeter
　See Spiegelman, Art

Granville-Barker, Harley
　1877-1946 .... TCLC 2
　See also Barker, Harley Granville
　See also CA 104; DAM DRAM

Grass, Guenter (Wilhelm)
　1927- ..... CLC 1, 2, 4, 6, 11, 15, 22, 32,
　　　　　　　　49, 88; DA; DAB; DAC; WLC
　See also CA 13-16R; CANR 20;
　DAM MST, NOV; DLB 75, 124; MTCW

Gratton, Thomas
　See Hulme, T(homas) E(rnest)

Grau, Shirley Ann
　1929- .... CLC 4, 9; SSC 15
　See also CA 89-92; CANR 22; DLB 2;
　INT CANR-22; MTCW

Gravel, Fern
　See Hall, James Norman

Graver, Elizabeth 1964- .... CLC 70
　See also CA 135

Graves, Richard Perceval 1945- .... CLC 44
　See also CA 65-68; CANR 9, 26, 51

Graves, Robert (von Ranke)
　1895-1985 ...... CLC 1, 2, 6, 11, 39, 44,
　　　　　　　　　45; DAB; DAC; PC 6
　See also CA 5-8R; 117; CANR 5, 36;
　CDBLB 1914-1945; DAM MST, POET;
　DLB 20, 100; DLBY 85; MTCW;
　SATA 45

Graves, Valerie
　See Bradley, Marion Zimmer

Gray, Alasdair (James) 1934- ...... CLC 41
　See also CA 126; CANR 47; INT 126;
　MTCW

Gray, Amlin 1946- .... CLC 29
　See also CA 138

Gray, Francine du Plessix 1930- .... CLC 22
　See also BEST 90:3; CA 61-64; CAAS 2;
　CANR 11, 33; DAM NOV;
　INT CANR-11; MTCW

Gray, John (Henry) 1866-1934 .... TCLC 19
　See also CA 119

Gray, Simon (James Holliday)
　1936- .... CLC 9, 14, 36
　See also AITN 1; CA 21-24R; CAAS 3;
　CANR 32; DLB 13; MTCW

Gray, Spalding 1941- .... CLC 49
　See also CA 128; DAM POP

Gray, Thomas
　1716-1771 ...... LC 4; DA; DAB; DAC;
　　　　　　　　　PC 2; WLC
　See also CDBLB 1660-1789; DAM MST;
　DLB 109

Grayson, David
　See Baker, Ray Stannard

Grayson, Richard (A.) 1951- .... CLC 38
　See also CA 85-88; CANR 14, 31

Greeley, Andrew M(oran) 1928- .... CLC 28
　See also CA 5-8R; CAAS 7; CANR 7, 43;
　DAM POP; MTCW

Green, Anna Katharine
　1846-1935 .... TCLC 63
　See also CA 112

Green, Brian
　See Card, Orson Scott

Green, Hannah
　See Greenberg, Joanne (Goldenberg)

Green, Hannah .... CLC 3
　See also CA 73-76

Green, Henry .... CLC 2, 13
　See also Yorke, Henry Vincent
　See also DLB 15

Green, Julian (Hartridge) 1900-
　See Green, Julien
　See also CA 21-24R; CANR 33; DLB 4, 72;
　MTCW

Green, Julien .... CLC 3, 11, 77
　See also Green, Julian (Hartridge)

Green, Paul (Eliot) 1894-1981 ...... CLC 25
　See also AITN 1; CA 5-8R; 103; CANR 3;
　DAM DRAM; DLB 7, 9; DLBY 81

Greenberg, Ivan 1908-1973
　See Rahv, Philip
　See also CA 85-88

Greenberg, Joanne (Goldenberg)
　1932- .... CLC 7, 30
　See also AAYA 12; CA 5-8R; CANR 14,
　32; SATA 25

Greenberg, Richard 1959(?)- .... CLC 57
　See also CA 138

Greene, Bette 1934- .... CLC 30
　See also AAYA 7; CA 53-56; CANR 4;
　CLR 2; JRDA; MAICYA; SAAS 16;
　SATA 8

Greene, Gael .... CLC 8
　See also CA 13-16R; CANR 10

Greene, Graham
1904-1991 .... CLC 1, 3, 6, 9, 14, 18, 27,
37, 70, 72; DA; DAB; DAC; WLC
See also AITN 2; CA 13-16R; 133;
CANR 35; CDBLB 1945-1960;
DAM MST, NOV; DLB 13, 15, 77, 100,
162; DLBY 91; MTCW; SATA 20

Greer, Richard
See Silverberg, Robert

Gregor, Arthur 1923- .... CLC 9
See also CA 25-28R; CAAS 10; CANR 11;
SATA 36

Gregor, Lee
See Pohl, Frederik

Gregory, Isabella Augusta (Persse)
1852-1932 .... TCLC 1
See also CA 104; DLB 10

Gregory, J. Dennis
See Williams, John A(lfred)

Grendon, Stephen
See Derleth, August (William)

Grenville, Kate 1950- .... CLC 61
See also CA 118; CANR 53

Grenville, Pelham
See Wodehouse, P(elham) G(renville)

Greve, Felix Paul (Berthold Friedrich)
1879-1948
See Grove, Frederick Philip
See also CA 104; 141; DAC; DAM MST

Grey, Zane 1872-1939 .... TCLC 6
See also CA 104; 132; DAM POP; DLB 9;
MTCW

Grieg, (Johan) Nordahl (Brun)
1902-1943 .... TCLC 10
See also CA 107

Grieve, C(hristopher) M(urray)
1892-1978 .... CLC 11, 19
See also MacDiarmid, Hugh; Pteleon
See also CA 5-8R; 85-88; CANR 33;
DAM POET; MTCW

Griffin, Gerald 1803-1840 .... NCLC 7
See also DLB 159

Griffin, John Howard 1920-1980.... CLC 68
See also AITN 1; CA 1-4R; 101; CANR 2

Griffin, Peter 1942- .... CLC 39
See also CA 136

Griffiths, Trevor 1935-........ CLC 13, 52
See also CA 97-100; CANR 45; DLB 13

Grigson, Geoffrey (Edward Harvey)
1905-1985 .... CLC 7, 39
See also CA 25-28R; 118; CANR 20, 33;
DLB 27; MTCW

Grillparzer, Franz 1791-1872...... NCLC 1
See also DLB 133

Grimble, Reverend Charles James
See Eliot, T(homas) S(tearns)

Grimke, Charlotte L(ottie) Forten
1837(?)-1914
See Forten, Charlotte L.
See also BW 1; CA 117; 124; DAM MULT,
POET

Grimm, Jacob Ludwig Karl
1785-1863 .... NCLC 3
See also DLB 90; MAICYA; SATA 22

Grimm, Wilhelm Karl 1786-1859 .. NCLC 3
See also DLB 90; MAICYA; SATA 22

**Grimmelshausen, Johann Jakob Christoffel
von** 1621-1676 .... LC 6

Grindel, Eugene 1895-1952
See Eluard, Paul
See also CA 104

Grisham, John 1955- .... CLC 84
See also AAYA 14; CA 138; CANR 47;
DAM POP

Grossman, David 1954- .... CLC 67
See also CA 138

Grossman, Vasily (Semenovich)
1905-1964 .... CLC 41
See also CA 124; 130; MTCW

Grove, Frederick Philip .... TCLC 4
See also Greve, Felix Paul (Berthold
Friedrich)
See also DLB 92

Grubb
See Crumb, R(obert)

Grumbach, Doris (Isaac)
1918- .... CLC 13, 22, 64
See also CA 5-8R; CAAS 2; CANR 9, 42;
INT CANR-9

Grundtvig, Nicolai Frederik Severin
1783-1872 .... NCLC 1

Grunge
See Crumb, R(obert)

Grunwald, Lisa 1959-............. CLC 44
See also CA 120

Guare, John 1938- .... CLC 8, 14, 29, 67
See also CA 73-76; CANR 21;
DAM DRAM; DLB 7; MTCW

Gudjonsson, Halldor Kiljan 1902-
See Laxness, Halldor
See also CA 103

Guenter, Erich
See Eich, Guenter

Guest, Barbara 1920-............. CLC 34
See also CA 25-28R; CANR 11, 44; DLB 5

Guest, Judith (Ann) 1936-....... CLC 8, 30
See also AAYA 7; CA 77-80; CANR 15;
DAM NOV, POP; INT CANR-15;
MTCW

Guevara, Che .... CLC 87; HLC
See also Guevara (Serna), Ernesto

Guevara (Serna), Ernesto 1928-1967
See Guevara, Che
See also CA 127; 111; DAM MULT; HW

Guild, Nicholas M. 1944-......... CLC 33
See also CA 93-96

Guillemin, Jacques
See Sartre, Jean-Paul

Guillen, Jorge 1893-1984.......... CLC 11
See also CA 89-92; 112; DAM MULT,
POET; DLB 108; HW

Guillen, Nicolas (Cristobal)
1902-1989 ..... CLC 48, 79; BLC; HLC
See also BW 2; CA 116; 125; 129;
DAM MST, MULT, POET; HW

Guillevic, (Eugene) 1907-......... CLC 33
See also CA 93-96

Guillois
See Desnos, Robert

Guillois, Valentin
See Desnos, Robert

Guiney, Louise Imogen
1861-1920 .... TCLC 41
See also DLB 54

Guiraldes, Ricardo (Guillermo)
1886-1927 .... TCLC 39
See also CA 131; HW; MTCW

Gumilev, Nikolai Stephanovich
1886-1921 .... TCLC 60

Gunesekera, Romesh............... CLC 91

Gunn, Bill .... CLC 5
See also Gunn, William Harrison
See also DLB 38

Gunn, Thom(son William)
1929- .... CLC 3, 6, 18, 32, 81
See also CA 17-20R; CANR 9, 33;
CDBLB 1960 to Present; DAM POET;
DLB 27; INT CANR-33; MTCW

Gunn, William Harrison 1934(?)-1989
See Gunn, Bill
See also AITN 1; BW 1; CA 13-16R; 128;
CANR 12, 25

Gunnars, Kristjana 1948-......... CLC 69
See also CA 113; DLB 60

Gurganus, Allan 1947-............ CLC 70
See also BEST 90:1; CA 135; DAM POP

Gurney, A(lbert) R(amsdell), Jr.
1930-................... CLC 32, 50, 54
See also CA 77-80; CANR 32;
DAM DRAM

Gurney, Ivor (Bertie) 1890-1937... TCLC 33

Gurney, Peter
See Gurney, A(lbert) R(amsdell), Jr.

Guro, Elena 1877-1913........... TCLC 56

Gustafson, Ralph (Barker) 1909-.... CLC 36
See also CA 21-24R; CANR 8, 45; DLB 88

Gut, Gom
See Simenon, Georges (Jacques Christian)

Guterson, David 1956-............ CLC 91
See also CA 132

Guthrie, A(lfred) B(ertram), Jr.
1901-1991 .... CLC 23
See also CA 57-60; 134; CANR 24; DLB 6;
SATA 62; SATA-Obit 67

Guthrie, Isobel
See Grieve, C(hristopher) M(urray)

Guthrie, Woodrow Wilson 1912-1967
See Guthrie, Woody
See also CA 113; 93-96

Guthrie, Woody.................... CLC 35
See also Guthrie, Woodrow Wilson

Guy, Rosa (Cuthbert) 1928-........ CLC 26
See also AAYA 4; BW 2; CA 17-20R;
CANR 14, 34; CLR 13; DLB 33; JRDA;
MAICYA; SATA 14, 62

Gwendolyn
See Bennett, (Enoch) Arnold

H. D. .... CLC 3, 8, 14, 31, 34, 73; PC 5
See also Doolittle, Hilda

H. de V.
See Buchan, John

Haavikko, Paavo Juhani
     1931- .... **CLC 18, 34**
     See also CA 106

Habbema, Koos
     See Heijermans, Herman

Hacker, Marilyn
     1942- .... **CLC 5, 9, 23, 72, 91**
     See also CA 77-80; DAM POET; DLB 120

Haggard, H(enry) Rider
     1856-1925 .... **TCLC 11**
     See also CA 108; 148; DLB 70, 156;
     SATA 16

Hagiwara Sakutaro 1886-1942 .... **TCLC 60**

Haig, Fenil
     See Ford, Ford Madox

Haig-Brown, Roderick (Langmere)
     1908-1976 .... **CLC 21**
     See also CA 5-8R; 69-72; CANR 4, 38;
     CLR 31; DLB 88; MAICYA; SATA 12

Hailey, Arthur 1920- .... **CLC 5**
     See also AITN 2; BEST 90:3; CA 1-4R;
     CANR 2, 36; DAM NOV, POP; DLB 88;
     DLBY 82; MTCW

Hailey, Elizabeth Forsythe 1938- ... **CLC 40**
     See also CA 93-96; CAAS 1; CANR 15, 48;
     INT CANR-15

Haines, John (Meade) 1924- .... **CLC 58**
     See also CA 17-20R; CANR 13, 34; DLB 5

Hakluyt, Richard 1552-1616 .... **LC 31**

Haldeman, Joe (William) 1943- ..... **CLC 61**
     See also CA 53-56; CANR 6; DLB 8;
     INT CANR-6

Haley, Alex(ander Murray Palmer)
     1921-1992 .... **CLC 8, 12, 76; BLC; DA;**
                                          DAB; DAC
     See also BW 2; CA 77-80; 136; DAM MST,
     MULT, POP; DLB 38; MTCW

Haliburton, Thomas Chandler
     1796-1865 .... **NCLC 15**
     See also DLB 11, 99

Hall, Donald (Andrew, Jr.)
     1928- .... **CLC 1, 13, 37, 59**
     See also CA 5-8R; CAAS 7; CANR 2, 44;
     DAM POET; DLB 5; SATA 23

Hall, Frederic Sauser
     See Sauser-Hall, Frederic

Hall, James
     See Kuttner, Henry

Hall, James Norman 1887-1951 ... **TCLC 23**
     See also CA 123; SATA 21

Hall, (Marguerite) Radclyffe
     1886-1943 .... **TCLC 12**
     See also CA 110; 150

Hall, Rodney 1935- .... **CLC 51**
     See also CA 109

Halleck, Fitz-Greene 1790-1867 .. **NCLC 47**
     See also DLB 3

Halliday, Michael
     See Creasey, John

Halpern, Daniel 1945- .... **CLC 14**
     See also CA 33-36R

Hamburger, Michael (Peter Leopold)
     1924- .... **CLC 5, 14**
     See also CA 5-8R; CAAS 4; CANR 2, 47;
     DLB 27

Hamill, Pete 1935- .... **CLC 10**
     See also CA 25-28R; CANR 18

Hamilton, Alexander
     1755(?)-1804 .... **NCLC 49**
     See also DLB 37

Hamilton, Clive
     See Lewis, C(live) S(taples)

Hamilton, Edmond 1904-1977 .... **CLC 1**
     See also CA 1-4R; CANR 3; DLB 8

Hamilton, Eugene (Jacob) Lee
     See Lee-Hamilton, Eugene (Jacob)

Hamilton, Franklin
     See Silverberg, Robert

Hamilton, Gail
     See Corcoran, Barbara

Hamilton, Mollie
     See Kaye, M(ary) M(argaret)

Hamilton, (Anthony Walter) Patrick
     1904-1962 .... **CLC 51**
     See also CA 113; DLB 10

Hamilton, Virginia 1936- .... **CLC 26**
     See also AAYA 2; BW 2; CA 25-28R;
     CANR 20, 37; CLR 1, 11, 40;
     DAM MULT; DLB 33, 52;
     INT CANR-20; JRDA; MAICYA;
     MTCW; SATA 4, 56, 79

Hammett, (Samuel) Dashiell
     1894-1961 .... **CLC 3, 5, 10, 19, 47;**
                                               SSC 17
     See also AITN 1; CA 81-84; CANR 42;
     CDALB 1929-1941; DLBD 6; MTCW

Hammon, Jupiter
     1711(?)-1800(?) ... **NCLC 5; BLC; PC 16**
     See also DAM MULT, POET; DLB 31, 50

Hammond, Keith
     See Kuttner, Henry

Hamner, Earl (Henry), Jr. 1923- ... **CLC 12**
     See also AITN 2; CA 73-76; DLB 6

Hampton, Christopher (James)
     1946- .... **CLC 4**
     See also CA 25-28R; DLB 13; MTCW

Hamsun, Knut .... **TCLC 2, 14, 49**
     See also Pedersen, Knut

Handke, Peter 1942- .. **CLC 5, 8, 10, 15, 38**
     See also CA 77-80; CANR 33;
     DAM DRAM, NOV; DLB 85, 124;
     MTCW

Hanley, James 1901-1985 ... **CLC 3, 5, 8, 13**
     See also CA 73-76; 117; CANR 36; MTCW

Hannah, Barry 1942- .... **CLC 23, 38, 90**
     See also CA 108; 110; CANR 43; DLB 6;
     INT 110; MTCW

Hannon, Ezra
     See Hunter, Evan

Hansberry, Lorraine (Vivian)
     1930-1965 ...... **CLC 17, 62; BLC; DA;**
                                          DAB; DAC; DC 2
     See also BW 1; CA 109; 25-28R; CABS 3;
     CDALB 1941-1968; DAM DRAM, MST,
     MULT; DLB 7, 38; MTCW

Hansen, Joseph 1923- .... **CLC 38**
     See also CA 29-32R; CAAS 17; CANR 16,
     44; INT CANR-16

Hansen, Martin A. 1909-1955 ..... **TCLC 32**

Hanson, Kenneth O(stlin) 1922- .... **CLC 13**
     See also CA 53-56; CANR 7

Hardwick, Elizabeth 1916- .... **CLC 13**
     See also CA 5-8R; CANR 3, 32;
     DAM NOV; DLB 6; MTCW

Hardy, Thomas
     1840-1928 ...... **TCLC 4, 10, 18, 32, 48,**
          53; DA; DAB; DAC; PC 8; SSC 2; WLC
     See also CA 104; 123; CDBLB 1890-1914;
     DAM MST, NOV, POET; DLB 18, 19,
     135; MTCW

Hare, David 1947- .... **CLC 29, 58**
     See also CA 97-100; CANR 39; DLB 13;
     MTCW

Harford, Henry
     See Hudson, W(illiam) H(enry)

Hargrave, Leonie
     See Disch, Thomas M(ichael)

Harjo, Joy 1951- .... **CLC 83**
     See also CA 114; CANR 35; DAM MULT;
     DLB 120; NNAL

Harlan, Louis R(udolph) 1922- ..... **CLC 34**
     See also CA 21-24R; CANR 25

Harling, Robert 1951(?)- .... **CLC 53**
     See also CA 147

Harmon, William (Ruth) 1938- ..... **CLC 38**
     See also CA 33-36R; CANR 14, 32, 35;
     SATA 65

Harper, F. E. W.
     See Harper, Frances Ellen Watkins

Harper, Frances E. W.
     See Harper, Frances Ellen Watkins

Harper, Frances E. Watkins
     See Harper, Frances Ellen Watkins

Harper, Frances Ellen
     See Harper, Frances Ellen Watkins

Harper, Frances Ellen Watkins
     1825-1911 .... **TCLC 14; BLC**
     See also BW 1; CA 111; 125; DAM MULT,
     POET; DLB 50

Harper, Michael S(teven) 1938- .. **CLC 7, 22**
     See also BW 1; CA 33-36R; CANR 24;
     DLB 41

Harper, Mrs. F. E. W.
     See Harper, Frances Ellen Watkins

Harris, Christie (Lucy) Irwin
     1907- .... **CLC 12**
     See also CA 5-8R; CANR 6; DLB 88;
     JRDA; MAICYA; SAAS 10; SATA 6, 74

Harris, Frank 1856-1931 .... **TCLC 24**
     See also CA 109; 150; DLB 156

Harris, George Washington
     1814-1869 .... **NCLC 23**
     See also DLB 3, 11

Harris, Joel Chandler
     1848-1908 .... **TCLC 2; SSC 19**
     See also CA 104; 137; DLB 11, 23, 42, 78,
     91; MAICYA; YABC 1

Harris, John (Wyndham Parkes Lucas)
     Beynon 1903-1969
     See Wyndham, John
     See also CA 102; 89-92

Harris, MacDonald .... **CLC 9**
     See also Heiney, Donald (William)

Harris, Mark 1922- . . . . **CLC 19**
See also CA 5-8R; CAAS 3; CANR 2;
DLB 2; DLBY 80

Harris, (Theodore) Wilson 1921- . . . . **CLC 25**
See also BW 2; CA 65-68; CAAS 16;
CANR 11, 27; DLB 117; MTCW

Harrison, Elizabeth Cavanna 1909-
See Cavanna, Betty
See also CA 9-12R; CANR 6, 27

Harrison, Harry (Max) 1925- . . . . . . **CLC 42**
See also CA 1-4R; CANR 5, 21; DLB 8;
SATA 4

Harrison, James (Thomas)
1937- . . . . **CLC 6, 14, 33, 66; SSC 19**
See also CA 13-16R; CANR 8, 51;
DLBY 82; INT CANR-8

Harrison, Jim
See Harrison, James (Thomas)

Harrison, Kathryn 1961- . . . . **CLC 70**
See also CA 144

Harrison, Tony 1937- . . . . **CLC 43**
See also CA 65-68; CANR 44; DLB 40;
MTCW

Harriss, Will(ard Irvin) 1922- . . . . . . **CLC 34**
See also CA 111

Harson, Sley
See Ellison, Harlan (Jay)

Hart, Ellis
See Ellison, Harlan (Jay)

Hart, Josephine 1942(?)- . . . . **CLC 70**
See also CA 138; DAM POP

Hart, Moss 1904-1961 . . . . **CLC 66**
See also CA 109; 89-92; DAM DRAM;
DLB 7

Harte, (Francis) Bret(t)
1836(?)-1902 . . . . **TCLC 1, 25; DA; DAC;
SSC 8; WLC**
See also CA 104; 140; CDALB 1865-1917;
DAM MST; DLB 12, 64, 74, 79;
SATA 26

Hartley, L(eslie) P(oles)
1895-1972 . . . . **CLC 2, 22**
See also CA 45-48; 37-40R; CANR 33;
DLB 15, 139; MTCW

Hartman, Geoffrey H. 1929- . . . . **CLC 27**
See also CA 117; 125; DLB 67

Hartmann von Aue
c. 1160-c. 1205 . . . . **CMLC 15**
See also DLB 138

Hartmann von Aue 1170-1210 . . . . **CMLC 15**

Haruf, Kent 1943- . . . . **CLC 34**
See also CA 149

Harwood, Ronald 1934- . . . . **CLC 32**
See also CA 1-4R; CANR 4; DAM DRAM,
MST; DLB 13

Hasek, Jaroslav (Matej Frantisek)
1883-1923 . . . . **TCLC 4**
See also CA 104; 129; MTCW

Hass, Robert 1941- . . . . . **CLC 18, 39; PC 16**
See also CA 111; CANR 30, 50; DLB 105

Hastings, Hudson
See Kuttner, Henry

Hastings, Selina . . . . **CLC 44**

Hatteras, Amelia
See Mencken, H(enry) L(ouis)

Hatteras, Owen . . . . **TCLC 18**
See also Mencken, H(enry) L(ouis); Nathan,
George Jean

Hauptmann, Gerhart (Johann Robert)
1862-1946 . . . . **TCLC 4**
See also CA 104; DAM DRAM; DLB 66,
118

Havel, Vaclav
1936- . . . . **CLC 25, 58, 65; DC 6**
See also CA 104; CANR 36; DAM DRAM;
MTCW

Haviaras, Stratis . . . . **CLC 33**
See also Chaviaras, Strates

Hawes, Stephen 1475(?)-1523(?) . . . . . **LC 17**

Hawkes, John (Clendennin Burne, Jr.)
1925- . . . . . . **CLC 1, 2, 3, 4, 7, 9, 14, 15,
27, 49**
See also CA 1-4R; CANR 2, 47; DLB 2, 7;
DLBY 80; MTCW

Hawking, S. W.
See Hawking, Stephen W(illiam)

Hawking, Stephen W(illiam)
1942- . . . . **CLC 63**
See also AAYA 13; BEST 89:1; CA 126;
129; CANR 48

Hawthorne, Julian 1846-1934 . . . . . **TCLC 25**

Hawthorne, Nathaniel
1804-1864 . . . . **NCLC 39; DA; DAB;
DAC; SSC 3; WLC**
See also AAYA 18; CDALB 1640-1865;
DAM MST, NOV; DLB 1, 74; YABC 2

Haxton, Josephine Ayres 1921-
See Douglas, Ellen
See also CA 115; CANR 41

Hayaseca y Eizaguirre, Jorge
See Echegaray (y Eizaguirre), Jose (Maria
Waldo)

Hayashi Fumiko 1904-1951 . . . . **TCLC 27**

Haycraft, Anna
See Ellis, Alice Thomas
See also CA 122

Hayden, Robert E(arl)
1913-1980 . . . . . . **CLC 5, 9, 14, 37; BLC;
DA; DAC; PC 6**
See also BW 1; CA 69-72; 97-100; CABS 2;
CANR 24; CDALB 1941-1968;
DAM MST, MULT, POET; DLB 5, 76;
MTCW; SATA 19; SATA-Obit 26

Hayford, J(oseph) E(phraim) Casely
See Casely-Hayford, J(oseph) E(phraim)

Hayman, Ronald 1932- . . . . **CLC 44**
See also CA 25-28R; CANR 18, 50;
DLB 155

Haywood, Eliza (Fowler)
1693(?)-1756 . . . . **LC 1**

Hazlitt, William 1778-1830 . . . . . . **NCLC 29**
See also DLB 110, 158

Hazzard, Shirley 1931- . . . . **CLC 18**
See also CA 9-12R; CANR 4; DLBY 82;
MTCW

Head, Bessie 1937-1986 . . . **CLC 25, 67; BLC**
See also BW 2; CA 29-32R; 119; CANR 25;
DAM MULT; DLB 117; MTCW

Headon, (Nicky) Topper 1956(?)- . . . **CLC 30**

Heaney, Seamus (Justin)
1939- . . . . . . **CLC 5, 7, 14, 25, 37, 74, 91;
DAB**
See also CA 85-88; CANR 25, 48;
CDBLB 1960 to Present; DAM POET;
DLB 40; DLBY 95; MTCW

Hearn, (Patricio) Lafcadio (Tessima Carlos)
1850-1904 . . . . **TCLC 9**
See also CA 105; DLB 12, 78

Hearne, Vicki 1946- . . . . **CLC 56**
See also CA 139

Hearon, Shelby 1931- . . . . **CLC 63**
See also AITN 2; CA 25-28R; CANR 18,
48

Heat-Moon, William Least . . . . **CLC 29**
See also Trogdon, William (Lewis)
See also AAYA 9

Hebbel, Friedrich 1813-1863 . . . . . **NCLC 43**
See also DAM DRAM; DLB 129

Hebert, Anne 1916- . . . **CLC 4, 13, 29; DAC**
See also CA 85-88; DAM MST, POET;
DLB 68; MTCW

Hecht, Anthony (Evan)
1923- . . . . **CLC 8, 13, 19**
See also CA 9-12R; CANR 6; DAM POET;
DLB 5

Hecht, Ben 1894-1964 . . . . **CLC 8**
See also CA 85-88; DLB 7, 9, 25, 26, 28, 86

Hedayat, Sadeq 1903-1951 . . . . **TCLC 21**
See also CA 120

Hegel, Georg Wilhelm Friedrich
1770-1831 . . . . **NCLC 46**
See also DLB 90

Heidegger, Martin 1889-1976 . . . . . . **CLC 24**
See also CA 81-84; 65-68; CANR 34;
MTCW

Heidenstam, (Carl Gustaf) Verner von
1859-1940 . . . . **TCLC 5**
See also CA 104

Heifner, Jack 1946- . . . . **CLC 11**
See also CA 105; CANR 47

Heijermans, Herman 1864-1924 . . . **TCLC 24**
See also CA 123

Heilbrun, Carolyn G(old) 1926- . . . . . **CLC 25**
See also CA 45-48; CANR 1, 28

Heine, Heinrich 1797-1856 . . . . **NCLC 4, 54**
See also DLB 90

Heinemann, Larry (Curtiss) 1944- . . **CLC 50**
See also CA 110; CAAS 21; CANR 31;
DLBD 9; INT CANR-31

Heiney, Donald (William) 1921-1993
See Harris, MacDonald
See also CA 1-4R; 142; CANR 3

Heinlein, Robert A(nson)
1907-1988 . . . . . . **CLC 1, 3, 8, 14, 26, 55**
See also AAYA 17; CA 1-4R; 125;
CANR 1, 20, 53; DAM POP; DLB 8;
JRDA; MAICYA; MTCW; SATA 9, 69;
SATA-Obit 56

Helforth, John
See Doolittle, Hilda

Hellenhofferu, Vojtech Kapristian z
See Hasek, Jaroslav (Matej Frantisek)

Heller, Joseph
1923- .... **CLC 1, 3, 5, 8, 11, 36, 63; DA;
DAB; DAC; WLC**
See also AITN 1; CA 5-8R; CABS 1;
CANR 8, 42; DAM MST, NOV, POP;
DLB 2, 28; DLBY 80; INT CANR-8;
MTCW

Hellman, Lillian (Florence)
1906-1984 ...... **CLC 2, 4, 8, 14, 18, 34,
44, 52; DC 1**
See also AITN 1, 2; CA 13-16R; 112;
CANR 33; DAM DRAM; DLB 7;
DLBY 84; MTCW

Helprin, Mark 1947- ..... **CLC 7, 10, 22, 32**
See also CA 81-84; CANR 47; DAM NOV,
POP; DLBY 85; MTCW

Helvetius, Claude-Adrien
1715-1771 .... **LC 26**

Helyar, Jane Penelope Josephine 1933-
See Poole, Josephine
See also CA 21-24R; CANR 10, 26;
SATA 82

Hemans, Felicia 1793-1835 ...... **NCLC 29**
See also DLB 96

Hemingway, Ernest (Miller)
1899-1961 .... **CLC 1, 3, 6, 8, 10, 13, 19,
30, 34, 39, 41, 44, 50, 61, 80; DA; DAB;
DAC; SSC 1; WLC**
See also CA 77-80; CANR 34;
CDALB 1917-1929; DAM MST, NOV;
DLB 4, 9, 102; DLBD 1; DLBY 81, 87;
MTCW

Hempel, Amy 1951- .... **CLC 39**
See also CA 118; 137

Henderson, F. C.
See Mencken, H(enry) L(ouis)

Henderson, Sylvia
See Ashton-Warner, Sylvia (Constance)

Henley, Beth .... **CLC 23; DC 6**
See also Henley, Elizabeth Becker
See also CABS 3; DLBY 86

Henley, Elizabeth Becker 1952-
See Henley, Beth
See also CA 107; CANR 32; DAM DRAM,
MST; MTCW

Henley, William Ernest
1849-1903 .... **TCLC 8**
See also CA 105; DLB 19

Hennissart, Martha
See Lathen, Emma
See also CA 85-88

Henry, O. .... **TCLC 1, 19; SSC 5; WLC**
See also Porter, William Sydney

Henry, Patrick 1736-1799 .... **LC 25**

Henryson, Robert 1430(?)-1506(?).... **LC 20**
See also DLB 146

Henry VIII 1491-1547 .... **LC 10**

Henschke, Alfred
See Klabund

Hentoff, Nat(han Irving) 1925- ..... **CLC 26**
See also AAYA 4; CA 1-4R; CAAS 6;
CANR 5, 25; CLR 1; INT CANR-25;
JRDA; MAICYA; SATA 42, 69;
SATA-Brief 27

Heppenstall, (John) Rayner
1911-1981 .... **CLC 10**
See also CA 1-4R; 103; CANR 29

Herbert, Frank (Patrick)
1920-1986 ...... **CLC 12, 23, 35, 44, 85**
See also CA 53-56; 118; CANR 5, 43;
DAM POP; DLB 8; INT CANR-5;
MTCW; SATA 9, 37; SATA-Obit 47

Herbert, George
1593-1633 .... **LC 24; DAB; PC 4**
See also CDBLB Before 1660; DAM POET;
DLB 126

Herbert, Zbigniew 1924- .... **CLC 9, 43**
See also CA 89-92; CANR 36;
DAM POET; MTCW

Herbst, Josephine (Frey)
1897-1969 .... **CLC 34**
See also CA 5-8R; 25-28R; DLB 9

Hergesheimer, Joseph
1880-1954 .... **TCLC 11**
See also CA 109; DLB 102, 9

Herlihy, James Leo 1927-1993 ...... **CLC 6**
See also CA 1-4R; 143; CANR 2

Hermogenes fl. c. 175- .... **CMLC 6**

Hernandez, Jose 1834-1886...... **NCLC 17**

Herodotus c. 484B.C.-429B.C..... **CMLC 17**

Herrick, Robert
1591-1674 ..... **LC 13; DA; DAB; DAC;
PC 9**
See also DAM MST, POP; DLB 126

Herring, Guilles
See Somerville, Edith

Herriot, James 1916-1995 .... **CLC 12**
See also Wight, James Alfred
See also AAYA 1; CA 148; CANR 40;
DAM POP; SATA 86

Herrmann, Dorothy 1941-........ **CLC 44**
See also CA 107

Herrmann, Taffy
See Herrmann, Dorothy

Hersey, John (Richard)
1914-1993 ...... **CLC 1, 2, 7, 9, 40, 81**
See also CA 17-20R; 140; CANR 33;
DAM POP; DLB 6; MTCW; SATA 25;
SATA-Obit 76

Herzen, Aleksandr Ivanovich
1812-1870 .... **NCLC 10**

Herzl, Theodor 1860-1904........ **TCLC 36**

Herzog, Werner 1942-............ **CLC 16**
See also CA 89-92

Hesiod c. 8th cent. B.C.-........ **CMLC 5**

Hesse, Hermann
1877-1962 .... **CLC 1, 2, 3, 6, 11, 17, 25,
69; DA; DAB; DAC; SSC 9; WLC**
See also CA 17-18; CAP 2; DAM MST,
NOV; DLB 66; MTCW; SATA 50

Hewes, Cady
See De Voto, Bernard (Augustine)

Heyen, William 1940- .... **CLC 13, 18**
See also CA 33-36R; CAAS 9; DLB 5

Heyerdahl, Thor 1914-............ **CLC 26**
See also CA 5-8R; CANR 5, 22; MTCW;
SATA 2, 52

Heym, Georg (Theodor Franz Arthur)
1887-1912 .... **TCLC 9**
See also CA 106

Heym, Stefan 1913-.............. **CLC 41**
See also CA 9-12R; CANR 4; DLB 69

Heyse, Paul (Johann Ludwig von)
1830-1914 .... **TCLC 8**
See also CA 104; DLB 129

Heyward, (Edwin) DuBose
1885-1940 .... **TCLC 59**
See also CA 108; DLB 7, 9, 45; SATA 21

Hibbert, Eleanor Alice Burford
1906-1993 .... **CLC 7**
See also BEST 90:4; CA 17-20R; 140;
CANR 9, 28; DAM POP; SATA 2;
SATA-Obit 74

Hichens, Robert S. 1864-1950..... **TCLC 64**
See also DLB 153

Higgins, George V(incent)
1939-................. **CLC 4, 7, 10, 18**
See also CA 77-80; CAAS 5; CANR 17, 51;
DLB 2; DLBY 81; INT CANR-17;
MTCW

Higginson, Thomas Wentworth
1823-1911 .... **TCLC 36**
See also DLB 1, 64

Highet, Helen
See MacInnes, Helen (Clark)

Highsmith, (Mary) Patricia
1921-1995 .... **CLC 2, 4, 14, 42**
See also CA 1-4R; 147; CANR 1, 20, 48;
DAM NOV, POP; MTCW

Highwater, Jamake (Mamake)
1942(?)- .... **CLC 12**
See also AAYA 7; CA 65-68; CAAS 7;
CANR 10, 34; CLR 17; DLB 52;
DLBY 85; JRDA; MAICYA; SATA 32,
69; SATA-Brief 30

Highway, Tomson 1951-...... **CLC 92; DAC**
See also CA 151; DAM MULT; NNAL

Higuchi, Ichiyo 1872-1896....... **NCLC 49**

Hijuelos, Oscar 1951- ...... **CLC 65; HLC**
See also BEST 90:1; CA 123; CANR 50;
DAM MULT, POP; DLB 145; HW

Hikmet, Nazim 1902(?)-1963....... **CLC 40**
See also CA 141; 93-96

Hildesheimer, Wolfgang
1916-1991 .... **CLC 49**
See also CA 101; 135; DLB 69, 124

Hill, Geoffrey (William)
1932-................. **CLC 5, 8, 18, 45**
See also CA 81-84; CANR 21;
CDBLB 1960 to Present; DAM POET;
DLB 40; MTCW

Hill, George Roy 1921-............ **CLC 26**
See also CA 110; 122

Hill, John
See Koontz, Dean R(ay)

Hill, Susan (Elizabeth)
1942-.................. **CLC 4; DAB**
See also CA 33-36R; CANR 29;
DAM MST, NOV; DLB 14, 139; MTCW

Hillerman, Tony 1925-............ **CLC 62**
See also AAYA 6; BEST 89:1; CA 29-32R;
CANR 21, 42; DAM POP; SATA 6

Hillesum, Etty 1914-1943 . . . . TCLC 49
See also CA 137

Hilliard, Noel (Harvey) 1929- . . . . . . CLC 15
See also CA 9-12R; CANR 7

Hillis, Rick 1956- . . . . CLC 66
See also CA 134

Hilton, James 1900-1954 . . . . TCLC 21
See also CA 108; DLB 34, 77; SATA 34

Himes, Chester (Bomar)
    1909-1984 . . . . CLC 2, 4, 7, 18, 58; BLC
See also BW 2; CA 25-28R; 114; CANR 22;
    DAM MULT; DLB 2, 76, 143; MTCW

Hinde, Thomas . . . . CLC 6, 11
See also Chitty, Thomas Willes

Hindin, Nathan
See Bloch, Robert (Albert)

Hine, (William) Daryl 1936- . . . . CLC 15
See also CA 1-4R; CAAS 15; CANR 1, 20;
    DLB 60

Hinkson, Katharine Tynan
See Tynan, Katharine

Hinton, S(usan) E(loise)
    1950- . . . . CLC 30; DA; DAB; DAC
See also AAYA 2; CA 81-84; CANR 32;
    CLR 3, 23; DAM MST, NOV; JRDA;
    MAICYA; MTCW; SATA 19, 58

Hippius, Zinaida . . . . TCLC 9
See also Gippius, Zinaida (Nikolayevna)

Hiraoka, Kimitake 1925-1970
See Mishima, Yukio
See also CA 97-100; 29-32R; DAM DRAM;
    MTCW

Hirsch, E(ric) D(onald), Jr. 1928- . . . CLC 79
See also CA 25-28R; CANR 27, 51;
    DLB 67; INT CANR-27; MTCW

Hirsch, Edward 1950- . . . . CLC 31, 50
See also CA 104; CANR 20, 42; DLB 120

Hitchcock, Alfred (Joseph)
    1899-1980 . . . . CLC 16
See also CA 97-100; SATA 27;
    SATA-Obit 24

Hitler, Adolf 1889-1945 . . . . TCLC 53
See also CA 117; 147

Hoagland, Edward 1932- . . . . CLC 28
See also CA 1-4R; CANR 2, 31; DLB 6;
    SATA 51

Hoban, Russell (Conwell) 1925- . . CLC 7, 25
See also CA 5-8R; CANR 23, 37; CLR 3;
    DAM NOV; DLB 52; MAICYA;
    MTCW; SATA 1, 40, 78

Hobbs, Perry
See Blackmur, R(ichard) P(almer)

Hobson, Laura Z(ametkin)
    1900-1986 . . . . CLC 7, 25
See also CA 17-20R; 118; DLB 28;
    SATA 52

Hochhuth, Rolf 1931- . . . . CLC 4, 11, 18
See also CA 5-8R; CANR 33;
    DAM DRAM; DLB 124; MTCW

Hochman, Sandra 1936- . . . . CLC 3, 8
See also CA 5-8R; DLB 5

Hochwaelder, Fritz 1911-1986 . . . . . . CLC 36
See also CA 29-32R; 120; CANR 42;
    DAM DRAM; MTCW

Hochwalder, Fritz
See Hochwaelder, Fritz

Hocking, Mary (Eunice) 1921- . . . . . CLC 13
See also CA 101; CANR 18, 40

Hodgins, Jack 1938- . . . . CLC 23
See also CA 93-96; DLB 60

Hodgson, William Hope
    1877(?)-1918 . . . . TCLC 13
See also CA 111; DLB 70, 153, 156

Hoeg, Peter 1957- . . . . CLC 95
See also CA 151

Hoffman, Alice 1952- . . . . CLC 51
See also CA 77-80; CANR 34; DAM NOV;
    MTCW

Hoffman, Daniel (Gerard)
    1923- . . . . CLC 6, 13, 23
See also CA 1-4R; CANR 4; DLB 5

Hoffman, Stanley 1944- . . . . CLC 5
See also CA 77-80

Hoffman, William M(oses) 1939- . . . CLC 40
See also CA 57-60; CANR 11

Hoffmann, E(rnst) T(heodor) A(madeus)
    1776-1822 . . . . NCLC 2; SSC 13
See also DLB 90; SATA 27

Hofmann, Gert 1931- . . . . CLC 54
See also CA 128

Hofmannsthal, Hugo von
    1874-1929 . . . . TCLC 11; DC 4
See also CA 106; DAM DRAM; DLB 81,
    118

Hogan, Linda 1947- . . . . CLC 73
See also CA 120; CANR 45; DAM MULT;
    NNAL

Hogarth, Charles
See Creasey, John

Hogarth, Emmett
See Polonsky, Abraham (Lincoln)

Hogg, James 1770-1835 . . . . NCLC 4
See also DLB 93, 116, 159

Holbach, Paul Henri Thiry Baron
    1723-1789 . . . . LC 14

Holberg, Ludvig 1684-1754 . . . . LC 6

Holden, Ursula 1921- . . . . CLC 18
See also CA 101; CAAS 8; CANR 22

Holderlin, (Johann Christian) Friedrich
    1770-1843 . . . . NCLC 16; PC 4

Holdstock, Robert
See Holdstock, Robert P.

Holdstock, Robert P. 1948- . . . . CLC 39
See also CA 131

Holland, Isabelle 1920- . . . . CLC 21
See also AAYA 11; CA 21-24R; CANR 10,
    25, 47; JRDA; MAICYA; SATA 8, 70

Holland, Marcus
See Caldwell, (Janet Miriam) Taylor
    (Holland)

Hollander, John 1929- . . . . . . CLC 2, 5, 8, 14
See also CA 1-4R; CANR 1, 52; DLB 5;
    SATA 13

Hollander, Paul
See Silverberg, Robert

Holleran, Andrew 1943(?)- . . . . CLC 38
See also CA 144

Hollinghurst, Alan 1954- . . . . CLC 55, 91
See also CA 114

Hollis, Jim
See Summers, Hollis (Spurgeon, Jr.)

Holly, Buddy 1936-1959 . . . . TCLC 65

Holmes, John
See Souster, (Holmes) Raymond

Holmes, John Clellon 1926-1988 . . . . CLC 56
See also CA 9-12R; 125; CANR 4; DLB 16

Holmes, Oliver Wendell
    1809-1894 . . . . NCLC 14
See also CDALB 1640-1865; DLB 1;
    SATA 34

Holmes, Raymond
See Souster, (Holmes) Raymond

Holt, Victoria
See Hibbert, Eleanor Alice Burford

Holub, Miroslav 1923- . . . . CLC 4
See also CA 21-24R; CANR 10

Homer
    c. 8th cent. B.C.- . . . . . CMLC 1, 16; DA;
                                DAB; DAC
See also DAM MST, POET

Honig, Edwin 1919- . . . . CLC 33
See also CA 5-8R; CAAS 8; CANR 4, 45;
    DLB 5

Hood, Hugh (John Blagdon)
    1928- . . . . CLC 15, 28
See also CA 49-52; CAAS 17; CANR 1, 33;
    DLB 53

Hood, Thomas 1799-1845 . . . . NCLC 16
See also DLB 96

Hooker, (Peter) Jeremy 1941- . . . . . . CLC 43
See also CA 77-80; CANR 22; DLB 40

hooks, bell . . . . CLC 94
See also Watkins, Gloria

Hope, A(lec) D(erwent) 1907- . . . . CLC 3, 51
See also CA 21-24R; CANR 33; MTCW

Hope, Brian
See Creasey, John

Hope, Christopher (David Tully)
    1944- . . . . CLC 52
See also CA 106; CANR 47; SATA 62

Hopkins, Gerard Manley
    1844-1889 . . . . NCLC 17; DA; DAB;
                            DAC; PC 15; WLC
See also CDBLB 1890-1914; DAM MST,
    POET; DLB 35, 57

Hopkins, John (Richard) 1931- . . . . . . CLC 4
See also CA 85-88

Hopkins, Pauline Elizabeth
    1859-1930 . . . . TCLC 28; BLC
See also BW 2; CA 141; DAM MULT;
    DLB 50

Hopkinson, Francis 1737-1791 . . . . . . LC 25
See also DLB 31

Hopley-Woolrich, Cornell George 1903-1968
See Woolrich, Cornell
See also CA 13-14; CAP 1

Horatio
See Proust, (Valentin-Louis-George-Eugene-)
    Marcel

Horgan, Paul (George Vincent O'Shaughnessy)
 1903-1995 . . . . **CLC 9, 53**
 See also CA 13-16R; 147; CANR 9, 35;
 DAM NOV; DLB 102; DLBY 85;
 INT CANR-9; MTCW; SATA 13;
 SATA-Obit 84

Horn, Peter
 See Kuttner, Henry

Hornem, Horace Esq.
 See Byron, George Gordon (Noel)

Hornung, E(rnest) W(illiam)
 1866-1921 . . . . **TCLC 59**
 See also CA 108; DLB 70

Horovitz, Israel (Arthur) 1939- . . . . . **CLC 56**
 See also CA 33-36R; CANR 46;
 DAM DRAM; DLB 7

Horvath, Odon von
 See Horvath, Oedoen von
 See also DLB 85, 124

Horvath, Oedoen von 1901-1938 . . . **TCLC 45**
 See also Horvath, Odon von
 See also CA 118

Horwitz, Julius 1920-1986 . . . . **CLC 14**
 See also CA 9-12R; 119; CANR 12

Hospital, Janette Turner 1942- . . . . . **CLC 42**
 See also CA 108; CANR 48

Hostos, E. M. de
 See Hostos (y Bonilla), Eugenio Maria de

Hostos, Eugenio M. de
 See Hostos (y Bonilla), Eugenio Maria de

Hostos, Eugenio Maria
 See Hostos (y Bonilla), Eugenio Maria de

Hostos (y Bonilla), Eugenio Maria de
 1839-1903 . . . . **TCLC 24**
 See also CA 123; 131; HW

Houdini
 See Lovecraft, H(oward) P(hillips)

Hougan, Carolyn 1943- . . . . **CLC 34**
 See also CA 139

Household, Geoffrey (Edward West)
 1900-1988 . . . . **CLC 11**
 See also CA 77-80; 126; DLB 87; SATA 14;
 SATA-Obit 59

Housman, A(lfred) E(dward)
 1859-1936 . . . . . . **TCLC 1, 10; DA; DAB;**
                                          DAC; PC 2
 See also CA 104; 125; DAM MST, POET;
 DLB 19; MTCW

Housman, Laurence 1865-1959 . . . . . **TCLC 7**
 See also CA 106; DLB 10; SATA 25

Howard, Elizabeth Jane 1923- . . . **CLC 7, 29**
 See also CA 5-8R; CANR 8

Howard, Maureen 1930- . . . . . **CLC 5, 14, 46**
 See also CA 53-56; CANR 31; DLBY 83;
 INT CANR-31; MTCW

Howard, Richard 1929- . . . . . . **CLC 7, 10, 47**
 See also AITN 1; CA 85-88; CANR 25;
 DLB 5; INT CANR-25

Howard, Robert Ervin 1906-1936 . . . **TCLC 8**
 See also CA 105

Howard, Warren F.
 See Pohl, Frederik

Howe, Fanny 1940- . . . . **CLC 47**
 See also CA 117; SATA-Brief 52

Howe, Irving 1920-1993 . . . . **CLC 85**
 See also CA 9-12R; 141; CANR 21, 50;
 DLB 67; MTCW

Howe, Julia Ward 1819-1910 . . . . . **TCLC 21**
 See also CA 117; DLB 1

Howe, Susan 1937- . . . . **CLC 72**
 See also DLB 120

Howe, Tina 1937- . . . . **CLC 48**
 See also CA 109

Howell, James 1594(?)-1666 . . . . **LC 13**
 See also DLB 151

Howells, W. D.
 See Howells, William Dean

Howells, William D.
 See Howells, William Dean

Howells, William Dean
 1837-1920 . . . . **TCLC 7, 17, 41**
 See also CA 104; 134; CDALB 1865-1917;
 DLB 12, 64, 74, 79

Howes, Barbara 1914-1996 . . . . **CLC 15**
 See also CA 9-12R; 151; CAAS 3;
 CANR 53; SATA 5

Hrabal, Bohumil 1914- . . . . **CLC 13, 67**
 See also CA 106; CAAS 12

Hsun, Lu
 See Lu Hsun

Hubbard, L(afayette) Ron(ald)
 1911-1986 . . . . **CLC 43**
 See also CA 77-80; 118; CANR 52;
 DAM POP

Huch, Ricarda (Octavia)
 1864-1947 . . . . **TCLC 13**
 See also CA 111; DLB 66

Huddle, David 1942- . . . . **CLC 49**
 See also CA 57-60; CAAS 20; DLB 130

Hudson, Jeffrey
 See Crichton, (John) Michael

Hudson, W(illiam) H(enry)
 1841-1922 . . . . **TCLC 29**
 See also CA 115; DLB 98, 153; SATA 35

Hueffer, Ford Madox
 See Ford, Ford Madox

Hughart, Barry 1934- . . . . **CLC 39**
 See also CA 137

Hughes, Colin
 See Creasey, John

Hughes, David (John) 1930- . . . . **CLC 48**
 See also CA 116; 129; DLB 14

Hughes, Edward James
 See Hughes, Ted
 See also DAM MST, POET

Hughes, (James) Langston
 1902-1967 . . . . . **CLC 1, 5, 10, 15, 35, 44;**
            BLC; DA; DAB; DAC; DC 3; PC 1;
                                          SSC 6; WLC
 See also AAYA 12; BW 1; CA 1-4R;
 25-28R; CANR 1, 34; CDALB 1929-1941;
 CLR 17; DAM DRAM, MST, MULT,
 POET; DLB 4, 7, 48, 51, 86; JRDA;
 MAICYA; MTCW; SATA 4, 33

Hughes, Richard (Arthur Warren)
 1900-1976 . . . . **CLC 1, 11**
 See also CA 5-8R; 65-68; CANR 4;
 DAM NOV; DLB 15, 161; MTCW;
 SATA 8; SATA-Obit 25

Hughes, Ted
 1930- . . . . . . **CLC 2, 4, 9, 14, 37; DAB;**
                                          DAC; PC 7
 See also Hughes, Edward James
 See also CA 1-4R; CANR 1, 33; CLR 3;
 DLB 40, 161; MAICYA; MTCW;
 SATA 49; SATA-Brief 27

Hugo, Richard F(ranklin)
 1923-1982 . . . . **CLC 6, 18, 32**
 See also CA 49-52; 108; CANR 3;
 DAM POET; DLB 5

Hugo, Victor (Marie)
 1802-1885 . . . . **NCLC 3, 10, 21; DA;**
                                          DAB; DAC; WLC
 See also DAM DRAM, MST, NOV, POET;
 DLB 119; SATA 47

Huidobro, Vicente
 See Huidobro Fernandez, Vicente Garcia

Huidobro Fernandez, Vicente Garcia
 1893-1948 . . . . **TCLC 31**
 See also CA 131; HW

Hulme, Keri 1947- . . . . **CLC 39**
 See also CA 125; INT 125

Hulme, T(homas) E(rnest)
 1883-1917 . . . . **TCLC 21**
 See also CA 117; DLB 19

Hume, David 1711-1776 . . . . **LC 7**
 See also DLB 104

Humphrey, William 1924- . . . . **CLC 45**
 See also CA 77-80; DLB 6

Humphreys, Emyr Owen 1919- . . . . . **CLC 47**
 See also CA 5-8R; CANR 3, 24; DLB 15

Humphreys, Josephine 1945- . . . . **CLC 34, 57**
 See also CA 121; 127; INT 127

Huneker, James Gibbons
 1857-1921 . . . . **TCLC 65**
 See also DLB 71

Hungerford, Pixie
 See Brinsmead, H(esba) F(ay)

Hunt, E(verette) Howard, (Jr.)
 1918- . . . . **CLC 3**
 See also AITN 1; CA 45-48; CANR 2, 47

Hunt, Kyle
 See Creasey, John

Hunt, (James Henry) Leigh
 1784-1859 . . . . **NCLC 1**
 See also DAM POET

Hunt, Marsha 1946- . . . . **CLC 70**
 See also BW 2; CA 143

Hunt, Violet 1866-1942 . . . . **TCLC 53**
 See also DLB 162

Hunter, E. Waldo
 See Sturgeon, Theodore (Hamilton)

Hunter, Evan 1926- . . . . **CLC 11, 31**
 See also CA 5-8R; CANR 5, 38;
 DAM POP; DLBY 82; INT CANR-5;
 MTCW; SATA 25

Hunter, Kristin (Eggleston) 1931- . . . **CLC 35**
 See also AITN 1; BW 1; CA 13-16R;
 CANR 13; CLR 3; DLB 33;
 INT CANR-13; MAICYA; SAAS 10;
 SATA 12

Hunter, Mollie 1922-............. **CLC 21**
See also McIlwraith, Maureen Mollie
Hunter
See also AAYA 13; CANR 37; CLR 25;
DLB 161; JRDA; MAICYA; SAAS 7;
SATA 54

Hunter, Robert (?)-1734............. **LC 7**

Hurston, Zora Neale
1903-1960 .... **CLC 7, 30, 61; BLC; DA;
DAC; SSC 4**
See also AAYA 15; BW 1; CA 85-88;
DAM MST, MULT, NOV; DLB 51, 86;
MTCW

Huston, John (Marcellus)
1906-1987 .... **CLC 20**
See also CA 73-76; 123; CANR 34; DLB 26

Hustvedt, Siri 1955-.............. **CLC 76**
See also CA 137

Hutten, Ulrich von 1488-1523...... **LC 16**

Huxley, Aldous (Leonard)
1894-1963 ..... **CLC 1, 3, 4, 5, 8, 11, 18,
35, 79; DA; DAB; DAC; WLC**
See also AAYA 11; CA 85-88; CANR 44;
CDBLB 1914-1945; DAM MST, NOV;
DLB 36, 100, 162; MTCW; SATA 63

Huysmans, Charles Marie Georges
1848-1907
See Huysmans, Joris-Karl
See also CA 104

Huysmans, Joris-Karl.............. **TCLC 7**
See also Huysmans, Charles Marie Georges
See also DLB 123

Hwang, David Henry
1957-................. **CLC 55; DC 4**
See also CA 127; 132; DAM DRAM;
INT 132

Hyde, Anthony 1946-............. **CLC 42**
See also CA 136

Hyde, Margaret O(ldroyd) 1917- ... **CLC 21**
See also CA 1-4R; CANR 1, 36; CLR 23;
JRDA; MAICYA; SAAS 8; SATA 1, 42,
76

Hynes, James 1956(?)-............ **CLC 65**

Ian, Janis 1951-................. **CLC 21**
See also CA 105

Ibanez, Vicente Blasco
See Blasco Ibanez, Vicente

Ibarguengoitia, Jorge 1928-1983.... **CLC 37**
See also CA 124; 113; HW

Ibsen, Henrik (Johan)
1828-1906 .... **TCLC 2, 8, 16, 37, 52;
DA; DAB; DAC; DC 2; WLC**
See also CA 104; 141; DAM DRAM, MST

Ibuse Masuji 1898-1993........... **CLC 22**
See also CA 127; 141

Ichikawa, Kon 1915-.............. **CLC 20**
See also CA 121

Idle, Eric 1943-................. **CLC 21**
See also Monty Python
See also CA 116; CANR 35

Ignatow, David 1914-...... **CLC 4, 7, 14, 40**
See also CA 9-12R; CAAS 3; CANR 31;
DLB 5

Ihimaera, Witi 1944- .... **CLC 46**
See also CA 77-80

Ilf, Ilya........................ **TCLC 21**
See also Fainzilberg, Ilya Arnoldovich

Illyes, Gyula 1902-1983........... **PC 16**
See also CA 114; 109

Immermann, Karl (Lebrecht)
1796-1840 .... **NCLC 4, 49**
See also DLB 133

Inclan, Ramon (Maria) del Valle
See Valle-Inclan, Ramon (Maria) del

Infante, G(uillermo) Cabrera
See Cabrera Infante, G(uillermo)

Ingalls, Rachel (Holmes) 1940-..... **CLC 42**
See also CA 123; 127

Ingamells, Rex 1913-1955 .... **TCLC 35**

Inge, William Motter
1913-1973 .... **CLC 1, 8, 19**
See also CA 9-12R; CDALB 1941-1968;
DAM DRAM; DLB 7; MTCW

Ingelow, Jean 1820-1897 .... **NCLC 39**
See also DLB 35, 163; SATA 33

Ingram, Willis J.
See Harris, Mark

Innaurato, Albert (F.) 1948(?)-... **CLC 21, 60**
See also CA 115; 122; INT 122

Innes, Michael
See Stewart, J(ohn) I(nnes) M(ackintosh)

Ionesco, Eugene
1909-1994 .... **CLC 1, 4, 6, 9, 11, 15, 41,
86; DA; DAB; DAC; WLC**
See also CA 9-12R; 144; DAM DRAM,
MST; MTCW; SATA 7; SATA-Obit 79

Iqbal, Muhammad 1873-1938 ..... **TCLC 28**

Ireland, Patrick
See O'Doherty, Brian

Iron, Ralph
See Schreiner, Olive (Emilie Albertina)

Irving, John (Winslow)
1942-................. **CLC 13, 23, 38**
See also AAYA 8; BEST 89:3; CA 25-28R;
CANR 28; DAM NOV, POP; DLB 6;
DLBY 82; MTCW

Irving, Washington
1783-1859 ..... **NCLC 2, 19; DA; DAB;
SSC 2; WLC**
See also CDALB 1640-1865; DAM MST;
DLB 3, 11, 30, 59, 73, 74; YABC 2

Irwin, P. K.
See Page, P(atricia) K(athleen)

Isaacs, Susan 1943- .... **CLC 32**
See also BEST 89:1; CA 89-92; CANR 20,
41; DAM POP; INT CANR-20; MTCW

Isherwood, Christopher (William Bradshaw)
1904-1986 .... **CLC 1, 9, 11, 14, 44**
See also CA 13-16R; 117; CANR 35;
DAM DRAM, NOV; DLB 15; DLBY 86;
MTCW

Ishiguro, Kazuo 1954- ...... **CLC 27, 56, 59**
See also BEST 90:2; CA 120; CANR 49;
DAM NOV; MTCW

Ishikawa, Takuboku
1886(?)-1912 .... **TCLC 15; PC 10**
See also CA 113; DAM POET

Iskander, Fazil 1929-............. **CLC 47**
See also CA 102

Isler, Alan .... **CLC 91**

Ivan IV 1530-1584 .... **LC 17**

Ivanov, Vyacheslav Ivanovich
1866-1949 .... **TCLC 33**
See also CA 122

Ivask, Ivar Vidrik 1927-1992....... **CLC 14**
See also CA 37-40R; 139; CANR 24

Ives, Morgan
See Bradley, Marion Zimmer

J. R. S.
See Gogarty, Oliver St. John

Jabran, Kahlil
See Gibran, Kahlil

Jabran, Khalil
See Gibran, Kahlil

Jackson, Daniel
See Wingrove, David (John)

Jackson, Jesse 1908-1983 .... **CLC 12**
See also BW 1; CA 25-28R; 109; CANR 27;
CLR 28; MAICYA; SATA 2, 29;
SATA-Obit 48

Jackson, Laura (Riding) 1901-1991
See Riding, Laura
See also CA 65-68; 135; CANR 28; DLB 48

Jackson, Sam
See Trumbo, Dalton

Jackson, Sara
See Wingrove, David (John)

Jackson, Shirley
1919-1965 .... **CLC 11, 60, 87; DA;
DAC; SSC 9; WLC**
See also AAYA 9; CA 1-4R; 25-28R;
CANR 4, 52; CDALB 1941-1968;
DAM MST; DLB 6; SATA 2

Jacob, (Cyprien-)Max 1876-1944 ... **TCLC 6**
See also CA 104

Jacobs, Jim 1942-................. **CLC 12**
See also CA 97-100; INT 97-100

Jacobs, W(illiam) W(ymark)
1863-1943 .... **TCLC 22**
See also CA 121; DLB 135

Jacobsen, Jens Peter 1847-1885 .. **NCLC 34**

Jacobsen, Josephine 1908-......... **CLC 48**
See also CA 33-36R; CAAS 18; CANR 23,
48

Jacobson, Dan 1929- .... **CLC 4, 14**
See also CA 1-4R; CANR 2, 25; DLB 14;
MTCW

Jacqueline
See Carpentier (y Valmont), Alejo

Jagger, Mick 1944-............... **CLC 17**

Jakes, John (William) 1932-....... **CLC 29**
See also BEST 89:4; CA 57-60; CANR 10,
43; DAM NOV, POP; DLBY 83;
INT CANR-10; MTCW; SATA 62

James, Andrew
See Kirkup, James

James, C(yril) L(ionel) R(obert)
1901-1989 .... **CLC 33**
See also BW 2; CA 117; 125; 128; DLB 125;
MTCW

James, Daniel (Lewis) 1911-1988
See Santiago, Danny
See also CA 125

James, Dynely
See Mayne, William (James Carter)

James, Henry Sr. 1811-1882 . . . . . **NCLC 53**

James, Henry
1843-1916 . . . . . . **TCLC 2, 11, 24, 40, 47,**
64; DA; DAB; DAC; SSC 8; WLC
See also CA 104; 132; CDALB 1865-1917;
DAM MST, NOV; DLB 12, 71, 74;
DLBD 13; MTCW

James, M. R.
See James, Montague (Rhodes)
See also DLB 156

James, Montague (Rhodes)
1862-1936 . . . . **TCLC 6; SSC 16**
See also CA 104

James, P. D. . . . . **CLC 18, 46**
See also White, Phyllis Dorothy James
See also BEST 90:2; CDBLB 1960 to
Present; DLB 87

James, Philip
See Moorcock, Michael (John)

James, William 1842-1910 . . . . . **TCLC 15, 32**
See also CA 109

James I 1394-1437 . . . . **LC 20**

Jameson, Anna 1794-1860 . . . . **NCLC 43**
See also DLB 99, 166

Jami, Nur al-Din 'Abd al-Rahman
1414-1492 . . . . **LC 9**

Jandl, Ernst 1925- . . . . **CLC 34**

Janowitz, Tama 1957- . . . . **CLC 43**
See also CA 106; CANR 52; DAM POP

Japrisot, Sebastien 1931- . . . . **CLC 90**

Jarrell, Randall
1914-1965 . . . . **CLC 1, 2, 6, 9, 13, 49**
See also CA 5-8R; 25-28R; CABS 2;
CANR 6, 34; CDALB 1941-1968; CLR 6;
DAM POET; DLB 48, 52; MAICYA;
MTCW; SATA 7

Jarry, Alfred
1873-1907 . . . . **TCLC 2, 14; SSC 20**
See also CA 104; DAM DRAM

Jarvis, E. K.
See Bloch, Robert (Albert); Ellison, Harlan
(Jay); Silverberg, Robert

Jeake, Samuel, Jr.
See Aiken, Conrad (Potter)

Jean Paul 1763-1825 . . . . **NCLC 7**

Jefferies, (John) Richard
1848-1887 . . . . **NCLC 47**
See also DLB 98, 141; SATA 16

Jeffers, (John) Robinson
1887-1962 . . . . **CLC 2, 3, 11, 15, 54; DA;**
DAC; WLC
See also CA 85-88; CANR 35;
CDALB 1917-1929; DAM MST, POET;
DLB 45; MTCW

Jefferson, Janet
See Mencken, H(enry) L(ouis)

Jefferson, Thomas 1743-1826 . . . . **NCLC 11**
See also CDALB 1640-1865; DLB 31

Jeffrey, Francis 1773-1850 . . . . **NCLC 33**
See also DLB 107

Jelakowitch, Ivan
See Heijermans, Herman

Jellicoe, (Patricia) Ann 1927- . . . . . . **CLC 27**
See also CA 85-88; DLB 13

Jen, Gish . . . . **CLC 70**
See also Jen, Lillian

Jen, Lillian 1956(?)-
See Jen, Gish
See also CA 135

Jenkins, (John) Robin 1912- . . . . **CLC 52**
See also CA 1-4R; CANR 1; DLB 14

Jennings, Elizabeth (Joan)
1926- . . . . **CLC 5, 14**
See also CA 61-64; CAAS 5; CANR 8, 39;
DLB 27; MTCW; SATA 66

Jennings, Waylon 1937- . . . . **CLC 21**

Jensen, Johannes V. 1873-1950 . . . . **TCLC 41**

Jensen, Laura (Linnea) 1948- . . . . . . **CLC 37**
See also CA 103

Jerome, Jerome K(lapka)
1859-1927 . . . . **TCLC 23**
See also CA 119; DLB 10, 34, 135

Jerrold, Douglas William
1803-1857 . . . . **NCLC 2**
See also DLB 158, 159

Jewett, (Theodora) Sarah Orne
1849-1909 . . . . **TCLC 1, 22; SSC 6**
See also CA 108; 127; DLB 12, 74;
SATA 15

Jewsbury, Geraldine (Endsor)
1812-1880 . . . . **NCLC 22**
See also DLB 21

Jhabvala, Ruth Prawer
1927- . . . . **CLC 4, 8, 29, 94; DAB**
See also CA 1-4R; CANR 2, 29, 51;
DAM NOV; DLB 139; INT CANR-29;
MTCW

Jibran, Kahlil
See Gibran, Kahlil

Jibran, Khalil
See Gibran, Kahlil

Jiles, Paulette 1943- . . . . **CLC 13, 58**
See also CA 101

Jimenez (Mantecon), Juan Ramon
1881-1958 . . . . **TCLC 4; HLC; PC 7**
See also CA 104; 131; DAM MULT,
POET; DLB 134; HW; MTCW

Jimenez, Ramon
See Jimenez (Mantecon), Juan Ramon

Jimenez Mantecon, Juan
See Jimenez (Mantecon), Juan Ramon

Joel, Billy . . . . **CLC 26**
See also Joel, William Martin

Joel, William Martin 1949-
See Joel, Billy
See also CA 108

John of the Cross, St. 1542-1591 . . . . **LC 18**

Johnson, B(ryan) S(tanley William)
1933-1973 . . . . **CLC 6, 9**
See also CA 9-12R; 53-56; CANR 9;
DLB 14, 40

Johnson, Benj. F. of Boo
See Riley, James Whitcomb

Johnson, Benjamin F. of Boo
See Riley, James Whitcomb

Johnson, Charles (Richard)
1948- . . . . **CLC 7, 51, 65; BLC**
See also BW 2; CA 116; CAAS 18;
CANR 42; DAM MULT; DLB 33

Johnson, Denis 1949- . . . . **CLC 52**
See also CA 117; 121; DLB 120

Johnson, Diane 1934- . . . . **CLC 5, 13, 48**
See also CA 41-44R; CANR 17, 40;
DLBY 80; INT CANR-17; MTCW

Johnson, Eyvind (Olof Verner)
1900-1976 . . . . **CLC 14**
See also CA 73-76; 69-72; CANR 34

Johnson, J. R.
See James, C(yril) L(ionel) R(obert)

Johnson, James Weldon
1871-1938 . . . . **TCLC 3, 19; BLC**
See also BW 1; CA 104; 125;
CDALB 1917-1929; CLR 32;
DAM MULT, POET; DLB 51; MTCW;
SATA 31

Johnson, Joyce 1935- . . . . **CLC 58**
See also CA 125; 129

Johnson, Lionel (Pigot)
1867-1902 . . . . **TCLC 19**
See also CA 117; DLB 19

Johnson, Mel
See Malzberg, Barry N(athaniel)

Johnson, Pamela Hansford
1912-1981 . . . . **CLC 1, 7, 27**
See also CA 1-4R; 104; CANR 2, 28;
DLB 15; MTCW

Johnson, Samuel
1709-1784 . . . . . **LC 15; DA; DAB; DAC;**
WLC
See also CDBLB 1660-1789; DAM MST;
DLB 39, 95, 104, 142

Johnson, Uwe
1934-1984 . . . . **CLC 5, 10, 15, 40**
See also CA 1-4R; 112; CANR 1, 39;
DLB 75; MTCW

Johnston, George (Benson) 1913- . . . **CLC 51**
See also CA 1-4R; CANR 5, 20; DLB 88

Johnston, Jennifer 1930- . . . . **CLC 7**
See also CA 85-88; DLB 14

Jolley, (Monica) Elizabeth
1923- . . . . **CLC 46; SSC 19**
See also CA 127; CAAS 13

Jones, Arthur Llewellyn 1863-1947
See Machen, Arthur
See also CA 104

Jones, D(ouglas) G(ordon) 1929- . . . . **CLC 10**
See also CA 29-32R; CANR 13; DLB 53

Jones, David (Michael)
1895-1974 . . . . **CLC 2, 4, 7, 13, 42**
See also CA 9-12R; 53-56; CANR 28;
CDBLB 1945-1960; DLB 20, 100; MTCW

Jones, David Robert 1947-
See Bowie, David
See also CA 103

Jones, Diana Wynne 1934- . . . . **CLC 26**
See also AAYA 12; CA 49-52; CANR 4,
26; CLR 23; DLB 161; JRDA; MAICYA;
SAAS 7; SATA 9, 70

Jones, Edward P. 1950- . . . . **CLC 76**
See also BW 2; CA 142

Jones, Gayl 1949- .... **CLC 6, 9; BLC**
See also BW 2; CA 77-80; CANR 27;
DAM MULT; DLB 33; MTCW

Jones, James 1921-1977.... **CLC 1, 3, 10, 39**
See also AITN 1, 2; CA 1-4R; 69-72;
CANR 6; DLB 2, 143; MTCW

Jones, John J.
See Lovecraft, H(oward) P(hillips)

Jones, LeRoi .... **CLC 1, 2, 3, 5, 10, 14**
See also Baraka, Amiri

Jones, Louis B. .... **CLC 65**
See also CA 141

Jones, Madison (Percy, Jr.) 1925- ... **CLC 4**
See also CA 13-16R; CAAS 11; CANR 7;
DLB 152

Jones, Mervyn 1922- .... **CLC 10, 52**
See also CA 45-48; CAAS 5; CANR 1;
MTCW

Jones, Mick 1956(?)- .... **CLC 30**

Jones, Nettie (Pearl) 1941- .... **CLC 34**
See also BW 2; CA 137; CAAS 20

Jones, Preston 1936-1979 .... **CLC 10**
See also CA 73-76; 89-92; DLB 7

Jones, Robert F(rancis) 1934- .... **CLC 7**
See also CA 49-52; CANR 2

Jones, Rod 1953- .... **CLC 50**
See also CA 128

Jones, Terence Graham Parry
1942- .... **CLC 21**
See also Jones, Terry; Monty Python
See also CA 112; 116; CANR 35; INT 116

Jones, Terry
See Jones, Terence Graham Parry
See also SATA 67; SATA-Brief 51

Jones, Thom 1945(?)- .... **CLC 81**

Jong, Erica 1942- ...... **CLC 4, 6, 8, 18, 83**
See also AITN 1; BEST 90:2; CA 73-76;
CANR 26, 52; DAM NOV, POP; DLB 2,
5, 28, 152; INT CANR-26; MTCW

Jonson, Ben(jamin)
1572(?)-1637 ...... **LC 6, 33; DA; DAB;**
DAC; DC 4; WLC
See also CDBLB Before 1660;
DAM DRAM, MST, POET; DLB 62,
121

Jordan, June 1936- .... **CLC 5, 11, 23**
See also AAYA 2; BW 2; CA 33-36R;
CANR 25; CLR 10; DAM MULT,
POET; DLB 38; MAICYA; MTCW;
SATA 4

Jordan, Pat(rick M.) 1941- .... **CLC 37**
See also CA 33-36R

Jorgensen, Ivar
See Ellison, Harlan (Jay)

Jorgenson, Ivar
See Silverberg, Robert

Josephus, Flavius c. 37-100 ...... **CMLC 13**

Josipovici, Gabriel 1940- .... **CLC 6, 43**
See also CA 37-40R; CAAS 8; CANR 47;
DLB 14

Joubert, Joseph 1754-1824 .... **NCLC 9**

Jouve, Pierre Jean 1887-1976 ...... **CLC 47**
See also CA 65-68

Joyce, James (Augustine Aloysius)
1882-1941 .... **TCLC 3, 8, 16, 35, 52;**
DA; DAB; DAC; SSC 3; WLC
See also CA 104; 126; CDBLB 1914-1945;
DAM MST, NOV, POET; DLB 10, 19,
36, 162; MTCW

Jozsef, Attila 1905-1937 .... **TCLC 22**
See also CA 116

Juana Ines de la Cruz 1651(?)-1695 ... **LC 5**

Judd, Cyril
See Kornbluth, C(yril) M.; Pohl, Frederik

Julian of Norwich 1342(?)-1416(?) .... **LC 6**
See also DLB 146

Juniper, Alex
See Hospital, Janette Turner

Junius
See Luxemburg, Rosa

Just, Ward (Swift) 1935- .... **CLC 4, 27**
See also CA 25-28R; CANR 32;
INT CANR-32

Justice, Donald (Rodney) 1925- .. **CLC 6, 19**
See also CA 5-8R; CANR 26; DAM POET;
DLBY 83; INT CANR-26

Juvenal c. 55-c. 127 .... **CMLC 8**

Juvenis
See Bourne, Randolph S(illiman)

Kacew, Romain 1914-1980
See Gary, Romain
See also CA 108; 102

Kadare, Ismail 1936- .... **CLC 52**

Kadohata, Cynthia .... **CLC 59**
See also CA 140

Kafka, Franz
1883-1924 .... **TCLC 2, 6, 13, 29, 47, 53;**
DA; DAB; DAC; SSC 5; WLC
See also CA 105; 126; DAM MST, NOV;
DLB 81; MTCW

Kahanovitsch, Pinkhes
See Der Nister

Kahn, Roger 1927- .... **CLC 30**
See also CA 25-28R; CANR 44; SATA 37

Kain, Saul
See Sassoon, Siegfried (Lorraine)

Kaiser, Georg 1878-1945 .... **TCLC 9**
See also CA 106; DLB 124

Kaletski, Alexander 1946- .... **CLC 39**
See also CA 118; 143

Kalidasa fl. c. 400- .... **CMLC 9**

Kallman, Chester (Simon)
1921-1975 .... **CLC 2**
See also CA 45-48; 53-56; CANR 3

Kaminsky, Melvin 1926-
See Brooks, Mel
See also CA 65-68; CANR 16

Kaminsky, Stuart M(elvin) 1934- ... **CLC 59**
See also CA 73-76; CANR 29, 53

Kane, Paul
See Simon, Paul

Kane, Wilson
See Bloch, Robert (Albert)

Kanin, Garson 1912- .... **CLC 22**
See also AITN 1; CA 5-8R; CANR 7;
DLB 7

Kaniuk, Yoram 1930- .... **CLC 19**
See also CA 134

Kant, Immanuel 1724-1804 ...... **NCLC 27**
See also DLB 94

Kantor, MacKinlay 1904-1977 ...... **CLC 7**
See also CA 61-64; 73-76; DLB 9, 102

Kaplan, David Michael 1946- ...... **CLC 50**

Kaplan, James 1951- .... **CLC 59**
See also CA 135

Karageorge, Michael
See Anderson, Poul (William)

Karamzin, Nikolai Mikhailovich
1766-1826 .... **NCLC 3**
See also DLB 150

Karapanou, Margarita 1946- .... **CLC 13**
See also CA 101

Karinthy, Frigyes 1887-1938 ...... **TCLC 47**

Karl, Frederick R(obert) 1927- ..... **CLC 34**
See also CA 5-8R; CANR 3, 44

Kastel, Warren
See Silverberg, Robert

Kataev, Evgeny Petrovich 1903-1942
See Petrov, Evgeny
See also CA 120

Kataphusin
See Ruskin, John

Katz, Steve 1935- .... **CLC 47**
See also CA 25-28R; CAAS 14; CANR 12;
DLBY 83

Kauffman, Janet 1945- .... **CLC 42**
See also CA 117; CANR 43; DLBY 86

Kaufman, Bob (Garnell)
1925-1986 .... **CLC 49**
See also BW 1; CA 41-44R; 118; CANR 22;
DLB 16, 41

Kaufman, George S. 1889-1961 ..... **CLC 38**
See also CA 108; 93-96; DAM DRAM;
DLB 7; INT 108

Kaufman, Sue .... **CLC 3, 8**
See also Barondess, Sue K(aufman)

Kavafis, Konstantinos Petrou 1863-1933
See Cavafy, C(onstantine) P(eter)
See also CA 104

Kavan, Anna 1901-1968 ...... **CLC 5, 13, 82**
See also CA 5-8R; CANR 6; MTCW

Kavanagh, Dan
See Barnes, Julian

Kavanagh, Patrick (Joseph)
1904-1967 .... **CLC 22**
See also CA 123; 25-28R; DLB 15, 20;
MTCW

Kawabata, Yasunari
1899-1972 ..... **CLC 2, 5, 9, 18; SSC 17**
See also CA 93-96; 33-36R; DAM MULT

Kaye, M(ary) M(argaret) 1909- ..... **CLC 28**
See also CA 89-92; CANR 24; MTCW;
SATA 62

Kaye, Mollie
See Kaye, M(ary) M(argaret)

Kaye-Smith, Sheila 1887-1956 ..... **TCLC 20**
See also CA 118; DLB 36

Kaymor, Patrice Maguilene
See Senghor, Leopold Sedar

Kazan, Elia 1909-.......... CLC **6, 16, 63**
See also CA 21-24R; CANR 32

Kazantzakis, Nikos
1883(?)-1957 .... TCLC **2, 5, 33**
See also CA 105; 132; MTCW

Kazin, Alfred 1915- .... CLC **34, 38**
See also CA 1-4R; CAAS 7; CANR 1, 45;
DLB 67

Keane, Mary Nesta (Skrine) 1904-1996
See Keane, Molly
See also CA 108; 114; 151

Keane, Molly.................... CLC **31**
See also Keane, Mary Nesta (Skrine)
See also INT 114

Keates, Jonathan 19(?)-........... CLC **34**

Keaton, Buster 1895-1966 .... CLC **20**

Keats, John
1795-1821 .... NCLC **8; DA; DAB;**
DAC; PC 1; WLC
See also CDBLB 1789-1832; DAM MST,
POET; DLB 96, 110

Keene, Donald 1922- .... CLC **34**
See also CA 1-4R; CANR 5

Keillor, Garrison................. CLC **40**
See also Keillor, Gary (Edward)
See also AAYA 2; BEST 89:3; DLBY 87;
SATA 58

Keillor, Gary (Edward) 1942-
See Keillor, Garrison
See also CA 111; 117; CANR 36;
DAM POP; MTCW

Keith, Michael
See Hubbard, L(afayette) Ron(ald)

Keller, Gottfried 1819-1890 .... NCLC **2**
See also DLB 129

Kellerman, Jonathan 1949- .... CLC **44**
See also BEST 90:1; CA 106; CANR 29, 51;
DAM POP; INT CANR-29

Kelley, William Melvin 1937-...... CLC **22**
See also BW 1; CA 77-80; CANR 27;
DLB 33

Kellogg, Marjorie 1922-............ CLC **2**
See also CA 81-84

Kellow, Kathleen
See Hibbert, Eleanor Alice Burford

Kelly, M(ilton) T(erry) 1947-....... CLC **55**
See also CA 97-100; CAAS 22; CANR 19,
43

Kelman, James 1946-.......... CLC **58, 86**
See also CA 148

Kemal, Yashar 1923- .... CLC **14, 29**
See also CA 89-92; CANR 44

Kemble, Fanny 1809-1893 .... NCLC **18**
See also DLB 32

Kemelman, Harry 1908-............ CLC **2**
See also AITN 1; CA 9-12R; CANR 6;
DLB 28

Kempe, Margery 1373(?)-1440(?) ..... LC **6**
See also DLB 146

Kempis, Thomas a 1380-1471 .... LC **11**

Kendall, Henry 1839-1882....... NCLC **12**

Keneally, Thomas (Michael)
1935-...... CLC **5, 8, 10, 14, 19, 27, 43**
See also CA 85-88; CANR 10, 50;
DAM NOV; MTCW

Kennedy, Adrienne (Lita)
1931- .... CLC **66; BLC; DC 5**
See also BW 2; CA 103; CAAS 20; CABS 3;
CANR 26, 53; DAM MULT; DLB 38

Kennedy, John Pendleton
1795-1870 .... NCLC **2**
See also DLB 3

Kennedy, Joseph Charles 1929-
See Kennedy, X. J.
See also CA 1-4R; CANR 4, 30, 40;
SATA 14, 86

Kennedy, William 1928-... CLC **6, 28, 34, 53**
See also AAYA 1; CA 85-88; CANR 14,
31; DAM NOV; DLB 143; DLBY 85;
INT CANR-31; MTCW; SATA 57

Kennedy, X. J................... CLC **8, 42**
See also Kennedy, Joseph Charles
See also CAAS 9; CLR 27; DLB 5;
SAAS 22

Kenny, Maurice (Francis) 1929-.... CLC **87**
See also CA 144; CAAS 22; DAM MULT;
NNAL

Kent, Kelvin
See Kuttner, Henry

Kenton, Maxwell
See Southern, Terry

Kenyon, Robert O.
See Kuttner, Henry

Kerouac, Jack ..... CLC **1, 2, 3, 5, 14, 29, 61**
See also Kerouac, Jean-Louis Lebris de
See also CDALB 1941-1968; DLB 2, 16;
DLBD 3; DLBY 95

Kerouac, Jean-Louis Lebris de 1922-1969
See Kerouac, Jack
See also AITN 1; CA 5-8R; 25-28R;
CANR 26; DA; DAB; DAC; DAM MST,
NOV, POET, POP; MTCW; WLC

Kerr, Jean 1923-................. CLC **22**
See also CA 5-8R; CANR 7; INT CANR-7

Kerr, M. E..................... CLC **12, 35**
See also Meaker, Marijane (Agnes)
See also AAYA 2; CLR 29; SAAS 1

Kerr, Robert .... CLC **55**

Kerrigan, (Thomas) Anthony
1918-.................... CLC **4, 6**
See also CA 49-52; CAAS 11; CANR 4

Kerry, Lois
See Duncan, Lois

Kesey, Ken (Elton)
1935-...... CLC **1, 3, 6, 11, 46, 64; DA;**
DAB; DAC; WLC
See also CA 1-4R; CANR 22, 38;
CDALB 1968-1988; DAM MST, NOV,
POP; DLB 2, 16; MTCW; SATA 66

Kesselring, Joseph (Otto)
1902-1967 .... CLC **45**
See also CA 150; DAM DRAM, MST

Kessler, Jascha (Frederick) 1929-.... CLC **4**
See also CA 17-20R; CANR 8, 48

Kettelkamp, Larry (Dale) 1933- .... CLC **12**
See also CA 29-32R; CANR 16; SAAS 3;
SATA 2

Key, Ellen 1849-1926........... TCLC **65**

Keyber, Conny
See Fielding, Henry

Keyes, Daniel 1927-.... CLC **80; DA; DAC**
See also CA 17-20R; CANR 10, 26;
DAM MST, NOV; SATA 37

Keynes, John Maynard
1883-1946 .... TCLC **64**
See also CA 114; DLBD 10

Khanshendel, Chiron
See Rose, Wendy

Khayyam, Omar
1048-1131 .... CMLC **11; PC 8**
See also DAM POET

Kherdian, David 1931-........... CLC **6, 9**
See also CA 21-24R; CAAS 2; CANR 39;
CLR 24; JRDA; MAICYA; SATA 16, 74

Khlebnikov, Velimir .... TCLC **20**
See also Khlebnikov, Viktor Vladimirovich

Khlebnikov, Viktor Vladimirovich 1885-1922
See Khlebnikov, Velimir
See also CA 117

Khodasevich, Vladislav (Felitsianovich)
1886-1939 .... TCLC **15**
See also CA 115

Kielland, Alexander Lange
1849-1906 .... TCLC **5**
See also CA 104

Kiely, Benedict 1919-.......... CLC **23, 43**
See also CA 1-4R; CANR 2; DLB 15

Kienzle, William X(avier) 1928- .... CLC **25**
See also CA 93-96; CAAS 1; CANR 9, 31;
DAM POP; INT CANR-31; MTCW

Kierkegaard, Soren 1813-1855.... NCLC **34**

Killens, John Oliver 1916-1987..... CLC **10**
See also BW 2; CA 77-80; 123; CAAS 2;
CANR 26; DLB 33

Killigrew, Anne 1660-1685.......... LC **4**
See also DLB 131

Kim
See Simenon, Georges (Jacques Christian)

Kincaid, Jamaica 1949-... CLC **43, 68; BLC**
See also AAYA 13; BW 2; CA 125;
CANR 47; DAM MULT, NOV;
DLB 157

King, Francis (Henry) 1923-...... CLC **8, 53**
See also CA 1-4R; CANR 1, 33;
DAM NOV; DLB 15, 139; MTCW

King, Martin Luther, Jr.
1929-1968 .... CLC **83; BLC; DA; DAB;**
DAC
See also BW 2; CA 25-28; CANR 27, 44;
CAP 2; DAM MST, MULT; MTCW;
SATA 14

King, Stephen (Edwin)
1947-...... CLC **12, 26, 37, 61; SSC 17**
See also AAYA 1, 17; BEST 90:1;
CA 61-64; CANR 1, 30, 52; DAM NOV,
POP; DLB 143; DLBY 80; JRDA;
MTCW; SATA 9, 55

King, Steve
See King, Stephen (Edwin)

King, Thomas 1943-......... CLC **89; DAC**
See also CA 144; DAM MULT; NNAL

Kingman, Lee................... CLC 17
See also Natti, (Mary) Lee
See also SAAS 3; SATA 1, 67

Kingsley, Charles 1819-1875..... NCLC 35
See also DLB 21, 32, 163; YABC 2

Kingsley, Sidney 1906-1995....... CLC 44
See also CA 85-88; 147; DLB 7

Kingsolver, Barbara 1955-...... CLC 55, 81
See also AAYA 15; CA 129; 134;
DAM POP; INT 134

Kingston, Maxine (Ting Ting) Hong
1940-................... CLC 12, 19, 58
See also AAYA 8; CA 69-72; CANR 13,
38; DAM MULT, NOV; DLBY 80;
INT CANR-13; MTCW; SATA 53

Kinnell, Galway
1927-.......... CLC 1, 2, 3, 5, 13, 29
See also CA 9-12R; CANR 10, 34; DLB 5;
DLBY 87; INT CANR-34; MTCW

Kinsella, Thomas 1928-......... CLC 4, 19
See also CA 17-20R; CANR 15; DLB 27;
MTCW

Kinsella, W(illiam) P(atrick)
1935-.............. CLC 27, 43; DAC
See also AAYA 7; CA 97-100; CAAS 7;
CANR 21, 35; DAM NOV, POP;
INT CANR-21; MTCW

Kipling, (Joseph) Rudyard
1865-1936..... TCLC 8, 17; DA; DAB;
DAC; PC 3; SSC 5; WLC
See also CA 105; 120; CANR 33;
CDBLB 1890-1914; CLR 39; DAM MST,
POET; DLB 19, 34, 141, 156; MAICYA;
MTCW; YABC 2

Kirkup, James 1918-............. CLC 1
See also CA 1-4R; CAAS 4; CANR 2;
DLB 27; SATA 12

Kirkwood, James 1930(?)-1989...... CLC 9
See also AITN 2; CA 1-4R; 128; CANR 6,
40

Kirshner, Sidney
See Kingsley, Sidney

Kis, Danilo 1935-1989........... CLC 57
See also CA 109; 118; 129; MTCW

Kivi, Aleksis 1834-1872........ NCLC 30

Kizer, Carolyn (Ashley)
1925-................ CLC 15, 39, 80
See also CA 65-68; CAAS 5; CANR 24;
DAM POET; DLB 5

Klabund 1890-1928.............. TCLC 44
See also DLB 66

Klappert, Peter 1942-............ CLC 57
See also CA 33-36R; DLB 5

Klein, A(braham) M(oses)
1909-1972........ CLC 19; DAB; DAC
See also CA 101; 37-40R; DAM MST;
DLB 68

Klein, Norma 1938-1989.......... CLC 30
See also AAYA 2; CA 41-44R; 128;
CANR 15, 37; CLR 2, 19;
INT CANR-15; JRDA; MAICYA;
SAAS 1; SATA 7, 57

Klein, T(heodore) E(ibon) D(onald)
1947-...................... CLC 34
See also CA 119; CANR 44

Kleist, Heinrich von
1777-1811........ NCLC 2, 37; SSC 22
See also DAM DRAM; DLB 90

Klima, Ivan 1931-................ CLC 56
See also CA 25-28R; CANR 17, 50;
DAM NOV

Klimentov, Andrei Platonovich 1899-1951
See Platonov, Andrei
See also CA 108

Klinger, Friedrich Maximilian von
1752-1831.................. NCLC 1
See also DLB 94

Klopstock, Friedrich Gottlieb
1724-1803................. NCLC 11
See also DLB 97

Knebel, Fletcher 1911-1993........ CLC 14
See also AITN 1; CA 1-4R; 140; CAAS 3;
CANR 1, 36; SATA 36; SATA-Obit 75

Knickerbocker, Diedrich
See Irving, Washington

Knight, Etheridge
1931-1991...... CLC 40; BLC; PC 14
See also BW 1; CA 21-24R; 133; CANR 23;
DAM POET; DLB 41

Knight, Sarah Kemble 1666-1727..... LC 7
See also DLB 24

Knister, Raymond 1899-1932...... TCLC 56
See also DLB 68

Knowles, John
1926-...... CLC 1, 4, 10, 26; DA; DAC
See also AAYA 10; CA 17-20R; CANR 40;
CDALB 1968-1988; DAM MST, NOV;
DLB 6; MTCW; SATA 8

Knox, Calvin M.
See Silverberg, Robert

Knye, Cassandra
See Disch, Thomas M(ichael)

Koch, C(hristopher) J(ohn) 1932-... CLC 42
See also CA 127

Koch, Christopher
See Koch, C(hristopher) J(ohn)

Koch, Kenneth 1925-......... CLC 5, 8, 44
See also CA 1-4R; CANR 6, 36;
DAM POET; DLB 5; INT CANR-36;
SATA 65

Kochanowski, Jan 1530-1584....... LC 10

Kock, Charles Paul de
1794-1871................. NCLC 16

Koda Shigeyuki 1867-1947
See Rohan, Koda
See also CA 121

Koestler, Arthur
1905-1983....... CLC 1, 3, 6, 8, 15, 33
See also CA 1-4R; 109; CANR 1, 33;
CDBLB 1945-1960; DLBY 83; MTCW

Kogawa, Joy Nozomi 1935-...CLC 78; DAC
See also CA 101; CANR 19; DAM MST,
MULT

Kohout, Pavel 1928-.............. CLC 13
See also CA 45-48; CANR 3

Koizumi, Yakumo
See Hearn, (Patricio) Lafcadio (Tessima
Carlos)

Kolmar, Gertrud 1894-1943....... TCLC 40

Komunyakaa, Yusef 1947...... CLC 86, 94
See also CA 147; DLB 120

Konrad, George
See Konrad, Gyoergy

Konrad, Gyoergy 1933-...... CLC 4, 10, 73
See also CA 85-88

Konwicki, Tadeusz 1926-..... CLC 8, 28, 54
See also CA 101; CAAS 9; CANR 39;
MTCW

Koontz, Dean R(ay) 1945-......... CLC 78
See also AAYA 9; BEST 89:3, 90:2;
CA 108; CANR 19, 36, 52; DAM NOV,
POP; MTCW

Kopit, Arthur (Lee) 1937-.... CLC 1, 18, 33
See also AITN 1; CA 81-84; CABS 3;
DAM DRAM; DLB 7; MTCW

Kops, Bernard 1926-.............. CLC 4
See also CA 5-8R; DLB 13

Kornbluth, C(yril) M. 1923-1958.... TCLC 8
See also CA 105; DLB 8

Korolenko, V. G.
See Korolenko, Vladimir Galaktionovich

Korolenko, Vladimir
See Korolenko, Vladimir Galaktionovich

Korolenko, Vladimir G.
See Korolenko, Vladimir Galaktionovich

Korolenko, Vladimir Galaktionovich
1853-1921................. TCLC 22
See also CA 121

Korzybski, Alfred (Habdank Skarbek)
1879-1950................. TCLC 61
See also CA 123

Kosinski, Jerzy (Nikodem)
1933-1991.... CLC 1, 2, 3, 6, 10, 15, 53,
70
See also CA 17-20R; 134; CANR 9, 46;
DAM NOV; DLB 2; DLBY 82; MTCW

Kostelanetz, Richard (Cory) 1940-.. CLC 28
See also CA 13-16R; CAAS 8; CANR 38

Kostrowitzki, Wilhelm Apollinaris de
1880-1918
See Apollinaire, Guillaume
See also CA 104

Kotlowitz, Robert 1924-............ CLC 4
See also CA 33-36R; CANR 36

Kotzebue, August (Friedrich Ferdinand) von
1761-1819................ NCLC 25
See also DLB 94

Kotzwinkle, William 1938-... CLC 5, 14, 35
See also CA 45-48; CANR 3, 44; CLR 6;
MAICYA; SATA 24, 70

Kozol, Jonathan 1936-............ CLC 17
See also CA 61-64; CANR 16, 45

Kozoll, Michael 1940(?)-.......... CLC 35

Kramer, Kathryn 19(?)-........... CLC 34

Kramer, Larry 1935-............. CLC 42
See also CA 124; 126; DAM POP

Krasicki, Ignacy 1735-1801....... NCLC 8

Krasinski, Zygmunt 1812-1859.... NCLC 4

Kraus, Karl 1874-1936........... TCLC 5
See also CA 104; DLB 118

Kreve (Mickevicius), Vincas
1882-1954................. TCLC 27

Kristeva, Julia 1941- . . . . CLC 77

Kristofferson, Kris 1936- . . . . CLC 26
See also CA 104

Krizanc, John 1956- . . . . CLC 57

Krleza, Miroslav 1893-1981 . . . . CLC 8
See also CA 97-100; 105; CANR 50;
DLB 147

Kroetsch, Robert
1927- . . . . CLC 5, 23, 57; DAC
See also CA 17-20R; CANR 8, 38;
DAM POET; DLB 53; MTCW

Kroetz, Franz
See Kroetz, Franz Xaver

Kroetz, Franz Xaver 1946- . . . . CLC 41
See also CA 130

Kroker, Arthur 1945- . . . . CLC 77

Kropotkin, Peter (Aleksieevich)
1842-1921 . . . . TCLC 36
See also CA 119

Krotkov, Yuri 1917- . . . . CLC 19
See also CA 102

Krumb
See Crumb, R(obert)

Krumgold, Joseph (Quincy)
1908-1980 . . . . CLC 12
See also CA 9-12R; 101; CANR 7;
MAICYA; SATA 1, 48; SATA-Obit 23

Krumwitz
See Crumb, R(obert)

Krutch, Joseph Wood 1893-1970 . . . . CLC 24
See also CA 1-4R; 25-28R; CANR 4;
DLB 63

Krutzch, Gus
See Eliot, T(homas) S(tearns)

Krylov, Ivan Andreevich
1768(?)-1844 . . . . NCLC 1
See also DLB 150

Kubin, Alfred (Leopold Isidor)
1877-1959 . . . . TCLC 23
See also CA 112; 149; DLB 81

Kubrick, Stanley 1928- . . . . CLC 16
See also CA 81-84; CANR 33; DLB 26

Kumin, Maxine (Winokur)
1925- . . . . CLC 5, 13, 28; PC 15
See also AITN 2; CA 1-4R; CAAS 8;
CANR 1, 21; DAM POET; DLB 5;
MTCW; SATA 12

Kundera, Milan
1929- . . . . CLC 4, 9, 19, 32, 68
See also AAYA 2; CA 85-88; CANR 19,
52; DAM NOV; MTCW

Kunene, Mazisi (Raymond) 1930- . . . CLC 85
See also BW 1; CA 125; DLB 117

Kunitz, Stanley (Jasspon)
1905- . . . . CLC 6, 11, 14
See also CA 41-44R; CANR 26; DLB 48;
INT CANR-26; MTCW

Kunze, Reiner 1933- . . . . CLC 10
See also CA 93-96; DLB 75

Kuprin, Aleksandr Ivanovich
1870-1938 . . . . TCLC 5
See also CA 104

Kureishi, Hanif 1954(?)- . . . . CLC 64
See also CA 139

Kurosawa, Akira 1910- . . . . CLC 16
See also AAYA 11; CA 101; CANR 46;
DAM MULT

Kushner, Tony 1957(?)- . . . . CLC 81
See also CA 144; DAM DRAM

Kuttner, Henry 1915-1958 . . . . TCLC 10
See also CA 107; DLB 8

Kuzma, Greg 1944- . . . . CLC 7
See also CA 33-36R

Kuzmin, Mikhail 1872(?)-1936 . . . . TCLC 40

Kyd, Thomas 1558-1594 . . . . . . LC 22; DC 3
See also DAM DRAM; DLB 62

Kyprianos, Iossif
See Samarakis, Antonis

La Bruyere, Jean de 1645-1696 . . . . . . LC 17

Lacan, Jacques (Marie Emile)
1901-1981 . . . . CLC 75
See also CA 121; 104

**Laclos, Pierre Ambroise Francois Choderlos
de** 1741-1803 . . . . NCLC 4

Lacolere, Francois
See Aragon, Louis

La Colere, Francois
See Aragon, Louis

La Deshabilleuse
See Simenon, Georges (Jacques Christian)

Lady Gregory
See Gregory, Isabella Augusta (Persse)

Lady of Quality, A
See Bagnold, Enid

**La Fayette, Marie (Madelaine Pioche de la
Vergne Comtes** 1634-1693 . . . . . . LC 2

Lafayette, Rene
See Hubbard, L(afayette) Ron(ald)

Laforgue, Jules
1860-1887 . . . . NCLC 5, 53; PC 14;
SSC 20

Lagerkvist, Paer (Fabian)
1891-1974 . . . . CLC 7, 10, 13, 54
See also Lagerkvist, Par
See also CA 85-88; 49-52; DAM DRAM,
NOV; MTCW

Lagerkvist, Par . . . . SSC 12
See also Lagerkvist, Paer (Fabian)

Lagerloef, Selma (Ottiliana Lovisa)
1858-1940 . . . . TCLC 4, 36
See also Lagerlof, Selma (Ottiliana Lovisa)
See also CA 108; SATA 15

Lagerlof, Selma (Ottiliana Lovisa)
See Lagerloef, Selma (Ottiliana Lovisa)
See also CLR 7; SATA 15

La Guma, (Justin) Alex(ander)
1925-1985 . . . . CLC 19
See also BW 1; CA 49-52; 118; CANR 25;
DAM NOV; DLB 117; MTCW

Laidlaw, A. K.
See Grieve, C(hristopher) M(urray)

Lainez, Manuel Mujica
See Mujica Lainez, Manuel
See also HW

Laing, R(onald) D(avid)
1927-1989 . . . . CLC 95
See also CA 107; 129; CANR 34; MTCW

Lamartine, Alphonse (Marie Louis Prat) de
1790-1869 . . . . NCLC 11; PC 16
See also DAM POET

Lamb, Charles
1775-1834 . . . . NCLC 10; DA; DAB;
DAC; WLC
See also CDBLB 1789-1832; DAM MST;
DLB 93, 107, 163; SATA 17

Lamb, Lady Caroline 1785-1828 . . NCLC 38
See also DLB 116

Lamming, George (William)
1927- . . . . CLC 2, 4, 66; BLC
See also BW 2; CA 85-88; CANR 26;
DAM MULT; DLB 125; MTCW

L'Amour, Louis (Dearborn)
1908-1988 . . . . CLC 25, 55
See also AAYA 16; AITN 2; BEST 89:2;
CA 1-4R; 125; CANR 3, 25, 40;
DAM NOV, POP; DLBY 80; MTCW

Lampedusa, Giuseppe (Tomasi) di . . . TCLC 13
See also Tomasi di Lampedusa, Giuseppe

Lampman, Archibald 1861-1899 . . NCLC 25
See also DLB 92

Lancaster, Bruce 1896-1963 . . . . CLC 36
See also CA 9-10; CAP 1; SATA 9

Landau, Mark Alexandrovich
See Aldanov, Mark (Alexandrovich)

Landau-Aldanov, Mark Alexandrovich
See Aldanov, Mark (Alexandrovich)

Landis, John 1950- . . . . CLC 26
See also CA 112; 122

Landolfi, Tommaso 1908-1979 . . . CLC 11, 49
See also CA 127; 117

Landon, Letitia Elizabeth
1802-1838 . . . . NCLC 15
See also DLB 96

Landor, Walter Savage
1775-1864 . . . . NCLC 14
See also DLB 93, 107

Landwirth, Heinz 1927-
See Lind, Jakov
See also CA 9-12R; CANR 7

Lane, Patrick 1939- . . . . CLC 25
See also CA 97-100; DAM POET; DLB 53;
INT 97-100

Lang, Andrew 1844-1912 . . . . TCLC 16
See also CA 114; 137; DLB 98, 141;
MAICYA; SATA 16

Lang, Fritz 1890-1976 . . . . CLC 20
See also CA 77-80; 69-72; CANR 30

Lange, John
See Crichton, (John) Michael

Langer, Elinor 1939- . . . . CLC 34
See also CA 121

Langland, William
1330(?)-1400(?) . . . . . . LC 19; DA; DAB;
DAC
See also DAM MST, POET; DLB 146

Langstaff, Launcelot
See Irving, Washington

Lanier, Sidney 1842-1881 . . . . NCLC 6
See also DAM POET; DLB 64; DLBD 13;
MAICYA; SATA 18

Lanyer, Aemilia 1569-1645 . . . . . . LC 10, 30
See also DLB 121

Lao Tzu . . . . **CMLC 7**

Lapine, James (Elliot) 1949- . . . . **CLC 39**
See also CA 123; 130; INT 130

Larbaud, Valery (Nicolas)
1881-1957 . . . . **TCLC 9**
See also CA 106; 152

Lardner, Ring
See Lardner, Ring(gold) W(ilmer)

Lardner, Ring W., Jr.
See Lardner, Ring(gold) W(ilmer)

Lardner, Ring(gold) W(ilmer)
1885-1933 . . . . **TCLC 2, 14**
See also CA 104; 131; CDALB 1917-1929;
DLB 11, 25, 86; MTCW

Laredo, Betty
See Codrescu, Andrei

Larkin, Maia
See Wojciechowska, Maia (Teresa)

Larkin, Philip (Arthur)
1922-1985 . . . . **CLC 3, 5, 8, 9, 13, 18, 33,**
                         39, 64; DAB
See also CA 5-8R; 117; CANR 24;
CDBLB 1960 to Present; DAM MST,
POET; DLB 27; MTCW

Larra (y Sanchez de Castro), Mariano Jose de
1809-1837 . . . . **NCLC 17**

Larsen, Eric 1941- . . . . **CLC 55**
See also CA 132

Larsen, Nella 1891-1964 . . . . . **CLC 37; BLC**
See also BW 1; CA 125; DAM MULT;
DLB 51

Larson, Charles R(aymond) 1938- . . . **CLC 31**
See also CA 53-56; CANR 4

Las Casas, Bartolome de 1474-1566 . . **LC 31**

Lasker-Schueler, Else 1869-1945 . . **TCLC 57**
See also DLB 66, 124

Latham, Jean Lee 1902- . . . . **CLC 12**
See also AITN 1; CA 5-8R; CANR 7;
MAICYA; SATA 2, 68

Latham, Mavis
See Clark, Mavis Thorpe

Lathen, Emma . . . . **CLC 2**
See also Hennissart, Martha; Latsis, Mary
J(ane)

Lathrop, Francis
See Leiber, Fritz (Reuter, Jr.)

Latsis, Mary J(ane)
See Lathen, Emma
See also CA 85-88

Lattimore, Richmond (Alexander)
1906-1984 . . . . **CLC 3**
See also CA 1-4R; 112; CANR 1

Laughlin, James 1914- . . . . **CLC 49**
See also CA 21-24R; CAAS 22; CANR 9,
47; DLB 48

Laurence, (Jean) Margaret (Wemyss)
1926-1987 . . . . **CLC 3, 6, 13, 50, 62;**
                             DAC; SSC 7
See also CA 5-8R; 121; CANR 33;
DAM MST; DLB 53; MTCW;
SATA-Obit 50

Laurent, Antoine 1952- . . . . **CLC 50**

Lauscher, Hermann
See Hesse, Hermann

Lautreamont, Comte de
1846-1870 . . . . **NCLC 12; SSC 14**

Laverty, Donald
See Blish, James (Benjamin)

Lavin, Mary 1912-1996 . . **CLC 4, 18; SSC 4**
See also CA 9-12R; 151; CANR 33;
DLB 15; MTCW

Lavond, Paul Dennis
See Kornbluth, C(yril) M.; Pohl, Frederik

Lawler, Raymond Evenor 1922- . . . . **CLC 58**
See also CA 103

Lawrence, D(avid) H(erbert Richards)
1885-1930 . . . . **TCLC 2, 9, 16, 33, 48, 61;**
                 DA; DAB; DAC; SSC 4, 19; WLC
See also CA 104; 121; CDBLB 1914-1945;
DAM MST, NOV, POET; DLB 10, 19,
36, 98, 162; MTCW

Lawrence, T(homas) E(dward)
1888-1935 . . . . **TCLC 18**
See also Dale, Colin
See also CA 115

Lawrence of Arabia
See Lawrence, T(homas) E(dward)

Lawson, Henry (Archibald Hertzberg)
1867-1922 . . . . **TCLC 27; SSC 18**
See also CA 120

Lawton, Dennis
See Faust, Frederick (Schiller)

Laxness, Halldor . . . . **CLC 25**
See also Gudjonsson, Halldor Kiljan

Layamon fl. c. 1200- . . . . **CMLC 10**
See also DLB 146

Laye, Camara 1928-1980 . . . **CLC 4, 38; BLC**
See also BW 1; CA 85-88; 97-100;
CANR 25; DAM MULT; MTCW

Layton, Irving (Peter)
1912- . . . . **CLC 2, 15; DAC**
See also CA 1-4R; CANR 2, 33, 43;
DAM MST, POET; DLB 88; MTCW

Lazarus, Emma 1849-1887 . . . . **NCLC 8**

Lazarus, Felix
See Cable, George Washington

Lazarus, Henry
See Slavitt, David R(ytman)

Lea, Joan
See Neufeld, John (Arthur)

Leacock, Stephen (Butler)
1869-1944 . . . . **TCLC 2; DAC**
See also CA 104; 141; DAM MST; DLB 92

Lear, Edward 1812-1888 . . . . **NCLC 3**
See also CLR 1; DLB 32, 163, 166;
MAICYA; SATA 18

Lear, Norman (Milton) 1922- . . . . . . **CLC 12**
See also CA 73-76

Leavis, F(rank) R(aymond)
1895-1978 . . . . **CLC 24**
See also CA 21-24R; 77-80; CANR 44;
MTCW

Leavitt, David 1961- . . . . **CLC 34**
See also CA 116; 122; CANR 50;
DAM POP; DLB 130; INT 122

Leblanc, Maurice (Marie Emile)
1864-1941 . . . . **TCLC 49**
See also CA 110

Lebowitz, Fran(ces Ann)
1951(?)- . . . . **CLC 11, 36**
See also CA 81-84; CANR 14;
INT CANR-14; MTCW

Lebrecht, Peter
See Tieck, (Johann) Ludwig

le Carre, John . . . . **CLC 3, 5, 9, 15, 28**
See also Cornwell, David (John Moore)
See also BEST 89:4; CDBLB 1960 to
Present; DLB 87

Le Clezio, J(ean) M(arie) G(ustave)
1940- . . . . **CLC 31**
See also CA 116; 128; DLB 83

Leconte de Lisle, Charles-Marie-Rene
1818-1894 . . . . **NCLC 29**

Le Coq, Monsieur
See Simenon, Georges (Jacques Christian)

Leduc, Violette 1907-1972 . . . . **CLC 22**
See also CA 13-14; 33-36R; CAP 1

Ledwidge, Francis 1887(?)-1917 . . . **TCLC 23**
See also CA 123; DLB 20

Lee, Andrea 1953- . . . . **CLC 36; BLC**
See also BW 1; CA 125; DAM MULT

Lee, Andrew
See Auchincloss, Louis (Stanton)

Lee, Chang-rae 1965- . . . . **CLC 91**
See also CA 148

Lee, Don L. . . . . **CLC 2**
See also Madhubuti, Haki R.

Lee, George W(ashington)
1894-1976 . . . . **CLC 52; BLC**
See also BW 1; CA 125; DAM MULT;
DLB 51

Lee, (Nelle) Harper
1926- . . . . **CLC 12, 60; DA; DAB; DAC;**
                                WLC
See also AAYA 13; CA 13-16R; CANR 51;
CDALB 1941-1968; DAM MST, NOV;
DLB 6; MTCW; SATA 11

Lee, Helen Elaine 1959(?)- . . . . **CLC 86**
See also CA 148

Lee, Julian
See Latham, Jean Lee

Lee, Larry
See Lee, Lawrence

Lee, Laurie 1914- . . . . **CLC 90; DAB**
See also CA 77-80; CANR 33; DAM POP;
DLB 27; MTCW

Lee, Lawrence 1941-1990 . . . . **CLC 34**
See also CA 131; CANR 43

Lee, Manfred B(ennington)
1905-1971 . . . . **CLC 11**
See also Queen, Ellery
See also CA 1-4R; 29-32R; CANR 2;
DLB 137

Lee, Stan 1922- . . . . **CLC 17**
See also AAYA 5; CA 108; 111; INT 111

Lee, Tanith 1947- . . . . **CLC 46**
See also AAYA 15; CA 37-40R; CANR 53;
SATA 8, 88

Lee, Vernon . . . . **TCLC 5**
See also Paget, Violet
See also DLB 57, 153, 156

Lee, William
See Burroughs, William S(eward)

Lee, Willy
　See Burroughs, William S(eward)

Lee-Hamilton, Eugene (Jacob)
　1845-1907 . . . . TCLC 22
　See also CA 117

Leet, Judith　1935- . . . . CLC 11

Le Fanu, Joseph Sheridan
　1814-1873 . . . . NCLC 9; SSC 14
　See also DAM POP; DLB 21, 70, 159

Leffland, Ella　1931- . . . . CLC 19
　See also CA 29-32R; CANR 35; DLBY 84;
　　INT CANR-35; SATA 65

Leger, Alexis
　See Leger, (Marie-Rene Auguste) Alexis
　Saint-Leger

Leger, (Marie-Rene Auguste) Alexis
　Saint-Leger　1887-1975. . . . . . . CLC 11
　See also Perse, St.-John
　See also CA 13-16R; 61-64; CANR 43;
　　DAM POET; MTCW

Leger, Saintleger
　See Leger, (Marie-Rene Auguste) Alexis
　Saint-Leger

Le Guin, Ursula K(roeber)
　1929- . . . . . . CLC 8, 13, 22, 45, 71; DAB;
　　　　　　　　　　　　　　DAC; SSC 12
　See also AAYA 9; AITN 1; CA 21-24R;
　　CANR 9, 32, 52; CDALB 1968-1988;
　　CLR 3, 28; DAM MST, POP; DLB 8, 52;
　　INT CANR-32; JRDA; MAICYA;
　　MTCW; SATA 4, 52

Lehmann, Rosamond (Nina)
　1901-1990 . . . . CLC 5
　See also CA 77-80; 131; CANR 8; DLB 15

Leiber, Fritz (Reuter, Jr.)
　1910-1992 . . . . CLC 25
　See also CA 45-48; 139; CANR 2, 40;
　　DLB 8; MTCW; SATA 45;
　　SATA-Obit 73

Leimbach, Martha　1963-
　See Leimbach, Marti
　See also CA 130

Leimbach, Marti . . . . CLC 65
　See also Leimbach, Martha

Leino, Eino . . . . TCLC 24
　See also Loennbohm, Armas Eino Leopold

Leiris, Michel (Julien)　1901-1990 . . . CLC 61
　See also CA 119; 128; 132

Leithauser, Brad　1953- . . . . CLC 27
　See also CA 107; CANR 27; DLB 120

Lelchuk, Alan　1938- . . . . CLC 5
　See also CA 45-48; CAAS 20; CANR 1

Lem, Stanislaw　1921- . . . . CLC 8, 15, 40
　See also CA 105; CAAS 1; CANR 32;
　　MTCW

Lemann, Nancy　1956- . . . . CLC 39
　See also CA 118; 136

Lemonnier, (Antoine Louis) Camille
　1844-1913 . . . . TCLC 22
　See also CA 121

Lenau, Nikolaus　1802-1850 . . . . . . NCLC 16

L'Engle, Madeleine (Camp Franklin)
　1918- . . . . CLC 12
　See also AAYA 1; AITN 2; CA 1-4R;
　　CANR 3, 21, 39; CLR 1, 14; DAM POP;
　　DLB 52; JRDA; MAICYA; MTCW;
　　SAAS 15; SATA 1, 27, 75

Lengyel, Jozsef　1896-1975. . . . . CLC 7
　See also CA 85-88; 57-60

Lennon, John (Ono)
　1940-1980 . . . . CLC 12, 35
　See also CA 102

Lennox, Charlotte Ramsay
　1729(?)-1804 . . . . NCLC 23
　See also DLB 39

Lentricchia, Frank (Jr.)　1940- . . . . . . CLC 34
　See also CA 25-28R; CANR 19

Lenz, Siegfried　1926- . . . . CLC 27
　See also CA 89-92; DLB 75

Leonard, Elmore (John, Jr.)
　1925- . . . . CLC 28, 34, 71
　See also AITN 1; BEST 89:1, 90:4;
　　CA 81-84; CANR 12, 28, 53; DAM POP;
　　INT CANR-28; MTCW

Leonard, Hugh . . . . CLC 19
　See also Byrne, John Keyes
　See also DLB 13

Leonov, Leonid (Maximovich)
　1899-1994 . . . . CLC 92
　See also CA 129; DAM NOV; MTCW

Leopardi, (Conte) Giacomo
　1798-1837 . . . . NCLC 22

Le Reveler
　See Artaud, Antonin (Marie Joseph)

Lerman, Eleanor　1952- . . . . CLC 9
　See also CA 85-88

Lerman, Rhoda　1936- . . . . CLC 56
　See also CA 49-52

Lermontov, Mikhail Yuryevich
　1814-1841 . . . . NCLC 47

Leroux, Gaston　1868-1927. . . . . . . TCLC 25
　See also CA 108; 136; SATA 65

Lesage, Alain-Rene　1668-1747 . . . . . . LC 28

Leskov, Nikolai (Semyonovich)
　1831-1895 . . . . NCLC 25

Lessing, Doris (May)
　1919- . . . . . CLC 1, 2, 3, 6, 10, 15, 22, 40,
　　　　　　　94; DA; DAB; DAC; SSC 6
　See also CA 9-12R; CAAS 14; CANR 33;
　　CDBLB 1960 to Present; DAM MST,
　　NOV; DLB 15, 139; DLBY 85; MTCW

Lessing, Gotthold Ephraim
　1729-1781 . . . . LC 8
　See also DLB 97

Lester, Richard　1932- . . . . CLC 20

Lever, Charles (James)
　1806-1872 . . . . NCLC 23
　See also DLB 21

Leverson, Ada　1865(?)-1936(?) . . . . TCLC 18
　See also Elaine
　See also CA 117; DLB 153

Levertov, Denise
　1923- . . . . . . CLC 1, 2, 3, 5, 8, 15, 28, 66;
　　　　　　　　　　　　　　　　PC 11
　See also CA 1-4R; CAAS 19; CANR 3, 29,
　　50; DAM POET; DLB 5, 165;
　　INT CANR-29; MTCW

Levi, Jonathan . . . . CLC 76

Levi, Peter (Chad Tigar)　1931- . . . . . CLC 41
　See also CA 5-8R; CANR 34; DLB 40

Levi, Primo
　1919-1987 . . . . CLC 37, 50; SSC 12
　See also CA 13-16R; 122; CANR 12, 33;
　　MTCW

Levin, Ira　1929- . . . . CLC 3, 6
　See also CA 21-24R; CANR 17, 44;
　　DAM POP; MTCW; SATA 66

Levin, Meyer　1905-1981 . . . . CLC 7
　See also AITN 1; CA 9-12R; 104;
　　CANR 15; DAM POP; DLB 9, 28;
　　DLBY 81; SATA 21; SATA-Obit 27

Levine, Norman　1924- . . . . CLC 54
　See also CA 73-76; CAAS 23; CANR 14;
　　DLB 88

Levine, Philip　1928- . . CLC 2, 4, 5, 9, 14, 33
　See also CA 9-12R; CANR 9, 37, 52;
　　DAM POET; DLB 5

Levinson, Deirdre　1931- . . . . CLC 49
　See also CA 73-76

Levi-Strauss, Claude　1908- . . . . CLC 38
　See also CA 1-4R; CANR 6, 32; MTCW

Levitin, Sonia (Wolff)　1934- . . . . CLC 17
　See also AAYA 13; CA 29-32R; CANR 14,
　　32; JRDA; MAICYA; SAAS 2; SATA 4,
　　68

Levon, O. U.
　See Kesey, Ken (Elton)

Lewes, George Henry
　1817-1878 . . . . NCLC 25
　See also DLB 55, 144

Lewis, Alun　1915-1944 . . . . TCLC 3
　See also CA 104; DLB 20, 162

Lewis, C. Day
　See Day Lewis, C(ecil)

Lewis, C(live) S(taples)
　1898-1963 . . . . . CLC 1, 3, 6, 14, 27; DA;
　　　　　　　　　　　DAB; DAC; WLC
　See also AAYA 3; CA 81-84; CANR 33;
　　CDBLB 1945-1960; CLR 3, 27;
　　DAM MST, NOV, POP; DLB 15, 100,
　　160; JRDA; MAICYA; MTCW;
　　SATA 13

Lewis, Janet　1899- . . . . CLC 41
　See also Winters, Janet Lewis
　See also CA 9-12R; CANR 29; CAP 1;
　　DLBY 87

Lewis, Matthew Gregory
　1775-1818 . . . . NCLC 11
　See also DLB 39, 158

Lewis, (Harry) Sinclair
　1885-1951 . . . . . TCLC 4, 13, 23, 39; DA;
　　　　　　　　　　　　　DAB; DAC; WLC
　See also CA 104; 133; CDALB 1917-1929;
　　DAM MST, NOV; DLB 9, 102; DLBD 1;
　　MTCW

Lewis, (Percy) Wyndham
1884(?)-1957 . . . . TCLC 2, 9
See also CA 104; DLB 15

Lewisohn, Ludwig 1883-1955 . . . . . . TCLC 19
See also CA 107; DLB 4, 9, 28, 102

Leyner, Mark 1956- . . . . CLC 92
See also CA 110; CANR 28, 53

Lezama Lima, Jose 1910-1976 . . . CLC 4, 10
See also CA 77-80; DAM MULT;
DLB 113; HW

L'Heureux, John (Clarke) 1934- . . . . CLC 52
See also CA 13-16R; CANR 23, 45

Liddell, C. H.
See Kuttner, Henry

Lie, Jonas (Lauritz Idemil)
1833-1908(?) . . . . TCLC 5
See also CA 115

Lieber, Joel 1937-1971 . . . . CLC 6
See also CA 73-76; 29-32R

Lieber, Stanley Martin
See Lee, Stan

Lieberman, Laurence (James)
1935- . . . . CLC 4, 36
See also CA 17-20R; CANR 8, 36

Lieksman, Anders
See Haavikko, Paavo Juhani

Li Fei-kan 1904-
See Pa Chin
See also CA 105

Lifton, Robert Jay 1926- . . . . CLC 67
See also CA 17-20R; CANR 27;
INT CANR-27; SATA 66

Lightfoot, Gordon 1938- . . . . CLC 26
See also CA 109

Lightman, Alan P. 1948- . . . . CLC 81
See also CA 141

Ligotti, Thomas (Robert)
1953- . . . . CLC 44; SSC 16
See also CA 123; CANR 49

Li Ho 791-817 . . . . PC 13

Liliencron, (Friedrich Adolf Axel) Detlev von
1844-1909 . . . . TCLC 18
See also CA 117

Lilly, William 1602-1681 . . . . LC 27

Lima, Jose Lezama
See Lezama Lima, Jose

Lima Barreto, Afonso Henrique de
1881-1922 . . . . TCLC 23
See also CA 117

Limonov, Edward 1944- . . . . CLC 67
See also CA 137

Lin, Frank
See Atherton, Gertrude (Franklin Horn)

Lincoln, Abraham 1809-1865 . . . . . NCLC 18

Lind, Jakov . . . . CLC 1, 2, 4, 27, 82
See also Landwirth, Heinz
See also CAAS 4

Lindbergh, Anne (Spencer) Morrow
1906- . . . . CLC 82
See also CA 17-20R; CANR 16;
DAM NOV; MTCW; SATA 33

Lindsay, David 1878-1945 . . . . TCLC 15
See also CA 113

Lindsay, (Nicholas) Vachel
1879-1931 . . . TCLC 17; DA; DAC; WLC
See also CA 114; 135; CDALB 1865-1917;
DAM MST, POET; DLB 54; SATA 40

Linke-Poot
See Doeblin, Alfred

Linney, Romulus 1930- . . . . CLC 51
See also CA 1-4R; CANR 40, 44

Linton, Eliza Lynn 1822-1898 . . . . NCLC 41
See also DLB 18

Li Po 701-763 . . . . CMLC 2

Lipsius, Justus 1547-1606 . . . . LC 16

Lipsyte, Robert (Michael)
1938- . . . . CLC 21; DA; DAC
See also AAYA 7; CA 17-20R; CANR 8;
CLR 23; DAM MST, NOV; JRDA;
MAICYA; SATA 5, 68

Lish, Gordon (Jay) 1934- . . CLC 45; SSC 18
See also CA 113; 117; DLB 130; INT 117

Lispector, Clarice 1925-1977 . . . . . . CLC 43
See also CA 139; 116; DLB 113

Littell, Robert 1935(?)- . . . . CLC 42
See also CA 109; 112

Little, Malcolm 1925-1965
See Malcolm X
See also BW 1; CA 125; 111; DA; DAB;
DAC; DAM MST, MULT; MTCW

Littlewit, Humphrey Gent.
See Lovecraft, H(oward) P(hillips)

Litwos
See Sienkiewicz, Henryk (Adam Alexander
Pius)

Liu E 1857-1909 . . . . TCLC 15
See also CA 115

Lively, Penelope (Margaret)
1933- . . . . CLC 32, 50
See also CA 41-44R; CANR 29; CLR 7;
DAM NOV; DLB 14, 161; JRDA;
MAICYA; MTCW; SATA 7, 60

Livesay, Dorothy (Kathleen)
1909- . . . . CLC 4, 15, 79; DAC
See also AITN 2; CA 25-28R; CAAS 8;
CANR 36; DAM MST, POET; DLB 68;
MTCW

Livy c. 59B.C.-c. 17 . . . . CMLC 11

Lizardi, Jose Joaquin Fernandez de
1776-1827 . . . . NCLC 30

Llewellyn, Richard
See Llewellyn Lloyd, Richard Dafydd
Vivian
See also DLB 15

Llewellyn Lloyd, Richard Dafydd Vivian
1906-1983 . . . . CLC 7, 80
See also Llewellyn, Richard
See also CA 53-56; 111; CANR 7;
SATA 11; SATA-Obit 37

Llosa, (Jorge) Mario (Pedro) Vargas
See Vargas Llosa, (Jorge) Mario (Pedro)

Lloyd Webber, Andrew 1948-
See Webber, Andrew Lloyd
See also AAYA 1; CA 116; 149;
DAM DRAM; SATA 56

Llull, Ramon c. 1235-c. 1316 . . . . . CMLC 12

Locke, Alain (Le Roy)
1886-1954 . . . . TCLC 43
See also BW 1; CA 106; 124; DLB 51

Locke, John 1632-1704 . . . . LC 7
See also DLB 101

Locke-Elliott, Sumner
See Elliott, Sumner Locke

Lockhart, John Gibson
1794-1854 . . . . NCLC 6
See also DLB 110, 116, 144

Lodge, David (John) 1935- . . . . CLC 36
See also BEST 90:1; CA 17-20R; CANR 19,
53; DAM POP; DLB 14; INT CANR-19;
MTCW

Loennbohm, Armas Eino Leopold 1878-1926
See Leino, Eino
See also CA 123

Loewinsohn, Ron(ald William)
1937- . . . . CLC 52
See also CA 25-28R

Logan, Jake
See Smith, Martin Cruz

Logan, John (Burton) 1923-1987 . . . . . CLC 5
See also CA 77-80; 124; CANR 45; DLB 5

Lo Kuan-chung 1330(?)-1400(?) . . . . . . LC 12

Lombard, Nap
See Johnson, Pamela Hansford

London, Jack . . TCLC 9, 15, 39; SSC 4; WLC
See also London, John Griffith
See also AAYA 13; AITN 2;
CDALB 1865-1917; DLB 8, 12, 78;
SATA 18

London, John Griffith 1876-1916
See London, Jack
See also CA 110; 119; DA; DAB; DAC;
DAM MST, NOV; JRDA; MAICYA;
MTCW

Long, Emmett
See Leonard, Elmore (John, Jr.)

Longbaugh, Harry
See Goldman, William (W.)

Longfellow, Henry Wadsworth
1807-1882 . . . . . NCLC 2, 45; DA; DAB;
DAC
See also CDALB 1640-1865; DAM MST,
POET; DLB 1, 59; SATA 19

Longley, Michael 1939- . . . . CLC 29
See also CA 102; DLB 40

Longus fl. c. 2nd cent. - . . . . CMLC 7

Longway, A. Hugh
See Lang, Andrew

Lonnrot, Elias 1802-1884 . . . . NCLC 53

Lopate, Phillip 1943- . . . . CLC 29
See also CA 97-100; DLBY 80; INT 97-100

Lopez Portillo (y Pacheco), Jose
1920- . . . . CLC 46
See also CA 129; HW

Lopez y Fuentes, Gregorio
1897(?)-1966 . . . . CLC 32
See also CA 131; HW

Lorca, Federico Garcia
See Garcia Lorca, Federico

Lord, Bette Bao 1938- . . . . **CLC 23**
See also BEST 90:3; CA 107; CANR 41;
INT 107; SATA 58

Lord Auch
See Bataille, Georges

Lord Byron
See Byron, George Gordon (Noel)

Lorde, Audre (Geraldine)
1934-1992 . . . . **CLC 18, 71; BLC; PC 12**
See also BW 1; CA 25-28R; 142; CANR 16,
26, 46; DAM MULT, POET; DLB 41;
MTCW

Lord Jeffrey
See Jeffrey, Francis

Lorenzini, Carlo 1826-1890
See Collodi, Carlo
See also MAICYA; SATA 29

Lorenzo, Heberto Padilla
See Padilla (Lorenzo), Heberto

Loris
See Hofmannsthal, Hugo von

Loti, Pierre . . . . **TCLC 11**
See also Viaud, (Louis Marie) Julien
See also DLB 123

Louie, David Wong 1954- . . . . **CLC 70**
See also CA 139

Louis, Father M.
See Merton, Thomas

Lovecraft, H(oward) P(hillips)
1890-1937 . . . . **TCLC 4, 22; SSC 3**
See also AAYA 14; CA 104; 133;
DAM POP; MTCW

Lovelace, Earl 1935- . . . . **CLC 51**
See also BW 2; CA 77-80; CANR 41;
DLB 125; MTCW

Lovelace, Richard 1618-1657 . . . . **LC 24**
See also DLB 131

Lowell, Amy 1874-1925 . . **TCLC 1, 8; PC 13**
See also CA 104; 151; DAM POET;
DLB 54, 140

Lowell, James Russell 1819-1891 . . **NCLC 2**
See also CDALB 1640-1865; DLB 1, 11, 64,
79

Lowell, Robert (Traill Spence, Jr.)
1917-1977 . . . **CLC 1, 2, 3, 4, 5, 8, 9, 11,**
15, 37; DA; DAB; DAC; PC 3; WLC
See also CA 9-12R; 73-76; CABS 2;
CANR 26; DAM MST, NOV; DLB 5;
MTCW

Lowndes, Marie Adelaide (Belloc)
1868-1947 . . . . **TCLC 12**
See also CA 107; DLB 70

Lowry, (Clarence) Malcolm
1909-1957 . . . . **TCLC 6, 40**
See also CA 105; 131; CDBLB 1945-1960;
DLB 15; MTCW

Lowry, Mina Gertrude 1882-1966
See Loy, Mina
See also CA 113

Loxsmith, John
See Brunner, John (Kilian Houston)

Loy, Mina . . . . **CLC 28; PC 16**
See also Lowry, Mina Gertrude
See also DAM POET; DLB 4, 54

Loyson-Bridet
See Schwob, (Mayer Andre) Marcel

Lucas, Craig 1951- . . . . **CLC 64**
See also CA 137

Lucas, George 1944- . . . . **CLC 16**
See also AAYA 1; CA 77-80; CANR 30;
SATA 56

Lucas, Hans
See Godard, Jean-Luc

Lucas, Victoria
See Plath, Sylvia

Ludlam, Charles 1943-1987 . . . . . **CLC 46, 50**
See also CA 85-88; 122

Ludlum, Robert 1927- . . . . **CLC 22, 43**
See also AAYA 10; BEST 89:1, 90:3;
CA 33-36R; CANR 25, 41; DAM NOV,
POP; DLBY 82; MTCW

Ludwig, Ken . . . . **CLC 60**

Ludwig, Otto 1813-1865 . . . . **NCLC 4**
See also DLB 129

Lugones, Leopoldo 1874-1938 . . . . . **TCLC 15**
See also CA 116; 131; HW

Lu Hsun 1881-1936 . . . . . . **TCLC 3; SSC 20**
See also Shu-Jen, Chou

Lukacs, George . . . . **CLC 24**
See also Lukacs, Gyorgy (Szegeny von)

Lukacs, Gyorgy (Szegeny von) 1885-1971
See Lukacs, George
See also CA 101; 29-32R

Luke, Peter (Ambrose Cyprian)
1919-1995 . . . . **CLC 38**
See also CA 81-84; 147; DLB 13

Lunar, Dennis
See Mungo, Raymond

Lurie, Alison 1926- . . . . **CLC 4, 5, 18, 39**
See also CA 1-4R; CANR 2, 17, 50; DLB 2;
MTCW; SATA 46

Lustig, Arnost 1926- . . . . **CLC 56**
See also AAYA 3; CA 69-72; CANR 47;
SATA 56

Luther, Martin 1483-1546 . . . . **LC 9**

Luxemburg, Rosa 1870(?)-1919 . . . . **TCLC 63**
See also CA 118

Luzi, Mario 1914- . . . . **CLC 13**
See also CA 61-64; CANR 9; DLB 128

L'Ymagier
See Gourmont, Remy (-Marie-Charles) de

Lynch, B. Suarez
See Bioy Casares, Adolfo; Borges, Jorge
Luis

Lynch, David (K.) 1946- . . . . **CLC 66**
See also CA 124; 129

Lynch, James
See Andreyev, Leonid (Nikolaevich)

Lynch Davis, B.
See Bioy Casares, Adolfo; Borges, Jorge
Luis

Lyndsay, Sir David 1490-1555 . . . . . . **LC 20**

Lynn, Kenneth S(chuyler) 1923- . . . . **CLC 50**
See also CA 1-4R; CANR 3, 27

Lynx
See West, Rebecca

Lyons, Marcus
See Blish, James (Benjamin)

Lyre, Pinchbeck
See Sassoon, Siegfried (Lorraine)

Lytle, Andrew (Nelson) 1902-1995 . . **CLC 22**
See also CA 9-12R; 150; DLB 6; DLBY 95

Lyttelton, George 1709-1773 . . . . **LC 10**

Maas, Peter 1929- . . . . **CLC 29**
See also CA 93-96; INT 93-96

Macaulay, Rose 1881-1958 . . . . . **TCLC 7, 44**
See also CA 104; DLB 36

Macaulay, Thomas Babington
1800-1859 . . . . **NCLC 42**
See also CDBLB 1832-1890; DLB 32, 55

MacBeth, George (Mann)
1932-1992 . . . . **CLC 2, 5, 9**
See also CA 25-28R; 136; DLB 40; MTCW;
SATA 4; SATA-Obit 70

MacCaig, Norman (Alexander)
1910- . . . . **CLC 36; DAB**
See also CA 9-12R; CANR 3, 34;
DAM POET; DLB 27

MacCarthy, (Sir Charles Otto) Desmond
1877-1952 . . . . **TCLC 36**

MacDiarmid, Hugh
. . . . **CLC 2, 4, 11, 19, 63; PC 9**
See also Grieve, C(hristopher) M(urray)
See also CDBLB 1945-1960; DLB 20

MacDonald, Anson
See Heinlein, Robert A(nson)

Macdonald, Cynthia 1928- . . . . . . **CLC 13, 19**
See also CA 49-52; CANR 4, 44; DLB 105

MacDonald, George 1824-1905 . . . . . **TCLC 9**
See also CA 106; 137; DLB 18, 163;
MAICYA; SATA 33

Macdonald, John
See Millar, Kenneth

MacDonald, John D(ann)
1916-1986 . . . . **CLC 3, 27, 44**
See also CA 1-4R; 121; CANR 1, 19;
DAM NOV, POP; DLB 8; DLBY 86;
MTCW

Macdonald, John Ross
See Millar, Kenneth

Macdonald, Ross . . . . . **CLC 1, 2, 3, 14, 34, 41**
See also Millar, Kenneth
See also DLBD 6

MacDougal, John
See Blish, James (Benjamin)

MacEwen, Gwendolyn (Margaret)
1941-1987 . . . . **CLC 13, 55**
See also CA 9-12R; 124; CANR 7, 22;
DLB 53; SATA 50; SATA-Obit 55

Macha, Karel Hynek 1810-1846 . . **NCLC 46**

Machado (y Ruiz), Antonio
1875-1939 . . . . **TCLC 3**
See also CA 104; DLB 108

Machado de Assis, Joaquim Maria
1839-1908 . . . . **TCLC 10; BLC**
See also CA 107

Machen, Arthur . . . . **TCLC 4; SSC 20**
See also Jones, Arthur Llewellyn
See also DLB 36, 156

Machiavelli, Niccolo
1469-1527 ...... **LC 8; DA; DAB; DAC**
See also DAM MST

MacInnes, Colin 1914-1976...... **CLC 4, 23**
See also CA 69-72; 65-68; CANR 21;
DLB 14; MTCW

MacInnes, Helen (Clark)
1907-1985 .... **CLC 27, 39**
See also CA 1-4R; 117; CANR 1, 28;
DAM POP; DLB 87; MTCW; SATA 22;
SATA-Obit 44

Mackay, Mary 1855-1924
See Corelli, Marie
See also CA 118

Mackenzie, Compton (Edward Montague)
1883-1972 .... **CLC 18**
See also CA 21-22; 37-40R; CAP 2;
DLB 34, 100

Mackenzie, Henry 1745-1831 .... **NCLC 41**
See also DLB 39

Mackintosh, Elizabeth 1896(?)-1952
See Tey, Josephine
See also CA 110

MacLaren, James
See Grieve, C(hristopher) M(urray)

Mac Laverty, Bernard 1942-....... **CLC 31**
See also CA 116; 118; CANR 43; INT 118

MacLean, Alistair (Stuart)
1922-1987 .... **CLC 3, 13, 50, 63**
See also CA 57-60; 121; CANR 28;
DAM POP; MTCW; SATA 23;
SATA-Obit 50

Maclean, Norman (Fitzroy)
1902-1990 .... **CLC 78; SSC 13**
See also CA 102; 132; CANR 49;
DAM POP

MacLeish, Archibald
1892-1982 .... **CLC 3, 8, 14, 68**
See also CA 9-12R; 106; CANR 33;
DAM POET; DLB 4, 7, 45; DLBY 82;
MTCW

MacLennan, (John) Hugh
1907-1990 .... **CLC 2, 14, 92; DAC**
See also CA 5-8R; 142; CANR 33;
DAM MST; DLB 68; MTCW

MacLeod, Alistair 1936- ..... **CLC 56; DAC**
See also CA 123; DAM MST; DLB 60

MacNeice, (Frederick) Louis
1907-1963 ...... **CLC 1, 4, 10, 53; DAB**
See also CA 85-88; DAM POET; DLB 10,
20; MTCW

MacNeill, Dand
See Fraser, George MacDonald

Macpherson, James 1736-1796 ...... **LC 29**
See also DLB 109

Macpherson, (Jean) Jay 1931-...... **CLC 14**
See also CA 5-8R; DLB 53

MacShane, Frank 1927-........... **CLC 39**
See also CA 9-12R; CANR 3, 33; DLB 111

Macumber, Mari
See Sandoz, Mari(e Susette)

Madach, Imre 1823-1864........ **NCLC 19**

Madden, (Jerry) David 1933- .... **CLC 5, 15**
See also CA 1-4R; CAAS 3; CANR 4, 45;
DLB 6; MTCW

Maddern, Al(an)
See Ellison, Harlan (Jay)

Madhubuti, Haki R.
1942- .... **CLC 6, 73; BLC; PC 5**
See also Lee, Don L.
See also BW 2; CA 73-76; CANR 24, 51;
DAM MULT, POET; DLB 5, 41;
DLBD 8

Maepenn, Hugh
See Kuttner, Henry

Maepenn, K. H.
See Kuttner, Henry

Maeterlinck, Maurice 1862-1949 ... **TCLC 3**
See also CA 104; 136; DAM DRAM;
SATA 66

Maginn, William 1794-1842....... **NCLC 8**
See also DLB 110, 159

Mahapatra, Jayanta 1928-......... **CLC 33**
See also CA 73-76; CAAS 9; CANR 15, 33;
DAM MULT

Mahfouz, Naguib (Abdel Aziz Al-Sabilgi)
1911(?)-
See Mahfuz, Najib
See also BEST 89:2; CA 128; DAM NOV;
MTCW

Mahfuz, Najib................ **CLC 52, 55**
See also Mahfouz, Naguib (Abdel Aziz
Al-Sabilgi)
See also DLBY 88

Mahon, Derek 1941-............. **CLC 27**
See also CA 113; 128; DLB 40

Mailer, Norman
1923- ...... **CLC 1, 2, 3, 4, 5, 8, 11, 14,
28, 39, 74; DA; DAB; DAC**
See also AITN 2; CA 9-12R; CABS 1;
CANR 28; CDALB 1968-1988;
DAM MST, NOV, POP; DLB 2, 16, 28;
DLBD 3; DLBY 80, 83; MTCW

Maillet, Antonine 1929-...... **CLC 54; DAC**
See also CA 115; 120; CANR 46; DLB 60;
INT 120

Mais, Roger 1905-1955 .... **TCLC 8**
See also BW 1; CA 105; 124; DLB 125;
MTCW

Maistre, Joseph de 1753-1821.... **NCLC 37**

Maitland, Frederic 1850-1906..... **TCLC 65**

Maitland, Sara (Louise) 1950-...... **CLC 49**
See also CA 69-72; CANR 13

Major, Clarence
1936- .... **CLC 3, 19, 48; BLC**
See also BW 2; CA 21-24R; CAAS 6;
CANR 13, 25, 53; DAM MULT; DLB 33

Major, Kevin (Gerald)
1949- .... **CLC 26; DAC**
See also AAYA 16; CA 97-100; CANR 21,
38; CLR 11; DLB 60; INT CANR-21;
JRDA; MAICYA; SATA 32, 82

Maki, James
See Ozu, Yasujiro

Malabaila, Damiano
See Levi, Primo

Malamud, Bernard
1914-1986 ..... **CLC 1, 2, 3, 5, 8, 9, 11,
18, 27, 44, 78, 85; DA; DAB; DAC;
SSC 15; WLC**
See also AAYA 16; CA 5-8R; 118; CABS 1;
CANR 28; CDALB 1941-1968;
DAM MST, NOV, POP; DLB 2, 28, 152;
DLBY 80, 86; MTCW

Malaparte, Curzio 1898-1957 ..... **TCLC 52**

Malcolm, Dan
See Silverberg, Robert

Malcolm X.................. **CLC 82; BLC**
See also Little, Malcolm

Malherbe, Francois de 1555-1628..... **LC 5**

Mallarme, Stephane
1842-1898 .... **NCLC 4, 41; PC 4**
See also DAM POET

Mallet-Joris, Francoise 1930-...... **CLC 11**
See also CA 65-68; CANR 17; DLB 83

Malley, Ern
See McAuley, James Phillip

Mallowan, Agatha Christie
See Christie, Agatha (Mary Clarissa)

Maloff, Saul 1922-................ **CLC 5**
See also CA 33-36R

Malone, Louis
See MacNeice, (Frederick) Louis

Malone, Michael (Christopher)
1942-....................... **CLC 43**
See also CA 77-80; CANR 14, 32

Malory, (Sir) Thomas
1410(?)-1471(?) ...... **LC 11; DA; DAB;
DAC**
See also CDBLB Before 1660; DAM MST;
DLB 146; SATA 59; SATA-Brief 33

Malouf, (George Joseph) David
1934- .... **CLC 28, 86**
See also CA 124; CANR 50

Malraux, (Georges-)Andre
1901-1976 ...... **CLC 1, 4, 9, 13, 15, 57**
See also CA 21-22; 69-72; CANR 34;
CAP 2; DAM NOV; DLB 72; MTCW

Malzberg, Barry N(athaniel) 1939-... **CLC 7**
See also CA 61-64; CAAS 4; CANR 16;
DLB 8

Mamet, David (Alan)
1947- ...... **CLC 9, 15, 34, 46, 91; DC 4**
See also AAYA 3; CA 81-84; CABS 3;
CANR 15, 41; DAM DRAM; DLB 7;
MTCW

Mamoulian, Rouben (Zachary)
1897-1987 .... **CLC 16**
See also CA 25-28R; 124

Mandelstam, Osip (Emilievich)
1891(?)-1938(?) ...... **TCLC 2, 6; PC 14**
See also CA 104; 150

Mander, (Mary) Jane 1877-1949... **TCLC 31**

Mandiargues, Andre Pieyre de....... **CLC 41**
See also Pieyre de Mandiargues, Andre
See also DLB 83

Mandrake, Ethel Belle
See Thurman, Wallace (Henry)

Mangan, James Clarence
1803-1849 .... **NCLC 27**

Maniere, J.-E.
See Giraudoux, (Hippolyte) Jean

Manley, (Mary) Delariviere
1672(?)-1724 . . . . **LC 1**
See also DLB 39, 80

Mann, Abel
See Creasey, John

Mann, (Luiz) Heinrich 1871-1950. . . **TCLC 9**
See also CA 106; DLB 66

Mann, (Paul) Thomas
1875-1955 . . . . **TCLC 2, 8, 14, 21, 35, 44,**
60; DA; DAB; DAC; SSC 5; WLC
See also CA 104; 128; DAM MST, NOV;
DLB 66; MTCW

Mannheim, Karl 1893-1947 . . . . . . **TCLC 65**

Manning, David
See Faust, Frederick (Schiller)

Manning, Frederic 1887(?)-1935 . . . **TCLC 25**
See also CA 124

Manning, Olivia 1915-1980 . . . . . . **CLC 5, 19**
See also CA 5-8R; 101; CANR 29; MTCW

Mano, D. Keith 1942- . . . . **CLC 2, 10**
See also CA 25-28R; CAAS 6; CANR 26;
DLB 6

Mansfield, Katherine
. . **TCLC 2, 8, 39; DAB; SSC 9, 23; WLC**
See also Beauchamp, Kathleen Mansfield
See also DLB 162

Manso, Peter 1940- . . . . **CLC 39**
See also CA 29-32R; CANR 44

Mantecon, Juan Jimenez
See Jimenez (Mantecon), Juan Ramon

Manton, Peter
See Creasey, John

Man Without a Spleen, A
See Chekhov, Anton (Pavlovich)

Manzoni, Alessandro 1785-1873 . . **NCLC 29**

Mapu, Abraham (ben Jekutiel)
1808-1867 . . . . **NCLC 18**

Mara, Sally
See Queneau, Raymond

Marat, Jean Paul 1743-1793 . . . . **LC 10**

Marcel, Gabriel Honore
1889-1973 . . . . **CLC 15**
See also CA 102; 45-48; MTCW

Marchbanks, Samuel
See Davies, (William) Robertson

Marchi, Giacomo
See Bassani, Giorgio

Margulies, Donald . . . . **CLC 76**

Marie de France c. 12th cent. -. . . . **CMLC 8**

Marie de l'Incarnation 1599-1672. . . . **LC 10**

Mariner, Scott
See Pohl, Frederik

Marinetti, Filippo Tommaso
1876-1944 . . . . **TCLC 10**
See also CA 107; DLB 114

Marivaux, Pierre Carlet de Chamblain de
1688-1763 . . . . **LC 4**

Markandaya, Kamala . . . . **CLC 8, 38**
See also Taylor, Kamala (Purnaiya)

Markfield, Wallace 1926-. . . . . **CLC 8**
See also CA 69-72; CAAS 3; DLB 2, 28

Markham, Edwin 1852-1940 . . . . . **TCLC 47**
See also DLB 54

Markham, Robert
See Amis, Kingsley (William)

Marks, J
See Highwater, Jamake (Mamake)

Marks-Highwater, J
See Highwater, Jamake (Mamake)

Markson, David M(errill) 1927- . . . . **CLC 67**
See also CA 49-52; CANR 1

Marley, Bob . . . . **CLC 17**
See also Marley, Robert Nesta

Marley, Robert Nesta 1945-1981
See Marley, Bob
See also CA 107; 103

Marlowe, Christopher
1564-1593 . . . . . **LC 22; DA; DAB; DAC;**
DC 1; WLC
See also CDBLB Before 1660;
DAM DRAM, MST; DLB 62

Marmontel, Jean-Francois
1723-1799 . . . . **LC 2**

Marquand, John P(hillips)
1893-1960 . . . . **CLC 2, 10**
See also CA 85-88; DLB 9, 102

Marquez, Gabriel (Jose) Garcia
See Garcia Marquez, Gabriel (Jose)

Marquis, Don(ald Robert Perry)
1878-1937 . . . . **TCLC 7**
See also CA 104; DLB 11, 25

Marric, J. J.
See Creasey, John

Marrow, Bernard
See Moore, Brian

Marryat, Frederick 1792-1848 . . . . **NCLC 3**
See also DLB 21, 163

Marsden, James
See Creasey, John

Marsh, (Edith) Ngaio
1899-1982 . . . . **CLC 7, 53**
See also CA 9-12R; CANR 6; DAM POP;
DLB 77; MTCW

Marshall, Garry 1934-. . . . . **CLC 17**
See also AAYA 3; CA 111; SATA 60

Marshall, Paule
1929- . . . . **CLC 27, 72; BLC; SSC 3**
See also BW 2; CA 77-80; CANR 25;
DAM MULT; DLB 157; MTCW

Marsten, Richard
See Hunter, Evan

Marston, John 1576-1634 . . . . **LC 33**
See also DAM DRAM; DLB 58

Martha, Henry
See Harris, Mark

Martial c. 40-c. 104 . . . . **PC 10**

Martin, Ken
See Hubbard, L(afayette) Ron(ald)

Martin, Richard
See Creasey, John

Martin, Steve 1945-. . . . . **CLC 30**
See also CA 97-100; CANR 30; MTCW

Martin, Valerie 1948-. . . . . **CLC 89**
See also BEST 90:2; CA 85-88; CANR 49

Martin, Violet Florence
1862-1915 . . . . **TCLC 51**

Martin, Webber
See Silverberg, Robert

Martindale, Patrick Victor
See White, Patrick (Victor Martindale)

Martin du Gard, Roger
1881-1958 . . . . **TCLC 24**
See also CA 118; DLB 65

Martineau, Harriet 1802-1876. . . . **NCLC 26**
See also DLB 21, 55, 159, 163, 166;
YABC 2

Martines, Julia
See O'Faolain, Julia

Martinez, Jacinto Benavente y
See Benavente (y Martinez), Jacinto

Martinez Ruiz, Jose 1873-1967
See Azorin; Ruiz, Jose Martinez
See also CA 93-96; HW

Martinez Sierra, Gregorio
1881-1947 . . . . **TCLC 6**
See also CA 115

Martinez Sierra, Maria (de la O'LeJarraga)
1874-1974 . . . . **TCLC 6**
See also CA 115

Martinsen, Martin
See Follett, Ken(neth Martin)

Martinson, Harry (Edmund)
1904-1978 . . . . **CLC 14**
See also CA 77-80; CANR 34

Marut, Ret
See Traven, B.

Marut, Robert
See Traven, B.

Marvell, Andrew
1621-1678 . . . . . . **LC 4; DA; DAB; DAC;**
PC 10; WLC
See also CDBLB 1660-1789; DAM MST,
POET; DLB 131

Marx, Karl (Heinrich)
1818-1883 . . . . **NCLC 17**
See also DLB 129

Masaoka Shiki . . . . **TCLC 18**
See also Masaoka Tsunenori

Masaoka Tsunenori 1867-1902
See Masaoka Shiki
See also CA 117

Masefield, John (Edward)
1878-1967 . . . . **CLC 11, 47**
See also CA 19-20; 25-28R; CANR 33;
CAP 2; CDBLB 1890-1914; DAM POET;
DLB 10, 19, 153, 160; MTCW; SATA 19

Maso, Carole 19(?)- . . . . **CLC 44**

Mason, Bobbie Ann
1940- . . . . **CLC 28, 43, 82; SSC 4**
See also AAYA 5; CA 53-56; CANR 11,
31; DLBY 87; INT CANR-31; MTCW

Mason, Ernst
See Pohl, Frederik

Mason, Lee W.
See Malzberg, Barry N(athaniel)

Mason, Nick 1945-. . . . . **CLC 35**

Mason, Tally
See Derleth, August (William)

Mass, William
See Gibson, William

Masters, Edgar Lee
1868-1950 . . . . . . **TCLC 2, 25; DA; DAC;**
PC 1
See also CA 104; 133; CDALB 1865-1917;
DAM MST, POET; DLB 54; MTCW

Masters, Hilary 1928- . . . . **CLC 48**
See also CA 25-28R; CANR 13, 47

Mastrosimone, William 19(?)- . . . . . . **CLC 36**

Mathe, Albert
See Camus, Albert

Matheson, Richard Burton 1926- . . . **CLC 37**
See also CA 97-100; DLB 8, 44; INT 97-100

Mathews, Harry 1930- . . . . **CLC 6, 52**
See also CA 21-24R; CAAS 6; CANR 18,
40

Mathews, John Joseph 1894-1979 . . . **CLC 84**
See also CA 19-20; 142; CANR 45; CAP 2;
DAM MULT; NNAL

Mathias, Roland (Glyn) 1915- . . . . . . **CLC 45**
See also CA 97-100; CANR 19, 41; DLB 27

Matsuo Basho 1644-1694 . . . . **PC 3**
See also DAM POET

Mattheson, Rodney
See Creasey, John

Matthews, Greg 1949- . . . . **CLC 45**
See also CA 135

Matthews, William 1942- . . . . **CLC 40**
See also CA 29-32R; CAAS 18; CANR 12;
DLB 5

Matthias, John (Edward) 1941- . . . . . . **CLC 9**
See also CA 33-36R

Matthiessen, Peter
1927- . . . . **CLC 5, 7, 11, 32, 64**
See also AAYA 6; BEST 90:4; CA 9-12R;
CANR 21, 50; DAM NOV; DLB 6;
MTCW; SATA 27

Maturin, Charles Robert
1780(?)-1824 . . . . **NCLC 6**

Matute (Ausejo), Ana Maria
1925- . . . . **CLC 11**
See also CA 89-92; MTCW

Maugham, W. S.
See Maugham, W(illiam) Somerset

Maugham, W(illiam) Somerset
1874-1965 . . . . . . **CLC 1, 11, 15, 67, 93;**
DA; DAB; DAC; SSC 8; WLC
See also CA 5-8R; 25-28R; CANR 40;
CDBLB 1914-1945; DAM DRAM, MST,
NOV; DLB 10, 36, 77, 100, 162; MTCW;
SATA 54

Maugham, William Somerset
See Maugham, W(illiam) Somerset

Maupassant, (Henri Rene Albert) Guy de
1850-1893 . . . . . **NCLC 1, 42; DA; DAB;**
DAC; SSC 1; WLC
See also DAM MST; DLB 123

Maupin, Armistead 1944- . . . . **CLC 95**
See also CA 125; 130; DAM POP; INT 130

Maurhut, Richard
See Traven, B.

Mauriac, Claude 1914- . . . . **CLC 9**
See also CA 89-92; DLB 83

Mauriac, Francois (Charles)
1885-1970 . . . . **CLC 4, 9, 56**
See also CA 25-28; CAP 2; DLB 65;
MTCW

Mavor, Osborne Henry 1888-1951
See Bridie, James
See also CA 104

Maxwell, William (Keepers, Jr.)
1908- . . . . **CLC 19**
See also CA 93-96; DLBY 80; INT 93-96

May, Elaine 1932- . . . . **CLC 16**
See also CA 124; 142; DLB 44

Mayakovski, Vladimir (Vladimirovich)
1893-1930 . . . . **TCLC 4, 18**
See also CA 104

Mayhew, Henry 1812-1887 . . . . . . **NCLC 31**
See also DLB 18, 55

Mayle, Peter 1939(?)- . . . . **CLC 89**
See also CA 139

Maynard, Joyce 1953- . . . . **CLC 23**
See also CA 111; 129

Mayne, William (James Carter)
1928- . . . . **CLC 12**
See also CA 9-12R; CANR 37; CLR 25;
JRDA; MAICYA; SAAS 11; SATA 6, 68

Mayo, Jim
See L'Amour, Louis (Dearborn)

Maysles, Albert 1926- . . . . **CLC 16**
See also CA 29-32R

Maysles, David 1932- . . . . **CLC 16**

Mazer, Norma Fox 1931- . . . . **CLC 26**
See also AAYA 5; CA 69-72; CANR 12,
32; CLR 23; JRDA; MAICYA; SAAS 1;
SATA 24, 67

Mazzini, Guiseppe 1805-1872 . . . . **NCLC 34**

McAuley, James Phillip
1917-1976 . . . . **CLC 45**
See also CA 97-100

McBain, Ed
See Hunter, Evan

McBrien, William Augustine
1930- . . . . **CLC 44**
See also CA 107

McCaffrey, Anne (Inez) 1926- . . . . . . **CLC 17**
See also AAYA 6; AITN 2; BEST 89:2;
CA 25-28R; CANR 15, 35; DAM NOV,
POP; DLB 8; JRDA; MAICYA; MTCW;
SAAS 11; SATA 8, 70

McCall, Nathan 1955(?)- . . . . **CLC 86**
See also CA 146

McCann, Arthur
See Campbell, John W(ood, Jr.)

McCann, Edson
See Pohl, Frederik

McCarthy, Charles, Jr. 1933-
See McCarthy, Cormac
See also CANR 42; DAM POP

McCarthy, Cormac 1933- . . . . . **CLC 4, 57, 59**
See also McCarthy, Charles, Jr.
See also DLB 6, 143

McCarthy, Mary (Therese)
1912-1989 . . . **CLC 1, 3, 5, 14, 24, 39, 59**
See also CA 5-8R; 129; CANR 16, 50;
DLB 2; DLBY 81; INT CANR-16;
MTCW

McCartney, (James) Paul
1942- . . . . **CLC 12, 35**
See also CA 146

McCauley, Stephen (D.) 1955- . . . . . **CLC 50**
See also CA 141

McClure, Michael (Thomas)
1932- . . . . **CLC 6, 10**
See also CA 21-24R; CANR 17, 46;
DLB 16

McCorkle, Jill (Collins) 1958- . . . . . . **CLC 51**
See also CA 121; DLBY 87

McCourt, James 1941- . . . . **CLC 5**
See also CA 57-60

McCoy, Horace (Stanley)
1897-1955 . . . . **TCLC 28**
See also CA 108; DLB 9

McCrae, John 1872-1918 . . . . **TCLC 12**
See also CA 109; DLB 92

McCreigh, James
See Pohl, Frederik

McCullers, (Lula) Carson (Smith)
1917-1967 . . . . **CLC 1, 4, 10, 12, 48; DA;**
DAB; DAC; SSC 9; WLC
See also CA 5-8R; 25-28R; CABS 1, 3;
CANR 18; CDALB 1941-1968;
DAM MST, NOV; DLB 2, 7; MTCW;
SATA 27

McCulloch, John Tyler
See Burroughs, Edgar Rice

McCullough, Colleen 1938(?)- . . . . . . **CLC 27**
See also CA 81-84; CANR 17, 46;
DAM NOV, POP; MTCW

McDermott, Alice 1953- . . . . **CLC 90**
See also CA 109; CANR 40

McElroy, Joseph 1930- . . . . **CLC 5, 47**
See also CA 17-20R

McEwan, Ian (Russell) 1948- . . . **CLC 13, 66**
See also BEST 90:4; CA 61-64; CANR 14,
41; DAM NOV; DLB 14; MTCW

McFadden, David 1940- . . . . **CLC 48**
See also CA 104; DLB 60; INT 104

McFarland, Dennis 1950- . . . . **CLC 65**

McGahern, John
1934- . . . . **CLC 5, 9, 48; SSC 17**
See also CA 17-20R; CANR 29; DLB 14;
MTCW

McGinley, Patrick (Anthony)
1937- . . . . **CLC 41**
See also CA 120; 127; INT 127

McGinley, Phyllis 1905-1978 . . . . . . **CLC 14**
See also CA 9-12R; 77-80; CANR 19;
DLB 11, 48; SATA 2, 44; SATA-Obit 24

McGinniss, Joe 1942- . . . . **CLC 32**
See also AITN 2; BEST 89:2; CA 25-28R;
CANR 26; INT CANR-26

McGivern, Maureen Daly
See Daly, Maureen

McGrath, Patrick 1950- . . . . **CLC 55**
See also CA 136

McGrath, Thomas (Matthew)
1916-1990 . . . . **CLC 28, 59**
See also CA 9-12R; 132; CANR 6, 33;
DAM POET; MTCW; SATA 41;
SATA-Obit 66

McGuane, Thomas (Francis III)
1939- . . . . **CLC 3, 7, 18, 45**
See also AITN 2; CA 49-52; CANR 5, 24,
49; DLB 2; DLBY 80; INT CANR-24;
MTCW

McGuckian, Medbh 1950- . . . . **CLC 48**
See also CA 143; DAM POET; DLB 40

McHale, Tom 1942(?)-1982 . . . . **CLC 3, 5**
See also AITN 1; CA 77-80; 106

McIlvanney, William 1936- . . . . **CLC 42**
See also CA 25-28R; DLB 14

McIlwraith, Maureen Mollie Hunter
See Hunter, Mollie
See also SATA 2

McInerney, Jay 1955- . . . . **CLC 34**
See also AAYA 18; CA 116; 123;
CANR 45; DAM POP; INT 123

McIntyre, Vonda N(eel) 1948- . . . . . **CLC 18**
See also CA 81-84; CANR 17, 34; MTCW

McKay, Claude
. . . . TCLC 7, 41; BLC; DAB; PC 2
See also McKay, Festus Claudius
See also DLB 4, 45, 51, 117

McKay, Festus Claudius 1889-1948
See McKay, Claude
See also BW 1; CA 104; 124; DA; DAC;
DAM MST, MULT, NOV, POET;
MTCW; WLC

McKuen, Rod 1933- . . . . **CLC 1, 3**
See also AITN 1; CA 41-44R; CANR 40

McLoughlin, R. B.
See Mencken, H(enry) L(ouis)

McLuhan, (Herbert) Marshall
1911-1980 . . . . **CLC 37, 83**
See also CA 9-12R; 102; CANR 12, 34;
DLB 88; INT CANR-12; MTCW

McMillan, Terry (L.) 1951- . . . . . **CLC 50, 61**
See also BW 2; CA 140; DAM MULT,
NOV, POP

McMurtry, Larry (Jeff)
1936- . . . . **CLC 2, 3, 7, 11, 27, 44**
See also AAYA 15; AITN 2; BEST 89:2;
CA 5-8R; CANR 19, 43;
CDALB 1968-1988; DAM NOV, POP;
DLB 2, 143; DLBY 80, 87; MTCW

McNally, T. M. 1961- . . . . **CLC 82**

McNally, Terrence 1939- . . . **CLC 4, 7, 41, 91**
See also CA 45-48; CANR 2;
DAM DRAM; DLB 7

McNamer, Deirdre 1950- . . . . **CLC 70**

McNeile, Herman Cyril 1888-1937
See Sapper
See also DLB 77

McNickle, (William) D'Arcy
1904-1977 . . . . **CLC 89**
See also CA 9-12R; 85-88; CANR 5, 45;
DAM MULT; NNAL; SATA-Obit 22

McPhee, John (Angus) 1931- . . . . . . **CLC 36**
See also BEST 90:1; CA 65-68; CANR 20,
46; MTCW

McPherson, James Alan
1943- . . . . **CLC 19, 77**
See also BW 1; CA 25-28R; CAAS 17;
CANR 24; DLB 38; MTCW

McPherson, William (Alexander)
1933- . . . . **CLC 34**
See also CA 69-72; CANR 28;
INT CANR-28

Mead, Margaret 1901-1978 . . . . **CLC 37**
See also AITN 1; CA 1-4R; 81-84;
CANR 4; MTCW; SATA-Obit 20

Meaker, Marijane (Agnes) 1927-
See Kerr, M. E.
See also CA 107; CANR 37; INT 107;
JRDA; MAICYA; MTCW; SATA 20, 61

Medoff, Mark (Howard) 1940- . . . **CLC 6, 23**
See also AITN 1; CA 53-56; CANR 5;
DAM DRAM; DLB 7; INT CANR-5

Medvedev, P. N.
See Bakhtin, Mikhail Mikhailovich

Meged, Aharon
See Megged, Aharon

Meged, Aron
See Megged, Aharon

Megged, Aharon 1920- . . . . **CLC 9**
See also CA 49-52; CAAS 13; CANR 1

Mehta, Ved (Parkash) 1934- . . . . **CLC 37**
See also CA 1-4R; CANR 2, 23; MTCW

Melanter
See Blackmore, R(ichard) D(oddridge)

Melikow, Loris
See Hofmannsthal, Hugo von

Melmoth, Sebastian
See Wilde, Oscar (Fingal O'Flahertie Wills)

Meltzer, Milton 1915- . . . . **CLC 26**
See also AAYA 8; CA 13-16R; CANR 38;
CLR 13; DLB 61; JRDA; MAICYA;
SAAS 1; SATA 1, 50, 80

Melville, Herman
1819-1891 . . . . . **NCLC 3, 12, 29, 45, 49;
DA; DAB; DAC; SSC 1, 17; WLC**
See also CDALB 1640-1865; DAM MST,
NOV; DLB 3, 74; SATA 59

Menander
c. 342B.C.-c. 292B.C. . . . . **CMLC 9; DC 3**
See also DAM DRAM

Mencken, H(enry) L(ouis)
1880-1956 . . . . **TCLC 13**
See also CA 105; 125; CDALB 1917-1929;
DLB 11, 29, 63, 137; MTCW

Mercer, David 1928-1980 . . . . **CLC 5**
See also CA 9-12R; 102; CANR 23;
DAM DRAM; DLB 13; MTCW

Merchant, Paul
See Ellison, Harlan (Jay)

Meredith, George 1828-1909 . . . **TCLC 17, 43**
See also CA 117; CDBLB 1832-1890;
DAM POET; DLB 18, 35, 57, 159

Meredith, William (Morris)
1919- . . . . **CLC 4, 13, 22, 55**
See also CA 9-12R; CAAS 14; CANR 6, 40;
DAM POET; DLB 5

Merezhkovsky, Dmitry Sergeyevich
1865-1941 . . . . **TCLC 29**

Merimee, Prosper
1803-1870 . . . . **NCLC 6; SSC 7**
See also DLB 119

Merkin, Daphne 1954- . . . . **CLC 44**
See also CA 123

Merlin, Arthur
See Blish, James (Benjamin)

Merrill, James (Ingram)
1926-1995 . . . . **CLC 2, 3, 6, 8, 13, 18, 34,
91**
See also CA 13-16R; 147; CANR 10, 49;
DAM POET; DLB 5, 165; DLBY 85;
INT CANR-10; MTCW

Merriman, Alex
See Silverberg, Robert

Merritt, E. B.
See Waddington, Miriam

Merton, Thomas
1915-1968 . . **CLC 1, 3, 11, 34, 83; PC 10**
See also CA 5-8R; 25-28R; CANR 22, 53;
DLB 48; DLBY 81; MTCW

Merwin, W(illiam) S(tanley)
1927- . . . **CLC 1, 2, 3, 5, 8, 13, 18, 45, 88**
See also CA 13-16R; CANR 15, 51;
DAM POET; DLB 5; INT CANR-15;
MTCW

Metcalf, John 1938- . . . . **CLC 37**
See also CA 113; DLB 60

Metcalf, Suzanne
See Baum, L(yman) Frank

Mew, Charlotte (Mary)
1870-1928 . . . . **TCLC 8**
See also CA 105; DLB 19, 135

Mewshaw, Michael 1943- . . . . **CLC 9**
See also CA 53-56; CANR 7, 47; DLBY 80

Meyer, June
See Jordan, June

Meyer, Lynn
See Slavitt, David R(ytman)

Meyer-Meyrink, Gustav 1868-1932
See Meyrink, Gustav
See also CA 117

Meyers, Jeffrey 1939- . . . . **CLC 39**
See also CA 73-76; DLB 111

Meynell, Alice (Christina Gertrude Thompson)
1847-1922 . . . . **TCLC 6**
See also CA 104; DLB 19, 98

Meyrink, Gustav . . . . **TCLC 21**
See also Meyer-Meyrink, Gustav
See also DLB 81

Michaels, Leonard
1933- . . . . **CLC 6, 25; SSC 16**
See also CA 61-64; CANR 21; DLB 130;
MTCW

Michaux, Henri 1899-1984 . . . . . . **CLC 8, 19**
See also CA 85-88; 114

Michelangelo 1475-1564 . . . . **LC 12**

Michelet, Jules 1798-1874 . . . . **NCLC 31**

Michener, James A(lbert)
1907(?)- . . . . **CLC 1, 5, 11, 29, 60**
See also AITN 1; BEST 90:1; CA 5-8R;
CANR 21, 45; DAM NOV, POP; DLB 6;
MTCW

Mickiewicz, Adam 1798-1855 . . . . . **NCLC 3**

Middleton, Christopher 1926- . . . . . . **CLC 13**
See also CA 13-16R; CANR 29; DLB 40

Middleton, Richard (Barham)
1882-1911 . . . . **TCLC 56**
See also DLB 156

Middleton, Stanley 1919-........ **CLC 7, 38**
See also CA 25-28R; CAAS 23; CANR 21,
46; DLB 14

Middleton, Thomas
1580-1627 .... **LC 33; DC 5**
See also DAM DRAM, MST; DLB 58

Migueis, Jose Rodrigues 1901-..... **CLC 10**

Mikszath, Kalman 1847-1910 ..... **TCLC 31**

Miles, Josephine
1911-1985 .... **CLC 1, 2, 14, 34, 39**
See also CA 1-4R; 116; CANR 2;
DAM POET; DLB 48

Militant
See Sandburg, Carl (August)

Mill, John Stuart 1806-1873..... **NCLC 11**
See also CDBLB 1832-1890; DLB 55

Millar, Kenneth 1915-1983 .... **CLC 14**
See also Macdonald, Ross
See also CA 9-12R; 110; CANR 16;
DAM POP; DLB 2; DLBD 6; DLBY 83;
MTCW

Millay, E. Vincent
See Millay, Edna St. Vincent

Millay, Edna St. Vincent
1892-1950 ...... **TCLC 4, 49; DA; DAB;
DAC; PC 6**
See also CA 104; 130; CDALB 1917-1929;
DAM MST, POET; DLB 45; MTCW

Miller, Arthur
1915- .... **CLC 1, 2, 6, 10, 15, 26, 47, 78;
DA; DAB; DAC; DC 1; WLC**
See also AAYA 15; AITN 1; CA 1-4R;
CABS 3; CANR 2, 30;
CDALB 1941-1968; DAM DRAM, MST;
DLB 7; MTCW

Miller, Henry (Valentine)
1891-1980 .... **CLC 1, 2, 4, 9, 14, 43, 84;
DA; DAB; DAC; WLC**
See also CA 9-12R; 97-100; CANR 33;
CDALB 1929-1941; DAM MST, NOV;
DLB 4, 9; DLBY 80; MTCW

Miller, Jason 1939(?)- .... **CLC 2**
See also AITN 1; CA 73-76; DLB 7

Miller, Sue 1943-................ **CLC 44**
See also BEST 90:3; CA 139; DAM POP;
DLB 143

Miller, Walter M(ichael, Jr.)
1923-..................... **CLC 4, 30**
See also CA 85-88; DLB 8

Millett, Kate 1934-............... **CLC 67**
See also AITN 1; CA 73-76; CANR 32, 53;
MTCW

Millhauser, Steven 1943-...... **CLC 21, 54**
See also CA 110; 111; DLB 2; INT 111

Millin, Sarah Gertrude 1889-1968 .. **CLC 49**
See also CA 102; 93-96

Milne, A(lan) A(lexander)
1882-1956 .... **TCLC 6; DAB; DAC**
See also CA 104; 133; CLR 1, 26;
DAM MST; DLB 10, 77, 100, 160;
MAICYA; MTCW; YABC 1

Milner, Ron(ald) 1938-....... **CLC 56; BLC**
See also AITN 1; BW 1; CA 73-76;
CANR 24; DAM MULT; DLB 38;
MTCW

Milosz, Czeslaw
1911- ... **CLC 5, 11, 22, 31, 56, 82; PC 8**
See also CA 81-84; CANR 23, 51;
DAM MST, POET; MTCW

Milton, John
1608-1674 ..... **LC 9; DA; DAB; DAC;
WLC**
See also CDBLB 1660-1789; DAM MST,
POET; DLB 131, 151

Min, Anchee 1957-............... **CLC 86**
See also CA 146

Minehaha, Cornelius
See Wedekind, (Benjamin) Frank(lin)

Miner, Valerie 1947- .... **CLC 40**
See also CA 97-100

Minimo, Duca
See D'Annunzio, Gabriele

Minot, Susan 1956- .... **CLC 44**
See also CA 134

Minus, Ed 1938-................. **CLC 39**

Miranda, Javier
See Bioy Casares, Adolfo

Mirbeau, Octave 1848-1917....... **TCLC 55**
See also DLB 123

Miro (Ferrer), Gabriel (Francisco Victor)
1879-1930 .... **TCLC 5**
See also CA 104

Mishima, Yukio
.... **CLC 2, 4, 6, 9, 27; DC 1; SSC 4**
See also Hiraoka, Kimitake

Mistral, Frederic 1830-1914 ...... **TCLC 51**
See also CA 122

Mistral, Gabriela........... **TCLC 2; HLC**
See also Godoy Alcayaga, Lucila

Mistry, Rohinton 1952-...... **CLC 71; DAC**
See also CA 141

Mitchell, Clyde
See Ellison, Harlan (Jay); Silverberg, Robert

Mitchell, James Leslie 1901-1935
See Gibbon, Lewis Grassic
See also CA 104; DLB 15

Mitchell, Joni 1943-............. **CLC 12**
See also CA 112

Mitchell, Margaret (Munnerlyn)
1900-1949 .... **TCLC 11**
See also CA 109; 125; DAM NOV, POP;
DLB 9; MTCW

Mitchell, Peggy
See Mitchell, Margaret (Munnerlyn)

Mitchell, S(ilas) Weir 1829-1914 .. **TCLC 36**

Mitchell, W(illiam) O(rmond)
1914-.................. **CLC 25; DAC**
See also CA 77-80; CANR 15, 43;
DAM MST; DLB 88

Mitford, Mary Russell 1787-1855.. **NCLC 4**
See also DLB 110, 116

Mitford, Nancy 1904-1973......... **CLC 44**
See also CA 9-12R

Miyamoto, Yuriko 1899-1951 ..... **TCLC 37**

Mo, Timothy (Peter) 1950(?)-...... **CLC 46**
See also CA 117; MTCW

Modarressi, Taghi (M.) 1931-...... **CLC 44**
See also CA 121; 134; INT 134

Modiano, Patrick (Jean) 1945-..... **CLC 18**
See also CA 85-88; CANR 17, 40; DLB 83

Moerck, Paal
See Roelvaag, O(le) E(dvart)

Mofolo, Thomas (Mokopu)
1875(?)-1948 .... **TCLC 22; BLC**
See also CA 121; DAM MULT

Mohr, Nicholasa 1935-...... **CLC 12; HLC**
See also AAYA 8; CA 49-52; CANR 1, 32;
CLR 22; DAM MULT; DLB 145; HW;
JRDA; SAAS 8; SATA 8

Mojtabai, A(nn) G(race)
1938- .... **CLC 5, 9, 15, 29**
See also CA 85-88

Moliere
1622-1673 ..... **LC 28; DA; DAB; DAC;
WLC**
See also DAM DRAM, MST

Molin, Charles
See Mayne, William (James Carter)

Molnar, Ferenc 1878-1952........ **TCLC 20**
See also CA 109; DAM DRAM

Momaday, N(avarre) Scott
1934- ..... **CLC 2, 19, 85, 95; DA; DAB;
DAC**
See also AAYA 11; CA 25-28R; CANR 14,
34; DAM MST, MULT, NOV, POP;
DLB 143; INT CANR-14; MTCW;
NNAL; SATA 48; SATA-Brief 30

Monette, Paul 1945-1995......... **CLC 82**
See also CA 139; 147

Monroe, Harriet 1860-1936....... **TCLC 12**
See also CA 109; DLB 54, 91

Monroe, Lyle
See Heinlein, Robert A(nson)

Montagu, Elizabeth 1917-........ **NCLC 7**
See also CA 9-12R

Montagu, Mary (Pierrepont) Wortley
1689-1762 .... **LC 9; PC 16**
See also DLB 95, 101

Montagu, W. H.
See Coleridge, Samuel Taylor

Montague, John (Patrick)
1929-.................... **CLC 13, 46**
See also CA 9-12R; CANR 9; DLB 40;
MTCW

Montaigne, Michel (Eyquem) de
1533-1592 ...... **LC 8; DA; DAB; DAC;
WLC**
See also DAM MST

Montale, Eugenio
1896-1981 .... **CLC 7, 9, 18; PC 13**
See also CA 17-20R; 104; CANR 30;
DLB 114; MTCW

Montesquieu, Charles-Louis de Secondat
1689-1755 .... **LC 7**

Montgomery, (Robert) Bruce 1921-1978
See Crispin, Edmund
See also CA 104

Montgomery, L(ucy) M(aud)
1874-1942 .... **TCLC 51; DAC**
See also AAYA 12; CA 108; 137; CLR 8;
DAM MST; DLB 92; JRDA; MAICYA;
YABC 1

Montgomery, Marion H., Jr. 1925- . . **CLC 7**
See also AITN 1; CA 1-4R; CANR 3, 48;
DLB 6

Montgomery, Max
See Davenport, Guy (Mattison, Jr.)

Montherlant, Henry (Milon) de
1896-1972 . . . . **CLC 8, 19**
See also CA 85-88; 37-40R; DAM DRAM;
DLB 72; MTCW

Monty Python
See Chapman, Graham; Cleese, John
(Marwood); Gilliam, Terry (Vance); Idle,
Eric; Jones, Terence Graham Parry; Palin,
Michael (Edward)
See also AAYA 7

Moodie, Susanna (Strickland)
1803-1885 . . . . **NCLC 14**
See also DLB 99

Mooney, Edward 1951-
See Mooney, Ted
See also CA 130

Mooney, Ted . . . . **CLC 25**
See also Mooney, Edward

Moorcock, Michael (John)
1939- . . . . **CLC 5, 27, 58**
See also CA 45-48; CAAS 5; CANR 2, 17,
38; DLB 14; MTCW

Moore, Brian
1921- . . . . . . **CLC 1, 3, 5, 7, 8, 19, 32, 90;**
DAB; DAC
See also CA 1-4R; CANR 1, 25, 42;
DAM MST; MTCW

Moore, Edward
See Muir, Edwin

Moore, George Augustus
1852-1933 . . . . **TCLC 7; SSC 19**
See also CA 104; DLB 10, 18, 57, 135

Moore, Lorrie . . . . **CLC 39, 45, 68**
See also Moore, Marie Lorena

Moore, Marianne (Craig)
1887-1972 . . . . **CLC 1, 2, 4, 8, 10, 13, 19,**
47; DA; DAB; DAC; PC 4
See also CA 1-4R; 33-36R; CANR 3;
CDALB 1929-1941; DAM MST, POET;
DLB 45; DLBD 7; MTCW; SATA 20

Moore, Marie Lorena 1957-
See Moore, Lorrie
See also CA 116; CANR 39

Moore, Thomas 1779-1852 . . . . **NCLC 6**
See also DLB 96, 144

Morand, Paul 1888-1976 . . **CLC 41; SSC 22**
See also CA 69-72; DLB 65

Morante, Elsa 1918-1985 . . . . **CLC 8, 47**
See also CA 85-88; 117; CANR 35; MTCW

Moravia, Alberto . . . . . . **CLC 2, 7, 11, 27, 46**
See also Pincherle, Alberto

More, Hannah 1745-1833 . . . . **NCLC 27**
See also DLB 107, 109, 116, 158

More, Henry 1614-1687 . . . . **LC 9**
See also DLB 126

More, Sir Thomas 1478-1535 . . . . **LC 10, 32**

Moreas, Jean . . . . **TCLC 18**
See also Papadiamantopoulos, Johannes

Morgan, Berry 1919- . . . . **CLC 6**
See also CA 49-52; DLB 6

Morgan, Claire
See Highsmith, (Mary) Patricia

Morgan, Edwin (George) 1920- . . . . . **CLC 31**
See also CA 5-8R; CANR 3, 43; DLB 27

Morgan, (George) Frederick
1922- . . . . **CLC 23**
See also CA 17-20R; CANR 21

Morgan, Harriet
See Mencken, H(enry) L(ouis)

Morgan, Jane
See Cooper, James Fenimore

Morgan, Janet 1945- . . . . **CLC 39**
See also CA 65-68

Morgan, Lady 1776(?)-1859 . . . . . . **NCLC 29**
See also DLB 116, 158

Morgan, Robin 1941- . . . . **CLC 2**
See also CA 69-72; CANR 29; MTCW;
SATA 80

Morgan, Scott
See Kuttner, Henry

Morgan, Seth 1949(?)-1990 . . . . **CLC 65**
See also CA 132

Morgenstern, Christian
1871-1914 . . . . **TCLC 8**
See also CA 105

Morgenstern, S.
See Goldman, William (W.)

Moricz, Zsigmond 1879-1942 . . . . . **TCLC 33**

Morike, Eduard (Friedrich)
1804-1875 . . . . **NCLC 10**
See also DLB 133

Mori Ogai . . . . **TCLC 14**
See also Mori Rintaro

Mori Rintaro 1862-1922
See Mori Ogai
See also CA 110

Moritz, Karl Philipp 1756-1793 . . . . . . **LC 2**
See also DLB 94

Morland, Peter Henry
See Faust, Frederick (Schiller)

Morren, Theophil
See Hofmannsthal, Hugo von

Morris, Bill 1952- . . . . **CLC 76**

Morris, Julian
See West, Morris L(anglo)

Morris, Steveland Judkins 1950(?)-
See Wonder, Stevie
See also CA 111

Morris, William 1834-1896 . . . . **NCLC 4**
See also CDBLB 1832-1890; DLB 18, 35,
57, 156

Morris, Wright 1910- . . . **CLC 1, 3, 7, 18, 37**
See also CA 9-12R; CANR 21; DLB 2;
DLBY 81; MTCW

Morrison, Chloe Anthony Wofford
See Morrison, Toni

Morrison, James Douglas 1943-1971
See Morrison, Jim
See also CA 73-76; CANR 40

Morrison, Jim . . . . **CLC 17**
See also Morrison, James Douglas

Morrison, Toni
1931- . . . . **CLC 4, 10, 22, 55, 81, 87;**
BLC; DA; DAB; DAC
See also AAYA 1; BW 2; CA 29-32R;
CANR 27, 42; CDALB 1968-1988;
DAM MST, MULT, NOV, POP; DLB 6,
33, 143; DLBY 81; MTCW; SATA 57

Morrison, Van 1945- . . . . **CLC 21**
See also CA 116

Mortimer, John (Clifford)
1923- . . . . **CLC 28, 43**
See also CA 13-16R; CANR 21;
CDBLB 1960 to Present; DAM DRAM,
POP; DLB 13; INT CANR-21; MTCW

Mortimer, Penelope (Ruth) 1918- . . . . **CLC 5**
See also CA 57-60; CANR 45

Morton, Anthony
See Creasey, John

Mosher, Howard Frank 1943- . . . . . . **CLC 62**
See also CA 139

Mosley, Nicholas 1923- . . . . **CLC 43, 70**
See also CA 69-72; CANR 41; DLB 14

Moss, Howard
1922-1987 . . . . **CLC 7, 14, 45, 50**
See also CA 1-4R; 123; CANR 1, 44;
DAM POET; DLB 5

Mossgiel, Rab
See Burns, Robert

Motion, Andrew (Peter) 1952- . . . . . . **CLC 47**
See also CA 146; DLB 40

Motley, Willard (Francis)
1909-1965 . . . . **CLC 18**
See also BW 1; CA 117; 106; DLB 76, 143

Motoori, Norinaga 1730-1801 . . . . **NCLC 45**

Mott, Michael (Charles Alston)
1930- . . . . **CLC 15, 34**
See also CA 5-8R; CAAS 7; CANR 7, 29

Mountain Wolf Woman
1884-1960 . . . . **CLC 92**
See also CA 144; NNAL

Moure, Erin 1955- . . . . **CLC 88**
See also CA 113; DLB 60

Mowat, Farley (McGill)
1921- . . . . **CLC 26; DAC**
See also AAYA 1; CA 1-4R; CANR 4, 24,
42; CLR 20; DAM MST; DLB 68;
INT CANAR-24; JRDA; MAICYA;
MTCW; SATA 3, 55

Moyers, Bill 1934- . . . . **CLC 74**
See also AITN 2; CA 61-64; CANR 31, 52

Mphahlele, Es'kia
See Mphahlele, Ezekiel
See also DLB 125

Mphahlele, Ezekiel 1919- . . . . . **CLC 25; BLC**
See also Mphahlele, Es'kia
See also BW 2; CA 81-84; CANR 26;
DAM MULT

Mqhayi, S(amuel) E(dward) K(rune Loliwe)
1875-1945 . . . . **TCLC 25; BLC**
See also DAM MULT

Mrozek, Slawomir 1930- . . . . **CLC 3, 13**
See also CA 13-16R; CAAS 10; CANR 29;
MTCW

Mrs. Belloc-Lowndes
See Lowndes, Marie Adelaide (Belloc)

Mtwa, Percy (?)-................ CLC 47

Mueller, Lisel 1924-........... CLC 13, 51
See also CA 93-96; DLB 105

Muir, Edwin 1887-1959.......... TCLC 2
See also CA 104; DLB 20, 100

Muir, John 1838-1914 .... TCLC 28

Mujica Lainez, Manuel
1910-1984 .... CLC 31
See also Lainez, Manuel Mujica
See also CA 81-84; 112; CANR 32; HW

Mukherjee, Bharati 1940-......... CLC 53
See also BEST 89:2; CA 107; CANR 45;
DAM NOV; DLB 60; MTCW

Muldoon, Paul 1951-.......... CLC 32, 72
See also CA 113; 129; CANR 52;
DAM POET; DLB 40; INT 129

Mulisch, Harry 1927-............. CLC 42
See also CA 9-12R; CANR 6, 26

Mull, Martin 1943-.............. CLC 17
See also CA 105

Mulock, Dinah Maria
See Craik, Dinah Maria (Mulock)

Munford, Robert 1737(?)-1783 .... LC 5
See also DLB 31

Mungo, Raymond 1946-........... CLC 72
See also CA 49-52; CANR 2

Munro, Alice
1931-......CLC 6, 10, 19, 50, 95; DAC;
SSC 3
See also AITN 2; CA 33-36R; CANR 33,
53; DAM MST, NOV; DLB 53; MTCW;
SATA 29

Munro, H(ector) H(ugh) 1870-1916
See Saki
See also CA 104; 130; CDBLB 1890-1914;
DA; DAB; DAC; DAM MST, NOV;
DLB 34, 162; MTCW; WLC

Murasaki, Lady................. CMLC 1

Murdoch, (Jean) Iris
1919-...... CLC 1, 2, 3, 4, 6, 8, 11, 15,
22, 31, 51; DAB; DAC
See also CA 13-16R; CANR 8, 43;
CDBLB 1960 to Present; DAM MST,
NOV; DLB 14; INT CANR-8; MTCW

Murfree, Mary Noailles
1850-1922 .... SSC 22
See also CA 122; DLB 12, 74

Murnau, Friedrich Wilhelm
See Plumpe, Friedrich Wilhelm

Murphy, Richard 1927-........... CLC 41
See also CA 29-32R; DLB 40

Murphy, Sylvia 1937-............. CLC 34
See also CA 121

Murphy, Thomas (Bernard) 1935-... CLC 51
See also CA 101

Murray, Albert L. 1916-.......... CLC 73
See also BW 2; CA 49-52; CANR 26, 52;
DLB 38

Murray, Les(lie) A(llan) 1938- ..... CLC 40
See also CA 21-24R; CANR 11, 27;
DAM POET

Murry, J. Middleton
See Murry, John Middleton

Murry, John Middleton
1889-1957 .... TCLC 16
See also CA 118; DLB 149

Musgrave, Susan 1951- .... CLC 13, 54
See also CA 69-72; CANR 45

Musil, Robert (Edler von)
1880-1942 .... TCLC 12; SSC 18
See also CA 109; DLB 81, 124

Muske, Carol 1945- .... CLC 90
See also Muske-Dukes, Carol (Anne)

Muske-Dukes, Carol (Anne) 1945-
See Muske, Carol
See also CA 65-68; CANR 32

Musset, (Louis Charles) Alfred de
1810-1857 .... NCLC 7

My Brother's Brother
See Chekhov, Anton (Pavlovich)

Myers, L. H. 1881-1944.......... TCLC 59
See also DLB 15

Myers, Walter Dean 1937- ... CLC 35; BLC
See also AAYA 4; BW 2; CA 33-36R;
CANR 20, 42; CLR 4, 16, 35;
DAM MULT, NOV; DLB 33;
INT CANR-20; JRDA; MAICYA;
SAAS 2; SATA 41, 71; SATA-Brief 27

Myers, Walter M.
See Myers, Walter Dean

Myles, Symon
See Follett, Ken(neth Martin)

Nabokov, Vladimir (Vladimirovich)
1899-1977 ..... CLC 1, 2, 3, 6, 8, 11, 15,
23, 44, 46, 64; DA; DAB; DAC; SSC 11;
WLC
See also CA 5-8R; 69-72; CANR 20;
CDALB 1941-1968; DAM MST, NOV;
DLB 2; DLBD 3; DLBY 80, 91; MTCW

Nagai Kafu.................... TCLC 51
See also Nagai Sokichi

Nagai Sokichi 1879-1959
See Nagai Kafu
See also CA 117

Nagy, Laszlo 1925-1978............ CLC 7
See also CA 129; 112

Naipaul, Shiva(dhar Srinivasa)
1945-1985 .... CLC 32, 39
See also CA 110; 112; 116; CANR 33;
DAM NOV; DLB 157; DLBY 85;
MTCW

Naipaul, V(idiadhar) S(urajprasad)
1932-.... CLC 4, 7, 9, 13, 18, 37; DAB;
DAC
See also CA 1-4R; CANR 1, 33, 51;
CDBLB 1960 to Present; DAM MST,
NOV; DLB 125; DLBY 85; MTCW

Nakos, Lilika 1899(?)-............ CLC 29

Narayan, R(asipuram) K(rishnaswami)
1906-............ CLC 7, 28, 47
See also CA 81-84; CANR 33; DAM NOV;
MTCW; SATA 62

Nash, (Frediric) Ogden 1902-1971 .. CLC 23
See also CA 13-14; 29-32R; CANR 34;
CAP 1; DAM POET; DLB 11;
MAICYA; MTCW; SATA 2, 46

Nathan, Daniel
See Dannay, Frederic

Nathan, George Jean 1882-1958 ... TCLC 18
See also Hatteras, Owen
See also CA 114; DLB 137

Natsume, Kinnosuke 1867-1916
See Natsume, Soseki
See also CA 104

Natsume, Soseki .... TCLC 2, 10
See also Natsume, Kinnosuke

Natti, (Mary) Lee 1919-
See Kingman, Lee
See also CA 5-8R; CANR 2

Naylor, Gloria
1950- ..... CLC 28, 52; BLC; DA; DAC
See also AAYA 6; BW 2; CA 107;
CANR 27, 51; DAM MST, MULT,
NOV, POP; MTCW

Neihardt, John Gneisenau
1881-1973 .... CLC 32
See also CA 13-14; CAP 1; DLB 9, 54

Nekrasov, Nikolai Alekseevich
1821-1878 .... NCLC 11

Nelligan, Emile 1879-1941....... TCLC 14
See also CA 114; DLB 92

Nelson, Willie 1933-.............. CLC 17
See also CA 107

Nemerov, Howard (Stanley)
1920-1991 .... CLC 2, 6, 9, 36
See also CA 1-4R; 134; CABS 2; CANR 1,
27, 53; DAM POET; DLB 5, 6;
DLBY 83; INT CANR-27; MTCW

Neruda, Pablo
1904-1973 ..... CLC 1, 2, 5, 7, 9, 28, 62;
DA; DAB; DAC; HLC; PC 4; WLC
See also CA 19-20; 45-48; CAP 2;
DAM MST, MULT, POET; HW; MTCW

Nerval, Gerard de
1808-1855 ..... NCLC 1; PC 13; SSC 18

Nervo, (Jose) Amado (Ruiz de)
1870-1919 .... TCLC 11
See also CA 109; 131; HW

Nessi, Pio Baroja y
See Baroja (y Nessi), Pio

Nestroy, Johann 1801-1862...... NCLC 42
See also DLB 133

Neufeld, John (Arthur) 1938- ...... CLC 17
See also AAYA 11; CA 25-28R; CANR 11,
37; MAICYA; SAAS 3; SATA 6, 81

Neville, Emily Cheney 1919-...... CLC 12
See also CA 5-8R; CANR 3, 37; JRDA;
MAICYA; SAAS 2; SATA 1

Newbound, Bernard Slade 1930-
See Slade, Bernard
See also CA 81-84; CANR 49;
DAM DRAM

Newby, P(ercy) H(oward)
1918- .... CLC 2, 13
See also CA 5-8R; CANR 32; DAM NOV;
DLB 15; MTCW

Newlove, Donald 1928- .... CLC 6
See also CA 29-32R; CANR 25

Newlove, John (Herbert) 1938-..... CLC 14
See also CA 21-24R; CANR 9, 25

Newman, Charles 1938-.......... CLC 2, 8
See also CA 21-24R

Newman, Edwin (Harold) 1919- .... **CLC 14**
See also AITN 1; CA 69-72; CANR 5

Newman, John Henry
1801-1890 .... **NCLC 38**
See also DLB 18, 32, 55

Newton, Suzanne 1936- .... **CLC 35**
See also CA 41-44R; CANR 14; JRDA;
SATA 5, 77

Nexo, Martin Andersen
1869-1954 .... **TCLC 43**

Nezval, Vitezslav 1900-1958 ..... **TCLC 44**
See also CA 123

Ng, Fae Myenne 1957(?)- .... **CLC 81**
See also CA 146

Ngema, Mbongeni 1955- .... **CLC 57**
See also BW 2; CA 143

Ngugi, James T(hiong'o)........ **CLC 3, 7, 13**
See also Ngugi wa Thiong'o

Ngugi wa Thiong'o 1938- ..... **CLC 36; BLC**
See also Ngugi, James T(hiong'o)
See also BW 2; CA 81-84; CANR 27;
DAM MULT, NOV; DLB 125; MTCW

Nichol, B(arrie) P(hillip)
1944-1988 .... **CLC 18**
See also CA 53-56; DLB 53; SATA 66

Nichols, John (Treadwell) 1940- .... **CLC 38**
See also CA 9-12R; CAAS 2; CANR 6;
DLBY 82

Nichols, Leigh
See Koontz, Dean R(ay)

Nichols, Peter (Richard)
1927- .... **CLC 5, 36, 65**
See also CA 104; CANR 33; DLB 13;
MTCW

Nicolas, F. R. E.
See Freeling, Nicolas

Niedecker, Lorine 1903-1970.... **CLC 10, 42**
See also CA 25-28; CAP 2; DAM POET;
DLB 48

Nietzsche, Friedrich (Wilhelm)
1844-1900 .... **TCLC 10, 18, 55**
See also CA 107; 121; DLB 129

Nievo, Ippolito 1831-1861 .... **NCLC 22**

Nightingale, Anne Redmon 1943-
See Redmon, Anne
See also CA 103

Nik. T. O.
See Annensky, Innokenty Fyodorovich

Nin, Anais
1903-1977 ...... **CLC 1, 4, 8, 11, 14, 60;**
SSC 10
See also AITN 2; CA 13-16R; 69-72;
CANR 22, 53; DAM NOV, POP; DLB 2,
4, 152; MTCW

Nishiwaki, Junzaburo 1894-1982 .... **PC 15**
See also CA 107

Nissenson, Hugh 1933- .... **CLC 4, 9**
See also CA 17-20R; CANR 27; DLB 28

Niven, Larry .... **CLC 8**
See also Niven, Laurence Van Cott
See also DLB 8

Niven, Laurence Van Cott 1938-
See Niven, Larry
See also CA 21-24R; CAAS 12; CANR 14,
44; DAM POP; MTCW

Nixon, Agnes Eckhardt 1927- ...... **CLC 21**
See also CA 110

Nizan, Paul 1905-1940 .... **TCLC 40**
See also DLB 72

Nkosi, Lewis 1936- .... **CLC 45; BLC**
See also BW 1; CA 65-68; CANR 27;
DAM MULT; DLB 157

Nodier, (Jean) Charles (Emmanuel)
1780-1844 .... **NCLC 19**
See also DLB 119

Nolan, Christopher 1965- .... **CLC 58**
See also CA 111

Noon, Jeff 1957- .... **CLC 91**
See also CA 148

Norden, Charles
See Durrell, Lawrence (George)

Nordhoff, Charles (Bernard)
1887-1947 .... **TCLC 23**
See also CA 108; DLB 9; SATA 23

Norfolk, Lawrence 1963- .... **CLC 76**
See also CA 144

Norman, Marsha 1947- .... **CLC 28**
See also CA 105; CABS 3; CANR 41;
DAM DRAM; DLBY 84

Norris, Benjamin Franklin, Jr.
1870-1902 .... **TCLC 24**
See also Norris, Frank
See also CA 110

Norris, Frank
See Norris, Benjamin Franklin, Jr.
See also CDALB 1865-1917; DLB 12, 71

Norris, Leslie 1921- .... **CLC 14**
See also CA 11-12; CANR 14; CAP 1;
DLB 27

North, Andrew
See Norton, Andre

North, Anthony
See Koontz, Dean R(ay)

North, Captain George
See Stevenson, Robert Louis (Balfour)

North, Milou
See Erdrich, Louise

Northrup, B. A.
See Hubbard, L(afayette) Ron(ald)

North Staffs
See Hulme, T(homas) E(rnest)

Norton, Alice Mary
See Norton, Andre
See also MAICYA; SATA 1, 43

Norton, Andre 1912- .... **CLC 12**
See also Norton, Alice Mary
See also AAYA 14; CA 1-4R; CANR 2, 31;
DLB 8, 52; JRDA; MTCW

Norton, Caroline 1808-1877...... **NCLC 47**
See also DLB 21, 159

Norway, Nevil Shute 1899-1960
See Shute, Nevil
See also CA 102; 93-96

Norwid, Cyprian Kamil
1821-1883 .... **NCLC 17**

Nosille, Nabrah
See Ellison, Harlan (Jay)

Nossack, Hans Erich 1901-1978 ..... **CLC 6**
See also CA 93-96; 85-88; DLB 69

Nostradamus 1503-1566........... **LC 27**

Nosu, Chuji
See Ozu, Yasujiro

Notenburg, Eleanora (Genrikhovna) von
See Guro, Elena

Nova, Craig 1945- .... **CLC 7, 31**
See also CA 45-48; CANR 2, 53

Novak, Joseph
See Kosinski, Jerzy (Nikodem)

Novalis 1772-1801 .... **NCLC 13**
See also DLB 90

Nowlan, Alden (Albert)
1933-1983 .... **CLC 15; DAC**
See also CA 9-12R; CANR 5; DAM MST;
DLB 53

Noyes, Alfred 1880-1958 .... **TCLC 7**
See also CA 104; DLB 20

Nunn, Kem 19(?)- .... **CLC 34**

Nye, Robert 1939- .... **CLC 13, 42**
See also CA 33-36R; CANR 29;
DAM NOV; DLB 14; MTCW; SATA 6

Nyro, Laura 1947- .... **CLC 17**

Oates, Joyce Carol
1938- ...... **CLC 1, 2, 3, 6, 9, 11, 15, 19,**
33, 52; DA; DAB; DAC; SSC 6; WLC
See also AAYA 15; AITN 1; BEST 89:2;
CA 5-8R; CANR 25, 45;
CDALB 1968-1988; DAM MST, NOV,
POP; DLB 2, 5, 130; DLBY 81;
INT CANR-25; MTCW

O'Brien, Darcy 1939- .... **CLC 11**
See also CA 21-24R; CANR 8

O'Brien, E. G.
See Clarke, Arthur C(harles)

O'Brien, Edna
1936- ... **CLC 3, 5, 8, 13, 36, 65; SSC 10**
See also CA 1-4R; CANR 6, 41;
CDBLB 1960 to Present; DAM NOV;
DLB 14; MTCW

O'Brien, Fitz-James 1828-1862... **NCLC 21**
See also DLB 74

O'Brien, Flann........ **CLC 1, 4, 5, 7, 10, 47**
See also O Nuallain, Brian

O'Brien, Richard 1942- .... **CLC 17**
See also CA 124

O'Brien, Tim 1946- .... **CLC 7, 19, 40**
See also AAYA 16; CA 85-88; CANR 40;
DAM POP; DLB 152; DLBD 9;
DLBY 80

Obstfelder, Sigbjoern 1866-1900... **TCLC 23**
See also CA 123

O'Casey, Sean
1880-1964 ...... **CLC 1, 5, 9, 11, 15, 88;**
DAB; DAC
See also CA 89-92; CDBLB 1914-1945;
DAM DRAM, MST; DLB 10; MTCW

O'Cathasaigh, Sean
See O'Casey, Sean

Ochs, Phil 1940-1976............. **CLC 17**
See also CA 65-68

O'Connor, Edwin (Greene)
1918-1968 .... **CLC 14**
See also CA 93-96; 25-28R

O'Connor, (Mary) Flannery
  1925-1964 .... **CLC 1, 2, 3, 6, 10, 13, 15,**
    21, 66; DA; DAB; DAC; SSC 1, 23; WLC
  See also AAYA 7; CA 1-4R; CANR 3, 41;
    CDALB 1941-1968; DAM MST, NOV;
    DLB 2, 152; DLBD 12; DLBY 80;
    MTCW

O'Connor, Frank .... **CLC 23; SSC 5**
  See also O'Donovan, Michael John
  See also DLB 162

O'Dell, Scott 1898-1989 .... **CLC 30**
  See also AAYA 3; CA 61-64; 129;
    CANR 12, 30; CLR 1, 16; DLB 52;
    JRDA; MAICYA; SATA 12, 60

Odets, Clifford
  1906-1963 .... **CLC 2, 28; DC 6**
  See also CA 85-88; DAM DRAM; DLB 7,
    26; MTCW

O'Doherty, Brian 1934- .... **CLC 76**
  See also CA 105

O'Donnell, K. M.
  See Malzberg, Barry N(athaniel)

O'Donnell, Lawrence
  See Kuttner, Henry

O'Donovan, Michael John
  1903-1966 .... **CLC 14**
  See also O'Connor, Frank
  See also CA 93-96

Oe, Kenzaburo
  1935- .... **CLC 10, 36, 86; SSC 20**
  See also CA 97-100; CANR 36, 50;
    DAM NOV; DLBY 94; MTCW

O'Faolain, Julia 1932- .... **CLC 6, 19, 47**
  See also CA 81-84; CAAS 2; CANR 12;
    DLB 14; MTCW

O'Faolain, Sean
  1900-1991 .... **CLC 1, 7, 14, 32, 70;**
                                    SSC 13
  See also CA 61-64; 134; CANR 12;
    DLB 15, 162; MTCW

O'Flaherty, Liam
  1896-1984 .... **CLC 5, 34; SSC 6**
  See also CA 101; 113; CANR 35; DLB 36,
    162; DLBY 84; MTCW

Ogilvy, Gavin
  See Barrie, J(ames) M(atthew)

O'Grady, Standish James
  1846-1928 .... **TCLC 5**
  See also CA 104

O'Grady, Timothy 1951- .... **CLC 59**
  See also CA 138

O'Hara, Frank
  1926-1966 .... **CLC 2, 5, 13, 78**
  See also CA 9-12R; 25-28R; CANR 33;
    DAM POET; DLB 5, 16; MTCW

O'Hara, John (Henry)
  1905-1970 .... **CLC 1, 2, 3, 6, 11, 42;**
                                    SSC 15
  See also CA 5-8R; 25-28R; CANR 31;
    CDALB 1929-1941; DAM NOV; DLB 9,
    86; DLBD 2; MTCW

O Hehir, Diana 1922- .... **CLC 41**
  See also CA 93-96

Okigbo, Christopher (Ifenayichukwu)
  1932-1967 ..... **CLC 25, 84; BLC; PC 7**
  See also BW 1; CA 77-80; DAM MULT,
    POET; DLB 125; MTCW

Okri, Ben 1959- .... **CLC 87**
  See also BW 2; CA 130; 138; DLB 157;
    INT 138

Olds, Sharon 1942- .... **CLC 32, 39, 85**
  See also CA 101; CANR 18, 41;
    DAM POET; DLB 120

Oldstyle, Jonathan
  See Irving, Washington

Olesha, Yuri (Karlovich)
  1899-1960 .... **CLC 8**
  See also CA 85-88

Oliphant, Laurence
  1829(?)-1888 .... **NCLC 47**
  See also DLB 18, 166

Oliphant, Margaret (Oliphant Wilson)
  1828-1897 .... **NCLC 11**
  See also DLB 18, 159

Oliver, Mary 1935- .... **CLC 19, 34**
  See also CA 21-24R; CANR 9, 43; DLB 5

Olivier, Laurence (Kerr)
  1907-1989 .... **CLC 20**
  See also CA 111; 150; 129

Olsen, Tillie
  1913- ..... **CLC 4, 13; DA; DAB; DAC;**
                                    SSC 11
  See also CA 1-4R; CANR 1, 43;
    DAM MST; DLB 28; DLBY 80; MTCW

Olson, Charles (John)
  1910-1970 ..... **CLC 1, 2, 5, 6, 9, 11, 29**
  See also CA 13-16; 25-28R; CABS 2;
    CANR 35; CAP 1; DAM POET; DLB 5,
    16; MTCW

Olson, Toby 1937- .... **CLC 28**
  See also CA 65-68; CANR 9, 31

Olyesha, Yuri
  See Olesha, Yuri (Karlovich)

Ondaatje, (Philip) Michael
  1943- ... **CLC 14, 29, 51, 76; DAB; DAC**
  See also CA 77-80; CANR 42; DAM MST;
    DLB 60

Oneal, Elizabeth 1934-
  See Oneal, Zibby
  See also CA 106; CANR 28; MAICYA;
    SATA 30, 82

Oneal, Zibby .... **CLC 30**
  See also Oneal, Elizabeth
  See also AAYA 5; CLR 13; JRDA

O'Neill, Eugene (Gladstone)
  1888-1953 ...... **TCLC 1, 6, 27, 49; DA;**
                                    DAB; DAC; WLC
  See also AITN 1; CA 110; 132;
    CDALB 1929-1941; DAM DRAM, MST;
    DLB 7; MTCW

Onetti, Juan Carlos
  1909-1994 .... **CLC 7, 10; SSC 23**
  See also CA 85-88; 145; CANR 32;
    DAM MULT, NOV; DLB 113; HW;
    MTCW

O Nuallain, Brian 1911-1966
  See O'Brien, Flann
  See also CA 21-22; 25-28R; CAP 2

Oppen, George 1908-1984 .... **CLC 7, 13, 34**
  See also CA 13-16R; 113; CANR 8; DLB 5,
    165

Oppenheim, E(dward) Phillips
  1866-1946 .... **TCLC 45**
  See also CA 111; DLB 70

Orlovitz, Gil 1918-1973 .... **CLC 22**
  See also CA 77-80; 45-48; DLB 2, 5

Orris
  See Ingelow, Jean

Ortega y Gasset, Jose
  1883-1955 .... **TCLC 9; HLC**
  See also CA 106; 130; DAM MULT; HW;
    MTCW

Ortese, Anna Maria 1914- .... **CLC 89**

Ortiz, Simon J(oseph) 1941- .... **CLC 45**
  See also CA 134; DAM MULT, POET;
    DLB 120; NNAL

Orton, Joe .... **CLC 4, 13, 43; DC 3**
  See also Orton, John Kingsley
  See also CDBLB 1960 to Present; DLB 13

Orton, John Kingsley 1933-1967
  See Orton, Joe
  See also CA 85-88; CANR 35;
    DAM DRAM; MTCW

Orwell, George
  ..... **TCLC 2, 6, 15, 31, 51; DAB; WLC**
  See also Blair, Eric (Arthur)
  See also CDBLB 1945-1960; DLB 15, 98

Osborne, David
  See Silverberg, Robert

Osborne, George
  See Silverberg, Robert

Osborne, John (James)
  1929-1994 ..... **CLC 1, 2, 5, 11, 45; DA;**
                                    DAB; DAC; WLC
  See also CA 13-16R; 147; CANR 21;
    CDBLB 1945-1960; DAM DRAM, MST;
    DLB 13; MTCW

Osborne, Lawrence 1958- .... **CLC 50**

Oshima, Nagisa 1932- .... **CLC 20**
  See also CA 116; 121

Oskison, John Milton
  1874-1947 .... **TCLC 35**
  See also CA 144; DAM MULT; NNAL

Ossoli, Sarah Margaret (Fuller marchesa d')
  1810-1850
  See Fuller, Margaret
  See also SATA 25

Ostrovsky, Alexander
  1823-1886 .... **NCLC 30, 57**

Otero, Blas de 1916-1979 .... **CLC 11**
  See also CA 89-92; DLB 134

Otto, Whitney 1955- .... **CLC 70**
  See also CA 140

Ouida .... **TCLC 43**
  See also De La Ramee, (Marie) Louise
  See also DLB 18, 156

Ousmane, Sembene 1923- .... **CLC 66; BLC**
  See also BW 1; CA 117; 125; MTCW

Ovid 43B.C.-18(?) .... **CMLC 7; PC 2**
  See also DAM POET

Owen, Hugh
  See Faust, Frederick (Schiller)

Owen, Wilfred (Edward Salter)
　　1893-1918 ..... TCLC **5, 27; DA; DAB;**
　　　　　　　　　　　　　　DAC; WLC
　　See also CA 104; 141; CDBLB 1914-1945;
　　DAM MST, POET; DLB 20

Owens, Rochelle 1936-............. CLC **8**
　　See also CA 17-20R; CAAS 2; CANR 39

Oz, Amos 1939- ... CLC **5, 8, 11, 27, 33, 54**
　　See also CA 53-56; CANR 27, 47;
　　DAM NOV; MTCW

Ozick, Cynthia
　　1928-........ CLC **3, 7, 28, 62; SSC 15**
　　See also BEST 90:1; CA 17-20R; CANR 23;
　　DAM NOV, POP; DLB 28, 152;
　　DLBY 82; INT CANR-23; MTCW

Ozu, Yasujiro 1903-1963.......... CLC **16**
　　See also CA 112

Pacheco, C.
　　See Pessoa, Fernando (Antonio Nogueira)

Pa Chin .... CLC **18**
　　See also Li Fei-kan

Pack, Robert 1929-.............. CLC **13**
　　See also CA 1-4R; CANR 3, 44; DLB 5

Padgett, Lewis
　　See Kuttner, Henry

Padilla (Lorenzo), Heberto 1932-... CLC **38**
　　See also AITN 1; CA 123; 131; HW

Page, Jimmy 1944-.............. CLC **12**

Page, Louise 1955-.............. CLC **40**
　　See also CA 140

Page, P(atricia) K(athleen)
　　1916-......... CLC **7, 18; DAC; PC 12**
　　See also CA 53-56; CANR 4, 22;
　　DAM MST; DLB 68; MTCW

Page, Thomas Nelson 1853-1922.... SSC **23**
　　See also CA 118; DLB 12, 78; DLBD 13

Paget, Violet 1856-1935
　　See Lee, Vernon
　　Sec also CA 104

Paget-Lowe, Henry
　　See Lovecraft, H(oward) P(hillips)

Paglia, Camille (Anna) 1947-....... CLC **68**
　　See also CA 140

Paige, Richard
　　See Koontz, Dean R(ay)

Pakenham, Antonia
　　See Fraser, (Lady) Antonia (Pakenham)

Palamas, Kostes 1859-1943........ TCLC **5**
　　See also CA 105

Palazzeschi, Aldo 1885-1974....... CLC **11**
　　See also CA 89-92; 53-56; DLB 114

Paley, Grace 1922-.... CLC **4, 6, 37; SSC 8**
　　See also CA 25-28R; CANR 13, 46;
　　DAM POP; DLB 28; INT CANR-13;
　　MTCW

Palin, Michael (Edward) 1943-..... CLC **21**
　　See also Monty Python
　　See also CA 107; CANR 35; SATA 67

Palliser, Charles 1947-............ CLC **65**
　　See also CA 136

Palma, Ricardo 1833-1919........ TCLC **29**

Pancake, Breece Dexter 1952-1979
　　See Pancake, Breece D'J
　　See also CA 123; 109

Pancake, Breece D'J.............. CLC **29**
　　See also Pancake, Breece Dexter
　　See also DLB 130

Panko, Rudy
　　See Gogol, Nikolai (Vasilyevich)

Papadiamantis, Alexandros
　　1851-1911 .... TCLC **29**

Papadiamantopoulos, Johannes 1856-1910
　　See Moreas, Jean
　　See also CA 117

Papini, Giovanni 1881-1956...... TCLC **22**
　　See also CA 121

Paracelsus 1493-1541............. LC **14**

Parasol, Peter
　　See Stevens, Wallace

Parfenie, Maria
　　See Codrescu, Andrei

Parini, Jay (Lee) 1948- .... CLC **54**
　　See also CA 97-100; CAAS 16; CANR 32

Park, Jordan
　　See Kornbluth, C(yril) M.; Pohl, Frederik

Parker, Bert
　　See Ellison, Harlan (Jay)

Parker, Dorothy (Rothschild)
　　1893-1967 .... CLC **15, 68; SSC 2**
　　See also CA 19-20; 25-28R; CAP 2;
　　DAM POET; DLB 11, 45, 86; MTCW

Parker, Robert B(rown) 1932-...... CLC **27**
　　See also BEST 89:4; CA 49-52; CANR 1,
　　26, 52; DAM NOV, POP;
　　INT CANR-26; MTCW

Parkin, Frank 1940-.............. CLC **43**
　　See also CA 147

Parkman, Francis, Jr.
　　1823-1893 .... NCLC **12**
　　See also DLB 1, 30

Parks, Gordon (Alexander Buchanan)
　　1912- .... CLC **1, 16; BLC**
　　See also AITN 2; BW 2; CA 41-44R;
　　CANR 26; DAM MULT; DLB 33;
　　SATA 8

Parnell, Thomas 1679-1718 .... LC **3**
　　See also DLB 94

Parra, Nicanor 1914-........ CLC **2; HLC**
　　See also CA 85-88; CANR 32;
　　DAM MULT; HW; MTCW

Parrish, Mary Frances
　　See Fisher, M(ary) F(rances) K(ennedy)

Parson
　　See Coleridge, Samuel Taylor

Parson Lot
　　See Kingsley, Charles

Partridge, Anthony
　　See Oppenheim, E(dward) Phillips

Pascoli, Giovanni 1855-1912 ...... TCLC **45**

Pasolini, Pier Paolo
　　1922-1975 .... CLC **20, 37**
　　See also CA 93-96; 61-64; DLB 128;
　　MTCW

Pasquini
　　See Silone, Ignazio

Pastan, Linda (Olenik) 1932- ...... CLC **27**
　　See also CA 61-64; CANR 18, 40;
　　DAM POET; DLB 5

Pasternak, Boris (Leonidovich)
　　1890-1960 ...... CLC **7, 10, 18, 63; DA;**
　　　　　　　　　　　　DAB; DAC; PC 6; WLC
　　See also CA 127; 116; DAM MST, NOV,
　　POET; MTCW

Patchen, Kenneth 1911-1972... CLC **1, 2, 18**
　　See also CA 1-4R; 33-36R; CANR 3, 35;
　　DAM POET; DLB 16, 48; MTCW

Pater, Walter (Horatio)
　　1839-1894 .... NCLC **7**
　　See also CDBLB 1832-1890; DLB 57, 156

Paterson, A(ndrew) B(arton)
　　1864-1941 .... TCLC **32**

Paterson, Katherine (Womeldorf)
　　1932-.................... CLC **12, 30**
　　See also AAYA 1; CA 21-24R; CANR 28;
　　CLR 7; DLB 52; JRDA; MAICYA;
　　MTCW; SATA 13, 53

Patmore, Coventry Kersey Dighton
　　1823-1896 .... NCLC **9**
　　See also DLB 35, 98

Paton, Alan (Stewart)
　　1903-1988 ...... CLC **4, 10, 25, 55; DA;**
　　　　　　　　　　　　DAB; DAC; WLC
　　See also CA 13-16; 125; CANR 22; CAP 1;
　　DAM MST, NOV; MTCW; SATA 11;
　　SATA-Obit 56

Paton Walsh, Gillian 1937-
　　See Walsh, Jill Paton
　　See also CANR 38; JRDA; MAICYA;
　　SAAS 3; SATA 4, 72

Paulding, James Kirke 1778-1860.. NCLC **2**
　　See also DLB 3, 59, 74

Paulin, Thomas Neilson 1949-
　　See Paulin, Tom
　　See also CA 123; 128

Paulin, Tom...................... CLC **37**
　　See also Paulin, Thomas Neilson
　　See also DLB 40

Paustovsky, Konstantin (Georgievich)
　　1892-1968 .... CLC **40**
　　See also CA 93-96; 25-28R

Pavese, Cesare
　　1908-1950 ..... TCLC **3; PC 13; SSC 19**
　　See also CA 104; DLB 128

Pavic, Milorad 1929-............. CLC **60**
　　See also CA 136

Payne, Alan
　　See Jakes, John (William)

Paz, Gil
　　See Lugones, Leopoldo

Paz, Octavio
　　1914- .... CLC **3, 4, 6, 10, 19, 51, 65;**
　　　　　　　　DA; DAB; DAC; HLC; PC 1; WLC
　　See also CA 73-76; CANR 32; DAM MST,
　　MULT, POET; DLBY 90; HW; MTCW

Peacock, Molly 1947-............. CLC **60**
　　See also CA 103; CAAS 21; CANR 52;
　　DLB 120

Peacock, Thomas Love
　　1785-1866 .... NCLC **22**
　　See also DLB 96, 116

Peake, Mervyn 1911-1968....... CLC **7, 54**
　　See also CA 5-8R; 25-28R; CANR 3;
　　DLB 15, 160; MTCW; SATA 23

Pearce, Philippa .... **CLC 21**
See also Christie, (Ann) Philippa
See also CLR 9; DLB 161; MAICYA;
SATA 1, 67

Pearl, Eric
See Elman, Richard

Pearson, T(homas) R(eid) 1956- .... **CLC 39**
See also CA 120; 130; INT 130

Peck, Dale 1967- .... **CLC 81**
See also CA 146

Peck, John 1941- .... **CLC 3**
See also CA 49-52; CANR 3

Peck, Richard (Wayne) 1934- ...... **CLC 21**
See also AAYA 1; CA 85-88; CANR 19,
38; CLR 15; INT CANR-19; JRDA;
MAICYA; SAAS 2; SATA 18, 55

Peck, Robert Newton
1928- .... **CLC 17; DA; DAC**
See also AAYA 3; CA 81-84; CANR 31;
DAM MST; JRDA; MAICYA; SAAS 1;
SATA 21, 62

Peckinpah, (David) Sam(uel)
1925-1984 .... **CLC 20**
See also CA 109; 114

Pedersen, Knut 1859-1952
See Hamsun, Knut
See also CA 104; 119; MTCW

Peeslake, Gaffer
See Durrell, Lawrence (George)

Peguy, Charles Pierre
1873-1914 .... **TCLC 10**
See also CA 107

Pena, Ramon del Valle y
See Valle-Inclan, Ramon (Maria) del

Pendennis, Arthur Esquir
See Thackeray, William Makepeace

Penn, William 1644-1718 .... **LC 25**
See also DLB 24

Pepys, Samuel
1633-1703 ..... **LC 11; DA; DAB; DAC; WLC**
See also CDBLB 1660-1789; DAM MST;
DLB 101

Percy, Walker
1916-1990 .... **CLC 2, 3, 6, 8, 14, 18, 47, 65**
See also CA 1-4R; 131; CANR 1, 23;
DAM NOV, POP; DLB 2; DLBY 80, 90;
MTCW

Perec, Georges 1936-1982 .... **CLC 56**
See also CA 141; DLB 83

Pereda (y Sanchez de Porrua), Jose Maria de
1833-1906 .... **TCLC 16**
See also CA 117

Pereda y Porrua, Jose Maria de
See Pereda (y Sanchez de Porrua), Jose
Maria de

Peregoy, George Weems
See Mencken, H(enry) L(ouis)

Perelman, S(idney) J(oseph)
1904-1979 ... **CLC 3, 5, 9, 15, 23, 44, 49**
See also AITN 1, 2; CA 73-76; 89-92;
CANR 18; DAM DRAM; DLB 11, 44;
MTCW

Peret, Benjamin 1899-1959 ...... **TCLC 20**
See also CA 117

Peretz, Isaac Loeb 1851(?)-1915... **TCLC 16**
See also CA 109

Peretz, Yitzkhok Leibush
See Peretz, Isaac Loeb

Perez Galdos, Benito 1843-1920 ... **TCLC 27**
See also CA 125; HW

Perrault, Charles 1628-1703 .... **LC 2**
See also MAICYA; SATA 25

Perry, Brighton
See Sherwood, Robert E(mmet)

Perse, St.-John .... **CLC 4, 11, 46**
See also Leger, (Marie-Rene Auguste) Alexis
Saint-Leger

Perutz, Leo 1882-1957 .... **TCLC 60**
See also DLB 81

Peseenz, Tulio F.
See Lopez y Fuentes, Gregorio

Pesetsky, Bette 1932- .... **CLC 28**
See also CA 133; DLB 130

Peshkov, Alexei Maximovich 1868-1936
See Gorky, Maxim
See also CA 105; 141; DA; DAC;
DAM DRAM, MST, NOV

Pessoa, Fernando (Antonio Nogueira)
1888-1935 .... **TCLC 27; HLC**
See also CA 125

Peterkin, Julia Mood 1880-1961.... **CLC 31**
See also CA 102; DLB 9

Peters, Joan K. 1945- .... **CLC 39**

Peters, Robert L(ouis) 1924- .... **CLC 7**
See also CA 13-16R; CAAS 8; DLB 105

Petofi, Sandor 1823-1849 .... **NCLC 21**

Petrakis, Harry Mark 1923- .... **CLC 3**
See also CA 9-12R; CANR 4, 30

Petrarch 1304-1374 .... **PC 8**
See also DAM POET

Petrov, Evgeny .... **TCLC 21**
See also Kataev, Evgeny Petrovich

Petry, Ann (Lane) 1908- ...... **CLC 1, 7, 18**
See also BW 1; CA 5-8R; CAAS 6;
CANR 4, 46; CLR 12; DLB 76; JRDA;
MAICYA; MTCW; SATA 5

Petursson, Halligrimur 1614-1674 .... **LC 8**

Philips, Katherine 1632-1664 .... **LC 30**
See also DLB 131

Philipson, Morris H. 1926- .... **CLC 53**
See also CA 1-4R; CANR 4

Phillips, David Graham
1867-1911 .... **TCLC 44**
See also CA 108; DLB 9, 12

Phillips, Jack
See Sandburg, Carl (August)

Phillips, Jayne Anne
1952- .... **CLC 15, 33; SSC 16**
See also CA 101; CANR 24, 50; DLBY 80;
INT CANR-24; MTCW

Phillips, Richard
See Dick, Philip K(indred)

Phillips, Robert (Schaeffer) 1938-... **CLC 28**
See also CA 17-20R; CAAS 13; CANR 8;
DLB 105

Phillips, Ward
See Lovecraft, H(oward) P(hillips)

Piccolo, Lucio 1901-1969 .... **CLC 13**
See also CA 97-100; DLB 114

Pickthall, Marjorie L(owry) C(hristie)
1883-1922 .... **TCLC 21**
See also CA 107; DLB 92

Pico della Mirandola, Giovanni
1463-1494 .... **LC 15**

Piercy, Marge
1936- .... **CLC 3, 6, 14, 18, 27, 62**
See also CA 21-24R; CAAS 1; CANR 13,
43; DLB 120; MTCW

Piers, Robert
See Anthony, Piers

Pieyre de Mandiargues, Andre 1909-1991
See Mandiargues, Andre Pieyre de
See also CA 103; 136; CANR 22

Pilnyak, Boris .... **TCLC 23**
See also Vogau, Boris Andreyevich

Pincherle, Alberto 1907-1990 ... **CLC 11, 18**
See also Moravia, Alberto
See also CA 25-28R; 132; CANR 33;
DAM NOV; MTCW

Pinckney, Darryl 1953- .... **CLC 76**
See also BW 2; CA 143

Pindar 518B.C.-446B.C. .... **CMLC 12**

Pineda, Cecile 1942- .... **CLC 39**
See also CA 118

Pinero, Arthur Wing 1855-1934 ... **TCLC 32**
See also CA 110; DAM DRAM; DLB 10

Pinero, Miguel (Antonio Gomez)
1946-1988 .... **CLC 4, 55**
See also CA 61-64; 125; CANR 29; HW

Pinget, Robert 1919- .... **CLC 7, 13, 37**
See also CA 85-88; DLB 83

Pink Floyd
See Barrett, (Roger) Syd; Gilmour, David;
Mason, Nick; Waters, Roger; Wright,
Rick

Pinkney, Edward 1802-1828 ..... **NCLC 31**

Pinkwater, Daniel Manus 1941- .... **CLC 35**
See also Pinkwater, Manus
See also AAYA 1; CA 29-32R; CANR 12,
38; CLR 4; JRDA; MAICYA; SAAS 3;
SATA 46, 76

Pinkwater, Manus
See Pinkwater, Daniel Manus
See also SATA 8

Pinsky, Robert 1940- ..... **CLC 9, 19, 38, 94**
See also CA 29-32R; CAAS 4;
DAM POET; DLBY 82

Pinta, Harold
See Pinter, Harold

Pinter, Harold
1930- ..... **CLC 1, 3, 6, 9, 11, 15, 27, 58, 73; DA; DAB; DAC; WLC**
See also CA 5-8R; CANR 33; CDBLB 1960
to Present; DAM DRAM, MST; DLB 13;
MTCW

Piozzi, Hester Lynch (Thrale)
1741-1821 .... **NCLC 57**
See also DLB 104, 142

Pirandello, Luigi
1867-1936 ..... **TCLC 4, 29; DA; DAB;**
DAC; DC 5; SSC 22; WLC
See also CA 104; DAM DRAM, MST

Pirsig, Robert M(aynard)
1928- .... **CLC 4, 6, 73**
See also CA 53-56; CANR 42; DAM POP;
MTCW; SATA 39

Pisarev, Dmitry Ivanovich
1840-1868 .... **NCLC 25**

Pix, Mary (Griffith) 1666-1709 .... **LC 8**
See also DLB 80

Pixerecourt, Guilbert de
1773-1844 .... **NCLC 39**

Plaidy, Jean
See Hibbert, Eleanor Alice Burford

Planche, James Robinson
1796-1880 .... **NCLC 42**

Plant, Robert 1948- .... **CLC 12**

Plante, David (Robert)
1940- .... **CLC 7, 23, 38**
See also CA 37-40R; CANR 12, 36;
DAM NOV; DLBY 83; INT CANR-12;
MTCW

Plath, Sylvia
1932-1963 ..... **CLC 1, 2, 3, 5, 9, 11, 14,**
17, 50, 51, 62; DA; DAB; DAC; PC 1;
WLC
See also AAYA 13; CA 19-20; CANR 34;
CAP 2; CDALB 1941-1968; DAM MST,
POET; DLB 5, 6, 152; MTCW

Plato
428(?)B.C.-348(?)B.C..... **CMLC 8; DA;**
DAB; DAC
See also DAM MST

Platonov, Andrei .... **TCLC 14**
See also Klimentov, Andrei Platonovich

Platt, Kin 1911- .... **CLC 26**
See also AAYA 11; CA 17-20R; CANR 11;
JRDA; SAAS 17; SATA 21, 86

Plautus c. 251B.C.-184B.C. .... **DC 6**

Plick et Plock
See Simenon, Georges (Jacques Christian)

Plimpton, George (Ames) 1927-..... **CLC 36**
See also AITN 1; CA 21-24R; CANR 32;
MTCW; SATA 10

Plomer, William Charles Franklin
1903-1973 .... **CLC 4, 8**
See also CA 21-22; CANR 34; CAP 2;
DLB 20, 162; MTCW; SATA 24

Plowman, Piers
See Kavanagh, Patrick (Joseph)

Plum, J.
See Wodehouse, P(elham) G(renville)

Plumly, Stanley (Ross) 1939- ...... **CLC 33**
See also CA 108; 110; DLB 5; INT 110

Plumpe, Friedrich Wilhelm
1888-1931 .... **TCLC 53**
See also CA 112

Poe, Edgar Allan
1809-1849 .... **NCLC 1, 16, 55; DA;**
DAB; DAC; PC 1; SSC 1, 22; WLC
See also AAYA 14; CDALB 1640-1865;
DAM MST, POET; DLB 3, 59, 73, 74;
SATA 23

Poet of Titchfield Street, The
See Pound, Ezra (Weston Loomis)

Pohl, Frederik 1919- .... **CLC 18**
See also CA 61-64; CAAS 1; CANR 11, 37;
DLB 8; INT CANR-11; MTCW;
SATA 24

Poirier, Louis 1910-
See Gracq, Julien
See also CA 122; 126

Poitier, Sidney 1927-.............. **CLC 26**
See also BW 1; CA 117

Polanski, Roman 1933- .... **CLC 16**
See also CA 77-80

Poliakoff, Stephen 1952- .... **CLC 38**
See also CA 106; DLB 13

Police, The
See Copeland, Stewart (Armstrong);
Summers, Andrew James; Sumner,
Gordon Matthew

Polidori, John William
1795-1821 .... **NCLC 51**
See also DLB 116

Pollitt, Katha 1949- .... **CLC 28**
See also CA 120; 122; MTCW

Pollock, (Mary) Sharon
1936- .... **CLC 50; DAC**
See also CA 141; DAM DRAM, MST;
DLB 60

Polo, Marco 1254-1324 .... **CMLC 15**

Polonsky, Abraham (Lincoln)
1910- .... **CLC 92**
See also CA 104; DLB 26; INT 104

Polybius c. 200B.C.-c. 118B.C. .... **CMLC 17**

Pomerance, Bernard 1940-........ **CLC 13**
See also CA 101; CANR 49; DAM DRAM

Ponge, Francis (Jean Gaston Alfred)
1899-1988 .... **CLC 6, 18**
See also CA 85-88; 126; CANR 40;
DAM POET

Pontoppidan, Henrik 1857-1943 ... **TCLC 29**

Poole, Josephine .... **CLC 17**
See also Helyar, Jane Penelope Josephine
See also SAAS 2; SATA 5

Popa, Vasko 1922-1991 .... **CLC 19**
See also CA 112; 148

Pope, Alexander
1688-1744 ...... **LC 3; DA; DAB; DAC;**
WLC
See also CDBLB 1660-1789; DAM MST,
POET; DLB 95, 101

Porter, Connie (Rose) 1959(?)- ..... **CLC 70**
See also BW 2; CA 142; SATA 81

Porter, Gene(va Grace) Stratton
1863(?)-1924 .... **TCLC 21**
See also CA 112

Porter, Katherine Anne
1890-1980 ...... **CLC 1, 3, 7, 10, 13, 15,**
27; DA; DAB; DAC; SSC 4
See also AITN 2; CA 1-4R; 101; CANR 1;
DAM MST, NOV; DLB 4, 9, 102;
DLBD 12; DLBY 80; MTCW; SATA 39;
SATA-Obit 23

Porter, Peter (Neville Frederick)
1929- .... **CLC 5, 13, 33**
See also CA 85-88; DLB 40

Porter, William Sydney 1862-1910
See Henry, O.
See also CA 104; 131; CDALB 1865-1917;
DA; DAB; DAC; DAM MST; DLB 12,
78, 79; MTCW; YABC 2

Portillo (y Pacheco), Jose Lopez
See Lopez Portillo (y Pacheco), Jose

Post, Melville Davisson
1869-1930 .... **TCLC 39**
See also CA 110

Potok, Chaim 1929- .... **CLC 2, 7, 14, 26**
See also AAYA 15; AITN 1, 2; CA 17-20R;
CANR 19, 35; DAM NOV; DLB 28, 152;
INT CANR-19; MTCW; SATA 33

Potter, Beatrice
See Webb, (Martha) Beatrice (Potter)
See also MAICYA

Potter, Dennis (Christopher George)
1935-1994 .... **CLC 58, 86**
See also CA 107; 145; CANR 33; MTCW

Pound, Ezra (Weston Loomis)
1885-1972 ...... **CLC 1, 2, 3, 4, 5, 7, 10,**
13, 18, 34, 48, 50; DA; DAB; DAC; PC 4;
WLC
See also CA 5-8R; 37-40R; CANR 40;
CDALB 1917-1929; DAM MST, POET;
DLB 4, 45, 63; MTCW

Povod, Reinaldo 1959-1994 .... **CLC 44**
See also CA 136; 146

Powell, Adam Clayton, Jr.
1908-1972 .... **CLC 89; BLC**
See also BW 1; CA 102; 33-36R;
DAM MULT

Powell, Anthony (Dymoke)
1905- .... **CLC 1, 3, 7, 9, 10, 31**
See also CA 1-4R; CANR 1, 32;
CDBLB 1945-1960; DLB 15; MTCW

Powell, Dawn 1897-1965 .... **CLC 66**
See also CA 5-8R

Powell, Padgett 1952-.............. **CLC 34**
See also CA 126

Power, Susan..................... **CLC 91**

Powers, J(ames) F(arl)
1917-.......... **CLC 1, 4, 8, 57; SSC 4**
See also CA 1-4R; CANR 2; DLB 130;
MTCW

Powers, John J(ames) 1945-
See Powers, John R.
See also CA 69-72

Powers, John R. .... **CLC 66**
See also Powers, John J(ames)

Powers, Richard (S.) 1957- .... **CLC 93**
See also CA 148

Pownall, David 1938-............. **CLC 10**
See also CA 89-92; CAAS 18; CANR 49;
DLB 14

Powys, John Cowper
1872-1963 .... **CLC 7, 9, 15, 46**
See also CA 85-88; DLB 15; MTCW

Powys, T(heodore) F(rancis)
1875-1953 .... **TCLC 9**
See also CA 106; DLB 36, 162

Prager, Emily 1952-............. **CLC 56**

Pratt, E(dwin) J(ohn)
1883(?)-1964 . . . . CLC 19; DAC
See also CA 141; 93-96; DAM POET;
DLB 92

Premchand . . . . TCLC 21
See also Srivastava, Dhanpat Rai

Preussler, Otfried 1923- . . . . CLC 17
See also CA 77-80; SATA 24

Prevert, Jacques (Henri Marie)
1900-1977 . . . . CLC 15
See also CA 77-80; 69-72; CANR 29;
MTCW; SATA-Obit 30

Prevost, Abbe (Antoine Francois)
1697-1763 . . . . LC 1

Price, (Edward) Reynolds
1933- . . CLC 3, 6, 13, 43, 50, 63; SSC 22
See also CA 1-4R; CANR 1, 37;
DAM NOV; DLB 2; INT CANR-37

Price, Richard 1949- . . . . CLC 6, 12
See also CA 49-52; CANR 3; DLBY 81

Prichard, Katharine Susannah
1883-1969 . . . . CLC 46
See also CA 11-12; CANR 33; CAP 1;
MTCW; SATA 66

Priestley, J(ohn) B(oynton)
1894-1984 . . . . CLC 2, 5, 9, 34
See also CA 9-12R; 113; CANR 33;
CDBLB 1914-1945; DAM DRAM, NOV;
DLB 10, 34, 77, 100, 139; DLBY 84;
MTCW

Prince 1958(?)- . . . . CLC 35

Prince, F(rank) T(empleton) 1912- . . CLC 22
See also CA 101; CANR 43; DLB 20

Prince Kropotkin
See Kropotkin, Peter (Aleksieevich)

Prior, Matthew 1664-1721 . . . . LC 4
See also DLB 95

Pritchard, William H(arrison)
1932- . . . . CLC 34
See also CA 65-68; CANR 23; DLB 111

Pritchett, V(ictor) S(awdon)
1900- . . . . CLC 5, 13, 15, 41; SSC 14
See also CA 61-64; CANR 31; DAM NOV;
DLB 15, 139; MTCW

Private 19022
See Manning, Frederic

Probst, Mark 1925- . . . . CLC 59
See also CA 130

Prokosch, Frederic 1908-1989 . . . . CLC 4, 48
See also CA 73-76; 128; DLB 48

Prophet, The
See Dreiser, Theodore (Herman Albert)

Prose, Francine 1947- . . . . CLC 45
See also CA 109; 112; CANR 46

Proudhon
See Cunha, Euclides (Rodrigues Pimenta) da

Proulx, E. Annie 1935- . . . . CLC 81

Proust, (Valentin-Louis-George-Eugene-)
Marcel
1871-1922 . . . . TCLC 7, 13, 33; DA;
DAB; DAC; WLC
See also CA 104; 120; DAM MST, NOV;
DLB 65; MTCW

Prowler, Harley
See Masters, Edgar Lee

Prus, Boleslaw 1845-1912 . . . . TCLC 48

Pryor, Richard (Franklin Lenox Thomas)
1940- . . . . CLC 26
See also CA 122

Przybyszewski, Stanislaw
1868-1927 . . . . TCLC 36
See also DLB 66

Pteleon
See Grieve, C(hristopher) M(urray)
See also DAM POET

Puckett, Lute
See Masters, Edgar Lee

Puig, Manuel
1932-1990 . . . CLC 3, 5, 10, 28, 65; HLC
See also CA 45-48; CANR 2, 32;
DAM MULT; DLB 113; HW; MTCW

Purdy, Al(fred Wellington)
1918- . . . . CLC 3, 6, 14, 50; DAC
See also CA 81-84; CAAS 17; CANR 42;
DAM MST, POET; DLB 88

Purdy, James (Amos)
1923- . . . . CLC 2, 4, 10, 28, 52
See also CA 33-36R; CAAS 1; CANR 19,
51; DLB 2; INT CANR-19; MTCW

Pure, Simon
See Swinnerton, Frank Arthur

Pushkin, Alexander (Sergeyevich)
1799-1837 . . . . . NCLC 3, 27; DA; DAB;
DAC; PC 10; WLC
See also DAM DRAM, MST, POET;
SATA 61

P'u Sung-ling 1640-1715 . . . . LC 3

Putnam, Arthur Lee
See Alger, Horatio, Jr.

Puzo, Mario 1920- . . . . CLC 1, 2, 6, 36
See also CA 65-68; CANR 4, 42;
DAM NOV, POP; DLB 6; MTCW

Pym, Barbara (Mary Crampton)
1913-1980 . . . . CLC 13, 19, 37
See also CA 13-14; 97-100; CANR 13, 34;
CAP 1; DLB 14; DLBY 87; MTCW

Pynchon, Thomas (Ruggles, Jr.)
1937- . . . . . CLC 2, 3, 6, 9, 11, 18, 33, 62,
72; DA; DAB; DAC; SSC 14; WLC
See also BEST 90:2; CA 17-20R; CANR 22,
46; DAM MST, NOV, POP; DLB 2;
MTCW

Qian Zhongshu
See Ch'ien Chung-shu

Qroll
See Dagerman, Stig (Halvard)

Quarrington, Paul (Lewis) 1953- . . . . CLC 65
See also CA 129

Quasimodo, Salvatore 1901-1968 . . . CLC 10
See also CA 13-16; 25-28R; CAP 1;
DLB 114; MTCW

Quay, Stephen 1947- . . . . CLC 95

Quay, The Brothers
See Quay, Stephen; Quay, Timothy

Quay, Timothy 1947- . . . . CLC 95

Queen, Ellery . . . . CLC 3, 11
See also Dannay, Frederic; Davidson,
Avram; Lee, Manfred B(ennington);
Sturgeon, Theodore (Hamilton); Vance,
John Holbrook

Queen, Ellery, Jr.
See Dannay, Frederic; Lee, Manfred
B(ennington)

Queneau, Raymond
1903-1976 . . . . CLC 2, 5, 10, 42
See also CA 77-80; 69-72; CANR 32;
DLB 72; MTCW

Quevedo, Francisco de 1580-1645 . . . . LC 23

Quiller-Couch, Arthur Thomas
1863-1944 . . . . TCLC 53
See also CA 118; DLB 135, 153

Quin, Ann (Marie) 1936-1973 . . . . CLC 6
See also CA 9-12R; 45-48; DLB 14

Quinn, Martin
See Smith, Martin Cruz

Quinn, Peter 1947- . . . . CLC 91

Quinn, Simon
See Smith, Martin Cruz

Quiroga, Horacio (Sylvestre)
1878-1937 . . . . TCLC 20; HLC
See also CA 117; 131; DAM MULT; HW;
MTCW

Quoirez, Francoise 1935- . . . . CLC 9
See also Sagan, Francoise
See also CA 49-52; CANR 6, 39; MTCW

Raabe, Wilhelm 1831-1910 . . . . TCLC 45
See also DLB 129

Rabe, David (William) 1940- . . . CLC 4, 8, 33
See also CA 85-88; CABS 3; DAM DRAM;
DLB 7

Rabelais, Francois
1483-1553 . . . . . . LC 5; DA; DAB; DAC;
WLC
See also DAM MST

Rabinovitch, Sholem 1859-1916
See Aleichem, Sholom
See also CA 104

Racine, Jean 1639-1699 . . . . LC 28; DAB
See also DAM MST

Radcliffe, Ann (Ward)
1764-1823 . . . . NCLC 6, 55
See also DLB 39

Radiguet, Raymond 1903-1923 . . . . TCLC 29
See also DLB 65

Radnoti, Miklos 1909-1944 . . . . TCLC 16
See also CA 118

Rado, James 1939- . . . . CLC 17
See also CA 105

Radvanyi, Netty 1900-1983
See Seghers, Anna
See also CA 85-88; 110

Rae, Ben
See Griffiths, Trevor

Raeburn, John (Hay) 1941- . . . . CLC 34
See also CA 57-60

Ragni, Gerome 1942-1991 . . . . CLC 17
See also CA 105; 134

Rahv, Philip 1908-1973 . . . . CLC 24
See also Greenberg, Ivan
See also DLB 137

Raine, Craig 1944- . . . . CLC 32
See also CA 108; CANR 29, 51; DLB 40

Raine, Kathleen (Jessie) 1908- ... **CLC 7, 45**
See also CA 85-88; CANR 46; DLB 20;
MTCW

Rainis, Janis 1865-1929 .... **TCLC 29**

Rakosi, Carl. .... **CLC 47**
See also Rawley, Callman
See also CAAS 5

Raleigh, Richard
See Lovecraft, H(oward) P(hillips)

Raleigh, Sir Walter 1554(?)-1618 .... **LC 31**
See also CDBLB Before 1660

Rallentando, H. P.
See Sayers, Dorothy L(eigh)

Ramal, Walter
See de la Mare, Walter (John)

Ramon, Juan
See Jimenez (Mantecon), Juan Ramon

Ramos, Graciliano 1892-1953 ..... **TCLC 32**

Rampersad, Arnold 1941-. .... **CLC 44**
See also BW 2; CA 127; 133; DLB 111;
INT 133

Rampling, Anne
See Rice, Anne

Ramsay, Allan 1684(?)-1758 .... **LC 29**
See also DLB 95

Ramuz, Charles-Ferdinand
1878-1947 .... **TCLC 33**

Rand, Ayn
1905-1982 ...... **CLC 3, 30, 44, 79; DA;**
DAC; WLC
See also AAYA 10; CA 13-16R; 105;
CANR 27; DAM MST, NOV, POP;
MTCW

Randall, Dudley (Felker)
1914- .... **CLC 1; BLC**
See also BW 1; CA 25-28R; CANR 23;
DAM MULT; DLB 41

Randall, Robert
See Silverberg, Robert

Ranger, Ken
See Creasey, John

Ransom, John Crowe
1888-1974 .... **CLC 2, 4, 5, 11, 24**
See also CA 5-8R; 49-52; CANR 6, 34;
DAM POET; DLB 45, 63; MTCW

Rao, Raja 1909- .... **CLC 25, 56**
See also CA 73-76; CANR 51; DAM NOV;
MTCW

Raphael, Frederic (Michael)
1931- .... **CLC 2, 14**
See also CA 1-4R; CANR 1; DLB 14

Ratcliffe, James P.
See Mencken, H(enry) L(ouis)

Rathbone, Julian 1935- .... **CLC 41**
See also CA 101; CANR 34

Rattigan, Terence (Mervyn)
1911-1977 .... **CLC 7**
See also CA 85-88; 73-76;
CDBLB 1945-1960; DAM DRAM;
DLB 13; MTCW

Ratushinskaya, Irina 1954- .... **CLC 54**
See also CA 129

Raven, Simon (Arthur Noel)
1927- .... **CLC 14**
See also CA 81-84

Rawley, Callman 1903-
See Rakosi, Carl
See also CA 21-24R; CANR 12, 32

Rawlings, Marjorie Kinnan
1896-1953 .... **TCLC 4**
See also CA 104; 137; DLB 9, 22, 102;
JRDA; MAICYA; YABC 1

Ray, Satyajit 1921-1992. .... **CLC 16, 76**
See also CA 114; 137; DAM MULT

Read, Herbert Edward 1893-1968. ... **CLC 4**
See also CA 85-88; 25-28R; DLB 20, 149

Read, Piers Paul 1941- ...... **CLC 4, 10, 25**
See also CA 21-24R; CANR 38; DLB 14;
SATA 21

Reade, Charles 1814-1884 .... **NCLC 2**
See also DLB 21

Reade, Hamish
See Gray, Simon (James Holliday)

Reading, Peter 1946- .... **CLC 47**
See also CA 103; CANR 46; DLB 40

Reaney, James 1926- .... **CLC 13; DAC**
See also CA 41-44R; CAAS 15; CANR 42;
DAM MST; DLB 68; SATA 43

Rebreanu, Liviu 1885-1944 ...... **TCLC 28**

Rechy, John (Francisco)
1934- .... **CLC 1, 7, 14, 18; HLC**
See also CA 5-8R; CAAS 4; CANR 6, 32;
DAM MULT; DLB 122; DLBY 82; HW;
INT CANR-6

Redcam, Tom 1870-1933 .... **TCLC 25**

Reddin, Keith. .... **CLC 67**

Redgrove, Peter (William)
1932- .... **CLC 6, 41**
See also CA 1-4R; CANR 3, 39; DLB 40

Redmon, Anne. .... **CLC 22**
See also Nightingale, Anne Redmon
See also DLBY 86

Reed, Eliot
See Ambler, Eric

Reed, Ishmael
1938- ... **CLC 2, 3, 5, 6, 13, 32, 60; BLC**
See also BW 2; CA 21-24R; CANR 25, 48;
DAM MULT; DLB 2, 5, 33; DLBD 8;
MTCW

Reed, John (Silas) 1887-1920 ...... **TCLC 9**
See also CA 106

Reed, Lou. .... **CLC 21**
See also Firbank, Louis

Reeve, Clara 1729-1807 .... **NCLC 19**
See also DLB 39

Reich, Wilhelm 1897-1957. .... **TCLC 57**

Reid, Christopher (John) 1949- ..... **CLC 33**
See also CA 140; DLB 40

Reid, Desmond
See Moorcock, Michael (John)

Reid Banks, Lynne 1929-
See Banks, Lynne Reid
See also CA 1-4R; CANR 6, 22, 38;
CLR 24; JRDA; MAICYA; SATA 22, 75

Reilly, William K.
See Creasey, John

Reiner, Max
See Caldwell, (Janet Miriam) Taylor
(Holland)

Reis, Ricardo
See Pessoa, Fernando (Antonio Nogueira)

Remarque, Erich Maria
1898-1970 .... **CLC 21; DA; DAB; DAC**
See also CA 77-80; 29-32R; DAM MST,
NOV; DLB 56; MTCW

Remizov, A.
See Remizov, Aleksei (Mikhailovich)

Remizov, A. M.
See Remizov, Aleksei (Mikhailovich)

Remizov, Aleksei (Mikhailovich)
1877-1957 .... **TCLC 27**
See also CA 125; 133

Renan, Joseph Ernest
1823-1892 .... **NCLC 26**

Renard, Jules 1864-1910 .... **TCLC 17**
See also CA 117

Renault, Mary. .... **CLC 3, 11, 17**
See also Challans, Mary
See also DLBY 83

Rendell, Ruth (Barbara) 1930- .. **CLC 28, 48**
See also Vine, Barbara
See also CA 109; CANR 32, 52;
DAM POP; DLB 87; INT CANR-32;
MTCW

Renoir, Jean 1894-1979 .... **CLC 20**
See also CA 129; 85-88

Resnais, Alain 1922-. .... **CLC 16**

Reverdy, Pierre 1889-1960 .... **CLC 53**
See also CA 97-100; 89-92

Rexroth, Kenneth
1905-1982 ...... **CLC 1, 2, 6, 11, 22, 49**
See also CA 5-8R; 107; CANR 14, 34;
CDALB 1941-1968; DAM POET;
DLB 16, 48, 165; DLBY 82;
INT CANR-14; MTCW

Reyes, Alfonso 1889-1959 .... **TCLC 33**
See also CA 131; HW

Reyes y Basoalto, Ricardo Eliecer Neftali
See Neruda, Pablo

Reymont, Wladyslaw (Stanislaw)
1868(?)-1925 .... **TCLC 5**
See also CA 104

Reynolds, Jonathan 1942-. .... **CLC 6, 38**
See also CA 65-68; CANR 28

Reynolds, Joshua 1723-1792 .... **LC 15**
See also DLB 104

Reynolds, Michael Shane 1937- .... **CLC 44**
See also CA 65-68; CANR 9

Reznikoff, Charles 1894-1976 .... **CLC 9**
See also CA 33-36; 61-64; CAP 2; DLB 28,
45

Rezzori (d'Arezzo), Gregor von
1914- .... **CLC 25**
See also CA 122; 136

Rhine, Richard
See Silverstein, Alvin

Rhodes, Eugene Manlove
1869-1934 .... **TCLC 53**

R'hoone
See Balzac, Honore de

Rhys, Jean
    1890(?)-1979 .... **CLC 2, 4, 6, 14, 19, 51;**
                                  SSC 21
    See also CA 25-28R; 85-88; CANR 35;
    CDBLB 1945-1960; DAM NOV; DLB 36,
    117, 162; MTCW

Ribeiro, Darcy 1922- .... **CLC 34**
    See also CA 33-36R

Ribeiro, Joao Ubaldo (Osorio Pimentel)
    1941- .... **CLC 10, 67**
    See also CA 81-84

Ribman, Ronald (Burt) 1932- .... **CLC 7**
    See also CA 21-24R; CANR 46

Ricci, Nino 1959- .... **CLC 70**
    See also CA 137

Rice, Anne 1941- .... **CLC 41**
    See also AAYA 9; BEST 89:2; CA 65-68;
    CANR 12, 36, 53; DAM POP

Rice, Elmer (Leopold)
    1892-1967 .... **CLC 7, 49**
    See also CA 21-22; 25-28R; CAP 2;
    DAM DRAM; DLB 4, 7; MTCW

Rice, Tim(othy Miles Bindon)
    1944- .... **CLC 21**
    See also CA 103; CANR 46

Rich, Adrienne (Cecile)
    1929- .... **CLC 3, 6, 7, 11, 18, 36, 73, 76;**
                                   PC 5
    See also CA 9-12R; CANR 20, 53;
    DAM POET; DLB 5, 67; MTCW

Rich, Barbara
    See Graves, Robert (von Ranke)

Rich, Robert
    See Trumbo, Dalton

Richard, Keith.................... **CLC 17**
    See also Richards, Keith

Richards, David Adams
    1950- .... **CLC 59; DAC**
    See also CA 93-96; DLB 53

Richards, I(vor) A(rmstrong)
    1893-1979 .... **CLC 14, 24**
    See also CA 41-44R; 89-92; CANR 34;
    DLB 27

Richards, Keith 1943-
    See Richard, Keith
    See also CA 107

Richardson, Anne
    See Roiphe, Anne (Richardson)

Richardson, Dorothy Miller
    1873-1957 .... **TCLC 3**
    See also CA 104; DLB 36

Richardson, Ethel Florence (Lindesay)
    1870-1946
    See Richardson, Henry Handel
    See also CA 105

Richardson, Henry Handel......... **TCLC 4**
    See also Richardson, Ethel Florence
    (Lindesay)

Richardson, John
    1796-1852 .... **NCLC 55; DAC**
    See also DLB 99

Richardson, Samuel
    1689-1761 ...... **LC 1; DA; DAB; DAC;**
                                    WLC
    See also CDBLB 1660-1789; DAM MST,
    NOV; DLB 39

Richler, Mordecai
    1931- .... **CLC 3, 5, 9, 13, 18, 46, 70;**
                                   DAC
    See also AITN 1; CA 65-68; CANR 31;
    CLR 17; DAM MST, NOV; DLB 53;
    MAICYA; MTCW; SATA 44;
    SATA-Brief 27

Richter, Conrad (Michael)
    1890-1968 .... **CLC 30**
    See also CA 5-8R; 25-28R; CANR 23;
    DLB 9; MTCW; SATA 3

Ricostranza, Tom
    See Ellis, Trey

Riddell, J. H. 1832-1906 .... **TCLC 40**

Riding, Laura.................... **CLC 3, 7**
    See also Jackson, Laura (Riding)

Riefenstahl, Berta Helene Amalia 1902-
    See Riefenstahl, Leni
    See also CA 108

Riefenstahl, Leni.................. **CLC 16**
    See also Riefenstahl, Berta Helene Amalia

Riffe, Ernest
    See Bergman, (Ernst) Ingmar

Riggs, (Rolla) Lynn 1899-1954 .... **TCLC 56**
    See also CA 144; DAM MULT; NNAL

Riley, James Whitcomb
    1849-1916 .... **TCLC 51**
    See also CA 118; 137; DAM POET;
    MAICYA; SATA 17

Riley, Tex
    See Creasey, John

Rilke, Rainer Maria
    1875-1926 .... **TCLC 1, 6, 19; PC 2**
    See also CA 104; 132; DAM POET;
    DLB 81; MTCW

Rimbaud, (Jean Nicolas) Arthur
    1854-1891 ..... **NCLC 4, 35; DA; DAB;**
                          DAC; PC 3; WLC
    See also DAM MST, POET

Rinehart, Mary Roberts
    1876-1958 .... **TCLC 52**
    See also CA 108

Ringmaster, The
    See Mencken, H(enry) L(ouis)

Ringwood, Gwen(dolyn Margaret) Pharis
    1910-1984 .... **CLC 48**
    See also CA 148; 112; DLB 88

Rio, Michel 19(?)-................. **CLC 43**

Ritsos, Giannes
    See Ritsos, Yannis

Ritsos, Yannis 1909-1990..... **CLC 6, 13, 31**
    See also CA 77-80; 133; CANR 39; MTCW

Ritter, Erika 1948(?)-............. **CLC 52**

Rivera, Jose Eustasio 1889-1928... **TCLC 35**
    See also HW

Rivers, Conrad Kent 1933-1968...... **CLC 1**
    See also BW 1; CA 85-88; DLB 41

Rivers, Elfrida
    See Bradley, Marion Zimmer

Riverside, John
    See Heinlein, Robert A(nson)

Rizal, Jose 1861-1896.......... **NCLC 27**

Roa Bastos, Augusto (Antonio)
    1917- .... **CLC 45; HLC**
    See also CA 131; DAM MULT; DLB 113;
    HW

Robbe-Grillet, Alain
    1922- ...... **CLC 1, 2, 4, 6, 8, 10, 14, 43**
    See also CA 9-12R; CANR 33; DLB 83;
    MTCW

Robbins, Harold 1916-............. **CLC 5**
    See also CA 73-76; CANR 26; DAM NOV;
    MTCW

Robbins, Thomas Eugene 1936-
    See Robbins, Tom
    See also CA 81-84; CANR 29; DAM NOV,
    POP; MTCW

Robbins, Tom................ **CLC 9, 32, 64**
    See also Robbins, Thomas Eugene
    See also BEST 90:3; DLBY 80

Robbins, Trina 1938-............. **CLC 21**
    See also CA 128

Roberts, Charles G(eorge) D(ouglas)
    1860-1943 .... **TCLC 8**
    See also CA 105; CLR 33; DLB 92;
    SATA 88; SATA-Brief 29

Roberts, Kate 1891-1985 .... **CLC 15**
    See also CA 107; 116

Roberts, Keith (John Kingston)
    1935- .... **CLC 14**
    See also CA 25-28R; CANR 46

Roberts, Kenneth (Lewis)
    1885-1957 .... **TCLC 23**
    See also CA 109; DLB 9

Roberts, Michele (B.) 1949-........ **CLC 48**
    See also CA 115

Robertson, Ellis
    See Ellison, Harlan (Jay); Silverberg, Robert

Robertson, Thomas William
    1829-1871 .... **NCLC 35**
    See also DAM DRAM

Robinson, Edwin Arlington
    1869-1935 .... **TCLC 5; DA; DAC; PC 1**
    See also CA 104; 133; CDALB 1865-1917;
    DAM MST, POET; DLB 54; MTCW

Robinson, Henry Crabb
    1775-1867 .... **NCLC 15**
    See also DLB 107

Robinson, Jill 1936-.............. **CLC 10**
    See also CA 102; INT 102

Robinson, Kim Stanley 1952- ...... **CLC 34**
    See also CA 126

Robinson, Lloyd
    See Silverberg, Robert

Robinson, Marilynne 1944-........ **CLC 25**
    See also CA 116

Robinson, Smokey................. **CLC 21**
    See also Robinson, William, Jr.

Robinson, William, Jr. 1940-
    See Robinson, Smokey
    See also CA 116

Robison, Mary 1949-............. **CLC 42**
    See also CA 113; 116; DLB 130; INT 116

Rod, Edouard 1857-1910 .... **TCLC 52**

Roddenberry, Eugene Wesley 1921-1991
See Roddenberry, Gene
See also CA 110; 135; CANR 37; SATA 45;
SATA-Obit 69

Roddenberry, Gene .... **CLC 17**
See also Roddenberry, Eugene Wesley
See also AAYA 5; SATA-Obit 69

Rodgers, Mary 1931- .... **CLC 12**
See also CA 49-52; CANR 8; CLR 20;
INT CANR-8; JRDA; MAICYA;
SATA 8

Rodgers, W(illiam) R(obert)
1909-1969 .... **CLC 7**
See also CA 85-88; DLB 20

Rodman, Eric
See Silverberg, Robert

Rodman, Howard 1920(?)-1985 ..... **CLC 65**
See also CA 118

Rodman, Maia
See Wojciechowska, Maia (Teresa)

Rodriguez, Claudio 1934- .... **CLC 10**
See also DLB 134

Roelvaag, O(le) E(dvart)
1876-1931 .... **TCLC 17**
See also CA 117; DLB 9

Roethke, Theodore (Huebner)
1908-1963 ...... **CLC 1, 3, 8, 11, 19, 46;**
PC 15
See also CA 81-84; CABS 2;
CDALB 1941-1968; DAM POET; DLB 5;
MTCW

Rogers, Thomas Hunton 1927- ..... **CLC 57**
See also CA 89-92; INT 89-92

Rogers, Will(iam Penn Adair)
1879-1935 .... **TCLC 8**
See also CA 105; 144; DAM MULT;
DLB 11; NNAL

Rogin, Gilbert 1929- .... **CLC 18**
See also CA 65-68; CANR 15

Rohan, Koda .... **TCLC 22**
See also Koda Shigeyuki

Rohmer, Eric .... **CLC 16**
See also Scherer, Jean-Marie Maurice

Rohmer, Sax .... **TCLC 28**
See also Ward, Arthur Henry Sarsfield
See also DLB 70

Roiphe, Anne (Richardson)
1935- .... **CLC 3, 9**
See also CA 89-92; CANR 45; DLBY 80;
INT 89-92

Rojas, Fernando de 1465-1541 ..... **LC 23**

**Rolfe, Frederick (William Serafino Austin
Lewis Mary)** 1860-1913 ...... **TCLC 12**
See also CA 107; DLB 34, 156

Rolland, Romain 1866-1944 .... **TCLC 23**
See also CA 118; DLB 65

Rolvaag, O(le) E(dvart)
See Roelvaag, O(le) E(dvart)

Romain Arnaud, Saint
See Aragon, Louis

Romains, Jules 1885-1972 .... **CLC 7**
See also CA 85-88; CANR 34; DLB 65;
MTCW

Romero, Jose Ruben 1890-1952 ... **TCLC 14**
See also CA 114; 131; HW

Ronsard, Pierre de
1524-1585 .... **LC 6; PC 11**

Rooke, Leon 1934- .... **CLC 25, 34**
See also CA 25-28R; CANR 23, 53;
DAM POP

Roper, William 1498-1578 .... **LC 10**

Roquelaure, A. N.
See Rice, Anne

Rosa, Joao Guimaraes 1908-1967 ... **CLC 23**
See also CA 89-92; DLB 113

Rose, Wendy 1948- .... **CLC 85; PC 13**
See also CA 53-56; CANR 5, 51;
DAM MULT; NNAL; SATA 12

Rosen, Richard (Dean) 1949- .... **CLC 39**
See also CA 77-80; INT CANR-30

Rosenberg, Isaac 1890-1918 ...... **TCLC 12**
See also CA 107; DLB 20

Rosenblatt, Joe .... **CLC 15**
See also Rosenblatt, Joseph

Rosenblatt, Joseph 1933-
See Rosenblatt, Joe
See also CA 89-92; INT 89-92

Rosenfeld, Samuel 1896-1963
See Tzara, Tristan
See also CA 89-92

Rosenthal, M(acha) L(ouis) 1917- ... **CLC 28**
See also CA 1-4R; CAAS 6; CANR 4, 51;
DLB 5; SATA 59

Ross, Barnaby
See Dannay, Frederic

Ross, Bernard L.
See Follett, Ken(neth Martin)

Ross, J. H.
See Lawrence, T(homas) E(dward)

Ross, Martin
See Martin, Violet Florence
See also DLB 135

Ross, (James) Sinclair
1908- .... **CLC 13; DAC**
See also CA 73-76; DAM MST; DLB 88

Rossetti, Christina (Georgina)
1830-1894 ..... **NCLC 2, 50; DA; DAB;**
DAC; PC 7; WLC
See also DAM MST, POET; DLB 35, 163;
MAICYA; SATA 20

Rossetti, Dante Gabriel
1828-1882 .... **NCLC 4; DA; DAB;**
DAC; WLC
See also CDBLB 1832-1890; DAM MST,
POET; DLB 35

Rossner, Judith (Perelman)
1935- .... **CLC 6, 9, 29**
See also AITN 2; BEST 90:3; CA 17-20R;
CANR 18, 51; DLB 6; INT CANR-18;
MTCW

Rostand, Edmond (Eugene Alexis)
1868-1918 ...... **TCLC 6, 37; DA; DAB;**
DAC
See also CA 104; 126; DAM DRAM, MST;
MTCW

Roth, Henry 1906-1995 .... **CLC 2, 6, 11**
See also CA 11-12; 149; CANR 38; CAP 1;
DLB 28; MTCW

Roth, Joseph 1894-1939 .... **TCLC 33**
See also DLB 85

Roth, Philip (Milton)
1933- ...... **CLC 1, 2, 3, 4, 6, 9, 15, 22,**
31, 47, 66, 86; DA; DAB; DAC; WLC
See also BEST 90:3; CA 1-4R; CANR 1, 22,
36; CDALB 1968-1988; DAM MST,
NOV, POP; DLB 2, 28; DLBY 82;
MTCW

Rothenberg, Jerome 1931- .... **CLC 6, 57**
See also CA 45-48; CANR 1; DLB 5

Roumain, Jacques (Jean Baptiste)
1907-1944 .... **TCLC 19; BLC**
See also BW 1; CA 117; 125; DAM MULT

Rourke, Constance (Mayfield)
1885-1941 .... **TCLC 12**
See also CA 107; YABC 1

Rousseau, Jean-Baptiste 1671-1741 ... **LC 9**

Rousseau, Jean-Jacques
1712-1778 ..... **LC 14; DA; DAB; DAC;**
WLC
See also DAM MST

Roussel, Raymond 1877-1933 ..... **TCLC 20**
See also CA 117

Rovit, Earl (Herbert) 1927- .... **CLC 7**
See also CA 5-8R; CANR 12

Rowe, Nicholas 1674-1718 .... **LC 8**
See also DLB 84

Rowley, Ames Dorrance
See Lovecraft, H(oward) P(hillips)

Rowson, Susanna Haswell
1762(?)-1824 .... **NCLC 5**
See also DLB 37

Roy, Gabrielle
1909-1983 ..... **CLC 10, 14; DAB; DAC**
See also CA 53-56; 110; CANR 5;
DAM MST; DLB 68; MTCW

Rozewicz, Tadeusz 1921- .... **CLC 9, 23**
See also CA 108; CANR 36; DAM POET;
MTCW

Ruark, Gibbons 1941- .... **CLC 3**
See also CA 33-36R; CAAS 23; CANR 14,
31; DLB 120

Rubens, Bernice (Ruth) 1923- .... **CLC 19, 31**
See also CA 25-28R; CANR 33; DLB 14;
MTCW

Rudkin, (James) David 1936- ...... **CLC 14**
See also CA 89-92; DLB 13

Rudnik, Raphael 1933- .... **CLC 7**
See also CA 29-32R

Ruffian, M.
See Hasek, Jaroslav (Matej Frantisek)

Ruiz, Jose Martinez .... **CLC 11**
See also Martinez Ruiz, Jose

Rukeyser, Muriel
1913-1980 .... **CLC 6, 10, 15, 27; PC 12**
See also CA 5-8R; 93-96; CANR 26;
DAM POET; DLB 48; MTCW;
SATA-Obit 22

Rule, Jane (Vance) 1931- .... **CLC 27**
See also CA 25-28R; CAAS 18; CANR 12;
DLB 60

Rulfo, Juan 1918-1986 .... **CLC 8, 80; HLC**
See also CA 85-88; 118; CANR 26;
DAM MULT; DLB 113; HW; MTCW

Runeberg, Johan 1804-1877 ...... **NCLC 41**

Runyon, (Alfred) Damon
1884(?)-1946 .... TCLC 10
See also CA 107; DLB 11, 86

Rush, Norman 1933- .... CLC 44
See also CA 121; 126; INT 126

Rushdie, (Ahmed) Salman
1947- ...... CLC 23, 31, 55; DAB; DAC
See also BEST 89:3; CA 108; 111;
CANR 33; DAM MST, NOV, POP;
INT 111; MTCW

Rushforth, Peter (Scott) 1945- ..... CLC 19
See also CA 101

Ruskin, John 1819-1900 .... TCLC 63
See also CA 114; 129; CDBLB 1832-1890;
DLB 55, 163; SATA 24

Russ, Joanna 1937- .... CLC 15
See also CA 25-28R; CANR 11, 31; DLB 8;
MTCW

Russell, George William 1867-1935
See A. E.
See also CA 104; CDBLB 1890-1914;
DAM POET

Russell, (Henry) Ken(neth Alfred)
1927- .... CLC 16
See also CA 105

Russell, Willy 1947- .... CLC 60

Rutherford, Mark .... TCLC 25
See also White, William Hale
See also DLB 18

Ruyslinck, Ward 1929- .... CLC 14
See also Belser, Reimond Karel Maria de

Ryan, Cornelius (John) 1920-1974 ... CLC 7
See also CA 69-72; 53-56; CANR 38

Ryan, Michael 1946- .... CLC 65
See also CA 49-52; DLBY 82

Rybakov, Anatoli (Naumovich)
1911- .... CLC 23, 53
See also CA 126; 135; SATA 79

Ryder, Jonathan
See Ludlum, Robert

Ryga, George 1932-1987 ..... CLC 14; DAC
See also CA 101; 124; CANR 43;
DAM MST; DLB 60

S. S.
See Sassoon, Siegfried (Lorraine)

Saba, Umberto 1883-1957 .... TCLC 33
See also CA 144; DLB 114

Sabatini, Rafael 1875-1950 .... TCLC 47

Sabato, Ernesto (R.)
1911- .... CLC 10, 23; HLC
See also CA 97-100; CANR 32;
DAM MULT; DLB 145; HW; MTCW

Sacastru, Martin
See Bioy Casares, Adolfo

Sacher-Masoch, Leopold von
1836(?)-1895 .... NCLC 31

Sachs, Marilyn (Stickle) 1927- ..... CLC 35
See also AAYA 2; CA 17-20R; CANR 13,
47; CLR 2; JRDA; MAICYA; SAAS 2;
SATA 3, 68

Sachs, Nelly 1891-1970 .... CLC 14
See also CA 17-18; 25-28R; CAP 2

Sackler, Howard (Oliver)
1929-1982 .... CLC 14
See also CA 61-64; 108; CANR 30; DLB 7

Sacks, Oliver (Wolf) 1933- .... CLC 67
See also CA 53-56; CANR 28, 50;
INT CANR-28; MTCW

Sade, Donatien Alphonse Francois Comte
1740-1814 .... NCLC 47

Sadoff, Ira 1945- .... CLC 9
See also CA 53-56; CANR 5, 21; DLB 120

Saetone
See Camus, Albert

Safire, William 1929- .... CLC 10
See also CA 17-20R; CANR 31

Sagan, Carl (Edward) 1934- .... CLC 30
See also AAYA 2; CA 25-28R; CANR 11,
36; MTCW; SATA 58

Sagan, Francoise .... CLC 3, 6, 9, 17, 36
See also Quoirez, Francoise
See also DLB 83

Sahgal, Nayantara (Pandit) 1927- ... CLC 41
See also CA 9-12R; CANR 11

Saint, H(arry) F. 1941- .... CLC 50
See also CA 127

St. Aubin de Teran, Lisa 1953-
See Teran, Lisa St. Aubin de
See also CA 118; 126; INT 126

Sainte-Beuve, Charles Augustin
1804-1869 .... NCLC 5

**Saint-Exupery, Antoine (Jean Baptiste Marie
Roger) de**
1900-1944 .... TCLC 2, 56; WLC
See also CA 108; 132; CLR 10; DAM NOV;
DLB 72; MAICYA; MTCW; SATA 20

St. John, David
See Hunt, E(verette) Howard, (Jr.)

Saint-John Perse
See Leger, (Marie-Rene Auguste) Alexis
Saint-Leger

Saintsbury, George (Edward Bateman)
1845-1933 .... TCLC 31
See also DLB 57, 149

Sait Faik .... TCLC 23
See also Abasiyanik, Sait Faik

Saki .... TCLC 3; SSC 12
See also Munro, H(ector) H(ugh)

Sala, George Augustus .... NCLC 46

Salama, Hannu 1936- .... CLC 18

Salamanca, J(ack) R(ichard)
1922- .... CLC 4, 15
See also CA 25-28R

Sale, J. Kirkpatrick
See Sale, Kirkpatrick

Sale, Kirkpatrick 1937- .... CLC 68
See also CA 13-16R; CANR 10

Salinas, Luis Omar 1937- ... CLC 90; HLC
See also CA 131; DAM MULT; DLB 82;
HW

Salinas (y Serrano), Pedro
1891(?)-1951 .... TCLC 17
See also CA 117; DLB 134

Salinger, J(erome) D(avid)
1919- ...... CLC 1, 3, 8, 12, 55, 56; DA;
DAB; DAC; SSC 2; WLC
See also AAYA 2; CA 5-8R; CANR 39;
CDALB 1941-1968; CLR 18; DAM MST,
NOV, POP; DLB 2, 102; MAICYA;
MTCW; SATA 67

Salisbury, John
See Caute, David

Salter, James 1925- .... CLC 7, 52, 59
See also CA 73-76; DLB 130

Saltus, Edgar (Everton)
1855-1921 .... TCLC 8
See also CA 105

Saltykov, Mikhail Evgrafovich
1826-1889 .... NCLC 16

Samarakis, Antonis 1919- .... CLC 5
See also CA 25-28R; CAAS 16; CANR 36

Sanchez, Florencio 1875-1910 ..... TCLC 37
See also HW

Sanchez, Luis Rafael 1936- .... CLC 23
See also CA 128; DLB 145; HW

Sanchez, Sonia 1934- ... CLC 5; BLC; PC 9
See also BW 2; CA 33-36R; CANR 24, 49;
CLR 18; DAM MULT; DLB 41;
DLBD 8; MAICYA; MTCW; SATA 22

Sand, George
1804-1876 .... NCLC 2, 42, 57; DA;
DAB; DAC; WLC
See also DAM MST, NOV; DLB 119

Sandburg, Carl (August)
1878-1967 .... CLC 1, 4, 10, 15, 35; DA;
DAB; DAC; PC 2; WLC
See also CA 5-8R; 25-28R; CANR 35;
CDALB 1865-1917; DAM MST, POET;
DLB 17, 54; MAICYA; MTCW; SATA 8

Sandburg, Charles
See Sandburg, Carl (August)

Sandburg, Charles A.
See Sandburg, Carl (August)

Sanders, (James) Ed(ward) 1939- ... CLC 53
See also CA 13-16R; CAAS 21; CANR 13,
44; DLB 16

Sanders, Lawrence 1920- .... CLC 41
See also BEST 89:4; CA 81-84; CANR 33;
DAM POP; MTCW

Sanders, Noah
See Blount, Roy (Alton), Jr.

Sanders, Winston P.
See Anderson, Poul (William)

Sandoz, Mari(e Susette)
1896-1966 .... CLC 28
See also CA 1-4R; 25-28R; CANR 17;
DLB 9; MTCW; SATA 5

Saner, Reg(inald Anthony) 1931- .... CLC 9
See also CA 65-68

Sannazaro, Jacopo 1456(?)-1530 ...... LC 8

Sansom, William
1912-1976 .... CLC 2, 6; SSC 21
See also CA 5-8R; 65-68; CANR 42;
DAM NOV; DLB 139; MTCW

Santayana, George 1863-1952 ..... TCLC 40
See also CA 115; DLB 54, 71; DLBD 13

Santiago, Danny .... **CLC 33**
See also James, Daniel (Lewis)
See also DLB 122

Santmyer, Helen Hoover
1895-1986 .... **CLC 33**
See also CA 1-4R; 118; CANR 15, 33;
DLBY 84; MTCW

Santos, Bienvenido N(uqui)
1911-1996 .... **CLC 22**
See also CA 101; 151; CANR 19, 46;
DAM MULT

Sapper .... **TCLC 44**
See also McNeile, Herman Cyril

Sappho fl. 6th cent. B.C.- .... **CMLC 3; PC 5**
See also DAM POET

Sarduy, Severo 1937-1993 .... **CLC 6**
See also CA 89-92; 142; DLB 113; HW

Sargeson, Frank 1903-1982 .... **CLC 31**
See also CA 25-28R; 106; CANR 38

Sarmiento, Felix Ruben Garcia
See Dario, Ruben

Saroyan, William
1908-1981 ..... **CLC 1, 8, 10, 29, 34, 56;**
DA; DAB; DAC; SSC 21; WLC
See also CA 5-8R; 103; CANR 30;
DAM DRAM, MST, NOV; DLB 7, 9, 86;
DLBY 81; MTCW; SATA 23;
SATA-Obit 24

Sarraute, Nathalie
1900- .... **CLC 1, 2, 4, 8, 10, 31, 80**
See also CA 9-12R; CANR 23; DLB 83;
MTCW

Sarton, (Eleanor) May
1912-1995 .... **CLC 4, 14, 49, 91**
See also CA 1-4R; 149; CANR 1, 34;
DAM POET; DLB 48; DLBY 81;
INT CANR-34; MTCW; SATA 36;
SATA-Obit 86

Sartre, Jean-Paul
1905-1980 .... **CLC 1, 4, 7, 9, 13, 18, 24,**
44, 50, 52; DA; DAB; DAC; DC 3; WLC
See also CA 9-12R; 97-100; CANR 21;
DAM DRAM, MST, NOV; DLB 72;
MTCW

Sassoon, Siegfried (Lorraine)
1886-1967 .... **CLC 36; DAB; PC 12**
See also CA 104; 25-28R; CANR 36;
DAM MST, NOV, POET; DLB 20;
MTCW

Satterfield, Charles
See Pohl, Frederik

Saul, John (W. III) 1942- .... **CLC 46**
See also AAYA 10; BEST 90:4; CA 81-84;
CANR 16, 40; DAM NOV, POP

Saunders, Caleb
See Heinlein, Robert A(nson)

Saura (Atares), Carlos 1932- .... **CLC 20**
See also CA 114; 131; HW

Sauser-Hall, Frederic 1887-1961.... **CLC 18**
See also Cendrars, Blaise
See also CA 102; 93-96; CANR 36; MTCW

Saussure, Ferdinand de
1857-1913 .... **TCLC 49**

Savage, Catharine
See Brosman, Catharine Savage

Savage, Thomas 1915- .... **CLC 40**
See also CA 126; 132; CAAS 15; INT 132

Savan, Glenn 19(?)- .... **CLC 50**

Sayers, Dorothy L(eigh)
1893-1957 .... **TCLC 2, 15**
See also CA 104; 119; CDBLB 1914-1945;
DAM POP; DLB 10, 36, 77, 100; MTCW

Sayers, Valerie 1952- .... **CLC 50**
See also CA 134

Sayles, John (Thomas)
1950- .... **CLC 7, 10, 14**
See also CA 57-60; CANR 41; DLB 44

Scammell, Michael .... **CLC 34**

Scannell, Vernon 1922- .... **CLC 49**
See also CA 5-8R; CANR 8, 24; DLB 27;
SATA 59

Scarlett, Susan
See Streatfeild, (Mary) Noel

Schaeffer, Susan Fromberg
1941- .... **CLC 6, 11, 22**
See also CA 49-52; CANR 18; DLB 28;
MTCW; SATA 22

Schary, Jill
See Robinson, Jill

Schell, Jonathan 1943- .... **CLC 35**
See also CA 73-76; CANR 12

Schelling, Friedrich Wilhelm Joseph von
1775-1854 .... **NCLC 30**
See also DLB 90

Schendel, Arthur van 1874-1946 ... **TCLC 56**

Scherer, Jean-Marie Maurice 1920-
See Rohmer, Eric
See also CA 110

Schevill, James (Erwin) 1920-....... **CLC 7**
See also CA 5-8R; CAAS 12

Schiller, Friedrich 1759-1805 .... **NCLC 39**
See also DAM DRAM; DLB 94

Schisgal, Murray (Joseph) 1926-..... **CLC 6**
See also CA 21-24R; CANR 48

Schlee, Ann 1934-................ **CLC 35**
See also CA 101; CANR 29; SATA 44;
SATA-Brief 36

Schlegel, August Wilhelm von
1767-1845 .... **NCLC 15**
See also DLB 94

Schlegel, Friedrich 1772-1829 .... **NCLC 45**
See also DLB 90

Schlegel, Johann Elias (von)
1719(?)-1749 .... **LC 5**

Schlesinger, Arthur M(eier), Jr.
1917- .... **CLC 84**
See also AITN 1; CA 1-4R; CANR 1, 28;
DLB 17; INT CANR-28; MTCW;
SATA 61

Schmidt, Arno (Otto) 1914-1979.... **CLC 56**
See also CA 128; 109; DLB 69

Schmitz, Aron Hector 1861-1928
See Svevo, Italo
See also CA 104; 122; MTCW

Schnackenberg, Gjertrud 1953-..... **CLC 40**
See also CA 116; DLB 120

Schneider, Leonard Alfred 1925-1966
See Bruce, Lenny
See also CA 89-92

Schnitzler, Arthur
1862-1931 .... **TCLC 4; SSC 15**
See also CA 104; DLB 81, 118

Schopenhauer, Arthur
1788-1860 .... **NCLC 51**
See also DLB 90

Schor, Sandra (M.) 1932(?)-1990 ... **CLC 65**
See also CA 132

Schorer, Mark 1908-1977 .... **CLC 9**
See also CA 5-8R; 73-76; CANR 7;
DLB 103

Schrader, Paul (Joseph) 1946-...... **CLC 26**
See also CA 37-40R; CANR 41; DLB 44

Schreiner, Olive (Emilie Albertina)
1855-1920 .... **TCLC 9**
See also CA 105; DLB 18, 156

Schulberg, Budd (Wilson)
1914- .... **CLC 7, 48**
See also CA 25-28R; CANR 19; DLB 6, 26,
28; DLBY 81

Schulz, Bruno
1892-1942 .... **TCLC 5, 51; SSC 13**
See also CA 115; 123

Schulz, Charles M(onroe) 1922- .... **CLC 12**
See also CA 9-12R; CANR 6;
INT CANR-6; SATA 10

Schumacher, E(rnst) F(riedrich)
1911-1977 .... **CLC 80**
See also CA 81-84; 73-76; CANR 34

Schuyler, James Marcus
1923-1991 .... **CLC 5, 23**
See also CA 101; 134; DAM POET; DLB 5;
INT 101

Schwartz, Delmore (David)
1913-1966 ... **CLC 2, 4, 10, 45, 87; PC 8**
See also CA 17-18; 25-28R; CANR 35;
CAP 2; DLB 28, 48; MTCW

Schwartz, Ernst
See Ozu, Yasujiro

Schwartz, John Burnham 1965- .... **CLC 59**
See also CA 132

Schwartz, Lynne Sharon 1939-..... **CLC 31**
See also CA 103; CANR 44

Schwartz, Muriel A.
See Eliot, T(homas) S(tearns)

Schwarz-Bart, Andre 1928-....... **CLC 2, 4**
See also CA 89-92

Schwarz-Bart, Simone 1938-........ **CLC 7**
See also BW 2; CA 97-100

Schwob, (Mayer Andre) Marcel
1867-1905 .... **TCLC 20**
See also CA 117; DLB 123

Sciascia, Leonardo
1921-1989 .... **CLC 8, 9, 41**
See also CA 85-88; 130; CANR 35; MTCW

Scoppettone, Sandra 1936-......... **CLC 26**
See also AAYA 11; CA 5-8R; CANR 41;
SATA 9

Scorsese, Martin 1942- .... **CLC 20, 89**
See also CA 110; 114; CANR 46

Scotland, Jay
See Jakes, John (William)

Scott, Duncan Campbell
1862-1947 .... **TCLC 6; DAC**
See also CA 104; DLB 92

Scott, Evelyn 1893-1963 .... CLC 43
See also CA 104; 112; DLB 9, 48

Scott, F(rancis) R(eginald)
1899-1985 .... CLC 22
See also CA 101; 114; DLB 88; INT 101

Scott, Frank
See Scott, F(rancis) R(eginald)

Scott, Joanna 1960- .... CLC 50
See also CA 126; CANR 53

Scott, Paul (Mark) 1920-1978 .... CLC 9, 60
See also CA 81-84; 77-80; CANR 33;
DLB 14; MTCW

Scott, Walter
1771-1832 .... NCLC 15; DA; DAB;
DAC; PC 13; WLC
See also CDBLB 1789-1832; DAM MST,
NOV, POET; DLB 93, 107, 116, 144, 159;
YABC 2

Scribe, (Augustin) Eugene
1791-1861 .... NCLC 16; DC 5
See also DAM DRAM

Scrum, R.
See Crumb, R(obert)

Scudery, Madeleine de 1607-1701..... LC 2

Scum
See Crumb, R(obert)

Scumbag, Little Bobby
See Crumb, R(obert)

Seabrook, John
See Hubbard, L(afayette) Ron(ald)

Sealy, I. Allan 1951- .... CLC 55

Search, Alexander
See Pessoa, Fernando (Antonio Nogueira)

Sebastian, Lee
See Silverberg, Robert

Sebastian Owl
See Thompson, Hunter S(tockton)

Sebestyen, Ouida 1924- .... CLC 30
See also AAYA 8; CA 107; CANR 40;
CLR 17; JRDA; MAICYA; SAAS 10;
SATA 39

Secundus, H. Scriblerus
See Fielding, Henry

Sedges, John
See Buck, Pearl S(ydenstricker)

Sedgwick, Catharine Maria
1789-1867 .... NCLC 19
See also DLB 1, 74

Seelye, John 1931- .... CLC 7

Seferiades, Giorgos Stylianou 1900-1971
See Seferis, George
See also CA 5-8R; 33-36R; CANR 5, 36;
MTCW

Seferis, George .... CLC 5, 11
See also Seferiades, Giorgos Stylianou

Segal, Erich (Wolf) 1937- .... CLC 3, 10
See also BEST 89:1; CA 25-28R; CANR 20,
36; DAM POP; DLBY 86;
INT CANR-20; MTCW

Seger, Bob 1945-................. CLC 35

Seghers, Anna .... CLC 7
See also Radvanyi, Netty
See also DLB 69

Seidel, Frederick (Lewis) 1936-..... CLC 18
See also CA 13-16R; CANR 8; DLBY 84

Seifert, Jaroslav
1901-1986 .... CLC 34, 44, 93
See also CA 127; MTCW

Sei Shonagon c. 966-1017(?) ...... CMLC 6

Selby, Hubert, Jr.
1928- .... CLC 1, 2, 4, 8; SSC 20
See also CA 13-16R; CANR 33; DLB 2

Selzer, Richard 1928-............. CLC 74
See also CA 65-68; CANR 14

Sembene, Ousmane
See Ousmane, Sembene

Senancour, Etienne Pivert de
1770-1846 .... NCLC 16
See also DLB 119

Sender, Ramon (Jose)
1902-1982 .... CLC 8; HLC
See also CA 5-8R; 105; CANR 8;
DAM MULT; HW; MTCW

Seneca, Lucius Annaeus
4B.C.-65.............. CMLC 6; DC 5
See also DAM DRAM

Senghor, Leopold Sedar
1906- .... CLC 54; BLC
See also BW 2; CA 116; 125; CANR 47;
DAM MULT, POET; MTCW

Serling, (Edward) Rod(man)
1924-1975 .... CLC 30
See also AAYA 14; AITN 1; CA 65-68;
57-60; DLB 26

Serna, Ramon Gomez de la
See Gomez de la Serna, Ramon

Serpieres
See Guillevic, (Eugene)

Service, Robert
See Service, Robert W(illiam)
See also DAB; DLB 92

Service, Robert W(illiam)
1874(?)-1958 ...... TCLC 15; DA; DAC;
WLC
See also Service, Robert
See also CA 115; 140; DAM MST, POET;
SATA 20

Seth, Vikram 1952-............ CLC 43, 90
See also CA 121; 127; CANR 50;
DAM MULT; DLB 120; INT 127

Seton, Cynthia Propper
1926-1982 .... CLC 27
See also CA 5-8R; 108; CANR 7

Seton, Ernest (Evan) Thompson
1860-1946 .... TCLC 31
See also CA 109; DLB 92; DLBD 13;
JRDA; SATA 18

Seton-Thompson, Ernest
See Seton, Ernest (Evan) Thompson

Settle, Mary Lee 1918- .... CLC 19, 61
See also CA 89-92; CAAS 1; CANR 44;
DLB 6; INT 89-92

Seuphor, Michel
See Arp, Jean

Sevigne, Marie (de Rabutin-Chantal) Marquise
de 1626-1696 .... LC 11

Sexton, Anne (Harvey)
1928-1974 .... CLC 2, 4, 6, 8, 10, 15, 53;
DA; DAB; DAC; PC 2; WLC
See also CA 1-4R; 53-56; CABS 2;
CANR 3, 36; CDALB 1941-1968;
DAM MST, POET; DLB 5; MTCW;
SATA 10

Shaara, Michael (Joseph, Jr.)
1929-1988 .... CLC 15
See also AITN 1; CA 102; 125; CANR 52;
DAM POP; DLBY 83

Shackleton, C. C.
See Aldiss, Brian W(ilson)

Shacochis, Bob .... CLC 39
See also Shacochis, Robert G.

Shacochis, Robert G. 1951-
See Shacochis, Bob
See also CA 119; 124; INT 124

Shaffer, Anthony (Joshua) 1926-.... CLC 19
See also CA 110; 116; DAM DRAM;
DLB 13

Shaffer, Peter (Levin)
1926- ...... CLC 5, 14, 18, 37, 60; DAB
See also CA 25-28R; CANR 25, 47;
CDBLB 1960 to Present; DAM DRAM,
MST; DLB 13; MTCW

Shakey, Bernard
See Young, Neil

Shalamov, Varlam (Tikhonovich)
1907(?)-1982 .... CLC 18
See also CA 129; 105

Shamlu, Ahmad 1925- .... CLC 10

Shammas, Anton 1951-........... CLC 55

Shange, Ntozake
1948- .... CLC 8, 25, 38, 74; BLC; DC 3
See also AAYA 9; BW 2; CA 85-88;
CABS 3; CANR 27, 48; DAM DRAM,
MULT; DLB 38; MTCW

Shanley, John Patrick 1950-....... CLC 75
See also CA 128; 133

Shapcott, Thomas W(illiam) 1935- .. CLC 38
See also CA 69-72; CANR 49

Shapiro, Jane..................... CLC 76

Shapiro, Karl (Jay) 1913- .. CLC 4, 8, 15, 53
See also CA 1-4R; CAAS 6; CANR 1, 36;
DLB 48; MTCW

Sharp, William 1855-1905 .... TCLC 39
See also DLB 156

Sharpe, Thomas Ridley 1928-
See Sharpe, Tom
See also CA 114; 122; INT 122

Sharpe, Tom..................... CLC 36
See also Sharpe, Thomas Ridley
See also DLB 14

Shaw, Bernard.................. TCLC 45
See also Shaw, George Bernard
See also BW 1

Shaw, G. Bernard
See Shaw, George Bernard

Shaw, George Bernard
1856-1950 ... **TCLC 3, 9, 21; DA; DAB;
DAC; WLC**
See also Shaw, Bernard
See also CA 104; 128; CDBLB 1914-1945;
DAM DRAM, MST; DLB 10, 57;
MTCW

Shaw, Henry Wheeler
1818-1885 .... **NCLC 15**
See also DLB 11

Shaw, Irwin 1913-1984 ...... **CLC 7, 23, 34**
See also AITN 1; CA 13-16R; 112;
CANR 21; CDALB 1941-1968;
DAM DRAM, POP; DLB 6, 102;
DLBY 84; MTCW

Shaw, Robert 1927-1978 .... **CLC 5**
See also AITN 1; CA 1-4R; 81-84;
CANR 4; DLB 13, 14

Shaw, T. E.
See Lawrence, T(homas) E(dward)

Shawn, Wallace 1943- .... **CLC 41**
See also CA 112

Shea, Lisa 1953- .... **CLC 86**
See also CA 147

Sheed, Wilfrid (John Joseph)
1930- .... **CLC 2, 4, 10, 53**
See also CA 65-68; CANR 30; DLB 6;
MTCW

Sheldon, Alice Hastings Bradley
1915(?)-1987
See Tiptree, James, Jr.
See also CA 108; 122; CANR 34; INT 108;
MTCW

Sheldon, John
See Bloch, Robert (Albert)

Shelley, Mary Wollstonecraft (Godwin)
1797-1851 .... **NCLC 14; DA; DAB;
DAC; WLC**
See also CDBLB 1789-1832; DAM MST,
NOV; DLB 110, 116, 159; SATA 29

Shelley, Percy Bysshe
1792-1822 .... **NCLC 18; DA; DAB;
DAC; PC 14; WLC**
See also CDBLB 1789-1832; DAM MST,
POET; DLB 96, 110, 158

Shepard, Jim 1956- .... **CLC 36**
See also CA 137

Shepard, Lucius 1947- .... **CLC 34**
See also CA 128; 141

Shepard, Sam
1943- .... **CLC 4, 6, 17, 34, 41, 44; DC 5**
See also AAYA 1; CA 69-72; CABS 3;
CANR 22; DAM DRAM; DLB 7;
MTCW

Shepherd, Michael
See Ludlum, Robert

Sherburne, Zoa (Morin) 1912- ...... **CLC 30**
See also AAYA 13; CA 1-4R; CANR 3, 37;
MAICYA; SAAS 18; SATA 3

Sheridan, Frances 1724-1766 .... **LC 7**
See also DLB 39, 84

Sheridan, Richard Brinsley
1751-1816 .... **NCLC 5; DA; DAB;
DAC; DC 1; WLC**
See also CDBLB 1660-1789; DAM DRAM,
MST; DLB 89

Sherman, Jonathan Marc .... **CLC 55**

Sherman, Martin 1941(?)- .... **CLC 19**
See also CA 116; 123

Sherwin, Judith Johnson 1936- ... **CLC 7, 15**
See also CA 25-28R; CANR 34

Sherwood, Frances 1940- .... **CLC 81**
See also CA 146

Sherwood, Robert E(mmet)
1896-1955 .... **TCLC 3**
See also CA 104; DAM DRAM; DLB 7, 26

Shestov, Lev 1866-1938 .... **TCLC 56**

Shevchenko, Taras 1814-1861 .... **NCLC 54**

Shiel, M(atthew) P(hipps)
1865-1947 .... **TCLC 8**
See also CA 106; DLB 153

Shields, Carol 1935- .... **CLC 91; DAC**
See also CA 81-84; CANR 51

Shiga, Naoya 1883-1971... **CLC 33; SSC 23**
See also CA 101; 33-36R

Shilts, Randy 1951-1994 .... **CLC 85**
See also CA 115; 127; 144; CANR 45;
INT 127

Shimazaki, Haruki 1872-1943
See Shimazaki Toson
See also CA 105; 134

Shimazaki Toson .... **TCLC 5**
See also Shimazaki, Haruki

Sholokhov, Mikhail (Aleksandrovich)
1905-1984 .... **CLC 7, 15**
See also CA 101; 112; MTCW;
SATA-Obit 36

Shone, Patric
See Hanley, James

Shreve, Susan Richards 1939- ...... **CLC 23**
See also CA 49-52; CAAS 5; CANR 5, 38;
MAICYA; SATA 46; SATA-Brief 41

Shue, Larry 1946-1985 .... **CLC 52**
See also CA 145; 117; DAM DRAM

Shu-Jen, Chou 1881-1936
See Lu Hsun
See also CA 104

Shulman, Alix Kates 1932- ...... **CLC 2, 10**
See also CA 29-32R; CANR 43; SATA 7

Shuster, Joe 1914- .... **CLC 21**

Shute, Nevil .... **CLC 30**
See also Norway, Nevil Shute

Shuttle, Penelope (Diane) 1947- ..... **CLC 7**
See also CA 93-96; CANR 39; DLB 14, 40

Sidney, Mary 1561-1621 .... **LC 19**

Sidney, Sir Philip
1554-1586 ..... **LC 19; DA; DAB; DAC**
See also CDBLB Before 1660; DAM MST,
POET; DLB 167

Siegel, Jerome 1914-1996 .... **CLC 21**
See also CA 116; 151

Siegel, Jerry
See Siegel, Jerome

Sienkiewicz, Henryk (Adam Alexander Pius)
1846-1916 .... **TCLC 3**
See also CA 104; 134

Sierra, Gregorio Martinez
See Martinez Sierra, Gregorio

Sierra, Maria (de la O'LeJarraga) Martinez
See Martinez Sierra, Maria (de la
O'LeJarraga)

Sigal, Clancy 1926- .... **CLC 7**
See also CA 1-4R

Sigourney, Lydia Howard (Huntley)
1791-1865 .... **NCLC 21**
See also DLB 1, 42, 73

Siguenza y Gongora, Carlos de
1645-1700 .... **LC 8**

Sigurjonsson, Johann 1880-1919... **TCLC 27**

Sikelianos, Angelos 1884-1951 .... **TCLC 39**

Silkin, Jon 1930- .... **CLC 2, 6, 43**
See also CA 5-8R; CAAS 5; DLB 27

Silko, Leslie (Marmon)
1948- .... **CLC 23, 74; DA; DAC**
See also AAYA 14; CA 115; 122;
CANR 45; DAM MST, MULT, POP;
DLB 143; NNAL

Sillanpaa, Frans Eemil 1888-1964... **CLC 19**
See also CA 129; 93-96; MTCW

Sillitoe, Alan
1928- .... **CLC 1, 3, 6, 10, 19, 57**
See also AITN 1; CA 9-12R; CAAS 2;
CANR 8, 26; CDBLB 1960 to Present;
DLB 14, 139; MTCW; SATA 61

Silone, Ignazio 1900-1978 .... **CLC 4**
See also CA 25-28; 81-84; CANR 34;
CAP 2; MTCW

Silver, Joan Micklin 1935- .... **CLC 20**
See also CA 114; 121; INT 121

Silver, Nicholas
See Faust, Frederick (Schiller)

Silverberg, Robert 1935- .... **CLC 7**
See also CA 1-4R; CAAS 3; CANR 1, 20,
36; DAM POP; DLB 8; INT CANR-20;
MAICYA; MTCW; SATA 13

Silverstein, Alvin 1933- .... **CLC 17**
See also CA 49-52; CANR 2; CLR 25;
JRDA; MAICYA; SATA 8, 69

Silverstein, Virginia B(arbara Opshelor)
1937- .... **CLC 17**
See also CA 49-52; CANR 2; CLR 25;
JRDA; MAICYA; SATA 8, 69

Sim, Georges
See Simenon, Georges (Jacques Christian)

Simak, Clifford D(onald)
1904-1988 .... **CLC 1, 55**
See also CA 1-4R; 125; CANR 1, 35;
DLB 8; MTCW; SATA-Obit 56

Simenon, Georges (Jacques Christian)
1903-1989 .... **CLC 1, 2, 3, 8, 18, 47**
See also CA 85-88; 129; CANR 35;
DAM POP; DLB 72; DLBY 89; MTCW

Simic, Charles 1938-... **CLC 6, 9, 22, 49, 68**
See also CA 29-32R; CAAS 4; CANR 12,
33, 52; DAM POET; DLB 105

Simmel, Georg 1858-1918 .... **TCLC 64**

Simmons, Charles (Paul) 1924- ..... **CLC 57**
See also CA 89-92; INT 89-92

Simmons, Dan 1948- .... **CLC 44**
See also AAYA 16; CA 138; CANR 53;
DAM POP

Simmons, James (Stewart Alexander)
1933- .... CLC 43
See also CA 105; CAAS 21; DLB 40

Simms, William Gilmore
1806-1870 .... NCLC 3
See also DLB 3, 30, 59, 73

Simon, Carly 1945-.............. CLC 26
See also CA 105

Simon, Claude 1913-...... CLC 4, 9, 15, 39
See also CA 89-92; CANR 33; DAM NOV;
DLB 83; MTCW

Simon, (Marvin) Neil
1927- .... CLC 6, 11, 31, 39, 70
See also AITN 1; CA 21-24R; CANR 26;
DAM DRAM; DLB 7; MTCW

Simon, Paul 1942(?)- .... CLC 17
See also CA 116

Simonon, Paul 1956(?)- .... CLC 30

Simpson, Harriette
See Arnow, Harriette (Louisa) Simpson

Simpson, Louis (Aston Marantz)
1923- .... CLC 4, 7, 9, 32
See also CA 1-4R; CAAS 4; CANR 1;
DAM POET; DLB 5; MTCW

Simpson, Mona (Elizabeth) 1957-... CLC 44
See also CA 122; 135

Simpson, N(orman) F(rederick)
1919- .... CLC 29
See also CA 13-16R; DLB 13

Sinclair, Andrew (Annandale)
1935- .... CLC 2, 14
See also CA 9-12R; CAAS 5; CANR 14, 38;
DLB 14; MTCW

Sinclair, Emil
See Hesse, Hermann

Sinclair, Iain 1943-.............. CLC 76
See also CA 132

Sinclair, Iain MacGregor
See Sinclair, Iain

Sinclair, Mary Amelia St. Clair 1865(?)-1946
See Sinclair, May
See also CA 104

Sinclair, May.................. TCLC 3, 11
See also Sinclair, Mary Amelia St. Clair
See also DLB 36, 135

Sinclair, Upton (Beall)
1878-1968 ...... CLC 1, 11, 15, 63; DA;
DAB; DAC; WLC
See also CA 5-8R; 25-28R; CANR 7;
CDALB 1929-1941; DAM MST, NOV;
DLB 9; INT CANR-7; MTCW; SATA 9

Singer, Isaac
See Singer, Isaac Bashevis

Singer, Isaac Bashevis
1904-1991 .... CLC 1, 3, 6, 9, 11, 15, 23,
38, 69; DA; DAB; DAC; SSC 3; WLC
See also AITN 1, 2; CA 1-4R; 134;
CANR 1, 39; CDALB 1941-1968; CLR 1;
DAM MST, NOV; DLB 6, 28, 52;
DLBY 91; JRDA; MAICYA; MTCW;
SATA 3, 27; SATA-Obit 68

Singer, Israel Joshua 1893-1944 ... TCLC 33

Singh, Khushwant 1915-........... CLC 11
See also CA 9-12R; CAAS 9; CANR 6

Sinjohn, John
See Galsworthy, John

Sinyavsky, Andrei (Donatevich)
1925- .... CLC 8
See also CA 85-88

Sirin, V.
See Nabokov, Vladimir (Vladimirovich)

Sissman, L(ouis) E(dward)
1928-1976 .... CLC 9, 18
See also CA 21-24R; 65-68; CANR 13;
DLB 5

Sisson, C(harles) H(ubert) 1914-..... CLC 8
See also CA 1-4R; CAAS 3; CANR 3, 48;
DLB 27

Sitwell, Dame Edith
1887-1964 .... CLC 2, 9, 67; PC 3
See also CA 9-12R; CANR 35;
CDBLB 1945-1960; DAM POET;
DLB 20; MTCW

Sjoewall, Maj 1935-.............. CLC 7
See also CA 65-68

Sjowall, Maj
See Sjoewall, Maj

Skelton, Robin 1925-............. CLC 13
See also AITN 2; CA 5-8R; CAAS 5;
CANR 28; DLB 27, 53

Skolimowski, Jerzy 1938-......... CLC 20
See also CA 128

Skram, Amalie (Bertha)
1847-1905 .... TCLC 25

Skvorecky, Josef (Vaclav)
1924- .... CLC 15, 39, 69; DAC
See also CA 61-64; CAAS 1; CANR 10, 34;
DAM NOV; MTCW

Slade, Bernard................. CLC 11, 46
See also Newbound, Bernard Slade
See also CAAS 9; DLB 53

Slaughter, Carolyn 1946-.......... CLC 56
See also CA 85-88

Slaughter, Frank G(ill) 1908- ...... CLC 29
See also AITN 2; CA 5-8R; CANR 5;
INT CANR-5

Slavitt, David R(ytman) 1935-.... CLC 5, 14
See also CA 21-24R; CAAS 3; CANR 41;
DLB 5, 6

Slesinger, Tess 1905-1945 .... TCLC 10
See also CA 107; DLB 102

Slessor, Kenneth 1901-1971........ CLC 14
See also CA 102; 89-92

Slowacki, Juliusz 1809-1849 ..... NCLC 15

Smart, Christopher
1722-1771 .... LC 3; PC 13
See also DAM POET; DLB 109

Smart, Elizabeth 1913-1986........ CLC 54
See also CA 81-84; 118; DLB 88

Smiley, Jane (Graves) 1949- .... CLC 53, 76
See also CA 104; CANR 30, 50;
DAM POP; INT CANR-30

Smith, A(rthur) J(ames) M(arshall)
1902-1980 .... CLC 15; DAC
See also CA 1-4R; 102; CANR 4; DLB 88

Smith, Anna Deavere 1950-........ CLC 86
See also CA 133

Smith, Betty (Wehner) 1896-1972... CLC 19
See also CA 5-8R; 33-36R; DLBY 82;
SATA 6

Smith, Charlotte (Turner)
1749-1806 .... NCLC 23
See also DLB 39, 109

Smith, Clark Ashton 1893-1961 .... CLC 43
See also CA 143

Smith, Dave................... CLC 22, 42
See also Smith, David (Jeddie)
See also CAAS 7; DLB 5

Smith, David (Jeddie) 1942-
See Smith, Dave
See also CA 49-52; CANR 1; DAM POET

Smith, Florence Margaret 1902-1971
See Smith, Stevie
See also CA 17-18; 29-32R; CANR 35;
CAP 2; DAM POET; MTCW

Smith, Iain Crichton 1928- .... CLC 64
See also CA 21-24R; DLB 40, 139

Smith, John 1580(?)-1631 .... LC 9

Smith, Johnston
See Crane, Stephen (Townley)

Smith, Joseph, Jr. 1805-1844 .... NCLC 53

Smith, Lee 1944-.............. CLC 25, 73
See also CA 114; 119; CANR 46; DLB 143;
DLBY 83; INT 119

Smith, Martin
See Smith, Martin Cruz

Smith, Martin Cruz 1942-......... CLC 25
See also BEST 89:4; CA 85-88; CANR 6,
23, 43; DAM MULT, POP;
INT CANR-23; NNAL

Smith, Mary-Ann Tirone 1944-..... CLC 39
See also CA 118; 136

Smith, Patti 1946- .... CLC 12
See also CA 93-96

Smith, Pauline (Urmson)
1882-1959 .... TCLC 25

Smith, Rosamond
See Oates, Joyce Carol

Smith, Sheila Kaye
See Kaye-Smith, Sheila

Smith, Stevie....... CLC 3, 8, 25, 44; PC 12
See also Smith, Florence Margaret
See also DLB 20

Smith, Wilbur (Addison) 1933-..... CLC 33
See also CA 13-16R; CANR 7, 46; MTCW

Smith, William Jay 1918- .... CLC 6
See also CA 5-8R; CANR 44; DLB 5;
MAICYA; SAAS 22; SATA 2, 68

Smith, Woodrow Wilson
See Kuttner, Henry

Smolenskin, Peretz 1842-1885.... NCLC 30

Smollett, Tobias (George) 1721-1771 .. LC 2
See also CDBLB 1660-1789; DLB 39, 104

Snodgrass, W(illiam) D(e Witt)
1926- .... CLC 2, 6, 10, 18, 68
See also CA 1-4R; CANR 6, 36;
DAM POET; DLB 5; MTCW

Snow, C(harles) P(ercy)
    1905-1980 ...... **CLC 1, 4, 6, 9, 13, 19**
    See also CA 5-8R; 101; CANR 28;
    CDBLB 1945-1960; DAM NOV; DLB 15,
    77; MTCW

Snow, Frances Compton
    See Adams, Henry (Brooks)

Snyder, Gary (Sherman)
    1930- .... **CLC 1, 2, 5, 9, 32**
    See also CA 17-20R; CANR 30;
    DAM POET; DLB 5, 16, 165

Snyder, Zilpha Keatley   1927- ...... **CLC 17**
    See also AAYA 15; CA 9-12R; CANR 38;
    CLR 31; JRDA; MAICYA; SAAS 2;
    SATA 1, 28, 75

Soares, Bernardo
    See Pessoa, Fernando (Antonio Nogueira)

Sobh, A.
    See Shamlu, Ahmad

Sobol, Joshua.................... **CLC 60**

Soderberg, Hjalmar   1869-1941 .... **TCLC 39**

Sodergran, Edith (Irene)
    See Soedergran, Edith (Irene)

Soedergran, Edith (Irene)
    1892-1923 .... **TCLC 31**

Softly, Edgar
    See Lovecraft, H(oward) P(hillips)

Softly, Edward
    See Lovecraft, H(oward) P(hillips)

Sokolov, Raymond   1941-.......... **CLC 7**
    See also CA 85-88

Solo, Jay
    See Ellison, Harlan (Jay)

Sologub, Fyodor .... **TCLC 9**
    See also Teternikov, Fyodor Kuzmich

Solomons, Ikey Esquir
    See Thackeray, William Makepeace

Solomos, Dionysios   1798-1857 ... **NCLC 15**

Solwoska, Mara
    See French, Marilyn

Solzhenitsyn, Aleksandr I(sayevich)
    1918- ...... **CLC 1, 2, 4, 7, 9, 10, 18, 26,
        34, 78; DA; DAB; DAC; WLC**
    See also AITN 1; CA 69-72; CANR 40;
    DAM MST, NOV; MTCW

Somers, Jane
    See Lessing, Doris (May)

Somerville, Edith   1858-1949 ...... **TCLC 51**
    See also DLB 135

Somerville & Ross
    See Martin, Violet Florence; Somerville,
    Edith

Sommer, Scott   1951- .... **CLC 25**
    See also CA 106

Sondheim, Stephen (Joshua)
    1930- .... **CLC 30, 39**
    See also AAYA 11; CA 103; CANR 47;
    DAM DRAM

Sontag, Susan   1933-... **CLC 1, 2, 10, 13, 31**
    See also CA 17-20R; CANR 25, 51;
    DAM POP; DLB 2, 67; MTCW

Sophocles
    496(?)B.C.-406(?)B.C..... **CMLC 2; DA;
        DAB; DAC; DC 1**
    See also DAM DRAM, MST

Sordello   1189-1269 .... **CMLC 15**

Sorel, Julia
    See Drexler, Rosalyn

Sorrentino, Gilbert
    1929- .... **CLC 3, 7, 14, 22, 40**
    See also CA 77-80; CANR 14, 33; DLB 5;
    DLBY 80; INT CANR-14

Soto, Gary   1952-........ **CLC 32, 80; HLC**
    See also AAYA 10; CA 119; 125;
    CANR 50; CLR 38; DAM MULT;
    DLB 82; HW; INT 125; JRDA; SATA 80

Soupault, Philippe   1897-1990 ...... **CLC 68**
    See also CA 116; 147; 131

Souster, (Holmes) Raymond
    1921- .... **CLC 5, 14; DAC**
    See also CA 13-16R; CAAS 14; CANR 13,
    29, 53; DAM POET; DLB 88; SATA 63

Southern, Terry   1924(?)-1995 .... **CLC 7**
    See also CA 1-4R; 150; CANR 1; DLB 2

Southey, Robert   1774-1843 .... **NCLC 8**
    See also DLB 93, 107, 142; SATA 54

Southworth, Emma Dorothy Eliza Nevitte
    1819-1899 .... **NCLC 26**

Souza, Ernest
    See Scott, Evelyn

Soyinka, Wole
    1934- .... **CLC 3, 5, 14, 36, 44; BLC;
        DA; DAB; DAC; DC 2; WLC**
    See also BW 2; CA 13-16R; CANR 27, 39;
    DAM DRAM, MST, MULT; DLB 125;
    MTCW

Spackman, W(illiam) M(ode)
    1905-1990 .... **CLC 46**
    See also CA 81-84; 132

Spacks, Barry   1931-.............. **CLC 14**
    See also CA 29-32R; CANR 33; DLB 105

Spanidou, Irini   1946- .... **CLC 44**

Spark, Muriel (Sarah)
    1918- ..... **CLC 2, 3, 5, 8, 13, 18, 40, 94;
        DAB; DAC; SSC 10**
    See also CA 5-8R; CANR 12, 36;
    CDBLB 1945-1960; DAM MST, NOV;
    DLB 15, 139; INT CANR-12; MTCW

Spaulding, Douglas
    See Bradbury, Ray (Douglas)

Spaulding, Leonard
    See Bradbury, Ray (Douglas)

Spence, J. A. D.
    See Eliot, T(homas) S(tearns)

Spencer, Elizabeth   1921-.......... **CLC 22**
    See also CA 13-16R; CANR 32; DLB 6;
    MTCW; SATA 14

Spencer, Leonard G.
    See Silverberg, Robert

Spencer, Scott   1945-.............. **CLC 30**
    See also CA 113; CANR 51; DLBY 86

Spender, Stephen (Harold)
    1909-1995 ...... **CLC 1, 2, 5, 10, 41, 91**
    See also CA 9-12R; 149; CANR 31;
    CDBLB 1945-1960; DAM POET;
    DLB 20; MTCW

Spengler, Oswald (Arnold Gottfried)
    1880-1936 .... **TCLC 25**
    See also CA 118

Spenser, Edmund
    1552(?)-1599 .... **LC 5; DA; DAB; DAC;
        PC 8; WLC**
    See also CDBLB Before 1660; DAM MST,
    POET; DLB 167

Spicer, Jack   1925-1965 ...... **CLC 8, 18, 72**
    See also CA 85-88; DAM POET; DLB 5, 16

Spiegelman, Art   1948- .... **CLC 76**
    See also AAYA 10; CA 125; CANR 41

Spielberg, Peter   1929- .... **CLC 6**
    See also CA 5-8R; CANR 4, 48; DLBY 81

Spielberg, Steven   1947- .... **CLC 20**
    See also AAYA 8; CA 77-80; CANR 32;
    SATA 32

Spillane, Frank Morrison   1918-
    See Spillane, Mickey
    See also CA 25-28R; CANR 28; MTCW;
    SATA 66

Spillane, Mickey .... **CLC 3, 13**
    See also Spillane, Frank Morrison

Spinoza, Benedictus de   1632-1677 .... **LC 9**

Spinrad, Norman (Richard)   1940-... **CLC 46**
    See also CA 37-40R; CAAS 19; CANR 20;
    DLB 8; INT CANR-20

Spitteler, Carl (Friedrich Georg)
    1845-1924 .... **TCLC 12**
    See also CA 109; DLB 129

Spivack, Kathleen (Romola Drucker)
    1938- .... **CLC 6**
    See also CA 49-52

Spoto, Donald   1941-............... **CLC 39**
    See also CA 65-68; CANR 11

Springsteen, Bruce (F.)   1949- ...... **CLC 17**
    See also CA 111

Spurling, Hilary   1940-............ **CLC 34**
    See also CA 104; CANR 25, 52

Spyker, John Howland
    See Elman, Richard

Squires, (James) Radcliffe
    1917-1993 .... **CLC 51**
    See also CA 1-4R; 140; CANR 6, 21

Srivastava, Dhanpat Rai   1880(?)-1936
    See Premchand
    See also CA 118

Stacy, Donald
    See Pohl, Frederik

Stael, Germaine de
    See Stael-Holstein, Anne Louise Germaine
    Necker Baronn
    See also DLB 119

Stael-Holstein, Anne Louise Germaine Necker
    Baronn   1766-1817 .... **NCLC 3**
    See also Stael, Germaine de

Stafford, Jean   1915-1979 ... **CLC 4, 7, 19, 68**
    See also CA 1-4R; 85-88; CANR 3; DLB 2;
    MTCW; SATA-Obit 22

Stafford, William (Edgar)
    1914-1993 .... **CLC 4, 7, 29**
    See also CA 5-8R; 142; CAAS 3; CANR 5,
    22; DAM POET; DLB 5; INT CANR-22

Staines, Trevor
    See Brunner, John (Kilian Houston)

Stairs, Gordon
See Austin, Mary (Hunter)

Stannard, Martin 1947-........... **CLC 44**
See also CA 142; DLB 155

Stanton, Maura 1946- .... **CLC 9**
See also CA 89-92; CANR 15; DLB 120

Stanton, Schuyler
See Baum, L(yman) Frank

Stapledon, (William) Olaf
1886-1950 .... **TCLC 22**
See also CA 111; DLB 15

Starbuck, George (Edwin) 1931-.... **CLC 53**
See also CA 21-24R; CANR 23;
DAM POET

Stark, Richard
See Westlake, Donald E(dwin)

Staunton, Schuyler
See Baum, L(yman) Frank

Stead, Christina (Ellen)
1902-1983 .... **CLC 2, 5, 8, 32, 80**
See also CA 13-16R; 109; CANR 33, 40;
MTCW

Stead, William Thomas
1849-1912 .... **TCLC 48**

Steele, Richard 1672-1729 .... **LC 18**
See also CDBLB 1660-1789; DLB 84, 101

Steele, Timothy (Reid) 1948-....... **CLC 45**
See also CA 93-96; CANR 16, 50; DLB 120

Steffens, (Joseph) Lincoln
1866-1936 .... **TCLC 20**
See also CA 117

Stegner, Wallace (Earle)
1909-1993 .... **CLC 9, 49, 81**
See also AITN 1; BEST 90:3; CA 1-4R;
141; CAAS 9; CANR 1, 21, 46;
DAM NOV; DLB 9; DLBY 93; MTCW

Stein, Gertrude
1874-1946 ...... **TCLC 1, 6, 28, 48; DA;**
DAB; DAC; WLC
See also CA 104; 132; CDALB 1917-1929;
DAM MST, NOV, POET; DLB 4, 54, 86;
MTCW

Steinbeck, John (Ernst)
1902-1968 ...... **CLC 1, 5, 9, 13, 21, 34,**
45, 75; DA; DAB; DAC; SSC 11; WLC
See also AAYA 12; CA 1-4R; 25-28R;
CANR 1, 35; CDALB 1929-1941;
DAM DRAM, MST, NOV; DLB 7, 9;
DLBD 2; MTCW; SATA 9

Steinem, Gloria 1934-............. **CLC 63**
See also CA 53-56; CANR 28, 51; MTCW

Steiner, George 1929-............. **CLC 24**
See also CA 73-76; CANR 31; DAM NOV;
DLB 67; MTCW; SATA 62

Steiner, K. Leslie
See Delany, Samuel R(ay, Jr.)

Steiner, Rudolf 1861-1925 .... **TCLC 13**
See also CA 107

Stendhal
1783-1842 .... **NCLC 23, 46; DA; DAB;**
DAC; WLC
See also DAM MST, NOV; DLB 119

Stephen, Leslie 1832-1904 .... **TCLC 23**
See also CA 123; DLB 57, 144

Stephen, Sir Leslie
See Stephen, Leslie

Stephen, Virginia
See Woolf, (Adeline) Virginia

Stephens, James 1882(?)-1950 ..... **TCLC 4**
See also CA 104; DLB 19, 153, 162

Stephens, Reed
See Donaldson, Stephen R.

Steptoe, Lydia
See Barnes, Djuna

Sterchi, Beat 1949-............... **CLC 65**

Sterling, Brett
See Bradbury, Ray (Douglas); Hamilton,
Edmond

Sterling, Bruce 1954-............. **CLC 72**
See also CA 119; CANR 44

Sterling, George 1869-1926 .... **TCLC 20**
See also CA 117; DLB 54

Stern, Gerald 1925- .... **CLC 40**
See also CA 81-84; CANR 28; DLB 105

Stern, Richard (Gustave) 1928-... **CLC 4, 39**
See also CA 1-4R; CANR 1, 25, 52;
DLBY 87; INT CANR-25

Sternberg, Josef von 1894-1969 ..... **CLC 20**
See also CA 81-84

Sterne, Laurence
1713-1768 ...... **LC 2; DA; DAB; DAC;**
WLC
See also CDBLB 1660-1789; DAM MST,
NOV; DLB 39

Sternheim, (William Adolf) Carl
1878-1942 .... **TCLC 8**
See also CA 105; DLB 56, 118

Stevens, Mark 1951- .... **CLC 34**
See also CA 122

Stevens, Wallace
1879-1955 .... **TCLC 3, 12, 45; DA;**
DAB; DAC; PC 6; WLC
See also CA 104; 124; CDALB 1929-1941;
DAM MST, POET; DLB 54; MTCW

Stevenson, Anne (Katharine)
1933-.................... **CLC 7, 33**
See also CA 17-20R; CAAS 9; CANR 9, 33;
DLB 40; MTCW

Stevenson, Robert Louis (Balfour)
1850-1894 ..... **NCLC 5, 14; DA; DAB;**
DAC; SSC 11; WLC
See also CDBLB 1890-1914; CLR 10, 11;
DAM MST, NOV; DLB 18, 57, 141, 156;
DLBD 13; JRDA; MAICYA; YABC 2

Stewart, J(ohn) I(nnes) M(ackintosh)
1906-1994 .... **CLC 7, 14, 32**
See also CA 85-88; 147; CAAS 3;
CANR 47; MTCW

Stewart, Mary (Florence Elinor)
1916-............... **CLC 7, 35; DAB**
See also CA 1-4R; CANR 1; SATA 12

Stewart, Mary Rainbow
See Stewart, Mary (Florence Elinor)

Stifle, June
See Campbell, Maria

Stifter, Adalbert 1805-1868 ...... **NCLC 41**
See also DLB 133

Still, James 1906-................ **CLC 49**
See also CA 65-68; CAAS 17; CANR 10,
26; DLB 9; SATA 29

Sting
See Sumner, Gordon Matthew

Stirling, Arthur
See Sinclair, Upton (Beall)

Stitt, Milan 1941-................ **CLC 29**
See also CA 69-72

Stockton, Francis Richard 1834-1902
See Stockton, Frank R.
See also CA 108; 137; MAICYA; SATA 44

Stockton, Frank R................ **TCLC 47**
See also Stockton, Francis Richard
See also DLB 42, 74; DLBD 13;
SATA-Brief 32

Stoddard, Charles
See Kuttner, Henry

Stoker, Abraham 1847-1912
See Stoker, Bram
See also CA 105; DA; DAC; DAM MST,
NOV; SATA 29

Stoker, Bram
1847-1912 .... **TCLC 8; DAB; WLC**
See also Stoker, Abraham
See also CA 150; CDBLB 1890-1914;
DLB 36, 70

Stolz, Mary (Slattery) 1920-....... **CLC 12**
See also AAYA 8; AITN 1; CA 5-8R;
CANR 13, 41; JRDA; MAICYA;
SAAS 3; SATA 10, 71

Stone, Irving 1903-1989............ **CLC 7**
See also AITN 1; CA 1-4R; 129; CAAS 3;
CANR 1, 23; DAM POP;
INT CANR-23; MTCW; SATA 3;
SATA-Obit 64

Stone, Oliver 1946-................ **CLC 73**
See also AAYA 15; CA 110

Stone, Robert (Anthony)
1937-.................... **CLC 5, 23, 42**
See also CA 85-88; CANR 23; DLB 152;
INT CANR-23; MTCW

Stone, Zachary
See Follett, Ken(neth Martin)

Stoppard, Tom
1937-...... **CLC 1, 3, 4, 5, 8, 15, 29, 34,**
63, 91; DA; DAB; DAC; DC 6; WLC
See also CA 81-84; CANR 39;
CDBLB 1960 to Present; DAM DRAM,
MST; DLB 13; DLBY 85; MTCW

Storey, David (Malcolm)
1933-.................... **CLC 2, 4, 5, 8**
See also CA 81-84; CANR 36;
DAM DRAM; DLB 13, 14; MTCW

Storm, Hyemeyohsts 1935-......... **CLC 3**
See also CA 81-84; CANR 45;
DAM MULT; NNAL

Storm, (Hans) Theodor (Woldsen)
1817-1888 .... **NCLC 1**

Storni, Alfonsina
1892-1938 .... **TCLC 5; HLC**
See also CA 104; 131; DAM MULT; HW

Stout, Rex (Todhunter) 1886-1975 ... **CLC 3**
See also AITN 2; CA 61-64

Stow, (Julian) Randolph 1935- .. **CLC 23, 48**
See also CA 13-16R; CANR 33; MTCW

Stowe, Harriet (Elizabeth) Beecher
1811-1896 ..... **NCLC 3, 50; DA; DAB;**
DAC; WLC
See also CDALB 1865-1917; DAM MST,
NOV; DLB 1, 12, 42, 74; JRDA;
MAICYA; YABC 1

Strachey, (Giles) Lytton
1880-1932 .... **TCLC 12**
See also CA 110; DLB 149; DLBD 10

Strand, Mark 1934- ...... **CLC 6, 18, 41, 71**
See also CA 21-24R; CANR 40;
DAM POET; DLB 5; SATA 41

Straub, Peter (Francis) 1943- ...... **CLC 28**
See also BEST 89:1; CA 85-88; CANR 28;
DAM POP; DLBY 84; MTCW

Strauss, Botho 1944- .... **CLC 22**
See also DLB 124

Streatfeild, (Mary) Noel
1895(?)-1986 .... **CLC 21**
See also CA 81-84; 120; CANR 31;
CLR 17; DLB 160; MAICYA; SATA 20;
SATA-Obit 48

Stribling, T(homas) S(igismund)
1881-1965 .... **CLC 23**
See also CA 107; DLB 9

Strindberg, (Johan) August
1849-1912 ...... **TCLC 1, 8, 21, 47; DA;**
DAB; DAC; WLC
See also CA 104; 135; DAM DRAM, MST

Stringer, Arthur 1874-1950 .... **TCLC 37**
See also DLB 92

Stringer, David
See Roberts, Keith (John Kingston)

Strugatskii, Arkadii (Natanovich)
1925-1991 .... **CLC 27**
See also CA 106; 135

Strugatskii, Boris (Natanovich)
1933- .... **CLC 27**
See also CA 106

Strummer, Joe 1953(?)- .... **CLC 30**

Stuart, Don A.
See Campbell, John W(ood, Jr.)

Stuart, Ian
See MacLean, Alistair (Stuart)

Stuart, Jesse (Hilton)
1906-1984 .... **CLC 1, 8, 11, 14, 34**
See also CA 5-8R; 112; CANR 31; DLB 9,
48, 102; DLBY 84; SATA 2;
SATA-Obit 36

Sturgeon, Theodore (Hamilton)
1918-1985 .... **CLC 22, 39**
See also Queen, Ellery
See also CA 81-84; 116; CANR 32; DLB 8;
DLBY 85; MTCW

Sturges, Preston 1898-1959 .... **TCLC 48**
See also CA 114; 149; DLB 26

Styron, William
1925- .... **CLC 1, 3, 5, 11, 15, 60**
See also BEST 90:4; CA 5-8R; CANR 6, 33;
CDALB 1968-1988; DAM NOV, POP;
DLB 2, 143; DLBY 80; INT CANR-6;
MTCW

Suarez Lynch, B.
See Bioy Casares, Adolfo; Borges, Jorge
Luis

Su Chien 1884-1918
See Su Man-shu
See also CA 123

Suckow, Ruth 1892-1960 .... **SSC 18**
See also CA 113; DLB 9, 102

Sudermann, Hermann 1857-1928 .. **TCLC 15**
See also CA 107; DLB 118

Sue, Eugene 1804-1857 .... **NCLC 1**
See also DLB 119

Sueskind, Patrick 1949- .... **CLC 44**
See also Suskind, Patrick

Sukenick, Ronald 1932- ..... **CLC 3, 4, 6, 48**
See also CA 25-28R; CAAS 8; CANR 32;
DLBY 81

Suknaski, Andrew 1942- .... **CLC 19**
See also CA 101; DLB 53

Sullivan, Vernon
See Vian, Boris

Sully Prudhomme 1839-1907 ...... **TCLC 31**

Su Man-shu .... **TCLC 24**
See also Su Chien

Summerforest, Ivy B.
See Kirkup, James

Summers, Andrew James 1942- ..... **CLC 26**

Summers, Andy
See Summers, Andrew James

Summers, Hollis (Spurgeon, Jr.)
1916- .... **CLC 10**
See also CA 5-8R; CANR 3; DLB 6

Summers, (Alphonsus Joseph-Mary Augustus)
Montague 1880-1948 .... **TCLC 16**
See also CA 118

Sumner, Gordon Matthew 1951- .... **CLC 26**

Surtees, Robert Smith
1803-1864 .... **NCLC 14**
See also DLB 21

Susann, Jacqueline 1921-1974 .... **CLC 3**
See also AITN 1; CA 65-68; 53-56; MTCW

Su Shih 1036-1101 .... **CMLC 15**

Suskind, Patrick
See Sueskind, Patrick
See also CA 145

Sutcliff, Rosemary
1920-1992 .... **CLC 26; DAB; DAC**
See also AAYA 10; CA 5-8R; 139;
CANR 37; CLR 1, 37; DAM MST, POP;
JRDA; MAICYA; SATA 6, 44, 78;
SATA-Obit 73

Sutro, Alfred 1863-1933 .... **TCLC 6**
See also CA 105; DLB 10

Sutton, Henry
See Slavitt, David R(ytman)

Svevo, Italo .... **TCLC 2, 35**
See also Schmitz, Aron Hector

Swados, Elizabeth (A.) 1951- .... **CLC 12**
See also CA 97-100; CANR 49; INT 97-100

Swados, Harvey 1920-1972 .... **CLC 5**
See also CA 5-8R; 37-40R; CANR 6;
DLB 2

Swan, Gladys 1934- .... **CLC 69**
See also CA 101; CANR 17, 39

Swarthout, Glendon (Fred)
1918-1992 .... **CLC 35**
See also CA 1-4R; 139; CANR 1, 47;
SATA 26

Sweet, Sarah C.
See Jewett, (Theodora) Sarah Orne

Swenson, May
1919-1989 .... **CLC 4, 14, 61; DA; DAB;**
DAC; PC 14
See also CA 5-8R; 130; CANR 36;
DAM MST, POET; DLB 5; MTCW;
SATA 15

Swift, Augustus
See Lovecraft, H(oward) P(hillips)

Swift, Graham (Colin) 1949- .... **CLC 41, 88**
See also CA 117; 122; CANR 46

Swift, Jonathan
1667-1745 ...... **LC 1; DA; DAB; DAC;**
PC 9; WLC
See also CDBLB 1660-1789; DAM MST,
NOV, POET; DLB 39, 95, 101; SATA 19

Swinburne, Algernon Charles
1837-1909 ...... **TCLC 8, 36; DA; DAB;**
DAC; WLC
See also CA 105; 140; CDBLB 1832-1890;
DAM MST, POET; DLB 35, 57

Swinfen, Ann .... **CLC 34**

Swinnerton, Frank Arthur
1884-1982 .... **CLC 31**
See also CA 108; DLB 34

Swithen, John
See King, Stephen (Edwin)

Sylvia
See Ashton-Warner, Sylvia (Constance)

Symmes, Robert Edward
See Duncan, Robert (Edward)

Symonds, John Addington
1840-1893 .... **NCLC 34**
See also DLB 57, 144

Symons, Arthur 1865-1945 .... **TCLC 11**
See also CA 107; DLB 19, 57, 149

Symons, Julian (Gustave)
1912-1994 .... **CLC 2, 14, 32**
See also CA 49-52; 147; CAAS 3; CANR 3,
33; DLB 87, 155; DLBY 92; MTCW

Synge, (Edmund) J(ohn) M(illington)
1871-1909 .... **TCLC 6, 37; DC 2**
See also CA 104; 141; CDBLB 1890-1914;
DAM DRAM; DLB 10, 19

Syruc, J.
See Milosz, Czeslaw

Szirtes, George 1948- .... **CLC 46**
See also CA 109; CANR 27

Tabori, George 1914- .... **CLC 19**
See also CA 49-52; CANR 4

Tagore, Rabindranath
1861-1941 .... **TCLC 3, 53; PC 8**
See also CA 104; 120; DAM DRAM,
POET; MTCW

Taine, Hippolyte Adolphe
1828-1893 .... **NCLC 15**

Talese, Gay 1932-................. **CLC 37**
See also AITN 1; CA 1-4R; CANR 9;
INT CANR-9; MTCW

Tallent, Elizabeth (Ann) 1954- ..... **CLC 45**
See also CA 117; DLB 130

Tally, Ted 1952- .... **CLC 42**
See also CA 120; 124; INT 124

Tamayo y Baus, Manuel
1829-1898 .... **NCLC 1**

Tammsaare, A(nton) H(ansen)
1878-1940 .... **TCLC 27**

Tan, Amy 1952- .... **CLC 59**
See also AAYA 9; BEST 89:3; CA 136;
DAM MULT, NOV, POP; SATA 75

Tandem, Felix
See Spitteler, Carl (Friedrich Georg)

Tanizaki, Jun'ichiro
1886-1965 ...... **CLC 8, 14, 28; SSC 21**
See also CA 93-96; 25-28R

Tanner, William
See Amis, Kingsley (William)

Tao Lao
See Storni, Alfonsina

Tarassoff, Lev
See Troyat, Henri

Tarbell, Ida M(inerva)
1857-1944 .... **TCLC 40**
See also CA 122; DLB 47

Tarkington, (Newton) Booth
1869-1946 .... **TCLC 9**
See also CA 110; 143; DLB 9, 102;
SATA 17

Tarkovsky, Andrei (Arsenyevich)
1932-1986 .... **CLC 75**
See also CA 127

Tartt, Donna 1964(?)- .... **CLC 76**
See also CA 142

Tasso, Torquato 1544-1595 .... **LC 5**

Tate, (John Orley) Allen
1899-1979 .... **CLC 2, 4, 6, 9, 11, 14, 24**
See also CA 5-8R; 85-88; CANR 32;
DLB 4, 45, 63; MTCW

Tate, Ellalice
See Hibbert, Eleanor Alice Burford

Tate, James (Vincent) 1943- ... **CLC 2, 6, 25**
See also CA 21-24R; CANR 29; DLB 5

Tavel, Ronald 1940- .... **CLC 6**
See also CA 21-24R; CANR 33

Taylor, C(ecil) P(hilip) 1929-1981... **CLC 27**
See also CA 25-28R; 105; CANR 47

Taylor, Edward
1642(?)-1729 ... **LC 11; DA; DAB; DAC**
See also DAM MST, POET; DLB 24

Taylor, Eleanor Ross 1920- .... **CLC 5**
See also CA 81-84

Taylor, Elizabeth 1912-1975 ... **CLC 2, 4, 29**
See also CA 13-16R; CANR 9; DLB 139;
MTCW; SATA 13

Taylor, Henry (Splawn) 1942- ...... **CLC 44**
See also CA 33-36R; CAAS 7; CANR 31;
DLB 5

Taylor, Kamala (Purnaiya) 1924-
See Markandaya, Kamala
See also CA 77-80

Taylor, Mildred D. .... **CLC 21**
See also AAYA 10; BW 1; CA 85-88;
CANR 25; CLR 9; DLB 52; JRDA;
MAICYA; SAAS 5; SATA 15, 70

Taylor, Peter (Hillsman)
1917-1994 ..... **CLC 1, 4, 18, 37, 44, 50,
71; SSC 10**
See also CA 13-16R; 147; CANR 9, 50;
DLBY 81, 94; INT CANR-9; MTCW

Taylor, Robert Lewis 1912- .... **CLC 14**
See also CA 1-4R; CANR 3; SATA 10

Tchekhov, Anton
See Chekhov, Anton (Pavlovich)

Teasdale, Sara 1884-1933 .... **TCLC 4**
See also CA 104; DLB 45; SATA 32

Tegner, Esaias 1782-1846 .... **NCLC 2**

Teilhard de Chardin, (Marie Joseph) Pierre
1881-1955 .... **TCLC 9**
See also CA 105

Temple, Ann
See Mortimer, Penelope (Ruth)

Tennant, Emma (Christina)
1937- .... **CLC 13, 52**
See also CA 65-68; CAAS 9; CANR 10, 38;
DLB 14

Tenneshaw, S. M.
See Silverberg, Robert

Tennyson, Alfred
1809-1892 .... **NCLC 30; DA; DAB;
DAC; PC 6; WLC**
See also CDBLB 1832-1890; DAM MST,
POET; DLB 32

Teran, Lisa St. Aubin de .... **CLC 36**
See also St. Aubin de Teran, Lisa

Terence 195(?)B.C.-159B.C. ...... **CMLC 14**

Teresa de Jesus, St. 1515-1582 ...... **LC 18**

Terkel, Louis 1912-
See Terkel, Studs
See also CA 57-60; CANR 18, 45; MTCW

Terkel, Studs .... **CLC 38**
See also Terkel, Louis
See also AITN 1

Terry, C. V.
See Slaughter, Frank G(ill)

Terry, Megan 1932- .... **CLC 19**
See also CA 77-80; CABS 3; CANR 43;
DLB 7

Tertz, Abram
See Sinyavsky, Andrei (Donatevich)

Tesich, Steve 1943(?)- .... **CLC 40, 69**
See also CA 105; DLBY 83

Teternikov, Fyodor Kuzmich 1863-1927
See Sologub, Fyodor
See also CA 104

Tevis, Walter 1928-1984 .... **CLC 42**
See also CA 113

Tey, Josephine .... **TCLC 14**
See also Mackintosh, Elizabeth
See also DLB 77

Thackeray, William Makepeace
1811-1863 .... **NCLC 5, 14, 22, 43; DA;
DAB; DAC; WLC**
See also CDBLB 1832-1890; DAM MST,
NOV; DLB 21, 55, 159, 163; SATA 23

Thakura, Ravindranatha
See Tagore, Rabindranath

Tharoor, Shashi 1956- .... **CLC 70**
See also CA 141

Thelwell, Michael Miles 1939- ..... **CLC 22**
See also BW 2; CA 101

Theobald, Lewis, Jr.
See Lovecraft, H(oward) P(hillips)

Theodorescu, Ion N. 1880-1967
See Arghezi, Tudor
See also CA 116

Theriault, Yves 1915-1983 .... **CLC 79; DAC**
See also CA 102; DAM MST; DLB 88

Theroux, Alexander (Louis)
1939- .... **CLC 2, 25**
See also CA 85-88; CANR 20

Theroux, Paul (Edward)
1941- .... **CLC 5, 8, 11, 15, 28, 46**
See also BEST 89:4; CA 33-36R; CANR 20,
45; DAM POP; DLB 2; MTCW;
SATA 44

Thesen, Sharon 1946- .... **CLC 56**

Thevenin, Denis
See Duhamel, Georges

Thibault, Jacques Anatole Francois
1844-1924
See France, Anatole
See also CA 106; 127; DAM NOV; MTCW

Thiele, Colin (Milton) 1920- .... **CLC 17**
See also CA 29-32R; CANR 12, 28, 53;
CLR 27; MAICYA; SAAS 2; SATA 14,
72

Thomas, Audrey (Callahan)
1935- .... **CLC 7, 13, 37; SSC 20**
See also AITN 2; CA 21-24R; CAAS 19;
CANR 36; DLB 60; MTCW

Thomas, D(onald) M(ichael)
1935- .... **CLC 13, 22, 31**
See also CA 61-64; CAAS 11; CANR 17,
45; CDBLB 1960 to Present; DLB 40;
INT CANR-17; MTCW

Thomas, Dylan (Marlais)
1914-1953 ... **TCLC 1, 8, 45; DA; DAB;
DAC; PC 2; SSC 3; WLC**
See also CA 104; 120; CDBLB 1945-1960;
DAM DRAM, MST, POET; DLB 13, 20,
139; MTCW; SATA 60

Thomas, (Philip) Edward
1878-1917 ....:. **TCLC 10**
See also CA 106; DAM POET; DLB 19

Thomas, Joyce Carol 1938- .... **CLC 35**
See also AAYA 12; BW 2; CA 113; 116;
CANR 48; CLR 19; DLB 33; INT 116;
JRDA; MAICYA; MTCW; SAAS 7;
SATA 40, 78

Thomas, Lewis 1913-1993 .... **CLC 35**
See also CA 85-88; 143; CANR 38; MTCW

Thomas, Paul
See Mann, (Paul) Thomas

Thomas, Piri 1928- .... **CLC 17**
See also CA 73-76; HW

Thomas, R(onald) S(tuart)
1913- .... **CLC 6, 13, 48; DAB**
See also CA 89-92; CAAS 4; CANR 30;
CDBLB 1960 to Present; DAM POET;
DLB 27; MTCW

Thomas, Ross (Elmore) 1926-1995 . . **CLC 39**
See also CA 33-36R; 150; CANR 22

Thompson, Francis Clegg
See Mencken, H(enry) L(ouis)

Thompson, Francis Joseph
1859-1907 . . . . **TCLC 4**
See also CA 104; CDBLB 1890-1914;
DLB 19

Thompson, Hunter S(tockton)
1939- . . . . **CLC 9, 17, 40**
See also BEST 89:1; CA 17-20R; CANR 23,
46; DAM POP; MTCW

Thompson, James Myers
See Thompson, Jim (Myers)

Thompson, Jim (Myers)
1906-1977(?) . . . . **CLC 69**
See also CA 140

Thompson, Judith . . . . **CLC 39**

Thomson, James 1700-1748 . . . . . . **LC 16, 29**
See also DAM POET; DLB 95

Thomson, James 1834-1882 . . . . . . **NCLC 18**
See also DAM POET; DLB 35

Thoreau, Henry David
1817-1862 . . . . . **NCLC 7, 21; DA; DAB;**
DAC; WLC
See also CDALB 1640-1865; DAM MST;
DLB 1

Thornton, Hall
See Silverberg, Robert

Thucydides c. 455B.C.-399B.C. . . . . **CMLC 17**

Thurber, James (Grover)
1894-1961 . . . . **CLC 5, 11, 25; DA; DAB;**
DAC; SSC 1
See also CA 73-76; CANR 17, 39;
CDALB 1929-1941; DAM DRAM, MST,
NOV; DLB 4, 11, 22, 102; MAICYA;
MTCW; SATA 13

Thurman, Wallace (Henry)
1902-1934 . . . . **TCLC 6; BLC**
See also BW 1; CA 104; 124; DAM MULT;
DLB 51

Ticheburn, Cheviot
See Ainsworth, William Harrison

Tieck, (Johann) Ludwig
1773-1853 . . . . **NCLC 5, 46**
See also DLB 90

Tiger, Derry
See Ellison, Harlan (Jay)

Tilghman, Christopher 1948(?)- . . . . . **CLC 65**

Tillinghast, Richard (Williford)
1940- . . . . **CLC 29**
See also CA 29-32R; CAAS 23; CANR 26,
51

Timrod, Henry 1828-1867 . . . . **NCLC 25**
See also DLB 3

Tindall, Gillian 1938- . . . . **CLC 7**
See also CA 21-24R; CANR 11

Tiptree, James, Jr. . . . . **CLC 48, 50**
See also Sheldon, Alice Hastings Bradley
See also DLB 8

Titmarsh, Michael Angelo
See Thackeray, William Makepeace

Tocqueville, Alexis (Charles Henri Maurice
Clerel Comte) 1805-1859 . . . . . **NCLC 7**

Tolkien, J(ohn) R(onald) R(euel)
1892-1973 . . . . . . **CLC 1, 2, 3, 8, 12, 38;**
DA; DAB; DAC; WLC
See also AAYA 10; AITN 1; CA 17-18;
45-48; CANR 36; CAP 2;
CDBLB 1914-1945; DAM MST, NOV,
POP; DLB 15, 160; JRDA; MAICYA;
MTCW; SATA 2, 32; SATA-Obit 24

Toller, Ernst 1893-1939 . . . . **TCLC 10**
See also CA 107; DLB 124

Tolson, M. B.
See Tolson, Melvin B(eaunorus)

Tolson, Melvin B(eaunorus)
1898(?)-1966 . . . . **CLC 36; BLC**
See also BW 1; CA 124; 89-92;
DAM MULT, POET; DLB 48, 76

Tolstoi, Aleksei Nikolaevich
See Tolstoy, Alexey Nikolaevich

Tolstoy, Alexey Nikolaevich
1882-1945 . . . . **TCLC 18**
See also CA 107

Tolstoy, Count Leo
See Tolstoy, Leo (Nikolaevich)

Tolstoy, Leo (Nikolaevich)
1828-1910 . . . . . . **TCLC 4, 11, 17, 28, 44;**
DA; DAB; DAC; SSC 9; WLC
See also CA 104; 123; DAM MST, NOV;
SATA 26

Tomasi di Lampedusa, Giuseppe 1896-1957
See Lampedusa, Giuseppe (Tomasi) di
See also CA 111

Tomlin, Lily . . . . **CLC 17**
See also Tomlin, Mary Jean

Tomlin, Mary Jean 1939(?)-
See Tomlin, Lily
See also CA 117

Tomlinson, (Alfred) Charles
1927- . . . . **CLC 2, 4, 6, 13, 45**
See also CA 5-8R; CANR 33; DAM POET;
DLB 40

Tonson, Jacob
See Bennett, (Enoch) Arnold

Toole, John Kennedy
1937-1969 . . . . **CLC 19, 64**
See also CA 104; DLBY 81

Toomer, Jean
1894-1967 . . . . . . **CLC 1, 4, 13, 22; BLC;**
PC 7; SSC 1
See also BW 1; CA 85-88;
CDALB 1917-1929; DAM MULT;
DLB 45, 51; MTCW

Torley, Luke
See Blish, James (Benjamin)

Tornimparte, Alessandra
See Ginzburg, Natalia

Torre, Raoul della
See Mencken, H(enry) L(ouis)

Torrey, E(dwin) Fuller 1937- . . . . **CLC 34**
See also CA 119

Torsvan, Ben Traven
See Traven, B.

Torsvan, Benno Traven
See Traven, B.

Torsvan, Berick Traven
See Traven, B.

Torsvan, Berwick Traven
See Traven, B.

Torsvan, Bruno Traven
See Traven, B.

Torsvan, Traven
See Traven, B.

Tournier, Michel (Edouard)
1924- . . . . **CLC 6, 23, 36, 95**
See also CA 49-52; CANR 3, 36; DLB 83;
MTCW; SATA 23

Tournimparte, Alessandra
See Ginzburg, Natalia

Towers, Ivar
See Kornbluth, C(yril) M.

Towne, Robert (Burton) 1936(?)- . . . . **CLC 87**
See also CA 108; DLB 44

Townsend, Sue 1946- . . **CLC 61; DAB; DAC**
See also CA 119; 127; INT 127; MTCW;
SATA 55; SATA-Brief 48

Townshend, Peter (Dennis Blandford)
1945- . . . . **CLC 17, 42**
See also CA 107

Tozzi, Federigo 1883-1920 . . . . **TCLC 31**

Traill, Catharine Parr
1802-1899 . . . . **NCLC 31**
See also DLB 99

Trakl, Georg 1887-1914 . . . . **TCLC 5**
See also CA 104

Transtroemer, Tomas (Goesta)
1931- . . . . **CLC 52, 65**
See also CA 117; 129; CAAS 17;
DAM POET

Transtromer, Tomas Gosta
See Transtroemer, Tomas (Goesta)

Traven, B. (?)-1969 . . . . **CLC 8, 11**
See also CA 19-20; 25-28R; CAP 2; DLB 9,
56; MTCW

Treitel, Jonathan 1959- . . . . **CLC 70**

Tremain, Rose 1943- . . . . **CLC 42**
See also CA 97-100; CANR 44; DLB 14

Tremblay, Michel 1942- . . . . . . **CLC 29; DAC**
See also CA 116; 128; DAM MST; DLB 60;
MTCW

Trevanian . . . . **CLC 29**
See also Whitaker, Rod(ney)

Trevor, Glen
See Hilton, James

Trevor, William
1928- . . . . . **CLC 7, 9, 14, 25, 71; SSC 21**
See also Cox, William Trevor
See also DLB 14, 139

Trifonov, Yuri (Valentinovich)
1925-1981 . . . . **CLC 45**
See also CA 126; 103; MTCW

Trilling, Lionel 1905-1975 . . . . **CLC 9, 11, 24**
See also CA 9-12R; 61-64; CANR 10;
DLB 28, 63; INT CANR-10; MTCW

Trimball, W. H.
See Mencken, H(enry) L(ouis)

Tristan
See Gomez de la Serna, Ramon

Tristram
See Housman, A(lfred) E(dward)

Trogdon, William (Lewis) 1939-
See Heat-Moon, William Least
See also CA 115; 119; CANR 47; INT 119

Trollope, Anthony
1815-1882 ..... NCLC 6, 33; DA; DAB;
DAC; WLC
See also CDBLB 1832-1890; DAM MST,
NOV; DLB 21, 57, 159; SATA 22

Trollope, Frances 1779-1863 ..... NCLC 30
See also DLB 21, 166

Trotsky, Leon 1879-1940 .... TCLC 22
See also CA 118

Trotter (Cockburn), Catharine
1679-1749 .... LC 8
See also DLB 84

Trout, Kilgore
See Farmer, Philip Jose

Trow, George W. S. 1943- .... CLC 52
See also CA 126

Troyat, Henri 1911- .... CLC 23
See also CA 45-48; CANR 2, 33; MTCW

Trudeau, G(arretson) B(eekman) 1948-
See Trudeau, Garry B.
See also CA 81-84; CANR 31; SATA 35

Trudeau, Garry B. .... CLC 12
See also Trudeau, G(arretson) B(eekman)
See also AAYA 10; AITN 2

Truffaut, Francois 1932-1984 ...... CLC 20
See also CA 81-84; 113; CANR 34

Trumbo, Dalton 1905-1976 .... CLC 19
See also CA 21-24R; 69-72; CANR 10;
DLB 26

Trumbull, John 1750-1831 .... NCLC 30
See also DLB 31

Trundlett, Helen B.
See Eliot, T(homas) S(tearns)

Tryon, Thomas 1926-1991 .... CLC 3, 11
See also AITN 1; CA 29-32R; 135;
CANR 32; DAM POP; MTCW

Tryon, Tom
See Tryon, Thomas

Ts'ao Hsueh-ch'in 1715(?)-1763 .... LC 1

Tsushima, Shuji 1909-1948
See Dazai, Osamu
See also CA 107

Tsvetaeva (Efron), Marina (Ivanovna)
1892-1941 .... TCLC 7, 35; PC 14
See also CA 104; 128; MTCW

Tuck, Lily 1938- .... CLC 70
See also CA 139

Tu Fu 712-770 .... PC 9
See also DAM MULT

Tunis, John R(oberts) 1889-1975 ... CLC 12
See also CA 61-64; DLB 22; JRDA;
MAICYA; SATA 37; SATA-Brief 30

Tuohy, Frank .... CLC 37
See also Tuohy, John Francis
See also DLB 14, 139

Tuohy, John Francis 1925-
See Tuohy, Frank
See also CA 5-8R; CANR 3, 47

Turco, Lewis (Putnam) 1934- ... CLC 11, 63
See also CA 13-16R; CAAS 22; CANR 24,
51; DLBY 84

Turgenev, Ivan
1818-1883 ...... NCLC 21; DA; DAB;
DAC; SSC 7; WLC
See also DAM MST, NOV

Turgot, Anne-Robert-Jacques
1727-1781 .... LC 26

Turner, Frederick 1943- .... CLC 48
See also CA 73-76; CAAS 10; CANR 12,
30; DLB 40

Tutu, Desmond M(pilo)
1931- .... CLC 80; BLC
See also BW 1; CA 125; DAM MULT

Tutuola, Amos 1920- ... CLC 5, 14, 29; BLC
See also BW 2; CA 9-12R; CANR 27;
DAM MULT; DLB 125; MTCW

Twain, Mark
..... TCLC 6, 12, 19, 36, 48, 59; SSC 6;
WLC
See also Clemens, Samuel Langhorne
See also DLB 11, 12, 23, 64, 74

Tyler, Anne
1941- .... CLC 7, 11, 18, 28, 44, 59
See also AAYA 18; BEST 89:1; CA 9-12R;
CANR 11, 33, 53; DAM NOV, POP;
DLB 6, 143; DLBY 82; MTCW; SATA 7

Tyler, Royall 1757-1826 .... NCLC 3
See also DLB 37

Tynan, Katharine 1861-1931 .... TCLC 3
See also CA 104; DLB 153

Tyutchev, Fyodor 1803-1873 ..... NCLC 34

Tzara, Tristan .... CLC 47
See also Rosenfeld, Samuel
See also DAM POET

Uhry, Alfred 1936- .... CLC 55
See also CA 127; 133; DAM DRAM, POP;
INT 133

Ulf, Haerved
See Strindberg, (Johan) August

Ulf, Harved
See Strindberg, (Johan) August

Ulibarri, Sabine R(eyes) 1919- ..... CLC 83
See also CA 131; DAM MULT; DLB 82;
HW

Unamuno (y Jugo), Miguel de
1864-1936 .... TCLC 2, 9; HLC; SSC 11
See also CA 104; 131; DAM MULT, NOV;
DLB 108; HW; MTCW

Undercliffe, Errol
See Campbell, (John) Ramsey

Underwood, Miles
See Glassco, John

Undset, Sigrid
1882-1949 .... TCLC 3; DA; DAB;
DAC; WLC
See also CA 104; 129; DAM MST, NOV;
MTCW

Ungaretti, Giuseppe
1888-1970 .... CLC 7, 11, 15
See also CA 19-20; 25-28R; CAP 2;
DLB 114

Unger, Douglas 1952- .... CLC 34
See also CA 130

Unsworth, Barry (Forster) 1930- .... CLC 76
See also CA 25-28R; CANR 30

Updike, John (Hoyer)
1932- ..... CLC 1, 2, 3, 5, 7, 9, 13, 15,
23, 34, 43, 70; DA; DAB; DAC; SSC 13;
WLC
See also CA 1-4R; CABS 1; CANR 4, 33,
51; CDALB 1968-1988; DAM MST,
NOV, POET, POP; DLB 2, 5, 143;
DLBD 3; DLBY 80, 82; MTCW

Upshaw, Margaret Mitchell
See Mitchell, Margaret (Munnerlyn)

Upton, Mark
See Sanders, Lawrence

Urdang, Constance (Henriette)
1922- .... CLC 47
See also CA 21-24R; CANR 9, 24

Uriel, Henry
See Faust, Frederick (Schiller)

Uris, Leon (Marcus) 1924- .... CLC 7, 32
See also AITN 1, 2; BEST 89:2; CA 1-4R;
CANR 1, 40; DAM NOV, POP; MTCW;
SATA 49

Urmuz
See Codrescu, Andrei

Urquhart, Jane 1949- .... CLC 90; DAC
See also CA 113; CANR 32

Ustinov, Peter (Alexander) 1921- .... CLC 1
See also AITN 1; CA 13-16R; CANR 25,
51; DLB 13

Vaculik, Ludvik 1926- .... CLC 7
See also CA 53-56

Valdez, Luis (Miguel)
1940- .... CLC 84; HLC
See also CA 101; CANR 32; DAM MULT;
DLB 122; HW

Valenzuela, Luisa 1938- ... CLC 31; SSC 14
See also CA 101; CANR 32; DAM MULT;
DLB 113; HW

Valera y Alcala-Galiano, Juan
1824-1905 .... TCLC 10
See also CA 106

Valery, (Ambroise) Paul (Toussaint Jules)
1871-1945 .... TCLC 4, 15; PC 9
See also CA 104; 122; DAM POET; MTCW

Valle-Inclan, Ramon (Maria) del
1866-1936 .... TCLC 5; HLC
See also CA 106; DAM MULT; DLB 134

Vallejo, Antonio Buero
See Buero Vallejo, Antonio

Vallejo, Cesar (Abraham)
1892-1938 .... TCLC 3, 56; HLC
See also CA 105; DAM MULT; HW

Valle Y Pena, Ramon del
See Valle-Inclan, Ramon (Maria) del

Van Ash, Cay 1918- .... CLC 34

Vanbrugh, Sir John 1664-1726 ...... LC 21
See also DAM DRAM; DLB 80

Van Campen, Karl
See Campbell, John W(ood, Jr.)

Vance, Gerald
See Silverberg, Robert

Vance, Jack .... CLC 35
See also Vance, John Holbrook
See also DLB 8

Vance, John Holbrook 1916-
See Queen, Ellery; Vance, Jack
See also CA 29-32R; CANR 17; MTCW

Van Den Bogarde, Derek Jules Gaspard Ulric
Niven 1921-
See Bogarde, Dirk
See also CA 77-80

Vandenburgh, Jane . . . . **CLC 59**

Vanderhaeghe, Guy 1951- . . . . **CLC 41**
See also CA 113

van der Post, Laurens (Jan) 1906- . . . **CLC 5**
See also CA 5-8R; CANR 35

van de Wetering, Janwillem 1931- . . **CLC 47**
See also CA 49-52; CANR 4

Van Dine, S. S. . . . . **TCLC 23**
See also Wright, Willard Huntington

Van Doren, Carl (Clinton)
1885-1950 . . . . **TCLC 18**
See also CA 111

Van Doren, Mark 1894-1972 . . . . . **CLC 6, 10**
See also CA 1-4R; 37-40R; CANR 3;
DLB 45; MTCW

Van Druten, John (William)
1901-1957 . . . . **TCLC 2**
See also CA 104; DLB 10

Van Duyn, Mona (Jane)
1921- . . . . **CLC 3, 7, 63**
See also CA 9-12R; CANR 7, 38;
DAM POET; DLB 5

Van Dyne, Edith
See Baum, L(yman) Frank

van Itallie, Jean-Claude 1936- . . . . . . **CLC 3**
See also CA 45-48; CAAS 2; CANR 1, 48;
DLB 7

van Ostaijen, Paul 1896-1928 . . . . . **TCLC 33**

Van Peebles, Melvin 1932- . . . . . . **CLC 2, 20**
See also BW 2; CA 85-88; CANR 27;
DAM MULT

Vansittart, Peter 1920- . . . . **CLC 42**
See also CA 1-4R; CANR 3, 49

Van Vechten, Carl 1880-1964 . . . . . . **CLC 33**
See also CA 89-92; DLB 4, 9, 51

Van Vogt, A(lfred) E(lton) 1912- . . . . . **CLC 1**
See also CA 21-24R; CANR 28; DLB 8;
SATA 14

Varda, Agnes 1928- . . . . **CLC 16**
See also CA 116; 122

Vargas Llosa, (Jorge) Mario (Pedro)
1936- . . . . **CLC 3, 6, 9, 10, 15, 31, 42, 85;
DA; DAB; DAC; HLC**
See also CA 73-76; CANR 18, 32, 42;
DAM MST, MULT, NOV; DLB 145;
HW; MTCW

Vasiliu, Gheorghe 1881-1957
See Bacovia, George
See also CA 123

Vassa, Gustavus
See Equiano, Olaudah

Vassilikos, Vassilis 1933- . . . . **CLC 4, 8**
See also CA 81-84

Vaughan, Henry 1621-1695 . . . . **LC 27**
See also DLB 131

Vaughn, Stephanie . . . . **CLC 62**

Vazov, Ivan (Minchov)
1850-1921 . . . . **TCLC 25**
See also CA 121; DLB 147

Veblen, Thorstein (Bunde)
1857-1929 . . . . **TCLC 31**
See also CA 115

Vega, Lope de 1562-1635 . . . . **LC 23**

Venison, Alfred
See Pound, Ezra (Weston Loomis)

Verdi, Marie de
See Mencken, H(enry) L(ouis)

Verdu, Matilde
See Cela, Camilo Jose

Verga, Giovanni (Carmelo)
1840-1922 . . . . **TCLC 3; SSC 21**
See also CA 104; 123

Vergil
70B.C.-19B.C. . . . . . **CMLC 9; DA; DAB;
DAC; PC 12**
See also DAM MST, POET

Verhaeren, Emile (Adolphe Gustave)
1855-1916 . . . . **TCLC 12**
See also CA 109

Verlaine, Paul (Marie)
1844-1896 . . . . **NCLC 2, 51; PC 2**
See also DAM POET

Verne, Jules (Gabriel)
1828-1905 . . . . **TCLC 6, 52**
See also AAYA 16; CA 110; 131; DLB 123;
JRDA; MAICYA; SATA 21

Very, Jones 1813-1880 . . . . **NCLC 9**
See also DLB 1

Vesaas, Tarjei 1897-1970 . . . . **CLC 48**
See also CA 29-32R

Vialis, Gaston
See Simenon, Georges (Jacques Christian)

Vian, Boris 1920-1959 . . . . **TCLC 9**
See also CA 106; DLB 72

Viaud, (Louis Marie) Julien 1850-1923
See Loti, Pierre
See also CA 107

Vicar, Henry
See Felsen, Henry Gregor

Vicker, Angus
See Felsen, Henry Gregor

Vidal, Gore
1925- . . . . . **CLC 2, 4, 6, 8, 10, 22, 33, 72**
See also AITN 1; BEST 90:2; CA 5-8R;
CANR 13, 45; DAM NOV, POP; DLB 6,
152; INT CANR-13; MTCW

Viereck, Peter (Robert Edwin)
1916- . . . . **CLC 4**
See also CA 1-4R; CANR 1, 47; DLB 5

Vigny, Alfred (Victor) de
1797-1863 . . . . **NCLC 7**
See also DAM POET; DLB 119

Vilakazi, Benedict Wallet
1906-1947 . . . . **TCLC 37**

Villiers de l'Isle Adam, Jean Marie Mathias
Philippe Auguste Comte
1838-1889 . . . . **NCLC 3; SSC 14**
See also DLB 123

Villon, Francois 1431-1463(?) . . . . **PC 13**

Vinci, Leonardo da 1452-1519 . . . . **LC 12**

Vine, Barbara . . . . **CLC 50**
See also Rendell, Ruth (Barbara)
See also BEST 90:4

Vinge, Joan D(ennison) 1948- . . . . . . **CLC 30**
See also CA 93-96; SATA 36

Violis, G.
See Simenon, Georges (Jacques Christian)

Visconti, Luchino 1906-1976 . . . . **CLC 16**
See also CA 81-84; 65-68; CANR 39

Vittorini, Elio 1908-1966 . . . . . . **CLC 6, 9, 14**
See also CA 133; 25-28R

Vizinczey, Stephen 1933- . . . . **CLC 40**
See also CA 128; INT 128

Vliet, R(ussell) G(ordon)
1929-1984 . . . . **CLC 22**
See also CA 37-40R; 112; CANR 18

Vogau, Boris Andreyevich 1894-1937(?)
See Pilnyak, Boris
See also CA 123

Vogel, Paula A(nne) 1951- . . . . **CLC 76**
See also CA 108

Voight, Ellen Bryant 1943- . . . . **CLC 54**
See also CA 69-72; CANR 11, 29; DLB 120

Voigt, Cynthia 1942- . . . . **CLC 30**
See also AAYA 3; CA 106; CANR 18, 37,
40; CLR 13; INT CANR-18; JRDA;
MAICYA; SATA 48, 79; SATA-Brief 33

Voinovich, Vladimir (Nikolaevich)
1932- . . . . **CLC 10, 49**
See also CA 81-84; CAAS 12; CANR 33;
MTCW

Vollmann, William T. 1959- . . . . **CLC 89**
See also CA 134; DAM NOV, POP

Voloshinov, V. N.
See Bakhtin, Mikhail Mikhailovich

Voltaire
1694-1778 . . . . . **LC 14; DA; DAB; DAC;
SSC 12; WLC**
See also DAM DRAM, MST

von Daeniken, Erich 1935- . . . . **CLC 30**
See also AITN 1; CA 37-40R; CANR 17,
44

von Daniken, Erich
See von Daeniken, Erich

von Heidenstam, (Carl Gustaf) Verner
See Heidenstam, (Carl Gustaf) Verner von

von Heyse, Paul (Johann Ludwig)
See Heyse, Paul (Johann Ludwig von)

von Hofmannsthal, Hugo
See Hofmannsthal, Hugo von

von Horvath, Odon
See Horvath, Oedoen von

von Horvath, Oedoen
See Horvath, Oedoen von

von Liliencron, (Friedrich Adolf Axel) Detlev
See Liliencron, (Friedrich Adolf Axel)
Detlev von

Vonnegut, Kurt, Jr.
1922- . . . . . . **CLC 1, 2, 3, 4, 5, 8, 12, 22,
40, 60; DA; DAB; DAC; SSC 8; WLC**
See also AAYA 6; AITN 1; BEST 90:4;
CA 1-4R; CANR 1, 25, 49;
CDALB 1968-1988; DAM MST, NOV,
POP; DLB 2, 8, 152; DLBD 3; DLBY 80;
MTCW

Von Rachen, Kurt
See Hubbard, L(afayette) Ron(ald)

von Rezzori (d'Arezzo), Gregor
See Rezzori (d'Arezzo), Gregor von

von Sternberg, Josef
See Sternberg, Josef von

Vorster, Gordon 1924- . . . . **CLC 34**
See also CA 133

Vosce, Trudie
See Ozick, Cynthia

Voznesensky, Andrei (Andreievich)
1933- . . . . **CLC 1, 15, 57**
See also CA 89-92; CANR 37;
DAM POET; MTCW

Waddington, Miriam 1917- . . . . **CLC 28**
See also CA 21-24R; CANR 12, 30;
DLB 68

Wagman, Fredrica 1937- . . . . **CLC 7**
See also CA 97-100; INT 97-100

Wagner, Richard 1813-1883 . . . . **NCLC 9**
See also DLB 129

Wagner-Martin, Linda 1936- . . . . **CLC 50**

Wagoner, David (Russell)
1926- . . . . **CLC 3, 5, 15**
See also CA 1-4R; CAAS 3; CANR 2;
DLB 5; SATA 14

Wah, Fred(erick James) 1939- . . . . . . **CLC 44**
See also CA 107; 141; DLB 60

Wahloo, Per 1926-1975 . . . . **CLC 7**
See also CA 61-64

Wahloo, Peter
See Wahloo, Per

Wain, John (Barrington)
1925-1994 . . . . **CLC 2, 11, 15, 46**
See also CA 5-8R; 145; CAAS 4; CANR 23;
CDBLB 1960 to Present; DLB 15, 27,
139, 155; MTCW

Wajda, Andrzej 1926- . . . . **CLC 16**
See also CA 102

Wakefield, Dan 1932- . . . . **CLC 7**
See also CA 21-24R; CAAS 7

Wakoski, Diane
1937- . . . . . **CLC 2, 4, 7, 9, 11, 40; PC 15**
See also CA 13-16R; CAAS 1; CANR 9;
DAM POET; DLB 5; INT CANR-9

Wakoski-Sherbell, Diane
See Wakoski, Diane

Walcott, Derek (Alton)
1930- . . . . **CLC 2, 4, 9, 14, 25, 42, 67, 76;**
BLC; DAB; DAC
See also BW 2; CA 89-92; CANR 26, 47;
DAM MST, MULT, POET; DLB 117;
DLBY 81; MTCW

Waldman, Anne 1945- . . . . **CLC 7**
See also CA 37-40R; CAAS 17; CANR 34;
DLB 16

Waldo, E. Hunter
See Sturgeon, Theodore (Hamilton)

Waldo, Edward Hamilton
See Sturgeon, Theodore (Hamilton)

Walker, Alice (Malsenior)
1944- . . . . **CLC 5, 6, 9, 19, 27, 46, 58;**
BLC; DA; DAB; DAC; SSC 5
See also AAYA 3; BEST 89:4; BW 2;
CA 37-40R; CANR 9, 27, 49;
CDALB 1968-1988; DAM MST, MULT,
NOV, POET, POP; DLB 6, 33, 143;
INT CANR-27; MTCW; SATA 31

Walker, David Harry 1911-1992 . . . . **CLC 14**
See also CA 1-4R; 137; CANR 1; SATA 8;
SATA-Obit 71

Walker, Edward Joseph 1934-
See Walker, Ted
See also CA 21-24R; CANR 12, 28, 53

Walker, George F.
1947- . . . . **CLC 44, 61; DAB; DAC**
See also CA 103; CANR 21, 43;
DAM MST; DLB 60

Walker, Joseph A. 1935- . . . . **CLC 19**
See also BW 1; CA 89-92; CANR 26;
DAM DRAM, MST; DLB 38

Walker, Margaret (Abigail)
1915- . . . . **CLC 1, 6; BLC**
See also BW 2; CA 73-76; CANR 26;
DAM MULT; DLB 76, 152; MTCW

Walker, Ted . . . . **CLC 13**
See also Walker, Edward Joseph
See also DLB 40

Wallace, David Foster 1962- . . . . **CLC 50**
See also CA 132

Wallace, Dexter
See Masters, Edgar Lee

Wallace, (Richard Horatio) Edgar
1875-1932 . . . . **TCLC 57**
See also CA 115; DLB 70

Wallace, Irving 1916-1990 . . . . . . **CLC 7, 13**
See also AITN 1; CA 1-4R; 132; CAAS 1;
CANR 1, 27; DAM NOV, POP;
INT CANR-27; MTCW

Wallant, Edward Lewis
1926-1962 . . . . **CLC 5, 10**
See also CA 1-4R; CANR 22; DLB 2, 28,
143; MTCW

Walley, Byron
See Card, Orson Scott

Walpole, Horace 1717-1797 . . . . **LC 2**
See also DLB 39, 104

Walpole, Hugh (Seymour)
1884-1941 . . . . **TCLC 5**
See also CA 104; DLB 34

Walser, Martin 1927- . . . . **CLC 27**
See also CA 57-60; CANR 8, 46; DLB 75,
124

Walser, Robert
1878-1956 . . . . **TCLC 18; SSC 20**
See also CA 118; DLB 66

Walsh, Jill Paton . . . . **CLC 35**
See also Paton Walsh, Gillian
See also AAYA 11; CLR 2; DLB 161;
SAAS 3

Walter, Villiam Christian
See Andersen, Hans Christian

Wambaugh, Joseph (Aloysius, Jr.)
1937- . . . . **CLC 3, 18**
See also AITN 1; BEST 89:3; CA 33-36R;
CANR 42; DAM NOV, POP; DLB 6;
DLBY 83; MTCW

Ward, Arthur Henry Sarsfield 1883-1959
See Rohmer, Sax
See also CA 108

Ward, Douglas Turner 1930- . . . . **CLC 19**
See also BW 1; CA 81-84; CANR 27;
DLB 7, 38

Ward, Mary Augusta
See Ward, Mrs. Humphry

Ward, Mrs. Humphry
1851-1920 . . . . **TCLC 55**
See also DLB 18

Ward, Peter
See Faust, Frederick (Schiller)

Warhol, Andy 1928(?)-1987 . . . . **CLC 20**
See also AAYA 12; BEST 89:4; CA 89-92;
121; CANR 34

Warner, Francis (Robert le Plastrier)
1937- . . . . **CLC 14**
See also CA 53-56; CANR 11

Warner, Marina 1946- . . . . **CLC 59**
See also CA 65-68; CANR 21

Warner, Rex (Ernest) 1905-1986 . . . . **CLC 45**
See also CA 89-92; 119; DLB 15

Warner, Susan (Bogert)
1819-1885 . . . . **NCLC 31**
See also DLB 3, 42

Warner, Sylvia (Constance) Ashton
See Ashton-Warner, Sylvia (Constance)

Warner, Sylvia Townsend
1893-1978 . . . . **CLC 7, 19; SSC 23**
See also CA 61-64; 77-80; CANR 16;
DLB 34, 139; MTCW

Warren, Mercy Otis 1728-1814 . . . **NCLC 13**
See also DLB 31

Warren, Robert Penn
1905-1989 . . . . **CLC 1, 4, 6, 8, 10, 13, 18,**
39, 53, 59; DA; DAB; DAC; SSC 4; WLC
See also AITN 1; CA 13-16R; 129;
CANR 10, 47; CDALB 1968-1988;
DAM MST, NOV, POET; DLB 2, 48,
152; DLBY 80, 89; INT CANR-10;
MTCW; SATA 46; SATA-Obit 63

Warshofsky, Isaac
See Singer, Isaac Bashevis

Warton, Thomas 1728-1790 . . . . **LC 15**
See also DAM POET; DLB 104, 109

Waruk, Kona
See Harris, (Theodore) Wilson

Warung, Price 1855-1911 . . . . **TCLC 45**

Warwick, Jarvis
See Garner, Hugh

Washington, Alex
See Harris, Mark

Washington, Booker T(aliaferro)
1856-1915 . . . . **TCLC 10; BLC**
See also BW 1; CA 114; 125; DAM MULT;
SATA 28

Washington, George 1732-1799 . . . . . . **LC 25**
See also DLB 31

Wassermann, (Karl) Jakob
1873-1934 .... TCLC **6**
See also CA 104; DLB 66

Wasserstein, Wendy
1950- .... CLC **32, 59, 90; DC 4**
See also CA 121; 129; CABS 3; CANR 53;
DAM DRAM; INT 129

Waterhouse, Keith (Spencer)
1929- .... CLC **47**
See also CA 5-8R; CANR 38; DLB 13, 15;
MTCW

Waters, Frank (Joseph)
1902-1995 .... CLC **88**
See also CA 5-8R; 149; CAAS 13; CANR 3,
18; DLBY 86

Waters, Roger 1944- .... CLC **35**

Watkins, Frances Ellen
See Harper, Frances Ellen Watkins

Watkins, Gerrold
See Malzberg, Barry N(athaniel)

Watkins, Gloria 1955(?)-
See hooks, bell
See also BW 2; CA 143

Watkins, Paul 1964- .... CLC **55**
See also CA 132

Watkins, Vernon Phillips
1906-1967 .... CLC **43**
See also CA 9-10; 25-28R; CAP 1; DLB 20

Watson, Irving S.
See Mencken, H(enry) L(ouis)

Watson, John H.
See Farmer, Philip Jose

Watson, Richard F.
See Silverberg, Robert

Waugh, Auberon (Alexander) 1939- .. CLC **7**
See also CA 45-48; CANR 6, 22; DLB 14

Waugh, Evelyn (Arthur St. John)
1903-1966 ...... CLC **1, 3, 8, 13, 19, 27,
44; DA; DAB; DAC; WLC**
See also CA 85-88; 25-28R; CANR 22;
CDBLB 1914-1945; DAM MST, NOV,
POP; DLB 15, 162; MTCW

Waugh, Harriet 1944- .... CLC **6**
See also CA 85-88; CANR 22

Ways, C. R.
See Blount, Roy (Alton), Jr.

Waystaff, Simon
See Swift, Jonathan

Webb, (Martha) Beatrice (Potter)
1858-1943 .... TCLC **22**
See also Potter, Beatrice
See also CA 117

Webb, Charles (Richard) 1939- ...... CLC **7**
See also CA 25-28R

Webb, James H(enry), Jr. 1946- .... CLC **22**
See also CA 81-84

Webb, Mary (Gladys Meredith)
1881-1927 .... TCLC **24**
See also CA 123; DLB 34

Webb, Mrs. Sidney
See Webb, (Martha) Beatrice (Potter)

Webb, Phyllis 1927- .... CLC **18**
See also CA 104; CANR 23; DLB 53

Webb, Sidney (James)
1859-1947 .... TCLC **22**
See also CA 117

Webber, Andrew Lloyd .... CLC **21**
See also Lloyd Webber, Andrew

Weber, Lenora Mattingly
1895-1971 .... CLC **12**
See also CA 19-20; 29-32R; CAP 1;
SATA 2; SATA-Obit 26

Webster, John
1579(?)-1634(?) ...... LC **33; DA; DAB;
DAC; DC 2; WLC**
See also CDBLB Before 1660;
DAM DRAM, MST; DLB 58

Webster, Noah 1758-1843 .... NCLC **30**

Wedekind, (Benjamin) Frank(lin)
1864-1918 .... TCLC **7**
See also CA 104; DAM DRAM; DLB 118

Weidman, Jerome 1913- .... CLC **7**
See also AITN 2; CA 1-4R; CANR 1;
DLB 28

Weil, Simone (Adolphine)
1909-1943 .... TCLC **23**
See also CA 117

Weinstein, Nathan
See West, Nathanael

Weinstein, Nathan von Wallenstein
See West, Nathanael

Weir, Peter (Lindsay) 1944- .... CLC **20**
See also CA 113; 123

Weiss, Peter (Ulrich)
1916-1982 .... CLC **3, 15, 51**
See also CA 45-48; 106; CANR 3;
DAM DRAM; DLB 69, 124

Weiss, Theodore (Russell)
1916- .... CLC **3, 8, 14**
See also CA 9-12R; CAAS 2; CANR 46;
DLB 5

Welch, (Maurice) Denton
1915-1948 .... TCLC **22**
See also CA 121; 148

Welch, James 1940- .... CLC **6, 14, 52**
See also CA 85-88; CANR 42;
DAM MULT, POP; NNAL

Weldon, Fay
1933- .... CLC **6, 9, 11, 19, 36, 59**
See also CA 21-24R; CANR 16, 46;
CDBLB 1960 to Present; DAM POP;
DLB 14; INT CANR-16; MTCW

Wellek, Rene 1903-1995 .... CLC **28**
See also CA 5-8R; 150; CAAS 7; CANR 8;
DLB 63; INT CANR-8

Weller, Michael 1942- .... CLC **10, 53**
See also CA 85-88

Weller, Paul 1958- .... CLC **26**

Wellershoff, Dieter 1925- .... CLC **46**
See also CA 89-92; CANR 16, 37

Welles, (George) Orson
1915-1985 .... CLC **20, 80**
See also CA 93-96; 117

Wellman, Mac 1945- .... CLC **65**

Wellman, Manly Wade 1903-1986 .. CLC **49**
See also CA 1-4R; 118; CANR 6, 16, 44;
SATA 6; SATA-Obit 47

Wells, Carolyn 1869(?)-1942 ...... TCLC **35**
See also CA 113; DLB 11

Wells, H(erbert) G(eorge)
1866-1946 .... TCLC **6, 12, 19; DA;
DAB; DAC; SSC 6; WLC**
See also AAYA 18; CA 110; 121;
CDBLB 1914-1945; DAM MST, NOV;
DLB 34, 70, 156; MTCW; SATA 20

Wells, Rosemary 1943- .... CLC **12**
See also AAYA 13; CA 85-88; CANR 48;
CLR 16; MAICYA; SAAS 1; SATA 18,
69

Welty, Eudora
1909- ...... CLC **1, 2, 5, 14, 22, 33; DA;
DAB; DAC; SSC 1; WLC**
See also CA 9-12R; CABS 1; CANR 32;
CDALB 1941-1968; DAM MST, NOV;
DLB 2, 102, 143; DLBD 12; DLBY 87;
MTCW

Wen I-to 1899-1946 .... TCLC **28**

Wentworth, Robert
See Hamilton, Edmond

Werfel, Franz (V.) 1890-1945 ...... TCLC **8**
See also CA 104; DLB 81, 124

Wergeland, Henrik Arnold
1808-1845 .... NCLC **5**

Wersba, Barbara 1932- .... CLC **30**
See also AAYA 2; CA 29-32R; CANR 16,
38; CLR 3; DLB 52; JRDA; MAICYA;
SAAS 2; SATA 1, 58

Wertmueller, Lina 1928- .... CLC **16**
See also CA 97-100; CANR 39

Wescott, Glenway 1901-1987....... CLC **13**
See also CA 13-16R; 121; CANR 23;
DLB 4, 9, 102

Wesker, Arnold 1932- .. CLC **3, 5, 42; DAB**
See also CA 1-4R; CAAS 7; CANR 1, 33;
CDBLB 1960 to Present; DAM DRAM;
DLB 13; MTCW

Wesley, Richard (Errol) 1945-....... CLC **7**
See also BW 1; CA 57-60; CANR 27;
DLB 38

Wessel, Johan Herman 1742-1785 .... LC **7**

West, Anthony (Panther)
1914-1987 .... CLC **50**
See also CA 45-48; 124; CANR 3, 19;
DLB 15

West, C. P.
See Wodehouse, P(elham) G(renville)

West, (Mary) Jessamyn
1902-1984 .... CLC **7, 17**
See also CA 9-12R; 112; CANR 27; DLB 6;
DLBY 84; MTCW; SATA-Obit 37

West, Morris L(anglo) 1916-..... CLC **6, 33**
See also CA 5-8R; CANR 24, 49; MTCW

West, Nathanael
1903-1940 ..... TCLC **1, 14, 44; SSC 16**
See also CA 104; 125; CDALB 1929-1941;
DLB 4, 9, 28; MTCW

West, Owen
See Koontz, Dean R(ay)

West, Paul 1930- .... CLC **7, 14**
See also CA 13-16R; CAAS 7; CANR 22,
53; DLB 14; INT CANR-22

West, Rebecca 1892-1983 . . CLC 7, 9, 31, 50
See also CA 5-8R; 109; CANR 19; DLB 36;
DLBY 83; MTCW

Westall, Robert (Atkinson)
1929-1993 . . . . CLC 17
See also AAYA 12; CA 69-72; 141;
CANR 18; CLR 13; JRDA; MAICYA;
SAAS 2; SATA 23, 69; SATA-Obit 75

Westlake, Donald E(dwin)
1933- . . . . CLC 7, 33
See also CA 17-20R; CAAS 13; CANR 16,
44; DAM POP; INT CANR-16

Westmacott, Mary
See Christie, Agatha (Mary Clarissa)

Weston, Allen
See Norton, Andre

Wetcheek, J. L.
See Feuchtwanger, Lion

Wetering, Janwillem van de
See van de Wetering, Janwillem

Wetherell, Elizabeth
See Warner, Susan (Bogert)

Whale, James 1889-1957 . . . . TCLC 63

Whalen, Philip 1923- . . . . CLC 6, 29
See also CA 9-12R; CANR 5, 39; DLB 16

Wharton, Edith (Newbold Jones)
1862-1937 . . . . . . TCLC 3, 9, 27, 53; DA;
DAB; DAC; SSC 6; WLC
See also CA 104; 132; CDALB 1865-1917;
DAM MST, NOV; DLB 4, 9, 12, 78;
DLBD 13; MTCW

Wharton, James
See Mencken, H(enry) L(ouis)

Wharton, William (a pseudonym)
. . . . CLC 18, 37
See also CA 93-96; DLBY 80; INT 93-96

Wheatley (Peters), Phillis
1754(?)-1784 . . . . LC 3; BLC; DA; DAC;
PC 3; WLC
See also CDALB 1640-1865; DAM MST,
MULT, POET; DLB 31, 50

Wheelock, John Hall 1886-1978 . . . . CLC 14
See also CA 13-16R; 77-80; CANR 14;
DLB 45

White, E(lwyn) B(rooks)
1899-1985 . . . . CLC 10, 34, 39
See also AITN 2; CA 13-16R; 116;
CANR 16, 37; CLR 1, 21; DAM POP;
DLB 11, 22; MAICYA; MTCW;
SATA 2, 29; SATA-Obit 44

White, Edmund (Valentine III)
1940- . . . . CLC 27
See also AAYA 7; CA 45-48; CANR 3, 19,
36; DAM POP; MTCW

White, Patrick (Victor Martindale)
1912-1990 . . CLC 3, 4, 5, 7, 9, 18, 65, 69
See also CA 81-84; 132; CANR 43; MTCW

White, Phyllis Dorothy James 1920-
See James, P. D.
See also CA 21-24R; CANR 17, 43;
DAM POP; MTCW

White, T(erence) H(anbury)
1906-1964 . . . . CLC 30
See also CA 73-76; CANR 37; DLB 160;
JRDA; MAICYA; SATA 12

White, Terence de Vere
1912-1994 . . . . CLC 49
See also CA 49-52; 145; CANR 3

White, Walter F(rancis)
1893-1955 . . . . TCLC 15
See also White, Walter
See also BW 1; CA 115; 124; DLB 51

White, William Hale 1831-1913
See Rutherford, Mark
See also CA 121

Whitehead, E(dward) A(nthony)
1933- . . . . CLC 5
See also CA 65-68

Whitemore, Hugh (John) 1936- . . . . . CLC 37
See also CA 132; INT 132

Whitman, Sarah Helen (Power)
1803-1878 . . . . NCLC 19
See also DLB 1

Whitman, Walt(er)
1819-1892 . . . . . NCLC 4, 31; DA; DAB;
DAC; PC 3; WLC
See also CDALB 1640-1865; DAM MST,
POET; DLB 3, 64; SATA 20

Whitney, Phyllis A(yame) 1903- . . . . CLC 42
See also AITN 2; BEST 90:3; CA 1-4R;
CANR 3, 25, 38; DAM POP; JRDA;
MAICYA; SATA 1, 30

Whittemore, (Edward) Reed (Jr.)
1919- . . . . CLC 4
See also CA 9-12R; CAAS 8; CANR 4;
DLB 5

Whittier, John Greenleaf
1807-1892 . . . . NCLC 8, 57
See also CDALB 1640-1865; DAM POET;
DLB 1

Whittlebot, Hernia
See Coward, Noel (Peirce)

Wicker, Thomas Grey 1926-
See Wicker, Tom
See also CA 65-68; CANR 21, 46

Wicker, Tom . . . . CLC 7
See also Wicker, Thomas Grey

Wideman, John Edgar
1941- . . . . CLC 5, 34, 36, 67; BLC
See also BW 2; CA 85-88; CANR 14, 42;
DAM MULT; DLB 33, 143

Wiebe, Rudy (Henry)
1934- . . . . CLC 6, 11, 14; DAC
See also CA 37-40R; CANR 42;
DAM MST; DLB 60

Wieland, Christoph Martin
1733-1813 . . . . NCLC 17
See also DLB 97

Wiene, Robert 1881-1938 . . . . TCLC 56

Wieners, John 1934- . . . . CLC 7
See also CA 13-16R; DLB 16

Wiesel, Elie(zer)
1928- . . . . . . CLC 3, 5, 11, 37; DA; DAB;
DAC
See also AAYA 7; AITN 1; CA 5-8R;
CAAS 4; CANR 8, 40; DAM MST,
NOV; DLB 83; DLBY 87; INT CANR-8;
MTCW; SATA 56

Wiggins, Marianne 1947- . . . . CLC 57
See also BEST 89:3; CA 130

Wight, James Alfred 1916-
See Herriot, James
See also CA 77-80; SATA 55;
SATA-Brief 44

Wilbur, Richard (Purdy)
1921- . . . CLC 3, 6, 9, 14, 53; DA; DAB;
DAC
See also CA 1-4R; CABS 2; CANR 2, 29;
DAM MST, POET; DLB 5;
INT CANR-29; MTCW; SATA 9

Wild, Peter 1940- . . . . CLC 14
See also CA 37-40R; DLB 5

Wilde, Oscar (Fingal O'Flahertie Wills)
1854(?)-1900 . . . . TCLC 1, 8, 23, 41; DA;
DAB; DAC; SSC 11; WLC
See also CA 104; 119; CDBLB 1890-1914;
DAM DRAM, MST, NOV; DLB 10, 19,
34, 57, 141, 156; SATA 24

Wilder, Billy . . . . CLC 20
See also Wilder, Samuel
See also DLB 26

Wilder, Samuel 1906-
See Wilder, Billy
See also CA 89-92

Wilder, Thornton (Niven)
1897-1975 . . . . . . CLC 1, 5, 6, 10, 15, 35,
82; DA; DAB; DAC; DC 1; WLC
See also AITN 2; CA 13-16R; 61-64;
CANR 40; DAM DRAM, MST, NOV;
DLB 4, 7, 9; MTCW

Wilding, Michael 1942- . . . . CLC 73
See also CA 104; CANR 24, 49

Wiley, Richard 1944- . . . . CLC 44
See also CA 121; 129

Wilhelm, Kate . . . . CLC 7
See also Wilhelm, Katie Gertrude
See also CAAS 5; DLB 8; INT CANR-17

Wilhelm, Katie Gertrude 1928-
See Wilhelm, Kate
See also CA 37-40R; CANR 17, 36; MTCW

Wilkins, Mary
See Freeman, Mary Eleanor Wilkins

Willard, Nancy 1936- . . . . CLC 7, 37
See also CA 89-92; CANR 10, 39; CLR 5;
DLB 5, 52; MAICYA; MTCW;
SATA 37, 71; SATA-Brief 30

Williams, C(harles) K(enneth)
1936- . . . . CLC 33, 56
See also CA 37-40R; DAM POET; DLB 5

Williams, Charles
See Collier, James L(incoln)

Williams, Charles (Walter Stansby)
1886-1945 . . . . TCLC 1, 11
See also CA 104; DLB 100, 153

Williams, (George) Emlyn
1905-1987 . . . . CLC 15
See also CA 104; 123; CANR 36;
DAM DRAM; DLB 10, 77; MTCW

Williams, Hugo 1942- . . . . CLC 42
See also CA 17-20R; CANR 45; DLB 40

Williams, J. Walker
See Wodehouse, P(elham) G(renville)

Williams, John A(lfred)
1925- . . . . CLC 5, 13; BLC
See also BW 2; CA 53-56; CAAS 3;
CANR 6, 26, 51; DAM MULT; DLB 2,
33; INT CANR-6

Williams, Jonathan (Chamberlain)
1929- . . . . CLC 13
See also CA 9-12R; CAAS 12; CANR 8;
DLB 5

Williams, Joy 1944- . . . . CLC 31
See also CA 41-44R; CANR 22, 48

Williams, Norman 1952- . . . . CLC 39
See also CA 118

Williams, Sherley Anne
1944- . . . . CLC 89; BLC
See also BW 2; CA 73-76; CANR 25;
DAM MULT, POET; DLB 41;
INT CANR-25; SATA 78

Williams, Shirley
See Williams, Sherley Anne

Williams, Tennessee
1911-1983 . . . . . CLC 1, 2, 5, 7, 8, 11, 15,
19, 30, 39, 45, 71; DA; DAB; DAC;
DC 4; WLC
See also AITN 1, 2; CA 5-8R; 108;
CABS 3; CANR 31; CDALB 1941-1968;
DAM DRAM, MST; DLB 7; DLBD 4;
DLBY 83; MTCW

Williams, Thomas (Alonzo)
1926-1990 . . . . CLC 14
See also CA 1-4R; 132; CANR 2

Williams, William C.
See Williams, William Carlos

Williams, William Carlos
1883-1963 . . . . CLC 1, 2, 5, 9, 13, 22, 42,
67; DA; DAB; DAC; PC 7
See also CA 89-92; CANR 34;
CDALB 1917-1929; DAM MST, POET;
DLB 4, 16, 54, 86; MTCW

Williamson, David (Keith) 1942- . . . . CLC 56
See also CA 103; CANR 41

Williamson, Ellen Douglas 1905-1984
See Douglas, Ellen
See also CA 17-20R; 114; CANR 39

Williamson, Jack . . . . CLC 29
See also Williamson, John Stewart
See also CAAS 8; DLB 8

Williamson, John Stewart 1908-
See Williamson, Jack
See also CA 17-20R; CANR 23

Willie, Frederick
See Lovecraft, H(oward) P(hillips)

Willingham, Calder (Baynard, Jr.)
1922-1995 . . . . CLC 5, 51
See also CA 5-8R; 147; CANR 3; DLB 2,
44; MTCW

Willis, Charles
See Clarke, Arthur C(harles)

Willy
See Colette, (Sidonie-Gabrielle)

Willy, Colette
See Colette, (Sidonie-Gabrielle)

Wilson, A(ndrew) N(orman) 1950- . . CLC 33
See also CA 112; 122; DLB 14, 155

Wilson, Angus (Frank Johnstone)
1913-1991 . . CLC 2, 3, 5, 25, 34; SSC 21
See also CA 5-8R; 134; CANR 21; DLB 15,
139, 155; MTCW

Wilson, August
1945- . . . . CLC 39, 50, 63; BLC; DA;
DAB; DAC; DC 2
See also AAYA 16; BW 2; CA 115; 122;
CANR 42; DAM DRAM, MST, MULT;
MTCW

Wilson, Brian 1942- . . . . CLC 12

Wilson, Colin 1931- . . . . CLC 3, 14
See also CA 1-4R; CAAS 5; CANR 1, 22,
33; DLB 14; MTCW

Wilson, Dirk
See Pohl, Frederik

Wilson, Edmund
1895-1972 . . . . CLC 1, 2, 3, 8, 24
See also CA 1-4R; 37-40R; CANR 1, 46;
DLB 63; MTCW

Wilson, Ethel Davis (Bryant)
1888(?)-1980 . . . . CLC 13; DAC
See also CA 102; DAM POET; DLB 68;
MTCW

Wilson, John 1785-1854 . . . . NCLC 5

Wilson, John (Anthony) Burgess 1917-1993
See Burgess, Anthony
See also CA 1-4R; 143; CANR 2, 46; DAC;
DAM NOV; MTCW

Wilson, Lanford 1937- . . . . CLC 7, 14, 36
See also CA 17-20R; CABS 3; CANR 45;
DAM DRAM; DLB 7

Wilson, Robert M. 1944- . . . . CLC 7, 9
See also CA 49-52; CANR 2, 41; MTCW

Wilson, Robert McLiam 1964- . . . . . CLC 59
See also CA 132

Wilson, Sloan 1920- . . . . CLC 32
See also CA 1-4R; CANR 1, 44

Wilson, Snoo 1948- . . . . CLC 33
See also CA 69-72

Wilson, William S(mith) 1932- . . . . . CLC 49
See also CA 81-84

Winchilsea, Anne (Kingsmill) Finch Counte
1661-1720 . . . . LC 3

Windham, Basil
See Wodehouse, P(elham) G(renville)

Wingrove, David (John) 1954- . . . . . . CLC 68
See also CA 133

Winters, Janet Lewis . . . . CLC 41
See also Lewis, Janet
See also DLBY 87

Winters, (Arthur) Yvor
1900-1968 . . . . CLC 4, 8, 32
See also CA 11-12; 25-28R; CAP 1;
DLB 48; MTCW

Winterson, Jeanette 1959- . . . . CLC 64
See also CA 136; DAM POP

Winthrop, John 1588-1649 . . . . LC 31
See also DLB 24, 30

Wiseman, Frederick 1930- . . . . CLC 20

Wister, Owen 1860-1938 . . . . TCLC 21
See also CA 108; DLB 9, 78; SATA 62

Witkacy
See Witkiewicz, Stanislaw Ignacy

Witkiewicz, Stanislaw Ignacy
1885-1939 . . . . TCLC 8
See also CA 105

Wittgenstein, Ludwig (Josef Johann)
1889-1951 . . . . TCLC 59
See also CA 113

Wittig, Monique 1935(?)- . . . . CLC 22
See also CA 116; 135; DLB 83

Wittlin, Jozef 1896-1976 . . . . CLC 25
See also CA 49-52; 65-68; CANR 3

Wodehouse, P(elham) G(renville)
1881-1975 . . . CLC 1, 2, 5, 10, 22; DAB;
DAC; SSC 2
See also AITN 2; CA 45-48; 57-60;
CANR 3, 33; CDBLB 1914-1945;
DAM NOV; DLB 34, 162; MTCW;
SATA 22

Woiwode, L.
See Woiwode, Larry (Alfred)

Woiwode, Larry (Alfred) 1941- . . . . CLC 6, 10
See also CA 73-76; CANR 16; DLB 6;
INT CANR-16

Wojciechowska, Maia (Teresa)
1927- . . . . CLC 26
See also AAYA 8; CA 9-12R; CANR 4, 41;
CLR 1; JRDA; MAICYA; SAAS 1;
SATA 1, 28, 83

Wolf, Christa 1929- . . . . CLC 14, 29, 58
See also CA 85-88; CANR 45; DLB 75;
MTCW

Wolfe, Gene (Rodman) 1931- . . . . CLC 25
See also CA 57-60; CAAS 9; CANR 6, 32;
DAM POP; DLB 8

Wolfe, George C. 1954- . . . . CLC 49
See also CA 149

Wolfe, Thomas (Clayton)
1900-1938 . . . . . TCLC 4, 13, 29, 61; DA;
DAB; DAC; WLC
See also CA 104; 132; CDALB 1929-1941;
DAM MST, NOV; DLB 9, 102; DLBD 2;
DLBY 85; MTCW

Wolfe, Thomas Kennerly, Jr. 1931-
See Wolfe, Tom
See also CA 13-16R; CANR 9, 33;
DAM POP; INT CANR-9; MTCW

Wolfe, Tom . . . . CLC 1, 2, 9, 15, 35, 51
See also Wolfe, Thomas Kennerly, Jr.
See also AAYA 8; AITN 2; BEST 89:1;
DLB 152

Wolff, Geoffrey (Ansell) 1937- . . . . . CLC 41
See also CA 29-32R; CANR 29, 43

Wolff, Sonia
See Levitin, Sonia (Wolff)

Wolff, Tobias (Jonathan Ansell)
1945- . . . . CLC 39, 64
See also AAYA 16; BEST 90:2; CA 114;
117; CAAS 22; DLB 130; INT 117

Wolfram von Eschenbach
c. 1170-c. 1220 . . . . CMLC 5
See also DLB 138

Wolitzer, Hilma 1930- . . . . CLC 17
See also CA 65-68; CANR 18, 40;
INT CANR-18; SATA 31

Wollstonecraft, Mary 1759-1797 . . . . . . LC 5
See also CDBLB 1789-1832; DLB 39, 104,
158

Wonder, Stevie .... CLC 12
See also Morris, Steveland Judkins

Wong, Jade Snow 1922- .... CLC 17
See also CA 109

Woodcott, Keith
See Brunner, John (Kilian Houston)

Woodruff, Robert W.
See Mencken, H(enry) L(ouis)

Woolf, (Adeline) Virginia
1882-1941 ...... TCLC 1, 5, 20, 43, 56;
DA; DAB; DAC; SSC 7; WLC
See also CA 104; 130; CDBLB 1914-1945;
DAM MST, NOV; DLB 36, 100, 162;
DLBD 10; MTCW

Woollcott, Alexander (Humphreys)
1887-1943 .... TCLC 5
See also CA 105; DLB 29

Woolrich, Cornell 1903-1968....... CLC 77
See also Hopley-Woolrich, Cornell George

Wordsworth, Dorothy
1771-1855 .... NCLC 25
See also DLB 107

Wordsworth, William
1770-1850 .... NCLC 12, 38; DA; DAB;
DAC; PC 4; WLC
See also CDBLB 1789-1832; DAM MST,
POET; DLB 93, 107

Wouk, Herman 1915- .... CLC 1, 9, 38
See also CA 5-8R; CANR 6, 33;
DAM NOV, POP; DLBY 82;
INT CANR-6; MTCW

Wright, Charles (Penzel, Jr.)
1935- .... CLC 6, 13, 28
See also CA 29-32R; CAAS 7; CANR 23,
36; DLB 165; DLBY 82; MTCW

Wright, Charles Stevenson
1932- .... CLC 49; BLC 3
See also BW 1; CA 9-12R; CANR 26;
DAM MULT, POET; DLB 33

Wright, Jack R.
See Harris, Mark

Wright, James (Arlington)
1927-1980 .... CLC 3, 5, 10, 28
See also AITN 2; CA 49-52; 97-100;
CANR 4, 34; DAM POET; DLB 5;
MTCW

Wright, Judith (Arandell)
1915- .... CLC 11, 53; PC 14
See also CA 13-16R; CANR 31; MTCW;
SATA 14

Wright, L(auralı) R. 1939- .... CLC 44
See also CA 138

Wright, Richard (Nathaniel)
1908-1960 .... CLC 1, 3, 4, 9, 14, 21, 48,
74; BLC; DA; DAB; DAC; SSC 2; WLC
See also AAYA 5; BW 1; CA 108;
CDALB 1929-1941; DAM MST, MULT,
NOV; DLB 76, 102; DLBD 2; MTCW

Wright, Richard B(ruce) 1937- ...... CLC 6
See also CA 85-88; DLB 53

Wright, Rick 1945- .... CLC 35

Wright, Rowland
See Wells, Carolyn

Wright, Stephen Caldwell 1946- .... CLC 33
See also BW 2

Wright, Willard Huntington 1888-1939
See Van Dine, S. S.
See also CA 115

Wright, William 1930- .... CLC 44
See also CA 53-56; CANR 7, 23

Wroth, LadyMary 1587-1653(?) ..... LC 30
See also DLB 121

Wu Ch'eng-en 1500(?)-1582(?)....... LC 7

Wu Ching-tzu 1701-1754 .... LC 2

Wurlitzer, Rudolph 1938(?)- ... CLC 2, 4, 15
See also CA 85-88

Wycherley, William 1641-1715.... LC 8, 21
See also CDBLB 1660-1789; DAM DRAM;
DLB 80

Wylie, Elinor (Morton Hoyt)
1885-1928 .... TCLC 8
See also CA 105; DLB 9, 45

Wylie, Philip (Gordon) 1902-1971... CLC 43
See also CA 21-22; 33-36R; CAP 2; DLB 9

Wyndham, John................... CLC 19
See also Harris, John (Wyndham Parkes
Lucas) Beynon

Wyss, Johann David Von
1743-1818 .... NCLC 10
See also JRDA; MAICYA; SATA 29;
SATA-Brief 27

Xenophon
c. 430B.C.-c. 354B.C......... CMLC 17

Yakumo Koizumi
See Hearn, (Patricio) Lafcadio (Tessima
Carlos)

Yanez, Jose Donoso
See Donoso (Yanez), Jose

Yanovsky, Basile S.
See Yanovsky, V(assily) S(emenovich)

Yanovsky, V(assily) S(emenovich)
1906-1989 .... CLC 2, 18
See also CA 97-100; 129

Yates, Richard 1926-1992 ..... CLC 7, 8, 23
See also CA 5-8R; 139; CANR 10, 43;
DLB 2; DLBY 81, 92; INT CANR-10

Yeats, W. B.
See Yeats, William Butler

Yeats, William Butler
1865-1939 ..... TCLC 1, 11, 18, 31; DA;
DAB; DAC; WLC
See also CA 104; 127; CANR 45;
CDBLB 1890-1914; DAM DRAM, MST,
POET; DLB 10, 19, 98, 156; MTCW

Yehoshua, A(braham) B.
1936- .... CLC 13, 31
See also CA 33-36R; CANR 43

Yep, Laurence Michael 1948- ...... CLC 35
See also AAYA 5; CA 49-52; CANR 1, 46;
CLR 3, 17; DLB 52; JRDA; MAICYA;
SATA 7, 69

Yerby, Frank G(arvin)
1916-1991 .... CLC 1, 7, 22; BLC
See also BW 1; CA 9-12R; 136; CANR 16,
52; DAM MULT; DLB 76;
INT CANR-16; MTCW

Yesenin, Sergei Alexandrovich
See Esenin, Sergei (Alexandrovich)

Yevtushenko, Yevgeny (Alexandrovich)
1933- .... CLC 1, 3, 13, 26, 51
See also CA 81-84; CANR 33;
DAM POET; MTCW

Yezierska, Anzia 1885(?)-1970 ..... CLC 46
See also CA 126; 89-92; DLB 28; MTCW

Yglesias, Helen 1915- .... CLC 7, 22
See also CA 37-40R; CAAS 20; CANR 15;
INT CANR-15; MTCW

Yokomitsu Riichi 1898-1947 ...... TCLC 47

Yonge, Charlotte (Mary)
1823-1901 .... TCLC 48
See also CA 109; DLB 18, 163; SATA 17

York, Jeremy
See Creasey, John

York, Simon
See Heinlein, Robert A(nson)

Yorke, Henry Vincent 1905-1974 ... CLC 13
See also Green, Henry
See also CA 85-88; 49-52

Yosano Akiko 1878-1942.. TCLC 59; PC 11

Yoshimoto, Banana .... CLC 84
See also Yoshimoto, Mahoko

Yoshimoto, Mahoko 1964-
See Yoshimoto, Banana
See also CA 144

Young, Al(bert James)
1939- .... CLC 19; BLC
See also BW 2; CA 29-32R; CANR 26;
DAM MULT; DLB 33

Young, Andrew (John) 1885-1971.... CLC 5
See also CA 5-8R; CANR 7, 29

Young, Collier
See Bloch, Robert (Albert)

Young, Edward 1683-1765........... LC 3
See also DLB 95

Young, Marguerite (Vivian)
1909-1995 .... CLC 82
See also CA 13-16; 150; CAP 1

Young, Neil 1945-................. CLC 17
See also CA 110

Young Bear, Ray A. 1950-......... CLC 94
See also CA 146; DAM MULT; NNAL

Yourcenar, Marguerite
1903-1987 .... CLC 19, 38, 50, 87
See also CA 69-72; CANR 23; DAM NOV;
DLB 72; DLBY 88; MTCW

Yurick, Sol 1925-................. CLC 6
See also CA 13-16R; CANR 25

Zabolotskii, Nikolai Alekseevich
1903-1958 .... TCLC 52
See also CA 116

Zamiatin, Yevgenii
See Zamyatin, Evgeny Ivanovich

Zamora, Bernice (B. Ortiz)
1938- .... CLC 89; HLC
See also CA 151; DAM MULT; DLB 82;
HW

Zamyatin, Evgeny Ivanovich
1884-1937 .... TCLC 8, 37
See also CA 105

Zangwill, Israel 1864-1926........ TCLC 16
See also CA 109; DLB 10, 135

Zappa, Francis Vincent, Jr. 1940-1993
See Zappa, Frank
See also CA 108; 143

Zappa, Frank . . . . **CLC 17**
See also Zappa, Francis Vincent, Jr.

Zaturenska, Marya 1902-1982 . . . . **CLC 6, 11**
See also CA 13-16R; 105; CANR 22

Zelazny, Roger (Joseph)
1937-1995 . . . . **CLC 21**
See also AAYA 7; CA 21-24R; 148;
CANR 26; DLB 8; MTCW; SATA 57;
SATA-Brief 39

Zhdanov, Andrei A(lexandrovich)
1896-1948 . . . . **TCLC 18**
See also CA 117

Zhukovsky, Vasily 1783-1852 . . . . **NCLC 35**

Ziegenhagen, Eric . . . . **CLC 55**

Zimmer, Jill Schary
See Robinson, Jill

Zimmerman, Robert
See Dylan, Bob

Zindel, Paul
1936- . . . . . **CLC 6, 26; DA; DAB; DAC;**
DC 5
See also AAYA 2; CA 73-76; CANR 31;
CLR 3; DAM DRAM, MST, NOV;
DLB 7, 52; JRDA; MAICYA; MTCW;
SATA 16, 58

Zinov'Ev, A. A.
See Zinoviev, Alexander (Aleksandrovich)

Zinoviev, Alexander (Aleksandrovich)
1922- . . . . **CLC 19**
See also CA 116; 133; CAAS 10

Zoilus
See Lovecraft, H(oward) P(hillips)

Zola, Emile (Edouard Charles Antoine)
1840-1902 . . . . . . **TCLC 1, 6, 21, 41; DA;**
DAB; DAC; WLC
See also CA 104; 138; DAM MST, NOV;
DLB 123

Zoline, Pamela 1941- . . . . **CLC 62**

Zorrilla y Moral, Jose 1817-1893 . . **NCLC 6**

Zoshchenko, Mikhail (Mikhailovich)
1895-1958 . . . . **TCLC 15; SSC 15**
See also CA 115

Zuckmayer, Carl 1896-1977 . . . . **CLC 18**
See also CA 69-72; DLB 56, 124

Zuk, Georges
See Skelton, Robin

Zukofsky, Louis
1904-1978 . . . . **CLC 1, 2, 4, 7, 11, 18;**
PC 11
See also CA 9-12R; 77-80; CANR 39;
DAM POET; DLB 5, 165; MTCW

Zweig, Paul 1935-1984 . . . . **CLC 34, 42**
See also CA 85-88; 113

Zweig, Stefan 1881-1942 . . . . **TCLC 17**
See also CA 112; DLB 81, 118

Literary Criticism Series
Cumulative Topic Index

This index lists all topic entries in Gale's *Classical and Medieval Literature Criticism, Contemporary Literary Criticism, Literature Criticism from 1400 to 1800, Nineteenth-Century Literature Criticism,* and *Twentieth-Century Literary Criticism.*

Age of Johnson LC 15: 1-87
Johnson's London, 3-15
aesthetics of neoclassicism, 15-36
"age of prose and reason," 36-45
clubmen and bluestockings, 45-56
printing technology, 56-62
periodicals: "a map of busy life," 62-74
transition, 74-86

AIDS in Literature CLC 81: 365-416

American Abolitionism NCLC 44: 1-73
overviews, 2-26
abolitionist ideals, 26-46
the literature of abolitionism, 46-72

American Black Humor Fiction TCLC 54: 1-85
characteristics of black humor, 2-13
origins and development, 13-38
black humor distinguished from related literary trends, 38-60
black humor and society, 60-75
black humor reconsidered, 75-83

American Civil War in Literature NCLC 32: 1-109
overviews, 2-20
regional perspectives, 20-54
fiction popular during the war, 54-79
the historical novel, 79-108

American Frontier in Literature NCLC 28: 1-103
definitions, 2-12
development, 12-17
nonfiction writing about the frontier, 17-30
frontier fiction, 30-45
frontier protagonists, 45-66
portrayals of Native Americans, 66-86
feminist readings, 86-98

twentieth-century reaction against frontier literature, 98-100

American Humor Writing NCLC 52: 1-59
overviews, 2-12
the Old Southwest, 12-42
broader impacts, 42-5
women humorists, 45-58

American Popular Song, Golden Age of TCLC 42: 1-49
background and major figures, 2-34
the lyrics of popular songs, 34-47

American Proletarian Literature TCLC 54: 86-175
overviews, 87-95
American proletarian literature and the American Communist Party, 95-111
ideology and literary merit, 111-7
novels, 117-36
Gastonia, 136-48
drama, 148-54
journalism, 154-9
proletarian literature in the United States, 159-74

American Romanticism NCLC 44: 74-138
overviews, 74-84
sociopolitical influences, 84-104
Romanticism and the American frontier, 104-15
thematic concerns, 115-37

American Western Literature TCLC 46: 1-100
definition and development of American Western literature, 2-7
characteristics of the Western novel, 8-23
Westerns as history and fiction, 23-34
critical reception of American Western

literature, 34-41
the Western hero, 41-73
women in Western fiction, 73-91
later Western fiction, 91-9

Art and Literature TCLC 54: 176-248
overviews, 176-93
definitions, 193-219
influence of visual arts on literature, 219-31
spatial form in literature, 231-47

Arthurian Literature CMLC 10: 1-127
historical context and literary beginnings, 2-27
development of the legend through Malory, 27-64
development of the legend from Malory to the Victorian Age, 65-81
themes and motifs, 81-95
principal characters, 95-125

Arthurian Revival NCLC 36: 1-77
overviews, 2-12
Tennyson and his influence, 12-43
other leading figures, 43-73
the Arthurian legend in the visual arts, 73-6

Australian Literature TCLC 50: 1-94
origins and development, 2-21
characteristics of Australian literature, 21-33
historical and critical perspectives, 33-41
poetry, 41-58
fiction, 58-76
drama, 76-82
Aboriginal literature, 82-91

Beat Generation, Literature of the TCLC 42: 50-102

overviews, 51-9
the Beat generation as a social phenomenon, 59-62
development, 62-5
Beat literature, 66-96
influence, 97-100

The Bell Curve Controversy CLC 91: 281-
330

Bildungsroman in Nineteenth-Century
Literature NCLC 20: 92-168
surveys, 93-113
in Germany, 113-40
in England, 140-56
female *Bildungsroman,* 156-67

Bloomsbury Group TCLC 34: 1-73
history and major figures, 2-13
definitions, 13-7
influences, 17-27
thought, 27-40
prose, 40-52
and literary criticism, 52-4
political ideals, 54-61
response to, 61-71

Bly, Robert, *Iron John: A Book about Men
and Men's Work* CLC 70: 414-62

The Book of J CLC 65: 289-311

Businessman in American Literature
TCLC 26: 1-48
portrayal of the businessman, 1-32
themes and techniques in business
fiction, 32-47

Celtic Twilight
See Irish Literary Renaissance

Children's Literature, Nineteenth-Century
NCLC 52: 60-135
overviews, 61-72
moral tales, 72-89
fairy tales and fantasy, 90-119
making men/making women, 119-34

Civic Critics, Russian NCLC 20: 402-46
principal figures and background, 402-9
and Russian Nihilism, 410-6
aesthetic and critical views, 416-45

Colonial America: The Intellectual
Background LC 25: 1-98
overviews, 2-17
philosophy and politics, 17-31
early religious influences in Colonial
America, 31-60
consequences of the Revolution, 60-78
religious influences in post-revolutionary America, 78-87
colonial literary genres, 87-97

Columbus, Christopher, Books on the
Quincentennial of His Arrival in the New
World CLC 70: 329-60

Connecticut Wits NCLC 48: 1-95
general overviews, 2-40
major works, 40-76
intellectual context, 76-95

Crime in Literature TCLC 54: 249-307
evolution of the criminal figure in
literature, 250-61
crime and society, 261-77
literary perspectives on crime and
punishment, 277-88
writings by criminals, 288-306

Czechoslovakian Literature of the
Twentieth Century TCLC 42: 103-96
through World War II, 104-35
de-Stalinization, the Prague Spring, and
contemporary literature, 135-72
Slovak literature, 172-85
Czech science fiction, 185-93

Dadaism TCLC 46: 101-71
background and major figures, 102-16
definitions, 116-26
manifestos and commentary by
Dadaists, 126-40
theater and film, 140-58
nature and characteristics of Dadaist
writing, 158-70

Darwinism and Literature NCLC 32: 110-
206
background, 110-31
direct responses to Darwin, 131-71
collateral effects of Darwinism, 171-205

de Man, Paul, Wartime Journalism of
CLC 55: 382-424

Detective Fiction, Nineteenth-Century
NCLC 36: 78-148
origins of the genre, 79-100
history of nineteenth-century detective
fiction, 101-33
significance of nineteenth-century
detective fiction, 133-46

Detective Fiction, Twentieth-Century
TCLC 38: 1-96
genesis and history of the detective
story, 3-22
defining detective fiction, 22-32
evolution and varieties, 32-77
the appeal of detective fiction, 77-90

The Double in Nineteenth-Century
Literature NCLC 40: 1-95
genesis and development of the theme,
2-15
the double and Romanticism, 16-27
sociological views, 27-52
psychological interpretations, 52-87
philosophical considerations, 87-95

Dramatic Realism NCLC 44: 139-202
overviews, 140-50
origins and definitions, 150-66
impact and influence, 166-93
realist drama and tragedy, 193-201

Electronic "Books": Hypertext and
Hyperfiction CLC 86: 367-404
books vs. CD-ROMS, 367-76
hypertext and hyperfiction, 376-95
implications for publishing, libraries,
and the public, 395-403

Eliot, T. S., Centenary of Birth CLC 55:
345-75

Elizabethan Drama LC 22: 140-240
origins and influences, 142-67
characteristics and conventions, 167-83
theatrical production, 184-200
histories, 200-12
comedy, 213-20
tragedy, 220-30

The Encyclopedists LC 26: 172-253
overviews, 173-210
intellectual background, 210-32
views on esthetics, 232-41

views on women, 241-52

English Caroline Literature LC 13: 221-307
    background, 222-41
    evolution and varieties, 241-62
    the Cavalier mode, 262-75
    court and society, 275-91
    politics and religion, 291-306

English Decadent Literature of the 1890s NCLC 28: 104-200
    fin de siècle: the Decadent period, 105-19
    definitions, 120-37
    major figures: "the tragic generation," 137-50
    French literature and English literary Decadence, 150-7
    themes, 157-61
    poetry, 161-82
    periodicals, 182-96

English Essay, Rise of the LC 18: 238-308
    definitions and origins, 236-54
    influence on the essay, 254-69
    historical background, 269-78
    the essay in the seventeenth century, 279-93
    the essay in the eighteenth century, 293-307

English Romantic Poetry NCLC 28: 201-327
    overviews and reputation, 202-37
    major subjects and themes, 237-67
    forms of Romantic poetry, 267-78
    politics, society, and Romantic poetry, 278-99
    philosophy, religion, and Romantic poetry, 299-324

Espionage Literature TCLC 50: 95-159
    overviews, 96-113
    espionage fiction/formula fiction, 113-26
    spies in fact and fiction, 126-38
    the female spy, 138-44
    social and psychological perspectives, 144-58

European Romanticism NCLC 36: 149-284
    definitions, 149-77
    origins of the movement, 177-82

    Romantic theory, 182-200
    themes and techniques, 200-23
    Romanticism in Germany, 223-39
    Romanticism in France, 240-61
    Romanticism in Italy, 261-4
    Romanticism in Spain, 264-8
    impact and legacy, 268-82

Existentialism and Literature TCLC 42: 197-268
    overviews and definitions, 198-209
    history and influences, 209-19
    Existentialism critiqued and defended, 220-35
    philosophical and religious perspectives, 235-41
    Existentialist fiction and drama, 241-67

Familiar Essay NCLC 48: 96-211
    definitions and origins, 97-130
    overview of the genre, 130-43
    elements of form and style, 143-59
    elements of content, 159-73
    the Cockneys: Hazlitt, Lamb, and Hunt, 173-91
    status of the genre, 191-210

Feminism in the 1990s: Commentary on Works by Naomi Wolf, Susan Faludi, and Camille Paglia CLC 76: 377-415

Feminist Criticism in 1990 CLC 65: 312-60

Fifteenth-Century English Literature LC 17: 248-334
    background, 249-72
    poetry, 272-315
    drama, 315-23
    prose, 323-33

Film and Literature TCLC 38: 97-226
    overviews, 97-119
    film and theater, 119-34
    film and the novel, 134-45
    the art of the screenplay, 145-66
    genre literature/genre film, 167-79
    the writer and the film industry, 179-90
    authors on film adaptations of their works, 190-200
    fiction into film: comparative essays, 200-23

French Drama in the Age of Louis XIV LC 28: 94-185

    overview, 95-127
    tragedy, 127-46
    comedy, 146-66
    tragicomedy, 166-84

French Enlightenment LC 14: 81-145
    the question of definition, 82-9
    Le siècle des lumières, 89-94
    women and the salons, 94-105
    censorship, 105-15
    the philosophy of reason, 115-31
    influence and legacy, 131-44

French Realism NCLC 52: 136-216
    origins and definitions, 137-70
    issues and influence, 170-98
    realism and representation, 198-215

French Revolution and English Literature NCLC 40: 96-195
    history and theory, 96-123
    romantic poetry, 123-50
    the novel, 150-81
    drama, 181-92
    children's literature, 192-5

Futurism, Italian TCLC 42: 269-354
    principles and formative influences, 271-9
    manifestos, 279-88
    literature, 288-303
    theater, 303-19
    art, 320-30
    music, 330-6
    architecture, 336-9
    and politics, 339-46
    reputation and significance, 346-51

Gaelic Revival
See **Irish Literary Renaissance**

Gates, Henry Louis, Jr., and African-American Literary Criticism CLC 65: 361-405

Gay and Lesbian Literature CLC 76: 416-39

German Exile Literature TCLC 30: 1-58
    the writer and the Nazi state, 1-10
    definition of, 10-4
    life in exile, 14-32

Topic Index

surveys, 32-50
Austrian literature in exile, 50-2
German publishing in the United States, 52-7

German Expressionism TCLC 34: 74-160
history and major figures, 76-85
aesthetic theories, 85-109
drama, 109-26
poetry, 126-38
film, 138-42
painting, 142-7
music, 147-53
and politics, 153-8

***Glasnost* and Contemporary Soviet Literature** CLC 59: 355-97

Gothic Novel NCLC 28: 328-402
development and major works, 328-34
definitions, 334-50
themes and techniques, 350-78
in America, 378-85
in Scotland, 385-91
influence and legacy, 391-400

Graphic Narratives CLC 86: 405-32
history and overviews, 406-21
the "Classics Illustrated" series, 421-2
reviews of recent works, 422-32

Greek Historiography CMLC 17: 1-49

Harlem Renaissance TCLC 26: 49-125
principal issues and figures, 50-67
the literature and its audience, 67-74
theme and technique in poetry, fiction, and drama, 74-115
and American society, 115-21
achievement and influence, 121-2

Havel, Václav, Playwright and President CLC 65: 406-63

Historical Fiction, Nineteenth-Century NCLC 48: 212-307
definitions and characteristics, 213-36
Victorian historical fiction, 236-65
American historical fiction, 265-88
realism in historical fiction, 288-306

Holocaust and the Atomic Bomb: Fifty Years Later CLC 91: 331-82
the Holocaust remembered, 333-52
Anne Frank revisited, 352-62
the atomic bomb and American memory, 362-81

Holocaust Denial Literature TCLC 58: 1-110
overviews, 1-30
Robert Faurisson and Noam Chomsky, 30-52
Holocaust denial literature in America, 52-71
library access to Holocaust denial literature, 72-5
the authenticity of Anne Frank's diary, 76-90
David Irving and the "normalization" of Hitler, 90-109

Holocaust, Literature of the TCLC 42: 355-450
historical overview, 357-61
critical overview, 361-70
diaries and memoirs, 370-95
novels and short stories, 395-425
poetry, 425-41
drama, 441-8

Hungarian Literature of the Twentieth Century TCLC 26: 126-88
surveys of, 126-47
Nyugat and early twentieth-century literature, 147-56
mid-century literature, 156-68
and politics, 168-78
since the 1956 revolt, 178-87

Indian Literature in English TCLC 54: 308-406
overview, 309-13
origins and major figures, 313-25
the Indo-English novel, 325-55
Indo-English poetry, 355-67
Indo-English drama, 367-72
critical perspectives on Indo-English literature, 372-80
modern Indo-English literature, 380-9
Indo-English authors on their work, 389-404

Irish Literary Renaissance TCLC 46: 172-287
overview, 173-83

development and major figures, 184-202
influence of Irish folklore and mythology, 202-22
Irish poetry, 222-34
Irish drama and the Abbey Theatre, 234-56
Irish fiction, 256-86

Irish Nationalism and Literature NCLC 44: 203-73
the Celtic element in literature, 203-19
anti-Irish sentiment and the Celtic response, 219-34
literary ideals in Ireland, 234-45
literary expressions, 245-73

Italian Futurism
See **Futurism, Italian**

Italian Humanism LC 12: 205-77
origins and early development, 206-18
revival of classical letters, 218-23
humanism and other philosophies, 224-39
humanisms and humanists, 239-46
the plastic arts, 246-57
achievement and significance, 258-76

Jacobean Drama LC 33: 1-37
the Jacobean worldview: an era of transition, 2-14
the moral vision of Jacobean drama, 14-22
Jacobean tragedy, 22-23
the Jacobean masque, 23-36

Jewish-American Fiction TCLC 62: 1-181
overviews, 2-24
major figures, 24-48
Jewish writers and American life, 48-78
Jewish characters in American fiction, 78-108
themes in Jewish-American fiction, 108-43
Jewish-American women writers, 143-59
the Holocaust and Jewish-American fiction, 159-81

Lake Poets, The NCLC 52: 217-304
characteristics of the Lake Poets and their works, 218-27
literary influences and collaborations, 227-66

defining and developing Romantic
   ideals, 266-84
embracing Conservatism, 284-303

Larkin, Philip, Controversy CLC 81: 417-
64

**Latin American Literature, Twentieth-
Century** TCLC 58: 111-98
   historical and critical perspectives, 112-
     36
   the novel, 136-45
   the short story, 145-9
   drama, 149-60
   poetry, 160-7
   the writer and society, 167-86
   Native Americans in Latin American
     literature, 186-97

Madness in Twentieth-Century Literature
TCLC 50: 160-225
   overviews, 161-71
   madness and the creative process, 171-
     86
   suicide, 186-91
   madness in American literature, 191-207
   madness in German literature, 207-13
   madness and feminist artists, 213-24

Metaphysical Poets LC 24: 356-439
   early definitions, 358-67
   surveys and overviews, 367-92
   cultural and social influences, 392-406
   stylistic and thematic variations, 407-38

Modern Essay, The TCLC 58: 199-273
   overview, 200-7
   the essay in the early twentieth century,
     207-19
   characteristics of the modern essay, 219-
     32
   modern essayists, 232-45
   the essay as a literary genre, 245-73

**Muckraking Movement in American
Journalism** TCLC 34: 161-242
   development, principles, and major
     figures, 162-70
   publications, 170-9
   social and political ideas, 179-86
   targets, 186-208
   fiction, 208-19
   decline, 219-29

impact and accomplishments, 229-40

**Multiculturalism in Literature and
Education** CLC 70: 361-413

Music and Modern Literature TCLC 62:
182-329
   overviews, 182-211
   musical form/literary form, 211-32
   music in literature, 232-50
   the influence of music on literature,
     250-73
   literature and popular music, 273-303
   jazz and poetry, 303-28

Native American Literature CLC 76: 440-
76

Natural School, Russian NCLC 24: 205-40
   history and characteristics, 205-25
   contemporary criticism, 225-40

Naturalism NCLC 36: 285-382
   definitions and theories, 286-305
   critical debates on Naturalism, 305-16
   Naturalism in theater, 316-32
   European Naturalism, 332-61
   American Naturalism, 361-72
   the legacy of Naturalism, 372-81

Negritude TCLC 50: 226-361
   origins and evolution, 227-56
   definitions, 256-91
   Negritude in literature, 291-343
   Negritude reconsidered, 343-58

New Criticism TCLC 34: 243-318
   development and ideas, 244-70
   debate and defense, 270-99
   influence and legacy, 299-315

The New World in Renaissance Literature
LC 31: 1-51
   overview, 1-18
   utopia vs. terror, 18-31
   explorers and Native Americans, 31-51

New York Intellectuals and *Partisan
Review* TCLC 30: 117-98
   development and major figures, 118-28
   influence of Judaism, 128-39

Partisan Review, 139-57
literary philosophy and practice, 157-75
political philosophy, 175-87
achievement and significance, 187-97

The New Yorker TCLC 58: 274-357
   overviews, 274-95
   major figures, 295-304
   New Yorker style, 304-33
   fiction, journalism, and humor at *The
     New Yorker,* 333-48
   the new *New Yorker,* 348-56

Newgate Novel NCLC 24: 166-204
   development of Newgate literature, 166-
     73
   Newgate Calendar, 173-7
   Newgate fiction, 177-95
   Newgate drama, 195-204

**Nigerian Literature of the Twentieth
Century** TCLC 30: 199-265
   surveys of, 199-227
   English language and African life, 227-
     45
   politics and the Nigerian writer, 245-54
   Nigerian writers and society, 255-62

Northern Humanism LC 16: 281-356
   background, 282-305
   precursor of the Reformation, 305-14
   the Brethren of the Common Life, the
     Devotio Moderna, and education,
     314-40
   the impact of printing, 340-56

**Nuclear Literature: Writings and
Criticism in the Nuclear Age** TCLC 46:
288-390
   overviews, 290-301
   fiction, 301-35
   poetry, 335-8
   nuclear war in Russo-Japanese litera-
     ture, 338-55
   nuclear war and women writers, 355-67
   the nuclear referent and literary
     criticism, 367-88

Occultism in Modern Literature TCLC 50:
362-406
   influence of occultism on literature,
     363-72
   occultism, literature, and society,
     372-87

Topic Index

fiction, 387-96
drama, 396-405

Opium and the Nineteenth-Century Literary Imagination NCLC 20: 250-301
original sources, 250-62
historical background, 262-71
and literary society, 271-9
and literary creativity, 279-300

Periodicals, Nineteenth-Century British NCLC 24: 100-65
overviews, 100-30
in the Romantic Age, 130-41
in the Victorian era, 142-54
and the reviewer, 154-64

Plath, Sylvia, and the Nature of Biography CLC 86: 433-62
the nature of biography, 433-52
reviews of *The Silent Woman,* 452-61

Polish Romanticism NCLC 52: 305-71
overviews, 306-26
major figures, 326-40
Polish Romantic drama, 340-62
influences, 362-71

Pre-Raphaelite Movement NCLC 20: 302-401
overview, 302-4
genesis, 304-12
Germ and *Oxford and Cambridge Magazine,* 312-20
Robert Buchanan and the "Fleshly School of Poetry," 320-31
satires and parodies, 331-4
surveys, 334-51
aesthetics, 351-75
sister arts of poetry and painting, 375-94
influence, 394-9

Psychoanalysis and Literature TCLC 38: 227-338
overviews, 227-46
Freud on literature, 246-51
psychoanalytic views of the literary process, 251-61
psychoanalytic theories of response to literature, 261-88
psychoanalysis and literary criticism, 288-312
psychoanalysis as literature/literature as psychoanalysis, 313-34

Rap Music CLC 76: 477-50

Renaissance Natural Philosophy LC 27: 201-87
cosmology, 201-28
astrology, 228-54
magic, 254-86

Restoration Drama LC 21: 184-275
general overviews, 185-230
Jeremy Collier stage controversy, 230-9
other critical interpretations, 240-75

Revising the Literary Canon CLC 81: 465-509

Robin Hood, Legend of LC 19: 205-58
origins and development of the Robin Hood legend, 206-20
representations of Robin Hood, 220-44
Robin Hood as hero, 244-56

Rushdie, Salman, *Satanic Verses* Controversy CLC 55: 214-63; 59: 404-56

Russian Nihilism NCLC 28: 403-47
definitions and overviews, 404-17
women and Nihilism, 417-27
literature as reform: the Civic Critics, 427-33
Nihilism and the Russian novel: Turgenev and Dostoevsky, 433-47

Russian Thaw TCLC 26: 189-247
literary history of the period, 190-206
theoretical debate of socialist realism, 206-11
Novy Mir, 211-7
Literary Moscow, 217-24
Pasternak, *Zhivago,* and the Nobel Prize, 224-7
poetry of liberation, 228-31
Brodsky trial and the end of the Thaw, 231-6
achievement and influence, 236-46

Salinger, J. D., Controversy Surrounding *In Search of J. D. Salinger* CLC 55: 325-44

Science Fiction, Nineteenth-Century

NCLC 24: 241-306
background, 242-50
definitions of the genre, 251-6
representative works and writers, 256-75
themes and conventions, 276-305

Scottish Chaucerians LC 20: 363-412

Scottish Poetry, Eighteenth-Century LC 29: 95-167
overviews, 96-114
the Scottish Augustans, 114-28
the Scots Vernacular Revival, 132-63
Scottish poetry after Burns, 163-6

Sherlock Holmes Centenary TCLC 26: 248-310
Doyle's life and the composition of the Holmes stories, 248-59
life and character of Holmes, 259-78
method, 278-9
Holmes and the Victorian world, 279-92
Sherlockian scholarship, 292-301
Doyle and the development of the detective story, 301-7
Holmes's continuing popularity, 307-9

Slave Narratives, American NCLC 20: 1-91
background, 2-9
overviews, 9-24
contemporary responses, 24-7
language, theme, and technique, 27-70
historical authenticity, 70-5
antecedents, 75-83
role in development of Black American literature, 83-8

Spanish Civil War Literature TCLC 26: 311-85
topics in, 312-33
British and American literature, 333-59
French literature, 359-62
Spanish literature, 362-73
German literature, 373-5
political idealism and war literature, 375-83

Spanish Golden Age Literature LC 23: 262-332
overviews, 263-81
verse drama, 281-304

prose fiction, 304-19
lyric poetry, 319-31

Spasmodic School of Poetry NCLC 24:
307-52
  history and major figures, 307-21
  the Spasmodics on poetry, 321-7
  Firmilian and critical disfavor, 327-39
  theme and technique, 339-47
  influence, 347-51

Steinbeck, John, Fiftieth Anniversary of
The Grapes of Wrath CLC 59: 311-54

Sturm und Drang NCLC 40: 196-276
  definitions, 197-238
  poetry and poetics, 238-58
  drama, 258-75

**Supernatural Fiction in the Nineteenth
Century** NCLC 32: 207-87
  major figures and influences, 208-35
  the Victorian ghost story, 236-54
  the influence of science and occultism,
    254-66
  supernatural fiction and society, 266-86

Supernatural Fiction, Modern TCLC 30:
59-116
  evolution and varieties, 60-74
  "decline" of the ghost story, 74-86
  as a literary genre, 86-92
  technique, 92-101
  nature and appeal, 101-15

Surrealism TCLC 30: 334-406
  history and formative influences, 335-43
  manifestos, 343-54
  philosophic, aesthetic, and political
    principles, 354-75
  poetry, 375-81
  novel, 381-6
  drama, 386-92
  film, 392-8
  painting and sculpture, 398-403
  achievement, 403-5

Symbolism, Russian TCLC 30: 266-333
  doctrines and major figures, 267-92
  theories, 293-8
  and French Symbolism, 298-310
  themes in poetry, 310-4
  theater, 314-20

and the fine arts, 320-32

Symbolist Movement, French NCLC 20:
169-249
  background and characteristics, 170-86
  principles, 186-91
  attacked and defended, 191-7
  influences and predecessors, 197-211
  and Decadence, 211-6
  theater, 216-26
  prose, 226-33
  decline and influence, 233-47

Theater of the Absurd TCLC 38: 339-415
  "The Theater of the Absurd," 340-7
  major plays and playwrights, 347-58
  and the concept of the absurd, 358-86
  theatrical techniques, 386-94
  predecessors of, 394-402
  influence of, 402-13

Tin Pan Alley
See **American Popular Song, Golden Age
of**

Transcendentalism, American NCLC 24:
1-99
  overviews, 3-23
  contemporary documents, 23-41
  theological aspects of, 42-52
  and social issues, 52-74
  literature of, 74-96

Travel Writing in the Nineteenth Century
NCLC 44: 274-392
  the European grand tour, 275-303
  the Orient, 303-47
  North America, 347-91

Travel Writing in the Twentieth Century
TCLC 30: 407-56
  conventions and traditions, 407-27
  and fiction writing, 427-43
  comparative essays on travel writers,
    443-54

Ulysses **and the Process of Textual
Reconstruction** TCLC 26: 386-416
  evaluations of the new *Ulysses,* 386-
    94
  editorial principles and procedures, 394-
    401
  theoretical issues, 401-16

Utopian Literature, Nineteenth-Century
NCLC 24: 353-473
  definitions, 354-74
  overviews, 374-88
  theory, 388-408
  communities, 409-26
  fiction, 426-53
  women and fiction, 454-71

Utopian Literature, Renaissance LC-32:
1-63
  overviews, 2-25
  classical background, 25-33
  utopia and the social contract, 33-9
  origins in mythology, 39-48
  utopia and the Renaissance country
    house, 48-52
  influence of millenarianism, 52-62

Vampire in Literature TCLC 46: 391-
454
  origins and evolution, 392-412
  social and psychological perspectives,
    413-44
  vampire fiction and science fiction, 445-
    53

Victorian Autobiography NCLC 40: 277-
363
  development and major characteristics,
    278-88
  themes and techniques, 289-313
  the autobiographical tendency in
    Victorian prose and poetry, 313-47
  Victorian women's autobiographies,
    347-62

Victorian Novel NCLC 32: 288-454
  development and major characteristics,
    290-310
  themes and techniques, 310-58
  social criticism in the Victorian novel,
    359-97
  urban and rural life in the Victorian
    novel, 397-406
  women in the Victorian novel, 406-25
  Mudie's Circulating Library, 425-34
  the late-Victorian novel, 434-51

Vietnam War in Literature and Film CLC
91: 383-437
  overview, 384-8
  prose, 388-412
  film and drama, 412-24
  poetry, 424-35

Topic Index

Vorticism TCLC 62: 330-426
    Wyndham Lewis and Vorticism, 330-8
    characteristics and principles of
        Vorticism, 338-65
    Lewis and Pound, 365-82
    Vorticist writing, 382-416
    Vorticist painting, 416-26

Women's Diaries, Nineteenth-Century
NCLC 48: 308-54
    overview, 308-13
    diary as history, 314-25
    sociology of diaries, 325-34
    diaries as psychological scholarship,
      334-43
    diary as autobiography, 343-8
    diary as literature, 348-53

Women Writers, Seventeenth-Century LC
30: 2-58
    overview, 2-15
    women and education, 15-9
    women and autobiography, 19-31
    women's diaries, 31-9
    early feminists, 39-58

World War I Literature TCLC 34: 392-
486
    overview, 393-403
    English, 403-27
    German, 427-50
    American, 450-66
    French, 466-74
    and modern history, 474-82

Yellow Journalism NCLC 36: 383-456
    overviews, 384-96
    major figures, 396-413

Young Playwrights Festival
    1988–CLC 55: 376-81
    1989–CLC 59: 398-403
    1990–CLC 65: 444-8

TCLC Cumulative Nationality Index

AMERICAN

Adams, Andy 56
Adams, Henry (Brooks) 4, 52
Agee, James (Rufus) 1, 19
Anderson, Maxwell 2
Anderson, Sherwood 1, 10, 24
Atherton, Gertrude (Franklin Horn) 2
Austin, Mary (Hunter) 25
Baker, Ray Stannard 47
Barry, Philip 11
Baum, L(yman) Frank 7
Beard, Charles A(ustin) 15
Becker, Carl 63:
Belasco, David 3
Bell, James Madison 43
Benchley, Robert (Charles) 1, 55
Benedict, Ruth 60
Benet, Stephen Vincent 7
Benet, William Rose 28
Bierce, Ambrose (Gwinett) 1, 7, 44
Biggers, Earl Derr 65
Black Elk 33
Boas, Franz 56
Bodenheim, Maxwell 44
Bourne, Randolph S(illiman) 16
Bradford, Gamaliel 36
Brennan, Christopher John 17
Bromfield, Louis (Brucker) 11
Burroughs, Edgar Rice 2, 32
Cabell, James Branch 6
Cable, George Washington 4
Cardozo, Benjamin N(athan) 65
Carnegie, Dale 53
Cather, Willa Sibert 1, 11, 31
Chambers, Robert W. 41
Chandler, Raymond (Thornton) 1, 7
Chapman, John Jay 7
Chesnutt, Charles W(addell) 5, 39
Chopin, Kate 5, 14

Cohan, George M. 60
Comstock, Anthony 13
Cotter, Joseph Seamon Sr. 28
Cram, Ralph Adams 45
Crane, (Harold) Hart 2, 5
Crane, Stephen (Townley) 11, 17, 32
Crawford, F(rancis) Marion 10
Crothers, Rachel 19
Cullen, Countee 4, 37
Davis, Rebecca (Blaine) Harding 6
Davis, Richard Harding 24
Day, Clarence (Shepard Jr.) 25
De Voto, Bernard (Augustine) 29
Dreiser, Theodore (Herman Albert) 10, 18, 35
Dunbar, Paul Laurence 2, 12
Dunne, Finley Peter 28
Eastman, Charles A(lexander) 55
Einstein, Albert 65
Faust, Frederick (Schiller) 49
Fisher, Rudolph 11
Fitzgerald, F(rancis) Scott (Key) 1, 6, 14, 28, 55
Fitzgerald, Zelda (Sayre) 52
Flecker, (Herman) James Elroy 43
Fletcher, John Gould 35
Forten, Charlotte L. 16
Freeman, Douglas Southall 11
Freeman, Mary Eleanor Wilkins 9
Futrelle, Jacques 19
Gale, Zona 7
Garland, (Hannibal) Hamlin 3
Gilman, Charlotte (Anna) Perkins (Stetson) 9, 37
Glasgow, Ellen (Anderson Gholson) 2, 7
Glaspell, Susan (Keating) 55
Goldman, Emma 13
Green, Anna Katharine 63
Grey, Zane 6

Guiney, Louise Imogen 41
Hall, James Norman 23
Harper, Frances Ellen Watkins 14
Harris, Joel Chandler 2
Harte, (Francis) Bret(t) 1, 25
Hatteras, Owen 18
Hawthorne, Julian 25
Hearn, (Patricio) Lafcadio (Tessima Carlos) 9
Henry, O. 1, 19
Hergesheimer, Joseph 11
Higginson, Thomas Wentworth 36
Holly, Buddy 65
Hopkins, Pauline Elizabeth 28
Howard, Robert Ervin 8
Howe, Julia Ward 21
Howells, William Dean 7, 17, 41
Huneker, James Gibbons 65
James, Henry 2, 11, 24, 40, 47, 64
James, William 15, 32
Jewett, (Theodora) Sarah Orne 1, 22
Johnson, James Weldon 3, 19
Kornbluth, C(yril) M. 8
Korzybski, Alfred (Habdank Skarbek) 61
Kuttner, Henry 10
Lardner, Ring(gold) W(ilmer) 2, 14
Lewis, (Harry) Sinclair 4, 13, 23, 39
Lewisohn, Ludwig 19
Lindsay, (Nicholas) Vachel 17
Locke, Alain (Le Roy) 43
London, Jack 9, 15, 39
Lovecraft, H(oward) P(hillips) 4, 22
Lowell, Amy 1, 8
Markham, Edwin 47
Marquis, Don(ald Robert Perry) 7
Masters, Edgar Lee 2, 25
McCoy, Horace (Stanley) 28
McKay, Claude 7, 41
Mencken, H(enry) L(ouis) 13

Millay, Edna St. Vincent **4, 49**
Mitchell, Margaret (Munnerlyn) **11**
Mitchell, S(ilas) Weir **36**
Monroe, Harriet **12**
Muir, John **28**
Nathan, George Jean **18**
Nordhoff, Charles (Bernard) **23**
Norris, Benjamin Franklin Jr. **24**
O'Neill, Eugene (Gladstone) **1, 6, 27, 49**
Oskison, John Milton **35**
Phillips, David Graham **44**
Porter, Gene(va Grace) Stratton **21**
Post, Melville Davisson **39**
Rawlings, Marjorie Kinnan **4**
Reed, John (Silas) **9**
Reich, Wilhelm **57**
Rhodes, Eugene Manlove **53**
Riggs, (Rolla) Lynn **56**
Riley, James Whitcomb **51**
Rinehart, Mary Roberts **52**
Roberts, Kenneth (Lewis) **23**
Robinson, Edwin Arlington **5**
Roelvaag, O(le) E(dvart) **17**
Rogers, Will(iam Penn Adair) **8**
Rourke, Constance (Mayfield) **12**
Runyon, (Alfred) Damon **10**
Saltus, Edgar (Everton) **8**
Santayana, George **40**
Sherwood, Robert E(mmet) **3**
Slesinger, Tess **10**
Steffens, (Joseph) Lincoln **20**
Stein, Gertrude **1, 6, 28, 48**
Sterling, George **20**
Stevens, Wallace **3, 12, 45**
Stockton, Frank R. **47**
Sturges, Preston **48**
Tarbell, Ida M(inerva) **40**
Tarkington, (Newton) Booth **9**
Teasdale, Sara **4**
Thurman, Wallace (Henry) **6**
Twain, Mark **6, 12, 19, 36, 48, 59**
Van Dine, S. S. **23**
Van Doren, Carl (Clinton) **18**
Veblen, Thorstein (Bunde) **31**
Washington, Booker T(aliaferro) **10**
Wells, Carolyn **35**
West, Nathanael **1, 14, 44**
Whale, James **63**
Wharton, Edith (Newbold Jones) **3, 9, 27, 53**
White, Walter F(rancis) **15**
Wister, Owen **21**
Wolfe, Thomas (Clayton) **4, 13, 29, 61**
Woollcott, Alexander (Humphreys) **5**
Wylie, Elinor (Morton Hoyt) **8**

ARGENTINIAN
Arlt, Roberto (Godofredo Christophersen) **29**
Guiraldes, Ricardo (Guillermo) **39**
Lugones, Leopoldo **15**
Storni, Alfonsina **5**

AUSTRALIAN
Baynton, Barbara **57**
Franklin, (Stella Maraia Sarah) Miles **7**
Furphy, Joseph **25**
Ingamells, Rex **35**
Lawson, Henry (Archibald Hertzberg) **27**
Paterson, A(ndrew) B(arton) **32**
Richardson, Henry Handel **4**
Warung, Price **45**

AUSTRIAN
Beer-Hofmann, Richard **60**
Broch, Hermann **20**
Freud, Sigmund **52**
Hofmannsthal, Hugo von **11**
Kafka, Franz **2, 6, 13, 29, 47, 53**
Kraus, Karl **5**
Kubin, Alfred (Leopold Isidor) **23**
Meyrink, Gustav **21**
Musil, Robert (Edler von) **12**
Perutz, Leo **60**
Roth, Joseph **33**
Schnitzler, Arthur **4**
Steiner, Rudolf **13**
Trakl, Georg **5**
Werfel, Franz (V.) **8**
Zweig, Stefan **17**

BELGIAN
Bosschere, Jean de **19**
Lemonnier, (Antoine Louis) Camille **22**
Maeterlinck, Maurice **3**
van Ostaijen, Paul **33**
Verhaeren, Emile (Adolphe Gustave) **12**

BRAZILIAN
Andrade, Mario de **43**
Cunha, Euclides (Rodrigues Pimenta) da **24**
Lima Barreto, Afonso Henrique de **23**
Machado de Assis, Joaquim Maria **10**
Ramos, Graciliano **32**

BULGARIAN
Vazov, Ivan (Minchov) **25**

CANADIAN
Campbell, Wilfred **9**
Carman, (William) Bliss **7**
Carr, Emily **32**
Connor, Ralph **31**
Drummond, William Henry **25**
Duncan, Sara Jeannette **60**
Garneau, (Hector de) Saint-Denys **13**
Grove, Frederick Philip **4**
Knister, Raymond **56**
Leacock, Stephen (Butler) **2**
McCrae, John **12**
Montgomery, L(ucy) M(aud) **51**
Nelligan, Emile **14**
Pickthall, Marjorie L(owry) C(hristie) **21**
Roberts, Charles G(eorge) D(ouglas) **8**
Scott, Duncan Campbell **6**
Service, Robert W(illiam) **15**
Seton, Ernest (Evan) Thompson **31**
Stringer, Arthur **37**

CHILEAN
Huidobro Fernandez, Vicente Garcia **31**
Mistral, Gabriela **2**

CHINESE
Liu E **15**
Lu Hsun **3**
Su Man-shu **24**
Wen I-to **28**

COLOMBIAN
Rivera, Jose Eustasio **35**

CZECH
Capek, Karel **6, 37**

Freud, Sigmund **52**
Hasek, Jaroslav (Matej Frantisek) **4**
Kafka, Franz **2, 6, 13, 29, 47, 53**
Nezval, Vitezslav **44**

DANISH
Brandes, Georg (Morris Cohen) **10**
Hansen, Martin A. **32**
Jensen, Johannes V. **41**
Nexo, Martin Andersen **43**
Pontoppidan, Henrik **29**

DUTCH
Couperus, Louis (Marie Anne) **15**
Frank, Anne(lies Marie) **17**
Heijermans, Herman **24**
Hillesum, Etty **49**
Schendel, Arthur van **56**

ENGLISH
Barbellion, W. N. P. **24**
Baring, Maurice **8**
Beerbohm, Henry Maximilian **1, 24**
Belloc, (Joseph) Hilaire (Pierre) **7, 18**
Bennett, (Enoch) Arnold **5, 20**
Benson, E(dward) F(rederic) **27**
Benson, Stella **17**
Bentley, E(dmund) C(lerihew) **12**
Besant, Annie (Wood) **9**
Blackmore, R(ichard) D(oddridge) **27**
Blackwood, Algernon (Henry) **5**
Bridges, Robert (Seymour) **1**
Brooke, Rupert (Chawner) **2, 7**
Burke, Thomas **63**
Butler, Samuel **1, 33**
Chesterton, G(ilbert) K(eith) **1, 6, 64**
Childers, (Robert) Erskine **65**
Conrad, Joseph **1, 6, 13, 25, 43, 57**
Coppard, A(lfred) E(dgar) **5**
Corelli, Marie **51**
Crofts, Freeman Wills **55**
Crowley, Aleister **7**
Dale, Colin **18**
Delafield, E. M. **61**
de la Mare, Walter (John) **4, 53**
Doughty, Charles M(ontagu) **27**
Douglas, Keith **40**
Dowson, Ernest (Christopher) **4**
Doyle, Arthur Conan **7**
Drinkwater, John **57**
Eddison, E(ric) R(ucker) **15**
Elaine **18**
Elizabeth **41**
Ellis, (Henry) Havelock **14**
Field, Michael **43**
Firbank, (Arthur Annesley) Ronald **1**
Ford, Ford Madox **1, 15, 39, 57**
Freeman, R(ichard) Austin **21**
Galsworthy, John **1, 45**
Gilbert, W(illiam) S(chwenck) **3**
Gissing, George (Robert) **3, 24, 47**
Gosse, Edmund (William) **28**
Grahame, Kenneth **64**
Granville-Barker, Harley **2**
Gray, John (Henry) **19**
Gurney, Ivor (Bertie) **33**
Haggard, H(enry) Rider **11**
Hall, (Marguerite) Radclyffe **12**
Hardy, Thomas **4, 10, 18, 32, 48, 53**
Henley, William Ernest **8**
Hichens, Robert S. **64**
Hilton, James **21**

Hodgson, William Hope **13**
Housman, A(lfred) E(dward) **1, 10**
Housman, Laurence **7**
Hudson, W(illiam) H(enry) **29**
Hulme, T(homas) E(rnest) **21**
Hunt, Violet **53**
Jacobs, W(illiam) W(ymark) **22**
James, Montague (Rhodes) **6**
Jerome, Jerome K(lapka) **23**
Johnson, Lionel (Pigot) **19**
Kaye-Smith, Sheila **20**
Keynes, John Maynard **64**
Kipling, (Joseph) Rudyard **8, 17**
Lawrence, D(avid) H(erbert Richards) **2, 9, 16, 33, 48, 61**
Lawrence, T(homas) E(dward) **18**
Lee, Vernon **5**
Lee-Hamilton, Eugene (Jacob) **22**
Leverson, Ada **18**
Lewis, (Percy) Wyndham **2, 9**
Lindsay, David **15**
Lowndes, Marie Adelaide (Belloc) **12**
Lowry, (Clarence) Malcolm **6, 40**
Macaulay, Rose **7, 44**
MacCarthy, (Sir Charles Otto) Desmond **36**
Maitland, Frederic **65**
Manning, Frederic **25**
Meredith, George **17, 43**
Mew, Charlotte (Mary) **8**
Meynell, Alice (Christina Gertrude Thompson) **6**
Middleton, Richard (Barham) **56**
Milne, A(lan) A(lexander) **6**
Murry, John Middleton **16**
Noyes, Alfred **7**
Oppenheim, E(dward) Phillips **45**
Orwell, George **2, 6, 15, 31, 51**
Ouida **43**
Owen, Wilfred (Edward Salter) **5, 27**
Pinero, Arthur Wing **32**
Powys, T(heodore) F(rancis) **9**
Quiller-Couch, Arthur Thomas **53**
Richardson, Dorothy Miller **3**
Rohmer, Sax **28**
Rolfe, Frederick (William Serafino Austin Lewis Mary) **12**
Rosenberg, Isaac **12**
Ruskin, John **20**
Rutherford, Mark **25**
Sabatini, Rafael **47**
Saintsbury, George (Edward Bateman) **31**
Saki **3**
Sapper **44**
Sayers, Dorothy L(eigh) **2, 15**
Shiel, M(atthew) P(hipps) **8**
Sinclair, May **3, 11**
Stapledon, (William) Olaf **22**
Stead, William Thomas **48**
Stephen, Leslie **23**
Strachey, (Giles) Lytton **12**
Summers, (Alphonsus Joseph-Mary Augustus) Montague **16**
Sutro, Alfred **6**
Swinburne, Algernon Charles **8, 36**
Symons, Arthur **11**
Thomas, (Philip) Edward **10**
Thompson, Francis Joseph **4**
Van Druten, John (William) **2**
Wallace, (Richard Horatio) Edgar **57**
Walpole, Hugh (Seymour) **5**
Ward, Mrs. Humphry **55**

Warung, Price **45**
Webb, (Martha) Beatrice (Potter) **22**
Webb, Mary (Gladys Meredith) **24**
Webb, Sidney (James) **22**
Welch, (Maurice) Denton **22**
Wells, H(erbert) G(eorge) **6, 12, 19**
Williams, Charles (Walter Stansby) **1, 11**
Woolf, (Adeline) Virginia **1, 5, 20, 43, 56**
Yonge, Charlotte (Mary) **48**
Zangwill, Israel **16**

ESTONIAN
Tammsaare, A(nton) H(ansen) **27**

FINNISH
Leino, Eino **24**
Soedergran, Edith (Irene) **31**

FRENCH
Alain **41**
Alain-Fournier **6**
Apollinaire, Guillaume **3, 8, 51**
Artaud, Antonin (Marie Joseph) **3, 36**
Barbusse, Henri **5**
Barres, Maurice **47**
Benda, Julien **60**
Bergson, Henri **32**
Bernanos, (Paul Louis) Georges **3**
Bloy, Leon **22**
Bourget, Paul (Charles Joseph) **12**
Claudel, Paul (Louis Charles Marie) **2, 10**
Colette, (Sidonie-Gabrielle) **1, 5, 16**
Coppee, Francois **25**
Daumal, Rene **14**
Desnos, Robert **22**
Drieu la Rochelle, Pierre(-Eugene) **21**
Dujardin, Edouard (Emile Louis) **13**
Durkheim, Emile **55**
Eluard, Paul **7, 41**
Fargue, Leon-Paul **11**
Feydeau, Georges (Leon Jules Marie) **22**
France, Anatole **9**
Gide, Andre (Paul Guillaume) **5, 12, 36**
Giraudoux, (Hippolyte) Jean **2, 7**
Gourmont, Remy (-Marie-Charles) de **17**
Huysmans, Joris-Karl **7**
Jacob, (Cyprien-)Max **6**
Jarry, Alfred **2, 14**
Larbaud, Valery (Nicolas) **9**
Leblanc, Maurice (Marie Emile) **49**
Leroux, Gaston **25**
Loti, Pierre **11**
Martin du Gard, Roger **24**
Mirbeau, Octave **55**
Mistral, Frederic **51**
Moreas, Jean **18**
Nizan, Paul **40**
Peguy, Charles Pierre **10**
Peret, Benjamin **20**
Proust, (Valentin-Louis-George-Eugene-) Marcel **7, 13, 33**
Radiguet, Raymond **29**
Renard, Jules **17**
Rolland, Romain **23**
Rostand, Edmond (Eugene Alexis) **6, 37**
Roussel, Raymond **20**
Saint-Exupery, Antoine (Jean Baptiste Marie Roger) de **2, 56**
Schwob, (Mayer Andre) Marcel **20**
Sully Prudhomme **31**
Teilhard de Chardin, (Marie Joseph) Pierre **9**

Valery, (Ambroise) Paul (Toussaint Jules) **4, 15**
Verne, Jules (Gabriel) **6, 52**
Vian, Boris **9**
Weil, Simone (Adolphine) **23**
Zola, Emile (Edouard Charles Antoine) **1, 6, 21, 41**

GERMAN
Andreas-Salome, Lou **56**
Auerbach, Erich **43**
Benjamin, Walter **39**
Benn, Gottfried **3**
Borchert, Wolfgang **5**
Brecht, Bertolt **1, 6, 13, 35**
Carossa, Hans **48**
Cassirer, Ernst **61**
Doblin, Alfred **13**
Doeblin, Alfred **13**
Einstein, Albert **65**
Ewers, Hanns Heinz **12**
Feuchtwanger, Lion **3**
George, Stefan (Anton) **2, 14**
Hauptmann, Gerhart (Johann Robert) **4**
Heym, Georg (Theodor Franz Arthur) **9**
Heyse, Paul (Johann Ludwig von) **8**
Hitler, Adolf **53**
Huch, Ricarda (Octavia) **13**
Kaiser, Georg **9**
Klabund **44**
Kolmar, Gertrud **40**
Lasker-Schueler, Else **57**
Liliencron, (Friedrich Adolf Axel) Detlev von **18**
Luxemburg, Rosa **63**
Mann, (Luiz) Heinrich **9**
Mann, (Paul) Thomas **2, 8, 14, 21, 35, 44, 60**
Mannheim, Karl **65**
Morgenstern, Christian **8**
Nietzsche, Friedrich (Wilhelm) **10, 18, 55**
Plumpe, Friedrich Wilhelm **53**
Raabe, Wilhelm **45**
Rilke, Rainer Maria **1, 6, 19**
Simmel, Georg **64**
Spengler, Oswald (Arnold Gottfried) **25**
Sternheim, (William Adolf) Carl **8**
Sudermann, Hermann **15**
Toller, Ernst **10**
Wassermann, (Karl) Jakob **6**
Wedekind, (Benjamin) Frank(lin) **7**
Wiene, Robert **56**

GHANIAN
Casely-Hayford, J(oseph) E(phraim) **24**

GREEK
Cavafy, C(onstantine) P(eter) **2, 7**
Kazantzakis, Nikos **2, 5, 33**
Palamas, Kostes **5**
Papadiamantis, Alexandros **29**
Sikelianos, Angelos **39**

HAITIAN
Roumain, Jacques (Jean Baptiste) **19**

HUNGARIAN
Ady, Endre **11**
Babits, Mihaly **14**
Csath, Geza **13**
Herzl, Theodor **36**
Horvath, Oedoen von **45**

Jozsef, Attila **22**
Karinthy, Frigyes **47**
Mikszath, Kalman **31**
Molnar, Ferenc **20**
Moricz, Zsigmond **33**
Radnoti, Miklos **16**

ICELANDIC
Sigurjonsson, Johann **27**

INDIAN
Aurobindo, Sri **63**
Chatterji, Saratchandra **13**
Gandhi, Mohandas Karamchand **59**
Iqbal, Muhammad **28**
Premchand **21**
Tagore, Rabindranath **3, 53**

INDONESIAN
Anwar, Chairil **22**

IRANIAN
Hedayat, Sadeq **21**

IRISH
Cary, (Arthur) Joyce (Lunel) **1, 29**
Dunsany, Lord **2, 59**
Gogarty, Oliver St. John **15**
Gregory, Isabella Augusta (Persse) **1**
Harris, Frank **24**
Joyce, James (Augustine Aloysius) **3, 8, 16, 35, 52**
Ledwidge, Francis **23**
Martin, Violet Florence **51**
Moore, George Augustus **7**
O'Grady, Standish James **5**
Riddell, J. H. **40**
Shaw, Bernard **45**
Shaw, George Bernard **3, 9, 21**
Somerville, Edith **51**
Stephens, James **4**
Stoker, Bram **8**
Synge, (Edmund) J(ohn) M(illington) **6, 37**
Tynan, Katharine **3**
Wilde, Oscar (Fingal O'Flahertie Wills) **1, 8, 23, 41**
Yeats, William Butler **1, 11, 18, 31**

ITALIAN
Alvaro, Corrado **60**
Betti, Ugo **5**
Brancati, Vitaliano **12**
Campana, Dino **20**
Carducci, Giosue **32**
Croce, Benedetto **37**
D'Annunzio, Gabriele **6, 40**
Deledda, Grazia (Cosima) **23**
Giacosa, Giuseppe **7**
Lampedusa, Giuseppe (Tomasi) di **13**
Malaparte, Curzio **52**
Marinetti, Filippo Tommaso **10**
Papini, Giovanni **22**
Pascoli, Giovanni **45**
Pavese, Cesare **3**
Pirandello, Luigi **4, 29**
Saba, Umberto **33**
Svevo, Italo **2, 35**
Tozzi, Federigo **31**
Verga, Giovanni (Carmelo) **3**

JAMAICAN
De Lisser, Herbert George **12**

Garvey, Marcus (Moziah Jr.) **41**
Mais, Roger **8**
McKay, Claude **7, 41**
Redcam, Tom **25**

JAPANESE
Akutagawa Ryunosuke **16**
Dazai, Osamu **11**
Futabatei, Shimei **44**
Hagiwara Sakutaro **60**
Hayashi Fumiko **27**
Ishikawa, Takuboku **15**
Masaoka Shiki **18**
Miyamoto, Yuriko **37**
Mori Ogai **14**
Nagai Kafu **51**
Natsume, Soseki **2, 10**
Rohan, Koda **22**
Shimazaki Toson **5**
Yokomitsu Riichi **47**
Yosano Akiko **59**

LATVIAN
Rainis, Janis **29**

LEBANESE
Gibran, Kahlil **1, 9**

LESOTHAN
Mofolo, Thomas (Mokopu) **22**

LITHUANIAN
Kreve (Mickevicius), Vincas **27**

MEXICAN
Azuela, Mariano **3**
Gamboa, Federico **36**
Nervo, (Jose) Amado (Ruiz de) **11**
Reyes, Alfonso **33**
Romero, Jose Ruben **14**

NEPALI
Devkota, Laxmiprasad **23**

NEW ZEALANDER
Mander, (Mary) Jane **31**
Mansfield, Katherine **2, 8, 39**

NICARAGUAN
Dario, Ruben **4**

NORWEGIAN
Bjornson, Bjornstjerne (Martinius) **7, 37**
Bojer, Johan **64**
Grieg, (Johan) Nordahl (Brun) **10**
Hamsun, Knut **2, 14, 49**
Ibsen, Henrik (Johan) **2, 8, 16, 37, 52**
Kielland, Alexander Lange **5**
Lie, Jonas (Lauritz Idemil) **5**
Obstfelder, Sigbjoern **23**
Skram, Amalie (Bertha) **25**
Undset, Sigrid **3**

PAKISTANI
Iqbal, Muhammad **28**

PERUVIAN
Palma, Ricardo **29**
Vallejo, Cesar (Abraham) **3, 56**

POLISH
Asch, Sholem **3**

Borowski, Tadeusz **9**
Conrad, Joseph **1, 6, 13, 25, 43, 57**
Peretz, Isaac Loeb **16**
Prus, Boleslaw **48**
Przybyszewski, Stanislaw **36**
Reymont, Wladyslaw (Stanislaw) **5**
Schulz, Bruno **5, 51**
Sienkiewicz, Henryk (Adam Alexander Pius) **3**
Singer, Israel Joshua **33**
Witkiewicz, Stanislaw Ignacy **8**

PORTUGUESE
Pessoa, Fernando (Antonio Nogueira) **27**

PUERTO RICAN
Hostos (y Bonilla), Eugenio Maria de **24**

ROMANIAN
Bacovia, George **24**
Rebreanu, Liviu **28**

RUSSIAN
Aldanov, Mark (Alexandrovich) **23**
Andreyev, Leonid (Nikolaevich) **3**
Annensky, Innokenty Fyodorovich **14**
Artsybashev, Mikhail (Petrovich) **31**
Babel, Isaak (Emmanuilovich) **2, 13**
Bagritsky, Eduard **60**
Balmont, Konstantin (Dmitriyevich) **11**
Bely, Andrey **7**
Blok, Alexander (Alexandrovich) **5**
Bryusov, Valery Yakovlevich **10**
Bulgakov, Mikhail (Afanas'evich) **2, 16**
Bulgya, Alexander Alexandrovich **53**
Bunin, Ivan Alexeyevich **6**
Chekhov, Anton (Pavlovich) **3, 10, 31, 55**
Der Nister **56**
Eisenstein, Sergei (Mikhailovich) **57**
Esenin, Sergei (Alexandrovich) **4**
Fadeyev, Alexander **53**
Gladkov, Fyodor (Vasilyevich) **27**
Gorky, Maxim **8**
Gumilev, Nikolai Stephanovich **60**
Guro, Elena **56**
Hippius, Zinaida **9**
Ilf, Ilya **21**
Ivanov, Vyacheslav Ivanovich **33**
Khlebnikov, Velimir **20**
Khodasevich, Vladislav (Felitsianovich) **15**
Korolenko, Vladimir Galaktionovich **22**
Kropotkin, Peter (Aleksieevich) **36**
Kuprin, Aleksandr Ivanovich **5**
Kuzmin, Mikhail **40**
Mandelstam, Osip (Emilievich) **2, 6**
Mayakovski, Vladimir (Vladimirovich) **4, 18**
Merezhkovsky, Dmitry Sergeyevich **29**
Petrov, Evgeny **21**
Pilnyak, Boris **23**
Platonov, Andrei **14**
Remizov, Aleksei (Mikhailovich) **27**
Shestov, Lev **56**
Sologub, Fyodor **9**
Tolstoy, Alexey Nikolaevich **18**
Tolstoy, Leo (Nikolaevich) **4, 11, 17, 28, 44**
Trotsky, Leon **22**
Tsvetaeva (Efron), Marina (Ivanovna) **7, 35**
Zabolotskii, Nikolai Alekseevich **52**
Zamyatin, Evgeny Ivanovich **8, 37**

Zhdanov, Andrei A(lexandrovich)   **18**
Zoshchenko, Mikhail (Mikhailovich)   **15**

SCOTTISH
Barrie, J(ames) M(atthew)   **2**
Bridie, James   **3**
Brown, George Douglas   **28**
Buchan, John   **41**
Cunninghame Graham, R(obert) B(ontine)   **19**
Davidson, John   **24**
Frazer, J(ames) G(eorge)   **32**
Gibbon, Lewis Grassic   **4**
Lang, Andrew   **16**
MacDonald, George   **9**
Muir, Edwin   **2**
Sharp, William   **39**
Tey, Josephine   **14**

SOUTH AFRICAN
Bosman, Herman Charles   **49**
Campbell, (Ignatius) Roy (Dunnachie)   **5**
Mqhayi, S(amuel) E(dward) K(rune Loliwe)   **25**
Schreiner, Olive (Emilie Albertina)   **9**
Smith, Pauline (Urmson)   **25**
Vilakazi, Benedict Wallet   **37**

SPANISH
Alas (y Urena), Leopoldo (Enrique Garcia)   **29**
Barea, Arturo   **14**
Baroja (y Nessi), Pio   **8**
Benavente (y Martinez), Jacinto   **3**
Blasco Ibanez, Vicente   **12**
Echegaray (y Eizaguirre), Jose (Maria Waldo)   **4**
Garcia Lorca, Federico   **1, 7, 49**
Jimenez (Mantecon), Juan Ramon   **4**
Machado (y Ruiz), Antonio   **3**
Martinez Sierra, Gregorio   **6**
Martinez Sierra, Maria (de la O'LeJarraga)   **6**
Miro (Ferrer), Gabriel (Francisco Victor)   **5**
Ortega y Gasset, Jose   **9**
Pereda (y Sanchez de Porrua), Jose Maria de   **16**
Perez Galdos, Benito   **27**
Salinas (y Serrano), Pedro   **17**
Unamuno (y Jugo), Miguel de   **2, 9**
Valera y Alcala-Galiano, Juan   **10**
Valle-Inclan, Ramon (Maria) del   **5**

SWEDISH
Bengtsson, Frans (Gunnar)   **48**
Dagerman, Stig (Halvard)   **17**
Heidenstam, (Carl Gustaf) Verner von   **5**
Key, Ellen   **65**
Lagerloef, Selma (Ottiliana Lovisa)   **4, 36**
Soderberg, Hjalmar   **39**
Strindberg, (Johan) August   **1, 8, 21, 47**

SWISS
Ramuz, Charles-Ferdinand   **33**
Rod, Edouard   **52**
Saussure, Ferdinand de   **49**
Spitteler, Carl (Friedrich Georg)   **12**
Walser, Robert   **18**

SYRIAN
Gibran, Kahlil   **1, 9**

TURKISH
Sait Faik   **23**

UKRAINIAN
Aleichem, Sholom   **1, 35**
Bialik, Chaim Nachman   **25**

URUGUAYAN
Quiroga, Horacio (Sylvestre)   **20**
Sanchez, Florencio   **37**

WELSH
Davies, W(illiam) H(enry)   **5**
Lewis, Alun   **3**
Machen, Arthur   **4**
Thomas, Dylan (Marlais)   **1, 8, 45**

Nationality Index

435

TCLC-65 Title Index

"The Abuse of Woman's Strength" (Key)
65:236

The Agony Column (Biggers) 65:4, 9

Albert Einstein: Philosopher-Scientist (*Einstein:
Philosopher-Scientist*) (Einstein) 65:81, 100,
126

"Antichrist" (Einstein) 65:169

Autobiographical Notes (Einstein)
See *Autobiographisches*

Autobiographisches (*Autobiographical Notes*)
(Einstein) 65:92, 122-26

"Baby, I Don't Care" (Holly) 65:138

"Baby, It's Love" (Holly) 65:149

"Baby, Won't You Come Out Tonight"
(Holly) 65:148

Barnets arhundrade (*The Century of the Child*)
(Key) 65:223-26, 233, 237-38

"Because I Love You" (Holly) 65:148

Bedouins (Huneker) 65:170, 179, 185, 187-88,
195

Behind That Curtain (Biggers) 65:5, 9

The Black Camel (Biggers) 65:5

Bracton's Note Book (Maitland) 65:249, 252,
276, 280, 282-83, 288

Buddy Holly: A Rock 'n' Roll Collection
(Holly) 65:153

Buddy Holly in 1958 (Holly) 65:137

Buddy Holly Showcase (Holly) 65:144

The Buddy Holly Story (Holly) 65:144-47,
151

The Buddy Holly Story, Volume II (Holly)
65:144, 147, 150

The Century of the Child (Key)
See *Barnets arhundrade*

Charlie Chan Carries On (Biggers) 65:2, 4, 9

The Chinese Parrot (Biggers) 65:4-5, 7

Chopin: The Man and His Music (Huneker)
65:157, 165, 170, 198, 205, 207

"Clerk Maxwell's Influence on the Evolution
of the Idea of Physical Reality" ("On Clerk
Maxwell's Influence") (Einstein) 65:73

Collected Papers (Maitland) 65:253

"Come Back Baby" (Holly) 65:137, 141, 148

"The Comet" (Huneker) 65:169

The Complete Buddy Holly (Holly) 65:144

"Considerations Concerning the Fundaments
of Theoretical Physics" (Einstein) 65:74

The Constitutional History of England
(Maitland) 65:259, 267

"The Corporation Sole" (Maitland) 65:267

"The Critic Who Gossips" (Huneker) 65:189

"Cross-Currents in Modern French Literature"
(Huneker) 65:189

"Crying, Waiting, Hoping" (Holly) 65:147

A Cure for Curables (Biggers) 65:2

"Dearest" ("Ummm Oh Yeah") (Holly)
65:138, 149-50

"Does the Inertia of a Body Depend on Its
Energy?" (Einstein) 65:88

Domesday Book and Beyond (Maitland)
65:253, 258, 260, 264, 269, 272, 275-76, 279,
281, 284, 291

"The Early History of Malice Aforethought"
(Maitland) 65:282

"Early in the Morning" (Holly) 65:139, 153

Egoists: A Book of Supermen (Huneker)
65:163, 167, 170, 179, 184-5, 188, 217

"The Eighth Deadly Sin" (Huneker) 65:156,
169, 197

Einstein: Philosopher-Scientist (Einstein)
See *Albert Einstein: Philosopher-Scientist*

"An Empty Cup" (Holly) 65:143

English Law and the Renaissance (Maitland)
65:265, 287

"Die Entfaltung der Seele durch Lebenskunst"
(Key) 65:238-41

Essays by James Huneker (Huneker) 65:199

"The Eternal Duel" (Huneker) 65:196

"Everyday" (Holly) 65:138-40, 142, 145, 153

"Faith and a Doubting World" (Cardozo)
65:41

"Fool's Paradise" (Holly) 65:149

"The Foundation of the General Theory of
Relativity" (Einstein) 65:92, 97

"Frank Wedekind" (Huneker) 65:199

Franz Liszt (Huneker) 65:165, 170

The General Theory of Relativity (Einstein)
65:111

Giant Buddy Holly (Holly) 65:144, 150

"Girl on My Mind" (Holly) 65:148

The Great Buddy Holly (Holly) 65:144

"The Greater Chopin" (Huneker) 65:199

The Growth of the Law (Cardozo) 65:22, 29,
32, 34-5, 39, 41

The HAC in Africa (Childers) 65:53

"Hall of the Missing Footsteps" (Huneker)
65:169, 196

"Have You Ever Been Lonely" (Holly)
65:150

"Heartbeat" (Holly) 65:137-38, 140-43, 152

*The History of English Law Before the Time of
Edward I* (Maitland) 65:262-64, 270-72,
274, 276, 279, 282, 284, 292

"Holly Hop" (Holly) 65:150

Holly in the Hills (Holly) 65:149

The House Without a Key (Biggers) 65:3-5,
8-9, 13

"I Guess I Was Just a Fool" (Holly) 65:149

"I Guess It Doesn't Matter Anymore" (Holly)
65:145-46, 150-51

Iconoclasts: A Book of Dramatists (Huneker)
65:157-59, 163, 165, 167, 170, 179, 185, 188,
217

Ideas and Opinions (Einstein) 65:133

Ideologie and Utopie (Ideology and Utopia) (Mannheim) **65**:295, 301-02, 307-08, 312, 319, 321-22, 333, 338

Ideology and Utopia (Mannheim)
See *Ideologie and Utopie*

If You're Only Human (Biggers) **65**:2

"I'm Changin' All Those Changes" (Holly) **65**:148

"I'm Gonna Love You Too" (Holly) **65**:138, 140, 153

"I'm Gonna Set My Foot Down" (Holly) **65**:148

Inside the Lines (Biggers) **65**:2

"The Iron Fan" (Huneker) **65**:198

"Isolde's Mother" (Huneker) **65**:169

"It's So Easy" (Holly) **65**:153

Ivory Apes and Peacocks (Huneker) **65**:161, 165, 170, 185, 193, 198, 203, 205-06, 218

"Jurisprudence" (Cardozo) **65**:35, 37, 39

Karleken och Aktenskapet (Key) **65**:242

Keeper of the Keys (Biggers) **65**:4, 8, 16

"Das Konservative Denken" (Maitland) **65**:310

Kvinnororelsen (Key) **65**:226, 234, 237-38

"Last Night" (Holly) **65**:143

Later Years (Einstein)
See *Out of His Later Years*

"Law and Literature" (Cardozo) **65**:46

Law and Literature and Other Essays and Addresses (Cardozo) **65**:41

"The Law of Real Property" (Maitland) **65**:274

"Learning the Game" (Holly) **65**:147, 151

Leslie Stephen (Maitland) **65**:276

The Letters of Frederic Willia Maitland (Maitland) **65**:276

Letters of James Huneker (Huneker) **65**:198

Life Lines (Key)
See *Lifslinjer*

Lifslinjer (Life Lines; Lines of Life) (Key) **65**:226-27

Lines of Life (Key)
See *Lifslinjer*

"Listen to Me" (Holly) **65**:138-43

"Little Baby" (Holly) **65**:138, 147

"Lonesome Tears" (Holly) **65**:149

"Look at Me" (Holly) **65**:138, 141

"The Lord's Prayer in B" (Huneker) **65**:196

Love and Ethics (Key) **65**:229

Love and Marriage (Key) **65**:225, 227, 229, 237-38

Love Insurance (Biggers) **65**:4

"Love's Made a Fool of You" (Holly) **65**:137-38, 141, 144, 148, 152-53

"The Magic Veimeer" (Huneker) **65**:161

"Mailman Bring Me No More Blues" (Holly) **65**:138-41

Man and Society in an Age of Reconstruction (Mannheim)
See *Mensch und Gesellschaft im Zeitalter des Umbaus*

"A Master of Cobwebs" (Huneker) **65**:156

"The Materials for English Legal History" (Maitland) **65**:281

"Max Liebermann and Some Phases of Modern German Art" (Huneker) **65**:161

"Maybe Baby" (Holly) **65**:145

The Meaning of Relativity (Einstein) **65**:91, 105

Melomaniacs (Huneker) **65**:156-58, 169-70, 195, 216

Memorunda de Parliamento (Maitland) **65**:282

"Memories" (Holly) **65**:149

Mensch und Gesellschaft im Zeitalter des Umbaus (Man and Society in an Age of Reconstruction) (Mannheim) **65**:303, 314, 333

Mezzotints in Modern Music (Huneker) **65**:157, 165, 170, 177, 188, 199, 215

"Midnight Shift" (Holly) **65**:151

Missbrukad Kvinnokraft och Naturenliga arbetsomraden for kvinnor (Misused Womanpower) (Key) **65**:242, 244

Misused Womanpower (Key)
See *Missbrukad Kvinnokraft och Naturenliga arbetsomraden for kvinnor*

"Moondreams" (Holly) **65**:147

The Morality of Women (Key) **65**:237

Motherliness and Education for Motherhood (Key) **65**:234

"The Music of the Future" (Huneker) **65**:215

"My Little Girl" (Holly) **65**:144

The Nature of the Judicial Process (Cardozo) **65**:21-2, 29, 32, 35, 39, 41, 43-5

New Cosmopolis (Huneker) **65**:168, 170

"Not Fade Away" (Holly) **65**:137, 144, 146, 151-52

"Now We're One" (Holly) **65**:147

"Oh Boy!" (Holly) **65**:143, 145, 148

Old Fogy (Huneker) **65**:165-67, 188, 205

"On Clerk Maxwell's Influence" (Einstein)
See "Clerk Maxwell's Influence on the Evolution of the Idea of Physical Reality"

"On Physical Reality" (Einstein) **65**:132

"On the Electrodynamics of Moving Bodies" (Einstein) **65**:86, 95, 106

"On the Method of Theoretical Physics" (Einstein) **65**:68, 95, 100

Out of His Later Years (Later Years) (Einstein) **65**:123, 131-34

Overtones: A Book of Temperaments (Huneker) **65**:157, 159, 170

The Painted Veil (Huneker) **65**:170, 185-87, 195-97, 205, 209-11, 213, 219

"Pan" (Huneker) **65**:196

The Paradoxes of Legal Science (Cardozo) **65**:32-3, 44

The Pathos of Distance (Huneker) **65**:164-65, 170, 185, 218

"Peggy Sue" (Holly) **65**:138-44

"Peggy Sue Got Married" (Holly) **65**:147

"Physics and Reality" (Einstein)
See "Physik and Realitat"

"Physik and Realitat" ("Physics and Reality") (Einstein) **65**:92, 94, 97, 101

Pleas of the Crown for the County of Gloucester, 1221 (Maitland) **65**:249, 260, 265, 274

"Poe and His Polish Contemporary" (Huneker) **65**:196

Political Theories of the Middle Age (Maitland) **65**:250, 253, 278

"Possession for Year and Day" (Maitland) **65**:282

The Principle of Relativity (Einstein) **65**:91, 97-8

"Principles of Research" (Einstein) **65**:73

"The Problem of Space, Ether, and the Field of Physics" (Einstein) **65**:70

Promenades of an Impressionists (Huneker) **65**:170, 188, 217

"The Purse of Aholibah" (Huneker) **65**:197

"Queen of Hearts" (Holly) **65**:145

"Queen of the Ballroom" (Holly) **65**:149

"Raining in My Heart" (Holly) **65**:146

"Rave On" (Holly) **65**:137-39, 142, 148, 153

"Ready Teddy" (Holly) **65**:138-39, 141

"Rebels of the Moon" (Huneker) **65**:169

"Remarks on Bertrand Russell's Theory of Knowledge" (Einstein) **65**:92

"Reminiscing" (Holly) **65**:137-38, 141

Reminiscing (Holly) **65**:147-48, 150

The Renaissance of Motherhood (Key) **65**:235, 237, 242

"Reply to Criticisms" (Einstein) **65**:126

The Riddle of the Sands (Childers) **65**:50-2, 54-61

"Rock Around with Ollie Vee" (Holly) **65**:148

"Rock-a-Bye Rock" (Holly) **65**:148

Roman Canon Law in the Church of England (Maitland) **65**:251, 259, 266

"Samhallsmoderlighet" (Key) **65**:243

See-Saw (Biggers) **65**:2

Select Passages from the Works of Bracton and Azo (Maitland) **65**:275

Selected Essays (Maitland) **65**:253, 257

Selected Writings of Benjamin Nathan Cardozo (Cardozo) **65**:32-3, 44

"A Sentimental Rebellion" (Huneker) **65**:197

Seven Keys to Baldpate (Biggers) **65**:2, 4, 9

Showcase (Holly) **65**:148-50

The Special Theory of Relativity (Einstein) **65**:111

"The Spiral Road" (Huneker) **65**:156, 195-96, 198

Steeplejack (Huneker) **65**:170-72, 178, 183-84, 186, 189, 205, 209, 211, 219-20

"The Supreme Sin" (Huneker) **65**:187, 197

"Take Your Time" (Holly) **65**:137-38, 141, 147

"Teardrops Fall Like Rain" (Holly) **65**:144

"Tell e How" (Holly) **65**:152

"That Makes It Tough" (Holly) **65**:147

"That'll Be the Day" (Holly) **65**:138, 143, 145, 150-51

"That's What They Say" (Holly) **65**:147, 151

"Think It Over" (Holly) **65**:153

"The Third Kingdom" (Huneker) **65**:158

"Three Disagreeable Girls" (Huneker) **65**:207

Three Rolls of the King's Court, 1194-1195 (Maitland) **65**:249

Three's a Crowd (Biggers) **65**:2

The Times History of the War in South Africa (Childers) **65**:55

"To the Heroes of the Battle of the Warsaw Ghetto" (Einstein) **65**:122

Township and Borough (Maitland) **65**:254, 276, 280, 284, 287

"True Love Ways" (Holly) **65**:144, 147, 151-53

"Ummm Oh Yeah" (Holly)
See "Dearest"

Unicorns (Huneker) **65**:170, 179, 185, 218

Variations (Huneker) **65**:185, 218-19

"The Vision Malefic" (Huneker) **65**:196

Visionaries (Huneker) **65**:156-58, 169-70, 195, 216

"A Visit to Walt Whitman" (Huneker) **65**:161

"Well...All Right" (Holly) **65**:137-38, 143, 145

"What I Believe" (Einstein) **65**:133

"What To Do" (Holly) **65**:147, 149, 151

"Why the History of English Law Remains
   Unwritten" (Maitland) **65**:281
"Wishing" (Holly) **65**:138, 149, 151
"The Woman Who Loved Chopin" (Huneker)
   65:169, 198
"Words of Love" (Holly) **65**:138, 140-42,
   145, 151-52
Year Books of Edward II (Maitland) **65**:252
"Year-One Atomic Age-A Message" (Einstein)
   65:122
The Younger Generation (Key) **65**:237
"You're the One" (Holly) **65**:138, 148, 150
"You've Got Love" (Holly) **65**:140